FOOTB REGIS

1986 EDITION

Editors/Football Register
HOWARD BALZER
BARRY SIEGEL

Contributing Editor/Football Register
DAVE SLOAN

President-Chief Executive Officer
RICHARD WATERS

Editor
TOM BARNIDGE

Director of Books and Periodicals
RON SMITH

Published by

The Sporting News

1212 North Lindbergh Boulevard
P.O. Box 56 — St. Louis, MO 63166

Copyright © 1986
The Sporting News Publishing Company

▼ A Times Mirror
◤ Company

ISBN 0-89204-217-6   ISSN 0071-7258

TABLE
of
CONTENTS

ON THE COVER: Cincinnati receiver Eddie Brown enjoyed a fine debut season in the National Football League, catching 53 passes for 942 yards and a 17.8-yard average while earning Rookie of the Year honors from The Sporting News.

Photo by Richard Pilling

EXPLANATION OF ABBREVIATIONS

AAFC—All America Football Conference. AFL—American Football League. CFL—Canadian Football League. CoFL—Continental Football League. EFL—Eastern Football League. NFL—National Football League. PFLA—Professional Football League of America. USFL—United States Football League. WFL—World Football League.

Att.—Attempts. Avg.—Average. Blk.—Blocked punts. Cmp.—Pass completions. F—Fumbles. FG—Field goals made. FGA—Field goal attempts. G—Games. Gain—Yards gained passing. No.—Number. P.C.—Passes caught. Pct.—Percentage completed. P.I.—Passes intercepted. Pts.—Total points scored. TD—Touchdowns. T.P.—Touchdown passes thrown. XP—Extra points made. XPM—Extra points missed. Yds.—Net yards gained.

Veteran Players

WALTER AUGUSTUS ABERCROMBIE
Running Back—Pittsburgh Steelers
Born September 26, 1959, at Waco, Tex.
Height, 6.00. Weight, 210.
High School—Waco, Tex., University.
Attended Baylor University.
Selected by Pittsburgh in 1st round (12th player selected) of 1982 NFL draft.
On injured reserve with knee injury, September 7 through November 26, 1982; activated, November 27, 1982.

| | | ——RUSHING—— | | | | PASS RECEIVING | | | | —TOTAL— | | |
Year	Club	G.	Att.	Yds.	Avg.	TD.	P.C.	Yds.	Avg.	TD.	TD.	Pts.	F.
1982—Pittsburgh NFL		6	21	100	4.8	2	1	14	14.0	0	2	12	0
1983—Pittsburgh NFL		15	112	446	4.0	4	26	391	15.0	3	7	42	2
1984—Pittsburgh NFL		14	145	610	4.2	1	16	135	8.4	0	1	6	0
1985—Pittsburgh NFL		16	227	851	3.7	7	24	209	8.7	2	9	54	5
Pro Totals—4 Years		51	505	2007	4.0	14	67	749	11.2	5	19	114	7

| | | | KICKOFF RETURNS | | |
Year	Club	G.	No.	Yds.	Avg.TD.
1982—Pittsburgh NFL		6	7	139	19.9 0
1983—Pittsburgh NFL		15		None	
1984—Pittsburgh NFL		14		None	
1985—Pittsburgh NFL		16		None	
Pro Totals—4 Years		51	7	139	19.9 0

Additional pro statistics: Recovered two fumbles, 1982; recovered one fumble, 1985.
Played in AFC Championship Game following 1984 season.

ROBERT ABRAHAM
Linebacker—Houston Oilers
Born July 13, 1960, at Myrtle Beach, S.C.
Height, 6.01. Weight, 230.
High School—Myrtle Beach, S.C.
Attended North Carolina State University.
Selected by Houston in 3rd round (77th player selected) of 1982 NFL draft.
On injured reserve with broken leg, December 7 through remainder of 1983 season.
Houston NFL, 1982 through 1985.
Games: 1982 (9), 1983 (14), 1984 (16), 1985 (16). Total—55.
Pro statistics: Recovered one fumble, 1982; intercepted one pass for no yards, 1983; intercepted one pass for one yard, 1984; recovered four fumbles, 1985.

GEORGE ACHICA
Defensive Tackle—New York Jets
Born December 19, 1961, at American Samoa.
Height, 6.05. Weight, 260.
High School—San Jose, Calif., Andrew Hill.
Attended University of Southern California.
Named as defensive tackle on THE SPORTING NEWS College All-America Team, 1982.
Selected by Los Angeles in 1983 USFL territorial draft.
Selected by Baltimore in 3rd round (57th player selected) of 1983 NFL draft.
Signed by Los Angeles Express, May 17, 1983.
Granted roster exemption, May 17, 1983; activated, May 21, 1983.
On developmental squad, June 25 through remainder of 1983 season.
Granted free agency, August 1, 1985; signed by Indianapolis Colts, August 3, 1985.
On injured reserve with knee injury, September 11 through October 10, 1985; activated, October 11, 1985.
Released by Indianapolis Colts, November 18, 1985; signed as free agent by New York Jets, March 25, 1986.
On developmental squad for 2 games with Los Angeles Express in 1983.
Los Angeles USFL, 1983 through 1985; Indianapolis NFL, 1985.
Games: 1983 (6), 1984 (18), 1985 USFL (18), 1985 NFL (4). Total USFL—42. Total Pro—46.
USFL statistics: Credited with five sacks for 32 yards, 1984; recovered one fumble and credited with seven sacks for 32 yards, 1985.

RICHARD CARL ACKERMAN
(Rick)
Defensive Tackle—Philadelphia Eagles
Born June 16, 1959, at LaGrange, Ill.
Height, 6.04. Weight, 250.
High School—Northbrook, Ill., Glenbard North.
Attended Memphis State University.
Signed as free agent by San Diego Chargers, June 11, 1981.

On injured reserve with neck and elbow injuries, August 25 through entire 1981 season.

Released by San Diego Chargers, November 2, 1984; signed as free agent by Los Angeles Raiders, November 6, 1984.

Released by Los Angeles Raiders, August 20, 1985; signed as free agent by Philadelphia Eagles, May 7, 1986.

San Diego NFL, 1982 and 1983; San Diego (9)-Los Angeles Raiders (6) NFL, 1984.

Games: 1982 (9), 1983 (15), 1984 (15). Total—39.

Pro statistics: Recovered two fumbles, 1983.

CURTIS LADONN ADAMS
Running Back—San Diego Chargers
Born April 30, 1962, at Muskegon, Mich.
Height, 5.11. Weight, 198.
High School—Muskegon, Mich., Orchard View.
Attended Central Michigan University.

Selected by Orlando in 9th round (117th player selected) of 1985 USFL draft.
Selected by San Diego in 8th round (207th player selected) of 1985 NFL draft.
Signed by San Diego Chargers, June 19, 1985.
On injured reserve with knee injury, September 12 through remainder of 1985 season.

		RUSHING				PASS RECEIVING				TOTAL		
Year Club	G.	Att.	Yds.	Avg.	TD.	P.C.	Yds.	Avg.	TD.	TD.	Pts.	F.
1985—San Diego NFL	1	16	49	3.1	1	1	12	12.0	0	1	6	0

Additional pro statistics: Returned two kickoffs for 50 yards, 1985.

GEORGE WALLACE ADAMS
Running Back—New York Giants
Born December 22, 1962, at Lexington, Ky.
Height, 6.01. Weight, 225.
High School—Lexington, Ky., Lafayette.
Attended University of Kentucky.

Selected by Orlando in 3rd round (33rd player selected) of 1985 USFL draft.
Selected by New York Giants in 1st round (19th player selected) of 1985 NFL draft.
Signed by New York Giants, July 22, 1985.

		RUSHING				PASS RECEIVING				TOTAL		
Year Club	G.	Att.	Yds.	Avg.	TD.	P.C.	Yds.	Avg.	TD.	TD.	Pts.	F.
1985—New York Giants NFL	16	128	498	3.9	2	31	389	12.5	2	4	24	7

		KICKOFF RETURNS			
Year Club	G.	No.	Yds.	Avg.	TD.
1985—N.Y. Giants NFL	16	14	241	17.2	0

Additional pro statistics: Attempted one pass with no completions and recovered two fumbles, 1985.

STEFON LEE ADAMS
Cornerback—Los Angeles Raiders
Born August 11, 1963, at High Point, N.C.
Height, 5.10. Weight, 195.
High School—High Point, N.C., Southwest Guilford.
Attended East Carolina University.
Brother of Amos Adams, wide receiver at East Carolina University.

Selected by Baltimore in 4th round (58th player selected) of 1985 USFL draft.
Selected by Los Angeles Raiders in 3rd round (80th player selected) of 1985 NFL draft.
Signed by Los Angeles Raiders, July 17, 1985.
On injured reserve with hamstring injury, September 2 through entire 1985 season.

WILLIS DEAN ADAMS
Wide Receiver
Born August 22, 1956, at Weimar, Tex.
Height, 6.02. Weight, 200.
High School—Schulenburg, Tex.
Attended Navarro Junior College and received bachelor of science degree
in physical education from University of Houston in 1982.

Selected by Cleveland in 1st round (20th player selected) of 1979 NFL draft.
On injured reserve with knee injury, October 22 through remainder of 1981 season.
On inactive list, September 19, 1982.
On injured reserve with knee injury, November 19 through remainder of 1982 season.
On injured reserve with knee injury, September 26 through remainder of 1985 season.
Granted free agency with no qualifying offer, February 1, 1986.

	PASS RECEIVING						PASS RECEIVING			
Year Club	G.	P.C.	Yds.	Avg.	TD.	Year Club	G.	P.C.	Yds.	Avg.	TD.
1979—Cleveland NFL	16	1	6	6.0	0	1983—Cleveland NFL	16	20	374	18.7	2
1980—Cleveland NFL	16	8	165	20.6	0	1984—Cleveland NFL	16	21	261	12.4	0
1981—Cleveland NFL	7	1	24	24.0	0	1985—Cleveland NFL	3	10	132	13.2	0
1982—Cleveland NFL	1		None			Pro Totals—7 Years	75	61	962	15.8	2

Additional pro statistics: Rushed twice for four yards, 1979; fumbled once, 1979, 1983 and 1984; rushed twice for seven yards, 1980; rushed once for two yards and recovered one fumble, 1983; recovered one fumble for four yards, 1985.

MARK ADICKES
Offensive Tackle—Kansas City Chiefs
Born April 22, 1961, at Badconstadt, West Germany.
Height, 6.05. Weight, 278.
High School—Killeen, Tex.
Attended Baylor University.
Brother of John Adickes, center at Baylor University.

Named as offensive tackle on THE SPORTING NEWS College All-America Team, 1983.
Selected by Houston in 1984 USFL territorial draft.
USFL rights traded with rights to center Mike Ruether by Houston Gamblers to Los Angeles Express for 2nd round pick in 1985 and 1986 draft, February 13, 1984.
Signed by Los Angeles Express, February 13, 1984.
Granted roster exemption, February 13, 1984; activated, February 24, 1984.
On injured reserve with knee injury, March 6 through remainder of 1984 season.
Selected by Kansas City in 1st round (5th player selected) of 1984 NFL supplemental draft.
Released by Los Angeles Express, August 1, 1985; re-signed by Express, August 2, 1985.
Released by Los Angeles Express, April 3, 1986; signed by Kansas City Chiefs, June 5, 1986.
Los Angeles USFL, 1984 and 1985.
Games: 1984 (2), 1985 (11). Total—13.

DAVID IVER AHRENS
Name pronounced AIR-ens.
(Dave)
Linebacker—Indianapolis Colts
Born December 5, 1958, at Cedar Falls, Iowa.
Height, 6.03. Weight, 247.
High School—Oregon, Wis.
Attended University of Wisconsin.

Selected by St. Louis in 6th round (143rd player selected) of 1981 NFL draft.
Traded by St. Louis Cardinals to Indianapolis Colts for 10th round pick in 1986 draft, August 27, 1985.
St. Louis NFL, 1981 through 1984; Indianapolis NFL, 1985.
Games: 1981 (16), 1982 (9), 1983 (16), 1984 (16), 1985 (16). Total—73.
Pro statistics: Intercepted one pass for 14 yards, 1981; returned one kickoff for five yards, 1982; recovered one fumble, 1982 and 1985; caught one pass for four yards, 1983.

MIKE AKIU
Name pronounced Ah-Q.
Wide Receiver—Houston Oilers
Born February 12, 1962, at Kailua, Haw.
Height, 5.09. Weight, 185.
High School—Kailua, Haw., Kalaheo.
Attended Washington State University and University of Hawaii.

Selected by Houston in 7th round (170th player selected) of 1985 NFL draft.
Signed by Houston Oilers, July 13, 1985.
On injured reserve with shoulder injury, November 9 through remainder of 1985 season.

Year Club	G.	P.C.	Yds.	Avg.	TD.
1985—Houston NFL	9	2	32	16.0	0

Additional pro statistics: Returned blocked punt 20 yards for a touchdown, 1985.

IRA LADOL ALBRIGHT
Fullback—Buffalo Bills
Born January 2, 1959, at Dallas, Tex.
Height, 6.00. Weight, 260.
High School—Dallas, Tex., South Cliff.
Attended Tyler Junior College and Northeastern Oklahoma State University.

Signed by Michigan Panthers, January 24, 1983.
Released by Michigan Panthers, February 27, 1983; re-signed by Panthers, March 1, 1983.
On developmental squad, March 4 through March 13, 1983; activated, March 14, 1983.
On developmental squad, April 21 through May 22, 1983; activated, May 23, 1983.
Selected by Pittsburgh Maulers in 11th round (61st player selected) of USFL expansion draft, September 6, 1983.
On developmental squad, March 29 through April 7, 1984; activated, April 8, 1984.
On developmental squad, April 12 through May 2, 1984; activated, May 3, 1984.
Franchise disbanded, October 25, 1984; not selected in USFL dispersal draft, December 6, 1984.
Signed as free agent by Houston Gamblers, January 21, 1985.
Released by Houston Gamblers, February 11, 1985; signed as free agent by Buffalo Bills, March 20, 1985.
Released by Buffalo Bills, August 26, 1985; re-signed by Bills, May 6, 1986.
On developmental squad for 6 games with Michigan Panthers in 1983.
On developmental squad for 4 games with Pittsburgh Maulers in 1984.
Michigan USFL, 1983; Pittsburgh USFL, 1984.
Games: 1983 (13), 1984 (14). Total—27.
Pro statistics: Credited with two sacks for six yards and recovered blocked kick in end zone for touchdown, 1983; rushed five times for 15 yards and recovered one fumble, 1984.
Played in USFL Championship Game following 1983 season.

VINCE DENADER ALBRITTON
Safety—Dallas Cowboys
Born July 23, 1962, at Oakland, Calif.
Height, 6.02. Weight, 213.
High School—Oakland, Calif., McClymond.
Attended University of Washington.

Selected by Philadelphia in 16th round (326th player selected) of 1984 USFL draft.
Signed as free agent by Dallas Cowboys, May 3, 1984.
On injured reserve with hamstring injury, August 20 through November 7, 1985; activated after clearing procedural waivers, November 9, 1985.
Dallas NFL, 1984 and 1985.
Games: 1984 (16), 1985 (7). Total—23.
Pro statistics: Recovered two fumbles, 1984.

CORWYN ALDREDGE
Tight End—Tampa Bay Buccaneers
Born September 6, 1963, at Natchitoches, La.
Height, 6.05. Weight, 225.
High School—Natchitoches, La., St. Mary's.
Attended Mississippi State University.

Signed as free agent by Tampa Bay Buccaneers, May 9, 1985.
On injured reserve with shoulder injury, August 20 through entire 1985 season.

CHARLES FRED ALEXANDER JR.
Running Back—Cincinnati Bengals
Born July 28, 1957, at Galveston, Tex.
Height, 6.01. Weight, 226.
High School—Galveston, Tex., Ball.
Attended Louisiana State University.
Cousin of Darrin Nelson, running back with Minnesota Vikings; and Kevin Nelson, running back with Los Angeles Express, 1984 and 1985.

Named as running back on THE SPORTING NEWS College All-America Team, 1978.
Selected by Cincinnati in 1st round (12th player selected) of 1979 NFL draft.

Year Club	G.	Att.	Yds.	Avg.	TD.	P.C.	Yds.	Avg.	TD.	TD.	Pts.	F.
			RUSHING				PASS RECEIVING				—TOTAL—	
1979—Cincinnati NFL	16	88	286	3.3	1	11	91	8.3	0	1	6	0
1980—Cincinnati NFL	16	169	702	4.2	2	36	192	5.3	0	2	12	2
1981—Cincinnati NFL	15	98	292	3.0	2	28	262	9.4	1	3	18	0
1982—Cincinnati NFL	9	64	207	3.2	1	14	85	6.1	1	2	12	1
1983—Cincinnati NFL	14	153	523	3.4	3	32	187	5.8	0	3	18	1
1984—Cincinnati NFL	16	132	479	3.6	2	29	203	7.0	0	2	12	2
1985—Cincinnati NFL	16	44	156	3.5	2	15	110	7.3	0	2	12	0
Pro Totals—7 Years	102	748	2645	3.5	13	165	1130	6.8	2	15	90	6

Additional pro statistics: Recovered one fumble, 1981 and 1985.
Played in AFC Championship Game following 1981 season.
Played in NFL Championship Game following 1981 season.

DAN LAMARR ALEXANDER
Guard—New York Jets
Born June 17, 1955, at Houston, Tex.
Height, 6.04. Weight, 260.
High School—Houston, Tex., Lamar.
Received degree in law enforcement from Louisiana State University.

Selected by New York Jets in 8th round (200th player selected) of 1977 NFL draft.
New York Jets NFL, 1977 through 1985.
Games: 1977 (14), 1978 (16), 1979 (16), 1980 (16), 1981 (16), 1982 (9), 1983 (16), 1984 (16), 1985 (16). Total—135.
Pro statistics: Recovered one fumble, 1978 and 1982.
Played in AFC Championship Game following 1982 season.

ALTON ALEXIS
Wide Receiver—Cleveland Browns
Born November 16, 1957, at New Iberia, La.
Height, 6.00. Weight, 184.
High School—New Iberia, La.
Received bachelor of science degree from Tulane University in 1980.
Related to Tony Hill, wide receiver with Dallas Cowboys;
and Whitney Paul, linebacker with New Orleans Saints.

Selected by Cincinnati in 11th round (281st player selected) of 1980 NFL draft.
Released by Cincinnati Bengals, August 26, 1980; re-signed by Bengals after clearing procedural waivers, December 10, 1980.
Released by Cincinnati Bengals, August 25, 1981; signed as free agent by Calgary Stampeders, October 22, 1981.
Released by Calgary Stampeders, June 18, 1983.
USFL rights traded by Birmingham Stallions to Jacksonville Bulls for draft choice, July 28, 1983.
Signed by Jacksonville Bulls, August 7, 1983.
On developmental squad, March 10 through March 22, 1984; activated, March 23, 1984.

Year Club	G.	P.C.	Yds.	Avg.	TD.	No.	Yds.	Avg.	TD.	No.	Yds.	Avg.	TD.	TD.	Pts.	F.
		PASS RECEIVING				—PUNT RETURNS—				—KICKOFF RET.—				—TOTAL—		
1980—Cincinnati NFL	1		None					None				None		0	0	0
1981—Calgary CFL	2	5	95	19.0	0			None				None		0	0	0
1982—Calgary CFL	16	25	440	17.6	5	18	96	5.3	0	15	380	25.3	0	5	30	2
1984—Jacksonville USFL	14	29	312	10.8	3			None				None		3	18	0
1985—Jacksonville USFL	18	83	1118	13.5	5			None				None		5	30	3
NFL Totals—1 Year	1	0	0	0.0	0	0	0	0.0	0	0	0	0.0	0	0	0	0
CFL Totals—2 Years	18	30	535	17.8	5	18	96	5.3	0	15	380	25.3	0	5	30	2
USFL Totals—2 Year	32	112	1430	12.8	8	0	0	0.0	0	0	0	0.0	0	8	48	3
Pro Totals—5 Years	51	142	1965	13.8	13	18	96	5.3	0	15	380	25.3	0	13	78	5

Additional CFL statistics: Rushed once for nine yards, 1982.
Additional USFL statistics: Recovered two fumbles, 1985.

RAUL ENRIQUE ALLEGRE
Placekicker—Indianapolis Colts

Born June 15, 1959, at Torreon, Coahuila, Mex.
Height, 5.10. Weight, 161.
High School—Shelton, Wash.
Attended University of Montana and received degree in civil engineering from University of Texas.

Signed as free agent by Dallas Cowboys, April 28, 1983.
Traded by Dallas Cowboys to Baltimore Colts for 9th round pick in 1984 draft, August 29, 1983.
Franchise transferred to Indianapolis, March 31, 1984.

Year Club	G.	XP.	XPM.	FG.	FGA.	Pts.
		—PLACE KICKING—				
1983—Baltimore NFL	16	22	2	30	35	112
1984—Indianapolis NFL	12	14	0	11	18	47
1985—Indianapolis NFL	16	36	3	16	26	84
Pro Totals—3 Years	44	72	5	57	79	243

ANTHONY DERRICK ALLEN
Wide Receiver—Atlanta Falcons

Born June 29, 1959, at McComb, Miss.
Height, 5.11. Weight, 185.
High School—Seattle, Wash., Garfield.
Attended University of Washington.
Brother of Patrick Allen, cornerback with Houston Oilers.

Selected by Tampa Bay in 3rd round (36th player selected) of 1983 USFL draft.
Selected by Atlanta in 6th round (156th player selected) of 1983 NFL draft.
USFL rights traded by Tampa Bay Bandits to Los Angeles Express for 4th round pick in 1984 draft, May 9, 1983.
Signed by Los Angeles Express, May 9, 1983.
Granted roster exemption, May 9, 1983; activated, May 14, 1983.
Traded by Los Angeles Express to Michigan Panthers for draft pick, April 18, 1984.
Not protected in merger of Michigan Panthers and Oakland Invaders; selected by Baltimore Stars in USFL dispersal draft, December 6, 1984.
Released by Baltimore Stars, February 18, 1985; signed as free agent by Portland Breakers, April 4, 1985.
Released by Portland Breakers, May 14, 1985; signed by Atlanta Falcons, July 18, 1985.

Year Club	G.	Att.	Yds.	Avg.	TD.	P.C.	Yds.	Avg.	TD.	TD.	Pts.	F.
		—RUSHING—				PASS RECEIVING				—TOTAL—		
1983—Los Angeles USFL	8	1	−6	−6.0	0	37	613	16.6	3	3	18	1
1984—Los Angeles (8)-Mich. (10) USFL	18	2	0	0.0	0	34	535	15.7	3	3	18	4
1985—Portland USFL	6		None			9	125	13.9	2	2	12	0
1985—Atlanta NFL	16		None			14	207	14.8	2	2	12	0
USFL Totals—3 Years	32	3	−6	−2.0	0	80	1273	15.9	8	8	48	5
NFL Totals—1 Year	16	0	0	0.0	0	14	207	14.8	2	2	12	0
Pro Totals—4 Years	48	3	−6	−2.0	0	94	1480	15.7	10	10	60	5

Year Club	G.	No.	Yds.	Avg.	TD.	No.	Yds.	Avg.	TD.
		—PUNT RETURNS—				—KICKOFF RET.—			
1983—Los Angeles USFL	8	15	105	7.0	0	11	211	19.2	0
1984—Los Angeles (8)-Michigan (10) USFL	18	36	233	6.5	0	2	31	15.5	0
1985—Portland USFL	6		None				None		
1985—Atlanta NFL	16	21	141	6.7	0	8	140	17.5	0
USFL Totals—3 Years	32	51	338	6.6	0	13	242	18.6	0
NFL Totals—1 Year	16	21	141	6.7	0	8	140	17.5	0
Pro Totals—4 Years	48	72	479	6.7	0	21	382	18.2	0

Additional USFL statistics: Attempted one pass with no completions and recovered one fumble, 1983.
Additional NFL statistics: Recovered one fumble, 1985.

—DID YOU KNOW—

That 49ers running back Roger Craig last season became the first player in NFL history to have 1,000 yards in both rushing and pass receiving in the same season?

GREG ALLEN
Running Back—Cleveland Browns
Born June 4, 1963, at Milton, Fla.
Height, 5.11. Weight, 200.
High School—Milton, Fla.
Attended Florida State University.

Selected by Tampa Bay in 1985 USFL territorial draft.
USFL rights traded with rights to running back Lorenzo Hampton by Tampa Bay Bandits to Orlando Renegades for rights to running back Jeff McCall, December 21, 1984.
Selected by Cleveland in 2nd round (35th player selected) of 1985 NFL draft.
Signed by Cleveland Browns, July 25, 1985.
On injured reserve with knee injury, October 25 through remainder of 1985 season.

Year Club	G.	Att.	Yds.	Avg.	TD.	P.C.	Yds.	Avg.	TD.	TD.	Pts.	F.
		—RUSHING—				PASS RECEIVING				—TOTAL—		
1985—Cleveland NFL	7	8	32	4.0	0		None			0	0	1

Additional pro statistics: Returned one kickoff for four yards, 1985.

KEVIN ALLEN
Offensive Tackle—Philadelphia Eagles
Born June 21, 1963, at Cincinnati, O.
Height, 6.05. Weight, 284.
High School—Cincinnati, O., Northwest.
Attended Indiana University.

Selected by Birmingham in 1st round (10th player selected) of 1985 USFL draft.
Selected by Philadelphia in 1st round (9th player selected) of 1985 NFL draft.
Signed by Philadelphia Eagles, August 20, 1985.
Philadelphia NFL, 1985.
Games: 1985 (16).
Pro statistics: Recovered one fumble, 1985.

LLOYD PATRICK ALLEN
(Known by middle name.)
Cornerback—Houston Oilers
Born August 26, 1961, at Seattle, Wash.
Height, 5.10. Weight, 185.
High School—Seattle, Wash., Garfield.
Attended Utah State University.
Brother of Anthony Allen, wide receiver with Atlanta Falcons.

Selected by Washington in 2nd round (27th player selected) of 1984 USFL draft.
Selected by Houston in 4th round (100th player selected) of 1984 NFL draft.
Signed by Houston Oilers, July 18, 1984.

Year Club	G.	No.	Yds.	Avg.	TD.	No.	Yds.	Avg.	TD.	TD.	Pts.	F.
		-INTERCEPTIONS-				—KICKOFF RET.—				—TOTAL—		
1984—Houston NFL	16	1	2	2.0	0	11	210	19.1	0	0	0	0
1985—Houston NFL	16		None				None			0	0	0
Pro Totals—2 Years	32	1	2	2.0	0	11	210	19.1	0	0	0	0

Additional pro statistics: Recovered two fumbles, 1985.

MARCUS ALLEN
Running Back—Los Angeles Raiders
Born March 26, 1960, at San Diego, Calif.
Height, 6.02. Weight, 205.
High School—San Diego, Calif., Lincoln.
Attended University of Southern California.
Brother of Damon Allen, quarterback with Edmonton Eskimos.

Named THE SPORTING NEWS NFL Player of the Year, 1985.
Named to THE SPORTING NEWS NFL All-Star Team, 1985.
Named THE SPORTING NEWS NFL Rookie of the Year, 1982.
Heisman Trophy winner, 1981.
Named THE SPORTING NEWS College Player of the Year, 1981.
Named as running back on THE SPORTING NEWS College All-America Team, 1981.
Established NFL record for most combined yards, season (2,314), 1985.
Tied NFL record for most consecutive games, 100 yards rushing (9), 1985.
Selected by Los Angeles Raiders in 1st round (10th player selected) of 1982 NFL draft.

Year Club	G.	Att.	Yds.	Avg.	TD.	P.C.	Yds.	Avg.	TD.	TD.	Pts.	F.
		—RUSHING—				PASS RECEIVING				—TOTAL—		
1982—Los Angeles Raiders NFL	9	160	697	4.4	*11	38	401	10.6	3	*14	*84	5
1983—Los Angeles Raiders NFL	15	266	1014	3.8	9	68	590	8.7	2	12	72	*14
1984—Los Angeles Raiders NFL	16	275	1168	4.2	13	64	758	11.8	5	*18	108	8
1985—Los Angeles Raiders NFL	16	380	*1759	4.6	11	67	555	8.3	3	14	84	3
Pro Totals—4 Years	56	1081	4638	4.3	44	237	2304	9.7	13	58	348	30

Additional pro statistics: Completed one of four pass attempts for 47 yards, 1982; recovered two fumbles, 1982 and 1985; attempted seven passes with four completions for 111 yards and three touchdowns and recovered two fumbles (including one in end zone for a touchdown), 1983; attempted four passes with one completion for 38 yards and recovered three fumbles, 1984; attempted two passes with one completion for 16 yards, 1985.

Played in AFC Championship Game following 1983 season.
Played in NFL Championship Game following 1983 season.
Played in Pro Bowl (NFL All-Star Game) following 1982, 1984 and 1985 seasons.

KURT DANIEL ALLERMAN
Linebacker—Detroit Lions
Born August 30, 1955, at Glennridge, N. J.
Height, 6.02. Weight, 232.
High School—Kinnelon, N. J.
Received bachelor of science degree in physical education and recreation from
Penn State University in 1977.

Selected by St. Louis in 3rd round (78th player selected) of 1977 NFL draft.
Released by St. Louis Cardinals, September 2, 1980; signed as free agent by Green Bay Packers, September 24, 1980.
Released by Green Bay Packers, September 6, 1982; claimed on waivers by St. Louis Cardinals, September 8, 1982.
Released by St. Louis Cardinals, August 26, 1985; signed as free agent by Detroit Lions, September 13, 1985.
On injured reserve with knee injury, December 3 through remainder of 1985 season.
St. Louis NFL, 1977 through 1979 and 1982 through 1984; Green Bay NFL, 1980 and 1981; Detroit NFL, 1985.
Games: 1977 (14), 1978 (15), 1979 (16), 1980 (13), 1981 (16), 1982 (9), 1983 (16), 1984 (16), 1985 (10). Total—125.
Pro statistics: Returned two kickoffs for 39 yards, 1977; recovered one fumble for 13 yards, 1978; returned two kickoffs for 16 yards and recovered two fumbles, 1979; recovered one fumble, 1981; returned one kickoff for 11 yards, 1983; recovered one fumble for two yards, 1984.

JOHN MICHAEL ALT
Offensive Tackle—Kansas City Chiefs
Born May 30, 1962, at Stuttgart, West Germany.
Height, 6.07. Weight, 278.
High School—Columbia Heights, Minn.
Attended University of Iowa.

Selected by Oklahoma in 3rd round (46th player selected) of 1984 USFL draft.
Selected by Kansas City in 1st round (21st player selected) of 1984 NFL draft.
Signed by Kansas City Chiefs, July 18, 1984.
On injured reserve with back injury, December 6 through remainder of 1985 season.
Kansas City NFL, 1984 and 1985.
Games: 1984 (15), 1985 (13). Total—28.

MORTEN ANDERSEN
Placekicker—New Orleans Saints
Born August 19, 1960, at Struer, Denmark.
Height, 6.02. Weight, 206.
High School—Indianapolis, Ind., Davis.
Attended Michigan State University.

Named to THE SPORTING NEWS NFL All-Star Team, 1985.
Named as placekicker on THE SPORTING NEWS College All-America Team, 1981.
Selected by New Orleans in 4th round (86th player selected) of 1982 NFL draft.
On injured reserve with sprained ankle, September 15 through November 19, 1982; activated, November 20, 1982.

Year Club	G.	XP.	XPM.	FG.	FGA.	Pts.
1982—New Orleans NFL...	8	6	0	2	5	12
1983—New Orleans NFL...	16	37	1	18	23	91
1984—New Orleans NFL...	16	34	0	20	27	94
1985—New Orleans NFL...	16	27	2	31	35	120
Pro Totals—4 Years.......	56	104	3	71	90	317

Played in Pro Bowl (NFL All-Star Game) following 1985 season.

ALFRED ANTHONY ANDERSON
Running Back—Minnesota Vikings
Born August 4, 1961, at Waco, Tex.
Height, 6.01. Weight, 213.
High School—Waco, Tex., Richfield.
Attended Baylor University.

Selected by San Antonio in 1984 USFL territorial draft.
Selected by Minnesota in 3rd round (67th player selected) of 1984 NFL draft.
Signed by Minnesota Vikings, May 18, 1984.

Year Club	G.	RUSHING Att.	Yds.	Avg.	TD.	PASS RECEIVING P.C.	Yds.	Avg.	TD.	TOTAL TD.	Pts.	F.
1984—Minnesota NFL..........................	16	201	773	3.8	2	17	102	6.0	1	3	18	8
1985—Minnesota NFL..........................	12	50	121	2.4	4	16	175	10.9	1	5	30	0
Pro Totals—2 Years	28	251	894	3.6	6	33	277	8.4	2	8	48	8

Year Club	G.	KICKOFF RETURNS No.	Yds.	Avg.	TD.
1984—Minnesota NFL.............	16	30	639	21.3	0
1985—Minnesota NFL.............	12		None		
Pro Totals—2 Years...........	28	30	639	21.3	0

Additional pro statistics: Attempted seven passes with three completions for 95 yards with two touchdowns and one interception and recovered two fumbles, 1984.

BRAD STEWART ANDERSON
Wide Receiver—Chicago Bears
Born January 21, 1961, at Glendale, Ariz.
Height, 6.02. Weight, 196.
High School—Phoenix, Ariz., Alhambra.
Attended Brigham Young University and received bachelor of arts degree in
accounting from University of Arizona.

Selected by Arizona in 1984 USFL territorial draft.
Selected by Chicago in 8th round (212th player selected) of 1984 NFL draft.
Signed by Chicago Bears, June 12, 1984.
On injured reserve with thumb injury, January 11 through remainder of 1985 season playoffs.

| | | | —PASS RECEIVING— | | | |
Year	Club	G.	P.C.	Yds.	Avg.	TD.
1984—Chicago NFL		12	3	77	25.7	1
1985—Chicago NFL		14	1	6	6.0	0
Pro Totals—2 Years		26	4	83	20.8	1

Played in NFC Championship Game following 1984 season.

DONALD CORTEZ ANDERSON
(Don)
Cornerback—Indianapolis Colts
Born July 8, 1963, at Detroit, Mich.
Height, 5.10. Weight, 185.
High School—Detroit, Mich., Cody.
Attended Purdue University.

Selected by Tampa Bay in 1st round (8th player selected) of 1985 USFL draft.
Selected by Indianapolis in 2nd round (32nd player selected) of 1985 NFL draft.
Signed by Indianapolis Colts, August 10, 1985.
On injured reserve with hamstring injury, September 12 through November 17, 1985; activated, November 18, 1985.
Indianapolis NFL, 1985.
Games: 1985 (5).
Pro statistics: Intercepted one pass for one yard and fumbled once, 1985.

GARY ALLAN ANDERSON
Placekicker—Pittsburgh Steelers
Born July 16, 1959, at Parys, Orange Free State, South Africa.
Height, 5.11. Weight, 170.
High School—Durban, South Africa, Brettonwood.
Received bachelor of science degree in management and accounting
from Syracuse University in 1982.
Son of Rev. Douglas Anderson, former pro soccer player in England.

Selected by Buffalo in 7th round (171st player selected) of 1982 NFL draft.
Released by Buffalo Bills, September 6, 1982; claimed on waivers by Pittsburgh Steelers, September 7, 1982.

| | | | —PLACE KICKING— | | | | |
Year	Club	G.	XP.	XPM.	FG.	FGA.	Pts.
1982—Pittsburgh NFL		9	22	0	10	12	52
1983—Pittsburgh NFL		16	38	1	27	31	119
1984—Pittsburgh NFL		16	45	0	24	32	117
1985—Pittsburgh NFL		16	40	0	*33	*42	139
Pro Totals—4 Years		57	145	1	94	117	427

Played in AFC Championship Game following 1984 season.
Played in Pro Bowl (NFL All-Star Game) following 1983 and 1985 seasons.

GARY WAYNE ANDERSON
Running Back—San Diego Chargers
Born April 18, 1961, at Columbia, Mo.
Height, 6.00. Weight, 190.
High School—Columbia, Mo., Hickman.
Attended University of Arkansas.

Named as running back on THE SPORTING NEWS USFL All-Star Team, 1985.
Selected by New Jersey in 1st round (5th player selected) of 1983 USFL draft.
Selected by San Diego in 1st round (20th player selected) of 1983 NFL draft.
USFL rights traded by New Jersey Generals to Tampa Bay Bandits for 1st round pick in 1984 draft, May 9, 1983.
Signed by Tampa Bay Bandits, May 9, 1983.
Granted roster exemption, May 9 through May 13, 1983; activated, May 14, 1983.
Released by Tampa Bay Bandits, September 27, 1985; signed by San Diego Chargers, September 30, 1985.
Granted roster exemption, September 30 through October 4, 1985; activated, October 5, 1985.

| | | | —RUSHING— | | | | PASS RECEIVING | | | | —TOTAL— | | |
Year	Club	G.	Att.	Yds.	Avg.	TD.	P.C.	Yds.	Avg.	TD.	TD.	Pts.	F.
1983—Tampa Bay USFL		8	97	516	5.3	4	29	347	12.0	0	4	24	7
1984—Tampa Bay USFL		18	268	1008	3.8	*19	66	682	10.3	2	*21	126	8
1985—Tampa Bay USFL		18	276	1207	4.4	16	72	678	9.4	4	20	120	11
1985—San Diego NFL		12	116	429	3.7	4	35	422	12.1	2	7	42	5
USFL Totals—3 Years		44	641	2731	4.3	39	167	1707	10.2	6	45	270	26
NFL Totals—1 Year		12	116	429	3.7	4	35	422	12.1	2	7	42	5
Pro Totals—4 Years		56	757	3160	4.2	43	202	2129	10.5	8	52	312	31

Year Club	G.	—PUNT RETURNS—				—KICKOFF RET.—		
		No.	Yds.	Avg.	TD.	No.	Yds.	Avg.TD.
1983—Tampa Bay USFL	8	2	—1	—0.5	0	3	47	15.7	0
1984—Tampa Day USFL	18	4	22	5.5	0			None
1985—Tampa Bay USFL	18			None		0	2	0.0	0
1985—San Diego NFL	12			None		13	302	23.2	1
USFL Totals—3 Years	44	6	21	3.5	0	3	49	16.3	0
NFL Totals—1 Year	12	0	0	0.0	0	13	302	23.2	1
Pro Totals—4 Years	56	6	21	3.5	0	16	351	21.9	1

Additional USFL statistics: Attempted one pass with no completions and recovered one fumble, 1983; attempted three passes with two completions for 44 yards, one touchdown and one interception and recovered two fumbles, 1984; attempted three passes with two completions for three yards and a touchdown and recovered five fumbles, 1985.

Additional NFL statistics: Recovered three fumbles, 1985.

GREGORY GERARD ANDERSON
(Greg)
Wide Receiver—Cleveland Browns
Born May 20, 1959, at New York, N.Y.
Height, 5.10. Weight, 170.
High School—Lakeland, Fla., Kathleen.
Received degree from Alabama State University.

Signed as free agent by New York Giants, May 4, 1982.
Released by New York Giants, August 31, 1982; signed by Birmingham Stallions, January 27, 1983.
Traded by Birmingham Stallions to Pittsburgh Maulers for draft pick, February 3, 1984.
Franchise disbanded, October 25, 1984.
Selected by Birmingham Stallions in USFL dispersal draft, December 6, 1984.
Traded by Birmingham Stallions to Arizona Outlaws for draft choice, February 20, 1985.
On developmental squad, February 24 through February 28, 1985; activated, March 1, 1985.
Released by Arizona Outlaws, August 16, 1985; signed as free agent by Cleveland Browns, April 20, 1986.
On developmental squad for 1 game with Arizona Outlaws in 1985.

Year Club	G.	P.C.	Yds.	Avg.	TD.
		—PASS RECEIVING—			
1983—Birmingham USFL	18	28	529	18.9	5
1984—Pittsburgh USFL	18	63	994	15.8	6
1985—Arizona USFL	17	51	915	17.9	5
Pro Totals—3 Years	53	142	2438	17.2	16

Additional pro statistics: Rushed three times for 39 yards, 1984; rushed once for minus 13 yards and fumbled once, 1985.

KENNETH ALLAN ANDERSON
(Ken)
Quarterback—Cincinnati Bengals
Born February 15, 1949, at Batavia, Ill.
Height, 6.03. Weight, 212.
High School—Batavia, Ill.
Received degree in mathematics from Augustana College and received degree from
Chase Law School at Northern Kentucky University in 1981.

Established NFL records for highest passing efficiency, game (20 or more attempts), 90.91 (20-22), November 10, 1974, against Pittsburgh Steelers; most consecutive seasons leading league in passing (2), 1974 and 1975; most consecutive completions, game (20), January 2, 1983, against Houston Oilers; highest completion percentage, season (70.55), 1982.

Led NFL quarterbacks in passing with 95.9 points in 1974, 94.1 points in 1975, 98.5 points in 1981 and 95.5 points in 1982.

Named THE SPORTING NEWS NFL Player of the Year, 1981.
Named to THE SPORTING NEWS AFC All-Star Team, 1975.
Named to THE SPORTING NEWS NFL All-Star Team, 1981.
Selected by Cincinnati in 3rd round (67th player selected) of 1971 NFL draft.

Year Club	G.	PASSING							RUSHING				—TOTAL—		
		Att.	Cmp.	Pct.	Gain	T.P.	P.I.	Avg.	Att.	Yds.	Avg.	TD.	TD.	Pts.	F.
1971—Cincinnati NFL	11	131	72	55.0	777	5	4	5.93	22	125	5.7	1	1	6	5
1972—Cincinnati NFL	13	301	171	56.8	1918	7	7	6.37	22	94	4.3	3	3	18	5
1973—Cincinnati NFL	14	329	179	54.4	2428	18	12	7.38	26	97	3.7	0	0	0	5
1974—Cincinnati NFL	13	328	*213	*64.9	*2667	18	10	*8.13	43	314	7.3	2	2	12	3
1975—Cincinnati NFL	13	377	228	60.5	*3169	21	11	8.41	49	188	3.8	2	2	12	4
1976—Cincinnati NFL	14	338	179	53.0	2367	19	14	7.00	31	134	4.3	1	1	6	3
1977—Cincinnati NFL	14	323	166	51.4	2145	11	11	6.64	26	128	4.9	2	2	12	5
1978—Cincinnati NFL	12	319	173	54.2	2219	10	22	6.96	29	167	5.8	1	1	6	8
1979—Cincinnati NFL	15	339	189	55.8	2340	16	10	6.90	28	235	8.4	2	2	12	1
1980—Cincinnati NFL	13	275	166	60.4	1778	6	13	6.47	16	122	7.6	0	0	0	1
1981—Cincinnati NFL	16	479	300	62.6	3754	29	10	7.84	46	320	7.0	1	1	6	5
1982—Cincinnati NFL	9	309	*218	*70.6	2495	12	9	8.07	25	85	3.4	4	4	24	1
1983—Cincinnati NFL	13	297	198	*66.7	2333	12	13	7.86	22	147	6.7	1	1	6	4
1984—Cincinnati NFL	11	275	175	63.6	2107	10	12	7.66	11	64	5.8	0	0	0	1
1985—Cincinnati NFL	3	32	16	50.0	170	2	0	5.31	1	0	0.0	0	0	0	1
Pro Totals—15 Years	184	4452	2643	59.4	32667	196	158	7.34	397	2220	5.6	20	20	120	52

Quarterback Rating Points: 1971 (53.4), 1972 (74.1), 1973 (81.5), 1974 (95.9), 1975 (94.1), 1976 (77.0), 1977 (69.8), 1978 (57.8), 1979 (80.9), 1980 (67.1), 1981 (98.5), 1982 (95.5), 1983 (85.6), 1984 (81.0), 1985 (86.7). Total—82.3.

Additional pro statistics: Recovered two fumbles and fumbled five times for minus nine yards, 1971; recovered three fumbles and fumbled five times for minus seven yards, 1973; recovered one fumble, 1974 and 1983; recovered one fumble and fumbled four times for minus eight yards, 1975; recovered two fumbles and fumbled five times for minus 13 yards, 1977; recovered three fumbles and fumbled eight times for minus eight yards, 1978; recovered two fumbles, 1980 and 1981; fumbled five times for minus 20 yards, 1981.

Played in AFC Championship Game following 1981 season.
Played in NFL Championship Game following 1981 season.
Played in Pro Bowl (NFL All-Star Game) following 1975, 1981 and 1982 seasons.

OTTIS JEROME ANDERSON
(O.J.)
Running Back—St. Louis Cardinals
Born January 19, 1957, at West Palm Beach, Fla.
Height, 6.02. Weight, 225.
High School—West Palm Beach, Fla., Forest Hill.
Received degree in physical education from University of Miami (Fla.).

Tied NFL record for most 100-yard games by rookie, season (9), 1979.
Named THE SPORTING NEWS NFL Rookie of the Year, 1979.
Named THE SPORTING NEWS NFC Player of the Year, 1979.
Named to THE SPORTING NEWS NFC All-Star Team, 1979.
Selected by St. Louis in 1st round (8th player selected) of 1979 NFL draft.

			—RUSHING—			PASS RECEIVING				—TOTAL—		
Year	Club	G.	Att.	Yds.	Avg.	TD.	P.C.	Yds.	Avg.	TD.	TD.	Pts.	F.
1979—St. Louis NFL		16	331	1605	4.8	8	41	308	7.5	2	10	60	10
1980—St. Louis NFL		16	301	1352	4.5	9	36	308	8.6	0	9	54	5
1981—St. Louis NFL		16	328	1376	4.2	9	51	387	7.6	0	9	54	13
1982—St. Louis NFL		8	145	587	4.0	3	14	106	7.6	0	3	18	2
1983—St. Louis NFL		15	296	1270	4.3	5	54	459	8.5	1	6	36	10
1984—St. Louis NFL		15	289	1174	4.1	6	70	611	8.7	2	8	48	8
1985—St. Louis NFL		9	117	479	4.1	4	23	225	9.8	0	4	24	3
Pro Totals—7 Years		95	1807	7843	4.3	44	289	2404	8.3	5	49	294	51

Additional pro statistics: Recovered one fumble, 1979, 1982, 1984 and 1985; attempted one pass with no completions, 1979; recovered four fumbles, 1980; recovered three fumbles, 1981 and 1983.
Played in Pro Bowl (NFL All-Star Game) following 1979 and 1980 seasons.

ROGER JOHN ANDERSON
(Known by middle name.)
Linebacker—Green Bay Packers
Born February 14, 1956, at Waukesha, Wis.
Height, 6.03. Weight, 229.
High School—Waukesha, Wis., South.
Received bachelor of arts degree in environmental studies from University of Michigan in 1978.

Selected by Green Bay in 1st round (26th player selected) of 1978 NFL draft.
On injured reserve with broken arm, December 6 through remainder of 1978 season.
On injured reserve with broken arm, August 28 through October 29, 1979; activated, October 30, 1979.
On injured reserve with broken arm, November 5 through remainder of 1980 season.

		—INTERCEPTIONS—				
Year	Club	G.	No.	Yds.	Avg.	TD.
1978—Green Bay NFL		13	5	27	5.4	0
1979—Green Bay NFL		7		None		
1980—Green Bay NFL		9		None		
1981—Green Bay NFL		16	3	12	4.0	0
1982—Green Bay NFL		9	3	22	7.3	0
1983—Green Bay NFL		16	5	54	10.8	1
1984—Green Bay NFL		16	3	24	8.0	0
1985—Green Bay NFL		16	2	2	1.0	0
Pro Totals—8 Years		102	21	141	6.7	1

Additional pro statistics: Recovered one fumble, 1978 through 1980 and 1983 through 1985; scored four points, kicking one field goal on one attempt and one extra point on two attempts, 1979; recovered four fumbles for 22 yards, 1981; recovered two fumbles, 1982; returned one kickoff for 14 yards, 1985.

STUART NOEL ANDERSON
Linebacker—Washington Redskins
Born December 25, 1959, at Mathews, Va.
Height, 6.01. Weight, 224.
High School—Cardinal, Va., Mathews.
Received bachelor of science degree in special education from University of Virginia in 1982.

Selected by Kansas City in 4th round (104th player selected) of 1982 NFL draft.
Released by Kansas City Chiefs, September 6, 1982; signed as free agent by Washington Redskins, December 23, 1982.
On injured reserve with knee injury, January 22, 1983 through remainder of 1982 season playoffs.
USFL rights traded with rights to linebacker Glenn Howard by Washington Federals to Philadelphia Stars for rights to wide receiver Walker Lee and defensive end Ron Estay, October 26, 1982.
Released by Washington Redskins, August 27, 1984; re-signed by Redskins, August 28, 1984.
On injured reserve with groin pull, September 12 through November 21, 1984.

Awarded on procedural waivers to Cleveland Browns, November 23, 1984.
Released by Cleveland Browns, August 5, 1985; signed as free agent by Washington Redskins, August 7, 1985.
Washington NFL, 1982, 1983 and 1985; Washington (2)-Cleveland (4) NFL, 1984.
Games: 1982 (2), 1983 (10), 1984 (0), 1985 (10). Total—40.
Pro statistics: Returned one kickoff for seven yards, 1982.
Played in NFC Championship Game following 1983 season.
Played in NFL Championship Game following 1983 season.

ALAN V. ANDREWS
Tight End—Pittsburgh Steelers
Born February 15, 1962, at Columbus, Ga.
Height, 6.05. Weight, 235.
High School—Roxbury, N.J., Succasunna.
Received bachelor of arts degree in communications
from Rutgers University in 1985.

Selected by New Jersey in 1985 USFL territorial draft.
Selected by Pittsburgh in 7th round (187th player selected) of 1985 NFL draft.
Signed by Pittsburgh Steelers, July 16, 1985.
On physically unable to perform/reserve with hamstring injury, July 27 through entire 1985 season.

GEORGE ELDON ANDREWS II
Linebacker—Los Angeles Rams
Born November 28, 1955, at Omaha, Neb.
Height, 6.03. Weight, 221.
High School—Omaha, Neb., Burke
Received bachelor of business administration degree from
University of Nebraska in 1978.

Selected by Los Angeles in 1st round (19th player selected) of 1979 NFL draft.
On injured reserve with knee injury, November 14 through remainder of 1984 season.
On injured reserve with knee injury, September 1 through entire 1985 season.
Los Angeles Rams NFL, 1979 through 1984.
Games: 1979 (16), 1980 (13), 1981 (15), 1982 (9), 1983 (16), 1984 (11). Total—80.
Pro statistics: Recovered one fumble, 1979, 1980 and 1982; caught one pass for two yards, 1979; intercepted one pass
for 22 yards, 1983; recovered four fumbles for nine yards, 1984.
Played in NFC Championship Game following 1979 season.
Played in NFL Championship Game following 1979 season.

THOMAS EDWARD ANDREWS
(Tom)
Offensive Tackle-Center—Chicago Bears
Born January 11, 1962, at Parma, O.
Height, 6.04. Weight, 267.
High School—Parma, O., Padua Franciscian.
Attended University of Louisville.

Selected by Memphis in 6th round (123rd player selected) of 1984 USFL draft.
Selected by Chicago in 4th round (98th player selected) of 1984 NFL draft.
Signed by Chicago Bears, July 2, 1984.
Released by Chicago Bears, August 27, 1985; re-signed by Bears, September 3, 1985.
Chicago NFL, 1984 and 1985.
Games: 1984 (7), 1985 (14). Total—21.
Played in NFC Championship Game following 1984 and 1985 seasons.
Played in NFL Championship Game following 1985 season.

WILLIAM L. ANDREWS
Running Back—Atlanta Falcons
Born December 25, 1955, at Thomasville, Ga.
Height, 6.00. Weight, 213.
High School—Thomasville, Ga.
Attended Auburn University

Tied NFL record for most seasons, 2,000 yards rushing and receiving combined (2).
Named to THE SPORTING NEWS NFL All-Star Team, 1983.
Selected by Atlanta in 3rd round (79th player selected) of 1979 NFL draft.
On injured reserve with knee injury, August 24 through entire 1984 season.
On physically unable to perform/reserve with knee injury, August 20 through entire 1985 season.

Year Club	G.	Att.	RUSHING Yds.	Avg.	TD.	PASS RECEIVING P.C.	Yds.	Avg.	TD.	TOTAL TD.	Pts.	F.
1979—Atlanta NFL	15	239	1023	4.3	3	39	309	7.9	2	5	30	5
1980—Atlanta NFL	16	265	1308	4.9	4	51	456	8.9	1	5	30	6
1981—Atlanta NFL	16	289	1301	4.5	10	81	735	9.1	2	12	72	12
1982—Atlanta NFL	9	139	573	4.1	5	42	503	12.0	2	7	42	1
1983—Atlanta NFL	16	331	1567	4.7	7	59	609	10.3	4	11	66	6
Pro Totals—5 Years	72	1263	5772	4.6	29	272	2612	9.6	11	40	240	30

Additional pro statistics: Recovered one fumble, 1979 and 1982; recovered two fumbles, 1980 and 1983; attempted
one pass with no completions, 1983.
Played in Pro Bowl (NFL All-Star Game) following 1980 through 1983 seasons.

TYRONE ANTHONY
Running Back
Born March 3, 1962, at Winston-Salem, N.C.
Height, 5.11. Weight, 212.
High School—Clemmons, N.C., West Forsythe.
Attended University of North Carolina.

Selected by Philadelphia in 1984 USFL territorial draft.
Selected by New Orleans in 3rd round (69th player selected) of 1984 NFL draft.
Signed by New Orleans Saints, June 26, 1984.
Released by New Orleans Saints after failing physical with back injury, May 19, 1986.

Year Club	G.	Att.	—RUSHING— Yds.	Avg.	TD.	P.C.	PASS RECEIVING Yds.	Avg.	TD.	TD.	—TOTAL— Pts.	F.
1984—New Orleans NFL	15	20	105	5.3	1	12	113	9.4	0	1	6	1
1985—New Orleans NFL	16	17	65	3.8	0	28	185	6.6	0	0	0	0
Pro Totals—2 Years	31	37	170	4.6	1	40	298	7.5	0	1	6	1

Year Club	G.	KICKOFF RETURNS No.	Yds.	Avg.	TD.
1984—New Orleans NFL	15	22	490	22.3	0
1985—New Orleans NFL	16	23	476	20.7	0
Pro Totals—2 Years	31	45	966	21.5	0

Additional pro statistics: Recovered one fumble, 1984.

DAVID ARCHER
(Dave)
Quarterback—Atlanta Falcons
Born February 15, 1962, at Fayetteville, N.C.
Height, 6.02. Weight, 203.
High School—Soda Springs, Ida.
Attended Snow College and Iowa State University.

Selected by Denver in 9th round (171st player selected) of 1984 USFL draft.
Signed as free agent by Atlanta Falcons, May 2, 1984.

Year Club	G.	Att.	Cmp.	—PASSING— Pct.	Gain	T.P.	P.I.	Avg.	Att.	—RUSHING— Yds.	Avg.	TD.	TD.	—TOTAL— Pts.	F.
1984—Atlanta NFL	2	18	11	61.1	181	1	1	10.06	6	38	6.3	0	0	0	1
1985—Atlanta NFL	16	312	161	51.6	1992	7	17	6.38	70	347	5.0	2	2	12	9
Pro Totals—2 Years	18	330	172	52.1	2173	8	18	6.58	76	385	5.1	2	2	12	10

Quarterback Rating Points: 1984 (90.3), 1985 (56.5). Total—58.0.
Additional pro statistics: Recovered two fumbles, 1985.

WILLIAM DONOVAN ARD
(Billy)
Guard—New York Giants
Born March 12, 1959, at East Orange, N.J.
Height, 6.03. Weight, 270.
High School—Watchung, N.J.
Attended Wake Forest University.
Brother of Pat Ard, defensive end at Boston College.

Named as guard on THE SPORTING NEWS College All-America Team, 1980.
Selected by New York Giants in 8th round (221st player selected) of 1981 NFL draft.
On injured reserve with knee injury, December 11 through remainder of 1984 season.
New York Giants NFL, 1981 through 1985.
Games: 1981 (13), 1982 (9), 1983 (16), 1984 (15), 1985 (16). Total—69.
Pro statistics: Recovered one fumble, 1981.

OBED CHUKWUMA ARIRI
Name pronounced Ah-REER-ee.

(Middle name means "God only knows" in Nigerian.)
Placekicker—Indianapolis Colts
Born April 7, 1956, at Owerri, Nigeria.
Height, 5.08. Weight, 165.
High School—Owerri, Nigeria, Holy Ghost College.
Received bachelor of science degree in industrial management and economics
from Clemson University in 1980.

Selected by Baltimore in 7th round (178th player selected) of 1981 NFL draft.
Released by Baltimore Colts, August 31, 1981; signed as free agent by Buffalo Bills, April 15, 1982.
Released by Buffalo Bills, August 23, 1982; signed by Washington Federals, October 27, 1982.
Released by Washington Federals, March 28, 1983; signed as free agent by New Jersey Generals, November 17, 1983.
Released by New Jersey Generals, February 13, 1984; signed as free agent by Tampa Bay Buccaneers, April 25, 1984.
Released by Tampa Bay Buccaneers, August 22, 1984; re-signed by Buccaneers, August 28, 1984.
Released by Tampa Bay Buccaneers, August 27, 1985; signed as free agent by Indianapolis Colts, April 1, 1986.

		—PLACE KICKING—					
Year	Club	G.	XP.	XPM.	FG.	FGA.	Pts.
1983—Washington USFL...		4	3	2	3	7	12
1984—Tampa Bay NFL.....		16	38	2	19	26	95
Pro Totals—2 Years.......		20	41	4	22	33	107

ADGER ARMSTRONG
Running Back—Tampa Bay Buccaneers
Born June 21, 1957, at Houston, Tex.
Height, 6.00. Weight, 230.
High Schools—Houston, Tex., Cyfair and Jersey Village.
Attended Texas A&M University.

Signed as free agent by Dallas Cowboys, May, 1979.
Released by Dallas Cowboys, July 30, 1979; signed as free agent by Houston Oilers, May 23, 1980.
Released by Houston Oilers, September 1, 1980; re-signed by Oilers, September 2, 1980.
On injured reserve with knee injury, September 7 through November 18, 1982; activated, November 19, 1982.
Released by Houston Oilers, August 29, 1983; signed as free agent by Tampa Bay Buccaneers, October 5, 1983.

			—RUSHING—			PASS RECEIVING				—TOTAL—		
Year	Club	G.	Att.	Yds.	Avg.	TD.	P.C.	Yds.	Avg.	TD.	TD.	Pts.	F.
1980—Houston NFL		16		None				None			0	0	0
1981—Houston NFL		16	31	146	4.7	0	29	278	9.6	1	1	6	2
1982—Houston NFL		6	8	15	1.9	0	12	75	6.3	0	0	0	0
1983—Tampa Bay NFL		11	7	30	4.3	0	15	173	11.5	2	2	12	0
1984—Tampa Bay NFL		15	10	34	3.4	2	22	180	8.2	3	5	30	1
1985—Tampa Bay NFL		16	2	6	3.0	0	2	4	2.0	1	1	6	0
Pro Totals—6 Years		80	58	231	4.0	2	80	710	8.9	7	9	54	3

Additional pro statistics: Returned three kickoffs for 36 yards, 1981; returned one kickoff for 10 yards, 1983; recovered one fumble, 1983 through 1985.

HARVEY LEE ARMSTRONG
Nose Tackle—Indianapolis Colts
Born December 29, 1959, at Houston, Tex.
Height, 6.02. Weight, 265.
High School—Houston, Tex., Kashmere.
Received degree in business from Southern Methodist University.

Selected by Philadelphia in 7th round (190th player selected) of 1982 NFL draft.
Released by Philadelphia Eagles, August 20, 1985; signed as free agent by Indianapolis Colts, May 21, 1986.
Philadelphia NFL, 1982 through 1984.
Games: 1982 (8), 1983 (16), 1984 (16). Total—40.
Pro statistics: Recovered two fumbles, 1983.

JAMES EDWARD ARNOLD
(Jim)
Punter—Kansas City Chiefs
Born January 31, 1961, at Dalton, Ga.
Height, 6.02. Weight, 220.
High School—Dalton, Ga.
Attended Vanderbilt University.

Named as punter on THE SPORTING NEWS College All-America Team, 1982.
Led NFL in punting yards with 4,397 in 1984.
Selected by Kansas City in 5th round (119th player selected) of 1983 NFL draft.

		—PUNTING—			
Year	Club	G.	No.	Avg.	Blk.
1983—Kansas City NFL		16	93	39.9	0
1984—Kansas City NFL		16	*98	*44.9	0
1985—Kansas City NFL		16	*93	41.2	*2
Pro Totals—3 Years		48	284	42.0	2

Additional pro statistics: Rushed once for no yards, recovered two fumbles and fumbled once for minus nine yards, 1984.

WALTER HENSLEE ARNOLD
(Walt)
Tight End—Kansas City Chiefs
Born August 31, 1958, at Galveston, Tex.
Height, 6.03. Weight, 221.
High School—Los Alamos, N. M.
Attended University of New Mexico.

Signed as free agent by Los Angeles Rams, May 29, 1980.
Released by Los Angeles Rams, August 31, 1982; signed as free agent by Houston Oilers, September 7, 1982.
Released by Houston Oilers, August 29, 1983; re-signed by Oilers, September 21, 1983.
Released by Houston Oilers, August 27, 1984; signed as free agent by Washington Redskins, September 5, 1984.
Released by Washington Redskins, October 3, 1984; signed as free agent by Kansas City Chiefs, October 9, 1984.

Year Club	G.	P.C.	Yds.	Avg.	TD.
				—PASS RECEIVING—	
1980—Los Angeles NFL..........	16	5	75	15.0	1
1981—Los Angeles NFL..........	16	20	212	10.6	2
1982—Houston NFL.................	9			None	
1983—Houston NFL.................	13	12	137	11.4	1
1984—Wa. (4)-KC (10) NFL...	14	11	95	8.6	1
1985—Kansas City NFL..........	16	28	339	12.1	1
Pro Totals—6 Years............	84	76	858	11.3	6

Additional pro statistics: Returned two kickoffs for nine yards, 1985.

WALKER LEE ASHLEY
(Walker Lee)
Linebacker—Minnesota Vikings
Born July 28, 1960, at Bayonne, N.J.
Height, 6.00. Weight, 231.
High School—Jersey City, N.J., Snyder.
Received degree in community development from Penn State University.

Selected by Philadelphia in 1983 USFL territorial draft.
Selected by Minnesota in 3rd round (73rd player selected) of 1983 NFL draft.
Signed by Minnesota Vikings, June 16, 1983.
On injured reserve with ruptured Achilles tendon, August 20 through entire 1985 season.
Minnesota NFL, 1983 and 1984.
Games: 1983 (15), 1984 (15). Total—30.

JIM VICTOR DANIEL ASMUS
Placekicker—Washington Redskins
Born December 2, 1958, at Meppal, Holland.
Height, 6.01. Weight, 195.
High School—La Puente, Calif.
Attended Mt. San Antonio College and University of Hawaii.

Signed as free agent by Philadelphia Eagles, May 16, 1981.
Released by Philadelphia Eagles, August 25, 1981; claimed on waivers by New Orleans Saints, August 27, 1981.
Released by New Orleans Saints, August 31, 1981; signed as free agent by Buffalo Bills, March 20, 1982.
Released by Buffalo Bills, August 17, 1982; claimed on waivers by Miami Dolphins, August 18, 1982.
Released by Miami Dolphins, August 25, 1982, signed as free agent by Arizona Wranglers, February 25, 1983.
Released by Arizona Wranglers, May 11, 1983; signed as free agent by Philadelphia Eagles, May 30, 1983.
Released by Philadelphia Eagles, August 22, 1983; re-signed by Eagles after clearing procedural waivers, May 7, 1984.
Released by Philadelphia Eagles, August 21, 1984; signed as free agent by Denver Gold, April 18, 1985.
Released by Denver Gold, July 31, 1985; signed as free agent by Washington Redskins, March 27, 1986.

Year Club	G.	No.	Avg.	Blk.	XP.	XPM.	FG.	FGA.	Pts.
		—PUNTING—				**——PLACE KICKING——**			
1983—Arizona USFL..	10	52	38.7	....	14	1	10	19	44
1985—Denver USFL	10	30	37.4	....	30	1	11	18	63
Pro Totals—2 Years..	20	82	38.2	....	44	2	21	37	107

Additional pro statistics: Attempted one pass with one completion for 28 yards and rushed once for minus 15 yards, 1983.

JESS GERALD ATKINSON
Placekicker—Washington Redskins
Born December 11, 1961, at Ann Arbor, Mich.
Height, 5.10. Weight, 162.
High School—Camy Springs, Md., Crossland.
Received bachelor of science degree in business from University of Maryland.

Selected by Baltimore in 6th round (87th player selected) of 1985 USFL draft.
Signed as free agent by New England Patriots, May 21, 1985.
Released by New England Patriots, August 19, 1985; signed as free agent by New York Giants, September 17, 1985.
Released by Ney York Giants, October 28, 1985; awarded on waivers to St. Louis Cardinals, October 29, 1985.
Released by St. Louis Cardinals, November 13, 1985; signed as free agent by Washington Redskins, May 8, 1986.

Year Club	G.	XP.	XPM.	FG.	FGA.	Pts.
			—PLACE KICKING—			
1985—NYG(6)-StL(2) NFL	8	17	1	10	18	†53

†Includes six points scored on a 14-yard run for a touchdown.

SCOTT EUGENE AUER
Name pronounced Our.
Guard-Offensive Tackle—Kansas City Chiefs
Born October 4, 1961, at Fort Wayne, Ind.
Height, 6.04. Weight, 255.
High School—Fort Wayne, Ind., Elmhurst.
Attended Michigan State University.

Selected by Michigan in 1984 USFL territorial draft.
Selected by Kansas City in 9th round (229th player selected) of 1984 NFL draft.

Signed by Kansas City Chiefs, July 9, 1984.
Released by Kansas City Chiefs, September 2, 1985; re-signed by Chiefs, October 9, 1985.
Kansas City NFL, 1984 and 1985.
Games: 1984 (16), 1985 (7). Total—23.

LORENZO DOWE AUGHTMAN

(Known by middle name.)

Offensive Lineman—Dallas Cowboys

Born January 28, 1961, at Brewton, Ala.
Height, 6.02. Weight, 258.
High School—Brewton, Ala., T.R. Miller.
Attended Auburn University.

Selected by Birmingham in 1984 USFL territorial draft.
Selected by Dallas in 11th round (304th player selected) of 1984 NFL draft.
Signed by Dallas Cowboys, June 7, 1984.
On injured reserve with shoulder injury, August 20 through entire 1985 season.
Dallas NFL, 1984.
Games: 1984 (7).

CLIFF AUSTIN

Running Back—Atlanta Falcons

Born March 2, 1960, at Atlanta, Ga.
Height, 6.00. Weight, 207.
High School—Avondale Estates, Ga.
Attended Clemson University.

Selected by Washington in 1983 USFL territorial draft.
Selected by New Orleans in 3rd round (66th player selected) of 1983 NFL draft.
Signed by New Orleans Saints, June 21, 1983.
On injured reserve with separated shoulder and hamstring injuries, August 30 through October 7, 1983; activated, October 8, 1983.
Released by New Orleans Saints, August 27, 1984; signed as free agent by Atlanta Falcons, September 4, 1984.
On injured reserve with sprained ankle, December 10 through remainder of 1985 season.

| | | —RUSHING— | | | PASS RECEIVING | | | | —TOTAL— | | |
Year Club	G.	Att.	Yds.	Avg.	TD.	P.C.	Yds.	Avg.	TD.	TD.	Pts.	F.
1983—New Orleans NFL	11	4	16	4.0	0	2	25	12.5	0	0	0	0
1984—Atlanta NFL	15	4	7	1.8	0		None			0	0	0
1985—Atlanta NFL	14	20	110	5.5	0	1	21	21.0	0	1	6	0
Pro Totals—3 Years	40	28	133	4.8	0	3	46	15.3	0	1	6	0

| | | KICKOFF RETURNS | | | |
Year Club	G.	No.	Yds.	Avg.	TD.
1983—New Orleans NFL	11	7	112	16.0	0
1984—Atlanta NFL	15	4	77	19.3	0
1985—Atlanta NFL	14	39	838	21.5	1
Pro Totals—3 Years	40	50	1027	20.5	1

JOHN G. AYERS

Cornerback—Atlanta Falcons

Born September 6, 1963, at Oakland, Calif.
Height, 5.11. Weight, 187.
High School—Richmond, Calif., Salesian.
Attended Contra Costa College and University of Illinois.

Selected by Atlanta in 11th round (284th player selected) of 1985 NFL draft.
Signed by Atlanta Falcons, July 8, 1985.
On injured reserve with shoulder injury, August 19 through entire 1985 season.

JOHN MILTON AYERS

Guard—San Francisco 49ers

Born April 14, 1953, at Carrizo Springs, Tex.
Height, 6.05. Weight, 265.
High School—Carrizo Springs, Tex.
Attended University of Texas and West Texas State University.

Selected by San Francisco in 8th round (223rd player selected) of 1976 NFL draft.
On injured reserve entire 1976 season.
On inactive list, September 19, 1982.
San Francisco NFL, 1977 through 1985.
Games: 1977 (14), 1978 (16), 1979 (16), 1980 (16), 1981 (16), 1982 (8), 1983 (16), 1984 (16), 1985 (16). Total—134.
Pro statistics: Recovered one fumble, 1978 and 1984.
Played in NFC Championship Game following 1981, 1983 and 1984 seasons.
Played in NFL Championship Game following 1981 and 1984 seasons.

—DID YOU KNOW—

That the Jets' 62 points on November 17 against Tampa Bay were the highest number of points scored in the NFL in a single game since 1973?

JOSEPH K. AZELBY
(Joe)
Linebacker—Indianapolis Colts
Born March 5, 1962, at New York, N.Y.
Height, 6.02. Weight, 230.
High School—Oradell, N.J., Bergen Catholic.
Received bachelor of arts degree in economics from Harvard University in 1984.

Selected by Buffalo in 10th round (263rd player selected) of 1984 NFL draft.
Released by Buffalo Bills, August 27, 1984; re-signed by Bills, September 12, 1984.
Released by Buffalo Bills, August 19, 1985; signed as free agent by San Francisco 49ers, February 17, 1986.
Released by San Francisco 49ers after failing physical, April 7, 1986; signed as free agent by Indianapolis Colts, May 12, 1986.
Buffalo NFL, 1984.
Games: 1984 (14).
Pro statistics: Recovered one fumble, 1984.

MICHEAL JAMES BAAB
(Mike)
Center—Cleveland Browns
Born December 6, 1959, at Fort Worth, Tex.
Height, 6.04. Weight, 270.
High School—Euless, Tex., Trinity.
Attended Tarrant County Junior College, Austin Community College
and University of Texas.

Selected by Cleveland in 5th round (115th player selected) of 1982 NFL draft.
Cleveland NFL, 1982 through 1985.
Games: 1982 (7), 1983 (15), 1984 (16), 1985 (16). Total—54.
Pro statistics: Fumbled once for minus 11 yards, 1984; rushed once for no yards and fumbled once for minus two yards, 1985.

STEVEN WILLIAM BAACK
Name pronounced Bock.
(Steve)
Nose Tackle-Defensive End—Detroit Lions
Born November 16, 1960, at Ames, Ia.
Height, 6.04. Weight, 265.
High School—John Day, Ore., Grant Union.
Received bachelor of science degree in psychology from University of Oregon in 1984.

Selected by Philadelphia in 9th round (184th player selected) of 1984 USFL draft.
Selected by Detroit in 3rd round (75th player selected) of 1984 NFL draft.
Signed by Detroit Lions, June 20, 1984.
Detroit NFL, 1984 and 1985.
Games: 1984 (16), 1985 (16). Total—32.
Pro statistics: Recovered one fumble, 1985.

CHRISTOPHER ROBERT BABYAR
Name pronounced Bab-YAR.
(Chris)
Guard—Buffalo Bills
Born June 1, 1962, at Bloomington, Ill.
Height, 6.04. Weight, 264.
High School—Roselle, Ill., Lake Park.
Received bachelor of science degree in political science
from University of Illinois in 1985.

Selected by Orlando in 9th round (124th player selected) of 1985 USFL draft.
Selected by Buffalo in 10th round (253rd player selected) of 1985 NFL draft.
Signed by Buffalo Bills, July 19, 1985.
On injured reserve with knee injury, September 3 through entire 1985 season.

CHRIS BAHR
Placekicker—Los Angeles Raiders
Born February 3, 1953, at State College, Pa.
Height, 5.10. Weight, 170.
High School—State College, Pa., Neshaminy.
Received bachelor of science degree in biology from Penn State University in 1976
and attending Chase Law School at Northern Kentucky University.
Brother of Matt Bahr, placekicker with Cleveland Browns.

Named to THE SPORTING NEWS AFC All-Star Team, 1977.
Named as placekicker on THE SPORTING NEWS College All-America Team, 1975.
Selected by Cincinnati in 2nd round (51st player selected) of 1976 NFL draft.
Released by Cincinnati Bengals, August 26, 1980; signed as free agent by Oakland Raiders, September 1, 1980.
Franchise transferred to Los Angeles, May 7, 1982.
Played with Philadelphia Atoms of North American Soccer League, 1975 (22 games, 11 goals, 2 assists).

Year Club	G.	XP.	XPM.	FG.	FGA.	Pts.
1976—Cincinnati NFL	14	39	3	14	27	81
1977—Cincinnati NFL	14	25	1	19	27	82
1978—Cincinnati NFL	16	26	3	16	30	74
1979—Cincinnati NFL	16	40	2	13	23	79
1980—Oakland NFL	16	41	3	19	37	98
1981—Oakland NFL	16	27	6	14	24	69
1982—L.A. Raiders NFL	9	*32	1	10	16	62
1983—L.A. Raiders NFL	16	51	2	21	27	114
1984—L.A. Raiders NFL	16	40	2	20	27	100
1985—L.A. Raiders NFL	16	40	2	20	32	100
Pro Totals—10 Years	149	361	25	166	270	859

Additional pro statistics: Punted twice for 44.0 average, 1977; punted four times for 27.0 average, 1978; punted twice for 21.5 average, 1981.

Played in AFC Championship Game following 1980 and 1983 seasons.

Played in NFL Championship Game following 1980 and 1983 seasons.

MATTHEW DAVID BAHR
(Matt)
Placekicker—Cleveland Browns

Born July 6, 1956, at Philadelphia; Pa.

Height, 5.10. Weight, 175.

High School—Langhorne, Pa., Neshaminy.

Received bachelor of science degree in electrical engineering from Penn State University in 1979; attending Carnegie-Mellon University for master's degree in industrial administration.

Brother of Chris Bahr, placekicker with Los Angeles Raiders.

Selected by Pittsburgh in 6th round (165th player selected) of 1979 NFL draft.

Released by Pittsburgh Steelers, August 31, 1981; signed as free agent by San Francisco 49ers, September 8, 1981.

Traded by San Francisco 49ers to Cleveland Browns for 9th round pick in 1983 draft, October 6, 1981.

Played with Colorado Caribous and Tulsa Roughnecks of North American Soccer League, 1978 (26 games, 3 assists).

Year Club	G.	XP.	XPM.	FG.	FGA.	Pts.
1979—Pittsburgh NFL	16	*50	2	18	30	104
1980—Pittsburgh NFL	16	39	3	19	28	96
1981—SF (4)-Cle (11) NFL	15	34	0	15	26	79
1982—Cleveland NFL	9	17	0	7	15	38
1983—Cleveland NFL	16	38	2	21	24	101
1984—Cleveland NFL	16	25	0	24	32	97
1985—Cleveland NFL	16	35	0	14	18	77
Pro Totals—7 Years	104	238	7	118	173	592

Played in AFC Championship Game following 1979 season.

Played in NFL Championship Game following 1979 season.

EDWIN RAYMOND BAILEY
Guard—Seattle Seahawks

Born May 15, 1959, at Savannah, Ga.

Height, 6.05. Weight, 265.

High School—Savannah, Ga., Tompkins.

Attended South Carolina State College.

Selected by Seattle in 5th round (114th player selected) of 1981 NFL draft.

On injured reserve with knee injury, November 10 through December 7, 1984; activated, December 8, 1984.

Seattle NFL, 1981 through 1985.

Games: 1981 (16), 1982 (9), 1983 (16), 1984 (12), 1985 (16). Total—69.

Pro statistics: Recovered one fumble, 1982.

Played in AFC Championship Game following 1983 season.

STACEY DWAYNE BAILEY
Wide Receiver—Atlanta Falcons

Born February 10, 1960, at San Rafael, Calif.

Height, 6.00. Weight, 160.

High School—San Rafael, Calif., Terra Linda.

Attended San Jose State University.

Selected by Atlanta in 3rd round (63rd player selected) of 1982 NFL draft.

On inactive list, September 12 and September 19, 1982.

Year Club	G.	P.C.	Yds.	Avg.	TD.
1982—Atlanta NFL	5	2	24	12.0	1
1983—Atlanta NFL	15	55	881	16.0	6
1984—Atlanta NFL	16	67	1138	17.0	6
1985—Atlanta NFL	15	30	364	12.1	0
Pro Totals—4 Years	51	154	2407	15.6	13

Additional pro statistics: Fumbled once, 1982 through 1985; rushed twice for minus five yards and recovered one fumble, 1983; rushed once for minus three yards, 1985.

—DID YOU KNOW—

That the 1985 season was the first since 1979 in which there were no tie games in the NFL?

WILLIAM DONALD BAILEY
(Don)
Center—Indianapolis Colts
Born March 24, 1961, at Miami, Fla.
Height, 6.04. Weight, 257.
High School—Hialeah, Fla., Miami Lakes.
Attended University of Miami (Fla.).

Selected by Tampa Bay in 9th round (108th player selected) of 1983 USFL draft.
Selected by Denver in 11th round (283rd player selected) of 1983 NFL draft.
Signed by Denver Broncos, May 18, 1983.
Released by Denver Broncos, August 22, 1983; signed as free agent by Tampa Bay Buccaneers, October 25, 1983.
On injured reserve with back injury, November 2 through remainder of 1983 season.
Released by Tampa Bay Buccaneers, August 20, 1984; signed as free agent by Indianapolis Colts, October 10, 1984.
Active for 1 game with Tampa Bay Buccaneers in 1983; did not play.
Tampa Bay NFL, 1983; Indianapolis NFL, 1984 and 1985.
Games: 1984 (10), 1985 (10). Total—20.
Pro statistics: Recovered one fumble and fumbled twice for minus 27 yards, 1984.

WILLIAM ERNEST BAIN
(Bill)
Offensive Tackle
Born August 9, 1952, at Los Angeles, Calif.
Height, 6.04. Weight, 285.
High School—Santa Fe Springs, Calif., St. Paul.
Attended University of Colorado, San Diego City College and received bachelor of arts degree
in public administration from University of Southern California.

Named as guard on THE SPORTING NEWS College All-America Team, 1974.
Selected by Green Bay in 2nd round (47th player selected) of 1975 NFL draft.
Traded by Green Bay Packers to Denver Broncos for a draft choice, August 31, 1976 (3rd round pick in 1977 draft).
On injured reserve with knee injury entire 1977 season.
Released by Denver Broncos, September 8, 1978; signed as free agent by New York Giants, October 30, 1978.
Released by New York Giants, November 9, 1978; re-signed by Giants, November 15, 1978.
Left New York Giants' camp voluntarily, July 17, 1979; signed as free agent by Washington Redskins, August 1, 1979.
Released by Washington Redskins, August 21, 1979; signed as free agent by Los Angeles Rams, September 28, 1979.
Released by Los Angeles Rams, October 23, 1979; re-signed by Rams, November 20, 1979.
Released by Los Angeles Rams, May 14, 1986.
Active for 7 games with New York Giants in 1978; did not play.
Green Bay NFL, 1975; Denver NFL, 1976; New York Giants (0)-Denver (1) NFL, 1978; Los Angeles Rams NFL, 1979 through 1985.
Games: 1975 (14), 1976 (14), 1978 (1), 1979 (8), 1980 (16), 1981 (16), 1982 (9), 1983 (16), 1984 (16), 1985 (15). Total—125.
Pro statistics: Returned one kickoff for 10 yards, 1975.
Played in NFC Championship Game following 1979 and 1985 seasons.
Played in NFL Championship Game following 1979 season.

CHARLES EDWARD BAKER
(Charlie)
Linebacker—St. Louis Cardinals
Born September 26, 1957, at Mt. Pleasant, Tex.
Height, 6.02. Weight, 234.
High School—Odessa, Tex., Ector.
Attended University of New Mexico.

Selected by St. Louis in 3rd round (81st player selected) of 1980 NFL draft.
On injured reserve with abdominal strain, October 5 through November 8, 1984; activated, November 9, 1984.
St. Louis NFL, 1980 through 1985.
Games: 1980 (16), 1981 (14), 1982 (9), 1983 (16), 1984 (9), 1985 (15). Total—79.
Pro statistics: Ran 27 yards with lateral on kickoff return, 1980; recovered one fumble, 1981; recovered two fumbles, 1982.

JAMES ALBERT LONDON BAKER
(Al or Bubba)
Defensive End—St. Louis Cardinals
Born December 9, 1956, at Jacksonville, Fla.
Height, 6.06. Weight, 270.
High School—Newark, N. J., Weequahic.
Attended Colorado State University.

Named THE SPORTING NEWS NFC Rookie of the Year, 1978.
Selected by Detroit in 2nd round (40th player selected) of 1978 NFL draft.
On reserve-retired list, August 19 through September 10, 1980; activated, September 11, 1980.
On physically unable to perform/active list with groin injury, July 29 through August 30, 1982; activated, August 31, 1982.
Traded by Detroit Lions to St. Louis Cardinals for defensive tackle Mike Dawson and 3rd round pick in 1984 draft, July 18, 1983.
Detroit NFL, 1978 through 1982; St. Louis NFL, 1983 through 1985.
Games: 1978 (16), 1979 (16), 1980 (15), 1981 (11), 1982 (9), 1983 (16), 1984 (15), 1985 (16). Total—114.

Pro statistics: Recovered one fumble, 1978 through 1980, 1982 and 1985; intercepted one pass for no yards, 1980; intercepted one pass for nine yards, 1981; intercepted two passes for 24 yards and recovered two fumbles, 1983.
Played in Pro Bowl (NFL All-Star Game) following 1978 through 1980 seasons.

JESSE BAKER
Defensive End—Houston Oilers
Born July 10, 1957, at Conyers, Ga.
Height, 6.05. Weight, 272.
High School—Conyers, Ga., Rockdale County.
Attended Jacksonville State University.

Selected by Houston in 2nd round (50th player selected) of 1979 NFL draft.
Houston NFL, 1979 through 1985.
Games: 1979 (16), 1980 (16), 1981 (16), 1982 (9), 1983 (16), 1984 (16), 1985 (16). Total—105.
Pro statistics: Recovered one fumble for 20 yards and one touchdown, 1979; recovered one fumble, 1980, 1981 and 1984; recovered one fumble for 56 yards, 1982.
Played in AFC Championship Game following 1979 season.

KEITH LEONARD BAKER
Wide Receiver—Philadelphia Eagles
Born June 4, 1957, at Dallas, Tex.
Height, 5.10. Weight, 187.
High School—Dallas, Tex., Franklin D. Roosevelt.
Attended Texas A&M University and Texas Southern University.

Signed as free agent by Montreal Alouettes, April, 1979.
Traded by Montreal Alouettes to Hamilton Tiger-Cats, June, 1981.
Traded by Hamilton Tiger-Cats to Ottawa Rough Riders, September 16, 1984.
Granted free agency, March 1, 1985; signed by San Francisco 49ers, April 10, 1985.
Traded by San Francisco 49ers to Philadelphia Eagles for 8th round pick in 1986 NFL draft, August 30, 1985.

		—RUSHING—			PASS RECEIVING				—TOTAL—		
Year Club	G.	Att.	Yds.	Avg.	TD.	P.C.	Yds.	Avg.	TD.	TD.	Pts.	F.
1979—Montreal CFL	12	3	42	14.0	0	29	571	19.7	5	5	30	0
1980—Montreal CFL	15	4	—20	—5.0	0	51	891	17.5	8	8	48	0
1981—Hamilton CFL	16	3	2	0.7	0	68	1218	17.9	11	11	66	0
1982—Hamilton CFL	16	5	19	3.8	0	80	1282	16.0	8	8	48	0
1983—Hamilton CFL	15	2	10	5.0	0	66	911	13.8	10	10	†62	0
1984—Hamilton (8)-Ottawa (4) CFL	12	2	27	13.5	0	39	623	16.0	5	5	30	1
1985—Philadelphia NFL	8			None		2	25	12.5	0	0	0	0
CFL Totals—6 Years	86	19	80	4.2	0	333	5496	16.5	47	47	284	1
NFL Totals—1 Year	8	0	0	0.0	0	2	25	12.5	0	0	0	0
Pro Totals—7 Years	94	19	80	4.2	0	335	5521	16.5	47	47	284	1

		—PUNT RETURNS—				—KICKOFF RET.—		
Year Club	G.	No.	Yds.	Avg.	TD.	No.	Yds.	Avg.TD.
1979—Montreal CFL	12	12	134	11.2	0	5	95	19.0 0
1980—Montreal CFL	15	11	85	7.7	0	3	48	16.0 0
1981—Hamilton CFL	16	9	80	8.9	0		None	
1982—Hamilton CFL	16	10	69	6.9	0	1	26	26.0 0
1983—Hamilton CFL	15	5	21	4.2	0		None	
1984—Hamilton (8)-Ottawa (4) CFL	12	5	18	3.6	0	2	32	16.0 0
1985—Philadelphia NFL	8		None				None	
CFL Totals—6 Years	86	52	407	7.8	0	11	201	18.3 0
NFL Totals—1 Year	8	0	0	0.0	0	0	0	0.0 0
Pro Totals—7 Years	94	52	407	7.8	0	11	201	18.3 0

†Includes one 2-point conversion.
Additional CFL statistics: Recovered one fumble, 1979; attempted one pass with no completions, 1979 and 1981; attempted two passes with one completion for 15 yards and a touchdown, 1982; attempted one pass with one interception, 1983.
Played in CFL Championship Game following 1979 season.

RONALD BAKER
(Ron)
Guard—Philadelphia Eagles
Born November 19, 1954, at Gary, Ind.
Height, 6.04. Weight, 274.
High School—Gary, Ind., Emerson.
Attended Indian Hills Junior College and Oklahoma State University.

Selected by Baltimore in 10th round (277th player selected) of 1977 NFL draft.
On injured reserve with ankle injury entire 1977 season.
Traded by Baltimore Colts to Philadelphia Eagles for 8th round pick in 1981 draft, August 26, 1980.
Baltimore NFL, 1978 and 1979; Philadelphia NFL, 1980 through 1985.
Games: 1978 (16), 1979 (16), 1980 (16), 1981 (16), 1982 (9), 1983 (16), 1984 (16), 1985 (15). Total—120.
Pro statistics: Returned one kickoff for six yards, 1980; recovered one fumble, 1982 through 1984.
Played in NFC Championship Game following 1980 season.
Played in NFL Championship Game following 1980 season.

BRIAN D. BALDINGER
Guard—Dallas Cowboys
Born January 7, 1959, at Pittsburgh, Pa.
Height, 6.04. Weight, 261.
High School—Massapequa, N.Y.
Attended Nassau Community College and received bachelor of science degree
in psychology from Duke University in 1982.
Brother of Rich Baldinger, guard-offensive tackle with Kansas City Chiefs; and
Gary Baldinger, rookie defensive lineman with Kansas City Chiefs.

Signed as free agent by Dallas Cowboys, April 30, 1982.
On inactive list, September 13 and September 19, 1982.
On injured reserve with knee injury, August 27 through entire 1985 season.
Dallas NFL, 1982 through 1984.
Games: 1982 (4), 1983 (16), 1984 (16). Total—36.
Played in NFC Championship Game following 1982 season.

RICHARD L. BALDINGER
(Rich)
Guard-Offensive Tackle—Kansas City Chiefs
Born December 31, 1959, at Camp Le Jeune, N.C.
Height, 6.04. Weight, 281.
High School—Massapequa, N.Y.
Attended Wake Forest University.
Brother of Brian Baldinger, guard with Dallas Cowboys; and
Gary Baldinger, rookie defensive lineman with Kansas City Chiefs.

Selected by New York Giants in 10th round (270th player selected) of 1982 NFL draft.
On inactive list, September 12, 1982.
Released by New York Giants, August 29, 1983; re-signed by Giants, September 8, 1983.
Released by New York Giants, October 7, 1983; signed as free agent by Kansas City Chiefs, October 26, 1983.
New York Giants NFL, 1982; New York Giants (2)-Kansas City (6) NFL, 1983; Kansas City NFL, 1984 and 1985.
Games: 1982 (1), 1983 (8), 1984 (14), 1985 (16). Total—39.

JOHN KARL BALDISCHWILER
(Known by middle name.)
Offensive Tackle—Indianapolis Colts
Born January 19, 1956, at Okmulgee, Okla.
Height, 6.05. Weight, 273.
High School—Okmulgee, Okla.
Attended University of Oklahoma.

Selected by Miami in 7th round (178th player selected) of 1978 NFL draft.
Traded by Miami Dolphins to Detroit Lions for 10th round pick in 1979 draft, August 28, 1978.
Traded by Detroit Lions to Baltimore Colts for 7th round pick in 1984 draft, July 28, 1983.
Franchise transferred to Indianapolis, March 31, 1984.
Released by Indianapolis Colts after failing physical with neck injury, June 15, 1984; re-signed by Colts, April 1,
1985.
Detroit NFL, 1978 through 1982; Baltimore NFL, 1983; Indianapolis NFL, 1985.
Games: 1978 (16), 1979 (16), 1980 (16), 1981 (16), 1982 (9), 1983 (14), 1985 (16). Total—103.

KEITH MANNING BALDWIN
Defensive End—Cleveland Browns
Born October 13, 1960, at Houston, Tex.
Height, 6.04. Weight, 270.
High School—Houston, Tex., M.B. Smiley.
Attended Texas A&M University.

Selected by Cleveland in 2nd round (31st player selected) of 1982 NFL draft.
Cleveland NFL, 1982 through 1985.
Games: 1982 (9), 1983 (16), 1984 (16), 1985 (10). Total—51.

THOMAS BURKE BALDWIN
(Tom)
Defensive Tackle—New York Jets
Born May 13, 1961, at Evergreen Park, Ill.
Height, 6.04. Weight, 275.
High School—Lansing, Ill., Thornton Fractional South.
Attended University of Wisconsin, Thornton Community College and
and received degree in education from The University of Tulsa.
Brother of Brian Baldwin, pitcher in Los Angeles Dodgers' organization, 1977 through 1979.

Selected by Oklahoma in 1984 USFL territorial draft.
Selected by New York Jets in 9th round (234th player selected) of 1984 NFL draft.
Signed by New York Jets, May 29, 1984.
New York Jets NFL, 1984 and 1985.
Games: 1984 (16), 1985 (16). Total—32.
Pro statistics: Recovered one fumble for nine yards and a touchdown, 1985.

QUINTON McCOY BALLARD
Defensive Tackle—Indianapolis Colts
Born November 18, 1960, at Ahoskie, N.C.
Height, 6.03. Weight, 289.
High School—Gatesville, N.C., Gates County.
Attended Elon College.
Brother of Joe Ballard, professional boxer.

Signed as free agent by Baltimore Colts, May 10, 1983.
Franchise transferred to Indianapolis, March 31, 1984.
On injured reserve with knee injury, August 27 through September 25, 1984.
Released by Indianapolis Colts, September 26, 1984; signed as free agent by Miami Dolphins, March 29, 1985.
Released by Miami Dolphins, August 19, 1985; signed as free agent by Indianapolis Colts, May 12, 1986.
Baltimore NFL, 1983.
Games: 1983 (15).

TED BANKER
Offensive Lineman—New York Jets
Born February 17, 1961, at Belleville, Ill.
Height, 6.02. Weight, 255.
High School—Belleville, Ill., Althoff.
Attended Southeast Missouri State University.

Signed as free agent by New York Jets, June 20, 1983.
On injured reserve with knee injury, August 12 through entire 1983 season.
On injured reserve with broken leg, December 24 through remainder of 1985 season playoffs.
New York Jets NFL, 1984 and 1985.
Games: 1984 (14), 1985 (16). Total—30.
Pro statistics: Returned one kickoff for five yards, 1984.

CARL BANKS
Linebacker—New York Giants
Born August 29, 1962, at Flint, Mich.
Height, 6.04. Weight, 235.
High School—Flint, Mich., Beecher.
Attended Michigan State University.

Named as linebacker on THE SPORTING NEWS College All-America Team, 1983.
Selected by Michigan in 1984 USFL territorial draft.
Selected by New York Giants in 1st round (3rd player selected) of 1984 NFL draft.
Signed by New York Giants, July 12, 1984.
On injured reserve with knee injury, October 12 through November 8, 1985; activated, November 9, 1985.
New York Giants NFL, 1984 and 1985.
Games: 1984 (16), 1985 (12). Total—28.
Pro statistics: Recovered one fumble, 1984 and 1985.

FREDERICK RAY BANKS
(Fred)
Wide Receiver—Cleveland Browns
Born May 26, 1962, at Columbus, Ga.
Height, 5.10. Weight, 177.
High School—Columbus, Ga., Baker.
Attended Chowan College and Liberty Baptist College.

Selected by Denver in 8th round (107th player selected) of 1985 USFL draft.
Selected by Cleveland in 8th round (203rd player selected) of 1985 NFL draft.
Signed by Cleveland Browns, July 11, 1985.
On injured reserve with pulled hamstring, October 9 through November 15, 1985; activated, November 16, 1985.

			—PASS RECEIVING—			
Year Club		G.	P.C.	Yds.	Avg.	TD.
1985—Cleveland NFL..............		10	5	62	12.4	2

GORDON GERARD BANKS
Wide Receiver—Dallas Cowboys
Born March 12, 1958, at Los Angeles, Calif.
Height 5.10. Weight, 173.
High School—Los Angeles, Calif., Loyola.
Received degree in political science from Stanford University.

Signed as free agent by New Orleans Saints, May 19, 1980.
Released by New Orleans Saints, August 26, 1980; re-signed by Saints after clearing procedural waivers, November 4, 1980.
Released by New Orleans Saints, Octoer 13, 1981; signed as free agent by San Diego Chargers, July 7, 1982.
Released by San Diego Chargers, August 31, 1982; signed as free agent by Oakland Invaders, January 26, 1983.
Placed on reserve/did not report list, January 30 through February 2, 1984; activated, February 3, 1984.
Protected in merger of Michigan Panthers and Oakland Invaders, December 6, 1984.
Released by Oakland Invaders, August 8, 1985; signed as free agent by Dallas Cowboys and placed on reserve/future list, November 6, 1985.
Activated from reserve/future list, December 5 1985

Year Club	G.	—RUSHING— Att.	Yds.	Avg.	TD.	PASS RECEIVING P.C.	Yds.	Avg.	TD.	—TOTAL— TD.	Pts.	F.
1980—New Orleans NFL	7	1	−5	−5.0	0	1	7	7.0	0	0	0	0
1981—New Orleans NFL	6		None			2	18	9.0	0	0	0	2
1983—Oakland USFL	18	5	20	4.0	0	61	855	14.0	2	2	12	5
1984—Oakland USFL	18	1	8	8.0	0	64	937	14.6	5	5	30	6
1985—Oakland USFL	18		None			62	1115	18.0	5	5	†32	1
1985—Dallas NFL	2	1	−1	−1.0	0		None			0	0	0
NFL Totals—3 Years	15	2	−6	−3.0	0	3	25	8.3	0	0	0	2
USFL Totals—3 Years	54	6	28	4.7	0	187	2907	15.5	12	12	74	12
Pro Totals—6 Years	69	8	22	2.8	0	190	2932	15.4	12	12	74	14

Year Club	G.	—PUNT RETURNS— No.	Yds.	Avg.	TD.
1980—New Orleans NFL	7		None		
1981—New Orleans NFL	6	2	0	0.0	0
1983—Oakland USFL	18	30	292	9.7	0
1984—Oakland USFL	18	25	147	5.9	0
1985—Oakland USFL	18	13	82	6.3	0
1985—Dallas NFL	2	3	27	9.0	0
NFL Totals—3 Years	15	5	27	5.4	0
USFL Totals—3 Years	54	68	521	7.7	0
Pro Totals—6 Years	69	73	548	7.5	0

†Includes one 2-point conversion.
Additional NFL statistics: Returned one kickoff for nine yards and recovered one fumble, 1981.
Additional USFL statistics: Returned three kickoffs for 27 yards and recovered one fumble, 1983; recovered two fumbles, 1984; recovered one fumble for minus eight yards, 1985.
Played in USFL Championship Game following 1985 season.

WILLIAM CHIP BANKS
(Known by middle name.)
Linebacker—Cleveland Browns
Born September 18, 1959, at Ft. Lawton, Okla.
Height, 6.04. Weight, 233.
High School—Augusta, Ga., Lucy Laney.
Attended University of Southern California.

Named as linebacker on THE SPORTING NEWS College All-America Team, 1981.
Selected by Cleveland in 1st round (3rd player selected) of 1982 NFL draft.
Traded with 3rd round pick in 1985 draft and 1st and 6th round picks in 1986 draft by Cleveland Browns to Buffalo Bills for 1st round pick in 1985 supplemental draft, April 9, 1985 (Bills received 1st round pick in 1985 draft from Browns when Banks did not report).

Year Club	G.	—INTERCEPTIONS— No.	Yds.	Avg.	TD.
1982—Cleveland NFL	9	1	14	14.0	0
1983—Cleveland NFL	16	3	95	31.7	1
1984—Cleveland NFL	16	1	8	8.0	0
1985—Cleveland NFL	16		None		
Pro Totals—4 Years	57	5	117	23.4	1

Additional pro statistics: Recovered one fumble, 1983; recovered three fumbles for 17 yards, 1984.
Played in Pro Bowl (NFL All-Star Game) following 1982 and 1983 seasons.
Named to play in Pro Bowl following 1985 season; replaced due to injury by Clay Matthews.

MARION BARBER
Fullback—New York Jets
Born December 6, 1959, at Fort Lauderdale, Fla.
Height, 6.02. Weight, 224.
High School—Detroit, Mich., Chadsey.
Received degree in juvenile behavior from University of Minnesota.

Selected by New York Jets in 2nd round (30th player selected) of 1981 NFL draft.
On injured reserve with concussion, August 17 through entire 1981 season.
On inactive list, September 12 and September 19, 1982.
On injured reserve with cracked rib, November 5 through remainder of 1985 season.

Year Club	G.	—RUSHING— Att.	Yds.	Avg.	TD.	PASS RECEIVING P.C.	Yds.	Avg.	TD.	—TOTAL— TD.	Pts.	F.
1982—New York Jets NFL	6	8	24	3.0	0		None			0	0	0
1983—New York Jets NFL	14	15	77	5.1	1	7	48	6.9	1	2	12	0
1984—New York Jets NFL	14	31	148	4.8	2	10	79	7.9	0	2	12	3
1985—New York Jets NFL	8	9	41	4.6	0	3	46	15.3	0	0	0	0
Pro Totals—4 Years	42	63	290	4.6	3	20	173	8.7	1	4	24	3

Additional pro statistics: Returned one kickoff for nine yards and recovered two fumbles, 1983; recovered one fumble, 1984.
Played in AFC Championship Game following 1982 season.

MIKE BARBER
Tight End—Denver Broncos
Born June 4, 1953, at Marshall, Tex.
Height, 6.03. Weight, 237.
High School—White Oak, Tex.
Attended Louisiana Tech University.

Selected by Houston in 2nd round (48th player selected) of 1976 NFL draft.
On injured reserve with tendinitis, September 15 through remainder of 1976 season.
Traded with 3rd and 8th round picks in 1982 draft by Houston Oilers to Los Angeles Rams for tight end Lewis Gilbert and 2nd and 3rd round picks in 1982 draft, April 27, 1982.
On injured reserve with knee injury, August 28 through September 28, 1984; activated, September 29, 1984.
Traded by Los Angeles Rams to Denver Broncos for 12th round pick in 1986 draft, October 9, 1985.

Year Club	G.	P.C.	Yds.	Avg.	TD.
1976—Houston NFL	1		None		
1977—Houston NFL	13	9	94	10.4	1
1978—Houston NFL	16	32	513	16.0	3
1979—Houston NFL	15	27	377	14.0	3
1980—Houston NFL	16	59	712	12.1	5
1981—Houston NFL	16	13	190	14.6	1
1982—L.A. Rams NFL	9	18	166	9.2	1
1983—L.A. Rams NFL	16	55	657	11.9	3
1984—L.A. Rams NFL	11	7	42	6.0	0
1985—Ram(5)-Den.(10) NFL.	15	2	37	18.5	0
Pro Totals—10 Years	128	222	2788	12.6	17

Additional pro statistics: Rushed twice for 14 yards and fumbled four times, 1978; rushed twice for four yards, 1979; fumbled once, 1979, 1983 and 1984; rushed once for one yard and returned one kickoff for 12 yards, 1980; recovered one fumble, 1980 and 1982.
Played in AFC Championship Game following 1978 and 1979 seasons.

LEO BARKER
Linebacker—Cincinnati Bengals
Born November 7, 1959, at Cristobal, Panama.
Height, 6.02. Weight, 227.
High School—Cristobal, Panama.
Attended New Mexico State University.

Selected by Arizona in 1984 USFL territorial draft.
Selected by Cincinnati in 7th round (177th player selected) of 1984 NFL draft.
Signed by Cincinnati Bengals, June 26, 1984.
Cincinnati NFL, 1984 and 1985.
Games: 1984 (16), 1985 (16). Total—32.

ROD DEAN BARKSDALE
Defensive Back—Los Angeles Raiders
Born September 8, 1962, at Los Angeles, Calif.
Height, 6.01. Weight, 182.
High School—Compton, Calif.
Received bachelor of science degree in political science
from University of Arizona in 1985.
Cousin of Jeremiah Castille, defensive back with Tampa Bay Buccaneers.

Signed as free agent by Los Angeles Raiders, May 11, 1985.
On injured reserve with ankle injury, August 20 through entire 1985 season.

JEFF BARNES
Linebacker—Los Angeles Raiders
Born March 1, 1955, at Philadelphia, Pa.
Height, 6.02. Weight, 225.
High School—Hayward, Calif.
Attended Chabot College and University of California.

Selected by Oakland in 5th round (139th player selected) of 1977 NFL draft.
Franchise transferred to Los Angeles, May 7, 1982.
Oakland NFL, 1977 through 1981; Los Angeles Raiders NFL, 1982 through 1985.
Games: 1977 (14), 1978 (16), 1979 (16), 1980 (16), 1981 (15), 1982 (9), 1983 (16), 1984 (16), 1985 (16). Total—134.
Pro statistics: Recovered two fumbles, 1977; intercepted one pass for eight yards, 1979; recovered one fumble, 1980 and 1984; intercepted one pass for 15 yards, 1984; intercepted one pass for no yards and recovered four fumbles for 14 yards, 1985.
Played in AFC Championship Game following 1977, 1980 and 1983 seasons.
Played in NFL Championship Game following 1980 and 1983 seasons.

ROOSEVELT BARNES JR.
Linebacker—Indianapolis Colts
Born August 3, 1958, at Fort Wayne, Ind.
Height, 6.02. Weight, 228.
High School—Fort Wayne, Ind.
Received bachelor's degree in management from Purdue University in 1981.

Selected by Detroit in 10th round (266th player selected) of 1982 NFL draft.

Granted free agency, February 1, 1986; re-signed by Lions and traded to Indianapolis Colts for conditional pick in 1987 draft, May 20, 1986.

Detroit NFL, 1982 through 1985.

Games: 1982 (9), 1983 (16), 1984 (16), 1985 (16). Total—57.

Pro statistics: Recovered one fumble, 1982 and 1983; intercepted two passes for 70 yards, 1983; intercepted one pass for minus one yard, 1985.

BUSTER BARNETT
Tight End—Los Angeles Raiders

Born November 24, 1958, at Macon, Miss.

Height, 6.05. Weight, 235.

High School—Macon, Miss., Noxubee.

Received bachelor of science degree in business management from Jackson State University in 1981.

Selected by Buffalo in 11th round (299th player selected) of 1981 NFL draft.

On injured reserve with knee injury, August 22 through September, 1985.

Released by Buffalo Bills, October 23, 1985; signed as free agent by Los Angeles Raiders, April 10, 1986.

| | | ——PASS RECEIVING—— | | | |
Year Club	G.	P.C.	Yds.	Avg.	TD.
1981—Buffalo NFL	16	4	36	9.0	1
1982—Buffalo NFL	9	4	39	9.8	0
1983—Buffalo NFL	15	10	94	9.4	0
1984—Buffalo NFL	16	8	67	8.4	0
Pro Totals—4 Years	56	26	236	9.1	1

Additional pro statistics: Recovered one fumble, 1984.

DOUGLAS SHIRL BARNETT JR.
(Doug)
Linebacker—Washington Redskins

Born April 12, 1960, at Montebello, Calif.

Height, 6.03. Weight, 250.

High School—West Covina, Calif., Edgewood.

Received bachelor of arts degree from Azusa Pacific College.

Selected by Los Angeles Rams in 5th round (118th player selected) of 1982 NFL draft.

On injured reserve with knee injury, August 10 through entire 1984 season.

Released by Los Angeles Rams, August 17, 1985; signed as free agent by Washington Redskins, October 7, 1985.

Released by Washington Redskins, October 19, 1985; re-signed by Redskins, April 16, 1986.

Los Angeles Rams NFL, 1982 and 1983; Washington NFL, 1985.

Games: 1982 (9), 1983 (16), 1985 (2). Total—27.

Pro statistics: Returned one kickoff for no yards and recovered one fumble, 1983.

WILLIAM PERRY BARNETT
(Bill)
Defensive End—Miami Dolphins

Born May 10, 1956, at St. Paul, Minn.

Height, 6.04. Weight, 260.

High School—Stillwater, Minn.

Received bachelor of arts degree in advertising from University of Nebraska in 1981.

Selected by Miami in 3rd round (75th player selected) of 1980 NFL draft.

On injured reserve with leg injury, September 18 through October 30, 1981; activated, October 31, 1981.

On injured reserve with torn ankle ligaments, December 7 through remainder of 1982 season.

On injured reserve with shoulder injury, January 3 through remainder of 1985 season playoffs.

Miami NFL, 1980 through 1985.

Games: 1980 (16), 1981 (9), 1982 (5), 1983 (15), 1984 (16), 1985 (16). Total—77.

Pro statistics: Returned one kickoff for seven yards, 1980; recovered one fumble for four yards, 1982; recovered one fumble, 1985.

Played in AFC Championship Game following 1984 season.

Played in NFL Championship Game following 1984 season.

STEVEN JOSEPH BARTKOWSKI
(Steve)
Quarterback—Los Angeles Rams

Born November 12, 1952, at Des Moines, Ia.

Height, 6.04. Weight, 218.

High School—Santa Clara, Calif., Buchser.

Attended University of California at Berkeley.

Son of Roman Bartkowski, former pitcher in Chicago Cubs' organization.

Led NFL quarterbacks in passing with 97.6 points in 1983.

Named NFC Rookie of the Year by THE SPORTING NEWS, 1975.

Selected by Atlanta in 1st round (1st player selected) of 1975 NFL draft.

On injured reserve with knee injury, October 12 through remainder of 1976 season.

On injured reserve with knee injury, November 23 through remainder of 1984 season.

On injured reserve with knee injury, October 23 through November 25, 1985.

Released by Atlanta Falcons, November 26, 1985; signed as free agent by Washington Redskins, December 12, 1985.

Granted free agency with no qualifying offer, February 1, 1986; signed by Los Angeles Rams, April 17, 1986.
Active for 2 games with Washington Redskins in 1985; did not play.

Year Club	G.	Att.	Cmp.	Pct.	Gain	T.P.	P.I.	Avg.	Att.	Yds.	Avg.	TD.	TD.	Pts.	F.
				PASSING						RUSHING			TOTAL		
1975—Atlanta NFL	11	255	115	45.1	1662	13	15	6.52	14	15	1.1	2	2	12	6
1976—Atlanta NFL	5	120	57	47.5	677	2	9	5.64	8	10	1.3	1	1	6	2
1977—Atlanta NFL	8	136	64	47.1	796	5	13	5.85	18	13	0.7	0	0	0	5
1978—Atlanta NFL	14	369	187	50.7	2489	10	18	6.75	33	60	1.8	2	2	12	7
1979—Atlanta NFL	14	380	204	53.7	2505	17	20	6.59	14	36	2.6	2	2	12	4
1980—Atlanta NFL	16	463	257	55.5	3544	*31	16	7.65	25	35	1.4	2	2	12	6
1981—Atlanta NFL	16	533	297	55.7	3829	30	23	7.18	11	2	0.2	0	0	0	4
1982—Atlanta NFL	9	262	166	63.4	1905	8	11	7.27	13	4	0.3	1	1	6	7
1983—Atlanta NFL	14	432	274	63.4	3167	22	5	7.33	16	38	2.4	1	1	6	7
1984—Atlanta NFL	11	269	181	*67.3	2158	11	10	8.02	15	34	2.3	0	0	0	7
1985—Atl. (5)-Wash. (0) NFL	5	111	69	62.2	738	5	1	6.65	5	9	1.8	0	0	0	3
Pro Totals—11 Years.........	123	3330	1871	56.2	23470	154	141	7.05	172	256	1.5	11	11	66	58

Quarterback Rating Points: 1975 (59.3), 1976 (39.6), 1977 (38.5), 1978 (61.1), 1979 (67.2), 1980 (88.0), 1981 (79.2), 1982 (78.1), 1983 (97.6), 1984 (89.7), 1985 (92.8). Total—76.1.

Additional pro statistics: Recovered four fumbles and fumbled six times for minus two yards, 1975; recovered one fumble and fumbled five times for minus one yard, 1977; recovered three fumbles and fumbled seven times for minus nine yards, 1978; fumbled once for minus one yard, 1979; recovered two fumbles, 1980; recovered three fumbles and fumbled four times for minus one yard, 1981; recovered one fumble and fumbled seven times for minus 10 yards, 1982; recovered one fumble, 1983; recovered four fumbles and fumbled seven times for minus 11 yards, 1984; recovered one fumble and fumbled three times for minus eight yards, 1985.

Played in Pro Bowl (NFL All-Star Game) following 1980 season.

BRIAN DALE BASCHNAGEL
Name pronounced BASH-nay-gull.
Wide Receiver—Chicago Bears
Born January 8, 1954, at Kingston, N. Y.
Height, 5.11. Weight, 184.
High School—Pittsburgh, Pa., North Allegheny.
Received bachelor of arts degree in finance from Ohio State University in 1976.

Selected by Chicago in 3rd round (66th player selected) of 1976 NFL draft.
On injured reserve with knee injury, November 21 through remainder of 1977 season.
On injured reserve with knee injury, August 19 through entire 1985 season.

Year Club	G.	P.C.	Yds.	Avg.	TD.	No.	Yds.	Avg.	TD.	No.	Yds.	Avg.	TD.	TD.	Pts.	F.
		PASS RECEIVING				PUNT RETURNS				KICKOFF RET.				TOTAL		
1976—Chicago NFL	14	13	226	17.4	0	2	2	1.0	0	29	754	26.0	0	0	0	1
1977—Chicago NFL	10	4	50	12.5	0	3	54	18.0	0	23	557	24.2	*1	1	6	1
1978—Chicago NFL	16	2	29	14.5	0	1	2	2.0	0	20	455	22.8	0	0	0	1
1979—Chicago NFL	16	30	452	15.1	2		None			12	260	21.7	0	2	12	0
1980—Chicago NFL	16	28	396	14.1	2		None				None			2	12	0
1981—Chicago NFL	16	34	554	16.3	3		None			2	34	17.0	0	3	18	2
1982—Chicago NFL	9	12	194	16.2	2		None				None			2	12	0
1983—Chicago NFL	16	5	70	14.0	0		None			3	42	14.0	0	0	0	1
1984—Chicago NFL	16	6	53	8.8	0		None				None			0	0	1
Pro Totals—9 Years.......	129	134	2024	15.1	9	6	58	9.7	0	89	2102	23.6	1	10	60	7

Additional pro statistics: Rushed once for no yards, 1977 and 1984; recovered one fumble for minus nine yards, 1977; attempted one pass with no completions, 1977, 1979 and 1982; recovered two fumbles, 1978, 1981 and 1984; rushed twice for no yards, 1978; recovered one fumble, 1979; rushed once for 10 yards and attempted one pass with one completion for 18 yards, 1981; rushed twice for two yards, 1983; attempted two passes with one completion for seven yards, 1984.

Played in NFC Championship Game following 1984 season.

WILLIAM FREDERICK BATES
(Bill)
Safety—Dallas Cowboys
Born June 6, 1961, at Knoxville, Tenn.
Height, 6.01. Weight, 201.
High School—Knoxville, Tenn., Farragut.
Attended University of Tennessee.

Selected by New Jersey in 1983 USFL territorial draft.
Signed as free agent by Dallas Cowboys, April 28, 1983.
On injured reserve with hip injury, September 3 through September 27, 1984; activated, September 28, 1984.

Year Club	G.	No.	Yds.	Avg.	TD.	No.	Yds.	Avg.	TD.	TD.	Pts.	F.
		INTERCEPTIONS				PUNT RETURNS				TOTAL		
1983—Dallas NFL	16	1	29	29.0	0		None			0	0	1
1984—Dallas NFL	12	1	3	3.0	0		None			0	0	0
1985—Dallas NFL	16	4	15	3.8	0	22	152	6.9	0	0	0	0
Pro Totals—3 Years....................	44	6	47	7.8	0	22	152	6.9	0	0	0	1

Additional pro statistics: Recovered two fumbles, 1983; recovered one fumble, 1984.
Played in Pro Bowl (NFL All-Star Game) following 1984 season.

ROBERT GLENN BAUMHOWER
(Bob)
Defensive Tackle—Miami Dolphins
Born August 4, 1955, at Portsmouth, Va.
Height, 6.05. Weight, 265.
High Schools—Palm Beach, Fla., Palm Beach Gardens and Tuscaloosa, Ala.
Attended University of Alabama.

Named to THE SPORTING NEWS AFC All-Star Team, 1979.
Named to THE SPORTING NEWS NFL All-Star Team, 1981.
Selected by Miami in 2nd round (40th player selected) of 1977 NFL draft.
On physically unable to perform/reserve with knee injury, July 24 through November 5, 1985.
On injured reserve with knee injury, November 6 through remainder of 1985 season.
Miami NFL, 1977 through 1984.
Games: 1977 (14), 1978 (16), 1979 (16), 1980 (16), 1981 (16), 1982 (9), 1983 (16), 1984 (15). Total—118.
Pro statistics: Recovered three fumbles, 1977; recovered two fumbles for 13 yards and one touchdown and intercepted one pass for no yards, 1978; recovered one fumble, 1979 and 1983; recovered four fumbles for 14 yards, 1980; recovered three fumbles for 10 yards, 1981; recovered two fumbles for 23 yards and a touchdown, 1984.
Played in AFC Championship Game following 1982 and 1984 seasons.
Played in NFL Championship Game following 1982 and 1984 seasons.
Played in Pro Bowl (NFL All-Star Game) following 1979 and 1981 through 1983 seasons.
Named to Pro Bowl following 1984 season; replaced due to injury by Joe Klecko.

MARK BAVARO
Tight End—New York Giants
Born April 28, 1963, at Winthrop, Mass.
Height, 6.04. Weight, 245.
High School—Danvers, Mass.
Attended University of Notre Dame.

Selected by Orlando in 15th round (212th player selected) of 1985 USFL draft.
Selected by New York Giants in 4th round (100th player selected) of 1985 NFL draft.
Signed by New York Giants, July 7, 1985.

| | | —PASS RECEIVING— | | | |
Year Club	G.	P.C.	Yds.	Avg.	TD.
1985—N.Y. Giants NFL	16	37	511	13.8	4

MARTIN BAYLESS
Safety—Buffalo Bills
Born October 11, 1962, at Dayton, O.
Height, 6.02. Weight, 195.
High School—Dayton, O., Belmont.
Attended Bowling Green State University.
Brother of Jerry Bayless, tight end at Bowling Green State University.

Selected by Memphis in 1st round (20th player selected) of 1984 USFL draft.
Selected by St. Louis in 4th round (101st player selected) of 1984 NFL draft.
Signed by St. Louis Cardinals, July 20, 1984.
Released by St. Louis Cardinals, September 19, 1984; awarded on waivers to Buffalo Bills, September 20, 1984.
On injured reserve with pinched nerve in neck, December 6 through remainder of 1985 season.
St. Louis (3)-Buffalo (13) NFL, 1984; Buffalo NFL, 1985.
Games: 1984 (16), 1985 (12). Total—28.
Pro statistics: Intercepted two passes for 10 yards and recovered one fumble, 1985.

PATRICK JESSE BEACH
(Pat)
Tight End—Indianapolis Colts
Born December 28, 1959, at Grant's Pass, Ore.
Height, 6.04. Weight, 243.
High School—Pullman, Wash.
Attended Washington State University.

Named as tight end on THE SPORTING NEWS College All-America team, 1981.
Selected by Baltimore in 6th round (140th player selected) of 1982 NFL draft.
Franchise transferred to Indianapolis, March 31, 1984.
On non-football injury list with ankle injury, August 10 through August 21, 1984.
On injured reserve with ankle injury, August 22 through entire 1984 season.

| | | —PASS RECEIVING— | | | |
Year Club	G.	P.C.	Yds.	Avg.	TD.
1982—Baltimore NFL	9	4	45	11.3	1
1983—Baltimore NFL	16	5	56	11.2	1
1985—Indianapolis NFL	16	36	376	10.4	6
Pro Totals—3 Years............	41	45	477	10.6	8

Additional pro statistics: Returned one kickoff for no yards, 1983; recovered one fumble for five yards and fumbled three times, 1985.

THOMAS LYNN BEASLEY
(Tom)
Defensive End—Washington Redskins

Born August 11, 1954, at Bluefield, W. Va.
Height, 6.05. Weight, 248.
High School—Northfork, W. Va.
Attended Virginia Polytechnic Institute.

Selected by Pittsburgh in 3rd round (60th player selected) of 1977 NFL draft.
On injured reserve entire 1977 season.
Released by Pittsburgh Steelers, August 27, 1984; signed as free agent by Washington Redskins, September 19, 1984.
Pittsburgh NFL, 1978 through 1983; Washington NFL, 1984 and 1985.
Games: 1978 (15), 1979 (13), 1980 (15), 1981 (13), 1982 (7), 1983 (16), 1984 (13), 1985 (12). Total—104.
Pro statistics: Recovered one fumble, 1982 and 1984; recovered two fumbles, 1983.
Played in AFC Championship Game following 1978 and 1979 seasons.
Played in NFL Championship Game following 1978 and 1979 seasons.

CLAYTON MAURICE BEAUFORD
Wide Receiver—Detroit Lions

Born March 1, 1963, at Palatka, Fla.
Height, 5.10. Weight, 173.
High School—Palatka, Fla.
Attended Auburn University.

Selected by Birmingham in 1985 USFL territorial draft.
Selected by Detroit in 10th round (258th player selected) of 1985 NFL draft.
Signed by Detroit Lions, July 21, 1985.
On non-football injury list with knee injury, August 20 through entire 1985 season.

KURT FRANK BECKER
Guard—Chicago Bears

Born December 22, 1958, at Aurora, Ill.
Height, 6.05. Weight, 270.
High School—Aurora, Ill., East.
Received bachelor of arts degree in business administration from University of Michigan.

Selected by Chicago in 6th round (146th player selected) of 1982 NFL draft.
On inactive list, September 12 and September 19, 1982.
On injured reserve with knee injury, October 4 through remainder of 1985 season.
Chicago NFL, 1982 through 1985.
Games: 1982 (5), 1983 (16), 1984 (16), 1985 (3). Total—40.
Played in NFC Championship Game following 1984 season.

MARK GERALD BEHNING

Name pronounced BEN-ing.

Offensive Tackle—Pittsburgh Steelers

Born September 26, 1961, at Alpena, Mich.
Height, 6.06. Weight, 291.
High School—Denton, Tex.
Attended University of Nebraska.

Selected by Pittsburgh in 2nd round (47th player selected) of 1985 NFL draft.
Signed by Pittsburgh Steelers, July 19, 1985.
On injured reserve with broken arm, August 20 through entire 1985 season.

KEVIN LEANDER BELCHER
Offensive Tackle—Los Angeles Raiders

Born November 9, 1961, at Bridgeport, Conn.
Height, 6.05. Weight, 310.
High School—Bridgeport, Conn., Basick.
Attended University of Wisconsin.

Selected by Oakland in 13th round (181st player selected) of 1985 USFL draft.
Selected by Los Angeles Raiders in 7th round (186th player selected) of 1985 NFL draft.
Signed by Los Angeles Raiders, July 10, 1985.
On non-football injury list with asthma, October 17 through remainder of 1985 season.
Los Angeles Raiders NFL, 1985.
Games: 1985 (4).

BOBBY LEE BELL JR.
Linebacker—Cleveland Browns

Born February 7, 1962, at St. Paul, Minn.
Height, 6.03. Weight, 217.
High School—Lee's Summit, Mo.
Received degree in food service and lodging management from University of Missouri.
Son of Bobby Bell Sr., Hall of Fame linebacker with Kansas City Chiefs, 1963 through 1974.

Selected by Chicago in 3rd round (43rd player selected) of 1984 USFL draft.
Selected by New York Jets in 4th round (91st player selected) of 1984 NFL draft.
Signed by New York Jets, May 29, 1984.

Released by New York Jets, August 19, 1985; signed as free agent by Cleveland Browns, May 4, 1986.
New York Jets NFL, 1984.
Games: 1984 (15).

GERARD ALFRED BELL
(Jerry)
Tight End—Tampa Bay Buccaneers
Born March 7, 1959, at Derby, Conn.
Height, 6.05. Weight, 230.
High School—El Cerrito, Calif.
Received bachelor of science degree in computer information systems
from Arizona State University in 1982.

Selected by Tampa Bay in 3rd round (74th player selected) of 1982 NFL draft.
On injured reserve with knee injury, November 4 through remainder of 1985 season.

		—PASS RECEIVING—			
Year Club	G.	P.C.	Yds.	Avg.	TD.
1982—Tampa Bay NFL	9	1	5	5.0	0
1983—Tampa Bay NFL	16	18	200	11.1	1
1984—Tampa Bay NFL	16	29	397	13.7	4
1985—Tampa Bay NFL	9	43	496	11.5	2
Pro Totals—4 Years	50	91	1098	12.1	7

Additional pro statistics: Recovered one fumble, 1983 and 1984; fumbled once, 1983; fumbled twice, 1985.

GREG LEON BELL
Running Back—Buffalo Bills
Born August 1, 1962, at Columbus, O.
Height, 5.10. Weight, 210.
High School—Columbus, O., South.
Received bachelor of arts degree in economics from University of Notre Dame in 1984.

Selected by Chicago in 1984 USFL territorial draft.
Selected by Buffalo in 1st round (26th player selected) of 1984 NFL draft.
Signed by Buffalo Bills, July 23, 1984.

		—RUSHING—				PASS RECEIVING			—TOTAL—		
Year Club	G.	Att.	Yds.	Avg.	TD.	P.C.	Yds.	Avg.	TD.	TD. Pts.	F.
1984—Buffalo NFL	16	262	1100	4.2	7	34	277	8.1	1	8 48	5
1985—Buffalo NFL	16	223	883	4.0	8	58	576	9.9	1	9 54	8
Pro Totals—2 Years	32	485	1983	4.1	15	92	853	9.3	2	17 102	13

Additional pro statistics: Returned one kickoff for 15 yards and recovered three fumbles, 1984; attempted one pass with no completions and recovered two fumbles, 1985.
Played in Pro Bowl (NFL All-Star Game) following 1984 season.

MIKE J. BELL
Defensive End—Kansas City Chiefs
Born August 30, 1957, at Wichita, Kan.
Height, 6.04. Weight, 250.
High School—Wichita, Kan., Bishop Carroll.
Attended Colorado State University.
Twin brother of Mark E. Bell, tight end with Seattle Seahawks and Baltimore-Indianapolis
Colts, 1979, 1980 and 1982 through 1984.

Named as defensive lineman on THE SPORTING NEWS College All-America Team, 1978.
Selected by Kansas City in 1st round (2nd player selected) of 1979 NFL draft.
On injured reserve with knee injury, October 9 through November 16, 1979; activated, November 17, 1979.
On injured reserve with torn bicep, September 20 through remainder of 1980 season.
On injured reserve with groin injury, December 14 through remainder of 1982 season.
On injured reserve with knee injury, December 13 through remainder of 1984 season.
Granted roster exemption/leave of absence with drug problem, November 20 through remainder of 1985 season.
Kansas City NFL, 1979 through 1985.
Games: 1979 (11), 1980 (2), 1981 (16), 1982 (6), 1983 (16), 1984 (15), 1985 (11). Total—77.
Pro statistics: Recovered one fumble, 1979, 1981, 1983 and 1985; recovered two fumbles and fumbled once, 1984.

TODD ANTHONY BELL
Safety—Chicago Bears
Born November 28, 1958, at Middletown, O.
Height, 6.01. Weight, 207.
High School—Middletown, O.
Attended Ohio State University.
Brother of Sean Bell, cornerback at Ohio State University.

Named to THE SPORTING NEWS NFL All-Star Team, 1984.
Selected by Chicago in 4th round (95th player selected) of 1981 NFL draft.
Granted free agency, February 1, 1985.
On reserve/unsigned free agency list, August 20 through remainder of 1985 season.

Year Club	G.	No.	Yds.	Avg.TD.	
1981—Chicago NFL	16	1	92	92.0	1
1982—Chicago NFL	9		None		
1983—Chicago NFL	15		None		
1984—Chicago NFL	16	4	46	11.5	1
Pro Totals—4 Years	56	5	138	27.6	2

Additional pro statistics: Recovered one fumble, 1981; returned one kickoff for 14 yards, 1982; returned two kickoffs for 18 yards and recovered one fumble for 10 yards, 1983; returned two kickoffs for 33 yards and recovered two fumbles for four yards, 1984.

Played in NFC Championship Game following 1984 season.
Played in Pro Bowl (NFL All-Star Game) following 1984 season.

RODNEY CARWELL BELLINGER
Cornerback—Buffalo Bills
Born June 4, 1962, at Miami, Fla.
Height, 5.08. Weight, 189.
High School—Coral Gables, Fla.
Attended University of Miami (Fla.).

Selected by Houston in 2nd round (40th player selected) of 1984 USFL draft.
Selected by Buffalo in 3rd round (77th player selected) of 1984 NFL draft.
Signed by Buffalo Bills, July 12, 1984.
On injured reserve with fractured cervical disc, September 13 through October 25, 1984; activated, October 26, 1984.

Year Club	G.	No.	Yds.	Avg.TD.	
1984—Buffalo NFL	10	1	0	0.0	0
1985—Buffalo NFL	16	2	64	32.0	0
Pro Totals—2 Years	26	3	64	21.3	0

Additional pro statistics: Recovered one fumble, 1985.

JESSE JAMES BENDROSS
Wide Receiver—Tampa Bay Buccaneers
Born July 19, 1962, at Hollywood, Fla.
Height, 6.00. Weight, 197.
High School—Miramar, Fla.
Attended Alabama University.

Selected by Birmingham in 1984 USFL territorial draft.
Selected by San Diego in 7th round (174th player selected) of 1984 NFL draft.
Signed by San Diego Chargers, July 12, 1984.
Traded by San Diego Chargers to Tampa Bay Buccaneers for conditional 12th round pick in 1987 draft, May 13, 1986.

Year Club	G.	P.C.	Yds.	Avg.	TD.
1984—San Diego NFL	16	16	213	13.3	0
1985—San Diego NFL	16	11	156	14.2	2
Pro Totals—2 Years	32	27	369	13.7	2

Additional pro statistics: Fumbled once, 1984; returned one kickoff for two yards, 1985.

ROLF JOACHIM BENIRSCHKE
Name pronounced Ben-ER-shka.
Placekicker—San Diego Chargers
Born February 7, 1955, at Boston, Mass.
Height, 6.01. Weight, 184.
High School—LaJolla, Calif.
Received bachelor of science degree in zoology from University of California at Davis in 1977.

Selected by Oakland in 12th round (334th player selected) of 1977 NFL draft.
Claimed on waivers from Oakland Raiders by San Diego Chargers, September 13, 1977.
On injured reserve with internal disorder, September 29 through remainder of 1979 season.
On injured reserve with groin injury, September 12 through remainder of 1985 season.

Year Club	G.	XP.	XPM.	FG.	FGA.	Pts.
1977—San Diego NFL	14	21	3	17	23	72
1978—San Diego NFL	15	37	*6	18	22	91
1979—San Diego NFL	4	12	1	4	4	24
1980—San Diego NFL	16	46	2	24	36	118
1981—San Diego NFL	16	*55	6	19	26	112
1982—San Diego NFL	9	*32	2	16	22	80
1983—San Diego NFL	16	43	2	15	24	88
1984—San Diego NFL	14	41	0	17	26	92
1985—San Diego NFL	1	2	0	0	0	2
Pro Totals—9 Years	105	289	22	130	183	679

Played in AFC Championship Game following 1980 and 1981 seasons.
Played in Pro Bowl (NFL All-Star Game) following 1982 season.

DAN BENISH
Defensive Tackle—Atlanta Falcons
Born November 21, 1961, at Youngstown, O.
Height, 6.05. Weight, 280.
High School—Hubbard, O.
Attended Clemson University.

Selected by Washington in 1983 USFL territorial draft.
Signed as free agent by Atlanta Falcons, May 3, 1983.
Atlanta NFL, 1983 through 1985.
Games: 1983 (16), 1984 (15), 1985 (16). Total—47.
Pro statistics: Recovered one fumble, 1985.

BARRY MARTIN BENNETT
Defensive End-Tackle—New York Jets
Born December 10, 1955, at St. Paul, Minn.
Height, 6.04. Weight, 257.
High School—St. Paul, Minn., North.
Received bachelor of science degree in physical education from Concordia College in 1977.

Selected by New Orleans in 3rd round (60th player selected) of 1978 NFL draft.
On injured reserve with neck injury, October 2 through remainder of 1981 season.
Released by New Orleans Saints, June 24, 1982; signed as free agent by Minnesota Vikings, July 20, 1982.
Released by Minnesota Vikings, September 6, 1982; signed as free agent by New York Jets, September 8, 1982.
On inactive list, September 19, 1982.
New Orleans NFL, 1978 through 1981; New York Jets NFL, 1982 through 1985.
Games: 1978 (16), 1979 (16), 1980 (15), 1981 (3), 1982 (7), 1983 (13), 1984 (15), 1985 (16). Total—101.
Pro statistics: Recovered four fumbles for six yards, 1984.
Member of New York Jets for AFC Championship Game following 1982 season; did not play.

BEN BENNETT
Quarterback—Houston Oilers
Born May 5, 1962, at Greensboro, N.C.
Height, 6.01. Weight, 195.
High School—Sunnyvale, Calif., Peterson.
Received bachelor of arts degree in history and psychology from Duke University.

Selected by Jacksonville in 1984 USFL territorial draft.
Selected by Atlanta in 6th round (148th player selected) of 1984 NFL draft.
Signed by Jacksonville Bulls, May 5, 1984.
Granted roster exemption, May 5 through May 31, 1984.
On developmental squad, June 1 through June 7, 1984; activated, June 8, 1984.
Released by Jacksonville Bulls, February 7, 1985; signed by Atlanta Falcons, February 26, 1985.
Released by Atlanta Falcons, August 5, 1985; signed as free agent by Houston Oilers, May 13, 1986.
On developmental squad for 1 game with Jacksonville Bulls in 1984.

		—————PASSING—————							—RUSHING—			—TOTAL—		
Year	Club	G.	Att.	Cmp.	Pct.	Gain	T.P.	P.I.	Avg.	Att.	Yds.	Avg. TD.	TD.	Pts.	F.
1984—Jacksonville USFL		2	13	7	53.8	113	1	0	8.69		None		0	0	0

USFL Quarterback Rating Points: 1984 (108.8).

ROB BENNETT
Tight End—New Orleans Saints
Born August 4, 1963, at Buckhannon, W. Va.
Height, 6.05. Weight, 250.
High School—Buckhannon, W. Va., Upshur.
Attended West Virginia University.

Selected by Birmingham in 1985 USFL territorial draft.
Signed as free agent by New Orleans Saints, June 5, 1985.
On injured reserve with knee injury, August 20 through entire 1985 season.

WOODROW BENNETT JR.
(Woody)
Fullback—Miami Dolphins
Born March 24, 1955, at York, Pa.
Height, 6.02. Weight, 222.
High School—York, Pa., William Penn.
Attended Arizona Western Junior College and University of Miami.

Signed as free agent by Montreal Alouettes, April, 1979.
Released by Montreal Alouettes, June 22, 1979; signed as free agent by New York Jets, July 9, 1979.
Released by New York Jets, November 17, 1980; claimed on waivers by Miami Dolphins, November 18, 1980.
On injured reserve with knee injury, September 22 through remainder of 1981 season.
On physically unable to perform/active list with knee injury, July 22 through August 23, 1982; activated, August 24, 1982.
On injured reserve with knee injury, September 7 through December 30, 1982; activated, December 31, 1982.

		————RUSHING————				PASS RECEIVING				—TOTAL—		
Year	Club	G.	Att.	Yds.	Avg. TD.	P.C.	Yds.	Avg. TD.		TD.	Pts.	F.
1979—New York Jets NFL		15	2	4	2.0 1	1	9	9.0 0		1	6	1
1980—New York Jets (8)-Miami (4) NFL		12	46	200	4.3 0	3	26	8.7 1		1	6	2

Year Club	G.	——RUSHING—— Att. Yds. Avg. TD.	PASS RECEIVING P.C. Yds. Avg. TD.	—TOTAL— TD. Pts. F.
1981—Miami NFL	3	28 104 3.7 0	4 22 5.5 0	0 0 1
1982—Miami NFL	1	9 15 1.7 0	None	0 0 0
1983—Miami NFL	16	49 197 4.0 2	6 35 5.8 0	2 12 1
1984—Miami NFL	16	144 606 4.2 7	6 44 7.3 1	8 48 4
1985—Miami NFL	16	54 256 4.7 0	10 101 10.1 1	1 6 0
Pro Totals—7 Years	79	332 1382 4.2 10	30 237 7.9 3	13 78 9

Additional pro statistics: Returned one kickoff for seven yards, 1979; recovered two fumbles, 1980 and 1984; returned six kickoffs for 88 yards, 1980; recovered one fumble, 1981 and 1983; returned one kickoff for six yards, 1983.

Played in AFC Championship Game following 1982, 1984 and 1985 seasons.

Played in NFL Championship Game following 1982 and 1984 seasons.

BRADLEY WILLIAM BENSON
(Brad)
Offensive Tackle—New York Giants
Born November 25, 1955, at Altoona, Pa.
Height, 6.03. Weight, 270.
High School—Altoona, Pa.
Attended Pennsylvania State University.

Selected by New England in 8th round (219th player selected) of 1977 NFL draft.

Released by New England Patriots, September 1, 1977; signed as free agent by New York Giants, November 15, 1977.

On injured reserve with knee injury, August 28 through September 27, 1979; activated, September 28, 1979.

Active for 5 games with New York Giants in 1977; did not play.

New York Giants NFL, 1977 through 1985.

Games: 1978 (16), 1979 (10), 1980 (15), 1981 (11), 1982 (9), 1983 (16), 1984 (16), 1985 (16). Total—109.

Pro statistics: Recovered one fumble, 1979.

CHARLES HENRY BENSON
Defensive End—Indianapolis Colts
Born November 21, 1960, at Houston, Tex.
Height, 6.03. Weight, 267.
High School—Houston, Tex., Aldine.
Attended Baylor University.

Selected by New Jersey in 10th round (118th player selected) of 1983 USFL draft.

Selected by Miami in 3rd round (76th player selected) of 1983 NFL draft.

Signed by Miami Dolphins, July 9, 1983.

On injured reserve with groin injury, August 30 through October 27, 1983; activated, October 28, 1983.

Released by Miami Dolphins, August 27, 1985; signed as free agent by Indianapolis Colts, December 19, 1985.

Miami NFL, 1983 and 1984; Indianapolis NFL, 1985.

Games: 1983 (8), 1984 (16), 1985 (1). Total—25.

Played in AFC Championship Game following 1984 season.

Played in NFL Championship Game following 1984 season.

CLIFFORD ANTHONY BENSON
(Cliff)
Tight End—Atlanta Falcons
Born August 28, 1961, at Chicago, Ill.
Height, 6.04. Weight, 238.
High School—Palos Heights, Ill., Alan B. Shepard.
Received bachelor of arts degree in social work from Purdue University in 1984.

Selected by Oakland in 1st round (11th player selected) of 1984 USFL draft.

Selected by Atlanta Falcons in 5th round (132nd player selected) of 1984 NFL draft.

Signed by Atlanta Falcons, July 12, 1984.

Year Club	G.	——PASS RECEIVING—— P.C. Yds. Avg. TD.
1984—Atlanta NFL	16	26 244 9.4 0
1985—Atlanta NFL	16	10 37 3.7 0
Pro Totals—2 Years	32	36 281 7.8 0

Additional pro statistics: Rushed three times for eight yards, 1984.

THOMAS CARL BENSON
Linebacker—Atlanta Falcons
Born September 6, 1961, at Ardmore, Okla.
Height, 6.02. Weight, 235.
High School—Ardmore, Okla.
Attended University of Oklahoma.
Cousin of Rich Turner, defensive tackle with Green Bay Packers, 1981 through 1983.

Selected by Oklahoma in 1984 USFL territorial draft.

Selected by Atlanta in 2nd round (36th player selected) of 1984 NFL draft.

Signed by Atlanta Falcons, July 22, 1984.

Atlanta NFL, 1984 and 1985.

Games: 1984 (16), 1985 (16). Total—32.

Pro statistics: Recovered two fumbles, 1985.

TROY B. BENSON
Linebacker—New York Jets
Born July 30, 1963, at Altoona, Pa.
Height, 6.02. Weight, 227.
High School—Altoona, Pa.
Attended University of Pittsburgh.
Brother of Brad Benson, offensive tackle with New York Giants.

Selected by Baltimore in 1985 USFL territorial draft.
Selected by New York Jets in 5th round (120th player selected) of 1985 NFL draft.
Signed by New York Jets, July 22, 1985.
On injured reserve with ankle injury, August 22 through entire 1985 season.

ALBERT TIMOTHY BENTLEY
Running Back—Indianapolis Colts
Born August 15, 1960, at Naples, Fla.
Height, 5.11. Weight, 205.
High School—Immokalee, Fla.
Attended University of Miami (Fla.).

Selected by Chicago in 1st round (7th player selected) of 1984 USFL draft.
USFL rights traded by Chicago Blitz to Michigan Panthers for safety John Arnaud, April 17, 1984.
Signed by Michigan Panthers, April 17, 1984.
Granted roster exemption, April 17 through May 4, 1984; activated, May 5, 1984.
Selected by Indianapolis in 2nd round (36th player selected) of 1984 NFL supplemental draft.
Not protected in merger of Michigan Panthers and Oakland Invaders; selected by Oakland Invaders in USFL dispersal draft, December 6, 1984.
Released by Oakland Invaders, August 1, 1985; signed by Indianapolis Colts, September 3, 1985.
Granted roster exemption, September 3 through September 11, 1985; activated, September 12, 1985.

Year Club	G.	Att.	Yds.	Avg.	TD.	P.C.	Yds.	Avg.	TD.	TD.	Pts.	F.
			RUSHING				PASS RECEIVING				TOTAL	
1984—Michigan USFL	8	18	60	3.3	0	2	7	3.5	0	0	0	1
1985—Oakland USFL	18	191	1020	5.3	4	42	441	10.5	3	7	42	6
1985—Indianapolis NFL	15	54	288	5.3	2	11	85	7.7	0	2	12	1
USFL Totals—2 Years	26	209	1080	5.2	4	44	448	10.2	3	7	42	7
NFL Totals—1 Year	15	54	288	5.3	2	11	85	7.7	0	2	12	1
Pro Totals—3 Years	41	263	1368	5.2	6	55	533	9.7	3	9	54	8

Year Club	G.	No.	Yds.	Avg.	TD.
		KICKOFF RETURNS			
1984—Michigan USFL	8	19	425	22.4	0
1985—Oakland USFL	18	7	177	25.3	0
1985—Indianapolis NFL	15	27	674	25.0	0
USFL Totals—2 Years	26	26	602	23.2	0
NFL Totals—1 Year	15	27	674	25.0	0
Pro Totals—3 Years	41	53	1276	24.1	0

Additional USFL statistics: Recovered two fumbles, 1984 and 1985; attempted one pass with no completions, 1985.
Additional NFL statistics: Attempted one pass with one completion for six yards and recovered one fumble, 1985.
Played in USFL Championship Game following 1985 season.

PAUL GEORGE BERGMANN
Tight End—Kansas City Chiefs
Born March 30, 1961, at Los Angeles, Calif.
Height, 6.02. Weight, 230.
High School—Granada Hills, Calif.
Attended University of California at Los Angeles.

Selected by Jacksonville in 3rd round (42nd player selected) of 1984 USFL draft.
Signed by Jacksonville Bulls, January 17, 1984.
On developmental squad, June 8 through June 11, 1984; activated, June 12, 1984.
Selected by Indianapolis in 1st round (8th player selected) of 1984 NFL supplemental draft.
On developmental squad, June 21 through remainder of 1984 season.
Released by Jacksonville Bulls, February 18, 1985; awarded on waivers to New Jersey Generals, February 19, 1985.
Released by New Jersey Generals, February 21, 1985; signed as free agent by Oakland Invaders, March 18, 1985.
On developmental squad, April 28 through May 4, 1985; activated, May 5, 1985.
Released by Oakland Invaders, July 31, 1985.
NFL rights released by Indianapolis Colts, November 6, 1985; signed as free agent by Kansas City Chiefs, April 14, 1986.
On developmental squad for 2 games with Jacksonville Bulls in 1984.
On developmental squad for 1 game with Oakland Invaders in 1985.

Year Club	G.	P.C.	Yds.	Avg.	TD.
		PASS RECEIVING			
1984—Jacksonville USFL	16	48	647	13.5	3
1985—Oakland USFL	13		None		
Pro Totals—2 Years	29	48	647	13.5	3

Additional pro statistics: Rushed once for six yards, recovered one fumble and fumbled once, 1984.
Played in USFL Championship Game following 1985 season.

SCOTT M. BERGOLD
Offensive Tackle—St. Louis Cardinals
Born November 19, 1961, at Milwaukee, Wis.
Height, 6.07. Weight, 263.
High School—Wauwatosa, Wis., West.
Received bachelor of science degree in history from University of Wisconsin in 1984.

Seclected by Jacksonville in 1985 USFL territorial draft.
Selected by St. Louis in 2nd round (51st player selected) of 1985 NFL draft.
Signed by St. Louis Cardinals, July 18, 1985.
St. Louis NFL, 1985.
Games: 1985 (16).

RUFUS T. BESS JR.
Cornerback—Minnesota Vikings
Born September 13, 1956, at Hartsville, S.C.
Height, 5.09. Weight, 185.
High School—Hartsville, S.C., Butler.
Received degree in industrial education from South Carolina State College.
Cousin of Rusty Russell, offensive tackle with Los Angeles Raiders.

Signed as free agent by Oakland Raiders, June 1, 1979.
Released by Oakland Raiders, August 18, 1980; claimed on waivers by Buffalo Bills, August 20, 1980.
Released by Buffalo Bills, September 6, 1982; claimed on waivers by Minnesota Vikings, September 7, 1982.
On inactive list, September 12, 1982.
On injured reserve with sprained shoulder, November 23 through remainder of 1985 season.

| | | –INTERCEPTIONS– | | | | –PUNT RETURNS– | | | | —TOTAL— | | |
Year Club	G.	No.	Yds.	Avg.	TD.	No.	Yds.	Avg.	TD.	TD.	Pts.	F.
1979—Oakland NFL	16	1	0	0.0	0		None			0	0	0
1980—Buffalo NFL	16		None				None			0	0	0
1981—Buffalo NFL	16	1	12	12.0	0		None			0	0	0
1982—Minnesota NFL	8		None			2	17	8.5	0	0	0	0
1983—Minnesota NFL	14	3	38	12.7	0	21	158	7.5	0	0	0	2
1984—Minnesota NFL	16	3	7	2.3	0	2	9	4.5	0	0	0	1
1985—Minnesota NFL	11	2	27	13.5	0		None			0	0	0
Pro Totals—7 Years	97	10	84	8.4	0	25	184	7.4	0	0	0	3

Additional pro statistics: Recovered one fumble, 1979; returned one kickoff for six yards and recovered two fumbles for four yards, 1981; returned two kickoffs for 44 yards, 1983; returned three kickoffs for 47 yards, 1984; recovered two fumbles, 1984 and 1985; returned two kickoffs for 33 yards, 1985.

DOUGLAS LLOYD BETTERS
(Doug)
Defensive End—Miami Dolphins
Born June 11, 1956, at Lincoln, Neb.
Height, 6.07. Weight, 265.
High School—Arlington Heights, Ill., Arlington.
Attended University of Montana and University of Nevada at Reno.

Named to THE SPORTING NEWS NFL All-Star Team, 1983.
Selected by Miami in 6th round (163rd player selected) of 1978 NFL draft.
Miami NFL, 1978 through 1985.
Games: 1978 (16), 1979 (16), 1980 (16), 1981 (15), 1982 (9), 1983 (16), 1984 (16), 1985 (14). Total—118.
Pro statistics: Recovered one fumble, 1980 and 1984; recovered four fumbles, 1983.
Played in AFC Championship Game following 1982, 1984 and 1985 seasons.
Played in NFL Championship Game following 1982 and 1984 seasons.
Played in Pro Bowl (NFL All-Star Game) following 1983 season.

DEAN BIASUCCI
Placekicker—Indianapolis Colts
Born July 25, 1962, at Niagara Falls, N.Y.
Height, 6.00. Weight, 188.
High School—Miramar, Fla.
Attended Western Carolina University.

Signed as free agent by Atlanta Falcons, May 16, 1984.
Released by Atlanta Falcons, August 14, 1984; signed as free agent by Indianapolis Colts, September 8, 1984.
Released by Indianapolis Colts, August 27, 1985; re-signed by Colts, April 22, 1986.

| | | | ——PLACE KICKING—— | | | |
Year Club	G.	XP.	XPM.	FG.	FGA.	Pts.
1984—Indianapolis NFL	15	13	1	3	5	22

DUANE CLAIR BICKETT
Name pronounced BIK-ett.
Linebacker—Indianapolis Colts
Born December 1, 1962, at Los Angeles, Calif.
Height, 6.05. Weight, 241.
High School—Glendale, Calif.
Received degree in accounting from University of Southern California in 1986.

Named as linebacker on THE SPORTING NEWS College All-America Team, 1984.
Selected by Los Angeles in 1985 USFL territorial draft.
Selected by Indianapolis in 1st round (5th player selected) of 1985 NFL draft.
Signed by Indianapolis Colts, August 7, 1985.
Indianapolis NFL, 1985.
Games: 1985 (16).
Pro statistics: Intercepted one pass for no yards and recovered two fumbles, 1985.

CRAIG MARLON BINGHAM
Linebacker—San Diego Chargers
Born September 29, 1959, at Kingston, Jamaica, West Indies.
Height, 6.02. Weight, 220.
High School—Stamford, Conn.
Received bachelor of science degree in speech communications
from Syracuse University in 1982.

Selected by Pittsburgh in 6th round (167th player selected) of 1982 NFL draft.
On injured reserve with dislocated thumb, August 28 through October 4, 1984; activated, October 5, 1984.
Released by Pittsburgh Steelers, September 2, 1985; signed as free agent by San Diego Chargers, September 18, 1985.
Released by San Diego Chargers, October 11, 1985; re-signed by Chargers, November 13, 1985.
On injured reserve with ankle injury, December 18 through remainder of 1985 season.
Pittsburgh NFL, 1982 through 1984; San Diego NFL, 1985.
Games: 1982 (6), 1983 (12), 1984 (11), 1985 (8). Total—37.
Pro statistics: Returned one kickoff for 15 yards, 1983; recovered one fumble, 1984.
Played in AFC Championship Game following 1984 season.

GUY RICHARD BINGHAM
Offensive Lineman—New York Jets
Born February 25, 1958, at Koiaumi Gumma Ken, Japan.
Height, 6.03. Weight, 255.
High School—Aberdeen, Wash., Weatherwax.
Received degree in physical education from University of Montana.

Selected by New York Jets in 10th round of 1980 NFL draft.
On injured reserve with knee injury, September 7 through November 18, 1982; activated, November 19, 1982.
New York Jets NFL, 1980 through 1985.
Games: 1980 (16), 1981 (16), 1982 (7), 1983 (16), 1984 (16), 1985 (16). Total—87.
Pro statistics: Returned one kickoff for 19 yards, 1980; recovered one fumble, 1984.
Played in AFC Championship Game following 1982 season.

CARL BIRDSONG
Punter—St. Louis Cardinals
Born January 1, 1959, at Kaufman, Tex.
Height, 6.00. Weight, 192.
High School—Amarillo, Tex.
Received bachelor of science degree in pharmacy
from Southwestern Oklahoma State University in 1983.

Signed as free agent by Buffalo Bills, May 10, 1981.
Released by Buffalo Bills, July 28, 1981; claimed on waivers by St. Louis Cardinals, July 29, 1981.

Year Club	G.	No.	Avg.	Blk.
1981—St. Louis NFL	16	69	41.8	0
1982—St. Louis NFL	9	54	43.8	0
1983—St. Louis NFL	16	85	41.5	0
1984—St. Louis NFL	16	67	38.7	1
1985—St. Louis NFL	16	85	41.7	★2
Pro Totals—5 Years	73	360	41.4	3

Additional pro statistics: Rushed once for minus two yards, 1981; attempted one pass with one completion for 11 yards, 1983; attempted one pass with no completions and recovered one fumble, 1985.
Played in Pro Bowl (NFL All-Star Game) following 1983 season.

KEITH BRYAN BISHOP
Center-Guard—Denver Broncos
Born March 10, 1957, at San Diego, Calif.
Height, 6.03. Weight, 265.
High School—Midland, Tex., Robert E. Lee.
Attended University of Nebraska and Baylor University.

Selected by Denver in 6th round (157th player selected) of 1980 NFL draft.
On injured reserve with ankle injury, August 18 through entire 1981 season.
Denver NFL, 1980 and 1982 through 1985.
Games: 1980 (16), 1982 (9), 1983 (16), 1984 (16), 1985 (14). Total—71.
Pro statistics: Recovered one fumble, 1982 and 1983.

PETER MICHAEL BLACK
(Mike)
Punter—Detroit Lions

Born January 18, 1961, at Glendale, Calif.
Height, 6.02. Weight, 197.
High School—Glendale, Calif.
Attended Arizona State University.
Nephew of Virgil Carter, quarterback with Chicago Bears, Cincinnati Bengals
and San Diego Chargers, 1968 through 1972, 1975 and 1976.

Selected by Arizona in 1983 USFL territorial draft.
Selected by Detroit in 7th round (181st player selected) of 1983 NFL draft.
Signed by Detroit Lions, June 2, 1983.

		—PUNTING—		
Year Club	G.	No.	Avg.	Blk.
1983—Detroit NFL	16	71	41.0	1
1984—Detroit NFL	16	76	41.6	0
1985—Detroit NFL	16	73	41.8	0
Pro Totals—3 Years	48	220	41.5	1

Additional pro statistics: Rushed twice for minus 10 yards, attempted one pass with one interception and fumbled once, 1983; rushed three times for minus six yards and recovered one fumble, 1984; rushed once for no yards and fumbled once for minus seven yards, 1985.

TODD ALAN BLACKLEDGE
Quarterback—Kansas City Chiefs

Born February 25, 1961, at Canton, O.
Height, 6.03. Weight, 225.
High School—North Canton, O., Hoover.
Received degree in speech communications from Penn State University in 1983.
Son of Ron Blackledge, offensive line coach with Pittsburgh Steelers.

Selected by Kansas City in 1st round (7th player selected) of 1983 NFL draft.
Selected by Philadelphia in 1984 USFL territorial draft.

		—PASSING—							—RUSHING—				—TOTAL—		
Year Club	G.	Att.	Cmp.	Pct.	Gain	T.P.	P.I.	Avg.	Att.	Yds.	Avg.	TD.	TD.	Pts.	F.
1983—Kansas City NFL	4	34	20	58.8	259	3	0	7.62	1	0	0.0	0	0	0	1
1984—Kansas City NFL	11	294	147	50.0	1707	6	11	5.81	18	102	5.7	1	1	6	8
1985—Kansas City NFL	12	172	86	50.0	1190	6	14	6.92	17	97	5.7	0	0	0	3
Pro Totals—3 Years	27	500	253	50.6	3156	15	25	6.31	36	199	5.5	1	1	6	12

Quarterback Rating Points: 1983 (112.3), 1984 (59.2), 1985 (50.3). Total—59.7.
Additional pro statistics: Recovered four fumbles and fumbled eight times for minus three yards, 1984; recovered one fumble, 1985.

DONALD KIRK BLACKMON
(Don)
Linebacker—New England Patriots

Born March 14, 1958, at Pompano Beach, Fla.
Height, 6.03. Weight, 235.
High School—Lauderdale Lakes, Fla., Boyd Anderson.
Attended University of Tulsa.

Selected by New England in 4th round (102nd player selected) of 1981 NFL draft.

		—INTERCEPTIONS—			
Year Club	G.	No.	Yds.	Avg.	TD.
1981—New England NFL	16		None		
1982—New England NFL	9	2	7	3.5	0
1983—New England NFL	15	1	39	39.0	0
1984—New England NFL	16	1	3	3.0	0
1985—New England NFL	14	1	14	14.0	0
Pro Totals—5 Years	70	5	63	12.6	0

Additional pro statistics: Recovered two fumbles for 47 yards, 1982; credited with two safeties and recovered two fumbles, 1985.
Played in AFC Championship Game following 1985 season.
Played in NFL Championship Game following 1985 season.

GLENN ALLEN BLACKWOOD
Safety—Miami Dolphins

Born February 23, 1957, at San Antonio, Tex.
Height, 6.00. Weight, 188.
High School—San Antonio, Tex., Churchill
Received bachelor of science degree in pre-dental studies from University of Texas in 1979.
Brother of Lyle Blackwood, safety with Miami Dolphins.

Selected by Miami in 8th round (215th player selected) of 1979 NFL draft.
On injured reserve with knee injury, November 19 through remainder of 1979 season.
Granted free agency, February 1, 1985; re-signed by Dolphins, September 12, 1985.
Granted roster exemption, September 12 through September 20, 1985; activated, September 21, 1985.

Year Club	G.	No.	Yds.	Avg.	TD.
		INTERCEPTIONS			
1979—Miami NFL	11		None		
1980—Miami NFL	16	3	0	0.0	0
1981—Miami NFL	16	4	124	31.0	0
1982—Miami NFL	9	2	42	21.0	*1
1983—Miami NFL	16	3	0	0.0	0
1984—Miami NFL	16	6	169	28.2	0
1985—Miami NFL	14	6	36	6.0	0
Pro Totals—7 Years............	98	24	371	15.5	1

Additional pro statistics: Returned one punt for no yards, 1980; recovered four fumbles, 1980 and 1983; returned two punts for eight yards and recovered one fumble for five yards, 1981; returned two punts for two yards, 1982; recovered one fumble, 1982, 1984 and 1985; fumbled once, 1982; returned one punt for 10 yards, 1983; returned three punts for 20 yards, 1985.

Played in AFC Championship Game following 1982, 1984 and 1985 seasons.

Played in NFL Championship Game following 1982 and 1984 seasons.

LYLE VERNON BLACKWOOD JR.
Safety—Miami Dolphins

Born May 24, 1951, at San Antonio, Tex.
Height, 6.01. Weight, 190.
High School—San Antonio, Tex., Churchill.
Attended Blinn Junior College and received bachelor of general studies degree
in government from Texas Christian University.
Brother of Glenn Blackwood, safety with Miami Dolphins.

Selected by Denver in 9th round (217th player selected) of 1973 NFL draft.
Claimed on waivers from Denver Broncos by Cincinnati Bengals, 1973.
Selected from Cincinnati Bengals by Seattle Seahawks in NFL expansion draft, March 30, 1976.
Claimed on waivers from Seattle Seahawks by Baltimore Colts, August 11, 1977.
Traded by Baltimore Colts to New York Giants for draft pick, July 15, 1981.
Released by New York Giants, August 31, 1981; signed as free agent by Miami Dolphins, September 30, 1981.

Year Club	G.	No.	Yds.	Avg.	TD.	No.	Yds.	Avg.	TD.	No.	Yds.	Avg.	TD.	TD.	Pts.	F.
		INTERCEPTIONS				—PUNT RETURNS—				—KICKOFF RET.—				—TOTAL—		
1973—Cincinnati NFL	7		None			4	12	3.0	0		None			0	0	0
1974—Cincinnati NFL	13		None			10	29	2.9	0	1	17	17.0	0	0	0	0
1975—Cincinnati NFL	14	2	44	22.0	0	23	123	5.3	0		None			0	0	1
1976—Seattle NFL	11		None			19	132	6.9	0	9	215	23.8	0	0	0	1
1977—Baltimore NFL	14	*10	163	16.3	0	7	22	3.1	0	1	24	24.0	0	0	0	3
1978—Baltimore NFL	16	4	146	36.5	2	1	2	2.0	0	1	18	18.0	0	2	12	0
1979—Baltimore NFL	16	4	63	15.8	0	4	−1	−0.3	0	3	41	13.7	0	0	0	0
1980—Baltimore NFL	11	1	0	0.0	0		None			2	41	20.5	0	0	0	0
1981—Miami NFL	12	3	12	4.0	0		None				None			0	0	0
1982—Miami NFL	9	2	41	20.5	0		None				None			0	0	0
1983—Miami NFL	16	4	77	19.3	0		None				None			0	0	0
1984—Miami NFL	16	3	29	9.7	0		None				None			0	0	0
1985—Miami NFL	16	1	0	0.0	0		None			2	32	16.0	0	0	0	0
Pro Totals—13 Years.....	171	34	575	16.9	2	68	319	4.7	0	19	388	20.4	0	2	12	5

Additional pro statistics: Recovered one fumble, 1975 and 1982; blocked two kicks and caught one pass for eight yards, 1976; recovered four fumbles for four yards, 1977; recovered three fumbles for seven yards, 1978; recovered two fumbles, 1979 and 1984.

Played in AFC Championship Game following 1982, 1984 and 1985 seasons.

Played in NFL Championship Game following 1982 and 1984 seasons.

BRIAN TIMOTHY BLADOS
Guard—Cincinnati Bengals

Born January 11, 1962, at Arlington, Va.
Height, 6.04. Weight, 295.
High School—Arlington, Va., Washington Lee.
Attended University of North Carolina.

Selected by Pittsburgh in 1984 USFL territorial draft.
Selected by Cincinnati in 1st round (28th player selected) of 1984 NFL draft.
Signed by Cincinnati Bengals, June 28, 1984.
Cincinnati NFL, 1984 and 1985.
Games: 1984 (16), 1985 (16). Total—32.
Pro statistics: Caught one pass for four yards, 1985.

ALBERT MATTHEW BLAIR
(Matt)
Linebacker—Minnesota Vikings

Born September 20, 1950, at Hilo, Hawaii.
Height, 6.05. Weight, 239.
High School—Dayton, O., Colonel White.
Attended Northeastern Oklahoma A&M and received degree in physical education
from Iowa State University.

Named to THE SPORTING NEWS NFC All-Star Team, 1977 and 1978.
Selected by Minnesota in 2nd round (51st player selected) of 1974 NFL draft.
On physically unable to perform/active with knee injury, July 21 through August 20, 1984; activated, August 21, 1984.

On injured reserve with knee injury, August 28 through September 27, 1984; activated, September 28, 1984.
On injured reserve with knee injury, September 9 through November 22, 1985; activated, November 23, 1985.

Year	Club	G.	No.	Yds.	Avg.TD.		Year	Club	G.	No.	Yds.	Avg.TD.
				—INTERCEPTIONS—							—INTERCEPTIONS—	
1974—Minnesota NFL		14	1	—3	—3.0 0		1981—Minnesota NFL		16	1	1	1.0 0
1975—Minnesota NFL		14	1	18	18.0 0		1982—Minnesota NFL		9		None	
1976—Minnesota NFL		14	2	25	12.5 0		1983—Minnesota NFL		16	1	0	0.0 0
1977—Minnesota NFL		14	1	18	18.0 0		1984—Minnesota NFL		11		None	
1978—Minnesota NFL		16	3	28	9.3 0		1985—Minnesota NFL		6		None	
1979—Minnesota NFL		16	3	32	10.7 0		Pro Totals—12 Years		160	16	119	7.4 0
1980—Minnesota NFL		14	3	0	0.0 0							

Additional pro statistics: Recovered one fumble for 13 yards, 1974; returned two punts for minus two yards, 1975; fumbled once, 1975 and 1981; recovered five fumbles for eight yards, 1976; returned one kickoff for no yards, 1976 and 1981; recovered two fumbles, 1977, 1981 and 1983; scored one touchdown after blocked kick, 1977; recovered three fumbles for 49 yards and one touchdown (touchdown was 49-yard run with lateral after fumble recovery), 1978; recovered two fumbles for 14 yards, 1979; recovered one fumble, 1980, 1984 and 1985.
Played in NFC Championship Game following 1974, 1976 and 1977 seasons.
Played in NFL Championship Game following 1974 and 1976 seasons.
Played in Pro Bowl (NFL All-Star Game) following 1977 through 1982 seasons.

CARL NATHANIEL BLAND
Wide Receiver—Detroit Lions
Born August 17, 1961, at Fluvanna County, Va.
Height, 5.11. Weight, 182.
High School—Richmond, Va., Thomas Jefferson.
Attended Virginia Union University.

Signed as free agent by Detroit Lions, May 3, 1984.
On injured reserve with hamstring injury, August 20 through November 7, 1984; activated after clearing procedural waivers, November 9, 1984.
Released by Detroit Lions, September 3, 1985; re-signed by Lions, October 17, 1985.
Released by Detroit Lions, October 31, 1985; re-signed by Lions, November 4, 1985.

Year	Club	G.	P.C.	Yds.	Avg.	TD.
				—PASS RECEIVING—		
1984—Detroit NFL		3		None		
1985—Detroit NFL		8	12	157	13.1	0
Pro Totals—2 Years		11	12	157	13.1	0

GERALD BLANTON
(Jerry)
Linebacker—Kansas City Chiefs
Born December 20, 1956, at Toledo, O.
Height, 6.01. Weight, 229.
High School—Toledo, O., Thomas A. Devilbiss.
Attended University of Kentucky.

Selected by Buffalo in 11th round (282nd player selected) of 1978 NFL draft.
Released by Buffalo Bills, August 24, 1978; signed as free agent by Hamilton Tiger-Cats, September 8, 1978.
Released by Hamilton Tiger-Cats, September 15, 1978; signed as free agent by Kansas City Chiefs, December 28, 1978.
On injured reserve with knee injury, September 1 through October 16, 1981; activated, October 17, 1981.
On injured reserve with knee injury, December 15 through remainder of 1981 season.
On injured reserve with ruptured disc in back, August 28 through October 12, 1984; activated, October 13, 1984.
Hamilton CFL, 1978; Kansas City NFL, 1979 through 1985.
Games: 1978 (1), 1979 (16), 1980 (16), 1981 (9), 1982 (9), 1983 (16), 1984 (10), 1985 (16). Total NFL—92. Total Pro—93.
Pro statistics: Recovered one fumble, 1979 and 1984; intercepted one pass for 14 yards, 1984.

DENNIS BLIGEN
Running Back—New York Jets
Born March 3, 1962, at New York, N.Y.
Height, 5.11. Weight, 209.
High School—New York, N.Y., Murray Bergtraum.
Attended St. John's University.

Signed as free agent by New York Jets, May 16, 1984.
On injured reserve with fractured thumb, July 31 through October 24, 1984; activated after clearing procedural waivers, October 26, 1984.
Released by New York Jets, November 24, 1984; re-signed by Jets, December 6, 1984.
On injured reserved with rib injury, August 27 through October 23, 1985; activated after clearing procedural waivers, October 25, 1985.

Year	Club	G.	Att.	Yds.	Avg.	TD.	P.C.	Yds.	Avg.	TD.	TD.	Pts.	F.
				—RUSHING—				PASS RECEIVING				—TOTAL—	
1984—N.Y. Jets NFL		1		None				None			0	0	0
1985—N.Y. Jets NFL		9	22	107	4.9	1	5	43	8.6	0	1	6	1
Pro Totals—2 Years		10	22	107	4.9	1	5	43	8.6	0	1	6	1

DWAINE P. BOARD
Defensive End—San Francisco 49ers
Born November 29, 1956, at Union Hall, Va.
Height, 6.05. Weight, 248.
High School—Rocky Mount, Va., Franklin County.
Received bachelor of science degree in industrial technology from
North Carolina A&T State University in 1979.

Selected by Pittsburgh in 5th round (137th player selected) of 1979 NFL draft.
Released by Pittsburgh Steelers, August 27, 1979; claimed on waivers by San Francisco 49ers, August 28, 1979.
On injured reserve with knee injury, September 23 through remainder of 1980 season.
On injured reserve with knee injury, September 16 through remainder of 1982 season.
San Francisco NFL, 1979 through 1985.
Games: 1979 (16), 1980 (3), 1981 (16), 1982 (1), 1983 (16), 1984 (16), 1985 (16). Total—84.
Pro statistics: Recovered five fumbles (including one in end zone for a touchdown), 1983; recovered one fumble, 1984 and 1985.
Played in NFC Championship Game following 1981, 1983 and 1984 seasons.
Played in NFL Championship Game following 1981 and 1984 seasons.

TONY L. BODDIE
Running Back—Denver Broncos
Born November 11, 1960, at Portsmouth, Va.
Height, 5.11. Weight, 195.
High School—Bremerton, Wash.
Attended Montana State University.

Selected by Los Angeles in 12th round (144th player selected) of 1983 USFL draft.
On developmental squad, March 23 through March 28, 1985; activated, March 29, 1985.
On developmental squad, April 26 through May 23, 1985; activated, May 24, 1985.
Released by Los Angeles Express, July 9, 1985; signed as free agent by Los Angeles Raiders, July 19, 1985.
Released by Los Angeles Raiders, July 25, 1985; signed as free agent by Denver Broncos, March 24, 1986.
On developmental squad for 5 games with Los Angeles Express in 1985.

		—RUSHING—				PASS RECEIVING				—TOTAL—		
Year Club	G.	Att.	Yds.	Avg.	TD.	P.C.	Yds.	Avg.	TD.	TD.	Pts.	F.
1983—Los Angeles USFL	18	109	403	3.7	3	46	434	9.4	2	5	30	7
1984—Los Angeles USFL	18	16	31	1.9	0	20	170	8.5	1	1	6	1
1985—Los Angeles USFL	13	49	208	4.2	1	17	124	7.3	1	2	12	3
Pro Totals—3 Years	49	174	642	3.7	4	83	728	8.8	4	8	48	11

		KICKOFF RETURNS			
Year Club	G.	No.	Yds.	Avg.	TD.
1983—Los Angeles USFL	18	7	132	18.9	0
1984—Los Angeles USFL	18	33	782	23.7	0
1985—Los Angeles USFL	13	29	517	17.8	0
Pro Totals—3 Years	49	69	1431	20.7	0

Additional pro statistics: Recovered two fumbles, 1983; attempted one pass with no completions, 1985.

KIM BOKAMPER
Defensive End—Miami Dolphins
Born September 25, 1954, at San Diego, Calif.
Height, 6.06. Weight, 255.
High School—Milpitas, Calif.
Attended Concordia College, San Jose City College and San Jose State University.

Selected by Miami in 1st round (19th player selected) of 1976 NFL draft.
On injured reserve with knee injury entire 1976 season.
On injured reserve with broken ankle, October 5 through Novenber 1, 1984; activated, November 2, 1984.

		—INTERCEPTIONS—			
Year Club	G.	No.	Yds.	Avg.	TD.
1977—Miami NFL	14		None		
1978—Miami NFL	16	1	2	2.0	0
1979—Miami NFL	14	1	3	3.0	0
1980—Miami NFL	16	1	6	6.0	0
1981—Miami NFL	16		None		
1982—Miami NFL	9	1	1	1.0	0
1983—Miami NFL	15	2	43	21.5	1
1984—Miami NFL	11		None		
1985—Miami NFL	16		None		
Pro Totals—9 Years	127	6	55	9.2	1

Additional pro statistics: Recovered two fumbles for two yards, 1977; credited with one safety, 1978; recovered one fumble and fumbled once, 1983.
Played in AFC Championship Game following 1982, 1984 and 1985 seasons.
Played in NFL Championship Game following 1982 and 1984 seasons.
Played in Pro Bowl (NFL All-Star Game) following 1979 season.

—DID YOU KNOW—
That the Dallas Cowboys have won their only two Super Bowls in New Orleans? Their three losses all came in Miami.

RICKEY ALLEN BOLDEN
Offensive Tackle—Cleveland Browns
Born September 8, 1961, at Dallas, Tex.
Height, 6.06. Weight, 280.
High School—Dallas, Tex., Hillcrest.
Attended Southern Methodist University.

Selected by Oakland in 4th round (72nd player selected) of 1984 USFL draft.
Selected by Cleveland in 4th round (96th player selected) of 1984 NFL draft.
Signed by Cleveland Browns, May 17, 1984.
On injured reserve with dislocated shoulder, November 21 through remainder of 1984 season.
Cleveland NFL, 1984 and 1985.
Games: 1984 (12), 1985 (16). Total—28.
Pro statistics: Caught one pass for 19 yards and fumbled once, 1984.

SCOTT LOUIS BOLZAN
Offensive Tackle—Cleveland Browns
Born July 25, 1962, at Chicago, Ill.
Height, 6.03. Weight, 280.
High School—South Holland, Ill., Thornwood.
Attended Northern Illinois University.

Selected by Chicago in 1984 USFL territotial draft.
Selected by New England in 9th round (238th player selected) of 1984 NFL draft.
Signed by New England Partiots, June 10, 1984.
Released by New England Patriots, August 21, 1984; signed by Chicago Blitz, October 15, 1984.
Franchise disbanded, November 20, 1984.
Selected by Memphis Showboats in USFL dispersal draft, December 6, 1984.
Released by Memphis Showboats, February 11, 1985; re-signed by Showboats, February 22, 1985.
On developmental squad, March 8 through March 15, 1985.
Released by Memphis Showboats, March 16, 1985; signed as free agent by Cleveland Browns, May 6, 1985.
Released by Cleveland Browns, September 2, 1985; re-signed by Browns, September 26, 1985.
Released by Cleveland Browns, October 2, 1985; re-signed by Browns, April 20, 1986.
On developmental squad for 1 game with Memphis Showboats in 1985.
Active for 1 game with Cleveland Browns in 1985; did not play.
Memphis USFL, 1985; Cleveland NFL, 1985.
Games: 1985 USFL (2).

STEVEN CHRISTOPHER BONO
(Steve)
Quarterback—Minnesota Vikings
Born May 11, 1962, at Norristown, Pa.
Height, 6.03. Weight, 211.
High School—Norristown, Pa.
Attended University of California at Los Angeles.

Selected by Memphis in 1985 USFL territorial draft.
Selected by Minnesota in 6th round (142nd player selected) of 1985 NFL draft.
Signed by Minnesota Vikings, July 10, 1985.

Year Club	G.	Att.	Cmp.	Pct.	Gain	T.P.	P.I.	Avg.	Att.	Yds.	Avg.	TD.	TD.	Pts.	F.
						PASSING				RUSHING				TOTAL	
1985—Minnesota NFL	1	10	1	10.0	5	0	0	0.50		None			0	0	0

Quarterback Rating Points: 1985 (39.6).

JON L. BORCHARDT
Guard—Seattle Seahawks
Born August 13, 1957, at Minneapolis, Minn.
Height, 6.05. Weight, 265.
High School—Brooklyn Park, Minn., Park Center.
Received bachelor of science degree in microbiology from Montana State University in 1979.

Selected by Buffalo in 3rd round (62nd player selected) of 1979 NFL draft.
Traded by Buffalo Bills to Seattle Seahawks for 7th round pick in 1986 draft, April 26, 1985.
Buffalo NFL, 1979 through 1984; Seattle NFL, 1985.
Games: 1979 (16), 1980 (16), 1981 (16), 1982 (9), 1983 (16), 1984 (16), 1985 (13). Total—102.
Pro statistics: Recovered one fumble, 1981.

MARK STEVEN BORTZ
Guard—Chicago Bears
Born February 12, 1961, at Pardeeville, Wis.
Height, 6.06. Weight, 271.
High School—Pardeeville, Wis.
Attended University of Iowa.

Selected by Los Angeles in 4th round (48th player selected) of 1983 USFL draft.
Selected by Chicago in 8th round (219th player selected) of 1983 NFL draft.
Signed by Chicago Bears, June 2, 1983.
Chicago NFL, 1983 through 1985.
Games: 1983 (16), 1984 (15), 1985 (16). Total—47.
Played in NFC Championship Game following 1984 and 1985 seasons.
Played in NFL Championship Game following 1985 season.

JEFF BOSTIC
Center—Washington Redskins
Born September 18, 1958, at Greensboro, N. C.
Height, 6.02. Weight, 260.
High School—Greensboro, N. C., Benjamin L. Smith.
Attended Clemson University.
Brother of Joe Bostic, guard with St. Louis Cardinals.

Signed as free agent by Philadelphia Eagles, May 20, 1980.
Released by Philadelphia Eagles, August 26, 1980; signed as free agent by Washington Redskins, September 1, 1984.
On injured reserve with knee injury, October 23 through remainder of 1984 season.
On injured reserve with knee injury, August 24 through October 18, 1985; activated, October 19, 1985.
Washington NFL, 1980 through 1985.
Games: 1980 (16), 1981 (16), 1982 (9), 1983 (16), 1984 (8), 1985 (10). Total—75.
Pro statistics: Recovered one fumble, 1981 and 1985; caught one pass for minus four yards, 1981; recovered three fumbles, 1983; recovered two fumbles, 1984.
Played in NFC Championship Game following 1982 and 1983 seasons.
Played in NFL Championship Game following 1982 and 1983 seasons.
Played in Pro Bowl (NFL All-Star Game) following 1983 season.

JOE EARL BOSTIC JR.
Guard—St. Louis Cardinals
Born April 20, 1957, at Greensboro, N.C.
Height, 6.03. Weight, 265.
High School—Greensboro, N.C., Benjamin L. Smith.
Attended Clemson University.
Brother of Jeff Bostic, center with Washington Redskins.

Selected by St. Louis in 3rd round (64th player selected) of 1979 NFL draft.
St. Louis NFL, 1979 through 1985.
Games: 1979 (16), 1980 (16), 1981 (14), 1982 (8), 1983 (14), 1984 (16), 1985 (16). Total—100.
Pro statistics: Recovered one fumble, 1983.

JOHN EARL BOSTIC
Cornerback—Detroit Lions
Born October 6, 1962, at Titusville, Fla.
Height, 5.10. Weight, 178.
High School—Titusville, Fla., Astronaut.
Received degree in pre-medicine from Bethune-Cookman College in 1985.

Selected by Tampa Bay in 1985 USFL territorial draft.
Selected by Kansas City in 6th round (149th player selected) of 1985 NFL draft.
Signed by Kansas City Chiefs, July 18, 1985.
Released by Kansas City Chiefs, August 12, 1985; signed as free agent by Detroit Lions, September 24, 1985.
Detroit NFL, 1985.
Games: 1985 (13).

KEITH BOSTIC
Safety—Houston Oilers
Born January 17, 1961, at Ann Arbor, Mich.
Height, 6.01. Weight, 212.
High School—Ann Arbor, Mich., Pioneer.
Attended University of Michigan.

Selected by Michigan in 1983 USFL territorial draft.
Selected by Houston in 2nd round (42nd player selected) of 1983 NFL draft.
Signed by Houston Oilers, June 27, 1983.

Year Club	G.	No.	Yds.	Avg.	TD.
1983—Houston NFL	16	2	0	0.0	0
1984—Houston NFL	16		None		
1985—Houston NFL	16	3	28	9.3	0
Pro Totals—3 Years	48	5	28	5.6	0

Additional pro statistics: Recovered two fumbles for 25 yards and a touchdown, 1984; recovered one fumble, 1985.

EMIL NICHOLAS BOURES
Name pronounced BORE-ees.
Guard-Center—Pittsburgh Steelers
Born January 29, 1960, at Bridgeport, Pa.
Height, 6.01. Weight, 257.
High School—Norristown, Pa., Bishop Kenrick.
Received bachelor of arts degree in communications from University of Pittsburgh in 1982.

Selected by Pittsburgh in 7th round (182nd player selected) of 1982 NFL draft.
On inactive list, September 13 and September 19, 1982.
On injured reserve with knee injury, November 16 through remainder of 1984 season.
On physically unable to perform/active with knee injury, July 20 through October 23, 1985; activated, October 24, 1985.
Pittsburgh NFL, 1982 through 1985.
Games: 1982 (5), 1983 (16), 1984 (8), 1985 (6). Total—35.
Pro statistics: Fumbled once, 1983.

MATTHEW KYLE BOUZA
(Matt)
Wide Receiver—Indianapolis Colts
Born April 8, 1959, at San Jose, Calif.
Height, 6.03. Weight, 211.
High School—Sacramento, Calif., Jesuit.
Received degree in political science from University of California at Berkeley.

Signed as free agent by San Francisco 49ers, May 8, 1981.
Released by San Francisco 49ers, August 31, 1981; re-signed by 49ers, September 1, 1981.
Released by San Francisco 49ers, September 9, 1981; signed as free agent by Baltimore Colts, May 15, 1982.
On injured reserve with separated shoulder, November 18 through remainder of 1983 season.
Franchise transferred to Indianapolis, March 31, 1984.
On injured reserve with knee injury, November 1 through November 28, 1985; activated, November 29, 1985.

| | | | —PASS RECEIVING— | | | |
Year Club	G.	P.C.	Yds.	Avg.	TD.	
1981—San Francisco NFL	1		None			
1982—Baltimore NFL	9	22	287	13.0	2	
1983—Baltimore NFL	11	25	385	15.4	0	
1984—Indianapolis NFL	16	22	270	12.3	0	
1985—Indianapolis NFL	12	27	381	14.1	2	
Pro Totals—5 Years............	49	96	1323	13.8	4	

Additional pro statistics: Returned three kickoffs for 31 yards, returned two punts for no yards and recovered one fumble, 1982; fumbled once, 1982 through 1984; returned one kickoff for minus four yards, 1983; returned three punts for 17 yards, 1984.

JAMES EDWIN BOWMAN
(Jim)
Safety—New England Patriots
Born October 26, 1963, at Cadillac, Mich.
Height, 6.02. Weight, 210.
High School—Cadillac, Mich.
Attended Central Michigan University.

Selected by Oakland in 11th round (153rd player selected) of 1985 USFL draft.
Selected by New England in 2nd round (52nd player selected) of 1985 NFL draft.
Signed by New England Patriots, July 23, 1985.
New England NFL, 1985.
Games: 1985 (16).
Pro statistics: Returned one punt for minus three yards, 1985.
Played in AFC Championship Game following 1985 season.
Played in NFL Championship Game following 1985 season.

CHARLES EMANUEL BOWSER
Linebacker—Miami Dolphins
Born October 2, 1959, at Plymouth, N.C.
Height, 6.03. Weight, 232.
High School—Plymouth, N.C.
Received bachelor of science degree in history from Duke University in 1982.

Selected by Miami in 4th round (108th player selected) of 1982 NFL draft.
On injured reserve with ankle injury, October 23 through remainder of 1985 season.
Miami NFL, 1982 through 1985.
Games: 1982 (9), 1983 (16), 1984 (15), 1985 (2). Total—42.
Pro statistics: Recovered one fumble, 1984.
Played in AFC Championship Game following 1982 and 1984 seasons.
Played in NFL Championship Game following 1982 and 1984 seasons.

WALTER NATHANIEL BOWYER JR.
Name pronounced BOY-er.
(Walt)
Defensive End—Denver Broncos
Born June 29, 1960, at Pittsburgh, Pa.
Height, 6.04. Weight, 252.
High School—Winkinsburg, Pa.
Attended Arizona State University.

Selected by Denver in 10th round (254th player selected) of 1983 NFL draft.
Released by Denver Broncos, August 27, 1985; re-signed by Broncos for 1986, December 14, 1985.
Denver NFL, 1983 and 1984.
Games: 1983 (14), 1984 (16). Total—30.
Pro statistics: Recovered one fumble, 1983 and 1984.

—DID YOU KNOW—
That Joe Morris of the Giants and Stump Mitchell of the Cardinals were the only non-kickers to lead their teams in scoring in 1985?

GERARD MARK JOSEPH BOYARSKY

Name pronounced Boy-ARE-ski.

(Jerry)

Nose Tackle—Cincinnati Bengals

Born May 15, 1959, at Scranton, Pa.
Height, 6.03. Weight, 290.
High School—Jermyn, Pa., Lakeland.
Received bachelor of arts degree in political science from University of Pittsburgh in 1981.

Selected by New Orleans in 5th round (128th player selected) of 1981 NFL draft.
On injured reserve with knee injury, September 1 through October 1, 1981; activated, October 2, 1981.
Released by New Orleans Saints, September 6, 1982; signed as free agent by Cincinnati Bengals, December 1, 1982 and 1983.
New Orleans NFL, 1981; Cincinnati NFL, 1982 through 1985.
Games: 1981 (11), 1982 (2), 1983 (15), 1984 (15), 1985 (16). Total—59.

BRENT VARNER BOYD

Guard—Minnesota Vikings

Born March 23, 1957, at Downey, Calif.
Height, 6.03. Weight, 275.
High School—La Habra, Calif., Lowell.
Received bachelor of arts degree in sociology from University of California at Los Angeles in 1980,
and attending UCLA for master's degree in business administration.

Selected by Minnesota in 3rd round (68th player selected) of 1980 NFL draft.
On injured reserve with knee injury, September 30 through remainder of 1981 season.
On physically unable to perform/active with knee injury, July 30 through September 1, 1982.
On physically unable to perform/reserve with knee injury, September 2 through November 19, 1982; activated, November 20, 1982.
On injured reserve with fractured fibula, August 27 through entire 1984 season.
Minnesota NFL, 1980 through 1983 and 1985.
Games: 1980 (16), 1981 (3), 1982 (4), 1983 (16), 1985 (15). Total—54.
Pro statistics: Returned one kickoff for 20 yards, 1980.

JEFFREY SANTEE BOYD

(Jeff)

Wide Receiver—Cleveland Browns

Born April 17, 1958, at Los Angeles, Calif.
Height, 6.02. Weight, 185.
High School—Inglewood, Calif., Morningside.
Attended Los Angeles Southwest Community College, University of Colorado and Chapman College.

Signed as free agent by Edmonton Eskimos, May 10, 1982.
Released by Edmonton Eskimos, June 20, 1982; signed as free agent by Minnesota Vikings, July 7, 1982.
Released by Minnesota Vikings, September 6, 1982; re-signed by Eskimos, November 15, 1982.
Released by Edmonton Eskimos, June 28, 1983; awarded on waivers to Winnipeg Blue Bombers, June 29, 1983.
Granted free agency, March 1, 1986; signed by Cleveland Browns, April 22, 1986.

Year Club	G.	Att.	Yds.	Avg.	TD.	P.C.	Yds.	Avg.	TD.	TD.	Pts.	F.
		—RUSHING—				PASS RECEIVING				—TOTAL—		
1983—Winnipeg CFL	14	2	9	4.5	0	50	974	19.5	7	7	42	1
1984—Winnipeg CFL	16	1	0	0.0	0	65	1106	17.0	11	11	66	0
1985—Winnipeg CFL	15	5	57	11.4	1	76	1372	18.1	14	15	90	2
Pro Totals—3 Years	45	8	66	8.3	1	191	3452	18.1	32	33	198	3

Additional pro statistics: Recovered one fumble, 1983 and 1985.

MARK HEARN BOYER

Tight End—Indianapolis Colts

Born September 16, 1962, at Huntington Beach, Calif.
Height, 6.04. Weight, 233.
High School—Huntington Beach, Calif., Edison.
Attended University of Southern California.

Selected by Los Angeles in 1985 USFL territorial draft.
Selected by Indianapolis in 9th round (229th player selected) of 1985 NFL draft.
Signed by Indianapolis Colts, July 18, 1985.

Year Club	G.	P.C.	Yds.	Avg.	TD.
		—PASS RECEIVING—			
1985—Indianapolis NFL	16	25	274	11.0	0

Additional pro statistics: Recovered one fumble, 1985.

DONALD CRAIG BRACKEN

(Don)

Punter—Green Bay Packers

Born February 16, 1962, at Coalinga, Calif.
Height, 6.00. Weight, 205.
High School—Thermopolis, Wyo., Hot Springs County.
Received bachelor of science degree in physical education from University of Michigan.

Selected by Michigan in 1984 USFL territorial draft.
Signed by Michigan Panthers, January 8, 1984.
Released by Michigan Panthers, February 16, 1984; signed as free agent by Kansas City Chiefs, May 4, 1984.
Released by Kansas City Chiefs, June 1, 1984; signed as free agent by Indianapolis Colts, June 14, 1984.
Released by Indianapolis Colts, August 6, 1984; signed as free agent by Denver Broncos, January 30, 1985.
Released by Denver Broncos, August 26, 1985; signed as free agent by Green Bay Packers, November 6, 1985.

Year Club	G.	No.	Avg.	Blk.
——PUNTING——				
1985—Green Bay NFL	7	26	40.5	0

CARLOS HUMBERTO BRADLEY
Linebacker—San Diego Chargers
Born April 27, 1960, at Philadelphia, Pa.
Height, 6.00. Weight, 222.
High School—Philadelphia, Pa., Germantown.
Received bachelor of science degree in physical education from Wake Forest University in 1981.

Selected by San Diego in 11th round (300th player selected) of 1981 NFL draft.
Released by San Diego Chargers, August 25, 1981; re-signed by Chargers after clearing procedural waivers, October 28, 1981.
On injured reserve with groin injury, December 31 through remainder of 1981 season playoffs.
On injured reserve with sprained ankle, October 9 through December 7, 1984; activated, December 8, 1984.
On injured reserve with foot injury, November 13 through remainder of 1985 season.
San Diego NFL, 1981 through 1985.
Games: 1981 (8), 1982 (9), 1983 (16), 1984 (8), 1985 (10). Total—51.
Pro statistics: Recovered one fumble, 1983; intercepted two passes for 36 yards, 1985.

DANNY BRADLEY
Wide Receiver—Los Angeles Rams
Born March 2, 1963, at Pine Bluff, Ark.
Height, 5.09. Weight, 186.
High School—Pine Bluff, Ark.
Attended University of Oklahoma.

Selected by San Antonio in 1985 USFL territorial draft.
Selected by Los Angeles Rams in 7th round (189th player selected) of 1985 NFL draft.
Signed by Los Angeles Rams, July 20, 1985.
On injured reserve with calf injury, August 14 through entire 1985 season.

ED JOHN BRADY
Linebacker—Los Angeles Rams
Born June 17, 1960, at Morris, Ill.
Height, 6.02. Weight, 235.
High School—Morris, Ill.
Attended University of Illinois.

Selected by Chicago in 1984 USFL territorial draft.
Selected by Los Angeles Rams in 8th round (215th player selected) of 1984 NFL draft.
Signed by Los Angeles Rams, July 14, 1984.
Released by Los Angeles Rams, August 27, 1984; re-signed by Rams, August 28, 1984.
Los Angeles Rams NFL, 1984 and 1985.
Games: 1984 (16), 1985 (16). Total—32.
Pro statistics: Recovered one fumble, 1985.
Played in NFC Championship Game following 1985 season.

MARK D. BRAMMER
Name pronounced BRAY-mer.
Tight End—Detroit Lions
Born May 3, 1958, at Traverse City, Mich.
Height, 6.03. Weight, 236.
High School—Traverse City, Mich.
Received degree in recreation from Michigan State University.

Selected by Buffalo in 3rd round (67th player selected) of 1980 NFL draft.
On injured reserve with ankle injury, August 28 through September 28, 1984; activated, September 29, 1984.
On injured reserve with hamstring injury, August 20 through September 23, 1985.
Released by Buffalo Bills, September 24, 1985; signed as free agent by Detroit Lions, March 6, 1986.

Year Club	G.	P.C.	Yds.	Avg.	TD.
——PASS RECEIVING——					
1980—Buffalo NFL	16	26	283	10.9	4
1981—Buffalo NFL	16	33	365	11.1	2
1982—Buffalo NFL	9	25	225	9.0	2
1983—Buffalo NFL	12	25	215	8.6	2
1984—Buffalo NFL	12	7	49	7.0	0
Pro Totals—5 Years	65	116	1137	9.8	10

Additional pro statistics: Rushed once for eight yards, 1980; rushed twice for 17 yards, recovered one fumble and fumbled three times, 1981; recovered two fumbles, 1982.

CLIFFORD BRANCH
(Cliff)
Wide Receiver—Los Angeles Raiders
Born August 1, 1948, at Houston, Tex.
Height, 5.11. Weight, 170.
High School—Houston, Tex., E. E. Worthing.
Attended Wharton County Junior College and University of Colorado.

Tied NFL record for longest completed passing play from scrimmage when he caught a 99-yard touchdown pass from quarterback Jim Plunkett against Washington Redskins, October 2, 1983.
Named as wide receiver on THE SPORTING NEWS AFC All-Star Team, 1974 and 1976.
Selected by Oakland in 4th round (98th player selected) of 1972 NFL draft.
Franchise transferred to Los Angeles, May 7, 1982.
On injured reserve with hamstring injury, August 23 through October 23, 1985; activated after clearing procedural waivers, October 25, 1985.

		—RUSHING—				PASS RECEIVING				—TOTAL—		
Year Club	G.	Att.	Yds.	Avg.	TD.	P.C.	Yds.	Avg.	TD.	TD.	Pts.	F.
1972—Oakland NFL	14	1	5	5.0	0	3	41	13.7	0	0	0	2
1973—Oakland NFL	13		None			19	290	15.3	3	3	18	0
1974—Oakland NFL	13		None			60	*1092	18.2	*13	13	78	1
1975—Oakland NFL	14	2	18	9.0	0	51	893	17.5	9	9	54	0
1976—Oakland NFL	14	3	12	4.0	0	46	1111	24.2	*12	12	72	0
1977—Oakland NFL	13		None			33	540	16.4	6	6	36	0
1978—Oakland NFL	16		None			49	709	14.5	1	1	6	2
1979—Oakland NFL	14	1	4	4.0	0	59	844	14.3	6	6	36	1
1980—Oakland NFL	16	1	1	1.0	0	44	858	19.5	7	7	42	0
1981—Oakland NFL	16		None			41	635	15.5	1	1	6	0
1982—Los Angeles Raiders NFL	9	2	10	5.0	0	30	575	19.2	4	4	24	0
1983—Los Angeles Raiders NFL	12	1	20	20.0	0	39	696	17.8	5	5	30	0
1984—Los Angeles Raiders NFL	14		None			27	401	14.9	0	0	0	0
1985—Los Angeles Raiders NFL	4		None				None			0	0	0
Pro Totals—14 Years	182	11	70	6.4	0	501	8685	17.3	67	67	402	6

Additional pro statistics: Returned 12 punts for 21 yards and nine kickoffs for 191 yards, 1972; recovered one fumble, 1974; recovered two fumbles, 1984.
Played in AFC Championship Game following 1973 through 1977, 1980 and 1983 seasons.
Played in NFL Championship Game following 1976, 1980 and 1983 seasons.
Played in Pro Bowl (NFL All-Star Game) following 1974 through 1977 seasons.

REGINALD ETOY BRANCH
(Reggie)
Running Back—Washington Redskins
Born October 22, 1962, at Sanford, Fla.
Height, 5.11. Weight, 227.
High School—Sanford, Fla., Seminole.
Attended West Virginia State College and East Carolina University.
Nephew of Tony Collins, running back with New England Patriots.

Signed as free agent by Washington Redskins, May 2, 1985.
Released by Washington Redskins, August 27, 1985; re-signed by Redskins, October 1, 1985.
Released by Washington Redskins, November 12, 1985; re-signed by Redskins, December 11, 1985.
Washington NFL, 1985.
Games: 1985 (8).

SCOT EUGENE BRANTLEY
Linebacker—Tampa Bay Buccaneers
Born February 24, 1958, at Chester, S. C.
Height, 6.01. Weight, 230.
High School—Ocala, Fla., Forest.
Attended University of Florida.

Selected by Tampa Bay in 3rd round (76th player selected) of 1980 NFL draft.
On injured reserve with shoulder injury, December 11 through remainder of 1985 season.
Selected by New York Mets' organization in 6th round of free-agent draft, June 8, 1976.

		—INTERCEPTIONS—			
Year Club	G.	No.	Yds.	Avg.	TD.
1980—Tampa Bay NFL	16	1	6	6.0	0
1981—Tampa Bay NFL	16	1	2	2.0	0
1982—Tampa Bay NFL	9		None		
1983—Tampa Bay NFL	16	1	0	0.0	0
1984—Tampa Bay NFL	16	3	55	18.3	0
1985—Tampa Bay NFL	13		None		
Pro Totals—6 Years	86	6	63	10.5	0

Additional pro statistics: Returned one kickoff for no yards, 1981; recovered one fumble, 1982; recovered two fumbles, 1984.

—DID YOU KNOW—
That seven of the top 12 leaders in sacks in 1985 played in the NFC East?

LARRY BRAZIEL
Name pronounced Bra-ZEAL.
Cornerback
Born September 25, 1954, at Fort Worth, Tex.
Height, 6.00. Weight, 184.
High School—Fort Worth, Tex., Dunbar.
Attended Compton Junior College and received bachelor of science degree in speech communications
from University of Southern California in 1980.
Selected by Baltimore in 5th round (115th player selected) of 1979 NFL draft.
Released by Baltimore Colts, September 8, 1982; signed as free agent by Cleveland Browns, September 16, 1982.
On inactive list, September 19, 1982.
Released by Cleveland Browns, August 28, 1984; re-signed by Browns, September 19, 1984.
Granted free agency, February 1, 1986; withdrew qualifying offer, April 7, 1986.

		—INTERCEPTIONS—			
Year Club	G.	No.	Yds.	Avg.	TD.
1979—Baltimore NFL	16	4	49	12.3	1
1980—Baltimore NFL	15	2	87	43.5	0
1981—Baltimore NFL	16	3	35	11.7	0
1982—Cleveland NFL	6		None		
1983—Cleveland NFL	13		None		
1984—Cleveland NFL	13		None		
1985—Cleveland NFL	16	2	40	20.0	0
Pro Totals—7 Years	95	11	211	19.2	1

Additional pro statistics: Recovered blocked punt in end zone for a touchdown, 1979; recovered one fumble, 1979, 1981 and 1985; fumbled once, 1981.

JAMES THOMAS BREECH
(Jim)
Placekicker—Cincinnati Bengals
Born April 11, 1956, at Sacramento, Calif.
Height 5.06. Weight, 161.
High School—Sacramento, Calif.
Attended University of California.
Selected by Detroit in 8th round (206th player selected) of 1978 NFL draft.
Released by Detroit Lions, August 23, 1978; signed as free agent by Oakland Raiders, December 12, 1978.
Released by Oakland Raiders, September 1, 1980; signed as free agent by Cincinnati Bengals, November 25, 1980.
Active for 1 game with Oakland Raiders in 1978; did not play.

		—PLACE KICKING—				
Year Club	G.	XP.	XPM.	FG.	FGA.	Pts.
1979—Oakland NFL	16	41	4	18	27	95
1980—Cincinnati NFL	4	11	1	4	7	23
1981—Cincinnati NFL	16	49	2	22	32	115
1982—Cincinnati NFL	9	25	1	14	18	67
1983—Cincinnati NFL	16	39	2	16	23	87
1984—Cincinnati NFL	16	37	0	22	31	103
1985—Cincinnati NFL	16	48	2	24	33	120
Pro Totals—8 Years	93	250	12	120	171	610

Additional pro statistics: Punted twice for 33.5 yard average, 1980; fumbled once, 1983; punted five times for 30.6 average, 1985.
Played in AFC Championship Game following 1981 season.
Played in NFL Championship Game following 1981 season.

LOUIS EVERETT BREEDEN
Cornerback—Cincinnati Bengals
Born October 26, 1953, at Hamlet, N. C.
Height, 5.11. Weight, 185.
High School—Hamlet., N. C.
Attended Richmond Technical Institute and received bachelor of science degree
from North Carolina Central University in 1977.
Tied NFL record for most yards, interception return (102), vs. San Diego Chargers, November 8, 1981.
Selected by Cincinnati in 7th round (187th player selected) of 1977 NFL draft.
On injured reserve, September 8 through entire 1977 season.
On injured reserve with shoulder injury, November 13 through remainder of 1979 season.

		—INTERCEPTIONS—			
Year Club	G.	No.	Yds.	Avg.	TD.
1978—Cincinnati NFL	16	3	25	8.3	0
1979—Cincinnati NFL	10		None		
1980—Cincinnati NFL	16	7	91	13.0	0
1981—Cincinnati NFL	16	4	145	★36.3	1
1982—Cincinnati NFL	6	2	9	4.5	0
1983—Cincinnati NFL	14	2	47	23.5	0
1984—Cincinnati NFL	16	4	96	24.0	0
1985—Cincinnati NFL	16	2	24	12.0	0
Pro Totals—8 Years	110	24	437	18.2	1

Additional pro statistics: Recovered one fumble, 1978 and 1983; returned six punts for minus 12 yards, returned one kickoff for 12 yards and fumbled twice, 1978; recovered one fumble for 10 yards, 1981; fumbled once, 1982 and 1984.
Played in AFC Championship Game following 1981 season.
Played in NFL Championship Game following 1981 season.

BRIAN MICHAEL BRENNAN
Wide Receiver—Cleveland Browns
Born February 15, 1962, at Bloomfield, Mich.
Height, 5.09. Weight, 178.
High School—Birmingham, Mich., Brother Rice.
Received bachelor of science degree in finance from Boston College in 1984.

Selected by Denver in 16th round (324th player selected) in 1984 USFL draft.
Selected by Cleveland in 4th round (104th player selected) of 1984 NFL draft.
Signed by Cleveland Browns, May 18, 1984.
On injured reserve with separated shoulder, September 4 through October 1, 1985; activated, October 2, 1985.

		-PASS RECEIVING-				-PUNT RETURNS-				—TOTAL—		
Year	Club	G.	P.C.	Yds.	Avg.	TD.	No.	Yds.	Avg.	TD.	TD.	Pts.	F.
1984—Cleveland NFL		15	35	455	13.0	3	25	199	8.0	0	3	18	1
1985—Cleveland NFL		12	32	487	15.2	0	19	153	8.1	1	1	6	3
Pro Totals—2 Years		27	67	942	14.1	3	44	352	8.0	1	4	24	4

Additional pro statistics: Attempted one pass with one completion for 33 yards and a touchdown, 1985.

HOBY F. J. BRENNER
Tight End—New Orleans Saints
Born June 2, 1959, at Linwood, Calif.
Height, 6.04. Weight, 245.
High School—Fullerton, Calif.
Attended University of Southern California.

Selected by New Orleans in 3rd round (71st player selected) of 1981 NFL draft.
On injured reserve with turf toe, September 1 through October 22, 1981; activated, October 23, 1981.
On injured reserve with knee injury, December 31 through remainder of 1982 season.

		——PASS RECEIVING——				
Year	Club	G.	P.C.	Yds.	Avg.	TD.
1981—New Orleans NFL		9	7	143	20.4	0
1982—New Orleans NFL		8	16	171	10.7	0
1983—New Orleans NFL		16	41	574	14.0	3
1984—New Orleans NFL		16	28	554	19.8	6
1985—New Orleans NFL		16	42	652	15.5	3
Pro Totals—5 Years		65	134	2094	15.6	12

Additional pro statistics: Fumbled once, 1981, 1982 and 1985; recovered one fumble, 1982.

TIM BREWSTER
Tight End—Indianapolis Colts
Born October 13, 1960, at Phillipsburg, N.J.
Height, 6.04. Weight, 220.
High School—Phillipsburg, N.J.
Attended Pasadena City College and University of Illinois.

Selected by Chicago in 1984 USFL territorial draft.
Signed as free agent by New York Giants, May 9, 1984.
Released by New York Giants, August 20, 1984; signed as free agent by Philadelphia Eagles, May 8, 1985.
Released by Philadelphia Eagles, August 26, 1985; signed as free agent by Indianapolis Colts, April 2, 1986.

TOM BRIEHL
Name pronounced Breel.
Linebacker—Houston Oilers
Born September 8, 1962, at Phoenix, Ariz.
Height, 6.03. Weight, 247.
High School—Phoenix, Ariz., Gerard Catholic.
Attended Stanford University.

Selected by Oakland in 1985 USFL territorial draft.
Selected by Houston in 4th round (87th player selected) of 1985 NFL draft.
Signed by Houston Oilers, July 19, 1985.
Houston NFL, 1985.
Games: 1985 (16).
Pro statistics: Returned one kickoff for five yards, 1985.

LEON BRIGHT
Running Back
Born May 19, 1955, at Starke, Fla.
Height, 5.09. Weight, 192.
High School—Merritt Island, Fla.
Attended Florida State University.

Signed as free agent by British Columbia Lions, March, 1977.
Released by British Columbia Lions, July 3, 1977; re-signed by Lions, July 14, 1977.

On injured list, August 10 through September 10, 1979; activated, September 11, 1979.
On injured list, October 2 through October 11, 1980; activated, October 12, 1980.
Granted free agency, April 1, 1981; signed as free agent by New York Giants, May 28, 1981.
On injured reserve with Achilles tendon injury, August 30 through September 30, 1983; activated, October 1, 1983.
Granted free agency, February 1, 1984.
Rights released by New York Giants, August 27, 1984; signed by Tampa Bay Buccaneers, September 29, 1984.
On injured reserve with knee injury, October 28 through remainder of 1985 season.
Granted free agency with no qualifying offer, February 1, 1986.

Year Club	G.	—RUSHING—				PASS RECEIVING				—TOTAL—		
		Att.	Yds.	Avg.	TD.	P.C.	Yds.	Avg.	TD.	TD.	Pts.	F.
1977—British Columbia CFL	15	6	43	7.2	0	45	816	18.1	7	9	54	4
1978—British Columbia CFL	15	4	90	22.5	1	52	781	15.0	2	3	18	0
1979—British Columbia CFL	11	2	7	3.5	0	36	569	15.8	3	5	30	5
1980—British Columbia CFL	15	1	1	1.0	0	13	204	15.7	1	3	18	3
1981—New York Giants NFL	15	51	197	3.9	2	28	291	10.4	0	2	12	3
1982—New York Giants NFL	8	1	5	5.0	0	2	19	9.5	0	0	0	0
1983—New York Giants NFL	7	1	2	2.0	0	2	33	16.5	0	0	0	2
1984—Tampa Bay NFL	12		None				None			0	0	2
1985—Tampa Bay NFL	8		None				None			0	0	4
NFL Totals—5 Years	50	53	204	3.8	2	32	343	10.7	0	2	12	11
CFL Totals—4 Years	56	13	141	10.8	1	146	2370	16.2	13	20	120	12
Pro Totals—9 Years	106	66	345	5.2	3	178	2713	15.2	13	22	132	23

Year Club	G.	—PUNT RETURNS—				—KICKOFF RET.—			
		No.	Yds.	Avg.	TD.	No.	Yds.	Avg.	TD.
1977—British Columbia CFL	15	29	419	*14.4	1	18	596	*33.1	1
1978—British Columbia CFL	15	40	498	*12.5	0	18	425	23.6	0
1979—British Columbia CFL	11	21	319	*15.2	2	27	*820	*30.4	0
1980—British Columbia CFL	15	47	*790	*16.8	1	25	635	25.4	0
1981—New York Giants NFL	15	52	410	7.9	0	25	481	19.2	0
1982—New York Giants NFL	8	*37	*325	8.8	0	4	72	18.0	0
1983—New York Giants NFL	7	17	117	6.9	0	21	475	22.6	0
1984—Tampa Bay NFL	12	23	173	7.5	0	16	303	18.9	0
1985—Tampa Bay NFL	8	12	124	10.3	0	11	213	19.4	0
NFL Totals—5 Years	50	141	1149	8.1	0	77	1544	20.1	0
CFL Totals—4 Years	56	137	2026	14.8	4	88	2476	28.1	1
Pro Totals—9 Years	106	278	3175	11.4	4	165	4020	24.4	1

Additional NFL statistics: Recovered four fumbles, 1981; recovered one fumble, 1984.
Additional CFL statistics: Recovered two fumbles, 1979; intercepted three passes for 94 yards and one touchdown and recovered three fumbles, 1980.

JAMES BRITT
Cornerback—Atlanta Falcons
Born September 12, 1960, at Minden, La.
Height, 6.00. Weight, 185.
High School—Minden, La.
Received degree in accounting from Louisiana State University.

Selected by New Jersey in 14th round (166th player selected) of 1983 USFL draft.
Selected by Atlanta in 2nd round (43rd player selected) of 1983 NFL draft.
Signed by Atlanta Falcons, July 16, 1983.
On injured reserve with broken leg, September 16 through remainder of 1985 season.
Atlanta NFL, 1983 through 1985.
Games: 1983 (14), 1984 (16), 1985 (2). Total—32.
Pro statistics: Intercepted one pass for 10 yards, 1984; intercepted one pass for eight yards, 1985.

PETER ANTHONY BROCK
(Pete)
Center—New England Patriots
Born July 14, 1954, at Portland, Ore.
Height, 6.05. Weight, 275.
High School—Beaverton, Ore., Jesuit.
Received bachelor of science degree in biology from University of Colorado in 1976.
Brother of Stan Brock, offensive tackle with New Orleans Saints;
and Willie Brock, center with Detroit Lions, 1978.

Named as center on THE SPORTING NEWS College All-America Team, 1975.
Selected by New England in 1st round (12th player selected) of 1976 NFL draft.
On injured reserve with knee injury, October 26 through November 29, 1985; activated, November 30, 1985.
New England NFL, 1976 through 1985.
Games: 1976 (14), 1977 (14), 1978 (15), 1979 (16), 1980 (16), 1981 (16), 1982 (9), 1983 (13), 1984 (12), 1985 (9).
Total—134.
Pro statistics: Recovered one fumble, 1976, 1980, 1981 and 1982; caught one pass for 6 yards and a touchdown, 1976; fumbled twice, 1979.
Played in AFC Championship Game following 1985 season.
Played in NFL Championship Game following 1985 season.

RALPH DIETER BROCK
(Known by middle name.)
Quarterback—Los Angeles Rams
Born February 12, 1951, at Birmingham, Ala.
Height, 6.00. Weight, 195.
High School—Birmingham, Ala., Jones Valley.
Attended Auburn University and Jacksonville State University.

Signed as free agent by Winnipeg Blue Bombers, 1974.
On suspended list, August 23 through September 19, 1983.
Traded by Winnipeg Blue Bombers to Hamilton Tiger-Cats for quarterback Tom Clements, September 20, 1983.
Granted free agency, March 1, 1985; signed by Los Angeles Rams, March 29, 1985.

Year Club	G.	Att.	Cmp.	Pct.	Gain	T.P.	P.I.	Avg.	Att.	Yds.	Avg.	TD.	TD.	Pts.	F.
				—PASSING—					—RUSHING—				—TOTAL—		
1974—Winnipeg CFL	16	27	12	44.4	176	0	2	6.52	2	6	3.0	0	0	0	1
1975—Winnipeg CFL	16	244	116	47.5	1911	11	9	7.83	36	173	4.8	2	2	12	8
1976—Winnipeg CFL	16	402	223	55.5	3101	17	18	7.71	46	72	1.6	2	2	12	7
1977—Winnipeg CFL	16	*418	242	57.9	3063	*23	19	7.33	62	220	3.6	6	6	36	7
1978—Winnipeg CFL	16	*486	*294	60.5	*3755	*23	18	7.73	28	47	1.7	3	3	18	4
1979—Winnipeg CFL	15	354	194	54.8	2383	15	12	6.73	30	97	3.2	1	1	6	2
1980—Winnipeg CFL	16	*514	304	59.1	*4252	*28	12	8.27	43	87	2.0	4	4	24	4
1981—Winnipeg CFL	16	*566	*354	62.5	*4796	*32	15	8.47	35	116	3.3	0	0	0	1
1982—Winnipeg CFL	16	543	314	57.8	4294	28	15	7.91	33	123	3.7	4	4	24	5
1983—Win. (6)-Ham. (6) CFL	12	420	229	54.5	3133	18	15	7.46	27	62	2.3	4	4	24	*10
1984—Hamilton CFL	15	*561	*320	57.0	*3966	15	*23	7.07	48	134	2.8	6	6	36	7
1985—Los Angeles NFL	15	365	218	59.7	2658	16	13	7.28	20	38	1.9	0	0	0	6
CFL Totals—11 Years	170	4535	2602	57.4	34830	210	158	7.68	390	1137	2.9	32	32	192	56
NFL Totals—1 Year	15	365	218	59.7	2658	16	13	7.28	20	38	1.9	0	0	0	6
Pro Totals—12 Years	185	4900	2820	57.6	37488	226	171	7.65	410	1175	2.9	32	32	192	62

NFL Quarterback Rating Points: 1985 (82.0).
Additional CFL statistics: Recovered one fumble for 13 yards, 1977; recovered one fumble, 1982.
Additional NFL statistics: Recovered one fumble and fumbled six times for minus seven yards, 1985.
Played in CFL Championship Game following 1984 season.
Played in NFC Championship Game following 1985 season.

STANLEY JAMES BROCK
(Stan)
Offensive Tackle—New Orleans Saints
Born June 8, 1958, at Portland, Ore.
Height, 6.06. Weight, 285.
High School—Beaverton, Ore., Jesuit.
Attended University of Colorado.
Brother of Pete Brock, center with New England Patriots; and
Willie Brock, center with Detroit Lions, 1978.

Named as offensive tackle on THE SPORTING NEWS College All-America Team, 1979.
Selected by New Orleans in 1st round (12th player selected) of 1980 NFL draft.
On injured reserve with knee injury, December 5 through remainder of 1984 season.
New Orleans NFL, 1980 through 1985.
Games: 1980 (16), 1981 (16), 1982 (9), 1983 (16), 1984 (14), 1985 (16). Total—87.
Pro statistics: Recovered one fumble, 1980, 1983 and 1985; returned two kickoffs for 18 yards and recovered two fumbles, 1981; returned one kickoff for 15 yards, 1983.

JEFF JEROME BROCKHAUS
Placekicker—Minnesota Vikings
Born April 15, 1959, at Fort Lauderdale, Fla.
Height, 6.03. Weight, 200.
High School—Brentwood, Mo.
Received bachelor of science degree in marketing from University of Missouri.

Signed as free agent by Atlanta Falcons, April 30, 1981.
Released by Atlanta Falcons, August 4, 1981; signed as free agent by New York Jets, March 22, 1982.
Released by New York Jets, August 17, 1982; signed as free agent by New Jersey Generals, November 18, 1982.
Released by New Jersey Generals, February 20, 1983; signed as free agent by New York Giants, March 21, 1983.
Released by New York Giants, July 23, 1983; signed as free agent by Chicag Blitz, November 12, 1983.
Released by Chicago Blitz, February 1, 1984; signed as free agent by Houston Gamblers, February 18, 1984.
Released by Houston Gamblers, March 9, 1984; signed as free agent by Jacksonville Bulls, Marh 22, 1984.
Released by Jacksonville Bulls, April 3, 1984; signed as free agent by Washington Federals, April 12, 1984.
Franchise transferred to Orlando, October 12, 1984.
Released by Orlando Renegades, June 24, 1985; signed as free agent by Minnesota Vikings, February 27, 1986.

Year Club	G.	No.	Avg.	Blk.	XP.	XPM.	FG.	FGA.	Pts.
		—PUNTING—			—PLACE KICKING—				
1984—Hou. (2)-Jack. (2)-Wash. (11) USFL	15	11	35.3	....	26	2	9	14	53
1985—Orlando USFL	18		None	....	37	1	11	20	70
Pro Totals—2 Years	33	11	35.3	....	63	3	20	34	123

MITCHELL EUGENE BROOKINS
Wide Receiver—Buffalo Bills
Born December 10, 1960, at Chicago, Ill.
Height, 5.11. Weight, 196.
High School—Chicago, Ill., Wendell Phillips.
Received bachelor of science degree in political science from University of Illinois in 1984.

Selected by Chicago in 1984 USFL territorial draft.
Selected by Buffalo in 4th round (95th player selected) of 1984 NFL draft.
Signed by Buffalo Bills, June 1, 1984.
On injured reserve with knee injury, October 12 through remainder of 1985 season.

					—PASS RECEIVING—
Year	Club	G.	P.C.	Yds.	Avg.	TD.
1984—Buffalo NFL		16	18	318	17.7	1
1985—Buffalo NFL		5	3	71	23.7	0
Pro Totals—2 Years		21	21	389	18.5	1

Additional pro statistics: Rushed twice for 27 yards, 1984; returned six kickoffs for 152 yards, 1985.

JAMES ROBERT BROOKS
Running Back—Cincinnati Bengals
Born December 28, 1958, at Warner Robins, Ga.
Height, 5.10. Weight, 182.
High School—Warner Robins, Ga.
Attended Auburn University.
Brother of Joe Brooks, safety at University of South Carolina.

Selected by San Diego in 1st round (24th player selected) of 1981 NFL draft.
Traded by San Diego Chargers to Cincinnati Bengals for running back Pete Johnson, May 29, 1984.

			—RUSHING—				PASS RECEIVING				—TOTAL—		
Year	Club	G.	Att.	Yds.	Avg.	TD.	P.C.	Yds.	Avg.	TD.	TD.	Pts.	F.
1981—San Diego NFL		14	109	525	4.8	3	46	329	7.2	3	6	36	7
1982—San Diego NFL		9	87	430	4.9	6	13	66	5.1	0	6	36	4
1983—San Diego NFL		15	127	516	4.1	3	25	215	8.6	0	3	18	8
1984—Cincinnati NFL		15	103	396	3.8	2	34	268	7.9	2	4	24	4
1985—Cincinnati NFL		16	192	929	4.8	7	55	576	10.5	5	12	72	7
Pro Totals—5 Years		69	618	2796	4.5	21	173	1454	8.4	10	31	186	30

			—PUNT RETURNS—				—KICKOFF RET.—			
Year	Club	G.	No.	Yds.	Avg.	TD.	No.	Yds.	Avg.	TD.
1981—San Diego NFL		14	22	290	13.2	0	40	949	23.7	0
1982—San Diego NFL		9	12	138	11.5	0	★33	★749	22.7	0
1983—San Diego NFL		15	18	137	7.6	0	32	607	19.0	0
1984—Cincinnati NFL		15	None				7	144	20.6	0
1985—Cincinnati NFL		16	None				3	38	12.7	0
Pro Totals—5 Years		69	52	565	10.9	0	115	2487	21.6	0

Additional pro statistics: Recovered two fumbles, 1981; recovered one fumble, 1982 and 1985; recovered three fumbles, 1983; attempted one pass with one completion for eight yards and a touchdown, 1985.
Played in AFC Championship Game following 1981 season.

KEVIN CRAIG BROOKS
Defensive End—Dallas Cowboys
Born February 9, 1963, at Detroit, Mich.
Height, 6.06. Weight, 270.
High School—Detroit, Mich., MacKenzie.
Received bachelor of general studies degree from University of Michigan in 1985.

Selected by Tampa Bay in 10th round (141st player selected) of 1985 USFL draft.
Selected by Dallas in 1st round (17th player selected) of 1985 NFL draft.
Signed by Dallas Cowboys, July 17, 1985.
Dallas NFL, 1985.
Games: 1985 (11).

TERRANCE AVERY BROOKS
(Terry)
Guard-Center—Cleveland Browns
Born December 12, 1963, at Frederick, Md.
Height, 6.01. Weight, 245.
High School—Frederick, Md., Linganore.
Attended Towson State University.

Signed as free agent by Cleveland Browns, June 21, 1985.
On injured reserve with knee injury, July 29 through entire 1985 season.

JAMES JAY BROPHY
(Known by middle name.)
Linebacker—Miami Dolphins
Born July 27, 1960, at Akron, O.
Height, 6.03. Weight, 233.
High School—Akron, O., John R. Buchtel.
Attended University of Miami (Fla.).

Selected by Tampa Bay in 4th round (73rd player selected) of 1984 USFL draft.
Selected by Miami in 2nd round (53rd player selected) of 1984 NFL draft.
Signed by Miami Dolphins, May 24, 1984.
Miami NFL, 1984 and 1985.
Games: 1984 (11), 1985 (16). Total—27.
Pro statistics: Intercepted one pass for 41 yards and recovered one fumble, 1985.
Played in AFC Championship Game following 1984 and 1985 seasons.
Played in NFL Championship Game following 1984 season.

WALTER CRAIG BROUGHTON
Running Back-Wide Receiver—Buffalo Bills
Born October 20, 1962, at Brewton, Ala.
Height, 5.10. Weight, 173.
High School—Brewton, Ala., T.R. Miller.
Attended Jacksonville State University.

Selected by Michigan in 2nd round (35th player selected) of 1984 USFL draft.
Signed by Michigan Panthers, February 6, 1984.
Not protected in merger of Michigan Panthers and Oakland Invaders; selected by Houston Gamblers in USFL dispersal draft, December 6, 1984.
Released by Houston Gamblers, February 18, 1985; awarded on waivers to New Jersey Generals, February 19, 1985.
On developmental squad, February 21 through March 18, 1985; activated, March 19, 1985.
Released by New Jersey Generals, July 31, 1985; awarded on waivers to Baltimore Stars, August 1, 1985.
Released by Baltimore Stars, August 2, 1985; signed as free agent by Buffalo Bills, May 10, 1986.
On developmental squad for 2 games with New Jersey Generals in 1985.

			PASS RECEIVING				–PUNT RETURNS–				—KICKOFF RET.—				—TOTAL—		
Year	Club	G.	P.C.	Yds.	Avg.	TD.	No.	Yds.	Avg.	TD.	No.	Yds.	Avg.	TD.	TD.	Pts.	F.
1984—Michigan USFL		18	35	593	16.9	5	16	110	6.9	0	11	220	20.0	0	5	30	2
1985—New Jersey USFL		15	21	359	17.1	3			None		1	0	0.0	0	3	18	1
Pro Totals—2 Years		33	56	952	17.0	8	16	110	6.9	0	12	220	18.3	0	8	48	3

Additional pro statistics: Recovered one fumble, 1984; recovered one fumble for five yards, 1985.

WILLIE LEE BROUGHTON
Defensive End—Indianapolis Colts
Born September 9, 1964, at Fort Pierce, Fla.
Height, 6.05. Weight, 245.
High School—Fort Pierce, Fla., Central.
Attended University of Miami (Fla.).
Brother of Dock Luckie, nose tackle with Winnipeg Blue Bombers, 1981.

Selected by Orlando in 1985 USFL territorial draft.
Selected by Indianapolis in 4th round (88th player selected) of 1985 NFL draft.
Signed by Indianapolis Colts, August 9, 1985.
Indianapolis NFL, 1985.
Games: 1985 (15).

AARON CEDRIC BROWN
Linebacker—Atlanta Falcons
Born January 13, 1956, at Warren, O.
Height, 6.02. Weight, 235.
High School—Warren, O., Western Reserve.
Attended Ohio State University.

Selected by Tampa Bay in 10th round of 1978 NFL draft.
On injured reserve with elbow injury, November 17, through December 13, 1979; activated, December 14, 1979.
Released by Tampa Bay Buccaneers, August 24, 1981; signed as free agent by Philadelphia Eagles, January 29, 1982.
Released by Philadelphia Eagles, September 6, 1982; signed as free agent by Winnipeg Blue Bombers, October 4, 1982.
Granted free agency, March 1, 1985; signed by Cleveland Browns, May 6, 1985.
Released by Cleveland Browns, September 2, 1985; signed as free agent by Philadelphia Eagles, September 19, 1985.
Released by Philadelphia Eagles, November 4, 1985; signed as free agent by Atlanta Falcons, February 10, 1986.

			——INTERCEPTIONS——			
Year	Club	G.	No.	Yds.	Avg.	TD.
1978—Tampa Bay NFL		16	1	10	10.0	0
1979—Tampa Bay NFL		12		None		
1980—Tampa Bay NFL		16		None		
1982—Winnipeg CFL		3		None		
1983—Winnipeg CFL		16		None		
1984—Winnipeg CFL		16	4	65	16.3	1
1985—Philadelphia NFL		7		None		
NFL Totals—4 Years		51	1	10	10.0	0
CFL Totals—3 Years		35	4	65	16.3	1
Pro Totals—7 Years		86	5	75	15.0	1

Additional NFL statistics: Recovered one fumble, 1978 and 1980.
Additional CFL statistics: Recovered one fumble, 1983 and 1984; returned one kickoff for nine yards, 1984.
Played in NFC Championship Game following 1979 season.

ARNOLD LEE BROWN
Cornerback—Detroit Lions
Born August 27, 1962, at Wilmington, N.C.
Height, 5.11. Weight, 185.
High School—Wilmington, N.C., E.A. Laney.
Attended North Carolina Central University.

Selected by Oakland in 8th round (108th player selected) of 1985 USFL draft.
Selected by Seattle in 5th round (128th player selected) of 1985 NFL draft.
Signed by Seattle Seahawks, July 21, 1985.
Released by Seattle Seahawks, August 27, 1985; signed as free agent by Detroit Lions, September 10, 1985.
On injured reserve with fractured elbow, November 2 through remainder of 1985 season.
Detroit NFL, 1985.
Games: 1985 (7).

CHARLES LEE BROWN
(Bud)
Safety—Miami Dolphins
Born April 19, 1961, at DeKalb, Miss.
Height, 6.00. Weight, 194.
High School—DeKalb, Miss., West Kemper.
Attended University of Southern Mississippi.

Selected by New Orleans in 1984 USFL territorial draft.
Selected by Miami in 11th round (305th player selected) of 1984 NFL draft.
Signed by Miami Dolphins, June 26, 1984.
Released by Miami Dolphins, August 27, 1984; re-signed by Dolphins, August 28, 1984.

		—INTERCEPTIONS—				
Year Club		G.	No.	Yds.	Avg.	TD.
1984—Miami NFL		16	1	53	53.0	0
1985—Miami NFL		16	2	40	20.0	0
Pro Totals—2 Years		32	3	93	31.0	0

Additional pro statistics: Recovered five fumbles for six yards, 1985.
Played in AFC Championship Game following 1984 and 1985 seasons.
Played in NFL Championship Game following 1984 season.

CHARLIE BROWN
Wide Receiver—Atlanta Falcons
Born October 29, 1958, at Charleston, S.C.
Height, 5.10. Weight, 184.
High School—St. John's Island, S.C.
Received bachelor's degree in physical education from South Carolina State College.

Selected by Washington in 8th round (201st player selected) of 1981 NFL draft.
On injured reserve with knee injury, September 1 through entire 1981 season.
On injured reserve with stress fracture in leg, October 23 through November 23, 1984; activated, November 24, 1984.
Traded by Washington Redskins to Atlanta Falcons for guard R.C. Thielemann, August 26, 1985.

		—PASS RECEIVING—				
Year Club		G.	P.C.	Yds.	Avg.	TD.
1982—Washington NFL		9	32	690	*21.6	8
1983—Washington NFL		15	78	1225	15.7	8
1984—Washington NFL		9	18	200	11.1	3
1985—Atlanta NFL		13	24	412	17.2	2
Pro Totals—4 Years		46	152	2527	16.6	21

Additional pro statistics: Recovered one fumble, 1982 and 1983; fumbled once, 1982; rushed four times for 53 yards, 1983.
Played in NFC Championship Game following 1982 and 1983 seasons.
Played in NFL Championship Game following 1982 and 1983 seasons.
Played in Pro Bowl (NFL All-Star Game) following 1982 and 1983 seasons.

CHRISTOPHER DUKE BROWN
(Chris)
Cornerback—Pittsburgh Steelers
Born April 11, 1962, at Owensboro, Ky.
Height, 6.00. Weight, 205.
High School—Owensboro, Ky., Catholic.
Received bachelor of business administration degree in accounting
from University of Notre Dame in 1984.

Selected by Chicago in 1984 USFL territorial draft.
Selected by Pittsburgh in 6th round (164th player selected) of 1984 NFL draft.
Signed by Pittsburgh Steelers, June 17, 1984.
On injured reserve with neck and back injuries, August 20 through October 17, 1985; activated, October 18, 1985.
On injured reserve with thigh injury, November 29 through remainder of 1985 season.
Pittsburgh NFL, 1984 and 1985.
Games: 1984 (16), 1985 (6). Total—22.
Pro statistics: Intercepted one pass for 31 yards, returned one kickoff for 11 yards and recovered one fumble, 1984.
Played in AFC Championship Game following 1984 season.

DAVID STEVEN BROWN
(Dave)
Cornerback—Seattle Seahawks
Born January 16, 1953, at Akron, O.
Height, 6.01. Weight, 195.
High School—Akron, O., Garfield.
Received bachelor of arts degree in speech from University of Michigan.

Tied NFL record for most touchdowns scored by interception, game (2), vs. Kansas City Chiefs, November 4, 1984.
Named as safety on THE SPORTING NEWS College All-America Team, 1974.
Selected by Pittsburgh in 1st round (26th player selected) of 1975 NFL draft.
Selected from Pittsburgh Steelers by Seattle Seahawks in NFL expansion draft, March 30, 1976.
Granted free agency, February 1, 1985; re-signed by Seahawks, August 19, 1985.
Granted roster exemption, August 19 through August 29, 1985; activated, August 30, 1985.

Year Club	G.	INTERCEPTIONS				PUNT RETURNS				—KICKOFF RET.—				—TOTAL—		
		No.	Yds.	Avg.	TD.	No.	Yds.	Avg.	TD.	No.	Yds.	Avg.	TD.	TD.	Pts.	F.
1975—Pittsburgh NFL	13		None			22	217	9.9	0	6	126	21.0	0	0	0	1
1976—Seattle NFL	14	4	70	17.5	0	13	74	5.6	0		None			0	2	0
1977—Seattle NFL	14	4	68	17.0	1		None				None			1	6	0
1978—Seattle NFL	16	3	44	14.7	0		None				None			0	0	0
1979—Seattle NFL	16	5	46	9.2	0		None				None			0	0	0
1980—Seattle NFL	16	6	32	5.3	0		None				None			0	0	0
1981—Seattle NFL	10	2	2	1.0	0		None				None			0	0	0
1982—Seattle NFL	9	1	3	3.0	0		None				None			0	0	0
1983—Seattle NFL	16	6	83	13.8	0		None				None			0	0	1
1984—Seattle NFL	16	8	179	22.4	*2		None				None			2	12	0
1985—Seattle NFL	16	6	58	9.7	*1		None				None			1	6	0
Pro Totals—11 Years	156	45	585	13.0	4	35	291	8.3	0	6	126	21.0	0	4	26	2

Additional pro statistics: Scored one safety, 1976; recovered one fumble for eight yards, 1981; recovered two fumbles for 15 yards, 1982; recovered three fumbles, 1983; recovered one fumble, 1984 and 1985.
Played in AFC Championship Game following 1975 and 1983 seasons.
Played in NFL Championship Game following 1975 season.
Played in Pro Bowl (NFL All-Star Game) following 1984 season.

EDDIE LEE BROWN
Wide Receiver—Cincinnati Bengals
Born December 17, 1962, at Miami, Fla.
Height, 6.00. Weight, 185.
High School—Miami, Fla., Senior.
Attended Navarro College and University of Miami (Fla.).

Named THE SPORTING NEWS NFL Rookie of the Year, 1985.
Selected by Orlando in 1985 USFL territorial draft.
Selected by Cincinnati in 1st round (13th player selected) of 1985 NFL draft.
Signed by Cincinnati Bengals, August 7, 1985.

Year Club	G.	——RUSHING——				PASS RECEIVING				—TOTAL—		
		Att.	Yds.	Avg.	TD.	P.C.	Yds.	Avg.	TD.	TD.	Pts.	F.
1985—Cincinnati NFL	16	14	129	9.2	0	53	942	17.8	8	8	48	2

Additional pro statistics: Returned one kickoff for six yards and recovered one fumble, 1985.

GREGORY LEE BROWN
(Greg)
Defensive End—Philadelphia Eagles
Born January 5, 1957, at Washington, D.C.
Height, 6.05. Weight, 265.
High School—Washington, D.C., Woodson.
Attended Kansas State University and Eastern Illinois University.

Signed as free agent by Philadelphia Eagles, May 16, 1981.
Philadelphia NFL, 1981 through 1985.
Games: 1981 (16), 1982 (9), 1983 (16), 1984 (16), 1985 (16). Total—73.
Pro statistics: Recovered two fumbles for seven yards and one touchdown, 1981; recovered two fumbles, one for a touchdown, 1982; recovered one fumble, 1984, recovered two fumbles, 1985.

LOMAS BROWN JR.
Offensive Tackle—Detroit Lions
Born March 30, 1963, at Miami, Fla.
Height, 6.04. Weight, 282.
High School—Miami Springs, Fla.
Attended University of Florida.
Cousin of Joe Taylor, defensive back with Chicago Bears, 1967 through 1974;
and Guy McIntyre, guard with San Francisco 49ers.

Named as tackle on THE SPORTING NEWS College All-America Team, 1984.
Selected by Orlando in 2nd round (18th player selected) of 1985 USFL draft.
Selected by Detroit in 1st round (6th player selected) of 1985 NFL draft.
Signed by Detroit Lions, August 9, 1985.
Detroit NFL, 1985.
Games: 1985 (16).

MARK ANTHONY BROWN
Linebacker—Miami Dolphins
Born July 18, 1961, at New Brunswick, N.J.
Height, 6.02. Weight, 225.
High School—Inglewood, Calif.
Attended Los Angeles Southwest Community College and Purdue University.

Selected by Boston in 10th round (115th player selected) of 1983 USFL draft.
Selected by Miami in 9th round (250th player selected) of 1983 NFL draft.
Signed by Miami Dolphins, June 15, 1983.
Miami NFL, 1983 through 1985.
Games: 1983 (14), 1984 (16), 1985 (15). Total—45.
Pro statistics: Intercepted one pass for no yards, returned one kickoff for no yards and recovered one fumble, 1983; intercepted one pass for five yards and recovered two fumbles, 1985.
Played in AFC Championship Game following 1984 and 1985 seasons.
Played in NFL Championship Game following 1984 season.

ROBERT LEE BROWN
Defensive End—Green Bay Packers
Born May 21, 1960, at Edenton, N.C.
Height, 6.02. Weight, 250.
High School—Edenton, N.C., John A. Holmes.
Attended Chowan Junior College and Virginia Polytechnic Institute and State University.

Selected by Green Bay in 4th round (98th player selected) of 1982 NFL draft.
On inactive list, September 20, 1982.
Green Bay NFL, 1982 through 1985.
Games: 1982 (8), 1983 (16), 1984 (16), 1985 (16). Total—56.
Pro statistics: Recovered one fumble, 1982; intercepted one pass for five yards and a touchdown, 1984; credited with one safety and recovered four fumbles, 1985.

RONALD JAMES BROWN
(Ron)
Wide Receiver-Kickoff Returner—Los Angeles Rams
Born March 31, 1961, at Los Angeles, Calif.
Height, 5.11. Weight, 181.
High School—Baldwin Park, Calif.
Attended Arizona State University.
Won gold medal in 4x100 relay during 1984 Olympics.

Tied NFL record for most touchdowns scored by kickoff return, game (2), against Green Bay Packers, November 24, 1985.
Named as kick returner to THE SPORTING NEWS NFL All-Star Team, 1985.
Selected by Arizona in 1983 USFL territorial draft.
Selected by Cleveland in 2nd round (41st player selected) of 1983 NFL draft.
NFL rights traded by Cleveland Browns to Los Angeles Rams for 2nd round pick in 1984 draft, April 27, 1984.
Signed by Los Angeles Rams, August 16, 1984.

		PASS RECEIVING				—KICKOFF RET.—				—TOTAL—		
Year Club	G.	P.C.	Yds.	Avg.	TD.	No.	Yds.	Avg.	TD.	TD.	Pts.	F.
1984—Los Angeles Rams NFL	16	23	478	20.8	4		None			0	0	0
1985—Los Angeles Rams NFL	13	14	215	15.4	3	28	918	*32.8	*3	6	36	2
Pro Totals—2 Years	29	37	693	18.7	7	28	918	32.8	3	6	36	2

Additional pro statistics: Rushed twice for 25 yards, 1984; rushed twice for 13 yards, 1985.
Played in NFC Championship Game following 1985 season.
Played in Pro Bowl (NFL All-Star Game) following 1985 season.

STEVE BROWN
Cornerback—Houston Oilers
Born March 20, 1960, at Sacramento, Calif.
Height, 5.11. Weight, 188.
High School—Sacramento, Calif., C.K. McClatchy.
Attended University of Oregon.

Selected by Arizona in 7th round (74th player selected) of 1983 USFL draft.
Selected by Houston in 3rd round (83rd player selected) of 1983 NFL draft.
Signed by Houston Oilers, June 28, 1983.

		-INTERCEPTIONS-				—KICKOFF RET.—				—TOTAL—		
Year Club	G.	No.	Yds.	Avg.	TD.	No.	Yds.	Avg.	TD.	TD.	Pts.	F.
1983—Houston NFL	16	1	16	16.0	0	31	795	25.6	*1	1	6	2
1984—Houston NFL	16	1	26	26.0	0	3	17	5.7	0	0	0	1
1985—Houston NFL	15	5	41	8.2	0	2	45	22.5	0	0	0	1
Pro Totals—3 Years	47	7	83	11.9	0	36	857	23.8	1	1	6	4

Additional pro statistics: Recovered one fumble, 1984 and 1985.

—DID YOU KNOW—

That the 1985 NFL draft was the first since 1968 where no quarterbacks, running backs or wide receivers were taken within the top seven picks of the draft?

THEOTIS BROWN II
Running Back—Kansas City Chiefs

Born April 20, 1957, at Chicago, Ill.
Height, 6.02. Weight, 225.
High School—Oakland, Calif., Skyline.
Attended University of California at Los Angeles.

Selected by St. Louis in 2nd round (35th player selected) of 1979 NFL draft.
Traded by St. Louis Cardinals to Seattle Seahawks for 4th round picks in 1982 and 1983 drafts, October 13, 1981.
Released by Seattle Seahawks, September 21, 1983; signed as free agent by Kansas City Chiefs, September 24, 1983.
On non-football injury list with heart condition, July 25 through entire 1985 season.

| | | —RUSHING— | | | | PASS RECEIVING | | | | —TOTAL— | | |
Year Club	G.	Att.	Yds.	Avg.	TD.	P.C.	Yds.	Avg.	TD.	TD.	Pts.	F.
1979—St. Louis NFL	16	73	318	4.4	7	25	191	7.6	0	7	42	3
1980—St. Louis NFL	16	40	186	4.7	1	21	290	13.8	1	2	12	2
1981—St. Louis (4)-Seattle (9) NFL	13	156	583	3.7	8	29	328	11.3	0	8	48	8
1982—Seattle NFL	9	53	141	2.7	2	12	95	7.9	0	2	12	3
1983—Seattle(3)-Kansas City(12) NFL	15	130	481	3.7	8	47	418	8.9	2	10	60	4
1984—Kansas City NFL	14	97	337	3.5	4	38	236	6.2	0	4	24	2
Pro Totals—6 Years	83	549	2046	3.7	30	172	1558	9.1	3	33	198	22

Additional pro statistics: Recovered two fumbles, 1979; returned two kickoffs for 26 yards, 1980; recovered three fumbles, 1981; returned two kickoffs for 33 yards, 1982; recovered one fumble, 1982 and 1983; attempted one pass with one completion for 11 yards and returned 15 kickoffs for 301 yards (20.1 avg.), 1983.

THOMAS EDWARD BROWN
(Ted)
Running Back—Minnesota Vikings

Born February 15, 1957, at High Point, N. C.
Height, 5.10. Weight, 206.
High School—High Point, N. C., T. W. Andrews.
Attended North Carolina State University.

Selected by Minnesota in 1st round (16th player selected) of 1979 NFL draft.
On suspended list, December 2 through December 6, 1983; reinstated, December 7, 1983.

| | | —RUSHING— | | | | PASS RECEIVING | | | | —TOTAL— | | |
Year Club	G.	Att.	Yds.	Avg.	TD.	P.C.	Yds.	Avg.	TD.	TD.	Pts.	F.
1979—Minnesota NFL	14	130	551	4.2	1	31	197	6.4	0	1	6	6
1980—Minnesota NFL	16	219	912	4.2	8	62	623	10.0	2	10	60	6
1981—Minnesota NFL	16	274	1063	3.9	6	83	694	8.4	2	8	48	3
1982—Minnesota NFL	8	120	515	4.3	1	31	207	6.7	2	3	18	0
1983—Minnesota NFL	10	120	476	4.0	10	41	357	8.7	1	11	66	2
1984—Minnesota NFL	13	98	442	4.5	3	46	349	7.6	3	6	36	2
1985—Minnesota NFL	14	93	336	3.6	7	30	291	9.7	3	10	60	1
Pro Totals—7 Years	91	1054	4295	4.1	36	324	2718	8.4	13	49	294	20

Additional pro statistics: Returned eight kickoffs for 186 yards (23.3 average) and recovered two fumbles, 1979; recovered three fumbles, 1980 and 1981; attempted one pass with one interception, 1981; recovered one fumble, 1982, 1983 and 1985; returned one kickoff for seven yards, 1985.

JOEY MATTHEW BROWNER
Safety—Minnesota Vikings

Born May 15, 1960, at Warren, O.
Height, 6.02. Weight, 205.
High Schools—Warren, O., Western Reserve; and Atlanta, Ga., Southwest.
Attended University of Southern California.
Brother of Ross Browner, defensive end with Cincinnati Bengals;
brother of Jim Browner, defensive back with Cincinnati Bengals,
1979 and 1980; and Keith Browner, linebacker with Tampa Bay Buccaneers.

Selected by Los Angeles in 1983 USFL territorial draft.
Selected by Minnesota in 1st round (19th player selected) of 1983 NFL draft.
Signed by Minnesota Vikings, April 30, 1983.

| | | —INTERCEPTIONS— | | | |
Year Club	G.	No.	Yds.	Avg.	TD.
1983—Minnesota NFL	16	2	0	0.0	0
1984—Minnesota NFL	16	1	20	20.0	0
1985—Minnesota NFL	16	2	17	8.5	*1
Pro Totals—3 Years	48	5	37	7.4	1

Additional pro statistics: Recovered four fumbles for four yards, 1983; fumbled once, 1983 and 1985; recovered three fumbles for 63 yards and a touchdown, 1984; returned one kickoff for no yards and recovered three fumbles for five yards, 1985.
Played in Pro Bowl (NFL All-Star Game) following 1985 season..

—DID YOU KNOW—

That Buffalo's Greg Bell scampered 77 yards for a score on the game's first play against Pittsburgh on December 15 last year? He scored on an 85-yard run on the opening play against the Cowboys on November 18, 1984.

KEITH TELLUS BROWNER
Linebacker—Tampa Bay Buccaneers
Born January 24, 1962, at Warren, O.
Height, 6.05. Weight, 240.
High School—Atlanta, Ga., Southwest.
Attended University of Southern California.
Brother of Ross Browner, defensive end with Cincinnati Bengals; Jim Browner, defensive back
with Cincinnati Bengals, 1979 and 1980; and Joey Browner, safety with Minnesota Vikings.

Selected by Los Angeles in 1984 USFL territorial draft.
Selected by Tampa Bay in 2nd round (30th player selected) of 1984 NFL draft.
Signed by Tampa Bay Buccaneers, May 30, 1984.
Tampa Bay NFL, 1984 and 1985.
Games: 1984 (16), 1985 (16). Total—32.
Pro statistics: Recovered one fumble, 1984 and 1985; intercepted one pass for 25 yards and fumbled once, 1985.

ROSS BROWNER
Defensive End—Cincinnati Bengals
Born March 22, 1954, at Warren, O.
Height, 6.03. Weight, 265.
High School—Warren, O., Western Reserve.
Received bachelor of arts degree in economics from University of Notre Dame in 1978.
Brother of Jim Browner, defensive back with Cincinnati Bengals, 1979 and 1980; Keith Browner,
linebacker with Tampa Bay Buccaneers; and Joey Browner, safety with Minnesota Vikings.

Outland Trophy winner, 1976.
Named defensive end on THE SPORTING NEWS College All-America Team, 1976 and 1977.
Selected by Cincinnati in 1st round (8th player selected) of 1978 NFL draft.
On suspended list for violating league drug policy, July 25 through September 25, 1983; reinstated, September 26, 1983.
Granted roster exemption, September 26, 1983; activated September 27, 1983.
Granted free agency, February 1, 1985; signed by Houston Gamblers, May 24, 1985.
Released by Houston Gamblers, July 23, 1985; re-signed by Bengals, August 27, 1985.
Granted roster exemption, August 27 through August 29, 1985; activated, August 30, 1985.
Cincinnati NFL, 1978 through 1985; Houston USFL, 1985.
Games: 1978 (11), 1979 (16), 1980 (15), 1981 (16), 1982 (9), 1983 (12), 1984 (16), 1985 USFL (5), 1985 NFL (16). Total NFL—111. Total Pro—116.
NFL statistics: recovered three fumbles for 21 yards, 1978; returned two kickoff for 29 yards, 1979; recovered one fumble, 1979 through 1984; intercepted one pass for 29 yards, 1982; credited with one extra point, 1983; recovered two fumbles and credited with one safety, 1985.
USFL statistics: Credited with ½ sack for 5½ yards, 1985.
Played in AFC Championship Game following 1981 season.
Played in NFL Championship Game following 1981 season.

NICHOLAS BRUCKNER
(Nick)
Wide Receiver—New York Jets
Born May 19, 1961, at Astoria, N.Y.
Height, 5.11. Weight, 185.
High School—Selden, N.Y., Newfield.
Attended Nassau Community College and received degree in speech and
communications from Syracuse University.
Son of Nick Bruckner Sr., former player in Eastern Basketball League.

Signed as free agent by New York Jets, May 20, 1983.
On injured reserve with knee injury, August 10 through November 1, 1983; activated after clearing procedural waivers, November 3, 1983.
Released by New York Jets, August 27, 1984; re-signed by Jets, August 28, 1984.
Released by New York Jets, August 27, 1985; re-signed by Jets, September 3, 1985.
Released by New York Jets, November 8, 1985; re-signed by Jets, March 25, 1986.
New York Jets NFL, 1983 through 1985.
Games: 1983 (7), 1984 (16), 1985 (9). Total—32.
Pro statistics: Caught one pass for 11 yards, returned two punts for 25 yards, returned one kickoff for 17 yards and recovered one fumble, 1984.

ROBERT LOUIS BRUDZINSKI
(Bob)
Linebacker—Miami Dolphins
Born January 1, 1955, at Fremont, O.
Height, 6.04. Weight, 223.
High School—Fremont, O., Ross.
Received bachelor of science degree in business (marketing) from Ohio State University in 1977.

Named as linebacker on THE SPORTING NEWS College All-America Team, 1976.
Selected by Los Angeles in 1st round (23rd player selected) of 1977 NFL draft.
Granted roster exemption when left camp, September 2, 1980; reinstated, September 6, 1980.
Left camp, November 5, 1980; granted roster exemption, November 6, 1980.
On retired-reserve list, November 12 through remainder of 1980 season.
Traded with 2nd round pick in 1981 draft by Los Angeles Rams to Miami Dolphins for 2nd and 3rd round picks in 1981 draft and 2nd round pick in 1982 draft, April 28, 1981.
Granted free agency, February 1, 1985; re-signed by Dolphins, September 21, 1985.

Year	Club		G.	No.	Yds.	Avg.	TD.
		—INTERCEPTIONS—					
1977—Los Angeles NFL			14	2	24	12.0	0
1978—Los Angeles NFL			16	1	31	31.0	1
1979—Los Angeles NFL			16	1	26	26.0	0
1980—Los Angeles NFL			9		None		
1981—Miami NFL			16	2	35	17.5	0
1982—Miami NFL			9	1	5	5.0	0
1983—Miami NFL			16		None		
1984—Miami NFL			16	1	0	0.0	0
1985—Miami NFL			14	1	6	6.0	0
Pro Totals—9 Years			126	9	127	14.1	1

Additional pro statistics: Recovered one fumble for three yards, 1979; recovered one fumble, 1982 and 1983; recovered two fumbles for seven yards and a touchdown, 1985.
Played in NFC Championship Game following 1978 and 1979 seasons.
Played in AFC Championship Game following 1982, 1984 and 1985 seasons.
Played in NFL Championship Game following 1979, 1982 and 1984 seasons.

SCOTT LEE BRUNNER
Quarterback—St. Louis Cardinals
Born March 24, 1957, at Sellersville, Pa.
Height, 6.05. Weight, 215.
High Schools—West Chester, Pa., Henderson and Lawrenceville, N. J.
Received degree in accounting from University of Delaware in 1980.
Son of John Brunner, assistant coach with Detroit Lions, Green Bay Packers and
Tampa Bay Buccaneers, 1980 through 1984.

Selected by New York Giants in 6th round (145th player selected) of 1980 NFL draft.
Traded by New York Giants to Denver Broncos for 4th round pick in 1984 draft, April 26, 1984.
On injured reserve with knee injury, August 28 through entire 1984 season.
Traded by Denver Broncos to Green Bay Packers for 6th round pick in 1986 draft, April 26, 1985.
Traded by Green Bay Packers to St. Louis Cardinals for 6th round pick in 1986 draft, August 26, 1985.

			—————PASSING—————							———RUSHING———				—TOTAL—		
Year	Club	G.	Att.	Cmp.	Pct.	Gain	T.P.	P.I.	Avg.	Att.	Yds.	Avg.	TD.	TD.	Pts.	F.
1980—N. Y. Giants NFL		6	112	52	46.4	610	4	6	5.45	10	18	1.8	0	0	0	3
1981—N. Y. Giants NFL		16	190	79	41.6	978	5	11	5.15	14	20	1.4	0	0	0	6
1982—N. Y. Giants NFL		9	298	161	54.0	2017	10	9	6.77	19	27	1.4	1	1	6	5
1983—N. Y. Giants NFL		16	386	190	49.2	2516	9	22	6.52	26	64	2.5	0	0	0	8
1985—St.Louis NFL		16	60	30	50.0	336	1	6	5.60	3	8	2.7	0	0	0	3
Pro Totals—5 Years		63	1046	512	48.9	6457	29	54	6.17	72	137	1.9	1	1	6	25

Quarterback Rating Points: 1980 (53.0), 1981 (42.7), 1982 (74.1), 1983 (54.3), 1985 (33.1). Total—56.2.
Additional pro statistics: Recovered one fumble, 1980; recovered two fumbles and fumbled six times for minus three yards, 1981; recovered three fumbles and fumbled five times for minus 12 yards, 1982; recovered three fumbles, 1983.

RICK DON BRYAN
Defensive Tackle—Atlanta Falcons
Born March 20, 1962, at Tulsa, Okla.
Height, 6.04. Weight, 270.
High School—Coweta, Okla.
Attended University of Oklahoma.

Named as defensive lineman on THE SPORTING NEWS College All-America Team, 1983.
Selected by Oklahoma in 1984 USFL territorial draft.
Selected by Atlanta in 1st round (9th player selected) of 1984 NFL draft.
Signed by Atlanta Falcons, July 20, 1984.
Atlanta NFL, 1984 and 1985.
Games: 1984 (16), 1985 (16). Total—32.
Pro statistics: Credited with one safety, 1984; caught extra point and ran four yards with lateral on fumble recovery, 1985.

WILLIAM KIRBY BRYAN
(Bill)
Center—Denver Broncos
Born June 21, 1955, at Burlington, N. C.
Height, 6.02. Weight, 258.
High School—Burlington, N. C., Walter Williams.
Received bachelor of arts degree in economics from Duke University in 1977.

Selected by Denver in 4th round (101st player selected) of 1977 NFL draft.
On injured reserve, October 3 through remainder of 1977 season.
Denver NFL, 1978 through 1985.
Games: 1978 (13), 1979 (16), 1980 (16), 1981 (14), 1982 (9), 1983 (16), 1984 (16), 1985 (16). Total—116.
Pro statistics: Recovered two fumbles, 1979; recovered one fumble, 1980 and 1985; fumbled twice for minus 20 yards, 1980; fumbled once, 1981 and 1984.

JEFF DWIGHT BRYANT
Defensive End—Seattle Seahawks
Born May 22, 1960, at Atlanta, Ga.
Height, 6.05. Weight, 270.
High School—Decatur, Ga., Gordon.
Attended Clemson University.

Selected by Seattle in 1st round (6th player selected) of 1982 NFL draft.
Seattle NFL, 1982 through 1985.
Games: 1982 (9), 1983 (16), 1984 (16), 1985 (16). Total—57.
Pro statistics: Recovered one fumble, 1983; intercepted one pass for one yard, credited with one safety and recovered two fumbles, 1984; recovered four fumbles, 1985.
Played in AFC Championship Game following 1983 season.

STEPHEN BRYANT
(Steve)
Wide Receiver—Indianapolis Colts
Born October 10, 1959, at Los Angeles, Calif.
Height, 6.02. Weight, 197.
High School—Los Angeles, Calif., Washington.
Attended Los Angeles Southwest Junior College and Purdue University.

Selected by Houston in 4th round (94th player selected) of 1982 NFL draft.
On injured reserve with knee injury, September 2 through October 22, 1985; activated, October 23, 1985.
Released by Houston Oilers, November 21, 1985; signed as free agent by Indianapolis Colts, March 24, 1986.

		——PASS RECEIVING——			
Year Club	G.	P.C.	Yds.	Avg.	TD.
1982—Houston NFL	7		None		
1983—Houston NFL	16	16	211	13.2	0
1984—Houston NFL	14	19	278	14.6	0
1985—Houston NFL	4		None		
Pro Totals—4 Years	41	35	489	14.0	0

Additional pro statistics: Recovered one fumble, 1982; attempted one pass with one completion for 24 yards and a touchdown, 1983; fumbled once, 1984.

BRAD EDWARD BUDDE
Name pronounced Buddy.
Guard—Kansas City Chiefs
Born May 9, 1958, at Detroit, Mich.
Height, 6.04. Weight, 260.
High School—Kansas City, Mo., Rockhurst.
Received bachelor of science degree in public administration from
University of Southern California.
Son of Ed Budde, guard with Kansas City Chiefs, 1963 through 1976;
and brother of John Budde, lineman at Michigan State University.

Named as guard on THE SPORTING NEWS College All-America Team, 1979.
Selected by Kansas City in 1st round (11th player selected) of 1980 NFL draft.
On injured reserve with knee injury, November 23 through remainder of 1983 season.
On injured reserve with shoulder injury, November 8 through remainder of 1985 season.
Kansas City NFL, 1980 through 1985.
Games: 1980 (16), 1981 (16), 1982 (9), 1983 (12), 1984 (16), 1985 (7). Total—76.
Pro statistics: Returned three kickoffs for 28 yards, 1980.

MAURY ANTHONY BUFORD
Punter—Chicago Bears
Born February 18, 1960, at Mount Pleasant, Tex.
Height, 6.01. Weight, 191.
High School—Mount Pleasant, Tex.
Received business degree from Texas Tech University in 1982.

Selected by San Diego in 8th round (215th player selected) of 1982 NFL draft.
Traded by San Diego Chargers to Chicago Bears for 12th round pick in 1986 draft, August 20, 1985.

		——PUNTING——		
Year Club	G.	No.	Avg.	Blk.
1982—San Diego NFL	9	21	41.3	*2
1983—San Diego NFL	16	63	43.9	0
1984—San Diego NFL	16	66	42.0	0
1985—Chicago NFL	16	68	42.2	1
Pro Totals—4 Years	57	218	42.5	3

Additional pro statistics: Attempted one pass with no completions, 1983; attempted one pass with one completion for five yards, 1985.
Played in NFC Championship Game following 1985 season.
Played in NFL Championship Game following 1985 season.

DAN BUNZ
Linebacker

Born October 7, 1955, at Roseville, Calif.
Height, 6.04. Weight, 225.
High School—Roseville, Calif., Oakmont.
Attended University of California at Riverside and received bachelor of arts degree in sociology
from California State University at Long Beach in 1978.

Selected by San Francisco in 1st round (24th player selected) of 1978 NFL draft.
On injured reserve with groin injury, November 20 through remainder of 1982 season.
On inactive list, September 19, 1982.
On physically unable to perform/active with groin injury, July 22 through August 15, 1983.
On physically unable to perform/reserve with groin injury, August 16 through October 21, 1983; activated, October 22, 1983.
Released by San Francisco 49ers, September 1, 1985; signed as free agent by Detroit Lions, December 3, 1985.
Granted free agency, February 1, 1986; withdrew qualifying offer, May 14, 1986.
San Francisco NFL, 1978 through 1984; Detroit NFL, 1985.
Games: 1978 (16), 1979 (14), 1980 (16), 1981 (14), 1982 (1), 1983 (9), 1984 (16), 1985 (2). Total—88.
Pro statistics: Intercepted one pass for 13 yards and recovered three fumbles for nine yards, 1978; intercepted one pass for two yards, 1979 and 1984; recovered five fumbles for five yards and fumbled once, 1979; recovered three fumbles for 24 yards, 1980; recovered two fumbles, 1981; recovered one fumble, 1983; intercepted one pass for 17 yards, 1985.
Played in NFC Championship Game following 1981, 1983 and 1984 seasons.
Played in NFL Championship Game following 1981 and 1984 seasons.

RONNIE BURGESS
Defensive Back—Green Bay Packers

Born March 7, 1963, at Sumter, S.C.
Height, 5.11. Weight, 175.
High School—Sumter, S.C.
Attended Wake Forest University.

Selected by Green Bay in 10th round (266th player selected) of 1985 NFL draft.
Signed as free agent by Ottawa Rough Riders, May 2, 1985.
Released by Ottawa Rough Riders, June 25, 1985; signed by Green Bay Packers, July 10, 1985.
On injured reserve with torn rib cartilage, September 16 through November 1, 1985; activated, November 2, 1985.
On injured reserve with pulled groin, December 7 through remainder of 1985 season.
Green Bay NFL, 1985.
Games: 1985 (7).

CHRIS BURKETT
Wide Receiver—Buffalo Bills

Born August 23, 1962, at Laurel, Miss.
Height, 6.04. Weight, 198.
High School—Collins, Miss.
Attended Jackson State University.

Selected by Baltimore in 1st round (14th player selected) of 1985 USFL draft.
Selected by Buffalo in 2nd round (42nd player selected) of 1985 NFL draft.
Signed by Buffalo Bills, July 23, 1985.

| | | ——PASS RECEIVING—— | | | |
Year Club	G.	P.C.	Yds.	Avg.	TD.
1985—Buffalo NFL..................	16	21	371	17.7	0

DERRICK D. BURROUGHS
Cornerback—Buffalo Bills

Born May 18, 1962, at Mobile, Ala.
Height, 6.01. Weight, 180.
High School—Prichard, Ala., M.T. Blount.
Attended Memphis State University.

Selected by Memphis in 1985 USFL territorial draft.
Selected by Buffalo in 1st round (14th player selected) of 1985 NFL draft.
Signed by Buffalo Bills, May 17, 1985.

| | | ——INTERCEPTIONS—— | | | |
Year Club	G.	No.	Yds.	Avg.	TD.
1985—Buffalo NFL..................	14	2	7	3.5	0

—DID YOU KNOW—

That Denver's Louie Wright returned blocked field goal attempts for touchdowns on consecutive plays in overtime against the San Diego Chargers on November 17? Rulon Jones blocked Bob Thomas' first field goal try and Wright had a 60-yard runback called back because of a timeout just before the play. Dennis Smith then blocked Thomas' next attempt, with Wright returning it for the winning points in the Broncos' 30-24 victory. It was Smith's second block of the game.

LLOYD EARL BURRUSS JR.
Safety—Kansas City Chiefs
Born October 31, 1957, at Charlottesville, Va.
Height, 6.00. Weight, 209.
High School—Charlottesville, Va.
Received bachelor of arts degree in general studies from University of Maryland in 1981.
Selected by Kansas City in 3rd round (78th player selected) 1981 NFL draft.

Year Club	G.	—INTERCEPTIONS— No.	Yds.	Avg.TD.	
1981—Kansas City NFL	14	4	75	18.8	1
1982—Kansas City NFL	9	1	25	25.0	0
1983—Kansas City NFL	12	4	46	11.5	0
1984—Kansas City NFL	16	2	16	8.0	0
1985—Kansas City NFL	15	1	0	0.0	0
Pro Totals—5 Years	66	12	162	13.5	1

Additional pro statistics: Returned five kickoffs for 91 yards, recovered one fumble for four yards and fumbled once, 1981; recovered two fumbles for 26 yards, 1983; recovered one fumble, 1984.

JAMES P. BURT
(Jim)
Nose Tackle—New York Giants
Born June 7, 1959, at Buffalo, N.Y.
Height, 6.01. Weight, 260.
High School—Orchard Park, N.Y.
Attended University of Miami (Fla.).
Signed as free agent by New York Giants, May 4, 1981.
On injured reserve with back injury, December 24 through remainder of 1982 season.
On injured reserve with back injury, November 2 through remainder of 1983 season.
New York Giants NFL, 1981 through 1985.
Games: 1981 (13), 1982 (4), 1983 (7), 1984 (16), 1985 (16). Total—56.
Pro statistics: Recovered one fumble, 1983; recovered two fumbles, 1984 and 1985.

BLAIR WALTER BUSH
Center—Seattle Seahawks
Born November 25, 1956, at Fort Hood, Tex.
Height, 6.03. Weight, 252.
High School—Palos Verdes, Calif.
Received degree in education from University of Washington.
Selected by Cincinnati in 1st round (16th player selected) of 1978 NFL draft.
Traded by Cincinnati Bengals to Seattle Seahawks for 1st round pick in 1985 draft, June 29, 1983.
Cincinnati NFL, 1978 through 1982; Seattle, NFL, 1983 through 1985.
Games: 1978 (16), 1979 (12), 1980 (16), 1981 (16), 1982 (8), 1983 (16), 1984 (16), 1985 (16). Total—116.
Pro statistics: Recovered one fumble for 12 yards, 1981; recovered one fumble, 1985.
Played in AFC Championship Game following 1981 and 1983 seasons.
Played in NFL Championship Game following 1981 season.

FRANK EVERETT BUSH
Linebacker—Houston Oilers
Born January 10, 1962, at Athens, Ga.
Height, 6.01. Weight, 218.
High School—Athens, Ga., Clarke Central.
Attended North Carolina State University.
Selected by Jacksonville in 1985 USFL territorial draft.
Selected by Houston in 5th round (133rd player selected) of 1985 NFL draft.
Signed by Houston Oilers, July 16, 1985.
Houston NFL, 1985.
Games: 1985 (16).
Pro statistics: Recovered three fumbles for three yards, 1985.

STEVE RAY BUSICK
Linebacker—Denver Broncos
Born December 10, 1958, at Los Angeles, Calif.
Height, 6.04. Weight, 227.
High School—Temple City, Calif.
Attended University of Southern California.
Selected by Denver in 7th round (181st player selected) of 1981 NFL draft.
Denver NFL, 1981 through 1985.
Games: 1981 (16), 1982 (9), 1983 (16), 1984 (16), 1985 (16). Total—73.
Pro statistics: Recovered two fumbles for three yards, 1981; intercepted two passes for 21 yards, 1984; recovered one fumble, 1984 and 1985.

JERRY O'DELL BUTLER
Wide Receiver—Buffalo Bills
Born October 2, 1957, at Ware Shoals, S.C.
Height, 6.00. Weight, 178.
High School—Ware Shoals, S.C.
Received bachelor of arts degree in recreation and parks administration
from Clemson University in 1980.

Named as wide receiver on THE SPORTING NEWS College All-America Team, 1978.
Named THE SPORTING NEWS AFC Rookie of the Year, 1979.
Selected by Buffalo in 1st round (5th player selected) of 1979 NFL draft.
On did not report list, August 24 through September 2, 1982.
Granted two-game roster exemption, September 3, 1982; activated, September 11, 1982.
On injured reserve with knee injury, November 4 through remainder of 1983 season.
On physically unable to perform/reserve with knee injury, August 14 through entire 1984 season.

		—PASS RECEIVING—			
Year Club	G.	P.C.	Yds.	Avg.	TD.
1979—Buffalo NFL	13	48	834	17.4	4
1980—Buffalo NFL	16	57	832	14.6	6
1981—Buffalo NFL	16	55	842	15.3	8
1982—Buffalo NFL	7	26	336	12.9	4
1983—Buffalo NFL	9	36	385	10.7	3
1985—Buffalo NFL	16	41	770	18.8	2
Pro Totals—6 Years	77	263	3999	15.2	27

Additional pro statistics: Rushed twice for 13 yards, 1979; fumbled once, 1979 and 1983; rushed once for 18 yards, 1980; rushed once for one yard and fumbled twice, 1981.

JOHN KEITH BUTLER
(Known by middle name.)
Linebacker—Seattle Seahawks
Born May 16, 1956, at Anniston, Ala.
Height, 6.04. Weight, 238.
High School—Huntsville, Ala., Lee.
Attending Memphis State University.

Selected by Seattle in 2nd round (36th player selected) of 1978 NFL draft.
Seattle NFL, 1978 through 1985.
Games: 1978 (16), 1979 (14), 1980 (16), 1981 (16), 1982 (8), 1983 (16), 1984 (16), 1985 (16). Total—118.
Pro statistics: Recovered two fumbles, 1978; intercepted one pass for four yards, 1979; intercepted two passes for 11 yards, 1980; intercepted two passes for no yards and fumbled once, 1981; intercepted one pass for no yards, 1983; intercepted two passes for 31 yards and recovered three fumbles, 1985.
Played in AFC Championship Game following 1983 season.

KEVIN GREGORY BUTLER
Kicker—Chicago Bears
Born July 24, 1962, at Savannah, Ga.
Height, 6.01. Weight, 204.
High School—Redan, Ga.
Attended University of Georgia.

Selected by Jacksonville in 1985 USFL territorial draft.
Selected by Chicago in 4th round (105th player selected) of 1985 NFL draft.
Signed by Chicago Bears, July 23, 1985.

		—PLACE KICKING—				
Year Club	G.	XP.	XPM.	FG.	FGA.	Pts.
1985—Chicago NFL	16	51	0	31	37	*144

Played in NFC Championship Game following 1985 season.
Played in NFL Championship Game following 1985 season.

MICHAEL ANTHONY BUTLER
(Mike)
Defensive End—Green Bay Packers
Born April 4, 1954, at Washington, D.C.
Height, 6.05. Weight, 269.
High School—Washington, D.C., Calvin Coolidge.
Attended University of Kansas.

Named as defensive end on THE SPORTING NEWS College All-America Team, 1976.
Selected by Green Bay in 1st round (9th player selected) of 1977 NFL draft.
Granted free agency, February 1, 1983; signed by Tampa Bay Bandits, July 31, 1983.
On developmental squad, March 17 through March 25, 1984; activated, March 26, 1984.
On developmental squad, May 3 through May 9, 1985; activated, May 10, 1985.
Released by Tampa Bay Bandits, July 17, 1985; re-signed by Green Bay Packers, July 25, 1985.
On non-football injury list with broken hand, July 30 through August 12, 1985; activated, August 13, 1985.
On injured reserve with shoulder injury, September 28 through November 8, 1985; activated, November 9, 1985.
On developmental squad for 1 game with Tampa Bay Bandits in 1984 and 1985.
Green Bay NFL, 1977 through 1982 and 1985; Tampa Bay USFL, 1984 and 1985.
Games: 1977 (14), 1978 (16), 1979 (14), 1980 (16), 1981 (16), 1982 (9), 1984 (17), 1985 USFL (17), 1985 NFL (10). Total NFL—95. Total USFL—34. Total Pro—129.
NFL statistics: Recovered one fumble, 1977 and 1982; recovered one fumble for 70 yards and one touchdown, 1979.
USFL statistics: Credited with 11 sacks for 90 yards, 1984; credited with five sacks for 18 yards, 1985.

RAYMOND LEONARD BUTLER
(Ray)
Wide Receiver—Seattle Seahawks
Born June 28, 1956, at Port Lavaca, Tex.
Height, 6.03. Weight, 195.
High School—Sweeny, Tex.
Attended Wharton County Junior College and received
degree in speech from University of Southern California in 1980.

Selected by Baltimore in 4th round (88th player selected) of 1980 NFL draft.
On injured reserve with broken arm, November 28 through remainder of 1983 season.
Franchise transferred to Indianapolis, March 31, 1984.
Released by Indianapolis Colts, November 18, 1985; signed as free agent by Seattle Seahawks, December 4, 1985.

			—PASS RECEIVING—			
Year	Club	G.	P.C.	Yds.	Avg.	TD.
1980—Baltimore NFL		16	34	574	16.9	2
1981—Baltimore NFL		16	46	832	18.1	9
1982—Baltimore NFL		9	17	268	15.8	2
1983—Baltimore NFL		11	10	207	20.7	3
1984—Indianapolis NFL		16	43	664	15.4	6
1985—Ind.(11)-Sea.(2) NFL		13	19	345	18.2	2
Pro Totals—6 Years		81	169	2890	17.1	24

Additional pro statistics: Rushed three times for 10 yards and recovered one fumble, 1982; rushed once for minus one yard, 1985.

ROBERT CALVIN BUTLER
(Bobby)
Cornerback—Atlanta Falcons
Born May 28, 1959, at Boynton Beach, Fla.
Height, 5.11. Weight, 170.
High School—Delray Beach, Fla., Atlantic.
Attended Florida State University.
Cousin of James (Cannonball) Butler, running back with Pittsburgh Steelers,
Atlanta Falcons and St. Louis Cardinals, 1965 through 1972.

Selected by Atlanta in 1st round (25th player selected) of 1981 NFL draft.

			—INTERCEPTIONS—			
Year	Club	G.	No.	Yds.	Avg.	TD.
1981—Atlanta NFL		16	5	86	17.2	0
1982—Atlanta NFL		9	2	0	0.0	0
1983—Atlanta NFL		16	4	12	3.0	0
1984—Atlanta NFL		15	2	25	12.5	0
1985—Atlanta NFL		16	5	—4	—0.8	0
Pro Totals—5 Years		72	18	119	6.6	0

Additional pro statistics: Returned one kickoff for 17 yards and recovered one fumble, 1983; recovered one fumble for 10 yards, 1984.

DAVID ROY BUTZ
(Dave)
Defensive Tackle—Washington Redskins
Born June 23, 1950, at Lafayette, Ala.
Height, 6.07. Weight, 295.
High School—Park Ridge, Ill., Maine South.
Received bachelor of science degree in physical education, health and safety from Purdue University in 1973.
Nephew of Earl Butz, former secretary of agriculture.

Named as defensive tackle on THE SPORTING NEWS College All-America Team, 1972.
Named to THE SPORTING NEWS NFL All-Star Team, 1983.
Selected by St. Louis in 1st round (5th player selected) of 1973 NFL draft.
Played out option with St. Louis Cardinals and signed by Washington Redskins, August 5, 1975; Cardinals received three draft choices (1st round picks in 1977 and 1978 and 2nd round pick in 1979) in exchange for three draft choices (5th and 15th round picks in 1976 and 6th round pick in 1977) as compensation, September 4, 1975.
St. Louis NFL, 1973 and 1974; Washington NFL, 1975 through 1985.
Games: 1973 (12), 1974 (1), 1975 (14), 1976 (14), 1977 (12), 1978 (16), 1979 (15), 1980 (16), 1981 (16), 1982 (9), 1983 (16), 1984 (15), 1985 (16). Total—172.
Pro statistics: Returned one kickoff for 23 yards, 1973; recovered one fumble, 1973, 1976 and 1982 through 1985; intercepted one pass for three yards, 1978; intercepted one pass for 26 yards, 1981.
Played in NFC Championship Game following 1982 and 1983 seasons.
Played in NFL Championship Game following 1982 and 1983 seasons.
Played in Pro Bowl (NFL All-Star Game) following 1983 season.

EARNEST ALEXANDER BYNER
Fullback—Cleveland Browns
Born September 15, 1962, at Milledgeville, Ga.
Height, 5.10. Weight, 215.
High School—Milledgeville, Ga., Baldwin.
Attended East Carolina University.

Selected by Cleveland in 10th round (280th player selected) of 1984 NFL draft.

Year Club	G.	RUSHING Att. Yds. Avg. TD.	PASS RECEIVING P.C. Yds. Avg. TD.	—TOTAL— TD. Pts. F.
1984—Cleveland NFL	16	72 426 5.9 2	11 118 10.7 0	3 18 3
1985—Cleveland NFL	16	244 1002 4.1 8	45 460 10.2 2	10 60 5
Pro Totals—2 Years	32	316 1428 4.5 10	56 578 10.3 2	13 78 8

Year Club	G.	KICKOFF RETURNS No. Yds. Avg.TD.
1984—Cleveland NFL	16	22 415 18.9 0
1985—Cleveland NFL	16	None
Pro Totals—2 Years	32	22 415 18.9 0

Additional pro statistics: Recovered two fumbles for 55 yards and a touchdown, 1984; recovered four fumbles, 1985.

DARRYL TERRENCE BYRD
Linebacker—San Francisco 49ers
Born September 3, 1960, at San Diego, Calif.
Height, 6.01. Weight, 224.
High School—Union City, Calif., James Logan.
Attended Chabot College and University of Illinois.

Selected by Chicago in 1983 USFL territorial draft.
Signed as free agent by Los Angeles Raiders, April 30, 1983.
Released by Los Angeles Raiders, August 29, 1983; re-signed by Raiders, August 30, 1983.
Released by Los Angeles Raiders, August 20, 1985; re-signed by Raiders, August 23, 1985.
Released by Los Angeles Raiders, August 27, 1985; signed as free agent by San Francisco 49ers, May 14, 1986.
Los Angeles Raiders NFL, 1983 and 1984.
Games: 1983 (16), 1984 (16). Total—32.
Played in AFC Championship Game following 1983 season.
Played in NFL Championship Game following 1983 season.

GILL ARNETTE BYRD
Cornerback—San Diego Chargers
Born February 20, 1961, at San Francisco, Calif.
Height, 5.10. Weight, 201.
High School—San Francisco, Calif., Lowell.
Received degree in business administration and finance
from San Jose State University in 1982.
Nephew of MacArthur Byrd, linebacker with Los Angeles Rams, 1965.

Selected by Oakland in 1983 USFL territorial draft.
Selected by San Diego in 1st round (22nd player selected) of 1983 NFL draft.
Signed by San Diego Chargers, May 20, 1983.
On injured reserve with pulled hamstring, December 12 through remainder of 1984 season.

Year Club	G.	INTERCEPTIONS No. Yds. Avg.TD.
1983—San Diego NFL	14	1 0 0.0 0
1984—San Diego NFL	13	4 157 39.3 *2
1985—San Diego NFL	16	1 25 25.0 0
Pro Totals—3 Years	43	6 182 30.3 2

Additional pro statistics: Recovered one fumble, 1985.

RICHARD BYRD
Nose Guard—Houston Oilers
Born March 20, 1962, at Natchez, Miss.
Height, 6.03. Weight, 255.
High School—Jackson, Miss., Jim Hill.
Attended University of Southern Mississippi.

Selected by Portland in 1985 USFL territorial draft.
Selected by Houston in 2nd round (36th player selected) of 1985 NFL draft.
Signed by Houston Oilers, July 19, 1985.
Houston NFL, 1985.
Games: 1985 (15).
Pro statistics: Recovered one fumble, 1985.

BRIAN DAVID CABRAL
Original Hawaiian surname is Kealiihaaheo (pronounced Kay-ah-lee-e-ha-hay-o).
Linebacker—Chicago Bears
Born June 23, 1956, at Fort Benning, Ga.
Height, 6.01. Weight, 224.
High School—Honolulu, Hawaii, St. Louis.
Received bachelor of science degree in therapeutic recreation from University of Colorado.

Selected by Atlanta in 4th round (95th player selected) of 1978 NFL draft.
On injured reserve with knee injury, August 12 through entire 1978 season.
Released by Atlanta Falcons, August 27, 1979; re-signed by Falcons, November 29, 1979.
Traded by Atlanta Falcons to Baltimore Colts for conditional future draft pick, August 14, 1980.
Released by Baltimore Colts, September 1, 1980; signed as free agent by Green Bay Packers, November 5, 1980.
Released by Green Bay Packers, August 17, 1981; signed as free agent by Chicago Bears, August 21, 1981.

Released by Chicago Bears, August 31, 1981; re-signed by Bears, September 1, 1981.
On inactive list, September 12, 1982.
On injured reserve with knee injury, September 10 through January 10, 1985; activated, January 11, 1985.
Atlanta NFL, 1979; Green Bay NFL, 1980; Chicago NFL, 1981 through 1985.
Games: 1979 (3), 1980 (7), 1981 (16), 1982 (8), 1983 (16), 1984 (16), 1985 (1). Total—67.
Pro statistics: Returned two kickoffs for 11 yards, 1983; caught one pass for seven yards, 1984.
Played in NFC Championship Game following 1984 and 1985 seasons.
Played in NFL Championship Game following 1985 season.

TOMMORIES CADE
(Mossy)
Cornerback—Green Bay Packers
Born December 26, 1961, at Eloy, Ariz.
Height, 6.01. Weight, 195.
High School—Eloy, Ariz., Santa Cruz Valley Union.
Attended University of Texas.

Named as defensive back on THE SPORTING NEWS College All-America Team, 1983.
Selected by San Antonio in 1984 USFL territorial draft.
Selected by San Diego in 1st round (6th player selected) of 1984 NFL draft.
USFL rights traded by San Antonio Gunslingers to Memphis Showboats for defensive back Vic Minor and draft choice, October 3, 1984.
Signed by Memphis Showboats, October 3, 1984.
On developmental squad, June 1 through June 14, 1984; activated, June 15, 1984.
On developmental squad, June 22 through June 29, 1984; activated, June 30, 1984.
Released by Memphis Showboats, September 5, 1984.
NFL rights traded by San Diego Chargers to Green Bay Packers for 1st round pick in 1986 draft and conditional pick in 1987 draft, September 6, 1985.
Signed by Green Bay Packers, September 5, 1985.
Granted roster exemption, September 5 through September 15, 1985; activated, September 16, 1985.
On developmental squad for 3 games with Memphis Showboats in 1984.

| | | —INTERCEPTIONS— | | | |
Year Club	G.	No.	Yds.	Avg.	TD.
1985—Memphis USFL............	15	2	0	0.0	0
1985—Green Bay NFL............	14	1	0	0.0	0
Pro Totals—2 Years............	29	3	0	0.0	0

Additional USFL statistics: Recovered two fumbles for 39 yards, 1985.
Additional NFL statistics: Recovered one fumble, 1985.

ANTHONY CALDWELL
(Tony)
Linebacker—Seattle Seahawks
Born April 1, 1961, at Los Angeles, Calif.
Height, 6.01. Weight, 220.
High School—Carson, Calif.
Attended University of Washington.

Selected by Philadelphia in 6th round (65th player selected) of 1983 USFL draft.
Selected by Los Angeles Raiders in 3rd round (82nd player selected) of 1983 NFL draft.
Signed by Los Angeles Raiders, June 10, 1983.
Released by Los Angeles Raiders, September 26, 1985; signed as free agent by Seattle Seahawks for 1986, November 8, 1985.
Los Angeles Raiders NFL, 1983 through 1985.
Games: 1983 (16), 1984 (16), 1985 (3). Total—35.
Played in AFC Championship Game following 1983 season.
Played in NFL Championship Game following 1983 season.

DARRYL CALDWELL
Offensive Tackle—Buffalo Bills
Born February 2, 1960, at Birmingham, Ala.
Height, 6.05. Weight, 245.
High School—Birmingham, Ala., C.W. Hayes.
Attended Tennessee State University.

Signed as free agent by Buffalo Bills, May 25, 1983.
Released by Buffalo Bills, August 27, 1984; signed as free agent by Memphis Showboats, September 18, 1984.
Released by Memphis Showboats, January 28, 1985; re-signed by Bills, May 6, 1986.
Buffalo NFL, 1983.
Games: 1983 (14).
Pro statistics: Recovered one fumble, 1983.

KEVIN BRADLEY CALL
Offensive Tackle—Indianapolis Colts
Born November 13, 1961, at Boulder, Colo.
Height, 6.07. Weight, 283.
High School—Boulder, Colo., Fairview.
Attended Colorado State University.

Selected by Denver in 1984 USFL territorial draft.
Selected by Indianapolis in 5th round (130th player selected) of 1984 NFL draft.

Signed by Indianapolis Colts, July 24, 1984.
Indianapolis NFL, 1984 and 1985.
Games: 1984 (15), 1985 (14). Total—29.

MITCHELL DAVID CALLAHAN
(Mitch)
Nose Tackle—Detroit Lions
Born February 19, 1961, at Phoenix, Ariz.
Height, 6.03. Weight, 243.
High School—Phoenix, Ariz., Alhambra.
Attended Phoenix College and Arizona State University.

Selected by Oakland in 5th round (89th player selected) of 1984 USFL draft.
Signed by Oakland Invaders, January 16, 1984.
On developmental squad, February 24 through March 2, 1984; activated, March 3, 1984.
On developmental squad, March 23 through April 27, 1984; activated, April 28, 1984.
Not protected in merger of Oakland Invaders and Michigan Panthers, December 6, 1984.
Signed as free agent by Portland Breakers, January 25, 1985.
Released by Portland Breakers, February 10, 1985; signed as free agent by Detroit Lions, March 10, 1986.
On developmental squad for 6 games with Oakland Invaders in 1984.
Oakland USFL, 1984.
Games: 1984 (11).

RICHARD JON CAMARILLO
(Rich)
Punter—New England Patriots
Born November 29, 1959, at Whittier, Calif.
Height, 5.11. Weight, 185.
High School—Pico Rivera, Calif., El Rancho.
Attended Cerritos Junior College and University of Washington.
Nephew of Leo Camarillo, professional on rodeo circuit.

Named to THE SPORTING NEWS NFL All-Star Team, 1983.
Led NFL in punting yards with 3,953 in 1985.
Led NFL in net punting average with 37.1 in 1983.
Signed as free agent by New England Patriots, May 11, 1981.
Released by New England Patriots, August 24, 1981; re-signed by Patriots after clearing procedural waivers, October 20, 1981.
On injured reserve with knee injury, August 28 through November 2, 1984; activated, November 3, 1984.

Year Club	G.	No.	Avg.	Blk.
1981—New England NFL	9	47	41.7	0
1982—New England NFL	9	49	43.7	0
1983—New England NFL	16	81	44.6	0
1984—New England NFL	7	48	42.1	0
1985—New England NFL	16	92	43.0	0
Pro Totals—5 Years	57	317	43.2	0

Additional pro statistics: Recovered one fumble and fumbled once, 1981.
Played in AFC Championship Game following 1985 season.
Played in NFL Championship Game following 1985 season.
Played in Pro Bowl (NFL All-Star Game) following 1983 season.

GLENN SCOTT CAMERON
Linebacker—Seattle Seahawks
Born February 21, 1953, at Miami, Fla.
Height, 6.02. Weight, 228.
High School—Coral Gables, Fla.
Received bachelor of science degree in business administration from University of Florida.

Selected by Cincinnati in 1st round (14th player selected) of 1975 NFL draft.
Released by Cincinnati Bengals, February 13, 1986; signed as free agent by Seattle Seahawks, May 14, 1986.
Cincinnati NFL, 1975 through 1985.
Games: 1975 (14), 1976 (14), 1977 (14), 1978 (15), 1979 (15), 1980 (14), 1981 (16), 1982 (9), 1983 (16), 1984 (16), 1985 (16). Total—159.
Pro statistics: Recovered one fumble, 1975 and 1980; intercepted three passes for 43 yards, 1980; intercepted one pass for no yards, 1981; recovered one fumble for one yard, 1983; intercepted one pass for 15 yards, 1984.
Played in AFC Championship Game following 1981 season.
Played in NFL Championship Game following 1981 season.

JACK LYNDON CAMERON
Defensive Back—Chicago Bears
Born November 5, 1961, at Roxboro, N.C.
Height, 6.00. Weight, 195.
High School—Roxboro, N.C., Person.
Attended Winston-Salem State University.

Signed as free agent by Chicago Bears, May 22, 1984.
Released by Chicago Bears, August 27, 1985; re-signed by Bears, May 21, 1986.

— 66 —

Year Club	PASS RECEIVING					—KICKOFF RET.—				—TOTAL—		
	G.	P.C.	Yds.	Avg.	TD.	No.	Yds.	Avg.	TD.	TD.	Pts.	F.
1984—Chicago NFL	16	1	13	13.0	0	26	485	18.7	0	0	0	0

Played in NFC Championship Game following 1984 season.

REGGIE LOUIS CAMP
Defensive End—Cleveland Browns
Born February 28, 1961, at San Francisco, Calif.
Height, 6.04. Weight, 270.
High School—Daly City, Calif., Jefferson.
Attended University of California at Berkley.

Selected by Oakland in 1983 USFL territorial draft.
Selected by Cleveland in 3rd round (68th player selected) of 1983 NFL draft.
Signed by Cleveland Browns, May 31, 1983.
Cleveland NFL, 1983 through 1985.
Games: 1983 (16), 1984 (16), 1985 (16). Total—48.
Pro statistics: Recovered one fumble, 1984 and 1985.

EARL CHRISTIAN CAMPBELL
Running Back—New Orleans Saints
Born March 29, 1955, at Tyler, Tex.
Height 5.11. Weight, 233.
High School—Tyler, Tex.
Received degree in speech communications from University of Texas in 1980.

Named as running back on THE SPORTING NEWS College All-America Team, 1977.
Named THE SPORTING NEWS College Player of the Year, 1977.
Heisman Trophy winner, 1977.
Established NFL record for most 200-yard games, season (4), 1980.
Tied NFL record for most consecutive games, 200 yards rushing (2), 1980.
Named THE SPORTING NEWS AFC Rookie and Player of the Year, 1978.
Named to THE SPORTING NEWS AFC All-Star Team, 1978 and 1979.
Named to THE SPORTING NEWS NFL All-Star Team, 1980.
Selected by Houston in 1st round (1st player selected) of 1978 NFL draft.
Traded by Houston Oilers to New Orleans Saints for 1st round pick in 1985 draft, October 9, 1984.

Year Club		RUSHING				PASS RECEIVING				—TOTAL—		
	G.	Att.	Yds.	Avg.	TD.	P.C.	Yds.	Avg.	TD.	TD.	Pts.	F.
1978—Houston NFL	15	302	*1450	4.8	13	12	48	4.0	0	13	78	9
1979—Houston NFL	16	368	*1697	4.6	*19	16	94	5.9	0	19	114	8
1980—Houston NFL	15	*373	*1934	*5.2	*13	11	47	4.3	0	13	78	4
1981—Houston NFL	16	361	1376	3.8	10	36	156	4.3	0	10	60	10
1982—Houston NFL	9	157	538	3.4	2	18	130	7.2	0	2	12	2
1983—Houston NFL	14	322	1301	4.0	12	19	216	11.4	0	12	72	4
1984—Houston (6)-New Orleans (8) NFL	14	146	468	3.2	4	3	27	9.0	0	4	24	2
1985—New Orleans NFL	16	158	643	4.1	1	6	88	14.7	0	1	6	4
Pro Totals—8 Years	115	2187	9407	4.3	74	121	806	6.7	0	74	444	43

Additional pro statistics: Recovered two fumbles, 1978, 1980 and 1981; recovered two fumbles for minus one yard, 1979; attempted two passes with one completion for 57 yards and a touchdown, 1980; attempted one pass with one interception and recovered one fumble, 1982; recovered two fumbles for one yard, 1984.
Played in AFC Championship Game following 1978 and 1979 seasons.
Played in Pro Bowl (NFL All-Star Game) following 1978 through 1983 seasons.

ROBERT SCOTT CAMPBELL
(Known by middle name.)
Quarterback—Pittsburgh Steelers
Born April 15, 1962, at Hershey, Pa.
Height, 6.00. Weight, 195.
High School—Hershey, Pa.
Attended Purdue University.
Son of Ken Campbell, wide receiver with New York Titans of AFL, 1960.

Selected by Philadelphia in 4th round (76th player selected) of 1984 USFL draft.
Selected by Pittsburgh in 7th round (191st player selected) of 1984 NFL draft.
Signed by Pittsburgh Steelers, May 19, 1984.

Year Club		PASSING							RUSHING				—TOTAL—		
	G.	Att.	Cmp.	Pct.	Gain	T.P.	P.I.	Avg.	Att.	Yds.	Avg.	TD.	TD.	Pts.	F.
1984—Pittsburgh NFL	5	15	8	53.3	109	1	1	7.27	3	−5	−1.7	0	0	0	1
1985—Pittsburgh NFL	16	96	43	44.8	612	4	6	6.38	9	28	3.1	0	0	0	3
Pro Totals—2 Years	21	111	51	45.9	721	5	7	6.50	12	23	1.9	0	0	0	4

Quarterback Rating Points: 1984 (71.3), 1985 (53.8). Total—56.2.
Additional pro statistics: Recovered one fumble, 1984; recovered three fumbles, 1985.
Member of Pittsburgh Steelers for AFC Championship Game following 1984 season; did not play.

JOHN RAYMOND CANNON
Defensive End—Tampa Bay Buccaneers
Born July 30, 1960, at Long Branch, N.J.
Height, 6.05. Weight, 265.
High School—Holmdel, N.J.
Received bachelor of business administration degree from
College of William & Mary in 1982.

Selected by Tampa Bay in 3rd round (83rd player selected) of 1982 NFL draft.
USFL rights traded by Memphis Showboats to Houston Gamblers for rights to defensive end Ray Yakavonis, February 13, 1985.
Tampa Bay NFL, 1982 through 1985.
Games: 1982 (9), 1983 (14), 1984 (16), 1985 (16). Total—55.
Pro statistics: Recovered one fumble, 1983 and 1984; intercepted one pass for no yards, 1984; recovered three fumbles, 1985.

MARK MAIDA CANNON
Center—Green Bay Packers
Born June 14, 1962, at Whittier, Calif.
Height, 6.03. Weight, 258.
High School—Austin, Tex., S.F. Austin.
Attended University of Texas at Arlington.

Selected by Tampa Bay in 3rd round (62nd player selected) of 1984 USFL draft.
Selected by Green Bay in 11th round (294th player selected) of 1984 NFL draft.
Signed by Green Bay Packers, July 12, 1984.
Green Bay NFL, 1984 and 1985.
Games: 1984 (16), 1985 (16). Total—32.
Pro statistics: Recovered two fumbles, 1985.

WAYNE ERWIN CAPERS
Wide Receiver—Indianapolis Colts
Born May 17, 1961, at Miami, Fla.
Height, 6.02. Weight, 193.
High School—Miami, Fla., South.
Attended Kansas University.

Selected by Pittsburgh in 2nd round (52nd player selected) of 1983 NFL draft.
Released by Pittsburgh Steelers, August 27, 1985; signed as free agent by Indianapolis Colts, September 11, 1985.

		—PASS RECEIVING—			
Year Club	G.	P.C.	Yds.	Avg.	TD.
1983—Pittsburgh NFL............	11	10	185	18.5	1
1984—Pittsburgh NFL............	16	7	81	11.6	0
1985—Indianapolis NFL.........	14	25	438	17.5	4
Pro Totals—3 Years............	41	42	704	16.8	5

Additional pro statistics: Rushed once for minus three yards and recovered two fumbles for two yards, 1984; fumbled once, 1984 and 1985; rushed three times for 18 yards and a touchdown, 1985.
Played in AFC Championship Game following 1984 season.

ROGER EUGENE CARON
Offensive Tackle—Indianapolis Colts
Born June 3, 1962, at Boston, Mass.
Height, 6.05. Weight, 270.
High School—Norwell, Mass.
Received bachelor of arts degree from Harvard University in 1985.

Selected by Baltimore in 2nd round (30th player selected) of 1985 USFL draft.
Selected by Indianapolis in 5th round (117th player selected) of 1985 NFL draft.
Signed by Indianapolis Colts, July 18, 1985.
Indianapolis NFL, 1985.
Games: 1985 (7).

ROBERT J. CARPENTER JR.
(Rob)
Running Back—New York Giants
Born April 20, 1955, at Lancaster, O.
Height, 6.01. Weight, 226.
High School—Lancaster, O.
Received bachelor of science degree in education from Miami University (O.) in 1977.

Selected by Houston in 3rd round (84th player selected) of 1977 NFL draft.
On injured reserve with knee injury, November 14 through remainder of 1978 season.
Traded by Houston Oilers to New York Giants for 3rd round pick in 1982 draft, September 29, 1981.
On did not report list, August 21 through November 28, 1982.
Granted two-game roster exemption, November 29, 1982; activated, December 3, 1982.
On injured reserve with knee injury, November 10 through remainder of 1983 season.

		—RUSHING—				PASS RECEIVING				—TOTAL—		
Year Club	G.	Att.	Yds.	Avg.	TD.	P.C.	Yds.	Avg.	TD.	TD.	Pts.	F.
1977—Houston NFL	11	144	652	4.5	1	23	156	6.8	0	1	6	3
1978—Houston NFL	11	82	348	4.2	5	17	150	8.8	0	5	30	0

Year	Club	G.	RUSHING				PASS RECEIVING				TOTAL		
			Att.	Yds.	Avg.	TD.	P.C.	Yds.	Avg.	TD.	TD.	Pts.	F.
1979—Houston NFL		16	92	355	3.9	3	16	116	7.3	1	4	24	3
1980—Houston NFL		15	97	359	3.7	3	43	346	8.0	0	3	18	4
1981—Houston (4)-N.Y. Giants (10) NFL		14	208	822	4.0	5	37	281	7.6	1	6	36	3
1982—New York Giants NFL		5	67	204	3.0	1	7	29	4.1	0	1	6	0
1983—New York Giants NFL		10	170	624	3.7	4	26	258	9.9	2	6	36	2
1984—New York Giants NFL		16	250	795	3.2	7	26	209	8.0	1	8	48	2
1985—New York Giants NFL		14	60	201	3.4	0	20	162	8.1	0	0	0	0
Pro Totals—9 Years		112	1170	4360	3.7	29	215	1707	7.9	5	34	204	17

Additional pro statistics: Recovered one fumble, 1977, 1980 and 1984; returned one kickoff for 11 yards, 1978; returned two kickoffs for 34 yards and recovered one fumble for minus two yards, 1979; returned one kickoff for seven yards, 1980.

Played in AFC Championship Game following 1979 season.

GREGG KEVIN CARR
Linebacker—Pittsburgh Steelers
Born March 31, 1962, at Birmingham, Ala.
Height, 6.01. Weight, 217.
High School—Birmingham, Ala., Woodlawn.
Attended Auburn University.

Selected by Birmingham in 1985 USFL territorial draft.
Selected by Pittsburgh in 6th round (160th player selected) of 1985 NFL draft.
Signed by Pittsburgh Steelers, July 19, 1985.
Pittsburgh NFL, 1985.
Games: 1985 (16).
Pro statistics: Recovered two fumbles, 1985.

ALPHONSO CARREKER
Name pronounced CARE-uh-ker.
Defensive End—Green Bay Packers
Born May 25, 1962, at Columbus, O.
Height, 6.06. Weight, 260.
High School—Columbus, O., Marion Franklin.
Attended Florida State University.

Selected by Tampa Bay in 1984 USFL territorial draft.
Selected by Green Bay in 1st round (12th player selected) of 1984 NFL draft.
Signed by Green Bay Packers, June 20, 1984.
Green Bay NFL, 1984 and 1985.
Games: 1984 (14), 1985 (16). Total—30.

JAY TIMOTHY CARROLL
Tight End—Minnesota Vikings
Born November 8, 1961, at Winona, Minn.
Height, 6.04. Weight, 230.
High School—Winona, Minn., Cotter.
Attended University of Minnesota.

Selected by Pittsburgh in 9th round (191st player selected) of 1984 USFL draft.
Selected by Tampa Bay in 7th round (169th player selected) of 1984 NFL draft.
Signed by Tampa Bay Buccaneers, June 21, 1984.
Released by Tampa Bay Buccaneers, September 2, 1985; awarded on waivers to Minnesota Vikings, September 3, 1985.

Year	Club	G.	PASS RECEIVING			
			P.C.	Yds.	Avg.	TD.
1984—Tampa Bay NFL		16	5	50	10.0	1
1985—Minnesota NFL		16	1	8	8.0	0
Pro Totals—2 Years		32	6	58	9.7	1

Additional pro statistics: Recovered one fumble, 1984 and 1985.

CARLOS A. CARSON
Wide Receiver—Kansas City Chiefs
Born December 28, 1958, at Lake Worth, Fla.
Height, 5.11. Weight, 180.
High School—Lake Worth, Fla., John I. Leonard.
Attended Louisana State University.
Cousin of Darrin Nelson, running back with Minnesota Vikings; and Kevin Nelson, running back with Los Angeles Express, 1984 and 1985.

Selected by Kansas City in 5th round (114th player selected) of 1980 NFL draft.
On injured reserve with broken foot, September 23 through December 11, 1981; activated, December 12, 1981.

Year	Club	G.	RUSHING				PASS RECEIVING				TOTAL		
			Att.	Yds.	Avg.	TD.	P.C.	Yds.	Avg.	TD.	TD.	Pts.	F.
1980—Kansas City NFL		16	2	41	20.5	0	5	68	13.6	0	0	0	1
1981—Kansas City NFL		5	1	—1	-1.0	0	7	179	25.6	1	1	6	1
1982—Kansas City NFL		9		None			27	494	18.3	2	2	12	1
1983—Kansas City NFL		16	2	20	10.0	0	80	1351	16.9	7	7	42	2

Year Club	G.	RUSHING				PASS RECEIVING					TOTAL		
		Att.	Yds.	Avg.	TD.	P.C.	Yds.	Avg.	TD.		TD.	Pts.	F.
1984—Kansas City NFL	16	1	—8	—8.0	0	57	1078	18.9	4		4	24	0
1985—Kansas City NFL	15	3	25	8.3	0	47	843	17.9	4		4	24	0
Pro Totals—6 Years	77	9	77	8.6	0	223	4013	18.0	18		18	108	5

Year Club	G.	KICKOFF RETURNS		
		No.	Yds.	Avg.TD.
1980—Kansas City NFL	16	40	917	22.9	0
1981—Kansas City NFL	5	10	227	22.7	0
1982—Kansas City NFL	9		None	
1983—Kansas City NFL	16	1	12	12.0	0
1984—Kansas City NFL	16	1	2	2.0	0
1985—Kansas City NFL	15		None	
Pro Totals—6 Years	77	52	1158	22.3	0

Additional pro statistics: Recovered one fumble, 1980 and 1981; attempted one pass with one completion for 48 yards and one touchdown, 1983; recovered two fumbles, 1984.

Played in Pro Bowl (NFL All-Star Game) following 1983 season.

HAROLD DONALD CARSON
(Harry)
Linebacker—New York Giants

Born November 26, 1953, at Florence, S. C.
Height, 6.02. Weight, 240.
High School—Florence, S. C., McClenaghan.
Received bachelor of science degree in physical education
from South Carolina State College.

Named to THE SPORTING NEWS NFL All-Star Team, 1984.
Named to THE SPORTING NEWS NFC All-Star Team, 1979.
Selected by New York Giants in 4th round (105th player selected) of 1976 NFL draft.
On injured reserve with knee injury, October 16 through November 13, 1980; activated, November 14, 1980.
On injured reserve, November 24 through remainder of 1980 season.
On injured reserve with knee injury, September 19 through October 28, 1983; activated, October 29, 1983.

Year Club	G.	INTERCEPTIONS				Year Club	G.	INTERCEPTIONS			
		No.	Yds.	Avg.TD.				No.	Yds.	Avg.TD.	
1976—N.Y. Giants NFL	12		None			1982—N.Y. Giants NFL	9	1	6	6.0	0
1977—N.Y. Giants NFL	14		None			1983—N.Y. Giants NFL	10		None		
1978—N.Y. Giants NFL	16	3	86	28.7	0	1984—N.Y. Giants NFL	16	1	6	6.0	0
1979—N.Y. Giants NFL	16	3	28	9.3	0	1985—N.Y. Giants NFL	16		None		
1980—N.Y. Giants NFL	8		None			Pro Totals—10 Years	133	8	126	15.8	0
1981—N.Y. Giants NFL	16		None								

Additional pro statistics: Recovered one fumble, 1976 through 1978, 1980 and 1984; returned one kickoff for five yards, 1976; recovered three fumbles for 22 yards and one touchdown, 1979; recovered one fumble for two yards, 1981.

Played in Pro Bowl (NFL All-Star Game) following 1978, 1979 and 1981 through 1985 seasons.

ANTHONY CARTER
Wide Receiver—Minnesota Vikings

Born September 17, 1960, at Riviera Beach, Fla.
Height, 5.11. Weight 162.
High School—Riviera Beach, Fla., Sun Coast.
Attended University of Michigan.
Cousin of Leonard Coleman, cornerback with Indianapolis Colts.

Named as wide receiver on THE SPORTING NEWS USFL All-Star Team, 1985.
Named as punt returner on THE SPORTING NEWS USFL All-Star Team, 1983.
Named as wide receiver on THE SPORTING NEWS College All-America Team, 1981 and 1982.
Selected by Michigan in 1983 USFL territorial draft.
Signed by Michigan Panthers, February 26, 1983.
Selected by Miami in 12th round (334th player selected) of 1983 NFL draft.
On injured reserve with broken arm, April 5 through remainder of 1984 season.
Protected in merger of Michigan Panthers and Oakland Invaders, December 6, 1984.
On developmental squad, June 24 through June 29, 1985; activated, June 30, 1985.
NFL rights traded by Miami Dolphins to Minnesota Vikings for linebacker Robin Sendlein and 2nd round pick in 1986 NFL draft, August 15, 1985.
Released by Oakland Invaders, August 23, 1985; signed by Minnesota Vikings, August 25, 1985.
Granted roster exemption, August 25 through August 28, 1985; activated, August 29, 1985.
On developmental squad for 1 game with Oakland Invaders in 1985.

Year Club	G.	PASS RECEIVING				PUNT RETURNS				TOTAL		
		P.C.	Yds.	Avg.	TD.	No.	Yds.	Avg.	TD.	TD.	Pts.	F.
1983—Michigan USFL	18	60	1181	19.7	9	40	387	9.7	*1	10	60	6
1984—Michigan USFL	6	30	538	17.9	4	5	21	4.2	0	4	24	2
1985—Oakland USFL	17	70	1323	18.9	14		None			15	90	0
1985—Minnesota NFL	16	43	821	19.1	8	9	117	13.0	0	8	48	1
USFL Totals—3 Years	41	160	3042	19.0	27	45	408	9.1	1	29	174	8
NFL Totals—1 Year	16	43	821	19.1	8	9	117	13.0	0	8	48	1
Pro Totals—4 Years	57	203	3863	19.0	35	54	525	9.7	1	37	222	9

Additional USFL statistics: Rushed three times for one yard and recovered three fumbles, 1983; recovered one fumble, 1984; recovered one fumble in end zone for a touchdown and attempted one pass with no completions, 1985.

Additional NFL statistics: Recovered one fumble, 1985.
Played in USFL Championship Game following 1983 and 1985 seasons.

GERALD LOUIS CARTER
Wide Receiver—Tampa Bay Buccaneers
Born June 19, 1957, at Bryan, Tex.
Height, 6.01. Weight, 190.
High School—Bryan, Tex.
Attended Tyler Junior College and Texas A&M University.

Selected by Tampa Bay in 9th round (240th player selected) of 1980 NFL draft
Released by Tampa Bay Buccaneers, August 25, 1980; claimed on procedural waivers by New York Jets, October 23, 1980.
Released by New York Jets, November 17, 1980; signed as free agent by Tampa Bay Buccaneers, December 12, 1980.
Active for 2 games with Tampa Bay Buccaneers in 1980; did not play.

| | | | ——PASS RECEIVING—— | | | |
Year Club	G.	P.C.	Yds.	Avg.	TD.
1980—N.Y.J. (3)-T.B. (0) NFL	3		None		
1981—Tampa Bay NFL	16	1	10	10.0	0
1982—Tampa Bay NFL	9	10	140	14.0	0
1983—Tampa Bay NFL	16	48	694	14.5	2
1984—Tampa Bay NFL	16	60	816	13.6	5
1985—Tampa Bay NFL	16	40	557	13.9	3
Pro Totals—6 Years............	76	159	2217	13.9	10

Additional pro statistics: Returned one kickoff for 12 yards, 1980; fumbled once, 1980, 1984 and 1985; fumbled three times and rushed once for no yards, 1983; recovered one fumble and rushed once for 16 yards, 1984; rushed once for 13 yards, 1985.

JOSEPH THOMAS CARTER
(Joe)
Running Back—Miami Dolphins
Born June 23, 1962, at Starkville, Miss.
Height, 5.11. Weight, 198.
High School—Starkville, Miss.
Attended University of Alabama.

Selected by Memphis in 5th round (104th player selected) of 1984 USFL draft.
Selected by Miami in 4th round (109th player selected) of 1984 NFL draft.
Signed by Miami Dolphins, July 18, 1984.
On injured reserve with knee injury, September 4 through October 18, 1985; activated, October 19, 1985.

| | | ——RUSHING—— | | | | PASS RECEIVING | | | | —TOTAL— | | |
Year Club	G.	Att.	Yds.	Avg.	TD.	P.C.	Yds.	Avg.	TD.	TD.	Pts.	F.
1984—Miami NFL	13	100	495	5.0	1	8	53	6.6	0	1	6	3
1985—Miami NFL	10	14	76	5.4	0	2	7	3.5	0	0	0	2
Pro Totals—2 Years....................	23	114	571	5.0	1	10	60	6.0	0	1	6	5

Additional pro statistics: Recovered two fumbles, 1984; returned four kickoffs for 82 yards and recovered one fumble, 1985.
Played in AFC Championship Game following 1985 season.
Member of Miami Dolphins for AFC Championship Game following 1984 season; did not play.
Played in NFL Championship Game following 1984 season.

MANSEL A. CARTER
Nose Tackle—Cleveland Browns
Born January 7, 1962, at East St. Louis, Ill.
Height, 6.08. Weight, 277.
High School—East St. Louis, Ill., Assumption.
Received degree from University of Notre Dame in 1983.

USFL rights traded by Chicago Blitz to Jacksonville Bulls for rights to wide receiver Kirk Pendleton, October 5, 1984.
Signed by Jacksonville Bulls, October 13, 1984.
On developmental squad, March 15 through March 19, 1985; activated, March 20, 1985.
On developmental squad, March 28 through April 5, 1985; activated, April 6, 1985.
On developmental squad, April 25 through May 9, 1985; activated, May 10, 1985.
Released by Jacksonville Bulls, July 11, 1985; signed as free agent by Cleveland Browns, May 4, 1986.
On developmental squad for 4 games with Jacksonville Bulls in 1985.
Jacksonville USFL, 1985.
Games: 1985 (11).
Pro statistics: Credited with one sack for six yards, 1985.

MICHAEL D'ANDREA CARTER
Nose Tackle—San Francisco 49ers
Born October 29, 1960, at Dallas, Tex.
Height, 6.02. Weight, 285.
High School—Dallas, Tex., Thomas Jefferson.
Received bachelor of science degree in sociology from Southern Methodist University in 1984.
Won silver medal in shot put during 1984 Olympics.

Selected by Los Angeles in 10th round (194th player selected) of 1984 USFL draft.
Selected by San Francisco in 5th round (121st player selected) of 1984 NFL draft.
USFL rights traded by Los Angeles Express to New Orleans Breakers for past considerations, June 19, 1984.
Signed by San Francisco 49ers, August 14, 1984.
On injured reserve with torn hamstring, September 28 through October 25, 1985; activated, October 26, 1985.
San Francisco NFL, 1984 and 1985.
Games: 1984 (16), 1985 (12). Total—28.
Played in NFC Championship Game following 1984 season.
Played in NFL Championship Game following 1984 season.
Played in Pro Bowl (NFL All-Star Game) following 1985 season.

RUBIN CARTER
Nose Tackle—Denver Broncos
Born December 12, 1952, at Pompano Beach, Fla.
Height, 6.00. Weight, 256.
High School—Fort Lauderdale, Fla., Stranahan.
Received bachelor of arts degree in business administration from University of Miami (Fla.).

Selected by Denver in 5th round (121st player selected) of 1975 NFL draft.
Denver NFL, 1975 through 1985.
Games: 1975 (14), 1976 (14), 1977 (14), 1978 (16), 1979 (15), 1980 (16), 1981 (16), 1982 (9), 1983 (16), 1984 (15), 1985 (16). Total—161.
Pro statistics: Recovered one fumble, 1976, 1978 and 1981; recovered two fumbles for two yards and one touchdown, 1979; recovered two fumbles, 1980 and 1984; recovered three fumbles, 1983; recovered one fumble for six yards, 1985.
Played in AFC Championship Game following 1977 season.
Played in NFL Championship Game following 1977 season.

RUSSELL EDMONDS CARTER JR.
Defensive Back—New York Jets
Born February 10, 1962, at Philadelphia, Pa.
Height, 6.02. Weight, 195.
High School—Ardmore, Pa., Lower Merion.
Attended Southern Methodist University.

Named as defensive back on THE SPORTING NEWS College All-America Team, 1983.
Selected by Denver in 1st round (9th player selected) of 1984 USFL draft.
Selected by New York Jets in 1st round (10th player selected) of 1984 NFL draft.
Signed by New York Jets, May 25, 1984.
On injured reserve with back injury, November 16 through December 26, 1985; activated, December 27, 1985.

		—INTERCEPTIONS—			
Year Club	G.	No.	Yds.	Avg.	TD.
1984—N.Y. Jets NFL	11	4	26	6.5	0
1985—N.Y. Jets NFL	8		None		
Pro Totals—2 Years	19	4	26	6.5	0

MAURICE CARTHON
Running Back—New York Giants
Born April 24, 1961, at Chicago, Ill.
Height, 6.01. Weight, 225.
High School—Osceola, Ark.
Attended Arkansas State University.

Selected by New Jersey in 8th round (94th player selected) of 1983 USFL draft.
Signed by New Jersey Generals, January 19, 1983.
On developmental squad, June 17 through remainder of 1983 season.
Signed by New York Giants, March 7, 1985, for contract to take effect after being granted free agency after 1985 USFL season.
Placed on did not report list, January 21 through January 27, 1985; activated, January 28, 1985.
Granted roster exemption, January 28 through February 3, 1985; activated, February 4, 1985.
On developmental squad for 3 games with New Jersey Generals in 1983.

		—RUSHING—				PASS RECEIVING				—TOTAL—		
Year Club	G.	Att.	Yds.	Avg.	TD.	P.C.	Yds.	Avg.	TD.	TD.	Pts.	F.
1983—New Jersey USFL	11	90	334	3.7	3	20	170	8.5	0	3	†24	4
1984—New Jersey USFL	18	238	1042	4.4	11	26	194	7.5	1	12	72	4
1985—New Jersey USFL	18	175	726	4.2	6	18	154	8.6	0	6	36	3
1985—New York Giants NFL	16	27	70	2.6	0	8	81	10.1	0	0	0	1
USFL Totals—3 Years	47	503	2102	4.2	20	64	518	8.1	1	21	132	11
NFL Totals—1 Year	16	27	70	2.6	0	8	81	10.1	0	0	0	1
Pro Totals—4 Years	63	530	2172	4.1	20	72	599	8.3	1	21	132	12

†Includes three 2-point conversions.
Additional pro statistics: Recovered one fumble, 1984.

—DID YOU KNOW—
That when Ethan Horton was the first draft pick of the Chiefs in 1985, it marked the first time since 1974 that Kansas City selected a running back in the opening round? Woody Green of Arizona State was the pick in 1974.

JEFFREY SCOTT CASE
(Known by middle name.)
Safety—Atlanta Falcons
Born May 17, 1962, at Waynoka, Okla.
Height, 6.00. Weight, 178.
High Schools—Alva, Okla. and Edmond, Okla., Memorial.
Attended Northeastern Oklahoma A&M and University of Oklahoma.

Selected by Oklahoma in 1984 USFL territorial draft.
Selected by Atlanta in 2nd round (32nd player selected) of 1984 NFL draft.
Signed by Atlanta Falcons, July 20, 1984.

Year Club	G.	No.	Yds.	Avg.	TD.
1984—Atlanta NFL	16		None		
1985—Atlanta NFL	14	4	78	19.5	0
Pro Totals—2 Years........	30	4	78	19.5	0

Additional pro statistics: Credited with one safety and recovered one fumble for 13 yards, 1985.

WENDELL B. CASON
Cornerback—Atlanta Falcons
Born January 22, 1963, at Lakewood, Calif.
Height, 5.11. Weight, 183.
High School—Carson, Calif.
Attended University of Oregon.

Signed as free agent by Atlanta Falcons, May 3, 1985.
Released by Atlanta Falcons, September 2, 1985; re-signed by Falcons, September 16, 1985.

Year Club	G.	No.	Yds.	Avg.	TD.
1985—Atlanta NFL	14	3	30	10.0	0

Additional pro statistics: Recovered two fumbles for two yards, 1985.

JEREMIAH CASTILLE
Name pronounced Cass-TEEL.
Defensive Back—Tampa Bay Buccaneers
Born January 15, 1961, at Columbus, Ga.
Height, 5.10. Weight, 175.
High School—Phenix City, Ala., Central.
Received degree in broadcasting from University of Alabama.

Selected by Birmingham in 1983 USFL territorial draft.
Selected by Tampa Bay in 3rd round (72nd player selected) of 1983 NFL draft.
Signed by Tampa Bay Buccaneers, May 18, 1983.

Year Club	G.	No.	Yds.	Avg.	TD.
1983—Tampa Bay NFL	15	1	69	69.0	1
1984—Tampa Bay NFL	16	3	38	12.7	0
1985—Tampa Bay NFL	16	7	49	7.0	0
Pro Totals—3 Years............	47	11	156	14.2	1

Additional pro statistics: Recovered two fumbles for 16 yards, 1984; recovered two fumbles and fumbled once, 1985.

MARK CATANO
Nose Tackle-Defensive Tackle—Pittsburgh Steelers
Born January 26, 1962, at Yonkers, N.Y.
Height, 6.03. Weight, 265.
High School—Montrose, N.Y., Hendrick Hudson.
Attended Hudson Valley Community College and Valdosta State College.

Selected by Memphis in 12th round (244th player selected) of 1984 USFL draft.
Signed as free agent by Pittsburgh Steelers, May 2, 1984.
Pittsburgh NFL, 1984 and 1985.
Games: 1984 (16), 1985 (15). Total—31.
Pro statistics: Returned one kickoff for no yards, 1984; recovered one fumble for 17 yards, 1985.
Played in AFC Championship Game following 1984 season.

DONALD RAY CATTAGE
(Known by middle name.)
Defensive End—New Orleans Saints
Born September 22, 1960, at Spokane, Wash.
Height, 6.03. Weight, 261.
High School—Spokane, Wash., Lewis & Clark.
Attended University of Washington.

Selected by Arizona in 17th round (194th player selected) of 1983 USFL draft.
Signed by Arizona Wranglers, January 27, 1983.
On developmental squad, May 2 through May 27, 1983; activated, May 28, 1983.
On developmental squad, July 2 through remainder of 1983 season.

Franchise transferred to Chicago, September 30, 1983.
Franchise disbanded, November 20, 1984.
Not selected in USFL dispersal draft, December 6, 1984; signed as free agent by Los Angeles Express, January 4, 1985.
On developmental squad, March 10 through March 28, 1985; activated, March 29, 1985.
Released by Los Angeles Express, August 2, 1985; signed as free agent by New Orleans Saints, May 13, 1986.
On developmental squad for 5 games with Arizona Wranglers in 1983.
On developmental squad for 3 games with Los Angeles Express in 1985.
Arizona USFL, 1983; Chicago USFL, 1984; Los Angeles USFL, 1985.
Games: 1983 (13), 1984 (18), 1985 (13). Total—44.
Pro statistics: Credited with three sacks for 32 yards, 1983; credited with three sacks for 17 yards and recovered two fumbles for 11 yards, 1984; credited with three sacks for 40 yards and recovered one fumble, 1985.

MATTHEW ANDREW CAVANAUGH
(Matt)
Quarterback—Philadelphia Eagles
Born October 27, 1956, at Youngstown, O.
Height, 6.02. Weight, 212.
High School—Youngstown, O., Chaney.
Received bachelor of science degree in administration of justice from University of Pittsburgh.

Selected by New England in 2nd round (50th player selected) of 1978 NFL draft.
Traded by New England Patriots to San Francisco 49ers for 7th round pick in 1984 draft, 8th round pick in 1985 draft and 7th round pick in 1986 draft, August 10, 1983.
Traded by San Francisco 49ers to Philadelphia Eagles for 3rd round pick in 1986 draft and 2nd round pick in 1987 draft, April 29, 1986.
Active for 16 games with New England Patriots in 1978; did not play.

Year Club	G.	Att.	Cmp.	Pct.	Gain	T.P.	P.I.	Avg.	Att.	Yds.	Avg.	TD.	TD.	Pts.	F.
					PASSING					RUSHING				TOTAL	
1979—New England NFL	13	1	1	100.0	10	0	0	10.00	1	—2	—2.0	0	0	0	0
1980—New England NFL	16	105	63	60.0	885	9	5	8.43	19	97	5.1	0	0	0	1
1981—New England NFL	16	219	115	52.5	1633	5	13	7.46	17	92	5.4	3	3	18	2
1982—New England NFL	7	60	27	45.0	490	5	5	8.17	2	3	1.5	0	0	0	1
1983—San Francisco NFL	5				None				1	8	8.0	0	0	0	0
1984—San Francisco NFL	8	61	33	54.1	449	4	0	7.36	4	—11	—2.8	0	0	0	0
1985—San Francisco NFL	16	54	28	51.9	334	1	1	6.19	4	5	1.3	0	0	0	0
Pro Totals—8 Years	81	500	267	53.4	3801	24	24	7.60	48	192	4.0	3	3	18	4

Quarterback Rating Points: 1979 (108.3), 1980 (95.9), 1981 (60.0), 1982 (66.7), 1984 (99.7), 1985 (69.5). Total—74.3.
Additional pro statistics: Recovered one fumble and fumbled once for minus four yards, 1980; caught one pass for nine yards, 1981.
Played in NFC Championship Game following 1984 season.
Member of San Francisco 49ers for NFC Championship Game following 1983 season; did not play.
Member of San Francisco 49ers for NFL Championship Game following 1984 season; did not play.

FRANK CEPHOUS III
Name pronounced See-fuss.
Running Back—Minnesota Vikings
Born July 4, 1961, at Philadelphia, Pa.
Height, 5.10. Weight, 205.
High School—Wilmington, Del., Saint Marks.
Attended University of California at Los Angeles.

Selected by San Antonio in 3rd round (45th player selected) of 1984 USFL draft.
Selected by New York Giants in 11th round (283rd player selected) of 1984 NFL draft.
Signed by New York Giants, May 28, 1984.
Released by New York Giants, August 19, 1985; signed as free agent by Minnesota Vikings, March 30, 1986.

Year Club	G.	Att.	Yds.	Avg.	TD.	P.C.	Yds.	Avg.	TD.	TD.	Pts.	F.
		RUSHING				PASS RECEIVING				TOTAL		
1984—New York Giants NFL	16	3	2	0.7	0		None			0	0	0

Year Club	G.	No.	Yds.	Avg.	TD.
	KICKOFF RETURNS				
1984—N.Y. Giants NFL	16	9	178	19.8	0

JEFFREY ALLAN CHADWICK
(Jeff)
Wide Receiver—Detroit Lions
Born December 16, 1960, at Detroit, Mich.
Height, 6.03. Weight, 190.
High School—Dearborn, Mich., Divine Child.
Attended Grand Valley State College.

Signed as free agent by Detroit Lions, May 15, 1983.
On injured reserve with broken collarbone, November 4 through remainder of 1985 season.

Year Club		—PASS RECEIVING—				
	G.	P.C.	Yds.	Avg.	TD.	
1983—Detroit NFL	16	40	617	15.4	4	
1984—Detroit NFL	16	37	540	14.6	2	
1985—Detroit NFL	7	25	478	19.1	3	
Pro Totals—3 Years	39	102	1635	16.0	9	

Additional pro statistics: Rushed once for 12 yards and a touchdown, 1984.

WESLEY SANDY CHANDLER
(Wes)
Wide Receiver—San Diego Chargers

Born August 22, 1956, at New Smyrna Beach, Fla.
Height, 6.00. Weight, 183.
High School—New Smyrna Beach, Fla.
Received degree in speech pathology from University of Florida.

Named as wide receiver on THE SPORTING NEWS College All-America Team, 1977.
Selected by New Orleans in 1st round (3rd player selected) of 1978 NFL draft.
Traded by New Orleans Saints to San Diego Chargers for wide receiver Aundra Thompson and 1st and 3rd round picks in 1982 draft, September 29, 1981.

Year Club		PASS RECEIVING				–PUNT RETURNS–				—KICKOFF RET.—				—TOTAL—		
	G.	P.C.	Yds.	Avg.	TD.	No.	Yds.	Avg.	TD.	No.	Yds.	Avg.	TD.	TD.	Pts.	F.
1978—New Orleans NFL	16	35	472	13.5	2	34	233	6.9	0	32	760	23.8	0	2	12	1
1979—New Orleans NFL	16	65	1069	16.4	6	3	13	4.3	0	7	136	19.4	0	6	36	0
1980—New Orleans NFL	16	65	975	15.0	6	8	36	4.5	0		None			6	36	2
1981—N.O. (4)-S.D. (12) NFL.	16	69	1142	16.6	6	5	79	15.8	0	8	125	15.6	0	6	36	1
1982—San Diego NFL	8	49	*1032	21.1	*9		None				None			9	54	0
1983—San Diego NFL	16	58	845	14.6	5	8	26	3.3	0		None			5	30	3
1984—San Diego NFL	15	52	708	13.6	6		None				None			6	36	0
1985—San Diego NFL	15	67	1199	17.9	10		None				None			10	60	1
Pro Totals—8 Years	118	460	7442	16.2	50	58	387	6.7	0	47	1021	21.7	0	50	300	8

Additional pro statistics: Rushed twice for 10 yards, 1978; punted eight times for 31.0 average, 1979; attempted one pass with one completion for 43 yards and recovered two fumbles, 1980; rushed once for nine yards, 1980 and 1985; recovered one fumble for 51 yards, rushed five times for minus one yard and attempted two passes with no completions, 1981; rushed five times for 32 yards, 1982; rushed twice for 25 yards and recovered one fumble, 1983.
Played in AFC Championship Game following 1981 season.
Played in Pro Bowl (NFL All-Star Game) following 1979, 1982, 1983 and 1985 seasons.

MICHAEL WILLIAM CHARLES
(Mike)
Defensive Tackle—Miami Dolphins

Born September 23, 1962, at Newark, N.J.
Height, 6.04. Weight, 283.
High School—Newark, N.J., Central.
Received bachelor of science degree in speech communications from Syracuse University.

Selected by New Jersey in 1983 USFL territorial draft.
Selected by Miami in 2nd round (55th player selected) of 1983 NFL draft.
Signed by Miami Dolphins, July 12, 1983.
On injured reserve with knee injury, November 17 through December 27, 1984; activated, December 28, 1984.
Miami NFL, 1983 through 1985.
Games: 1983 (16), 1984 (10), 1985 (16). Total—42.
Pro statistics: Recovered one fumble and credited with one safety, 1983.
Played in AFC Championship Game following 1984 and 1985 seasons.
Played in NFL Championship Game following 1984 season.

BARNEY LEWIS CHAVOUS
Name pronounced CHAY-vus.
Defensive End—Denver Broncos

Born March 22, 1951, at Aiken, S. C.
Height, 6.03. Weight, 258.
High School—Aiken, S. C., Schofield.
Received bachelor of science degree in physical education from South Carolina State University in 1973.

Selected by Denver in 2nd round (36th player selected) of 1973 NFL draft.
Denver NFL, 1973 through 1985.
Games: 1973 (14), 1974 (14), 1975 (9), 1976 (13), 1977 (13), 1978 (16), 1979 (16), 1980 (16), 1981 (16), 1982 (9), 1983 (15), 1984 (15), 1985 (16). Total—182.
Pro statistics: Recovered two fumbles, 1973 and 1974; recovered one fumble, 1980, 1981 and 1985; credited with one safety, 1982; recovered one fumble in end zone for touchdown, 1983.
Played in AFC Championship Game following 1977 season.
Played in NFL Championship Game following 1977 season.

—DID YOU KNOW—

That although the San Diego Chargers were 0-8 against their AFC Western Division rivals in 1984, their record against all other opponents was 7-1?

DERON LEIGH CHERRY
Safety—Kansas City Chiefs
Born September 12, 1959, at Riverside, N.J.
Height, 5.11. Weight, 196.
High School—Palmyra, N.J.
Attended Rutgers University.
Related to Raphel Cherry, safety with Washington Redskins.

Tied NFL record for most interceptions, game (4), against Seattle Seahawks, September 29, 1985.
Signed as free agent by Kansas City Chiefs, May 4, 1981.
Released by Kansas City Chiefs, August 31, 1981; re-signed by Chiefs, September 23, 1981.
On inactive list, September 19, 1982.
On injured reserve with shoulder separation, December 30 through remainder of 1982 season.

Year Club	G.	No.	Yds.	Avg.	TD.
1981—Kansas City NFL	13	1	4	4.0	0
1982—Kansas City NFL	7			None	
1983—Kansas City NFL	16	7	100	14.3	0
1984—Kansas City NFL	16	7	140	20.0	0
1985—Kansas City NFL	16	7	87	12.4	*1
Pro Totals—5 Years	68	22	331	15.0	1

Additional pro statistics: Returned three kickoffs for 52 yards, 1981; returned one kickoff for 39 yards, 1982; returned two kickoffs for 54 yards, recovered two fumbles for four yards and fumbled twice, 1983; returned one kickoff for no yards, 1984.
Played in Pro Bowl (NFL All-Star Game) following 1983 through 1985 seasons.

RAPHEL JEROME CHERRY

First name pronounced RA-fehl.

Safety—Washington Redskins
Born December 19, 1961, at Little Rock, Ark.
Height, 6.00. Weight, 194.
High School—Los Angeles, Calif., Washington.
Attended University of Hawaii.
Related to Deron Cherry, safety with Kansas City Chiefs.

Selected by Houston in 1st round (6th player selected) of 1985 USFL draft.
Selected by Washington in 5th round (122nd player selected) of 1985 NFL draft.
Signed by Washington Redskins, July 18, 1985.

Year Club	G.	No.	Yds.	Avg.	TD.
1985—Washington NFL	16	2	29	14.5	0

Additional pro statistics: Returned four punts for 22 yards, returned one kickoff for nine yards and caught one pass for 11 yards, 1985.

JOHN CHESLEY
Tight End—Denver Broncos
Born July 2, 1962, at Washington, D.C.
Height, 6.05. Weight, 225.
High School—Washington, D.C.
Attended Oklahoma State University.
Brother of Al Chesley, linebacker with Philadelphia Eagles, 1979 through 1982.

Selected by Oklahoma in 1984 USFL territorial draft.
Selected by Miami in 10th round (277th player selected) of 1984 NFL draft.
Signed by Miami Dolphins, July 9, 1984.
Released by Miami Dolphins, August 27, 1984; re-signed by Dolphins, October 19, 1984.
Released by Miami Dolphins, November 2, 1984; re-signed by Dolphins, April 11, 1985.
Released by Miami Dolphins, September 2, 1985; signed as free agent by Denver Broncos, April 23, 1986.
Miami NFL, 1984.
Games: 1984 (1).

ANTHONY PAUL CHICKILLO

Name pronounced CHI-kill-o.

(Tony)
Nose Tackle—Miami Dolphins
Born July 8, 1960, at Miami, Fla.
Height, 6.03. Weight, 257.
High School—Miami, Fla., Southwest.
Received degree in recreational therapy from University of Miami (Fla.) in 1983.
Son of Nick Chickillo, guard with Chicago Cardinals, 1953.

Selected by New Jersey in 16th round (191st player selected) of 1983 USFL draft.
Selected by Tampa Bay in 5th round (131st player selected) of 1983 NFL draft.
Signed by Tampa Bay Buccaneers, June 6, 1983.
On injured reserve with ankle injury, August 22 through entire 1983 season.
Released by Tampa Bay Buccaneers, August 20, 1984; awarded on waivers to Indianapolis Colts, August 21, 1984.
Released by Indianapolis Colts, August 27, 1984.
USFL rights traded by New Jersey Generals to Orlando Renegades for rights to defensive tackle Charles Cook, October 31, 1984.

Signed as free agent by San Diego Chargers, December 13, 1984.
Released by San Diego Chargers, October 5, 1985; signed as free agent by Miami Dolphins, April 30, 1986.
San Diego NFL, 1984 and 1985.
Game: 1984 (1), 1985 (4). Total—5.

RAY CHILDRESS
Defensive End—Houston Oilers
Born October 20, 1962, at Memphis, Tenn.
Height, 6.06. Weight, 267.
High School—Richardson, Tex., J.J. Pearce.
Attended Texas A&M University.

Named as defensive lineman on THE SPORTING NEWS College All-America Team, 1984.
Selected by Houston in 1985 USFL territorial draft.
Selected by Houston in 1st round (3rd player selected) of 1985 NFL draft.
Signed by Houston Oilers, August 24, 1985.
Granted roster exemption, August 24 through August 29, 1985; activated, August 30, 1985.
Houston NFL, 1985.
Games: 1985 (16).
Pro statistics: Recovered one fumble, 1985.

JEFFREY BRUCE CHRISTENSEN
(Jeff)
Quarterback—Cleveland Browns
Born January 8, 1960, at Gibson City, Ill.
Height, 6.03. Weight, 202.
High School—Gibson City, Ill.
Attended Eastern Illinois University.

Selected by New Jersey in 17th round (195th player selected) of 1983 USFL draft.
Selected by Cincinnati in 5th round (137th player selected) of 1983 NFL draft.
Signed by Cincinnati Bengals, June 2, 1983.
Traded by Cincinnati Bengals to Los Angeles Rams for draft choice, July 25, 1984.
Released by Los Angeles Rams, August 15, 1984; signed as free agent by Philadelphia Eagles for 1985, October 23, 1984.
Signed for 1984 season, November 27, 1984.
Released by Philadelphia Eagles, September 2, 1985; re-signed by Eagles, November 20, 1985.
Released by Philadelphia Eagles, November 25, 1985; signed as free agent by Cleveland Browns, April 20, 1986.
Active for 3 games with Philadelphia Eagles in 1984; did not play.
Active for 1 game with Philadelphia Eagles in 1985; did not play.
Cincinnati NFL, 1983; Philadelphia NFL, 1984 and 1985.
Games: 1983 (1).
Pro statistics: Rushed once for minus two yards, 1983.

TODD JAY CHRISTENSEN
Tight End—Los Angeles Raiders
Born August 3, 1956, at Bellefonte, Pa.
Height, 6.03. Weight, 230.
High School—Eugene, Ore., Sheldon.
Attended Brigham Young University.

Named to THE SPORTING NEWS NFL All-Star Team, 1983 and 1985.
Selected by Dallas in 2nd round (56th player selected) of 1978 NFL draft.
On injured reserve with broken foot, August 28 through entire 1978 season.
Released by Dallas Cowboys, August 27, 1979; claimed on waivers by New York Giants, August 28, 1979.
Released by New York Giants, September 4, 1979; signed as free agent by Oakland Raiders, September 26, 1979.
Franchise transferred to Los Angeles, May 7, 1982.
On did not report list, August 14 through August 22, 1984.
Reported and granted roster exemption, August 23 through August 31, 1984; activated, September 1, 1984.

| | | ——PASS RECEIVING—— | | | | |
Year Club	G.	P.C.	Yds.	Avg.	TD.
1979—NYG (1)-Oak (12) NFL	13	None			
1980—Oakland NFL................	16	None			
1981—Oakland NFL................	16	8	115	14.4	2
1982—L.A. Raiders NFL........	9	42	510	12.1	4
1983—L.A. Raiders NFL........	16	*92	1247	13.6	12
1984—L.A. Raiders NFL........	16	80	1007	12.6	7
1985—L.A. Raiders NFL........	16	82	987	12.0	6
Pro Totals—7 Years...........	102	304	3866	12.7	31

Additional pro statistics: Recovered two fumbles for one yard, 1979; recovered one fumble in end zone for a touchdown and returned one kickoff for 10 yards, 1980; returned four kickoffs for 54 yards and credited with one safety, 1981; recovered one fumble, 1981 and 1983 through 1985; rushed once for minus six yards and fumbled three times, 1982; fumbled once, 1983 and 1984.
Played in AFC Championship Game following 1980 and 1983 seasons.
Played in NFC Championship Game following 1980 and 1983 seasons.
Played in Pro Bowl (NFL All-Star Game) following 1983 through 1985 seasons.

GREG A. CHRISTY
Offensive Tackle—Buffalo Bills
Born April 29, 1962, at Freeport, Pa.
Height, 6.04. Weight, 279.
High School—Freeport, Pa.
Attended University of Pittsburgh.

Selected by Baltimore in 1985 USFL territorial draft.
Signed as free agent by Buffalo Bills, May 10, 1985.
On injured reserve with knee injury, August 26 through October 23, 1985; activated after clearing procedural waivers, October 25, 1985.
Buffalo NFL, 1985.
Games: 1985 (7).

SAM CLANCY
Defensive End—Cleveland Browns
Born May 29, 1958, at Pittsburgh, Pa.
Height, 6.07. Weight, 260.
High School—Pittsburgh, Pa., Brashear.
Attended University of Pittsburgh.

Selected by Phoenix in 3rd round (62nd player selected) of 1981 NBA draft.
Released by Phoenix Suns, October 19, 1981; signed by Billings Volcanos (CBA), November 12, 1981.
Selected by Seattle in 11th round (284th player selected) of 1982 NFL draft.
On injured reserve with knee injury, August 16 through entire 1982 season.
Granted free agency, February 1, 1984; signed by Pittsburgh Maulers, February 10, 1984.
Franchise disbanded, October 25, 1984.
Selected by Memphis Showboats in USFL dispersal draft, December 6, 1984.
Granted free agency, August 1, 1985; re-signed by Seahawks and traded to Cleveland Browns for 7th round pick in 1986 draft, August 27, 1985.
Granted roster exemption, August 27 through September 5, 1985; activated, September 6, 1985.
Seattle NFL, 1983; Pittsburgh USFL, 1984; Memphis USFL, 1985; Cleveland NFL, 1985.
Games: 1983 (13), 1984 (18), 1985 USFL (18), 1985 NFL (14). Total NFL—27. Total USFL—36. Total Pro—63.
USFL Statistics: Credited with 15 sacks for 136 yards and recovered two fumbles, 1984; credited with four sacks for 28 yards, 1985.

BASKETBALL RECORD AS PLAYER

Year—Team	G	Min.	FGM	FGA	Pct.	FTM	FTA	Pct.	3-pt. Made	3-pt. Att.	Pts.	Avg.	Reb.	Avg.	Ast.	PF	Blk. Shots	Steals
81-82 Billings CBA	41	1170	190	355	53.5	89	128	69.5	1	5	472	11.5	342	8.3	50	144	41	67

PLAYOFF RECORD

Year—Team	G	Min.	FGM	FGA	Pct.	FTM	FTA	Pct.	3-pt. Made	3-pt. Att.	Pts.	Avg.	Reb.	Avg.	Ast.	PF	Blk. Shots	Steals
81-82 Billings CBA	5	167	24	46	52.1	12	19	63.1	1	1	63	12.6	54	10.8	8	23	5	8

CLEVELAND E. CLANTON III
(Chuck)
Defensive Back—Green Bay Packers
Born July 15, 1962, at Richmond, Va.
Height, 5.11. Weight, 192.
High School—Pensacola, Fla., Pine Forest.
Attended Auburn University.

Named as safety on THE SPORTING NEWS USFL All-Star Team, 1985.
Selected by Birmingham in 1984 USFL territorial draft.
Signed by Birmingham Stallions, January 11, 1984.
On developmental squad, June 16 through remainder of 1984 season.
Selected by Green Bay in 2nd round (39th player selected) of 1984 NFL supplemental draft.
Granted free agency, July 31, 1985; signed by Green Bay Packers, December 3, 1985.
Granted roster exemption, December 3 through December 6, 1985; activated, December 7, 1985.
On developmental squad for 2 games with Birmingham Stallions in 1984.

Year Club	G.	No.	Yds.	—INTERCEPTIONS— Avg.TD.	
1984—Birmingham USFL	16	10	*249	*24.9	*3
1985—Birmingham USFL	18	*16	*275	17.2	*1
1985—Green Bay NFL	3			None	
USFL Totals—2 Years	34	26	524	20.2	4
NFL Totals—1 Year	3	0	0	0.0	0
Pro Totals—3 Years	37	26	524	20.2	4

Additional USFL statistics: Recovered two fumbles for 40 yards, 1985.

SAM JACK CLAPHAN
Name pronounced Clap-in.
Offensive Tackle—San Diego Chargers
Born October 10, 1956, at Tahlequah, Okla.
Height, 6.06. Weight, 282.
High School—Stillwell, Okla.
Received bachelor of science degree in special education from University of Oklahoma in 1979.

Selected by Cleveland in 2nd round (47th player selected) of 1979 NFL draft.
On injured reserve with back injury, August 27 through entire 1979 season.
Released by Cleveland Browns, August 26, 1980; signed as free agent by San Diego Chargers, May 1, 1981.
On inactive list, September 12 and September 19, 1982.
On injured reserve with knee injury, December 4 through remainder of 1985 season.
San Diego NFL, 1981 through 1985.
Games: 1981 (16), 1982 (2), 1983 (16), 1984 (16), 1985 (12). Total—62.
Pro statistics: Recovered one fumble, 1985.
Played in AFC Championship Game following 1981 season.

BRET CLARK
Safety
Born February 24, 1961, at Nebraska City, Neb.
Height, 6.02. Weight, 200.
High School—Nebraska City, Neb.
Attended University of Nebraska.

Selected by Denver in 1985 USFL territorial draft.
USFL rights traded by Denver Gold to Tampa Bay Bandits for pick in 1986 draft and $5,000, May 10, 1985.
Signed by Tampa Bay Bandits, May 10, 1985.
Selected by Los Angeles Raiders in 7th round (191st player selected) of 1985 NFL draft.
Released by Tampa Bay Bandits, March 7, 1986.
NFL rights traded by Los Angeles Raiders to Atlanta Falcons for 4th round pick in 1986 draft, April 29, 1986.
Tampa Bay USFL, 1985.
Games: 1985 (7).
Pro statistics: Intercepted one pass for no yards, credited with one sack for nine yards and returned two kickoffs for 19 yards, 1985.

BRUCE CLARK
Defensive End—New Orleans Saints
Born March 31, 1958, at New Castle, Pa.
Height, 6.03. Weight, 281.
High School—New Castle, Pa.
Attended Penn State University.

Selected by Green Bay in 1st round (4th player selected) of 1980 NFL draft.
Signed by Toronto Argonauts, May 26, 1980.
Granted free agency, March 1, 1982; traded by Green Bay Packers to New Orleans Saints for 1st round pick in 1983 draft, June 10, 1982.
Toronto CFL, 1980 and 1981; New Orleans NFL, 1982 through 1985.
Games: 1980 (16), 1981 (16), 1982 (9), 1983 (15), 1984 (15), 1985 (16). Total CFL—32. Total NFL—55. Pro Total—87.
CFL statistics: Intercepted one pass for no yards and recovered four fumbles for six yards, 1980; recovered one fumble, 1981.
NFL statistics: Recovered one fumble, 1983; intercepted one pass for nine yards and recovered two fumbles for five yards, 1984; recovered one fumble for four yards, 1985.
Played in Pro Bowl (NFL All-Star Game) following 1984 season.

DWIGHT EDWARD CLARK
Wide Receiver—San Francisco 49ers
Born January 8, 1957, at Kinston, N. C.
Height, 6.04. Weight, 215.
High School—Charlotte, N. C., Garinger.
Received bachelor of arts degree in history from Clemson University in 1980.

Selected by San Francisco in 10th round (249th player selected) of 1979 NFL draft.
On injured reserve with knee injury, December 21 through remainder of 1983 season.

| | | ——PASS RECEIVING—— | | | |
Year Club	G.	P.C.	Yds.	Avg.	TD.
1979—San Francisco NFL	16	18	232	12.9	0
1980—San Francisco NFL	16	82	991	12.1	8
1981—San Francisco NFL	16	85	1105	13.0	4
1982—San Francisco NFL	9	*60	913	15.2	5
1983—San Francisco NFL	16	70	840	12.0	8
1984—San Francisco NFL	16	52	880	16.9	6
1985—San Francisco NFL	16	54	705	13.1	10
Pro Totals—7 Years............	105	421	5666	13.5	41

Additional pro statistics: Recovered one fumble, 1979; fumbled twice, 1980; rushed three times for 32 yards, 1981; attempted one pass with no completions, 1981, 1983 and 1984; fumbled once, 1982; rushed three times for 18 yards, 1983.
Played in NFC Championship Game following 1981 and 1984 seasons.
Played in NFL Championship Game following 1981 and 1984 seasons.
Played in Pro Bowl (NFL All-Star Game) following 1981 and 1982 seasons.

GARY C. CLARK
Wide Receiver—Washington Redskins
Born May 1, 1962, at Radford, Va.
Height, 5.09. Weight, 175.
High School—Dublin, Va., Pulaski County.
Attended James Madison University.

Selected by Jacksonville in 1st round (6th player selected) of 1984 USFL draft.

Signed by Jacksonville Bulls, January 16, 1984.
On developmental squad, May 9 through May 15, 1984; activated, May 16, 1984.
On developmental squad, June 4 through June 11, 1984; activated, June 12, 1984.
Selected by Washington in 2nd round (55th player selected) of 1984 NFL supplemental draft.
On developmental squad, March 17 through March 19, 1985; activated, March 20, 1985.
Released by Jacksonville Bulls, May 1, 1985; signed by Washington Redskins, May 13, 1985.
On developmental squad for 2 games with Jacksonville Bulls in 1984.
On developmental squad for 1 game with Jacksonville Bulls in 1985.

		PASS RECEIVING				-PUNT RETURNS-				—KICKOFF RET.—				—TOTAL—		
Year	Club	G.	P.C.	Yds.	Avg. TD.	No.	Yds.	Avg. TD.		No.	Yds.	Avg. TD.		TD.	Pts.	F.
1984—Jacksonville USFL		16	56	760	13.6	2	20	84	4.2	0	19	341	18.0	0	2	12	5
1985—Jacksonville USFL		9	10	61	6.1	1	7	44	6.3	0	3	56	18.7	0	1	6	1
1985—Washington NFL		16	72	926	12.9	5	None				None				5	30	0
USFL Totals—2 Years		25	66	821	12.4	3	27	128	4.7	0	22	397	18.0	0	3	18	6
NFL Totals—1 Year		16	72	926	12.9	5	0	0	0.0	0	0	0	0.0	0	5	30	0
Pro Totals—3 Years		41	138	1747	12.7	8	27	128	4.7	0	22	397	18.0	0	8	48	6

Additional USFL statistics: Rushed twice for nine yards and recovered four fumbles, 1984; recovered one fumble, 1985.
Additional NFL statistics: Rushed twice for 10 yards, 1985.

JESSIE L. CLARK
Fullback—Green Bay Packers
Born January 3, 1960, at Thebes, Ark.
Height, 6.00. Weight, 233.
High School—Crossett, Ark.
Attended Louisiana Tech University and received bachelor of arts
degree in criminal justice from University of Arkansas in 1983.
Cousin of Dennis Woodberry, cornerback with Birmingham Stallions.

Selected by Green Bay in 7th round (188th player selected) of 1983 NFL draft.
On injured reserve with muscle tear in elbow, November 16 through remainder of 1984 season.

		——RUSHING——				PASS RECEIVING			—TOTAL—		
Year	Club	G.	Att.	Yds.	Avg. TD.	P.C.	Yds.	Avg. TD.	TD.	Pts.	F.
1983—Green Bay NFL		16	71	328	4.6	0	18	279	15.5	1	1	6	2
1984—Green Bay NFL		11	87	375	4.3	4	29	234	8.1	2	6	36	2
1985—Green Bay NFL		16	147	633	4.3	5	24	252	10.5	2	7	42	4
Pro Totals—3 Years		43	305	1336	4.4	9	71	765	10.8	5	14	84	8

Additional pro statistics: Recovered one fumble, 1983; recovered two fumbles, 1985.

KELVIN CLARK
Guard—New Orleans Saints
Born January 30, 1956, at Odessa, Tex.
Height, 6.03. Weight, 273.
High School—Odessa, Tex.
Attended University of Nebraska.

Selected by Denver in 1st round (22nd player selected) of 1979 NFL draft.
Traded by Denver Broncos to New Orleans Saints for 4th round pick in 1984 draft, August 30, 1982.
On injured reserve with broken ankle, September 24 through remainder of 1985 season.
Denver NFL, 1979 through 1981; New Orleans NFL, 1982 through 1985.
Games: 1979 (15), 1980 (14), 1981 (16), 1982 (9), 1983 (16), 1984 (16), 1985 (2). Total—88.
Pro statistics: Recovered fumble in end zone for a touchdown, 1983.

MONTE BRYAN CLARK
(Known by middle name.)
Quarterback—Buffalo Bills
Born July 27, 1960, at Redwood City, Calif.
Height, 6.02. Weight, 196.
High School—Los Altos, Calif.
Received bachelor of arts degree in communications from Michigan State University.
Son of Monte Clark, offensive lineman with San Francisco 49ers, Dallas Cowboys and Cleveland Browns,
1959 through 1969; head coach with San Francisco 49ers, 1976, and Detroit Lions, 1978 through 1984.

Selected by San Francisco in 9th round (251st player selected) of 1982 NFL draft.
On inactive list, September 12 and September 19, 1982.
On injured reserve with separated shoulder, August 23 through entire 1983 season.
Released by San Francisco 49ers, September 4, 1984; re-signed by 49ers, September 18, 1984.
Released by San Francisco 49ers, September 29, 1984; signed as free agent by Cincinnati Bengals, December 5, 1984.
Traded by Cincinnati Bengals to Miami Dolphins for draft choice, May 6, 1985.
On injured waivers with shoulder injury, August 26 through September 23, 1985.
Released by Miami Dolphins, September 24, 1985; signed as free agent by Buffalo Bills, May 19, 1986.
Active for 7 games with San Francisco 49ers in 1982; did not play.
Active for 2 games with San Francisco 49ers in 1984; did not play.
San Francisco NFL, 1982; San Francisco (0)-Cincinnati (1) NFL, 1984.
Games: 1984 (1).

RANDALL BYRON CLARK
(Randy)
Center—St. Louis Cardinals
Born July 27, 1957, at Chicago, Ill.
Height, 6.04. Weight, 270.
High School—Mount Prospect, Ill., Prospect.
Received bachelor of science degree in marketing from Northern Illinois University in 1980.

Selected by Chicago in 8th round (215th player selected) of 1980 NFL draft.
Released by Chicago Bears, August 26, 1980; signed as free agent by St. Louis Cardinals, October 27, 1980.
St. Louis NFL, 1980 through 1985.
Games: 1980 (8), 1981 (16), 1982 (9), 1983 (14), 1984 (16), 1985 (16). Total—79.
Pro statistics: Returned two kickoffs for 14 yards, 1980; fumbled once, 1983; recovered two fumbles, 1984.

STEPHEN SPENCE CLARK
(Steve)
Guard—Miami Dolphins
Born August 2, 1960, at Salt Lake City, Utah.
Height, 6.04. Weight, 255.
High School—Salt Lake City, Utah, Skyline.
Attended University of Utah.

Selected by Miami in 9th round (239th player selected) of 1982 NFL draft.
Released by Miami Dolphins, August 30, 1982; re-signed by Dolphins, December 7, 1982.
Released by Miami Dolphins, August 29, 1983; re-signed by Dolphins, August 30, 1983.
On injured reserve with broken ankle, August 28 through September 27, 1984; activated, September 28, 1984.
Miami NFL, 1982 through 1985.
Games: 1982 (2), 1983 (11), 1984 (12), 1985 (16). Total—41.
Pro statistics: Recovered one fumble, 1982 and 1985.
Played in AFC Championship Game following 1984 and 1985 seasons.
Member of Miami Dolphins for AFC Championship Game following 1982 season; did not play.
Played in NFL Championship Game following 1984 season.
Member of Miami Dolphins for NFL Championship Game following 1982 season; did not play.

KENNETH MAURICE CLARKE
(Ken)
Nose Tackle—Philadelphia Eagles
Born August 28, 1956, at Savannah, Ga.
Height, 6.02. Weight, 272.
High School—Boston, Mass., English.
Received bachelor of science degree in psychology from Syracuse University in 1978.

Signed as free agent by Philadelphia Eagles, May 4, 1978.
Philadelphia NFL, 1978 through 1985.
Games: 1978 (16), 1979 (16), 1980 (16), 1981 (16), 1982 (9), 1983 (16), 1984 (16), 1985 (16). Total—121.
Pro statistics: Recovered one fumble, 1978 and 1982; returned one kickoff for no yards and fumbled once, 1980; credited with one safety and returned one kickoff for no yards, 1981; recovered three fumbles for five yards, 1983; recovered two fumbles, 1985.
Played in NFC Championship Game following 1980 season.
Played in NFL Championship Game following 1980 season.

RAYMOND DE WAYNE CLAYBORN
(Ray)
Cornerback—New England Patriots
Born January 2, 1955, at Fort Worth, Tex.
Height, 6.00. Weight, 186.
High School—Fort Worth, Tex., Trimble.
Received degree in communications from University of Texas.

Named as cornerback on THE SPORTING NEWS College All-America Team, 1976.
Named to THE SPORTING NEWS NFL All-Star Team, 1983.
Selected by New England in 1st round (16th player selected) of 1977 NFL draft.

		-INTERCEPTIONS-				—KICKOFF RET.—				—TOTAL—		
Year Club	G.	No.	Yds.	Avg.	TD.	No.	Yds.	Avg.	TD.	TD.	Pts.	F.
1977—New England NFL	14		None			28	869	★31.0	★3	3	†20	1
1978—New England NFL	16	4	72	18.0	0	27	636	23.6	0	0	0	0
1979—New England NFL	16	5	56	11.2	0	2	33	16.5	0	0	0	0
1980—New England NFL	16	5	87	17.4	0		None			0	0	0
1981—New England NFL	16	2	39	19.5	0		None			0	0	0
1982—New England NFL	9	1	26	26.0	0		None			0	0	0
1983—New England NFL	16		None				None			0	0	0
1984—New England NFL	16	3	102	34.0	0		None			0	0	0
1985—New England NFL	16	6	80	13.3	★1		None			1	6	0
Pro Totals—9 Years	135	26	462	17.8	1	57	1538	27.0	3	4	26	1

†Includes one safety.
Additional pro statistics: Recovered one fumble, 1978, 1980 and 1982; recovered two fumbles for four yards, 1981.
Played in AFC Championship Game following 1985 season.
Played in NFL Championship Game following 1985 season.
Played in Pro Bowl (NFL All-Star Game) following 1983 and 1985 seasons.

HARVEY JEROME CLAYTON
Cornerback—Pittsburgh Steelers
Born April 4, 1961, at Kendall, Fla.
Height, 5.09. Weight, 180.
High School—Miami, Fla., South Dade.
Attended Florida State University.

Selected by Tampa Bay in 1983 USFL territorial draft.
Signed as free agent by Pittsburgh Steelers, May 19, 1983.

Year Club	G.	No.	Yds.	Avg.TD.	
		—INTERCEPTIONS—			
1983—Pittsburgh NFL............	14	1	70	70.0	1
1984—Pittsburgh NFL............	14	1	0	0.0	0
1985—Pittsburgh NFL............	14			None	
Pro Totals—3 Years............	42	2	70	35.0	1

Additional pro statistics: Returned one punt for no yards and recovered one fumble, 1984.
Played in AFC Championship Game following 1984 season.

MARK GREGORY CLAYTON
Wide Receiver—Miami Dolphins
Born April 8, 1961, at Indianapolis, Ind.
Height, 5.09. Weight, 172.
High School—Indianapolis, Ind., Cathedral.
Attended University of Louisville.

Established NFL record for most touchdown receptions, season (18), 1984.
Selected by Miami in 8th round (223rd player selected) of 1983 NFL draft.

Year Club		-PASS RECEIVING-				-PUNT RETURNS-				—TOTAL—		
	G.	P.C.	Yds.	Avg.	TD.	No.	Yds.	Avg.	TD.	TD.	Pts.	F.
1983—Miami NFL	14	6	114	19.0	1	41	392	9.6	*1	2	12	3
1984—Miami NFL	15	73	1389	19.0	*18	8	79	9.9	0	*18	108	2
1985—Miami NFL	16	70	996	14.2	4	2	14	7.0	0	4	24	2
Pro Totals—3 Years....................	45	149	2499	16.8	23	51	485	9.5	1	24	144	7·

Additional pro statistics: Rushed twice for nine yards, returned one kickoff for 25 yards, attempted one pass with one completion for 48 yards and a touchdown, 1983; recovered one fumble, 1983 through 1985; rushed three times for 35 yards, returned two kickoffs for 15 yards and attempted one pass with one interception, 1984; rushed once for 10 yards, 1985.
Played in AFC Championship Game following 1984 and 1985 seasons.
Played in NFL Championship Game following 1984 season.
Played in Pro Bowl (NFL All-Star Game) following 1984 and 1985 seasons.

KYLE CLIFTON
Linebacker—New York Jets
Born August 23, 1962, at Onley, Tex.
Height, 6.04. Weight, 233.
High School—Bridgeport, Tex.
Received degree in business management from Texas Christian University.

Selected by Birmingham in 1st round (12th player selected) of 1984 USFL draft.
Selected by New York Jets in 3rd round (64th player selected) of 1984 NFL draft.
Signed by New York Jets, July 12, 1984.

Year Club	G.	No.	Yds.	Avg.TD.	
		—INTERCEPTIONS—			
1984—N.Y. Jets NFL	16	1	0	0.0	0
1985—N.Y. Jets NFL	16	3	10	3.3	0
Pro Totals—2 Years............	32	4	10	2.5	0

Additional pro statistics: Intercepted one pass for no yards and recovered one fumble, 1984; recovered two fumbles, 1985.

FREDERICK DEXTOR CLINKSCALE
(Known by middle name.)
Safety—Dallas Cowboys
Born April 13, 1958, at Greenville, S.C.
Height, 5.11. Weight, 195.
High School—Greenville, S.C., J.L. Mann.
Received degree in business administration from South Carolina State College.

Signed as free agent by Dallas Cowboys, May, 1980.
On injured reserved with Achilles tendon injury, August 31 through entire 1981 season.

Year Club	G.	No.	Yds.	Avg.TD.	
		—INTERCEPTIONS—			
1980—Dallas NFL	16			None	
1982—Dallas NFL	9	1	0	0.0	0
1983—Dallas NFL	15	2	68	34.0	1
1984—Dallas NFL	15	3	32	10.7	0
1985—Dallas NFL	16	3	16	5.3	0
Pro Totals—5 Years............	71	9	116	12.9	1

Additional pro statistics: Recovered one fumble, 1980; recovered four fumbles, 1983; recovered two fumbles, 1984 and 1985.

Played in NFC Championship Game following 1980 and 1982 seasons.

GARRY WILBERT COBB
Linebacker—Philadelphia Eagles
Born March 16, 1957, at Carthage, N. C.
Height, 6.02. Weight, 227.
High School—Stamford, Conn.
Attended University of Southern California.

Selected by Dallas in 9th round (247th player selected) of 1979 NFL draft.
Released by Dallas Cowboys, August 21, 1979; signed as free agent by Detroit Lions, October 24, 1979.
Granted free agency, February 1, 1985; re-signed by Lions and traded to Philadelphia Eagles for running back Wilbert Montgomery, August 21, 1985.

| | | —INTERCEPTIONS— | | | |
Year Club	G.	No.	Yds.	Avg.	TD.
1979—Detroit NFL	8		None		
1980—Detroit NFL	16		None		
1981—Detroit NFL	16	3	32	10.7	0
1982—Detroit NFL	6	2	12	6.0	0
1983—Detroit NFL	15	4	19	4.8	0
1984—Detroit NFL	16		None		
1985—Philadelphia NFL	16		None		
Pro Totals—7 Years	93	9	63	7.0	0

Additional pro statistics: Caught one pass for 19 yards and recovered three fumbles, 1981; caught one pass for 25 yards, 1982; recovered two fumbles, 1983.

SHERMAN COCROFT
Safety—Kansas City Chiefs
Born August 29, 1961, at Watsonville, Calif.
Height, 6.01. Weight, 188.
High School—Watsonville, Calif.
Attended Cabrillo College and San Jose State University.

Selected by Oakland in 1984 USFL territorial draft.
Signed as free agent by Seattle Seahawks, May 3, 1984.
Released by Seattle Seahawks, August 21, 1984; signed as free agent by Kansas City Chiefs for 1985, October 15, 1984.

| | | —INTERCEPTIONS— | | | |
Year Club	G.	No.	Yds.	Avg.	TD.
1985—Kansas City NFL	16	3	27	9.0	0

Additional pro statistics: Recovered two fumbles, 1985.

MICHAEL LYNN COFER
(Mike)
Linebacker—Detroit Lions
Born April 7, 1960, at Knoxville, Tenn.
Height, 6.05. Weight, 245.
High School—Knoxville, Tenn., Rule.
Attended University of Tennessee.

Selected by New Jersey in 1983 USFL territorial draft.
Selected by Detroit in 3rd round (67th player selected) of 1983 NFL draft.
Signed by Detroit Lions, July 1, 1983.
On injured reserve with hip injury, October 25 through remainder of 1985 season.
Detroit NFL, 1983 through 1985.
Games: 1983 (16), 1984 (16), 1985 (7). Total—39.
Pro statistics: Recovered one fumble, 1983 and 1984.

KEN COFFEY
Safety—Washington Redskins
Born July 11, 1960, at Rantoul, Ill.
Height, 6.00. Weight, 190.
High School—Big Spring, Tex.
Attended Tyler Junior College and received degree in finance from Southwest Texas State University.
Brother of Wayne Coffey, rookie wide receiver with New England Patriots.

Selected by Washington in 9th round (226th player selected) of 1982 NFL draft.
On injured reserve with blood disorder, August 24 through entire 1982 season.
On injured reserve with dislocated shoulder, August 28 through September 28, 1984; activated, September 29, 1984.
On injured reserve with knee injury, August 20 through entire 1985 season.

| | | —INTERCEPTIONS— | | | |
Year Club	G.	No.	Yds.	Avg.	TD.
1983—Washington NFL	13	4	62	15.5	0
1984—Washington NFL	12	1	15	15.0	0
Pro Totals—2 Years	25	5	77	15.4	0

Additional pro statistics: Recovered one fumble, 1983 and 1984; returned one punt for six yards, 1984.
Played in NFC Championship Game following 1983 season.
Played in NFL Championship Game following 1983 season.

PAUL RANDOLPH COFFMAN
Tight End—Green Bay Packers

Born March 29, 1956, at St. Louis, Mo.
Height, 6.03. Weight, 225.
High School—Chase, Kan.
Received degree in grain milling science from Kansas State University in 1982.
Signed as free agent by Green Bay Packers, May 18, 1978.

Year Club	G.	P.C.	Yds.	Avg.	TD.
1978—Green Bay NFL	16			None	
1979—Green Bay NFL	16	56	711	12.7	4
1980—Green Bay NFL	16	42	496	11.8	3
1981—Green Bay NFL	16	55	687	12.5	4
1982—Green Bay NFL	9	23	287	12.5	2
1983—Green Bay NFL	16	54	814	15.1	11
1984—Green Bay NFL	14	43	562	13.1	9
1985—Green Bay NFL	16	49	666	13.6	6
Pro Totals—8 Years	119	322	4223	13.1	39

Additional pro statistics: Fumbled four times, 1979; rushed once for three yards, 1980; returned three kickoffs for 77 yards, 1981; recovered one fumble, 1981 and 1984; fumbled once, 1981 and 1983 through 1985.
Played in Pro Bowl (NFL All-Star Game) following 1982 through 1984 seasons.

ROBIN COLE
Linebacker—Pittsburgh Steelers

Born September 11, 1955, at Los Angeles, Calif.
Height, 6.02. Weight, 229.
High School—Compton, Calif.
Attended University of New Mexico.
Cousin of Willie Davis, Hall of Fame defensive end with Cleveland Browns and Green Bay Packers, 1958 through 1969.
Selected by Pittsburgh in 1st round (21st player selected) of 1977 NFL draft.
Pittsburgh NFL, 1977 through 1985.
Games: 1977 (8), 1978 (16), 1979 (13), 1980 (14), 1981 (14), 1982 (9), 1983 (16), 1984 (16), 1985 (16). Total—122.
Pro statistics: Recovered two fumbles, 1977; recovered one fumble, 1979 and 1981; returned one kickoff for three yards, 1979; intercepted one pass for 34 yards and recovered one fumble for 14 yards, 1980; intercepted one pass for 29 yards, 1981; recovered two fumbles for 20 yards, 1983; intercepted one pass for 12 yards and recovered one fumble for eight yards, 1984; intercepted one pass for four yards and recovered three fumbles, 1985.
Played in AFC Championship Game following 1978, 1979 and 1984 seasons.
Played in NFL Championship Game following 1978 and 1979 seasons.
Played in Pro Bowl (NFL All-Star Game) following 1984 season.

GREG JEROME COLEMAN
Punter—Minnesota Vikings

Born September 9, 1954, at Jacksonville, Fla.
Height, 6.00. Weight, 180.
High School—Jacksonville, Fla., William M. Raines.
Received degree in criminology from Florida A&M University.
Cousin of Vince Coleman, outfielder with St. Louis Cardinals.
Selected by Cincinnati in 14th round (398th player selected) of 1976 NFL draft.
Released by Cincinnati Bengals, August, 1976; signed as free agent by Cleveland Browns, March, 1977.
Released by Cleveland Browns, August 30, 1978; signed as free agent by Minnesota Vikings, October 20, 1978.

Year Club	G.	No.	Avg.	Blk.
1977—Cleveland NFL	14	61	39.2	0
1978—Minnesota NFL	9	51	39.0	1
1979—Minnesota NFL	16	90	39.5	1
1980—Minnesota NFL	16	81	38.8	0
1981—Minnesota NFL	15	88	41.4	0
1982—Minnesota NFL	9	*58	41.1	0
1983—Minnesota NFL	16	91	41.5	0
1984—Minnesota NFL	16	82	42.4	0
1985—Minnesota NFL	16	67	42.8	0
Pro Totals—9 Years	127	669	40.7	2

Additional pro statistics: Rushed once for minus three yards, 1977; rushed twice for 22 yards, 1978; recovered one fumble, 1981 and 1985; rushed once for 15 yards, 1982; rushed once for minus nine yards, 1983; rushed twice for 11 yards and attempted one pass with no completions, 1984; rushed twice for no yards and fumbled once, 1985.

LEONARD DAVID COLEMAN
Cornerback—Indianapolis Colts

Born January 30, 1962, at Boynton Beach, Fla.
Height, 6.02. Weight, 208.
High School—Lake Worth, Fla.
Attended Vanderbilt University.
Cousin of Anthony Carter, wide receiver with Minnesota Vikings.
Selected by Memphis in 1984 USFL territorial draft.
Selected by Indianapolis in 1st round (8th player selected) of 1984 NFL draft.

Signed by Memphis Showboats, September 13, 1984.
Released by Memphis Showboats, September 18, 1985; signed by Indianapolis Colts, September 18, 1985.
Granted roster exemption, September 18 through September 29, 1985; activated, September 30, 1985.

		—INTERCEPTIONS—			
Year Club	G.	No.	Yds.	Avg.	TD.
1985—Memphis USFL.............	18	2	6	3.0	0
1985—Indianapolis NFL	12		None		
Pro Totals—2 Years............	30	2	6	3.0	0

Additional USFL statistics: Credited with one sack for nine yards and recovered four fumbles for 31 yards and a touchdown, 1985.

MONTE COLEMAN
Linebacker—Washington Redskins
Born November 4, 1957, at Pine Bluff, Ark.
Height, 6.02. Weight, 230.
High School—Pine Bluff, Ark.
Attended Central Arkansas University.

Selected by Washington in 11th round (289th player selected) of 1979 NFL draft.
On injured reserve with thigh injury, September 16 through October 16, 1983; activated, October 17, 1983.
On injured reserve with strained hamstring, September 25 through November 8, 1985; activated, November 9, 1985.

		—INTERCEPTIONS—			
Year Club	G.	No.	Yds.	Avg.	TD.
1979—Washington NFL..........	16	1	13	13.0	0
1980—Washington NFL..........	16	3	92	30.7	0
1981—Washington NFL..........	12	3	52	17.3	1
1982—Washington NFL..........	8		None		
1983—Washington NFL..........	10		None		
1984—Washington NFL..........	16	1	49	49.0	1
1985—Washington NFL..........	10		None		
Pro Totals—7 Years............	88	8	206	25.8	2

Additional pro statistics: Recovered three fumbles, 1979; caught one pass for 12 yards, 1980; recovered two fumbles, 1980 and 1983; recovered one fumble for two yards, 1981; ran 27 yards with lateral on punt return and recovered one fumble, 1984.
Played in NFC Championship Game following 1982 and 1983 seasons.
Played in NFL Championship Game following 1982 and 1983 seasons.

BRUCE STOKES COLLIE
Offensive Tackle—San Francisco 49ers
Born June 27, 1962, at Nuremburg, Germany.
Height, 6.06. Weight, 275.
High School—San Antonio, Tex., Robert E. Lee.
Attended University of Texas at Arlington.

Selected by Baltimore in 6th round (78th player selected) of 1985 USFL draft.
Selected by San Francisco in 5th round (140th player selected) of 1985 NFL draft.
Signed by San Francisco 49ers, June 25, 1985.
San Francisco NFL, 1985.
Games: 1985 (16).

REGINALD C. COLLIER
(Reggie)
Quarterback—Dallas Cowboys
Born May 14, 1961, at Biloxi, Miss.
Height, 6.03. Weight, 207.
High School—Biloxi, Miss., D'Iberville.
Attended University of Southern Mississippi.

Selected by Birmingham in 1st round (3rd player selected) of 1983 USFL draft.
Signed by Birmingham Stallions, January 13, 1983.
Selected by Dallas in 6th round (162nd player selected) of 1983 NFL draft.
On developmental squad, March 26 through March 29, 1983; activated, March 30, 1983.
On developmental squad, May 1 through May 8, 1983; activated, May 9, 1983.
On developmental squad, May 14 through May 19, 1983.
On injured reserve with knee injury, May 20 through remainder of 1983 season.
Traded by Birmingham Stallions to Washington Federals for rights to center Joel Hilgenberg and 1st round pick in 1985 draft, January 12, 1984.
Franchise transferred to Orlando, October 12, 1984.
On developmental squad, February 22 through February 27, 1985; activated, February 28, 1985.
Released by Orlando Renegades, May 22, 1986; signed by Dallas Cowboys, May 23, 1986.
On developmental squad for 3 games with Birmingham Stallions in 1983.
On developmental squad for 1 game with Orlando Renegades in 1985.

		—PASSING—							—RUSHING—				—TOTAL—		
Year Club	G.	Att.	Cmp.	Pct.	Gain	T.P.	P.I.	Avg.	Att.	Yds.	Avg.	TD.	TD.	Pts.	F.
1983—Birmingham USFL	7	108	47	43.5	604	1	7	5.59	39	253	6.5	4	4	24	1
1984—Washington USFL	9	160	82	51.3	969	6	12	6.06	24	174	7.3	1	1	6	2
1985—Orlando USFL	16	427	229	53.6	2578	13	16	6.04	92	606	6.6	12	12	†74	11
Pro Totals—3 Years..........	32	695	358	51.5	4151	20	35	5.97	155	1033	6.7	17	17	104	14

†Includes one 2-point conversion.
Quarterback Rating Points: 1983 (37.6), 1984 (51.3), 1985 (66.5). Total—58.7.
Additional pro statistics: Recovered two fumbles, 1984; recovered six fumbles, 1985.

TIMOTHY COLLIER
(Tim)
Cornerback
Born May 31, 1954, at Dallas, Tex.
Height, 6.00. Weight, 176.
High School—Dallas, Tex., South Oak Cliff.
Attended East Texas State University.

Selected by Kansas City in 9th round (249th player selected) of 1976 NFL draft.
Traded by Kansas City Chiefs to St. Louis Cardinals for 5th round choice in 1980 draft, February 15, 1980.
Released by St. Louis Cardinals, December 8, 1982; signed as free agent by San Francisco 49ers, December 14, 1982.
On injured reserve with Achilles tendon injury, July 29 through entire 1984 season.
Released by San Francisco 49ers, September 2, 1985; re-signed by 49ers, December 24, 1985.
Granted free agency with no qualifying offer, February 1, 1986.

Year Club	G.	No.	Yds.	Avg.	TD.
1976—Kansas City NFL	13	2	10	5.0	0
1977—Kansas City NFL	9	2	134	67.0	1
1978—Kansas City NFL..........	15	3	38	12.7	0
1979—Kansas City NFL..........	14	2	45	22.5	0
1980—St. Louis NFL................	12	2	22	11.0	
1981—St. Louis NFL................	14	1	17	17.0	0
1982—St. L. (4)-S.F. (2) NFL..	6		None		
1983—San Francisco NFL	10	3	32	10.7	1
Pro Totals—8 Years	93	15	298	19.9	2

Additional pro statistics: Recovered one fumble, 1976; fumbled once and returned one kickoff for no yards, 1979.
Played in NFC Championship Game following 1983 season.

ANTHONY COLLINS
(Tony)
Running Back—New England Patriots
Born May 27, 1959, at Sanford, Fla.
Height, 5.11. Weight, 212.
High School—Penn Yan, N.Y., Penn Yan Academy.
Attended East Carolina University.
Cousin of Kenny Jackson, wide receiver with Philadelphia Eagles;
and uncle of Reggie Branch, running back at University of Washington.

Selected by New England in 2nd round (47th player selected) of 1981 NFL draft.

Year Club	G.	Att.	Yds.	Avg.	TD.	P.C.	Yds.	Avg.	TD.	TD.	Pts.	F.
		—RUSHING—				PASS RECEIVING				—TOTAL—		
1981—New England NFL....................	16	204	873	4.3	7	26	232	8.9	0	7	42	8
1982—New England NFL....................	9	164	632	3.9	1	19	187	9.8	2	3	18	5
1983—New England NFL....................	16	219	1049	4.8	10	27	257	9.5	0	10	60	10
1984—New England NFL....................	16	138	550	4.0	5	16	100	6.3	0	5	30	3
1985—New England NFL....................	16	163	657	4.0	3	52	549	10.6	2	5	30	6
Pro Totals—5 Years....................	73	888	3761	4.2	26	140	1325	9.5	4	30	180	32

Year Club	G.	No.	Yds.	Avg.	TD.
		KICKOFF RETURNS			
1981—New England NFL.......	16	39	773	19.8	0
1982—New England NFL.......	9		None		
1983—New England NFL.......	16		None		
1984—New England NFL.......	16	25	544	21.8	0
1985—New England NFL.......	16		None		
Pro Totals—5 Years............	73	64	1317	20.6	0

Additional pro statistics: Returned three punts for 15 yards and attempted one pass with no completions, 1981; recovered two fumbles, 1981 through 1983 and 1985.
Played in AFC Championship Game following 1985 season.
Played in NFL Championship Game following 1985 season.
Played in Pro Bowl (NFL All-Star Game) following 1983 season.

DWIGHT DEAN COLLINS
Wide Receiver—Detroit Lions
Born August 23, 1961, at Rochester, N.Y.
Height, 6.01. Weight, 208.
High School—Beaver Falls, Pa.
Attended University of Pittsburgh.

Selected by Pittsburgh in 1984 USFL territorial draft.
Selected by Minnesota in 6th round (154th player selected) of 1984 NFL draft.
Signed by Minnesota Vikings, June 2, 1984.
Placed on did not report list, August 20 through September 16, 1985.
Released by Minnesota Vikings, September 17, 1985; signed as free agent by Detroit Lions, March 6, 1986.

Year Club	G.	P.C.	Yds.	Avg.	TD.
		—PASS RECEIVING—			
1984—Minnesota NFL.............	16	11	143	13.0	1

Additional pro statistics: Rushed three times for minus 14 yards, 1984.

GLEN LEON COLLINS
Defensive End—Green Bay Packers
Born July 10, 1959, at Jackson, Miss.
Height, 6.06. Weight, 265.
High School—Jackson, Miss., Jim Hill.
Attended Mississippi State University.

Named as defensive tackle on THE SPORTING NEWS College All-America Team, 1981.
Selected by Cincinnati in 1st round (26th player selected) of 1982 NFL draft.
On inactive list, September 19, 1982.
Traded by Cincinnati Bengals to Green Bay Packers for draft choice, May 12, 1986.
Cincinnati NFL, 1982 through 1985.
Games: 1982 (7), 1983 (16), 1984 (16), 1985 (16). Total—55.
Pro statistics: Recovered one fumble, 1983 and 1984.

JAMES BRIAN COLLINS
(Jim)
Linebacker—Los Angeles Rams
Born June 11, 1958, at Orange, N.J.
Height, 6.02. Weight, 235.
High School—Mendham, N.J.
Received bachelor of science degree in psychology from Syracuse University in 1981.

Named to THE SPORTING NEWS NFL All-Star Team, 1985.
Selected by Los Angeles in 2nd round (43rd player selected) of 1981 NFL draft.
On injured reserve with pulled stomach muscle, September 1 through October 2, 1981; activated October 3, 1981.
On injured reserve with knee injury, December 4 through remainder of 1981 season.

		—INTERCEPTIONS—			
Year Club	G.	No.	Yds.	Avg.	TD.
1981—L.A. Rams NFL	7		None		
1982—L.A. Rams NFL	6		None		
1983—L.A. Rams NFL	16	2	46	23.0	0
1984—L.A. Rams NFL	16	2	43	21.5	0
1985—L.A. Rams NFL	16	2	8	4.0	0
Pro Totals—5 Years	61	6	97	16.2	0

Additional pro statistics: Recovered one fumble, 1983 and 1985; recovered two fumbles for 17 yards and fumbled once, 1984.
Played in NFC Championship Game following 1985 season.
Played in Pro Bowl (NFL All-Star Game) following 1985 season.

SCOTT NEAL COLLINS
Linebacker
Born November 10, 1960, at San Diego, Calif.
Height, 6.01. Weight, 220.
High School—Huntington Beach, Calif., Edison.
Attended Orange Coast College and Oregon Tech.

Signed as free agent by New York Jets, May 20, 1984.
On injured reserve with knee injury, July 27 through entire 1984 season.
On injured reserve with neck injury, August 15 through entire 1985 season.
Granted free agency with no qualifying offer, February 1, 1986.

ANTHONY CRIS COLLINSWORTH
(Known by middle name.)
Wide Receiver—Cincinnati Bengals
Born January 27, 1959, at Dayton, O.
Height, 6.05. Weight, 192.
High School—Titusville, Fla., Astronaut.
Received degree in accounting from University of Florida in 1981.

Selected by Cincinnati in 2nd round (37th player selected) of 1981 NFL draft.
Signed by Tampa Bay Bandits, June 27, 1983, for contract to take effect after being granted free agency, February 1, 1985.
Released by Tampa Bay Bandits, February 18, 1984; re-signed by Bengals, February 21, 1984.

		—PASS RECEIVING—			
Year Club	G.	P.C.	Yds.	Avg.	TD.
1981—Cincinnati NFL	16	67	1009	15.1	8
1982—Cincinnati NFL	9	49	700	14.3	1
1983—Cincinnati NFL	14	66	1130	17.1	5
1984—Cincinnati NFL	15	64	989	15.5	6
1985—Cincinnati NFL	16	65	1125	17.3	5
Pro Totals—5 Years	70	311	4953	15.9	25

Additional pro statistics: Recovered one fumble, 1981, 1983 and 1984; fumbled three times, 1981; rushed once for minus 11 yards, 1982; fumbled once, 1982 and 1985; rushed twice for two yards and fumbled twice, 1983; rushed once for seven yards, 1984; rushed once for three yards and attempted one pass with one interception, 1985.
Played in AFC Championship Game following 1981 season.
Played in NFL Championship Game following 1981 season.
Played in Pro Bowl (NFL All-Star Game) following 1981 through 1983 seasons.

JAMES MICHAEL COLQUITT
(Jimmy)
Punter—Tampa Bay Buccaneers
Born January 17, 1963, at Knoxville, Tenn.
Height, 6.04. Weight, 208.
High School—Knoxville, Tenn., Doyle.
Attended University of Tennessee.
Nephew of Craig Colquitt, punter with Green Bay Packers.

Signed as free agent by New York Giants, May 3, 1985.
Released by New York Giants, July 29, 1985; signed as free agent by Seattle Seahawks, August 14, 1985.
Released by Seattle Seahawks, September 2, 1985; re-signed by Seahawks, September 17, 1985.
Released by Seattle Seahawks, October 1, 1985; signed as free agent by Tampa Bay Buccaneers, March 21, 1986.

		——PUNTING——		
Year Club	G.	No.	Avg.	Blk.
1985—Seattle NFL	2	12	40.1	0

JOSEPH CRAIG COLQUITT
(Known by middle name.)
Punter—Green Bay Packers
Born June 9, 1954, at Knoxville, Tenn.
Height, 6.01. Weight, 182.
High School—Knoxville, Tenn., South
Attended Cleveland State Community College and received degree
in fine arts from University of Tennessee.
Uncle of Jimmy Colquitt, punter with Tampa Bay Buccaneers.

Selected by Pittsburgh in 3rd round (79th player selected) of 1978 NFL draft.
On physically unable to perform/active list with torn Achilles tendon, July 30 through August 23, 1982.
Placed on reserve, August 24 through entire 1982 season.
Released by Pittsburgh Steelers, August 19, 1985; signed as free agent by Green Bay Packers, May 23, 1986.

		——PUNTING——		
Year Club	G.	No.	Avg.	Blk.
1978—Pittsburgh NFL	16	66	40.0	0
1979—Pittsburgh NFL	16	68	40.2	0
1980—Pittsburgh NFL	16	61	40.7	0
1981—Pittsburgh NFL	16	84	43.3	0
1983—Pittsburgh NFL	16	80	41.9	0
1984—Pittsburgh NFL	16	70	41.2	0
Pro Totals—6 Years	96	429	41.4	0

Additional pro statistics: Rushed for 17 yards, fumbled once and recovered one fumble, 1980; rushed once for eight yards, 1981; rushed once for no yards, 1984.
Played in AFC Championship Game following 1978, 1979 and 1984 seasons.
Played in NFL Championship Game following 1978 and 1979 seasons.

EDDIE COLSON
Running Back—Cleveland Browns
Born September 8, 1963, at Oahu, Haw.
Height, 5.10. Weight, 228.
High School—Jacksonville, N.C.
Attended University of North Carolina.

Selected by Baltimore in 1985 USFL territorial draft.
Signed as free agent by Cleveland Browns, May 6, 1985.
On injured reserve with knee injury, August 20 through entire 1985 season.

DARREN COMEAUX
Linebacker—Denver Broncos
Born April 15, 1960, at San Diego, Calif.
Height, 6.01. Weight, 227.
High School—San Diego, Calif.
Attended San Diego Mesa College and Arizona State University.

Signed as free agent by Denver Broncos, April 30, 1982.
On injured reserve with broken foot, September 7 through December 15, 1982; activated, December 16, 1982.
Released by Denver Broncos, August 29, 1983; re-signed by Broncos, September 13, 1983.
Released by Denver Broncos, September 2, 1985; re-signed by Broncos, September 3, 1985.
On injured reserve with broken thumb, October 16 through November 21, 1985; activated, November 22, 1985.
Denver NFL, 1982 through 1985.
Games: 1982 (3), 1983 (14), 1984 (16), 1985 (11). Total—44.
Pro statistics: Intercepted one pass for five yards and recovered one fumble, 1984.

WILLIAM CONTZ
(Bill)
Offensive Tackle—Cleveland Browns
Born May 12, 1961, at Belle Vernon, Pa.
Height, 6.05. Weight, 270.
High School—Belle Vernon, Pa.
Received bachelor of science degree in business logistics
from Penn State University in 1983.

Selected by Philadelphia in 1983 USFL territorial draft.
Selected by Cleveland in 5th round (122nd player selected) of 1983 NFL draft.
Signed by Cleveland Browns, May 31, 1983.
On injured reserve with knee injury, December 12 through remainder of 1984 season.
On physically unable to perform/active with knee injury, August 20 through October 18, 1985; activated, October 19, 1985.
Cleveland NFL, 1983 through 1985.
Games: 1983 (16), 1984 (15), 1985 (4). Total—35.
Pro statistics: Returned one kickoff for three yards, 1983; returned one kickoff for 10 yards, 1984.

JOHNIE EARL COOKS
Linebacker—Indianapolis Colts
Born November 23, 1958, at Leland, Miss.
Height, 6.04. Weight, 243.
High School—Leland, Miss.
Received degree in physical education from Mississippi State University.

Named as linebacker on THE SPORTING NEWS College All-America Team, 1981.
Selected by Baltimore in 1st round (2nd player selected) of 1982 NFL draft.
Franchise transferred to Indianapolis, March 31, 1984.
Baltimore NFL, 1982 and 1983; Indianapolis NFL, 1984 and 1985.
Games: 1982 (9), 1983 (16), 1984 (16), 1985 (16). Total—57.
Pro statistics: Recovered one fumble, 1982; intercepted one pass for 15 yards, recovered two fumbles for 52 yards and a touchdown and fumbled once, 1983; intercepted one pass for seven yards, 1985.

EVAN COOPER
Defensive Back-Kick Returner—Philadelphia Eagles
Born June 28, 1962, at Miami, Fla.
Height, 5.11. Weight, 184.
High School—Miami, Fla., Killian.
Received bachelor of science degree in communications
from University of Michigan in 1984.

Selected by Michigan in 1984 USFL territorial draft.
Selected by Philadelphia in 4th round (88th player selected) of 1984 NFL draft.
Signed by Philadelphia Eagles, June 11, 1984.

		INTERCEPTIONS			–PUNT RETURNS–				—KICKOFF RET.—				—TOTAL—		
Year	Club	G.	No.	Yds.	Avg. TD.	No.	Yds.	Avg.	TD.	No.	Yds.	Avg.	TD.	TD.	Pts. F.
1984—Philadelphia NFL		16	None			40	250	6.3	0	17	299	17.6	0	0	0 0
1985—Philadelphia NFL		16	2	13	6.5 0	43	364	8.5	0	3	32	10.7	0	0	0 1
Pro Totals—2 Years		32	2	13	6.5 0	83	614	7.4	0	20	331	16.6	0	0	0 1

Additional pro statistics: Recovered one fumble, 1985.

JAMES ALBERT COOPER
(Jim)
Offensive Tackle—Dallas Cowboys
Born September 28, 1955, at Philadelphia, Pa.
Height, 6.05. Weight, 274.
High School—Philadelphia, Pa., Cardinal Dougherty.
Attended Temple University.

Selected by Dallas in 6th round (164th player selected) of 1977 NFL draft.
On injured reserve with broken ankle, October 20 through remainder of 1984 season.
Dallas NFL, 1977 through 1985.
Games: 1977 (14), 1978 (14), 1979 (15), 1980 (15), 1981 (16), 1982 (9), 1983 (16), 1984 (7), 1985 (15). Total—121.
Pro statistics: Recovered one fumble, 1979, 1980 and 1982.
Played in NFC Championship Game following 1977, 1978, and 1980 through 1982 seasons.
Played in NFL Championship Game following 1977 and 1978 seasons.

LOUIS COOPER
Linebacker—Kansas City Chiefs
Born August 5, 1963, at Marion, S.C.
Height, 6.02. Weight, 235.
High School—Marion, S.C.
Attended West Carolina University.

Selected by Orlando in 6th round (76th player selected) of 1985 USFL draft.
Selected by Seattle in 11th round (305th player selected) of 1985 NFL draft.
Signed by Seattle Seahawks, July 17, 1985.
Released by Seattle Seahawks, August 27, 1985; signed as free agent by Kansas City Chiefs, September 17, 1985.
On injured reserve with ankle injury, October 14 through November 20, 1985; activated after clearing procedural waivers, November 22, 1985.
Kansas City NFL, 1985.
Games: 1985 (8).

MARION EARL COOPER
(Known by middle name.)
Tight End—Los Angeles Raiders
Born September 17, 1957, at Giddings, Tex.
Height, 6.02. Weight, 227.
High School—Lexington, Tex., Lincoln.
Received bachelor of science degree in physical education from Rice University in 1981.

Selected by San Francisco in 1st round (13th player selected) of 1980 NFL draft.
On injured reserve with headaches, December 16 through remainder of 1985 season.
Traded by San Francisco 49ers to Los Angeles Raiders for conditional 6th round pick in 1987 draft, May 14, 1986.

		—RUSHING—				PASS RECEIVING				—TOTAL—		
Year Club	G.	Att.	Yds.	Avg.	TD.	P.C.	Yds.	Avg.	TD.	TD.	Pts.	F.
1980—San Francisco NFL	16	171	720	4.2	5	83	567	6.8	4	9	54	8
1981—San Francisco NFL	16	98	330	3.4	1	51	477	9.4	0	1	6	3
1982—San Francisco NFL	9	24	77	3.2	0	19	153	8.1	1	1	6	1
1983—San Francisco NFL	16		None			15	207	13.8	3	3	18	1
1984—San Francisco NFL	16	3	13	4.3	0	41	459	11.2	4	4	24	0
1985—San Francisco NFL	15	2	12	6.0	0	4	45	11.3	0	0	0	0
Pro Totals—6 Years	88	298	1152	3.9	6	213	1908	9.0	12	18	108	13

Additional pro statistics: Recovered three fumbles, 1980; recovered one fumble, 1981 and 1984; returned three kickoffs for 45 yards, 1983; returned one kickoff for no yards, 1984.
Played in NFC Championship Game following 1981, 1983 and 1984 seasons.
Played in NFL Championship Game following 1981 and 1984 seasons.

MARK SAMUEL COOPER
Guard—Denver Broncos
Born February 14, 1960, at Camden, N.J.
Height, 6.05. Weight, 267.
High School—Miami, Fla., Killian.
Received bachelor of arts degree in communications
from University of Miami (Fla.) in 1983.

Selected by New Jersey in 5th round (60th player selected) of 1983 USFL draft.
Selected by Denver in 2nd round (31st player selected) of 1983 NFL draft.
Signed by Denver Broncos, June 26, 1983.
On injured reserve with sprained ankle, December 13 through remainder of 1984 season.
Denver NFL, 1983 through 1985.
Games: 1983 (10), 1984 (15), 1985 (15). Total—40.
Pro statistics: Caught one pass for 13 yards, 1985.

JOHN CORKER
Linebacker—Miami Dolphins
Born December 29, 1958, at Miami, Fla.
Height, 6.05. Weight, 240.
High School—Miami, Fla., South.
Attended Oklahoma State University.

Named as outside linebacker on THE SPORTING NEWS USFL All-Star Team, 1983 and 1984.
Led USFL in sacks with 28 and yards lost with 199 in 1983.
Selected by Houston in 5th round (134th player selected) on 1980 NFL draft.
On injured reserve with headaches, November 20 through remainder of 1981 season.
Released by Houston Oilers, December 3, 1982.
USFL rights traded by Washington Federals to Michigan Panthers for 5th round pick in 1983 draft, December 16, 1982.
Signed by Michigan Panthers, December 20, 1982.
On developmental squad, April 4 through April 6, 1983; activated, April 7, 1983.
On developmental squad, March 18 through March 23, 1984; activated, March 24, 1984.
On developmental squad, June 10 through June 29, 1984; activated, June 30, 1984.
Granted free agency, November 30, 1984 and not protected in merger of Michigan Panthers and Oakland Invaders; selected by Memphis Showboats in USFL dispersal draft, December 6, 1984.
Signed by Memphis Showboats, December 12, 1984.
On developmental squad, February 25 through March 3, 1985; activated, March 4, 1985.
Released by Memphis Showboats, July 31, 1985; re-signed by Showboats, August 1, 1985.
Released by Memphis Showboats, January 25, 1986; signed as free agent by Miami Dolphins, May 20, 1986.
On developmental squad for 1 game with Michigan Panthers in 1983.
On developmental squad for 4 games with Michigan Panthers in 1984.
On developmental squad for 1 game with Memphis Showboats in 1985.
Houston NFL, 1980 through 1982; Michigan USFL, 1983 and 1984; Memphis USFL, 1985.
Games: 1980 (16), 1981 (11), 1982 (3), 1983 (17), 1984 (14), 1985 (18). Total NFL—30. Total USFL—49. Total Pro—79.
NFL statistics: Recovered one fumble for 43 yards and a touchdown, 1980.
USFL statistics: Credited with 28 sacks for 199 yards, intercepted two passes for 22 yards, recovered six fumbles for 100 yards and a touchdown and fumbled twice, 1983; credited with eight sacks for 52½ yards, intercepted two passes for 22 yards and recovered two fumbles, 1984; credited with 5½ sacks for 43½ yards, 1985.
Played in USFL Championship Game following 1983 season.

—DID YOU KNOW—
That the Cleveland Browns became the first NFL team to win a division championship with a non-winning record when their 8-8 mark led the AFC Central Division last season?

ANTHONY GEORGE CORLEY
Running Back—New York Jets
Born August 10, 1960, at Reno, Nev.
Height, 6.00. Weight, 210.
High School—Reno, Nev., Hug.
Attended University of Nevada at Reno.

Selected by Michigan in 7th round (143rd player selected) in 1984 USFL draft.
Signed as free agent by Pittsburgh Steelers, May 22, 1984.
Released by Pittsburgh Steelers, September 2, 1985; signed as free agent by San Diego Chargers, September 12, 1985.
Released by San Diego Chargers, October 1, 1985; re-signed by Chargers, December 20, 1985.
Released by San Diego Chargers, April 23, 1985; awarded on waivers to New York Jets, May 6, 1985.

Year	Club		G.	Att.	Yds.	Avg.	TD.	P.C.	Yds.	Avg.	TD.	TD.	Pts.	F.
					RUSHING				PASS RECEIVING				—TOTAL—		
1984—Pittsburgh NFL			14	18	89	4.9	0		None			0	0	0
1985—San Diego NFL			4		None				None			0	0	0
Pro Totals—2 Years			18	18	89	4.9	0	0	0	0.0	0	0	0	0

Additional pro statistics: Returned one kickoff for 15 yards and recovered two fumbles, 1984.
Played in AFC Championship Game following 1984 season.

FREDERICK KEITH CORNWELL
(Fred)
Tight End—Dallas Cowboys
Born August 7, 1961, at Osborne, Kan.
Height, 6.06. Weight, 233.
High School—Canyon Country, Calif., Canyon.
Received bachelor of science degree in civil engineering
from University of California in 1984.

Selected by Los Angeles in 1984 USFL territorial draft.
Selected by Dallas in 3rd round (81st player selected) of 1984 NFL draft.
Signed by Dallas Cowboys, July 8, 1984.

		PASS RECEIVING			
Year	Club	G.	P.C.	Yds.	Avg.	TD.
1984—Dallas NFL	14	2	23	11.5	1
1985—Dallas NFL	16	6	77	12.8	1
Pro Totals—2 Years	30	8	100	12.5	2

DOUGLAS DURANT COSBIE
(Doug)
Tight End—Dallas Cowboys
Born March 27, 1956, at Palo Alto, Calif.
Height, 6.06. Weight, 245.
High School—Mt. View, Calif., St. Francis.
Attended College of the Holy Cross, DeAnza College and received bachelor of science degree
in marketing from University of Santa Clara in 1979.

Selected by Dallas in 3rd round (76th player selected) of 1979 NFL draft.
USFL rights traded by Michigan Panthers to Oakland Invaders for rights to placekicker Wilson Alvarez, September 2, 1982.

		PASS RECEIVING			
Year	Club	G.	P.C.	Yds.	Avg.	TD.
1979—Dallas NFL	16	5	36	7.2	0
1980—Dallas NFL	16	2	11	5.5	1
1981—Dallas NFL	16	17	225	13.2	5
1982—Dallas NFL	9	30	441	14.7	4
1983—Dallas NFL	16	46	588	12.8	6
1984—Dallas NFL	16	60	789	13.2	4
1985—Dallas NFL	16	64	793	12.4	6
Pro Totals—7 Years	105	224	2883	12.9	26

Additional pro statistics: Fumbled once, 1979, 1981 and 1984; returned one kickoff for 13 yards and recovered two fumbles, 1980; rushed four times for 33 yards and returned one kickoff for no yards, 1981; rushed once for minus two yards and returned one kickoff for four yards, 1982; returned two kickoffs for 17 yards, 1983; fumbled twice, 1985.
Played in NFC Championship Game following 1980 through 1982 seasons.
Played in Pro Bowl (NFL All-Star Game) following 1983 through 1985 seasons.

JOSEPH PATRICK COSTELLO JR.
(Joe)
Defensive End—Cleveland Browns
Born June 1, 1960, at New York, N.Y.
Height, 6.03. Weight, 255.
High School—Stratford, Conn.
Received bachelor of science degree in accounting from Central Connecticut State University in 1982.

Signed as free agent by Montreal Concordes, March, 1982.
Released by Montreal Concordes, June 30, 1983; signed by Jacksonville Bulls, October 20, 1983.

Released by Jacksonville Bulls, February 28, 1986; signed as free agent by Cleveland Browns, April 21, 1986.
Montreal CFL, 1982; Jacksonville USFL, 1984 and 1985.
Games: 1982 (2), 1984 (18), 1985 (18). Total—38.
Pro statistics: Credited with 4½ sacks for 40½ yards, 1984; credited with 4½ sacks for 36 yards, 1985.

STEPHEN PAUL COURSON
Name pronounced CORE-sin.
(Steve)
Guard—Tampa Bay Buccaneers
Born October 1, 1955, at Philadelphia, Pa.
Height, 6.01. Weight, 275.
High School—Gettysburg, Pa.
Attended University of South Carolina.

Selected by Pittsburgh in 5th round (125th player selected) of 1977 NFL draft.
On injured reserve entire 1977 season.
On injured reserve with ankle injury, October 15 through December 2, 1180; activated, December 3, 1980.
USFL rights traded by Washington Federals to Houston Gamblers for rights to quarterback Dieter Brock, August 4, 1983.
Traded by Pittsburgh Steelers to Tampa Bay Buccaneers for guard Ray Snell, July 30, 1984.
Pitttsburgh NFL, 1978 through 1983; Tampa Bay NFL, 1984 and 1985.
Games: 1978 (16), 1979 (16), 1980 (8), 1981 (16), 1982 (8), 1983 (9), 1984 (14), 1985 (16). Total—103.
Pro statistics: Recovered one fumble, 1978, 1979 and 1982; recovered two fumbles, 1981; recovered one fumble for two yards, 1985.
Played in AFC Championship Game following 1978 and 1979 seasons.
Played in NFL Championship Game following 1978 and 1979 seasons.

MATTHEW CARTER COURTNEY
(Matt)
Cornerback—New York Jets
Born December 21, 1961, at Greeley, Colo.
Height, 5.11. Weight, 188.
High School—Arapahoe, Colo.
Attended Idaho State University.

Selected by Jacksonville in 4th round (78th player selected) of 1984 USFL draft.
Signed by Jacksonville Bulls, January 12, 1984.
On developmental squad, June 15 through June 19, 1984; activated, June 20, 1984.
Released by Jacksonville Bulls, October 15, 1984; signed as free agent by Kansas City Chiefs, April 20, 1985.
Released by Kansas City Chiefs, August 26, 1985; signed as free agent by New York Jets, March 25, 1986.
On developmental squad for 1 game with Jacksonville Bulls in 1984.
Jacksonville USFL, 1984.
Games: 1984 (16).
Pro statistics: Credited with one sack for six yards, intercepted two passes for 14 yards and recovered one fumble, 1984.

TOM COUSINEAU
Linebacker—Cleveland Browns
Born May 6, 1957, at Fairview Park, O.
Height, 6.03. Weight, 225.
High School—Lakewood, O., St. Edwards.
Received bachelor of arts degree in marketing from Ohio State University in 1979.

Selected by Buffalo in 1st round (1st player selected) of 1979 NFL draft.
Signed by Montreal Alouettes, July 19, 1979.
On reserve list, July 14 through July 27, 1981; activated, July 28, 1981.
On reserve list, August 8 through August 21, 1981; activated, August 22, 1981.
On injured list with elbow injury, August 27 through October 27, 1981; activated, October 28, 1981.
Granted free agency, March 1, 1982; received offer sheet from Houston Oilers, April 19, 1982.
Offer matched by Buffalo Bills and traded to Cleveland Browns for 1st round pick in 1983 draft, 3rd round pick in 1984 draft and 5th round pick in 1985 draft, April 23, 1982.

Year Club	G.	No.	Yds.	Avg.	TD.
1979—Montreal CFL	14		None		
1980—Montreal CFL	16	1	33	33.0	0
1981—Montreal CFL	4		None		
1982—Cleveland NFL	9	1	6	6.0	0
1983—Cleveland NFL	16	4	47	11.8	0
1984—Cleveland NFL	16	2	9	4.5	0
1985—Cleveland NFL	16	1	0	0.0	0
CFL Totals—3 Years	34	1	33	33.0	0
NFL Totals—4 Years	57	8	62	7.8	0
Pro Totals—7 Years	91	9	95	10.6	0

Additional CFL statistics: Recovered two fumbles, 1979; recovered one fumble, 1980.
Additional NFL statistics: Recovered two fumbles for 14 yards, 1983; recovered two fumbles, 1984; recovered one fumble, 1985.
Played in CFL Championship Game following 1979 season.

JAMES PAUL COVERT
(Jim)
Offensive Tackle—Chicago Bears
Born March 22, 1960, at Conway, Pa.
Height, 6.04. Weight, 271.
High School—Freedom, Pa., Area.
Attended University of Pittsburgh.

Named to THE SPORTING NEWS NFL All-Star Team, 1985.
Selected by Tampa Bay in 1st round (12th player selected) of 1983 USFL draft.
Selected by Chicago in 1st round (6th player selected) of 1983 NFL draft.
Signed by Chicago Bears, July 20, 1983.
Chicago NFL, 1983 through 1985.
Games: 1983 (16), 1984 (16), 1985 (15). Total—47.
Pro statistics: Recovered one fumble, 1983; recovered two fumbles, 1984.
Played in NFC Championship Game following 1984 and 1985 seasons.
Played in NFL Championship Game following 1985 season.
Played in Pro Bowl (NFL All-Star Game) following 1985 season.

ARTHUR COX
Tight End—Atlanta Falcons
Born February 5, 1961, at Plant City, Fla.
Height, 6.02. Weight, 255.
High School—Plant City, Fla.
Attended Texas Southern University.

Signed as free agent by Atlanta Falcons, May 4, 1983.

		—PASS RECEIVING—				
Year Club		G.	P.C.	Yds.	Avg.	TD.
1983—Atlanta NFL		15	9	83	9.2	1
1984—Atlanta NFL		16	34	329	9.7	3
1985—Atlanta NFL		16	33	454	13.8	2
Pro Totals—3 Years		47	76	866	11.4	6

Additional pro statistics: Fumbled once, 1983 and 1984.

STEVE COX
Punter-Placekicker—Washington Redskins
Born May 11, 1958, at Shreveport, La.
Height, 6.04. Weight, 195.
High School—Charleston, Ark.
Received bachelor of science degree in banking and finance from University of Arkansas in 1982.

Selected by Cleveland in 5th round (134th player selected) of 1981 NFL draft.
On injured reserve with head injury, August 30 through November 1, 1983; activated, November 2, 1983.
Released by Cleveland Browns, August 27, 1985; signed as free agent by Washington Redskins, October 1, 1985.

		—PUNTING—			
Year Club		G.	No.	Avg.	Blk.
1981—Cleveland NFL		16	68	42.4	*2
1982—Cleveland NFL		9	48	39.1	1
1983—Cleveland NFL		7		None	
1984—Cleveland NFL		16	74	43.4	2
1985—Washington NFL		12	52	41.8	0
Pro Totals—5 Years		60	242	41.9	5

Additional pro statistics: Attempted one field goal and missed, 1981, 1982 and 1985; rushed twice for minus 11 yards and recovered one fumble, 1982; successful on only field goal attempt, 1983; made one of three field goal attempts and attempted one pass with one completion for 16 yards, 1984; attempted one pass with one completion for 11 yards, 1985.

ROBERT EDWARD CRABLE
(Bob)
Linebacker—New York Jets
Born September 22, 1959, at Cincinnati, O.
Height, 6.03. Weight, 228.
High School—Cincinnati, O., Moeller.
Received bachelor of science degree in business administration from
University of Notre Dame in 1982.

Named as linebacker on THE SPORTING NEWS College All-America Team, 1980 and 1981.
Selected by New York Jets in 1st round (23rd player selected) of 1982 NFL draft.
On physically unable to perform/active with knee injury, July 14 through August 20, 1984; activated, August 21, 1984.
On injured reserve with knee injury, August 28 through September 27, 1984; activated, September 28, 1984.
On injured reserve with knee injury, November 5 through remainder of 1984 season.
On physically unable to perform/active with knee injury, July 25 through October 13, 1985; activated, October 14, 1985.
New York Jets NFL, 1982 through 1985.
Games: 1982 (9), 1983 (14), 1984 (5), 1985 (10). Total—38.
Pro statistics: Intercepted one pass for no yards, 1983; recovered one fumble, 1985.

ROGER TIMOTHY CRAIG
Fullback—San Francisco 49ers
Born July 10, 1960, at Davenport, Ia.
Height, 6.00. Weight, 222.
High School—Davenport, Ia., Central.
Attended University of Nebraska.

Established NFL record for most pass receptions by running back, season (92), 1985.
Selected by Boston in 1983 USFL territorial draft.
Selected by San Francisco in 2nd round (49th player selected) of 1983 NFL draft.
Signed by San Francisco 49ers, June 13, 1983.

Year Club	G.	RUSHING				PASS RECEIVING				—TOTAL—		
		Att.	Yds.	Avg.	TD.	P.C.	Yds.	Avg.	TD.	TD.	Pts.	F.
1983—San Francisco NFL	16	176	725	4.1	8	48	427	8.9	4	12	72	6
1984—San Francisco NFL	16	155	649	4.2	7	71	675	9.5	3	10	60	3
1985—San Francisco NFL	16	214	1050	4.9	9	*92	1016	11.0	6	15	90	5
Pro Totals—3 Years	48	545	2424	4.4	24	211	2118	10.0	13	37	222	14

Additional pro statistics: Recovered one fumble, 1983 and 1984.
Played in NFC Championship Game following 1983 and 1984 seasons.
Played in NFL Championship Game following 1984 season.
Played in Pro Bowl (NFL All-Star Game) following 1985 season.

SMILEY LAWRENCE CRESWELL III
Defensive End—New England Patriots
Born December 11, 1959, at Monroe, Wash.
Height, 6.04. Weight, 250.
High School—Monroe, Wash.
Attended Columbia Basin Community College and Michigan State University.

Selected by Michigan in 1983 USFL territorial draft.
Selected by New England in 5th round (118th player selected) of 1983 NFL draft.
Signed by New England Patriots, May 16, 1983.
On injured reserve with thumb injury, August 23 through entire 1983 season.
On injured reserve with knee injury, July 25 through entire 1984 season.
Released by New England Patriots, August 28, 1985; signed as free agent by Philadelphia Eagles, September 13, 1985.
Released by Philadelphia Eagles, November 5, 1985; signed as free agent by New England Patriots, December 3, 1985.
Active for 3 games with New England Patriots in 1985; did not play.
Philadelphia (3)-New England (0) NFL, 1985.
Games: 1985 (3).
Played in AFC Championship Game following 1985 season.
Played in NFL Championship Game following 1985 season.

JOE STANIER CRIBBS
Running Back—Buffalo Bills
Born January 5, 1958, at Sulligent, Ala.
Height, 5.11. Weight, 190.
High School—Sulligent, Ala.
Attended Auburn University.

Named as running back on THE SPORTING NEWS USFL All-Star Team, 1984.
Selected by Buffalo in 2nd round (29th player selected) of 1980 NFL draft.
On did not report list, August 24 through November 19, 1982; activated, November 20, 1982.
Signed by Birmingham Stallions, July 2, 1983, for contract to take affect after being granted free agency, February 1, 1984.
Granted roster exemption, February 15, 1984; activated, February 25, 1984.
On suspended list, May 9 through May 22, 1984; activated, May 23, 1984.
On developmental squad, June 3 through June 7, 1985; activated, June 8, 1985.
Released by Birmingham Stallions, October 14, 1985; re-signed by Buffalo Bills, October 11, 1985.
Granted roster exemption, October 11 through October 18, 1985; activated, October 19, 1985.
On developmental squad for 1 game with Birmingham Stallions in 1985.

Year Club	G.	RUSHING				PASS RECEIVING				—TOTAL—		
		Att.	Yds.	Avg.	TD.	P.C.	Yds.	Avg.	TD.	TD.	Pts.	F.
1980—Buffalo NFL	16	306	1185	3.9	11	52	415	8.0	1	12	72	*16
1981—Buffalo NFL	15	257	1097	4.3	3	40	603	15.1	7	10	60	12
1982—Buffalo NFL	7	134	633	4.7	3	13	99	7.6	0	3	18	5
1983—Buffalo NFL	16	263	1131	4.3	3	57	524	9.2	7	10	60	6
1984—Birmingham USFL	16	*297	*1467	4.9	8	39	500	12.8	5	13	78	7
1985—Birmingham USFL	17	267	1047	3.9	7	41	287	7.0	1	8	48	3
1985—Buffalo NFL	10	122	399	3.3	1	18	142	7.9	0	1	6	5
NFL Totals—5 Years	64	1072	4445	4.1	21	180	1783	9.9	15	36	216	44
USFL Totals—2 Years	33	564	2514	4.5	15	80	787	9.8	6	21	126	10
Pro Totals—7 Years	97	1636	6959	4.3	36	260	2570	9.9	21	57	342	54

—DID YOU KNOW—
That in a December 1 game against Pittsburgh, Denver's Karl Mecklenburg played seven different defensive positions and recorded four sacks?

Year Club	—PUNT RETURNS— G.	No.	Yds.	Avg.	TD.
1980 Buffalo NFL	16	29	154	5.3	0
1981—Buffalo NFL	15	None			
1982—Buffalo NFL	7	None			
1983—Buffalo NFL	16	None			
1984—Birmingham USFL	16	None			

Year Club	—PUNT RETURNS— G.	No.	Yds.	Avg.	TD.
1985—Birmingham USFL	17	None			
1985—Buffalo NFL	10	None			
NFL Totals—5 Years	64	29	154	5.3	0
USFL Totals—2 Years	33	0	0	0.0	0
Pro Totals—7 Years	97	29	154	5.3	0

Additional NFL statistics: Attempted one pass with one completion for 13 yards; returned two kickoffs for 39 yards (19.5 average), and recovered one fumble for minus seven yards, 1980; attempted one pass with one completion for nine yards and a touchdown, 1981; attempted one pass with one interception and recovered two fumbles, 1982; recovered one fumble, 1981, 1983 and 1985; attempted two passes with one completion for three yards, 1983.

Additional USFL statistics: Recovered one fumble, 1984 and 1985.

Played in Pro Bowl (NFL All-Star Game) following 1980 and 1983 seasons.

Named to Pro Bowl following 1981 season (replaced due to injury by Pete Johnson).

NOLAN NEIL CROMWELL
Safety—Los Angeles Rams
Born January 30, 1955, at Smith Center, Kan.
Height, 6.01. Weight, 200.
High School—Ransom, Kan.
Attended University of Kansas.

Named to THE SPORTING NEWS NFL All-Star Team, 1980.
Selected by Los Angeles in 2nd round (31st player selected) of 1977 NFL draft.
On injured reserve with knee injury, November 13 through remainder of 1984 season.

Year Club	—INTERCEPTIONS— G.	No.	Yds.	Avg.	TD.
1977—L.A. Rams NFL	14	None			
1978—L.A. Rams NFL	16	1	31	31.0	0
1979—L.A. Rams NFL	16	5	109	21.8	0
1980—L.A. Rams NFL	16	8	140	17.5	1
1981—L.A. Rams NFL	16	5	94	18.8	0

Year Club	—INTERCEPTIONS— G.	No.	Yds.	Avg.	TD.
1982—L.A. Rams NFL	9	3	33	11.0	0
1983—L.A. Rams NFL	16	3	76	25.3	1
1984—L.A. Rams NFL	11	3	54	18.0	1
1985—L.A. Rams NFL	16	2	5	2.5	0
Pro Totals—9 Years	130	30	542	18.1	3

Additional pro statistics: Recovered two fumbles for three yards, 1977; returned one punt for eight yards, recovered one fumble in end zone for a touchdown and rushed once for 16 yards and a touchdown, 1978; rushed once for five yards and a touchdown and recovered three fumbles, 1979; scored one point on run for extra point, rushed twice for no yards, attempted one pass with no completions, fumbled twice and recovered one fumble for minus one yard, 1980; rushed once for 17 yards and recovered three fumbles for four yards, 1981; rushed once for 17 yards and a touchdown and recovered one fumble for six yards, 1982; rushed once for no yards and recovered two fumbles, 1983; recovered one fumble, 1984; returned one kickoff for three yards and recovered four fumbles for 12 yards, 1985. Total—Rushed eight times for 55 yards and three touchdowns, scored one point on run for extra point, returned one punt for eight yards, returned one kickoff for three yards, recovered 18 fumbles for 24 yards and one touchdown, attempted one pass with no completions and fumbled twice.

Played in NFC Championship Game following 1978, 1979 and 1985 seasons.

Played in NFL Championship Game following 1979 season.

Played in Pro Bowl (NFL All-Star Game) following 1980 through 1983 seasons.

JUSTIN ALLEN CROSS
Offensive Tackle—Buffalo Bills
Born April 29, 1959, at Montreal, Quebec, Canada.
Height, 6.06. Weight, 265.
High School—Portsmouth, N.H.
Received bachelor of science degree in biology from Western State (Colo.) College in 1981.
Brother of Jeff Cross, center-forward with Los Angeles Clippers.

Selected by Buffalo in 10th round (272nd player selected) of 1981 NFL draft.
On injured reserve with back injury, August 29 through entire 1981 season.
On injured reserve with ankle injury, October 22 through remainder of 1984 season.
On injured reserve with broken arm, September 17 through November 28, 1985; activated, November 29, 1985.
Buffalo NFL, 1982 through 1985.
Games: 1982 (9), 1983 (15), 1984 (7), 1985 (3). Total—34.
Pro statistics: Recovered one fumble, 1983.

RANDALL LAUREAT CROSS
(Randy)
Guard—San Francisco 49ers
Born April 25, 1954, at Brooklyn, N.Y.
Height, 6.03. Weight, 265.
High School—Encino, Calif., Crespi.
Received degree in political science from University of California at Los Angeles in 1976.
Son of Dennis Cross, former television actor.

Selected by San Francisco in 2nd round (42nd player selected) of 1976 NFL draft.
On injured reserve with ankle injury, November 3 through remainder of 1978 season.
On injured reserve with knee injury, December 18 through remainder of 1985 season.
San Francisco NFL, 1976 through 1985.
Games: 1976 (14), 1977 (14), 1978 (9), 1979 (16), 1980 (16), 1981 (16), 1982 (9), 1983 (16), 1984 (16), 1985 (15). Total—141.
Pro statistics: Recovered one fumble, 1976 and 1982; fumbled once for minus 37 yards; 1977; fumbled once, 1978; recovered two fumbles, 1979.

Played in NFC Championship Game following 1981, 1983 and 1984 seasons.
Played in NFL Championship Game following 1981 and 1984 seasons.
Played in Pro Bowl (NFL All-Star Game) following 1981, 1982 and 1984 seasons.

DAVID RODNEY CROUDIP
Defensive Back—Atlanta Falcons
Born January 25, 1959, at Indianapolis, Ind.
Height, 5.08. Weight, 183.
High School—Compton, Calif.
Attended Ventura College and San Diego State University.

Selected by Los Angeles in 7th round (78th player selected) of 1983 USFL draft.
Selected by Houston in 18th round (107th player selected) of USFL expansion draft, September 6, 1983.
Released by Houston Gamblers, February 29, 1984; signed as free agent by Los Angeles Rams, April 2, 1984.
Released by Los Angeles Rams, August 27, 1984; re-signed by Rams, August 28, 1984.
Released by Los Angeles Rams, September 19, 1984; re-signed by Rams, September 21, 1984.
Released by Los Angeles Rams, September 2, 1985; re-signed by Rams, September 3, 1985.
Released by Los Angeles Rams, September 5, 1985; signed as free agent by San Diego Chargers, September 10, 1985.
Released by San Diego Chargers, October 5, 1985; signed as free agent by Atlanta Falcons, October 8, 1985.
Los Angeles USFL, 1983; Houston USFL, 1984; Los Angeles Rams NFL, 1984; San Diego (2)-Atlanta (11) NFL, 1985.
Games: 1983 (18), 1984 USFL (1), 1984 NFL (16), 1985 (13). Total USFL—19. Total NFL—29. Total Pro—48.
Pro statistics: Recovered one fumble, 1983 and 1985; recovered two fumbles, 1984.

DWAYNE CRUTCHFIELD
Fullback—Houston Oilers
Born September 30, 1959, at Cincinnati, O.
Height, 6.00. Weight, 245.
High School—Cincinnati, O., North College Hill.
Attended Iowa State University.

Selected by New York Jets in 3rd round (79th player selected) of 1982 NFL draft.
Released by New York Jets, November 18, 1983; awarded on waivers to Houston Oilers, November 21, 1983.
Traded by Houston Oilers to Los Angeles Rams for 6th round pick in 1984 draft, April 9, 1984.
Released by Los Angeles Rams, July 9, 1985; signed as free agent by Miami Dolphins, July 19, 1985.
Released by Miami Dolphins, August 5, 1985; signed as free agent by Houston Oilers, August 10, 1985.
On injured reserve with knee injury, September 2 through entire 1985 season.

Year Club	G.	Att.	Yds.	Avg.	TD.	P.C.	Yds.	Avg.	TD.	TD.	Pts.	F.
			RUSHING				PASS RECEIVING				TOTAL	
1982—New York Jets NFL	6	22	78	3.5	1		None			1	6	1
1983—N.Y.J. (11)-Hou. (2) NFL	13	140	578	4.1	3	19	133	7.0	0	3	18	2
1984—Los Angeles Rams NFL	15	73	337	4.6	1	2	11	5.5	1	2	12	1
Pro Totals—3 Years	34	235	993	4.2	5	21	144	6.9	1	6	36	4

Additional pro statistics: Returned one kickoff for 20 yards, 1984.
Member of New York Jets for AFC Championship Game following 1982 season; did not play.

ROBERT JOSEPH CRYDER
(Bob)
Offensive Tackle—Seattle Seahawks
Born September 7, 1956, at O'Fallon, Ill.
Height, 6.04. Weight, 282.
High School—O'Fallon, Ill.
Received degree in recreation and park management from University of Alabama in 1978.

Selected by New England in 1st round (18th player selected) of 1978 NFL draft.
On injured reserve with broken wrist, October 6 through remainder of 1978 season.
Traded by New England Patriots to Seattle Seahawks for 3rd round pick in 1985 draft and conditional 2nd round pick in 1986 draft, July 31, 1984.
New England NFL, 1978 through 1983; Seattle NFL, 1984 and 1985.
Games: 1978 (5), 1979 (16), 1980 (16), 1981 (15), 1982 (9), 1983 (14), 1984 (16), 1985 (15). Total—106.
Pro statistics: Recovered one fumble, 1979; recovered three fumbles, 1983.

GEORGE EDWARD CUMBY
Linebacker—Green Bay Packers
Born July 5, 1956, at Gorman, Tex.
Height, 6.00. Weight, 224.
High School—Gorman, Tex.
Attended University of Oklahoma.
Cousin of Kenneth Cumby, linebacker at Oklahoma State University;
and Garry Cumby, defensive end at Tulane University.

Named as linebacker on THE SPORTING NEWS College All-America Team, 1979.
Selected by Green Bay in 1st round (26th player selected) of 1980 NFL draft.
On injured reserve with knee injury, November 5 through remainder of 1980 season.

Year	Club	G.	No.	Yds.	Avg.	TD.
			—INTER	CEPTION	S—	
1980—Green Bay NFL		9		None		
1981—Green Bay NFL		16	3	22	7.3	0
1982—Green Bay NFL		9	1	4	4.0	0
1983—Green Bay NFL		15		None		
1984—Green Bay NFL		16	1	7	7.0	0
1985—Green Bay NFL		15		None		
Pro Totals—6 Years		80	5	33	6.6	0

Additional pro statistics: Recovered two fumbles for 70 yards, 1981; recovered one fumble, 1982; recovered two fumbles, 1984.

BENNIE LEE CUNNINGHAM JR.
Tight End—Pittsburgh Steelers
Born December 23, 1954, at Laurens, S. C.
Height, 6.05. Weight, 265.
High School—Seneca, S. C.
Received bachelor of arts degree in secondary education from Clemson University in 1976.

Named as tight end on THE SPORTING NEWS College All-America Team, 1975.
Selected by Pittsburgh in 1st round (28th player selected) of 1976 NFL draft.
On injured reserve with hip injury, October 12 through November 30, 1984; activated, December 1, 1984.
On injured reserve with knee injury, September 3 through October 10, 1985; activated, October 11, 1985.

Year	Club	G.	P.C.	Yds.	Avg.	TD.
			—PASS	RECEIVIN	G—	
1976—Pittsburgh NFL		12	5	49	9.8	1
1977—Pittsburgh NFL		12	20	347	17.4	2
1978—Pittsburgh NFL		6	16	321	20.1	2
1979—Pittsburgh NFL		15	36	512	14.2	4
1980—Pittsburgh NFL		15	18	232	12.9	2
1981—Pittsburgh NFL		15	41	574	14.0	3
1982—Pittsburgh NFL		9	21	277	13.2	2
1983—Pittsburgh NFL		16	35	442	12.6	3
1984—Pittsburgh NFL		7	4	64	16.0	1
1985—Pittsburgh NFL		11	6	61	10.2	0
Pro Totals—10 Years		118	202	2879	14.3	20

Additional pro statistics: Recovered one fumble, 1976, 1979, 1981 and 1983; fumbled once, 1978; fumbled four times, 1983.
Played in AFC Championship Game following 1976, 1979 and 1984 seasons.
Played in NFL Championship Game following 1979 season.
Member of Pittsburgh Steelers for AFC Championship Game following 1978 season; did not play.
Member of Pittsburgh Steelers for NFL Championship Game following 1978 season; did not play.

RANDALL CUNNINGHAM
Quarterback—Philadelphia Eagles
Born March 27, 1963, at Santa Barbara, Calif.
Height, 6.04. Weight, 192.
High School—Santa Barbara, Calif.
Attended University of Nevada at Las Vegas.
Brother of Sam Cunningham, running back with New England Patriots,
1973 through 1979, 1981 and 1982.

Named as punter on THE SPORTING NEWS College All-America Team, 1984.
Selected by Arizona in 1985 USFL territorial draft.
Selected by Philadelphia in 2nd round (37th player selected) of 1985 NFL draft.
Signed by Philadelphia Eagles, July 22, 1985.

Year	Club	G.	Att.	Cmp.	Pct.	Gain	T.P.	P.I.	Avg.	Att.	Yds.	Avg.	TD.	TD.	Pts.	F.
				—PASSING						—RUSHING—				—TOTAL—		
1985—Philadelphia NFL		6	81	34	42.0	548	1	8	6.77	29	205	7.1	0	0	0	3

Quarterback Rating Points: 1985 (29.8).

AUGUST ONORATO CURLEY
Linebacker—Detroit Lions
Born January 24, 1960, at Little Rock, Ark.
Height, 6.03. Weight, 226.
High School—Atlanta, Ga., Southwest.
Received degree in marketing from University of Southern California.

Selected by Los Angeles in 1983 USFL territorial draft.
Selected by Detroit in 4th round (94th player selected) of 1983 NFL draft.
Signed by Detroit Lions, June 1, 1983.
On injured reserve with knee injury, November 9 through remainder of 1983 season.
On physically unable to perform/active with knee injury, July 22 through August 19, 1984.
On physically unable to perform/reserve with knee injury, August 20 through October 23, 1984; activated, October 24, 1984.
Detroit NFL, 1983 through 1985.
Games: 1983 (10), 1984 (8), 1985 (16). Total—34.
Pro statistics: Returned one kickoff for seven yards, 1983.

CRAIG ANTHONY CURRY
Safety—Tampa Bay Buccaneers
Born July 20, 1961, at Houston, Tex.
Height, 6.00. Weight, 187.
High School—Houston, Tex., Kashmere.
Attended University of Texas.

Selected by San Antonio in 1984 USFL territorial draft.
Selected by Indianapolis in 4th round (93rd player selected) of 1984 NFL draft.
Signed by Indianapolis Colts, May 24, 1984.
Released by Indianapolis Colts, August 20, 1984; signed as free agent by Tampa Bay Buccaneers, November 12, 1984.
Tampa Bay NFL, 1984 and 1985.
Games: 1984 (5), 1985 (16). Total—21.

GEORGE JESSEL CURRY
(Buddy)
Linebacker—Atlanta Falcons
Born June 4, 1958, at Greenville, N.C.
Height, 6.04. Weight, 222.
High School—Danville, Va., George Washington.
Received bachelor of science degree in business administration from
University of North Carolina in 1980.

Selected by Atlanta in 2nd round (36th player selected) of 1980 NFL draft.
On injured reserve with knee injury, January 7 through remainder of 1982 season playoffs.

		——INTERCEPTIONS——			
Year Club	G.	No.	Yds.	Avg.	TD.
1980—Atlanta NFL	16	3	13	4.3	0
1981—Atlanta NFL	16	1	35	35.0	1
1982—Atlanta NFL	9	1	0	0.0	0
1983—Atlanta NFL	16		None		
1984—Atlanta NFL	16		None		
1985—Atlanta NFL	16	1	0	0.0	0
Pro Totals—6 Years	89	6	48	8.0	1

Additional pro statistics: Recovered one fumble for 30 yards and a touchdown and fumbled once, 1980; recovered one fumble, 1983; recovered one fumble for four yards, 1984.

DAVID JOHN D'ADDIO
Name pronounced DAD-ee-oh.
(Dave)
Running Back—Detroit Lions
Born July 13, 1961, at Newark, N.J.
Height, 6.02. Weight, 229.
High School—Union, N.J.
Attended University of Maryland.

Selected by Washington in 1984 USFL territorial draft.
Selected by Detroit in 4th round (106th player selected) of 1984 NFL draft.
Signed by Detroit Lions, July 14, 1984.
On injured reserve with ankle injury, August 27 through entire 1985 season.

		——RUSHING——				PASS RECEIVING				—TOTAL—		
Year Club	G.	Att.	Yds.	Avg.	TD.	P.C.	Yds.	Avg.	TD.	TD.	Pts.	F.
1984—Detroit NFL	16	7	46	6.6	0	1	12	12.0	0	0	0	0

Additional pro statistics: Returned one kickoff for no yards, 1984.

DARNELL LEUGTIG DAILEY
Linebacker—Washington Redskins
Born September 8, 1959, at Baltimore, Md.
Height, 6.03. Weight, 238.
High School—Baltimore, Md., Baltimore Polytechnic School of Engineering.
Received bachelor of science degree in general studies from University of Maryland in 1982.
Related to Quintin Dailey, guard with Chicago Bulls.

Selected by St. Louis in 9th round (232nd player selected) of 1982 NFL draft.
On injured reserve with Achilles tendon injury, August 25 through entire 1982 season.
Released by St. Louis Cardinals, August 16, 1983; signed by Washington Federals, September 29, 1983.
On developmental squad, March 24 through May 5, 1984; activated, May 6, 1984.
Franchise transferred to Orlando, October 12, 1984.
Released by Orlando Renegades, January 28, 1985; signed as free agent by Washington Redskins, March 23, 1985.
On injured reserve with neck injury, August 20 through entire 1985 season.
On developmental squad for 6 games with Washington Federals in 1984.
Washington USFL, 1984.
Games: 1984 (12).

DAVID MERLE DALBY
(Dave)
Center—Los Angeles Raiders
Born October 19, 1950, at Alexandria, Minn.
Height, 6.03. Weight, 255.
High School—Whittier, Calif., La Serna.
Attended University of California at Los Angeles.

Named as center on THE SPORTING NEWS College All-America Team, 1971.
Selected by Oakland in 4th round (100th player selected) of 1972 NFL draft.
Franchise transferred to Los Angeles, May 7, 1982.
Oakland NFL, 1972 through 1981; Los Angeles Raiders, 1982 through 1985.
Games: 1972 (14), 1973 (14), 1974 (14), 1975 (14), 1976 (14), 1977 (14), 1978 (16), 1979 (16), 1980 (16), 1981 (16), 1982 (9), 1983 (16), 1984 (16), 1985 (16). Total—205.
Pro statistics: Fumbled once, 1973; recovered one fumble, 1973, 1974, 1978, 1979, 1983 and 1984; caught one pass for one yard, 1979; fumbled once for minus one yard, 1980.
Played in AFC Championship Game following 1973 through 1977, 1980 and 1983 seasons.
Played in NFL Championship Game following 1976, 1980 and 1983 seasons.
Played in Pro Bowl (NFL All-Star Game) following 1977 season.

JEFFERY DWAYNE DALE
Safety—San Diego Chargers
Born October 6, 1962, at Pineville, La.
Height, 6.03. Weight, 214.
High School—Winnfield, La.
Attended Louisiana State University.

Selected by Portland in 1985 USFL territorial draft.
Selected by San Diego in 2nd round (55th player selected) of 1985 NFL draft.
Signed by San Diego Chargers, July 26, 1985.

Year Club	G.	No.	Yds.	Avg.	TD.
1985—San Diego NFL	16	2	83	41.5	*1

KENNETH RAY DALLAFIOR
Offensive Tackle—San Diego Chargers
Born August 26, 1959, at Royal Oak, Mich.
Height, 6.03. Weight, 265.
High School—Madison Heights, Mich., Madison.
Received bachelor of arts and science degree in business studies
from University of Minnesota in 1982.

Selected by Pittsburgh in 5th round (124th player selected) of 1982 NFL draft.
On injured reserve with sprained neck, September 6 through entire 1982 season.
Released by Pittsburgh Steelers, August 29, 1983; signed as free agent by Michigan Panthers, October 26, 1983.
Not protected in merger of Michigan Panthers and Oakland Invaders; selected by New Jersey Generals, December 6, 1984.
Released by New Jersey Generals, January 28, 1985; signed as free agent by San Diego Chargers, June 21, 1985.
Released by San Diego Chargers, September 2, 1985; re-signed by Chargers, December 4, 1985.
Michigan USFL, 1984: San Diego NFL, 1985.
Games: 1984 (18), 1985 (3). Total—21.

COACHING RECORD
Assistant coach at Madison High School, Madison Heights, Mich., 1985.

EUGENE DANIEL JR.
Cornerback—Indianapolis Colts
Born May 4, 1961, at Baton Rouge, La.
Height, 5.11. Weight, 179.
High School—Baton Rouge, La., Robert E. Lee.
Received degree in marketing from Louisiana State University.

Selected by New Orleans in 1984 USFL territorial draft.
Selected by Indianapolis in 8th round (205th player selected) of 1984 NFL draft.
Signed by Indianapolis Colts, June 21, 1984.

Year Club	G.	No.	Yds.	Avg.	TD.
1984—Indianapolis NFL	15	6	25	4.2	0
1985—Indianapolis NFL	16	8	53	6.6	0
Pro Totals—2 Years............	31	14	78	5.6	0

Additional pro statistics: Returned one punt for six yards, recovered three fumbles for 25 yards and fumbled once, 1985.

—DID YOU KNOW—
That only hours after the Giants' Joe Morris posted the NFL's first 200-yard rushing performance (202 yards) against Pittsburgh on December 21, Washington's George Rogers topped Morris' total with a 206-yard game against St. Louis?

KENNETH RAY DANIEL
(Kenny)
Cornerback—New York Giants
Born June 1, 1960, at Martinez, Calif.
Height, 5.10. Weight, 180.
High School—Richmond, Calif., Kennedy.
Attended Contra Costa College and San Jose State University.

Signed as free agent by Washington Redskins, May 24, 1982.
Released by Washington Redskins, August 19, 1982; signed by Oakland Invaders, October 26, 1982.
Signed by New York Giants, March 8, 1984, for contract to take effect after being granted free agency, November 30, 1984.
On injured reserve with broken hand, August 26 through entire 1985 season.

| | | —INTERCEPTIONS— | | | |
Year Club	G.	No.	Yds.	Avg.TD.	
1983—Oakland USFL.............	18	4	51	12.8	0
1984—Oakland USFL.............	18	6	28	4.7	0
1984—N.Y. Giants NFL	15		None		
USFL Totals—2 Years........	36	10	79	7.9	0
NFL Totals—1 Year...........	15	0	0	0.0	0
Pro Totals—3 Years............	51	10	79	7.9	0

Additional USFL statistics: Recovered two fumbles for one yards, 1983; recovered two fumbles for 68 yards, 1984.
Additional NFL statistics: Returned one kickoff for 52 yards, 1984.

CALVIN RICHARD DANIELS
Linebacker—Kansas City Chiefs
Born December 26, 1958, at Morehead City, N.C.
Height, 6.03. Weight, 241.
High School—Goldsboro, N.C.
Attended University of North Carolina.

Selected by Kansas City in 2nd round (46th player selected) of 1982 NFL draft.
Kansas City NFL, 1982 through 1985.
Games: 1982 (9), 1983 (16), 1984 (16), 1985 (16). Total—57.
Pro statistics: Returned one kickoff for no yards and recovered one fumble, 1983; intercepted two passes for 11 yards, 1984; recovered two fumbles, 1984 and 1985.

GARY DENNIS DANIELSON
Quarterback—Cleveland Browns
Born September 10, 1951, at Detroit, Mich.
Height, 6.02. Weight, 196.
High School—Dearborn, Mich., Divine Child.
Received bachelor of arts degree in business management and master's degree
in sports administration, both from Purdue University.

Signed as free agent by New York Stars (WFL), 1974.
Traded by Charlotte Hornets (WFL) to Chicago Winds (WFL) for future considerations, 1975.
Signed as free agent by Detroit Lions after World Football League folded, 1976.
On injured reserve with knee injury, August 28 through entire 1979 season.
On injured reserve with broken wrist, October 8 through November 24, 1981; activated, November 25, 1981.
USFL rights traded by Michigan Panthers to Arizona Wranglers for 4th round pick in 1984 draft, April 4, 1983.
Traded by Detroit Lions to Cleveland Browns for 3rd round pick in 1986 draft, May 1, 1985.

| | | —PASSING— | | | | | | —RUSHING— | | | —TOTAL— | | |
Year Club	G.	Att.	Cmp.	Pct.	Gain	T.P.	P.I.	Avg.	Att.	Yds.	Avg.	TD.	TD.	Pts.	F.
1974—N.Y.-Char. WFL..............	....	60	28	46.7	305	1	0	5.08	10	51	5.1	3	3	21	....
1975—Chicago WFL	....	15	9	60.0	107	0	2	7.13		None			0	0	....
1976—Detroit NFL.....................	1			None						None			0	0	0
1977—Detroit NFL.....................	13	100	42	42.0	445	1	5	4.45	7	62	8.9	0	0	0	0
1978—Detroit NFL.....................	16	351	199	56.7	2294	18	17	6.54	22	93	4.2	0	0	0	5
1980—Detroit NFL.....................	16	417	244	58.5	3223	13	11	7.73	48	232	4.8	2	2	12	11
1981—Detroit NFL.....................	6	96	56	58.3	784	3	5	8.17	9	23	2.6	2	2	12	2
1982—Detroit NFL.....................	8	197	100	50.8	1343	10	14	6.82	23	92	4.0	0	0	0	6
1983—Detroit NFL.....................	10	113	59	52.2	720	7	4	6.37	6	8	1.3	0	0	0	2
1984—Detroit NFL.....................	15	410	252	61.5	3076	17	15	7.50	41	218	5.3	3	4	24	7
1985—Cleveland NFL.................	8	163	97	59.5	1274	8	6	7.82	25	126	5.0	0	0	0	5
WFL Totals—2 Years........	....	75	37	49.3	412	1	2	5.49	10	51	5.1	3	3	21	....
NFL Totals—9 Years.........	93	1847	1049	56.8	13159	77	77	7.12	181	854	4.7	7	8	48	38
Pro Totals—11 Years.........	....	1922	1086	56.5	13571	78	79	7.06	191	905	4.7	10	11	69	....

NFL Quarterback Rating Points: 1977 (38.1), 1978 (73.6), 1980 (82.6), 1981 (73.4), 1982 (60.3), 1983 (78.0), 1984 (83.1), 1985 (85.3). Total—75.6.
Additional pro statistics: Recovered one fumble, 1977, 1982 and 1983; recovered two fumbles and fumbled five times for minus 12 yards, 1978; recovered four fumbles and fumbled 11 times for minus two yards, 1980; fumbled six times for minus 11 yards, 1982; caught one pass for 22 yards and a touchdown, recovered two fumbles and fumbled seven times for minus five yards, 1984; recovered one fumble and fumbled five times for minus 17 yards, 1985.

BYRON DARBY
Defensive End—Philadelphia Eagles
Born June 4, 1960, at Los Angeles, Calif.
Height, 6.04. Weight, 260.
High School—Inglewood, Calif.
Attended University of Southern California.

Selected by Los Angeles in 1983 USFL territorial draft.
Selected by Philadelphia in 5th round (120th player selected) of 1983 NFL draft.
Signed by Philadelphia Eagles, May 25, 1983.
On injured reserve with knee injury, September 25 through November 4, 1985; activated, November 5, 1985.
Philadelphia NFL, 1983 through 1985.
Games: 1983 (16), 1984 (16), 1985 (10). Total—42.
Pro statistics: Returned two kickoffs for three yards and fumbled once, 1983.

RAMSEY DARDAR
Defensive Tackle—New York Giants
Born October 3, 1959, at Cecilia, La.
Height, 6.02. Weight, 264.
High School—Cecilia, La.
Attended Louisiana State University.

Selected by New Jersey in 3rd round (27th player selected) of 1983 USFL draft.
Selected by St. Louis in 3rd round (71st player selected) of 1983 NFL draft.
Signed by St. Louis Cardinals, June 28, 1983.
On injured reserve with knee injury, August 30 through entire 1983 season.
Released by St. Louis Cardinals, September 2, 1985; signed as free agent by New York Giants, April 10, 1986.
St. Louis NFL, 1984.
Games: 1984 (16).

BRYAN F. DAUSIN
Offensive Tackle—Indianapolis Colts
Born January 28, 1960, at San Antonio, Tex.
Height, 6.04. Weight, 260.
High School—San Antonio, Tex., Roosevelt.
Received bachelor of science degree in physical education from Texas A&M University.

Signed as free agent by Houston Oilers, June 15, 1983.
Released by Houston Oilers, August 15, 1983; signed by Houston Gamblers, September 9, 1983.
On developmental squad, May 24 through June 9, 1984; activated, June 10, 1984.
On developmental squad, June 18 through remainder of 1984 season.
Traded by Houston Gamblers to San Antonio Gunslingers for defensive end Mike St. Clair, December 12, 1984.
Released by San Antonio Gunslingers, February 18, 1985; signed as free agent by Denver Gold, April 24, 1985.
Released by Denver Gold, May 24, 1985; signed as free agent by Houston Gamblers, June 1, 1985.
Granted free agency with option not exercised, August 2, 1985; signed by Indianapolis Colts, May 12, 1986.
On developmental squad for 4 games with Houston Gamblers in 1984.
Houston USFL, 1984; Denver (5)-Houston (3) USFL, 1985.
Games: 1984 (13), 1985 (8). Total—21.

RONALD DONOVAN DAVENPORT
(Ron)
Fullback—Miami Dolphins
Born December 22, 1962, at Summerset, Bermuda.
Height, 6.02. Weight, 230.
High School—Atlanta, Ga., Walter F. George.
Attended University of Louisville.

Selected by Memphis in 9th round (120th player selected) of 1985 USFL draft.
Selected by Miami in 6th round (167th player selected) of 1985 NFL draft.
Signed by Miami Dolphins, July 15, 1985.

Year Club	RUSHING					PASS RECEIVING				—TOTAL—		
	G.	Att.	Yds.	Avg.	TD.	P.C.	Yds.	Avg.	TD.	TD.	Pts.	F.
1985—Miami NFL	16	98	370	3.8	11	13	74	5.7	2	13	78	2

Played in AFC Championship Game following 1985 season.

STANLEY CHAUNCE DAVID
(Stan)
Linebacker—Buffalo Bills
Born February 17, 1962, at North Platte, Neb.
Height, 6.03. Weight, 210.
High School—Tucumcari, N.M.
Received degree in mechanical engineering from Texas Tech University in 1984.

Selected by Denver in 1984 USFL territorial draft.
Selected by Buffalo in 7th round (182nd player selected) of 1984 NFL draft.
Signed by Buffalo Bills, July 9, 1984.
On injured reserve with torn muscle in back, August 23 through entire 1985 season.
Buffalo NFL, 1984.
Games: 1984 (16).
Pro statistics: Returned one kickoff for six yards and ran 36 yards with a blocked punt for a touchdown, 1984.

BRUCE E. DAVIS
Wide Receiver—Los Angeles Raiders
Born February 25, 1963, at Dallas, Tex.
Height, 5.08. Weight, 170.
High School—Dallas, Tex., Franklin D. Roosevelt.
Received bachelor of arts degree in radio and television communications from Baylor University.

Selected by San Antonio in 1984 USFL territorial draft.
Selected by Cleveland in 2nd round (50th player selected) of 1984 NFL draft.
Signed by Cleveland Browns, June 6, 1984.
Released by Cleveland Browns, August 30, 1985; signed as free agent by Los Angeles Raiders for 1986, November 29, 1985.

		PASS RECEIVING				—KICKOFF RET.—				—TOTAL—		
Year	Club	G.	P.C.	Yds.	Avg.	TD.	No.	Yds.	Avg.	TD.	TD.	Pts.	F.
1984—Cleveland NFL		14	7	119	17.0	2	18	369	20.5	0	2	12	2

Additional pro statistics: Rushed once for six yards, 1984.

BRUCE EDWARD DAVIS
Offensive Tackle—Los Angeles Raiders
Born June 21, 1956, at Rutherfordton, N.C.
Height, 6.06, Weight, 285.
High School—Marbury, Md., Lackey.
Attended University of California at Los Angeles.

Selected by Oakland in 11th round (294th player selected) of 1979 NFL draft.
Franchise transferred to Los Angeles, May 7, 1982.
Oakland NFL, 1979 through 1981; Los Angeles Raiders NFL, 1982 through 1985.
Games: 1979 (12), 1980 (16), 1981 (16), 1982 (9), 1983 (16), 1984 (16), 1985 (16). Total—101.
Pro statistics: Recovered one fumble, 1982 and 1983.
Played in AFC Championship Game following 1980 and 1983 seasons.
Played in NFL Championship Game following 1980 and 1983 seasons.

JAMES STEVEN DAVIS
Cornerback—Los Angeles Raiders
Born June 12, 1957, at Los Angeles, Calif.
Height, 6.00. Weight, 195.
High School—Los Angeles, Calif., Crenshaw.
Attended Los Angeles Southwest Junior College and Southern University.

Selected by Oakland in 5th round (118th player selected) of 1981 NFL draft.
On injured reserve, August 25 through entire 1981 season.
Franchise transferred to Los Angeles, May 7, 1982.

		——INTERCEPTIONS——			
Year	Club	G.	No.	Yds.	Avg. TD.
1982—L.A. Raiders NFL		9	2	*107	53.5 *1
1983—L.A. Raiders NFL		16	1	10	10.0 0
1984—L.A. Raiders NFL		15	1	8	8.0 0
1985—L.A. Raiders NFL		15		None	
Pro Totals—4 Years		55	4	125	31.3 1

Additional pro statistics: Recovered one fumble, 1982 and 1983; recovered two fumbles, 1984.
Played in AFC Championship Game following 1983 season.
Played in NFL Championship Game following 1983 season.

JEFFERY EUGENE DAVIS
(Jeff)
Linebacker—Tampa Bay Buccaneers
Born January 26, 1960, at Greensboro, N.C.
Height, 6.00. Weight, 230.
High School—Greensboro, N.C., Dudley.
Received degree in industrial management from Clemson University in 1984.

Selected by Tampa Bay in 5th round (128th player selected) of 1982 NFL draft.
Tampa Bay NFL, 1982 through 1985.
Games: 1982 (9), 1983 (15), 1984 (16), 1985 (16). Total—56.
Pro statistics: Returned one kickoff for no yards and fumbled once, 1982; recovered one fumble, 1982 and 1984; intercepted one pass for no yards, 1984; intercepted one pass for 22 yards and recovered two fumbles, 1985.

JOHNNY LEE DAVIS
Fullback—Cleveland Browns
Born July 17, 1956, at Montgomery, Ala.
Height, 6.01. Weight, 235.
High School—Montgomery, Ala., Sidney Lanier.
Received bachelor of science degree in recreation and park management
from University of Alabama in 1978.

Selected by Tampa Bay in 2nd round (30th player selected) of 1978 NFL draft.
Traded by Tampa Bay Buccaneers to San Francisco 49ers for running back James Owens, August 31, 1981.
Released by San Francisco 49ers, August 30, 1982; signed as free agent by Cleveland Browns, December 2, 1982.
USFL rights traded by Birmingham Stallions to Memphis Showboats for rights to defensive back Fred Bohannon, December 21, 1983.

Year	Club	G.	Att.	RUSHING Yds.	Avg.	TD.	P.C.	PASS RECEIVING Yds.	Avg.	TD.	TD.	TOTAL Pts.	F.
1978—Tampa Bay NFL		16	97	370	3.8	3	5	13	2.6	0	3	18	2
1979—Tampa Bay NFL		16	59	221	3.7	2	5	57	11.4	0	2	12	0
1980—Tampa Bay NFL		14	39	130	3.3	1	4	17	4.3	0	1	6	1
1981—San Francisco NFL		16	94	297	3.2	7	3	—1	—0.3	0	7	42	1
1982—Cleveland NFL		2	4	3	0.8	1		None			1	6	0
1983—Cleveland NFL		16	13	42	3.2	0	5	20	4.0	0	0	0	0
1984—Cleveland NFL		16	3	15	5.0	1		None			1	6	0
1985—Cleveland NFL		16	4	9	2.3	0		None			0	0	0
Pro Totals—8 Years		112	313	1087	3.5	15	22	106	4.8	0	15	90	4

Additional pro statistics: Recovered one fumble, 1979; returned one kickoff for no yards, 1981; returned one kickoff for eight yards, 1983.
Played in NFC Championship Game following 1979 and 1981 seasons.
Played in NFL Championship Game following 1981 season.

LEE DAVIS
Cornerback—Seattle Seahawks
Born December 18, 1962, at Okolona, Miss.
Height, 5.11. Weight, 198.
High School—Amory, Miss.
Attended University of Mississippi.

Selected by Cincinnati in 5th round (129th player selected) of 1985 NFL draft.
Signed by Cincinnati Bengals, June 25, 1985.
Released by Cincinnati Bengals, September 2, 1985; re-signed by Bengals, September 3, 1985.
Released by Cincinnati Bengals, October 24, 1985; signed as free agent by Seattle Seahawks, April 15, 1986.
Cincinnati NFL, 1985.
Games: 1985 (7).

MICHAEL LEONAR DAVIS
(Mike)
Safety—Los Angeles Raiders
Born April 15, 1956, at Los Angeles, Calif.
Height, 6.03. Weight, 205.
High School—Los Angeles, Calif., Alain Leroy Locke.
Attended East Los Angeles Junior College and received bachelor of science degree
in communications from University of Colorado in 1977.

Selected by Oakland in 2nd round (35th player selected) of 1977 NFL draft.
On injured reserve entire 1977 season.
On injured reserve with knee and ankle injuries, September 23 through November 20, 1981; activated, November 21, 1981.
Franchise transferred to Los Angeles, May 7, 1982.
On injured reserve with knee injury, November 13 through December 22, 1985; activated, December 23, 1985.

Year	Club	G.	No.	INTERCEPTIONS Yds.	Avg.	TD.
1978—Oakland NFL		16	1	0	0.0	0
1979—Oakland NFL		16	2	22	11.0	0
1980—Oakland NFL		16	3	88	29.3	0
1981—Oakland NFL		7	1	0	0.0	0
1982—L.A. Raiders NFL		9	1	56	56.0	*1
1983—L.A. Raiders NFL		16	1	3	3.0	0
1984—L.A. Raiders NFL		16	2	11	5.5	0
1985—L.A. Raiders NFL		11		None		
Pro Totals—8 Years		107	11	180	16.4	1

Additional pro statistics: Recovered one fumble, 1978, 1982, 1984 and 1985; returned one punt for six yards and recovered three fumbles for 14 yards, 1979; recovered three fumbles for 35 yards, 1980; recovered two fumbles, 1983.
Played in AFC Championship Game following 1980 and 1983 seasons.
Played in NFL Championship Game following 1980 and 1983 seasons.

PRESTON DAVIS
Cornerback—Indianapolis Colts
Born March 10, 1962, at Lubbock, Tex.
Height, 5.11. Weight, 173.
High School—Lubbock, Tex., Estacado.
Attended Baylor University.

Selected by San Antonio in 1984 USFL territorial draft.
Signed as free agent by New England Patriots, July 6, 1984.
Released by New England Patriots, August 27, 1984.
USFL rights traded by San Antonio Gunslingers to Denver Gold for rights to running back James Hadnot, September 5, 1984.
Signed as free agent by Indianapolis Colts, September 18, 1984.

Year	Club	G.	No.	INTERCEPTIONS Yds.	Avg.	TD.
1984—Indianapolis NFL		12	1	3	3.0	0
1985—Indianapolis NFL		16	2	14	7.0	0
Pro Totals—2 Years		28	3	17	5.7	0

Additional pro statistics: Recovered two fumbles, 1985

RUSSELL ALAN DAVIS
Tight End—Indianapolis Colts

Born June 16, 1960 at Harrisburg, Pa.
Height, 6.05. Weight, 230.
High School—Harrisburg, Pa., Central Dauphin East.
Received bachelor of arts degree in communications from University of Maryland.

Selected by Buffalo in 12th round (322nd player selected) of 1984 NFL draft.
Released by Buffalo Bills, August 28, 1984; re-signed by Bills, May 10, 1985.
Released by Buffalo Bills, August 10, 1985; signed as free agent by Indianapolis Colts, April 2, 1986.

TONY DAVIS
Tight End—Seattle Seahawks

Born February 11, 1962, at Colorado Springs, Colo.
Height, 6.05. Weight, 248.
High School—Colorado Springs, Colo., Air Academy.
Attended University of Missouri.

Selected by Baltimore in 5th round (73rd player selected) of 1985 USFL draft.
Selected by Seattle in 4th round (109th player selected) of 1985 NFL draft.
Signed by Seattle Seahawks, July 21, 1985.
On injured reserve with foot injury, August 27 through entire 1985 season.

TYRONE DAVIS
(Ty)
Cornerback—New York Giants

Born November 17, 1961, at Athens, Ga.
Height, 6.01. Weight, 190.
High School—Athens, Ga., Cedar Shoals.
Attended Clemson University.

Selected by Orlando in 1985 USFL territorial draft.
Selected by New York Giants in 3rd round (58th player selected) of 1985 NFL draft.
Signed by New York Giants, June 4, 1985.
On injured reserve with back injury, November 1 through remainder of 1985 season.
New York Giants NFL, 1985.
Games: 1985 (7).

WAYNE ELLIOT DAVIS
Cornerback—San Diego Chargers

Born July 17, 1963, at Cincinnati, O.
Height, 5.11. Weight, 175.
High School—Cincinnati, O., Mount Healthy.
Attended Indiana State University.

Selected by Baltimore in 2nd round (21st player selected) of 1985 USFL draft.
Selected by San Diego in 2nd round (39th player selected) of 1985 NFL draft.
Signed by San Diego Chargers, June 14, 1985.

| | | —INTERCEPTIONS— | | | |
Year Club	G.	No.	Yds.	Avg.	TD.
1985—San Diego NFL	16	2	29	14.5	0

Additional pro statistics: Recovered one fumble, 1985.

DOUGLAS ARLIN DAWSON
(Doug)
Guard—St. Louis Cardinals

Born December 27, 1961, at Houston, Tex.
Height, 6.03. Weight, 267.
High School—Houston, Tex., Memorial.
Attended University of Texas.

Selected by San Antonio in 1984 USFL territorial draft.
Selected by St. Louis in 2nd round (45th player selected) of 1984 NFL draft.
Signed by St. Louis Cardinals, July 28, 1984.
St. Louis NFL, 1984 and 1985.
Games: 1984 (15), 1985 (16). Total—31.
Pro statistics: Recovered one fumble, 1985.

JAMES LINWOOD DAWSON
(Lin)
Tight End—New England Patriots

Born June 24, 1959, at Norfolk, Va.
Height, 6.03. Weight, 240.
High School—Kinston, N.C.
Attended North Carolina State University.

Selected by New England in 8th round (212th player selected) of 1981 NFL draft.
On inactive list, September 19, 1982.

Year Club		—PASS RECEIVING—			
	G.	P.C.	Yds.	Avg.	TD.
1981—New England NFL.......	15	7	126	18.0	0
1982—New England NFL.......	8	13	160	12.3	1
1983—New England NFL.......	13	9	84	9.3	1
1984—New England NFL.......	16	39	427	10.9	4
1985—New England NFL.......	16	17	148	8.7	0
Pro Totals—5 Years............	68	85	945	11.1	6

Additional pro statistics: Recovered one fumble, 1984 and 1985; fumbled once, 1985.
Played in AFC Championship Game following 1985 season.
Played in NFL Championship Game following 1985 season.

FREDERICK RUDOLPH DEAN
(Fred)
Defensive End—San Francisco 49ers
Born February 24, 1952, at Arcadia, La.
Height, 6.02. Weight, 232.
High School—Ruston, La.
Attended Louisiana Tech University.

Named to THE SPORTING NEWS AFC All-Star Team, 1979.
Named to THE SPORTING NEWS NFL All-Star Team, 1981.
Selected by San Diego in 2nd round (33rd player selected) of 1975 NFL draft.
On did not report list, August 18 through September 15, 1980; activated, September 16, 1980.
Traded with 1st round pick in 1983 draft by San Diego Chargers to San Francisco 49ers for 1st and 2nd round picks in 1983 draft, October 2, 1981.
Placed on did not report list, August 21 through November 12, 1984.
Reported and granted roster exemption, November 13 through November 15, 1984; activated, November 16, 1984.
San Diego NFL, 1975 through 1980; San Diego (3)-San Francisco (11) NFL, 1981; San Francisco NFL, 1982 through 1985.
Games: 1975 (14), 1976 (14), 1977 (11), 1978 (15), 1979 (13), 1980 (14), 1981 (14), 1982 (9), 1983 (16), 1984 (5), 1985 (16). Total—141.
Pro statistics: Recovered four fumbles, 1975; recovered two fumbles for 11 yards and one touchdown and intercepted one pass for 22 yards and one touchdown (tied for league lead in touchdowns on interceptions), 1977; recovered one fumble, 1978, 1980, 1982 and 1985; recovered three fumbles for two yards, 1979.
Played in AFC Championship Game following 1980 season.
Played in NFC Championship Game following 1981, 1983 and 1984 seasons.
Played in NFL Championship Game following 1981 and 1984 seasons.
Played in Pro Bowl (NFL All-Star Game) following 1979 through 1981 seasons.
Named to Pro Bowl following 1983 season; replaced due to injury by William Gay.

VERNON DEAN
Cornerback—Washington Redskins
Born May 5, 1959, at Los Angeles, Calif.
Height, 5.11. Weight, 178.
High School—Los Angeles, Calif.
Attended Los Angeles Valley Junior College, U.S. International University
and San Diego State University.

Selected by Washington in 2nd round (49th player selected) of 1982 NFL draft.

Year Club		—INTERCEPTIONS—			
	G.	No.	Yds.	Avg.	TD.
1982—Washington NFL..........	9	3	62	20.7	0
1983—Washington NFL..........	16	5	54	10.8	0
1984—Washington NFL..........	16	7	114	16.3	*2
1985—Washington NFL..........	16	5	8	1.6	0
Pro Totals—4 Years............	57	20	238	11.9	2

Additional pro statistics: Recovered three fumbles (including one in end zone for a touchdown), 1983; recovered one fumble for six yards, 1984; returned one punt for no yards and recovered one fumble, 1985.
Played in NFC Championship Game following 1982 and 1983 seasons.
Played in NFL Championship Game following 1982 and 1983 seasons.

STEVEN L. DeBERG
(Steve)
Quarterback—Tampa Bay Buccaneers
Born January 19, 1954, at Oakland, Calif.
Height, 6.03. Weight, 210.
High School—Anaheim, Calif., Savanna.
Attended Fullerton Junior College and received bachelor of science degree
from San Jose State University in 1980.

Selected by Dallas in 10th round (275th player selected) of 1977 NFL draft.
Claimed on waivers from Dallas Cowboys by San Francisco 49ers, September 12, 1977.
Traded by San Francisco 49ers to Denver Broncos for 4th round pick in 1983 draft, August 31, 1981.
USFL rights traded by Oakland Invaders to Denver Gold for rights to tight end John Thompson and offensive tackle Randy Van Divier, October 7, 1983.
On injured reserve with separated shoulder, November 16 through December 21, 1983; activated, December 22, 1983.

Granted free agency, February 1, 1984; re-signed by Broncos and traded to Tampa Bay Buccaneers for 4th round pick in 1984 draft and 2nd round pick in 1985 draft, April 24, 1984.

Active for 5 games with San Francisco 49ers in 1977; did not play.

Year	Club	G.	Att.	Cmp.	Pct.	Gain	T.P.	P.I.	Avg.	Att.	Yds.	Avg.	TD.	TD.	Pts.	F.
					PASSING						RUSHING				TOTAL	
1978—San Francisco NFL		12	302	137	45.4	1570	8	22	5.20	15	20	1.3	1	1	6	9
1979—San Francisco NFL		16	*578	*347	60.0	3652	17	21	6.32	17	10	0.6	0	0	0	6
1980—San Francisco NFL		11	321	186	57.9	1998	12	17	6.22	6	4	0.7	0	0	0	4
1981—Denver NFL		14	108	64	59.3	797	6	6	7.38	9	40	4.4	0	0	0	2
1982—Denver NFL		9	223	131	58.7	1405	7	11	6.30	8	27	3.4	1	1	6	4
1983—Denver NFL		10	215	119	55.3	1617	9	7	7.52	13	28	2.2	1	1	6	5
1984—Tampa Bay NFL		16	509	308	60.5	3554	19	18	6.98	28	59	2.1	2	2	12	15
1985—Tampa Bay NFL		11	370	197	53.2	2488	19	18	6.72	9	28	3.1	0	0	0	3
Pro Totals—9 Years		99	2626	1489	56.7	17081	97	120	6.50	105	216	2.1	5	5	30	48

Quarterback Rating Points: 1978 (39.8), 1979 (73.1), 1980 (66.5), 1981 (77.6), 1982 (67.2), 1983 (79.9), 1984 (79.3), 1985 (71.3). Total—69.6.

Additional pro statistics: Recovered two fumbles, 1978 and 1979; fumbled nine times for minus five yards, 1978; fumbled six times for minus 17 yards, 1979; fumbled four times for minus six yards, 1980; recovered two fumbles and fumbled 15 times for minus eight yards, 1984.

TONY DEGRATE
Defensive Tackle—Tampa Bay Buccaneers
Born April 25, 1962, at Snyder, Tex.
Height, 6.04. Weight, 280.
High School—Snyder, Tex.
Attended University of Texas.

Selected by San Antonio in 1985 USFL territorial draft.
Selected by Cincinnati in 5th round (127th player selected) of 1985 NFL draft.
Signed by Cincinnati Bengals, July 21, 1985.
Released by Cincinnati Bengals, August 21, 1985; signed as free agent by Green Bay Packers, October 1, 1985.
Released by Green Bay Packers, October 8, 1985; signed as free agent by Tampa Bay Buccaneers, March 20, 1986.
Green Bay NFL, 1985.
Games: 1985 (1).

CHARLES RAY DeJURNETT
Name pronounced Dee-Scher-NAY.
Nose Tackle—Los Angeles Rams
Born June 17, 1952, at Picayune, Miss.
Height, 6.04. Weight, 260.
High School—Los Angeles, Calif., Crenshaw.
Attended West Los Angeles College and San Jose State University.

Selected by San Diego in 17th round (418th player selected) of 1974 NFL draft.
Signed as free agent by Southern California Sun (WFL), 1974.
Signed by San Diego Chargers after World Football League folded, 1976.
On injured reserve with broken leg, January 10 through remainder of 1980 season playoffs.
On physically unable to perform/active list with leg injury, July 24 through August 16, 1981.
On physically unable to perform/reserve list with leg injury, August 17 through November 4, 1981; transferred to injury reserve November 5 through remainder of 1981 season.
Released by San Diego Chargers, September 6, 1982; signed as free agent by Los Angeles Rams, November 26, 1982.
On injured reserve with pulled groin, September 6 through October 3, 1983; activated, October 4, 1983.
Southern California WFL, 1974 and 1975; San Diego NFL, 1976 through 1980; Los Angeles Rams NFL, 1982 through 1985.
Games: 1974 (20), 1975 (12), 1976 (13), 1977 (11), 1978 (15), 1979 (12), 1980 (15), 1981 (4), 1982 (4), 1983 (10), 1984 (16), 1985 (15). Total WFL—32. Total NFL—115. Total Pro—147.
WFL statistics: Intercepted one pass for one yard and recovered one fumble, 1975.
NFL statistics: Recovered one fumble, 1980.
Played in NFC Championship Game following 1985 season.

ALBERT LOUIS DEL GRECO JR.
(Al)
Placekicker—Green Bay Packers
Born March 2, 1962, at Providence, R. I.
Height, 5.10. Weight, 195.
High School—Coral Gables, Fla.
Attended Auburn University.

Signed as free agent by Miami Dolphins, May 17, 1984.
Released by Miami Dolphins, August 27, 1984; signed as free agent by Green Bay Packers, October 17, 1984.

Year	Club	G.	XP.	XPM.	FG.	FGA.	Pts.
			PLACE KICKING				
1984—Green Bay NFL		9	34	0	9	12	61
1985—Green Bay NFL		16	38	2	19	26	95
Pro Totals—2 Years		25	72	2	28	38	156

JEFFREY ALAN DELLENBACH
(Jeff)
Offensive Tackle—Miami Dolphins
Born February 14, 1963, at Wausau, Wis.
Height, 6.06. Weight, 280.
High School—Wausau, Wis., East.
Attended University of Wisconsin.

Selected by Jacksonville in 1985 USFL territorial draft.
Selected by Miami in 4th round (111th player selected) of 1985 NFL draft.
Signed by Miami Dolphins, July 15, 1985.
Miami NFL, 1985.
Games: 1985 (11).
Played in AFC Championship Game following 1985 season.

JACK DEL RIO
Linebacker—New Orleans Saints
Born April 4, 1963, at Castro Valley, Calif.
Height, 6.04. Weight, 235.
High School—Hayward, Calif.
Attended University of Southern California.

Selected by Los Angeles in 1985 USFL territorial draft.
Selected by New Orleans in 3rd round (68th player selected) of 1985 NFL draft.
Signed by New Orleans Saints, July 31, 1985.
Selected by Toronto Blue Jays' organization in 22nd round of free-agent draft, June 8, 1981.
New Orleans NFL, 1985.
Games: 1985 (16).
Pro statistics: Recovered five fumbles for 22 yards and a touchdown and intercepted two passes for 13 yards, 1985.

TONY LAWRENCE DE LUCA
Nose Tackle—San Diego Chargers
Born November 16, 1960, at Greenwich, Conn.
Height, 6.04. Weight, 250.
High Schools—Greenwich, Conn.; and Milford, Conn., Academy.
Attended University of Rhode Island.

Signed as free agent by Los Angeles Rams, May 5, 1984.
Released by Los Angeles Rams, August 21, 1984; awarded on waivers to Green Bay Packers, August 22, 1984.
Released by Green Bay Packers, August 27, 1984; re-signed by Packers, December 12, 1984.
On non-football injury list with bleeding ulcer, August 20 through September 10, 1985.
Released by Green Bay Packers, September 11, 1985.
USFL rights traded by Tampa Bay Bandits to Arizona Outlaws for past consideration, February 24, 1986.
Signed as free agent by San Diego Chargers, May 8, 1986.
Green Bay NFL, 1984.
Games: 1984 (1).

MARK WESLEY DENNARD
Center—Miami Dolphins
Born November 2, 1955, at Bay City, Tex.
Height, 6.01. Weight, 262.
High School—Bay City, Tex.
Received bachelor of arts degree in marketing from Texas A&M University in 1978.

Selected by Miami in 10th round (274th player selected) of 1978 NFL draft.
On injured reserve with broken wrist, August 2 through entire 1978 season.
On injured reserve with calf injury, November 17 through December 17, 1981; activated, December 18, 1981.
On inactive list, September 12, 1982.
On injured reserve with shoulder injury, October 28 through remainder of 1983 season.
Traded by Miami Dolphins to Philadelphia Eagles for 3rd round pick in 1985 draft, March 7, 1984.
Released by Philadelphia Eagles, April 11, 1986; signed as free agent by Miami Dolphins, April 30, 1986.
Miami NFL, 1979 through 1983; Philadelphia NFL, 1984 and 1985.
Games: 1979 (16), 1980 (16), 1981 (11), 1982 (8), 1983 (8), 1984 (16), 1985 (16). Total—91.
Pro statistics: Recovered one fumble, 1979 and 1980; recovered one fumble for minus 19 yards, 1985.
Played in AFC Championship Game following 1982 season.
Played in NFL Championship Game following 1982 season.

PRESTON JACKSON DENNARD
Wide Receiver—Green Bay Packers
Born November 28, 1955, at Cordele, Ga.
Height, 6.01. Weight, 183.
High Schools—Phoenix, Ariz., South Mountain; and Tempe, Ariz., Marcos de Niza.
Attended University of New Mexico.
Brother of Glenn Dennard, wide receiver at Arizona State University.

Signed as free agent by Los Angeles Rams, May 16, 1978.
Released by Los Angeles Rams, August 22, 1978; re-signed by Rams, September 30, 1978.
Traded by Los Angeles Rams to Buffalo Bills for 5th round pick in 1985 draft, August 1, 1984.
Traded by Buffalo Bills to Green Bay Packers for 12th round pick in 1986 draft, August 20, 1985.

Year Club	—PASS RECEIVING—				
	G.	P.C.	Yds.	Avg.	TD.
1978—L.A. Rams NFL............	11	3	35	11.7	0
1979—L.A. Rams NFL............	15	43	766	17.8	4
1980—L.A. Rams NFL............	16	36	596	16.6	6
1981—L.A. Rams NFL............	15	49	821	16.8	4
1982—L.A. Rams NFL............	9	25	383	15.3	2
1983—L.A. Rams NFL............	14	33	465	14.1	5
1984—Buffalo NFL................	16	30	417	13.9	7
1985—Green Bay NFL...........	16	13	182	14.0	2
Pro Totals—8 Years...........	112	232	3665	15.8	30

Additional pro statistics: Rushed four times for 32 yards, 1979; recovered one fumble, 1979 and 1981; fumbled once, 1979, 1981, 1984 and 1985; rushed twice for 20 yards and recovered two fumbles, 1980; rushed six times for 29 yards, 1981.
Played in NFC Championship Game following 1978 and 1979 seasons.
Played in NFL Championship Game following 1979 season.

GLENN DENNISON
Tight End—New York Jets
Born November 17, 1961, at Beaver Falls, Pa.
Height, 6.03. Weight, 225.
High School—Beaver Falls, Pa.
Attended University of Miami (Fla.).

Selected by Houston in 3rd round (64th player selected) in 1984 USFL draft.
Selected by New York Jets in 2nd round (39th player selected) of 1984 NFL draft.
Signed by New York Jets, May 29, 1984.
On physically unable to perform/reserve with back injury, July 27 through August 18, 1985.
On injured reserve with back injury, August 19 through entire 1985 season.

Year Club	—PASS RECEIVING—				
	G.	P.C.	Yds.	Avg.	TD.
1984—N.Y. Jets NFL	16	16	141	8.8	1

Additional pro statistics: Rushed once for four yards, 1984.

RICK STEVEN DENNISON
Linebacker—Denver Broncos
Born June 22, 1958, at Kalispell, Mont.
Height, 6.03. Weight, 220.
High School—Fort Collins, Colo., Rocky Mountain.
Received bachelor of science degree in civil engineering from Colorado State University in 1980.

Signed as free agent by Buffalo Bills, May 9, 1980.
Released by Buffalo Bills, August 20, 1980; signed as free agent by Denver Broncos, December 29, 1980.
Released by Denver Broncos, August 31, 1981; signed as free agent by Buffalo Bills, February 26, 1982.
Released by Buffalo Bills, August 31, 1982; signed as free agent by Denver Broncos, September 7, 1982.
Denver NFL, 1982 through 1985.
Games: 1982 (9), 1983 (16), 1984 (16), 1985 (15). Total—56.
Pro statistics: Returned two kickoffs for 27 yards and recovered one fumble, 1984.

RICHARD LAMAR DENT
Defensive End—Chicago Bears
Born December 13, 1960, at Atlanta, Ga.
Height, 6.05. Weight, 263.
High School—Atlanta, Ga., Murphy.
Attended Tennessee State University.

Selected by Philadelphia in 8th round (89th player selected) of 1983 USFL draft.
Selected by Chicago in 8th round (203rd player selected) of 1983 NFL draft.
Signed by Chicago Bears, May 12, 1983.
Chicago NFL, 1983 through 1985.
Games: 1983 (16), 1984 (16), 1985 (16). Total—48.
Pro statistics: Recovered one fumble, 1984; intercepted two passes for 10 yards and a touchdown and recovered two fumbles, 1985.
Played in NFC Championship Game following 1984 and 1985 seasons.
Played in NFL Championship Game following 1985 season.
Played in Pro Bowl (NFL All-Star Game) following 1984 and 1985 seasons.

STEVEN LEONARD DeOSSIE
(Steve)
Linebacker—Dallas Cowboys
Born November 22, 1962, at Tacoma, Wash.
Height, 6.02. Weight, 248.
High School—Boston, Mass., Don Bosco Technical.
Received bachelor of science degree in communications from Boston College in 1984.

Selected by New Jersey in 1st round (14th player selected) of 1984 USFL draft.
Selected by Dallas in 4th round (110th player selected) of 1984 NFL draft.
Signed by Dallas Cowboys, May 3, 1984.
Dallas NFL, 1984 and 1985.
Games: 1984 (16), 1985 (16). Total—32.

JOSEPH DEVLIN
(Joe)
Offensive Tackle—Buffalo Bills
Born February 23, 1954 at Phoenixville, Pa.
Height, 6.05. Weight, 267.
High School—Frazer, Pa., Great Valley.
Attended University of Iowa.

Named as guard on THE SPORTING NEWS College All-America Team, 1975.
Selected by Buffalo in 2nd round (52nd player selected) of 1976 NFL draft.
On injured reserve with knee injury, December 13 through remainder of 1978 season.
On injured reserve with broken ankle, August 22 through entire 1983 season.
Buffalo NFL, 1976 through 1982, 1984 and 1985.
Games: 1976 (14), 1977 (14), 1978 (14), 1979 (16), 1980 (16), 1981 (16), 1982 (9), 1984 (16), 1985 (16). Total—131.
Pro statistics: Recovered one fumble, 1978 and 1982; recovered two fumbles, 1979.

ANTHONY CHARLES DICKERSON
Linebacker—Buffalo Bills
Born June 9, 1957, at Texas City, Tex.
Height, 6.02. Weight, 219.
High School—Pearland, Tex.
Attended Henderson County Junior College and Southern Methodist University.

Signed as free agent by Calgary Stampeders, April, 1978.
Released by Calgary Stampeders, August 20, 1978; signed as free agent by Toronto Argonauts, September 28, 1978.
Released by Toronto Argonauts, October 6, 1978; signed as free agent by Dallas Cowboys, May 15, 1980.
Traded by Dallas Cowboys to Buffalo Bills for 12th round pick in 1986 draft, August 27, 1985.

	—INTERCEPTIONS—						—INTERCEPTIONS—			
Year Club	G.	No.	Yds.	Avg.TD.	Year Club		G.	No.	Yds.	Avg.TD.
1978—Cal.(2)-Tor. (1) CFL	3	1	0	0.0	0	1984—Dallas NFL	16	1	0	0.0	0
1980—Dallas NFL	16	2	46	23.0	0	1985—Buffalo NFL	16		None		
1981—Dallas NFL	16		None			CFL Totals—1 Year	3	1	0	0.0	0
1982—Dallas NFL	9	1	4	4.0	0	NFL Totals—6 Years	89	5	58	11.6	0
1983—Dallas NFL	16	1	8	8.0	0	Pro Totals—7 Years	92	6	58	9.7	0

Additional CFL statistics: Returned one kickoff for no yards and recovered one fumble, 1978.
Additional NFL statistics: Recovered one fumble, 1980 and 1984; recovered two fumbles, 1981; credited with one safety and recovered three fumbles, 1983.
Played in NFC Championship Game following 1980 through 1982 seasons.

ERIC DEMETRIC DICKERSON
Running Back—Los Angeles Rams
Born September 2, 1960, at Sealy, Tex.
Height, 6.03. Weight, 218.
High School—Sealy, Tex.
Attended Southern Methodist University.
Cousin of Dexter Manley, defensive end with Washington Redskins; and Robert Dickerson,
running back at University of Texas at El Paso.

Named as running back on THE SPORTING NEWS College All-America Team, 1982.
Named THE SPORTING NEWS NFL Player of the Year, 1983.
Named to THE SPORTING NEWS NFL All-Star Team, 1983 and 1984.
Established NFL records for most yards rushing by rookie (1,808), 1983; most touchdowns rushing by rookie (18),
1983; most yards rushing, season (2,105), 1984; most games, 100 yards rushing, season (12), 1984.
Selected by Arizona in 1st round (6th player selected) of 1983 USFL draft.
Selected by Los Angeles Rams in 1st round (2nd player selected) of 1983 NFL draft.
Signed by Los Angeles Rams, July 12, 1983.
On did not report list, August 20 through September 12, 1985.
Reported and granted roster exemption, September 13 through Setpember 19, 1985; activated, September 20, 1985.

	—RUSHING—				PASS RECEIVING				—TOTAL—		
Year Club	G.	Att.	Yds.	Avg.	TD.	P.C.	Yds.	Avg.	TD.	TD. Pts. F.
1983—Los Angeles Rams NFL	16	*390	*1808	4.6	18	51	404	7.9	2	20 120 13
1984—Los Angeles Rams NFL	16	379	*2105	5.6	*14	21	139	6.6	0	14 84 14
1985—Los Angeles Rams NFL	14	292	1234	4.2	12	20	126	6.3	0	12 72 10
Pro Totals—3 Years	46	1061	5147	4.9	44	92	669	7.3	2	46 276 37

Additional pro statistics: Recovered one fumble, 1983; attempted one pass with one interception and recovered
four fumbles, 1984; recovered three fumbles, 1985.
Played in NFC Championship Game following 1985 season.
Played in Pro Bowl (NFL All-Star Game) following 1983 and 1984 seasons.

—DID YOU KNOW—

That Pittsburgh wide receiver John Stallworth, who didn't catch three touchdown passes in one game during his first 10 years with the Steelers, had two such games in the same month in 1984? Stallworth caught three scoring passes from Mark Malone in Pittsburgh's 35-7 victory over Houston on November 4 and caught three more in the Steelers' 52-24 rout of San Diego on November 25.

CLIFFORD LYNN DICKEY
(Known by middle name.)
Quarterback—Green Bay Packers
Born October 19, 1949, at Paola, Kan.
Height, 6.04. Weight, 203.
High School—Osawatomie, Kan.
Received bachelor of science degree in physical education from Kansas State University in 1971.

Selected by Houston in 3rd round (56th player selected) of 1971 NFL draft.
Missed entire season due to hip injury, 1972.
Traded by Houston Oilers to Green Bay Packers for quarterback John Hadl, defensive back Ken Ellis, two draft choices (4th round pick in 1976 and 3rd round pick in 1977) and cash, April 2, 1976.
Placed on physically unable to perform list with broken leg, July 21, 1978; transferred to injured reserve, October 4, 1978.

				—PASSING—						—RUSHING—				—TOTAL—		
Year Club	G.	Att.	Cmp.	Pct.	Gain	T.P.	P.I.	Avg.	Att.	Yds.	Avg.	TD.	TD.	Pts.	F.
1971—Houston NFL	6	57	19	33.3	315	0	9	5.53	1	4	4.0	0	0	0	1
1973—Houston NFL	14	120	71	59.2	888	6	10	7.40	6	9	1.5	0	0	†1	5
1974—Houston NFL	14	113	63	55.8	704	2	8	6.23	3	7	2.3	0	0	0	2
1975—Houston NFL	14	4	2	50.0	46	1	4	11.50	1	3	3.0	0	0	0	0
1976—Green Bay NFL	10	243	115	47.3	1465	7	14	6.03	11	19	1.8	1	1	6	7
1977—Green Bay NFL	9	220	113	51.4	1346	5	14	6.12	5	24	4.8	0	0	0	1
1979—Green Bay NFL	5	119	60	50.4	787	5	4	6.61	5	13	2.6	0	0	0	2
1980—Green Bay NFL	16	478	278	58.2	3529	15	25	7.38	19	11	0.6	1	1	6	13
1981—Green Bay NFL	13	354	204	57.6	2593	17	15	7.32	19	6	0.3	0	0	0	8
1982—Green Bay NFL	9	218	124	56.9	1790	12	14	8.21	13	19	1.5	0	0	0	5
1983—Green Bay NFL	16	484	289	59.7	*4458	*32	*29	*9.21	21	12	0.6	3	3	18	9
1984—Green Bay NFL	15	401	237	59.1	3195	25	19	7.97	18	6	0.3	3	3	18	3
1985—Green Bay NFL	12	314	172	54.8	2206	15	17	7.03	18	—12	—0.7	1	1	6	8
Pro Totals—13 Years	153	3125	1747	55.9	23322	141	179	7.46	140	121	0.9	9	9	55	64

Quarterback Rating Points: 1971 (13.3), 1973 (64.3), 1974 (51.0), 1975 (52.1), 1976 (52.1), 1977 (51.4), 1979 (71.5), 1980 (70.0), 1981 (79.1), 1982 (75.4), 1983 (87.3), 1984 (85.6), 1985 (70.4). Total—71.0.
†Scored an extra point.
Additional pro statistics: Recovered three fumbles, 1976 and 1981; recovered one fumble and fumbled twice for minus one yard, 1979; recovered five fumbles and fumbled 13 times for minus seven yards, 1980; fumbled eight times for minus 26 yards, 1981; recovered two fumbles and fumbled five times for minus one yard, 1982; recovered six fumbles, 1983; recovered one fumble and fumbled three times for minus 11 yards, 1984; recovered five fumbles and fumbled eight times for minus 18 yards, 1985.

CURTIS RAYMOND DICKEY
Running Back—Cleveland Browns
Born November 27, 1956, at Madisonville, Tex.
Height, 6.01. Weight, 222.
High School—Bryan, Tex.
Attended Texas A&M University.

Selected by Baltimore in 1st round (5th player selected) of 1980 NFL draft.
On inactive list, September 19, 1982.
Franchise transferred to Indianapolis, March 31, 1984.
On injured reserve with knee injury, December 13 through remainder of 1984 season.
On injured reserve with knee injury, September 11 through October 17, 1985; activated, October 18, 1985.
Released by Indianapolis Colts, November 25, 1985; awarded on waivers to Cleveland Browns, November 26, 1985.

			—RUSHING—				PASS RECEIVING				—TOTAL—		
Year Club	G.	Att.	Yds.	Avg.	TD.	P.C.	Yds.	Avg.	TD.	TD.	Pts.	F.
1980—Baltimore NFL	15	176	800	4.5	11	25	204	8.2	2	13	78	3
1981—Baltimore NFL	15	164	779	4.8	7	37	419	11.3	3	10	60	8
1982—Baltimore NFL	8	66	232	3.5	1	21	228	10.9	0	1	6	3
1983—Baltimore NFL	16	254	1122	4.4	4	24	483	20.1	3	7	42	7
1984—Indianapolis NFL	10	131	523	4.0	3	14	135	9.6	0	3	18	6
1985—Ind.(6)-Cle.(1) NFL	7	11	40	3.6	0	3	30	10.0	0	0	0	0
Pro Totals—6 Years	71	802	3496	4.4	26	124	1499	12.1	8	34	204	29

Additional pro statistics: Returned four kickoffs for 86 yards, 1980; recovered one fumble, 1983 and 1984; attempted one pass with one completion for 63 yards and a touchdown, 1984.

CLINT DIDIER
Tight End—Washington Redskins
Born April 4, 1959, at Connell, Wash.
Height, 6.05. Weight, 240.
High School—Connell, Wash.
Attended Columbia Basin Junior College and Portland State University.

Selected by Washington in 12th round (314th player selected) of 1981 NFL draft.
On injured reserve with pulled hamstring, August 18 through entire 1981 season.
On injured reserve with fractured leg, August 28 through September 28, 1984; activated, September 29, 1984.

Year Club	G.	P.C.	Yds.	Avg.	TD.
1982—Washington NFL	8	2	10	5.0	1
1983—Washington NFL	16	9	153	17.0	4
1984—Washington NFL	11	30	350	11.7	5
1985—Washington NFL	16	41	433	10.6	4
Pro Totals—4 Years	51	82	946	11.5	14

Additional pro statistics: Recovered one fumble in end zone for a touchdown and fumbled once, 1983.
Played in NFC Championship Game following 1982 and 1983 seasons.
Played in NFL Championship Game following 1982 and 1983 seasons.

CHRISTIAN JEFFERY DIETERICH

Name pronounced DEE-trick.

(Chris)

Guard-Offensive Tackle—Detroit Lions

Born July 27, 1958, at Freeport, N.Y.
Height, 6.03. Weight, 260.
High School—East Setauket, N.Y., Ward Melville.
Attended North Carolina State University and Suffolk Community College.

Selected by Detroit in 6th round (140th player selected) of 1980 NFL draft.
Released by Detroit Lions, August 26, 1980; re-signed by Lions, October 15, 1980.
On injured reserve with knee injury, November 18 through remainder of 1981 season.
On injured reserve with knee injury, October 17 through November 15, 1985; activated, November 16, 1985.
Detroit NFL, 1980 through 1985.
Games: 1980 (8), 1981 (7), 1982 (5), 1983 (16), 1984 (16), 1985 (9). Total—61.
Pro statistics: Recovered one fumble, 1980 and 1983.

STEPHEN WHITFIELD DILS

(Steve)

Quarterback—Los Angeles Rams

Born December 8, 1955, at Seattle, Wash.
Height, 6.01. Weight, 191.
High School—Vancouver, Wash., Fort Vancouver.
Received bachelor of arts degree in economics from Stanford University in 1979. .

Selected by Minnesota in 4th round (97th player selected) of 1979 NFL draft.
Traded by Minnesota Vikings to Los Angeles Rams for 4th round pick in 1985 draft, September 18, 1984.

Year Club	G.	Att.	Cmp.	Pct.	Gain	T.P.	P.I.	Avg.	Att.	Yds.	Avg.	TD.	TD.	Pts.	F.
				PASSING						RUSHING			TOTAL		
1979—Minnesota NFL	1				None						None		0	0	0
1980—Minnesota NFL	16	51	32	62.7	352	3	0	6.90	3	26	8.7	0	0	0	0
1981—Minnesota NFL	2	102	54	52.9	607	1	2	5.95	4	14	3.5	0	0	0	3
1982—Minnesota NFL	9	26	11	42.3	68	0	0	2.62	1	5	5.0	0	0	0	0
1983—Minnesota NFL	16	444	239	53.8	2840	11	16	6.40	16	28	1.8	0	0	0	13
1984—Min. (3)-Rams (7) NFL	10	7	4	57.1	44	1	1	6.29			None		0	0	0
1985—Los Angeles Rams NFL	15				None				2	—4	—2.0	0	0	0	0
Pro Totals—7 Years	69	630	340	54.0	3911	16	19	6.21	26	69	2.7	0	0	0	16

Quarterback Rating Points: 1980 (102.8), 1981 (66.0), 1982 (49.8), 1983 (66.8), 1984 (75.9). Total—68.8.
Additional pro statistics: Recovered two fumbles, 1981; recovered six fumbles, 1983.
Member of Los Angeles Rams for NFC Championship Game following 1985 season; did not play.

ANGELO JAMES DILULO

Nose Tackle—Seattle Seahawks

Born May 11, 1962, at Boise, Ida.
Height, 6.01. Weigh, 264.
High School—Boise, Ida.
Attended Oregon State University.

Signed as free agent by Seattle Seahawks, July 10, 1985.
On injured reserve with knee injury, August 20 through entire 1985 season.

DWAYNE K. DIXON

Wide Receiver—San Diego Chargers

Born August 2, 1962, at Gainesville, Fla.
Height, 6.02. Weight, 207.
High School—Alachua, Fla., Santa Fe.
Received bachelor of arts degree in liberal arts and science (criminology) from University of Florida.
Brother of Hewritt Dixon, fullback-tight end with Denver Broncos
and Oakland Raiders, 1963 through 1970.

Selected by Tampa Bay in 1984 USFL territorial draft.
Signed as free agent by Kansas City Chiefs, June 20, 1984.
Released by Kansas City Chiefs, August 13, 1984; signed as free agent by Tampa Bay Buccaneers, October 9, 1984.
Released by Tampa Bay Buccaneers, August 13, 1985; signed as free agent by San Diego Chargers, April 15, 1986.

Year Club	G.	P.C.	Yds.	Avg.	TD.
1984—Tampa Bay NFL	10	5	69	13.8	0

HANFORD DIXON
Cornerback—Cleveland Browns
Born December 25, 1958, at Mobile, Ala.
Height, 5.11. Weight, 186.
High School—Theodore, Ala.
Attended University of Southern Mississippi.
Cousin of Lyneal Alston, wide receiver at University of Southern Mississippi.

Named as defensive back on THE SPORTING NEWS College All-America Team, 1980.
Selected by Cleveland in 1st round (22nd player selected) of 1981 NFL draft.

| | | | —INTERCEPTIONS— | | |
Year Club	G.	No.	Yds.	Avg.	TD.
1981—Cleveland NFL............	16		None		
1982—Cleveland NFL............	9	4	22	5.5	0
1983—Cleveland NFL............	16	3	41	13.7	0
1984—Cleveland NFL............	16	5	31	6.2	0
1985—Cleveland NFL............	16	3	65	21.7	0
Pro Totals—5 Years...........	73	15	159	10.6	0

Additional pro statistics: Fumbled once, 1982; recovered one fumble, 1984.

KIRK JAMES DODGE
Linebacker—Detroit Lions
Born June 4, 1962, at Whittier, Calif.
Height, 6.01. Weight, 231.
High School—San Francisco, Calif., Lowell.
Attended Fullerton College and University of Nevada at Las Vegas.

Selected by Los Angeles in 6th round (112th player selected) of 1984 USFL draft.
Selected by Atlanta in 7th round (175th player selected) of 1984 NFL draft.
Signed by Atlanta Falcons, June 10, 1984.
Released by Atlanta Falcons, August 26, 1984; signed as free agent by Detroit Lions, October 2, 1984
On injured reserve with shoulder injury, August 20 through entire 1985 season.
Detroit NFL, 1984.
Games: 1984 (11).
Pro statistics: Recovered one fumble, 1984.

JEROME WILLIAM DOERGER
(Jerry)
Center-Offensive Tackle—San Diego Chargers
Born July 18, 1960, at Cincinnati, O.
Height, 6.05. Weight, 270.
High School—Cincinnati, O., LaSalle.
Received bachelor of science degree in mechanical engineering from University of Wisconsin in 1984.

Selected by Chicago in 8th round (200th player selected) of 1982 NFL draft.
Released by Chicago Bears, August 16, 1983.
USFL rights traded by Washington Federals to Chicago Blitz for two 6th round picks in 1984 draft, January 3, 1984.
Signed by Chicago Blitz, January 10, 1984.
On developmental squad, April 28 through May 4, 1984; activated, May 5, 1984.
Franchise disbanded, November 20, 1984.
Selected by Orlando in USFL dispersal draft, December 6, 1984.
On developmental squad, March 19 through April 25, 1985; activated, April 26, 1985.
Granted free agency, August 1, 1985; signed by San Diego Chargers, August 5, 1985.
On injured reserve with back injury, October 26 through December 6, 1985; activated, December 7, 1985.
On developmental squad for 1 game with Chicago Blitz in 1984.
On developmental squad for 5 games with Orlando Renegades in 1985.
Chicago NFL, 1982; Chicago USFL, 1984; Orlando USFL, 1985; San Diego NFL, 1985.
Games: 1982 (1), 1984 (17), 1985 USFL (13), 1985 NFL (8). Total NFL—9. Total USFL—30. Total Pro—39.
USFL statistics: Recovered one fumble and fumbled twice, 1985.

STEPHEN GUGEL DOIG
(Steve)
Linebacker—New England Patriots
Born March 28, 1960, at Melrose, Mass.
Height, 6.02. Weight, 242.
High School—North Reading, Mass.
Attended University of New Hampshire.

Selected by Detroit in 3rd round (69th player selected) of 1982 NFL draft.
On injured reserve with ankle injury, October 8 through November 11, 1983; activated, November 12, 1983.
Released by Detroit Lions, August 27, 1985; signed as free agent by New England Patriots, February 24, 1986.
Detroit NFL, 1982 through 1984.
Games: 1982 (9), 1983 (9), 1984 (16). Total—34.

—DID YOU KNOW—
That Vikings rookie nose tackle Tim Newton set a club record for interceptions by a defensive lineman with two in 1985?

CHRISTOPHER JOHN DOLEMAN
(Chris)
Linebacker—Minnesota Vikings
Born October 16, 1961, at Indianapolis, Ind.
Height, 6.05. Weight, 250.
High Schools—Wayne, Pa., Valley Forge Military Academy;
and York, Pa., William Penn.
Attended University of Pittsburgh.

Selected by Baltimore in 1985 USFL territorial draft.
Selected by Minnesota in 1st round (4th player selected) of 1985 NFL draft.
Signed by Minnesota Vikings, August 8, 1985.
Minnesota NFL, 1985.
Games: 1985 (16).
Pro statistics: Intercepted one pass for five yards and recovered three fumbles, 1985.

PAUL MATTHEW DOMBROSKI
Cornerback—Tampa Bay Buccaneers
Born August 8, 1956, at Sumter, S. C.
Height, 6.00. Weight, 185.
High School—Wahiawa, Hawaii, Lei-Le-Hall.
Attended University of Hawaii and Linfield College.

Signed as free agent by Kansas City Chiefs, May 10, 1980.
On injured reserve with shoulder injury, October 9 through November 10, 1981; claimed on procedural waivers by New England Patriots, November 12, 1981.
On injured reserve with concussion, September 6 through November 3, 1983; activated, November 4, 1983.
USFL rights traded by Memphis Showboats to Pittsburgh Maulers for rights to defensive back Mark Young, January 30, 1984.
Released by New England Patriots, August 27, 1984; re-signed by Patriots, August 28, 1984.
On injured reserve with knee injury, December 8 through remainder of 1984 season.
Released by New England Patriots, August 27, 1985; signed as free agent by Tampa Bay Buccaneers, August 29, 1985.
On injured reserve with thigh injury, October 14 through remainder of 1985 season.

Year Club	G.	No.	Yds.	Avg.	TD.
1980—Kansas City NFL..........	16	1	6	6.0	0
1981—K.C.(5)-N.E.(6) NFL.....	11		None		
1982—New England NFL.......	9		None		
1983—New England NFL.......	7		None		
1984—New England NFL.......	14	1	23	23.0	0
1985—Tampa Bay NFL	6		None		
Pro Totals—6 Years............	63	2	29	14.5	0

Additional pro statistics: Returned three kickoffs for 66 yards, 1981; returned one kickoff for 19 yards and recovered one fumble, 1982.

JEFF DONALDSON
Safety—Houston Oilers
Born April 19, 1962, at Fort Collins, Colo.
Height, 6.00. Weight, 193.
High School—Fort Collins, Colo.
Attended University of Colorado.

Selected by Denver in 1984 USFL territorial draft.
Selected by Houston in 9th round (228th player selected) of 1984 NFL draft.
Signed by Houston Oilers, July 17, 1984.

Year Club	G.	No.	Yds.	Avg.	TD.	No.	Yds.	Avg.	TD.	TD.	Pts.	F.
			–PUNT RETURNS–				—KICKOFF RET.—				—TOTAL—	
1984—Houston NFL...............................	16		None				None			0	0	0
1985—Houston NFL...............................	16	6	35	5.8	0	5	93	18.6	0	0	0	0
Pro Totals—2 Years.................................	32	6	35	5.8	0	5	93	18.6	0	0	0	0

Additional pro statistics: Recovered two fumbles and fumbled once, 1985.

RAYMOND CANUTE DONALDSON
(Ray)
Center—Indianapolis Colts
Born May 17, 1958, at Rome, Ga.
Height, 6.04. Weight, 274.
High School—Rome, Ga., East.
Attended University of Georgia.
Step-brother of John Tutt, outfielder in San Diego Padres' organization;
and cousin of Robert Lavette, running back with Dallas Cowboys.

Selected by Baltimore in 2nd round (32nd player selected) of 1980 NFL draft.
Franchise transferred to Indianapolis, March 31, 1984.
Baltimore NFL, 1980 through 1983; Indianapolis NFL, 1984 and 1985.
Games: 1980 (16), 1981 (16), 1982 (9), 1983 (16), 1984 (16), 1985 (16). Total—89.
Pro statistics: Recovered one fumble, 1981, 1982 and 1985; fumbled once, 1983.

DOUGLAS MAX DONLEY
(Doug)
Wide Receiver—Chicago Bears
Born February 6, 1959, at Cambridge O.
Height, 6.00. Weight, 178.
High School—Cambridge, O.
Attended Ohio State University.

Selected by Dallas in 2nd round (53rd player selected) of 1981 NFL draft.
Released by Dallas Cowboys, July 9, 1985; signed as free agent by Chicago Bears, May 21, 1986.

Year Club		—PASS RECEIVING—			
	G.	P.C.	Yds.	Avg.	TD.
1981—Dallas NFL	11	3	32	10.7	0
1982—Dallas NFL	6	2	23	11.5	0
1983—Dallas NFL	11	18	370	20.6	2
1984—Dallas NFL	15	32	473	14.8	2
Pro Totals—4 Years	43	55	898	16.3	4

Additional pro statistics: Returned one punt for three yards, 1981; returned eight kickoffs for 151 yards, one punt for 14 yards and fumbled twice, 1982; returned one punt for one yard, 1983; rushed twice for five yards, 1984.
Played in NFC Championship Game following 1981 and 1982 seasons.

WILLIAM FREDERICK DONNALLEY
(Rick)
Center-Guard—Kansas City Chiefs
Born December 11, 1958, at Wilmington, Del.
Height, 6.02. Weight, 257.
High School—Raleigh, N.C., Sanderson.
Received bachelor of science degree in business administration from
University of North Carolina in 1981.

Selected by Pittsburgh in 3rd round (73rd player selected) of 1981 NFL draft.
On injured reserve with broken hand, August 25 through entire 1981 season.
Traded by Pittsburgh Steelers to Washington Redskins for 5th round pick in 1985 draft, August 20, 1984.
On injured reserve with knee injury, November 18 through remainder of 1985 season.
Traded by Washington Redskins to Kansas City Chiefs for 6th round pick in 1986 draft, April 29, 1986.
Pittsburgh NFL, 1982 and 1983; Washington NFL, 1984 and 1985.
Games: 1982 (5), 1983 (16), 1984 (15), 1985 (13). Total—49.
Pro statistics: Returned one kickoff for eight yards, 1982; ran two yards with lateral on kickoff return, 1983.

RICK DONNELLY
Punter—Atlanta Falcons
Born May 17, 1962, at Miller Place, N.Y.
Height, 6.00. Weight, 184.
High School—Miller Place, N.Y.
Attended University of Wyoming.

Selected by San Antonio in 14th round (192nd player selected) of 1985 USFL draft.
Signed as free agent by New England Patriots, May 8, 1985.
Released by New England Patriots, August 19, 1985; signed as free agent by Atlanta Falcons, August 23, 1985.
On injured reserve with knee injury, November 18 through remainder of 1985 season.

Year Club		—PUNTING—		
	G.	No.	Avg.	Blk.
1985—Atlanta NFL	11	59	43.6	0

Additional pro statistics: Rushed twice for minus five yards and recovered one fumble, 1985.

DANIEL E. DOORNINK
(Dan)
Fullback—Seattle Seahawks
Born February 1, 1956, at Yakima, Wash.
Height, 6.03. Weight, 210.
High School—Wapato, Wash.
Received degree from Washington State University; attending
medical school at University of Washington.

Selected by New York Giants in 7th round (174th player selected) of 1978 NFL draft.
Traded by New York Giants to Seattle Seahawks for 7th round pick in 1980 draft, August 21, 1979.
On injured reserve with knee injury, October 9 through November 7, 1985; activated, November 8, 1985.
On injured reserve with fractured fibula, November 11 through remainder of 1985 season.

Year Club		—RUSHING—				PASS RECEIVING				—TOTAL—		
	G.	Att.	Yds.	Avg.	TD.	P.C.	Yds.	Avg.	TD.	TD.	Pts.	F.
1978—New York Giants NFL	12	60	306	5.1	1	12	66	5.5	0	1	6	2
1979—Seattle NFL	16	152	500	3.3	8	54	432	8.0	1	9	54	6
1980—Seattle NFL	15	100	344	3.4	3	31	237	7.6	2	5	30	2
1981—Seattle NFL	15	65	194	3.0	1	27	350	13.0	4	5	30	3
1982—Seattle NFL	8	45	178	4.0	0	22	176	8.0	0	0	0	2
1983—Seattle NFL	16	40	99	2.5	2	24	328	13.7	2	4	24	1
1984—Seattle NFL	16	57	215	3.8	0	31	365	11.8	2	2	12	0
1985—Seattle NFL	6	4	0	0.0	0	8	52	6.5	0	0	0	0
Pro Totals—8 Years	104	523	1836	3.5	15	209	2006	9.6	11	26	156	16

Additional pro statistics: Returned one kickoff for 13 yards, 1979; recovered one fumble, 1980 through 1983; punted once for 54 yards, 1982.
Played in AFC Championship Game following 1983 season.

KEITH ROBERT DORNEY
Offensive Tackle—Detroit Lions
Born December 3, 1957, at Allentown, Pa.
Height, 6.05. Weight, 270.
High School—Emmaus, Pa.
Received bachelor of science degree in business from Penn State University in 1979.

Named as offensive tackle on THE SPORTING NEWS College All-America Team, 1978.
Selected by Detroit in 1st round (10th player selected) of 1979 NFL draft.
On injured reserve with knee injury, October 15 through December 5, 1980; activated, December 6, 1980.
Detroit NFL, 1979 through 1985.
Games: 1979 (16), 1980 (9), 1981 (16), 1982 (9), 1983 (13), 1984 (16), 1985 (16). Total—95.
Pro statistics: Recovered one fumble, 1981.
Played in Pro Bowl (NFL All-Star Game) following 1982 season.

ANTHONY DREW DORSETT
Name pronounced Dor-SETT.
(Tony)
Running Back—Dallas Cowboys
Born April 7, 1954, at Rochester, Pa.
Height, 5.11. Weight, 185.
High School—Aliquippa, Pa., Hopewell.
Attended University of Pittsburgh.

Established NFL record for longest run from scrimmage (99 yards), January 3, 1983, against Minnesota Vikings.
Named THE SPORTING NEWS NFC Rookie of the Year, 1977.
Named to THE SPORTING NEWS NFL All-Star Team, 1981.
Named as running back on THE SPORTING NEWS College All-America Team, 1976.
Named THE SPORTING NEWS College Player of the Year, 1976.
Heisman Trophy winner, 1976.
Selected by Dallas in 1st round (2nd player selected) of 1977 NFL draft.

Year Club	G.	RUSHING				PASS RECEIVING				TOTAL		
		Att.	Yds.	Avg.	TD.	P.C.	Yds.	Avg.	TD.	TD.	Pts.	F.
1977—Dallas NFL	14	208	1007	4.8	12	29	273	9.4	1	13	78	7
1978—Dallas NFL	16	290	1325	4.6	7	37	378	10.2	2	10	60	12
1979—Dallas NFL	14	250	1107	4.4	6	45	375	8.3	1	7	42	9
1980—Dallas NFL	15	278	1185	4.3	11	34	263	7.7	0	11	66	8
1981—Dallas NFL	16	342	1646	4.8	4	32	325	10.2	2	6	36	10
1982—Dallas NFL	9	*177	745	4.2	5	24	179	7.5	0	5	30	6
1983—Dallas NFL	16	289	1321	4.6	8	40	287	7.2	1	9	54	5
1984—Dallas NFL	16	302	1189	3.9	6	51	459	9.0	1	7	42	12
1985—Dallas NFL	16	305	1307	4.3	7	46	449	9.8	3	10	60	7
Pro Totals—9 Years	132	2441	10832	4.4	66	338	2988	8.8	11	78	468	76

Additional pro statistics: Attempted one pass with one completion for 34 yards, 1977; recovered four fumbles for 54 yards and one touchdown, 1978; attempted one pass with no completions, 1978, 1980, 1982 and 1983; recovered one fumble, 1979, 1980 and 1982 through 1984; recovered two fumbles, 1981; attempted one pass with one interception, 1984; recovered three fumbles, 1985.
Played in NFC Championship Game following 1977, 1978 and 1980 through 1982 seasons.
Played in NFL Championship Game following 1977 and 1978 seasons.
Played in Pro Bowl (NFL All-Star Game) following 1978 and 1981 through 1983 seasons.

JOHN MICHAEL DORSEY
Linebacker—Green Bay Packers
Born August 31, 1960, at Leonardtown, Md.
Height, 6.02. Weight, 235.
High School—Leonardtown, Md., Fort Union.
Attended University of Connecticut.

Selected by Philadelphia in 7th round (142nd player selected) of 1984 USFL draft.
Selected by Green Bay in 4th round (99th player selected) of 1984 NFL draft.
Signed by Green Bay Packers, July 12, 1984.
Green Bay NFL, 1984 and 1985.
Games: 1984 (16), 1985 (16). Total—32.
Pro statistics: Recovered two fumbles, 1985.

REGINALD LEE DOSS
(Reggie)
Defensive End—Los Angeles Rams
Born December 7, 1956, at Mobile, Ala.
Height, 6.04. Weight, 263.
High School—San Antonio, Tex., Sam Houston.
Attended Hampton Institute.

Selected by Los Angeles in 7th round (189th player selected) of 1978 NFL draft.
Los Angeles Rams NFL, 1978 through 1985.

Games: 1978 (16), 1979 (16), 1980 (16), 1981 (16), 1982 (9), 1983 (16), 1984 (16), 1985 (16). Total—121.
Pro statistics: Recovered one fumble, 1980 through 1984; credited with one safety and recovered two fumbles, 1985.
Played in NFC Championship Game following 1978, 1979 and 1985 seasons.
Played in NFL Championship Game following 1979 season.

MICHAEL REESE DOUGLASS
(Mike)
Linebacker
Born March 15, 1955, at St. Louis, Mo.
Height, 6.00. Weight, 214.
High School—Los Angeles, Calif., Jordan.
Attended Arizona State University, Los Angeles City College and
San Diego State University.

Selected by Green Bay in 5th round (116th player selected) of 1978 NFL draft.
On suspended list, November 30 through December 4, 1983; reinstated, December 5, 1983.
Released by Green Bay Packers, May 27, 1986.

Year Club	G.	No.	Yds.	Avg.TD.		Year Club	G.	No.	Yds.	Avg.TD.
1978—Green Bay NFL	16		None			1983—Green Bay NFL	15		None	
1979—Green Bay NFL	16	3	73	24.3 0		1984—Green Bay NFL	16		None	
1980—Green Bay NFL	16		None			1985—Green Bay NFL	15	2	126	63.0 ★1
1981—Green Bay NFL	16	3	20	6.7 0		Pro Totals—8 Years	119	10	274	27.4 1
1982—Green Bay NFL	9	2	55	27.5 0						

Additional pro statistics: Recovered two fumbles, 1978, 1980, 1984 and 1985; recovered three fumbles, 1981; recovered one fumble for six yards, 1982; recovered four fumbles for 57 yards and two touchdowns, 1983; fumbled once, 1985.

MICHAEL LYNN DOWNS
(Mike)
Safety—Dallas Cowboys
Born June 9, 1959, at Dallas, Tex.
Height, 6.03. Weight, 204.
High School—Dallas, Tex., South Oak Cliff.
Received degree in business, political science and physical education from Rice University in 1981.
Signed as free agent by Dallas Cowboys, May, 1981.

Year Club	G.	No.	Yds.	Avg.TD.
1981—Dallas NFL	15	7	81	11.6 0
1982—Dallas NFL	9	1	22	22.0 0
1983—Dallas NFL	16	4	80	20.0 0
1984—Dallas NFL	16	7	126	18.0 1
1985—Dallas NFL	16	3	11	3.7 0
Pro Totals—5 Years	72	22	320	14.5 1

Additional pro statistics: Recovered one fumble, 1981; recovered three fumbles for 87 yards and one touchdown, 1982; recovered two fumbles for 10 yards and a touchdown, 1983; recovered two fumbles for 28 yards, 1984; recovered three fumbles, 1985.
Played in NFC Championship Game following 1981 and 1982 seasons.

JOE LYNN DRAKE
Nose Tackle—Philadelphia Eagles
Born May 28, 1963, at San Francisco, Calif.
Height, 6.02. Weight, 290.
High School—San Francisco, Calif., Galileo.
Attended University of Arizona.

Selected by Arizona in 1985 USFL territorial draft.
Selected by Philadelphia in 9th round (233rd player selected) of 1985 NFL draft.
Signed by Philadelphia Eagles, July 21, 1985.
Philadelphia NFL, 1985.
Games: 1985 (16).

CHRIS DRESSEL
Tight End—Houston Oilers
Born February 7, 1961, at Placentia, Calif.
Height, 6.04. Weight, 238.
High School—Placentia, Calif., El Dorado.
Attended Stanford University.

Selected by Oakland in 1983 USFL territorial draft.
Selected by Houston in 3rd round (69th player selected) of 1983 NFL draft.
Signed by Houston Oilers, June 22, 1983.

Year Club	G.	P.C.	Yds.	Avg.	TD.
1983—Houston NFL	16	32	316	9.9	4
1984—Houston NFL	16	40	378	9.5	2
1985—Houston NFL	16	3	17	5.7	1
Pro Totals—3 Years	48	75	711	9.5	7

Additional pro statistics: Returned four kickoffs for 40 yards and rushed once for three yards, 1983; fumbled once, 1984; recovered one fumble, 1985.

WILLIE DREWREY
Wide Receiver-Kick Returner—Houston Oilers

Born April 28, 1963, at Columbus, N.J.
Height, 5.07. Weight, 158.
High School—Columbus, N.J., Northern Burlington.
Attended West Virginia University.

Named as kick returner on THE SPORTING NEWS College All-America Team, 1984.
Selected by Birmingham in 1985 USFL territorial draft.
Selected by Houston in 11th round (281st player selected) of 1985 NFL draft.
Signed by Houston Oilers, July 18, 1985.

		PASS RECEIVING				–PUNT RETURNS–				—KICKOFF RET.—				—TOTAL—		
Year	Club	G.	P.C.	Yds.	Avg.	TD.	No.	Yds.	Avg.	TD.	No.	Yds.	Avg.	TD.	TD.	Pts.	F.
1985—Houston NFL		14	2	28	14.0	0	24	215	9.0	0	26	642	24.7	0	0	0	2

Additional pro statistics: Rushed twice for minus four yards, 1985.

KENNY WAYNE DUCKETT
Wide Receiver—Dallas Cowboys

Born October 1, 1959, at Winston-Salem, N.C.
Height, 5.11. Weight, 182.
High School—Winston-Salem, N.C., Reynolds.
Attended Wake Forest University.

Selected by New Orleans in 3rd round (68th player selected) of 1982 NFL draft.
On non-football injury list with diabetes, November 19 through remainder of 1984 season.
On injured reserve with broken thumb, August 28 through October 9, 1985; activated after clearing procedural waivers, October 11, 1985.
Released by New Orleans Saints, October 15, 1985; signed as free agent by Dallas Cowboys, December 5, 1985.

		PASS RECEIVING					—KICKOFF RET.—				—TOTAL—		
Year	Club	G.	P.C.	Yds.	Avg.	TD.	No.	Yds.	Avg.	TD.	TD.	Pts.	F.
1982—New Orleans NFL		7	12	196	16.3	2	2	39	19.5	0	2	12	0
1983—New Orleans NFL		14	19	283	14.9	2	33	719	21.8	0	2	12	1
1984—New Orleans NFL		11	3	24	8.0	0	29	580	20.0	0	0	0	0
1985—N.O.(1)-Dal.(3) NFL		4		None			9	173	19.2	0	0	0	1
Pro Totals—4 Years		36	34	503	14.8	4	73	1511	20.7	0	4	24	2

Additional pro statistics: Rushed twice for minus 16 yards, 1983; rushed once for minus three yards, 1984; recovered one fumble, 1985.

BOBBY RAY DUCKWORTH
Wide Receiver—Los Angeles Rams

Born November 27, 1958, at Crossett, Ark.
Height, 6.03. Weight, 197.
High School—Hamburg, Ark.
Attended University of Arkansas.

Selected by San Diego in 6th round (162nd player selected) of 1981 NFL draft.
On non-football injury list with toe injury, August 5 through entire 1981 season.
On inactive list, September 12 and September 19, 1982.
Traded by San Diego Chargers to Los Angeles Rams for offensive tackle Gary Kowalski and 5th round pick in 1986 draft, September 2, 1985.
On suspended list, December 3 through December 9, 1985; activated, December 10, 1985.

		——PASS RECEIVING——				
Year	Club	G.	P.C.	Yds.	Avg.	TD.
1982—San Diego NFL		5	2	77	38.5	0
1983—San Diego NFL		16	20	422	21.1	5
1984—San Diego NFL		16	25	715	28.6	4
1985—L.A. Rams NFL		14	25	422	16.9	3
Pro Totals—4 Years		51	72	1636	22.7	12

Additional pro statistics: Fumbled once, 1984.
Played in NFC Championship Game following 1985 season.

MARK DAVID DUDA
Defensive Tackle—St. Louis Cardinals

Born February 4, 1961, at Wilkes Barre, Pa.
Height, 6.03. Weight, 279.
High School—Plymouth, Pa., Wyoming Valley West.
Attended University of Maryland.

Selected by Washington in 1983 USFL territorial draft.
Selected by St. Louis in 4th round (96th player selected) of 1983 NFL draft.
Signed by St. Louis Cardinals, May 9, 1983.
On injured reserve with dislocated kneecap, November 6 through remainder of 1984 season.
St. Louis NFL, 1983 through 1985.
Games: 1983 (14), 1984 (8), 1985 (16). Total—38.
Pro statistics: Returned one kickoff for 12 yards and recovered two fumbles, 1983; recovered one fumble, 1984 and 1985.

DAVID RUSSELL DUERSON
(Dave)
Safety—Chicago Bears

Born November 28, 1960, at Muncie, Ind.
Height, 6.01. Weight, 202.
High School—Muncie, Ind., Northside.
Received bachelor of arts degree in economics and communications from
University of Notre Dame in 1983.
Cousin of Allen Leavell, guard with Houston Rockets.

Selected by Chicago in 1983 USFL territorial draft.
Selected by Chicago in 3rd round (64th player selected) of 1983 NFL draft.
Signed by Chicago Bears, June 25, 1983.

Year Club	G.	No.	Yds.	Avg.	TD.	No.	Yds.	Avg.	TD.	TD.	Pts.	F.
		-INTERCEPTIONS-				-PUNT RETURNS-				—TOTAL—		
1983—Chicago NFL	16		None				None			0	0	0
1984—Chicago NFL	16	1	9	9.0	0	1	4	4.0	0	0	0	0
1985—Chicago NFL	15	5	53	10.6	0	6	47	7.8	0	0	0	1
Pro Totals—3 Years	47	6	62	10.3	0	7	51	7.3	0	0	0	1

Additional pro statistics: Returned three kickoffs for 66 yards, 1983; returned four kickoffs for 95 yards, 1984; recovered one fumble, 1985.
Played in NFC Championship Game following 1984 and 1985 seasons.
Played in NFL Championship Game following 1985 season.
Played in Pro Bowl (NFL All-Star Game) following 1985 season.

CLYDE LEWIS DUNCAN
Wide Receiver—St. Louis Cardinals

Born February 5, 1961, at Oxon Hill, Md.
Height, 6.02. Weight, 211.
High School—Oxon Hill, Md.
Received degree in political science from University of Tennessee in 1984.

Selected by Memphis in 1984 USFL territorial draft.
Selected by St. Louis in 1st round (17th player selected) of 1984 NFL draft.
Signed by St. Louis Cardinals, September 10, 1984.
Granted roster exemption, September 10 through September 20, 1984; activated, September 21, 1984.
On injured reserve with dislocated shoulder, October 19 through November 22, 1984; activated, November 23, 1984.

Year Club	G.	P.C.	Yds.	Avg.	TD.	No.	Yds.	Avg.	TD.	TD.	Pts.	F.
		PASS RECEIVING				—KICKOFF RET.—				—TOTAL—		
1984—St. Louis NFL	8		None				None			0	0	0
1985—St. Louis NFL	11	4	39	9.8	1	28	550	19.6	0	1	6	3
Pro Totals—2 Years	19	4	39	9.8	1	28	550	19.6	0	1	6	3

Additional pro statistics: Recovered one fumble, 1985.

GARY EDWARD DUNN
Nose Tackle—Pittsburgh Steelers

Born August 24, 1953, at Coral Gables, Fla.
Height, 6.03. Weight, 265.
High School—Coral Gables, Fla.
Received bachelor of business administration degree from University of Miami (Fla.) in 1976.
Son of Eddie Dunn, head coach at University of Miami (Fla.), 1943 and 1944.

Selected by Pittsburgh in 6th round (159th player selected) of 1976 NFL draft.
On injured reserve entire 1977 season.
Pittsburgh NFL, 1976 and 1978 through 1985.
Games: 1976 (5), 1978 (16), 1979 (16), 1980 (16), 1981 (16), 1982 (9), 1983 (13), 1984 (16), 1985 (10). Total—117.
Pro statistics: Recovered one fumble, 1978; recovered two fumbles, 1979; recovered one fumble for one yard, 1981; recovered three fumbles, 1985.
Played in AFC Championship Game following 1978, 1979 and 1984 seasons.
Played in NFL Championship Game following 1978 and 1979 seasons.

KELDRICK A. DUNN
(K. D.)
Tight End—Tampa Bay Buccaneers

Born April 28, 1963, at Fort Hood, Tex.
Height, 6.03. Weight, 235.
High School—Decatur, Ga., Gordon.
Attended Clemson University.

Selected by Orlando in 1985 USFL territorial draft.
Selected by St. Louis in 5th round (116th player selected) of 1985 NFL draft.
Signed by St. Louis Cardinals, July 3, 1985.
Released by St. Louis Cardinals, August 26, 1985; signed as free agent by Tampa Bay Buccaneers, November 5, 1985.
Tampa Bay NFL, 1985.
Games: 1985 (7).

PATRICK NEIL DUNSMORE
(Pat)
Tight End—Chicago Bears
Born October 2, 1959, at Duluth, Minn.
Height, 6.03. Weight, 237.
High School—Ankeny, Ia.
Received bachelor of science degree in physical education from Drake University in 1983.

Selected by Chicago in 11th round (126th player selected) of 1983 USFL draft.
Selected by Chicago in 4th round (107th player selected) of 1983 NFL draft.
Signed by Chicago Bears, June 25, 1983.
On injured reserve with groin injury, August 28 through September 27, 1984; activated, September 28, 1984.
On injured reserve with thigh injury, September 3 through entire 1985 season.

| | | —PASS RECEIVING— | | | |
Year Club	G.	P.C.	Yds.	Avg.	TD.
1983—Chicago NFL	16	8	102	12.8	0
1984—Chicago NFL	12	9	106	11.8	1
Pro Totals—2 Years	28	17	208	12.2	1

Played in NFC Championship Game following 1984 season.

MARK SUPER DUPER
(Given name at birth was Mark Kirby Dupas.)
Wide Receiver—Miami Dolphins
Born January 25, 1959, at Pineville, La.
Height, 5.09. Weight, 187.
High School—Moreauville, La.
Attended Northwestern (La.) State University.

Selected by Miami in 2nd round (52nd player selected) of 1982 NFL draft.
On inactive list, September 12 and September 19, 1982.
On injured reserve with broken leg, September 16 through November 8, 1985; activated, November 9, 1985.

| | | —PASS RECEIVING— | | | |
Year Club	G.	P.C.	Yds.	Avg.	TD.
1982—Miami NFL	2		None		
1983—Miami NFL	16	51	1003	19.7	10
1984—Miami NFL	16	71	1306	18.4	8
1985—Miami NFL	9	35	650	18.6	3
Pro Totals—4 Years	43	157	2959	18.8	21

Additional pro statistics: Recovered one fumble, 1984; recovered one fumble for three yards and fumbled once, 1985.
Played in AFC Championship Game following 1984 and 1985 seasons.
Played in NFL Championship Game following 1984 season.
Member of Miami Dolphins for AFC and NFL Championship Game following 1982 season; did not play.
Played in Pro Bowl (NFL All-Star Game) following 1983 and 1984 seasons.

MICHAEL RAY DURRETTE
(Mike)
Guard—San Francisco 49ers
Born August 11, 1957, at Charlottesville, Va.
Height, 6.04. Weight, 280.
High School—Charlottesville, Va., Miller Military of Albemarle.
Attended Ferrum Junior College and West Virginia University.
Related to Walter White, tight end with Kansas City Chiefs, 1975 through 1979.

Signed by Los Angeles Express, January 10, 1983.
On developmental squad, May 18 through June 8, 1985; activated, June 9, 1985.
Released by Los Angeles Express, August 1, 1985; signed as free agent by San Francisco 49ers, February 7, 1986.
On developmental squad for 3 games with Los Angeles Express in 1985.
Los Angeles USFL, 1983 through 1985.
Games: 1983 (17), 1984 (18), 1985 (16). Total—51.
Pro statistics: Rushed twice for no yards, caught one pass for four yards and recovered two fumbles, 1983; returned one kickoff for five yards and fumbled once, 1984.

JOHN OWEN DUTTON
Defensive Tackle—Dallas Cowboys
Born February 6, 1951, at Rapid City, S. D.
Height, 6.07. Weight, 267.
High School—Rapid City, S. D.
Received degree in business administration from University of Nebraska.

Named to THE SPORTING NEWS AFC All-Star Team, 1975 and 1976.
Named as defensive tackle on THE SPORTING NEWS College All-America Team, 1973.
Selected by Baltimore in 1st round (5th player selected) of 1974 NFL draft.
Placed on retired reserve list by Baltimore Colts, August 21, 1979.
Traded by Baltimore Colts to Dallas Cowboys for 1st and 2nd round picks in 1980 draft, October 9, 1979; activated, October 22, 1979.
Baltimore NFL, 1974 through 1978; Dallas NFL, 1979 through 1985.

Games: 1974 (14), 1975 (14), 1976 (14), 1977 (12), 1978 (14), 1979 (8), 1980 (16), 1981 (16), 1982 (9), 1983 (16), 1984 (16), 1985 (16). Total—165.

Pro statistics: Recovered one fumble, 1974, 1975, 1977, 1983 and 1985; recovered three fumbles for 10 yards, 1978; intercepted one pass for 38 yards and a touchdown and recovered two fumbles, 1980; credited with one safety, 1981 and 1984.

Played in NFC Championship Game following 1980 and 1982 seasons.
Member of Dallas Cowboys for NFC Championship Game following 1981 season; did not play.
Played in Pro Bowl (NFL All-Star Game) following 1975 through 1977 seasons.

KENNY EASLEY
Safety—Seattle Seahawks
Born January 15, 1959, at Chesapeake, Va.
Height, 6.03. Weight, 206.
High School—Chesapeake, Va., Oscar Smith.
Received degree in political science from University of California at Los Angeles.
Cousin of Walt Easley, running back with San Francisco 49ers, Chicago Blitz
and Pittsburgh Maulers, 1981 through 1984.
Named to The Sporting News NFL All-Star Team, 1984 and 1985.
Named as defensive back on The Sporting News College All-America Team, 1978 through 1980.
Selected by Chicago Bulls in 10th round of 1981 NBA draft.
Selected by Seattle in 1st round (4th player selected) of 1981 NFL draft.

		-INTERCEPTIONS-				-PUNT RETURNS-				—TOTAL—		
Year Club	G.	No.	Yds.	Avg.	TD.	No.	Yds.	Avg.	TD.	TD.	Pts.	F.
1981—Seattle NFL	14	3	155	51.7	1		None			1	6	0
1982—Seattle NFL	8	4	48	12.0	0	1	15	15.0	0	0	0	0
1983—Seattle NFL	16	7	106	15.1	0	1	6	6.0	0	0	0	0
1984—Seattle NFL	16	*10	126	12.6	*2	16	194	12.1	0	2	12	0
1985—Seattle NFL	13	2	22	11.0	0	8	87	10.9	0	0	0	2
Pro Totals—5 Years	67	26	457	17.6	3	26	302	11.6	0	3	18	2

Additional pro statistics: Recovered four fumbles for 25 yards, 1981; recovered one fumble, 1982, 1984 and 1985; recovered three fumbles for 29 yards, 1983.
Played in AFC Championship Game following 1983 season.
Played in Pro Bowl (NFL All-Star Game) following 1982 through 1985 seasons.

WILLIE CHARLES EASMON
(Ricky)
Defensive Back—Tampa Bay Buccaneers
Born July 3, 1963, at Inverness, Fla.
Height, 5.10. Weight, 160.
High School—Dunnellon, Fla.
Attended University of Florida.
Selected by Tampa Bay in 1985 USFL territorial draft.
Signed as free agent by Dallas Cowboys, May 2, 1985.
Released by Dallas Cowboys, September 2, 1985; re-signed by Cowboys, September 10, 1985.
Released by Dallas Cowboys, November 9, 1985; awarded on waivers to Tampa Bay Buccaneers, November 11, 1985.
Dallas (8)-Tampa Bay (6) NFL, 1985.
Games: 1985 (14).

BO EASON
Safety—Houston Oilers
Born March 10, 1961, at Walnut Grove, Calif.
Height, 6.02. Weight, 200.
High School—Walnut Grove, Calif., Delta.
Attended University of California at Davis.
Brother of Tony Eason, quarterback with New England Patriots.
Selected by Oakland in 1st round (18th player selected) of 1984 USFL draft.
Selected by Houston in 2nd round (54th player selected) of 1984 NFL draft.
Signed by Houston Oilers, July 22, 1984.
On injured reserve with knee injury, October 25 through November 23, 1984; activated, November 24, 1984.

		——INTERCEPTIONS——			
Year Club	G.	No.	Yds.	Avg.	TD.
1984—Houston NFL	10	1	20	20.0	0
1985—Houston NFL	16	3	55	18.3	0
Pro Totals—2 Years	26	4	75	18.8	0

Additional pro statistics: Recovered one fumble, 1984; fumbled once, 1985.

CHARLES CARROLL EASON IV
(Tony)
Quarterback—New England Patriots
Born October 8, 1959, at Blythe, Calif.
Height, 6.04. Weight, 212.
High School—Clarksburg, Calif., Delta.
Attended American River College and received bachelor of science degree
in physical education from University of Illinois in 1983.
Brother of Bo Eason, safety with Houston Oilers.

Selected by Chicago in 1983 USFL territorial draft.
USFL rights traded with running back Calvin Murray and 1st round pick in 1983 draft by Chicago Blitz to Arizona Wranglers for rights to placekicker Frank Corral and 1st round pick in 1983 draft, January 4, 1983.
Selected by New England in 1st round (15th player selected) of 1983 NFL draft.
Signed by New England Patriots, June 2, 1983.

Year Club	G.	Att.	Cmp.	Pct.	Gain	T.P.	P.I.	Avg.	Att.	Yds.	Avg.	TD.	TD.	Pts.	F.
				PASSING						RUSHING			TOTAL		
1983—New England NFL............	16	95	46	48.4	557	1	5	5.86	19	39	2.1	0	0	0	5
1984—New England NFL............	16	431	259	60.1	3228	23	8	7.49	40	154	3.9	5	5	30	7
1985—New England NFL............	16	299	168	56.2	2156	11	17	7.21	22	70	3.2	1	1	6	4
Pro Totals—3 Years............	48	825	473	57.3	5941	35	30	7.20	81	263	3.2	6	6	36	16

Quarterback Rating Points: 1983 (48.4), 1984 (93.4), 1985 (67.5). Total—78.8.
Additional pro statistics: Recovered one fumble, 1983; recovered two fumbles and fumbled seven times for minus five yards, 1984; recovered one fumble and fumbled four times for minus 19 yards, 1985.
Played in AFC Championship Game following 1985 season.
Played in NFL Championship Game following 1985 season.

BRAD M. EDELMAN
Guard—New Orleans Saints
Born September 3, 1960, at Jacksonville, Fla.
Height, 6.06. Weight, 265.
High School—Creve Coeur, Mo., Parkway North.
Attended University of Missouri.

Named as center on THE SPORTING NEWS College All-America Team, 1981.
Selected by New Orleans on 2nd round (30th player selected) of 1982 NFL draft.
On injured reserve with knee injury, October 9 through November 18, 1984; activated, November 19, 1984.
On injured reserve with knee injury, September 24 through November 15, 1985; activated, November 16, 1985.
New Orleans NFL, 1982 through 1985.
Games: 1982 (9), 1983 (16), 1984 (11), 1985 (8). Total—44.

DAVID LEE EDWARDS
(Dave)
Safety—Pittsburgh Steelers
Born March 31, 1962, at Senoia, Ga.
Height, 6.00. Weight, 196.
High School—Decatur, Ga., Columbia.
Received bachelor of arts degree in history from University of Illinois in 1985.

Selected by Baltimore in 13th round (188th player selected) of 1985 USFL draft.
Signed as free agent by Pittsburgh Steelers, May 3, 1985.
On injured reserve with foot injury, December 10 through remainder of 1985 season.
Pittsburgh NFL, 1985.
Games: 1985 (14).

DENNIS RAY EDWARDS
Defensive End—Los Angeles Rams
Born October 6, 1959, Stockton, Calif.
Height, 6.04. Weight, 250.
High School—Stockton, Calif., Edison.
Received bachelor of arts degree from University of Southern California.

Selected by Buffalo in 9th round (245th player selected) of 1982 NFL draft.
Released by Buffalo Bills, September 6, 1982; signed by Los Angeles Express, January 10, 1983.
On injured reserve with shoulder injury, May 6 through remainder of 1983 season.
On developmental squad, March 16 through March 22, 1984; activated, March 23, 1984.
Traded by Los Angeles Express to Denver Gold for draft choice, March 28, 1984.
On developmental squad, March 31 through April 8, 1984; activated, April 9, 1984.
On developmental squad, June 2 through remainder of 1984 season.
Released by Denver Gold, February 18, 1985; signed as free agent by Winnipeg Blue Bombers, April 10, 1985.
Released by Winnipeg Blue Bombers, July 2, 1985; signed as free agent by Los Angeles Rams, March 21, 1986.
On developmental squad for 1 game with Los Angeles Express and 5 games with Denver Gold in 1984.
Los Angeles USFL, 1983; Los Angeles (5)-Denver (8) USFL, 1984.
Games: 1983 (9), 1984 (13). Total—22.
Pro statistics: Credited with six sacks for 51 yards, credited with one safety and recovered two fumbles, 1983; credited with one sack for two yards, 1984.

EDDIE EDWARDS
Defensive End—Cincinnati Bengals
Born April 25, 1954, at Sumter, S. C.
Height, 6.05. Weight, 256.
High School—Fort Pierce, Fla., Central.
Attended Arizona Western College and University of Miami.

Selected by Cincinnati in 1st round (3rd player selected) of 1977 NFL draft.
Cincinnati NFL, 1977 through 1985.
Games: 1977 (12), 1978, (16), 1979 (14), 1980 (16), 1981 (14), 1982 (9), 1983 (16), 1984 (16), 1985 (16). Total—129.
Pro statistics: Recovered one fumble for three yards, 1977; recovered two fumbles, 1978, 1979 and 1985; intercepted one pass for two yards, 1978; recovered one fumble, 1980 through 1983; recovered three fumbles for minus two yards, 1984.

Played in AFC Championship Game following 1981 season.
Played in NFL Championship Game following 1981 season.

HERMAN LEE EDWARDS
Cornerback—Philadelphia Eagles
Born April 27, 1954, at Fort Monmouth, N. J.
Height, 6.00. Weight, 194.
High School—Monterey, Calif.
Attended Monterey Peninsula College, University of California at Berkeley and received
bachelor of science degree in criminal justice from San Diego State University in 1976.
Signed as free agent by Philadelphia Eagles, May, 1977.

Year	Club	G.	No.	Yds.	Avg.	TD.	Year	Club	G.	No.	Yds.	Avg.	TD.
		—INTERCEPTIONS—							—INTERCEPTIONS—				
1977—Philadelphia NFL		14	6	9	1.5	0	1982—Philadelphia NFL		9	5	3	0.6	0
1978—Philadelphia NFL		16	7	59	8.4	0	1983—Philadelphia NFL		16	1	0	0.0	0
1979—Philadelphia NFL		16	3	6	2.0	0	1984—Philadelphia NFL		16	2	0	0.0	0
1980—Philadelphia NFL		16	3	12	4.0	0	1985—Philadelphia NFL		16	3	8	2.7	*1
1981—Philadelphia NFL		16	3	1	0.3	0	Pro Totals—9 Years		135	33	98	3.0	1

Additional pro statistics: Recovered two fumbles and fumbled once, 1977; recovered one fumble for 26 yards and a touchdown and fumbled once, 1978; recovered one fumble, 1979; recovered one fumble for four yards, 1981 and 1985.
Played in NFC Championship Game following 1980 season.
Played in NFL Championship Game following 1980 season.

RICHARD RANDOLPH EDWARDS
(Randy)
Defensive End—Seattle Seahawks
Born March 9, 1961, at Marietta, Ga.
Height, 6.04. Weight, 255.
High School—Marietta, Ga., Wheeler.
Received degree in corporate finance from University of Alabama.
Selected by Birmingham in 1984 USFL territorial draft.
Signed as free agent by Seattle Seahawks, May 2, 1984.
Seattle NFL, 1984 and 1985.
Games: 1984 (13), 1985 (16). Total—29.
Pro statistics: Recovered one fumble, 1985.

STANLEY EDWARDS
(Stan)
Running Back—Houston Oilers
Born May 20, 1960, at Detroit, Mich.
Height, 6.00. Weight, 210.
High School—Detroit, Mich., Kettering.
Attended University of Michigan.
Selected by Houston in 3rd round (72nd player selected) of 1982 NFL draft.
On injured reserve with dislocated shoulder, September 7 through November 18, 1982; activated, November 19, 1982.
Released by Houston Oilers, August 27, 1984; re-signed by Oilers, September 12, 1984.

			—RUSHING—				PASS RECEIVING				—TOTAL—		
Year	Club	G.	Att.	Yds.	Avg.	TD.	P.C.	Yds.	Avg.	TD.	TD.	Pts.	F.
1982—Houston NFL		7	15	58	3.9	0	9	53	5.9	0	0	0	0
1983—Houston NFL		14	16	40	2.5	0	9	79	8.8	1	1	6	0
1984—Houston NFL		14	60	267	4.5	1	20	151	7.6	0	1	6	2
1985—Houston NFL		15	25	96	3.8	1	7	71	10.1	0	1	6	0
Pro Totals—4 Years		50	116	461	4.0	2	45	354	7.9	1	3	18	2

CHARLES KALEV EHIN
(Middle name is an Estonian name meaning Atlas, or great person.)
(Chuck)
Defensive End—San Diego Chargers
Born July 1, 1961, at Marysville, Calif.
Height, 6.04. Weight, 265.
High School—Layton, Utah.
Attended Brigham Young University.
Selected by Chicago in 17th round (198th player selected) of 1983 USFL draft.
Selected by San Diego in 12th round (329th player selected) of 1983 NFL draft.
Signed by San Diego Chargers, June 6, 1983.
San Diego NFL, 1983 through 1985.
Games: 1983 (9), 1984 (16), 1985 (16). Total—41.
Pro statistics: Recovered one fumble, 1984 and 1985.

CARL FREDERICK EKERN
Name pronounced EH-kern.
Linebacker—Los Angeles Rams
Born May 27, 1954, at Richland, Wash.
Height, 6.03. Weight, 230.
High School—Sunnyvale, Calif., Fremont.
Received bachelor of business administration degree from San Jose State University and attending
California State University at Long Beach for master's degree in business administration.
Cousin of Andy Ekern, offensive tackle with Indianapolis Colts, 1984.

Selected by Los Angeles in 5th round (128th player selected) of 1976 NFL draft.
On injured reserve with knee injury, August 20 through entire 1979 season.
On injured reserve with knee injury, November 23 through remainder of 1982 season.
Los Angeles Rams NFL, 1976 through 1978 and 1980 through 1985.
Games: 1976 (14), 1977 (14), 1978 (16), 1980 (15), 1981 (16), 1982 (3), 1983 (16), 1984 (16), 1985 (16). Total—126.
Pro statistics: Returned one kickoff for eight yards, 1977; intercepted one pass for nine yards, 1982; intercepted one pass for one yard and recovered two fumbles, 1983; recovered one fumble, 1984; intercepted two passes for 55 yards and a touchdown, 1985.
Played in NFC Championship Game following 1976, 1978 and 1985 seasons.

DONALD EUGENE ELDER
(Donnie)
Cornerback—New York Jets
Born December 13, 1962, at Chattanooga, Tenn.
Height, 5.09. Weight, 175.
High School—Chattanooga, Tenn., Brainerd.
Attended Memphis State University.

Selected by Memphis in 1985 USFL territorial draft.
Selected by New York Jets in 3rd round (67th player selected) of 1985 NFL draft.
Signed by New York Jets, July 17, 1985.
On injured reserve with hip injury, November 16 through remainder of 1985 season.
New York Jets NFL, 1985.
Games: 1985 (10).
Pro statistics: Returned three kickoffs for 42 yards and fumbled once, 1985.

HENRY ELLARD
Wide Receiver—Los Angeles Rams
Born July 21, 1961, at Fresno, Calif.
Height, 5.11. Weight, 170.
High School—Fresno, Calif., Hoover.
Attended Fresno State University.

Established NFL record for highest punt return average, career, 75 or more attempts (13.51).
Named as punt returner to THE SPORTING NEWS NFL All-Star Team, 1984 and 1985.
Selected by Oakland in 1983 USFL territorial draft.
Selected by Los Angeles Rams in 2nd round (32nd player selected) of 1983 NFL draft.
Signed by Los Angeles Rams, July 22, 1983.

		PASS RECEIVING				–PUNT RETURNS–				—KICKOFF RET.—				—TOTAL—		
Year Club	G.	P.C.	Yds.	Avg.	TD.	No.	Yds.	Avg.	TD.	No.	Yds.	Avg.	TD.	TD.	Pts.	F.
1983—L.A. Rams NFL	12	16	268	16.8	0	16	217	*13.6	*1	15	314	20.9	0	1	6	2
1984—L.A. Rams NFL	16	34	622	18.3	6	30	403	13.4	*2	2	24	12.0	0	8	48	4
1985—L.A. Rams NFL	16	54	811	15.0	5	37	501	13.5	1		None			6	36	5
Pro Totals—3 Years	44	104	1701	16.4	11	83	1121	13.5	4	17	338	19.9	0	15	90	11

Additional pro statistics: Rushed three times for seven yards, 1983; recovered two fumbles, 1983 and 1984; rushed three times for minus five yards, 1984; rushed three times for eight yards and recovered five fumbles, 1985.
Played in NFC Championship Game following 1985 season.
Played in Pro Bowl (NFL All-Star Game) following 1984 season.

GARY ELLERSON
Running Back—Green Bay Packers
Born July 17, 1963, at Albany, Ga.
Height, 5.11. Weight, 220.
High School—Albany, Ga., Monroe.
Attended University of Wisconsin.

Selected by Green Bay in 7th round (182nd player selected) of 1985 NFL draft.
Signed by Green Bay Packers, July 19, 1985.

		——RUSHING——				PASS RECEIVING				—TOTAL—		
Year Club	G.	Att.	Yds.	Avg.	TD.	P.C.	Yds.	Avg.	TD.	TD.	Pts.	F.
1985—Green Bay NFL	15	32	205	6.4	2	2	15	7.5	0	2	12	3

		KICKOFF RETURNS		
Year Club	G.	No.	Yds.	Avg.TD.
1985—Green Bay NFL	15	29	521	18.0 0

Additional pro statistics: Recovered three fumbles, 1985.

ANTHONY ROBERT ELLIOTT
(Tony)
Nose Tackle—New Orleans Saints

Born April 23, 1959, at New York, N.Y.
Height, 6.02. Weight, 300.
High School—Bridgeport, Conn., Harding.
Attended University of Wisconsin and North Texas State University.

Selected by New Orleans in 5th round (114th player selected) of 1982 NFL draft.
On reserve/non-football injury, November 11 through December 8, 1983; activated, December 9, 1983.
Released by New Orleans Saints, July 12, 1984; re-signed by Saints, October 26, 1984.
Granted roster exemption, October 26 through November 23, 1984; activated, November 24, 1984.
New Orleans NFL, 1982 through 1985.
Games: 1982 (9), 1983 (12), 1984 (4), 1985 (16). Total—41.
Pro statistics: Recovered one fumble, 1982; recovered two fumbles, 1985.

GERRY LYNN ELLIS
First name pronounced Gary.
Fullback—Green Bay Packers

Born November 12, 1957, at Columbia, Mo.
Height, 5.11. Weight, 225.
High School—Columbia, Mo., Hickman.
Attended Fort Scott Junior College and University of Missouri.

Selected by Los Angeles in 7th round (192nd player selected) of 1980 NFL draft.
Released by Los Angeles Rams, September 1, 1980; signed as free agent by Green Bay Packers, September 10, 1980.

Year Club	G.	—RUSHING— Att.	Yds.	Avg.	TD.	PASS RECEIVING P.C.	Yds.	Avg.	TD.	—TOTAL— TD.	Pts.	F.
1980—Green Bay NFL	15	126	545	4.3	5	48	496	10.3	3	8	48	7
1981—Green Bay NFL	15	196	860	4.4	4	65	499	7.7	3	7	42	5
1982—Green Bay NFL	9	62	228	3.7	1	18	140	7.8	0	1	6	6
1983—Green Bay NFL	15	141	696	4.9	4	52	603	11.6	2	6	36	7
1984—Green Bay NFL	16	123	581	4.7	4	36	312	8.7	2	6	36	2
1985—Green Bay NFL	16	104	571	5.5	5	24	206	8.6	0	5	30	2
Pro Totals—6 Years	86	752	3481	4.6	23	243	2256	9.3	10	33	198	29

Additional pro statistics: Recovered five fumbles, 1980; attempted two passes with one completion for 23 yards 1981; recovered one fumble, 1981, 1983 and 1985; attempted five passes with two completions for 31 yards and one touchdown and one interception, 1983; attempted four passes with one completion for 17 yards, 1984; returned 13 kickoffs for 247 yards and attempted one pass with no completions, 1985.

KERWIN RAY ELLIS
(Known by middle name.)
Safety—Philadelphia Eagles

Born April 27, 1959, at Canton, O.
Height, 6.01. Weight, 196.
High School—Canton, O., McKinley.
Attended Ohio State University.

Selected by Philadelphia in 12th round (331st player selected) of 1981 NFL draft.

Year Club	G.	—INTERCEPTIONS— No.	Yds.	Avg.	TD.
1981—Philadelphia NFL	16	None			
1982—Philadelphia NFL	9	None			
1983—Philadelphia NFL	16	1	18	18.0	0
1984—Philadelphia NFL	16	7	119	17.0	0
1985—Philadelphia NFL	16	4	32	8.0	0
Pro Totals—5 Years	73	12	169	14.1	0

Additional pro statistics: Recovered one fumble, 1981, 1983 and 1984; returned seven kickoffs for 119 yards, 1983; returned two kickoffs for 25 yards and fumbled once, 1984; recovered three fumbles for eight yards, 1985.

RIKI MORGAN ELLISON
(Formerly known as Riki Gray.)
Linebacker—San Francisco 49ers

Born August 15, 1960, at Christchurch, New Zealand.
Height, 6.02. Weight, 225.
High School—Tucson, Ariz., Amphitheater.
Received bachelor of arts degree in international relations, certificate of defense and strategic studies
and physical education from University of Southern California in 1983; and attending
University of Southern California for master's degree in international relations and foreign policy.

Selected by Los Angeles in 1983 USFL territorial draft.
Selected by San Francisco in 5th round (117th player selected) of 1983 NFL draft.
Signed by San Francisco 49ers, June 1, 1983.
San Francisco NFL, 1983 through 1985.
Games: 1983 (16), 1984 (16), 1985 (16). Total—48.
Pro statistics: Recovered two fumbles for seven yards, 1985.
Played in NFC Championship Game following 1983 and 1984 seasons.
Played in NFL Championship Game following 1984 season.

NEIL JAMES ELSHIRE
Defensive End—Minnesota Vikings
Born March 8, 1958, at Salem, Ore.
Height, 6.06. Weight, 260.
High School—Albany, Ore., South.
Received degree in political science from University of Oregon.

Signed as free agent by Washington Redskins, May 1, 1981.
On injured reserve with knee injury, August 17 through October 14, 1981; claimed on procedural waivers by Minnesota Vikings, October 16, 1981.
On injured reserve with knee injury, December 8 through remainder of 1982 season.
On injured reserve with knee injury, August 28 through September 27, 1984; activated, September 28, 1984.
Granted free agency, February 1, 1985; re-signed by Vikings, August 16, 1985.
Granted roster exemption, August 16 through August 30, 1985; activated, August 31, 1985.
Minnesota NFL, 1981 through 1985.
Games: 1981 (4), 1982 (5), 1983 (16), 1984 (12), 1985 (16). Total—53.
Pro statistics: Returned one kickoff for seven yards, 1982; recovered three fumbles, 1983; recovered one fumble, 1984; credited with one safety, 1985.

JOHN ALBERT ELWAY
Quarterback—Denver Broncos
Born June 28, 1960, at Port Angeles, Wash.
Height, 6.03. Weight, 210.
High School—Granada Hills, Calif.
Received bachelor of arts degree in economics from Stanford University in 1983.
Son of Jack Elway, head football coach at Stanford University.

Named as quarterback on THE SPORTING NEWS College All-America Team, 1980 and 1982.
Selected by Oakland in 1983 USFL territorial draft.
Selected by Baltimore in 1st round (1st player selected) of 1983 NFL draft.
Rights traded by Baltimore Colts to Denver Broncos for quarterback Mark Herrmann, rights to offensive lineman Chris Hinton and 1st round pick in 1984 draft, May 2, 1983.
Signed by Denver Broncos, May 2, 1983.

Year Club	G.	Att.	Cmp.	Pct.	Gain	T.P.	P.I.	Avg.	Att.	Yds.	Avg.	TD.	TD.	Pts.	F.
				PASSING						RUSHING			TOTAL		
1983—Denver NFL	11	259	123	47.5	1663	7	14	6.42	28	146	5.2	1	1	6	6
1984—Denver NFL	15	380	214	56.3	2598	18	15	6.84	56	237	4.2	1	1	6	14
1985—Denver NFL	16	*605	327	54.0	3891	22	23	6.43	51	253	5.0	0	0	0	7
Pro Totals—3 Years	42	1244	664	53.4	8152	47	52	6.55	135	636	4.7	2	2	12	27

Quarterback Rating Points: 1983 (54.9), 1984 (76.8), 1985 (70.2). Total—69.1.
Additional pro statistics: Recovered three fumbles, 1983; recovered five fumbles and fumbled 14 times for minus 10 yards, 1984; recovered two fumbles and fumbled seven times for minus 35 yards, 1985.

RECORD AS BASEBALL PLAYER

Year Club	League	Pos.	G.	AB.	R.	H.	2B.	3B.	HR.	RBI.	B.A.	PO.	A.	E.	F.A.
1982—Oneonta	NYP	OF	42	151	26	48	6	2	4	25	.318	69	8	0	1.000

Selected by Kansas City Royals' organization in 18th round of free-agent draft, June 5, 1979.
Selected by New York Yankees' organization in 2nd round of free-agent draft, June 8, 1981.

PHILLIP EARL EPPS
(Phil)
Wide Receiver—Green Bay Packers
Born November 11, 1959, at Atlanta, Tex.
Height, 5.10. Weight, 165.
High School—Atlanta, Tex.
Received bachelor of science degree in criminal justice from Texas Christian University.
Cousin of Cedric Mack, cornerback with St. Louis Cardinals.

Selected by Green Bay in 12th round (321st player selected) of 1982 NFL draft.
USFL rights traded with future draft picks by San Antonio Gunslingers to Philadelphia Stars for rights to running back Billy Campfield, March 5, 1984.

Year Club	G.	P.C.	Yds.	Avg.	TD.	No.	Yds.	Avg.	TD.	No.	Yds.	Avg.	TD.	TD.	Pts.	F.
		PASS RECEIVING				PUNT RETURNS				KICKOFF RET.				TOTAL		
1982—Green Bay NFL	9	10	226	22.6	2	20	150	7.5	0		None			2	12	1
1983—Green Bay NFL	16	18	313	17.4	0	36	324	9.0	*1		None			1	6	2
1984—Green Bay NFL	16	26	435	16.7	3	29	199	6.9	0	12	232	19.3	0	3	18	1
1985—Green Bay NFL	16	44	683	15.5	3	15	146	9.7	0	12	279	23.3	0	4	24	1
Pro Totals—4 Years	57	98	1657	16.9	8	100	819	8.2	1	24	511	21.3	0	10	60	5

Additional pro statistics: Recovered one fumble, 1984; rushed five times for 103 yards and a touchdown, 1985.

RICHARD MARK ERENBERG
(Rich)
Running Back-Kick Returner—Pittsburgh Steelers
Born April 17, 1962, at Chappaqua, N.Y.
Height, 5.10. Weight, 200.
High School—Chappaqua, N.Y., Horace Greeley.
Received degree in geography from Colgate University.

Selected by New Jersey in 1984 USFL territorial draft.
Selected by Pittsburgh in 9th round (247th player selected) of 1984 NFL draft.
Signed by Pittsburgh Steelers, June 16, 1984.

		RUSHING				PASS RECEIVING				−TOTAL−		
Year Club	G.	Att.	Yds.	Avg.	TD.	P.C.	Yds.	Avg.	TD.	TD.	Pts.	F.
1984—Pittsburgh NFL	16	115	405	3.5	2	38	358	9.4	1	3	18	3
1985—Pittsburgh NFL	14	17	67	3.9	0	33	326	9.9	3	3	18	1
Pro Totals—2 Years	30	132	472	3.6	2	71	684	9.6	4	6	36	4

		KICKOFF RETURNS			
Year Club	G.	No.	Yds.	Avg.	TD.
1984—Pittsburgh NFL	16	28	575	20.5	0
1985—Pittsburgh NFL	14	21	441	21.0	0
Pro Totals—2 Years	30	49	1016	20.7	0

Additional pro statistics: Recovered three fumbles, 1984.
Played in AFC Championship Game following 1984 season.

NORMAN JULIUS ESIASON
(Boomer)

Quarterback—Cincinnati Bengals
Born April 17, 1961, at West Islip, N.Y.
Height, 6.04. Weight, 220.
High School—Islip Terrace, N.Y., East Islip.
Attended University of Maryland.

Selected by Washington in 1984 USFL territorial draft.
Selected by Cincinnati in 2nd round (38th player selected) of 1984 NFL draft.
Signed by Cincinnati Bengals, June 19, 1984.

		PASSING							RUSHING				−TOTAL−		
Year Club	G.	Att.	Cmp.	Pct.	Gain	T.P.	P.I.	Avg.	Att.	Yds.	Avg.	TD.	TD.	Pts.	F.
1984—Cincinnati NFL	10	102	51	50.0	530	3	3	5.20	19	63	3.3	2	2	12	4
1985—Cincinnati NFL	15	431	251	58.2	3443	27	12	7.99	33	79	2.4	1	1	6	9
Pro Totals—2 Years	25	533	302	56.7	3973	30	15	7.45	52	142	2.7	3	3	18	13

Quarterback Rating Points: 1984 (62.9), 1985 (93.2). Total—87.4.
Additional pro statistics: Recovered two fumbles and fumbled four times for minus two yards, 1984; recovered four fumbles and fumbled nine times for minus five yards, 1985.

RONALD ARDEN ESSINK
(Ron)

Offensive Tackle—Seattle Seahawks
Born July 30, 1958, at Zeeland, Mich.
Height, 6.06. Weight, 275.
High School—Zeeland, Mich.
Attended Grand Valley State College.

Selected by Seattle in 10th round (265th player selected) of 1980 NFL draft.
On inactive list, September 12 and September 19, 1982.
On injured reserve with pulled groin, December 7 through remainder of 1985 season.
Seattle NFL, 1980 through 1985.
Games: 1980 (16), 1981 (16), 1982 (7), 1983 (16), 1984 (16), 1985 (12). Total—83.
Pro statistics: Caught one pass for two yards and a touchdown, 1980; recovered one fumble, 1980 and 1983.
Played in AFC Championship Game following 1983 season.'

LEON EVANS
Defensive End—Detroit Lions
Born October 12, 1961, at Silver Spring, Md.
Height, 6.05. Weight, 282.
High School—Silver Spring, Md., Montgomery Blair.
Attended University of Miami (Fla.).

Signed as free agent by Washington Redskins, July 15, 1983.
Released by Washington Redskins, August 21, 1983; signed as free agent by Philadelphia Eagles, February 15, 1984.
On injured reserve with knee injury, August 27 through entire 1984 season.
On injured reserve with foot and groin injuries, August 27 through October 7, 1985.
Released by Philadelphia Eagles, October 8, 1985; signed as free agent by Detroit Lions, October 16, 1985.
Released by Detroit Lions, October 17, 1985; re-signed by Lions, October 24, 1985.
Detroit NFL, 1985.
Games: 1985 (8).

MAJOR DONEL EVERETT
Fullback—Philadelphia Eagles
Born January 4, 1960, at New Hebron, Miss.
Height, 5.11. Weight, 215.
High School—New Hebron, Miss.
Received degree in mathematics from Mississippi College.

Selected by Birmingham in 13th round (149th player selected) of 1983 NFL draft.
Signed by Birmingham Stallions, January 21, 1983.

Released by Birmingham Stallions, February 7, 1983; signed as free agent by Philadelphia Eagles, May 12, 1983.

		——RUSHING——				PASS RECEIVING				—TOTAL—		
Year Club	G.	Att.	Yds.	Avg.	TD.	P.C.	Yds.	Avg.	TD.	TD.	Pts.	F.
1983—Philadelphia NFL	16	5	7	1.4	0	2	18	9.0	0	0	0	0
1984—Philadelphia NFL	16		None				None			0	0	0
1985—Philadelphia NFL	15	4	13	3.3	0	4	25	6.3	0	0	0	2
Pro Totals—3 Years	47	9	20	2.2	0	6	43	7.2	0	0	0	2

		KICKOFF RETURNS			
Year Club	G.	No.	Yds.	Avg.	TD.
1983—Philadelphia NFL	16	14	275	19.6	0
1984—Philadelphia NFL	16	3	40	13.3	0
1985—Philadelphia NFL	15		None		
Pro Totals—3 Years	47	17	315	18.5	0

Additional pro statistics: Recovered one fumble, 1983; recovered two fumbles, 1985.

ROBERT ALAN FADA
(Rob)
Guard—Kansas City Chiefs
Born May 7, 1961, at Fairborn, O.
Height, 6.02. Weight, 259.
High School—Fairborn, O., Parks Hills.
Received bachelor of science degree in behavioral neuoscience from University of Pittsburgh in 1983.

Selected by Arizona in 4th round (47th player selected) of 1983 USFL draft.
Selected by Chicago in 9th round (230th player selected) of 1983 NFL draft.
Signed by Chicago Bears, June 10, 1983.
On injured reserve with knee injury, September 21 through November 11, 1983; activated, November 12, 1983.
Released by Chicago Bears, August 28, 1985; signed as free agent by Kansas City Chiefs, November 5, 1985.
Chicago NFL, 1983 and 1984; Kansas City NFL, 1985.
Games: 1983 (5), 1984 (13), 1985 (5). Total—23.
Played in NFC Championship Game following 1984 season.

JAMES JOHN FAHNHORST
(Jim)
Linebacker—San Francisco 49ers
Born November 8, 1958, at St. Cloud, Minn.
Height, 6.04. Weight, 230.
High School—St. Cloud, Minn., Technical.
Attended University of Minnesota.
Brother of Keith Fahnhorst, offensive tackle with San Francisco 49ers.

Selected by Minnesota in 4th round (92nd player selected) of 1982 NFL draft.
Signed by Chicago Blitz, August 16, 1982.
USFL rights subsequently traded by Los Angeles Express to Chicago Blitz for rights to tight end Mike Sherrod and wide receiver Kris Haines and 6th, 7th and 8th round picks in 1983 draft, November 2, 1982.
Franchise transferred to Arizona, September 30, 1983.
Signed by San Francisco 49ers, June 13, 1984; Minnesota Vikings did not exercise right of first refusal, June 28, 1984.
On injured reserve with knee injury, December 5 through remainder of 1984 season.
Chicago USFL, 1983; Arizona USFL, 1984; San Francisco NFL, 1984 and 1985.
Games: 1983 (18), 1984 USFL (18), 1984 NFL (14), 1985 (15). Total USFL—36. Total NFL—29. Total Pro—65.
USFL statistics: Intercepted one pass for 19 yards, recovered three fumbles for six yards and credited with one sack for nine yards, 1983; intercepted one pass for no yards, credited with one sack for seven yards and recovered one fumble, 1984.
NFL statistics: Intercepted two passes for nine yards, 1984.
Played in USFL Championship Game following 1984 season.

KEITH VICTOR FAHNHORST
Offensive Tackle—San Francisco 49ers
Born February 6, 1952, at St. Cloud, Minn.
Height, 6.06. Weight, 273.
High School—St. Cloud, Minn., Tech.
Received degree in psychology from University of Minnesota.
Brother of Jim Fahnhorst, linebacker with San Francisco 49ers.

Selected by San Francisco in 2nd round (35th player selected) of 1974 NFL draft.
San Francisco NFL, 1974 through 1985.
Games: 1974 (14), 1975 (14), 1976 (13), 1977 (14), 1978 (15), 1979 (16), 1980 (16), 1981 (16), 1982 (9), 1983 (16), 1984 (15), 1985 (16). Total—174.
Pro statistics: Recovered two fumbles, 1974 and 1981; caught one pass for one yard and returned one kickoff for 13 yards, 1975; recovered one fumble, 1975, 1977, 1978 and 1983.
Played in NFC Championship Game following 1981, 1983 and 1984 seasons.
Played in NFL Championship Game following 1981 and 1984 seasons.
Played in Pro Bowl (NFL All-Star Game) following 1984 season.

PAUL JAY FAIRCHILD
Guard—New England Patriots
Born September 14, 1961, at Carroll, Ia.
Height, 6.04. Weight, 270.
High School—Glidden, Ia., Ralston.
Attended Ellsworth Junior College and received bachelor of
general science degree in liberal arts from University of Kansas in 1984.

Selected by Houston in 6th round (124th player selected) of 1984 USFL draft.
Selected by New England in 5th round (124th player selected) of 1984 NFL draft.
Signed by New England Patriots, June 18, 1984.
New England NFL, 1984 and 1985.
Games: 1984 (7), 1985 (16). Total—23.
Played in AFC Championship Game following 1985 season.
Played in NFL Championship Game following 1985 season.

KEN MARK FANTETTI
Linebacker—Cleveland Browns
Born April 7, 1957, at Toledo, Ore.
Height, 6.02. Weight, 232.
High School—Gresham, Ore.
Received degree in communications from University of Wyoming.

Selected by Detroit in 2nd round (37th player selected) of 1979 NFL draft.
Placed on did not report list, August 20 through August 27, 1984.
Reported and granted roster exemption, August 28 through September 7, 1984; activated, September 8, 1984.
On injured reserve with broken thumb, September 11 through November 7, 1985; activated, November 8, 1985.
Granted free agency with no qualifying offer, February 1, 1986; signed by Cleveland Browns, May 4, 1986.
Detroit NFL, 1979 through 1985.
Games: 1979 (16), 1980 (16), 1981 (16), 1982 (9), 1983 (16), 1984 (14), 1985 (8). Total—95.
Pro statistics: Returned two kickoffs for 18 yards, 1979; intercepted one pass for 10 yards, 1980; intercepted two passes for 18 yards, 1981; recovered one fumble, 1981 and 1983; intercepted two passes for no yards, 1983; intercepted one pass for one yard, 1984.

JOHN HOWARD FARLEY
Running Back—Green Bay Packers
Born August 11, 1961, at Stockton, Calif.
Height, 5.10. Weight, 202.
High School—Stockton, Calif., A.A. Stagg.
Attended California State University at Sacramento.

Selected by New Orleans in 7th round (139th player selected) of 1984 USFL draft.
Selected by Cincinnati in 4th round (92nd player selected) of 1984 NFL draft.
Signed by Cincinnati Bengals, June 25, 1984.
On injured reserve with knee injury, August 27 through October 22, 1985.
Released by Cincinnati Bengals, October 23, 1985; signed as free agent by Green Bay Packers, March 10, 1986.

Year Club	G.	Att.	Yds.	Avg.	TD.	P.C.	Yds.	Avg.	TD.	TD.	Pts.	F.
		RUSHING				PASS RECEIVING				—TOTAL—		
1984—Cincinnati NFL	13	7	11	1.6	0	2	11	5.5	0	0	0	1

Year Club	G.	No.	Yds.	Avg.TD.
	KICKOFF RETURNS			
1984—Cincinnati NFL	13	6	93	15.5 0

Additional pro statistics: Recovered one fumble, 1984.

GEORGE FARMER III
Wide Receiver—Miami Dolphins
Born December 5, 1958, at Los Angeles, Calif.
Height, 5.10. Weight, 175.
High School—Gardena, Calif.
Attended Santa Monica City College and Southern University.

Selected by Los Angeles in 9th round (248th player selected) of 1980 NFL draft.
On injured reserve, August 18 through entire 1980 season.
On injured reserve with knee injury, August 18 through entire 1981 season.
Released by Los Angeles Rams, August 27, 1985; signed as free agent by Miami Dolphins for 1986, November 1, 1985.

Year Club	G.	P.C.	Yds.	Avg.	TD.
	PASS RECEIVING				
1982—L.A. Rams NFL	8	17	344	20.2	2
1983—L.A. Rams NFL	16	40	556	13.9	5
1984—L.A. Rams NFL	14	7	75	10.7	0
Pro Totals—3 Years	38	64	975	15.2	7

Additional pro statistics: Recovered one fumble, 1982; rushed once for minus nine yards, 1983.

—DID YOU KNOW—
That in an October 13 game at New England, Buffalo's Greg Bell was the only Bills' player to attempt a rush? Bell carried 23 times for 72 yards.

SEAN WARD FARRELL
Guard—Tampa Bay Buccaneers
Born May 25, 1960, at Southampton, N.Y.
Height, 6.03. Weight, 260.
High School—Westhampton Beach, N.Y.
Received bachelor of arts degree in general arts and sciences from Penn State University in 1982.

Named to THE SPORTING NEWS NFL All-Star Team, 1984.
Named as guard on THE SPORTING NEWS College All-America Team, 1981.
Selected by Tampa Bay in 1st round (17th player selected) of 1982 NFL draft.
Tampa Bay NFL, 1982 through 1985.
Games: 1982 (9), 1983 (10), 1984 (15), 1985 (14). Total—48.
Pro statistics: Recovered one fumble, 1983; recovered two fumbles, 1984.

PAUL V. FARREN
Offensive Tackle—Cleveland Browns
Born December 24, 1960, at Weymouth, Mass.
Height, 6.05. Weight, 270.
High School—Cohasset, Mass.
Received bachelor of arts degree in marketing finance from Boston University in 1983.

Selected by Boston in 1983 USFL territorial draft.
Selected by Cleveland in 12th round (316th player selected) of 1983 NFL draft.
Signed by Cleveland Browns, May 31, 1983.
On injured reserve with knee injury, December 30 through remainder of 1985 season playoffs.
Cleveland NFL, 1983 through 1985.
Games: 1983 (16), 1984 (15), 1985 (13). Total—44.
Pro statistics: Recovered one fumble, 1984.

CHRISTOPHER ALAN FAULKNER
(Chris)
Tight End—San Diego Chargers
Born April 13, 1960, at Tipton, Ind.
Height, 6.04. Weight, 250.
High School—Arcadia, Ind., Hamilton Heights.
Attended University of Florida.

Selected by Tampa Bay in 1983 USFL territorial draft.
Selected by Dallas in 4th round (108th player selected) of 1983 NFL draft.
Signed by Dallas Cowboys, July 10, 1983.
Released by Dallas Cowboys, August 22, 1983; signed as free agent by Los Angeles Rams, January 31, 1984.
On non-football injury list, November 26 through remainder of 1984 season.
Released by Los Angeles Rams, August 27, 1985; signed as free agent by San Diego Chargers, August 30, 1985.
On injured reserve with knee injury, November 6 through remainder of 1985 season.
Los Angeles Rams NFL, 1984; San Diego NFL, 1985.
Games: 1984 (8), 1985 (9). Total—17.
Pro statistics: Caught one pass for six yards, 1984; caught one pass for 12 yards and recovered one fumble, 1985.

RON EDWARD FAUROT
Name pronounced Fa-ROW.
Defensive End—San Diego Chargers
Born January 27, 1962, at Wichita, Kan.
Height, 6.07. Weight, 262.
High School—Hurst, Tex., L.D. Bell.
Received bachelor of science degree in personnel management
from University of Arkansas in 1984.

Selected by Oklahoma in 1st round (2nd player selected) of 1984 USFL draft.
Selected by New York Jets in 1st round (15th player selected) of 1984 NFL draft.
Signed by New York Jets, May 31, 1984.
Released by New York Jets, October 10, 1985; signed as free agent by San Diego Chargers, November 6, 1985.
On injured reserve with knee injury, November 7 through remainder of 1985 season.
New York Jets NFL, 1984 and 1985.
Games: 1984 (15), 1985 (5). Total—20.
Pro statistics: Recovered one fumble, 1984.

GRANT EARL FEASEL
Center
Born June 28, 1960, at Barstow, Calif.
Height, 6.08. Weight, 278.
High School—Barstow, Calif.
Received bachelor of science degree in biology from Abilene Christian University in 1983.
Brother of Greg Feasel, offensive tackle with Jacksonville Bulls.

Selected by Baltimore in 6th round (161st player selected) of 1983 NFL draft.
Franchise transferred to Indianapolis, March 31, 1984.
Released by Indianapolis Colts, October 10, 1984; signed as free agent by Minnesota Vikings, October 17, 1984.
On injured reserve with knee injury, August 29 through entire 1985 season.
Granted free agency with option not exercised, February 1, 1986.
Baltimore NFL, 1983; Indianapolis (6)-Minnesota (9) NFL, 1984.
Games: 1983 (11), 1984 (15). Total—26.

GERRY FEEHERY

Name pronounced FEER-ee.

Center—Philadelphia Eagles

Born March 9, 1960, at Philadelphia, Pa.
Height, 6.02. Weight, 268.
High School—Springfield, Pa., Cardinal O'Hara.
Received bachelor of science degree in marketing from Syracuse University.

Selected by New Jersey in 1983 USFL territorial draft.
Signed as free agent by Philadelphia Eagles, May 4, 1983.
On injured reserve with knee injury, November 4 through remainder of 1983 season.
Philadelphia NFL, 1983 through 1985.
Games: 1983 (2), 1984 (6), 1985 (15). Total—23.

CHARLES MARK FELLOWS

(Known by middle name.)

Linebacker—San Diego Chargers

Born February 26, 1963, at Billings, Mont.
Height, 6.01. Weight, 222.
High School—Choteau, Mont.
Attended Montana State University.

Selected by San Diego in 7th round (196th player selected) of 1985 NFL draft.
Signed by San Diego Chargers, July 15, 1985.
On injured reserve with fractured hip, September 18 through remainder of 1985 season.
San Diego NFL, 1985.
Games: 1985 (2).

RONALD LEE FELLOWS

(Ron)

Cornerback—Dallas Cowboys

Born November 7, 1958, at South Bend, Ind.
Height, 6.00. Weight, 180.
High School—South Bend, Ind., Washington.
Attended Butler (Kan.) County Community College and University of Missouri.

Selected by Dallas in 7th round (173rd player selected) of 1981 NFL draft.

		-PUNT RETURNS-				—KICKOFF RET.—				—TOTAL—		
Year Club	G.	No.	Yds.	Avg.	TD.	No.	Yds.	Avg.	TD.	TD.	Pts.	F.
1981—Dallas NFL	16	11	44	4.0	0	8	170	21.3	0	0	0	0
1982—Dallas NFL	9	25	189	7.6	0	16	359	22.4	0	0	0	3
1983—Dallas NFL	16	10	75	7.5	0	43	855	19.9	0	2	12	4
1984—Dallas NFL	16		None			6	94	15.7	0	0	0	3
1985—Dallas NFL	13		None				None			0	0	0
Pro Totals—5 Years	70	46	308	6.7	0	73	1478	20.2	0	2	12	10

		—INTERCEPTIONS—			
Year Club	G.	No.	Yds.	Avg.	TD.
1981—Dallas NFL	16		None		
1982—Dallas NFL	9		None		
1983—Dallas NFL	16	5	139	27.8	1
1984—Dallas NFL	16	3	3	1.0	0
1985—Dallas NFL	13	4	52	13.0	0
Pro Totals—5 Years	70	12	194	16.2	1

Additional pro statistics: Recovered one fumble, 1982; returned blocked field goal attempt 62 yards for a touchdown and recovered three fumbles, 1983; recovered one fumble for 12 yards, 1984.
Played in NFC Championship Game following 1981 and 1982 seasons.

JOHN GARY FENCIK

(Known by middle name.)

Safety—Chicago Bears

Born June 11, 1954, at Chicago, Ill.
Height, 6.01. Weight 197.
High School—Barrington, Ill.
Received bachelor of arts degree in history from Yale University; attending
Northwestern University for master's degree in management.

Named to THE SPORTING NEWS NFC All-Star Team, 1979.
Named to THE SPORTING NEWS NFL All-Star Team, 1981.
Selected by Miami in 10th round (281st player selected) of 1976 NFL draft.
Released by Miami Dolphins, September 6, 1976; signed as free agent by Chicago Bears, September 15, 1976.

		—INTERCEPTIONS—						—INTERCEPTIONS—			
Year Club	G.	No.	Yds.	Avg.	TD.	Year Club	G.	No.	Yds.	Avg.	TD.
1976—Chicago NFL	13		None			1982—Chicago NFL	9	2	2	1.0	0
1977—Chicago NFL	14	4	33	8.3	0	1983—Chicago NFL	7	2	34	17.0	0
1978—Chicago NFL	16	4	77	19.3	0	1984—Chicago NFL	16	5	102	20.4	0
1979—Chicago NFL	14	6	31	5.2	0	1985—Chicago NFL	16	5	43	8.6	0
1980—Chicago NFL	15	1	8	8.0	0	Pro Totals—10 Years	136	35	451	12.9	1
1981—Chicago NFL	16	6	121	20.2	1						

Additional pro statistics: Recovered one fumble, 1976, 1981 and 1983 through 1985; recovered two fumbles for 13 yards, 1978; recovered two fumbles, 1979; recovered three fumbles for 52 yards, 1980; fumbled once, 1984.

Played in NFC Championship Game following 1984 and 1985 seasons.

Played in NFL Championship Game following 1985 season.

Played in Pro Bowl (NFL All-Star Game) following 1980 and 1981 seasons.

JOE CARLTON FERGUSON JR.
Quarterback—Detroit Lions
Born April 23, 1950, at Alvin, Tex.
Height, 6.01. Weight, 195.
High School—Shreveport, La., Woodlawn.
Received bachelor of science degree in physical education from
University of Arkansas in 1973.

Established NFL record for fewest passes intercepted among qualifiers, season (1), 1976.

Tied NFL records for most fumbles and most own fumbles recovered, game (4), September 18, 1977, against Miami Dolphins.

Selected by Buffalo in 3rd round (57th player selected) of 1973 NFL draft.

Traded by Buffalo Bills to Detroit Lions for 7th round pick in 1986 draft, April 30, 1985.

Year Club	G.	PASSING Att.	Cmp.	Pct.	Gain	T.P.	P.I.	Avg.	RUSHING Att.	Yds.	Avg.	TD.	TOTAL TD.	Pts.	F.
1973—Buffalo NFL	14	164	73	44.5	939	4	10	5.73	48	147	3.1	2	2	12	7
1974—Buffalo NFL	14	232	119	51.3	1588	12	12	6.84	54	111	2.1	2	2	12	*14
1975—Buffalo NFL	14	321	169	52.6	2426	*25	17	7.56	23	82	3.6	1	1	6	4
1976—Buffalo NFL	7	151	74	49.0	1086	9	1	7.19	18	81	4.5	0	0	0	2
1977—Buffalo NFL	14	*457	221	48.4	*2803	12	*24	6.13	41	279	6.8	2	2	12	12
1978—Buffalo NFL	16	330	175	53.0	2136	16	15	6.47	27	76	2.8	0	0	0	5
1979—Buffalo NFL	16	458	238	52.0	3572	14	15	7.80	22	68	3.1	1	1	6	5
1980—Buffalo NFL	16	439	251	57.2	2805	20	18	6.39	31	65	2.1	0	0	0	9
1981—Buffalo NFL	16	498	252	50.6	3652	24	20	7.33	20	29	1.5	1	1	6	2
1982—Buffalo NFL	9	264	144	54.5	1597	7	*16	6.05	16	46	2.9	1	2	12	5
1983—Buffalo NFL	16	508	281	55.3	2995	26	25	5.90	20	88	4.4	0	0	0	3
1984—Buffalo NFL	12	344	191	55.5	1991	12	17	5.79	19	102	5.4	0	0	0	8
1985—Detroit NFL	8	54	31	57.4	364	2	3	6.74	4	12	3.0	1	1	6	1
Pro Totals—13 Years	172	4220	2219	52.6	27954	183	193	6.62	343	1186	3.5	11	12	72	77

Quarterback Rating Points: 1973 (45.6), 1974 (69.0), 1975 (81.3), 1976 (90.0), 1977 (54.6), 1978 (70.5), 1979 (74.5), 1980 (74.6), 1981 (74.1), 1982 (56.3), 1983 (69.3), 1984 (63.5), 1985 (67.2). Total—68.7.

Additional pro statistics: Recovered four fumbles, fumbled seven times for minus three yards and caught one pass for minus three yards, 1973; recovered five fumbles and fumbled 14 times for minus 13 yards, 1974; recovered three fumbles, 1975, 1978, 1979 and 1983; fumbled four times for minus one yard, 1975; recovered seven fumbles and fumbled 12 times for minus seven yards, 1977; fumbled five times for minus three yards and caught one pass for minus six yards, 1978; recovered one fumble and fumbled nine times for minus 12 yards, 1980; recovered two fumbles, one for a touchdown and fumbled five times for minus 10 yards, 1982; recovered two fumbles and fumbled eight times for minus 26 yards, 1984.

KEITH TYRONE FERGUSON
Defensive End—Detroit Lions
Born April 3, 1959, at Miami, Fla.
Height, 6.05. Weight, 260.
High School—Miami, Fla., Edison.
Attended Ohio State University.

Selected by San Diego in 5th round (131st player selected) of 1981 NFL draft.

Released by San Diego Chargers, November 20, 1985; awarded on waivers to Detroit Lions, November 21, 1985.

San Diego NFL, 1981 through 1984; San Diego (10)-Detroit (5) NFL, 1985.

Games: 1981 (16), 1982 (9), 1983 (16), 1984 (16), 1985 (15). Total—72.

Pro statistics: Recovered one fumble, 1982, 1984 and 1985; recovered two fumbles, 1983.

Played in AFC Championship Game following 1981 season.

VINCE FERRAGAMO
Quarterback—Green Bay Packers
Born April 24, 1954, at Torrance, Calif.
Height, 6.03. Weight, 217.
High School—Wilmington, Calif., Banning.
Attended University of California, received bachelor of science degree in pre-med from
University of Nebraska in 1977 and attends Creighton University medical school.

Selected by Los Angeles in 4th round (91st player selected) of 1977 NFL draft.

Granted free agency, February 2, 1981; signed by Montreal Alouettes, April 27, 1981.

On reserve list, October 15 through remainder of 1981 season.

Released by Montreal Concordes, June 5, 1982; re-signed by Los Angeles Rams, July 7, 1982.

Traded with 3rd round pick in 1986 draft by Los Angeles Rams to Buffalo Bills for tight end Tony Hunter, July 18, 1985.

Released by Buffalo Bills, December 3, 1985; signed as free agent by Green Bay Packers, December 11, 1985.

Active for 2 games with Green Bay Packers in 1985; did not play.

Year Club	G.	PASSING Att.	Cmp.	Pct.	Gain	T.P.	P.I.	Avg.	RUSHING Att.	Yds.	Avg.	TD.	TOTAL TD.	Pts.	F.
1977—L.A. Rams NFL	3	15	9	60.0	83	2	0	5.53	1	0	0.0	0	0	0	0
1978—L.A. Rams NFL	9	20	7	35.0	114	0	2	5.70	2	10	5.0	0	0	0	0
1979—L.A. Rams NFL	8	110	53	48.2	778	5	10	7.07	3	—2	—0.7	0	0	0	2

Year Club	G.	Att.	Cmp.	Pct.	Gain	T.P.	P.I.	Avg.	Att.	Yds.	Avg.	TD.	TD.	Pts.	F.
					PASSING					RUSHING				TOTAL	
1980—L.A. Rams NFL	16	404	240	59.4	3199	30	19	7.92	15	34	2.3	1	1	6	4
1981—Montreal CFL	13	342	175	51.2	2182	7	*25	6.38	15	57	3.8	0	0	0	5
1982—L.A. Rams NFL	7	209	118	56.5	1609	9	9	7.70	4	3	0.8	1	1	6	1
1983—L.A. Rams NFL	16	464	274	59.1	3276	22	23	7.06	22	17	0.8	0	0	0	8
1984—L.A. Rams NFL	3	66	29	43.9	317	2	8	4.80	4	0	0.0	0	0	0	0
1985—Buff. (10)-G.B. (0) NFL	10	287	149	51.9	1677	5	17	5.84	8	15	1.9	1	1	6	1
CFL Total—1 Year	13	342	175	51.2	2182	7	25	6.38	15	57	3.8	0	0	0	5
NFL Totals—8 Years	72	1575	879	55.8	11053	75	88	7.02	59	77	1.3	3	3	18	16
Pro Totals—9 Years	85	1917	1054	55.0	13235	82	113	6.90	74	134	1.8	3	3	18	21

NFL Quarterback Rating Points: 1977 (114.7), 1978 (15.4), 1979 (48.8), 1980 (89.7), 1982 (77.7), 1983 (75.9), 1984 (29.2), 1985 (50.8). Total—70.5.
Additional NFL statistics: Recovered one fumble, 1979; recovered two fumbles, 1980 and 1983.
Additional CFL statistics: Recovered one fumble, 1981.
Played in NFC Championship Game following 1978 and 1979 seasons.
Played in NFL Championship Game following 1979 season.

RONALD LEE FERRARI
(Ron)
Linebacker—San Francisco 49ers
Born July 30, 1959, at Springfield, Ill.
Height, 6.00. Weight, 212.
High School—Moweaqua, Ill.
Attended Lake Land College and received bachelor of science degree in agricultural economics
from University of Illinois in 1982.

Selected by San Francisco in 7th round (195th player selected) of 1982 NFL draft.
On injured reserve with knee injury, November 12 through remainder of 1984 season.
San Francisco NFL, 1982 through 1985.
Games: 1982 (9), 1983 (16), 1984 (11), 1985 (16). Total—52.
Pro statistics: Returned two kickoffs for 19 yards, 1982.
Played in NFC Championship Game following 1983 season.

EARL THOMAS FERRELL
Running Back—St. Louis Cardinals
Born March 27, 1958, at Halifax, Va.
Height, 6.00. Weight, 215.
High School—South Boston, Va., Halifax County.
Received degree in physical education from East Tennessee State University.

Selected by St. Louis in 5th round (125th player selected) of 1982 NFL draft.
On non-football injury list with drug problems, November 21 through remainder of 1985 season.

Year Club	G.	Att.	Yds.	Avg.	TD.	P.C.	Yds.	Avg.	TD.	TD.	Pts.	F.
		RUSHING				PASS RECEIVING				TOTAL		
1982—St. Louis NFL	9		None				None			0	0	0
1983—St. Louis NFL	16	7	53	7.6	1		None			1	6	2
1984—St. Louis NFL	16	41	190	4.6	1	26	218	8.4	1	2	12	3
1985—St. Louis NFL	11	46	208	4.5	2	25	277	11.1	2	4	24	2
Pro Totals—4 Years	52	94	451	4.8	4	51	495	9.7	3	7	42	7

Year Club	G.	No.	Yds.	Avg.	TD.
		KICKOFF RETURNS			
1982—St. Louis NFL	9	4	88	22.0	0
1983—St. Louis NFL	16	13	257	19.8	0
1984—St. Louis NFL	16	1	0	0.0	0
1985—St. Louis NFL	11		None		
Pro Totals—4 Years	52	18	345	19.2	0

Additional pro statistics: Returned one punt for six yards, 1982; returned one punt for 17 yards, 1983; recovered one fumble, 1985.

DON SINCLAIR FIELDER
Defensive End—Tampa Bay Buccaneers
Born October 20, 1959, at Las Cruces, N.M.
Height, 6.03. Weight, 240.
High School—Garden Grove, Calif., Rancho Alamitos.
Attended Golden West Junior College and University of Kentucky.

Signed as free agent by Pittsburgh Steelers, May 5, 1982.
Released by Pittsburgh Steelers, August 10, 1982; signed by Philadelphia Stars, October 7, 1982.
Franchise transferred to Baltimore, November 1, 1984.
On developmental squad, May 31 through June 5, 1985; activated, June 6, 1985.
Granted free agency, August 1, 1985; signed by Tampa Bay Buccaneers, August 7, 1985.
On injured reserve with knee injury, November 27 through remainder of 1985 season.
On developmental squad for 1 game with Baltimore Stars in 1985.
Philadelphia USFL, 1983 and 1984; Baltimore USFL, 1985; Tampa Bay NFL, 1985.
Games: 1983 (18), 1984 (18), 1985 USFL (17), 1985 NFL (11). Total USFL—53. Total Pro—64.
USFL statistics: Credited with 8½ sacks for 45½ yards and recovered one fumble, 1983; credited with six sacks for 51 yards, 1984; credited with nine sacks for 71½ yards, 1985.
Played in USFL Championship Game following 1983 through 1985 seasons.

JOSEPH CHARLES FIELDS JR.
(Joe)
Center—New York Jets

Born November 14, 1953, at Woodbury, N. J.
Height, 6.02. Weight, 253.
High School—Gloucester City, N. J., Catholic.
Attended University of Rutgers at Camden and received bachelor of science degree
in accounting from Widener College.

Selected by New York Jets in 14th round (349th player selected) of 1975 NFL draft.
New York Jets NFL, 1975 through 1985.
Games: 1975 (14), 1976 (14), 1977 (14), 1978 (16), 1979 (15), 1980 (13), 1981 (16), 1982 (9), 1983 (12), 1984 (16), 1985 (15). Total—154.
Pro statistics: Fumbled once for minus 21 yards and recovered one fumble for four yards, 1975; fumbled once for minus 14 yards, 1976; recovered one fumble, 1977, 1980, 1984 and 1985; fumbled once for minus 15 yards, 1981.
Played in AFC Championship Game following 1982 season.
Played in Pro Bowl (NFL All-Star Game) following 1981 and 1982 seasons.

DAN CLEMENT FIKE JR.
Guard-Offensive Tackle—Cleveland Browns

Born June 16, 1961, at Mobile, Ala.
Height, 6.07. Weight, 280.
High School—Pensacola, Fla., Pine Forest.
Attended University of Florida.

Selected by Tampa Bay in 1984 USFL territorial draft.
Selected by New York Jets in 10th round (274th player selected) of 1983 NFL draft.
Signed by New York Jets, June 10, 1983.
Released by New York Jets, August 29, 1983; signed by Tampa Bay Bandits, November 13, 1983.
Signed by Cleveland Browns, January 20, 1985, to take affect after being granted free agency following 1985 USFL season.
Tampa Bay USFL, 1984 and 1985; Cleveland NFL, 1985.
Games: 1984 (18), 1985 USFL (18), 1985 NFL (13). Total USFL—36. Total Pro—49.
USFL statistics: Recovered one fumble, 1985.

DAVID M. FINZER
Punter—Seattle Seahawks

Born February 3, 1959, at Chicago, Ill.
Height, 6.01. Weight, 195.
High School—Wilmette, Ill., Loyola Academy.
Attended University of Illinois and DePauw University.

Signed as free agent by Dallas Cowboys, April 30, 1982.
Released by Dallas Cowboys, August 31, 1982; signed as free agent by Chicago Bears, April 7, 1983.
Released by Chicago Bears, August 16, 1983; signed by Chicago Blitz, November 7, 1983.
Released by Chicago Blitz, January 30, 1984; signed as free agent by San Diego Chargers, May 20, 1984.
Traded by San Diego Chargers to Chicago Bears for 12th round pick in 1985 draft, August 15, 1984.
Released by Chicago Bears, August 27, 1985; signed as free agent by Seattle Seahawks, October 1, 1985.

| | | | ——PUNTING—— | | |
Year	Club	G.	No.	Avg.	Blk.
1984—Chicago NFL		16	83	40.1	2
1985—Seattle NFL		12	68	40.7	0
Pro Totals—2 Years		28	151	40.4	2

Additional pro statistics: Rushed twice for no yards, 1984; rushed once for minus two yards and attempted one pass with one interception, 1985.
Played in NFC Championship Game following 1984 season.

JEFFREY MICHAEL FISHER
(Jeff)
Safety—Chicago Bears

Born February 25, 1958, at Culver City, Calif.
Height, 5.11. Weight, 188.
High School—Woodland Hills, Calif., Taft.
Received bachelor of science degree in public administration
from University of Southern California in 1981.

Selected by Chicago in 7th round (177th player selected) of 1981 NFL draft.
On injured reserve with broken leg, October 24 through remainder of 1983 season.
On injured reserve with ankle injury, August 19 through entire 1985 season.

| | | | INTERCEPTIONS | | | | -PUNT RETURNS- | | | | —KICKOFF RET.— | | | | —TOTAL— | | |
Year	Club	G.	No.	Yds.	Avg.	TD.	No.	Yds.	Avg.	TD.	No.	Yds.	Avg.	TD.	TD.	Pts.	F.
1981—Chicago NFL		16	2	3	1.5	0	43	509	11.8	1	7	102	14.6	0	1	6	3
1982—Chicago NFL		9	3	19	6.3	0	7	53	7.6	0	7	102	14.6	0	0	0	2
1983—Chicago NFL		8		None			13	71	5.5	0		None			0	0	0
1984—Chicago NFL		16		None			*57	492	8.6	0		None			0	0	4
Pro Totals—4 Years		49	5	22	4.4	0	120	1125	9.4	1	14	204	14.6	0	1	6	5

Additional pro statistics: Recovered one fumble, 1981 and 1984.
Played in NFC Championship Game following 1984 season.

SIMON RAYNARD FLETCHER
Defensive End—Denver Broncos
Born February 18, 1962, at Bay City, Tex.
Height, 6.05. Weight, 240.
High School—Bay City, Tex.
Attended University of Houston.

Selected by Houston in 1985 USFL territorial draft.
Selected by Denver in 2nd round (54th player selected) of 1985 NFL draft.
Signed by Denver Broncos, July 16, 1985.
Denver NFL, 1985.
Games: 1985 (16).

TOM FLICK
Quarterback—San Diego Chargers
Born August 30, 1958, at Patuxent River, Md.
Height, 6.03. Weight, 190.
High School—Belleville, Wash.
Received bachelor of arts degree in communications from University of Washington in 1981.

Selected by Washington in 4th round (90th player selected) of 1981 NFL draft.
Traded by Washington Redskins to New England Patriots for quarterback Tom Owen, August 25, 1982.
On inactive list, September 12 and September 19, 1982.
On injured reserve with elbow injury, August 16 through September 28, 1983.
Released by New England Patriots, September 29, 1983; signed as free agent by Cleveland Browns, January 3, 1984.
Released by Cleveland Browns, July 28, 1985; signed as free agent by San Diego Chargers, May 15, 1986.

Year	Club	G.	Att.	Cmp.	Pct.	Gain	T.P.	P.I.	Avg.	Att.	Yds.	Avg.	TD.	TD.	Pts.	F.
					PASSING							RUSHING			TOTAL	
1981—Washington NFL		6	27	13	48.1	143	0	2	5.30		None			0	0	2
1982—New England NFL		3	5	0	0.0	0	0	0	0.00		None			0	0	0
1984—Cleveland NFL		1	1	1	100.0	2	0	0	2.00		None			0	0	1
Pro Totals—3 Years		10	33	14	42.4	145	0	2	4.39	0	0	0.0	0	0	0	3

Quarterback Rating Points: 1981 (33.4), 1982 (0.0), 1984 (79.2). Total—30.3.
Additional pro statistics: Recovered one fumble, 1981.

LARRY DARNELL FLOWERS
Safety—New York Jets
Born April 19, 1958, at Temple, Tex.
Height, 6.01. Weight, 195.
High School—Temple, Tex.
Attended Texas Tech University.

Selected by Tampa Bay in 4th round (102nd player selected) of 1980 NFL draft.
Released by Tampa Bay Buccaneers, August 6, 1980; claimed on waivers by New York Giants, August 8, 1980.
On injured reserve with concussion, August 26 through entire 1980 season.
Released by New York Giants, September 8, 1982; re-signed by Giants, November 23, 1982.
Released by New York Giants, September 2, 1985; re-signed by Giants, September 4, 1985.
Released by New York Giants, November 9, 1985; signed as free agent by New York Jets, November 14, 1985.
New York Giants NFL, 1981 through 1984; New York Giants (9)-New York Jets (6) NFL, 1985.
Games: 1981 (16), 1982 (6), 1983 (14), 1984 (16), 1985 (15). Total—67.
Pro statistics: Intercepted one pass for nine yards, 1981; recovered one fumble, 1981, 1983 and 1985; intercepted one pass for 19 yards, 1983.

THOMAS JEFFERY FLYNN
(Tom)
Safety—Green Bay Packers
Born March 24, 1962, at Verona, Pa.
Height, 6.00. Weight, 195.
High School—Pittsburgh, Pa., Penn Hills.
Attended University of Pittsburgh.

Selected by Pittsburgh in 1984 USFL territorial draft.
Selected by Green Bay in 5th round (126th player selected) of 1984 NFL draft.
Signed by Green Bay Packers, July 1, 1984.

Year	Club	G.	No.	Yds.	Avg.	TD.	No.	Yds.	Avg.	TD.	TD.	Pts.	F.
			INTERCEPTIONS				PUNT RETURNS				TOTAL		
1984—Green Bay NFL		16	9	106	11.8	0	15	128	8.5	0	0	0	1
1985—Green Bay NFL		16	1	7	7.0	0	7	41	5.9	0	0	0	0
Pro Total—2 Years		32	10	113	11.3	0	22	169	7.7	0	0	0	0

Additional pro statistics: Recovered three fumbles for three yards, 1984; returned one kickoff for 20 yards and recovered one fumble, 1985.

STEPHEN JAMES FOLEY
(Steve)
Safety—Denver Broncos
Born November 11, 1953, at New Orleans, La.
Height, 6.03. Weight, 190.
High School—New Orleans, La., Jesuit.
Received degree in business administration from Tulane University.

Selected by Denver in 8th round (199th player selected) of 1975 NFL draft.
Signed as free agent by Jacksonville Express (WFL), 1975.
Signed by Denver Broncos after World Football League folded, May 1976.
On injured reserve with fractured arm, September 14 through remainder of 1982 season.
On injured reserve with separated shoulder, October 9 through November 10, 1985; activated, November 11, 1985.

Year Club	—INTERCEPTIONS—					Year Club	—INTERCEPTIONS—				
	G.	No.	Yds.	Avg.	TD.		G.	No.	Yds.	Avg.	TD.
1975—Jacksonville WFL	10	1	30	30.0	0	1982—Denver NFL	1		None		
1976—Denver NFL	14	4	95	23.8	0	1983—Denver NFL	14	5	28	5.6	0
1977—Denver NFL	13	3	22	7.3	0	1984—Denver NFL	16	6	97	16.2	1
1978—Denver NFL	16	6	84	14.0	0	1985—Denver NFL	12	3	47	15.7	0
1979—Denver NFL	16	6	14	2.3	0						
1980—Denver NFL	16	4	115	*28.8	0	WFL Totals—1 Year	10	1	30	30.0	0
1981—Denver NFL	16	5	81	16.2	0	NFL Totals—10 Years	134	42	583	13.9	1
						Pro Totals—11 Years	144	43	613	14.3	1

Additional WFL statistics: Returned one punt for two yards, 1975.
Additional NFL statistics: Fumbled once, 1976, 1979 and 1983; rushed once for 14 yards, 1978; recovered one fumble, 1981 and 1983; recovered two fumbles for 22 yards and a touchdown, 1984.
Played in AFC Championship Game following 1977 season.
Played in NFL Championship Game following 1977 season.

HERMAN FONTENOT
Running Back-Kick Returner—Cleveland Browns
Born September 12, 1963, at St. Elizabeth, Tex.
Height, 6.00. Weight, 206.
High School—Beaumont, Tex., Charlton-Pollard.
Attended Louisiana State University.

Selected by New Jersey in 9th round (127th player selected) of 1985 USFL draft.
Signed as free agent by Cleveland Browns, May 6, 1985.
On injured reserve with broken bone in back, August 27 through October 24, 1985; activated, October 25, 1985.

Year Club	PASS RECEIVING				—KICKOFF RET.—				—TOTAL—		
	G.	P.C.	Yds.	Avg.	TD.	No.	Yds.	Avg.	TD.	TD.	Pts.	F.
1985—Cleveland NFL	9	2	19	9.5	0	8	215	26.9	0	0	0	1

Additional pro statistics: Attempted one pass with no completions, 1985.

DEWEY FORTE
Defensive Tackle—Pittsburgh Steelers
Born October 31, 1961, at Lakeland, Fla.
Height, 6.05. Weight, 270.
High School—Lakeland, Fla., Kathleen.
Attended Bethune-Cookman College.

Selected by Tampa Bay in 1984 USFL territorial draft.
USFL rights traded with rights to defensive tackle Lee Williams by Tampa Bay Bandits to Los Angeles Express for draft choice, March 2, 1984.
Signed by Los Angeles Express, March 6, 1984.
Granted roster exemption, March 6 through March 15, 1984; activated, March 16, 1984.
On developmental squad, March 16 through March 29, 1984; activated, March 30, 1984.
On developmental squad, April 28 through May 3, 1984; activated, May 4, 1984.
Selected by Miami in 2nd round (53rd player selected) of 1984 NFL supplemental draft.
NFL rights traded with 2nd round pick in 1985 draft by Miami Dolphins to San Diego Chargers for running back Pete Johnson, September 22, 1984.
Released by Los Angeles Express, October 20, 1984; signed by San Diego Chargers for 1985, October 24, 1984.
Released by San Diego Chargers, August 19, 1985; signed as free agent by Pittsburgh Steelers, May 13, 1986.
On developmental squad for 3 games with Los Angeles Express in 1984.
Los Angeles USFL, 1984.
Games: 1984 (13).
Pro statistics: Credited with three sacks for 22 yards, 1984.

JEROME FOSTER
Defensive End—Miami Dolphins
Born July 25, 1960, at Detroit, Mich.
Height, 6.02. Weight, 263.
High School—Detroit, Mich., Kettering.
Attended Ohio State University.

Selected by Oakland in 5th round (55th player selected) of 1983 USFL draft.
Selected by Houston in 5th round (139th player selected) of 1983 NFL draft.
Signed by Houston Oilers, June 22, 1983.
On injured reserve with knee injury, September 20 through November 9, 1984; activated, November 10, 1984.
Released by Houston Oilers, September 2, 1985; signed as free agent by Miami Dolphins, March 6, 1986.
Houston NFL, 1983 and 1984.
Games: 1983 (16), 1984 (9). Total—25.

—DID YOU KNOW—
That when the Patriots signed free-agent punter Jack Fahey, he was the first player ever signed from Assumption, where only club football is played?

ROY ALLEN FOSTER
Guard-Offensive Tackle—Miami Dolphins
Born May 24, 1960, at Los Angeles, Calif.
Height, 6.04. Weight, 272.
High Schools—Woodland Hills, Calif., Taft; and Shawnee Mission, Kan., West.
Attended University of Southern California.

Named as guard on THE SPORTING NEWS College All-America Team, 1981.
Selected by Miami in 1st round (24th player selected) of 1982 NFL draft.
Miami NFL, 1982 through 1985.
Games: 1982 (9), 1983 (16), 1984 (16), 1985 (16). Total—57.
Pro statistics: Recovered one fumble, 1984.
Played in AFC Championship Game following 1982, 1984 and 1985 seasons.
Played in NFL Championship Game following 1982 and 1984 seasons.
Played in Pro Bowl (NFL All-Star Game) following 1985 season.

ELBERT FOULES
Cornerback—Philadelphia Eagles
Born July 4, 1961, at Greenville, Miss.
Height, 5.11. Weight, 185.
High School—Greenville, Miss.
Attended Alcorn State University.
Cousin of Wilbert Montgomery, running back with Detroit Lions;
and Cle Montgomery, wide receiver with Los Angeles Raiders

Signed as free agent by Philadelphia Eagles, May 12, 1983.

Year Club	G.	No.	Yds.	Avg.	TD.
		—INTERCEPTIONS—			
1983—Philadelphia NFL	16	1	0	0.0	0
1984—Philadelphia NFL	16	4	27	6.8	0
1985—Philadelphia NFL	16			None	
Pro Totals—3 Years............	48	5	27	5.4	0

Additional pro statistics: Returned one punt for seven yards, 1983; returned one kickoff for seven yards and recovered one fumble, 1985.

JOHN CHARLES FOURCADE
Quarterback—New Orleans Saints
Born October 11, 1960, at Gretna, La.
Height, 6.01. Weight, 200.
High School—Marrero, La., Archbishop Shaw.
Attended University of Mississippi.

Signed as free agent by Toronto Argonauts, May 5, 1982.
Traded by Toronto Argonauts to British Columbia Lions, May 20, 1982.
Released by British Columbia Lions, July 4, 1982; re-signed by Lions, July 8, 1982.
Released by British Columbia Lions, June 30, 1983; signed by Birmingham Stallions, October 10, 1983.
Released by Birmingham Stallions, February 13, 1984; signed as free agent by Memphis Showboats, May 31, 1984.
On developmental squad, May 31 through remainder of 1984 season.
Released by Memphis Showboats, January 23, 1985; signed as free agent by New York Giants, May 3, 1985.
Released by New York Giants, July 22, 1985; signed as free agent by New Orleans Saints, May 13, 1986.
On developmental squad for 4 games with Memphis Showboats in 1984.

Year Club	G.	Att.	Cmp.	Pct.	Gain	T.P.	P.I.	Avg.	Att.	Yds.	Avg.	TD.	TD.	Pts.	F.
		—PASSING—							—RUSHING—				—TOTAL—		
1982—British Columbia CFL.....	4	14	5	35.7	55	0	3	3.93	2	37	18.5	0	0	0	0

DANIEL FRANCIS FOUTS
(Dan)
Quarterback—San Diego Chargers
Born June 10, 1951, at San Francisco, Calif.
Height, 6.03. Weight, 205.
High School—San Francisco, Calif., St. Ignatius Prep.
Received bachelor of science degree in political science from University
of Oregon in 1973 and attended University of California at San Diego.

Established NFL records for most 4,000-yard seasons (3); most 300-yard passing games, career (47); most 400-yard passing games, career (6); most passes attempted, season (609), 1981.
Tied NFL record for most consecutive games, 400 yards passing (2), 1984; most 3,000-yard seasons (5).
Named THE SPORTING NEWS NFL Player of the Year, 1979.
Named THE SPORTING NEWS AFC Player of the Year, 1979.
Named to THE SPORTING NEWS AFC All-Star Team, 1979.
Selected by San Diego in 3rd round (64th player selected) of 1973 NFL draft.
On injured reserve with knee and groin injuries, December 8 through remainder of 1984 season.

Year Club	G.	Att.	Cmp.	Pct.	Gain	T.P.	P.I.	Avg.	Att.	Yds.	Avg.	TD.	TD.	Pts.	F.
		—PASSING—							—RUSHING—				—TOTAL—		
1973—San Diego NFL	10	194	87	44.8	1126	6	13	5.80	7	32	4.6	0	0	0	2
1974—San Diego NFL	11	237	115	48.5	1732	8	13	7.31	19	63	3.3	1	1	6	4
1975—San Diego NFL	10	195	106	54.4	1396	2	10	7.16	23	170	7.4	2	2	12	3
1976—San Diego NFL	14	359	208	57.9	2535	14	15	7.06	18	65	3.6	0	0	0	8
1977—San Diego NFL	4	109	69	63.3	869	4	6	7.97	6	13	2.2	0	0	0	4
1978—San Diego NFL	15	381	224	58.8	2999	24	20	7.87	20	43	2.2	2	2	12	10

Year Club	G.	Att.	Cmp.	Pct.	Gain	T.P.	P.I.	Avg.	Att.	Yds.	Avg.	TD.	TD.	Pts.	F.
				—PASSING—					—RUSHING—				—TOTAL—		
1979—San Diego NFL	16	530	332	*62.6	*4082	24	24	7.70	26	49	1.9	2	2	12	13
1980—San Diego NFL	16	*589	*348	59.1	*4715	30	24	8.01	23	15	0.7	2	2	12	11
1981—San Diego NFL	16	*609	*360	59.1	*4802	*33	17	7.89	22	56	2.5	0	0	0	9
1982—San Diego NFL	9	330	204	61.8	*2883	*17	11	*8.74	9	8	0.9	1	1	6	2
1983—San Diego NFL	10	340	215	63.2	2975	20	15	8.75	12	—5	—0.4	1	1	6	5
1984—San Diego NFL	13	507	317	62.5	3740	19	17	7.38	12	—29	—2.4	0	0	0	8
1985—San Diego NFL	14	430	254	59.1	3638	27	20	*8.46	11	—1	—0.1	0	0	0	13
Pro Totals—13 Years	158	4810	2839	59.0	37492	228	205	7.79	208	479	2.3	11	11	66	92

Quarterback Rating Points: 1973 (46.0), 1974 (61.4), 1975 (59.3), 1976 (75.3), 1977 (77.5), 1978 (83.2), 1979 (82.6), 1980 (84.6), 1981 (90.6), 1982 (93.6), 1983 (92.5), 1984 (83.4), 1985 (88.1). Total—81.5.

Additional pro statistics: Recovered one fumble, 1973, 1975 and 1984; recovered four fumbles, 1976; recovered three fumbles, 1978, 1980 and 1982; fumbled 10 times for minus four yards, 1978; recovered six fumbles and fumbled 13 times for minus 20 yards, 1979; fumbled 11 times for minus five yards, 1980; recovered two fumbles and fumbled nine times for minus 22 yards, 1981; recovered two fumbles, 1983; caught one pass for no yards, 1984; recovered six fumbles and fumbled 13 times for minus 11 yards, 1985.

Played in AFC Championship Game following 1980 and 1981 seasons.

Played in Pro Bowl (NFL All-Star Game) following 1979 through 1983 and 1985 seasons.

BOBBY LANE FOWLER
Fullback—New Orleans Saints

Born September 11, 1960, at Temple, Tex.
Height, 6.02. Weight, 230.
High School—Angleton, Tex.
Attended University of Texas-El Paso and Louisiana Tech University.

Signed as free agent by New Orleans Saints, June 20, 1984.
Released by New Orleans Saints, August 27, 1984; re-signed by Saints, May 9, 1985.
On injured reserve with knee injury, September 2 through October 13, 1985; activated after clearing procedural waivers, October 15, 1985.

Year Club	G.	Att.	Yds.	Avg.	TD.	P.C.	Yds.	Avg.	TD.	TD.	Pts.	F.
		—RUSHING—				PASS RECEIVING				—TOTAL—		
1985—New Orleans NFL	10	2	4	2.0	0	5	43	8.6	0	0	0	0

Year Club	G.	No.	Yds.	Avg.	TD.
	KICKOFF RETURNS				
1985—New Orleans NFL	10	4	78	19.5	0

COACHING RECORD

Graduate assistant at Louisiana Tech University, 1984.

STEVEN TODD FOWLER
(Known by middle name.)
Fullback—Dallas Cowboys

Born June 9, 1962, at Van, Tex.
Height, 6.03. Weight, 218.
High School—Van, Tex.
Attended Henderson County Junior College and Stephen F. Austin State Univesity

Selected by Houston in 16th round (329th player selected) of 1984 USFL draft.
Signed by Houston Gamblers, January 20, 1984.
Selected by Dallas in 1st round (25th player selected) of 1984 NFL supplemental draft.
Signed by Dallas Cowboys, September 24, 1984, for contract to take effect after being granted free agency after 1985 USFL season.
On developmental squad, February 21 through March 30, 1985; activated, March 31, 1985.
On injured reserve with knee injury, August 27 through October 28, 1985; activated, October 29, 1985.
On developmental squad for 5 games with Houston Gamblers in 1985.

Year Club	G.	Att.	Yds.	Avg.	TD.	P.C.	Yds.	Avg.	TD.	TD.	Pts.	F.
		—RUSHING—				PASS RECEIVING				—TOTAL—		
1984—Houston USFL	18	170	1003	5.9	11	24	301	12.5	2	13	78	4
1985—Houston USFL	13	92	402	4.4	3	27	239	8.9	1	4	†26	5
1985—Dallas NFL	8	7	25	3.6	0	5	24	4.8	0	0	0	0
USFL Totals—2 Years	31	262	1405	5.4	14	51	540	10.6	3	17	104	9
NFL Totals—1 Year	8	7	25	3.6	0	5	24	4.8	0	0	0	0
Pro Totals—3 Years	39	269	1430	5.3	14	56	564	10.1	3	17	104	9

†Includes one 2-point conversion.
Additional USFL statistics: Recovered four fumbles, 1984; recovered two fumbles, 1985.
Additional NFL statistics: Returned three kickoffs for 48 yards, 1985.

DENNIS JAMES FOWLKES
Linebacker—Minnesota Vikings

Born March 11, 1961, at Columbus, O.
Height, 6.02. Weight, 236.
High School—Columbus, O., East.
Attended West Virginia University.

Selected by Washington in 10th round (117th player selected) of 1983 USFL draft.
Signed as free agent by Pittsburgh Steelers, May 5, 1983.
On injured reserve with concussion, August 23, 1983 through September 4, 1983.

Released by Pittsburgh Steelers, September 5, 1983; signed as free agent by Minnesota Vikings, October 6, 1983.
Released by Minnesota Vikings, September 2, 1985; re-signed by Vikings, September 12, 1985.
Minnesota NFL, 1983 through 1985.
Games: 1983 (11), 1984 (14), 1985 (15). Total—40.
Pro statistics: Recovered two fumbles for five yards, 1983; recovered one fumble, 1985.

TIMOTHY RICHARD FOX
(Tim)
Safety—Los Angeles Rams
Born November 1, 1953, at Canton, O.
Height, 5.11. Weight, 186.
High School—Canton, O., Glenwood.
Received bachelor of arts degree in communications from Ohio State University in 1976.

Named as safety on THE SPORTING NEWS College All-America Team, 1975.
Selected by New England in 1st round (21st player selected) of 1976 NFL draft.
Traded by New England Patriots to San Diego Chargers for 2nd round pick in 1982 draft and 3rd round pick in 1983 draft, April 27, 1982.
On inactive list, September 12, 1982.
On injured reserve with fractured ankle, October 1 through October 30, 1983; activated, October 31, 1983.
On physically unable to perform/active with ankle injury, July 21 through August 20, 1984; activated, August 21, 1984.
On injured reserve with ankle injury, August 28 through September 27, 1984; activated, September 28, 1984.
Released by San Diego Chargers, August 13, 1985; signed as free agent by Los Angeles Rams, November 14, 1985.

| | | —INTERCEPTIONS— | | | | | | —INTERCEPTIONS— | | |
Year Club	G.	No.	Yds.	Avg.TD.		Year Club	G.	No.	Yds.	Avg.TD.
1976—New England NFL	13	3	67	22.3	0	1982—San Diego NFL	7	4	103	25.8	0
1977—New England NFL	14	3	39	13.0	0	1983—San Diego NFL	12	2	14	7.0	0
1978—New England NFL	16	2	10	5.0	0	1984—San Diego NFL	11	1	36	36.0	0
1979—New England NFL	16	2	38	19.0	0	1985—L.A. Rams NFL	6	2	8	4.0	0
1980—New England NFL	16	4	41	10.3	0	Pro Totals—10 Years	127	26	376	14.5	0
1981—New England NFL	16	3	20	6.7	0						

Additional pro statistics: Recovered four fumbles for 11 yards, 1976; recovered one fumble, 1977, 1978 and 1984; credited with one safety, 1978; recovered one fumble for four yards, 1979; fumbled once, 1982.
Played in NFC Championship Game following 1985 season.
Played in Pro Bowl (NFL All-Star Game) following 1980 season.

WILLIAM P. FRALIC
(Bill)
Guard—Atlanta Falcons
Born October 31, 1962, at Penn Hills, Pa.
Height, 6.05. Weight, 280.
High School—Pittsburgh, Pa., Penn Hills.
Attended University of Pittsburgh.

Named as offensive tackle on THE SPORTING NEWS College Football All-America Team, 1983 and 1984.
Selected by Baltimore in 1985 USFL territorial draft.
Selected by Atlanta in 1st round (2nd player selected) of 1985 NFL draft.
Signed by Atlanta Falcons, July 22, 1985.
Atlanta NFL, 1985.
Games: 1985 (15).

ANDRE S. FRANCIS
Cornerback—New York Jets
Born October 5, 1960, at Kingston, Jamaica.
Height, 5.09. Weight, 170.
High School—Miami, Fla., Central.
Attended New Mexico State University.

Signed as free agent by Montreal Concordes, February 15, 1983.
Traded by Montreal Concordes to Saskatchewan Roughriders for draft choice, September 12, 1985.
Released by Saskatchewan Roughriders, September 21, 1985; signed as free agent by New York Jets, April 3, 1986.

| | | —INTERCEPTIONS— | | |
Year Club	G.	No.	Yds.	Avg.TD.
1983—Montreal CFL	16	5	108	21.6	0
1984—Montreal CFL	16	3	84	28.0	0
1985—Mon (9)-Sas (1) CFL	10		None		
Pro Totals—3 Years	42	8	192	24.0	0

Additional pro statistics: Returned seven kickoffs for 143 yards and ran 34 yards with a lateral on punt return, 1984.

RUSSELL ROSS FRANCIS
(Russ)
Tight End—San Francisco 49ers
Born April 3, 1953, at Seattle, Wash.
Height, 6.06. Weight, 242.
High Schools—Kailua, Oahu, Hawaii; and Pleasant Hill, Ore.
Attended University of Oregon.
Son of Ed Francis, part-time scout with New England Patriots.

Selected by New England in 1st round (16th player selected) of 1975 NFL draft.
On did not report list, August 18 through entire 1981 season.
Traded with 2nd round pick in 1982 draft by New England Patriots to San Francisco 49ers for 1st, 4th and two 2nd round picks in 1982 draft, April 27, 1982.
On injured reserve with neck injury, October 23 through December 6, 1984; activated, December 7, 1984.
Selected by Kansas City Royals in 9th round of free-agent draft, June 5, 1974.

| | —PASS RECEIVING— | | | | | —PASS RECEIVING— | | | |
Year Club	G.	P.C.	Yds.	Avg. TD.	Year Club	G.	P.C.	Yds.	Avg. TD.
1975—New England NFL	14	35	636	18.2	4	1982—San Francisco NFL	9	23	278	12.1	2
1976—New England NFL	13	26	367	14.1	3	1983—San Francisco NFL	16	33	357	10.8	4
1977—New England NFL	10	16	229	14.3	4	1984—San Francisco NFL	10	23	285	12.4	2
1978—New England NFL	15	39	543	13.9	4	1985—San Francisco NFL	16	44	478	10.9	3
1979—New England NFL	12	39	557	14.3	5	Pro Totals—10 Years..........	130	319	4335	13.6	39
1980—New England NFL........	15	41	664	16.2	8						

Additional pro statistics: Fumbled once, 1975, 1976, 1978 and 1984; rushed twice for 12 yards and recovered one fumble, 1976 and 1978; recovered one fumble for three yards, 1977; attempted one pass with one completion for 45 yards, 1982; fumbled twice, 1982, 1983 and 1985; recovered two fumbles, 1984.
Played in NFC Championship Game following 1983 and 1984 seasons.
Played in NFL Championship Game following 1984 season.
Played in Pro Bowl (NFL All-Star Game) following 1976 and 1977 seasons.
Named to play in Pro Bowl following 1978 season; replaced due to injury by Riley Odoms.

JOHN E. FRANK
Tight End—San Francisco 49ers
Born April 17, 1962, at Pittsburgh, Pa.
Height, 6.03. Weight, 225.
High School—Pittsburgh, Pa., Mount Lebanon.
Received bachelor of arts degree in pre-med from Ohio State University in 1984.

Selected by New Jersey in 1984 USFL territorial draft.
USFL rights traded with rights to guard Joe Lukens by New Jersey Generals to Pittsburgh Maulers for cornerback Kerry Justin, November 15, 1983.
Selected by San Francisco in 2nd round (56th player selected) of 1984 NFL draft.
Signed by San Francisco 49ers, July 16, 1984.

| | —PASS RECEIVING— | | | | |
Year Club	G.	P.C.	Yds.	Avg.	TD.
1984—San Francisco NFL	15	7	60	8.6	1
1985—San Francisco NFL	16	7	50	7.1	1
Pro Totals—2 Years............	31	14	110	7.9	2

Additional pro statistics: Returned one kickoff for one yard, 1985.
Played in NFC Championship Game following 1984 season.
Member of San Francisco 49ers for NFL Championship Game following 1984 season; did not play.

ANTHONY RAY FRANKLIN
(Tony)
Placekicker—New England Patriots
Born November 18, 1956, at Big Spring, Tex.
Height, 5.08. Weight, 182.
High School—Fort Worth, Tex., Arlington Heights.
Attended Texas A&M University.
Brother of Eric Franklin, placekicker at Texas A&M University.

Selected by Philadelphia in 3rd round (74th player selected) of 1979 NFL draft.
Traded by Philadelphia Eagles to New England Patriots for 6th round pick in 1985 draft, February 21, 1984.

| | —PLACE KICKING— | | | | | |
Year Club	G.	XP.	XPM.	FG.	FGA.	Pts.
1979—Philadelphia NFL ...	16	36	3	23	31	105
1980—Philadelphia NFL ...	16	48	0	16	31	96
1981—Philadelphia NFL ...	16	41	2	20	31	101
1982—Philadelphia NFL ...	9	23	2	6	9	41
1983—Philadelphia NFL ...	16	24	3	15	26	69
1984—New England NFL..	16	42	0	22	28	108
1985—New England NFL..	16	40	1	24	30	112
Pro Totals—7 Years.......	105	254	11	126	186	632

Additional pro statistics: Punted once for 32 yards, 1979; punted once for 13 yards, 1981, rushed once for minus five yards, 1985.
Played in NFC Championship Game following 1980 season.
Played in AFC Championship Game following 1985 season.
Played in NFL Championship Game following 1980 and 1985 seasons.

BYRON PAUL FRANKLIN
Wide Receiver—Seattle Seahawks
Born September 3, 1958, at Florence, Ala.
Height, 6.01. Weight, 179.
High School—Sheffield, Ala.
Attended Auburn University.

Selected by Buffalo in 2nd round (50th player selected) of 1981 NFL draft.
On injured reserve with sciatic nerve injury, September 6 through entire 1982 season.

Traded by Buffalo Bills to Seattle Seahawks for tight end Pete Metzelaars, August 20, 1985.
On injured reserve with knee injury, December 4 through remainder of 1985 season.

		PASS RECEIVING				—KICKOFF RET.—				—TOTAL—		
Year	Club	G.	P.C.	Yds.	Avg.	TD.	No.	Yds.	Avg.	TD.	TD.	Pts.	F.
1981—Buffalo NFL		13	2	29	14.5	0	21	436	20.8	0	0	0	2
1983—Buffalo NFL		15	30	452	15.1	4	None				4	24	0
1984—Buffalo NFL		16	69	862	12.5	4	None				4	24	4
1985—Seattle NFL		13	10	119	11.9	0	None				0	0	0
Pro Totals—4 Years		57	111	1462	13.2	8	21	436	20.8	0	8	48	6

Additional pro statistics: Rushed once for minus 11 yards and returned five punts for 45 yards, 1981; rushed once for three yards, 1983; rushed once for minus seven yards, 1984; rushed once for five yards, 1985.

ELVIS FRANKS
Defensive End—Los Angeles Raiders
Born July 9, 1957, at Doucette, Tex.
Height, 6.04. Weight, 270.
High School—Woodville, Tex., Kirby.
Attended Morgan State University.

Selected by Cleveland in 5th round (116th player selected) of 1980 NFL draft.
On injured reserve with knee injury, August 20 through October 29, 1985.
Released by Cleveland Browns, October 30, 1985; signed as free agent by Los Angeles Raiders, November 25, 1985.
Cleveland NFL, 1980 through 1984; Los Angeles Raiders NFL, 1985.
Games: 1980 (16), 1981 (16), 1982 (9), 1983 (16), 1984 (16), 1985 (3). Total—76.
Pro statistics: Recovered one fumble, 1980 and 1983; recovered one fumble for three yards, 1982.

GUY SHELTON FRAZIER
Linebacker—Buffalo Bills
Born July 20, 1959, at Detroit, Mich.
Height, 6.02. Weight, 217.
High School—Detroit, Mich., Cass Tech.
Attended University of Wyoming.

Selected by Cincinnati in 4th round (93rd player selected) of 1981 NFL draft.
On injured reserve with broken hand, October 10 through November 16, 1983; activated, November 17, 1983.
Released by Cincinnati Bengals, August 27, 1985; awarded on waivers to Buffalo Bills, August 28, 1985.
Cincinnati NFL, 1981 through 1984; Buffalo NFL, 1985.
Games: 1981 (16), 1982 (9), 1983 (10), 1984 (16), 1985 (16). Total—67.
Pro statistics: Intercepted one pass for eight yards, 1984.
Played in AFC Championship Game following 1981 season.
Played in NFL Championship Game following 1981 season.

LESLIE ANTONIO FRAZIER
Cornerback—Chicago Bears
Born April 3, 1959, at Columbus, Miss.
Height, 6.00. Weight, 189.
High School—Columbus, Miss., Lee.
Received bachelor of arts degree in business administration from Alcorn State University.

Signed as free agent by Chicago Bears, July 18, 1981.

		-INTERCEPTIONS-				—KICKOFF RET.—				—TOTAL—		
Year	Club	G.	No.	Yds.	Avg.	TD.	No.	Yds.	Avg.	TD.	TD.	Pts.	F.
1981—Chicago NFL		13	None				6	77	12.8	0	0	0	0
1982—Chicago NFL		9	None				2	0	0.0	0	0	0	0
1983—Chicago NFL		16	7	135	19.3	1	None				1	6	0
1984—Chicago NFL		11	5	89	17.8	0	None				0	0	0
1985—Chicago NFL		16	6	119	19.8	*1	None				1	6	0
Pro Totals—5 Years		65	18	343	19.1	2	8	77	9.6	0	2	12	0

Additional pro statistics: Recovered one fumble for seven yards, 1982; recovered one fumble for three yards, 1983.
Played in NFC Championship Game following 1984 and 1985 seasons.
Played in NFL Championship Game following 1985 season.

ANDREW BRIAN FREDERICK
(Andy)
Offensive Tackle—Chicago Bears
Born July 25, 1954, at Oak Park, Ill.
Height, 6.06. Weight, 265.
High School—Westchester, Ill., St. Joseph
Received bachelor of science degree in business from University of New Mexico in 1977.

Selected by Dallas in 5th round (137th player selected) of 1977 NFL draft.
Released by Dallas Cowboys, August 21, 1979; re-signed by Cowboys, August 31, 1979.
Released by Dallas Cowboys, September 6, 1982; claimed on waivers by Cleveland Browns, September 7, 1982.
On inactive list, September 12, 1982.
Traded by Cleveland Browns to Chicago Bears for past consideration, April 28, 1983 (Bears had acquired offensive lineman Gerry Sullivan from Browns in 1982 for 6th round pick in 1983 but Sullivan retired three days after reporting).
Released by Chicago Bears, August 29, 1983; re-signed by Bears, August 30, 1983.
Dallas NFL, 1977 through 1981; Cleveland NFL, 1982; Chicago NFL, 1983 through 1985.
Games: 1977 (14), 1978 (16), 1979 (16), 1980 (16), 1981 (16), 1982 (7), 1983 (16), 1984 (16), 1985 (16). Total—133.

Pro statistics: Recovered one fumble, 1978.
Played in NFC Championship Game following 1977, 1978, 1980, 1984 and 1985 seasons.
Member of Dallas Cowboys for NFC Championship Game following 1981 season; did not play.
Played in NFL Championship Game following 1977, 1978 and 1985 seasons.

MICHAEL JOSEPH FREEMAN
(Mike)
Guard—Denver Broncos
Born October 13, 1961, at Mt. Holly, N.J.
Height, 6.03. Weight, 256.
High Schools—Tucson, Ariz., Sahuaro and Fountain Valley, Calif.
Attended University of Arizona.
Nephew of Bob Freeman, defensive back with Cleveland Browns, Green Bay Packers,
Philadelphia Eagles and Washington Redskins, 1957 through 1962.

Signed as free agent by Denver Broncos, May 2, 1984.
On injured reserve with sprained knee, August 20 through entire 1985 season.
Denver NFL, 1984.
Games: 1984 (9).

PHILLIP EMERY FREEMAN
(Phil)
Wide Receiver—Tampa Bay Buccaneers
Born December 9, 1962, at St. Paul, Minn.
Height, 5.11. Weight, 185.
High School—Santa Monica, Calif., St. Monica.
Attended University of Arizona.

Selected by Arizona in 1985 USFL territorial draft.
Selected by Tampa Bay in 8th round (204th player selected) of 1985 NFL draft.
Signed by Tampa Bay Buccaneers, June 24, 1985.
On injured reserve with broken wrist, December 10 through remainder of 1985 season.

		KICKOFF RETURNS			
Year Club	G.	No.	Yds.	Avg.	TD.
1985—Tampa Bay NFL	14	48	1085	22.6	0

Additional pro statistics: Fumbled once, 1985.

STEVEN JAY FREEMAN
(Steve)
Safety—Buffalo Bills
Born May 8, 1953, at Lamesa, Tex.
Height, 5.11. Weight, 185.
High School—Memphis, Tenn., Whitehaven.
Received degree in agricultural economics from Mississippi State University.

Named to THE SPORTING NEWS NFL All-Star Team, 1983.
Selected by New England in 5th round (117th player selected) of 1975 NFL draft.
Claimed on waivers from New England Patriots by Buffalo Bills, August 21, 1975.

		—INTERCEPTIONS—						—INTERCEPTIONS—			
Year Club	G.	No.	Yds.	Avg.	TD.	Year Club	G.	No.	Yds.	Avg.	TD.
1975—Buffalo NFL	14	2	44	22.0	1	1981—Buffalo NFL..................	16		None		
1976—Buffalo NFL	14		None			1982—Buffalo NFL..................	9	3	27	9.0	0
1977—Buffalo NFL	14	1	4	4.0	0	1983—Buffalo NFL..................	16	3	40	13.3	0
1978—Buffalo NFL	16		None			1984—Buffalo NFL..................	15	3	45	15.0	0
1979—Buffalo NFL	16	3	62	20.7	1	1985—Buffalo NFL..................	16		None		
1980—Buffalo NFL	16	7	107	15.3	1	Pro Totals—11 Years	162	22	329	15.0	3

Additional pro statistics: Recovered one fumble, 1975, 1976, 1982 and 1984; recovered two fumbles, 1979; returned
one kickoff for no yards, 1981; recovered two fumbles for 31 yards, 1983.

WILLIAM JASPER FRIZZELL
Defensive Back—Detroit Lions
Born September 8, 1962, at Greenville, N.C.
Height, 6.03. Weight, 198.
High School—Greenville, N.C., J.H. Rose.
Attended North Carolina Central University.

Selected by Detroit in 10th round (259th player selected) of 1984 NFL draft.
On injured reserve with ankle injury, September 2 through November 1, 1985; activated, November 2, 1985.
Detroit NFL, 1984 and 1985.
Games: 1984 (16), 1985 (8). Total—24.
Pro statistics: Intercepted one pass for three yards, 1985.

IRVING DALE FRYAR
Wide Receiver-Punt Returner—New England Patriots
Born September 28, 1962, at Mount Holly, N.J.
Height, 6.00. Weight, 200.
High School—Mount Holly, N.J., Rancocas Valley Regional.
Attended University of Nebraska.

Named as wide receiver on THE SPORTING NEWS College All-America Team, 1983.
Selected by Chicago in 1st round (3rd player selected) of 1984 USFL draft.
Signed by New England Patriots, April 11, 1984.
Selected officially by New England in 1st round (1st player selected) of 1984 NFL draft.

Year Club	G.	—RUSHING—				PASS RECEIVING				—TOTAL—		
		Att.	Yds.	Avg.	TD.	P.C.	Yds.	Avg.	TD.	TD.	Pts.	F.
1984—New England NFL	14	2	—11	—5.5	0	11	164	14.9	1	1	6	4
1985—New England NFL	16	7	27	3.9	1	39	670	17.2	7	10	60	4
Pro Totals—2 Years	30	9	16	1.8	1	50	834	16.7	8	11	66	8

Year Club	G.	—PUNT RETURNS—				—KICKOFF RET.—			
		No.	Yds.	Avg.	TD.	No.	Yds.	Avg.	TD.
1984—New England NFL	14	36	347	9.6	0	5	95	19.0	0
1985—New England NFL	16	37	520	*14.1	*2	3	39	13.0	0
Pro Totals—2 Years	30	73	867	11.9	2	8	134	16.8	0

Additional pro statistics: Recovered one fumble, 1984.
Played in NFL Championship Game following 1985 season.
Played in Pro Bowl (NFL All-Star Game) following 1985 season.

DAVID FRYE
(Dave)
Linebacker—Atlanta Falcons
Born June 21, 1961, at Cincinnati, O.
Height, 6.02. Weight, 218.
High School—Cincinnati, O., Woodward.
Attended Santa Ana College and Purdue University.

Signed as free agent by Atlanta Falcons, May 9, 1983.
On non-football injury list with drug problem, September 27 through October 8, 1985; activated, October 9, 1985.
Atlanta NFL, 1983 through 1985.
Games: 1983 (16), 1984 (16), 1985 (14). Total—46.
Pro statistics: Recovered two fumbles, 1983 and 1984; intercepted one pass for 20 yards and recovered one fumble for 13 yards, 1985.

JEFFERY AVERY FULLER
(Jeff)
Safety—San Francisco 49ers
Born August 8, 1962, at Dallas, Tex.
Height, 6.02. Weight, 216.
High School—Dallas, Tex., Franklin D. Roosevelt.
Attended Texas A&M University.

Selected by Houston in 1984 USFL territorial draft.
Selected by San Francisco in 5th round (139th player selected) of 1984 NFL draft.
Signed by San Francisco 49ers, May 29, 1984.
San Francisco NFL, 1984 and 1985.
Games: 1984 (13), 1985 (16). Total—29.
Pro statistics: Intercepted one pass for 38 yards, 1984; intercepted one pass for four yards, 1985.
Played in NFC Championship Game following 1984 season.
Played in NFL Championship Game following 1984 season.

STEPHEN RAY FULLER
(Steve)
Quarterback—Chicago Bears
Born January 5, 1957, at Enid, Okla.
Height, 6.04. Weight, 198.
High School—Spartanburg, S.C.
Received degree from Clemson University.

Selected by Kansas City in 1st round (23rd player selected) of 1979 NFL draft.
On injured reserve with knee injury, December 18 through remainder of 1980 season.
Traded by Kansas City Chiefs to Los Angeles Rams for cornerback Lucious Smith and 5th round pick in 1985 draft, August 19, 1983.
Traded by Los Angeles Rams to Chicago Bears for 11th round pick in 1984 draft and 6th round pick in 1985 draft, April 30, 1984.
On injured reserve with separated shoulder, August 28 through October 5, 1984; activated, October 6, 1984.
Active for 16 games with Los Angeles Rams in 1983; did not play.

Year Club	G.	—PASSING—							—RUSHING—				—TOTAL—		
		Att.	Cmp.	Pct.	Gain	T.P.	P.I.	Avg.	Att.	Yds.	Avg.	TD.	TD.	Pts.	F.
1979—Kansas City NFL	16	270	146	54.1	1484	6	14	5.50	50	264	5.3	1	1	6	6
1980—Kansas City NFL	14	320	193	60.3	2250	10	12	7.03	60	274	4.6	4	4	24	*16
1981—Kansas City NFL	13	134	77	57.5	934	3	4	6.97	19	118	6.2	0	0	0	4
1982—Kansas City NFL	9	93	49	52.7	665	3	2	7.15	10	56	5.6	0	0	0	3
1984—Chicago NFL	6	78	53	67.9	595	3	0	7.63	15	89	5.9	1	1	6	0
1985—Chicago NFL	16	107	53	49.5	777	1	5	7.26	24	77	3.2	5	5	30	3
Pro Totals—7 Years	74	1002	571	57.0	6705	26	37	6.69	178	878	4.9	11	11	66	32

Quarterback Rating Points: 1979 (55.8), 1980 (76.1), 1981 (73.9), 1982 (77.3), 1984 (103.3), 1985 (57.3). Total—70.7.
Additional pro statistics: Recovered three fumbles and fumbled six times for minus four yards, 1979; recovered

seven fumbles and fumbled 16 times for minus 43 yards, 1980; recovered one fumble and fumbled four times for minus six yards, 1981; recovered two fumbles, 1982; recovered one fumble and fumbled three times for minus 15 yards, 1985.

Played in NFC Championship Game following 1984 and 1985 seasons.

Played in NFL Championship Game following 1985 season.

BOBBY LEE FUTRELL
Cornerback—Tampa Bay Buccaneers
Born August 4, 1962, at Ahoskie, N.C.
Height, 5.11. Weight, 178.
High School—Ahoskie, N.C.
Attended Elizabeth City State University.

Selected by Michigan in 5th round (93rd player selected) of 1984 USFL draft.

Signed by Michigan Panthers, January 23, 1984.

Not protected in merger of Michigan Panthers and Oakland Invaders; selected by Tampa Bay Bandits in USFL dispersal draft, December 6, 1984.

Released by Tampa Bay Bandits, February 18, 1985; re-signed by Bandits, February 19, 1985.

Released by Tampa Bay Bandits, April 19, 1985; awarded on waivers to Oakland Invaders, April 23, 1985.

On developmental squad, May 23 through June 14, 1985; activated, June 15, 1985.

Released by Oakland Invaders, August 2, 1985; signed as free agent by Tampa Bay Buccaneers, April 2, 1986.

On developmental squad for 3 games with Oakland Invaders in 1985.

		INTERCEPTIONS				–PUNT RETURNS–				—KICKOFF RET.—				—TOTAL—		
Year Club	G.	No.	Yds.	Avg.	TD.	No.	Yds.	Avg.	TD.	No.	Yds.	Avg.	TD.	TD.	Pts.	F.
1984—Michigan USFL............	18	1	29	29.0	0	3	17	5.7	0	27	576	21.3	0	0	0	4
1985—TB (8)-Oak. (6) USFL..	14			None				None		10	199	19.9	0	0	0	0
Pro Totals—2 Years.......	32	1	29	29.0	0	3	17	5.7	0	37	775	20.9	0	0	0	4

Additional pro statistics: Recovered two fumbles, 1984.

On developmental squad for USFL Championship Game following 1985 season.

GREGORY SCOTT GAINES
(Greg)
Linebacker—Seattle Seahawks
Born October 16, 1958, at Martinsville, Va.
Height, 6.03. Weight, 220.
High School—Hermitage, Tenn., DuPont.
Attended University of Tennessee.
Nephew of Ray Oldham, safety with Baltimore Colts, Pittsburgh Steelers,
New York Giants and Detroit Lions, 1973 through 1982.

Signed as free agent by Seattle Seahawks, May 6, 1981.

On injured reserve with knee injury, October 28 through remainder of 1981 season.

On injured reserve with knee injury, August 31 through entire 1982 season.

Seattle NFL, 1981 and 1983 through 1985.

Games: 1981 (8), 1983 (16), 1984 (16), 1985 (16). Total—56.

Pro statistics: Recovered one fumble, 1981; recovered four fumbles, 1983; intercepted one pass for 18 yards, 1984; recovered two fumbles for seven yards, 1985.

Played in AFC Championship Game following 1983 season.

HOWARD LEE GAJAN JR.
Name pronounced Guy-jawn.
(Hokie)
Running Back—New Orleans Saints
Born September 6, 1959, at Baton Rouge, La.
Height, 5.11. Weight, 225.
High School—Baker, La.
Attended Louisiana State University.

Selected by New Orleans in 10th round (249th player selected) of 1981 NFL draft.

On injured reserve with head injuries suffered in car accident, August 18 through entire 1981 season.

Released by New Orleans Saints, September 6, 1982; re-signed by Saints, September 7, 1982.

On injured reserve with knee injury, November 14 through remainder of 1985 season.

		——RUSHING——				PASS RECEIVING				—TOTAL—		
Year Club	G.	Att.	Yds.	Avg.	TD.	P.C.	Yds.	Avg.	TD.	TD.	Pts.	F.
1982—New Orleans NFL.................................	9	19	77	4.1	0	3	10	3.3	0	0	0	0
1983—New Orleans NFL.................................	16	81	415	5.1	4	17	130	7.6	0	4	24	3
1984—New Orleans NFL.................................	14	102	615	*6.0	5	35	288	8.2	2	7	42	0
1985—New Orleans NFL.................................	6	50	251	5.0	2	8	87	10.9	0	2	12	3
Pro Totals—4 Years.................................	45	252	1358	5.4	11	63	515	8.2	2	13	78	6

Additional pro statistics: Returned one kickoff for 18 yards, 1982; recovered one fumble, 1982 and 1983; attempted one pass with no completions, 1983; attempted one pass with one completion for 34 yards and a touchdown, 1984.

—DID YOU KNOW—

That when three Iowa players were selected on the first round of the 1986 NFL draft, it marked the sixth time in the 1980s that at least one school had more than two players selected on the first round?

ANTHONY DALE GALBREATH

Name pronounced GALL-breath.

(Tony)
Running Back—New York Giants

Born January 29, 1954, at Fulton, Mo.
Height, 6.00. Weight, 228.
High School—Fulton, Mo.
Attended Centerville Community College and University of Missouri.

Established NFL record for pass receptions by running back, career (431).
Selected by New Orleans in 2nd round (32nd player selected) of 1976 NFL draft.
On injured reserve with knee injury, December 16 through remainder of 1979 season.
Traded by New Orleans Saints to Minnesota Vikings for 3rd round pick in 1982 draft, August 31, 1981.
On inactive list, September 19, 1982.
Traded by Minnesota Vikings to New York Giants for linebacker Brad Van Pelt, July 12, 1984.

Year	Club	G.	Att.	Yds.	Avg.	TD.	P.C.	Yds.	Avg.	TD.	TD.	Pts.	F.
1976—New Orleans NFL		14	136	570	4.2	7	54	420	7.8	1	8	48	7
1977—New Orleans NFL		14	168	644	3.8	3	41	265	6.5	0	3	18	3
1978—New Orleans NFL		16	186	635	3.4	5	74	582	7.9	2	7	42	6
1979—New Orleans NFL		15	189	708	3.7	9	58	484	8.3	1	10	67	5
1980—New Orleans NFL		16	81	308	3.8	3	57	470	8.2	2	5	30	3
1981—Minnesota NFL		14	42	198	4.7	2	18	144	8.0	0	2	12	2
1982—Minnesota NFL		8	39	116	3.0	1	17	153	9.0	0	1	6	1
1983—Minnesota NFL		13	113	474	4.2	4	45	348	7.7	2	6	36	4
1984—New York Giants NFL		16	22	97	4.4	0	37	357	9.6	0	0	0	0
1985—New York Giants NFL		16	29	187	6.4	0	30	327	10.9	1	1	6	2
Pro Totals—10 Years		142	1005	3937	3.9	34	431	3550	8.2	9	43	265	33

Additional pro statistics: Recovered one fumble, 1976 and 1979; returned 20 kickoffs for 399 yards and returned two punts for eight yards, 1976; recovered two fumbles for one yard, 1978; made one of two extra points and two of three field goals for seven points and attempted three passes with two completions for 70 yards and one interception, 1979; recovered two fumbles, 1980 and 1983; returned six kickoffs for 86 yards and attempted two passes with no completions, 1980; returned one kickoff for 16 yards, 1981; attempted one pass with one completion for 13 yards, 1984; returned seven kickoffs for 120 yards, 1985.

DAVID LAWRENCE GALLOWAY
Defensive Tackle—St. Louis Cardinals

Born February 16, 1959, at Tampa, Fla.
Height, 6.03. Weight, 277.
High School—Brandon, Fla.
Attended University of Florida.

Selected by St. Louis in 2nd round (38th player selected) of 1982 NFL draft.
On injured reserve with dislocated shoulder, September 8 through November 30, 1982; activated, December 1, 1982.
St. Louis NFL, 1982 through 1985.
Games: 1982 (5), 1983 (16), 1984 (14), 1985 (16). Total—51.
Pro statistics: Intercepted one pass for 17 yards and credited with one safety, 1983; recovered one fumble, 1983 and 1985.

DUANE KEITH GALLOWAY
Cornerback—Detroit Lions

Born November 7, 1961, at Los Angeles, Calif.
Height, 5.08. Weight 181.
High School—Los Angeles, Calif., Crenshaw.
Attended Santa Monica City College and Arizona State University.

Selected by Los Angeles in 19th round (217th player selected) of 1983 USFL draft.
Signed by Los Angeles Express, January 26, 1983.
Released by Los Angeles Express, February 20, 1983; signed as free agent by Saskatchewan Roughriders, March 15, 1983.
Released by Saskatchewan Roughriders, June 28, 1983; re-signed by Roughriders, July 27, 1983.
Released by Saskatchewan Roughriders, September 11, 1983; signed as free agent by Indianapolis Colts, May 15, 1984.
On injured reserve with thigh injury, August 13 through September 17, 1984.
Released by Indianapolis Colts, September 18, 1984; signed as free agent by Detroit Lions, May 9, 1985.
On injured reserve with broken arm, September 10 through December 20, 1985; activated, December 21, 1985.
Saskatchewan CFL, 1983; Detroit NFL, 1985.
Games: 1983 (6), 1985 (2). Total—8.

MIKE ALAN GANN
Defensive End—Atlanta Falcons

Born October 19, 1963, at Stillwater, Okla.
Height, 6.05. Weight, 265.
High School—Lakewood, Colo.
Received bachelor of business administration degree
from University of Notre Dame in 1985.

Selected by Tampa Bay in 1st round (12th player selected) of 1985 USFL draft.
Selected by Atlanta in 2nd round (45th player selected) of 1985 NFL draft.

Signed by Atlanta Falcons, July 23, 1985.
Atlanta NFL, 1985.
Games: 1985 (16).
Pro statistics: Recovered one fumble for 42 yards and a touchdown, 1985.

FRANK BENITEZ GARCIA
Punter—Tampa Bay Buccaneers
Born June 5, 1957, at Tucson, Ariz.
Height, 6.00. Weight, 210.
High School—Tucson, Ariz., Salpointe.
Attended Arizona State University, University of Nevada at Las Vegas,
received bachelor of science degree in secondary education from University of Arizona and
attending Arizona for master's degree in special education.

Signed as free agent by Atlanta Falcons, May 5, 1979.
Released by Atlanta Falcons, July 26, 1979; signed as free agent by San Diego Chargers, June, 1980.
Released by San Diego Chargers, July 28, 1980; signed as free agent by Green Bay Packers, March 11, 1981.
Released by Green Bay Packers, August 17, 1981; signed as free agent by Tampa Bay Buccaneers, August 21, 1981.
Released by Tampa Bay Buccaneers, August 24, 1981; signed as free agent by Seattle Seahawks, December 16, 1981.
Released by Seattle Seahawks, August 31, 1982; signed as free agent by Chicago Blitz, March 19, 1983.
On developmental squad, April 10, 1983.
Released by Chicago Blitz, April 11, 1983; signed as free agent by Tampa Bay Buccaneers, May 11, 1983.
On developmental squad for 1 game with Chicago Blitz in 1983.

		—PUNTING—		
Year Club	G.	No.	Avg.	Blk.
1981—Seattle NFL	1	2	37.0	0
1983—Chicago USFL	3	18	37.5	0
1983—Tampa Bay NFL	16	*95	42.2	1
1984—Tampa Bay NFL	16	68	41.9	0
1985—Tampa Bay NFL	16	77	42.0	*2
NFL Totals—4 Years	49	242	42.0	3
USFL Totals—1 Year	3	18	37.5	0
Pro Totals—5 Years	52	260	41.7	3

Additional pro statistics: Attempted one pass with no completions, 1984.

HAL E. GARDNER JR.
Linebacker—Buffalo Bills
Born January 18, 1962, at New Iberia, La.
Height, 6.04. Weight, 220.
High School—Logan, Utah.
Attended Utah State University.

Selected by Baltimore in 3rd round (44th player selected) of 1985 USFL draft.
Selected by Buffalo in 3rd round (63rd player selected) of 1985 NFL draft.
Signed by Buffalo Bills, July 19, 1985.
On injured reserve with toe injury, December 6 through remainder of 1985 season.
Buffalo NFL, 1985.
Games: 1985 (13).

SCOTT AARON GARNETT
Nose Tackle—San Diego Chargers
Born December 3, 1962, at Harrisburg, Pa.
Height, 6.02. Weight, 271.
High School—Pasadena, Calif., John Muir.
Attended University of Washington.

Selected by Washington in 4th round (66th player selected) of 1984 USFL draft.
Selected by Denver in 8th round (218th player selected) of 1984 NFL draft.
Signed by Denver Broncos, May 15, 1984.
Released by Denver Broncos, September 3, 1985; signed as free agent by San Francisco 49ers, September 28, 1985.
Released by San Francisco 49ers, October 26, 1985; signed as free agent by San Diego Chargers, November 20, 1985.
Denver NFL, 1984; San Francisco (3)-San Diego (5) NFL, 1985.
Games: 1984 (16), 1985 (8). Total—24.
Pro statistics: Recovered one fumble, 1984.

GREGG DAVID GARRITY
Wide Receiver—Philadelphia Eagles
Born November 24, 1960, at Pittsburgh, Pa.
Height, 5.10. Weight, 171.
High School—Wexford, Pa., North Allegheny.
Received bachelor of science degree in industrial arts education
from Penn State University in 1983.

Selected by Philadelphia in 1983 USFL territorial draft.
Selected by Pittsburgh in 5th round (140th player selected) of 1983 NFL draft.
Signed by Pittsburgh Steelers, May 20, 1983.
Released by Pittsburgh Steelers, October 23, 1984; awarded on waivers to Philadelphia Eagles, October 24, 1984.

Year Club	—PASS RECEIVING—				
	G.	P.C.	Yds.	Avg.	TD.
1983—Pittsburgh NFL............	15	19	279	14.7	1
1984—Pitt. (6)-Phi. (4) NFL...	10	2	22	11.0	0
1985—Philadelphia NFL	12	7	142	20.3	0
Pro Totals—3 Years............	37	28	443	15.8	1

Additional pro statistics: Recovered one fumble and fumbled once, 1983.

KEITH JERROLD GARY
Defensive End—Pittsburgh Steelers
Born September 14, 1959, at Bethesda, Md.
Height, 6.03. Weight, 264.
High School—Fairfax, Va., Chantilly.
Attended Ferrum Junior College and University of Oklahoma.

Selected by Pittsburgh in 1st round (17th player selected) of 1981 NFL draft.
Signed by Montreal Alouettes, July 7, 1981.
On reserve, August 30 through September 4, 1982.
On injured list, September 5 through remainder of 1982 season.
Granted free agency, March 11, 1983; signed by Pittsburgh Steelers, April 15, 1983.
On injured reserve with hamstring and knee injuries, October 22 through November 22, 1985; activated, November 23, 1985.
Montreal CFL, 1981 and 1982; Pittsburgh NFL, 1983 through 1985.
Games: 1981 (13), 1982 (7), 1983 (16), 1984 (16), 1985 (12). Total CFL—20. Total NFL—44. Total Pro—64.
CFL statistics: Recovered one fumble for 20 yards, 1982.
NFL statistics: Recovered two fumbles for 17 yards, 1983; recovered one fumble for six yards, 1984; recovered one fumble, 1985.
Played in AFC Championship Game following 1984 season.

RUSSELL CRAIG GARY
Safety—New Orleans Saints
Born July 31, 1959, at Minneapolis, Minn.
Height, 5.11. Weight, 195.
High School—Minneapolis, Minn., Central.
Attended University of Nebraska.

Selected by New Orleans in 2nd round (29th player selected) of 1981 NFL draft.
On injured reserve with knee injury, September 25 through remainder of 1985 season.

Year Club	—INTERCEPTIONS—				
	G.	No.	Yds.	Avg.	TD.
1981—New Orleans NFL........	14	1	0	0.0	0
1982—New Orleans NFL........	9	2	25	12.5	0
1983—New Orleans NFL........	14	3	70	23.3	0
1984—New Orleans NFL........	16		None		
1985—New Orleans NFL........	2		None		
Pro Totals—5 Years............	55	6	95	15.8	0

Additional pro statistics: Recovered two fumbles, 1982; fumbled once, 1983; recovered one fumble for five yards, 1984.

MARCUS D. GASTINEAU
Name pronounced GAS-tin-oh.
(Mark)
Defensive End—New York Jets
Born November 20, 1956, at Ardmore, Okla.
Height, 6.05. Weight, 265.
High School—Springerville, Ariz., Round Valley.
Attended Eastern Arizona Junior College, Arizona State University and
East Central (Okla.) University
Son of Ernie Gastineau, former professional boxer.

Named to THE SPORTING NEWS NFL All-Star Team, 1984 and 1985.
Selected by New York Jets in 2nd round (41st player selected) of 1979 NFL draft.
New York Jets NFL, 1979 through 1985.
Games: 1979 (16), 1980 (16), 1981 (16), 1982 (9), 1983 (16), 1984 (16), 1985 (16). Total—105.
Pro statistics: Recovered two fumbles, 1981; recovered two fumbles (including one in end zone for a touchdown), 1983; recovered one fumble in end zone for a touchdown, 1984; recovered three fumbles, 1985.
Played in AFC Championship Game following 1982 season.
Played in Pro Bowl (NFL All-Star Game) following 1981 through 1985 seasons.

WILLIE JAMES GAULT
Wide Receiver—Chicago Bears
Born September 5, 1960, at Griffin, Ga.
Height, 6.01. Weight, 183.
High School—Griffin, Ga.
Attended University of Tennessee.

Selected by New Jersey in 1983 USFL territorial draft.
Selected by Chicago in 1st round (18th player selected) of 1983 NFL draft.
Signed by Chicago Bears, August 16, 1983.

Year Club	G.	Att.	RUSHING Yds.	Avg.	TD.	PASS RECEIVING P.C. Yds.	Avg.	TD.	TOTAL TD.	Pts.	F.
1983—Chicago NFL	16	4	31	7.8	0	40 836	20.9	8	8	48	1
1984—Chicago NFL	16		None			34 587	17.3	6	6	36	1
1985—Chicago NFL	16	5	18	3.6	0	33 704	21.3	1	2	12	0
Pro Totals—3 Years	48	9	49	5.4	0	107 2127	19.9	15	16	96	2

Year Club	G.	PUNT RETURNS No. Yds.	Avg.	TD.	KICKOFF RET. No. Yds.	Avg.	TD.
1983—Chicago NFL	16	9 60	6.7	0	13 276	21.2	0
1984—Chicago NFL	16	None			1 12	12.0	0
1985—Chicago NFL	16	None			22 577	26.2	1
Pro Totals—3 Years	48	9 60	6.7	0	36 865	24.0	1

Additional pro statistics: Recovered one fumble, 1983.
Played in NFC Championship Game following 1984 and 1985 seasons.
Played in NFL Championship Game following 1985 season.

WILLIAM H. GAY
(Bill)
Defensive Lineman—Detroit Lions
Born May 28, 1955, at San Francisco, Calif.
Height, 6.05. Weight, 260.
High School—San Diego, Calif., Herbert Hoover.
Attended San Diego City College and University of Southern California.
Related to Dwight McDonald, wide receiver with San Diego Chargers, 1975 through 1978.

Selected by Denver in 2nd round (55th player selected) of 1978 NFL draft.
Traded by Denver Broncos to Detroit Lions for defensive back Charlie West and 6th round pick in 1979 draft, August 14, 1978.
Detroit NFL, 1978 through 1985.
Games: 1978 (16), 1979 (15), 1980 (16), 1981 (16), 1982 (9), 1983 (15), 1984 (16), 1985 (16). Total—119.
Pro statistics: Recovered one fumble, 1978, 1981 and 1982; returned one kickoff for no yards, recovered one fumble in end zone for a touchdown and fumbled once, 1979; intercepted one pass for seven yards, 1982 and 1985; recovered one fumble for 11 yards, 1983; recovered two fumbles for 30 yards, 1984; recovered six fumbles for three yards, 1985.
Played in Pro Bowl (NFL All-Star Game) following 1983 season.

SHAUN LaNARD GAYLE
Defensive Back—Chicago Bears
Born March 8, 1962, at Newport News, Va.
Height, 5.11. Weight, 195.
High School—Hampton, Va., Bethel.
Received bachelor of science degree in education from Ohio State University in 1984.

Selected by Michigan in 14th round (288th player selected) of 1984 USFL draft.
Selected by Chicago in 10th round (271st player selected) of 1984 NFL draft.
Signed by Chicago Bears, June 21, 1984.
On injured reserve with broken ankle, December 12 through remainder of 1984 season.
Chicago NFL, 1984 and 1985.
Games: 1984 (15), 1985 (16). Total—31.
Pro statistics: Intercepted one pass for minus one yard, 1984; recovered one fumble, 1985.
Played in NFC Championship Game following 1985 season.
Played in NFL Championship Game following 1985 season.

JAMES GEATHERS
Defensive End—New Orleans Saints
Born June 26, 1960, at Georgetown, S.C.
Height, 6.07. Weight, 267.
High School—Georgetown, S.C., Choppee.
Attended Paducah Community College and Wichita State University.
Brother of Robert Geathers, defensive end with Boston Breakers, 1983.

Selected by Oklahoma in 1984 USFL territorial draft.
Selected by New Orleans in 2nd round (42nd player selected) of 1984 NFL draft.
Signed by New Orleans Saints, May 30, 1984.
New Orleans NFL, 1984 and 1985.
Games: 1984 (16), 1985 (16). Total—32.

DENNIS LOUIS GENTRY
Running Back—Chicago Bears
Born February 10, 1959, at Lubbock, Tex.
Height, 5.08. Weight, 184.
High School—Lubbock, Tex., Dunbar.
Attended Baylor University.

Selected by Chicago in 4th round (89th player selected) of 1982 NFL draft.

Year Club	G.	Att.	RUSHING Yds.	Avg.	TD.	PASS RECEIVING P.C. Yds.	Avg.	TD.	TOTAL TD.	Pts.	F.
1982—Chicago NFL	9	4	21	5.3	0	1 9	9.0	0	0	0	4
1983—Chicago NFL	15	16	65	4.1	0	2 8	4.0	0	0	0	1

Year Club	G.	RUSHING				PASS RECEIVING				TOTAL		
		Att.	Yds.	Avg.	TD.	P.C.	Yds.	Avg.	TD.	TD.	Pts.	F.
1984—Chicago NFL	16	21	79	3.8	1	4	29	7.3	0	1	6	0
1985—Chicago NFL	16	30	160	5.3	2	5	77	15.4	0	3	18	0
Pro Totals—4 Years	56	71	325	4.6	3	12	123	10.3	0	4	24	5

Year Club	G.	PUNT RETURNS				KICKOFF RET.			
		No.	Yds.	Avg.	TD.	No.	Yds.	Avg.	TD.
1982—Chicago NFL	9	17	89	5.2	0	9	161	17.9	0
1983—Chicago NFL	15		None			7	130	18.6	0
1984—Chicago NFL	16		None			11	209	19.0	0
1985—Chicago NFL	16	0	47	....	0	18	466	25.9	1
Pro Totals—4 Years	56	17	136	8.0	0	45	966	21.5	1

Additional pro statistics: Recovered one fumble, 1982.
Played in NFC Championship Game following 1984 and 1985 seasons
Played in NFL Championship Game following 1985 season.

ERNEST GERARD GIBSON
Defensive Back—New England Patriots
Born October 3, 1961, at Jacksonville, Fla.
Height, 5.10. Weight, 185.
High School—Jacksonville, Fla., Bishop Kenny.
Received bachelor of arts degree in political science from Furman University in 1984.

Selected by Memphis in 3rd round (44th player selected) of 1984 USFL draft.
USFL rights traded by Memphis Showboats to Birmingham Stallions for rights to quarterback Walter Lewis, January 16, 1984.
Selected by New England in 6th round (151st player selected) of 1984 NFL draft.
Signed by New England Patriots, June 6, 1984.
On injured reserve with chest injury, September 2 through October 3, 1985; activated, October 4, 1985.

Year Club	G.	INTERCEPTIONS			
		No.	Yds.	Avg.	TD.
1984—New England NFL	15	2	4	2.0	0
1985—New England NFL	9		None		
Pro Totals—2 Years	24	2	4	2.0	0

Additional pro statistics: Returned one punt for three yards and recovered one fumble, 1984.
Played in AFC Championship Game following 1985 season.
Played in NFL Championship Game following 1985 season.

JON WILLIAM GIESLER
Name pronounced Geese-ler.
Offensive Tackle—Miami Dolphins
Born December 23, 1956, at Toledo, O.
Height, 6.05. Weight, 260.
High School—Elmore, O., Woodmore.
Received bachelor of science degree in education from University of Michigan in 1979.

Selected by Miami in 1st round (24th player selected) of 1979 NFL draft.
On injured reserve with shoulder injury, September 2 through October 9, 1980; activated, October 10, 1980.
Miami NFL, 1979 through 1985.
Games: 1979 (16), 1980 (10), 1981 (16), 1982 (9), 1983 (16), 1984 (16), 1985 (13). Total—96.
Pro statistics: Recovered one fumble, 1981 and 1985.
Played in AFC Championship Game following 1982, 1984 and 1985 seasons.
Played in NFL Championship Game following 1982 and 1984 seasons.

DAREN GILBERT
Offensive Tackle—New Orleans Saints
Born October 3, 1963, at San Diego, Calif.
Height, 6.06. Weight, 285.
High School—Compton, Calif., Dominguez.
Attended California State University at Fullerton.

Selected by Los Angeles in 1985 USFL territorial draft.
Selected by New Orleans in 2nd round (38th player selected) of 1985 NFL draft.
Signed by New Orleans Saints, August 5, 1985.
New Orleans NFL, 1985.
Games: 1985 (16).

GALE GILBERT
Quarterback—Seattle Seahawks
Born December 20, 1961, at Red Bluff, Calif.
Height, 6.03. Weight, 215.
High School—Red Bluff, Calif.
Attended University of California at Berkeley.

Selected by Oakland in 1985 USFL territorial draft.
Signed as free agent by Seattle Seahawks, May 2, 1985.

Year	Club	G.	Att.	Cmp.	Pct.	—PASSING— Gain	T.P.	P.I.	Avg.	—RUSHING— Att.	Yds.	Avg.	TD.	—TOTAL— TD.	Pts.	F.
1985—Seattle NFL		9	40	19	47.5	218	1	2	5.45	7	4	0.6	0	0	0	1

Quarterback Rating Points: 1985 (51.9).

Additional pro statistics: Recovered one fumble and fumbled once for minus five yards, 1985.

JIMMIE GILES JR.
Tight End—Tampa Bay Buccaneers
Born November 8, 1954, at Natchez, Miss.
Height, 6.03. Weight, 240.
High School—Greenville, Miss.
Received bachelor of science degree in business administration from Alcorn State University in 1977.
Related to Sammy White, wide receiver with Minnesota Vikings.

Selected by Houston in 3rd round (70th player selected) of 1977 NFL draft.
Traded with four draft choices (1st and 2nd round in 1978 and 3rd and 5th round in 1979) by Houston Oilers to Tampa Bay Buccaneers for 1st round pick in 1978 draft, April 24, 1978.
On reserve/did not report, August 16 through August 26, 1983.
Reinstated and granted roster exemption, August 27 through September 1, 1983; activated, September 2, 1983.

Year	Club	—PASS RECEIVING— G.	P.C.	Yds.	Avg.	TD.
1977—Houston NFL		14	17	147	8.6	0
1978—Tampa Bay NFL		16	23	324	14.1	2
1979—Tampa Bay NFL		16	40	579	14.5	7
1980—Tampa Bay NFL		16	33	602	18.2	4
1981—Tampa Bay NFL		16	45	786	17.5	6
1982—Tampa Bay NFL		9	28	499	17.8	3
1983—Tampa Bay NFL		11	25	349	14.0	1
1984—Tampa Bay NFL		14	24	310	12.9	2
1985—Tampa Bay NFL		16	43	673	15.7	8
Pro Totals—9 Years		128	278	4269	15.4	33

Additional pro statistics: Rushed once for minus 10 yards, 1977; returned five kickoffs for 60 yards, rushed once for minus one yard, 1978; fumbled once, 1978 and 1983; rushed twice for seven yards, 1979; recovered one fumble, 1979, 1980 and 1982; fumbled twice, 1980 and 1982; rushed once for one yard, 1982; fumbled three times, 1985.
Played in NFC Championship Game following 1979 season.
Played in Pro Bowl (NFL All-Star Game) following 1980 through 1982 and 1985 seasons.

RECORD AS BASEBALL PLAYER
Selected by Los Angeles Dodgers' organization in 12th round of free-agent draft, June 8, 1976.
Placed on restricted list, July 14, 1977.

Year	Club	League	Pos.	G.	AB.	R.	H.	2B.	3B.	HR.	RBI.	B.A.	PO.	A.	E.	F.A.
1976—Bellingham		Northw.	O-1-3	29	51	4	4	0	0	0	0	.078	16	5	2	.913

OWEN GILL
Fullback—Indianapolis Colts
Born February 19, 1962, at London, England.
Height, 6.01. Weight, 230.
High School—Brooklyn, N.Y., Samuel J. Tilden.
Attended University of Iowa.

Selected by Oakland in 1985 USFL territorial draft.
Selected by Seattle in 2nd round (53rd player selected) of 1985 NFL draft.
Signed by Seattle Seahawks, June 3, 1985.
Released by Seattle Seahawks, September 4, 1985; awarded on waivers to Indianapolis Colts, September 5, 1985.

Year	Club	—RUSHING— G.	Att.	Yds.	Avg.	TD.	PASS RECEIVING P.C.	Yds.	Avg.	TD.	—TOTAL— TD.	Pts.	F.
1985—Indianapolis NFL		15	45	262	5.8	2	5	52	10.4	0	2	12	1

Additional pro statistics: Returned one kickoff for six yards, 1985.

NESBY LEE GLASGOW
Safety—Indianapolis Colts
Born April 15, 1957, at Los Angeles, Calif.
Height, 5.10. Weight, 188.
High School—Gardena, Calif.
Attended University of Washington.

Tied NFL record for most combined kick returns, game (12), September 2, 1979, vs. Denver Broncos.
Selected by Baltimore in 8th round (207th player selected) of 1979 NFL draft.
Franchise transferred to Indianapolis, March 31, 1984.

Year	Club	INTERCEPTIONS G.	No.	Yds.	Avg.	TD.	-PUNT RETURNS- No.	Yds.	Avg.	TD.	—KICKOFF RET.— No.	Yds.	Avg.	TD.	—TOTAL— TD.	Pts.	F.
1979—Baltimore NFL		16	1	—1	-1.0	0	44	352	8.0	1	50	1126	22.5	0	1	6	8
1980—Baltimore NFL		16	4	65	16.3	0	23	187	8.1	0	33	743	22.5	0	0	0	5
1981—Baltimore NFL		14	2	35	17.5	0		None			1	35	35.0	0	0	0	0
1982—Baltimore NFL		9		None			4	24	6.0	0		None			0	0	0
1983—Baltimore NFL		16	3	35	11.7	0	1	9	9.0	0		None			0	0	0
1984—Indianapolis NFL		16	1	8	8.0	0	7	79	11.3	0		None			0	0	1
1985—Indianapolis NFL		16		None				None				None			0	0	0
Pro Totals—7 Years		103	11	142	12.9	0	79	651	8.2	1	84	1904	22.7	0	1	6	14

Additional pro statistics: Recovered two fumbles, 1979 through 1981; recovered one fumble, 1984.

KERRY R. GLENN
Cornerback—New York Jets
Born March 31, 1962, at St. Louis, Mo.
Height, 5.09. Weight, 175.
High School—East St. Louis, Ill.
Attended University of Minnesota.

Selected by Orlando in 4th round (46th player selected) of 1985 USFL draft.
Selected by New York Jets in 10th round (262nd player selected) of 1985 NFL draft.
Signed by New York Jets, July 26, 1985.

			——INTERCEPTIONS——			
Year	Club	G.	No.	Yds.	Avg.	TD.
1985—N.Y. Jets NFL		16	4	15	3.8	*1

Additional pro statistics: Returned five kickoffs for 71 yards and recovered two fumbles for 31 yards, 1985.

CLYDE M. GLOVER
Defensive End—San Francisco 49ers
Born July 16, 1960, at New Orleans, La.
Height, 6.06. Weight, 266.
High School—Las Vegas, Nev., Sunset.
Attended Walla Walla Community College and Fresno State University.

Selected by Oakland in 1984 USFL territorial draft.
Signed as free agent by New England Patriots, May 14, 1984.
Released by New England Patriots, August 21, 1984; signed as free agent by Kansas City Chiefs for 1985, October 15, 1984.
Released by Kansas City Chiefs, August 10, 1985; signed as free agent by San Francisco 49ers, March 10, 1986.

KEVIN BERNARD GLOVER
Center—Detroit Lions
Born June 17, 1963, at Washington, D.C.
Height, 6.02. Weight, 262.
High School—Largo, Md.
Attended University of Maryland.

Named as center on THE SPORTING NEWS College All-America Team, 1984.
Selected by Tampa Bay in 1985 USFL territorial draft.
Selected by Detroit in 2nd round (34th player selected) of 1985 NFL draft.
Signed by Detroit Lions, July 23, 1985.
On injured reserve with knee injury, December 7 through remainder of 1985 season.
Detroit NFL, 1985.
Games: 1985 (10).

CHRISTOPHER JAMES GODFREY
(Chris)
Guard—New York Giants
Born May 17, 1958, at Detroit, Mich.
Height, 6.03. Weight, 265.
High Schools—Detroit, Mich., De LaSalle and Miami, Fla., Lake.
Received bachelor of science degree in business from University of Michigan in 1980.

Signed as free agent by Washington Redskins, May 20, 1980.
Released by Washington Redskins, August 26, 1980; signed as free agent by New York Jets, September 23, 1980.
On physically unable to perform/active list with knee injury, July 17 through August 10, 1981.
Released by New York Jets, August 11, 1981; claimed on waivers by Green Bay Packers, August 13, 1981.
On injured reserve with knee injury, August 31 through entire 1981 season.
Released by Green Bay Packers, August 30, 1982; signed by Michigan Panthers, January 24, 1983.
Signed by New York Giants, April 28, 1984, to contract to take effect after being granted free agency, November 30, 1984.
On developmental squad, May 13 through May 19, 1984; activated, May 20, 1984.
On developmental squad, June 2 through remainder of 1984 season.
On developmental squad for 5 games with Michigan Panthers in 1984.
New York Jets NFL, 1980; Michigan USFL, 1983 and 1984; New York Giants NFL, 1984 and 1985.
Games: 1980 (6), 1983 (18), 1984 USFL (13), 1984 NFL (10), 1985 (16). Total NFL—32. Total USFL—31. Total Pro—63.
Pro statistics: Recovered two fumbles, 1983.
Played in USFL Championship Game following 1983 season.

WILLARD E. GOFF JR.
Defensive Tackle—Atlanta Falcons
Born October 17, 1961, at Lamar, Colo.
Height, 6.03. Weight, 265.
High School—Springfield, Colo.
Attended Dodge City Community College, University of Illinois
and West Texas State University.

Selected by Orlando in 15th round (221st player selected) of 1985 USFL draft.
Signed as free agent by Atlanta Falcons, May 3, 1985.
Released by Atlanta Falcons, August 27, 1985; re-signed by Falcons, November 7, 1985.
Atlanta NFL, 1985.
Games: 1985 (7).

MIKE GOLIC

Name pronounced Go-lick.

Defensive End—Houston Oilers

Born December 12, 1962, at Willowick, O.
Height, 6.05. Weight, 265.
High School—Cleveland, O., St. Joseph.
Attended University of Notre Dame.
Son of Louis Golic, former player with Montreal Alouettes, Hamilton Tiger-Cats and Saskatchewan
Roughriders; and brother of Bob Golic, nose tackle with Cleveland Browns.

Selected by Orlando in 15th round (204th player selected) of 1985 USFL draft.
Selected by Houston in 10th round (255th player selected) of 1985 NFL draft.
Signed by Houston Oilers, July 18, 1985.
On injured reserve with ankle injury, August 27 through entire 1985 season.

ROBERT PERRY GOLIC

Name pronounced Go-lick.

(Bob)

Nose Tackle—Cleveland Browns

Born October 26, 1957, at Cleveland, O.
Height, 6.02. Weight, 260.
High School—Cleveland, O., St. Joseph.
Received bachelor of business administration degree in management from
University of Notre Dame in 1979.
Son of Louis Golic, former player with Montreal Alouettes, Hamilton Tiger-Cats and Saskatchewan
Roughriders; and brother of Mike Golic, defensive end with Houston Oilers.

Named to THE SPORTING NEWS NFL All-Star Team, 1985.
Selected by New England in 2nd round (52nd player selected) of 1979 NFL draft.
On injured reserve with shoulder injury, August 28 through December 14, 1979; activated, December 15, 1979.
Released by New England Patriots, August 31, 1982; signed as free agent by Cleveland Browns, September 2, 1982.
On inactive list, September 12, 1982.
New England NFL, 1979 through 1982; Cleveland NFL, 1983 through 1985.
Games: 1979 (1), 1980 (16), 1981 (16), 1982 (6), 1983 (16), 1984 (15), 1985 (16). Total—86.
Pro statistics: Recovered one fumble, 1981; intercepted one pass for seven yards and a touchdown, 1983; recovered
one fumble for 18 yards, 1984.
Played in Pro Bowl (NFL All-Star Game) following 1985 season.

LEON EUGENE GONZALEZ III

Wide Receiver—Dallas Cowboys

Born September 21, 1963, at Jacksonville, Fla.
Height, 5.10. Weight, 162.
High School—Jacksonville, Fla., Ribault.
Received business administration degree from Bethune-Cookman College in 1985.

Selected by Orlando in 11th round (147th player selected) of 1985 USFL draft.
Selected by Dallas in 8th round (216th player selected) of 1985 NFL draft.
Signed by Dallas Cowboys, July 14, 1985.
On injured reserve with foot injury, December 5 through remainder of 1985 season.

		-PASS RECEIVING-				-PUNT RETURNS-				—TOTAL—		
Year Club	G.	P.C.	Yds.	Avg.	TD.	No.	Yds.	Avg.	TD.	TD.	Pts.	F.
1985—Dallas NFL	11	3	28	9.3	0	15	58	3.9	0	0	0	1

CONRAD LAWRENCE GOODE

Name pronounced Goodie.

Offensive Tackle—New York Giants

Born January 19, 1962, at St. Louis, Mo.
Height, 6.06. Weight, 285.
High School—Creve Coeur, Mo., Parkway Central.
Attended University of Missouri.
Stepson of Irv Goode, guard-center with St. Louis Cardinals, Buffalo Bills and
Miami Dolphins, 1962 thrugh 1974.

Selected by Oklahoma in 1st round (22nd player selected) of 1984 USFL draft.
Selected by New York Giants in 4th round (87th player selected) of 1984 NFL draft.
Signed by New York Giants, June 8, 1984.
New York Giants NFL, 1984 and 1985.
Games: 1984 (8), 1985 (16). Total—24.

JOHN TIMOTHY GOODE

Tight End—Philadelphia Eagles

Born November 5, 1962, at Cleveland Heights, O.
Height, 6.02. Weight, 243.
High School—Cleveland, O., Benedictine.
Attended Youngstown State University.

Selected by Oklahoma in 5th round (85th player selected) of 1984 USFL draft.
Selected by St. Louis in 5th round (136th player selected) of 1984 NFL draft.
Signed by St. Louis Cardinals, July 19, 1984.

Released by St. Louis Cardinals, September 2, 1985; signed as free agent by Philadelphia Eagles, September 13, 1985.

		—PASS RECEIVING—				
Year	Club	G.	P.C.	Yds.	Avg.	TD.
1984—St. Louis NFL		16	3	23	7.7	0
1985—Philadelphia NFL		14			None	
Pro Totals—2 Years		30	3	23	7.7	0

EUGENE GOODLOW
Wide Receiver—New Orleans Saints
Born December 19, 1958, at St. Louis, Mo.
Height, 6.02. Weight, 181.
High School—Rochester, N.Y., McQuaid Jesuit.
Attended Kansas State University.

Signed by Winnipeg Blue Bombers, September 22, 1980.
Selected by New Orleans in 3rd round (66th player selected) of 1982 NFL draft.
On injured list with neck injury, August 20 through remainder of 1982 season.
Granted free agency, March 1, 1983; signed by New Orleans Saints, March 2, 1983.
On injured reserve with pulled hamstring, October 5 through November 18, 1984; activated, November 19, 1984.
On injured reserve with knee injury, October 11 through November 7, 1985; activated, November 8, 1985.

		—PASS RECEIVING—				
Year	Club	G.	P.C.	Yds.	Avg.	TD.
1980—Winnipeg CFL		5	17	206	12.1	1
1981—Winnipeg CFL		16	*100	1494	14.9	4
1982—Winnipeg CFL		6	30	515	17.2	8
1983—New Orleans NFL		16	41	487	11.9	2
1984—New Orleans NFL		10	22	281	12.8	3
1985—New Orleans NFL		12	32	603	18.8	3
CFL Totals—3 Years		27	147	2215	15.1	13
NFL Totals—3 Years		38	95	1371	14.4	8
Pro Totals—6 Years		65	242	3586	14.8	21

Additional CFL statistics: Returned three punts for 22 yards, two kickoffs for 38 yards and fumbled once, 1980; returned four kickoffs for 72 yards and recovered two fumbles, 1981.
Additional NFL statistics: Rushed once for three yards, 1983 and 1985; rushed once for five yards, 1984.

JOHN RICHARD GOODMAN
Defensive End-Nose Tackle—Pittsburgh Steelers
Born November 12, 1958, at Oklahoma City, Okla.
Height, 6.06. Weight, 255.
High School—Richardson, Tex., L. V. Berkner.
Attended University of Oklahoma.

Selected by Pittsburgh in 2nd round (56th player selected) of 1980 NFL draft.
On injured reserve with knee injury, September 2 through entire 1980 season.
On injured reserve with knee injury, September 3 through October 3, 1985; activated, October 4, 1985.
Pittsburgh NFL, 1981 through 1985.
Games: 1981 (15), 1982 (9), 1983 (14), 1984 (14), 1985 (12). Total—64.
Played in AFC Championship Game following 1984 season.

JEFFERY ALAN GOSSETT
(Jeff)
Punter—Cleveland Browns
Born January 25, 1957, at Charleston, Ill.
Height, 6.02. Weight, 197.
High School—Charleston, Ill.
Received bachelor of science degree in physical education from Eastern Illinois University in 1982.

Signed as free agent by Dallas Cowboys, May, 1980.
Released by Dallas Cowboys, August 25, 1980; signed as free agent by San Diego Chargers, April 6, 1981.
Released by San Diego Chargers, August 31, 1981; signed as free agent by Kansas City Chiefs, November 5, 1981.
Released by Kansas City Chiefs, December 14, 1982; re-signed by Chiefs, December 21, 1982.
Released by Kansas City Chiefs, August 29, 1983; awarded on waivers to Cleveland Browns, August 30, 1983.
Signed by Chicago Blitz, December 20, 1983, for contract to take effect after being granted free agency, February 1, 1984.
USFL rights traded with placekicker Efren Herrera by Pittsburgh Maulers to Chicago Blitz for rights to linebacker Bruce Huther, December 30, 1983.
Franchise disbanded, November 20, 1984; signed as free agent by Portland Breakers, February 4, 1985.
Signed by Cleveland Browns for 1985 season, May 20, 1985.
Released by Portland Breakers, June 26, 1985.

—DID YOU KNOW—
That when John L. Williams and Neal Anderson of Florida were both taken in the 1986 NFL draft, it marked the first time since 1971 that two running backs were selected from the same school on the first round? John Brockington and Leo Hayden were both selected out of the same Ohio State backfield on round one fifteen years earlier.

Year Club	G.	No.	Avg.	Blk.
1981—Kansas City NFL	7	29	39.3	0
1982—Kansas City NFL	8	33	41.4	0
1983—Cleveland NFL	16	70	40.8	0
1984—Chicago USFL	18	85	*42.5	....
1985—Portland USFL	18	74	42.2	....
1985—Cleveland NFL	16	81	40.3	0
NFL Totals—4 Years	47	213	40.5	0
USFL Totals—2 Years	36	159	42.3	....
Pro Totals—6 Years	83	372	41.3	....

Additional NFL statistics: Recovered one fumble, 1982; attempted one pass with no completions, 1985.

Additional USFL statistics: Rushed once for no yards, 1984; attempted one pass with one interception, rushed once for minus four yards, recovered one fumble and fumbled once, 1985.

RECORD AS BASEBALL PLAYER

Selected by New York Mets' organization in 5th round of free-agent draft, June 6, 1978.
Placed on restricted list, April 30, 1980.

Year Club	League	Pos.	G.	AB.	R.	H.	2B.	3B.	HR.	RBI.	B.A.	PO.	A.	E.	F.A.
1978—Lynchburg	Carol.	3B-OF	10	21	1	5	1	0	0	4	.238	6	8	6	.700
1978—Little Falls	NYP	3B-OF	61	233	30	59	12	4	4	36	.253	54	102	19	.891
1979—Lynchburg	Carol.	3B	112	386	56	98	25	2	13	53	.254	71	200	*32	.894

PRESTON GOTHARD
Tight End—Pittsburgh Steelers
Born February 23, 1962, at Montgomery, Ala.
Height, 6.04. Weight, 235.
High School—Montgomery, Ala., Lowndes Academy.
Attended University of Alabama.

Signed as free agent by Pittsburgh Steelers, May 3, 1985.

		PASS RECEIVING			
Year Club	G.	P.C.	Yds.	Avg.	TD.
1985—Pittsburgh NFL	16	6	83	13.8	0

Additional pro statistics: Recovered one fumble, 1985.

RUSSELL CRAIG GRAHAM
(Russ)
Offensive Tackle—Pittsburgh Steelers
Born May 5, 1961, at Borger, Tex.
Height, 6.02. Weight, 245.
High School—Borger, Tex.
Attended Oklahoma State University.

Selected by Michigan in 10th round (111th player selected) of 1983 USFL draft.
Signed by Michigan Panthers, January 12, 1983.
On developmental squad, April 21 through April 26, 1983.
Released by Michigan Panthers, April 27, 1983; signed as free agent by Pittsburgh Steelers, May 10, 1983.
Released by Pittsburgh Steelers after not reporting, July 15, 1983; re-signed by Steelers, June 15, 1984.
On injured reserve with knee injury, August 27 through entire 1984 season.
On injured reserve with knee injury, August 25 through entire 1985 season.
Michigan USFL, 1983.
Games: 1983 (4).

WILLIAM ROGER GRAHAM
Safety—Detroit Lions
Born September 27, 1959, at Silsbee, Tex.
Height, 5.11. Weight, 190.
High School—Silsbee, Tex.
Received degree in sociology from University of Texas.

Selected by Detroit in 5th round (127th player selected) of 1982 NFL draft.
On injured reserve with broken foot, September 7 through November 19, 1982; activated, November 20, 1982.

		INTERCEPTIONS		
Year Club	G.	No.	Yds.	Avg. TD.
1982—Detroit NFL	7		None	
1983—Detroit NFL	14		None	
1984—Detroit NFL	14	3	22	7.3 0
1985—Detroit NFL	16	3	22	7.3 0
Pro Totals—4 Years	51	6	44	7.3 0

Additional pro statistics: Recovered three fumbles, 1983; recovered two fumbles, 1984; recovered one fumble, 1985.

NORMAN LANCE GRANGER
(Norm)
Running Back—Dallas Cowboys
Born September 14, 1961, at Newark, N.J.
Height, 5.09. Weight, 220.
High School—Newark, N.J., Barringer.
Attended University of Iowa.

Selected by Oklahoma in 2nd round (37th player selected) of 1984 USFL draft.
Selected by Dallas in 5th round (137th player selected) of 1984 NFL draft.
Signed by Dallas Cowboys, May 16, 1984.
Released by Dallas Cowboys, August 27, 1985; re-signed by Cowboys, March 12, 1986.
Dallas NFL, 1984.
Games: 1984 (15).
Pro statistics: Returned two kickoffs for six yards and recovered one fumble, 1984.

DARRYL GRANT
Defensive Tackle—Washington Redskins
Born November 22, 1959, at San Antonio, Tex.
Height, 6.01. Weight, 275.
High School—San Antonio, Tex., Highlands.
Attended Rice University.

Selected by Washington in 9th round (231st player selected) of 1981 NFL draft.
On injured reserve with knee injury, November 2 through remainder of 1985 season.
Washington NFL, 1981 through 1985.
Games: 1981 (15), 1982 (9), 1983 (16), 1984 (15), 1985 (8). Total—63.
Pro statistics: Returned one kickoff for 20 yards, 1981; recovered two fumbles, 1983; recovered four fumbles for 22 yards and a touchdown, 1984.
Played in NFC Championship Game following 1982 and 1983 seasons.
Played in NFL Championship Game following 1982 and 1983 seasons.

OTIS GRANT
Wide Receiver—Detroit Lions
Born August 13, 1961, at Atlanta, Ga.
Height, 6.03. Weight, 197.
High School—Atlanta, Ga., Carver.
Attended Michigan State University.

Selected by Michigan in 1983 USFL territorial draft.
Selected by Los Angeles Rams in 5th round (134th player selected) of 1983 NFL draft.
Signed by Los Angeles Rams, June 28, 1983.
On non-football injury list, December 7 through remainder of 1984 season.
Selected by Pittsburgh Pirates' organization in 6th round of free-agent draft, June 6, 1979.
Released by Los Angeles Rams, August 27, 1985; signed as free agent by Detroit Lions, May 7, 1986.

		——PASS RECEIVING——			
Year Club		G.	P.C.	Yds.	Avg. TD.
1983—L.A. Rams NFL.............		16	12	221	18.4	1
1984—L.A. Rams NFL.............		14	9	64	7.1	0
Pro Totals—2 Years............		30	21	285	13.6	1

Additional pro statistics: Rushed twice for minus 10 yards, recovered one fumble and fumbled once, 1983.

WILFRED L. GRANT
(Will)
Center—Buffalo Bills
Born March 7, 1954, at Boston, Mass.
Height, 6.03. Weight, 264.
High Schools—Braintree, Mass., Thayer Academy; and Milford, Conn., Academy.
Attended Idaho State University and University of Kentucky.

Selected by Buffalo in 10th round (255th player selected) of 1978 NFL draft.
Buffalo NFL, 1978 through 1985.
Games: 1978 (16), 1979 (16), 1980 (16), 1981 (16), 1982 (9), 1983 (16), 1984 (16), 1985 (16). Total—121.
Pro statistics: Recovered one fumble, 1980, 1981 and 1985.

MARSHARNE DeWAYNE GRAVES
Offensive Tackle—Denver Broncos
Born July 8, 1962, at Memphis, Tenn.
Height, 6.03. Weight, 272.
High School—San Francisco, Calif., Lincoln.
Attended University of Arizona.
Cousin of Henry Lawrence, offensive tackle with Los Angeles Raiders.

Selected by Arizona in 1984 USFL territorial draft.
Signed as free agent by Denver Broncos, May 2, 1984.
Released by Denver Broncos, August 27, 1984; re-signed by Broncos for 1985, October 9, 1984.
Signed for 1984 season, November 5, 1984.
On injured reserve with knee injury, August 26 through entire 1985 season.
Denver NFL, 1984.
Games: 1984 (1).

EARNEST GRAY
Wide Receiver—St. Louis Cardinals
Born March 2, 1957, at Greenwood, Miss.
Height, 6.03. Weight, 195.
High School—Greenwood, Miss.
Attended Memphis State University.

Selected by New York Giants in 2nd round (36th player selected) of 1979 NFL draft.
On injured reserve with broken hand, November 17 through December 13, 1984; activated, December 14, 1984.
Granted free agency, February 1, 1985; re-signed by Giants, November 5, 1985.
Granted roster exemption, November 5 through November 18, 1985.
Released by New York Giants, November 19, 1985; awarded on waivers to St. Louis Cardinals, November 20, 1985.

			——PASS RECEIVING——			
Year	Club	G.	P.C.	Yds.	Avg.	TD.
1979—N.Y. Giants NFL		16	28	537	19.2	4
1980—N.Y. Giants NFL		16	52	777	14.9	10
1981—N.Y. Giants NFL		16	22	360	16.4	2
1982—N.Y. Giants NFL		9	25	426	17.0	4
1983—N.Y. Giants NFL		16	78	1139	14.6	5
1984—N.Y. Giants NFL		12	38	529	13.9	2
1985—St. Louis NFL		5	3	22	7.3	0
Pro Totals—7 Years		90	246	3790	15.4	27

Additional pro statistics: Rushed twice for two yards and returned one kickoff for no yards, 1979; fumbled once, 1979 through 1981; recovered one fumble, 1980.

JERRY GRAY
Defensive Back—Los Angeles Rams
Born December 2, 1962, at Lubbock, Tex.
Height, 6.00. Weight, 185.
High School—Lubbock, Tex., Estacado.
Attended University of Texas.

Named as defensive back on THE SPORTING NEWS College All-America Team, 1984.
Selected by San Antonio in 1985 USFL territorial draft.
Selected by Los Angeles Rams in 1st round (21st player selected) of 1985 NFL draft.
Signed by Los Angeles Rams, August 1, 1985.
Los Angeles Rams NFL, 1985.
Games: 1985 (16).
Played in NFC Championship Game following 1985 season.

DONALD GRECO
(Don)
Guard—Detroit Lions
Born April 1, 1959, at St. Louis, Mo.
Height, 6.03. Weight, 265.
High School—St. Louis, Mo., Riverview Gardens.
Attended Western Illinois University.

Selected by Detroit in 3rd round (72nd player selected) of 1981 NFL draft.
On injured reserve with pinched nerve, August 31 through entire 1981 season.
On injured reserve with shoulder injury, September 10 through October 10, 1985; activated, October 11, 1985.
Detroit NFL, 1982 through 1985.
Games: 1982 (9), 1983 (12), 1984 (16), 1985 (8). Total—45.
Pro statistics: Recovered one fumble, 1983 and 1984.

BOYCE K. GREEN
Running Back—Kansas City Chiefs
Born June 24, 1960, at Beaufort, S.C.
Height, 5.11. Weight, 215.
High School—Beaufort, S.C.
Received bachelor of science degree in physical education from Carson-Newman College in 1984.

Selected by Cleveland in 11th round (288th player selected) of 1983 NFL draft.
Traded by Cleveland Browns to Kansas City Chiefs for 7th round pick in 1986 draft, April 29, 1986.

			——RUSHING——				PASS RECEIVING				—TOTAL—		
Year	Club	G.	Att.	Yds.	Avg.	TD.	P.C.	Yds.	Avg.	TD.	TD.	Pts.	F.
1983—Cleveland NFL		13	104	497	4.8	3	25	167	6.7	1	4	24	4
1984—Cleveland NFL		16	202	673	3.3	0	12	124	10.3	1	1	6	3
1985—Cleveland NFL		13		None				None			0	0	0
Pro Totals—3 Years		42	306	1170	3.8	3	37	291	7.9	2	5	30	7

			KICKOFF RETURNS			
Year	Club	G.	No.	Yds.	Avg.	TD.
1983—Cleveland NFL		13	17	350	20.6	0
1984—Cleveland NFL		16		None		
1985—Cleveland NFL		13	2	20	10.0	0
Pro Totals—3 Years		42	19	370	19.5	0

Additional pro statistics: Recovered two fumbles, 1984.

CLEVELAND CARL GREEN
Offensive Tackle—Miami Dolphins
Born September 11, 1957, at Bolton, Miss.
Height, 6.03. Weight, 262.
High School—Utica, Miss., Hinds County.
Received degree in plant and soil science from Southern University.

— 155 —

Signed as free agent by Miami Dolphins, May, 1979.
On injured reserve with broken hand, October 10 through November 6, 1980; activated, November 7, 1980.
On inactive list, September 19, 1982.
Miami NFL, 1979 through 1985.
Games: 1979 (16), 1980 (12), 1981 (6), 1982 (3), 1983 (16), 1984 (16), 1985 (12). Total—81.
Pro statistics: Recovered one fumble, 1980.
Played in AFC Championship Game following 1982, 1984 and 1985 seasons.
Played in NFL Championship Game following 1982 and 1984 seasons.

CURTIS GREEN
Defensive End—Detroit Lions
Born June 3, 1957, at Quincy, Fla.
Height, 6.03. Weight, 258.
High School—Quincy, Fla., James A. Shanks.
Attended Alabama State University.

Selected by Detroit in 2nd round (46th player selected) of 1981 NFL draft.
On inactive list, September 19, 1982.
Detroit NFL, 1981 through 1985.
Games: 1981 (14), 1982 (7), 1983 (16), 1984 (16), 1985 (15). Total—68.
Pro statistics: Recovered one fumble, 1981 and 1985.

DARRELL GREEN
Cornerback—Washington Redskins
Born February 15, 1960, at Houston, Tex.
Height, 5.08. Weight, 170.
High School—Houston, Tex., Jesse Jones.
Attended Texas A&I University.

Selected by Denver in 10th round (112th player selected) of 1983 USFL draft.
Selected by Washington in 1st round (28th player selected) of 1983 NFL draft.
Signed by Washington Redskins, June 10, 1983.

Year Club	G.	-INTERCEPTIONS-				-PUNT RETURNS-				—TOTAL—		
		No.	Yds.	Avg.	TD.	No.	Yds.	Avg.	TD.	TD.	Pts.	F.
1983—Washington NFL	16	2	7	3.5	0	4	29	7.3	0	0	0	1
1984—Washington NFL	16	5	91	18.2	1	2	13	6.5	0	1	6	0
1985—Washington NFL	16	2	0	0.0	0	16	214	13.4	0	0	0	2
Pro Totals—3 Years	48	9	98	10.9	1	22	256	11.6	0	1	6	3

Additional pro statistics: Recovered one fumble, 1983 and 1985; rushed once for six yards, 1985.
Played in NFC Championship Game following 1983 season.
Played in NFL Championship Game following 1983 season.
Played in Pro Bowl (NFL All-Star Game) following 1984 season.

GARY F. GREEN
Cornerback—Los Angeles Rams
Born October 22, 1955, at San Antonio, Tex.
Height, 5.11. Weight, 191.
High School—San Antonio, Tex., Sam Houston.
Received bachelor of science degree in physical education from Baylor University in 1977.
Cousin of David Hill, tight end with Los Angeles Rams; and Jim Hill, defensive back with
San Diego Chargers, Green Bay Packers and Cleveland Browns, 1969 through 1975.

Named as cornerback on THE SPORTING NEWS College All-America Team, 1976.
Selected by Kansas City in 1st round (10th player selected) of 1977 NFL draft.
Traded by Kansas City Chiefs to Los Angeles Rams for 1st and 5th round picks in 1984 draft, May 1, 1984.

Year Club	G.	-INTERCEPTIONS-				-PUNT RETURNS-				—TOTAL—		
		No.	Yds.	Avg.	TD.	No.	Yds.	Avg.	TD.	TD.	Pts.	F.
1977—Kansas City NFL	11	3	19	6.3	0	14	115	8.2	0	0	0	3
1978—Kansas City NFL	16	1	0	0.0	0	1	6	6.0	0	0	0	0
1979—Kansas City NFL	16	5	148	29.6	0	None				0	0	0
1980—Kansas City NFL	16	2	25	12.5	0	None				0	0	1
1981—Kansas City NFL	16	5	37	7.4	0	None				0	0	0
1982—Kansas City NFL	9	2	42	21.0	*1	None				1	6	0
1983—Kansas City NFL	16	6	59	9.8	0	None				0	0	0
1984—Los Angeles Rams NFL	16	3	88	29.3	0	None				0	0	0
1985—Los Angeles Rams NFL	16	6	84	14.0	*1	None				1	6	0
Pro Totals—9 Years	132	33	502	15.2	2	15	121	8.1	0	2	12	4

Additional pro statistics: Recovered two fumbles, 1977 through 1979 and 1983; returned one kickoff for 27 yards, 1978; recovered one fumble, 1981 and 1984; recovered one fumble for 18 yards, 1982.
Played in NFC Championship Game following 1985 season.
Played in Pro Bowl (NFL All-Star Game) following 1981 through 1983 and 1985 seasons.

HUGH DONELL GREEN
Linebacker—Miami Dolphins
Born July 27, 1959, at Natchez, Miss.
Height, 6.02. Weight, 225.
High School—Natchez, Miss., North.
Attended University of Pittsburgh.

Named THE SPORTING NEWS College Player of the Year, 1980.

Named as defensive end on THE SPORTING NEWS College All-America Team, 1979 and 1980.
Named to THE SPORTING NEWS NFL All-Star Team, 1983.
Selected by Tampa Bay in 1st round (7th player selected) of 1981 NFL draft.
On non-football injury list with eye and wrist injury, November 1 through November 29, 1984; activated, November 30, 1984.
Traded by Tampa Bay Buccaneers to Miami Dolphins for 1st and 2nd round picks in 1986 draft, October 9, 1985.

			—INTERCEPTIONS—			
Year Club	G.	No.	Yds.	Avg.	TD.	
1981—Tampa Bay NFL	16	2	56	28.0	0	
1982—Tampa Bay NFL	9	1	31	31.0	0	
1983—Tampa Bay NFL	16	2	54	27.0	*2	
1984—Tampa Bay NFL	8		None			
1985—T.B.(5)-Mia.(11) NFL...	16	1	28	28.0	0	
Pro Totals—5 Years............	65	6	169	28.2	2	

Additional pro statistics: Recovered one fumble, 1981 and 1985; recovered two fumbles for 11 yards and fumbled once, 1983.
Played in AFC Championship Game following 1985 season.
Played in Pro Bowl (NFL All-Star Game) following 1982 and 1983 seasons.

JACOB CARL GREEN
Defensive End—Seattle Seahawks
Born January 21, 1957, at Pasadena, Tex.
Height, 6.03. Weight, 255.
High School—Houston, Tex., Kashmere.
Attended Texas A&M University.
Cousin of George Small, defensive tackle with New York Giants and
Calgary Stampeders, 1980 through 1983.

Named to THE SPORTING NEWS NFL All-Star Team, 1984.
Selected by Seattle in 1st round (10th player selected) of 1980 NFL draft.
Seattle NFL, 1980 through 1985.
Games: 1980 (14), 1981 (16), 1982 (9), 1983 (16), 1984 (16), 1985 (16). Total—87.
Pro statistics: Recovered one fumble, 1981; intercepted one pass for 73 yards and a touchdown and recovered two fumbles, 1983; recovered four fumbles, 1984; recovered two fumbles for 79 yards and a touchdown and intercepted one pass for 19 yards and a touchdown, 1985.
Played in AFC Championship Game following 1983 season.

LAWRENCE CHRISTOPHER GREEN
Linebacker—Indianapolis Colts
Born May 15, 1962, at Florence, Ala.
Height, 6.02. Weight, 230.
High School—Florence, Ala., Bradshaw.
Attended University of Tennessee-Chattanooga.

Selected by Washington in 7th round (135th player selected) of 1984 USFL draft.
Selected by New York Giants in 12th round (311th player selected) of 1984 NFL draft.
Signed by New York Giants, June 5, 1984.
On injured reserve with hamstring injury, August 28 through entire 1984 season.
Released by New York Giants, August 26, 1985; signed as free agent by Indianapolis Colts, March 24, 1986.

MICHAEL JAMES GREEN
(Mike)
Linebacker
Born June 29, 1961, at Port Arthur, Tex.
Height, 6.00. Weight, 239.
High School—Port Arthur, Tex., Lincoln.
Received degree in business from Oklahoma State University.

Selected by Michigan in 15th round (178th player selected) of 1983 USFL draft.
Selected by San Diego in 9th round (245th player selected) of 1983 NFL draft.
Signed by San Diego Chargers, May 26, 1983.
Released by San Diego Chargers after failing physical, May 23, 1986.
San Diego NFL, 1983 through 1985.
Games: 1983 (16), 1984 (16), 1985 (15). Total—47.
Pro statistics: Intercepted one pass for three yards, 1983; recovered one fumble, 1984; intercepted two passes for 17 yards and recovered two fumbles, 1985.

ROY GREEN
Wide Receiver—St. Louis Cardinals
Born June 30, 1957, at Magnolia, Ark.
Height, 6.00. Weight, 195.
High School—Magnolia, Ark.
Attended Henderson State University

Tied NFL record for longest kickoff return, game (106 yards), against Dallas Cowboys, October 21, 1979.
Named as kick returner to THE SPORTING NEWS NFC All-Star Team, 1979.
Named to THE SPORTING NEWS NFL All-Star Team, 1983 and 1984.
Selected by St. Louis in 4th round (89th player selected) of 1979 NFL draft.
On injured reserve with knee injury, December 15 through remainder of 1980 season.

Year Club	G.	INTERCEPTIONS No.	Yds.	Avg.	TD.	-PUNT RETURNS- No.	Yds.	Avg.	TD.	—KICKOFF RET.— No.	Yds.	Avg.	TD.	—TOTAL— TD.	Pts.	F.
1979—St. Louis NFL	16	None				8	42	5.3	0	41	1005	24.5	*1	1	6	4
1980—St. Louis NFL	15	1	10	10.0	0	16	168	10.5	1	32	745	23.3	0	1	6	2
1981—St. Louis NFL	16	3	44	14.7	0	None				8	135	16.9	0	5	30	2
1982—St. Louis NFL	9	None				3	20	6.7	0	None				3	18	1
1983—St. Louis NFL	16	None				None				1	14	14.0	0	14	84	3
1984—St. Louis NFL	16	None				None				1	18	18.0	0	12	72	1
1985—St. Louis NFL	13	None				None				None				5	30	2
Pro Totals—7 Years	101	4	54	13.5	0	27	230	8.5	1	83	1917	23.1	1	41	246	15

Year Club	G.	——PASS RECEIVING—— P.C.	Yds.	Avg.	TD.
1979—St. Louis NFL	16	1	15	15.0	0
1980—St. Louis NFL	15	None			
1981—St. Louis NFL	16	33	708	21.5	4
1982—St. Louis NFL	9	32	453	14.2	3
1983—St. Louis NFL	16	78	1227	15.7	*14
1984—St. Louis NFL	16	78	*1555	19.9	12
1985—St. Louis NFL	13	50	693	13.9	5
Pro Totals—7 Years	101	272	4651	17.1	38

Additional pro statistics: Recovered two fumbles, 1979; rushed three times for 60 yards and one touchdown, 1981; rushed six times for eight yards, attempted one pass with no completions and recovered one fumble for two yards, 1982; rushed four times for 49 yards and recovered one fumble, 1983; rushed once for minus 10 yards, 1984; rushed once for two yards, 1985.

Played in Pro Bowl (NFL All-Star Game) following 1983 and 1984 seasons.

GEORGE GREENE
(Tiger)
Cornerback—Atlanta Falcons
Born February 15, 1962, at Hendersonville, N.C.
Height, 5.10. Weight, 184.
High School—Flat Rock, N.C., East Henderson.
Attended Western Carolina University.

Selected by Memphis in 14th round (191st player selected) of 1985 USFL draft.
Signed as free agent by Atlanta Falcons, May 3, 1985.
On injured reserve with knee injury, September 16 through October 18, 1985; activated, October 19, 1985.
On injured reserve with ankle injury, December 10 through remainder of 1985 season.

Year Club	G.	——INTERCEPTIONS—— No.	Yds.	Avg.	TD.
1985—Atlanta NFL	10	2	27	13.5	0

KEVIN DARWIN GREENE
Linebacker—Los Angeles Rams
Born July 31, 1962, at New York, N.Y.
Height, 6.03. Weight, 238.
High School—Granite City, Ill., South.
Attended Auburn University.

Selected by Birmingham in 1985 USFL territorial draft.
Selected by Los Angeles Rams in 5th round (113th player selected) of 1985 NFL draft.
Signed by Los Angeles Rams, July 12, 1985.
Los Angeles Rams NFL, 1985.
Games: 1985 (15).
Played in NFC Championship Game following 1985 season.

THEODORE DANIEL GREENE II
(Danny)
Wide Receiver—Seattle Seahawks
Born December 26, 1961, at Compton, Calif.
Height, 5.11. Weight, 195.
High School—Compton, Calif.
Attended University of Washington.

Selected by Portland in 1985 USFL territorial draft.
Selected by Seattle in 3rd round (81st player selected) of 1985 NFL draft.
Signed by Seattle Seahawks, July 21, 1985.
On injured reserve with hamstring injury, October 2 through remainder of season.

Year Club	G.	PASS RECEIVING P.C.	Yds.	Avg.	TD.	-PUNT RETURNS- No.	Yds.	Avg.	TD.	—KICKOFF RET.— No.	Yds.	Avg.	TD.	—TOTAL— TD.	Pts.	F.
1985—Seattle NFL	4	2	10	5.0	1	11	60	5.5	0	5	144	28.8	0	1	6	1

DAVID MARK GREENWOOD
Defensive Back—Tampa Bay Buccaneers
Born March 25, 1960, at Park Falls, Wis.
Height, 6.03. Weight, 210.
High School—Park Falls, Wis.
Attended University of Wisconsin.

Named as safety on THE SPORTING NEWS USFL All-Star Team, 1983.
Selected by Michigan in 1st round (10th player selected) of 1983 USFL draft.
Signed by Michigan Panthers, January 14, 1983.
Selected by New Orleans in 8th round (206th player selected) of 1983 NFL draft.
On developmental squad, April 10 through April 20, 1983; activated, April 21, 1983.
On developmental squad, May 13 through June 7, 1984.
On injured reserve with knee injury, June 8 through remainder of 1984 season.
Protected in merger of Michigan Panthers and Oakland Invaders, December 6, 1984.
On developmental squad, February 21 through March 7, 1985; activated, March 8, 1985.
Released by Oakland Invaders, July 24, 1985.
NFL rights traded by New Orleans Saints to Tampa Bay Buccaneers for 3rd round pick in 1986 draft, August 30, 1985.
Signed by Tampa Bay Buccaneers, August 30, 1985.
Granted roster exemption, August 30 through September 5, 1985; activated, September 6, 1985.
On developmental squad for 2 games with Michigan Panthers in 1983.
On developmental squad for 4 games with Michigan Panthers in 1984.
On developmental squad for 2 games with Oakland Invaders in 1985.

		INTERCEPTIONS				—PUNTING—		
Year Club	G.	No.	Yds.	Avg.	TD.	No.	Avg.	Blk.
1983—Michigan USFL	16	2	31	15.5	0	37	41.4	....
1984—Michigan USFL	11	4	10	2.5	0	38	36.6	....
1985—Oakland USFL	16	3	21	7.0	0	None		
1985—Tampa Bay NFL	16	5	15	3.0	0	None		
USFL Totals—3 Years	43	9	62	6.9	0	75	38.9	....
NFL Totals—1 Year	16	5	15	3.0	0	0	0.0	0
Pro Totals—4 Years	59	14	77	5.5	0	75	38.9	....

Additional USFL statistics: Returned one kickoff for three yards, recovered two fumbles for four yards, fumbled twice and credited with one sack for nine yards, 1983; credited with two sacks for 35 yards, ran once for minus seven yards and attempted one pass with one completion for six yards, 1984; credited with two sacks for 13 yards, 1985.
Additional NFL statistics: Recovered one fumble for nine yards and fumbled twice, 1985.
Played in USFL Championship Game following 1983 and 1985 seasons.

CURTIS WILLIAM GREER
Defensive End—St. Louis Cardinals
Born November 10, 1957, at Detroit, Mich.
Height, 6.04. Weight, 258.
High School—Detroit, Mich., Cass Tech.
Received bachelor of science degree in speech communication
from University of Michigan in 1979.

Selected by St. Louis in 1st round (6th player selected) of 1980 NFL draft.
On injured reserve with concussion, September 9 through October 9, 1980; activated, October 10, 1980.
On injured reserve with broken thumb, December 15 through remainder of 1980 season.
St. Louis NFL, 1980 through 1985.
Games: 1980 (11), 1981 (16), 1982 (9), 1983 (16), 1984 (16), 1985 (16). Total—84.
Pro statistics: Recovered four fumbles for two yards, 1981; recovered three fumbles, 1982; recovered one fumble for five yards, 1983; recovered one fumble, 1985.

TERRY LEE GREER
Wide Receiver—Cleveland Browns
Born September 27, 1957, at Memphis, Tenn.
Height, 6.01. Weight, 192.
High School—Memphis, Tenn., Messick.
Received bachelor of science degree in business from Alabama State University in 1980.

Signed as free agent by Toronto Argonauts, March 21, 1980.
Selected by Los Angeles Rams in 11th round (304th player selected) of 1980 NFL draft.
On injured reserve, August 10 through remainder of 1981 season.
Granted free agency, March 1, 1986.
Los Angeles Rams matched Cleveland Browns offer sheet and traded him to Cleveland Browns for 4th round pick in 1986 draft, April 18, 1986.

		—RUSHING—				PASS RECEIVING				—TOTAL—		
Year Club	G.	Att.	Yds.	Avg.	TD.	P.C.	Yds.	Avg.	TD.	TD.	Pts.	F.
1980—Toronto CFL	14	2	38	19.0	1	37	552	14.9	2	3	18	0
1981—Toronto CFL	6	1	22	22.0	0	21	284	13.5	3	4	24	1
1982—Toronto CFL	15	7	52	7.4	1	85	1466	17.2	11	12	†74	1
1983—Toronto CFL	16	2	15	7.5	0	★113	★2003	17.7	8	8	48	1
1984—Toronto CFL	15	2	13	6.5	0	70	1189	17.0	14	14	84	1
1985—Toronto CFL	16	3	45	15.0	0	78	1323	17.0	9	9	54	0
Pro Totals—6 Years	82	17	185	10.9	2	404	6817	16.9	47	50	302	4

		KICKOFF RETURNS			
Year Club	G.	No.	Yds.	Avg.	TD.
1980—Toronto CFL	14	23	533	23.2	0
1981—Toronto CFL	6	11	418	38.0	1
1982—Toronto CFL	15	12	285	23.8	0
1983—Toronto CFL	16	1	0	0.0	0
1984—Toronto CFL	15	3	31	10.3	0
1985—Toronto CFL	16	None			
Pro Totals—6 Years	82	50	1267	25.3	1

†Scored one 2-point conversion.

Additional pro statistics: Attempted one pass with one completion for 39 yards and a touchdown, 1982; attempted two passes with one completion for 39 yards with one touchdown and one interception, 1983; attempted three passes with one completion for 42 yards and a touchdown, 1984; attempted two passes with one completion for minus one yard and recovered one fumble for two yards, 1985.

Played in CFL Championship Game following 1982 and 1983 seasons.

JAMES VICTOR GRIFFIN
Safety—Cincinnati Bengals

Born September 7, 1961, at Camilla, Ga.
Height, 6.02. Weight, 197.
High School—Camilla, Ga., Mitchell.
Attended Middle Tennessee State University.

Selected by Cincinnati in 7th round (193rd player selected) of 1983 NFL draft.

			—INTERCEPTIONS—			
Year	Club	G.	No.	Yds.	Avg.	TD.
1983—Cincinnati NFL		16	1	41	41.0	1
1984—Cincinnati NFL		16	1	57	57.0	1
1985—Cincinnati NFL		16	7	116	16.6	∗1
Pro Totals—3 Years		48	9	214	23.8	3

Additional pro statistics: Recovered two fumbles, 1984; returned one kickoff for no yards and recovered one fumble for 29 yards, 1985.

JEFF GRIFFIN
Cornerback—St. Louis Cardinals

Born July 19, 1958, at Carson, Calif.
Height, 6.00. Weight, 185.
High School—Wilmington, Calif., Banning.
Attended University of Utah.

Selected by St. Louis in 3rd round (61st player selected) of 1981 NFL draft.
On injured reserve with broken arm, August 30 through October 3, 1983; activated, October 4, 1983.
On injured reserve with broken arm, October 27 through remainder of 1983 season.
On injured reserve with broken arm, August 28 through October 18, 1984; activated, October 19, 1984.
On injured reserve with knee injury, September 10 through October 9, 1985; activated, October 10, 1985.

			—INTERCEPTIONS—			
Year	Club	G.	No.	Yds.	Avg.	TD.
1981—St. Louis NFL		16	1	4	4.0	0
1982—St. Louis NFL		8	1	8	8.0	0
1983—St. Louis NFL		3		None		
1984—St. Louis NFL		8	2	0	0.0	0
1985—St. Louis NFL		12		None		
Pro Totals—5 Years		47	4	12	3.0	0

Additional pro statistics: Returned two kickoffs for 34 yards, 1981; returned one kickoff for 12 yards, 1982; recovered one fumble, 1985.

KEITH GRIFFIN
Running Back—Washington Redskins

Born October 26, 1961, at Columbus, O.
Height, 5.08. Weight, 185.
High School—Columbus, O., Eastmoor.
Attended University of Miami (Fla.).
Brother of Archie Griffin, running back with Cincinnati Bengals and Jacksonville Bulls,
1976 through 1982 and 1984; and Ray Griffin, defensive back with Cincinnati Bengals, 1978 through 1984.

Selected by Oklahoma in 11th round (212th player selected) of 1984 USFL draft.
Selected by Washington in 10th round (279th player selected) of 1984 NFL draft.
Signed by Washington Redskins, July 13, 1984.

			—RUSHING—				PASS RECEIVING				—TOTAL—		
Year	Club	G.	Att.	Yds.	Avg.	TD.	P.C.	Yds.	Avg.	TD.	TD.	Pts.	F.
1984—Washington NFL		16	97	408	4.2	0	8	43	5.4	0	0	0	7
1985—Washington NFL		16	102	473	4.6	3	37	285	7.7	0	3	18	1
Pro Totals—2 Years		32	199	881	4.4	3	45	328	7.3	0	3	18	8

			KICKOFF RETURNS			
Year	Club	G.	No.	Yds.	Avg.	TD.
1984—Washington NFL		16	9	164	18.2	0
1985—Washington NFL		16	7	142	20.3	0
Pro Totals—2 Years		32	16	306	19.1	0

ANTHONY GRIGGS
Linebacker—Cleveland Browns

Born February 12, 1960, at Lawton, Okla.
Height, 6.03. Weight, 230.
High School—Willingboro, N.J., John F. Kennedy.
Attended Ohio State University and received degree in communications from Villanova University.
Cousin of Billy Griggs, tight end with New York Jets.

Selected by Philadelphia in 4th round (104th player selected) of 1982 NFL draft.
Traded by Philadelphia Eagles to Cleveland Browns for 8th round pick in 1986 draft, April 29, 1986.

			—INTERCEPTIONS—		
Year	Club	G.	No.	Yds.	Avg.TD.
1982—Philadelphia NFL		9			None
1983—Philadelphia NFL		16	3	61	20.3	0
1984—Philadelphia NFL		16			None
1985—Philadelphia NFL		16			None
Pro Totals—4 Years............		57	3	61	20.3	0

Additional pro statistics: Recovered one fumble, 1982.

WILLIAM EDWARD GRIGGS
(Billy)
Tight End—New York Jets

Born August 4, 1962, at Camden, N.J.
Height, 6.03. Weight, 230.
High School—Pennsauken, N.J.
Received bachelor of arts degree in sociology from University of Virginia in 1984.
Cousin of Anthony Griggs, linebacker with Cleveland Browns.

Selected by New York Jets in 8th round (203rd player selected) of 1984 NFL draft.
On injured reserve with ankle injury, August 14 through entire 1984 season.
New York Jets NFL, 1985.
Games: 1985 (16).

RANDALL COLLINS GRIMES
(Randy)
Offensive Lineman—Tampa Bay Buccaneers

Born July 20, 1960, at Tyler, Tex.
Height, 6.04. Weight, 270.
High School—Tyler, Tex., Robert E. Lee.
Attended Baylor University.

Selected by New Jersey in 6th round (70th player selected) of 1983 USFL draft.
Selected by Tampa Bay in 2nd round (45th player selected) of 1983 NFL draft.
Signed by Tampa Bay Buccaneers, June 6, 1983.
Tampa Bay NFL, 1983 through 1985.
Games: 1983 (15), 1984 (10), 1985 (16). Total—41.
Pro statistics: Recovered one fumble, 1983.

RUSS GRIMM
Guard—Washington Redskins

Born May 2, 1959, at Scottsdale, Pa.
Height, 6.03. Weight, 275.
High School—Southmoreland, Pa.
Attended University of Pittsburgh.

Named to THE SPORTING NEWS NFL All-Star Team, 1985.
Selected by Washington in 3rd round (69th player selected) of 1981 NFL draft.
Washington NFL, 1981 through 1985.
Games: 1981 (14), 1982 (9), 1983 (16), 1984 (16), 1985 (16). Total—71.
Pro statistics: Recovered one fumble, 1981 and 1982; recovered two fumbles, 1984.
Played in NFC Championship Game following 1982 and 1983 seasons.
Played in NFL Championship Game following 1982 and 1983 seasons.
Played in Pro Bowl (NFL All-Star Game) following 1983 through 1985 seasons.

JOHN GLENN GRIMSLEY
Linebacker—Houston Oilers

Born February 25, 1962, at Canton, O.
Height, 6.02. Weight, 232.
High School—Canton, O., McKinley.
Attended University of Kentucky.

Selected by Denver in 3rd round (59th player selected) of 1984 USFL draft.
Selected by Houston in 6th round (141st player selected) of 1984 NFL draft.
Signed by Houston Oilers, July 7, 1984.
Houston NFL, 1984 and 1985.
Games: 1984 (16), 1985 (15). Total—31.
Pro statistics: Recovered one fumble for five yards, 1985.

STEVEN JAMES GROGAN
(Steve)
Quarterback—New England Patriots

Born July 24, 1953, at San Antonio, Tex.
Height, 6.04. Weight, 210.
High School—Ottawa, Kan.
Received bachelor of science degree in physical education from Kansas State University in 1975.
Son of Jim Grogan, assistant coach at Ottawa College; and brother of Scott Grogan,
assistant coach at University of Nebraska at Omaha.

Selected by New England in 5th round (116th player selected) of 1975 NFL draft.
On injured reserve with broken leg, November 30, 1985 through January 3, 1986; activated, January 4, 1986.

| | | | —PASSING— | | | | | | —RUSHING— | | | | —TOTAL— | | |
Year Club	G.	Att.	Cmp.	Pct.	Gain	T.P.	P.I.	Avg.	Att.	Yds.	Avg.	TD.	TD.	Pts.	F.
1975—New England NFL...........	13	274	139	50.7	1976	11	18	7.21	30	110	3.7	3	3	18	6
1976—New England NFL...........	14	302	145	48.0	1903	18	20	6.30	60	397	6.6	12	13	78	6
1977—New England NFL...........	14	305	160	52.5	2162	17	21	7.09	61	324	5.3	1	1	6	7
1978—New England NFL...........	16	362	181	50.0	2824	15	23	7.80	81	539	*6.7	5	5	30	9
1979—New England NFL...........	16	423	206	48.7	3286	*28	20	7.77	64	368	5.8	2	2	12	12
1980—New England NFL...........	12	306	175	57.2	2475	18	22	*8.09	30	112	3.7	1	1	6	4
1981—New England NFL...........	8	216	117	54.2	1859	7	16	*8.61	12	49	4.1	2	2	12	5
1982—New England NFL...........	6	122	66	54.1	930	7	4	7.62	9	42	4.7	1	1	6	2
1983—New England NFL...........	12	303	168	55.4	2411	15	12	7.96	23	108	4.7	2	2	12	4
1984—New England NFL...........	3	68	32	47.1	444	3	6	6.53	7	12	1.7	0	0	0	4
1985—New England NFL...........	7	156	85	54.5	1311	7	5	8.40	20	29	1.5	2	2	12	6
Pro Totals—11 Years.........	121	2837	1474	52.0	21581	146	167	7.61	397	2090	5.3	31	32	192	65

Quarterback Rating Points: 1975 (60.2), 1976 (60.8), 1977 (65.3), 1978 (63.3), 1979 (77.5), 1980 (73.1), 1981 (63.0), 1982 (84.2), 1983 (81.4), 1984 (46.4), 1985 (84.1). Total—69.6.

Additional pro statistics: Recovered four fumbles and fumbled six times for minus 12 yards, 1975; recovered four fumbles and one touchdown and fumbled six times for minus 18 yards, 1976; recovered two fumbles and fumbled seven times for minus 41 yards, 1977; recovered two fumbles and fumbled nine times for minus 24 yards, 1978; recovered four fumbles and fumbled 12 times for minus 12 yards, 1979; recovered one fumble and fumbled four times for minus 10 yards, 1980; recovered two fumbles, caught two passes for 27 yards and fumbled five times for minus eight yards, 1981; recovered one fumble 1982 and 1983; caught one pass for minus eight yards, 1983; recovered two fumbles and fumbled four times for minus three yards, 1984; recovered one fumble and fumbled six times for minus 10 yards, 1985.

Member of New England Patriots for AFC Championship Game following 1985 season; did not play.
Played in NFL Championship Game following 1985 season.

ELOIS GROOMS

First name pronounced Eh-LOYS.

Defensive Tackle

Born May 20, 1953, at Tompkinsville, Ky.
Height, 6.04. Weight, 250.
High School—Tompkinsville, Ky.
Received bachelor of science degree in health and physical education
from Tennessee Tech University in 1975.

Selected by New Orleans in 3rd round (63rd player selected) of 1975 NFL draft.
Traded by New Orleans Saints to St. Louis Cardinals for 3rd round pick in 1983 draft, August 3, 1982.
On injured reserve with separated shoulder, October 10 through remainder of 1985 season.
Granted free agency with no qualifying offer, February 1, 1986.
New Orleans NFL, 1975 through 1981; St. Louis NFL, 1982 through 1985.
Games: 1975 (10), 1976 (11), 1977 (14), 1978 (16), 1979 (16), 1980 (16), 1981 (16), 1982 (9), 1983 (11), 1984 (11), 1985 (5). Total—135.

Pro statistics: Recovered two fumbles, 1977 and 1979; caught one pass for three yards and one touchdown, 1977; recovered one fumble, 1978, 1980 and 1982; intercepted one pass for minus two yards and credited with one safety, 1979; intercepted one pass for 37 yards, 1980; recovered one fumble for 20 yards, 1981; intercepted one pass for 10 yards and recovered one fumble for 40 yards and a touchdown, 1983.

ALFRED E. GROSS

(Al)

Safety—Cleveland Browns

Born January 4, 1961, at Stockton, Calif.
Height, 6.03. Weight, 195.
High School—Stockton, Calif., Franklin.
Attended University of Arizona.

Selected by Arizona in 1983 USFL territorial draft.
Selected by Dallas in 9th round (246th player selected) of 1983 NFL draft.
Signed by Dallas Cowboys, June 20, 1983.
Released by Dallas Cowboys, August 2, 1983; awarded on waivers to Cleveland Browns, August 4, 1983.

| | | —INTERCEPTIONS— | | | |
Year Club	G.	No.	Yds.	Avg.	TD.
1983—Cleveland NFL..............	16	1	18	18.0	0
1984—Cleveland NFL..............	16	5	103	20.6	0
1985—Cleveland NFL..............	16	5	109	21.8	*1
Pro Totals—3 Years...........	48	11	230	20.9	1

Additional pro statistics: Recovered one fumble for four yards, 1983; recovered two fumbles for 28 yards, 1984; recovered two fumbles for two yards, 1985.

JEFFREY EUGENE GROTH

(Jeff)

Wide Receiver—New Orleans Saints

Born July 2, 1957, at Mankato, Minn.
Height, 5.10. Weight, 182.
High School—Chagrin Falls, O.
Received degree in business administration from Bowling Green State University.
Brother of Jon Groth, outfielder in Cincinnati Reds' organization.

Selected by Miami in 8th round (206th player selected) of 1979 NFL draft.
Released by Miami Dolphins, August 27, 1979; re-signed by Dolphins, August 28, 1979.
Released by Miami Dolphins, September 29, 1979; re-signed by Dolphins, October 2, 1979.
Released by Miami Dolphins, October 13, 1979; claimed on waivers by Houston Oilers, October 16, 1979.
Released by Houston Oilers, August 31, 1981; signed as free agent by New Orleans Saints, September 9, 1981.
On injured reserve with hamstring injury, October 16 through November 15, 1985; activated, November 16, 1985.
Selected by Chicago Cubs' organization in 9th round of free-agent draft, June 5, 1978.
Selected by Atlanta Braves' organization in 32nd round of free-agent draft, June 5, 1979.
Selected by Texas Rangers' organization in secondary phase of free-agent draft, January 8, 1980.

Year Club	G.	PASS RECEIVING P.C.	Yds.	Avg.	TD.	–PUNT RETURNS– No.	Yds.	Avg.	TD.	—KICKOFF RET.— No.	Yds.	Avg.	TD.	—TOTAL— TD.	Pts.	F.
1979—Mia. (4)-Hou. (6) NFL	10	1	6	6.0	0			None		1	21	21.0	0	0	0	0
1980—Houston NFL	16	4	57	11.8	0	1	0	0.0	0	12	216	18.0	0	0	0	2
1981—New Orleans NFL	15	20	380	19.0	1	37	436	11.8	0	3	50	16.7	0	1	6	0
1982—New Orleans NFL	9	30	383	12.8	1	21	144	6.9	0			None		1	6	1
1983—New Orleans NFL	16	49	585	11.9	1	39	275	7.1	0			None		1	6	3
1984—New Orleans NFL	16	33	487	14.8	0	6	32	5.3	0			None		0	0	0
1985—New Orleans NFL	12	15	238	15.9	2	1	0	0.0	0			None		2	12	0
Pro Totals—7 Years	94	152	2126	14.0	5	105	887	8.4	0	16	287	17.9	0	5	30	6

Additional pro statistics: Recovered one fumble, 1980 and 1982; rushed twice for 27 yards, 1981; rushed once for one yard, 1982; rushed once for 15 yards and recovered two fumbles, 1983.
Played in AFC Championship Game following 1979 season.

MICHAEL ANTHONY GUENDLING
(Mike)
Linebacker—San Diego Chargers
Born June 18, 1962, at Chicago, Ill.
Height, 6.03. Weight, 241.
High School—Arlington Heights, Ill., St. Viator.
Attended Northwestern University.

Selected by Philadelphia in 13th round (266th player selected) of 1983 USFL draft.
Selected by San Diego in 2nd round (33rd player selected) of 1984 NFL draft.
Signed by San Diego Chargers, June 15, 1984.
On injured reserve with knee injury, July 21 through entire 1984 season.
On injured reserve with knee injury, August 20 through October 25, 1985; activated, October 26, 1985.
San Diego NFL, 1985.
Games: 1985 (9).

DAVID RUSTON GUILBEAU
(Rusty)
Linebacker—New York Jets
Born November 20, 1958, at Opalousas, Fla.
Height, 6.04. Weight, 237.
High School—Sunset, La.
Attended McNeese State University.

Selected by St. Louis in 3rd round (73rd player selected) of 1982 NFL draft.
Released by St. Louis Cardinals, September 6, 1982; signed as free agent by New York Jets, November 23, 1982.
On injured reserve with knee injury, December 9 through remainder of 1985 season.
New York Jets NFL, 1982 through 1985.
Games: 1982 (4), 1983 (16), 1984 (16), 1985 (14). Total—50.
Pro statistics: Recovered one fumble, 1985.
Played in AFC Championship Game following 1982 season.

MICHAEL DONALD GUMAN
(Mike)
Running Back—Los Angeles Rams
Born April 21, 1958, at Allentown, Pa.
Height, 6.02. Weight, 218.
High School—Bethlehem, Pa., Catholic.
Received bachelor of science degree in marketing from Penn State University in 1980.

Selected by Los Angeles in 6th round (154th player selected) of 1980 NFL draft.
On injured reserve with knee injury, September 19 through November 14, 1985; activated, November 15, 1985.

Year Club	G.	——RUSHING—— Att.	Yds.	Avg.	TD.	PASS RECEIVING P.C.	Yds.	Avg.	TD.	—TOTAL— TD.	Pts.	F.
1980—Los Angeles Rams NFL	16	100	410	4.1	4	14	131	9.4	0	4	24	4
1981—Los Angeles Rams NFL	16	115	433	3.8	4	18	130	7.2	0	4	24	2
1982—Los Angeles Rams NFL	9	69	266	3.9	2	31	310	10.0	0	2	12	3
1983—Los Angeles Rams NFL	16	7	42	6.0	0	34	347	10.2	4	4	24	0
1984—Los Angeles Rams NFL	16	1	2	2.0	0	19	161	8.5	0	1	6	0
1985—Los Angeles Rams NFL	8	11	32	2.9	0	3	23	7.7	0	0	0	0
Pro Totals—6 Years	81	303	1185	3.9	10	119	1102	9.3	4	15	90	9

Additional pro statistics: Attempted one pass with one completion for 31 yards and a touchdown, returned two punts for six yards and returned two kickoffs for 25 yards, 1980; attempted one pass with one completion for seven yards and a touchdown and returned one kickoff for 10 yards, 1981; attempted one pass with one interception and returned eight kickoffs for 102 yards, 1982; returned two kickoffs for 30 yards, 1983 and 1985; returned one kickoff for 43 yards and a touchdown and recovered one fumble, 1984.
Played in NFC Championship Game following 1985 season.

DUANE N. GUNN
Wide Receiver—Washington Redskins
Born November 17, 1961, at Ispwich, England.
Height, 6.00. Weight, 170.
High School—Indianapolis, Ind., North Central.
Attended Northeastern Oklahoma A&M Junior College and Indiana University.

Selected by Washington in 6th round (119th player selected) of 1984 USFL draft.
Rights traded by Washington Federals to Los Angeles Express for draft choice, March 9, 1984.
Signed by Los Angeles Express, March 9, 1984.
Granted roster exemption, March 9, 1984; activated, March 23, 1984.
Selected by Pittsburgh in 1st round (23rd player selected) of 1984 NFL supplemental draft.
On suspended list, March 22 through March 28, 1985; activated, March 29, 1985.
Released by Los Angeles Express, June 12, 1985.
NFL rights released by Pittsburgh Steelers, August 7, 1985; signed as free agent by Washington Redskins, April 16, 1986.

		PASS RECEIVING				–PUNT RETURNS–				—KICKOFF RET.—				—TOTAL—		
Year Club	G.	P.C.	Yds.	Avg.	TD.	No.	Yds.	Avg.	TD.	No.	Yds.	Avg.	TD.	TD.	Pts.	F.
1984—Los Angeles USFL	14	10	117	11.7	1	17	155	9.1	*1	12	259	21.6	0	2	12	3
1985—Los Angeles USFL	14	32	585	18.3	1	17	171	10.1	1	9	212	23.6	0	2	12	2
Pro Totals—2 Years	28	42	702	16.7	2	34	326	9.6	2	21	471	22.4	0	4	24	5

Additional pro statistics: Recovered two fumbles, 1984; rushed once for 47 yards and recovered one fumble, 1985.

GREGORY LAWSON GUNTER
(Greg)
Center—New York Jets
Born May 16, 1962, at Glen Cove, N.Y.
Height, 6.03. Weight, 265.
High School—Glen Head, N.Y., North Shore.
Attended Nassau Community College, Wake Forest University and C.W. Post College.

Signed as free agent by New York Jets, May 10, 1985.
Released by New York Jets, September 2, 1985; re-signed by Jets, September 3, 1985.
Released by New York Jets, September 12, 1985; re-signed by Jets, December 24, 1985.
Active for 1 game with New York Jets in 1985; did not play.

JAMES JOEL GUSTAFSON
(Jim)
Wide Receiver—Minnesota Vikings
Born March 16, 1961, at Minneapolis, Minn.
Height, 6.01. Weight, 185.
High School—Bloomington, Minn., Lincoln.
Received degree in finance from St. Thomas College in 1983.

Signed as free agent by Cincinnati Bengals, April 28, 1983.
Released by Cincinnati Bengals, August 29, 1983; signed as free agent by Minnesota Vikings, March 3, 1984.
Released by Minnesota Vikings, August 13, 1984; re-signed by Vikings, April 21, 1985.
On injured reserve with separated shoulder, August 20 through entire 1985 season.

WILLIAM RAY GUY
(Known by middle name.)
Punter—Los Angeles Raiders
Born December 22, 1949, at Swainsboro, Ga.
Height, 6.03. Weight, 205.
High School—Thomson, Ga.
Attended University of Southern Mississippi.

Named as punter on THE SPORTING NEWS College All-America Team, 1972.
Named to THE SPORTING NEWS AFC All-Star Team, 1973 through 1978.
Selected by Oakland in 1st round (23rd player selected) of 1973 NFL draft.
Franchise transferred to Los Angeles, May 7, 1982.
Selected by Cincinnati Reds' organization in 14th round of free-agent draft, June 5, 1969.
Selected by Houston Astros' organization in secondary phase of free-agent draft, June 8, 1971.
Selected by Atlanta Braves' organization in 17th round of free-agent draft, June 6, 1972.
Selected by Cincinnati Reds' organization in secondary phase of free-agent draft, January 10, 1973.

	—PUNTING—					—PUNTING—		
Year Club	G.	No.	Avg.	Blk.	Year Club	G.	No.	Avg. Blk.
1973—Oakland NFL	14	69	45.3	0	1980—Oakland NFL	16	71	43.6 0
1974—Oakland NFL	14	74	*42.2	0	1981—Oakland NFL	16	96	43.7 0
1975—Oakland NFL	14	68	*43.8	0	1982—Los Angeles Raiders NFL ...	9	47	39.1 0
1976—Oakland NFL	14	67	41.6	0	1983—Los Angeles Raiders NFL ...	16	78	42.8 0
1977—Oakland NFL	14	59	*43.3	0	1984—Los Angeles Raiders NFL ...	16	91	41.9 0
1978—Oakland NFL	16	81	42.7	*2	1985—Los Angeles Raiders NFL ...	16	89	40.8 0
1979—Oakland NFL	16	69	42.6	1	Pro Totals—13 Years	191	959	42.6 3

Additional pro statistics: Rushed once for 21 yards, 1973; fumbled once for seven yard loss and attempted one pass with one interception, 1974; attempted one pass with one completion for 22 yards, 1975; rushed once for no yards, 1976 and 1985; fumbled once for 14 yard loss and kicked one extra point after touchdown, 1976; recovered one fumble, 1976 and 1980; rushed three times for 38 yards and attempted one pass with one completion for 32 yards, 1980; fumbled once,

1981; rushed two times for minus three yards, 1982; rushed twice for minus 13 yards, 1983; fumbled once for 28 yard loss, 1985.

Played in AFC Championship Game following 1973 through 1977, 1980 and 1983 seasons.
Played in NFL Championship Game following 1976, 1980 and 1983 seasons.
Played in Pro Bowl (NFL All-Star Game) following 1973 through 1978 and 1980 seasons.

JOSEPH GLENN HACKETT
(Joey)
Tight End—Denver Broncos
Born September 29, 1958, at Greensboro, N.C.
Height, 6.05. Weight, 230.
High School—Greensboro, N.C., Southern Guilford.
Received degree from Elon College in 1980.

Signed as free agent by Dallas Cowboys, May, 1981.
Released by Dallas Cowboys, August 24, 1981; signed as free agent by Washington Redskins, April 2, 1982.
Released by Washington Redskins, June 21, 1982; signed by New Jersey Generals, November 11, 1982.
Released by New Jersey Generals, February 20, 1983; re-signed by Generals, March 2, 1983.
On developmental squad, March 4 through March 18, 1983; activated, March 19, 1983.
On developmental squad, March 26 through May 17, 1983.
On injured reserve with broken hand, May 18 through June 26, 1983; activated from injured reserve after clearing procedural waivers, June 28, 1983.
On developmental squad, June 28 through remainder of 1983 season.
Selected by San Antonio Gunslingers in 14th round (81st player selected) of USFL expansion draft, September 6, 1983.
Released by San Antonio Gunslingers, July 23, 1985; signed as free agent by Denver Broncos, May 17, 1986.
On developmental squad for 11 games with New Jersey Generals in 1983.

		—PASS RECEIVING—				
Year	Club	G.	P.C.	Yds.	Avg.	TD.
1984—San Antonio USFL........		18	29	431	14.9	5
1985—San Antonio USFL........		18	34	515	15.2	3
Pro Totals—2 Years............		36	63	946	15.0	8

Additional pro statistics: Recovered one fumble, 1984; fumbled twice, 1985.

MICHAEL HADDIX
Fullback—Philadelphia Eagles
Born December 27, 1961, at Tippah County, Miss.
Height, 6.02. Weight, 225.
High School—Walnut, Miss.
Attended Mississippi State University.

Selected by Denver in 2nd round (16th player selected) of 1983 USFL draft.
Selected by Philadelphia in 1st round (8th player selected) of 1983 NFL draft.
Signed by Philadelphia Eagles, May 13, 1983.

			—RUSHING—			PASS RECEIVING			—TOTAL—		
Year	Club	G.	Att.	Yds.	Avg.	TD.	P.C.	Yds.	Avg.	TD.	TD.	Pts.	F.
1983—Philadelphia NFL		14	91	220	2.4	2	23	254	11.0	0	2	12	4
1984—Philadelphia NFL		14	48	130	2.7	1	33	231	7.0	0	1	6	2
1985—Philadelphia NFL		16	67	213	3.2	0	43	330	7.7	0	0	0	2
Pro Totals—3 Years.....................		44	206	563	2.7	3	99	815	8.2	0	3	18	8

Additional pro statistics: Returned three kickoffs for 51 yards, 1983.

NICHOLAS SCOTT HADEN
(Nick)
Center—Los Angeles Raiders
Born November 7, 1962, at Pittsburgh, Pa.
Height, 6.02. Weight, 270.
High School—McKees Rocks, Pa., Montour.
Received bachelor of arts degree in labor relations from Penn State University in 1985.

Selected by Baltimore in 1985 USFL territorial draft.
Selected by Los Angeles Raiders in 7th round (192nd player selected) of 1985 NFL draft.
Signed by Los Angeles Raiders, July 17, 1985.
On injured reserve with hand injury, August 27 through entire 1985 season.

JOHN YANCY HAINES
Defensive Tackle—Indianapolis Colts
Born December 16, 1961, at Fort Worth, Tex.
Height, 6.06. Weight, 260.
High School—Fort Worth, Tex., Arlington Heights.
Attended University of Texas.

Selected by San Antonio in 1984 USFL territorial draft.
Selected by Minnesota in 7th round (180th player selected) of 1984 NFL draft.
Signed by Minnesota Vikings, June 26, 1984.
On physically unable to perform/reserve with knee injury, August 8 through October 23, 1984; activated, October 24, 1984.
Released by Minnesota Vikings, August 14, 1985; signed as free agent by Indianapolis Colts, March 24, 1986.

Minnesota NFL, 1984.
Games: 1984 (8).
Pro statistics: Recovered one fumble for six yards, 1984.

CARL BLAKE HAIRSTON
Defensive End—Cleveland Browns
Born December 15, 1952, at Martinsville, Va.
Height, 6.04. Weight, 260.
High School—Martinsville, Va.
Received bachelor of arts degree in education from University of Maryland (Eastern Shore) in 1985.

Selected by Philadelphia in 7th round (191st player selected) of 1976 NFL draft.
Traded by Philadelphia Eagles to Cleveland Browns for 9th round pick in 1985 draft, February 9, 1984.
Philadelphia NFL, 1976 through 1983; Cleveland NFL, 1984 and 1985.
Games: 1976 (14), 1977 (14), 1978 (16), 1979 (15), 1980 (16), 1981 (16), 1982 (9), 1983 (16), 1984 (16), 1985 (16). Total—148.
Pro statistics: Recovered one fumble, 1977, 1980, 1981 and 1985; intercepted one pass for no yards, 1980; recovered two fumbles for 24 yards, 1982; recovered two fumbles, 1983.
Played in NFC Championship Game following 1980 season.
Played in NFL Championship Game following 1980 season.

ALI HAJI-SHEIKH
Name pronounced Hodgie-Sheek.
Placekicker—New York Giants
Born January 11, 1961, at Ann Arbor, Mich.
Height, 6.00. Weight, 172.
High School—Arlington, Tex.
Attended University of Michigan.

Established NFL record for most field goals, season (35), 1983.
Named to THE SPORTING NEWS NFL All-Star Team, 1983.
Selected by Michigan in 1983 USFL territorial draft.
Selected by New York Giants in 9th round (237th player selected) of 1983 NFL draft.
Signed by New York Giants, June 13, 1983.
On injured reserve with hamstring injury, September 17 through remainder of 1985 season.

| | ——PLACE KICKING—— | | | | | |
Year Club	G.	XP.	XPM.	FG.	FGA.	Pts.
1983—N.Y. Giants NFL	16	22	1	*35	42	127
1984—N.Y. Giants NFL	16	32	3	17	33	83
1985—N.Y. Giants NFL	2	5	0	2	5	11
Pro Totals—3 Years.......	34	59	4	54	80	221

Additional pro statistics: Had only attempted punt blocked, 1984.
Played in Pro Bowl (NFL All-Star Game) following 1983 season.

DARRYL HALEY
Offensive Tackle—New England Patriots
Born February 16, 1961, at Los Angeles, Calif.
Height, 6.04. Weight, 275.
High School—Los Angeles, Calif., Alin Leroy Locke.
Attended University of Utah.
Cousin of Darrell Jackson, pitcher with Minnesota Twins, 1978 through 1982.

Selected by New England in 2nd round (55th player selected) of 1982 NFL draft.
On non-football injury list with colitis, August 28 through entire 1985 season.
New England NFL, 1982 through 1984.
Games: 1982 (9), 1983 (16), 1984 (16). Total—41.

ALVIN EUGENE HALL
Defensive Back—Detroit Lions
Born August 12, 1958, at Dayton, O.
Height, 5.10. Weight, 184.
High School—Dayton, O., Fairview.
Attended Miami (O.) University.

Signed as free agent by Cleveland Browns, May 7, 1980.
Released by Cleveland Browns, August 20, 1980; signed as free agent by Detroit Lions, May 8, 1981.

| | | -INTERCEPTIONS- | | | | —KICKOFF RET.— | | | | —TOTAL— | | |
Year Club	G.	No.	Yds.	Avg.	TD.	No.	Yds.	Avg.	TD.	TD.	Pts.	F.
1981—Detroit NFL...............	16	1	60	60.0	1	25	525	21.0	0	1	6	1
1982—Detroit NFL...............	9	1	2	2.0	0	16	426	26.6	*1	1	6	1
1983—Detroit NFL...............	16	2	18	9.0	0	23	492	21.4	0	0	0	1
1984—Detroit NFL...............	16	2	64	32.0	0	19	385	20.3	0	0	0	3
1985—Detroit NFL...............	16			None		39	886	22.7	0	0	0	2
Pro Totals—4 Years...................	73	6	144	24.0	1	122	2714	22.2	1	2	12	8

Additional pro statistics: Recovered one fumble, 1982 and 1984; returned eight punts for 109 yards, 1983; recovered two fumbles, 1983 and 1985; returned seven punts for 30 yards, 1984.

RONALD DAVID HALLSTROM
(Ron)
Guard—Green Bay Packers
Born June 11, 1959, at Holden, Mass.
Height, 6.06. Weight, 283.
High School—Moline, Ill.
Attended Iowa Central Junior College and University of Iowa.

Selected by Green Bay in 1st round (22nd player selected) of 1982 NFL draft.
On inactive list, September 12 and September 20, 1982.
Green Bay NFL, 1982 through 1985.
Games: 1982 (6), 1983 (16), 1984 (16), 1985 (16). Total—54.
Pro statistics: Recovered two fumbles for one yard, 1984; recovered one fumble, 1985.

MIKE HAMBY
Defensive Tackle—Buffalo Bills
Born November 2, 1962, at Salt Lake City, Utah.
Height, 6.04. Weight, 253.
High School—Lehi, Utah.
Attended Utah State University.

Selected by Jacksonville in 2nd round (27th player selected) of 1985 USFL draft.
Selected by Buffalo in 6th round (141st player selected) of 1985 NFL draft.
Signed by Buffalo Bills, July 19, 1985.
On injured reserve with knee injury, August 19 through entire 1985 season.

DEAN HAMEL
Defensive Tackle—Washington Redskins
Born July 7, 1961, at Detroit, Mich.
Height, 6.03. Weight, 275.
High School—Warren, Mich., Mott.
Attended Coffeyville Community College and University of Tulsa.

Selected by Washington in 12th round (309th player selected) in 1985 NFL draft.
Signed by Washington Redskins, June 14, 1985.
Washington NFL, 1985.
Games: 1985 (16).
Pro statistics: Returned one kickoff for 14 yards, 1985.

HARRY E. HAMILTON
Safety—New York Jets
Born November 29, 1962, at Jamaica, N.Y.
Height, 6.00. Weight, 193.
High School—Nanticoke, Pa., John S. Fine.
Received bachelor of arts degree in pre-law and liberal arts from Penn State University in 1984.
Brother of Lance Hamilton, rookie defensive back with New York Giants;
and Darren Hamilton, wide receiver at Penn State University.

Selected by Philadelphia in 1984 USFL territorial draft.
Selected by New York Jets in 7th round (176th player selected) of 1984 NFL draft.
Signed by New York Jets, May 29, 1984.
On injured reserve with knee injury, October 22 through remainder of 1984 season.
On injured reserve with shoulder injury, October 14 through November 15, 1985; activated, November 16, 1985.
New York Jets NFL, 1984 and 1985.
Games: 1984 (8), 1985 (11). Total—19.
Pro statistics: Intercepted two passes for 14 yards and recovered one fumble, 1985.

STEVEN HAMILTON
(Steve)
Defensive End—Washington Redskins
Born September 28, 1961, at Niagara Falls, N.Y.
Height, 6.04. Weight, 253.
High School—Williamsville, N.Y., East
Attended Fork Union Military Academy and East Carolina University.

Selected by Michigan in 4th round (79th player selected) of 1984 USFL draft.
Selected by Washington in 2nd round (55th player selected) of 1984 NFL draft.
Signed by Washington Redskins, June 5, 1984.
On injured reserve with fractured ankle, August 20 through entire 1984 season.
On injured reserve with shoulder injury, September 3, through November 1, 1985; activated, November 2, 1985.
Washington NFL, 1985.
Games: 1985 (7).

WESLEY DEAN HAMILTON
(Wes)
Guard—Minnesota Vikings
Born April 24, 1953, at Texas City, Tex.
Height, 6.03. Weight, 270.
High School—Flossmoor, Ill., Homewood-Flossmoor.
Received bachelor of science degree in education from University of Tulsa in 1976.

Selected by Minnesota in 3rd round (85th player selected) of 1976 NFL draft.
On injured reserve with knee injury, August 28 through October 5, 1984; activated, October 6, 1984.
On injured reserve with back injury, August 27 through entire 1985 season.
Minnesota NFL, 1976 through 1984.
Games: 1976 (13), 1977 (14), 1978 (16), 1979 (16), 1980 (13), 1981 (16), 1982 (9), 1983 (15), 1984 (4). Total—116.
Pro statistics: Recovered one fumble, 1979.
Played in NFC Championship Game following 1977 season.

BOB HAMM
Defensive End—Kansas City Chiefs
Born April 24, 1959, at Kansas City, Mo.
Height, 6.04. Weight, 263.
High School—Mountain View, Calif., St. Francis.
Attended University of Nevada at Reno.

Signed as free agent by Kansas City Chiefs, May 9, 1983.
On injured reserve with knee injury, August 28 through September 27, 1984; activated, September 28, 1984.
Released by Kansas City Chiefs, August 29, 1983; awarded on waivers to Houston Oilers, August 30, 1983.
Traded with 4th round pick in 1986 draft by Houston Oilers to Kansas City Chiefs for 5th and 6th round picks in 1985 draft, April 30, 1985.
On injured reserve with knee injury, December 11 through remainder of 1985 season.
Houston NFL, 1983 through 1985.
Games: 1983 (16), 1984 (12), 1985 (14). Total—42.
Pro statistics: Recovered one fumble, 1984.

DANIEL OLIVER HAMPTON
(Dan)
Defensive Lineman—Chicago Bears
Born September 19, 1957, at Oklahoma City, Okla.
Height, 6.05. Weight, 270.
High School—Jacksonville, Ark.
Attended University of Arkansas.

Named to THE SPORTING NEWS NFL All-Star Team, 1984.
Selected by Chicago in 1st round (4th player selected) of 1979 NFL draft.
Chicago NFL, 1979 through 1985.
Games: 1979 (16), 1980 (16), 1981 (16), 1982 (9), 1983 (11), 1984 (15), 1985 (16). Total—99.
Pro statistics: Recovered two fumbles, 1979; recovered three fumbles, 1984 and 1985.
Played in NFC Championship Game following 1984 and 1985 seasons.
Played in NFL Championship Game following 1985 season.
Played in Pro Bowl (NFL All-Star Game) following 1980, 1982, 1984 and 1985 seasons.

LORENZO TIMOTHY HAMPTON
Running Back—Miami Dolphins
Born March 12, 1962, at Lake Wales, Fla.
Height, 6.00. Weight, 212.
High School—Lake Wales, Fla.
Attended University of Florida.

Selected by Tampa Bay in 1985 USFL territorial draft.
USFL rights traded with rights to running back Greg Allen by Tampa Bay Bandits to Orlando Renegades for rights to running back Jeff McCall, December 21, 1984.
Selected by Miami in 1st round (27th player selected) of 1985 NFL draft.
Signed by Miami Dolphins, July 19, 1985.

		RUSHING				PASS RECEIVING			—TOTAL—		
Year Club	G.	Att.	Yds.	Avg.	TD.	P.C.	Yds.	Avg. TD.	TD.	Pts.	F.
1985—Miami NFL	16	105	369	3.5	3	8	56	7.0 0	3	18	3

		KICKOFF RETURNS		
Year Club	G.	No.	Yds.	Avg.TD.
1985—Miami NFL	16	45	1020	22.7 0

Additional pro statistics: Recovered one fumble, 1985.
Played in AFC Championship Game following 1985 season.

ANTHONY DUANE HANCOCK
Wide Receiver—Kansas City Chiefs
Born June 10, 1960, at Cleveland, O.
Height, 6.00. Weight, 204.
High School—Cleveland, O., John Hay.
Received degree in sociology from University of Tennessee.
Cousin of Von Mansfield, safety with Arizona Outlaws.

Selected by Kansas City in 1st round (11th player selected) of 1982 NFL draft.

		PASS RECEIVING			—PUNT RETURNS—				—KICKOFF RET.—				—TOTAL—		
Year Club	G.	P.C.	Yds.	Avg. TD.	No.	Yds.	Avg.	TD.	No.	Yds.	Avg.	TD.	TD.	Pts.	F.
1982—Kansas City NFL	9	7	116	16.6 1	12	103	8.6	0	27	609	22.6	0	1	6	1
1983—Kansas City NFL	16	37	584	15.8 1	14	81	5.8	0	29	515	17.8	0	1	6	2
1984—Kansas City NFL	14	10	217	21.7 1	3	14	4.7	0	2	32	16.0	0	1	6	1
1985—Kansas City NFL	16	15	286	19.1 2			None		6	125	20.8	0	2	12	1
Pro Totals—4 Years	55	69	1203	17.4 5	29	198	6.8	0	64	1281	20.0	0	5	30	5

Additional pro statistics: Recovered one fumble, 1984.

KEVIN DREW HANCOCK
Linebacker—Detroit Lions
Born January 6, 1962, at Longview, Tex.
Height, 6.02. Weight, 224.
High School—Texas City, Tex.
Attended Baylor University.

Selected by San Antonio in 1985 USFL territorial draft.
Selected by Detroit in 4th round (90th player selected) of 1985 NFL draft.
Signed by Detroit Lions, July 21, 1985.
On injured reserve with knee injury, August 13 through entire 1985 season.

DUAN EDWARD HANKS
Wide Receiver—Miami Dolphins
Born July 28, 1961, at Detroit, Mich.
Height, 6.00. Weight, 180.
High School—Detroit, Mich., Cass Tech.
Attended Stephen F. Austin State University.

Selected by Philadelphia in 14th round (283rd player selected) of 1984 USFL draft.
Signed by Philadelphia Stars, January 27, 1984.
On injured reserve, February 20 through February 23, 1984.
Released by Philadelphia Stars, February 24, 1984.
Selected by Miami in 3rd round (82nd player selected) of 1984 NFL supplemental draft.
Signed by Miami Dolphins, July 5, 1984.
On injured reserve with shoulder injury, August 1 through September 11, 1984.
Released by Miami Dolphins, September 12, 1984; re-signed by Baltimore Stars, October 26, 1984.
Released by Baltimore Stars, February 11, 1985; re-signed by Dolphins, April 20, 1985.
On injured reserve with knee injury, August 19 through entire 1985 season.

PAUL EDWARD HANNA
Nose Tackle—Cleveland Browns
Born September 14, 1959, at Lakewood, O.
Height, 6.04. Weight, 251.
High School—West Lake, O.
Received degree from Purdue University in 1982.

Signed by San Antonio Gunslingers, October 22, 1983.
On developmental squad, April 13 through April 21, 1984; activated, April 22, 1984.
Traded by San Antonio Gunslingers to Memphis Showboats for defensive back Leon Williams, February 13, 1985.
On developmental squad, March 29 through April 3, 1985; activated, April 4, 1985.
Traded by Memphis Showboats to Arizona Outlaws for linebacker Daryl Goodlow, April 10, 1985.
Traded by Arizona Outlaws to San Antonio Gunslingers for wide receiver Al Hill, April 15, 1985.
Released by San Antonio Gunslingers, July 23, 1985; signed as free agent by Cleveland Browns, May 4, 1986.
On developmental squad for 1 game with San Antonio Gunslingers in 1984.
On developmental squad for 1 game with Memphis Showboats in 1985.
San Antonio USFL, 1984; Memphis (5)-Arizona (1)-San Antonio (10) USFL, 1985.
Games: 1984 (17), 1985 (16). Total—33..
Pro statistics: Credited with four sacks for 28 yards and recovered one fumble, 1984; credited with four sacks for 20 yards and recovered two fumbles, 1985.

CHARLES ALVIN HANNAH
(Charley)
Guard—Los Angeles Raiders
Born July 26, 1955, at Albertville, Ala.
Height, 6.05. Weight, 260.
High School—Chattanooga, Tenn., Baylor.
Attended University of Alabama.
Son of Herb Hannah, tackle with New York Giants, 1951, and brother
of John Hannah, guard with New England Patriots.

Selected by Tampa Bay in 3rd round (56th player selected) of 1977 NFL draft.
On injured reserve, November 14 through remainder of 1977 season.
On injured reserve with knee injury, December 7 through December 26, 1979; activated, December 27, 1979.
Traded by Tampa Bay Buccaneers to Los Angeles Raiders for defensive end Dave Browning and 4th round pick in 1984 draft, July 18, 1983.
Tampa Bay NFL, 1977 through 1982; Los Angeles Raiders NFL, 1983 through 1985.
Games: 1977 (9), 1978 (16), 1979 (14), 1980 (16), 1981 (15), 1982 (7), 1983 (16), 1984 (15), 1985 (15). Total—123.
Pro statistics: Recovered one fumble for eight yards and fumbled once for minus 32 yards, 1978; attempted one pass with no completions, 1980; recovered one fumble, 1985.
Played in NFC Championship Game following 1979 season.
Played in AFC Championship Game following 1983 season.
Played in NFL Championship Game following 1983 season.

JOHN ALLEN HANNAH
Guard—New England Patriots
Born April 4, 1951, at Canton, Ga.
Height, 6.03. Weight, 265.
High Schools—Chattanooga, Tenn., Baylor and Albertville, Tenn.
Attended University of Alabama.
Son of Herb Hannah, tackle with New York Giants, 1951, and brother of
Charley Hannah, guard with Los Angeles Raiders.

Named to THE SPORTING NEWS AFC All-Star Team, 1974, 1976, 1978 and 1979.
Named to THE SPORTING NEWS NFL All-Star Team, 1980, 1981, 1984 and 1985.
Named as center on THE SPORTING NEWS College All-America Team, 1972.
Selected by New England in 1st round (4th player selected) of 1973 NFL draft.
New England NFL, 1973 through 1985.
Games: 1973 (13), 1974 (14), 1975 (14), 1976 (14), 1977 (11), 1978 (16), 1979 (16), 1980 (16), 1981 (16), 1982 (8), 1983 (16), 1984 (15), 1985 (14). Total—183.
Pro statistics: Recovered one fumble, 1973 and 1979; returned one kickoff for no yards, 1973; recovered one fumble in end zone for a touchdown, 1974; recovered two fumbles, 1978 and 1981; recovered three fumbles, 1983.
Played in AFC Championship Game following 1985 season.
Played in NFL Championship Game following 1985 season.
Played in Pro Bowl (NFL All-Star Game) following 1976, 1978 through 1982, 1984 and 1985 seasons.
Named to play in Pro Bowl following 1983 season; replaced due to injury by Bob Kuechenberg.

BRIAN HANSEN
Punter—New Orleans Saints
Born October 26, 1960, at Hawarden, Ia.
Height, 6.03. Weight, 218.
High School—Hawarden, Ia., West Sioux Community.
Attended Sioux Falls College.

Selected by New Orleans in 9th round (237th player selected) of 1984 NFL draft.

		—PUNTING—		
Year Club	G.	No.	Avg.	Blk.
1984—New Orleans NFL	16	69	43.8	1
1985—New Orleans NFL	16	89	42.3	0
Pro Totals—2 Years	32	158	42.9	1

Additional pro statistics: Rushed twice for minus 27 yards, 1984; attempted one pass with one completion for eight yards, 1985.
Played in Pro Bowl (NFL All-Star Game) following 1984 season.

CHARLES EDWARD HARBISON
Safety—Buffalo Bills
Born October 27, 1959, at Gaston County, N.C.
Height, 6.01. Weight, 185.
High School—Boiling Springs, N.C., Crest.
Attended Gardner-Webb College.

Signed as free agent by Buffalo Bills, May 1, 1982.
Released by Buffalo Bills, August 9, 1982; signed by Boston Breakers, November 16, 1982.
Franchise transferred to New Orleans, October 18, 1983.
On developmental squad, April 7 through April 13, 1984; activated, April 14, 1984.
Franchise transferred to Portland, November 13, 1984.
Released by Portland Breakers, February 18, 1985; signed as free agent by Buffalo Bills, March 22, 1985.
Released by Buffalo Bills, August 26, 1985; re-signed by Bills, May 6, 1986.
On developmental squad for 1 game with New Orleans Breakers in 1984.

		—INTERCEPTIONS—			
Year Club	G.	No.	Yds.	Avg.	TD.
1983—Boston USFL	18	2	66	33.0	0
1984—New Orleans USFL	17	1	0	0.0	0
Pro Totals—2 Years	35	3	66	22.0	0

Additional pro statistics: Recovered three fumbles for one yard, credited with two sacks for 13 yards and returned two kickoffs for 18 yards, 1983; recovered two fumbles, 1984.

JAMES EDWARD HARBOUR
Wide Receiver—Indianapolis Colts
Born November 10, 1962, at Meridian, Miss.
Height, 6.00. Weight, 192.
High School—Meridian, Miss.
Attended University of Mississippi.

Selected by Tampa Bay in 4th round (56th player selected) of 1985 USFL draft.
Selected by Indianapolis in 7th round (173rd player selected) of 1985 NFL draft.
Signed by Indianapolis Colts, July 18, 1985.
On injured reserve with dislocated kneecap, August 27 through entire 1985 season.

MICHAEL HARDEN
(Mike)
Cornerback—Denver Broncos
Born February 16, 1958, at Memphis, Tenn.
Height, 6.01. Weight, 190.
High School—Detroit, Mich., Central.
Received bachelor of arts degree in political science from University of Michigan in 1980.

Selected by Denver in 5th round (131st player selected) of 1980 NFL draft.
On injured reserve with knee injury, December 16 through remainder of 1982 season.

Year—Club	G.	No.	Yds.	Avg.	TD.	No.	Yds.	Avg.	TD.	TD.	Pts.	F.
		-INTERCEPTIONS-				—KICKOFF RET.—				—TOTAL—		
1980—Denver NFL	16	None				12	214	17.8	0	0	0	1
1981—Denver NFL	16	2	34	17.0	0	11	178	16.2	0	0	0	0
1982—Denver NFL	5	2	3	1.5	0	None				0	0	0
1983—Denver NFL	15	4	127	31.8	0	1	9	9.0	0	0	0	0
1984—Denver NFL	16	6	79	13.2	1	1	4	4.0	0	1	6	1
1985—Denver NFL	16	5	100	20.0	*1	None				1	6	0
Pro Totals—6 Years	84	19	343	18.1	2	25	405	16.2	0	2	12	2

Additional pro statistics: Returned two punts for 36 yards and recovered one fumble, 1981; recovered one fumble for 13 yards, 1982; recovered three fumbles, 1983; recovered two fumbles, 1984; recovered two fumbles for five yards, 1985.

WILLIAM DAVID HARDISON
(Dee)
Defensive End—New York Giants

Born May 2, 1956, at Jacksonville, N. C.
Height, 6.04. Weight, 274.
High School—Newton Grove, N. C., Hobbton.
Attended University of North Carolina.

Selected by Buffalo in 2nd round (32nd player selected) of 1978 NFL draft.
Released by Buffalo Bills, August 25, 1981; signed as free agent by New York Giants, December 8, 1981.
On injured reserve with hip injury, November 30 through December 30, 1982; activated, December 31, 1982.
Active for 2 games with New York Giants in 1981; did not play.
Buffalo NFL, 1978 through 1980; New York Giants NFL, 1981 through 1985.
Games: 1978 (16), 1979 (16), 1980 (16), 1982 (5), 1983 (16), 1984 (15), 1985 (13). Total—97.
Pro statistics: Recovered one fumble, 1983.

ANDRE HARDY
Running Back-Kick Returner—San Francisco 49ers

Born November 28, 1961, at San Diego, Calif.
Height, 6.01. Weight, 233.
High School—San Diego, Calif., Herbert Hoover.
Attended San Diego City College, Weber State College and received
bachelor of science degree in communications from St. Mary's College (Cal.) in 1984.

Selected by San Antonio in 5th round (86th player selected) of 1984 USFL draft.
Selected by Philadelphia in 5th round (116th player selected) of 1984 NFL draft.
Signed by Philadelphia Eagles, May 31, 1984.
Released by Philadelphia Eagles, September 4, 1985; signed as free agent by Seattle Seahawks, October 9, 1985.
Released by Seattle Seahawks, November 6, 1985; re-signed by Seahawks, November 11, 1985.
Released by Seattle Seahawks, November 21, 1985; signed as free agent by San Francisco 49ers, March 7, 1986.

Year Club	G.	Att.	Yds.	Avg.	TD.	P.C.	Yds.	Avg.	TD.	TD.	Pts.	F.
		——RUSHING——				PASS RECEIVING				—TOTAL—		
1984—Philadelphia NFL	6	14	41	2.9	0	2	22	11.0	0	0	0	0
1985—Seattle NFL	3	5	5	1.0	0	3	7	2.3	0	0	0	1
Pro Totals—2 Years	9	19	46	2.4	0	5	29	5.8	0	0	0	1

Additional pro statistics: Returned one kickoff for 20 yards, 1984; recovered one fumble, 1985.

BRUCE ALAN HARDY
Tight End—Miami Dolphins

Born June 1, 1956, at Murray, Utah.
Height, 6.05. Weight, 232.
High School—Copperton, Utah, Bingham.
Received bachelor of science degree in business administration
from Arizona State University.
Brother of Bryan Hardy, pitcher in Chicago Cubs' organization, 1979, 1980 and 1982.

Selected by Miami in 9th round (247th player selected) of 1978 NFL draft.

Year Club	G.	P.C.	Yds.	Avg.	TD.
		——PASS RECEIVING——			
1978—Miami NFL	16	4	32	8.0	2
1979—Miami NFL	16	30	386	12.9	3
1980—Miami NFL	16	19	159	8.4	2
1981—Miami NFL	16	15	174	11.6	0
1982—Miami NFL	9	12	66	5.5	2
1983—Miami NFL	15	22	202	9.2	0
1984—Miami NFL	16	28	257	9.2	5
1985—Miami NFL	16	39	409	10.5	4
Pro Totals—8 Years	120	169	1685	10.0	18

Additional pro statistics: Returned two kickoffs for 27 yards, 1978; attempted one pass with no completions, 1979; fumbled once, 1980, 1981 and 1985; rushed once for two yards, 1983; returned one kickoff for 11 yards, 1985.
Played in AFC Championship Game following 1982, 1984 and 1985 seasons.
Played in NFL Championship Game following 1982 and 1984 seasons.

LARRY HARDY
Tight End—New Orleans Saints
Born July 9, 1956, at Mendenhall, Miss.
Height, 6.03. Weight, 246.
High School—Mendenhall, Miss.
Attended Jackson State University.
Brother of Edgar Hardy, guard with San Francisco 49ers, 1973; and Bertha Hardy, former player with
New Orleans Pride of the Women's Professional Basketball League.

Selected by New Orleans in 12th round (309th player selected) of 1978 NFL draft.
On injured reserve with thigh injury, October 28 through remainder of 1983 season.
On injured reserve with thigh injury, August 27 through November 6, 1984; activated after clearing procedural waivers, November 8, 1984.

| | | —PASS RECEIVING— | | | |
Year	Club	G.	P.C.	Yds.	Avg.	TD.
1978—New Orleans NFL		16	5	131	26.2	1
1979—New Orleans NFL		16	1	3	3.0	1
1980—New Orleans NFL		16	13	197	15.2	0
1981—New Orleans NFL		16	23	275	12.0	1
1982—New Orleans NFL		9	8	67	8.4	1
1983—New Orleans NFL		6	2	29	14.5	0
1984—New Orleans NFL		6	4	50	12.5	1
1985—New Orleans NFL		16	15	208	13.9	2
Pro Totals—8 Years		101	71	960	13.5	7

Additional pro statistics: Returned two kickoffs for three yards, 1978; recovered two fumbles and fumbled twice, 1981; fumbled once, 1982.

FRANK COLE HARE
Nose Tackle—Houston Oilers
Born February 13, 1963, at Atlanta, Ga.
Height, 6.02. Weight, 244.
High School—Lexington, Ky., Henry Clay.
Attended University of Kentucky.

Signed as free agent by Houston Oilers, May 6, 1985.
On injured reserve with knee injury, August 15 through entire 1985 season.

DERRICK TODD HARMON
Running Back-Kick Returner—San Francisco 49ers
Born April 26, 1963, at New York, N.Y.
Height, 5.10. Weight, 202.
High School—Queens, N.Y., Bayside.
Received bachelor of science degree in engineering physics from Cornell University in 1984.
Brother of Ronnie Harmon, rookie running back with Buffalo Bills;
and Kevin Harmon, tailback at University of Iowa.

Selected by Oklahoma in 17th round (335th player selected) of 1984 USFL draft.
Selected by San Francisco in 9th round (248th player selected) of 1984 NFL draft.
Signed by San Francisco 49ers, May 4, 1984.

| | | | —RUSHING— | | | | PASS RECEIVING | | | | —TOTAL— | | |
Year	Club	G.	Att.	Yds.	Avg.	TD.	P.C.	Yds.	Avg.	TD.	TD.	Pts.	F.
1984—San Francisco NFL		16	39	192	4.9	1	1	2	2.0	0	1	6	1
1985—San Francisco NFL		15	28	92	3.3	0	14	123	8.8	0	0	0	2
Pro Totals—2 Years		31	67	284	4.2	1	15	125	8.3	0	1	6	3

| | | KICKOFF RETURNS | | | |
Year	Club	G.	No.	Yds.	Avg.TD.
1984—San Francisco NFL		16	13	357	27.5	0
1985—San Francisco NFL		15	23	467	20.3	0
Pro Totals—2 Years		31	36	824	22.9	0

Additional pro statistics: Attempted two passes with no completions and recovered two fumbles, 1984; attempted one pass with no completions and recovered one fumble, 1985.
Played in NFC Championship Game following 1984 season.
Played in NFL Championship Game following 1984 season.

MARK HARPER
Defensive Back—Cleveland Browns
Born November 5, 1961, at Memphis, Tenn.
Height, 5.09. Weight, 174.
High School—Memphis, Tenn., Northside.
Received degree from Alcorn State University in 1982.

Signed by Chicago Blitz, July 31, 1983.
Franchise transferred to Arizona, September 30, 1983.
Traded by Arizona Wranglers to Pittsburgh Maulers for draft choice, February 13, 1984.
On developmental squad, February 24 through March 28, 1984; activated, March 29, 1984.
Franchise disbanded, October 25, 1984.
Selected by Jacksonville Bulls in USFL dispersal draft, December 6, 1984.
On developmental squad, April 25 through June 13, 1985; activated, June 14, 1985.
Released by Jacksonville Bulls, February 28, 1986; signed as free agent by Cleveland Browns, April 7, 1986.

On developmental squad for 5 games with Pittsburgh Maulers in 1984.
On developmental squad for 7 games with Jacksonville Bulls in 1985.

		PUNT RETURNS				KICKOFF RET.—				—TOTAL—		
Year Club	G.	No.	Yds.	Avg.	TD.	No.	Yds.	Avg.	TD.	TD.	Pts.	F.
1984—Pittsburgh USFL	12	22	157	7.1	0	7	130	18.6	0	0	0	1
1985—Jacksonville USFL	11			None				None		0	0	0
Pro Totals—2 Years	23	22	157	7.1	0	7	130	18.6	0	0	0	1

Additional pro statistics: Recovered three fumbles, 1984; intercepted one pass for 10 yards, 1985.

DENNIS WAYNE HARRAH
Guard—Los Angeles Rams
Born March 9, 1953, at Charleston, W. Va.
Height, 6.05. Weight, 265.
High School—Charleston, W. Va., Stonewall Jackson.
Attended University of Miami (Fla.).

Named as offensive tackle on THE SPORTING NEWS College All-America Team, 1974.
Selected by Los Angeles in 1st round (11th player selected) of 1975 NFL draft.
On injured reserve with knee injury, November 8 through remainder of 1977 season.
On did not report list, August 19 through September 7, 1980; activated, September 8, 1980.
On injured reserve with thigh injury, October 4 through October 31, 1985; activated, November 1, 1985.
Los Angeles Rams NFL, 1975 through 1985.
Games: 1975 (14), 1976 (14), 1977 (8), 1978 (15), 1979 (13), 1980 (15), 1981 (15), 1982 (9), 1983 (15), 1984 (16), 1985 (10). Total—144.
Pro statistics: Recovered one fumble, 1982.
Played in NFC Championship Game following 1975, 1976, 1978, 1979 and 1985 seasons.
Played in NFL Championship Game following 1979 season.
Played in Pro Bowl (NFL All-Star Game) following 1978 through 1980 and 1985 seasons.

JAMES CLEARANCE HARRELL JR.
Linebacker—Detroit Lions
Born July 19, 1957, at Tampa, Fla.
Height, 6.01. Weight, 220.
High School—Tampa, Fla., Chamberlain.
Received bachelor of science degree in public relations from University of Florida.

Named as outside linebacker on THE SPORTING NEWS USFL All-Star Team, 1984.
Signed as free agent by Denver Broncos, May 12, 1979.
Released by Denver Broncos, August 27, 1979; claimed on waivers by Detroit Lions, August 28, 1979.
On injured reserve with shoulder injury, August 29 through October 19, 1979; activated, October 20, 1979.
On injured reserve with knee injury, October 15 through remainder of 1980 season.
Granted free agency, February 1, 1984; signed by Tampa Bay Bandits, March 23, 1984.
On developmental squad, June 7 through June 27, 1985; activated, June 28, 1985.
Granted free agency, August 1, 1985; signed by Detroit Lions, August 13, 1985.
On injured reserve with back injury, October 24 through remainder of 1985 season.
On developmental squad for 3 games with Tampa Bay Bandits in 1985.
Detroit NFL, 1979 through 1983; Tampa Bay USFL, 1984 and 1985; Detroit NFL, 1985.
Games: 1979 (9), 1980 (5), 1981 (16), 1982 (9), 1983 (16), 1984 (14), 1985 USFL (15), 1985 NFL (7). Total NFL—62. Total USFL—29. Total Pro—91.
NFL statistics: Returned one kickoff for no yards, 1981; intercepted one pass for 20 yards, 1985.
USFL statistics: Intercepted one pass for eight yards, credited with 1½ sacks for 14 yards and recovered one fumble for 18 yards, 1984; intercepted two passes for 19 yards and credited with four sacks for 33 yards, 1985.

PERRY DONELL HARRINGTON
Running Back
Born May 13, 1958, at Bentonia, Miss.
Height, 5.11. Weight, 210.
High School—Jackson, Miss., Lanier.
Received bachelor of science degree in finance from Jackson State University in 1980.

Selected by Philadelphia in 2nd round (53rd player selected) of 1980 NFL draft.
On injured reserve with broken leg, September 28 through remainder of 1981 season.
Granted free agency, February 1, 1984; re-signed by Eagles and traded to Cleveland Browns for conditional pick in 1985 draft, July 23, 1984.
Released by Cleveland Browns, August 27, 1984; signed as free agent by St. Louis Cardinals, November 8, 1984.
On injured reserve with knee injury, November 20 through remainder of 1985 season.
Granted free agency with no qualifying offer, February 1, 1986.

		—RUSHING—				PASS RECEIVING				—TOTAL—		
Year Club	G.	Att.	Yds.	Avg.	TD.	P.C.	Yds.	Avg.	TD.	TD.	Pts.	F.
1980—Philadelphia NFL	14	32	166	5.2	1	3	24	8.0	0	1	6	1
1981—Philadelphia NFL	4	34	140	4.1	2	9	27	3.0	0	2	12	1
1982—Philadelphia NFL	9	56	231	4.1	1	13	74	5.7	0	1	6	2
1983—Philadelphia NFL	15	23	98	4.3	1	1	19	19.0	0	1	6	1
1984—St. Louis NFL	6	3	6	2.0	0			None		0	0	0
1985—St. Louis NFL	11	7	42	6.0	1			None		1	6	1
Pro Totals—6 Years	59	155	683	4.4	6	26	144	5.5	0	6	36	6

Year	Club	G.	No.	Yds.	Avg.TD.	
		KICKOFF RETURNS				
1980—Philadelphia NFL		14	6	104	17.3	0
1981—Philadelphia NFL		4		None		
1982—Philadelphia NFL		9		None		
1983—Philadelphia NFL		15	4	79	19.8	0
1984—St. Louis NFL		6		None		
1985—St. Louis NFL		11	4	77	19.3	0
Pro Totals—6 Years		59	14	260	18.6	0

Played in NFC Championship Game following 1980 season.
Played in NFL Championship Game following 1980 season.

ALFRED CARL HARRIS
(Al)
Linebacker—Chicago Bears
Born December 31, 1956, at Bangor, Me.
Height, 6.05. Weight, 250.
High School—Wahiawa, Hawaii, Leilehua.
Received bachelor of science degree in communications from Arizona State University.
Cousin of Ricky Bell, running back with Tampa Bay Buccaneers and San Diego Chargers,
1977 through 1982; and Archie Bell, lead singer of Archie Bell and the Drells.

Named as defensive lineman on THE SPORTING NEWS College All-America Team, 1978.
Selected by Chicago in 1st round (9th player selected) of 1979 NFL draft.
On injured reserve with knee injury, August 28 through October 25, 1979; activated, October 26, 1979.
On inactive list, September 19, 1982.
Granted free agency, February 1, 1985.
On reserve/unsigned free agency list, August 20 through entire 1985 season.
Chicago NFL, 1979 through 1984.
Games: 1979 (4), 1980 (16), 1981 (16), 1982 (8), 1983 (13), 1984 (16). Total—73.
Pro statistics: Caught one pass for 18 yards, intercepted one pass for 44 yards and a touchdown and recovered three fumbles for five yards, 1981; recovered two fumbles, 1983; intercepted one pass for 34 yards, 1984.
Played in NFC Championship Game following 1984 season.

BOB HARRIS
Linebacker—St. Louis Cardinals
Born November 11, 1960, at Everett, Wash.
Height, 6.02. Weight, 223.
High School—Decatur, Ga., Cedar Grove.
Received degree in organizational management from Auburn University in 1983.

Selected by Birmingham in 1983 USFL territorial draft.
Selected by St. Louis in 8th round (211th player selected) of 1983 NFL draft.
Signed by St. Louis Cardinals, June 7, 1983.
On injured reserve with knee injury, November 9 through remainder of 1983 season.
On injured reserve with dislocated elbow, August 19 through October 17, 1985; activated, October 18, 1985.

Year	Club	G.	No.	Yds.	Avg.TD.	
		—INTERCEPTIONS—				
1983—St. Louis NFL		8	3	10	3.3	0
1984—St. Louis NFL		16		None		
1985—St. Louis NFL		10		None		
Pro Totals—3 Years		34	3	10	3.3	0

ERIC WAYNE HARRIS
Cornerback—Los Angeles Rams
Born August 11, 1955, at Memphis, Tenn.
Height, 6.03. Weight, 202.
High School—Memphis, Tenn., Hamilton.
Attended Memphis State University.

Selected by Kansas City in 4th round (104th player selected) of 1977 NFL draft.
Signed by Toronto Argonauts, April, 1977.
Granted free agency, April 15, 1980; given offer sheet by New Orleans Saints, April 26, 1980.
Offer matched by Kansas City Chiefs, April 28, 1980; signed by Chiefs, May 16, 1980.
Traded by Kansas City Chiefs to Los Angeles Rams for running back Jewerl Thomas, August 19, 1983.
On injured reserve with ankle injury, November 2 through December 7, 1984; activated, December 8, 1984.
On injured reserve with back injury, November 14 through remainder of 1985 season.

Year	Club	G.	No.	Yds.	Avg.TD.		Year	Club	G.	No.	Yds.	Avg.TD.	
		—INTERCEPTIONS—							—INTERCEPTIONS—				
1977—Toronto CFL		16	7	166	23.7	1	1983—L.A. Rams NFL		16	4	100	25.0	0
1978—Toronto CFL		16	3	27	9.0	0	1984—L.A. Rams NFL		7		None		
1979—Toronto CFL		16	3	12	4.0	0	1985—L.A. Rams NFL		9		None		
1980—Kansas City NFL		15	7	54	7.7	0	CFL Totals—3 Years		48	13	205	15.8	1
1981—Kansas City NFL		16	7	109	15.6	0	NFL Totals—6 Years		71	21	329	15.7	1
1982—Kansas City NFL		8	3	66	22.0	*1	Pro Totals—9 Years		119	34	534	15.7	2

Additional CFL statistics: Returned three punts for no yards and recovered four fumbles for two yards, 1977; fumbled once, 1977 and 1978; returned one kickoff for no yards and recovered two fumbles for 12 yards, 1978; recovered two fumbles, 1979.
Additional NFL statistics: Recovered two fumbles for 20 yards, 1981; recovered one fumble, 1983 and 1984.

HERBERT H. HARRIS
Wide Receiver—New Orleans Saints

Born May 4, 1961, at Houston, Tex.
Height, 6.01. Weight, 195.
High School—Houston, Tex., Kashmere.
Received bachelor of science degree in secondary education from Lamar University.

Signed as free agent by Tampa Bay Buccaneers, May 3, 1983.
Released by Tampa Bay Buccaneers, August 23, 1983; signed by Houston Gamblers, October 28, 1983.
Released by Houston Gamblers, November 15, 1983; awarded on waivers to Philadelphia Stars, November 22, 1983.
Franchise transferred to Baltimore, November 1, 1984.
On developmental squad, April 13 through April 25, 1985; activated, April 26, 1985.
On developmental squad, May 31 through June 13, 1985; activated, June 14, 1985.
On developmental squad, June 21 through remainder of 1985 season.
Granted free agency, August 1, 1985; signed as free agent by Philadelphia Eagles, August 5, 1985.
Released by Philadelphia Eagles, September 2, 1985; signed as free agent by New Orleans Saints, May 15, 1986.
On developmental squad for 5 games with Baltimore Stars in 1985.

		—PASS RECEIVING—			
Year Club	G.	P.C.	Yds.	Avg.	TD.
1984—Philadelphia USFL	17	18	309	17.2	2
1985—Baltimore USFL	12	16	210	13.1	3
Pro Totals—2 Years	29	34	519	15.3	5

Additional pro statistics: Ran 33 yards with lateral on punt return, returned four kickoffs for 73 yards and recovered three fumbles for seven yards, 1984; fumbled once, 1984 and 1985; returned nine kickoffs for 199 yards, 1985.
Played in USFL Championship Game following 1984 season.
On developmental squad for USFL Championship Game following 1985 season.

JOHN EDWARD HARRIS
Safety—Seattle Seahawks

Born June 13, 1956, at Fort Benning, Ga.
Height, 6.02. Weight, 200.
High School—Miami, Fla., Jackson.
Received bachelor of science degree in political science from Arizona State University in 1978.

Selected by Seattle in 7th round (173rd player selected) of 1978 NFL draft.
On did not report list, August 31 through September 1, 1982; activated and granted two-game roster exemption, September 2, 1982.
Activated, September 10, 1982.

		—INTERCEPTIONS—			
Year Club	G.	No.	Yds.	Avg.	TD.
1978—Seattle NFL	16	4	65	16.3	0
1979—Seattle NFL	14	2	30	15.0	0
1980—Seattle NFL	16	6	28	4.7	0
1981—Seattle NFL	16	10	155	15.5	2
1982—Seattle NFL	9	4	33	8.3	0
1983—Seattle NFL	16	2	15	7.5	0
1984—Seattle NFL	16	6	79	13.2	0
1985—Seattle NFL	16	7	20	2.9	0
Pro Totals—8 Years	119	41	425	10.4	2

Additional pro statistics: Returned five punts for 58 yards, 1978; fumbled once, 1978, 1979 and 1981; returned eight punts for 70 yards and returned one kickoff for 21 yards, 1979; recovered one fumble, 1979, 1980 and 1984; recovered three fumbles, 1981; returned two punts for 27 yards and recovered three fumbles for 62 yards, 1983; returned one kickoff for seven yards, 1984; returned three punts for 24 yards and recovered two fumbles, 1985.
Played in AFC Championship Game following 1983 season.

LESLIE WAYNE HARRIS

(Known by middle name.)

Guard—Buffalo Bills

Born November 7, 1961, at Water Valley, Miss.
Height, 6.02. Weight, 269.
High School—Water Valley, Miss.
Attended Mississippi State University.

Selected by New Jersey in 5th round (51st player selected) of 1983 USFL draft.
Signed by New Jersey Generals, January 31, 1983.
On developmental squad, April 20 through April 28, 1984; activated, April 29, 1984.
On developmental squad, May 21 through June 8, 1984; activated, June 9, 1984.
Granted free agency, August 1, 1985; signed by Buffalo Bills, May 6, 1986.
On developmental squad for 5 games with New Jersey Generals in 1984.
New Jersey USFL, 1983 through 1985.
Games: 1983 (18), 1984 (14), 1985 (18). Total—50.
Pro statistics: Recovered one fumble, 1985.

—DID YOU KNOW—

That when Tampa Bay quarterback Steve Young won his first NFL start against Detroit on November 24, he was the first of Tampa Bay's 13 starting quarterbacks since 1976 to win his debut game?

MICHAEL LEE HARRIS
(M.L.)
Tight End—Cincinnati Bengals
Born January 16, 1954, at Columbus, O.
Height, 6.05. Weight, 238.
High School—Columbus, O., North.
Attended University of Tampa and Kansas State University

Signed by Hamilton Tiger-Cats, April, 1976.
Granted free agency, April, 1978; signed by Toronto Argonauts, May, 1978 (Argonauts sent linebacker Ray Nettles to Tiger-Cats as compensation).
Granted free agency, April 1, 1980; signed as free agent by Cincinnati Bengals, April 30, 1980.
On injured reserve with broken thumb, October 29 through November 27, 1980; activated, November 28, 1980.
On injured reserve with knee injury, November 28 through remainder of 1983 season.
On injured reserve with broken wrist, September 3 through October 11, 1985; activated, October 12, 1985.

		—RUSHING—				PASS RECEIVING				—TOTAL—		
Year Club	G.	Att.	Yds.	Avg.	TD.	P.C.	Yds.	Avg.	TD.	TD.	Pts.	F.
1976—Hamilton CFL	11	5	—1	—0.2	1	24	550	22.9	3	4	24	2
1977—Hamilton CFL	16	4	12	3.0	2	43	771	17.9	6	8	48	1
1978—Toronto CFL	12	5	16	3.2	0	32	496	15.5	3	3	18	0
1979—Toronto CFL	12	3	13	4.3	0	46	530	11.5	1	1	6	1
1980—Cincinnati NFL	12	1	0	0.0	0	10	137	13.7	0	0	0	0
1981—Cincinnati NFL	15			None		13	181	13.9	2	2	12	1
1982—Cincinnati NFL	9	2	—3	—1.5	0	10	103	10.3	3	3	18	0
1983—Cincinnati NFL	12			None		8	66	8.3	2	2	12	0
1984—Cincinnati NFL	16	1	—2	—2.0	0	48	759	15.8	2	2	12	2
1985—Cincinnati NFL	10			None		10	123	12.3	1	1	6	0
CFL Totals—4 Years	51	17	40	2.4	3	145	2347	16.2	13	16	96	4
NFL Totals—6 Years	74	3	—5	—1.7	0	99	1369	13.8	10	10	60	3
Pro Totals—10 Years	125	20	35	1.8	3	244	3716	15.2	23	26	156	7

Additional CFL statistics: Returned three kickoffs for 51 yards, 1976; recovered one fumble, 1976 and 1977; returned one kickoff for 20 yards, 1978.
Additional NFL statistics: Recovered two fumbles for three yards, 1981; returned one kickoff for 12 yards and recovered one fumble, 1984.
Played in AFC Championship Game following 1981 season.
Played in NFL Championship Game following 1981 season.

NATHAN HARRIS
(Nate)
Wide Receiver—Washington Redskins
Born September 28, 1962, at Longview, Tex.
Height, 5.09. Weight, 172.
High School—Longview, Tex.
Received bachelor of science degree in business administration from The University of Tulsa.

Selected by Denver in 14th round (194th player selected) of 1985 USFL draft.
Signed by Denver Gold, January 21, 1985.
Released by Denver Gold, July 31, 1985; signed as free agent by Washington Redskins, April 16, 1986.

		–PUNT RETURNS–				—KICKOFF RET.—				—TOTAL—		
Year Club	G.	No.	Yds.	Avg.	TD.	No.	Yds.	Avg.	TD.	TD.	Pts.	F.
1985—Denver USFL	18	5	8	1.6	0	2	14	7.0	0	0	0	0

DENNIS HARRISON
Defensive End—Los Angeles Rams
Born July 31, 1956, at Cleveland, O.
Height, 6.08. Weight, 280.
High School—Murfreesboro, Tenn., Riverdale.
Received bachelor of science degree in education from Vanderbilt University in 1978.

Selected by Philadelphia in 4th round (92nd player selected) of 1978 draft.
On injured reserve with knee injury, August 28 through September 28, 1979; activated, September 29, 1979.
Placed on did not report list, August 20 through September 27, 1985; activated, September 28, 1985.
Traded by Philadelphia Eagles to Los Angeles Rams for 4th round pick in 1986 draft and 7th round pick in 1987 draft, September 28, 1985.
Granted roster exemption, September 28 through October 3, 1985; activated, October 4, 1985.
Philadelphia NFL, 1978 through 1984; Los Angeles Rams NFL, 1985.
Games: 1978 (16), 1979 (12), 1980 (15), 1981 (13), 1982 (9), 1983 (16), 1984 (16), 1985 (12). Total—109.
Pro statistics: Intercepted one pass for 12 yards, 1978; recovered three fumbles, 1981; recovered one fumble, 1982 and 1984; recovered one fumble for 16 yards, 1983.
Played in NFC Championship Game following 1980 and 1985 seasons.
Played in NFL Championship Game following 1980 season.
Played in Pro Bowl (NFL All-Star Game) following 1982 season.

—DID YOU KNOW—
That Rams running back Eric Dickerson has averaged 8.1 yards a carry in his career against the St. Louis Cardinals? Dickerson carried 21 times for 208 yards in a 1984 game and 20 times for 124 yards in a game last season. The Rams won both games.

MARCK HARRISON
Running Back—Cleveland Browns
Born April 20, 1961, at Columbus, O.
Height, 5.08. Weight, 195.
High School—Columbus, O., Eastmoor.
Attended University of Wisconsin.

Selected by Jacksonville in 1985 USFL territorial draft.
USFL rights traded with rights to center Dan Turk and tight end Kay Whisenhunt by Jacksonville Bulls to Tampa Bay Bandits for rights to running back Cedric Jones, placekicker Bobby Raymond and defensive back Eric Riley, January 3, 1985.
USFL rights traded by Tampa Bay Bandits to Orlando Renegades for draft choice, March 7, 1985.
Signed by Orlando Renegades and granted roster exemption, March 7 through March 13, 1985; activated, March 14, 1985.
On developmental squad, April 12 through April 17, 1985, activated, April 18, 1985.
Released by Orlando Renegades, April 24, 1985; signed as free agent by Cleveland Browns, May 6, 1985.
Released by Cleveland Browns, August 20, 1985; re-signed by Browns, May 2, 1986.
On developmental squad for 1 game with Orlando Renegades in 1985.

		—RUSHING—				PASS RECEIVING				—TOTAL—		
Year	Club	G.	Att.	Yds.	Avg.	TD.	P.C.	Yds.	Avg.	TD.	TD.	Pts.	F.
1985—Orlando USFL		3	3	5	1.7	0	1	5	5.0	0	0	0	0

Additional pro statistics: Returned one kickoff for nine yards, 1985.

DARYL KEITH HART
Cornerback—Buffalo Bills
Born January 10, 1961, at Memphis, Tenn.
Height, 5.10. Weight, 172.
High School—Memphis, Tenn., Douglass.
Attended Alcorn State University and Lane College.

Selected by Oakland in 3rd round (53rd player selected) of 1984 USFL draft.
Signed by Oakland Invaders, January 15, 1984.
On developmental squad, April 21 through May 10, 1984; activated, May 11, 1984.
Selected by Buffalo in 2nd round (41st player selected) of 1984 NFL supplemental draft.
Protected in merger of Oakland Invaders and Michigan Panthers, December 6, 1984.
On developmental squad, April 28 through May 22, 1985; activated, May 23, 1985.
Released by Oakland Invaders, July 31, 1985; signed by Buffalo Bills, May 19, 1986.
On developmental squad for 3 games with Oakland Invaders in 1984 and 1985.
Oakland USFL, 1984 and 1985.
Games: 1984 (15), 1985 (14). Total—29.
Pro statistics: Returned six kickoffs for 94 yards and recovered one fumble, 1985.
Played in USFL Championship Game following 1985 season.

MICHAEL ALBERT HARTENSTINE
(Mike)
Defensive End—Chicago Bears
Born July 27, 1953, at Bethlehem, Pa.
Height, 6.03. Weight, 258.
High School—Bethlehem, Pa., Liberty.
Attended Penn State University.

Selected by Chicago in 2nd round (31st player selected) of 1975 NFL draft.
Chicago NFL, 1975 through 1985.
Games: 1975 (14), 1976 (14), 1977 (14), 1978 (16), 1979 (16), 1980 (16), 1981 (16), 1982 (9), 1983 (16), 1984 (16), 1985 (16). Total—163.
Pro statistics: Scored a safety and recovered two fumbles for five yards, 1975; recovered three fumbles for three yards and scored one touchdown on a 12 yard lateral, 1976; recovered three fumbles, 1977; recovered three fumbles for 10 yards, 1978; recovered one fumble, 1979 and 1985; recovered one fumble for four yards, 1981; recovered one fumble for 10 yards and a touchdown, 1983; recovered two fumbles, 1984.
Played in NFC Championship Game following 1984 and 1985 seasons.
Played in NFL Championship Game following 1985 season.

JOHN DANIEL HARTY
Defensive End—San Francisco 49ers
Born December 17, 1958, at Sioux City, Ia.
Height, 6.04. Weight, 263.
High School—Sioux City, Ia., Heelan.
Attended University of Iowa.

Selected by San Francisco in 2nd round (36th player selected) of 1981 NFL draft.
On injured reserve with foot injury, November 23 through remainder of 1983 season.
On physically unable to perform/active with fractured foot, July 19 through August 12, 1984.
On physically unable to perform/reserve with fractured foot, August 13 through entire 1984 season.
On physically unable to perfom/active with foot injury, August 2 through November 5, 1985; activated, November 6, 1985.
San Francisco NFL, 1981 through 1983 and 1985.
Games: 1981 (14), 1982 (9), 1983 (5), 1985 (7). Total—35.
Pro statistics: Credited with one safety, 1985.
Played in NFC Championship Game following 1981 season.
Played in NFL Championship Game following 1981 season.

JAMES DONALD HASLETT
(Jim)
Linebacker—Buffalo Bills

Born December 9, 1957, at Pittsburgh, Pa.
Height, 6.03. Weight, 228.
High School—Pittsburgh, Pa., Avalon.
Attended Indiana (Pa.) University.
Brother of Jon Haslett, rookie linebacker with Pittsburgh Steelers; and cousin of Hal Stringert, defensive back with The Hawaiians (WFL) and San Diego Chargers, 1974 through 1980.

Selected by Buffalo in 2nd round (51st player selected) of 1979 NFL draft.
On injured reserve with back injury, September 13 through November 17, 1983; activated, November 18, 1983.

			—INTERCEPTIONS—		
Year Club	G.	No.	Yds.	Avg.	TD.
1979—Buffalo NFL	16	2	15	7.5	0
1980—Buffalo NFL	16	2	30	15.0	0
1981—Buffalo NFL	16		None		
1982—Buffalo NFL	6		None		
1983—Buffalo NFL	5		None		
1984—Buffalo NFL	15		None		
1985—Buffalo NFL	16	1	40	40.0	0
Pro Totals—7 Years	90	5	85	17.0	0

Additional pro statistics: Recovered two fumbles, 1979; recovered one fumble, 1980 through 1982; caught one pass for four yards, 1982; recovered three fumbles for 10 yards, 1984; recovered three fumbles and fumbled once, 1985.

DONALD WILLIAM HASSELBECK
(Don)
Tight End—New York Giants

Born April 1, 1955, at Cincinnati, O.
Height, 6.07. Weight, 245.
High School—Cincinnati, O., LaSalle.
Attended University of Colorado.

Named as tight end on THE SPORTING NEWS College All-America Team, 1976.
Selected by New England in 2nd round (52nd player selected) of 1977 NFL draft.
Granted roster exemption, August 18, 1981; activated August 29, 1981.
On injured reserve with knee injury, December 11 through remainder of 1981 season.
Traded by New England Patriots to Los Angeles Raiders for tight end Derrick Ramsey, September 13, 1983.
Released by Los Angeles Raiders, August 27, 1984; awarded on waivers to Minnesota Vikings, August 28, 1984.
Granted free agency after not receiving qualifying offer, February 1, 1985; signed by New York Giants, May 21, 1985.
Released by New York Giants, August 26, 1985; re-signed by Giants, September 3, 1985.
On injured reserve with hamstring injury, October 10 through December 13, 1985; activated, December 14, 1985.

			—PASS RECEIVING—		
Year Club	G.	P.C.	Yds.	Avg.	TD.
1977—New England NFL	14	9	76	8.4	4
1978—New England NFL	16	7	107	15.3	0
1979—New England NFL	16	13	158	12.2	0
1980—New England NFL	16	8	130	16.3	4
1981—New England NFL	14	46	808	17.6	6
1982—New England NFL	9	15	158	10.5	1
1983—N.E. (1)-Rai. (14) NFL.	15	3	24	8.0	2
1984—Minnesota NFL	16	1	10	10.0	0
1985—N.Y. Giants NFL	7	5	71	14.2	1
Pro Totals—9 Years	123	107	1542	14.4	18

Additional pro statistics: Fumbled once, 1979; returned one kickoff for seven yards and fumbled twice, 1981; recovered one fumble, 1984; returned one kickoff for 21 yards, 1985.
Played in AFC Championship Game following 1983 season.
Played in NFL Championship Game following 1983 season.

ROGER DALE HATCHER
(Known by middle name.)
Punter—Los Angeles Rams

Born April 5, 1963, at Cheraw, S.C.
Height, 6.02. Weight, 200.
High School—Cheraw, S.C.
Attended Clemson University.

Named to THE SPORTING NEWS NFL All-Star Team, 1985.
Led NFL in net punting average with 38.0 in 1985.
Selected by Orlando in 8th round (114th player selected) of 1985 USFL draft.
Selected by Los Angeles Rams in 3rd round (77th player selected) of 1985 NFL draft.
Signed by Los Angeles Rams, July 12, 1985.

			—PUNTING—	
Year Club	G.	No.	Avg.	Blk.
1985—L.A. Rams NFL	16	87	43.2	1

Played in NFC Championship Game following 1985 season.
Played in Pro Bowl (NFL All-Star Game) following 1985 season.

RON CARL HAUSAUER
Guard—Green Bay Packers
Born August 16, 1959, at Hazen, N.D.
Height, 6.04. Weight, 270.
High School—Beulah, N.D.
Attended University of North Dakota and Jamestown College.

Signed as free agent by Cincinnati Bengals, April 30, 1982.
Released by Cincinnati Bengals, August 30, 1982; signed by Denver Gold, December 10, 1982.
On injured reserve with knee injury, June 16 through remainder of 1983 season.
Released by Denver Gold, February 20, 1984; signed as free agent by Pittsburgh Maulers, March 20, 1984.
On developmental squad, March 20 through April 11, 1984; activated, April 12, 1984.
On developmental squad, April 20 through May 10, 1984; activated, May 11, 1984.
On developmental squad, June 4 through June 7, 1984; activated, June 8, 1984.
On developmental squad, June 15 through June 21, 1984; activated, June 22, 1984.
Franchise disbanded, October 25, 1984.
Selected by Denver Gold in USFL dispersal draft, December 6, 1984.
Released by Denver Gold, March 20, 1985; signed as free agent by Green Bay Packers, April 22, 1986.
On developmental squad for 8 games with Pittsburgh Maulers in 1984.
Denver USFL, 1983; Pittsburgh USFL, 1984; Denver USFL, 1985.
Games: 1983 (15), 1984 (3), 1985 (4). Total—22.

FRANK HAWKINS
Running Back—Los Angeles Raiders
Born July 3, 1959, at Las Vegas, Nev.
Height, 5.09. Weight, 210.
High School—Las Vegas, Nev., Western.
Received degree in criminal justice from University of Nevada at Reno in 1981.
Cousin of Larry Heater, running back with New York Giants, 1980 through 1983.

Selected by Oakland in 10th round (276th player selected) of 1981 NFL draft.
Released by Oakland Raiders, August 25, 1981; re-signed by Raiders, September 23, 1981.
Franchise transferred to Los Angeles, May 7, 1982.

Year	Club	G.	Att.	Yds.	Avg.	TD.	P.C.	Yds.	Avg.	TD.	TD.	Pts.	F.
			—RUSHING—				PASS RECEIVING				—TOTAL—		
1981—Oakland NFL		13	40	165	4.1	0	10	109	10.9	0	0	0	1
1982—Los Angeles Raiders NFL		9	27	54	2.0	2	7	35	5.0	1	3	18	1
1983—Los Angeles Raiders NFL		16	110	526	4.8	6	20	150	7.5	2	8	48	2
1984—Los Angeles Raiders NFL		16	108	376	3.5	3	7	51	7.3	0	3	18	3
1985—Los Angeles Raiders NFL		16	84	269	3.2	4	27	174	6.4	0	4	24	0
Pro Totals—5 Years		70	369	1390	3.8	15	71	519	7.3	3	18	108	7

Additional pro statistics: Recovered one fumble, 1981, 1983 and 1984; returned one kickoff for seven yards, 1981; returned one kickoff for 14 yards, 1985.
Played in AFC Championship Game following 1983 season.
Played in NFL Championship Game following 1983 season.

GREGORY DALE HAWTHORNE
(Greg)
Wide Receiver—New England Patriots
Born September 5, 1956, at Fort Worth, Tex.
Height, 6.02. Weight, 225.
High School—Fort Worth, Tex., Poly.
Attended Baylor University.

Selected by Pittsburgh in 1st round (28th player selected) of 1979 NFL draft.
Traded by Pittsburgh Steelers to New England Patriots for 9th round pick in 1985 draft, August 21, 1984.
Released by New England Patriots, October 17, 1985; re-signed by Patriots, October 26, 1985.

Year	Club	G.	Att.	Yds.	Avg.	TD.	P.C.	Yds.	Avg.	TD.	TD.	Pts.	F.
			—RUSHING—				PASS RECEIVING				—TOTAL—		
1979—Pittsburgh NFL		15	28	123	4.4	1	8	47	5.9	0	1	6	2
1980—Pittsburgh NFL		15	63	226	3.6	4	12	158	13.2	0	4	24	6
1981—Pittsburgh NFL		10	25	58	2.3	2	4	23	5.8	0	2	12	1
1982—Pittsburgh NFL		9	15	68	4.5	0	12	182	15.2	3	3	18	0
1983—Pittsburgh NFL		10	5	47	9.4	0	19	300	15.8	0	0	0	0
1984—New England NFL		14		None			7	127	18.1	0	0	0	0
1985—New England NFL		15		None			3	42	14.0	1	1	6	0
Pro Totals—7 Years		88	136	522	3.8	7	65	879	13.5	4	11	66	9

	KICKOFF RETURNS				
Year	Club	G.	No.	Yds.	Avg.TD.
1979—Pittsburgh NFL		15	2	46	23.0	0
1980—Pittsburgh NFL		15	9	169	18.8	0
1981—Pittsburgh NFL		10	7	138	19.7	0
1982—Pittsburgh NFL		9		None	
1983—Pittsburgh NFL		10		None	
1984—New England NFL		14	1	14	14.0	0
1985—New England NFL		15	1	13	13.0	0
Pro Totals—7 Years		88	20	380	19.0	0

Additional pro statistics: Recovered one fumble, 1979 and 1983; recovered three fumbles, 1980.
Played in AFC Championship Game following 1979 and 1985 seasons.
Played in NFL Championship Game following 1979 and 1985 seasons.

GARY L. HAYES
Defensive Back—Green Bay Packers

Born August 19, 1957, at Tuscon, Ariz.
Height, 5.10. Weight, 180.
High School—El Cerrito, Calif.
Attended Fresno State University.

Signed as free agent by St. Louis Cardinals, May 29, 1980.
Released by St. Louis Cardinals, August 26, 1980; signed as free agent by Edmonton Eskimos, February 15, 1981.
USFL rights traded by Oakland Invaders to Los Angeles Express for rights to defensive end Chris Lindstrom and cornerback Jeff Allen, September 27, 1983.
Granted free agency, March 1, 1984; signed by Green Bay Packers, March 21, 1984.

		INTERCEPTIONS				–PUNT RETURNS–				—KICKOFF RET.—				—TOTAL—		
Year Club	G.	No.	Yds.	Avg.	TD.	No.	Yds.	Avg.	TD.	No.	Yds.	Avg.	TD.	TD.	Pts.	F.
1981—Edmonton CFL	15	2	39	19.5	0	71	601	8.5	0	9	209	23.2	0	0	0	2
1982—Edmonton CFL	16	2	27	13.5	0	*100	818	8.2	0	5	95	19.0	0	0	0	2
1983—Edmonton CFL	16	1	34	34.0	0	61	380	6.2	0	13	269	20.7	0	0	0	2
1984—Green Bay NFL	16		None			4	24	6.0	0		None			0	0	0
1985—Green Bay NFL	16		None			1	0	0.0	0		None			0	0	1
CFL Totals—3 Years	47	5	100	20.0	0	232	1799	7.8	0	27	573	21.2	0	0	0	6
NFL Totals—2 Years.....	32	0	0	0.0	0	5	24	4.8	0	0	0	0.0	0	0	0	1
Pro Totals—5 Years.......	79	5	100	20.0	0	237	1823	7.7	0	27	573	21.2	0	0	0	7

Additional CFL statistics: Recovered one fumble, 1983.
Additional NFL statistics: Recovered three fumbles, 1985.
Played in CFL Championship Game following 1981 and 1982 seasons.

JEFFREY HAYES
(Jeff)
Punter—Washington Redskins

Born August 19, 1959, at Elkin, N.C.
Height, 5.11. Weight, 175.
High School—Elkin, N.C.
Attended University of North Carolina.

Signed as free agent by Washington Redskins, May 24, 1982.
On injured reserve with torn thigh muscle, October 1 through remainder of 1985 season.

	——PUNTING——			
Year Club	G.	No.	Avg.	Blk.
1982—Washington NFL..................	9	51	38.0	1
1983—Washington NFL..................	16	72	38.8	0
1984—Washington NFL..................	16	72	39.4	1
1985—Washington NFL..................	4	16	41.6	0
Pro Totals—4 Years....................	45	211	39.0	2

Additional pro statistics: Rushed twice for 63 yards, 1983; rushed twice for 13 yards, recovered one fumble and fumbled twice, 1984.
Played in NFC Championship Game following 1982 and 1983 seasons.
Played in NFL Championship Game following 1982 and 1983 seasons.

JONATHAN MICHAEL HAYES
Tight End—Kansas City Chiefs

Born August 11, 1962, at South Fayette, Pa.
Height, 6.05. Weight, 234.
High School—McDonald, Pa., South Fayette.
Attended University of Iowa.
Brother of Jay Hayes, defensive end with Memphis Showboats.

Selected by Kansas City in 2nd round (41st player selected) of 1985 NFL draft.
Signed by Kansas City Chiefs, June 19, 1985.

	——PASS RECEIVING——				
Year Club	G.	P.C.	Yds.	Avg.	TD.
1985—Kansas City NFL..........	16	5	39	7.8	1

Additional pro statistics: Returned one kickoff for no yards, 1985.

LESTER HAYES
Cornerback—Los Angeles Raiders

Born January 22, 1955, at Houston, Tex.
Height, 6.00. Weight, 200.
High School—Houston, Tex., Wheatley.
Attended Texas A&M University.

Named to THE SPORTING NEWS NFL All-Star Team, 1980 and 1981.
Named as safety on THE SPORTING NEWS College All-America Team, 1976.
Selected by Oakland in 5th round (126th player selected) of 1977 NFL draft.
Franchise transferred to Los Angeles, May 7, 1982.

		INTERCEPTIONS				—KICKOFF RET.—				—TOTAL—		
Year Club	G.	No.	Yds.	Avg.	TD.	No.	Yds.	Avg.	TD.	TD.	Pts.	F.
1977—Oakland NFL.............................	14	1	27	27.0	0	3	57	19.0	0	0	0	1
1978—Oakland NFL.............................	16	4	86	21.5	0		None			0	0	0

Year Club	G.	INTERCEPTIONS				KICKOFF RET.				TOTAL		
		No.	Yds.	Avg.	TD.	No.	Yds.	Avg.	TD.	TD.	Pts.	F.
1979—Oakland NFL	16	7	100	14.3	*2		None			2	12	0
1980—Oakland NFL	16	*13	*273	21.0	1	1	0	0.0	0	1	6	0
1981—Oakland NFL	16	3	0	0.0	0		None			0	0	0
1982—Los Angeles Raiders NFL	9	2	0	0.0	0		None			0	0	0
1983—Los Angeles Raiders NFL	16	2	49	24.5	0		None			0	0	0
1984—Los Angeles Raiders NFL	16	1	3	3.0	0		None			0	0	0
1985—Los Angeles Raiders NFL	16	4	27	6.8	*1	1	0	0.0	0	1	6	0
Pro Totals—9 Years	135	37	565	15.3	4	5	57	11.4	0	4	24	1

Additional pro statistics: Recovered two fumbles for minus three yards, 1977; recovered two fumbles, 1980; recovered one fumble, 1985.

Played in AFC Championship Game following 1977, 1980 and 1983 seasons.

Played in NFL Championship Game following 1980 and 1983 seasons.

Played in Pro Bowl (NFL All-Star Game) following 1980 through 1984 seasons.

JAMES HAYNES
Linebacker—New Orleans Saints
Born August 9, 1960, at Tallulah, La.
Height, 6.02. Weight, 227.
High School—Tallulah, La.
Attended Coahoma Junior College and Mississippi Valley State University.

Signed as free agent by New Orleans Saints, June 20, 1984.

On injured reserve with rotator cuff injury, August 27 through October 4, 1984; activated after clearing procedural waivers, October 5, 1984.

New Orleans NFL, 1984 and 1985.

Games: 1984 (10), 1985 (16). Total—26.

Pro statistics: Caught one pass for eight yards and recovered two fumbles, 1985.

MARK HAYNES
Cornerback—Denver Broncos
Born November 6, 1958, at Kansas City, Kan.
Height, 5.11. Weight, 198.
High School—Kansas City, Kan., Harmon.
Attended University of Colorado.

Selected by New York Giants in 1st round (8th player selected) of 1980 NFL draft.

Left camp voluntarily and granted roster exemption, August 21 through August 27, 1984; returned and activated, August 28, 1984.

On injured reserve with knee injury, December 14 through remainder of 1984 season.

Granted free agency, February 1, 1985; re-signed by Giants, October 16, 1985.

Granted roster exemption, October 16 through October 27, 1985; activated, October 28, 1985.

On injured reserve with groin injury, December 14 through remainder of 1985 season.

Traded by New York Giants to Denver Broncos for 2nd and 6th round picks in 1986 draft and 2nd round pick in 1987 draft, April 29, 1986.

Year Club	G.	INTERCEPTIONS			
		No.	Yds.	Avg.	TD.
1980—N.Y. Giants NFL	15	1	6	6.0	0
1981—N.Y. Giants NFL	16	1	9	9.0	0
1982—N.Y. Giants NFL	9	1	0	0.0	0
1983—N.Y. Giants NFL	15	3	18	6.0	0
1984—N.Y. Giants NFL	15	7	90	12.9	0
1985—N.Y. Giants NFL	5		None		
Pro Totals—6 Years	75	13	123	9.5	0

Additional pro statistics: Returned two kickoffs for 40 yards, 1980; recovered one fumble, 1981; recovered two fumbles for four yards, 1983; recovered two fumbles for 12 yards, 1984.

Played in Pro Bowl (NFL All-Star Game) following 1982 and 1983 seasons.

Named to play in Pro Bowl following 1984 season; replaced due to injury by Eric Wright.

MICHAEL JAMES HAYNES
(Mike)
Cornerback—Los Angeles Raiders
Born July 1, 1953, at Denison, Tex.
Height, 6.02. Weight, 190.
High School—Los Angeles, Calif., John Marshall.
Attending Arizona State University.
Brother of Reggie Haynes, tight end with Washington Redskins, 1978.

Named to THE SPORTING NEWS NFL All-Star Team, 1984 and 1985.

Named to THE SPORTING NEWS AFC All-Star Team, 1976, 1978 and 1979.

Named by THE SPORTING NEWS as AFC Rookie of the Year, 1976.

Named as defensive back on THE SPORTING NEWS College All-America Team, 1975.

Selected by New England in 1st round (5th player selected) of 1976 NFL draft.

On did not report list, September 1 through September 22, 1980.

Granted roster exemption, September 23 through September 28, 1980; activated, September 29, 1980.

On injured reserve with collapsed lung, November 6 through December 10, 1981; activated, December 11, 1981.

Granted free agency, February 1, 1983; signed by Los Angeles Raiders, November 2, 1983 (Haynes had sued NFL when trade to Raiders was voided because it was after trading deadline).

Contract awarded to Raiders in settlement, November 10, 1983, with Patriots receiving 1st round pick in 1984 draft and 2nd round pick in 1985 draft and Raiders receiving 7th round pick in 1985 draft.

Granted roster exemption, November 10, 1983; activated, November 18, 1983.

Year Club	G.	INTERCEPTIONS				PUNT RETURNS				—TOTAL—		
		No.	Yds.	Avg.	TD.	No.	Yds.	Avg.	TD.	TD.	Pts.	F.
1976—New England NFL	14	8	90	11.3	0	45	608	13.5	2	2	12	3
1977—New England NFL	14	5	54	10.8	0	24	200	8.3	0	0	0	4
1978—New England NFL	16	6	123	20.5	1	14	183	13.1	0	1	6	1
1979—New England NFL	16	3	66	22.0	0	5	16	3.2	0	0	0	1
1980—New England NFL	13	1	31	31.0	0	17	140	8.2	0	1	6	2
1981—New England NFL	8	1	3	3.0	0	6	12	2.0	0	0	0	0
1982—New England NFL	9	4	26	6.5	0	None				0	0	0
1983—Los Angeles Raiders NFL	5	1	0	0.0	0	None				0	0	0
1984—Los Angeles Raiders NFL	16	6	*220	36.7	1	None				1	6	0
1985—Los Angeles Raiders NFL	16	4	8	2.0	0	1	9	9.0	0	0	0	0
Pro Totals—10 Years	127	39	621	15.9	2	112	1168	10.4	2	5	30	11

Additional pro statistics: Recovered three fumbles, 1976 and 1979; recovered two fumbles, 1977; ran 65 yards with blocked field goal for a touchdown and recovered three fumbles for six yards, 1980.

Played in AFC Championship Game following 1983 season.

Played in NFL Championship Game following 1983 season.

Played in Pro Bowl (NFL All-Star Game) following 1976 through 1980, 1982 and 1985 seasons.

Member of Pro Bowl following 1984 season; did not play.

THOMAS W. HAYNES JR.
(Tommy)
Defensive Back—Dallas Cowboys
Born February 6, 1963, at Chicago, Ill.
Height, 6.02. Weight, 190.
High School—Covina, Calif.
Attended Mt. San Antonio College and University of Southern California.

Selected by Los Angeles in 1985 USFL territorial draft.

USFL rights traded by Los Angeles Express to Portland Breakers for draft choice, February 19, 1985.

Signed by Portland Breakers, February 20, 1985.

Granted roster exemption, February 20 through February 22, 1985; activated, February 23, 1985.

Released by Portland Breakers, July 31, 1985; signed as free agent by Dallas Cowboys, August 2, 1985.

Released by Dallas Cowboys, August 20, 1985; re-signed by Cowboys, March 7, 1986.

Portland USFL, 1985.

Games: 1985 (16).

Pro statistics: Intercepted one pass for 29 yards, 1985.

ANDREW ROOSEVELT HEADEN
(Andy)
Linebacker—New York Giants
Born July 8, 1960, at Asheboro, N.C.
Height, 6.05. Weight, 242.
High School—Asheboro, N.C., Eastern Randolph.
Attended Clemson University.

Selected by Washington in 1983 USFL territorial draft.

Selected by New York Giants in 8th round (205th player selected) of 1983 NFL draft.

Signed by New York Giants, June 13, 1983.

On injured reserve with sprained foot, October 10 through November 16, 1984; activated, November 17, 1984.

New York Giants NFL, 1983 through 1985.

Games: 1983 (16), 1984 (11), 1985 (16). Total—43.

Pro statistics: Intercepted one pass for four yards and recovered one fumble for 81 yards and a touchdown, 1984; intercepted two passes for seven yards, 1985.

HERMAN WILLIE HEARD JR.
Running Back—Kansas City Chiefs
Born November 24, 1961, at Denver, Colo.
Height, 5.10. Weight, 184.
High School—Denver, Colo., South.
Attended Fort Lewis College and University of Southern Colorado.

Selected by Kansas City in 3rd round (61st player selected) of 1984 NFL draft.

Year Club	G.	RUSHING				PASS RECEIVING				—TOTAL—		
		Att.	Yds.	Avg.	TD.	P.C.	Yds.	Avg.	TD.	TD.	Pts.	F.
1984—Kansas City NFL	16	165	684	4.1	4	25	223	8.9	0	4	24	5
1985—Kansas City NFL	16	164	595	3.6	4	31	257	8.3	2	6	36	4
Pro Totals—2 Years	32	329	1279	3.9	8	56	480	8.6	2	10	60	9

Additional pro statistics: Recovered three fumbles, 1984; recovered one fumble, 1985.

—DID YOU KNOW—
That in Week 9 of the 1985 season, a record 13 NFL running backs rushed for more than 100 yards?

BOBBY JOSEPH HEBERT JR.

Name pronounced A-bear.

Quarterback—New Orleans Saints

Born August 19, 1960, at Baton Rouge, La.
Height, 6.04. Weight, 215.
High School—Galliano, La., South Lafourche.
Received degree in business administration from Northwestern Louisiana State University in 1983.
Brother of Billy Bob Herbert, quarterback at Nichols State University.

Named THE SPORTING NEWS USFL Player of the Year, 1983.
Named as quarterback on THE SPORTING NEWS USFL All-Star Team, 1983.
Selected by Michigan in 3rd round (34th player selected) of 1983 USFL draft.
Signed by Michigan Panthers, January 22, 1983.
On reserve/did not report, January 23 through February 15, 1984; activated, February 16, 1984.
Protected in merger of Michigan Panthers and Oakland Invaders, December 6, 1984.
Granted free agency, July 15, 1985; signed by New Orleans Saints, August 7, 1985.

			PASSING						RUSHING				TOTAL		
Year Club	G.	Att.	Cmp.	Pct.	Gain	T.P.	P.I.	Avg.	Att.	Yds.	Avg.	TD.	TD.	Pts.	F.
1983—Michigan USFL	18	451	257	57.0	3568	⋆27	17	⋆7.91	28	35	1.3	3	3	†20	8
1984—Michigan USFL	17	500	272	54.4	3758	24	22	7.52	18	76	4.2	1	1	6	8
1985—Oakland USFL	18	456	244	53.5	3811	30	19	8.36	12	31	2.6	1	1	6	5
1985—New Orleans NFL	6	181	97	53.6	1208	5	4	6.67	12	26	2.2	0	1	6	1
USFL Totals—3 Years	53	1407	773	54.9	11137	81	58	7.92	58	142	2.4	5	5	32	21
NFL Totals—1 Year	6	181	97	53.6	1208	5	4	6.67	12	26	2.2	0	1	6	1
Pro Totals—4 Years	59	1588	870	54.8	12345	86	62	7.77	70	168	2.4	5	6	38	22

†Includes one 2-point conversion.
USFL Quarterback Rating Points: 1983 (86.7), 1984 (76.4), 1985 (86.1). Total—83.1.
NFL Quarterback Rating Points: 1985 (74.6).
Additional USFL statistics: Recovered two fumbles, 1983; recovered three fumbles, 1984; recovered three fumbles and fumbled five times for minus two yards, 1985.
Additional NFL statistics: Caught one pass for seven yards and a touchdown and recovered one fumble, 1985.
Played in USFL Championship Game following 1983 and 1985 seasons.

JOHNNY LYNDELL HECTOR

Running Back—New York Jets

Born November 26, 1960, at Lafayette, La.
Height, 5.11. Weight, 197.
High School—New Iberia, La.
Attended Texas A&M University.

Selected by Chicago in 2nd round (19th player selected) of 1983 USFL draft.
Selected by New York Jets in 2nd round (51st player selected) of 1983 NFL draft.
Signed by New York Jets, June 9, 1983.

		RUSHING				PASS RECEIVING				TOTAL		
Year Club	G.	Att.	Yds.	Avg.	TD.	P.C.	Yds.	Avg.	TD.	TD.	Pts.	F.
1983—New York Jets NFL	10	16	85	5.3	0	5	61	12.2	1	1	6	2
1984—New York Jets NFL	13	124	531	4.3	1	20	182	9.1	0	1	6	2
1985—New York Jets NFL	14	145	572	3.9	6	17	164	9.6	0	6	36	2
Pro Totals—3 Years	37	285	1188	4.2	7	42	407	9.7	1	8	48	6

		KICKOFF RETURNS			
Year Club	G.	No.	Yds.	Avg.	TD.
1983—New York Jets NFL	10	14	274	19.6	0
1984—New York Jets NFL	13		None		
1985—New York Jets NFL	14	11	274	24.9	0
Pro Totals—3 Years	37	25	548	21.9	0

Additional pro statistics: Recovered one fumble, 1985.

VINCENT GEORGE HEFLIN

(Vince)

Wide Receiver—Miami Dolphins

Born July 7, 1959, at Dayton, O.
Height, 6.00. Weight, 185.
High School—Dayton, Ohio, Wayne.
Attended Central State (O.) University.
Brother of Victor Heflin, cornerback with St. Louis Cardinals, 1983 and 1984.

Signed as free agent by Miami Dolphins, July 1, 1982.
Released by Miami Dolphins, August 29, 1983; re-signed by Dolphins, September 6, 1983.
Released by Miami Dolphins, September 2, 1985; re-signed by Dolphins, September 3, 1985.
On injured reserve with hip injury, October 19 through remainder of 1985 season.

		PASS RECEIVING				PUNT RETURNS				KICKOFF RET.				TOTAL		
Year Club	G.	P.C.	Yds.	Avg.	TD.	No.	Yds.	Avg.	TD.	No.	Yds.	Avg.	TD.	TD.	Pts.	F.
1982—Miami NFL	6		None				None			2	49	24.5	0	0	0	0
1983—Miami NFL	14		None			1	19	19.0	0	1	27	27.0	0	0	0	0
1984—Miami NFL	16		None			6	76	12.7	0	9	130	14.4	0	0	0	1
1985—Miami NFL	5	6	98	16.3	1		None				None			0	0	0
Pro Totals—4 Years	41	6	98	16.3	1	7	95	13.6	0	12	206	17.2	0	0	0	1

Played in AFC Championship Game following 1982 and 1984 seasons.
Played in NFL Championship Game following 1982 and 1984 seasons.

MICHAEL WILLIAM HEGMAN
(Mike)
Linebacker—Dallas Cowboys
Born January 17, 1953, at Memphis, Tenn.
Height, 6.01. Weight, 225.
High School—Memphis, Tenn., Northside.
Attended Alabama A&M University and received degree in physical education
from Tennessee State University.

Selected by Dallas in 7th round (173rd player selected) of 1975 NFL draft.
On injured reserve with broken arm, September 8 through October 14, 1981; activated, October 15, 1981.
Did not play in 1975.
Dallas NFL, 1976 through 1985.
Games: 1976 (14), 1977 (14), 1978 (16), 1979 (16), 1980 (16), 1981 (11), 1982 (9), 1983 (16), 1984 (16), 1985 (16). Total—144.
Pro statistics: Recovered one fumble, 1976, 1977, 1984 and 1985; intercepted one pass for no yards, 1977; recovered two fumbles, 1978; intercepted two passes for two yards and recovered one fumble in end zone for a touchdown, 1980; recovered one fumble for nine yards and a touchdown, 1983; intercepted three passes for three yards, 1984; intercepted one pass for seven yards, 1985.
Played in NFC Championship Game following 1977, 1978, 1981 and 1982 seasons.
Member of Dallas Cowboys for NFC Championship Game following 1980 season; did not play.
Played in NFL Championship Game following 1977 and 1978 seasons.

RONALD RAMON HELLER
(Ron)
Offensive Tackle—Tampa Bay Buccaneers
Born August 25, 1962, at East Meadow, N.Y.
Height, 6.06. Weight, 280.
High School—Farming Dale, N.Y.
Received bachelor of science degree in administration of justice
from Penn State University in 1984.

Selected by Philadelphia in 1984 USFL territorial draft.
Selected by Tampa Bay in 4th round (112th player selected) of 1984 NFL draft.
Signed by Tampa Bay Buccaneers, June 6, 1984.
Tampa Bay NFL, 1984 and 1985.
Games: 1984 (14), 1985 (16). Total—30.

DALE ROBERT HELLESTRAE
Name pronounced Hellus-TRAY.
Offensive Tackle—Buffalo Bills
Born July 11, 1962, at Phoenix, Ariz.
Height, 6.05. Weight, 265.
High School—Scottsdale, Ariz., Saguaro.
Attended Southern Methodist University.

Selected by Houston in 1985 USFL territorial draft.
Selected by Buffalo in 4th round (112th player selected) of 1985 NFL draft.
Signed by Buffalo Bills, July 19, 1985.
On injured reserve with broken thumb, October 4 through remainder of 1985 season.
Buffalo NFL, 1985.
Games: 1985 (4).

ANDREW CAREY HENDEL
(Andy)
Linebacker—Miami Dolphins
Born March 4, 1961, at Rochester, N.Y.
Height 6.01. Weight, 230.
High School—Irondequoit, N.Y.
Attended North Carolina State University.

Selected by Jacksonville in 1984 USFL territorial draft.
Signed by Jacksonville Bulls, January 16, 1984.
On developmental squad, May 16 through May 30, 1984; activated, May 31, 1984.
On developmental squad, June 20 through remainder of 1984 season.
Released injured by Jacksonville Bulls, February 23, 1985; signed as free agent by Miami Dolphins, March 6, 1986.
On developmental squad for 3 games with Jacksonville Bulls in 1984.

| | | | —INTERCEPTIONS— | | |
Year Club	G.	No.	Yds.	Avg.	TD.
1984—Jacksonville USFL.......	15	3	84	28.0	0

Additional pro statistics: Credited with one sack for three yards, 1984.

—DID YOU KNOW—
That when the Oilers were shut out on November 10 by Buffalo, 20-0, it marked the first time since December 11, 1976 that they were whitewashed? Pittsburgh performed the feat nine years earlier, 21-0.

WYMON HENDERSON
Defensive Back—San Francisco 49ers
Born December 15, 1961, at North Miami Beach, Fla.
Height, 5.10. Weight, 190.
High School—Miami Beach, Fla., North.
Attended Hancock Junior College and University of Nevada at Las Vegas.

Selected by Los Angeles in 8th round (96th player selected) of 1983 USFL draft.
Signed by Los Angeles Express, January 20, 1983.
Granted free agency, August 1, 1985; signed by San Francisco 49ers, August 7, 1985.
Released by San Francisco 49ers, August 20, 1985; re-signed by 49ers, February 3, 1986.

			——INTERCEPTIONS——			
Year	Club	G.	No.	Yds.	Avg.	TD.
1983—Los Angeles USFL		16		None		
1984—Los Angeles USFL		18	3	23	7.7	0
1985—Los Angeles USFL		18	4	44	11.0	0
Pro Totals—3 Years		52	7	67	9.6	0

Additional pro statistics: Recovered one fumble for 30 yards and one touchdown, 1983; returned one punt for three yards and recovered two fumbles, 1984; recovered one fumble and fumbled three times, 1985.

JOHN HERALD HENDY
Cornerback—San Diego Chargers
Born October 9, 1962, at Guatamala City, Guatamala.
Height, 5.10. Weight, 196.
High School—Santa Clara, Calif., Wilcox.
Attended California State University at Long Beach.

Selected by Los Angeles in 1985 USFL territorial draft.
Selected by San Diego in 3rd round (69th player selected) of 1985 NFL draft.
Signed by San Diego Chargers, July 17, 1985.

			——INTERCEPTIONS——			
Year	Club	G.	No.	Yds.	Avg.	TD.
1985—San Diego NFL		16	4	139	34.8	*1

Additional pro statistics: Recovered one fumble, 1985.

MATTHEW BERNARD HERKENHOFF
(Matt)
Offensive Tackle—Kansas City Chiefs
Born April 2, 1951, at Melrose, Minn.
Height, 6.04. Weight, 286.
High School—Melrose, Minn.
Attended University of Minnesota.

Selected by Kansas City in 4th round (94th player selected) of 1974 NFL draft.
Selected by New York in 9th round of 1974 WFL draft.
Contract breached by Charlotte Hornets (WFL) and signed by Kansas City Chiefs, June, 1975.
Missed entire 1975 season due to leg injuries.
On injured reserve with knee injury, October 2 through remainder of 1979 season.
On injured reserve with knee injury, December 9 through remainder of 1980 season.
On injured reserve with pulled groin, October 9 through November 15, 1985; activated, November 16, 1985.
New York-Charlotte WFL, 1974; Kansas City NFL, 1976 through 1985.
Games: 1974 (?), 1976 (14), 1977 (14), 1978 (16), 1979 (5), 1980 (14), 1981 (16), 1982 (9), 1983 (12), 1984 (15), 1985 (10).
Total NFL—125.
Pro statistics: Recovered one fumble, 1976 and 1981.

MATT HERNANDEZ
Defensive End—Seattle Seahawks
Born October 16, 1961, at Detroit, Mich.
Height, 6.06. Weight, 260.
High School—East Detroit, Mich.
Attended Purdue University.

Selected by Chicago in 15th round (174th player selected) of 1983 USFL draft.
Selected by Seattle in 8th round (210th player selected) of 1983 NFL draft.
Signed by Seattle Seahawks, May 6, 1983.
Released by Seattle Seahawks, August 27, 1984; signed as free agent by Minnesota Vikings, September 12, 1984.
Left Minnesota Vikings camp voluntarily and released, August 4, 1985; signed as free agent by Seattle Seahawks, May 14, 1986.
Seattle NFL, 1983; Minnesota NFL, 1984.
Games: 1983 (8), 1984 (13). Total—21.
Played in AFC Championship Game following 1983 season.

MARK DONALD HERRMANN
Quarterback—San Diego Chargers
Born January 8, 1959, at Cincinnati, O.
Height, 6.04. Weight, 206.
High School—Carmel, Ind.
Received bachelor of science degree in business management from Purdue University in 1981.

Selected by Denver in 4th round (98th player selected) of 1981 NFL draft.
On inactive list, September 19, 1982.
Traded with rights to offensive tackle Chris Hinton and 1st round pick in 1984 draft by Denver Broncos to Baltimore Colts for rights to quarterback John Elway, May 2, 1983.
On injured reserve with broken collarbone, August 30 through October 27, 1983; activated, October 28, 1983.
Franchise transferred to Indianapolis, March 31, 1984.
On injured reserve with broken thumb, August 28 through October 19, 1984; activated, October 20, 1984.
Granted free agency, February 1, 1985; re-signed by Colts and traded to San Diego Chargers for 10th round pick in 1986 draft, March 27, 1985.
Active for 16 games with Denver Broncos in 1981; did not play.

			PASSING						RUSHING				TOTAL		
Year Club	G.	Att.	Cmp.	Pct.	Gain	T.P.	P.I.	Avg.	Att.	Yds.	Avg.	TD.	TD.	Pts.	F.
1982—Denver NFL	2	60	32	53.3	421	1	4	7.02	3	7	2.3	1	1	6	1
1983—Baltimore NFL	2	36	18	50.0	256	0	3	7.11	1	0	0.0	0	0	0	2
1984—Indianapolis NFL	3	56	29	51.8	352	1	6	6.29		None			0	0	0
1985—San Diego NFL	9	201	132	65.7	1537	10	10	7.65	18	—8	—0.4	0	0	0	0
Pro Totals—5 Years	16	353	211	59.8	2566	12	23	7.27	22	—1	—0.1	1	1	6	3

Quarterback Rating Points: 1982 (53.5), 1983 (38.7), 1984 (37.8), 1985 (84.5). Total—66.5.
Additional pro statistics: Recovered one fumble, 1983; recovered two fumbles and fumbled eight times for minus 26 yards, 1985.

JESSE LEE HESTER
Wide Receiver—Los Angeles Raiders
Born January 21, 1963, at Belle Glade, Fla.
Height, 5.11. Weight, 170.
High School—Belle Glade, Fla., Central.
Received degree in social science from Florida State University.
Selected by Tampa Bay in 1985 USFL territorial draft.
Selected by Los Angeles Raiders in 1st round (23rd player selected) of 1985 NFL draft.
Signed by Los Angeles Raiders, July 23, 1985.

		PASS RECEIVING			
Year Club	G.	P.C.	Yds.	Avg.	TD.
1985—L.A. Raiders NFL	16	32	665	20.8	4

Additional pro statistics: Rushed once for 13 yards and a touchdown, and recovered one fumble, 1985.

DWIGHT HICKS
Defensive Back—San Francisco 49ers
Born April 5, 1956, at Mount Holly, N. J.
Height, 6.01. Weight, 192.
High School—Pennsauken, N. J.
Attended University of Michigan.
Brother of Jason Hicks, defensive back at University of Miami (Fla.).
Selected by Detroit in 6th round (150th player selected) of 1978 NFL draft.
Released by Detroit Lions, August 15, 1978; signed as free agent by Toronto Argonauts, September 16, 1978.
Released by Toronto Argonauts, October 14, 1978; signed as free agent by Philadelphia Eagles, December 28, 1978.
Released by Philadelphia Eagles, August 28, 1979; signed as free agent by San Francisco 49ers, October 24, 1979.

		INTERCEPTIONS				PUNT RETURNS				TOTAL		
Year Club	G.	No.	Yds.	Avg.	TD.	No.	Yds.	Avg.	TD.	TD.	Pts.	F.
1978—Toronto CFL	3	2	0	0.0	0	6	60	10.0	0	0	0	0
1979—San Francisco NFL	8	5	57	11.4	0	13	120	9.2	0	0	0	0
1980—San Francisco NFL	16	4	73	18.3	0	12	58	4.8	0	0	0	0
1981—San Francisco NFL	16	9	*239	26.6	1	19	171	9.0	0	2	12	1
1982—San Francisco NFL	9	3	5	1.7	0	10	54	5.4	0	0	0	0
1983—San Francisco NFL	15	2	102	51.0	*2		None			2	12	0
1984—San Francisco NFL	16	3	42	14.0	0		None			0	0	1
1985—San Francisco NFL	16	4	68	17.0	0		None			0	0	0
CFL Totals—1 Year	3	2	0	0.0	0	6	60	10.0	0	0	0	0
NFL Totals—7 Years	96	30	586	19.5	3	54	403	7.5	0	4	24	2
Pro Totals—8 Years	99	32	586	18.3	3	60	463	7.7	0	4	24	2

Additional pro statistics: Returned two kickoffs for 36 yards and recovered one fumble for two yards, 1979; recovered two fumbles, 1980; returned one kickoff for 22 yards, recovered four fumbles for 80 yards and a touchdown, 1981; fumbled once, 1981 and 1985; recovered two fumbles for five yards, 1983; recovered three fumbles for six yards, 1984; recovered two fumbles for 19 yards, 1985.
Played in NFC Championship Game following 1981, 1983 and 1984 seasons.
Played in NFL Championship Game following 1981 and 1984 seasons.
Played in Pro Bowl (NFL All-Star Game) following 1981 through 1984 seasons.

JAY WALTER HILGENBERG
Center—Chicago Bears
Born March 21, 1959, at Iowa City, Ia.
Height, 6.03. Weight, 255.
High School—Iowa City, Ia., City.
Attended University of Iowa.
Brother of Joel Hilgenberg, center-guard with New Orleans Saints; and nephew of Wally Hilgenberg, linebacker with Detroit Lions and Minnesota Vikings, 1964 through 1979.

Signed as free agent by Chicago Bears, May 8, 1981.
Chicago NFL, 1981 through 1985.
Games: 1981 (16), 1982 (9), 1983 (16), 1984 (16), 1985 (16). Total—73.
Pro statistics: Recovered one fumble for five yards, 1982; recovered one fumble, 1983 and 1985.
Played in NFC Championship Game following 1984 and 1985 seasons.
Played in NFL Championship Game following 1985 season.
Played in Pro Bowl (NFL All-Star Game) following 1985 season.

JOEL HILGENBERG
Center-Guard—New Orleans Saints
Born July 10, 1962, at Iowa City, Ia.
Height, 6.03. Weight, 253.
High School—Iowa City, Ia., City.
Attended University of Iowa.
Brother of Jay Hilgenberg, center with Chicago Bears; and nephew of Wally Hilgenberg,
linebacker with Detroit Lions and Minnesota Vikings, 1964 through 1979.
Selected by Washington in 6th round (109th player selected) of 1984 USFL draft.
USFL rights traded with 1st round pick in 1985 draft by Washington Federals to Birmingham Stallions for quarterback Reggie Collier, January 12, 1984.
Selected by New Orleans in 4th round (97th player selected) of 1984 NFL draft.
Signed by New Orleans Saints, July 24, 1984.
On injured reserve with dislocated elbow, October 30 through December 6, 1984; activated, December 7, 1984.
New Orleans NFL, 1984 and 1985.
Games: 1984 (10), 1985 (15). Total—25.
Pro statistics: Recovered one fumble, 1985.

RUSSELL TODD HILGER
(Rusty)
Quarterback—Los Angeles Raiders
Born May 9, 1962, at Oklahoma City, Okla.
Height, 6.04. Weight, 200.
High School—Oklahoma City, Okla., Southeast.
Attended Oklahoma State University.
Selected by Denver in 1985 USFL territorial draft.
Selected by Los Angeles Raiders in 6th round (143rd player selected) of 1985 NFL draft.
Signed by Los Angeles Raiders, July 21, 1985.

| | | | |PASSING| | | | | |RUSHING| | |—TOTAL—| |
Year Club	G.	Att.	Cmp.	Pct.	Gain	T.P.	P.I.	Avg.	Att.	Yds.	Avg.	TD.	TD.	Pts.	F.
1985—L.A. Raiders NFL..............	4	13	4	30.8	54	1	0	4.15	3	8	2.7	0	0	0	1

Quarterback Rating Points: 1985 (70.7).
Additional pro statistics: Recovered one fumble, 1985.

ALFONDIA HILL
(Al)
Wide Receiver—Denver Broncos
Born July 17, 1960, at Kansas City, Mo.
Height, 6.03. Weight, 205.
High School—Kansas City, Mo., Lincoln.
Attended Coffeyville Junior College and received bachelor's degree
in finance from University of Arizona.
Signed as free agent by New Orleans Saints, May 27, 1982.
Released by New Orleans Saints, July 30, 1982.
USFL rights traded by Oakland Invaders to Denver Gold for rights to linebacker Dean Moore, September 9, 1982.
Signed by Denver Gold, October 15, 1982.
Released by Denver Gold, February 7, 1983; re-signed by Gold, February 14, 1983.
Released injured by Denver Gold, February 17, 1983; signed as free agent by Winnipeg Blue Bombers, May 3, 1983.
Released by Winnipeg Blue Bombers, June 16, 1983; signed as free agent by Baltimore Colts, July 13, 1983.
Released by Baltimore Colts, August 16, 1983; signed as free agent by Arizona Wranglers, October 12, 1983.
Released by Arizona Wranglers, February 20, 1984; re-signed by Wranglers, February 24, 1984.
On developmental squad, February 24 through April 19, 1984.
Released by Arizona Wranglers, April 20, 1984; awarded on waivers to Oakland Invaders, April 23, 1984.
Not protected in merger of Oakland Invaders and Michigan Panthers; selected by Oakland Invaders in USFL dispersal draft, December 6, 1984.
Traded by Oakland Invaders to San Antonio Gunslingers for draft choice, February 12, 1985.
Released by San Antonio Gunslingers, February 18, 1985; re-signed by Gunslingers, February 19, 1985.
On developmental squad, February 21 through March 31, 1985; activated, April 1, 1985.
On developmental squad, April 6 through April 14, 1985.
Traded by San Antonio Gunslingers to Arizona Outlaws for defensive tackle Paul Hanna, April 15, 1985.
On developmental squad, April 15 through May 17, 1985; activated, May 18, 1985.
On developmental squad, May 24 through June 6, 1985; activated, June 7, 1985.
Released by Arizona Outlaws, June 24, 1985; signed as free agent by Denver Broncos, July 17, 1985.
On injured reserve with shoulder injury, August 15 through entire 1985 season.
On developmental squad for 8 games with Arizona Wranglers in 1984.
On developmental squad for 7 games with San Antonio Gunslingers and 6 games with Arizona Outlaws in 1985.

Year Club	——PASS RECEIVING——				
	G.	P.C.	Yds.	Avg.	TD.
1984—Oakland USFL..............	8	1	10	10.0	0
1985—S.A.(1)-Ariz.(4) USFL...	5		None		
Pro Totals—2 Years............	13	1	10	10.0	0

ANDREW HILL
(Drew)
Wide Receiver—Houston Oilers
Born October 5, 1956, at Newman, Ga.
Height, 5.09. Weight, 170.
High School—Newman, Ga.
Received bachelor of arts degree in industrial management from Georgia Tech in 1981.
Established NFL record for most kickoff returns, season (60), 1981.
Selected by Los Angeles in 12th round (328th player selected) of 1979 NFL draft.
On injured reserve with back injury, August 24 through entire 1983 season.
Traded by Los Angeles Rams to Houston Oilers for 7th round pick in 1986 draft and 4th round pick in 1987 draft, July 3, 1985.

Year Club	G.	PASS RECEIVING				—KICKOFF RET.—				—TOTAL—		
		P.C.	Yds.	Avg.	TD.	No.	Yds.	Avg.	TD.	TD.	Pts.	F.
1979—Los Angeles Rams NFL	16	4	94	23.5	1	40	803	20.1	0	1	6	2
1980—Los Angeles Rams NFL	16	19	416	21.9	2	43	880	20.5	★1	3	18	2
1981—Los Angeles Rams NFL	16	16	355	22.2	3	★60	1170	19.5	0	3	18	1
1982—Los Angeles Rams NFL	9	7	92	13.1	0	2	42	21.0	0	0	0	0
1984—Los Angeles Rams NFL	16	14	390	27.9	4	26	543	20.9	0	4	24	0
1985—Houston NFL	16	64	1169	18.3	9	1	22	22.0	0	9	54	0
Pro Totals—6 Years	89	124	2516	20.3	19	172	3460	20.1	1	20	120	5

Additional pro statistics: Returned one punt for no yards, 1979; recovered one fumble and rushed once for four yards, 1980; rushed once for 14 yards, returned two punts for 22 yards and recovered one fumble, 1981.
Played in NFC Championship Game following 1979 season.
Played in NFL Championship Game following 1979 season.

DAVID HILL
Tight End—Los Angeles Rams
Born January 1, 1954, at San Antonio, Tex.
Height, 6.02. Weight, 240.
High School—San Antonio, Tex., Highlands.
Attended Texas A&I University.
Brother of Jim Hill, defensive back with San Diego Chargers, Green Bay Packers and Cleveland Browns, 1969 through 1975; cousin of Gary Green, cornerback back with Los Angeles Rams.
Selected by Detroit in 2nd round (46th player selected) of 1976 NFL draft.
Traded by Detroit Lions to Los Angeles Rams for cornerback Rod Perry and 3rd round pick in 1984 draft, August 19, 1983.

Year Club	G.	——RUSHING——				PASS RECEIVING				—TOTAL—		
		Att.	Yds.	Avg.	TD.	P.C.	Yds.	Avg.	TD.	TD.	Pts.	F.
1976—Detroit NFL	14		None			19	249	13.1	5	5	30	2
1977—Detroit NFL	14	4	10	2.5	0	32	465	14.5	2	2	12	1
1978—Detroit NFL	16	3	12	4.0	0	53	633	11.9	4	4	24	1
1979—Detroit NFL	16	1	15	15.0	0	47	569	12.1	3	3	18	1
1980—Detroit NFL	16		None			39	424	10.9	1	1	6	1
1981—Detroit NFL	15		None			33	462	14.0	4	4	24	1
1982—Detroit NFL	9		None			22	252	11.5	4	4	24	0
1983—Los Angeles Rams NFL	16		None			28	280	10.0	2	2	12	1
1984—Los Angeles Rams NFL	16		None			31	300	9.7	1	1	6	2
1985—Los Angeles Rams NFL	16		None			29	271	9.3	1	1	6	2
Pro Totals—10 Years	148	8	37	4.6	0	333	3905	11.7	27	27	162	12

Additional pro statistics: Attempted one pass which was intercepted, 1976; recovered one fumble, 1976 through 1979, 1983 and 1984; attempted one pass with no completions, 1977.
Played in NFC Championship Game following 1985 season.
Played in Pro Bowl (NFL All-Star Game) following 1979 season.

GREG HILL
Cornerback—Kansas City Chiefs
Born February 12, 1961, at Orange, Tex.
Height, 6.01. Weight, 199.
High School—West Orange, Tex., Stark.
Attended Oklahoma State University.
Selected by Philadelphia in 3rd round (32nd player selected) of 1983 USFL draft.
Selected by Houston in 4th round (86th player selected) of 1983 NFL draft.
Signed by Houston Oilers, June 25, 1983.
Released by Houston Oilers, August 27, 1984; awarded on waivers to Kansas City Chiefs, August 28, 1984.

Year Club	—INTERCEPTIONS—			
	G.	No.	Yds.	Avg.TD.
1983—Houston NFL..................	14	None		
1984—Kansas City NFL..........	15	2	—1	—0.5	0
1985—Kansas City NFL..........	16	3	37	12.3	0
Pro Totals—3 Years............	45	5	36	7.2	0

Additional pro statistics: Fumbled once, 1984.

JOHN STARK HILL
Center
Born April 16, 1950, at East Orange, N. J.
Height, 6.02. Weight, 264.
High School—Somerset, N. J., Franklin.
Received bachelor of science degree in industrial engineering
from Lehigh University in 1972.

Selected by New York Giants in 6th round (132nd player selected) of 1972 NFL draft.
Claimed on waivers from New York Giants by New Orleans Saints, September 19, 1975.
Released by New Orleans Saints, April 3, 1985; signed as free agent by Seattle Seahawks, July 10, 1985.
Released by Seattle Seahawks, August 27, 1985; signed as free agent by San Francisco 49ers, November 26, 1985.
Released by San Francisco 49ers, December 14, 1985; re-signed by 49ers, December 16, 1985.
Granted free agency with no qualifying offer, February 1, 1986.
New York Giants NFL, 1972 through 1974; New Orleans NFL, 1975 through 1984; San Francisco, 1985.
Games: 1972 (14), 1973 (12), 1974 (12), 1975 (14), 1976 (14), 1977 (14), 1978 (16), 1979 (16), 1980 (15), 1981 (13), 1982 (9), 1983 (16), 1984 (11), 1985 (1). Total—177.
Pro statistics: Fumbled once and recovered one fumble for minus 13 yards, 1973; recovered one fumble for one yard, 1975; recovered one fumble, 1977 and 1980.

KENNETH HILL
(Kenny)
Safety—New York Giants
Born July 25, 1958, at Oak Grove, La.
Height, 6.00. Weight, 195.
High School—Oak Grove, La.
Received bachelor of science degree in molecular biophysics from Yale University in 1980.

Selected by Oakland in 8th round (194th player selected) of 1980 NFL draft.
On injured reserve with hip pointer, August 26 through entire 1980 season.
On injured reserve with pulled hamstring, August 31 through October 18, 1981; activated after clearing procedural waivers, October 20, 1981.
Franchise transferred to Los Angeles, May 7, 1982.
Traded by Los Angeles Raiders to New York Giants for 7th round pick in 1985 draft, August 27, 1984.
On injured reserve with hamstring injury, September 3 through October 3, 1985; activated, October 4, 1985.
Oakland NFL, 1981; Los Angeles Raiders NFL, 1982 and 1983; New York Giants NFL, 1984 and 1985.
Games: 1981 (9), 1982 (9), 1983 (16), 1984 (12), 1985 (12). Total—58.
Pro statistics: Returned one kickoff for 21 yards, 1981; returned two kickoffs for 20 yards, 1982; fumbled once, 1982 and 1985; returned one kickoff for 27 yards, 1984; intercepted two passes for 30 yards, returned 11 kickoffs for 186 yards and recovered two fumbles, 1985.
Played in AFC Championship Game following 1983 season.
Played in NFL Championship Game following 1983 season.

KENT ANGELO HILL
Guard—Los Angeles Rams
Born March 7, 1957, at Americus, Ga.
Height, 6.05. Weight, 260.
High School—Americus, Ga.
Received bachelor of science degree in industrial management from Georgia Tech in 1979.

Named to THE SPORTING NEWS NFL All-Star Team, 1983.
Selected by Los Angeles in 1st round (26th player selected) of 1979 NFL draft.
Los Angeles Rams NFL, 1979 through 1985.
Games: 1979 (16), 1980 (16), 1981 (16), 1982 (9), 1983 (16), 1984 (16), 1985 (16). Total—105.
Pro statistics: Recovered two fumbles, 1982.
Played in NFC Championship Game following 1979 and 1985 seasons.
Played in NFL Championship Game following 1979 season.
Played in Pro Bowl (NFL All-Star Game) following 1980 and 1982 through 1985 seasons.

LEROY ANTHONY HILL JR.
(Tony)
Wide Receiver—Dallas Cowboys
Born June 23, 1956, at San Diego, Calif.
Height, 6.02. Weight, 202.
High School—Long Beach, Calif., Long Beach Polytechnic.
Received bachelor of science degree in political science from Stanford University in 1977.
Related to Alton Alexis, wide receiver with Cleveland Browns.

Selected by Dallas in 3rd round (62nd player selected) of 1977 NFL draft.
On injured reserve with shoulder separation, September 6 through October 12, 1984; activated, October 13, 1984.

Year Club	G.	PASS RECEIVING P.C.	Yds.	Avg.	TD.	PUNT RETURNS No.	Yds.	Avg.	TD.	—KICKOFF RET.— No.	Yds.	Avg.	TD.	—TOTAL— TD.	Pts.	F.
1977—Dallas NFL	14	2	21	10.5	0	10	124	12.4	0	3	64	21.3	0	0	0	0
1978—Dallas NFL	16	46	823	17.9	6	11	101	9.2	0		None			6	36	1
1979—Dallas NFL	16	60	1062	17.7	10	6	43	7.2	0	1	32	32.0	0	10	60	1
1980—Dallas NFL	16	60	1055	17.6	8		None				None			8	48	0
1981—Dallas NFL	16	46	953	20.7	4		None				None			4	24	1
1982—Dallas NFL	9	35	526	15.0	1		None				None			1	6	0
1983—Dallas NFL	12	49	801	16.3	7		None				None			7	42	1
1984—Dallas NFL	11	58	864	14.9	5		None				None			5	30	0
1985—Dallas NFL	15	74	1113	15.0	7		None				None			7	42	2
Pro Totals—9 Years	125	430	7218	16.8	48	27	268	9.9	0	4	96	24.0	0	48	288	6

Additional pro statistics: Rushed three times for 17 yards and attempted one pass with no completions, 1978; rushed twice for 18 yards, 1979; rushed four times for 27 yards, 1980; rushed once for minus three yards, 1981; rushed once for 22 yards, 1982; rushed once for two yards, 1983; rushed once for seven yards, 1984; rushed once for minus six yards and attempted one pass with one completion for 42 yards, 1985.

Played in NFC Championship Game following 1977, 1978 and 1980 through 1982 seasons.

Played in NFL Championship Game following 1977 and 1978 seasons.

Played in Pro Bowl (NFL All-Star Game) following 1978, 1979 and 1985 seasons.

RODRICK HILL
(Rod)
Cornerback—Buffalo Bills

Born March 14, 1959, at Detroit, Mich.
Height, 6.00. Weight, 188.
High School—Detroit, Mich., M.L. King.
Attended Kentucky State University.

Selected by Dallas in 1st round (25th player selected) of 1982 NFL draft.
Traded with 5th round pick in 1985 draft by Dallas Cowboys to Buffalo Bills for 5th round pick in 1985 draft and 6th round pick in 1986 draft, August 23, 1984.
On injured reserve with fractured ankle, September 12 through remainder of 1984 season.
On injured reserve with broken hand, October 25 through December 5, 1985; activated, December 6, 1985.

Year Club	G.	INTERCEPTIONS No.	Yds.	Avg.	TD.	-PUNT RETURNS- No.	Yds.	Avg.	TD.	—KICKOFF RET.— No.	Yds.	Avg.	TD.	—TOTAL— TD.	Pts.	F.
1982—Dallas NFL	9		None			4	39	9.8	0		None			0	0	1
1983—Dallas NFL	14	2	12	6.0	0	30	232	7.7	0	14	243	17.4	0	0	0	2
1984—Buffalo NFL	2		None				None				None			0	0	0
1985—Buffalo NFL	10	2	17	8.5	0	16	120	7.5	0		None			0	0	1
Pro Totals—4 Years	35	4	29	7.3	0	50	391	7.8	0	14	243	17.4	0	0	0	4

Additional pro statistics: Recovered three fumbles, 1982; recovered two fumbles, 1983.

Played in NFC Championship Game following 1982 season.

TROY J. HILL
Defensive Back—Cleveland Browns

Born February 18, 1962, at South River, N.J.
Height, 5.11. Weight, 180.
High School—South River, N.J.
Attended University of Pittsburgh.
Brother-in-law of Drew Pearson, wide receiver with Dallas Cowboys, 1973 through 1983.

Selected by Pittsburgh in 1984 USFL territorial draft.
Signed by Pittsburgh Maulers, May 4, 1984.
Granted roster exemption, May 4, 1984; activated, May 9, 1984.
Franchise disbanded, October 25, 1984.
Selected by Baltimore Stars in USFL dispersal draft, December 6, 1984.
Released by Baltimore Stars, January 28, 1985; signed as free agent by Cleveland Browns, May 6, 1985.
On injured reserve with shoulder injury, August 20 through entire 1985 season.

Year Club	KICKOFF RETURNS G.	No.	Yds.	Avg.	TD.
1984—Pittsburgh USFL	7	7	141	20.1	0

Additional pro statistics: Credited with one sack for 11 yards, recovered one fumble and fumbled once, 1984.

BRYAN ERIC HINKLE
Linebacker—Pittsburgh Steelers

Born June 4, 1959, at Long Beach, Calif.
Height, 6.02. Weight, 220.
High School—Silverdale, Wash., Central Kitsap.
Received degree in business from University of Oregon.

Selected by Pittsburgh in 6th round (156th player selected) of 1981 NFL draft.
On injured reserve with ankle injury and concussion, August 31 through entire 1981 season.
On injured reserve with torn quadricep, January 7 through remainder of 1982 season playoffs.

Year Club	G.	No.	Yds.	Avg.	TD.
1982—Pittsburgh NFL............	9		None		
1983—Pittsburgh NFL............	16	1	14	14.0	1
1984—Pittsburgh NFL............	15	3	77	25.7	0
1985—Pittsburgh NFL............	14		None		
Pro Totals—4 Years............	54	4	91	22.8	1

Additional pro statistics: Recovered two fumbles for four yards, 1983; recovered two fumbles for 21 yards and a touchdown, 1984.

Played in AFC Championship Game following 1984 season.

WILLIAM DEWAYNE HINSON
(Billy)
Guard—Denver Broncos
Born January 8, 1963, at Folkston, Ga.
Height, 6.01. Weight, 278.
High School—Hilliard, Fla.
Attended University of Florida.

Selected by Tampa Bay in 1985 USFL territorial draft.
Selected by Denver in 5th round (139th player selected) of 1985 NFL draft.
Signed by Denver Broncos, July 11, 1985.
On injured reserve with hand injury, August 26 through entire 1985 season.

CHRISTOPHER JERROD HINTON
(Chris)
Guard—Indianapolis Colts
Born July 31, 1961, at Chicago, Ill.
Height, 6.04. Weight, 289.
High School—Chicago, Ill., Wendell Phillips.
Received degree in sociology from Northwestern University.

Named as offensive tackle on THE SPORTING NEWS All-America Team, 1982.
Selected by Chicago in 1983 USFL territorial draft.
Selected by Denver in 1st round (4th player selected) of 1983 NFL draft.
Rights traded with quarterback Mark Herrmann, and 1st round pick in 1984 draft by Denver Broncos to Baltimore Colts for rights to quarterback John Elway, May 2, 1983.
Signed by Baltimore Colts, May 12, 1983.
Franchise transferred to Indianapolis, March 31, 1984.
On injured reserve with fractured fibula, October 8 through remainder of 1984 season.
Baltimore NFL, 1983; Indianapolis NFL, 1984 and 1985.
Games: 1983 (16), 1984 (6), 1985 (16). Total—38.
Pro statistics: Recovered one fumble, 1983.
Played in Pro Bowl (NFL All-Star Game) following 1983 and 1985 seasons.

ERIC ELLSWORTH HIPPLE
Quarterback—Detroit Lions
Born September 16, 1957, at Lubbock, Tex.
Height, 6.02. Weight, 196.
High School—Downey, Calif., Warren.
Received bachelor of science degree in business administration from
Utah State University in 1980.

Selected by Detroit in 4th round (85th player selected) of 1980 NFL draft.
On injured reserve with knee injury, October 18 through December 13, 1984; activated, December 14, 1984.

Year Club	G.	Att.	Cmp.	Pct.	Gain	T.P.	P.I.	Avg.	Att.	Yds.	Avg.	TD.	TD.	Pts.	F.
1980—Detroit NFL......................	15		None							None			0	0	0
1981—Detroit NFL......................	16	279	140	50.2	2358	14	15	8.45	41	168	4.1	7	7	42	*14
1982—Detroit NFL......................	9	86	36	41.9	411	2	4	4.78	10	57	5.7	0	0	0	1
1983—Detroit NFL......................	16	387	204	52.7	2577	12	18	6.66	41	171	4.2	3	3	18	12
1984—Detroit NFL......................	8	38	16	42.1	246	1	1	6.47	2	3	1.5	0	0	0	0
1985—Detroit NFL......................	16	406	223	54.9	2952	17	18	7.27	32	89	2.8	2	2	12	13
Pro Totals—6 Years..........	80	1196	619	51.8	8544	46	56	7.14	126	488	3.9	12	12	72	40

Quarterback Rating Points: 1981 (73.3), 1982 (66.9), 1983 (64.7), 1984 (62.0), 1985 (73.6). Total—68.1.

Additional pro statistics: Recovered four fumbles and fumbled 14 times for minus 10 yards; recovered six fumbles, 1983; recovered three fumbles and fumbled 13 times for minus three yards, 1985.

TERRELL LEE HOAGE
(Terry)
Safety—New Orleans Saints
Born April 11, 1962, at Ames, Iowa.
Height, 6.03. Weight, 199.
High School—Huntsville, Tex.
Received degree in genetics from University of Georgia.

Named as defensive back on THE SPORTING NEWS College All-America Team, 1983.
Selected by Jacksonville in 1984 USFL territorial draft.
Selected by New Orleans in 3rd round (68th player selected) of 1984 NFL draft.

Signed by New Orleans Saints, July 25, 1984.

			—INTERCEPTIONS—				
Year	Club	G.	No.	Yds.	Avg.	TD.	
1984—New Orleans NFL		14		None			
1985—New Orleans NFL		16	4	79	19.8	⋆1	
Pro Totals—2 Years		30	4	79	19.8	1	

Additional pro statistics: Recovered one fumble, 1984; recovered two fumbles, 1985.

LIFFORT HOBLEY
Safety—Miami Dolphins
Born October 12, 1962, at Shreveport, La.
Height, 6.00. Weight, 207.
High School—Shreveport, La., C.E. Byrd.
Attended Louisiana State University.

Selected by Portland in 1985 USFL territorial draft.
Selected by Pittsburgh in 3rd round (74th player selected) of 1985 NFL draft.
Signed by Pittsburgh Steelers, June 5, 1985.
Released by Pittsburgh Steelers, August 25, 1985; signed as free agent by San Diego Chargers, August 28, 1985.
Released by San Diego Chargers after failing physical, August 29, 1985; signed as free agent by St. Louis Cardinals September 11, 1985.
Released by St. Louis Cardinals, October 15, 1985; signed as free agent by Miami Dolphins, March 6, 1986.
St. Louis NFL, 1985.
Games: 1985 (5).

GARY E. HOFFMAN
Offensive Tackle—San Francisco 49ers
Born September 28, 1961, at Sacramento, Calif.
Height, 6.07. Weight, 285.
High School—Sacramento, Calif., Christian Brothers.
Received degree in science from University of Santa Clara.

Selected by San Antonio in 9th round (189th player selected) of 1984 USFL draft.
Selected by Green Bay in 10th round (267th player selected) of 1984 NFL draft.
Signed by Green Bay Packers, June 6, 1984.
On injured reserve with eye injury, August 27 through December 13, 1984; activated after clearing procedural waivers, December 15, 1984.
Released by Green Bay Packers, August 12, 1985; re-signed by Packers, August 13, 1985.
Released by Green Bay Packers, September 2, 1985; signed as free agent by San Francisco 49ers, February 17, 1986.
Green Bay NFL, 1984.
Games: 1984 (1).

GARY KEITH HOGEBOOM
Name pronounced HOAG-ih-boom.
Quarterback—Indianapolis Colts
Born August 21, 1958, at Grand Rapids, Mich.
Height, 6.04. Weight, 207.
High School—Grand Rapids, Mich., Northview.
Attended Central Michigan University.

Selected by Dallas in 5th round (133rd player selected) of 1980 NFL draft.
Traded with 2nd round pick in 1986 draft by Dallas Cowboys to Indianapolis Colts for 2nd round pick in 1986 draft and conditional 1987 pick, April 28, 1986.

			—PASSING—							—RUSHING—				—TOTAL—		
Year	Club	G.	Att.	Cmp.	Pct.	Gain	T.P.	P.I.	Avg.	Att.	Yds.	Avg.	TD.	TD.	Pts.	F.
1980—Dallas NFL		2			None						None			0	0	0
1981—Dallas NFL		1			None						None			0	0	0
1982—Dallas NFL		4	8	3	37.5	45	0	1	5.63	3	0	0.0	0	0	0	0
1983—Dallas NFL		6	17	11	64.7	161	1	1	9.47	6	−10	−1.7	0	0	0	0
1984—Dallas NFL		16	367	195	53.1	2366	7	14	6.45	15	19	1.3	0	0	0	8
1985—Dallas NFL		16	126	70	55.6	978	5	7	7.76	8	48	6.0	1	1	6	2
Pro Totals—6 Years		45	518	279	53.9	3550	13	23	6.85	32	57	1.8	1	1	6	10

Quarterback Rating Points: 1982 (17.2), 1983 (90.6), 1984 (63.7), 1985 (70.8). Total—65.6.
Additional pro statistics: Recovered four fumbles and fumbled eight times for minus three yards, 1984.
Member of Dallas Cowboys for NFC Championship Game following 1980 and 1981 seasons; did not play.
Played in NFC Championship Game following 1982 season.

WILLIAM BENJAMIN HOGGARD
(D. D.)
Cornerback—Cleveland Browns
Born May 20, 1961, at Windsor, N.C.
Height, 6.00. Weight, 188.
High School—Windsor, N.C., Bertie.
Attended North Carolina State University.

Selected by Washington in 12th round (141st player selected) of 1983 USFL draft.
Signed as free agent by Washington Redskins, April 28, 1983.
Released by Washington Redskins, July 30, 1983; signed by Washington Federals, October 21, 1983.

On developmental squad, March 2 through March 6, 1984.
Released by Washington Federals, March 7, 1984; signed by Cleveland Browns, May 6, 1985.
Released by Cleveland Browns, September 2, 1985; re-signed by Browns, October 9, 1985.
Released by Cleveland Browns, October 23, 1985; re-signed by Browns for 1986 season, November 1, 1985.
On developmental squad for 1 game with Washington Federals in 1984.
Washington USFL, 1984; Cleveland NFL, 1985.
Games: 1984 (1), 1985 (2). Total—3.

ERIC W. HOLLE
Defensive Lineman—Kansas City Chiefs
Born September 5, 1960, at Houston, Tex.
Height, 6.04. Weight, 258.
High School—Austin, Tex., LBJ.
Attended University of Texas.

Selected by San Antonio in 1984 USFL territorial draft.
Selected by Kansas City in 5th round (117th player selected) of 1984 NFL draft.
Signed by Kansas City Chiefs, July 12, 1984.
Kansas City NFL, 1984 and 1985.
Games: 1984 (16), 1985 (16). Total—32.
Pro statistics: Recovered one fumble for two yards, 1984.

BRIAN DOUGLASS HOLLOWAY
Offensive Tackle—New England Patriots
Born July 25, 1959, at Omaha, Neb.
Height, 6.07. Weight, 288.
High School—Potomac, Md., Winston Churchill.
Received bachelor of arts degree in economics from Stanford University in 1981.
Son-in-law of John McKenzie, forward with Chicago Black Hawks, Detroit Red Wings, New York Rangers,
Boston Bruins, Philadelphia/Vancouver Blazers, Minnesota Fighting Saints, Cincinnati Stingers and
New England Whalers, 1958 through 1961 and 1963 through 1979;
and brother of Jonathan Holloway, defensive back at Stanford University.

Selected by New England in 1st round (19th player selected) of 1981 NFL draft.
New England NFL, 1981 through 1985.
Games: 1981 (16), 1982 (9), 1983 (16), 1984 (16), 1985 (16). Total—73.
Pro statistics: Recovered one fumble, 1981; recovered two fumbles, 1985.
Played in AFC Championship Game following 1985 season.
Played in NFL Championship Game following 1985 season.
Played in Pro Bowl (NFL All-Star Game) following 1983 through 1985 seasons.

ROBERT HOLLY
(Bob)
Quarterback—Atlanta Falcons
Born June 1, 1960, at Clifton, N.J.
Height, 6.02. Weight, 190.
High School—Clifton, N.J.
Received bachelor of arts degree in history from Princeton University.

Selected by Washington in 11th round (291st player selected) of 1982 NFL draft.
Traded by Washington Redskins to Philadelphia Eagles for 7th round pick in 1985 draft, August 14, 1984.
Released by Philadelphia Eagles, August 27, 1984; re-signed by Eagles, August 28, 1984.
Released by Philadelphia Eagles, October 16, 1984; signed as free agent by Atlanta Falcons, November 23, 1984.
Released by Atlanta Falcons, September 2, 1985; re-signed by Falcons, October 1, 1985.
Active for 9 games with Washington Redskins in 1982; did not play.
Active for 7 games with Philadelphia Eagles in 1984; did not play.
Active for 4 games with Atlanta Falcons in 1984; did not play.

| | | —————PASSING————— | | | | | | | —RUSHING— | | | —TOTAL— | | |
Year Club	G.	Att.	Cmp.	Pct.	Gain	T.P.	P.I.	Avg.	Att.	Yds.	Avg.	TD.	TD.	Pts.	F.
1983—Washington NFL	5	1	1	100.0	5	0	0	5.00	4	13	3.3	0	0	0	2
1985—Atlanta NFL	4	39	24	61.5	295	1	2	7.56	3	36	12.0	1	1	6	1
Pro Totals—4 Years	9	40	25	62.5	300	1	2	7.50	7	49	7.0	1	1	6	3

Quarterback Rating Points: 1983 (87.5), 1985 (72.1). Total—72.9.
Member of Washington Redskins for NFC Championship Game following 1982 and 1983 seasons; did not play.
Member of Washington Redskins for NFL Championship Game following 1982 and 1983 seasons; did not play.

RODNEY A. HOLMAN
Tight End—Cincinnati Bengals
Born April 20, 1960, at Ypsilanti, Mich.
Height, 6.03. Weight, 232.
High School—Ypsilanti, Mich.
Received degree from Tulane University in 1981.
Cousin of Preston Pearson, running back with Baltimore Colts,
Pittsburgh Steelers and Dallas Cowboys, 1967 through 1980.

Selected by Cincinnati in 3rd round (82nd player selected) of 1982 NFL draft.

Year Club	—PASS RECEIVING—				
	G.	P.C.	Yds.	Avg.	TD.
1982—Cincinnati NFL	9	3	18	6.0	1
1983—Cincinnati NFL	16	2	15	7.5	0
1984—Cincinnati NFL	16	21	239	11.4	1
1985—Cincinnati NFL	16	38	479	12.6	7
Pro Totals—4 Years	57	64	751	11.7	9

Additional pro statistics: Recovered one fumble and fumbled once, 1984 and 1985.

RONALD HOLMES
(Ron)
Defensive End—Tampa Bay Buccaneers
Born August 26, 1963, at Fort Benning, Ga.
Height, 6.04. Weight, 255.
High School—Lacey, Wash., Timberline.
Attended University of Washington.

Selected by Portland in 1985 USFL territorial draft.
USFL rights traded with rights to linebacker Tim Meamber by Portland Breakers to Baltimore Stars for rights to defensive end Kenny Neil, February 13, 1985.
Selected by Tampa Bay in 1st round (8th player selected) of 1985 NFL draft.
Signed by Tampa Bay Buccaneers, August 4, 1985.
Tampa Bay NFL, 1985.
Games: 1985 (16).
Pro statistics: Recovered two fumbles, 1985.

TOM HOLMOE
Safety—San Francisco 49ers
Born March 7, 1960, at Los Angeles, Calif.
Height, 6.02. Weight, 180.
High School—La Crescenta, Calif., Valley.
Attended Brigham Young University.

Selected by Boston in 9th round (102nd player selected) of 1983 USFL draft.
Selected by San Francisco in 4th round (90th player selected) of 1983 NFL draft.
Signed by San Francisco 49ers, July 16, 1983.
On injured reserve with separated shoulder, September 1 through entire 1985 season.
San Francisco NFL, 1983 and 1984.
Games: 1983 (16), 1984 (16). Total—32.
Pro statistics: Recovered one fumble, 1983.
Played in NFC Championship Game following 1983 and 1984 seasons.
Played in NFL Championship Game following 1984 season.

PETER JOSEPH HOLOHAN
(Pete)
Tight End—San Diego Chargers
Born July 25, 1959, at Albany, N.Y.
Height, 6.04. Weight, 244.
High School—Liverpool, N.Y.
Attended University of Notre Dame.

Selected by San Diego in 7th round (189th player selected) of 1981 NFL draft.
Left San Diego Chargers voluntarily and placed on left-camp retired list; October 28, 1981; reinstated, April 30, 1982.
USFL rights traded with wide receiver Neil Balholm, defensive end Bill Purifoy, tight end Mike Hirn and linebacker Orlando Flanagan by Chicago Blitz to Denver Gold for center Glenn Hyde and defensive end Larry White, December 28, 1983.

Year Club	—PASS RECEIVING—				
	G.	P.C.	Yds.	Avg.	TD.
1981—San Diego NFL	7	1	14	14.0	0
1982—San Diego NFL	9		None		
1983—San Diego NFL	16	23	272	11.8	2
1984—San Diego NFL	15	56	734	13.1	1
1985—San Diego NFL	15	42	458	10.9	3
Pro Totals—5 Years	62	122	1478	12.1	6

Additional pro statistics: Recovered one fumble, 1982; attempted one pass with no completions, 1983 and 1985; attempted two passes with one completion for 25 yards and a touchdown and recovered two fumbles for 19 yards, 1984; returned one kickoff for no yards and fumbled once, 1985.

MICHAEL HOLSTON
(Mike)
Wide Receiver—Indianapolis Colts
Born January 8, 1958, at Seat Pleasant, Md.
Height, 6.03. Weight, 188.
High School—Blandensburg, Md.
Attended Hagerstown Junior College and Morgan State University.

Selected by Houston in 3rd round (79th player selected) of 1981 NFL draft.

Released by Houston Oilers, September 25, 1985; signed as free agent by Kansas City Chiefs, November 5, 1985.
Released by Kansas Chiefs, December 11, 1985; signed as free agent by Indianapolis Colts, March 24, 1986.

——PASS RECEIVING——

Year Club	G.	P.C.	Yds.	Avg.	TD.
1981—Houston NFL	16	27	427	15.8	2
1982—Houston NFL	9	5	116	23.2	1
1983—Houston NFL	16	14	205	14.6	0
1984—Houston NFL	16	22	287	13.0	1
1985—Hou. (3)-K.C. (4) NFL..	7	6	76	12.7	0
Pro Totals—5 Years	64	74	1111	15.0	4

Additional pro statistics: Recovered one fumble, 1983 and 1984.

HARRY THOMPSON HOLT III
Tight End—Cleveland Browns
Born December 29, 1957, at Harlingen, Tex.
Height, 6.04. Weight, 230.
High Schools—Harlingen, Tex. and Tucson, Ariz., Sunnyside.
Attended University of Arizona.

Signed as free agent by British Columbia Lions, September 13, 1978.
Released by British Columbia Lions, September 14, 1978; re-signed by Lions, September 21, 1978.
On injured list, November 2 through remainder of 1978 season.
On injured list, November 1 through remainder of 1979 season.
On injured list, October 19 through remainder of 1980 season.
Placed on retired list, June 20 through July 12, 1981.
Activated and placed on reserve, July 13 through July 20, 1981; activated, July 21, 1981.
On reserve, August 20 through September 1, 1981; activated, September 2, 1981.
On reserve, September 9 through September 28, 1981; activated, September 29, 1981.
On reserve, October 21 through October 27, 1981; activated, October 28, 1981.
On reserve, August 30 through September 10, 1982; activated, September 11, 1982.
On reserve, October 3 through October 29, 1982; activated, October 30, 1982.
On injured list, October 30 through remainder of 1982 season.
Granted free agency, March 1, 1983.
USFL rights traded with wide receiver Jerome Stelly and future draft picks by Chicago Blitz to Michigan Panthers for center Tom Piette, April 28, 1983.
Signed by Cleveland Browns, May 19, 1983.
On injured reserve with rib injury, October 6 through November 1, 1984; activated, November 2, 1984.
On injured reserve with knee injury, November 22, 1985 through January 2, 1986; activated, January 3, 1986.

Year Club	G.	——RUSHING——				PASS RECEIVING				—TOTAL—		
		Att.	Yds.	Avg.	TD.	P.C.	Yds.	Avg.	TD.	TD.	Pts.	F.
1978—British Columbia CFL	7	27	107	4.0	1	14	201	14.4	1	2	12	2
1979—British Columbia CFL	15	7	51	7.3	1	32	560	17.5	2	3	18	1
1980—British Columbia CFL	14	12	103	8.6	0	38	648	17.1	5	6	36	2
1981—British Columbia CFL	8	3	4	1.3	0	18	367	20.4	2	2	12	0
1982—British Columbia CFL	10	4	21	5.3	0	35	588	16.8	4	4	24	0
1983—Cleveland NFL	15	3	8	2.7	0	29	420	14.5	3	3	18	1
1984—Cleveland NFL	12	1	12	12.0	0	20	261	13.1	0	0	0	0
1985—Cleveland NFL	11		None			10	95	9.5	1	1	6	1
CFL Totals—5 Years	54	53	286	5.4	2	137	2364	17.3	14	17	102	5
NFL Totals—3 Years	38	4	20	5.0	0	59	776	13.2	4	4	24	2
Pro Totals—8 Years	92	57	306	5.4	2	196	3140	16.0	18	21	126	7

——PUNT RETURNS——

Year Club	G.	No.	Yds.	Avg.	TD.
1978—British Columbia CFL.	7	6	62	10.3	0
1979—British Columbia CFL.	15		None		
1980—British Columbia CFL.	14	21	258	12.3	1
1981—British Columbia CFL.	8		None		
1982—British Columbia CFL.	10	1	5	5.0	0
1983—Cleveland NFL	15		None		
1984—Cleveland NFL	12		None		
1985—Cleveland NFL	11		None		
CFL Totals—5 Years	54	28	325	11.6	1
NFL Totals—3 Years	38		None		
Pro Totals—8 Years	92	28	325	11.6	1

Additional CFL statistics: Returned five kickoffs for 127 yards (25.4-yard average, 1978; recovered one fumble, 1979, 1980 and 1982; attempted one pass with no completions, 1982.
Additional NFL statistics: Recovered one fumble, 1983; returned one kickoff for one yard, 1984.

—DID YOU KNOW—

That when San Diego's Lionel James caught eight passes for 42 yards in the Chargers' final regular-season game against Kansas City, he ended the season with 1,027 yards in receptions, thus becoming the first running back in NFL history to surpass the 1,000-yard mark? A few hours later, San Francisco's Roger Craig caught five passes for 50 yards against Dallas to become the second. Craig finished with 1,016 receiving yards.

ISSIAC HOLT III
Cornerback—Minnesota Vikings
Born October 4, 1962, at Birmingham, Ala.
Height, 6.01. Weight, 197.
High School—Birmingham, Ala., Carver.
Attended Alcorn State University.

Selected by San Antonio in 1st round (3rd player selected) of 1985 USFL draft.
Selected by Minnesota in 2nd round (30th player selected) of 1985 NFL draft.
Signed by Minnesota Vikings, May 24, 1985.
Minnesota NFL, 1985.
Games: 1985 (15).
Pro statistics: Intercepted one pass for no yards, 1985.

JOHN STEPHANIE HOLT
Cornerback—Tampa Bay Buccaneers
Born May 14, 1959, at Lawton, Okla.
Height, 5.11. Weight, 180.
High School—Enid, Okla.
Attended West Texas State University.

Selected by Tampa Bay in 4th round (89th player selected) of 1981 NFL draft.
USFL rights traded with rights to defensive end Clenzie Pierson by Denver Gold to Houston Gamblers for rights to center George Yarno, September 23, 1983.

		—INTERCEPTIONS—				—PUNT RETURNS—				—TOTAL—	
Year Club	G.	No.	Yds.	Avg.	TD.	No.	Yds.	Avg.	TD.	TD.	Pts.	F.
1981—Tampa Bay NFL	16	1	13	13.0	0	9	100	11.1	0	0	0	1
1982—Tampa Bay NFL	9		None			16	81	5.1	0	0	0	2
1983—Tampa Bay NFL	16	3	43	14.3	0	5	43	8.6	0	0	0	1
1984—Tampa Bay NFL	15	1	25	25.0	0	6	17	2.8	0	0	0	0
1985—Tampa Bay NFL	16	1	3	3.0	0		None			0	0	0
Pro Totals—5 Years	72	6	84	14.0	0	36	241	6.7	0	0	0	4

		KICKOFF RETURNS			
Year Club	G.	No.	Yds.	Avg.TD.	
1981—Tampa Bay NFL	16	11	274	24.9	0
1982—Tampa Bay NFL	9		None		
1983—Tampa Bay NFL	16		None		
1984—Tampa Bay NFL	15		None		
1985—Tampa Bay NFL	16		None		
Pro Totals—5 Years	72	11	274	24.9	0

Additional pro statistics: Recovered one fumble, 1982 through 1984; recovered two fumbles, 1985.

WINFORD DeWAYNE HOOD
Offensive Tackle—Denver Broncos
Born March 29, 1962, at Atlanta, Ga.
Height, 6.03. Weight, 262.
High School—Atlanta, Ga., Therrell.
Attended University of Georgia.

Selected by Jacksonville in 1984 USFL territorial draft.
Selected by Denver in 8th round (207th player selected) of 1984 NFL draft.
Signed by Denver Broncos, May 21, 1984.
Denver NFL, 1984 and 1985.
Games: 1984 (16), 1985 (16). Total—32.

DWAYNE BARRETT HOOPER
Running Back—Pittsburgh Steelers
Born July 19, 1963, at Baltimore, Md.
Height, 6.00. Weight, 208.
High School—Baltimore, Md., Woodlawn.
Attended Rutgers University.

Selected by New Jersey in 1985 USFL territorial draft.
Signed as free agent by Pittsburgh Steelers, June 21, 1985.
On injured reserve with hamstring injury, August 20 through entire 1985 season.

WES HOPKINS
Safety—Philadelphia Eagles
Born September 26, 1961, at Birmingham, Ala.
Height, 6.01. Weight, 210.
High School—Birmingham, Ala., John Carroll.
Attended Southern Methodist University.

Named to THE SPORTING NEWS NFL All-Star Team, 1985.
Selected by New Jersey in 4th round (46th player selected) of 1983 USFL draft.
Selected by Philadelphia in 2nd round (35th player selected) of 1983 NFL draft.
Signed by Philadelphia Eagles, May 26, 1983.

		INTERCEPTIONS			
Year Club	G.	No.	Yds.	Avg.	TD.
1983—Philadelphia NFL	11			None	
1984—Philadelphia NFL	16	5	107	21.4	0
1985—Philadelphia NFL	15	6	36	6.0	*1
Pro Totals—3 Years	45	11	143	13.0	1

Additional pro statistics: Recovered three fumbles, 1984; recovered two fumbles for 42 yards and fumbled once, 1985.

Played in Pro Bowl (NFL All-Star Game) following 1985 season.

MICHAEL HORAN

Name pronounced Hor-RAN.

(Mike)

Punter—Philadelphia Eagles

Born February 1, 1959, at Orange, Calif.
Height, 5.11. Weight, 190.
High School—Fullerton, Calif., Sunny Hills.
Attended Fullerton College and received degree in mechanical engineering from California State University at Long Beach.

Selected by Atlanta in 9th round (235th player selected) of 1982 NFL draft.

Released by Atlanta Falcons, September 4, 1982; signed as free agent by Green Bay Packers, March 15, 1983.

Released by Green Bay Packers after failing physical, May 6, 1983; signed as free agent by Buffalo Bills, May 25, 1983.

Released by Buffalo Bills, August 22, 1983; signed as free agent by Philadelphia Eagles, May 7, 1984.

		PUNTING		
Year Club	G.	No.	Avg.	Blk.
1984—Philadelphia NFL	16	92	42.2	0
1985—Philadelphia NFL	16	91	41.5	0
Pro Totals—2 Years	32	183	41.9	0

Additional pro statistics: Rushed once for 12 yards, 1985.

ETHAN SHANE HORTON

Running Back—Kansas City Chiefs

Born December 19, 1962, at Kannapolis, N.C.
Height, 6.03. Weight, 228.
High School—Kannapolis, N.C., A.L. Brown.
Attended University of North Carolina.

Selected by Baltimore in 1985 USFL territorial draft.

Selected by Kansas City in 1st round (15th player selected) of 1985 NFL draft.

Signed by Kansas City Chiefs, July 26, 1985.

		RUSHING				PASS RECEIVING				TOTAL		
Year Club	G.	Att.	Yds.	Avg.	TD.	P.C.	Yds.	Avg.	TD.	TD.	Pts.	F.
1985—Kansas City NFL	16	48	146	3.0	3	28	185	6.6	1	4	24	2

Additional pro statistics: Attempted one pass with no completions, 1985.

RAYMOND ANTHONY HORTON

(Ray)

Cornerback—Cincinnati Bengals

Born April 12, 1960, at Tacoma, Wash.
Height, 5.11. Weight, 190.
High School—Tacoma, Wash., Mt. Tahoma.
Received bachelor of arts degree in sociology from University of Washington in 1983.

Selected by Los Angeles in 3rd round (25th player selected) of 1983 USFL draft.

Selected by Cincinnati in 2nd round (53rd player selected) of 1983 NFL draft.

Signed by Cincinnati Bengals, May 21, 1983.

		INTERCEPTIONS				PUNT RETURNS				KICKOFF RET.				TOTAL		
Year Club	G.	No.	Yds.	Avg.	TD.	No.	Yds.	Avg.	TD.	No.	Yds.	Avg.	TD.	TD.	Pts.	F.
1983—Cincinnati NFL	16	5	121	24.2	1	1	10	10.0	0	5	128	25.6	0	1	6	1
1984—Cincinnati NFL	15	3	48	16.0	1	2	—1	—0.5	0			None		1	6	0
1985—Cincinnati NFL	16	2	3	1.5	0			None				None		0	0	1
Pro Totals—3 Years	47	10	172	17.2	2	3	9	3.0	0	5	128	25.6	0	2	12	2

Additional pro statistics: Recovered one fumble, 1983 and 1984; recovered two fumbles, 1985.

JEFF W. HOSTETLER

Quarterback—New York Giants

Born April 22, 1961, at Hollsopple, Pa.
Height, 6.03. Weight, 212.
High School—Johnstown, Pa., Conemaugh Valley.
Attended West Virginia University.
Son-in-law of Don Nehlen, head coach at West Virginia University.

Selected by Pittsburgh in 1984 USFL territorial draft.

Selected by New York Giants in 3rd round (59th player selected) of 1984 NFL draft.

USFL rights traded with rights to cornerback Dwayne Woodruff by Pittsburgh Maulers to Arizona Wranglers for draft choice, May 2, 1984.

Signed by New York Giants, June 12, 1984.
On injured reserve with pulled hamstring, December 14 through remainder of 1985 season.
Active for 16 games with New York Giants in 1984; did not play.
New York Giants NFL, 1985.
Games: 1985 (5).

JAMES HUSEN HOUGH
(Jim)
Center—Minnesota Vikings
Born August 4, 1956, at Lynwood, Calif.
Height, 6.02. Weight, 268.
High School—La Mirada, Calif.
Attended Utah State University.

Selected by Minnesota in 4th round (100th player selected) of 1978 NFL draft.
On injured reserve with knee injury, September 24 through October 23, 1980; activated, October 24, 1980.
On injured reserve with knee injury, December 11 through remainder of 1980 season.
On injured reserve with knee injury, October 31 through remainder of 1984 season.
On injured reserve with torn tricep, September 14 through December 6, 1985; activated, December 7, 1985.
Minnesota NFL, 1978 through 1985.
Games: 1978 (15), 1979 (16), 1980 (10), 1981 (16), 1982 (9), 1983 (16), 1984 (9), 1985 (4). Total—95.
Pro statistics: Recovered one fumble, 1979 and 1982.

KEVIN NATHANIEL HOUSE
Wide Receiver—Tampa Bay Buccaneers
Born December 20, 1957, at St. Louis, Mo.
Height, 6.01. Weight, 185.
High School—University City, Mo.
Attended Southern Illinois University.

Selected by Tampa Bay in 2nd round (49th player selected) of 1980 NFL draft.
Selected by St. Louis (baseball) Cardinals' organization in 27th round of free-agent draft, June 5, 1979.
Selected by Chicago White Sox' organization in 20th round of free-agent draft, June 3, 1980.

| | | | —PASS RECEIVING— | | |
Year Club	G.	P.C.	Yds.	Avg.	TD.
1980—Tampa Bay NFL	14	24	531	22.1	5
1981—Tampa Bay NFL	16	56	1176	21.0	9
1982—Tampa Bay NFL	9	28	438	15.6	2
1983—Tampa Bay NFL	16	47	769	16.4	5
1984—Tampa Bay NFL	16	76	1005	13.2	5
1985—Tampa Bay NFL	16	44	803	18.3	5
Pro Totals—6 Years	87	275	4722	17.2	31

Additional pro statistics: Rushed once for 32 yards, 1980; fumbled once, 1980 and 1982; rushed twice for nine yards, attempted one pass with no completions and fumbled twice, 1981; rushed once for minus one yard, 1982; rushed once for minus four yards, 1983; recovered one fumble, 1984 and 1985.

CARL DELANO HOWARD JR.
Cornerback—New York Jets
Born September 20, 1961, at Newark, N.J.
Height, 6.02. Weight, 177.
High School—Irvington, N.J., Technical.
Received degree in economics from Rutgers University.

Selected by New Jersey in 1984 USFL territorial draft.
Signed as free agent by Dallas Cowboys, May 3, 1984.
On injured reserve with knee injury, November 20 through remainder of 1984 season.
Released by Dallas Cowboys, September 2, 1985; awarded on waivers to Houston Oilers, September 3, 1985.
Released by Houston Oilers, September 7, 1985; signed as free agent by Tampa Bay Buccaneers, October 15, 1985.
Released by Tampa Bay Buccaneers, November 12, 1985; signed as free agent by New York Jets, December 5, 1985.
Dallas NFL, 1984; Tampa Bay (4)-New York Jets (3) NFL, 1985.
Games: 1984 (10), 1985 (7). Total—17.

DAVID HOWARD
Linebacker—Minnesota Vikings
Born December 8, 1961, at Enterprise, Ala.
Height, 6.02. Weight, 225.
High School—Long Beach, Calif., Poly.
Attended Oregon State University and California State University at Long Beach.

Selected by Los Angeles in 1984 USFL territorial draft.
Signed by Los Angeles Express, February 10, 1984.
On developmental squad, April 28 through May 10, 1984; activated, May 11, 1984.
Selected by Minnesota in 3rd round (67th player selected) of 1984 NFL supplemental draft.
Released by Los Angeles Express, August 22, 1985; signed by Minnesota Vikings, August 25, 1985.
Granted roster exemption, August 25 through September 6, 1985; activated, September 7, 1985.
On developmental squad for 2 games with Los Angeles Express in 1984.
Los Angeles USFL, 1984 and 1985; Minnesota NFL, 1985.
Games: 1984 (15), 1985 USFL (18), 1985 NFL (16). Total USFL—33. Total Pro—49.

USFL statistics: Intercepted two passes for 14 yards, credited with 4½ sacks for 39 yards, recovered three fumbles and fumbled once, 1984; intercepted one pass for six yards, recovered four fumbles for 12 yards, credited with three sacks for 30 yards and returned two kickoffs for 10 yards, 1985.

JAMES THOMAS HOWARD
(Known by middle name.)
Linebacker—St. Louis Cardinals
Born August 18, 1954, at Lubbock, Tex.
Height, 6.02. Weight, 220.
High School—Lubbock, Tex., Dunbar.
Attended Texas Tech University.

Selected by Kansas City in 3rd round (67th player selected) of 1977 NFL draft.
On injured reserve with separated shoulder, December 9 through remainder of 1981 season.
Granted free agency, February 1, 1984.
Placed on did not report list, August 20 through August 31, 1984.
Traded by Kansas City Chiefs to St. Louis Cardinals for 7th round pick in 1985 draft and granted roster exemption, September 1, 1984; activated; September 6, 1984.
On injured reserve with knee injury, September 17 through December 9, 1985; activated, December 10, 1985.

		—INTERCEPTIONS—						—INTERCEPTIONS—			
Year Club	G.	No.	Yds.	Avg.	TD.	Year Club	G.	No.	Yds.	Avg.	TD.
1977—Kansas City NFL	13	1	0	0.0	0	1982—Kansas City NFL	9	2	10	5.0	0
1978—Kansas City NFL	16	1	0	0.0	0	1983—Kansas City NFL	16		None		
1979—Kansas City NFL	16	1	19	19.0	0	1984—St. Louis NFL	15	2	—4	—2.0	0
1980—Kansas City NFL	16		None			1985—St. Louis NFL	3		None		
1981—Kansas City NFL	9		None			Pro Totals—9 Years	113	7	25	3.6	0

Additional pro statistics: Recovered one fumble, 1978 and 1982; recovered three fumbles for 18 yards and one touchdown, 1980; recovered two fumbles for 65 yards and one touchdown, 1981; recovered one fumble for 29 yards and a touchdown, 1984.

PAUL EUGENE HOWARD
Guard—Denver Broncos
Born September 12, 1950, at San Jose, Calif.
Height, 6.03. Weight, 260.
High School—Central Valley, Calif.
Attended Brigham Young University.

Selected by Denver in 3rd round (54th player selected) of 1973 NFL draft.
Missed entire 1976 season due to injury.
Denver NFL, 1973 through 1975 and 1977 through 1985.
Games: 1973 (14), 1974 (14), 1975 (14), 1977 (14), 1978 (13), 1979 (16), 1980 (14), 1981 (16), 1982 (9), 1983 (16), 1984 (16), 1985 (16). Total—172.
Pro statistics: Recovered one fumble, 1975 and 1977.
Played in AFC Championship Game following 1977 season.
Played in NFL Championship Game following 1977 season.

BOBBY GLEN HOWE
(Known by middle name.)
Offensive Tackle—Atlanta Falcons
Born October 18, 1961, at New Albany, Miss.
Height, 6.06. Weight, 292.
High School—New Albany, Miss., W.P. Daniel.
Attended University of Southern Mississippi.

Selected by New Orleans in 1984 USFL territorial draft.
Selected by Atlanta in 9th round (233rd player selected) of 1984 NFL draft.
Signed by Atlanta Falcons, June 4, 1984.
Released by Atlanta Falcons, August 26, 1984; signed as free agent by Pittsburgh Steelers, May 9, 1985.
Released by Pittsburgh Steelers, September 2, 1985; re-signed by Steelers, September 3, 1985.
Released by Pittsburgh Steelers, October 4, 1985; signed as free agent by Atlanta Falcons, November 19, 1985.
Pittsburgh (2)-Atlanta (5) NFL, 1985.
Games: 1985 (7).

LEROY HOWELL
Defensive End—Seattle Seahawks
Born November 4, 1962, at Columbus, S.C.
Height, 6.04. Weight, 235.
High School—Columbus, S.C., Richland Northeast.
Attended Appalachian State University.

Selected by New Orleans in 7th round (133rd player selected) of 1984 USFL draft.
Selected by Buffalo in 9th round (236th player selected) of 1984 NFL draft.
Signed by Buffalo Bills, July 9, 1984.
On injured reserve with knee injury, August 28 through December 13, 1984; activated, December 14, 1984.
Released by Buffalo Bills, August 27, 1985; signed as free agent by Seattle Seahawks, May 14, 1986.
Active for 1 game with Buffalo Bills in 1984; did not play.

PAT GERRAD HOWELL
Guard—Houston Oilers
Born March 12, 1957, at Fresno, Calif.
Height, 6.06. Weight, 265.
High School—Fresno, Calif.
Received bachelor of arts degree in speech communication from
University of Southern California in 1979.

Named as guard on THE SPORTING NEWS College All-America Team, 1978.
Selected by Atlanta in 2nd round (49th player selected) of 1979 NFL draft.
Released by Atlanta Falcons, September 14, 1983; signed as free agent by Houston Oilers, October 19, 1983.
On injured reserve with shoulder injury, August 15 through October 14, 1985.
Awarded on procedural waivers to Detroit Lions, October 16, 1985.
Released by Detroit Lions after failing physical, October 16, 1985; signed as free agent by Houston Oilers, October 18, 1985.
Atlanta NFL, 1979 through 1982; Atlanta (2)-Houston (7) NFL, 1983; Houston NFL, 1984 and 1985.
Games: 1979 (15), 1980 (5), 1981 (16), 1982 (9), 1983 (9), 1984 (11), 1985 (2). Total—67.

HARLAN CHARLES HUCKLEBY
Running Back—Green Bay Packers
Born December 30, 1957, at Detroit, Mich.
Height, 6.01. Weight, 201.
High School—Detroit, Mich., Cass Tech.
Attended University of Michigan.

Selected by New Orleans in 5th round (120th player selected) of 1979 NFL draft.
Released by New Orleans Saints, August 27, 1979; signed as free agent by Saskatchewan Roughriders, September 2, 1979.
Released by Saskatchewan Roughriders, June 25, 1980; signed as free agent by Green Bay Packers, July 17, 1980.
On injured reserve with knee injury, November 21 through remainder of 1985 season.

Year Club	G.	Att.	—RUSHING— Yds.	Avg.	TD.	PASS RECEIVING P.C. Yds. Avg. TD.				—TOTAL— TD. Pts. F.		
1979—Saskatchewan CFL	8	58	259	4.5	1	10	37	3.7	0	1	6	1
1980—Green Bay NFL	16	6	11	1.8	1	3	11	3.7	0	1	6	0
1981—Green Bay NFL	16	139	381	2.7	5	27	221	8.2	3	8	48	3
1982—Green Bay NFL	9	4	19	4.8	0		None			0	0	0
1983—Green Bay NFL	16	50	182	3.6	4	10	87	8.7	0	4	24	4
1984—Green Bay NFL	16	35	145	4.1	0	8	65	8.1	0	0	0	1
1985—Green Bay NFL	11	8	41	5.1	0	5	27	5.4	0	0	0	0
NFL Totals—6 Years	84	242	779	3.2	10	53	411	7.8	3	13	78	8
CFL Totals—1 Year	8	58	259	4.5	1	10	37	3.7	0	1	6	1
Pro Totals—7 Years	92	300	1038	3.5	11	63	448	7.1	3	14	84	9

		KICKOFF RETURNS			
Year Club	G.	No.	Yds.	Avg.	TD.
1979—Saskatchewan CFL	8	11	212	19.3	0
1980—Green Bay NFL	16	3	59	19.7	0
1981—Green Bay NFL	16	7	134	19.1	0
1982—Green Bay NFL	9	5	89	17.8	0
1983—Green Bay NFL	16	41	757	18.5	0
1984—Green Bay NFL	16	14	261	18.6	0
1985—Green Bay NFL	11		None		
NFL Totals—6 Years	84	70	1300	18.6	0
CFL Totals—1 Year	8	11	212	19.3	0
Pro Totals—7 Years	92	81	1512	18.7	0

Additional CFL statistics: Recovered one fumble, 1979.
Additional NFL statistics: Recovered one fumble, 1983 and 1984.

GORDON HUDSON
Tight End—Seattle Seahawks
Born June 22, 1962, at Kennewick, Wash.
Height, 6.03. Weight, 235.
High School—Kennewick, Wash.
Attended Brigham Young University.

Named as tight end on THE SPORTING NEWS USFL All-Star Team, 1985.
Selected by Los Angeles in 8th round (154th player selected) of 1984 USFL draft.
Signed by Los Angeles Express, January 16, 1984.
On reserve/did not report, February 14 through entire 1984 season.
Selected by Seattle in 1st round (22nd player selected) of 1984 NFL supplemental draft.
Activated from did not report, January 26, 1985.
On developmental squad, May 19 through remainder of 1985 season.
Released by Los Angeles Express, November 13, 1985; signed by Seattle Seahawks for 1986, November 14, 1985.
On developmental squad for 6 games with Los Angeles Express in 1985.

		—PASS RECEIVING—			
Year Club	G.	P.C.	Yds.	Avg.	TD.
1985—Los Angeles USFL	11	34	476	14.0	0

Additional USFL statistics: Recovered one fumble and fumbled once, 1985.

CHARLES HUFF
Defensive Back—San Francisco 49ers
Born February 24, 1963, at Statesboro, Ga.
Height, 5.11. Weight, 195.
High School—Portal, Ga.
Received degree from Presbyterian College in 1985.

Signed as free agent by San Francisco 49ers, May 14, 1985.
On injured reserve with knee injury, August 26 through entire 1985 season.

KENNETH WAYNE HUFF
(Ken)
Guard—Washington Redskins
Born February 21, 1953, at Hutchinson, Kan.
Height, 6.04. Weight, 265.
High Schools—Deerfield, Mass., Deerfield Academy and Coronado, Calif.
Received bachelor of arts degree in psychology from University of North Carolina.

Named as guard on THE SPORTING NEWS College All-America Team, 1974.
Selected by Baltimore in 1st round (3rd player selected) of 1975 NFL draft.
Granted free agency, February 1, 1983; Colts withdrew offer August 23, 1983 and signed by Washington Redskins, August 25, 1983.
Baltimore NFL, 1975 through 1982; Washington NFL, 1983 through 1985.
Games: 1975 (9), 1976 (8), 1977 (14), 1978 (16), 1979 (14), 1980 (16), 1981 (16), 1982 (9), 1983 (13), 1984 (15), 1985 (16). Total—146.
Pro statistics: Returned one kickoff for 15 yards, 1977; recovered one fumble, 1980; caught one pass for minus one yard, 1981; recovered three fumbles, 1984.
Member of Washington Redskins for NFC Championship Game following 1983 season; did not play.
Played in NFL Championship Game following 1983 season.

DAVID LAMBERT HUFFMAN
(Dave)
Guard—Minnesota Vikings
Born April 4, 1957, at Canton, O.
Height, 6.06. Weight, 255.
High School—Dallas, Tex., Thomas Jefferson.
Recieved bachelor of arts degree in anthropology from
University of Notre Dame in 1979.
Brother of Tim Huffman, guard with Green Bay Packers, 1981 through 1985; and Steve Huffman,
center at University of Notre Dame.

Named as center on THE SPORTING NEWS College All-America Team, 1978.
Selected by Minnesota in 2nd round (43rd player selected) of 1979 NFL draft.
Signed by Arizona Wranglers, January 6, 1984, for contract to take effect after being granted free agency, February 1, 1984.
Traded by Arizona Wranglers to Memphis Showboats for past consideration, December 6, 1984.
Released by Memphis Showboats, August 20, 1985; re-signed by Minnesota Vikings, September 5, 1985.
Granted roster exemption, September 5 through September 13, 1985; activated, September 14, 1985.
Minnesota NFL, 1979 through 1983 and 1985; Arizona USFL, 1984; Memphis USFL, 1985.
Games: 1979 (13), 1980 (16), 1981 (13), 1982 (9), 1983 (15), 1984 (18), 1985 USFL (18), 1985 NFL (15). Total NFL—81. Total USFL—36. Total Pro—117.
NFL statistics: Recovered blocked fumble in end zone for a touchdown, returned three kickoffs for 42 yards and recovered two fumbles, 1983; fumbled once for minus 26 yards, 1985.
USFL statistics: Returned one kickoff for eight yards, 1984; caught one pass for two yards and a touchdown and recovered two fumbles, 1985.
Played in USFL Championship Game following 1984 season.

TIMOTHY PATRICK HUFFMAN
(Tim)
Guard
Born August 31, 1959, at Canton, O.
Height, 6.05. Weight, 282.
High School—Dallas, Tex., Thomas Jefferson.
Attended University of Notre Dame.
Brother of Dave Huffman, guard with Minnesota Vikings;
and Steve Huffman, center at University of Notre Dame.

Selected by Green Bay in 9th round (227th player selected) of 1981 NFL draft.
On injured reserve with foot injury, September 1 through September 28, 1981; activated, September 29, 1981.
On injured reserve with ankle injury, November 13 through remainder of 1981 season.
On injured reserve with back injury, September 4 through November 1, 1985; activated, November 2, 1985.
On injured reserve with back injury, November 20 through remainder of 1985 season.
Granted free agency with no qualifying offer, February 1, 1986.
Green Bay NFL, 1981 through 1985.
Games: 1981 (6), 1982 (9), 1983 (15), 1984 (16), 1985 (2). Total—48.

ALLEN JEFFRIES HUGHES
Defensive Tackle—Detroit Lions
Born September 8, 1959, at Detroit, Mich.
Height, 6.03. Weight, 254.
High School—Detroit, Mich., Benedictine.
Received bachelor of science degree in communications and
criminal justice from Western Michigan University.
Son of Allen Hughes, player with Harlem Globetrotters, 1959 through 1964.

Selected by Pittsburgh in 12th round (320th player selected) of 1982 NFL draft.
Released by Pittsburgh Steelers, August 19, 1983; signed as free agent by Ottawa Rough Riders, September 3, 1982.
Released by Ottawa Rough Riders, September 10, 1983; signed by Chicago Blitz, November 11, 1982.
Released by Chicago Blitz, February 27, 1983; awarded on waivers to Michigan Panthers, March 1, 1983.
On injured reserve, March 3 through April 11, 1983; awarded on procedural waivers to New Jersey Generals, April 13, 1983.
Released by New Jersey Generals, April 14, 1983; awarded on waivers to Michigan Panthers, April 15, 1983.
Not protected in merger of Michigan Panthers and Oakland Invaders; selected by Portland Breakers in USFL dispersal draft, December 6, 1984.
Released by Portland Breakers, July 18, 1985; signed as free agent by Detroit Lions, March 6, 1986.
Ottawa CFL, 1982; Michigan USFL, 1983 and 1984; Portland USFL, 1985.
Games: 1982 (1), 1983 (12), 1984 (18), 1985 (17). Total USFL—47. Total Pro—48.
Pro statistics: Recovered one fumble for six yards and credited with four sacks for 27½ yards, 1983; credited with two sacks for 14 yards, 1984; recovered one fumble, 1984 and 1985; credited with five sacks for 32 yards, 1985.
Played in USFL Championship Game following 1983 season.

DAVID A. HUGHES
Fullback—Seattle Seahawks
Born June 1, 1959, at Honolulu, Hawaii.
Height, 6.00. Weight, 220.
High School—Pearl City, Hawaii, Kamehameha.
Attended Boise State University.

Selected by Seattle in 2nd round (31st player selected) of 1981 NFL draft.
On injured reserve with neck injury, November 8 through December 6, 1985; activated, December 7, 1985.

| | | —RUSHING— | | | | PASS RECEIVING | | | | —TOTAL— | | |
Year Club	G.	Att.	Yds.	Avg.	TD.	P.C.	Yds.	Avg.	TD.	TD.	Pts.	F.
1981—Seattle NFL	16	47	135	2.9	0	35	263	7.5	2	2	12	4
1982—Seattle NFL	9	30	106	3.5	0	11	98	8.9	1	1	6	0
1983—Seattle NFL	16	83	313	3.8	1	10	100	10.0	1	2	12	2
1984—Seattle NFL	16	94	327	3.5	1	22	121	5.5	1	2	12	4
1985—Seattle NFL	12	40	128	3.2	0	19	184	9.7	0	0	0	2
Pro Totals—5 Years	69	294	1009	3.4	2	97	766	7.9	5	7	42	12

| | | KICKOFF RETURNS | | | |
Year Club	G.	No.	Yds.	Avg.	TD.
1981—Seattle NFL	16		None		
1982—Seattle NFL	9	1	17	17.0	0
1983—Seattle NFL	16	12	282	23.5	0
1984—Seattle NFL	16	17	348	20.5	0
1985—Seattle NFL	12		None		
Pro Totals—5 Years	69	30	647	21.6	0

Additional pro statistics: Recovered one fumble, 1981 and 1985; recovered three fumbles, 1984.
Played in AFC Championship Game following 1983 season.

ROBERT CHARLES HUMPHERY
(Bobby)
Wide Receiver—New York Jets
Born August 23, 1961, at Lubbock, Tex.
Height 5.10. Weight, 180.
High School—Lubbock, Tex., Estacado.
Received degree in social work from New Mexico State University.

Named as kick returner to THE SPORTING NEWS NFL All-Star Team, 1984.
Selected by New York Jets in 9th round (247th player selected) of 1983 NFL draft.
On injured reserve with broken finger, August 1 through entire 1983 season.
On injured reserve with fractured wrist, September 3 through October 4, 1985; activated, October 5, 1985.

| | | PASS RECEIVING | | | | —KICKOFF RET.— | | | | —TOTAL— | | |
Year Club	G.	P.C.	Yds.	Avg.	TD.	No.	Yds.	Avg.	TD.	TD.	Pts.	F.
1984—New York Jets NFL	16	14	206	14.7	1	22	675	*30.7	*1	2	12	1
1985—New York Jets NFL	12		None			17	363	21.4	0	0	0	2
Pro Totals—2 Years	28	14	206	14.7	1	39	1038	26.6	1	2	12	4

Additional pro statistics: Recovered two fumbles, 1984; returned one punt for no yards, ran once for 10 yards and recovered one fumble, 1985.

—DID YOU KNOW—
That rookie punters Harry Newsome of Pittsburgh and Dale Hatcher of the Rams were teammates at Cheraw High School in South Carolina?

DONNIE RAY HUMPHREY
Defensive End—Green Bay Packers
Born April 20, 1961, at Huntsville, Ala.
Height, 6.03. Weight, 275.
High School—Huntsville, Ala., J.O. Johnson.
Attended Auburn University.

Selected by Birmingham in 1984 USFL territorial draft.
Selected by Green Bay in 3rd round (72nd player selected) of 1984 NFL draft.
Signed by Green Bay Packers, July 12, 1984.
Green Bay NFL, 1984 and 1985.
Games: 1984 (16), 1985 (16). Total—32.

STEFAN GOVAN HUMPHRIES
Guard—Chicago Bears
Born January 20, 1962, at Fort Lauderdale, Fla.
Height, 6.04. Weight, 265.
High School—Fort Lauderdale, Fla., St. Thomas Aquinas.
Received bachelor of science degree in engineering science
from University of Michigan in 1984.

Named as guard on THE SPORTING NEWS College All-America Team, 1983.
Selected by Michigan in 1984 USFL territorial draft.
Selected by Chicago in 3rd round (71st player selected) of 1984 NFL draft.
Signed by Chicago Bears, July 2, 1984.
On injured reserve with knee injury, December 5 through remainder of 1984 season.
On injured reserve with knee injury, September 3 through October 3, 1985; activated, October 4, 1985.
Chicago NFL, 1984 and 1985.
Games: 1984 (9), 1985 (11). Total—20.
Played in NFC Championship Game following 1985 season.
Played in NFL Championship Game following 1985 season.

KENNETH LaMONTE HUNLEY
(Known by middle name.)
Linebacker—Indianapolis Colts
Born January 31, 1963, at Richmond, Va.
Height, 6.02. Weight, 232.
High School—Petersburg, Pa.
Attended University of Arizona.
Brother of Ricky Hunley, linebacker with Denver Broncos.

Selected by Arizona in 1985 USFL territorial draft.
Signed as free agent by Indianapolis Colts, May 14, 1985.
Indianapolis NFL, 1985.
Games: 1985 (16).

RICKY CARDELL HUNLEY
Linebacker—Denver Broncos
Born November 11, 1961, at Petersburg, Va.
Height, 6.02. Weight, 238.
High School—Petersburg, Va.
Received degree in business from University of Arizona in 1984.
Brother of Lamonte Hunley, linebacker with Indianapolis Colts.

Selected by Arizona in 1984 USFL territorial draft.
Selected by Cincinnati in 1st round (7th player selected) in 1984 NFL draft.
NFL rights traded by Cincinnati Bengals to Denver Broncos for 1st and 3rd round picks in 1986 draft and 5th round
pick in 1987 draft, October 9, 1984.
Signed by Denver Broncos, October 16, 1984.
Granted roster exemption, October 16 though October 25, 1984; activated, October 26, 1984.
Selected by Pittsburgh Pirates' organization in 26th round of free-agent draft, June 3, 1980.
Denver NFL, 1984 and 1985.
Games: 1984 (8), 1985 (16). Total—24.

BYRON RAY HUNT
Linebacker—New York Giants
Born December 17, 1958, at Longview, Tex.
Height, 6.05. Weight, 242.
High School—Longview, Tex., White Oak.
Received degree in political science from Southern Methodist University.
Brother of Sam Hunt, defensive end with New England Patriots
and Green Bay Packers, 1974 through 1980.

Selected by New York Giants in 9th round (224th player selected) of 1981 NFL draft.

Year Club	G.	No.	Yds.	Avg.TD.
1981—N.Y. Giants NFL	16	1	7	7.0 0
1982—N.Y. Giants NFL	9		None	
1983—N.Y. Giants NFL	16		None	
1984—N.Y. Giants NFL	13	1	14	14.0 0
1985—N.Y. Giants NFL	16		None	
Pro Totals—5 Years	70	2	21	10.5 0

Additional pro statistics: Recovered two fumbles, 1984; recovered one fumble, 1985.

DANIEL LEWIS HUNTER
Cornerback—Denver Broncos
Born September 1, 1962, at Arkadelphia, Ark.
Height, 5.11. Weight, 175.
High School—Arkadelphia, Ark.
Attended Henderson State University.

Signed as free agent by Los Angeles Express, January 13, 1984.
Released by Los Angeles Express, February 22, 1984; signed as free agent by Dallas Cowboys, May 10, 1984.
Released by Dallas Cowboys, August 13, 1984; signed as free agent by Denver Broncos, February 27, 1985.

Year Club	G.	No.	Yds.	Avg.TD.
1985—Denver NFL	16	1	20	20.0 0

Additional pro statistics: Returned two kickoffs for 32 yards, 1985.

HERMAN HUNTER
Running Back-Kick Returner—Philadelphia Eagles
Born February 14, 1961, at Columbus, Ga.
Height, 6.01. Weight, 193.
High School—Columbus, Ga., Hardaway.
Attended Tennessee State University.

Selected by Memphis in 1985 USFL territorial draft.
Selected by Philadelphia in 11th round (289th player selected) of 1985 NFL draft.
Signed by Philadelphia Eagles, July 19, 1985.

Year Club	G.	Att.	Yds.	Avg.	TD.	P.C.	Yds.	Avg.	TD.	TD.	Pts.	F.
		RUSHING				PASS RECEIVING				TOTAL		
1985—Philadelphia NFL	16	27	121	4.5	1	28	405	14.5	1	2	12	4

Year Club	G.	No.	Yds.	Avg.TD.
		KICKOFF RETURNS		
1985—Philadelphia NFL	16	48	1047	21.8 0

Additional pro statistics: Attempted two passes with one completion for 38 yards and a touchdown, returned one punt for six yards and recovered two fumbles, 1985.

TONY WAYNE HUNTER
Tight End—Los Angeles Rams
Born May 22, 1960, at Cincinnati, O.
Height, 6.04. Weight, 235.
High School—Cincinnati, O., Moeller.
Received bachelor of science degree in economics from University of Notre Dame in 1984.

Selected by Chicago in 1983 USFL territorial draft.
Selected by Buffalo in 1st round (12th player selected) of 1983 NFL draft.
Signed by Buffalo Bills, June 17, 1983.
On injured reserve with back injury, September 29 through October 25, 1984; activated, October 26, 1984.
Traded by Buffalo Bills to Los Angeles Rams for quarterback Vince Ferragamo and 3rd round pick in 1986 draft, July 18, 1985.

Year Club	G.	P.C.	Yds.	Avg.	TD.
		PASS RECEIVING			
1983—Buffalo NFL	13	36	402	11.2	3
1984—Buffalo NFL	11	33	331	10.0	2
1985—L.A. Rams NFL	16	50	562	11.2	4
Pro Totals—3 Years	40	119	1295	10.9	9

Additional pro statistics: Rushed twice for 28 yards, 1983; recovered one fumble, 1983 through 1985; fumbled once, 1983 and 1984; rushed once for six yards, 1984; fumbled three times, 1985.
Played in NFC Championship Game following 1985 season.

ANTHONY LaRUE HUTCHISON
Running Back—Buffalo Bills
Born February 4, 1961, at Houston, Tex.
Height, 5.10. Weight, 186.
High School—Converse, Tex., Judson.
Attended Texas Tech University.

Selected by Denver in 1983 USFL territorial draft.
Selected by Chicago in 10th round (256th player selected) of 1983 NFL draft.
Signed by Chicago Bears, May 12, 1983.

Released by Chicago Bears, September 2, 1985; awarded on waivers to Buffalo Bills, September 3, 1985.
On injured reserve with knee injury, October 12 through remainder of 1985 season.

Year Club	G.	Att.	Yds.	Avg.	TD.	P.C.	Yds.	Avg.	TD.	TD.	Pts.	F.
		—RUSHING—				PASS RECEIVING				—TOTAL—		
1983—Chicago NFL	16	6	13	2.2	1	None				1	6	1
1984—Chicago NFL	12	14	39	2.8	1	1	7	7.0	0	1	6	0
1985—Buffalo NFL	5	2	11	5.5	0	None				0	0	0
Pro Totals—3 Years	33	22	63	2.9	2	1	7	7.0	0	2	12	1

		KICKOFF RETURNS			
Year Club	G.	No.	Yds.	Avg.	TD.
1983—Chicago NFL	16	17	259	15.2	0
1984—Chicago NFL	12	None			
1985—Buffalo NFL	5	12	239	19.9	0
Pro Totals—3 Years	33	29	498	17.2	0

Played in NFC Championship Game following 1984 season.

DONALD AMECHI IGWEBUIKE

Name pronounced Ig-way-BWEE-kay.

(Middle name means "You can't predict tomorrow.")

Placekicker—Tampa Bay Buccaneers

Born December 27, 1960, at Anambra, Nigeria.
Height, 5.09. Weight, 185.
High School—Anambra, Nigeria, Immaculate Conception.
Attended Clemson University.

Selected by Tampa Bay in 10th round (260th player selected) of 1985 NFL draft.
Signed by Tampa Bay Buccaneers, June 6, 1985.

		—PLACE KICKING—				
Year Club	G.	XP.	XPM.	FG.	FGA.	Pts.
1985—Tampa Bay NFL	16	30	2	22	32	96

TUNCH ALI ILKIN

Name pronounced TOON-ch ILL-kin.

Offensive Tackle—Pittsburgh Steelers

Born September 23, 1957, at Istanbul, Turkey.
Height, 6.03. Weight, 265.
High School—Highland Park, Ill.
Received bachelor of science degree in broadcasting from Indiana State University in 1980.

Selected by Pittsburgh in 6th round (165th player selected) of 1980 NFL draft.
Released by Pittsburgh Steelers, August 25, 1980; re-signed by Steelers, October 15, 1983.
On injured reserve with shoulder injury, August 30 through September 29, 1983; activated, September 30, 1983.
Pittsburgh NFL, 1980 through 1985.
Games: 1980 (10), 1981 (16), 1982 (8), 1983 (11), 1984 (16), 1985 (16). Total—77.
Pro statistics: Recovered one fumble, 1981, 1983 and 1985.
Played in AFC Championship Game following 1984 season.

BRIAN DeWAYNE INGRAM

Linebacker—New England Patriots

Born October 31, 1959, at Memphis, Tenn.
Height, 6.04. Weight, 235.
High School—Memphis, Tenn., Hamilton.
Attended University of Tennessee.

Selected by New England in 4th round (111th player selected) of 1982 NFL draft.
On inactive list, September 12, 1982.
On injured reserve with knee injury, September 28 through remainder of 1983 season.
New England NFL, 1982 through 1985.
Games: 1982 (8), 1983 (4), 1984 (12), 1985 (15). Total—39.
Played in AFC Championship Game following 1985 season.
Played in NFL Championship Game following 1985 season.

LeROY IRVIN JR.

Cornerback—Los Angeles Rams

Born September 15, 1957, at Fort Dix, N.J.
Height, 5.11. Weight, 184.
High School—Augusta, Ga., Glenn Hills.
Attended University of Kansas.

Established NFL record for most punt return yards, game (207), against Atlanta Falcons, October 11, 1981.
Tied NFL record for most touchdowns, punt returns, game (2), against Atlanta Falcons, October 11, 1981.
Named as punt returner to THE SPORTING NEWS NFL All-Star Team, 1981.
Selected by Los Angeles in 3rd round (70th player selected) of 1980 NFL draft.

Year Club	G.	No.	Yds.	Avg.	TD.	No.	Yds.	Avg.	TD.	TD.	Pts.	F.
		-INTERCEPTIONS-				-PUNT RETURNS-				—TOTAL—		
1980—Los Angeles Rams NFL	16	2	80	40.0	0	42	296	7.0	0	0	0	5
1981—Los Angeles Rams NFL	16	3	18	6.0	0	46	*615	*13.4	*3	3	18	3

Year Club	G.	No.	-INTERCEPTIONS- Yds.	Avg.	TD.	No.	-PUNT RETURNS- Yds.	Avg.	TD.	—TOTAL— TD.	Pts.	F.
1982—Los Angeles Rams NFL	9		None			22	242	11.0	1	1	6	4
1983—Los Angeles Rams NFL	15	4	42	10.5	0	25	212	8.5	0	0	0	4
1984—Los Angeles Rams NFL	16	5	166	33.2	*2	9	83	9.2	0	2	12	0
1985—Los Angeles Rams NFL	16	6	83	13.8	*1		None			1	6	0
Pro Totals—6 Years	88	20	389	19.5	3	144	1448	10.1	4	7	42	16

Additional pro statistics: Returned one kickoff for five yards and recovered three fumbles, 1980; recovered three fumbles for 14 yards, 1981; recovered two fumbles, 1982 and 1983; returned one kickoff for 22 yards, 1983; returned two kickoffs for 33 yards, 1984.

Played in NFC Championship Game following 1985 season.

Played in Pro Bowl (NFL All-Star Game) following 1985 season.

TIMOTHY EDWARD IRWIN
(Tim)
Offensive Tackle—Minnesota Vikings
Born December 13, 1958, at Knoxville, Tenn.
Height, 6.07. Weight, 285.
High School—Knoxville, Tenn., Central.
Received degree in political science from University of Tennessee in 1981.

Selected by Minnesota in 3rd round (74th player selected) of 1981 NFL draft.
Minnesota NFL, 1981 through 1985.
Games: 1981 (7), 1982 (9), 1983 (16), 1984 (16), 1985 (16). Total—64.
Pro statistics: Recovered one fumble, 1983; recovered one fumble for two yards, 1984.

EDDIE LEE IVERY
(Eddie Lee)
Running Back—Green Bay Packers
Born July 30, 1957, at McDuffie, Ga.
Height, 6.00. Weight, 214.
High School—Thomson, Ga.
Attended Georgia Tech.

Selected by Green Bay in 1st round (15th player selected) of 1979 NFL draft.
On injured reserve with knee injury, September 5 through remainder of 1979 NFL season.
On injured reserve with knee injury, September 8 through remainder of 1981 season.
On reserve/non-football injury with drug problems, October 28 through remainder of 1983 season.
On injured reserve with knee injury, August 29 through October 5, 1984; activated, October 6, 1984.

Year Club	G.	Att.	——RUSHING—— Yds.	Avg.	TD.	P.C.	PASS RECEIVING Yds.	Avg.	TD.	—TOTAL— TD.	Pts.	F.
1979—Green Bay NFL	1	3	24	8.0	0		None			0	0	1
1980—Green Bay NFL	16	202	831	4.1	3	50	481	9.6	1	4	24	3
1981—Green Bay NFL	1	14	72	5.1	1	2	10	5.0	0	1	6	0
1982—Green Bay NFL	9	127	453	3.6	9	16	186	11.6	1	10	60	2
1983—Green Bay NFL	8	86	340	4.0	2	16	139	8.7	1	3	18	1
1984—Green Bay NFL	10	99	552	5.6	6	19	141	7.4	1	7	42	1
1985—Green Bay NFL	15	132	636	4.8	2	28	270	9.6	2	4	24	1
Pro Totals—7 Years	60	663	2908	4.4	23	131	1227	9.4	6	29	174	9

Additional pro statistics: Recovered two fumbles, 1980; attempted one pass with no completions, 1982 and 1985; returned one kickoff for 17 yards and attempted two passes with two completions for 50 yards, 1983; recovered one fumble, 1985.

CHARLES MELVIN JACKSON
Linebacker—New York Jets
Born March 22, 1955, at Los Angeles, Calif.
Height, 6.02. Weight, 222.
High School—Berkeley, Calif.
Attended University of Washington.
Cousin of Odell Jones, pitcher in Baltimore Orioles' organization.

Selected by Denver in 9th round (241st player selected) of 1977 NFL draft.
On injured reserve, August 30 through 1977 season.
Released by Denver Broncos, August 29, 1978; claimed on waivers by Kansas City Chiefs, August 30, 1978.
On injured reserve with rib injury, November 2 through November 29, 1979; activated, November 30, 1979.
Granted free agency, February 2, 1981; signed as free agent by Edmonton Eskimos, May 4, 1981.
Released by Edmonton Eskimos, June 29, 1981; signed as free agent by Kansas City Chiefs, July 4, 1981.
Left Kansas City Chiefs voluntarily and granted roster exemption, October 3 through October 9, 1984.
Placed on reserve/left squad, October 10 through remainder of 1984 season.
Traded by Kansas City Chiefs to New York Jets for 7th round pick in 1985 draft, April 25, 1985.
Kansas City NFL, 1978 through 1984; New York Jets NFL, 1985.
Games: 1978 (16), 1979 (12), 1980 (16), 1981 (14), 1982 (9), 1983 (15), 1984 (4), 1985 (16). Total—102.
Pro statistics: Recovered one fumble, 1979 and 1985; recovered three fumbles for 33 yards, 1981; recovered two fumbles for four yards, 1982; recovered four fumbles for 47 yards and a touchdown, 1983; intercepted one pass for 16 yards, 1984.

EARNEST JACKSON
Running Back—Philadelphia Eagles

Born December 18, 1959, at Needville, Tex.
Height, 5.09. Weight, 208.
High School—Rosenburg, Tex., Lamar.
Attended Texas A&M University.

Selected by Oakland in 9th round (103rd player selected) of 1983 USFL draft.
USFL rights traded by Oakland Invaders to Michigan Panthers for 8th round pick in 1984 draft, March 24, 1983.
Selected by San Diego in 8th round (202nd player selected) of 1983 NFL draft.
Signed by San Diego Chargers, July 11, 1983.
Traded by San Diego Chargers to Philadelphia Eagles for 4th round pick in 1986 draft and 8th round pick in 1987 draft, September 2, 1985.

		—RUSHING—				PASS RECEIVING				—TOTAL—		
Year Club	G.	Att.	Yds.	Avg.	TD.	P.C.	Yds.	Avg.	TD.	TD.	Pts.	F.
1983—San Diego NFL	12	11	39	3.5	0	5	42	8.4	0	0	0	1
1984—San Diego NFL	16	296	1179	4.0	8	39	222	5.7	1	9	54	3
1985—Philadelphia NFL	16	282	1028	3.6	5	10	126	12.6	1	6	36	3
Pro Totals—3 Years	44	589	2246	3.8	13	54	390	7.2	2	15	90	7

		KICKOFF RETURNS		
Year Club	G.	No.	Yds.	Avg.TD.
1983—San Diego NFL	12	11	201	18.3 0
1984—San Diego NFL	16	1	10	10.0 0
1985—Philadelphia NFL	16		None	
Pro Totals—3 Years	44	12	211	17.6 0

Additional pro statistics: Recovered one fumble, 1983; recovered two fumbles, 1984.
Played in Pro Bowl (NFL All-Star Game) following 1984 season.

JEFFERY PAUL JACKSON
(Jeff)
Linebacker—Atlanta Falcons

Born October 9, 1961, at Shreveport, Ga.
Height, 6.01. Weight, 228.
High School—Griffin, Ga.
Attended Auburn University.

Selected by Birmingham in 1984 USFL territorial draft.
Selected by Atlanta in 8th round (206th player selected) of 1984 NFL draft.
Signed by Atlanta Falcons, June 10, 1984.
Released by Atlanta Falcons, November 21, 1985; re-signed by Falcons, January 21, 1986.
Atlanta NFL, 1984 and 1985.
Games: 1984 (16), 1985 (11). Total—27.
Pro statistics: Intercepted one pass for 35 yards and a touchdown and recovered one fumble, 1984.

KENNY JACKSON
Wide Receiver—Philadelphia Eagles

Born February 15, 1962, at Neptune, N.J.
Height, 6.00. Weight, 180.
High School—South River, N.J.
Received degree in finance from Penn State University.
Cousin of Tony Collins, running back with New England Patriots.

Selected by Philadelphia in 1984 USFL territorial draft.
Selected by Philadelphia in 1st round (4th player selected) of 1984 NFL draft.
Signed by Philadelphia Eagles, May 1, 1984.
On injured reserve with separated shoulder, October 22 through November 22, 1984; activated, November 23, 1984.

		—PASS RECEIVING—			
Year Club	G.	P.C.	Yds.	Avg.	TD.
1984—Philadelphia NFL	11	26	398	15.3	1
1985—Philadelphia NFL	16	40	692	17.3	1
Pro Totals—2 Years	27	66	1090	16.5	2

MICHAEL ANTHONY JACKSON
Linebacker—Seattle Seahawks

Born July 15, 1957, at Pasco, Wash.
Height, 6.01. Weight, 220.
High School—Pasco, Wash.
Attended University of Washington.

Selected by Seattle in 3rd round (57th player selected) of 1979 NFL draft.
On suspended list, December 26, 1982.
On injured reserve with knee injury, October 19 through November 25, 1983; activated, November 26, 1983.
On injured reserve with knee injury, October 5 through November 11, 1984; activated, November 12, 1984.

Year Club	—INTERCEPTIONS—			
	G.	No.	Yds.	Avg.TD.
1979—Seattle NFL	15			None
1980—Seattle NFL	15	2	9	4.5 0
1981—Seattle NFL	16	2	51	25.5 0
1982—Seattle NFL	8	2	29	14.5 0
1983—Seattle NFL	11			None
1984—Seattle NFL	8			None
1985—Seattle NFL	16			None
Pro Totals—7 Years	89	6	89	14.8 0

Additional pro statistics: Recovered one fumble, 1979, 1982 and 1983; recovered two fumbles, 1980 and 1981.
Played in AFC Championship Game following 1983 season.

RICKEY ANDERSON JACKSON
Linebacker—New Orleans Saints
Born March 20, 1958, at Pahokee, Fla.
Height, 6.02. Weight, 236.
High School—Pahokee, Fla.
Attended University of Pittsburgh.

Selected by New Orleans in 2nd round (51st player selected) of 1981 NFL draft.
New Orleans NFL, 1981 through 1985.
Games: 1981 (16), 1982 (9), 1983 (16), 1984 (16), 1985 (16). Total—73.
Pro statistics: Recovered one fumble, 1981; intercepted one pass for 32 yards and recovered two fumbles, 1982; intercepted one pass for no yards and recovered two fumbles for minus two yards, 1983; fumbled once, 1983 and 1984; recovered four fumbles for four yards and intercepted one pass for 14 yards, 1984.
Played in Pro Bowl (NFL All-Star Game) following 1983 through 1985 seasons.

ROBERT CHARLES JACKSON
(Bobby)
Cornerback—New York Jets
Born December 23, 1956, at Albany, Ga.
Height, 5.10. Weight, 180.
High School—Albany, Ga.
Received degree in criminology from Florida State University.
Cousin of Alfred Jenkins, wide receiver with Birmingham Express (WFL)
and Atlanta Falcons, 1974 through 1983.

Selected by New York Jets in 6th round (140th player selected) of 1978 NFL draft.
On injured reserve with broken arm, November 17 through December 25, 1981; activated, December 26, 1981.
On injured reserve with pulled hamstring, October 3 through remainder of 1984 season.
On injured reserve with back injury, December 27 through remainder of 1985 season playoffs.

Year Club	—INTERCEPTIONS—			
	G.	No.	Yds.	Avg.TD.
1978—New York Jets NFL	16	5	26	5.2 0
1979—New York Jets NFL	16	4	63	15.8 1
1980—New York Jets NFL	15	1	7	7.0 0
1981—New York Jets NFL	9			None
1982—New York Jets NFL	9	5	84	16.8 *1
1983—New York Jets NFL	15	2	8	4.0 0
1984—New York Jets NFL	3			None
1985—New York Jets NFL	12	4	8	2.0 0
Pro Totals—8 Years	95	21	196	9.3 2

Additional pro statistics: Recovered one fumble, 1978; recovered two fumbles for 80 yards and returned a blocked field goal 95 yards for a touchdown, 1982.
Played in AFC Championship Game following 1982 season.

ROBERT MICHAEL JACKSON
Safety—Cincinnati Bengals
Born October 10, 1958, at Grand Rapids, Mich.
Height, 5.10. Weight, 186.
High School—Allendale, Mich.
Attended Central Michigan University.

Selected by Cincinnati in 11th round (285th player selected) of 1981 NFL draft.
On injured reserve with knee injury, August 10 through entire 1981 season.

Year Club	—INTERCEPTIONS—			
	G.	No.	Yds.	Avg.TD.
1982—Cincinnati NFL	9			None
1983—Cincinnati NFL	16	2	21	10.5 0
1984—Cincinnati NFL	16	4	32	8.0 1
1985—Cincinnati NFL	16	6	100	16.7 *1
Pro Totals—4 Years	57	12	153	12.8 2

Additional pro statistics: Recovered one fumble, 1982 and 1985; recovered three fumbles, 1984.

TERENCE LEON JACKSON
(Terry)
Cornerback—Seattle Seahawks

Born December 9, 1955, at Sherman, Tex.
Height, 5.11. Weight, 197.
High School—San Diego, Calif., St. Augustine's.
Attended San Diego City College, San Diego State University and attending
Bergen County Community College.
Brother of Monte Jackson, cornerback with Los Angeles Rams and
Oakland-Los Angeles Raiders, 1975 through 1983.

Selected by New York Giants in 5th round (120th player selected) of 1978 NFL draft.
On injured reserve with dislocated shoulder, October 29 through remainder of 1980 season.
On inactive list, September 20, 1982.
Traded by New York Giants to Seattle Seahawks for 6th round pick in 1985 draft, March 12, 1984.

Year Club	G.	No.	Yds.	Avg.	TD.
1978—N.Y. Giants NFL	15	7	115	16.4	1
1979—N.Y. Giants NFL	16	3	10	3.3	0
1980—N.Y. Giants NFL	8	1	5	5.0	0
1981—N.Y. Giants NFL	16	3	57	19.0	1
1982—N.Y. Giants NFL	8	4	75	18.8	0
1983—N.Y. Giants NFL	12	6	20	3.3	0
1984—Seattle NFL	16	4	78	19.5	1
1985—Seattle NFL	16			None	
Pro Totals—8 Years	107	28	360	12.9	3

Additional pro statistics: Returned four punts for one yard, 1978; recovered one fumble, 1978 and 1981; ran 47 yards with blocked punt for a touchdown, returned one punt for five yards and recovered one fumble for minus two yards, 1979; recovered three fumbles for 11 yards, 1980; returned two punts for 22 yards, 1981; recovered one fumble for 35 yards and a touchdown, 1983.

THOMAS JACKSON
(Tom)
Linebacker—Denver Broncos

Born April 4, 1951, at Cleveland, O.
Height, 5.11. Weight, 220.
High School—Cleveland, O., John Adams.
Attended University of Louisville.

Named to THE SPORTING NEWS AFC All-Star Team, 1977.
Selected by Denver in 4th round (88th player selected) of 1973 NFL draft.
On injured reserve with knee injury, September 3 through October 3, 1985; activated, October 4, 1985.

Year Club	G.	No.	Yds.	Avg.	TD.	Year Club	G.	No.	Yds.	Avg.	TD.
1973—Denver NFL	8			None		1980—Denver NFL	16			None	
1974—Denver NFL	13	1	39	39.0	0	1981—Denver NFL	16			None	
1975—Denver NFL	14	2	0	0.0	0	1982—Denver NFL	9	1	8	8.0	0
1976—Denver NFL	14	7	136	19.4	1	1983—Denver NFL	15	1	0	0.0	0
1977—Denver NFL	13	4	95	23.8	*1	1984—Denver NFL	16			None	
1978—Denver NFL	16	3	28	9.3	1	1985—Denver NFL	12			None	
1979—Denver NFL	13	1	34	34.0	0	Pro Totals—13 Years	175	20	340	17.0	3

Additional pro statistics: Fumbled once and recovered two fumbles, 1976; fumbled once, 1977; recovered two fumbles for 70 yards, 1979; recovered one fumble, 1981 and 1984; returned one kickoff for two yards and recovered two fumbles for 34 yards, 1983.
Played in AFC Championship Game following 1977 season.
Played in NFL Championship Game following 1977 season.
Played in Pro Bowl (NFL All-Star Game) following 1977 through 1979 seasons.

THOMAS CAMERON JACOBS
(Cam)
Linebacker—Pittsburgh Steelers

Born March 10, 1962, at Oklahoma City, Okla.
Height, 6.01. Weight, 218.
High School—Coral Gables, Fla.
Received bachelor of arts degree in office administration
from University of Kentucky in 1985.

Selected by Tampa Bay in 2nd round (28th player selected) of 1985 USFL draft.
Selected by Pittsburgh in 5th round (136th player selected) of 1985 NFL draft.
Signed by Pittsburgh Steelers, July 20, 1985.
On injured reserve with broken thumb, August 25 through entire 1985 season.

JOE JACOBY
Offensive Tackle—Washington Redskins

Born July 6, 1959, at Louisville, Ky.
Height, 6.07. Weight, 305.
High School—Louisville, Ky., Western.
Attended University of Louisville.

Named to THE SPORTING NEWS NFL All-Star Team, 1983 and 1984.
Signed as free agent by Washington Redskins, May 1, 1981.
Washington NFL, 1981 through 1985.
Games: 1981 (14), 1982 (9), 1983 (16), 1984 (16), 1985 (11). Total—66.
Pro statistics: Recovered one fumble, 1981 and 1982; recovered fumble in end zone for a touchdown, 1984.
Played in NFC Championship Game following 1982 and 1983 seasons.
Played in NFL Championship Game following 1982 and 1983 seasons.
Played in Pro Bowl (NFL All-Star Game) following 1983 through 1985 seasons.

JESSE CRAIG JAMES
(Known by middle name.)
Fullback—New England Patriots
Born January 2, 1961, at Jacksonville, Tex.
Height, 6.00. Weight, 215.
High School—Houston, Tex., Stratford.
Received degree in history from Southern Methodist University.
Brother of Chris James, outfielder with Philadelphia Phillies.

Selected by Washington in 1st round (4th player selected) of 1983 USFL draft.
Signed by Washington Federals, January 12, 1983.
Selected by New England in 7th round (187th player selected) of 1983 NFL draft.
On developmental squad, March 19 through April 14, 1983; activated, April 15, 1983.
On developmental squad, March 9 through April 11, 1984.
Released with knee injury by Washington Federals, April 12, 1984; signed by New England Patriots, April 20, 1984.
On developmental squad for 4 games with Washington Federals in 1983.
On developmental squad for 5 games with Washington Federals in 1984.

		—RUSHING—				PASS RECEIVING				—TOTAL—		
Year Club	G.	Att.	Yds.	Avg.	TD.	P.C.	Yds.	Avg.	TD.	TD.	Pts.	F.
1983—Washington USFL	14	202	823	4.1	4	40	342	8.6	2	6	36	6
1984—Washington USFL	2	16	61	3.8	0	1	13	13.0	0	0	0	0
1984—New England NFL	15	160	790	4.9	1	22	159	7.2	0	1	6	4
1985—New England NFL	16	263	1227	4.7	5	27	360	13.3	2	7	42	8
USFL Totals—2 Years	16	218	884	4.1	4	41	355	8.7	2	6	36	6
NFL Totals—2 Years	31	423	2017	4.8	6	49	519	10.6	2	8	48	12
Pro Totals—4 Years	47	641	2901	4.5	10	90	874	9.7	4	14	84	18

Additional pro statistics: Returned one kickoff for no yards, attempted two passes with two completions for 16 yards and two touchdowns and recovered four fumbles, 1985.
Played in AFC Championship Game following 1985 season.
Played in NFL Championship Game following 1985 season.
Played in Pro Bowl (NFL All-Star Game) following 1985 season.

JUNE JAMES IV
Linebacker—Detroit Lions
Born December 2, 1962, at Jennings, La.
Height, 6.01. Weight, 218.
High School—Kansas City, Mo., Southeast.
Attended University of Texas.

Selected by San Antonio in 1985 USFL territorial draft.
Selected by Detroit in 9th round (230th player selected) of 1985 NFL draft.
Signed by Detroit Lions, July 21, 1985.
Detroit NFL, 1985.
Games: 1985 (16).
Pro statistics: Recovered one fumble, 1985.

LIONEL JAMES
Running Back-Kick Returner—San Diego Chargers
Born May 25, 1962, at Albany, Ga.
Height, 5.06. Weight, 172.
High School—Albany, Ga., Dougherty.
Attended Auburn University.

Established NFL records for most combined yards gained, season (2,535), 1985; most 300-yard combined yardage games, season (2), 1985; most pass reception yards by running back, season (1,027), 1985.
Selected by Birmingham in 1984 USFL territorial draft.
Selected by San Diego in 5th round (118th player selected) of 1984 NFL draft.
Signed by San Diego Chargers, June 8, 1984.

		—RUSHING—				PASS RECEIVING				—TOTAL—		
Year Club	G.	Att.	Yds.	Avg.	TD.	P.C.	Yds.	Avg.	TD.	TD.	Pts.	F.
1984—San Diego NFL	16	25	115	4.6	0	23	206	9.0	0	1	6	9
1985—San Diego NFL	16	105	516	4.9	2	86	1027	11.9	6	8	48	9
Pro Totals—2 Years	32	130	631	4.9	2	109	1233	11.3	6	9	54	18

		—PUNT RETURNS—				—KICKOFF RET.—		
Year Club	G.	No.	Yds.	Avg.	TD.	No.	Yds.	Avg.TD.
1984—San Diego NFL	16	30	208	6.9	1	*43	*959	22.3 0
1985—San Diego NFL	16	25	213	8.5	0	36	779	21.6 0
Pro Totals—2 Years	32	55	421	7.7	1	79	1738	22.0 0

Additional pro statistics: Attempted two passes with no completions and one interception and recovered four fumbles, 1984; recovered one fumble, 1985.

ROLAND ORLANDO JAMES
Safety—New England Patriots
Born February 18, 1958, at Xenia, O.
Height, 6.02. Weight, 191.
High School—Jamestown, O., Greenview.
Attended University of Tennessee.

Named as cornerback on THE SPORTING NEWS College All-America Team, 1979.
Selected by New England in 1st round (14th player selected) of 1980 NFL draft.
On injured reserve with knee injury, January 6, 1983 through remainder of 1982 season playoffs.

		—INTERCEPTIONS—				-PUNT RETURNS-				—TOTAL—		
Year Club	G.	No.	Yds.	Avg.	TD.	No.	Yds.	Avg.	TD.	TD.	Pts.	F.
1980—New England NFL	16	4	32	8.0	0	33	331	10.0	1	1	6	2
1981—New England NFL	16	2	29	14.5	0	7	56	8.0	0	0	0	1
1982—New England NFL	7	3	12	4.0	0		None			0	0	1
1983—New England NFL	16	5	99	19.8	0		None			0	0	0
1984—New England NFL	15	2	14	7.0	0		None			0	0	0
1985—New England NFL	16	4	51	12.8	0	2	13	6.5	0	0	0	1
Pro Totals—6 Years	86	20	237	11.9	0	42	400	9.5	1	1	6	5

Additional pro statistics: Recovered one fumble, 1980, 1981 and 1984; recovered four fumbles, 1983; credited with one safety, 1984.
Played in AFC Championship Game following 1985 season.
Played in NFL Championship Game following 1985 season.

RONNIE NATHANIEL JAMES
Fullback—Los Angeles Raiders
Born January 2, 1961, at Los Angeles, Calif.
Height, 6.02. Weight, 230.
High School—Houston, Tex., Jack Yates.
Attended Texas A&M University and Grambling State University.

Signed as free agent by Los Angeles Express, March 28, 1984.
On developmental squad, March 28 through May 10, 1984; activated, May 11, 1984.
On developmental squad, June 9 through remainder of 1984 season.
Released by Los Angeles Express, January 11, 1985; signed as free agent by Los Angeles Raiders, February 21, 1985.
Released by Los Angeles Raiders, August 20, 1985; re-signed by Raiders, May 2, 1986.
On developmental squad for 9 games with Los Angeles Express in 1984.
Los Angeles USFL, 1984.
Games: 1984 (5).
Pro statistics: Returned one kickoff for seven yards, 1984.

JOHN MICHAEL JANATA
Offensive Tackle—Tampa Bay Buccaneers
Born April 10, 1961, at Chicago, Ill.
Height, 6.07. Weight, 255.
High School—Las Vegas, Nev., Bonanza.
Attended Antelope Valley College and University of Illinois.

Signed as free agent by Chicago Bears, May 4, 1983.
Released by Chicago Bears, August 27, 1984; signed as free agent by Tampa Bay Buccaneers, February 17, 1985.
On injured reserve with elbow and wrist injuries, August 20 through entire 1985 season.
Chicago NFL, 1983.
Games: 1983 (15).
Pro statistics: Returned one kickoff for two yards and recovered one fumble, 1983.

RONALD VINCENT JAWORSKI
(Ron)
Quarterback—Philadelphia Eagles
Born March 23, 1951, at Lackawanna, N. Y.
Height, 6.02. Weight, 196.
High School—Lackawanna, N. Y.
Attended Youngstown State University.

Tied NFL record for longest completed passing play from scrimmage when he threw a 99-yard touchdown pass to wide receiver Mike Quick against Atlanta Falcons, November 10, 1985.
Selected by Los Angeles in 2nd round (37th player selected) of 1973 NFL draft.
Member of Los Angeles Rams' taxi squad, 1973.
Traded by Los Angeles Rams to Philadelphia Eagles for tight end Charle Young, March 10, 1977.
On injured reserve with broken fibula, November 27 through remainder of 1984 season.

		——PASSING——							——RUSHING——				—TOTAL—		
Year Club	G.	Att.	Cmp.	Pct.	Gain	T.P.	P.I.	Avg.	Att.	Yds.	Avg.	TD.	TD.	Pts.	F.
1974—Los Angeles NFL	5	24	10	41.7	144	0	1	6.00	7	34	4.9	1	1	6	1
1975—Los Angeles NFL	14	48	24	50.0	302	0	2	6.29	12	33	2.8	2	2	12	1
1976—Los Angeles NFL	5	52	20	28.5	273	1	5	5.25	2	15	7.5	1	1	6	0
1977—Philadelphia NFL	14	346	166	48.0	2183	18	21	6.31	40	127	3.2	5	5	30	6
1978—Philadelphia NFL	16	398	206	51.8	2487	16	16	6.25	30	79	2.6	0	0	0	7
1979—Philadelphia NFL	16	374	190	50.8	2669	18	12	7.14	43	119	2.8	2	2	12	12
1980—Philadelphia NFL	16	451	257	57.0	3529	27	12	7.82	27	95	3.5	1	1	6	6
1981—Philadelphia NFL	16	461	250	54.2	3095	23	20	6.71	22	128	5.8	0	0	0	3

Year Club	G.	Att.	Cmp.	Pct.	—PASSING—Gain	T.P.	P.I.	Avg.	—RUSHING—Att.	Yds.	Avg.	TD.	—TOTAL—TD.	Pts.	F.
1982—Philadelphia NFL	9	286	167	58.4	2076	12	12	7.26	10	9	0.9	0	0	0	9
1983—Philadelphia NFL	16	446	235	52.7	3315	20	18	7.43	25	129	5.2	1	1	6	11
1984—Philadelphia NFL	13	427	234	54.8	2754	16	14	6.45	5	18	3.6	1	1	6	5
1985—Philadelphia NFL	16	484	255	52.7	3450	17	20	7.13	17	35	2.1	2	2	12	5
Pro Totals—12 Years.........	156	3797	2014	53.0	26277	168	153	6.92	240	821	3.4	16	16	96	66

Quarterback Rating Points: 1974 (44.3), 1975 (52.5), 1976 (22.8), 1977 (60.3), 1978 (68.0), 1979 (76.8), 1980 (90.9), 1981 (74.0), 1982 (77.5), 1983 (75.1), 1984 (73.5), 1985 (70.2). Total—73.1.

Additional pro statistics: Recovered two fumbles and fumbled once for minus three yards, 1975; recovered three fumbles and fumbled six times for minus four yards, 1977; recovered three fumbles and fumbled seven times for minus one yard, 1978; recovered five fumbles and fumbled 12 times for minus 23 yards, 1979; recovered four fumbles, 1980 and 1983; recovered three fumbles and fumbled three times for minus two yards, 1981; recovered four fumbles and fumbled nine times for minus 11 yards, 1982; recovered two fumbles, 1984 and 1985.

Played in NFC Championship Game following 1975 and 1980 seasons.
Member of Los Angeles Rams for NFC Championship Game following 1974 and 1976 seasons; did not play.
Played in NFL Championship Game following 1980 season.
Played in Pro Bowl (NFL All-Star Game) following 1980 season.

JAMES WILSON JEFFCOAT JR.
(Jim)
Defensive End—Dallas Cowboys
Born April 1, 1961, at Long Branch, N.J.
Height, 6.05. Weight, 263.
High School—Matawan, N.J., Regional.
Received bachelor of arts degree in communications
from Arizona State University in 1983.

Selected by Arizona in 1983 USFL territorial draft.
Selected by Dallas in 1st round (23rd player selected) of 1983 NFL draft.
Signed by Dallas Cowboys, May 24, 1983.
Dallas NFL, 1983 through 1985.
Games: 1983 (16), 1984 (16), 1985 (16). Total—48.
Pro statistics: Recovered fumble in end zone for a touchdown, 1984; intercepted one pass for 65 yards and a touchdown and recovered two fumbles, 1985.

JOHN LARRY JEFFERSON
Wide Receiver—Houston Oilers
Born February 3, 1956, Dallas, Tex.
Height, 6.01. Weight, 204.
High School—Dallas, Tex., Roosevelt.
Attended Arizona State University.

Named to THE SPORTING NEWS AFC All-Star Team, 1979.
Named to THE SPORTING NEWS NFL All-Star Team, 1980.
Selected by San Diego in 1st round (14th player selected) of 1978 NFL draft.
On did not report list, August 17 through September 16, 1981.
Traded with 1st round pick in 1982 draft by San Diego Chargers to Green Bay Packers for wide receiver Aundra Thompson, 1st round pick in 1982 and 1983 drafts and 2nd round picks in 1982 and 1984 drafts, September 17, 1981.
Granted free agency, February 1, 1985; re-signed by Green Bay Packers, September 18, 1985.
Granted roster exemption, September 18 through September 25, 1985; activated, September 26, 1985.
Traded by Green Bay Packers to Cleveland Browns for rights to offensive tackle Tommy Robison and 7th round pick in 1987 draft, September 19, 1985.
Released by Cleveland Browns, November 12, 1985; signed as free agent by Houston Oilers, May 21, 1986.

Year Club	G.	P.C.	—PASS RECEIVING—Yds.	Avg.	TD.
1978—San Diego NFL	14	56	1001	17.9	*13
1979—San Diego NFL	15	61	1090	17.9	10
1980—San Diego NFL	16	82	*1340	16.3	*13
1981—Green Bay NFL.............	13	39	632	16.2	4
1982—Green Bay NFL.............	8	27	452	16.7	0
1983—Green Bay NFL...........	16	57	830	14.6	7
1984—Green Bay NFL...........	13	26	339	13.0	0
1985—Cleveland NFL.............	7	3	30	10.0	0
Pro Totals—8 Years...........	102	351	5714	16.3	47

Additional pro statistics: Rushed once for seven yards and recovered one fumble, 1978; rushed once for 16 yards and returned one kickoff for no yards, 1980; rushed twice for 22 yards and returned one kickoff for three yards, 1981; rushed two times for 16 yards, 1982; fumbled once, 1983.
Played in AFC Championship Game following 1980 season.
Played in Pro Bowl (NFL All-Star Game) following 1978 through 1980 and 1982 seasons.

THOMAS JOHN JELESKY
(Tom)
Offensive Tackle—Philadelphia Eagles
Born October 4, 1960, at Merrillville, Ind.
Height, 6.06. Weight, 275.
High School—Merrillville, Ind.
Attended Purdue University.

Signed as free agent by Philadelphia Eagles, December 14, 1983.
Selected by Denver in 14th round (277th player selected) of 1984 USFL draft.
On injured reserve with knee injury, August 27 through entire 1984 season.
Active for 1 game with Philadelphia Eagles in 1983, did not play.
Philadephia NFL, 1983 and 1985.
Games: 1985 (16).

FLETCHER JENKINS
Defensive End—New Orleans Saints
Born November 4, 1959, at Tacoma, Wash.
Height, 6.02. Weight, 258.
High School—Tacoma, Wash., Lakes.
Attended University of Washington.

Selected by Baltimore in 7th round (169th player selected) of 1982 NFL draft.
Released by Baltimore Colts, August 29, 1983; signed by Los Angeles Express, October 25, 1983.
On developmental squad, June 15 through June 26, 1984; activated, June 27, 1984.
Granted free agency, August 1, 1985; signed as free agent by New Orleans Saints, May 13, 1986.
On developmental squad for 2 games with Los Angeles Express in 1984.
Baltimore NFL, 1982; Los Angeles USFL, 1984 and 1985.
Games: 1982 (9), 1984 (16), 1985 (17). Total—42.
NFL statistics: Recovered one fumble, 1982.
USFL statistics: Credited with five sacks for 35 yards, 1984; credited with three sacks for 13 yards and recovered one fumble, 1985.

KENNETH WALTON JENKINS
(Ken)
Kick Returner—Washington Redskins
Born May 8, 1959, at Washington, D.C.
Height, 5.08. Weight, 183.
High School—Bethesda, Md., Landon.
Received degree in business administration from Bucknell University.

Signed as free agent by Philadelphia Eagles, May 8, 1982.
On injured reserve with broken toe, September 6 through entire 1982 season.
Released by Philadelphia Eagles, August 29, 1983; signed as free agent by Detroit Lions, September 29, 1983.
Released by Detroit Lions, September 2, 1985; signed as free agent by Washington Redskins, September 11, 1985.
On injured reserve with dislocated shoulder, December 11 through remainder of 1985 season.

			—RUSHING—			PASS RECEIVING				—TOTAL—		
Year Club	G.	Att.	Yds.	Avg.	TD.	P.C.	Yds.	Avg.	TD.	TD.	Pts.	F.
1983—Detroit NFL	12		None				None			0	0	2
1984—Detroit NFL	14	78	358	4.6	1	21	246	11.7	0	1	6	0
1985—Washington NFL	13	2	39	19.5	0		None			0	0	1
Pro Totals—3 Years	39	80	397	5.0	1	21	246	11.7	0	1	6	3

		—PUNT RETURNS—				—KICKOFF RET.—			
Year Club	G.	No.	Yds.	Avg.	TD.	No.	Yds.	Avg.	TD.
1983—Detroit NFL	12	23	230	10.0	0	22	459	20.9	0
1984—Detroit NFL	14	1	1	1.0	0	18	396	22.0	0
1985—Washington NFL	13	26	272	10.5	0	41	1018	24.8	0
Pro Totals—3 Years	39	50	503	10.1	0	81	1873	23.1	0

Additional pro statistics: Recovered one fumble, 1983 through 1985; attempted one pass with no completions, 1984.

DAVID TUTHILL JENNINGS
(Dave)
Punter—New York Jets
Born June 8, 1952, at New York, N. Y.
Height, 6.04. Weight, 200.
High School—Garden City, N. Y.
Received bachelor of arts degree in economics from St. Lawrence University in 1974.
Cousin of Carlton Fisk, outfielder-catcher with Chicago White Sox.

Named to The Sporting News NFC All-Star Team, 1979.
Named to The Sporting News NFL All-Star Team, 1980.
Led NFL punters in yards with 4,445 in 1979 and 4,211 in 1980.
Signed as free agent by Houston Oilers, 1974.
Released by Houston Oilers and signed as free agent by New York Giants, July, 1974.
Released by New York Giants, August 27, 1985; awarded on waivers to New York Jets, August 28, 1985.

	—PUNTING—					—PUNTING—			
Year Club	G.	No.	Avg.	Blk.	Year Club	G.	No.	Avg.	Blk.
1974—New York Giants NFL	14	68	39.8	*2	1981—New York Giants NFL	16	97	43.3	0
1975—New York Giants NFL	14	76	40.9	0	1982—New York Giants NFL	9	49	42.8	0
1976—New York Giants NFL	14	74	41.3	3	1983—New York Giants NFL	16	84	40.3	1
1977—New York Giants NFL	14	100	39.9	0	1984—New York Giants NFL	16	90	40.0	*3
1978—New York Giants NFL	16	95	42.1	0	1985—New York Jets NFL	16	74	40.2	0
1979—New York Giants NFL	16	*104	42.7	0	Pro Totals—12 Years	177	1005	41.5	9
1980—New York Giants NFL	16	94	*44.8	0					

Additional pro statistics: Rushed once for no yards, recovered two fumbles, fumbled once for minus 13 yards and attempted one pass with one completion for minus one yard, 1978; rushed twice for 11 yards and attempted two passes with two completions for 48 yards, 1979; attempted one pass with no completions, 1983.
Played in Pro Bowl (NFL All-Star Game) following 1978 through 1980 and 1982 seasons.

STANFORD JAMISON JENNINGS
Running Back—Cincinnati Bengals
Born March 12, 1962, at Summerville, S.C.
Height, 6.01. Weight, 205.
High School—Summerville, S.C.
Attended Furman University.

Selected by Michigan in 1st round (17th player selected) of 1984 USFL draft.
Selected by Cincinnati in 3rd round (65th player selected) of 1984 NFL draft.
Signed by Cincinnati Bengals, July 2, 1984.

		—RUSHING—				PASS RECEIVING				—TOTAL—		
Year Club	G.	Att.	Yds.	Avg.	TD.	P.C.	Yds.	Avg.	TD.	TD.	Pts.	F.
1984—Cincinnati NFL	15	79	379	4.8	2	35	346	9.9	3	5	30	3
1985—Cincinnati NFL	16	31	92	3.0	1	12	101	8.4	3	4	24	1
Pro Totals—2 Years	31	110	471	4.3	3	47	447	9.5	6	9	54	4

		KICKOFF RETURNS			
Year Club	G.	No.	Yds.	Avg.	TD.
1984—Cincinnati NFL	15	22	452	20.5	0
1985—Cincinnati NFL	16	13	218	16.8	0
Pro Totals—2 Years	31	35	670	19.1	0

Additional pro statistics: Recovered two fumbles, 1984; recovered one fumble, 1985.

DERRICK JENSEN
Running Back—Los Angeles Raiders
Born April 27, 1956, at Waukegan, Ill.
Height, 6.01. Weight, 220.
High Schools—Waukegan, Ill. and Osawatomie, Kan.
Attended University of Texas at Arlington.

Selected by Oakland in 3rd round (57th player selected) of 1978 NFL draft.
On injured reserve, August 29 through entire 1978 season.
Franchise transferred to Los Angeles, May 7, 1982.

		—RUSHING—				PASS RECEIVING				—TOTAL—		
Year Club	G.	Att.	Yds.	Avg.	TD.	P.C.	Yds.	Avg.	TD.	TD.	Pts.	F.
1979—Oakland NFL	16	73	251	3.4	0	7	23	3.3	1	1	6	6
1980—Oakland NFL	16	14	30	2.1	0	7	87	12.4	0	1	6	1
1981—Oakland NFL	16	117	456	3.9	4	28	271	9.7	0	4	24	0
1982—Los Angeles Raiders NFL	9		None				None			0	0	0
1983—Los Angeles Raiders NFL	16	1	5	5.0	0	1	2	2.0	1	1	6	1
1984—Los Angeles Raiders NFL	16	3	3	1.0	1	1	1	1.0	1	2	12	0
1985—Los Angeles Raiders NFL	16	16	35	2.2	0		None			0	0	0
Pro Totals—7 Years	105	224	780	3.5	5	44	384	8.7	3	9	54	8

Additional pro statistics: Recovered three fumbles, 1979, returned one kickoff for no yards, 1979 and 1983; returned one kickoff for 33 yards and a touchdown, 1980; recovered one fumble, 1981; returned one kickoff for 27 yards, 1982; returned one kickoff for 11 yards, 1984.
Played in AFC Championship Game following 1980 and 1983 seasons.
Played in NFL Championship Game following 1980 and 1983 seasons.

JAMES CHRISTOPHER JENSEN
(Jim)
Wide Receiver—Miami Dolphins
Born November 14, 1958, at Abington, Pa.
Height, 6.04. Weight, 215.
High School—Doylestown, Pa., Central Bucks.
Received bachelor of science degree in special education from Boston University in 1981.

Selected by Miami in 11th round (291st player selected) of 1981 NFL draft.
On inactive list, September 12 and September 19, 1982.
Granted free agency, February 1, 1985; re-signed by Dolphins, August 31, 1985.
Granted roster exemption, August 31 through September 6, 1985; activated, September 7, 1985.

		—PASS RECEIVING—			
Year Club	G.	P.C.	Yds.	Avg.	TD.
1981—Miami NFL	16		None		
1982—Miami NFL	6		None		
1983—Miami NFL	16		None		
1984—Miami NFL	16	13	139	10.7	2
1985—Miami NFL	16	1	4	4.0	1
Pro Totals—5 Years	70	14	143	10.2	3

Additional pro statistics: Attempted one pass with no completions, 1982; attempted one pass with one completion for 35 yards and a touchdown, 1984.
Played in AFC Championship Game following 1982, 1984 and 1985 seasons.
Played in NFL Championship Game following 1982 and 1984 seasons.

RUSSELL D. JENSEN
(Russ)
Quarterback—Los Angeles Raiders
Born July 13, 1961, at Whittier, Calif.
Height, 6.03. Weight, 215.
High School—La Mirada, Calif.
Attended San Francisco State University and received bachelor of arts degree
in psychology from California Lutheran College.

Selected by Los Angeles in 1983 USFL territorial draft.
Signed by Los Angeles Express, January 20, 1983.
On developmental squad, March 4 through July 1, 1983; activated, July 2, 1983.
On developmental squad, February 24 through June 21, 1984; activated, June 22, 1984.
On developmental squad, February 24 through February 27, 1985.
Left Los Angeles Express voluntarily and granted roster exemption, February 28 through March 3, 1985.
Released by Los Angeles Express, March 4, 1985; signed as free agent by Los Angeles Raiders, March 20, 1985.
On injured reserve with broken thumb, August 20 through September 27, 1985; activated after clearing procedural waivers, September 29, 1985.
Released by Los Angeles Raiders, October 8, 1985; re-signed by Raiders, October 23, 1985.
On injured reserve with broken thumb, October 23 through remainder of 1985 season.
On developmental squad for 17 games with Los Angeles Express in 1983 and 1984.
On developmental squad for 1 game with Los Angeles Express in 1985.
Active for 1 game with Los Angeles Raiders in 1985; did not play.

				—PASSING—					—RUSHING—			—TOTAL—		
Year	Club	G.	Att.	Cmp.	Pct.	Gain	T.P.	P.I.	Avg.	Att. Yds.	Avg. TD.	TD.	Pts.	F.
1984—Los Angeles USFL............		1	6	2	33.3	33	0	1	5.50	None		0	0	0

Quarterback Rating Points: 1984 (13.2).

MARK DARRELL JERUE
Linebacker—Los Angeles Rams
Born January 15, 1960, at Seattle, Wash.
Height, 6.03. Weight, 229.
High School—Mercer Island, Wash.
Attended University of Washington.

Selected by New York Jets in 5th round (135th player selected) of 1982 NFL draft.
On injured reserve with heart irregularity, August 24 through entire 1982 season.
Released by New York Jets, August 29, 1983; awarded on waivers to Baltimore Colts, August 30, 1983.
Traded by Baltimore Colts to Los Angeles Rams for quarterback Mark Reed, August 30, 1983.
USFL rights traded with rights to running back Ted McKnight and 1st and 5th round picks in 1984 draft by Jacksonville Bulls to Oakland Invaders for rights to quarterback Turk Schonert, October 24, 1983.
Los Angeles Rams NFL, 1983 through 1985.
Games: 1983 (16), 1984 (16), 1985 (16). Total—48.
Pro statistics: Recovered one fumble, 1985.
Played in NFC Championship Game following 1985 season.

GARY MICHAEL JETER
Defensive End—Los Angeles Rams
Born January 24, 1955, at Weirton, W. Va.
Height, 6.04. Weight, 260.
High School—Cleveland, O., Cathedral Latin.
Attended University of Southern California.
Nephew of Bob Jeter, back with Green Bay Packers and Chicago Bears, 1963 through 1973;
and Tony Jeter, end with Pittsburgh Steelers, 1966 and 1968.

Selected by New York Giants in 1st round (5th player selected) of 1977 NFL draft.
On injured reserve with knee injury, December 8 through remainder of 1978 season.
On injured reserve with knee injury, September 1 through October 1, 1981; activated, October 2, 1981.
On inactive list, September 20, 1982.
On injured reserve with knee injury, November 24 through December 23, 1982; activated, December 24, 1982.
Traded by New York Giants to Los Angeles Rams for 3rd and 6th round picks in 1983 draft, April 13, 1983.
On injured reserve with herniated disc, August 28 through November 8, 1984; activated, November 9, 1984.
New York Giants NFL, 1977 through 1982; Los Angeles Rams NFL, 1983 through 1985.
Games: 1977 (14), 1978 (13), 1979 (16), 1980 (16), 1981 (12), 1982 (4), 1983 (16), 1984 (5), 1985 (16). Total—112.
Pro statistics: Recovered one fumble, 1978, 1979 and 1985; recovered three fumbles for seven yards, 1980.
Played in NFC Championship Game following 1985 season.

DWAYNE JILES
Name pronounced Giles.
Linebacker—Philadelphia Eagles
Born November 23, 1961, at Linden, Tex.
Height, 6.04. Weight, 242.
High School—Linden, Tex., Kildare.
Attended Texas Tech University.

Selected by Denver in 1985 USFL territorial draft.
Selected by Philadelphia in 5th round (121st player selected) of 1985 NFL draft.
Signed by Philadelphia Eagles, July 23, 1985.
On injured reserve with cracked vertebra, August 27 through October 17, 1985; activated, October 18, 1985.
Philadelphia NFL, 1985.
Games: 1985 (10).

BOBBY CHARLES JOHNSON
Safety—St. Louis Cardinals
Born September 1, 1960, at La Grange, Tex.
Height, 6.00. Weight, 186.
High School—La Grange, Tex.
Attended University of Texas.
Brother of Johnnie Johnson, safety with Los Angeles Rams.

Signed as free agent by Dallas Cowboys, May 4, 1982.
Released by Dallas Cowboys, September 6, 1982; signed as free agent by New Orleans Saints, June 27, 1983.
Released by New Orleans Saints, August 29, 1983; re-signed by Saints, August 30, 1983.
Released by New Orleans Saints, August 26, 1985; signed as free agent by St. Louis Cardinals, August 29, 1985.
On injured reserve with knee injury, September 10 through October 17, 1985; activated, October 18, 1985.

Year Club	G.	No.	Yds.	Avg.	TD.
1983—New Orleans NFL	16	2	80	40.0	1
1984—New Orleans NFL	16	1	7	7.0	0
1985—St. Louis NFL	11		None		
Pro Totals—3 Years	43	3	87	29.0	1

Additional pro statistics: Recovered one fumble, 1983 and 1985; fumbled once, 1983.

BOBBY LEE JOHNSON
Wide Receiver—New York Giants
Born December 14, 1961, at East St. Louis, Ill.
Height, 5.11. Weight, 171.
High School—East St. Louis, Ill., Assumption.
Attended Independence Junior College and Kansas University.

Selected by Philadelphia in 3rd round (65th player selected) of 1984 USFL draft.
Signed by Philadelphia Stars, February 7, 1984.
Released by Philadelphia Stars, February 20, 1984; signed as free agent by New York Giants, May 16, 1984.

Year Club	G.	P.C.	Yds.	Avg.	TD.
1984—N.Y. Giants NFL	16	48	795	16.6	7
1985—N.Y. Giants NFL	16	33	533	16.2	8
Pro Totals—2 Years	32	81	1328	16.4	15

CECIL ELLORD JOHNSON
Linebacker
Born August 19, 1955, at Miami, Fla.
Height, 6.02. Weight, 235.
High School—Miami, Fla., Jackson.
Received bachelor of arts degree in sociology from University of Pittsburgh.
Brother of Robert Johnson, drummer with K.C. and the Sunshine Band.

Signed as free agent by Tampa Bay Buccaneers, May, 1977.
On injured reserve with foot and back injuries, October 5 through remainder of 1983 season.
On injured reserve with knee injury, October 26 through remainder of 1984 season.
Granted free agency with no qualifying offer, February 1, 1986.

Year Club	G.	No.	Yds.	Avg.	TD.
1977—Tampa Bay NFL	13	1	0	0.0	0
1978—Tampa Bay NFL	13	2	5	2.5	0
1979—Tampa Bay NFL	15		None		
1980—Tampa Bay NFL	16		None		
1981—Tampa Bay NFL	16	5	84	16.8	0
1982—Tampa Bay NFL	9		None		
1983—Tampa Bay NFL	5		None		
1984—Tampa Bay NFL	8		None		
1985—Tampa Bay NFL	16	1	12	12.0	0
Pro Totals—9 Years	111	9	101	11.2	0

Additional pro statistics: Fumbled once, 1977 and 1981; recovered four fumbles, 1977 and 1979; recovered two fumbles, 1978; recovered one fumble, 1985.
Played in NFC Championship Game following 1979 season.

DAMIAN JOHNSON
Offensive Tackle—New York Giants
Born December 18, 1962, at Great Bend, Kan.
Height, 6.05. Weight, 290.
High School—Great Bend, Kan.
Attended Kansas State University.

Selected by Jacksonville in 15th round (205th player selected) of 1985 USFL draft.
Signed as free agent by New York Giants, May 7, 1985.
On injured reserve with knee injury, September 2 through entire 1985 season.

DANIEL JEROME JOHNSON
(Dan)
Tight End—Miami Dolphins
Born May 17, 1960, at Minneapolis, Minn.
Height, 6.03. Weight, 240.
High School—New Hope, Minn., Cooper.
Attended Golden Valley Lutheran Junior College and Iowa State University.

Selected by Miami in 7th round (170th player selected) of 1982 NFL draft.
On injured reserve with shin splints, September 6 through entire 1982 season.
Granted free agency, February 1, 1985; re-signed by Dolphins, August 25, 1985.
Granted roster exemption, August 25 and August 26, 1985.
On non-football injury list with appendectomy, August 27 through October 4, 1985; activated, October 5, 1985.

| | | —PASS RECEIVING— | | | |
Year Club	G.	P.C.	Yds.	Avg.	TD.
1983—Miami NFL	16	24	189	7.9	4
1984—Miami NFL	16	34	426	12.5	3
1985—Miami NFL	12	13	192	14.8	3
Pro Totals—3 Years	44	71	807	11.4	10

Additional pro statistics: Fumbled once, 1983.
Played in AFC Championship Game following 1984 and 1985 seasons.
Played in NFL Championship Game following 1984 season.

DEMETRIOUS JOHNSON
Safety—Detroit Lions
Born July 21, 1961, at St. Louis, Mo.
Height, 5.11. Weight, 190.
High School—St. Louis, Mo., McKinley.
Received degree in counseling psychology from University of Missouri.

Selected by Denver in 1st round (9th player selected) of 1983 USFL draft.
Selected by Detroit in 5th round (115th player selected) of 1983 NFL draft.
Signed by Detroit Lions, June 1, 1983.
Detroit NFL, 1983 through 1985.
Games: 1983 (14), 1984 (16), 1985 (16). Total—46.
Pro statistics: Recovered one fumble, 1983 and 1984; returned one punt for no yards, 1984; intercepted three passes for 39 yards, recovered five fumbles for 24 yards and fumbled once, 1985.

DENNIS CRAIG JOHNSON
Linebacker—Tampa Bay Buccaneers
Born June 19, 1958, at Flint, Mich.
Height, 6.03. Weight, 235.
High School—Flint, Mich., Northwestern.
Attended University of Southern California.

Named as linebacker on THE SPORTING NEWS College All-America Team, 1979.
Selected by Minnesota in 4th round (92nd player selected) of 1980 NFL draft.
On injured reserve with knee injury, September 2 through October 3, 1980; activated, October 4, 1980.
Released by Minnesota Vikings, October 29, 1985; awarded on waivers to Tampa Bay Buccaneers, October 30, 1985.
Minnesota NFL, 1980 through 1984; Minnesota (8)-Tampa Bay (8) NFL, 1985.
Games: 1980 (12), 1981 (16), 1982 (9), 1983 (16), 1984 (16), 1985 (16). Total—85.
Pro statistics: Recovered one fumble, 1980, 1984 and 1985; recovered two fumbles, 1982.

EARL JOHNSON
Cornerback—New Orleans Saints
Born October 20, 1963, at Daytona Beach, Fla.
Height, 6.00. Weight, 190.
High School—Daytona Beach, Fla., Seabreeze.
Attended University of South Carolina.

Selected by Los Angeles in 1985 USFL territorial draft.
Selected by New Orleans in 9th round (236th player selected) of 1985 NFL draft.
Signed by New Orleans Saints, July 16, 1985.
On injured reserve with knee injury, August 20 through December 12, 1985; activated, December 13, 1985.
New Orleans NFL, 1985.
Games: 1985 (2).

EDDIE JOHNSON
Linebacker—Cleveland Browns
Born February 3, 1959, at Albany, Ga.
Height, 6.01. Weight, 225.
High School—Albany, Ga., Daughtery.
Attended University of Louisville.

Selected by Cleveland in 7th round (187th player selected) of 1981 NFL draft.
Cleveland NFL, 1981 through 1985.
Games: 1981 (16), 1982 (9), 1983 (16), 1984 (16), 1985 (16). Total—73.
Pro statistics: Returned one kickoff for seven yards and recovered one fumble, 1981; intercepted two passes for three yards, 1984; intercepted one pass for six yards, 1985.

EZRA RAY JOHNSON
Defensive End—Green Bay Packers
Born October 2, 1955, at Shreveport, La.
Height, 6.04. Weight, 259.
High School—Shreveport, La., Green Oaks.
Attended Morris Brown College.

Selected by Green Bay in 1st round (28th player selected) of 1977 NFL draft.
On injured reserve with knee injury, December 14 through remainder of 1984 season.
Green Bay NFL, 1977 through 1985.
Games: 1977 (14), 1978 (16), 1979 (11), 1980 (15), 1981 (16), 1982 (9), 1983 (16), 1984 (13), 1985 (16). Total—126.
Pro statistics: Recovered one fumble, 1977; recovered two fumbles, 1978 and 1985; returned one kickoff for 14 yards, 1978; recovered two fumbles, 1983.
Played in Pro Bowl (NFL All-Star Game) following 1978 season.

GARY LYNN JOHNSON
Defensive Tackle—San Francisco 49ers
Born August 31, 1952, at Shreveport, La.
Height, 6.02. Weight, 251.
High School—Bossier City, La., Mitchell.
Attended Grambling State University.

Named to THE SPORTING NEWS NFL All-Star Team, 1980.
Selected by San Diego in 1st round (8th player selected) of 1975 NFL draft.
Traded by San Diego Chargers to San Francisco 49ers for 5th and 11th picks in 1986 draft, September 28, 1984.
On injured reserve with pulled chest muscle, November 26 through remainder of 1985 season.
San Diego NFL, 1975 through 1983; San Diego (4)-San Francisco (12) NFL, 1984; San Francisco NFL, 1985.
Games: 1975 (14), 1976 (14), 1977 (14), 1978 (15), 1979 (16), 1980 (16), 1981 (16), 1982 (9), 1983 (16), 1984 (16), 1985 (11). Total—157.
Pro statistics: Recovered one fumble, 1975, 1977 and 1981; intercepted one pass for 52 yards and a touchdown, 1978; recovered two fumbles for 36 yards and fumbled once, 1979; recovered three fumbles, 1980; intercepted one pass for 41 yards and a touchdown, 1981; credited with one safety, 1982 and 1984; recovered two fumbles, 1983; recovered three fumbles for 36 yards and a touchdown, 1984.
Played in AFC Championship Game following 1980 and 1981 seasons.
Played in NFC Championship Game following 1984 season.
Played in NFL Championship Game following 1984 season.
Played in Pro Bowl (NFL All-Star Game) following 1979 through 1982 seasons.

JAMES L. JOHNSON
Linebacker—Detroit Lions
Born June 21, 1962, at Los Angeles, Calif.
Height, 6.02. Weight, 235.
High School—Lake Elsinore, Calif.
Attended Orange Coast College and San Diego State University.

Selected by Portland in 4th round (50th player selected) of 1985 USFL draft.
Selected by Detroit in 3rd round (62nd player selected) of 1985 NFL draft.
Signed by Detroit Lions, July 26, 1985.
On injured reserve with back injury, September 2 through entire 1985 season.

JOHNNIE JOHNSON JR.
Safety—Los Angeles Rams
Born October 8, 1956, at La Grange, Tex.
Height, 6.01. Weight, 183.
High School—La Grange, Tex.
Attended University of Texas.
Brother of Bobby Johnson, safety with St. Louis Cardinals.

Named as safety on THE SPORTING NEWS College All-America Team, 1980.
Selected by Los Angeles in 1st round (17th player selected) of 1980 NFL draft.
On injured reserve with broken ankle, August 28 through October 16, 1984; activated, October 17, 1984.

| | | —INTERCEPTIONS— | | | |
Year Club	G.	No.	Yds.	Avg.	TD.
1980—L.A. Rams NFL.............	16	3	102	34.0	1
1981—L.A. Rams NFL.............	16		None		
1982—L.A. Rams NFL.............	9	1	7	7.0	0
1983—L.A. Rams NFL.............	16	4	115	28.8	★2
1984—L.A. Rams NFL.............	9	2	21	10.5	0
1985—L.A. Rams NFL.............	16	5	96	19.2	★1
Pro Totals—6 Years............	82	15	341	22.7	4

Additional pro statistics: Returned one punt for three yards, 1980 and 1984; recovered five fumbles for 16 yards, 1980; returned one punt for 39 yards and recovered five fumbles for five yards, 1981; recovered two fumbles for nine yards, 1982; returned 14 punts for 109 yards, recovered two fumbles for four yards and fumbled once, 1983; recovered one fumble, 1985.
Played in NFC Championship Game following 1985 season.

KENNETH RAY JOHNSON
(Kenny)
Safety—Atlanta Falcons
Born January 7, 1958, at Columbia, Miss.
Height, 5.11. Weight, 167.
High School—Moss Point, Miss.
Attended Mississippi State University.

Selected by Atlanta in 5th round (137th player selected) of 1980 NFL draft.
Tied NFL record for most touchdowns scored by interception, game (2), against Green Bay Packers, November 27, 1983.
On injured reserve with fractured shoulder blade, September 16 through December 6, 1985; activated, December 7, 1985.

Year Club	G.	INTERCEPTIONS No.	Yds.	Avg.	TD.	–PUNT RETURNS– No.	Yds.	Avg.	TD.	–KICKOFF RET.– No.	Yds.	Avg.	TD.	–TOTAL– TD.	Pts.	F.
1980—Atlanta NFL	16	4	49	12.3	0	23	281	12.2	0	None				0	0	2
1981—Atlanta NFL	16	3	35	11.7	0	4	6	1.5	0	None				2	12	1
1982—Atlanta NFL	9	2	30	15.0	0	None				None				0	0	0
1983—Atlanta NFL	16	2	57	28.5	*2	None				11	224	20.4	0	2	12	1
1984—Atlanta NFL	16	5	75	15.0	0	10	79	7.9	0	19	359	18.9	0	0	0	2
1985—Atlanta NFL	5	None				None				1	20	20.0	0	0	0	0
Pro Totals—6 Years	78	16	246	15.4	2	37	366	9.9	0	31	603	19.5	0	4	24	6

Additional pro statistics: Recovered four fumbles for seven yards, 1980; recovered two fumbles for 55 yards and two touchdowns, 1981; recovered one fumble, 1983.

LAWRENCE WENDELL JOHNSON
Cornerback—Buffalo Bills
Born September 11, 1957, at Gary, Ind.
Height, 5.11. Weight, 204.
High School—Gary, Ind., Roosevelt.
Attended University of Wisconsin.

Named as cornerback on THE SPORTING NEWS College All-America Team, 1978.
Selected by Cleveland in 2nd round (40th player selected) of 1979 NFL draft.
On injured reserve with shoulder injury, September 17 through remainder of 1980 season.
On injured reserve with knee injury, December 29 through remainder of 1982 season.
Traded by Cleveland Browns to Buffalo Bills for draft choice, October 9, 1984.

Year Club	G.	——INTERCEPTIONS—— No.	Yds.	Avg.	TD.
1979—Cleveland NFL	16	None			
1980—Cleveland NFL	2	1	3	3.0	0
1981—Cleveland NFL	16	None			
1982—Cleveland NFL	8	4	17	4.3	0
1983—Cleveland NFL	16	2	0	0.0	0
1984—Cle. (6)-Buf. (10) NFL..	16	1	0	0.0	0
1985—Buffalo NFL	16	1	0	0.0	0
Pro Totals—7 Years	90	9	20	2.2	0

Additional pro statistics: Recovered one fumble, 1980 and 1982.

LEE JOHNSON
Punter-Placekicker—Houston Oilers
Born November 2, 1961, at Dallas, Tex.
Height, 6.01. Weight, 204.
High School—The Woodlands, Tex., McCullough.
Attended Brigham Young University.

Selected by Houston in 9th round (125th player selected) of 1985 USFL draft.
Selected by Houston in 5th round (138th player selected) of 1985 NFL draft.
Signed by Houston Oilers, June 25, 1985.

Year Club	G.	——PUNTING—— No.	Avg.	Blk.
1985—Houston NFL	16	83	41.7	0

Additional pro statistics: Rushed once for no yards, recovered one fumble for seven yards and fumbled twice, 1985.

MICHAEL McCOLLY JOHNSON
(Butch)
Wide Receiver—Denver Broncos
Born May 28, 1954, at Los Angeles, Calif.
Height, 6.01. Weight, 187.
High School—Los Angeles, Calif., Dorsey.
Attended University of California at Riverside.
Brother-in-law of singer-songwriter Bill Withers;
cousin of former Massachusetts Senator Edward Brooke.

Tied NFL record for most punt returns, game (9), against Buffalo Bills, November 15, 1976.
Selected by Dallas in 3rd round (87th player selected) of 1976 NFL draft.
On injured reserve with broken finger, August 29 through October 4, 1979; activated, October 5, 1979.

Traded with 2nd round pick in 1984 draft by Dallas Cowboys to Houston Oilers for wide receiver Mike Renfro, 2nd round pick in 1984 draft and 5th round pick in 1985 draft, April 13, 1984.

Traded by Houston Oilers to Denver Broncos for 3rd round pick in 1985 draft, August 20, 1984.

			PASS RECEIVING			–PUNT RETURNS–				—KICKOFF RET.—				—TOTAL—		
Year	Club	G.	P.C.	Yds.	Avg. TD.	No.	Yds.	Avg.	TD.	No.	Yds.	Avg.	TD.	TD.	Pts.	F.
1976—Dallas NFL		14	5	84	16.8	2	45	489	10.9	0	28	693	24.8	0	2	12	5
1977—Dallas NFL		14	12	135	11.3	1	50	423	8.5	0	22	536	24.4	0	1	6	4
1978—Dallas NFL		16	12	155	12.9	0	51	401	7.9	0	29	603	20.8	0	0	0	5
1979—Dallas NFL		11	6	105	17.5	1	None				None				1	6	0
1980—Dallas NFL		16	19	263	13.8	4	None				None				4	24	0
1981—Dallas NFL		16	25	552	22.1	5	None				None				5	30	0
1982—Dallas NFL		9	12	269	22.4	3	None				None				3	18	0
1983—Dallas NFL		16	41	561	13.7	3	None				None				3	18	0
1984—Denver NFL		16	42	587	14.0	6	None				None				6	36	1
1985—Denver NFL		16	19	380	20.0	3	None				None				3	18	0
Pro Totals—10 Years		144	193	3091	16.0	28	146	1313	9.0	0	79	1832	23.2	0	28	168	15

Additional pro statistics: Recovered two fumbles, 1976 and 1977; rushed once for minus three yards, 1977; recovered one fumble, 1978; rushed once for 13 yards, 1979; rushed once for nine yards, 1982; rushed once for no yards, 1983; rushed once for three yards, 1984.

Played in NFC Championship Game following 1977, 1978 and 1980 through 1982 seasons.

Played in NFL Championship Game following 1977 and 1978 seasons.

MIKE JOHNSON
Defensive End—Houston Oilers
Born April 24, 1962, at Chicago, Ill.
Height, 6.05, Weight, 253.
High School—Chicago, Ill., South Shore.
Attended Arizona Western College and University of Illinois.

Selected by Chicago in 1984 USFL territorial draft.
Selected by Houston in 9th round (228th player selected) of 1984 NFL draft.
Signed by Houston Oilers, July 7, 1984.
On injured reserve with knee injury, August 19 through entire 1985 season.
Houston NFL, 1984.
Games: 1984 (16).
Pro statistics: Recovered one fumble, 1984.

NORM JOHNSON
Placekicker—Seattle Seahawks
Born May 31, 1960, at Inglewood, Calif.
Height, 6.02, Weight, 193.
High School—Garden Grove, Calif., Pacifica.
Attended University of California at Los Angeles.
Brother of Mitch Johnson, offensive lineman at University of California at Los Angeles.

Named to THE SPORTING NEWS NFL All-Star Team, 1984.
Signed as free agent by Seattle Seahawks, May 4, 1982.

			PLACE KICKING				
Year	Club	G.	XP.	XPM.	FG.	FGA.	Pts.
1982—Seattle NFL		9	13	1	10	14	43
1983—Seattle NFL		16	49	1	18	25	103
1984—Seattle NFL		16	50	1	20	24	110
1985—Seattle NFL		16	40	1	14	25	82
Pro Totals—4 Years		57	152	4	62	88	338

Additional pro statistics: Attempted one pass with one completion for 27 yards, 1982.
Played in AFC Championship Game following 1983 season.
Played in Pro Bowl (NFL All-Star Game) following 1984 season.

RICHARD JOHNSON
Cornerback—Houston Oilers
Born September 16, 1963, at Harvey, Ill.
Height, 6.01. Weight, 195.
High School—Harvey, Ill., Thornton.
Attended University of Wisconsin.

Named as defensive back on THE SPORTING NEWS College All-America Team, 1984.
Selected by Jacksonville in 1985 USFL territorial draft.
Selected by Houston in 1st round (11th player selected) of 1985 NFL draft.
Signed by Houston Oilers, August 22, 1985.
Granted roster exemption, August 22 through August 29, 1985; activated, August 30, 1985.
Houston NFL, 1985.
Games: 1985 (16).
Pro statistics: Recovered one fumble, 1985.

RON JOHNSON
Wide Receiver—Philadelphia Eagles
Born September 21, 1958, at Monterey, Calif.
Height, 6.03. Weight, 186.
High School—Monterey, Calif.
Attended California State University at Long Beach.

Selected by Seattle in 7th round (170th player selected) of 1981 NFL draft.
Released by Seattle Seahawks, August 17, 1981; claimed on waivers by Baltimore Colts, August 19, 1981.
Released by Baltimore Colts, August 25, 1981; signed as free agent by Hamilton Tiger-Cats, March 10, 1982.
Granted free agency, March 1, 1985.
USFL rights traded by Los Angeles Express to Portland Breakers for past considerations, May 15, 1985.
Signed by Portland Breakers, May 15, 1985.
Released by Portland Breakers, June 26, 1985; signed as free agent by Philadelphia Eagles, July 22, 1985.
On injured reserve with dislocated shoulder, November 19 through remainder of 1985 season.

Year Club	G.	Att.	Yds.	Avg.	TD.	P.C.	Yds.	Avg.	TD.	TD.	Pts.	F.
			—RUSHING—			PASS RECEIVING				—TOTAL—		
1982—Hamilton CFL	11	1	—3	—3.0	0	37	505	13.6	5	5	30	1
1983—Hamilton CFL	16		None			53	914	17.2	6	6	36	1
1984—Hamilton CFL	15		None			50	684	13.6	2	2	12	0
1985—Portland USFL	6	4	15	3.8	0	22	476	21.6	2	2	12	0
1985—Philadelphia NFL	8		None			11	186	16.9	0	0	0	0
CFL Totals—3 Years	42	1	—3	—3.0	0	140	2103	15.0	13	13	78	2
USFL Totals—1 Year	6	4	15	3.8	0	22	476	21.6	2	2	12	0
NFL Totals—1 Year	8	0	0	0.0	0	11	186	16.9	0	0	0	0
Pro Totals—5 Years	56	5	12	2.4	0	173	2765	16.0	15	15	90	2

TRUMAINE JOHNSON
Wide Receiver—San Diego Chargers
Born November 16, 1960, at Bogaloosa, La.
Height, 6.03. Weight, 196.
High School—Baker, La.
Attended Grambling State University.

Named as wide receiver on THE SPORTING NEWS USFL All-Star Team, 1983 and 1984.
Selected by Chicago in 1st round (11th player selected) of 1983 USFL draft.
Signed by Chicago Blitz, January 14, 1983.
Selected by San Diego in 6th round (141st player selected) of 1983 NFL draft.
Franchise transferred to Arizona, September 30, 1983.
Protected in merger of Arizona Wranglers and Oklahoma Outlaws, December 6, 1984.
Left Arizona Outlaws camp voluntarily, January 23, 1985.
On suspended list, February 22 through entire 1985 season.
Released by Arizona Outlaws, July 10, 1985; signed by San Diego Chargers, July 12, 1985.

Year Club	G.	Att.	Yds.	Avg.	TD.	P.C.	Yds.	Avg.	TD.	TD.	Pts.	F.
			—RUSHING—			PASS RECEIVING				—TOTAL—		
1983—Chicago USFL	18	7	40	5.7	0	∗81	∗1322	16.3	10	10	60	3
1984—Arizona USFL	18	1	3	3.0	0	90	1268	14.1	13	13	78	3
1985—San Diego NFL	11		None			4	51	12.8	1	1	6	0
USFL Totals—2 Years	36	8	43	5.4	0	171	2590	15.1	23	23	138	6
NFL Totals—1 Year	11	0	0	0.0	0	4	51	12.8	1	1	6	0
Pro Totals—3 Years	47	8	43	5.4	0	175	2641	15.1	24	24	144	6

Additional pro statistics: Returned one punt for 26 yards, recovered two fumbles and attempted one pass with no completions, 1983; recovered one fumble and returned two punts for four yards, 1984.
Played in USFL Championship Game following 1984 season.

VANCE EDWARD JOHNSON
Wide Receiver—Denver Broncos
Born March 13, 1963, at Trenton, N.J.
Height, 5.11. Weight, 174.
High School—Tucson, Ariz., Cholla.
Attended University of Arizona.

Selected by Arizona in 1985 USFL territorial draft.
Selected by Denver in 2nd round (31st player selected) of 1985 NFL draft.
Signed by Denver Broncos, July 16, 1985.

Year Club	G.	Att.	Yds.	Avg.	TD.	P.C.	Yds.	Avg.	TD.	TD.	Pts.	F.
			—RUSHING—			PASS RECEIVING				—TOTAL—		
1985—Denver NFL	16	10	36	3.6	0	51	721	14.1	3	3	18	5

Year Club	G.	No.	Yds.	Avg.	TD.	No.	Yds.	Avg.TD.
			—PUNT RETURNS—			—KICKOFF RET.—		
1985—Denver NFL	16	30	260	8.7	0	30	740	24.7 0

Additional pro statistics: Attempted one pass with no completions and recovered two fumbles, 1985.

WILLIAM ARTHUR JOHNSON
(Billy White Shoes)
Wide Receiver—Atlanta Falcons
Born January 27, 1952, at Bouthwyn, Pa.
Height, 5.09. Weight, 170.
High School—Boothwyn, Pa., Chichester.
Attended Widener College.

Established NFL record for punt return yards, career (3,036).
Tied NFL record for most touchdowns, combined returns, season (4), 1975.
Named as punt returner to THE SPORTING NEWS NFL All-Star Team, 1983.

Selected by Houston in 15th round (365th player selected) of 1974 NFL draft.
On injured reserve with knee injury, November 10 through remainder of 1978 season.
On injured reserve with knee injury, September 11 through remainder of 1979 season.
Granted free agency, February 2, 1981; signed by Montreal Alouettes, May 19, 1981.
Released by Montreal Concordes, April 15, 1982; signed as free agent by Atlanta Falcons, July 20, 1982.
On injured reserve with knee injury, October 9 through remainder of 1984 season.
Played for Philadelphia Athletics of American Professional Slo-Pitch Softball League, 1978.

		——RUSHING——				PASS RECEIVING				—TOTAL—		
Year Club	G.	Att.	Yds.	Avg.	TD.	P.C.	Yds.	Avg.	TD.	TD.	Pts.	F.
1974—Houston NFL	14	5	82	16.4	1	29	388	13.4	2	3	18	1
1975—Houston NFL	14	5	17	3.4	0	37	393	10.6	1	5	30	5
1976—Houston NFL	14	6	6	1.0	0	47	495	10.5	4	4	24	3
1977—Houston NFL	14	6	102	17.0	1	20	412	20.6	3	7	42	2
1978—Houston NFL	5		None			1	10	10.0	0	0	0	0
1979—Houston NFL	2		None			6	108	18.0	1	1	6	0
1980—Houston NFL	16	2	1	0.5	0	31	343	11.1	2	2	12	1
1981—Montreal CFL	16	1	—9	—9.0	0	65	1060	16.3	5	5	30	3
1982—Atlanta NFL	9		None			2	11	5.5	0	0	0	1
1983—Atlanta NFL	16	15	83	5.5	0	64	709	11.1	4	5	30	4
1984—Atlanta NFL	6	3	8	2.7	0	24	371	15.5	3	3	18	1
1985—Atlanta NFL	16	8	—8	—1.0	0	62	830	13.4	5	5	30	4
NFL Totals—11 Years	126	50	291	5.8	2	323	4070	12.6	25	35	210	22
CFL Totals—1 Year	16	1	—9	—9.0	0	65	1060	16.3	5	5	30	3
Pro Totals—12 Years	142	51	282	5.5	2	388	5130	13.2	30	40	240	25

		—PUNT RETURNS—				—KICKOFF RET.—			
Year Club	G.	No.	Yds.	Avg.	TD.	No.	Yds.	Avg.	TD.
1974—Houston NFL	14	30	409	13.6	0	29	785	27.1	0
1975—Houston NFL	14	40	612	★15.3	★3	33	798	24.2	★1
1976—Houston NFL	14	38	403	10.6	0	26	579	22.3	0
1977—Houston NFL	14	35	539	★15.4	★2	25	630	25.2	1
1978—Houston NFL	5	8	60	7.5	0	4	73	18.3	0
1979—Houston NFL	2	4	17	4.3	0	4	37	9.3	0
1980—Houston NFL	16		None				None		
1981—Montreal CFL	16	59	597	10.1	0		None		
1982—Atlanta NFL	9	24	273	11.4	0		None		
1983—Atlanta NFL	16	46	489	10.6	★1		None		
1984—Atlanta NFL	6	15	152	10.1	0	2	39	19.5	0
1985—Atlanta NFL	16	10	82	8.2	0		None		
NFL Totals—11 Years	126	250	3036	12.1	6	123	2941	23.9	2
CFL Totals—1 Year	16	59	597	10.1	0	0	0	0.0	0
Pro Totals—12 Years	142	309	3633	11.8	6	123	2941	23.9	2

Additional pro statistics: Recovered one fumble, 1975 and 1976; attempted one pass with no completions and recovered two fumbles, 1983.
Played in Pro Bowl (NFL All-Star Game) following 1975, 1977 and 1983 seasons.

WILLIAM THOMAS JOHNSON
(Bill)
Running Back—Cincinnati Bengals
Born October 31, 1960, at Poughkeepsie, N.Y.
Height, 6.02. Weight, 230.
High School—Freedom Plains, N.Y., Arlington.
Attended Arkansas State University.

Selected by Denver in 17th round (343rd player selected) of 1984 USFL draft.
Signed by Denver Gold, January 29, 1984.
On developmental squad, February 24 through March 23, 1984; activated, March 24, 1984.
On developmental squad, June 8 through June 14, 1984; activated, June 15, 1984.
Selected by Cincinnati in 2nd round (35th player selected) of 1984 NFL supplemental draft.
Granted free agency, August 1, 1985; signed by Cincinnati Bengals, August 9, 1985.
On injured reserve with hamstring injury, December 20 through remainder of 1985 season.
On developmental squad for 5 games with Denver Gold in 1984.

		——RUSHING——				PASS RECEIVING				—TOTAL—		
Year Club	G.	Att.	Yds.	Avg.	TD.	P.C.	Yds.	Avg.	TD.	TD.	Pts.	F.
1984—Denver USFL	13	36	132	3.7	2	10	135	13.5	1	3	18	4
1985—Denver USFL	18	212	1261	★6.0	15	29	337	11.6	1	16	96	8
1985—Cincinnati NFL	13	8	44	5.5	0		None			0	0	0
USFL Totals—2 Years	31	248	1393	5.6	17	39	472	12.1	2	19	114	12
NFL Totals—1 Year	13	8	144	5.5	0	0	0	0.0	0	0	0	0
Pro Totals—3 Years	44	256	1537	6.0	17	39	472	12.1	2	19	114	12

Additional pro statistics: Recovered four fumbles, 1984.

BRIAN JOHNSTON
Center—New York Giants
Born November 26, 1962, at Highland, Md.
Height, 6.03. Weight, 275.
High School—Glenelg, Md.
Attended University of North Carolina.

Selected by New York Giants in 3rd round (73rd player selected) of 1985 NFL draft.
Signed by New York Giants, July 15, 1985.
On non-football injury list with back injury, August 14 through entire 1985 season.

CHARLES JOINER JR.
(Charlie)
Wide Receiver—San Diego Chargers
Born October 14, 1947, at Many, La.
Height, 5.11. Weight, 180.
High School—Lake Charles, La., W. O. Boston.
Received bachelor of science degree in business administration from
Grambling College in 1969.
Cousin of Tom Woodland, defensive tackle with New Jersey Generals.

Established NFL record for most pass receptions, career (716).
Selected by Houston AFL in 4th round (93rd player selected) of 1969 AFL-NFL draft.
Traded with linebacker Ron Pritchard by Houston Oilers to Cincinnati Bengals for running backs Fred Willis and Paul Robinson, October 25, 1972.
Traded by Cincinnati Bengals to San Diego Chargers for defensive end Coy Bacon, April 2, 1976.

		—RUSHING—				PASS RECEIVING				—TOTAL—		
Year Club	G.	Att.	Yds.	Avg.	TD.	P.C.	Yds.	Avg.	TD.	TD.	Pts.	F.
1969—Houston AFL	7		None			7	77	11.0	0	0	0	0
1970—Houston NFL	9		None			28	416	14.9	3	3	18	0
1971—Houston NFL	14		None			31	681	22.0	7	7	42	1
1972—Houston (6)-Cin. (6) NFL	12	3	14	4.7	0	24	439	18.3	2	2	12	2
1973—Cincinnati NFL	5		None			13	214	16.5	0	0	0	1
1974—Cincinnati NFL	14	4	20	5.0	0	24	390	16.3	1	1	6	3
1975—Cincinnati NFL	14		None			37	726	19.6	5	5	30	1
1976—San Diego NFL	14		None			50	1056	20.1	7	7	42	0
1977—San Diego NFL	14		None			35	542	15.5	6	6	36	1
1978—San Diego NFL	16		None			33	607	18.4	1	1	6	2
1979—San Diego NFL	16	1	—12	—12.0	0	72	1008	14.0	4	4	24	1
1980—San Diego NFL	16		None			71	1132	15.9	4	4	24	3
1981—San Diego NFL	16		None			70	1188	17.0	7	7	42	2
1982—San Diego NFL	9		None			36	545	15.1	0	0	0	1
1983—San Diego NFL	16		None			65	960	14.8	3	3	18	2
1984—San Diego NFL	16		None			61	793	13.0	6	6	36	0
1985—San Diego NFL	16		None			59	932	15.8	7	7	42	1
Pro Totals—17 Years	224	8	22	2.8	1	716	11706	16.3	63	63	378	21

		KICKOFF RETURNS						KICKOFF RETURNS		
Year Club	G.	No.	Yds.	Avg.TD.		Year Club	G.	No.	Yds.	Avg.TD.
1969—Houston AFL	7	3	73	24.3	0	1978—San Diego NFL	16		None	
1970—Houston NFL	9		None			1979—San Diego NFL	16		None	
1971—Houston NFL	14	1	25	25.0	0	1980—San Diego NFL	16		None	
1972—Hou.(6)-Cin.(6) NFL	12	5	88	17.6	0	1981—San Diego NFL	16		None	
1973—Cincinnati NFL	5		None			1982—San Diego NFL	9		None	
1974—Cincinnati NFL	14		None			1983—San Diego NFL	16		None	
1975—Cincinnati NFL	14		None			1984—San Diego NFL	16		None	
1976—San Diego NFL	14		None			1985—San Diego NFL	16		None	
1977—San Diego NFL	14	1	8	8.0	0	Pro Totals—17 Years	224	10	194	19.4 0

Additional pro statistics: Recovered one fumble, 1975 and 1976.
Played in AFC Championship Game following 1980 and 1981 seasons.
Played in Pro Bowl (NFL All-Star Game) following 1976, 1979 and 1980 seasons.

TIM JOINER
Linebacker—New Orleans Saints
Born January 7, 1961, at Los Angeles, Calif.
Height, 6.04. Weight, 248.
High School—Baton Rouge, La., Catholic.
Attended Louisiana State University.

Selected by Arizona in 10th round (119th player selected) of 1983 USFL draft.
Selected by Houston in 3rd round (58th player selected) of 1983 NFL draft.
Signed by Houston Oilers, July 12, 1983.
On injured reserve with knee injury, August 28 through October 4, 1984; activated, October 5, 1984.
On injured reserve with knee injury, August 15 through October 21, 1985.
Released by Houston Oilers, October 22, 1985; signed as free agent by New Orleans Saints, May 9, 1986.
Houston NFL, 1983 and 1984.
Games: 1983 (15), 1984 (11). Total—26.
Pro statistics: Recovered one fumble, 1984.

KENNETH CLAY JOLLY
(Ken)
Linebacker—Kansas City Chiefs
Born February 28, 1962, at Dallas, Tex.
Height, 6.02. Weight, 220.
High School—Dallas, Tex., Bryan Adams.
Attended Dallas County Community College, Johnson County Community College,
Park College, Cleveland Chiropractic College and Mid-America Nazarene.

Signed as free agent by Kansas City Chiefs, May 22, 1984.
Kansas City NFL, 1984 and 1985.
Games: 1984 (16), 1985 (16). Total—32.
Pro statistics: Recovered one fumble, 1985.

ANTHONY JONES
Tight End—Washington Redskins
Born May 16, 1960, at Baltimore, Md.
Height, 6.03. Weight, 248.
High School—Baltimore, Md., Patterson.
Attended University of Maryland (Eastern Shore) and Wichita State University.

Selected by Oklahoma in 1984 USFL territorial draft.
Selected by Washington in 11th round (306th player selected) of 1984 NFL draft.
Signed by Washington Redskins, June 21, 1984.
On injured reserve with neck injury, December 21 through remainder of 1984 season.
Washington NFL, 1984 and 1985.
Games: 1984 (16), 1985 (16). Total—32.
Pro statistics: Caught one pass for six yards, 1984; returned one kickoff for no yards, 1985.

ANTHONY LEVINE JONES
(A. J.)
Running Back—Detroit Lions
Born May 30, 1959, at Youngstown, O.
Height, 6.01. Weight, 215.
High School—Youngstown, O., North.
Attended University of Texas.
Brother of Mike Jones, running back with Oakland Invaders, 1985.

Selected by Los Angeles Rams in 8th round (202nd player selected) of 1982 NFL draft.
On inactive list, September 12 and September 19, 1982.
On injured reserve with chest injury, November 2 through December 13, 1983; activated, December 14, 1983.
On injured reserve with pulled groin, November 30 through remainder of 1984 season.
Released by Los Angeles Rams, September 18, 1985; signed as free agent by Detroit Lions, October 30, 1985.
Los Angeles Rams NFL, 1982 through 1984; Los Angeles Rams (1)-Detroit (8) NFL, 1985.
Games: 1982 (6), 1983 (9), 1984 (13), 1985 (9). Total—37.
Pro statistics: Recovered one fumble, 1984; returned 10 kickoffs for 226 yards and rushed once for two yards, 1985.

CEDRIC DECORRUS JONES
Wide Receiver—New England Patriots
Born June 1, 1960, at Norfolk, Va.
Height, 6.01. Weight, 184.
High School—Weldon, N.C.
Received bachelor of arts degree in history and political science from
Duke University in 1982.

Selected by New England in 3rd round (56th player selected) of 1982 NFL draft.
On inactive list, September 19, 1982.

Year Club	G.	P.C.	Yds.	Avg.	TD.
1982—New England NFL.......	2	1	5	5.0	0
1983—New England NFL.......	15	20	323	16.2	1
1984—New England NFL.......	14	19	244	12.8	2
1985—New England NFL.......	16	21	237	11.3	2
Pro Totals—4 Years............	47	61	809	13.3	5

Additional pro statistics: Returned four kickoffs for 63 yards, 1983; fumbled once, 1983 and 1984; returned one kickoff for 20 yards and recovered fumble in end zone for a touchdown, 1984; returned three kickoffs for 37 yards and recovered one fumble for 15 yards and a touchdown, 1985.
Played in AFC Championship Game following 1985 season.
Played in NFL Championship Game following 1985 season.

DARYLL KEITH JONES
Defensive Back—Green Bay Packers
Born March 23, 1962, at Columbia, Ga.
Height, 6.00. Weight, 190.
High School—Columbus, Ga., Carver.
Attended University of Georgia.

Selected by Jacksonville in 1984 USFL territorial draft.
Selected by Green Bay in 7th round (181st player selected) of 1984 NFL draft.
Signed by Green Bay Packers, June 6, 1984.
On injured reserve with neck injury, October 30 through remainder of 1985 season.
Selected by Pittsburgh Pirates' organization in 17th round of free-agent draft, June 3, 1980.
Green Bay NFL, 1984 and 1985.
Games: 1984 (16), 1985 (8). Total—24.
Pro statistics: Returned one kickoff for 19 yards and recovered three fumbles, 1984; returned one kickoff for 11 yards, 1985.

DAVID J. JONES
Center—Detroit Lions
Born October 25, 1961, at Taipei, Taiwan.
Height, 6.03. Weight, 266.
High School—Austin, Tex., David Crockett.
Attended University of Texas.

Selected by Houston in 1984 USFL territorial draft.
Selected by Detroit in 8th round (214th player selected) of 1984 NFL draft.
Signed by Detroit Lions, June 4, 1984.
On injured reserve with pulled hamstring, September 8 through October 12, 1984; activated, October 13, 1984.
On injured reserve with back injury, December 14 through remainder of 1984 season.
On injured reserve with neck injury, November 8 through remainder of 1985 season.
Detroit NFL, 1984 and 1985.
Games: 1984 (10), 1985 (9). Total—19.
Pro statistics: Recovered one fumble, 1985.

DWIGHT SEAN JONES
(Known by middle name.)
Defensive End—Los Angeles Raiders
Born December 19, 1962, at Kingston, Jamaica.
Height, 6.07. Weight, 275.
High School—Montclair, N.J., Kimberly Academy.
Attended Northeastern University.
Brother of Max Jones, linebacker with Birmingham Stallions, 1984.

Selected by Washington in 5th round (91st player selected) of 1984 USFL draft.
Selected by Los Angeles Raiders in 2nd round (51st player selected) of 1984 NFL draft.
Signed by Los Angeles Raiders, July 12, 1984.
Los Angeles Raiders NFL, 1984 and 1985.
Games: 1984 (16), 1985 (15). Total—31.
Pro statistics: Recovered one fumble, 1985.

EDWARD LEE JONES
(Too Tall)
Defensive End—Dallas Cowboys
Born February 23, 1951, at Jackson, Tenn.
Height, 6.09. Weight, 287.
High School—Jackson, Tenn., Central-Merry.
Received degree in health and physical education from Tennessee State University.

Named as defensive end on THE SPORTING NEWS College All-America Team, 1973.
Placed on retired reserve, June 19, 1979.
Selected by Dallas in 1st round (1st player selected) of 1974 NFL draft.
Dallas NFL, 1974 through 1978 and 1980 through 1985.
Games: 1974 (14), 1975 (14), 1976 (14), 1977 (14), 1978 (16), 1980 (16), 1981 (16), 1982 (9), 1983 (16), 1984 (16), 1985 (16). Total—161.
Pro statistics: Intercepted one pass for two yards, 1975; recovered one fumble, 1975, 1976 and 1982; recovered three fumbles, 1980 and 1981; intercepted one pass for no yards, 1982; intercepted one pass for 12 yards, 1983; recovered two fumbles, 1983 and 1984.
Played in NFC Championship Game following 1975, 1977, 1978 and 1980 through 1982 seasons.
Played in NFL Championship Game following 1975, 1977 and 1978 seasons.
Played in Pro Bowl (NFL All-Star Game) following 1981 through 1983 seasons.

GORDON JONES
Wide Receiver—Chicago Bears
Born July 25, 1957, at Buffalo, N.Y.
Height, 6.00. Weight, 190.
High School—N. Versailles, Pa., East Allegheny.
Attended University of Pittsburgh.

Selected by Tampa Bay in 2nd round (34th player selected) of 1979 NFL draft.
Released by Tampa Bay Buccaneers, August 29, 1983; signed as free agent by Los Angeles Rams, September 8, 1983.
On injured reserve with broken foot, November 21 through remainder of 1983 season.
Released by Los Angeles Rams, September 4, 1984; signed as free agent by Los Angeles Raiders, March 15, 1985.
Released by Los Angeles Raiders, September 2, 1985; signed as free agent by Chicago Bears, May 21, 1986.
Active for 1 game with Los Angeles Rams in 1984; did not play.

| | | —PASS RECEIVING— | | | |
Year Club	G.	P.C.	Yds.	Avg.	TD.
1979—Tampa Bay NFL	12	4	80	20.0	1
1980—Tampa Bay NFL	16	48	669	13.9	5
1981—Tampa Bay NFL	13	20	276	13.8	1
1982—Tampa Bay NFL	9	14	205	14.6	1
1983—L.A. Rams NFL	11	11	172	15.6	0
Pro Totals—6 Years	61	97	1402	14.5	8

Additional pro statistics: Rushed once for 12 yards, 1979; rushed once for minus 10 yards, 1980; fumbled once, 1980 and 1982.
Played in NFC Championship Game following 1979 season.

JAMES ROOSEVELT JONES
Fullback—Detroit Lions
Born March 21, 1961, at Pompano Beach, Fla.
Height, 6.02. Weight, 228.
High School—Pompano Beach, Fla., Ely.
Attended University of Florida.

Selected by Tampa Bay in 1983 USFL territorial draft.
Selected by Detroit in 1st round (13th player selected) of 1983 NFL draft.
Signed by Detroit Lions, May 12, 1983.

		——RUSHING——				PASS RECEIVING				—TOTAL—		
Year Club	G.	Att.	Yds.	Avg.	TD.	P.C.	Yds.	Avg.	TD.	TD.	Pts.	F.
1983—Detroit NFL	14	135	475	3.5	6	46	467	10.2	1	7	42	4
1984—Detroit NFL	16	137	532	3.9	3	77	662	8.6	5	8	48	6
1985—Detroit NFL	14	244	886	3.6	6	45	334	7.4	3	9	54	7
Pro Totals—3 Years	44	516	1893	3.7	15	168	1463	8.7	9	24	144	17

Additional pro statistics: Recovered one fumble, 1983 and 1985; attempted two passes with no completions, 1983; attempted five passes with three completions for 62 yards and a touchdown and recovered three fumbles, 1984; attempted one pass with no completions, 1985.

JAMES JONES JR.
Running Back—Dallas Cowboys
Born December 6, 1958, at Vicksburg, Miss.
Height, 5.10. Weight, 203.
High School—Vicksburg, Miss.
Attended Mississippi State University.

Selected by Dallas in 3rd round (80th player selected) of 1980 NFL draft.
On injured reserve with knee injury, August 30 through entire 1983 season.
On physically unable to perform/active with knee injury, July 19 through August 20, 1984.
On physically unable to perform/reserve with knee injury, August 21 through October 19, 1984; activated, October 20, 1984.

		——RUSHING——				PASS RECEIVING				—TOTAL—		
Year Club	G.	Att.	Yds.	Avg.	TD.	P.C.	Yds.	Avg.	TD.	TD.	Pts.	F.
1980—Dallas NFL	16	41	135	3.3	0	5	39	7.8	0	0	0	5
1981—Dallas NFL	16	34	183	5.4	1	6	37	6.2	0	1	6	4
1982—Dallas NFL	5		None				None			0	0	0
1984—Dallas NFL	9	8	13	1.6	0	7	57	8.1	1	1	6	0
1985—Dallas NFL	16	1	0	0.0	0	24	179	7.5	0	0	0	0
Pro Totals—5 Years	62	84	331	3.9	1	42	312	7.4	1	2	12	9

		—PUNT RETURNS—				—KICKOFF RET.—			
Year Club	G.	No.	Yds.	Avg.	TD.	No.	Yds.	Avg.TD.	
1980—Dallas NFL	16	54	548	10.1	0	32	720	22.5	0
1981—Dallas NFL	16	33	188	5.7	0	27	517	19.1	0
1982—Dallas NFL	5		None			2	46	23.0	0
1984—Dallas NFL	9		None				None		
1985—Dallas NFL	16		None			9	161	17.9	0
Pro Totals—5 Years	62	87	736	8.5	0	70	1444	20.6	0

Additional pro statistics: Recovered two fumbles, 1981; attempted two passes with one completion for 12 yards with one touchdown and one interception, 1985.
Played in NFC Championship Game following 1980 and 1981 seasons.
Member of Dallas Cowboys for NFC Championship Game following 1982 season; did not play.

JOHNNY JONES
(Lam)
Wide Receiver—New York Jets
Born April 4, 1958, at Lawton, Okla.
Height, 5.11. Weight, 180.
High School—Lampasas, Tex.
Attended University of Texas.

Named as wide receiver on THE SPORTING NEWS College All-America Team, 1979.
Selected by New York Jets in 1st round (2nd player selected) of 1980 NFL draft.
On injured reserve with broken collarbone, August 28 through October 25, 1984; activated, October 26, 1984.
On injured reserve with finger injury, August 15 through entire 1985 season.

		——RUSHING——				PASS RECEIVING				—TOTAL—		
Year Club	G.	Att.	Yds.	Avg.	TD.	P.C.	Yds.	Avg.	TD.	TD.	Pts.	F.
1980—New York Jets NFL	16	2	5	2.5	0	25	482	19.3	3	3	18	1
1981—New York Jets NFL	15	2	0	0.0	0	20	342	17.1	3	3	18	2
1982—New York Jets NFL	8	1	2	2.0	0	18	294	16.3	2	2	12	0
1983—New York Jets NFL	14	4	10	2.5	0	43	734	17.1	4	4	24	2
1984—New York Jets NFL	8		None			32	470	14.7	1	1	6	1
Pro Totals—5 Years	61	9	17	1.9	0	138	2322	16.8	13	13	78	6

Additional pro statistics: Returned four kickoffs for 67 yards, 1980; recovered one fumble, 1980 and 1982; returned one kickoff for six yards and recovered two fumbles, 1981.
Played in AFC Championship Game following 1982 season.

KENNETH EUGENE JONES
(Ken)
Offensive Tackle—Buffalo Bills
Born December 1, 1952, at St. Louis, Mo.
Height, 6.05. Weight, 279.
High School—Bridgeton, Mo., Pattonville.
Attended Arkansas State University.

Named as guard on THE SPORTING NEWS College All-America Team, 1975.
Selected by Buffalo in 2nd round (45th player selected) of 1976 NFL draft.
Buffalo NFL, 1976 through 1985.
Games: 1976 (12), 1977 (14), 1978 (16), 1979 (16), 1980 (16), 1981 (15), 1982 (9), 1983 (16), 1984 (16), 1985 (16). Total—146.
Pro statistics: Recovered two fumbles, 1976 and 1981; recovered one fumble, 1978 through 1980 and 1983.

MICHAEL ANTHONY JONES
(Mike)
Wide Receiver—Minnesota Vikings
Born April 14, 1960, at Chattanooga, Tenn.
Height, 5.11. Weight, 180.
High School—Chattanooga, Tenn., Riverside.
Attended Tennessee State University.

Selected by Minnesota in 6th round (159th player selected) of 1983 NFL draft.

			—PASS RECEIVING—			
Year	Club	G.	P.C.	Yds.	Avg.	TD.
1983—Minnesota NFL		16	6	95	15.8	0
1984—Minnesota NFL		16	38	591	15.6	1
1985—Minnesota NFL		16	46	641	13.9	4
Pro Totals—3 Years		48	90	1327	14.7	5

Additional pro statistics: Rushed once for nine yards and returned two kickoffs for 31 yards, 1983; rushed four times for 45 yards, recovered two fumbles and fumbled once, 1984; rushed twice for six yards, 1985.

ROBERT WASHINGTON JONES
(Robbie)
Linebacker—New York Giants
Born December 25, 1959, at Demopolis, Ala.
Height, 6.02. Weight, 230.
High School—Demopolis, Ala.
Attended University of Alabama.

Selected by Birmingham in 1983 USFL territorial draft.
Selected by New York Giants in 12th round (309th player selected) of 1983 NFL draft.
Signed by New York Giants, July 6, 1983.
On injured reserve with abrasion to spinal cord, August 22 through entire 1983 season.
New York Giants NFL, 1984 and 1985.
Games: 1984 (16), 1985 (16). Total—32.

RULON KENT JONES
Defensive End—Denver Broncos
Born March 25, 1958, at Salt Lake City, Utah.
Height, 6.06. Weight, 260.
High School—Ogden, Utah, Weber.
Attended Utah State University.

Named to THE SPORTING NEWS NFL All-Star Team, 1985.
Named as defensive tackle on THE SPORTING NEWS College All-America Team, 1979.
Selected by Denver in 2nd round (42nd player selected) of 1980 NFL draft.
On injured reserve with knee injury, September 21 through October 20, 1983; activated, October 21, 1983.
Denver NFL, 1980 through 1985.
Games: 1980 (16), 1981 (16), 1982 (9), 1983 (12), 1984 (16), 1985 (16). Total—85.
Pro statistics: Credited with one safety, 1980 and 1983; recovered one fumble, 1980 and 1981; recovered two fumbles for four yards, 1983; recovered two fumbles for five yards and a touchdown, 1984; recovered three fumbles, 1985.
Played in Pro Bowl (NFL All-Star Game) following 1985 season.

TERRY WAYNE JONES
Defensive Tackle
Born November 8, 1956, at Sandersville, Ga.
Height, 6.02. Weight, 253.
High School—Sandersville, Ga., Washington County.
Received bachelor of science degree in industrial arts and physical education from University of Alabama.

Selected by Green Bay in 11th round (287th player selected) of 1978 NFL draft.
On injured reserve with knee injury, September 12 through October 11, 1979; activated, October 12, 1979.
Released by Green Bay Packers, September 1, 1980; re-signed by Packers, September 5, 1980.
On injured reserve with Achilles tendon injury, September 6 through remainder of 1983 season.
On injured reserve with Achilles tendon injury, August 5 through entire 1985 season.
Granted free agency with no qualifying offer, February 1, 1986.

Green Bay NFL, 1978 through 1984.
Games: 1978 (16), 1979 (12), 1980 (15), 1981 (16), 1982 (9), 1983 (1), 1984 (16). Total—85.
Pro statistics: Recovered one fumble, 1979, 1980 and 1984; recovered two fumbles, 1981.

CURTIS WAYNE JORDAN
Safety—Washington Redskins
Born January 25, 1954, at Lubbock, Tex.
Height, 6.02. Weight, 205.
High School—Lubbock, Tex., Monterey.
Received degree in advertising and public relations from Texas Tech University.

Selected by Tampa Bay in 6th round (158th player selected) of 1976 NFL draft.
On injured reserve with broken collarbone, August 17 through December 9, 1981; claimed on procedural waivers by Washington Redskins, December 11, 1981.

		—INTERCEPTIONS—			
Year Club	G.	No.	Yds.	Avg.TD.	
1976—Tampa Bay NFL	11	2	10	5.0	0
1977—Tampa Bay NFL	12	1	0	0.0	0
1978—Tampa Bay NFL	16	3	23	7.7	0
1979—Tampa Bay NFL	16	None			
1980—Tampa Bay NFL	16	None			
1981—Washington NFL	2	None			
1982—Washington NFL	9	None			
1983—Washington NFL	15	1	20	20.0	0
1984—Washington NFL	16	2	18	9.0	0
1985—Washington NFL	16	5	88	17.6	0
Pro Totals—10 Years	129	14	159	11.4	0

Additional pro statistics: Recovered one fumble, 1976, 1977, 1979 and 1980; returned one kickoff for no yards, 1980; recovered blocked punt in end zone for a touchdown, 1982; recovered two fumbles for 20 yards, 1983; recovered one fumble for 29 yards and a touchdown, 1984; recovered two fumbles, 1985.
Played in NFC Championship Game following 1979, 1982 and 1983 seasons.
Played in NFL Championship Game following 1982 and 1983 seasons.

DAVID TURNER JORDAN
Guard—New York Giants
Born July 14, 1962, at Birmingham, Ala.
Height, 6.06. Weight, 276.
High School—Vestavia Hills, Ala.
Attended Auburn University.

Selected by Birmingham in 1984 USFL territorial draft.
Selected by New York Giants in 10th round (255th player selected) of 1984 NFL draft.
Signed by New York Giants, June 3, 1984.
New York Giants NFL, 1984 and 1985.
Games: 1984 (14), 1985 (16). Total—30.

ERIC RONDELL JORDAN
Running Back—New England Patriots
Born November 17, 1961, at Pineville, La.
Height, 6.00. Weight, 190.
High School—Las Vegas, Nev., Chaparral.
Attended Purdue University and Northeastern University.

Selected by Oakland in 6th round (114th player selected) of 1984 USFL draft.
Signed by Oakland Invaders, January 20, 1984.
On developmental squad, February 24 through March 15, 1984; activated, March 16, 1984.
Selected by New England in 2nd round (43rd player selected) of 1984 NFL supplemental draft.
Protected in merger of Oakland Invaders and Michigan Panthers, December 6, 1984.
Placed on did not report list, January 25 through February 27, 1985.
Granted roster exemption, February 28 through March 7, 1985; activated, March 8, 1985.
On developmental squad, April 6 through April 12, 1985; activated, April 13, 1985.
Granted free agency, August 1, 1985; signed by New England Patriots, August 15, 1985.
On non-football injury list with broken jaw, August 16 through entire 1985 season.
On developmental squad for 3 games with Oakland Invaders in 1984.
On developmental squad for 1 game with Oakland Invaders in 1985.
Selected by Cincinnati Reds' organization in 15th round of free-agent draft, June 5, 1979.

		—RUSHING—				PASS RECEIVING				—TOTAL—		
Year Club	G.	Att.	Yds.	Avg.	TD.	P.C.	Yds.	Avg.	TD.	TD.	Pts.	F.
1984—Oakland USFL	14	135	744	5.5	6	19	140	7.4	0	6	36	2
1985—Oakland USFL	15	60	204	3.4	3	3	33	11.0	0	3	18	4
Pro Totals—2 Years	29	195	948	4.9	9	22	173	7.9	0	9	54	6

		KICKOFF RETURNS			
Year Club	G.	No.	Yds.	Avg.TD.	
1984—Oakland USFL	14	4	83	20.8	0
1985—Oakland USFL	15	16	372	23.3	0
Pro Totals—2 Years	29	20	455	22.8	0

Additional pro statistics: Recovered one fumble for minus one yard, 1984; sacked in only pass attempt and recovered one fumble, 1985.
On developmental squad for USFL Championship Game following 1985 season.

PAUL BUFORD JORDAN
(Known by middle name.)
Running Back—New Orleans Saints
Born June 26, 1962, at Lafayette, La.
Height, 6.00. Weight, 222.
High School—Iota, La.
Attended McNeese State University.

Selected by New Orleans in 1st round (13th player selected) of 1984 USFL draft.
Signed by New Orleans Breakers, January 9, 1984.
Selected by Green Bay in 1st round (12th player selected) of 1984 NFL supplemental draft.
Franchise transferred to Portland, November 13, 1984.
On developmental squad, April 6 through April 20, 1985; activated, April 21, 1985.
Released, July 31, 1985; signed by Green Bay Packers, September 2, 1985.
Granted roster exemption, September 2 through September 15, 1985.
Released by Green Bay Packers, September 16, 1985; signed as free agent by New Orleans Saints, March 6, 1986.
On developmental squad for 2 games with Portland Breakers in 1985.

| | | —RUSHING— | | | | PASS RECEIVING | | | | —TOTAL— | | |
Year Club	G.	Att.	Yds.	Avg.	TD.	P.C.	Yds.	Avg.	TD.	TD.	Pts.	F.
1984—New Orleans USFL	18	214	1276	*6.0	8	45	427	9.5	4	12	72	9
1985—Portland USFL	15	165	817	5.0	5	12	192	16.0	1	6	†38	11
Pro Totals—2 Years	33	379	2093	5.5	13	57	619	10.9	5	18	110	20

†Includes one 2-point conversion.
Additional pro statistics: Recovered four fumbles, 1984 and 1985.

SHELBY LEWIS JORDAN
Offensive Tackle—Los Angeles Raiders
Born January 23, 1952, at East St. Louis, Ill.
Height, 6.07. Weight, 280.
High School—East St. Louis, Ill.
Received degree from Washington (Mo.) University and attending
Bryant College for master's degree in marketing.

Selected by Houston in 7th round (157th player selected) of 1973 NFL draft.
Released by Houston Oilers, 1973; signed as free agent by New England Patriots, April 2, 1974.
Missed entire 1974 and 1976 seasons due to injury.
On reserve/did not report, August 16 through August 28, 1983; reinstated, August 29, 1983.
Granted roster exemption, August 29 through September 5, 1983.
Traded by New England Patriots to Los Angeles Raiders for 4th round pick in 1985 draft, September 6, 1983.
Granted roster exemption, September 6 through September 19, 1983; activated, September 20, 1983.
On injured reserve with knee injury, November 15 through remainder of 1984 season.
New England NFL, 1975 and 1977 through 1982; Los Angeles Raiders NFL, 1983 through 1985.
Games: 1975 (14), 1977 (10), 1978 (16), 1979 (14), 1980 (16), 1981 (16), 1982 (9), 1983 (13), 1984 (11), 1985 (16).
Total—135.
Pro statistics: Recovered two fumbles for 12 yards, 1975; recovered one fumble, 1979.
Played in AFC Championship Game following 1983 season.
Played in NFL Championship Game following 1983 season.

STEVEN RUSSELL JORDAN
(Steve)
Tight End—Minnesota Vikings
Born January 10, 1961, at Phoenix, Ariz.
Height, 6.03. Weight, 230.
High School—Phoenix, Ariz., South Mountain.
Received bachelor of science degree in civil engineering from Brown University in 1982.

Selected by Minnesota in 7th round (179th player selected) of 1982 NFL draft.

| | | —PASS RECEIVING— | | | |
Year Club	G.	P.C.	Yds.	Avg.	TD.
1982—Minnesota NFL	9	3	42	14.0	0
1983—Minnesota NFL	13	15	212	14.1	2
1984—Minnesota NFL	14	38	414	10.9	2
1985—Minnesota NFL	16	68	795	11.7	0
Pro Totals—4 Years	52	124	1463	11.8	4

Additional pro statistics: Rushed once for four yards and a touchdown and recovered one fumble, 1984; fumbled twice, 1985.

WILLIAM THADIUS JUDSON
Cornerback—Miami Dolphins
Born March 26, 1959, at Detroit, Mich.
Height, 6.01. Weight, 187.
High School—Atlanta, Ga., Sylvan Hills.
Received bachelor of science degree in business administration
from South Carolina State College in 1981.

Selected by Miami in 8th round (208th player selected) of 1981 NFL draft.
On injured reserve with hamstring injury, August 31 through entire 1981 season.

Year Club	G.	No.	Yds.	Avg.	TD.
			—INTERCEPTIONS—		
1982—Miami NFL	9		None		
1983—Miami NFL	16	6	60	10.0	0
1984—Miami NFL	16	4	121	30.3	1
1985—Miami NFL	16	4	88	22.0	*1
Pro Totals—4 Years	57	14	269	19.2	2

Additional pro statistics: Recovered two fumbles for 37 yards, 1984.
Played in AFC Championship Game following 1982, 1984 and 1985 seasons.
Played in NFL Championship Game following 1982 and 1984 seasons.

ESTER JAMES JUNIOR III
(E.J.)
Linebacker—St. Louis Cardinals
Born December 8, 1959, at Sallsburg, N.C.
Height, 6.03. Weight, 235.
High School—Nashville, Tenn., Maplewood.
Received degree in public relations from University of Alabama.

Named as defensive end on THE SPORTING NEWS College All-America Team, 1980.
Selected by St. Louis in 1st round (5th player selected) of 1981 NFL draft.
On suspended list for drug use, July 25 through September 25, 1983; reinstated, September 26, 1983.

Year Club	G.	No.	Yds.	Avg.	TD.
			—INTERCEPTIONS—		
1981—St. Louis NFL	16	1	5	5.0	0
1982—St. Louis NFL	9		None		
1983—St. Louis NFL	12	3	27	9.0	0
1984—St. Louis NFL	16	1	18	18.0	0
1985—St. Louis NFL	16	5	109	21.8	0
Pro Totals—5 Years	69	10	159	15.9	0

Additional pro statistics: Recovered one fumble, 1982; recovered one fumble for one yard, 1983.
Played in Pro Bowl (NFL All-Star Game) following 1984 and 1985 seasons.

ABNER KIRK JUNKIN
(Trey)
Tight End—Los Angeles Raiders
Born January 23, 1961, at Conway, Ark.
Height, 6.02. Weight, 225.
High School—North Little Rock, Ark., Northeast.
Attended Louisiana Tech University.
Brother of Mike Junkin, linebacker at Duke University.

Selected by Buffalo in 4th round (93rd player selected) of 1983 NFL draft.
Released by Buffalo Bills, September 12, 1984; signed as free agent by Washington Redskins, September 25, 1984.
Granted free agency after not receiving qualifying offer, February 1, 1985; signed by Los Angeles Raiders, March 10, 1985.
Buffalo NFL, 1983; Buffalo (2)-Washington (12) NFL, 1984; Los Angeles Raiders NFL, 1985.
Games: 1983 (16), 1984 (14), 1985 (16). Total—46.
Pro statistics: Recovered one fumble, 1983 and 1984; caught two passes for eight yards and a touchdown, 1985.

VYTO KAB
Tight End—New York Giants
Born December 23, 1959, at Albany, Ga.
Height, 6.05. Weight, 240.
High School—Wayne, N.J., DePaul.
Received degree in food service and housing administration from Penn State University.

Selected by Philadelphia in 3rd round (78th player selected) of 1982 NFL draft.
On injured reserve with ankle injury, December 14 through remainder of 1983 season.
On injured reserve with hamstring injury, September 13 through October 7, 1985.
Released by Philadelphia Eagles, October 8, 1985; awarded on waivers to New York Giants, October 9, 1985.
(Philadelphia subsequently acquired 12th round pick in 1986 draft from New York Giants for past consideration for waiving Kab).
On injured reserve with foot injury, December 28 through remainder of 1985 season playoffs.

Year Club	G.	P.C.	Yds.	Avg.	TD.
			—PASS RECEIVING—		
1982—Philadelphia NFL	9	4	35	8.8	1
1983—Philadelphia NFL	14	18	195	10.8	1
1984—Philadelphia NFL	16	9	102	11.3	3
1985—Phi.(1)-NYG(11) NFL..	12		None		
Pro Totals—4 Years	51	31	332	10.7	5

—DID YOU KNOW—

That the Detroit Lions defeated the previous year's Super Bowl contenders at home on consecutive weekends in 1985? On October 20, they defeated the 49ers, 23-21, and the following week beat the Dolphins, 31-21.

JOHN FREDERICK KAISER
Linebacker—Seattle Seahawks
Born June 6, 1962, at Oconomowoc, Wis.
Height, 6.03. Weight, 221.
High School—Hartland, Wis., Arrowhead.
Attended College of the Sequoias and University of Arizona.
Cousin of Billy McCool, pitcher with Cincinnati Reds, San Diego Padres
and St. Louis Cardinals, 1964 through 1970.

Selected by Arizona in 1984 USFL territorial draft.
Selected by Seattle in 6th round (162nd player selected) of 1984 NFL draft.
Signed by Seattle Seahawks, June 15, 1984.
Seattle NFL, 1984 and 1985.
Games: 1984 (16), 1985 (16). Total—32.

RICHARD JAMES KANE
(Rick)
Running Back
Born November 12, 1954, at Lincoln, Neb.
Height, 6.00. Weight, 200.
High School—Pleasanton, Calif., Amador Valley.
Attended University of Oregon and San Jose State University.

Selected by Detroit in 3rd round (69th player selected) of 1977 NFL draft.
On inactive list, September 12 and September 19, 1982.
On reserve/did not report, August 16 through August 28, 1983; activated, August 29, 1983.
Released by Detroit Lions, August 28, 1984; signed as free agent by Washington Redskins, September 4, 1984.
Released by Washington Redskins, November 28, 1984; re-signed by Redskins, December 21, 1984.
Released by Washington Redskins, May 16, 1985; signed as free agent by Detroit Lions, May 29, 1985.
Granted free agency with no qualifying offer, February 1, 1986.

		——RUSHING——				PASS RECEIVING				—TOTAL—		
Year Club	G.	Att.	Yds.	Avg.	TD.	P.C.	Yds.	Avg.	TD.	TD.	Pts.	F.
1977—Detroit NFL	14	124	421	3.4	4	18	186	10.3	0	4	24	10
1978—Detroit NFL	15	44	153	3.5	2	16	161	10.1	0	2	12	1
1979—Detroit NFL	16	94	332	3.5	4	9	104	11.6	1	5	30	4
1980—Detroit NFL	16	31	125	4.0	0	5	26	5.2	0	0	0	3
1981—Detroit NFL	16	77	332	4.3	2	18	187	10.4	1	3	18	2
1982—Detroit NFL	6	7	17	2.4	0	3	25	8.3	0	0	0	0
1983—Detroit NFL	14	4	19	4.8	0	2	15	7.5	0	0	0	0
1984—Washington NFL	12	17	43	2.5	0	1	7	7.0	0	0	0	3
1985—Detroit NFL	16	11	44	4.0	0	5	56	11.2	0	0	0	1
Pro Totals—9 Years	125	409	1486	3.6	12	77	767	10.0	2	14	84	24

		KICKOFF RETURNS			
Year Club	G.	No.	Yds.	Avg.	TD.
1977—Detroit NFL	14	16	376	23.5	0
1978—Detroit NFL	15	8	156	19.5	0
1979—Detroit NFL	16	13	281	21.6	0
1980—Detroit NFL	16	23	495	21.5	0
1981—Detroit NFL	16		None		
1982—Detroit NFL	6	1	19	19.0	0
1983—Detroit NFL	14		None		
1984—Washington NFL	12	3	43	14.3	0
1985—Detroit NFL	16		None		
Pro Totals—9 Years	125	64	1370	21.4	0

Additional pro statistics: Returned one punt for 13 yards and recovered three fumbles, 1977; recovered two fumbles, 1979.

KENNETH SCOTT KAPLAN
(Ken)
Offensive Tackle—Tampa Bay Buccaneers
Born January 12, 1960, at Boston, Mass.
Height, 6.04. Weight, 275.
High School—Brockton, Mass.
Attended University of New Hampshire.

Selected by Tampa Bay in 6th round (158th player selected) of 1983 NFL draft.
On injured reserve with back injury, August 29 through entire 1983 season.
Tampa Bay NFL, 1984 and 1985.
Games: 1984 (16), 1985 (16). Total—32.

RICHARD JOHN KARLIS
(Rich)
Placekicker—Denver Broncos
Born May 23, 1959, at Salem, O.
Height, 6.00. Weight, 180.
High School—Salem, O.
Received degree in economics from University of Cincinnati.

Signed as free agent by Houston Oilers, June 5, 1981.
Released by Houston Oilers, July 31, 1981; signed as free agent by Denver Broncos, June 4, 1982.

		—PLACE KICKING—					
Year	Club	G.	XP.	XPM.	FG.	FGA.	Pts.
1982—Denver NFL		9	15	1	11	13	48
1983—Denver NFL		16	33	1	21	25	96
1984—Denver NFL		16	38	3	21	28	101
1985—Denver NFL		16	41	3	23	38	110
Pro Totals—4 Years		57	127	8	76	104	355

KANI KAUAHI
Name pronounced Ka-WAH-he.
Center—Seattle Seahawks
Born September 6, 1959, at Kekaha, Hawaii.
Height, 6.02. Weight, 260.
High School—Honolulu, Hawaii, Kamehameha.
Attended Arizona State University and University of Hawaii.

Signed as free agent by Seattle Seahawks, April 30, 1982.
Seattle NFL, 1982 through 1985.
Games: 1982 (2), 1983 (10), 1984 (16), 1985 (16). Total—44.
Pro statistics: Recovered two fumbles, 1984.
Member of Seattle Seahawks for AFC Championship Game following 1983 season; did not play.

MEL KAUFMAN
Linebacker—Washington Redskins
Born February 24, 1958, at Los Angeles, Calif.
Height, 6.02. Weight, 218.
High School—Santa Monica, Calif.
Attended California Poly State University at San Luis Obispo.
Son-in-law of Billie Matthews, assistant coach with Indianapolis Colts.

Signed as free agent by Washington Redskins, May 6, 1981.
On injured reserve with shoulder injury, November 19 through remainder of 1981 season.

		—INTERCEPTIONS—				
Year	Club	G.	No.	Yds.	Avg.	TD.
1981—Washington NFL		11	2	25	12.5	0
1982—Washington NFL		9		None		
1983—Washington NFL		16	2	93	46.5	1
1984—Washington NFL		15		None		
1985—Washington NFL		15	3	10	3.3	0
Pro Totals—5 Years		66	7	128	18.3	1

Additional pro statistics: Recovered one fumble, 1982 and 1984; recovered one fumble for 30 yards and a touchdown, 1983; recovered two fumbles, 1985.
Played in NFC Championship Game following 1982 and 1983 seasons.
Played in NFL Championship Game following 1982 and 1983 seasons.

CLARENCE HUBERT KAY
Tight End—Denver Broncos
Born July 30, 1961, at Seneca, S.C.
Height, 6.02. Weight, 237.
High School—Seneca, S.C.
Attended University of Georgia.

Selected by Jacksonville in 1984 USFL territorial draft.
Selected by Denver in 7th round (186th player selected) of 1984 NFL draft.
Signed by Denver Broncos, May 17, 1984.

		—PASS RECEIVING—				
Year	Club	G.	P.C.	Yds.	Avg.	TD.
1984—Denver NFL		16	16	136	8.5	3
1985—Denver NFL		16	29	339	11.7	3
Pro Totals—2 Years		32	45	475	10.6	6

Additional pro statistics: Fumbled once, 1984 and 1985; recovered one fumble, 1985.

TIM ALLYNN KEARSE
Wide Receiver—Detroit Lions
Born October 24, 1959, at York, Pa.
Height, 5.10. Weight, 193.
High School—York, Pa.
Attended San Jose State University.

Selected by Oakland in 1983 USFL territorial draft.
Selected by San Diego in 11th round (303rd player selected) of 1983 NFL draft.
Signed with British Columbia Lions, June 1, 1983.
Traded with defensive back Ken Hinton by British Columbia Lions to Saskatchewan Roughriders for draft pick, August 28, 1983.
Released by Saskatchewan Roughriders, April 29, 1985; signed by San Diego Chargers, May 7, 1985.
Released by San Diego Chargers, July 28, 1985; signed as free agent by Detroit Lions, May 29, 1986.

Year	Club	G.	P.C.	Yds.	Avg.	TD.	No.	Yds.	Avg.	TD.	TD.	Pts.	F.
			-PASS RECEIVING-				-PUNT RETURNS-				—TOTAL—		
1983—B.C. (1)-Sask (6) CFL		7	9	144	16.0	1	15	201	13.4	1	2	12	0
1984—Saskatchewan CFL		8	19	240	12.6	0	11	125	11.4	1	1	6	3
Pro Totals—2 Years		15	28	384	13.7	1	26	326	12.5	2	3	18	3

Additional CFL statistics: Returned one kickoff for 24 yards, 1983; rushed once for five yards and ran for seven yards with lateral on kickoff return, 1984.

MIKE KELLEY
Center-Guard—Houston Oilers

Born August 27, 1962, at Westfield, Mass.
Height, 6.05. Weight, 266.
High School—Westfield, Mass.
Attended University of Notre Dame.

Selected by Jacksonville in 4th round (47th player selected) of 1985 USFL draft.
Selected by Houston in 3rd round (82nd player selected) of 1985 NFL draft.
Signed by Houston Oilers, July 25, 1985.
Houston NFL, 1985.
Games: 1985 (16).

BOBBY KEMP
Safety—Cincinnati Bengals

Born May 29, 1959, at Oakland, Calif.
Height, 6.00. Weight, 191.
High School—North Miami Beach, Fla.
Attended Taft Junior College and California State University at Fullerton.

Selected by Cincinnati in 8th round (202nd player selected) of 1981 NFL draft.
On injured reserve with dislocated shoulder, August 28 through October 12, 1984; activated, October 13, 1984.

Year Club	G.	No.	Yds.	Avg.	TD.
		——INTERCEPTIONS——			
1981—Cincinnati NFL	16		None		
1982—Cincinnati NFL	9	1	0	0.0	0
1983—Cincinnati NFL	16	3	26	8.7	0
1984—Cincinnati NFL	10	4	27	6.8	0
1985—Cincinnati NFL	16	1	0	0.0	0
Pro Totals—5 Years	67	9	53	5.9	0

Additional pro statistics: Returned one kickoff for no yards, 1981; recovered one fumble, 1983 and 1984; fumbled once, 1984.
Played in AFC Championship Game following 1981 season.
Played in NFL Championship Game following 1981 season.

JEFFREY ALLAN KEMP
(Jeff)
Quarterback—San Francisco 49ers

Born July 11, 1959, at Santa Ana, Calif.
Height, 6.01. Weight, 201.
High School—Potomac, Md., Winston Churchill.
Received bachelor of arts degree in economics from Dartmouth College in 1981;
and received master's in business administration degree from Pepperdine University in 1986.
Son of Jack Kemp, quarterback with Pittsburgh Steelers, Los Angeles and San Diego Chargers and Buffalo Bills, 1957, 1960 through 1967 and 1969; currently Republican Congressman from New York.

Signed as free agent by Los Angeles Rams, May 11, 1981.
Released by Los Angeles Rams, August 31, 1981; re-signed by Rams, September 1, 1981.
On injured reserve with back injury, October 3 through December 1, 1981; activated, December 2, 1981.
On inactive list, September 12 and September 19, 1982.
Granted free agency, February 1, 1986; re-signed by Rams and traded to San Francisco 49ers, May 26, 1986. (This completed deal of April 29, 1986 in which 49ers traded 3rd round pick in 1986 draft to Rams for two 4th round picks in 1986 draft.)
Active for 7 games with Los Angeles Rams in 1982; did not play.

Year	Club	G.	Att.	Cmp.	Pct.	Gain	T.P.	P.I.	Avg.	Att.	Yds.	Avg.	TD.	TD.	Pts.	F.
			——PASSING——							——RUSHING——				—TOTAL—		
1981—L.A. Rams NFL		1	6	2	33.3	25	0	1	4.17	2	9	4.5	0	0	0	0
1983—L.A. Rams NFL		4	25	12	48.0	135	1	0	5.40	3	—2	-0.7	0	0	0	2
1984—L.A. Rams NFL		14	284	143	50.4	2021	13	7	7.12	34	153	4.5	1	1	6	8
1985—L.A. Rams NFL		5	38	16	42.1	214	0	1	5.63	5	0	0.0	0	0	0	2
Pro Totals—5 Years		24	353	173	49.0	2395	14	9	6.78	44	160	3.6	1	1	6	12

Quarterback Rating Points: 1981 (7.6), 1983 (77.9), 1984 (78.7), 1985 (49.7). Total—74.1.
Additional pro statistics: Recovered three fumbles and fumbled eight times for minus 16 yards, 1984.
Member of Los Angeles Rams for 1985 Championship Game following 1985 season; did not play.

—DID YOU KNOW—

That entering the 1986 season, no National Football League team has a winning record in regular-season games against the Los Angeles Raiders?

MICHAEL LEE KENN
(Mike)
Offensive Tackle—Atlanta Falcons
Born February 9, 1956, at Evanston, Ill.
Height, 6.07. Weight, 277.
High School—Evanston, Ill.
Received bachelor of arts degree in general studies from University of Michigan in 1978.

Named to THE SPORTING NEWS NFL All-Star Team, 1980.
Selected by Atlanta in 1st round (13th player selected) of 1978 NFL draft.
On injured reserve with knee injury, November 18 through remainder of 1985 season.
Atlanta NFL, 1978 through 1985.
Games: 1978 (16), 1979 (16), 1980 (16), 1981 (16), 1982 (9), 1983 (16), 1984 (14), 1985 (11). Total—114.
Pro statistics: Recovered two fumbles, 1978 and 1979; recovered three fumbles, 1980; recovered one fumble, 1981 through 1983.
Played in Pro Bowl (NFL All-Star Game) following 1980 through 1984 seasons.

DEREK KENNARD
Guard—St. Louis Cardinals
Born September 9, 1962, at Stockton, Calif.
Height, 6.03. Weight, 265.
High School—Stockton, Calif., Edison.
Attended University of Nevada at Reno.

Selected by Los Angeles in 3rd round (52nd player selected) of 1984 USFL draft.
Signed by Los Angeles Express, March 22, 1984.
Granted roster exemption, March 22, 1984; activated, April 13, 1984.
On developmental squad, April 13 through April 27, 1984; activated, April 28, 1984.
Selected by St. Louis in 2nd round (45th player selected) of 1984 NFL supplemental draft.
On developmental squad, March 15 through April 12, 1985; activated, April 13, 1985.
Released by Los Angeles Express, August 1, 1985; re-signed by Express, August 2, 1985.
Released by Los Angeles Express, April 29, 1986; signed by St. Louis Cardinals, May 29, 1986.
On developmental squad for 2 games with Los Angeles Express in 1984.
On developmental squad for 4 games with Los Angeles Express in 1985.
Los Angeles USFL, 1984 and 1985.
Games: 1984 (6), 1985 (14). Total—20.
Pro statistics: Returned one kickoff for no yards, 1985.

ALLAN STEPHEN KENNEDY
Offensive Tackle—San Francisco 49ers
Born January 8, 1958, at Vancouver, British Columbia.
Height, 6.07. Weight, 275.
High School—Woodland Hills, Calif., El Camino Real.
Received bachelor of arts degree in criminal justice from Washington State University in 1981.

Selected by Washington in 10th round (267th player selected) of 1981 NFL draft.
Released by Washington Redskins, August 24, 1981; signed as free agent by San Francisco 49ers, September 9, 1981.
On injured reserve with broken finger, September 10 through December 3, 1981; activated, December 4, 1981.
On injured reserve with ankle injury, September 7 through entire 1982 season.
On injured reserve with knee injury, September 1 through entire 1985 season.
San Francisco NFL, 1981, 1983 and 1984.
Games: 1981 (3), 1983 (16), 1984 (15). Total—34.
Played in NFC Championship Game following 1981, 1983 and 1984 seasons.
Played in NFL Championship Game following 1981 and 1984 seasons.

STEVEN FAUCETTE KENNEY
(Steve)
Guard—Philadelphia Eagles
Born December 26, 1955, at Wilmington, N. C.
Height, 6.04. Weight, 274.
High School—Raleigh, N. C., Sanderson.
Received bachelor of science degree in administration management from Clemson University.

Signed as free agent by Philadelphia Eagles, May 14, 1979.
On injured reserve with knee injury, August 21 through entire 1979 season.
Philadelphia NFL, 1980 through 1985.
Games: 1980 (15), 1981 (13), 1982 (9), 1983 (16), 1984 (11), 1985 (16). Total—80.
Pro statistics: Recovered two fumbles, 1981; recovered one fumble, 1982.
Played in NFC Championship Game following 1980 season.
Played in NFL Championship Game following 1980 season.

—DID YOU KNOW—
That on November 10, the Colts scored nine points against the Patriots with only one second ticking off the clock? Indianapolis' Owen Gill scored at 14:04 of the fourth quarter and Irving Fryar of New England was caught by Tate Randle for a safety on the kickoff at 14:05.

WILLIAM PATRICK KENNEY
(Bill)
Quarterback—Kansas City Chiefs

Born January 20, 1955, at San Francisco, Calif.
Height, 6.04. Weight, 211.
High School—San Clemente, Calif.
Attended Arizona State University, Saddleback Community College and received bachelor of science degree
in business management from University of Northern Colorado in 1978.
Son of Charles Kenney, guard with San Francisco 49ers, 1947.

Selected by Miami in 12th round (333rd player selected) of 1978 NFL draft.
Traded by Miami Dolphins to Washington Redskins for 6th round pick in 1979 draft, August 1, 1978.
Released by Washington Redskins, August 21, 1978; signed as free agent by Kansas City Chiefs, January 19, 1979.
On injured reserve with broken thumb, August 28 through October 5, 1984; activated, October 6, 1984.
Active for 16 games with Kansas City Chiefs in 1979; did not play.

					—PASSING—					—RUSHING—			—TOTAL—	
Year	Club	G.	Att.	Cmp.	Pct.	Gain	T.P.	P.I.	Avg.	Att.	Yds.	Avg. TD.	TD.	Pts.	F.
1980—Kansas City NFL		3	69	37	53.6	542	5	2	7.86	8	8	1.0	0	0	0	1
1981—Kansas City NFL		13	274	147	53.6	1983	9	16	7.24	24	89	3.7	1	1	6	4
1982—Kansas City NFL		7	169	95	56.2	1192	7	6	7.05	13	40	3.1	0	0	0	3
1983—Kansas City NFL		16	*603	*346	57.4	4348	24	18	7.21	23	59	2.6	3	3	18	7
1984—Kansas City NFL		9	282	151	53.5	2098	15	10	7.44	9	—8	—0.9	0	0	0	8
1985—Kansas City NFL		16	338	181	53.6	2536	17	9	7.50	14	1	0.1	1	1	6	6
Pro Totals—7 Years		64	1735	957	55.2	12699	77	61	7.32	91	189	2.1	5	5	30	29

Quarterback Rating Points: 1980 (91.4), 1981 (63.8), 1982 (77.0), 1983 (80.8), 1984 (80.7), 1985 (83.6). Total—78.7.
Additional pro statistics: Fumbled once for minus six yards, 1980; fumbled four times for minus two yards, 1981;
recovered two fumbles, 1982; caught one pass for no yards and recovered four fumbles, 1983; recovered three fumbles
and fumbled eight times for minus 34 yards, 1984; recovered five fumbles and fumbled six times for minus 18 yards,
1985.
Played in Pro Bowl (NFL All-Star Game) following 1983 season.

CRAWFORD FRANCIS KER
Guard—Dallas Cowboys

Born May 5, 1962, at Philadelphia, Pa.
Height, 6.03. Weight, 293.
High School—Dunedin, Fla.
Attended Arizona Western College and University of Florida.

Selected by Tampa Bay in 1985 USFL territorial draft.
Selected by Dallas in 3rd round (76th player selected) of 1985 NFL draft.
Signed by Dallas Cowboys, July 12, 1985.
On injured reserve with back injury, October 23 through remainder of 1985 season.
Dallas NFL, 1985.
Games: 1985 (5).

DON EMIT KERN III
Tight End—Cincinnati Bengals

Born August 25, 1962, at Los Gatos, Calif.
Height, 6.04. Weight, 225.
High School—Saratoga, Calif.
Attended West Valley College and Arizona State University.

Selected by Arizona in 1984 USFL territorial draft.
Selected by Cincinnati in 6th round (150th player selected) of 1984 NFL draft.
Signed by Cincinnati Bengals, June 11, 1984.
On injured reserve with broken leg, October 29 through remainder of 1985 season.

		—PASS RECEIVING—			
Year	Club	G.	P.C.	Yds.	Avg. TD.
1984—Cincinnati NFL		16	2	14	7.0	0
1985—Cincinnati NFL		8		None		
Pro Totals—2 Years		24	2	14	7.0	0

WALLACE TODD KERSTEN
(Wally)
Offensive Tackle—Indianapolis Colts

Born December 8, 1959, at Minneapolis, Minn.
Height, 6.05. Weight, 270.
High School—Minneapolis, Minn., Roosevelt.
Attended Normandale Junior College and University of Minnesota.

Selected by Los Angeles Rams in 5th round (117th player selected) of 1982 NFL draft.
On inactive list, September 12 and September 19, 1982.
On injured reserve with knee injury, August 22 through September 26, 1983.
Released by Los Angeles Rams, September 27, 1983; signed by Oklahoma Outlaws, September 7, 1984.
Protected in merger of Oklahoma Outlaws and Arizona Wranglers, December 6, 1984.
Released by Arizona Outlaws, February 11, 1985; signed as free agent by Minnesota Vikings, May 10, 1985.
Released by Minnesota Vikings, May 20, 1985; signed as free agent by San Francisco 49ers, June 27, 1985.
Released by San Francisco 49ers, August 20, 1985; signed as free agent by Tampa Bay Buccaneers, October 29,
1985.

Released by Tampa Bay Buccaneers, November 19, 1985; signed as free agent by Indianapolis Colts, May 12, 1986.
Active for 3 games with Tampa Bay Buccaneers in 1985; did not play.
Los Angeles Rams NFL, 1982; Tampa Bay NFL, 1985.
Games: 1982 (3).

TYRONE P. KEYS
Defensive End—Chicago Bears
Born October 24, 1959, at Brookhaven, Miss.
Height, 6.07. Weight, 267.
High School—Jackson, Miss., Callaway.
Received bachelor of science degree in physical education
from Mississippi State University.

Selected by New York Jets in 5th round (113th player selected) of 1981 NFL draft.
Signed as free agent by British Columbia Lions, May 20, 1981.
On reserve list, July 12 through July 18, 1981; activated, July 19, 1981.
On reserve list, July 25 through August 2, 1981; activated, August 3, 1981.
On reserve list, August 16 through September 12, 1981; activated, September 13, 1981.
On reserve list, September 21 through remainder of 1981 season.
On reserve list, July 2 through July 17, 1982; activated, July 18, 1982.
On reserve list, August 15 through August 31, 1982; activated, September 1, 1982.
On reserve list, September 12 through September 18, 1982; activated, September 19, 1982.
On reserve list, October 17 through October 23, 1982; activated, October 24, 1982.
Traded by British Columbia Lions to Toronto Argonauts for defensive back Jo Jo Heath, April 25, 1983.
Released by Toronto Argonauts, July 2, 1983.
NFL rights traded by New York Jets to Chicago Bears for 5th round pick in 1985 draft, July 13, 1983.
Signed by Chicago Bears, July 10, 1983.
British Columbia CFL, 1981 and 1982; Chicago NFL, 1983 through 1985.
Games: 1981 (5), 1982 (10), 1983 (14), 1984 (15), 1985 (16). Total CFL—15. Total NFL—45. Total Pro—60.
Played in NFC Championship Game following 1984 and 1985 seasons.
Played in NFL Championship Game following 1985 season.

MAX JOHN KIDD
(Known by middle name.)
Punter—Buffalo Bills
Born August 22, 1961, at Springfield, Ill.
Height, 6.03. Weight, 208.
High School—Findlay, O.
Received bachelor of science degree in industrial engineering and
management science from Northwestern University in 1984.

Selected by Chicago in 1984 USFL territorial draft.
Selected by Buffalo in 5th round (128th player selected) of 1984 NFL draft.
Signed by Buffalo Bills, June 1, 1984.

Year Club	G.	No.	Avg.	Blk.
1984—Buffalo NFL	16	88	42.0	2
1985—Buffalo NFL	16	92	41.5	0
Pro Totals—2 Years	32	180	41.7	2

BLAIR ARMSTRONG KIEL
Quarterback—Indianapolis Colts
Born November 29, 1961, at Columbus, Ind.
Height, 6.00. Weight, 200.
High School—Columbus, Ind., East.
Received degree in marketing from University of Notre Dame in 1984.

Selected by Chicago in 1984 USFL territorial draft.
Selected by Tampa Bay in 11th round (281st player selected) of 1984 NFL draft.
Signed by Tampa Bay Buccaneers, June 5, 1984.
On non-football injury list with ulcerative colitis, November 13 through remainder of 1984 season.
On non-football injury with Crohn's Disease, August 12 through September 30, 1985.
Released by Tampa Bay Buccaneers, October 1, 1985; signed as free agent by Indianapolis Colts, February 13, 1986.

Year Club	G.	Att.	Cmp.	Pct.	Gain	T.P.	P.I.	Avg.	Att.	Yds.	Avg.	TD.	TD.	Pts.	F.
		←——————PASSING——————→							←——RUSHING——→				←—TOTAL—→		
1984—Tampa Bay NFL	10	None							None				0	0	0

JEFF C. KIEWEL
Name pronounced KEY-well.
Guard—Atlanta Falcons
Born September 27, 1960, at Phoenix, Ariz.
Height, 6.04. Weight, 265.
High School—Tucson, Ariz., Sabino.
Attended University of Arizona.

Selected by Arizona in 1983 USFL territorial draft.
Signed by Arizona Wranglers, February 26, 1983.
On developmental squad, May 28 through June 3, 1983; activated, June 4, 1983.
On developmental squad, February 24 through entire 1984 season.

Not protected in merger of Arizona Wranglers and Oklahoma Outlaws; selected by Houston Gamblers in USFL dispersal draft, December 6, 1984.
Released by Houston Gamblers, February 18, 1985; re-signed by Gamblers, February 19, 1985.
On developmental squad, February 21 through February 25, 1985.
Contract voided by USFL, February 26, 1985; signed as free agent by Atlanta Falcons, March 16, 1985.
On developmental squad for 1 game with Arizona Wranglers in 1983.
On developmental squad for 18 games with Arizona Wranglers in 1984.
On developmental squad for 1 game with Houston Gamblers in 1985.
Arizona USFL, 1983; Atlanta NFL, 1985.
Games: 1983 (16), 1985 (16). Total—32.
Pro statistics: Recovered two fumbles, 1985.
On developmental squad for USFL Championship Game following 1984 season.

TOM JOSEPH KILKENNY
Linebacker—Philadelphia Eagles
Born August 27, 1958, at Philadelphia, Pa.
Height, 6.03. Weight, 235.
High School—Philadelphia, Pa., Father Judge.
Attended Temple University.

Selected by Philadelphia in 1984 USFL territorial draft.
Signed by Philadelphia Stars, January 24, 1984.
Released by Philadelphia Stars, February 13, 1984; awarded on waivers to Chicago Blitz, February 14, 1984.
On developmental squad, February 24 through March 10, 1984; activated, March 11, 1984.
Selected by Cincinnati in 3rd round (65th player selected) of 1984 NFL supplemental draft.
Franchise disbanded, November 20, 1984.
Selected by Denver Gold in USFL dispersal draft, December 6, 1984.
Granted free agency, August 1, 1985; signed by Cincinnati Bengals, August 9, 1985.
Released by Cincinnati Bengals, August 19, 1985; signed as free agent by Philadelphia Eagles, March 12, 1986.
On developmental squad for 2 games with Chicago Blitz in 1984.
Chicago USFL, 1984; Denver USFL, 1985.
Games: 1984 (16), 1985 (18). Total—34.
Pro statistics: Intercepted one pass for five yards, credited with two sacks for 15 yards and recovered two fumbles, 1984; returned one kickoff for 12 yards, credited with one sack for seven yards and recovered one fumble, 1985.

BRUCE MICHAEL KIMBALL
Guard
Born August 19, 1959, at Beverly, Mass.
Height, 6.02. Weight, 260.
High School—Byfield, Mass., Triton.
Attended Bridgeton (Mass.) Academy Prep School and received bachelor of science degree
in physical education from University of Massachusetts in 1979.

Selected by Pittsburgh in 7th round (192nd player selected) of 1979 NFL draft.
Released by Pittsburgh Steelers, August 20, 1979; signed as free agent by Toronto Argonauts, September 6, 1979.
On injured reserve, September 22 through remainder of 1980 season.
Granted free agency, March 1, 1981; signed as free agent by New York Giants, March 27, 1981.
On injured reserve with knee injury, July 24 through entire 1981 season.
On injured reserve with fractured leg, September 13 through remainder of 1982 season.
Released by New York Giants, August 15, 1983; signed as free agent by Washington Redskins, August 25, 1983.
Released by Washington Redskins, August 27, 1984; re-signed by Redskins, October 23, 1984.
On injured reserve with back injury, August 20 through entire 1985 season.
Granted free agency with no qualifying offer, February 1, 1986.
Toronto CFL, 1979 and 1980; New York Giants NFL, 1982; Washington NFL, 1983 and 1984.
Games: 1979 (8), 1980 (11), 1982 (1), 1983 (16), 1984 (8). Total CFL—19. Total NFL—25. Total Pro—44.
Pro statistics: Recovered two fumbles, 1980.
Played in NFC Championship Game following 1983 season.
Played in NFL Championship Game following 1983 season.

JAMIE KIMMEL
Linebacker—Los Angeles Raiders
Born March 28, 1962, at Johnson City, N.Y.
Height, 6.03. Weight, 240.
High School—Conklin, N.Y., Susquehanna Valley.
Attended Syracuse University.

Selected by New Jersey in 1985 USFL territorial draft.
Selected by Los Angeles Raiders in 4th round (107th player selected) of 1985 NFL draft.
Signed by Los Angeles Raiders, July 22, 1985.
On injured reserve with hamstring injury, August 27 through entire 1985 season.

ALFRED TERANCE KINARD
(Terry)
Safety—New York Giants
Born November 24, 1959, at Bitburg, West Germany.
Height, 6.01. Weight, 200.
High School—Sumter, S.C.
Attended Clemson University.

Named as defensive back on The Sporting News College All-America Team, 1982.
Selected by Washington in 1983 USFL territorial draft.

Selected by New York Giants in 1st round (10th player selected) of 1983 NFL draft.
Signed by New York Giants, May 17, 1983.

		—INTERCEPTIONS—			
Year Club	G.	No.	Yds.	Avg.	TD.
1983—N. Y. Giants NFL	16	3	49	16.3	0
1984—N. Y. Giants NFL	15	2	29	14.5	0
1985—N. Y. Giants NFL	16	5	100	20.0	0
Pro Totals—3 Years...........	47	10	178	17.8	0

Additional pro statistics: Recovered one fumble for 10 yards, 1983; returned one punt for no yards and fumbled once, 1984; recovered one fumble, 1984 and 1985.

ANGELO TYRONE KING
Linebacker—Detroit Lions
Born February 10, 1958, at Columbia, S.C.
Height, 6.01. Weight, 222.
High School—Columbia, S.C.
Received degree in health and physical education
from South Carolina State College.

Signed as free agent by Dallas Cowboys, May, 1981.
Released by Dallas Cowboys, August 25, 1981; re-signed by Cowboys, September 8, 1981.
Traded by Dallas Cowboys to Detroit Lions for 6th round pick in 1986 draft, August 27, 1984.
Dallas NFL, 1981 through 1983; Detroit NFL, 1984 and 1985.
Games: 1981 (15), 1982 (9), 1983 (16), 1984 (16), 1985 (16). Total—72.
Pro statistics: Recovered two fumbles, 1981.
Played in NFC Championship Game following 1981 and 1982 seasons.

BRUCE ERIC KING
Running Back—Kansas City Chiefs
Born January 7, 1963, at Clarksville, Ind.
Height, 6.01. Weight, 219.
High School—Lincoln City, Ind., Heritage Hills.
Attended Purdue University.

Selected by Oakland in 8th round (105th player selected) of 1985 USFL draft.
Selected by Kansas City in 5th round (126th player selected) of 1985 NFL draft.
Signed by Kansas City Chiefs, July 15, 1985.

		—RUSHING—				PASS RECEIVING				—TOTAL—		
Year Club	G.	Att.	Yds.	Avg.	TD.	P.C.	Yds.	Avg.	TD.	TD.	Pts.	F.
1985—Kansas City NFL.....................................	16	28	83	3.0	0	7	45	6.4	0	0	0	0

Additional pro statistics: Returned one kickoff for 13 yards and recovered one fumble, 1985.

DAVID JOEL KING
Cornerback—San Diego Chargers
Born May 19, 1963, at Mobile, Ala.
Height, 5.08. Weight, 176.
High School—Fairhope, Ala.
Attended Auburn University.

Selected by Birmingham in 1985 USFL territorial draft.
Selected by San Diego in 10th round (264th player selected) of 1985 NFL draft.
Signed by San Diego Chargers, July 10, 1985.
On injured reserve with ankle injury, September 10 through remainder of 1985 season.
San Diego NFL, 1985.
Games: 1985 (1).

EMANUEL KING
Linebacker—Cincinnati Bengals
Born August 15, 1963, at Leroy, Ala.
Height, 6.04. Weight, 245.
High School—Leroy, Ala.
Attended University of Alabama.

Selected by Birmingham in 1985 USFL territorial draft.
Selected by Cincinnati in 1st round (25th player selected) of 1985 NFL draft.
Signed by Cincinnati Bengals, May 30, 1985.
Cincinnati NFL, 1985.
Games: 1985 (16).
Pro statistics: Recovered one fumble, 1985.

GORDON DAVID KING
Offensive Tackle—New York Giants
Born February 3, 1956, at Madison, Wis.
Height, 6.06. Weight, 275.
High School—Fair Oaks, Calif., Bella Vista.
Received bachelor of arts degree in communications/psychology from
Stanford University in 1978.

Named as offensive tackle on THE SPORTING NEWS College All-America Team, 1977.

Selected by New York Giants in 1st round (10th player selected) of 1978 NFL draft.
On injured reserve with ankle injury, November 29 through remainder of 1978 season.
On injured reserve with dislocated elbow, August 29 through October 18, 1979; activated, October 19, 1979.
On injured reserve with broken arm, December 6 through remainder of 1983 season.
On physically unable to perform/reserve with broken arm, July 19 through entire 1984 season.
New York Giants NFL, 1978 through 1983 and 1985.
Games: 1978 (11), 1979 (7), 1980 (12), 1981 (16), 1982 (9), 1983 (14), 1985 (15). Total—84.
Pro statistics: Recovered one fumble, 1979, 1981 and 1982.

KENNETH L. KING
(Kenny)
Running Back—Los Angeles Raiders
Born March 7, 1957, at Clarendon, Tex.
Height, 5.11. Weight, 205.
High School—Clarendon, Tex.
Attended University of Oklahoma.

Selected by Houston in 3rd round (72nd player selected) of 1979 NFL draft.
On injured reserve with rib injury, November 21 through remainder of 1979 season.
Traded by Houston Oilers to Oakland Raiders for safety Jack Tatum and 7th round picks in 1980 and 1981 draft, April 30, 1980.
On injured reserve with bruised sternum, December 21 through remainder of 1981 season.
Franchise transferred to Los Angeles, May 7, 1982.

Year Club	G.	Att.	Yds.	Avg.	TD.	P.C.	Yds.	Avg.	TD.	TD.	Pts.	F.
1979—Houston NFL	12	3	9	3.0	0		None			0	0	0
1980—Oakland NFL	15	172	761	4.4	4	22	145	6.6	0	4	24	6
1981—Oakland NFL	14	170	828	4.9	0	27	216	8.0	0	0	0	10
1982—Los Angeles Raiders NFL	9	69	264	3.8	2	9	57	6.3	0	2	12	1
1983—Los Angeles Raiders NFL	15	82	294	3.6	1	14	149	10.6	1	2	12	1
1984—Los Angeles Raiders NFL	16	67	254	3.8	0	14	99	7.1	0	0	0	3
1985—Los Angeles Raiders NFL	16	16	67	4.2	0	3	49	16.3	0	0	0	1
Pro Totals—7 Years	97	579	2477	4.3	7	89	715	8.0	1	8	48	22

Additional pro statistics: Returned one kickoff for 17 yards, 1979; recovered two fumbles, 1981; recovered one fumble, 1984.
Played in AFC Championship Game following 1980 and 1983 seasons.
Played in NFL Championship Game following 1980 and 1983 seasons.
Named to play in Pro Bowl (NFL All-Star Game) following 1980 season; replaced due to injury by Franco Harris.

LINDEN KEITH KING
Linebacker—San Diego Chargers
Born June 28, 1955, at Memphis, Tenn.
Height, 6.04. Weight, 250.
High School—Colorado Springs, Colo., Air Academy.
Attended Colorado State University.

Selected by San Diego in 3rd round (77th player selected) of 1977 NFL draft.
On injured reserve, September 12 through 1977 season.
On injured reserve with ankle injury, November 5, 1980, through January 9, 1981; activated, January 10, 1981.
San Diego NFL, 1978 through 1985.
Games: 1978 (14), 1979 (16), 1980 (5), 1981 (16), 1982 (9), 1983 (16), 1984 (16), 1985 (16). Total—108.
Pro statistics: Intercepted one pass for three yards and recovered one fumble for 14 yards, 1978; recovered two fumbles, 1979, 1983 and 1984; intercepted one pass for 28 yards, 1981; recovered one fumble, 1982; intercepted one pass for 19 yards, 1983; intercepted two passes for 52 yards and fumbled once, 1984; intercepted two passes for eight yards, 1985.
Played in AFC Championship Game following 1980 and 1981 seasons.

REGGIE KINLAW
Defensive Tackle—Seattle Seahawks
Born January 9, 1957, at Miami, Fla.
Height, 6.02. Weight, 245.
High School—Miami, Fla., Springs.
Attended University of Oklahoma.
Brother of Marcus Kinlaw, offensive lineman at University of Miami (Fla.); and cousin of Dan Driessen, first baseman with San Francisco Giants.

Selected by Oakland in 12th round (320th player selected) of 1979 NFL draft.
On injured reserve with knee injury, September 9 through remainder of 1981 season.
Franchise transferred to Los Angeles, May 7, 1982.
Released by Los Angeles Raiders, August 27, 1985; awarded on waivers to Seattle Seahawks, August 28, 1985.
Oakland NFL, 1979 through 1981; Los Angeles Raiders NFL, 1982 through 1984; Seattle NFL, 1985.
Games: 1979 (16), 1980 (14), 1981 (1), 1982 (9), 1983 (16), 1984 (13), 1985 (16). Total—85.
Pro statistics: Recovered one fumble, 1982.
Played in AFC Championship Game following 1980 and 1983 seasons.
Played in NFL Championship Game following 1980 and 1983 seasons.

LARRY D. KINNEBREW
Running Back—Cincinnati Bengals
Born June 11, 1959, at Rome, Ga.
Height, 6.01. Weight, 252.
High School—Rome, Ga., East.
Attended Tennessee State University.

Selected by Cincinnati in 6th round (165th player selected) of 1983 NFL draft.
On injured reserve with broken hand, September 24 through October 25, 1985; activated, October 26, 1985.

| | | | —RUSHING— | | | | PASS RECEIVING | | | | —TOTAL— | |
Year	Club	G.	Att.	Yds.	Avg.	TD.	P.C.	Yds.	Avg.	TD.	TD.	Pts.	F.
1983—Cincinnati NFL		16	39	156	4.0	3	2	4	2.0	0	3	18	3
1984—Cincinnati NFL		16	154	623	4.0	9	19	159	8.4	1	10	60	4
1985—Cincinnati NFL		12	170	714	4.2	9	22	187	8.5	1	10	60	4
Pro Totals—3 Years		44	363	1493	4.1	21	43	350	8.1	2	23	138	11

Additional pro statistics: Recovered one fumble, 1983 and 1985; returned one kickoff for seven yards, 1984.

JOSEPH EDWARD KLECKO
(Joe)
Defensive Tackle-Defensive End—New York Jets
Born October 15, 1953, at Chester, Pa.
Height, 6.03. Weight, 263.
High School—Chester, Pa., St. James.
Received bachelor of arts degree in history from Temple University in 1977.

Named to THE SPORTING NEWS NFL All-Star Team, 1981.
Selected by New York Jets in 6th round (144th player selected) of 1977 NFL draft.
On injured reserve with knee injury, November 26, 1982 through January 4, 1983; activated, January 5, 1983.
Played semi-pro football with Ridley Township Green Knights, 1971 and 1972.
New York Jets NFL, 1977 through 1985.
Games: 1977 (13), 1978 (16), 1979 (16), 1980 (15), 1981 (16), 1982 (2), 1983 (16), 1984 (12), 1985 (16). Total—122.
Pro statistics: Recovered one fumble, 1978, 1983 and 1985; recovered two fumbles, 1981 and 1984.
Played in AFC Championship Game following 1982 season.
Played in Pro Bowl (NFL All-Star Game) following 1981 and 1983 through 1985 seasons.

VICTOR K. KLEVER
(Rocky)
Tight End—New York Jets
Born July 10, 1959, at Portland, Ore.
Height, 6.03. Weight, 225.
High School—Anchorage, Alaska, West.
Received degree in business management from University of Montana in 1982.

Selected by New York Jets in 9th round (247th player selected) of 1982 NFL draft.
On injured reserve with broken hand, August 24 through entire 1982 season.
Released by New York Jets, August 29, 1983; re-signed by Jets after clearing procedural waivers, November 3, 1983.

| | | | —PASS RECEIVING— | | | |
Year	Club	G.	P.C.	Yds.	Avg.	TD.
1983—New York Jets NFL		5		None		
1984—New York Jets NFL		16	3	29	9.7	1
1985—New York Jets NFL		16	14	183	13.1	2
Pro Totals—3 Years		37	17	212	12.5	3

Additional pro statistics: Returned one kickoff for three yards and recovered one fumble, 1985.

DANNY LEE KNIGHT
Wide Receiver—Buffalo Bills
Born May 30, 1960, at Natchez, Miss.
Height, 5.11. Weight, 205.
High School—Natchez, Miss., North.
Attended Mississippi State University.

Selected by New Jersey in 1984 USFL territorial draft.
Signed by New Jersey Generals, January 4, 1984.
On injured reserve with groin injury, February 22 through March 23, 1984; activated, March 24, 1984.
On developmental squad, April 7 through April 19, 1984; activated, April 20, 1984.
Selected by Miami in 1st round (26th player selected) of 1984 NFL supplemental draft.
Released by New Jersey Generals, July 31, 1985; signed by Miami Dolphins, August 7, 1985.
Released by Miami Dolphins, August 19, 1985; signed as free agent by Buffalo Bills, May 6, 1986.
On developmental squad for 2 games with New Jersey Generals in 1984.

| | | | PASS RECEIVING | | | | -PUNT RETURNS- | | | | —KICKOFF RET.— | | | | —TOTAL— | |
Year	Club	G.	P.C.	Yds.	Avg.	TD.	No.	Yds.	Avg.	TD.	No.	Yds.	Avg.	TD.	TD.	Pts.	F.
1984—New Jersey USFL		12	17	287	16.9	1		None				None			1	6	0
1985—New Jersey USFL		18	7	97	13.9	1	26	240	9.2	0	9	200	22.2	0	1	6	4
Pro Totals—2 Years		30	24	384	16.0	2	26	240	9.2	0	9	200	22.0	0	2	12	4

Additional pro statistics: Rushed twice for no yards, 1984; recovered two fumbles, 1985.

GREGORY MICHAEL KOCH

Name pronounced Cook.

(Greg)

Offensive Tackle—Green Bay Packers

Born June 14, 1955, at Bethesda, Md.
Height, 6.04. Weight, 276.
High School—Houston, Tex., Spring Woods.
Attended University of Arkansas.

Selected by Green Bay in 2nd round (39th player selected) of 1977 NFL draft.
Left Green Bay Packers camp voluntarily, August 19 through September 4, 1985; activated, September 5, 1985.
Green Bay NFL, 1977 through 1985.
Games: 1977 (14), 1978 (16), 1979 (16), 1980 (16), 1981 (16), 1982 (9), 1983 (15), 1984 (15), 1985 (16). Total—133.
Pro statistics: Recovered one fumble, 1985.

PETER ALAN KOCH

(Pete)

Defensive End—Kansas City Chiefs

Born January 23, 1962, at Nassau County, N.Y.
Height, 6.06. Weight, 265.
High School—New Hyde Park, N.Y., Memorial.
Attended University of Maryland.
Brother of Larry Koch, pitcher in St. Louis Cardinals' organization, 1967, 1968, 1970 and 1971.

Selected by Washington in 1984 USFL territorial draft.
Selected by Cincinnati in 1st round (16th player selected) of 1984 NFL draft.
Signed by Cincinnati Bengals, July 30, 1984.
Released by Cincinnati Bengals, September 2, 1985; awarded on waivers to Kansas City Chiefs, September 3, 1985.
Cincinnati NFL, 1984; Kansas City NFL, 1985.
Games: 1984 (16), 1985 (16). Total—32.

VICTOR E. KOENNING

(Vic)

Linebacker—Green Bay Packers

Born February 26, 1960, at Midwest City, Okla.
Height, 6.03. Weight, 230.
High School—Owasso, Okla.
Received bachelor of science degree in communications
from Kansas State University in 1983.

Signed as free agent by Denver Broncos, April 28, 1983.
Released by Denver Broncos, August 16, 1983.
USFL rights traded by Denver Gold to Oklahoma Outlaws for rights to linebacker Bob Kardoes, September 2, 1983.
Signed by Oklahoma Outlaws, October 11, 1983.
Protected in merger of Oklahoma Outlaws and Arizona Wranglers, December 6, 1983.
Released by Arizona Outlaws, August 21, 1985; signed as free agent by Green Bay Packers, April 20, 1986.

		—INTERCEPTIONS—			
Year Club	G.	No.	Yds.	Avg.	TD.
1984—Oklahoma USFL	18	3	26	8.7	1
1985—Arizona USFL	17	2	91	45.5	*1
Pro Totals—2 Years	35	5	117	23.4	2

Additional pro statistics: Credited with 5½ sacks for 54 yards and recovered two fumbles for minus five yards, 1984; recovered one fumble and credited with one sack for 11 yards, 1985.

MATTHEW JOSEPH KOFLER

(Matt)

Quarterback—Indianapolis Colts

Born August 30, 1959, at Longview, Wash.
Height, 6.03. Weight, 192.
High School—San Diego, Calif., Patrick Henry.
Attended San Diego Mesa Junior College and San Diego State University.
Son of Otto Kofler, assistant coach at Stanford University.

Selected by Buffalo in 2nd round (48th player selected) of 1982 NFL draft.
On inactive list, September 12 and September 19, 1982.
Traded by Buffalo Bills to Indianapolis Colts for 11th round pick in 1986 draft, August 14, 1985.

		—PASSING—							—RUSHING—				—TOTAL—		
Year Club	G.	Att.	Cmp.	Pct.	Gain	T.P.	P.I.	Avg.	Att.	Yds.	Avg.	TD.	TD.	Pts.	F.
1982—Buffalo NFL	4			None					2	21	10.5	0	0	0	0
1983—Buffalo NFL	16	61	35	57.4	440	4	3	7.21	4	25	6.3	0	0	0	0
1984—Buffalo NFL	16	93	33	35.5	432	2	5	4.65	10	80	8.0	0	0	0	1
1985—Indianapolis NFL	5	48	23	47.9	284	1	3	5.92	4	33	8.3	1	1	6	0
Pro Totals—4 Years	41	202	91	45.0	1156	7	11	5.72	20	159	8.0	1	1	6	1

Quarterback Rating Points: 1983 (81.3), 1984 (35.8), 1985 (47.6). Total—52.6.
Additional pro statistics: Recovered one fumble, 1984.

JOE KOHLBRAND
Linebacker—New Orleans Saints
Born March 18, 1963, at Merritt Island, Fla.
Height, 6.04. Weight, 242.
High School—Merritt Island, Fla.
Attended University of Miami (Fla.).

Selected by New Orleans in 8th round (206th player selected) of 1985 NFL draft.
Signed by New Orleans Saints, July 25, 1985.
On injured reserve with knee injury, August 28 through October 3, 1985; activated after clearing procedural waivers, October 4, 1985.
New Orleans NFL, 1985.
Games: 1985 (12).

ROBERT HENRY KOHRS
(Bob)
Linebacker—Pittsburgh Steelers
Born November 8, 1958, at Phoenix, Ariz.
Height, 6.03. Weight, 235.
High School—Phoenix, Ariz., Brophy Prep.
Attended Arizona State University.

Selected by Pittsburgh in 2nd round (35th player selected) of 1980 NFL draft.
On injured reserve with broken foot, September 1 through entire 1980 season.
On injured reserve with knee injury, November 4 through remainder of 1983 season.
On physically unable to perform/reserve with knee injury, August 21 through October 11, 1984; activated, October 12, 1984.
On injured reserve with knee injury, November 23 through remainder of 1985 season.
Pittsburgh NFL, 1981 through 1985.
Games: 1981 (16), 1982 (9), 1983 (9), 1984 (10), 1985 (11). Total—55.
Pro statistics: Recovered one fumble, 1981 through 1983; returned one kickoff for six yards and credited with one safety, 1983.
Played in AFC Championship Game following 1984 season.

CHRISTOPHER JAMES KOLODZIEJSKI
Name pronounced Ko-la-JESS-skee.
(Chris)
Tight End—Pittsburgh Steelers
Born January 5, 1961, at Augsburg, Germany.
Height, 6.03. Weight, 231.
High School—Santa Monica, Calif.
Received bachelor of science degree in finance from University of Wyoming in 1984.

Selected by Denver in 1984 USFL territorial draft.
Selected by Pittsburgh in 2nd round (52nd player selected) of 1984 NFL draft.
Signed by Pittsburgh Steelers, July 20, 1984.
On injured reserve with knee injury, October 15 through remainder of 1984 season.
On physically unable to perform/reserve with knee injury, July 19 through entire 1985 season.

		—PASS RECEIVING—				
Year	Club	G.	P.C.	Yds.	Avg.	TD.
1984—Pittsburgh NFL		7	5	59	11.8	0

WILLIAM JEFFREY KOMLO
(Jeff)
Quarterback
Born July 30, 1956, at Cleverly, Md.
Height, 6.02. Weight, 200.
High School—Hyattsville, Md., DeMatha.
Attended University of Delaware and attending Villanova University.
Brother of Drew Komlo, quarterback at University of Delaware.

Selected by Detroit in 9th round (231st player selected) of 1979 NFL draft.
Released by Detroit Lions, September 6, 1982; claimed on waivers by Atlanta Falcons, September 7, 1982.
On inactive list, September 12 and September 19, 1982.
Released by Atlanta Falcons, August 22, 1983; signed as free agent by Tampa Bay Buccaneers, October 7, 1983.
On injured reserve with elbow injury, August 20 through entire 1984 season.
Granted free agency after not receiving qualifying offer, February 1, 1985; signed by Seattle Seahawks, February 28, 1985.
On injured reserve with elbow injury, August 20 through entire 1985 season.
Granted free agency with no qualifying offer, February 1, 1986.
Active for 7 games with Atlanta Falcons in 1982; did not play.

			—PASSING—							—RUSHING—				—TOTAL—		
Year	Club	G.	Att.	Cmp.	Pct.	Gain	T.P.	P.I.	Avg.	Att.	Yds.	Avg.	TD.	TD.	Pts.	F.
1979—Detroit NFL		16	368	183	49.7	2238	11	23	6.08	30	107	3.6	2	2	12	11
1980—Detroit NFL		4	4	2	50.0	26	0	1	6.50		None			0	0	0
1981—Detroit NFL		3	57	29	50.9	290	1	3	5.09	6	3	0.5	0	0	0	2
1983—Tampa Bay NFL		2	8	4	50.0	49	0	1	6.13	2	11	5.5	0	0	0	2
Pro Totals—5 Years		25	437	218	49.9	2603	12	28	5.96	38	121	3.2	2	2	12	15

Quarterback Rating Points: 1979 (52.6), 1980 (31.3), 1981 (49.6), 1983 (29.7). Total—50.8.
Additional pro statistics: Recovered six fumbles and fumbled 11 times for minus 22 yards, 1979; recovered two fumbles, 1981.

STEVE KORTE
Center—New Orleans Saints
Born January 15, 1960, at Denver, Colo.
Height, 6.02. Weight, 272.
High School—Littleton, Colo., Arapahoe.
Received degree in physical education from University of Arkansas.

Named as guard on THE SPORTING NEWS College All-America Team, 1982.
Selected by Birmingham in 2nd round (20th player selected) of 1983 USFL draft.
Selected by New Orleans in 2nd round (38th player selected) of 1983 NFL draft.
Signed by New Orleans Saints, June 20, 1983.
USFL rights traded by Birmingham Stallions to Memphis Showboats for offensive tackle Phil McKinnely, January 22, 1985.
On injured reserve with knee injury, September 25 through October 24, 1985; activated, October 25, 1985.
New Orleans NFL, 1983 through 1985.
Games: 1983 (16), 1984 (15), 1985 (12). Total—43.
Pro statistics: Recovered one fumble in end zone for a touchdown, 1983; recovered one fumble, 1984; fumbled once for minus 18 yards, 1985.

BERNIE KOSAR
Quarterback—Cleveland Browns
Born November 25, 1963, at Boardman, O.
Height, 6.05. Weight, 210.
High School—Boardman, O.
Received degree in finance and economics from University of Miami (Fla.) in 1985.

Selected by Cleveland in 1st round of NFL supplemental draft, July 2, 1985.
Signed by Cleveland Browns, July 2, 1985.

		—————PASSING—————							——RUSHING——				—TOTAL—		
Year	Club	G.	Att.	Cmp.	Pct.	Gain	T.P.	P.I.	Avg.	Att.	Yds.	Avg.	TD.	TD.	Pts.	F.
1985—Cleveland NFL..............		12	248	124	50.0	1578	8	7	6.36	26	—12	—0.5	1	1	6	14

Quarterback Rating Points: 1985 (69.3).
Additional pro statistics: Recovered two fumbles and fumbled 14 times for minus 25 yards, 1985.

JIM KOVACH
Name pronounced KOE-vawch.
Linebacker—San Francisco 49ers
Born May 1, 1956, at Parma Heights, O.
Height, 6.02. Weight, 239.
High School—Parma Heights, O., Valley Forge.
Received bachelor of science degree in pre-med from University of Kentucky in 1979; attending medical school at University of Kentucky.

Selected by New Orleans in 4th round (93rd player selected) of 1979 NFL draft.
On injured reserve with dislocated shoulder, December 3 through remainder of 1980 season.
On injured reserve with knee injury, September 17 through November 13, 1985.
Awarded on procedural waivers to San Francisco 49ers, November 15, 1985.
New Orleans NFL, 1979 through 1984; New Orleans (2)-San Francisco (4) NFL, 1985.
Games: 1979 (16), 1980 (11), 1981 (15), 1982 (8), 1983 (16), 1984 (15), 1985 (6). Total—87.
Pro statistics: Returned one kickoff for 10 yards, 1979; intercepted one pass for no yards, 1980; intercepted one pass for 13 yards, 1981; recovered one fumble, 1981 and 1982; intercepted one pass for 16 yards, 1984; intercepted one pass for 53 yards, 1985.

GARY STUART KOWALSKI
Offensive Tackle—San Diego Chargers
Born July 2, 1960, at New Haven, Conn.
Height, 6.05. Weight, 290.
High School—Clinton, Conn., Morgan.
Attended Boston College.

Selected by Boston in 1983 USFL territorial draft.
Selected by Los Angeles Rams in 6th round (144th player selected) of 1983 NFL draft.
Signed by Los Angeles Rams, June 3, 1983.
On injured reserve with knee injury, August 28 through entire 1984 season.
Traded with 5th round pick in 1986 draft by Los Angeles Rams to San Diego Chargers for wide receiver Bobby Duckworth, September 2, 1985.
On injured reserve with knee injury, December 7 through remainder of 1985 season.
Los Angeles Rams NFL, 1983; San Diego NFL, 1985.
Games: 1983 (15), 1985 (13). Total—28.

BRUCE KOZERSKI
Center—Cincinnati Bengals
Born April 2, 1962, at Plains, Pa.
Height, 6.04. Weight, 275.
High School—Wilkes-Barre, Pa., James M. Coughlin.
Attended Holy Cross College.

Selected by Houston in 12th round (245th player selected) of 1984 USFL draft.
Selected by Cincinnati in 9th round (231st player selected) of 1984 NFL draft.
Signed by Cincinnati Bengals, June 10, 1984.
Cincinnati NFL, 1984 and 1985.
Games: 1984 (16), 1985 (14). Total—30.

MICHAEL JOHN KOZLOWSKI
(Mike)
Safety—Miami Dolphins
Born February 24, 1956, at Newark, N. J.
Height, 6.01. Weight, 198.
High School—Encinitas, Calif., San Dieguito.
Attended San Diego State University (on volleyball scholarship), Brigham Young University,
Mira Costa Junior College and University of Colorado.
Brother of Glen Kozlowski, rookie wide receiver with Chicago Bears.

Selected by Miami in 10th round (272nd player selected) of 1979 NFL draft.
On injured reserve with ankle injury, August 30 through entire 1980 season.
Tied NFL record for most touchdowns scored by interception, game (2), against New York Jets, December 16, 1983.
On injured reserve with torn ankle ligament, October 9, 1985 through January 2, 1986, activated, January 3, 1986.

| | | INTERCEPTIONS | | | –PUNT RETURNS– | | | —KICKOFF RET.— | | | —TOTAL— | | |
Year Club	G.	No.	Yds.	Avg. TD.	No.	Yds.	Avg. TD.	No.	Yds.	Avg. TD.	TD.	Pts.	F.
1979—Miami NFL	16		None		3	21	7.0 0	4	85	21.3 0	0	0	0
1981—Miami NFL	14	3	37	12.3 0	1	9	9.0 0	1	40	40.0 0	1	6	0
1982—Miami NFL	9	1	36	36.0 0		None		1	10	10.0 0	0	0	0
1983—Miami NFL	16	2	73	36.5 *2	2	10	6.0 0	4	50	12.5 0	2	12	2
1984—Miami NFL	16	1	26	26.0 0	4	41	10.3 0	2	23	11.5 0	0	0	0
1985—Miami NFL	5		None		7	65	9.3 0	0	32	 0	0	0	0
Pro Totals—6 Years	76	7	172	24.6 2	17	146	8.6 0	12	240	20.0 0	3	18	2

Additional pro statistics: Recovered one fumble, 1979 and 1983; recovered one fumble for 25 yards and a touchdown, 1981; recovered two fumbles for 30 yards, 1982.
Played in AFC Championship Game following 1982, 1984 and 1985 seasons.
Played in NFL Championship Game following 1982 and 1984 seasons.

GREG J. KRAGEN
Nose Tackle—Denver Broncos
Born March 4, 1962, at Chicago, Ill.
Height, 6.03. Weight, 245.
High School—Pleasanton, Calif., Amador.
Attended Utah State University.

Selected by Oklahoma in 15th round (296th player selected) of 1984 USFL draft.
Signed as free agent by Denver Broncos, May 2, 1984.
Released by Denver Broncos, August 27, 1984; re-signed by Broncos, January 20, 1985.
Denver NFL, 1985.
Games: 1985 (16).

THOMAS FRANCIS KRAMER
(Tommy)
Quarterback—Minnesota Vikings
Born March 7, 1955, at San Antonio, Tex.
Height, 6.02. Weight, 200.
High School—San Antonio, Tex., Robert E. Lee.
Received bachelor of business administration degree from Rice University.
Son of Colonel John J. Kramer, head coach at Texas Lutheran College, 1953 through 1958.

Selected by Minnesota in 1st round (27th player selected) of 1977 NFL draft.
On injured reserve with knee injury, September 20 through remainder of 1983 season.

| | | ——PASSING—— | | | | | | | ——RUSHING—— | | | | —TOTAL— | | |
Year Club	G.	Att.	Cmp.	Pct.	Gain	T.P.	P.I.	Avg.	Att.	Yds.	Avg. TD.	TD.	Pts.	F.
1977—Minnesota NFL	6	57	30	52.6	425	5	4	7.46	10	3	0.3 0	0	0	3
1978—Minnesota NFL	4	16	5	31.3	50	0	1	3.13	1	10	10.0 0	0	0	0
1979—Minnesota NFL	16	566	315	55.7	3397	23	24	6.00	32	138	4.3 1	1	6	9
1980—Minnesota NFL	15	522	299	57.3	3582	19	23	6.86	31	115	3.7 1	1	6	2
1981—Minnesota NFL	14	593	322	54.3	3912	26	24	6.60	10	13	1.3 0	0	0	8
1982—Minnesota NFL	9	308	176	57.1	2037	15	12	6.61	21	77	3.7 3	3	18	3
1983—Minnesota NFL	3	82	55	67.1	550	3	4	6.71	8	3	0.4 0	0	0	2
1984—Minnesota NFL	9	236	124	52.5	1678	9	10	7.11	15	9	0.6 0	1	6	10
1985—Minnesota NFL	15	506	277	54.7	3522	19	*26	6.96	27	54	2.0 0	0	0	9
Pro Totals—9 Years	91	2886	1603	55.5	19153	119	128	6.64	155	422	2.7 5	6	36	46

Quarterback Rating Points: 1977 (77.2), 1978 (15.0), 1979 (69.7), 1980 (72.1), 1981 (72.8), 1982 (77.3), 1983 (77.8), 1984 (70.6), 1985 (67.8). Total—71.3.
Additional pro statistics: Fumbled three times for minus three yards, 1977; ran three yards with lateral on pass reception and fumbled nine times for minus six yards, 1979; recovered two fumbles, 1979 and 1980; recovered three fumbles, 1981; recovered one fumble and fumbled three times for minus 21 yards, 1982; recovered one fumble, 1983; caught one pass for 20 yards and a touchdown, recovered three fumbles and fumbled 10 times for minus five yards, 1984; fumbled nine times for minus 16 yards, 1985.
Member of Minnesota Vikings for NFC Championship Game following 1977 season; did not play.

RICHARD BARRY KRAUSS
(Known by middle name.)
Linebacker—Indianapolis Colts
Born March 17, 1957, at Pompano Beach, Fla.
Height, 6.03. Weight, 247.
High School—Pompano Beach, Fla.
Received bachelor of science degree in education from University of Alabama.

Named as linebacker on THE SPORTING NEWS College All-America Team, 1978.
Selected by Baltimore in 1st round (6th player selected) of 1979 NFL draft.
Franchise transferred to Indianapolis, March 31, 1984.
Baltimore NFL, 1979 through 1983; Indianapolis NFL, 1984 and 1985.
Games: 1979 (15), 1980 (16), 1981 (16), 1982 (9), 1983 (16), 1984 (16), 1985 (16). Total—104.
Pro statistics: Recovered two fumbles, 1979, 1981, 1983 and 1985; recovered one fumble, 1980; intercepted one pass for 10 yards, 1981; caught one pass for five yards and a touchdown, 1982; rushed once for minus one yard, 1983; intercepted three passes for 20 yards, recovered two fumbles for minus five yards and fumbled once, 1984; intercepted one pass for no yards, 1985.

RICH KRAYNAK
Linebacker—Philadelphia Eagles
Born January 20, 1961, at Phoenixville, Pa.
Height, 6.01. Weight, 230.
High School—Phoenixville, Pa.
Attended University of Pittsburgh.

Selected by Philadelphia in 8th round (93rd player selected) of 1983 USFL draft.
Selected by Philadelphia in 8th round (201st player selected) of 1983 NFL draft.
Signed by Philadelphia Eagles, May 25, 1983.
Philadelphia NFL, 1983 through 1985.
Games: 1983 (16), 1984 (14), 1985 (16). Total—46.
Pro statistics: Recovered one fumble, 1983; returned blocked punt eight yards for a touchdown, 1984; intercepted one pass for 26 yards, 1985.

STEVE KENNETH KREIDER
Wide Receiver—Cincinnati Bengals
Born May 12, 1958, at Reading, Pa.
Height, 6.03. Weight, 192.
High School—Leesport, Pa., Schuylkill Valley.
Received bachelor of science degree in electrical engineering from Lehigh University in 1979
and received master's degree in electrical engineering from Lehigh.

Selected by Cincinnati in 6th round (139th player selected) of 1979 NFL draft.

Year Club	G.	P.C.	Yds.	Avg.	TD.
1979—Cincinnati NFL	15	3	20	6.7	0
1980—Cincinnati NFL	16	17	272	16.0	0
1981—Cincinnati NFL	16	37	520	14.1	5
1982—Cincinnati NFL	9	16	230	14.4	1
1983—Cincinnati NFL	16	42	554	13.2	1
1984—Cincinnati NFL	16	20	243	12.2	1
1985—Cincinnati NFL	16	10	184	18.4	1
Pro Totals—7 Years	104	145	2023	14.0	9

Additional pro statistics: Fumbled once, 1979, 1980 and 1984; rushed twice for no yards, 1979; returned one kickoff for 19 yards and recovered one fumble, 1980; attempted one pass with no completions, 1980 and 1983; rushed once for 21 yards, attempted three passes with one completion for 13 yards and fumbled twice, 1981; scored extra point on run, 1982 and 1985; rushed once for two yards, 1983; attempted one pass with one completion for one yard, 1985.
Played in AFC Championship Game following 1981 season.
Played in NFL Championship Game following 1981 season.

MITCH KRENK
Tight End—Chicago Bears
Born November 19, 1959, at Crete, Neb.
Height, 6.02. Weight, 225.
High School—Nebraska City, Neb.
Attended University of Nebraska.

Selected by Boston in 1983 USFL territorial draft.
Signed as free agent by Seattle Seahawks, April 28, 1983.
Released by Seattle Seahawks, August 29, 1983; signed as free agent by Dallas Cowboys, March 3, 1984.
Released by Dallas Cowboys, August 27, 1984; awarded on waivers to Chicago Bears, August 28, 1984.
On injured reserve with neck injury, September 28 through November 8, 1984; activated, November 9, 1984.
On injured reserve with ruptured disc, August 19 through entire 1985 season.

Year Club	G.	P.C.	Yds.	Avg.	TD.
1984—Chicago NFL	8	2	31	15.5	0

Played in NFC Championship Game following 1984 season.

MARK KREROWICZ
Offensive Tackle—Buffalo Bills
Born March 1, 1963, at Toledo, O.
Height, 6.04. Weight, 282.
High School—Toledo, O., St. John's.
Attended Ohio State University.

Selected by New Jersey in 1985 USFL territorial draft.
Selected by Cleveland in 6th round (147th player selected) of 1985 NFL draft.
Signed by Cleveland Browns, July 15, 1985.
Released by Cleveland Browns, October 19, 1985; signed as free agent by Buffalo Bills, May 6, 1986.
Active for 6 games with Cleveland Browns in 1985; did not play.
Cleveland NFL, 1985.

DAVID M. KRIEG
Name pronounced Craig.
(Dave)
Quarterback—Seattle Seahawks
Born October 20, 1958, at Iola, Wis.
Height, 6.01. Weight, 185.
High School—Schofield, Wis., D.C. Everest.
Received bachelor of science degree in marketing management from Milton College in 1980.

Signed as free agent by Seattle Seahawks, May 6, 1980.

				—PASSING—					—RUSHING—				—TOTAL—		
Year Club	G.	Att.	Cmp.	Pct.	Gain	T.P.	P.I.	Avg.	Att.	Yds.	Avg.	TD.	TD.	Pts.	F.
1980—Seattle NFL	1	2	0	0.0	0	0	0	0.00		None			0	0	0
1981—Seattle NFL	7	112	64	57.1	843	7	5	7.53	11	56	5.1	1	1	6	4
1982—Seattle NFL	3	78	49	62.8	501	2	2	6.42	6	—3	—0.5	0	0	0	5
1983—Seattle NFL	9	243	147	60.5	2139	18	11	8.80	16	55	3.4	2	2	12	10
1984—Seattle NFL	16	480	276	57.5	3671	32	*24	7.65	46	186	4.0	3	3	18	11
1985—Seattle NFL	16	532	285	53.6	3602	27	20	6.77	35	121	3.5	1	1	6	11
Pro Totals—6 Years	52	1447	821	56.7	10756	86	62	7.43	114	415	3.6	7	7	42	41

Quarterback Rating Points: 1980 (39.6), 1981 (83.3), 1982 (79.0), 1983 (95.0), 1984 (83.3), 1985 (76.2). Total—82.1.
Additional pro statistics: Recovered one fumble and fumbled twice for minus 14 yards, 1982; caught one pass for 11 yards and recovered two fumbles, 1983; recovered three fumbles and fumbled 11 times for minus 24 yards, 1984; recovered three fumbles and fumbled 11 times for minus two yards, 1985.
Played in AFC Championship Game following 1983 season.
Played in Pro Bowl (NFL All-Star Game) following 1984 season.

TIMOTHY A. KRUMRIE
Name pronounced KRUM-RYG.
(Tim)
Nose Tackle—Cincinnati Bengals
Born May 20, 1960, at Eau Claire, Wis.
Height, 6.02. Weight, 262.
High School—Mondovi, Wis.
Attended University of Wisconsin.

Selected by Tampa Bay in 7th round (84th player selected) of 1983 USFL draft.
Selected by Cincinnati in 10th round (276th player selected) of 1983 NFL draft.
Signed by Cincinnati Bengals, May 19, 1983.
Cincinnati NFL, 1983 through 1985.
Games: 1983 (16), 1984 (16), 1985 (16). Total—48.
Pro statistics: Recovered one fumble, 1983; recovered one fumble for eight yards, 1984; recovered two fumbles, 1985.

GARY WAYNE KUBIAK
Quarterback—Denver Broncos
Born August 15, 1961, at Houston, Tex.
Height, 6.00. Weight, 192.
High School—Houston, Tex., Saint Pius X.
Received degree in physical education from Texas A&M University.

Selected by Denver in 8th round (197th player selected) of 1983 NFL draft.

				—PASSING—					—RUSHING—				—TOTAL—		
Year Club	G.	Att.	Cmp.	Pct.	Gain	T.P.	P.I.	Avg.	Att.	Yds.	Avg.	TD.	TD.	Pts.	F.
1983—Denver NFL	4	22	12	54.5	186	1	1	8.45	4	17	4.3	1	1	6	0
1984—Denver NFL	7	75	44	58.7	440	4	1	5.87	9	27	3.0	1	1	6	1
1985—Denver NFL	16	5	2	40.0	61	1	0	12.20	1	6	6.0	0	0	0	0
Pro Totals—3 Years	27	102	58	56.9	687	6	2	6.74	14	50	3.6	2	2	12	1

Quarterback Rating Points: 1983 (78.9), 1984 (87.6), 1985 (125.8). Total—88.9.
Additional pro statistics: Caught one pass for 20 yards, 1984.

LARRY KUBIN
Linebacker—Kansas City Chiefs
Born February 26, 1959, at Union, N.J.
Height, 6.02. Weight, 238.
High School—Union, N.J.
Received bachelor of arts degree in philosophy from Penn State University in 1980.

Selected by Washington in 6th round (148th player selected) of 1981 NFL draft.
On injured reserve with knee injury, September 1 through entire 1981 season.
Traded by Washington Redskins to Buffalo Bills for conditional draft choice, September 2, 1985.
Released by Buffalo Bills, September 17, 1985; signed as free agent by Tampa Bay Buccaneers, October 10, 1985.
On injured reserve with knee injury, November 4 through remainder of 1985 season.
Granted free agency with no qualifying offer, February 1, 1986; signed by Kansas City Chiefs, May 12, 1986.
Washington NFL, 1982 through 1984; Buffalo (2)-Tampa Bay (4) NFL, 1985.
Games: 1982 (9), 1983 (12), 1984 (16), 1985 (6). Total—43.
Pro statistics: Recovered one fumble, 1982.
Played in NFC Championship Game following 1982 and 1983 seasons.
Played in NFL Championship Game following 1982 and 1983 seasons.

ROD RANDLE KUSH
Safety—Houston Oilers
Born December 29, 1956, at Omaha, Neb.
Height, 6.00. Weight, 188.
High School—Omaha, Neb., Harry A. Burke.
Received bachelor of science degree in criminal justice from
University of Nebraska at Omaha in 1979.

Selected by Buffalo in 5th round (114th player selected) of 1979 NFL draft.
On injured reserve with foot injury, August 22 through entire 1979 season.
On injured reserve with knee injury, October 8 through remainder of 1980 season.
On injured reserve with knee injury, October 12 through remainder of 1983 season.
Granted free agency, February 1, 1985; withdrew qualifying offer, June 11, 1985.
Signed by Houston Oilers, July 10, 1985.

Year Club	G.	No.	Yds.	Avg.	TD.
1980—Buffalo NFL	5		None		
1981—Buffalo NFL	16	1	19	19.0	0
1982—Buffalo NFL	9		None		
1983—Buffalo NFL	4		None		
1984—Buffalo NFL	16	1	15	15.0	0
1985—Houston NFL	16	2	6	3.0	0
Pro Totals—6 Years	66	4	40	10.0	0

Additional pro statistics: Recovered five fumbles, 1980; rushed once for minus six yards and recovered three fumbles for five yards, 1981; fumbled once, 1981 and 1984; recovered one fumble, 1984.

FULTON GERALD KUYKENDALL
Linebacker
Born June 10, 1953, at Coronado, Calif.
Height, 6.04. Weight, 228.
High School—Vallejo, Calif., St. Patrick's.
Received bachelor of science degree in kinesiology from University of California at Los Angeles.

Selected by Atlanta in 6th round (132nd player selected) of 1975 NFL draft.
On injured reserve with back injury, October 26 through remainder of 1976 season.
On injured reserve with broken arm, October 18 through remainder of 1977 season.
On injured reserve with shoulder injury, September 29 through November 13, 1980; activated, November 14, 1980.
Traded by Atlanta Falcons to San Francisco 49ers for defensive end Lawrence Pillers, July 19, 1985.
On injured reserve with knee injury, August 26 through October 17, 1985; activated, October 18, 1985.
On injured reserve with ruptured bicep, October 24 through remainder of 1985 season.
Granted free agency with no qualifying offer, February 1, 1986.
Atlanta NFL, 1975 through 1984; San Francisco NFL, 1985.
Games: 1975 (14), 1976 (7), 1977 (5), 1978 (16), 1979 (16), 1980 (10), 1981 (16), 1982 (9), 1983 (14), 1984 (16), 1985 (1). Total—124.
Pro statistics: Recovered two fumbles, 1975; recovered one fumble, 1976, 1978, 1979, 1981 and 1983; intercepted one pass for 20 yards and a touchdown, 1981; intercepted two passes for 22 yards, 1982; recovered two fumbles for nine yards, 1984.

JAMES MICHAEL LACHEY
Name pronounced Luh-SHAY.
(Jim)
Offensive Tackle—San Diego Chargers
Born June 4, 1963, at St. Henry, O.
Height, 6.06. Weight, 288.
High School—St. Henry, O.
Received degree in marketing from Ohio State University in 1985.

Selected by New Jersey in 1985 USFL territorial draft.
Selected by San Diego in 1st round (12th player selected) of 1985 NFL draft.
Signed by San Diego Chargers, July 28, 1985.
San Diego NFL, 1985.
Games: 1985 (16).

DAVID WALTER LAFARY
Name pronounced La-FARR-ee.
(Dave)
Offensive Tackle—New Orleans Saints
Born January 13, 1955, at Cincinnati, O.
Height, 6.07. Weight, 285.
High School—Cincinnati, O., LaSalle.
Received degree in health and physical education from Purdue University.

Selected by New Orleans in 5th round (118th player selected) of 1977 NFL draft.
On injured reserve with broken ankle, September 3 through remainder of 1984 season.
New Orleans NFL, 1977 through 1983 and 1985.
Games: 1977 (10), 1978 (15), 1979 (16), 1980 (15), 1981 (16), 1982 (9), 1983 (16), 1984 (1), 1985 (11). Total—109.
Pro statistics: Caught one pass for five yards, 1981; recovered one fumble, 1981, 1983 and 1985.

GREG LaFLEUR
Tight End—St. Louis Cardinals
Born September 16, 1958, at Lafayette, La.
Height, 6.04. Weight, 236.
High School—Ville Platt, La.
Received bachelor of arts degree in sociology from Louisiana State University in 1981.

Selected by Philadelphia in 3rd round (82nd player selected) of 1981 NFL draft.
Released by Philadelphia Eagles, August 31, 1981; claimed on waivers by St. Louis Cardinals, September 1, 1981.

| | | —PASS RECEIVING— | | | |
Year	Club	G.	P.C.	Yds.	Avg.	TD.
1981—St. Louis NFL		16	14	190	13.6	2
1982—St. Louis NFL		9	5	67	13.4	1
1983—St. Louis NFL		16	12	99	8.3	0
1984—St. Louis NFL		16	17	198	11.6	0
1985—St. Louis NFL		16	9	119	13.2	0
Pro Totals—5 Years		73	57	673	11.8	3

Additional pro statistics: Fumbled three times, 1983.

SEAN EDWARD LANDETA
Punter—New York Giants
Born January 6, 1962, at Baltimore, Md.
Height, 6.00. Weight, 200.
High School—Baltimore, Md., Loch Raven.
Attended Towson State University.

Named as punter on THE SPORTING NEWS USFL All-Star Team, 1983 and 1984.
Led USFL in net punting average with 38.1 in 1984.
Selected by Philadelphia in 14th round (161st player selected) of 1983 USFL draft.
Signed by Philadelphia Stars, January 24, 1983.
Franchise transferred to Baltimore, November 1, 1984.
Granted free agency, August 1, 1985; signed by New York Giants, August 5, 1985.

| | | —PUNTING— | | | |
Year	Club	G.	No.	Avg.	Blk.
1983—Philadelphia USFL		18	86	41.9	....
1984—Philadelphia USFL		18	53	41.0	....
1985—Baltimore USFL		18	65	41.8	....
1985—N. Y. Giants NFL		16	81	42.9	0
USFL Totals—3 Years		54	204	41.6	....
NFL Totals—1 Year		16	81	42.9	0
Pro Totals—4 Years		70	285	42.0	....

Additional USFL statistics: Rushed once for minus five yards and fumbled once, 1983; recovered one fumble, 1983 and 1984.
Additional NFL statistics: Attempted one pass with no completions, 1985.
Played in USFL Championship Game following 1983 through 1985 seasons.

MICHAEL GEDDIE LANDRUM
(Mike)
Tight End—Atlanta Falcons
Born November 6, 1961, at Laurel, Miss.
Height, 6.02. Weight, 231.
High School—Columbia, Miss.
Attended University of Southern Mississippi.

Selected by Birmingham in 10th round (195th player selected) of 1984 USFL draft.
Signed by Birmingham Stallions, January 9, 1984.
Released by Birmingham Stallions, January 26, 1984; signed as free agent by Atlanta Falcons, May 2, 1984.
On injured reserve with knee injury, August 26 through entire 1985 season.

| | | —PASS RECEIVING— | | | |
Year	Club	G.	P.C.	Yds.	Avg.	TD.
1984—Atlanta NFL		15	6	66	11.0	0

Additional pro statistics: Recovered one fumble, 1984.

ERIC LANE
Running Back—Seattle Seahawks
Born January 6, 1959, at Oakland, Calif.
Height, 6.00. Weight, 195.
High School—Hayward, Calif.
Attended Chabot Junior College and Brigham Young University.
Nephew of MacArthur Lane, running back with St. Louis Cardinals,
Green Bay Packers and Kansas City Chiefs, 1968 through 1978.
Selected by Seattle in 8th round (196th player selected) of 1981 NFL draft.

Year Club	G.	Att.	RUSHING Yds.	Avg.	TD.	PASS RECEIVING P.C.	Yds.	Avg.	TD.	TOTAL TD.	Pts.	F.
1981—Seattle NFL	14	8	22	2.8	0	7	58	8.3	0	0	0	0
1982—Seattle NFL	9		None				None			0	0	1
1983—Seattle NFL	16	3	1	0.3	0	2	9	4.5	0	0	0	2
1984—Seattle NFL	15	80	299	3.7	4	11	101	9.2	1	5	30	1
1985—Seattle NFL	16	14	32	2.3	0	15	153	10.2	0	0	0	0
Pro Totals—5 Years	70	105	354	3.4	4	35	321	9.2	1	5	30	4

Year Club	G.	No.	KICKOFF RETURNS Yds.	Avg.	TD.
1981—Seattle NFL	14	10	208	20.8	0
1982—Seattle NFL	9	11	172	15.6	0
1983—Seattle NFL	16	4	58	14.5	0
1984—Seattle NFL	15		None		
1985—Seattle NFL	16	1	1	1.0	0
Pro Totals—5 Years	70	26	439	16.9	0

Additional pro statistics: Recovered one fumble, 1981 through 1983; attempted one pass with no completions, 1982; recovered three fumbles, 1984; recovered two fumbles, 1985.
Played in AFC Championship Game following 1983 season.

GARCIA R. LANE
Cornerback-Kick Returner—Kansas City Chiefs
Born December 31, 1961, at Youngstown, O.
Height, 5.09. Weight, 180.
High School—Youngstown, O., South.
Attended Ohio State University.
Selected by New Jersey in 1984 USFL territorial draft.
USFL rights traded with linebacker Orlando Lowry by New Jersey Generals to Philadelphia Stars for past consideration involving rights of linebacker Lawrence Taylor, January 9, 1984.
Signed by Philadelphia Stars, January 27, 1984.
Selected by Kansas City in 3rd round (61st player selected) of 1984 NFL supplemental draft.
Franchise transferred to Baltimore, November 1, 1984.
Granted free agency, August 1, 1985; signed by Kansas City Chiefs, August 6, 1985.

Year Club	G.	INTERCEPTIONS No.	Yds.	Avg.	TD.	PUNT RETURNS No.	Yds.	Avg.	TD.	KICKOFF RET. No.	Yds.	Avg.	TD.	TOTAL TD.	Pts.	F.
1984—Philadelphia USFL	17	5	82	16.4	0	*48	*418	8.7	0		None			0	0	4
1985—Baltimore USFL	18	3	47	15.7	0	*46	403	8.8	0	1	39	39.0	0	0	0	3
1985—Kansas City NFL	16		None			43	381	8.9	0	13	269	20.7	0	0	0	3
USFL Totals—2 Years	35	8	129	16.1	0	94	821	8.7	0	1	39	39.0	0	0	0	7
NFL Totals—1 Year	16	0	0.0		0	43	381	8.9	0	13	269	20.7	0	0	0	3
Pro Totals—3 Years	51	8	129	16.1	0	137	1202	8.8	0	14	308	22.0	0	0	0	10

Additional USFL statistics: Recovered one fumble, 1984; recovered one fumble for seven yards, 1985.
Additional NFL statistics: Recovered one fumble, 1985.
Played in USFL Championship Game following 1984 and 1985 seasons.

GENE ERIC LANG
Running Back—Denver Broncos
Born March 15, 1962, at Pass Christian, Miss.
Height, 5.10. Weight, 196.
High School—Pass Christian, Miss.
Attended Louisiana State University.
Selected by Denver in 11th round (298th player selected of 1984 NFL draft.
On injured reserve with broken hand, December 3 through remainder of 1985 season.

Year Club	G.	Att.	RUSHING Yds.	Avg.	TD.	PASS RECEIVING P.C.	Yds.	Avg.	TD.	TOTAL TD.	Pts.	F.
1984—Denver NFL	16	8	42	5.3	2	4	24	6.0	1	3	18	0
1985—Denver NFL	12	84	318	3.8	5	23	180	7.8	2	7	42	3
Pro Totals—2 Years	28	92	360	3.9	7	27	204	7.6	3	10	60	3

Year Club	G.	No.	KICKOFF RETURNS Yds.	Avg.	TD.
1984—Denver NFL	16	19	404	21.3	0
1985—Denver NFL	12	17	361	21.2	0
Pro Totals—2 Years	28	36	765	21.3	0

Additional pro statistics: Recovered one fumble for six yards, 1984; recovered one fumble, 1985.

REGINALD DEVAN LANGHORNE
(Reggie)
Wide Receiver—Cleveland Browns
Born April 7, 1963, at Suffolk, Va.
Height, 6.02. Weight, 195.
High School—Smithfield, Va.
Attended Elizabeth City State University.
Selected by Oakland in 4th round (52nd player selected) of 1985 USFL draft.
Selected by Cleveland in 7th round (175th player selected) of 1985 NFL draft.
Signed by Cleveland Browns, July 15, 1985.

		—PASS RECEIVING—				
Year	Club	G.	P.C.	Yds.	Avg.	TD.
1985—Cleveland NFL		16	1	12	12.0	0

Additional pro statistics: Returned three kickoffs for 46 yards, recovered one fumble and fumbled once, 1985.

KENNETH WAYNE LANIER
(Ken)
Offensive Tackle—Denver Broncos
Born July 8, 1959, at Columbus, O.
Height, 6.03. Weight, 269.
High School—Columbus, O., Marion Franklin.
Received degree in industrial arts from Florida State University in 1981.
Selected by Denver in 5th round (125th player selected) of 1981 NFL draft.
Denver NFL, 1981 through 1985.
Games: 1981 (8), 1982 (9), 1983 (16), 1984 (16), 1985 (16). Total—65.
Pro statistics: Recovered one fumble, 1982 and 1984.

PAUL JAY LANKFORD
Cornerback—Miami Dolphins
Born June 15, 1958, at New York, N.Y.
Height, 6.02. Weight, 182.
High School—Farmingdale, N.Y.
Received bachelor of science degree in health planning and administration
from Penn State University in 1982.
Selected by Miami in 3rd round (80th player selected) of 1982 NFL draft.
On inactive list, September 12 and September 19, 1982.

		—INTERCEPTIONS—				
Year	Club	G.	No.	Yds.	Avg.	TD.
1982—Miami NFL		7		None		
1983—Miami NFL		16	1	10	10.0	0
1984—Miami NFL		16	3	25	8.3	0
1985—Miami NFL		16	4	10	2.5	0
Pro Totals—4 Years		55	8	45	5.6	0

Additional pro statistics: Recovered one fumble, 1984.
Played in AFC Championship Game following 1982, 1984 and 1985 seasons.
Played in NFL Championship Game following 1982 and 1984 seasons.

MICHAEL JOHN LANSFORD
(Mike)
Placekicker—Los Angeles Rams
Born July 20, 1958, at Monterrey Park, Calif.
Height, 6.00. Weight, 183.
High School—Arcadia, Calif.
Attended Pasadena City College and University of Washington.
Selected by New York Giants in 12th round (312th player selected) of 1980 NFL draft.
Released by New York Giants, August 3, 1980; claimed on waivers by San Francisco 49ers, August 5, 1980.
Released by San Francisco 49ers, August 18, 1980; signed as free agent by Oakland Raiders, June, 1981.
Released by Oakland Raiders, August 18, 1981; signed as free agent by Los Angeles Rams, July 1, 1982.
On injured reserve with knee injury, August 24 through November 23, 1983; activated after clearing procedural waivers, November 25, 1983.

		—PLACE KICKING—					
Year	Club	G.	XP.	XPM.	FG.	FGA.	Pts.
1982—L.A. Rams NFL		9	23	1	9	15	50
1983—L.A. Rams NFL		4	9	0	6	9	27
1984—L.A. Rams NFL		16	37	1	25	33	112
1985—L.A. Rams NFL		16	38	1	22	29	104
Pro Totals—4 Years		45	107	3	62	86	293

Played in NFC Championship Game following 1985 season.

STEVE M. LARGENT
Wide Receiver—Seattle Seahawks

Born September 28, 1954, at Tulsa, Okla.
Height, 5.11. Weight 184.
High School—Oklahoma City, Okla., Putnam.
Received bachelor of science degree in biology from University of Tulsa in 1976.
Established NFL record for most seasons, 50 or more pass receptions (8).
Tied NFL record for most seasons, 1,000 or more yards in pass receptions (7).
Named to THE SPORTING NEWS NFL All-Star Team, 1983.
Named to THE SPORTING NEWS AFC All-Star Team, 1978.
Selected by Houston in 4th round (117th player selected) of 1976 NFL draft.
Traded by Houston Oilers to Seattle Seahawks for 8th round pick in 1977 draft, August 26, 1976.
On injured reserve with broken wrist, December 16 through remainder of 1979 season.

		PASS RECEIVING				PUNT RETURNS				—KICKOFF RET.—				—TOTAL—		
Year Club	G.	P.C.	Yds.	Avg.	TD.	No.	Yds.	Avg.	TD.	No.	Yds.	Avg.	TD.	TD.	Pts.	F.
1976—Seattle NFL	14	54	705	13.0	4	4	36	9.0	0	8	156	19.5	0	4	24	2
1977—Seattle NFL	14	33	643	19.5	10	4	32	8.0	0		None			10	60	0
1978—Seattle NFL	16	71	1168	16.5	8		None				None			8	48	0
1979—Seattle NFL	15	66	1237	18.7	9		None				None			9	54	0
1980—Seattle NFL	16	66	1064	16.1	6		None				None			6	36	1
1981—Seattle NFL	16	75	1224	16.3	9		None				None			10	60	2
1982—Seattle NFL	8	34	493	14.5	3		None				None			3	18	0
1983—Seattle NFL	15	72	1074	14.9	11		None				None			11	66	3
1984—Seattle NFL	16	74	1164	15.7	12		None				None			12	72	1
1985—Seattle NFL	16	79	★1287	16.3	6		None				None			6	†37	0
Pro Totals—10 Years	146	624	10059	16.1	78	8	68	8.5	0	8	156	19.5	0	79	475	9

†Scored an extra point.
Additional pro statistics: Rushed four times for minus 14 yards, 1976; recovered one fumble, 1978; rushed once for two yards and recovered two fumbles, 1980; rushed six times for 47 yards and one touchdown, 1981; attempted one pass with no completions, 1981 and 1985; rushed once for eight yards, 1982; attempted one pass with one completion for 11 yards, 1983; rushed twice for 10 yards, 1984.
Played in AFC Championship Game following 1983 season.
Played in Pro Bowl (NFL All-Star Game) following 1978, 1981, 1984 and 1985 seasons.
Named in Pro Bowl following 1979 season; replaced due to wrist injury.

BRANDON HUGH LAUFENBERG
(Babe)
Quarterback—Washington Redskins

Born December 5, 1959, at Burbank, Calif.
Height, 6.02. Weight, 195.
High School—Encino, Calif., Crespi Carmelite.
Attended Stanford University, University of Missouri,
Los Angeles Pierce College and Indiana University.
Selected by Chicago in 20th round (235th player selected) of 1983 USFL draft.
Selected by Washington in 6th round (168th player selected) of 1983 NFL draft.
Signed by Washington Redskins, June 17, 1983.
On injured reserve with rotator cuff injury, August 27 through entire 1984 season.
Released by Washington Redskins, September 2, 1985; signed as free agent by San Diego Chargers, September 30, 1985.
Released by San Diego Chargers, October 15, 1985.
USFL rights traded by Arizona Outlaws to Memphis Showboats for quarterback John Conner, November 1, 1985.
Signed as free agent by Washington Redskins, November 20, 1985.
Active for 16 games with Washington Redskins in 1983; did not play.
Active for 2 games with San Diego Chargers in 1985; did not play.
Active for 5 games with Washington Redskins in 1985; did not play.
Member of Washington Redskins for NFC and NFL Championship Games following 1983 season; did not play.

JAMES DAVID LAUGHLIN
(Jim)
Linebacker—Los Angeles Rams

Born July 5, 1958, at Euclid, O.
Height, 6.01. Weight, 222.
High School—Lyndhurst, O., Charles F. Brush.
Received bachelor of science degree in business administration from Ohio State University in 1980.
Selected by Atlanta in 4th round (91st player selected) of 1980 NFL draft.
Released by Atlanta Falcons, August 28, 1983; signed as free agent by Green Bay Packers, September 6, 1983.
Released by Green Bay Packers, August 27, 1984; signed as free agent by Los Angeles Rams, November 30, 1984.
Released by Los Angeles Rams, August 27, 1985; re-signed by Rams, October 9, 1985.
Released by Los Angeles Rams, October 15, 1985; re-signed by Rams, October 21, 1985.

	—INTERCEPTIONS—						—INTERCEPTIONS—			
Year Club	G.	No.	Yds.	Avg.	TD.	Year Club	G.	No.	Yds.	Avg. TD.
1980—Atlanta NFL	16	1	7	7.0	0	1984—L.A. Rams NFL	3		None	
1981—Atlanta NFL	14		None			1985—L.A. Rams NFL	10		None	
1982—Atlanta NFL	9		None			Pro Totals—6 Years	67	2	29	14.5 0
1983—Green Bay NFL	15	1	22	22.0	0					

Additional pro statistics: Recovered one fumble, 1981; returned one kickoff for 10 yards, 1982.
Played in NFC Championship Game following 1985 season.

ROBERT L. LAVETTE
Running Back—Dallas Cowboys
Born September 8, 1963, at Cartersville, Ga.
Height, 5.11. Weight, 199.
High School—Cartersville, Ga.
Attended Georgia Tech.
Cousin of Ray Donaldson, center with Indianapolis Colts.

Selected by Jacksonville in 1985 USFL territorial draft.
Selected by Dallas in 4th round (103rd player selected) of 1985 NFL draft.
Signed by Dallas Cowboys, July 14, 1985.
On injured reserve with knee injury, December 5 through remainder of 1985 season.

		—————RUSHING—————				PASS RECEIVING				—TOTAL—		
Year Club	G.	Att.	Yds.	Avg.	TD.	P.C.	Yds.	Avg.	TD.	TD.	Pts.	F.
1985—Dallas NFL	12	13	34	2.6	0	1	8	8.0	0	0	0	0

		KICKOFF RETURNS			
Year Club	G.	No.	Yds.	Avg.	TD.
1985—Dallas NFL	12	34	682	20.1	0

HENRY LAWRENCE
Offensive Tackle—Los Angeles Raiders
Born September 26, 1951, at Danville, Pa.
Height, 6.04. Weight, 275.
High Schools—Palmetto, Fla., Lincoln; Bradenton, Fla., Manatee; and Wyoming, N.Y., Central.
Received bachelor of science degree in political science from Florida A&M University in 1974.
Cousin of Marsharne Graves, offensive tackle with Denver Broncos.

Selected by Oakland in 1st round (19th player selected) of 1974 NFL draft.
Franchise transferred to Los Angeles, May 7, 1982.
Oakland NFL, 1974 through 1981; Los Angeles Raiders NFL, 1982 through 1985.
Games: 1974 (14), 1975 (14), 1976 (8), 1977 (14), 1978 (16), 1979 (16), 1980 (16), 1981 (16), 1982 (9), 1983 (16), 1984 (16), 1985 (16). Total—171.
Pro statistics: Recovered one fumble, 1975, 1977 through 1979 and 1982; recovered two fumbles, 1980 and 1981.
Played in AFC Championship Game following 1974 through 1977, 1980 and 1983 seasons.
Played in NFL Championship Game following 1976, 1980 and 1983 seasons.
Played in Pro Bowl (NFL All- Star Game) following 1983 and 1984 seasons.

PATRICK JOSEPH LEAHY
(Pat)
Placekicker—New York Jets
Born March 19, 1951, at St. Louis, Mo.
Height, 6.00. Weight, 193.
High School—St. Louis, Mo., Augustinian Academy.
Received degree in marketing and business administration from St. Louis University
(did not play college football).

Named to THE SPORTING NEWS AFC All-Star Team, 1978.
Signed as free agent by St. Louis Cardinals, 1974.
Released by St. Louis Cardinals and signed as free agent by New York Jets, November 8, 1974.
On injured reserve with knee injury, October 13 through remainder of 1979 season.

		———PLACE KICKING———							———PLACE KICKING———			
Year Club	G.	XP.	XPM.	FG.	FGA.	Pts.	Year Club	G.	XP.	XPM.	FG.	FGA.	Pts.
1974—N.Y. Jets NFL	6	18	1	6	11	36	1981—N.Y. Jets NFL	16	38	1	25	36	113
1975—N.Y. Jets NFL	14	27	3	13	21	66	1982—N.Y. Jets NFL	9	26	*5	11	17	59
1976—N.Y. Jets NFL	14	16	4	11	16	49	1983—N.Y. Jets NFL	16	36	1	16	24	84
1977—N.Y. Jets NFL	14	18	3	15	25	63	1984—N.Y. Jets NFL	16	38	1	17	24	89
1978—N.Y. Jets NFL	16	41	1	22	30	107	1985—N.Y. Jets NFL	16	43	2	26	34	121
1979—N.Y. Jets NFL	6	12	3	8	13	36	Pro Totals—12 Years	159	349	25	184	273	901
1980—N.Y. Jets NFL	16	36	0	14	22	78							

Additional pro statistics: Recovered one fumble, 1975.
Played in AFC Championship Game following 1982 season.

CARL LEE III
Defensive Back—Minnesota Vikings
Born April 6, 1961, at South Charleston, W. Va.
Height, 5.11. Weight, 185.
High School—South Charleston, W. Va.
Attended Marshall University.

Selected by Minnesota in 7th round (186th player selected) of 1983 NFL draft.
Released by Minnesota Vikings, August 27, 1985; re-signed by Vikings, September 2, 1985.

		———INTERCEPTIONS———			
Year Club	G.	No.	Yds.	Avg.	TD.
1983—Minnesota NFL	16	1	31	31.0	0
1984—Minnesota NFL	16	1	0	0.0	0
1985—Minnesota NFL	15	3	68	22.7	0
Pro Totals—3 Years	47	5	99	19.8	0

Additional pro statistics: Recovered one fumble, 1984.

DANZELL IVAN LEE
Tight End—Washington Redskins
Born March 16, 1963, at Corsicana, Tex.
Height, 6.02. Weight, 232.
High School—Corsicana, Tex.
Attended Lamar University.

Selected by Washington in 6th round (163rd player selected) of 1985 NFL draft.
Signed by Washington Redskins, July 18, 1985.
On injured reserve with sprained back, August 27 through entire 1985 season.

KEITH LAMAR LEE
Defensive Back—Indianapolis Colts
Born December 22, 1957, at San Antonio, Tex.
Height, 5.11. Weight, 193.
High School—Los Angeles, Calif., Gardena.
Attended Santa Monica City College and Colorado State University.

Selected by Buffalo in 5th round (129th player selected) of 1980 NFL draft.
On injured reserve with knee injury, August 21 through entire 1980 season.
Released by Buffalo Bills, August 25, 1981; signed as free agent by New England Patriots, August 28, 1981.
Released by New England Patriots, August 19, 1985; signed as free agent by Indianapolis Colts, September 12, 1985.
New England NFL, 1981 through 1984; Indianapolis NFL, 1985.
Games: 1981 (15), 1982 (9), 1983 (15), 1984 (15), 1985 (14). Total—68.
Pro statistics: Returned two kickoffs for 20 yards and intercepted one pass for no yards, 1981; returned one kickoff for 14 yards, 1982; returned four kickoffs for 40 yards, returned one punt for no yards, recovered two fumbles and fumbled once, 1983; returned three kickoffs for 43 yards, 1984; returned one kickoff for six yards, 1985.

LARRY DWAYNE LEE
Guard-Center—Miami Dolphins
Born September 10, 1959, at Dayton, O.
Height, 6.02. Weight, 260.
High School—Dayton, O., Roth.
Attended University of California at Los Angeles.
Cousin of Rick Porter, running back with Memphis Showboats.

Selected by Detroit in 5th round (129th player selected) of 1981 NFL draft.
Released by Detroit Lions, September 2, 1985; re-signed by Lions, September 10, 1985.
Released by Detroit Lions, November 16, 1985; awarded on waivers to Miami Dolphins, November 18, 1985.
Detroit NFL, 1981 through 1984; Detroit (6)-Miami (5) NFL, 1985.
Games: 1981 (16), 1982 (9), 1983 (16), 1984 (15), 1985 (11). Total—67.
Pro statistics: Returned one kickoff for no yards, 1981; returned one kickoff for 14 yards, 1982; returned one kickoff for 11 yards, 1983; recovered one fumble and fumbled twice for minus 24 yards, 1984.
Played in AFC Championship Game following 1985 season.

MARK ANTHONY LEE
Cornerback—Green Bay Packers
Born March 20, 1958, at Hanford, Calif.
Height, 5.11. Weight, 187.
High School—Hanford, Calif.
Attended University of Washington.

Selected by Green Bay in 2nd round (34th player selected) of 1980 NFL draft.

Year Club	G.	INTERCEPTIONS				-PUNT RETURNS-				—KICKOFF RET.—				—TOTAL—		
		No.	Yds.	Avg.	TD.	No.	Yds.	Avg.	TD.	No.	Yds.	Avg.	TD.	TD.	Pts.	F.
1980—Green Bay NFL	15		None			5	32	6.4	0	30	589	19.6	0	0	0	1
1981—Green Bay NFL	16	6	50	8.3	0	20	187	9.4	1	14	270	19.3	0	1	6	0
1982—Green Bay NFL	9	1	40	40.0	0		None				None			0	0	0
1983—Green Bay NFL	16	4	23	5.8	0	1	—4	—4.0	0	1	0	0	0	0	0	1
1984—Green Bay NFL	16	3	33	11.0	0		None				None			0	0	0
1985—Green Bay NFL	14	1	23	23.0	0		None				None			0	0	0
Pro Totals—6 Years	86	15	169	11.3	0	26	215	8.3	1	45	859	19.1	0	1	6	2

Additional pro statistics: Recovered one fumble, 1981; recovered one fumble for 15 yards, 1983; recovered two fumbles, 1984.

RONALD VAN LEE
(Ronnie)
Guard—Miami Dolphins
Born December 24, 1956, at Pine Bluff, Ark.
Height, 6.04. Weight, 265.
High School—Tyler, Tex.
Attended Baylor University.

Selected by Miami in 3rd round (65th player selected) of 1979 NFL draft.
Released by Miami Dolphins, August 29, 1983; signed as free agent by Atlanta Falcons, September 14, 1983.
Traded with 6th round pick in 1985 draft by Atlanta Falcons to Miami Dolphins for cornerback Gerald Small, August 26, 1984.

Year	Club	—PASS RECEIVING—				
		G.	P.C.	Yds.	Avg.	TD.
1979—Miami NFL		16	2	14	7.0	0
1980—Miami NFL		16	7	83	11.9	2
1981—Miami NFL		16	14	64	4.6	1
1982—Miami NFL		9	2	6	3.0	0
1983—Atlanta NFL		14		None		
1984—Miami NFL		16		None		
1985—Miami NFL		15		None		
Pro Totals—7 Years		102	25	167	6.7	3

Played in AFC Championship Game following 1982, 1984 and 1985 seasons.
Played in NFL Championship Game following 1982 and 1984 seasons.

JEFF JAMES LEIDING
Linebacker—Indianapolis Colts
Born October 28, 1961, at Kansas City, Mo.
Height, 6.04. Weight, 240.
High Schools—Tulsa, Okla., Union; and Kansas City, Mo., Hickman Mills.
Attended University of Texas.

Selected by San Antonio in 1984 USFL territorial draft.
Selected by St. Louis in 5th round (129th player selected) of 1984 NFL draft.
Signed by St. Louis Cardinals, July 16, 1984.
Released by St. Louis Cardinals, August 27, 1984; signed by San Antonio Gunslingers, January 21, 1985.
On developmental squad, March 9 through April 5, 1985; activated, April 6, 1985.
On developmental squad, May 30 through July 22, 1985.
Released by San Antonio Gunslingers, July 23, 1985; signed as free agent by Indianapolis Colts, May 12, 1986.
On developmental squad for 8 games with San Antonio Gunslingers in 1985.
San Antonio USFL, 1985.
Games: 1985 (10).

JAMES FRANCIS LEONARD
(Jim)
Center—San Diego Chargers
Born October 19, 1957, at Santa Cruz, Calif.
Height, 6.03. Weight, 260.
High School—Santa Cruz, Calif., Harbor.
Received bachelor of business administration degree from University of Santa Clara in 1979.

Selected by Tampa Bay in 7th round (186th player selected) of 1980 NFL draft.
Granted free agency, February 1, 1984; signed by Oakland Invaders, February 10, 1984.
On developmental squad, March 30 through April 27, 1984; activated, April 28, 1984.
Protected in merger of Oakland Invaders and Michigan Panthers, December 6, 1984.
Released by Oakland Invaders, July 31, 1985; re-signed by Buccaneers and traded to San Francisco 49ers for 12th round pick in 1986 draft, August 9, 1985.
Released by San Francisco 49ers, November 6, 1985; awarded on waivers to San Diego Chargers, November 7, 1985.
On developmental squad for 4 games with Oakland Invaders in 1984.
Tampa Bay NFL, 1980 through 1982; Oakland USFL, 1984 and 1985; San Francisco (9)-San Diego (7) NFL, 1985.
Games: 1980 (16), 1981 (16), 1982 (9), 1984 (14), 1985 USFL (18), 1985 NFL (16). Total NFL—57. Total USFL—32. Total Pro—89.
Pro statistics: Fumbled once for minus six yards, 1981; fumbled once for minus 15 yards, 1985.
Played in USFL Championship Game following 1985 season.

ALBERT RAY LEWIS
Cornerback—Kansas City Chiefs
Born October 6, 1960, at Mansfield, La.
Height, 6.02. Weight, 190.
High School—Mansfield, La., DeSoto.
Attended Grambling State University.

Selected by Philadelphia in 15th round (175th player selected) of 1983 USFL draft.
Selected by Kansas City in 3rd round (61st player selected) of 1983 NFL draft.
Signed by Kansas City Chiefs, May 19, 1983.
On injured reserve with knee injury, December 10 through remainder of 1984 season.

Year	Club	—INTERCEPTIONS—				
		G.	No.	Yds.	Avg.	TD.
1983—Kansas City NFL		16	4	42	10.5	0
1984—Kansas City NFL		15	4	57	14.3	0
1985—Kansas City NFL		16	8	59	7.4	0
Pro Totals—3 Years		47	16	158	9.9	0

Additional pro statistics: Recovered two fumbles, 1983; recovered one fumble in end zone for a touchdown, 1985.

—DID YOU KNOW—
That Mike Ditka is the only man to have both played for and coached a Super Bowl winner? Ditka was the Cowboys' starting tight end in Dallas' 24-3 victory over Miami in Super Bowl VI and the coach of the Super Bowl XX champion Bears.

DAVID WAYNE LEWIS
Tight End—Detroit Lions
Born June 8, 1961, at Portland, Ore.
Height, 6.03. Weight, 235.
High School—Portland, Ore., U.S. Grant.
Received bachelor of science degree in political science
from University of California at Berkeley in 1984.

Selected by Oakland in 1984 USFL territorial draft.
Selected by Detroit in 1st round (20th player selected) of 1984 NFL draft.
Signed by Detroit Lions, July 19, 1984.

Year Club	G.	P.C.	Yds.	Avg.	TD.
1984—Detroit NFL	16	16	236	14.8	3
1985—Detroit NFL	15	28	354	12.6	3
Pro Totals—2 Years	31	44	590	13.4	6

(—PASS RECEIVING—)

Additional pro statistics: Recovered two fumbles and fumbled twice, 1984; fumbled once, 1985.

LEO E. LEWIS III
Wide Receiver—Minnesota Vikings
Born September 17, 1956, at Columbia, Mo.
Height, 5.08. Weight, 170.
High School—Columbia, Mo., Hickman.
Received degree in education from University of Missouri.
Son of Leo Lewis, member of Canadian Football League Hall of Fame and running back with
Winnipeg Blue Bombers,1955 through 1966; brother of Marc Lewis, wide receiver with Denver Gold.

Signed as free agent by St. Louis Cardinals, May 21, 1979.
On injured reserve with ankle injury, August 21 through November 15, 1979.
Released by St. Louis Cardinals, November 16, 1979; signed as free agent by Calgary Stampeders, March, 1980.
Released by Calgary Stampeders, August 7, 1980; signed as free agent by Hamilton Tiger-Cats, August 13, 1980.
Released by Hamilton Tiger-Cats, August 20, 1980; signed as free agent by Minnesota Vikings, May 10, 1981.
Released by Minnesota Vikings, August 25, 1981; re-signed after clearing procedural waivers, November 11, 1981.

		—RUSHING—				PASS RECEIVING				—TOTAL—		
Year Club	G.	Att.	Yds.	Avg.	TD.	P.C.	Yds.	Avg.	TD.	TD.	Pts.	F.
1980—Calgary (5)-Hamilton (1) CFL	6	1	62	62.0	1	8	91	11.4	1	2	12	0
1981—Minnesota NFL	4	1	16	16.0	0	2	58	29.0	0	0	0	0
1982—Minnesota NFL	9		None			8	150	18.8	3	3	18	0
1983—Minnesota NFL	14	1	2	2.0	0	12	127	10.6	0	0	0	0
1984—Minnesota NFL	16	2	11	5.5	0	47	830	17.7	4	4	24	1
1985—Minnesota NFL	10	1	2	2.0	0	29	442	15.2	3	3	18	1
NFL Totals—5 Years	53	5	31	6.2	0	98	1607	16.4	10	10	60	2
CFL Total—1 Year	6	1	62	62.0	1	8	91	11.4	1	2	12	0
Pro Totals—6 Years	59	6	93	15.5	1	106	1698	16.0	11	12	72	2

		—PUNT RETURNS—				—KICKOFF RET.—			
Year Club	G.	No.	Yds.	Avg.	TD.	No.	Yds.	Avg.	TD.
1980—Calgary (5)-Hamilton (1) CFL	6	22	163	7.4	0	15	345	23.0	0
1981—Minnesota NFL	4		None				None		
1982—Minnesota NFL	9		None				None		
1983—Minnesota NFL	14	3	52	17.3	0	1	25	25.0	0
1984—Minnesota NFL	16	4	31	7.8	0	1	31	31.0	0
1985—Minnesota NFL	10		None				None		
NFL Totals—5 Years	53	7	83	11.9	0	2	56	28.0	0
CFL Total—1 Year	6	22	163	7.4	0	15	345	23.0	0
Pro Totals—6 Years	59	29	246	8.5	0	17	401	23.6	0

Additional pro statistics: Recovered three fumbles, 1984; recovered one fumble, 1985.

MARK JOSEPH LEWIS
Tight End—Green Bay Packers
Born May 20, 1961, at Houston, Tex.
Height, 6.02. Weight, 218.
High School—Houston, Tex., Kashmere.
Attended Texas A&M University.

Selected by Houston in 1985 USFL territorial draft.
Selected by Green Bay in 6th round (155th player selected) of 1985 NFL draft.
Signed by Green Bay Packers, July 19, 1985.
On injured reserve with knee injury, August 27 through December 20, 1985; activated, December 21, 1985.
Green Bay NFL, 1985.
Games: 1985 (1).

—DID YOU KNOW—

That the Green Bay Packers have finished the last four complete NFL seasons with a record of 8-8? The Packers finished at .500 in 1981, 1983, 1984 and 1985. In the strike-shortened 1982 season, Green Bay was 5-3-1.

TIMOTHY JAY LEWIS
(Tim)
Defensive Back—Green Bay Packers
Born December 18, 1961, at Quakertown, Pa.
Height, 5.11. Weight, 191.
High School—Perkasie, Pa., Pennridge.
Received bachelor of arts degree in economics from University of Pittsburgh in 1983.
Brother of Will Lewis, cornerback with New Jersey Generals; cousin of Robb Riddick,
running back with Buffalo Bills; cousin of Alan Page, defensive tackle with
Minnesota Vikings and Chicago Bears, 1967 through 1981.
Selected by Washington in 2nd round (21st player selected) of 1983 USFL draft.
Selected by Green Bay in 1st round (11th player selected) of 1983 NFL draft.
Signed by Green Bay Packers, July 21, 1983.

| | | -INTERCEPTIONS- | | | | —KICKOFF RET.— | | | —TOTAL— | | |
Year Club	G.	No.	Yds.	Avg.	TD.	No.	Yds.	Avg.	TD.	TD.	Pts.	F.
1983—Green Bay NFL	16	5	111	22.2	0	20	358	17.9	0	0	0	3
1984—Green Bay NFL	16	7	151	21.6	1		None			1	6	0
1985—Green Bay NFL	16	4	4	1.0	0		None			1	6	0
Pro Totals—3 Years	48	16	266	16.6	1	20	358	17.9	0	2	12	3

Additional pro statistics: Recovered one fumble, 1983; recovered one fumble for six yards and a touchdown, 1985.

GEORGE VINCENT LILJA
Guard-Center—Cleveland Browns
Born March 3, 1958, at Evergreen Park, Ill.
Height, 6.04. Weight, 270.
High School—Orland Park, Ill., Carl Sandburg.
Received bachelor of arts degree in general studies from University of Michigan in 1981.
Brother of Larry Lilja, strength coach at Northwestern University;
and Dave Lilja, tight end at Indiana University.
Selected by Los Angeles in 4th round (104th player selected) of 1981 NFL draft.
On injured reserve with ankle injury, August 31 through entire 1981 season.
Released by Los Angeles Rams, September 8, 1983; signed as free agent by New York Jets, September 27, 1983.
Released by New York Jets, November 15, 1984; signed as free agent by Cleveland Browns, November 21, 1984.
Active for 1 game with Los Angeles Rams in 1983; did not play.
Los Angeles Rams NFL, 1982; Los Angeles Rams (0)-New York Jets (1) NFL, 1983; New York Jets (3)-Cleveland (4) NFL, 1984; Cleveland NFL, 1985.
Games: 1982 (9), 1983 (1), 1984 (7), 1985 (16). Total—33.
Pro statistics: Recovered one fumble, 1985.

ROBERT ANTHONEY LILLY
(Tony)
Safety—Denver Broncos
Born February 16, 1962, at Alexandria, Va.
Height, 6.00. Weight, 199.
High School—Woodbridge, Va.
Attended University of Florida.
Selected by Tampa Bay in 1984 USFL territorial draft.
Selected by Denver in 3rd round (78th player selected) of 1984 NFL draft.
Signed by Denver Broncos, May 23, 1984.
Denver NFL, 1984 and 1985.
Games: 1984 (13), 1985 (16). Total—29.
Pro statistics: Intercepted one pass for five yards, recovered one fumble for three yards and fumbled once, 1984; intercepted two passes for four yards and recovered one fumble, 1985.

CHRISTOPHER ANDREW LINDSTROM
(Chris)
Defensive End—Tampa Bay Buccaneers
Born August 3, 1960, at Weymouth, Mass.
Height, 6.07. Weight, 260.
High School—Weymouth, Mass., South.
Received bachelor of science degree in physical education
from Boston University in 1982.
Brother of Dave Lindstrom, defensive end with Kansas City Chiefs.
Selected by St. Louis in 8th round (205th player selected) of 1982 NFL draft.
Left St. Louis Cardinals' camp voluntarily, July 22, 1982; returned, July 27, 1982.
Left St. Louis Cardinals' camp voluntarily and released, July 28, 1982; claimed on procedural waivers by Baltimore Colts, May 10, 1983.
Released by Baltimore Colts, August 22, 1983; signed as free agent by Cincinnati Bengals, September 6, 1983.
Released by Cincinnati Bengals, September 27, 1983.
USFL rights traded by New Orleans Breakers to Chicago Blitz for draft pick, December 1, 1983.
Signed as free agent by San Francisco 49ers, December 21, 1983.
Released by San Francisco 49ers, February 8, 1984; awarded on procedural waivers to Houston Oilers, April 6, 1984.
Signed by Chicago Blitz, April 27, 1984, after restraining order issued negating option year in NFL contract.
On developmental squad, May 25 through May 30, 1984; activated, May 31, 1984.

Franchise disbanded, November 20, 1984; signed as free agent by Tampa Bay Buccaneers, March 23, 1985.
On developmental squad for 1 game with Chicago Blitz in 1984.
Cincinnati NFL, 1983; Chicago USFL, 1984; Tampa Bay NFL, 1985.
Games: 1983 (1), 1984 (8), 1985 (15). Total NFL 16. Total Pro 24.
Pro statistics: Recovered one fumble, 1985.

COACHING RECORD
Assistant coach at Colby College, 1982.

DAVID ALAN LINDSTROM
(Dave)
Defensive End—Kansas City Chiefs
Born November 16, 1954, at Cambridge, Mass.
Height, 6.06. Weight, 255.
High School—Weymouth, Mass., South.
Attended Boston University.
Brother of Chris Lindstrom, defensive end with Tampa Bay Buccaneers.

Selected by San Diego in 6th round (146th player selected) of 1977 NFL draft.
On injured reserve, September 12 through 1977 season.
Released by San Diego Chargers, August 28, 1978; claimed on waivers by Kansas City Chiefs, August 30, 1978.
On injured reserve with knee injury, November 30 through remainder of 1979 season.
Kansas City NFL, 1978 through 1985.
Games: 1978 (16), 1979 (13), 1980 (16), 1981 (16), 1982 (9), 1983 (16), 1984 (16), 1985 (16). Total—118.
Pro statistics: Recovered one fumble, 1980; returned one kickoff for one yard, 1982; returned one kickoff for no yards, 1983.

ADAM JAMES LINGNER
Center-Guard—Kansas City Chiefs
Born November 2, 1960, at Indianapolis, Ill.
Height, 6.04. Weight, 260.
High School—Rock Island, Ill.,Alleman.
Attended University of Illinois.

Selected by Chicago in 1983 USFL territorial draft.
Selected by Kansas City in 9th round (231st player selected) of 1983 NFL draft.
Signed by Kansas City Chiefs, June 1, 1983.
Kansas City NFL, 1983 through 1985.
Games: 1983 (16), 1984 (16), 1985 (16). Total—48.

RONNIE LEON LIPPETT
Cornerback—New England Patriots
Born December 10, 1960, at Melborne, Fla.
Height, 5.11. Weight, 180.
High School—Sebring, Fla.
Attended University of Miami (Fla.).

Selected by New England in 8th round (214th player selected) of 1983 NFL draft.

		—INTERCEPTIONS—			
Year Club	G.	No.	Yds.	Avg.	TD.
1983—New England NFL.......	16		None		
1984—New England NFL.......	16	3	23	7.7	0
1985—New England NFL.......	16	3	93	31.0	0
Pro Totals—3 Years...........	48	6	116	19.3	0

Additional pro statistics: Recovered one fumble, 1983 and 1984; fumbled once, 1984.
Played in AFC Championship Game following 1985 season.
Played in NFL Championship Game following 1985 season.

LOUIS ADAM LIPPS
Wide Receiver-Kick Returner—Pittsburgh Steelers
Born August 9, 1962, at New Orleans, La.
Height, 5.10. Weight, 186.
High School—Reserve, La., East St. John's.
Attended University of Southern Mississippi.

Named THE SPORTING NEWS NFL Rookie of the Year, 1984.
Selected by Arizona in 8th round (155th player selected) of 1984 USFL draft.
Selected by Pittsburgh in 1st round (23rd player selected) of 1984 NFL draft.
Signed by Pittsburgh Steelers, May 19, 1984.

		—RUSHING—				PASS RECEIVING				—TOTAL—		
Year Club	G.	Att.	Yds.	Avg.	TD.	P.C.	Yds.	Avg.	TD.	TD.	Pts.	F.
1984—Pittsburgh NFL.....................................	14	3	71	23.7	1	45	860	19.1	9	11	66	8
1985—Pittsburgh NFL.....................................	16	2	16	8.0	1	59	1134	19.2	12	15	90	5
Pro Totals—2 Years.....................	30	5	87	17.4	2	104	1994	19.2	21	26	156	13

		—PUNT RETURNS—				—KICKOFF RET.—		
Year Club	G.	No.	Yds.	Avg.	TD.	No.	Yds.	Avg.TD.
1984—Pittsburgh NFL.................................	14	53	*656	12.4	1		None	
1985—Pittsburgh NFL.................................	16	36	437	12.1	*2	13	237	18.2 0
Pro Totals—2 Years.................................	30	89	1093	12.3	3	13	237	18.2 0

Additional pro statistics: Recovered two fumbles, 1984; recovered four fumbles for three yards, 1985.
Played in AFC Championship Game following 1984 season.
Played in Pro Bowl (NFL All-Star Game) following 1984 and 1985 seasons.

DAVID GENE LITTLE
(Dave)
Tight End—Philadelphia Eagles
Born April 18, 1961, at Selma, Calif.
Height, 6.02. Weight, 232.
High School—Fresno, Calif., Roosevelt.
Attended Kings River College and Middle Tennessee State University.

Signed as free agent by Memphis Showboats, January 11, 1984.
Released by Memphis Showboats, February 20, 1984; signed as free agent by Kansas City Chiefs, June 21, 1984.
On injured reserve with knee injury, November 6 through remainder of 1984 season.
Released by Kansas City Chiefs, August 19, 1985; signed as free agent by Philadelphia Eagles, September 11, 1985.

Year Club	G.	P.C.	Yds.	Avg.	TD.
1984—Kansas City NFL	10	1	13	13.0	0
1985—Philadelphia NFL	15	7	82	11.7	0
Pro Totals—2 Years	25	8	95	11.9	0

Additional pro statistics: Recovered fumble in end zone for a touchdown, 1985.

DAVID LAMAR LITTLE
Linebacker—Pittsburgh Steelers
Born January 3, 1959, at Miami, Fla.
Height, 6.01. Weight, 240.
High School—Miami, Fla., Jackson.
Received degree in sociology from University of Florida.
Brother of Larry Little, guard with San Diego Chargers
and Miami Dolphins, 1967 through 1980; currently head coach at Bethune-Cookman College.

Selected by Pittsburgh in 7th round (183rd player selected) of 1981 NFL draft.
Pittsburgh NFL, 1981 through 1985.
Games: 1981 (16), 1982 (9), 1983 (16), 1984 (16), 1985 (16). Total—73.
Pro statistics: Recovered one fumble, 1981; recovered one fumble for two yards, 1982; intercepted two passes for no yards and recovered two fumbles for 11 yards, 1985.
Played in AFC Championship Game following 1984 season.

GEORGE WILLARD LITTLE
Defensive Tackle—Miami Dolphins
Born June 27, 1963, at Duquesne, Pa.
Height, 6.04. Weight, 278.
High School—Duquesne, Pa.
Attended University of Iowa.

Selected by Oakland in 1985 USFL territorial draft.
Selected by Miami in 3rd round (65th player selected) of 1985 NFL draft.
Signed by Miami Dolphins, July 18, 1985.
Miami NFL, 1985.
Games: 1985 (14).
Played in AFC Championship Game following 1985 season.

GREG LOBERG
Center—New Orleans Saints
Born December 7, 1961, at San Rafael, Calif.
Height, 6.04. Weight, 250.
High School—San Rafael, Calif., Terra Linda.
Attended University of California at Berkeley.

Selected by Oakland in 1984 USFL territorial draft.
Signed by Oakland Invaders, January 7, 1984.
Released by Oakland Invaders, January 30, 1984; awarded on waivers to San Antonio Gunslingers, January 31, 1984.
Traded by San Antonio Gunslingers to Los Angeles Express for past considerations, February 8, 1984.
Released by Los Angeles Express, February 21, 1984; re-signed by Express, March 15, 1984.
On developmental squad, March 15, 1984.
Released injured with broken leg by Los Angeles Express, May 16, 1984; re-signed by Express, February 10, 1985.
Released by Los Angeles Express, March 6, 1985; signed as free agent by Denver Gold, March 20, 1985.
Released by Denver Gold, July 31, 1985; signed as free agent by New Orleans Saints, May 14, 1986.
Los Angeles USFL, 1984; Denver USFL, 1985.
Games: 1984 (6), 1985 (14). Total—20.

JAMES LOCKETTE
Defensive End—San Diego Chargers
Born April 7, 1960, at St. Louis, Mo.
Height, 6.04. Weight, 259.
High School—St. Louis, Mo., Sumner.
Attended University of Missouri.

Selected by Birmingham in 6th round (68th player selected) of 1983 USFL draft.
USFL rights traded by Birmingham Stallions to New Jersey Generals for 7th round pick in 1984 draft, January 27, 1983.
Signed by New Jersey Generals, January 31, 1983.
Granted free agency, August 1, 1985; signed by San Diego Chargers, August 5, 1985.
On injured reserve with knee injury, August 20 through entire 1985 season.
New Jersey USFL, 1983 through 1985.
Games: 1983 (18), 1984 (18), 1985 (18). Total—54.
Pro statistics: Credited with 4½ sacks for 36½ yards, 1983; intercepted one pass for four yards and credited with 5½ sacks for 33½ yards, 1984; credited with 13 sacks for 108 yards, 1985.

EUGENE LOCKHART JR.
Linebacker—Dallas Cowboys
Born March 8, 1961, at Crockett, Tex.
Height, 6.02. Weight, 233.
High School—Crockett, Tex.
Received bachelor of arts degree in marketing from University of Houston in 1983.
Selected by Houston in 1984 USFL territorial draft.
Selected by Dallas in 6th round (152nd player selected) of 1984 NFL draft.
Signed by Dallas Cowboys, May 8, 1984.
Dallas NFL, 1984 and 1985.
Games: 1984 (15), 1985 (16). Total—31.
Pro statistics: Intercepted one pass for 32 yards and recovered one fumble, 1984; intercepted one pass for 19 yards and a touchdown and recovered four fumbles for 17 yards, 1985.

JAMES DAVID LOFTON
Wide Receiver—Green Bay Packers
Born July 5, 1956, at Fort Ord, Calif.
Height, 6.03. Weight, 197.
High School—Los Angeles, Calif., Washington.
Received bachelor of science degree in industrial engineering from
Stanford University in 1978.
Cousin of Kevin Bass, outfielder with Houston Astros;
and cousin of Tron Armstrong, wide receiver with Miami Dolphins.
Named to THE SPORTING NEWS NFL All-Star Team, 1980 and 1981.
Selected by Green Bay in 1st round (6th player selected) of 1978 NFL draft.

Year Club	G.	Att.	Yds.	Avg.	TD.	P.C.	Yds.	Avg.	TD.	TD.	Pts.	F.
			—RUSHING—				PASS RECEIVING			—TOTAL—		
1978—Green Bay NFL	16	3	13	4.3	0	46	818	17.8	6	6	36	2
1979—Green Bay NFL	15	1	—1	—1.0	0	54	968	17.9	4	4	24	5
1980—Green Bay NFL	16		None			71	1226	17.3	4	4	24	0
1981—Green Bay NFL	16		None			71	1294	18.2	8	8	48	0
1982—Green Bay NFL	9	4	101	25.3	1	35	696	19.9	4	5	30	0
1983—Green Bay NFL	16	9	36	4.0	0	58	1300	*22.4	8	8	48	0
1984—Green Bay NFL	16	10	82	8.2	0	62	1361	*22.0	7	7	42	1
1985—Green Bay NFL	16	4	14	3.5	0	69	1153	16.7	4	4	24	3
Pro Totals—8 Years	120	31	245	7.9	1	466	8816	18.9	45	46	276	11

Additional pro statistics: Returned one kickoff for no yards and attempted two passes with no completions, 1978; attempted one pass with no completions, 1979; recovered one fumble, 1981; attempted one pass with one completion for 43 yards, 1982.
Played in Pro Bowl (NFL All-Star Game) following 1978 and 1980 through 1985 seasons.

DAVID LOGAN
Nose Tackle—Tampa Bay Buccaneers
Born October 25, 1956, at Pittsburgh, Pa.
Height, 6.02. Weight, 250.
High School—East Liberty, Pa., Peabody.
Received bachelor of arts and science degree in urban and black studies from
University of Pittsburgh in 1979.
Related to Bill Cartwright, center with New York Knicks.
Named to THE SPORTING NEWS NFL All-Star Team, 1984.
Selected by Tampa Bay in 12th round (307th player selected) of 1979 NFL draft.
On injured reserve with knee injury, August 28 through November 16, 1979; activated, November 17, 1979.
On injured reserve with back injury, December 27 through remainder of 1979 playoffs.
Tampa Bay NFL, 1979 through 1985.
Games: 1979 (5), 1980 (16), 1981 (16), 1982 (9), 1983 (16), 1984 (16), 1985 (16). Total—94.
Pro statistics: Recovered one fumble for 60 yards and a touchdown, 1980; recovered one fumble for 21 yards and a touchdown, 1981; recovered one fumble for 54 yards and a touchdown, 1983; intercepted one pass for 27 yards and a touchdown, 1984; recovered one fumble for two yards, 1985.

NEIL VINCENT LOMAX
Quarterback—St. Louis Cardinals
Born February 17, 1959, at Portland, Ore.
Height, 6.03. Weight, 215.
High School—Lake Oswego, Ore.
Received degree in communications from Portland State University.
Selected by St. Louis in 2nd round (33rd player selected) of 1981 NFL draft.

Year Club	G.	Att.	Cmp.	Pct.	Gain	T.P.	P.I.	Avg.	Att.	Yds.	Avg.	TD.	TD.	Pts.	F.
				PASSING						RUSHING				TOTAL	
1981—St. Louis NFL	14	236	119	50.4	1575	4	10	6.67	19	104	5.5	2	2	12	6
1982—St. Louis NFL	9	205	109	53.2	1367	5	6	6.67	28	119	4.3	1	1	6	8
1983—St. Louis NFL	13	354	209	59.0	2636	24	11	7.45	27	127	4.7	2	2	12	9
1984—St. Louis NFL	16	560	345	61.6	4614	28	16	8.24	35	184	5.3	3	3	18	11
1985—St. Louis NFL	16	471	265	56.3	3214	18	12	6.82	32	125	3.9	0	0	0	10
Pro Totals—5 Years	68	1826	1047	57.3	13406	79	55	7.34	141	659	4.7	8	8	48	44

Quarterback Rating Points: 1981 (60.1), 1982 (70.1), 1983 (92.0), 1984 (92.5), 1985 (79.5). Total—82.3.

Additional pro statistics: Caught one pass for 10 yards, recovered one fumble and fumbled eight times for minus one yard, 1982; recovered three fumbles, 1983; recovered two fumbles and fumbled 11 times for minus five yards, 1984; recovered four fumbles and fumbled 10 times for minus one yard, 1985.

Played in Pro Bowl (NFL All-Star Game) following 1984 season.

DARREN M. LONG
Tight End—Los Angeles Rams
Born July 12, 1959, at Exeter, Calif.
Height, 6.03. Weight, 236.
High School—Exeter, Calif., Union.
Attended College of the Sequoias and California State University at Long Beach.

Selected by Los Angeles in 1983 USFL territorial draft.
Signed as free agent by Green Bay Packers, May 5, 1983.
Released by Green Bay Packers, August 15, 1983; signed by Los Angeles Express, September 23, 1983.
On developmental squad, February 24 through April 12, 1984; activated, April 13, 1984.
On developmental squad, June 22 through remainder of 1984 season.
Released by Los Angeles Express, February 4, 1985; re-signed by Express, June 14, 1985.
Released by Los Angeles Express, June 24, 1985; signed as free agent by Los Angeles Rams, March 10, 1986.
On developmental squad for 8 games with Los Angeles Express in 1984.

Year Club	G.	P.C.	Yds.	Avg.	TD.
		PASS RECEIVING			
1984—Los Angeles USFL	10	6	99	16.5	0
1985—Los Angeles USFL	1	3	28	9.3	0
Pro Totals—2 Years	11	9	127	14.1	0

Additional pro statistics: Recovered one fumble and fumbled once, 1984.

HOWARD M. LONG
(Howie)
Defensive End—Los Angeles Raiders
Born January 6, 1960, at Somerville, Mass.
Height, 6.05. Weight, 270.
High School—Milford, Mass.
Received bachelor of arts degree in communications from Villanova University in 1981.

Named to THE SPORTING NEWS NFL All-Star Team, 1983.
Selected by Oakland in 2nd round (48th player selected) of 1981 NFL draft.
Franchise transferred to Los Angeles, May 7, 1982.
Left Los Angeles Raiders camp voluntarily, July 30 through August 2, 1984; returned, August 3, 1984.
Oakland NFL, 1981; Los Angeles Raiders NFL, 1982 through 1985.
Games: 1981 (16), 1982 (9), 1983 (16), 1984 (16), 1985 (16). Total—73.
Pro statistics: Recovered two fumbles, 1983; recovered two fumbles for four yards, 1984.
Played in AFC Championship Game following 1983 season.
Played in NFL Championship Game following 1983 season.
Played in Pro Bowl (NFL All-Star Game) following 1983 through 1985 seasons.

TERRY LUTHER LONG
Guard—Pittsburgh Steelers
Born July 21, 1959, at Columbia, S.C.
Height, 5.11. Weight, 260.
High School—Columbia, S.C., Eau Claire.
Attended East Carolina University.
Spent two years in Army before entering college.

Selected by Washington in 4th round (76th player selected) of 1984 USFL draft.
Selected by Pittsburgh in 4th round (111th player selected) of 1984 NFL draft.
Signed by Pittsburgh Steelers, July 10, 1984.
Pittsburgh NFL, 1984 and 1985.
Games: 1984 (12), 1985 (15). Total—27.
Pro statistics: Returned one punt for no yards and fumbled once, 1984.
Played in AFC Championship Game following 1984 season.

RONALD MANDEL LOTT
(Ronnie)
Defensive Back—San Francisco 49ers
Born May 8, 1959, at Albuquerque, N.M.
Height, 6.00. Weight, 199.
High School—Rialto, Calif., Eisenhower.
Received bachelor of science degree in public administration
from University of Southern California in 1981.

Named as defensive back on THE SPORTING NEWS College All-America Team, 1980.
Named to THE SPORTING NEWS NFL All-Star Team, 1981.
Selected by San Francisco in 1st round (8th player selected) of 1981 NFL draft.

			—INTERCEPTIONS—			
Year	Club	G.	No.	Yds.	Avg.TD.	
1981—San Francisco NFL		16	7	117	16.7	*3
1982—San Francisco NFL		9	2	95	47.5	*1
1983—San Francisco NFL		15	4	22	5.5	0
1984—San Francisco NFL		12	4	26	6.5	0
1985—San Francisco NFL		16	6	68	11.3	0
Pro Totals—5 Years............		68	23	328	14.3	4

Additional pro statistics: Returned seven kickoffs for 111 yards and fumbled once, 1981; recovered two fumbles, 1981 and 1985; recovered one fumble, 1983; returned one kickoff for two yards, 1985.
Played in NFC Championship Game following 1981, 1983 and 1984 seasons.
Played in NFL Championship Game following 1981 and 1984 seasons.
Played in Pro Bowl (NFL All-Star Game) following 1981 through 1984 seasons.

DUVAL LEE LOVE
Offensive Tackle—Los Angeles Rams
Born June 24, 1963, at Los Angeles, Calif.
Height, 6.03. Weight, 263.
High School—Fountain Valley, Calif.
Attended University of California at Los Angeles.

Selected by Memphis in 1985 USFL territorial draft.
Selected by Los Angeles Rams in 10th round (274th player selected) of 1985 NFL draft.
Signed by Los Angeles Rams, July 16, 1985.
On injured reserve with shoulder injury, September 2 through October 3, 1985; activated, October 4, 1985.
On injured reserve with pinched nerve in neck, November 15 through remainder of 1985 season.
Los Angeles Rams NFL, 1985.
Games: 1985 (6).

RANDY LOVE
Running Back—St. Louis Cardinals
Born September 30, 1956, at Garland, Tex.
Height, 6.01. Weight, 224.
High School—Garland, Tex.
Attended University of Houston.
Cousin of Brig Owens, defensive back with Washington Redskins, 1966 through 1977.

Selected by New England in 8th round (216th player selected) of 1979 NFL draft.
Released by New England Patriots, August 16, 1979; signed as free agent by St. Louis Cardinals, November 15, 1979.

			—RUSHING—				PASS RECEIVING				—TOTAL—		
Year	Club	G.	Att.	Yds.	Avg.	TD.	P.C.	Yds.	Avg.	TD.	TD.	Pts.	F.
1979—St. Louis NFL..............................		4		None				None			0	0	0
1980—St. Louis NFL..............................		16	1	3	3.0	0		None			0	0	3
1981—St. Louis NFL..............................		16	3	11	3.7	0		None			0	0	0
1982—St. Louis NFL..............................		9		None				None			0	0	1
1983—St. Louis NFL..............................		16	35	103	2.9	2	6	58	9.7	1	3	18	4
1984—St. Louis NFL..............................		16	25	90	3.6	1	7	33	4.7	1	2	12	1
1985—St. Louis NFL..............................		12	1	4	4.0	0	2	4	2.0	0	0	0	0
Pro Totals—7 Years.................................		89	65	211	3.2	3	15	95	6.3	2	5	30	9

Additional pro statistics: Returned three kickoffs for 46 yards, 1980 and 1981; recovered two fumbles, 1980 and 1981; returned four kickoffs for 69 yards, 1982; recovered one fumble, 1982 and 1983; returned three kickoffs for 71 yards, 1983; returned one kickoff for one yard, 1984.

ROBERT KIRK LOWDERMILK
(Known by middle name.)
Center—Minnesota Vikings
Born April 10, 1963, at Canton, O.
Height, 6.03. Weight, 265.
High School—Salem, O.
Attended Ohio State University.

Selected by New Jersey in 1985 USFL territorial draft.
Selected by Minnesota in 3rd round (59th player selected) of 1985 NFL draft.
Signed by Minnesota Vikings, August 12, 1985.
Minnesota NFL, 1985.
Games: 1985 (16).

WOODROW LOWE
Linebacker—San Diego Chargers
Born June 9, 1954, at Columbus, Ga.
Height, 6.00. Weight, 229.
High School—Phenix City, Ala.
Attended University of Alabama.

Selected by San Diego in 5th round (131st player selected) of 1976 NFL draft.

Year Club	—INTERCEPTIONS— G.	No.	Yds.	Avg.	TD.	Year Club	—INTERCEPTIONS— G.	No.	Yds.	Avg.	TD.
1976—San Diego NFL	14	1	8	8.0	0	1982—San Diego NFL	9	1	2	2.0	0
1977—San Diego NFL	14	1	28	28.0	0	1983—San Diego NFL	16	None			
1978—San Diego NFL	16	1	16	16.0	0	1984—San Diego NFL	15	3	61	20.3	1
1979—San Diego NFL	16	5	150	*30.0	*2	1985—San Diego NFL	16	3	6	2.0	0
1980—San Diego NFL	16	3	72	24.0	1	Pro Totals—10 Years	148	21	343	16.3	4
1981—San Diego NFL	16	3	0	0.0	0						

Additional pro statistics: Recovered two fumbles, 1976; recovered one fumble, 1978, 1980 and 1983; recovered one fumble for two yards, 1979; fumbled once, 1984.
Played in AFC Championship Game following 1980 and 1981 seasons.

DOMINIC GERALD LOWERY
(Nick)
Placekicker—Kansas City Chiefs
Born May 27, 1956, at Munich, Germany
Height, 6.04. Weight, 189.
High School—Washington, D. C., St. Albans.
Received bachelor of arts degree in government from Dartmouth College in 1978.

Established NFL record for highest field goal percentage, career (76.8).
Signed as free agent by New York Jets, May 17, 1978.
Released by New York Jets, August 21, 1978; signed as free agent by New England Patriots, September 19, 1978.
Released by New England Patriots, October 6, 1978; signed as free agent by Cincinnati Bengals, July 2, 1979.
Released by Cincinnati Bengals, August 13, 1979; signed as free agent by Washington Redskins, August 18, 1979.
Released by Washington Redskins, August 20, 1979; re-signed by Redskins, August 25, 1979.
Released by Washington Redskins, August 27, 1979; signed as free agent by Kansas City Chiefs, February 16, 1980.

Year Club	—PLACE KICKING— G.	XP.	XPM.	FG.	FGA.	Pts.
1978—New England NFL..	2	7	0	0	1	7
1980—Kansas City NFL.....	16	37	0	20	26	97
1981—Kansas City NFL.....	16	37	1	26	36	115
1982—Kansas City NFL.....	9	17	0	19	*24	74
1983—Kansas City NFL.....	16	44	1	24	30	116
1984—Kansas City NFL.....	16	35	0	23	33	104
1985—Kansas City NFL.....	16	35	0	24	27	107
Pro Totals—7 Years	91	212	2	136	177	620

Additional pro statistics: Recovered one fumble, 1981.
Played in Pro Bowl (NFL All-Star Game) following 1981 season.

ORLANDO DEWEY LOWRY
Linebacker—Indianapolis Colts
Born August 14, 1961, at Cleveland, O.
Height, 6.04. Weight, 234.
High School—Shaker Heights, O.
Attended Ohio State University.
Brother of Quentin Lowry; linebacker with Washington Redskins
and Tampa Bay Buccaneers, 1981 through 1983.

Selected by New Jersey in 1984 USFL territorial draft.
USFL rights traded with rights to defensive back Garcia Lane by New Jersey Generals to Philadelphia Stars for past considerations involving linebacker Lawrence Taylor, January 9, 1984.
Signed as free agent by Washington Redskins, May 3, 1984.
Released by Washington Redskins, August 27, 1984; signed as free agent by Indianapolis Colts, March 20, 1985.
Indianapolis NFL, 1985.
Games: 1985 (16).
Pro statistics: Returned one punt for no yards, 1985.

OLIVER LUCK
Quarterback—Houston Oilers
Born April 5, 1960, at Cleveland, O.
Height, 6.02. Weight, 193.
High School—Cleveland, O., St. Ignacius.
Received bachelor of arts degree in history from West Virginia University in 1982.

Selected by Houston in 2nd round (44th player selected) of 1982 NFL draft.
On injured reserve with broken leg, September 4 through October 15, 1985; activated, October 16, 1985.
Active for 9 games with Houston Oilers in 1982; did not play.

Year Club	G.	—PASSING— Att.	Cmp.	Pct.	Gain	T.P.	P.I.	Avg.	—RUSHING— Att.	Yds.	Avg.	TD.	—TOTAL— TD.	Pts.	F.
1983—Houston NFL	7	217	124	57.1	1375	8	13	6.34	17	55	3.2	0	0	0	5
1984—Houston NFL	4	36	22	61.1	256	2	1	7.11	10	75	7.5	1	1	6	2
1985—Houston NFL	5	100	56	56.0	572	2	2	5.72	15	95	6.3	0	0	0	9
Pro Totals—4 Years	16	353	202	57.2	2203	12	16	6.24	42	225	5.4	1	1	6	16

Quarterback Rating Points: 1983 (63.4), 1984 (89.6), 1985 (70.9). Total—68.3.
Additional pro statistics: Recovered one fumble, 1983; recovered two fumbles, 1984; recovered three fumbles, 1985.

MICHAEL CHRISTOPHER WILBERT LUCKHURST
(Mick)
Placekicker—Atlanta Falcons
Born March 31, 1958, at Redbourn, England.
Height, 6.02. Weight, 180.
High School—Redbourn, England, St. Columbus College.
Attended St. Cloud State University and University of California.
Husband of Terri Moody Luckhurst, professional golfer.
Signed as free agent by Atlanta Falcons, May 5, 1981.

| | | —PLACE KICKING— | | | | |
Year Club	G.	XP.	XPM.	FG.	FGA.	Pts.
1981—Atlanta NFL	16	51	0	21	33	114
1982—Atlanta NFL	9	21	1	10	14	51
1983—Atlanta NFL	16	43	2	17	22	94
1984—Atlanta NFL	16	31	0	20	27	91
1985—Atlanta NFL	16	29	0	24	31	101
Pro Totals—5 Years.......	73	175	3	92	127	451

Additional pro statistics: Punted once for 26 yards, 1985.

BRIAN KEITH LUFT
Offensive Tackle—New York Jets
Born September 5, 1963, at Fresno, Calif.
Height, 6.06. Weight, 263.
High School—Fresno, Calif., Bullard.
Attended University of Southern California.
Selected by New York Jets in 5th round (124th player selected) of 1985 NFL draft.
Signed by New York Jets, July 23, 1985.
On injured reserve with shoulder injury, August 15 through entire 1985 season.

DAVID GRAHAM LUTZ
Offensive Tackle—Kansas City Chiefs
Born December 30, 1959, at Monroe, N.C.
Height, 6.05. Weight, 285.
High School—Wadesboro, N.C., Bowman.
Attended Georgia Tech.
Selected by Oakland in 3rd round (31st player selected) of 1983 USFL draft.
Selected by Kansas City in 2nd round (34th player selected) of 1983 NFL draft.
Signed by Kansas City Chiefs, June 1, 1983.
On injured reserve with knee injury, September 4 through November 8, 1984; activated, November 9, 1984.
Kansas City NFL, 1983 through 1985.
Games: 1983 (16), 1984 (7), 1985 (16). Total—39.
Pro statistics: Recovered one fumble, 1985.

ALLEN LYDAY
Safety—Houston Oilers
Born September 16, 1960, at Wichita, Kan.
Height, 5.10. Weight, 186.
High School—Wichita, Kan., South.
Attended Texas Southern University and University of Nebraska.
Selected by Boston in 1983 USFL territorial draft.
Signed as free agent by Kansas City Chiefs, April 28, 1983.
Released by Kansas City Chiefs, August 29, 1983; signed by New Orleans Breakers, November 7, 1983.
Released by New Orleans Breakers, January 27, 1984; awarded on procedural waivers to Houston Oilers, April 6, 1984.
Released by Houston Oilers, August 20, 1984; re-signed by Oilers after clearing procedural waivers, October 25, 1984.
On injured reserve with knee injury, November 21 through remainder of 1984 season.
Released by Houston Oilers, September 3, 1985; re-signed by Oilers, September 26, 1985.
Houston NFL, 1984 and 1985.
Games: 1984 (4), 1985 (13). Total—17.
Pro statistics: Intercepted one pass for 12 yards, 1984; returned one kickoff for six yards, recovered one fumble and fumbled once, 1985.

LESTER EVERETT LYLES
Safety—New York Jets
Born December 27, 1962, at Washington, D.C.
Height, 6.03. Weight, 209.
High School—Washington, D.C., St. Albans.
Attended University of Virginia.
Selected by Orlando in 1985 USFL territorial draft.
Selected by New York Jets in 2nd round (40th player selected) of 1985 NFL draft.
Signed by New York Jets, July 3, 1985.
On injured reserve with hip injury, August 27 through November 15, 1985; activated, November 16, 1985.
New York Jets NFL, 1985.
Games: 1985 (6).
Pro statistics: Recovered one fumble for 13 yards, 1985.

ROBERT LYLES
Linebacker—Houston Oilers
Born March 21, 1961, at Los Angeles, Calif.
Height, 6.01. Weight, 223.
High School—Los Angeles, Calif., Belmont.
Attended Texas Christian University.

Selected by Houston in 5th round (114th player selected) of 1984 NFL draft.
On injured reserve with knee injury, September 25 through December 6, 1984; activated, December 7, 1984.
Houston NFL, 1984 and 1985.
Games: 1984 (6), 1985 (16). Total—22.

JOHNNY ROSS LYNN
Defensive Back—New York Jets
Born December 19, 1956, at Los Angeles, Calif.
Height, 6.00. Weight, 198.
High School—Pasadena, Calif., John Muir.
Received degree in history from University of California at Los Angeles.

Selected by New York Jets in 4th round (98th player selected) of 1979 NFL draft.
On injured reserve with knee injury, September 1 through entire 1980 season.
USFL rights traded by Washington Federals to Los Angeles Express for rights to quarterback Vince Evans, November 11, 1983.
Signed by Los Angeles Express, November 21, 1983, for contract to take effect after being granted free agency, February 1, 1984.
Re-signed by New York Jets after exercising buyout option in contract with Los Angeles Express, February, 1984.

		—INTERCEPTIONS—			
Year Club	G.	No.	Yds.	Avg.	TD.
1979—N.Y. Jets NFL	16	2	46	23.0	0
1981—N.Y. Jets NFL	13	3	76	25.3	0
1982—N.Y. Jets NFL	8	1	3	3.0	0
1983—N.Y. Jets NFL	16	3	70	23.3	1
1984—N.Y. Jets NFL	14	2	16	8.0	0
1985—N.Y. Jets NFL	14	1	24	24.0	0
Pro Totals—6 Years	81	12	235	19.6	1

Additional pro statistics: Recovered blocked punt in end zone for a touchdown and recovered two fumbles, 1979; recovered one fumble, 1982; ran two yards with lateral on fumble recovery, 1984; recovered one fumble for seven yards, 1985.
Played in AFC Championship Game following 1982 season.

MARTY LYONS
Defensive End-Defensive Tackle—New York Jets
Born January 15, 1957, at Tokoma Park, Md.
Height, 6.05. Weight, 269.
High School—St. Petersburg, Fla., Catholic.
Attended University of Alabama.

Named as defensive lineman on THE SPORTING NEWS College All-America Team, 1978.
Selected by New York Jets in 1st round (14th player selected) of 1979 NFL draft.
New York Jets NFL, 1979 through 1985.
Games: 1979 (16), 1980 (16), 1981 (12), 1982 (7), 1983 (16), 1984 (13), 1985 (16). Total—96.
Pro statistics: Recovered three fumbles, 1979; recovered one fumble, 1981; recovered one fumble for 10 yards, 1982.
Played in AFC Championship Game following 1982 season.

WILLIAM THOMAS MAAS
(Bill)
Nose Tackle-Defensive End—Kansas City Chiefs
Born March 2, 1962, at Newton Square, Pa.
Height, 6.04. Weight, 259.
High School—Newton Square, Pa., Marple Newtown.
Attended University of Pittsburgh.
Brother-in-law of Dan Marino, quarterback with Miami Dolphins.

Selected by Pittsburgh in 1984 USFL territorial draft.
Selected by Kansas City in 1st round (5th player selected) of 1984 NFL draft.
Signed by Kansas City Chiefs, July 13, 1984.
Kansas City NFL, 1984 and 1985.
Games: 1984 (14), 1985 (16). Total—30.
Pro statistics: Recovered one fumble, 1985.

MARK GOODWIN MacDONALD
Guard—Minnesota Vikings
Born April 30, 1961, at West Roxbury, Mass.
Height, 6.04. Weight, 267.
High School—Boston, Mass., Catholic Memorial.
Attended Boston College.

Selected by Pittsburgh in 4th round (84th player selected) of 1984 USFL draft (elected to return to college for final year of eligibility).

Selected by Minnesota in 5th round (115th player selected) of 1985 NFL draft.
Signed by Minnesota Vikings, July 25, 1985.
Minnesota NFL, 1985.
Games: 1985 (16).

DONALD MATTHEW MACEK
Name pronounced MAY-sick.
(Don)
Center—San Diego Chargers
Born July 21, 1954, at Manchester, N. H.
Height, 6.02. Weight, 260.
High School—Manchester, N. H., Central.
Received bachelor of science degree in marketing from Boston College and
attending National University for master's degree in marketing.
Selected by San Diego in 2nd round (31st player selected) of 1976 NFL draft.
On injured reserve with neck injury, December 7 through remainder of 1979 season.
Left San Diego Chargers camp voluntarily, August 7 through August 21, 1984; returned, August 22, 1984.
San Diego NFL, 1976 through 1985.
Games: 1976 (14), 1977 (14), 1978 (14), 1979 (10), 1980 (16), 1981 (15), 1982 (9), 1983 (11), 1984 (13), 1985 (15).
Total—131.
Pro statistics: Recovered one fumble, 1976, 1977, 1980, 1981 and 1983; returned one kickoff for six yards, 1978;
fumbled once, 1978 and 1982; fumbled twice for minus 23 yards, 1980.
Played in AFC Championship Game following 1980 and 1981 seasons.

MICHAEL BRUCE MACHUREK
Name pronounced Ma-CHUR-ek.
(Mike)
Quarterback
Born July 22, 1960, at Las Vegas, Nev.
Height, 6.01. Weight, 205.
High School—San Diego, Calif., Madison.
Attended San Diego Community College and Idaho State University.
Selected by Detroit in 6th round (154th player selected) of 1982 NFL draft.
Released by Detroit Lions, September 6, 1982; re-signed by Lions, September 7, 1982.
On inactive list, September 12 and 19, 1982.
On commissioner's exempt list, November 20 through November 29, 1982; activated, November 30, 1982.
On physically unable to perform/active with cancer surgery, July 21 through August 7, 1983; activated, August 8,
1983.
On injured reserve with shoulder injury, August 20 through entire 1985 season.
Granted free agency with no qualifying offer, February 1, 1986.
Active for 5 games with Detroit Lions in 1982; did not play.
Active for 16 games with Detroit Lions in 1983; did not play.

			PASSING						RUSHING			TOTAL		
Year Club	G.	Att.	Cmp.	Pct.	Gain	T.P.	P.I.	Avg.	Att.	Yds.	Avg. TD.	TD.	Pts.	F.
1984—Detroit NFL	4	43	14	32.6	193	0	6	4.49	1	9	9.0 0	0	0	0

Quarterback Rating Points: 1984 (8.3).

CEDRIC MANUEL MACK
Cornerback—St. Louis Cardinals
Born September 14, 1960, at Freeport, Tex.
Height, 6.00. Weight, 194.
High School—Freeport, Tex., Brazosport.
Attended Baylor University.
Cousin of Phillip Epps, wide receiver with Green Bay Packers.
Selected by Oakland in 12th round (138th player selected) of 1983 USFL draft.
Selected by St. Louis in 2nd round (44th player selected) of 1983 NFL draft.
Signed by St. Louis Cardinals, July 11, 1983.
On injured reserve with dislocated shoulder, September 28 through October 25, 1984; activated, October 26, 1984.
Selected by New York Yankees' organization in 22nd round of free-agent draft, June 5, 1979.

		INTERCEPTIONS				PASS RECEIVING				TOTAL		
Year Club	G.	No.	Yds.	Avg.	TD.	P.C.	Yds.	Avg.	TD.	TD.	Pts.	F.
1983—St. Louis NFL	16	3	25	8.3	0		None			0	0	0
1984—St. Louis NFL	12		None			5	61	12.2	0	0	0	0
1985—St. Louis NFL	16	2	10	5.0	0	1	16	16.0	0	0	0	0
Pro Totals—3 Years	44	5	35	7.0	0	6	77	12.8	0	0	0	0

Additional pro statistics: Recovered two fumbles, 1985.

KEVIN MACK
Running Back—Cleveland Browns
Born August 9, 1962, at Kings Mountain, N.C.
Height, 6.00. Weight, 212.
High School—Kings Mountain, N.C.
Attended Clemson University.
Selected by Washington in 1984 USFL territorial draft.

Rights traded with rights to defensive tackle James Robinson by Washington Federals to Los Angeles Express for draft choices, March 16, 1984.
Signed by Los Angeles Express, March 16, 1984.
Granted roster exemption, March 16, 1984; activated, March 23, 1984.
On developmental squad, March 30 through April 6, 1984; activated, April 7, 1984.
On developmental squad, April 28 through May 10, 1984; activated, May 11, 1984.
Selected by Cleveland in 1st round (11th player selected) of 1984 NFL supplemental draft.
Released by Los Angeles Express, January 31, 1985; signed by Cleveland Browns, February 1, 1985.
On developmental squad for 3 games with Los Angeles Express in 1984.

| Year Club | G. | RUSHING | | | | PASS RECEIVING | | | | —TOTAL— | | |
		Att.	Yds.	Avg.	TD.	P.C.	Yds.	Avg.	TD.	TD.	Pts.	F.
1984—Los Angeles USFL	12	73	330	4.5	4	6	38	6.3	0	4	24	3
1985—Cleveland NFL	16	222	1104	5.0	7	29	297	10.2	3	10	60	4
Pro Totals—2 Years	28	295	1434	4.9	11	35	335	9.6	3	14	84	7

Additional USFL statistics: Returned three kickoffs for 20 yards and recovered four fumbles, 1984.
Additional NFL statistics: Recovered three fumbles, 1985.
Played in Pro Bowl (NFL All-Star Game) following 1985 season.

KYLE ERICKSON MACKEY
Quarterback—Philadelphia Eagles
Born March 2, 1962, at Alpine, Tex.
Height, 6.02. Weight, 220.
High School—Alpine, Tex.
Attended East Texas State University.
Son of Dee Mackey, tight end with San Francisco 49ers, Baltimore Colts
and New York Jets, 1960 through 1965.

Selected by Washington in 11th round (215th player selected) of 1984 USFL draft.
Selected by St. Louis in 11th round (296th player selected) of 1984 NFL draft.
Signed by St. Louis Cardinals, July 16, 1984.
Released by St. Louis Cardinals, August 26, 1985; signed as free agent by Philadelphia Eagles, March 10, 1986.
Active for 16 games with St. Louis Cardinals in 1984; did not play.

DOUGLAS BRIAN MACKIE
(Doug)
Offensive Tackle—New Orleans Saints
Born February 18, 1957, at Saugus, Mass.
Height, 6.04. Weight, 262.
High School—Saugus, Mass.
Attended Ohio State University.

Signed as free agent by New York Giants, April 12, 1982.
Released by New York Giants, June 23, 1982; signed by Boston Breakers, September 16, 1982.
Traded by Boston Breakers to Tampa Bay Bandits for past consideration, January 27, 1983.
On developmental squad, March 25 through April 7, 1983; activated, April 8, 1983.
On developmental squad, June 3 through June 16, 1983; activated, June 17, 1983.
Traded by Tampa Bay Bandits to New Jersey Generals for rights to safety Zac Henderson, September 8, 1983.
On developmental squad, February 23 through March 15, 1985; activated, March 16, 1986.
On developmental squad, June 10 through June 14, 1985; activated, June 15, 1985.
Granted free agency, August 1, 1985; signed as free agent by New Orleans Saints, May 9, 1986.
On developmental squad for 4 games with Tampa Bay Bandits in 1983.
On developmental squad for 4 games with New Jersey Generals in 1985.
Played with West Virginia Rockets of American Football Association, 1981.
Tampa Bay USFL, 1983; New Jersey USFL, 1984 and 1985.
Games: 1983 (13), 1984 (18), 1985 (14). Total—45.

CALVIN MAGEE
Tight End—Tampa Bay Buccaneers
Born April 23, 1963, at New Orleans, La.
Height, 6.03. Weight, 240.
High School—New Orleans, La., Booker T. Washington.
Attended Southern University.

Selected by Portland in 1985 USFL territorial draft.
Signed as free agent by Tampa Bay Buccaneers, May 9, 1985.

| Year Club | G. | PASS RECEIVING | | | |
		P.C.	Yds.	Avg.	TD.
1985—Tampa Bay NFL	16	26	288	11.1	3

Additional pro statistics: Returned two kickoffs for 20 yards and fumbled once, 1985.

STEVEN KENNETH MAIDLOW
(Steve)
Linebacker—Buffalo Bills
Born June 6, 1960, at Lansing, Mich.
Height, 6.02. Weight, 238.
High School—East Lansing, Mich.
Attended Michigan State University.

Selected by Michigan in 1983 USFL territorial draft.

Selected by Cincinnati in 4th round (109th player selected) of 1983 NFL draft.
Signed by Cincinnati Bengals, May 19, 1983.
Released by Cincinnati Bengals, September 2, 1985; awarded on waivers to Buffalo Bills, September 3, 1985.
Cincinnati NFL, 1983 and 1984; Buffalo NFL, 1985.
Games: 1983 (16), 1984 (16), 1985 (16). Total—48.
Pro statistics: Recovered one fumble, 1985.

DORAN OLIVER MAJOR
Defensive Back—Philadelphia Eagles
Born May 20, 1961, at Honolulu, Hawaii.
Height, 5.10. Weight, 175.
High School—Biloxi, Miss.
Attended Memphis State University.
Related to Bill Triplett, back with St. Louis Cardinals,
New York Giants and Detroit Lions, 1962 through 1972.
Signed by Memphis Showboats, January 20, 1984.
On developmental squad, February 24 through March 10, 1984; activated, March 11, 1984.
On developmental squad, March 25 through March 28, 1985; activated, March 29, 1985.
Released by Memphis Showboats, July 31, 1985; re-signed by Showboats, August 1, 1985.
Released by Memphis Showboats, August 2, 1985; signed as free agent by Philadelphia Eagles, May 7, 1986.
On developmental squad for 2 games with Memphis Showboats in 1984.
On developmental squad for 1 game with Memphis Showboats in 1985.

		—INTERCEPTIONS—			
Year Club	G.	No.	Yds.	Avg.	TD.
1984—Memphis USFL	16	2	20	10.0	0
1985—Memphis USFL	17	None			
Pro Totals—2 Years	33	2	20	10.0	0

Additional pro statistics: Recovered three fumbles and credited with one sack for 10 yards, 1984; recovered one fumble, 1985.

RYDELL MALANCON
Name pronounced Mah-LOHN-sohn.
Linebacker—Atlanta Falcons
Born January 10, 1962, at New Orleans, La.
Height, 6.01. Weight, 227.
High School—St. James, La.
Attended Louisiana State University.
Selected by New Orleans in 1984 USFL territorial draft.
Selected by Atlanta in 4th round (94th player selected) of 1984 NFL draft.
Signed by Atlanta Falcons, July 15, 1984.
On injured reserved with ankle injury, September 28 through November 30, 1984; activated, December 1, 1984.
On injured reserve with knee injury, August 19 through entire 1985 season.
Atlanta NFL, 1984.
Games: 1984 (7).
Pro statistics: Returned one kickoff for no yards, 1984.

RICK LEROY MALLORY
Offensive Lineman—Tampa Bay Buccaneers
Born October 21, 1960, at Seattle, Wash.
Height, 6.02. Weight, 260.
High School—Renton, Wash., Lindbergh.
Attended University of Washington.
Selected by Arizona in 11th round (221st player selected) of 1984 USFL draft.
Selected by Tampa Bay in 9th round (225th player selected) of 1984 NFL draft.
Signed by Tampa Bay Buccaneers, June 21, 1984.
On injured reserve with ankle injury, August 27 through entire 1984 season.
Tampa Bay NFL, 1985.
Games: 1985 (13).

MARK M. MALONE
Quarterback—Pittsburgh Steelers
Born November 22, 1958, at El Cajon, Calif.
Height, 6.04. Weight, 222.
High School—El Cajon, Calif., Valley.
Attended Arizona State University.
Selected by Pittsburgh in 1st round (28th player selected) of 1980 NFL draft.
On physically unable to perform/active with knee injury, July 29 through August 23, 1982.
On reserve, August 24 through December 13, 1982; activated, December 14, 1982.
Active for 3 games with Pittsburgh Steelers in 1982; did not play.

		—PASSING—							—RUSHING—				—TOTAL—		
Year Club	G.	Att.	Cmp.	Pct.	Gain	T.P.	P.I.	Avg.	Att.	Yds.	Avg.	TD.	TD.	Pts.	F.
1980—Pittsburgh NFL	1	None							None				0	0	0
1981—Pittsburgh NFL	8	88	45	51.1	553	3	5	6.28	16	68	4.3	2	3	18	2
1983—Pittsburgh NFL	2	20	9	45.0	124	1	2	6.20	None				0	0	0
1984—Pittsburgh NFL	13	272	147	54.0	2137	16	17	7.86	25	42	1.7	3	3	18	4
1985—Pittsburgh NFL	10	233	117	50.2	1428	13	7	6.13	15	80	5.3	1	1	6	3
Pro Totals—6 Years	34	613	318	51.9	4242	33	31	6.92	56	190	3.4	6	7	42	9

Quarterback Rating Points: 1981 (58.4), 1983 (42.5), 1984 (73.4), 1985 (75.5). Total—70.9.

Additional pro statistics: Caught one pass for 90 yards and a touchdown and returned one kickoff for three yards, 1981; recovered one fumble, 1983; recovered two fumbles, 1984; recovered three fumbles and fumbled three times for minus five yards, 1985.

Played in AFC Championship Game following 1984 season.

WILLIAM H. MANDLEY
(Pete)
Wide Receiver-Punt Returner—Detroit Lions
Born July 29, 1961, at Mesa, Ariz.
Height, 5.10. Weight, 191.
High School—Mesa, Ariz., Westwood.
Attended Northern Arizona University.

Selected by Arizona in 1984 USFL territorial draft.
Selected by Detroit in 2nd round (47th player selected) of 1984 NFL draft.
Signed by Detroit Lions, July 10, 1984.

Year Club		PASS RECEIVING				-PUNT RETURNS-				—KICKOFF RET.—				—TOTAL—		
	G.	P.C.	Yds.	Avg.	TD.	No.	Yds.	Avg.	TD.	No.	Yds.	Avg.	TD.	TD.	Pts.	F.
1984—Detroit NFL	15	3	38	12.7	0	2	0	0.0	0	22	390	17.7	0	0	0	2
1985—Detroit NFL	16	18	316	17.6	0	38	403	10.6	1	6	152	25.3	0	1	6	3
Pro Totals—2 Years	31	21	354	16.9	0	40	403	10.1	1	28	542	19.4	0	1	6	5

Additional pro statistics: Recovered two fumbles, 1984 and 1985.

JAMES MANESS
Name pronounced MAY-niss.
Wide Receiver
Born May 1, 1963, at Decatur, Tex.
Height, 6.01. Weight, 174.
High School—Decatur, Tex.
Attended Texas Christian University.

Selected by Los Angeles in 1st round (17th player selected) of 1985 USFL draft.
Selected by Chicago in 3rd round (78th player selected) of 1985 NFL draft.
Signed by Chicago Bears, July 23, 1985.
On injured reserve with pulled groin, November 8 through remainder of 1985 season.
Released by Chicago Bears, May 23, 1986.
Chicago NFL, 1985.
Games: 1985 (8).
Pro statistics: Caught one pass for 34 yards and returned two punts for nine yards, 1985.

DINO M. MANGIERO
Name pronounced Man-gee-air-oh.
Nose Tackle—San Francisco 49ers
Born December 29, 1958, at New York, N.Y.
Height, 6.02. Weight, 270.
High School—Staten Island, N.Y., Curtis.
Received bachelor of science degree in physical education from Rutgers University in 1980.

Signed as free agent by Kansas City Chiefs, May, 1980.
Released by Kansas City Chiefs, August 26, 1980; re-signed by Chiefs, September 3, 1980.
On injured reserve with knee injury, August 11 through October 19, 1981; activated after clearing procedural waivers, October 21, 1981.
On injured reserve with hand injury, September 6 through November 22, 1982; re-signed after clearing procedural waivers, November 24, 1982.
Released by Kansas City Chiefs, August 27, 1984; awarded on waivers to Seattle Seahawks, August 28, 1984.
Released by Seattle Seahawks, September 2, 1985; signed as free agent by San Francisco 49ers, May 15, 1986.
Kansas City NFL, 1980 through 1983; Seattle NFL, 1984.
Games: 1980 (16), 1981 (9), 1982 (6), 1983 (16), 1984 (15). Total—62.
Pro statistics: Intercepted one pass for no yards and recovered one fumble, 1980; returned one kickoff for eight yards, 1982; recovered one fumble for 32 yards, 1983.

DEXTER MANLEY
Defensive End—Washington Redskins
Born February 2, 1959, at Houston, Tex.
Height, 6.03. Weight, 253.
High School—Houston, Tex., Yates.
Attended Oklahoma State University.
Cousin of Eric Dickerson, running back with Los Angeles Rams.

Selected by Washington in 5th round (119th player selected) of 1981 NFL draft.
Washington NFL, 1981 through 1985.
Games: 1981 (16), 1982 (9), 1983 (16), 1984 (15), 1985 (16). Total—72.
Pro statistics: Intercepted one pass for minus two yards and recovered three fumbles for three yards, 1982; intercepted one pass for one yard, 1983; recovered one fumble, 1984.
Played in NFC Championship Game following 1982 and 1983 seasons.
Played in NFL Championship Game following 1982 and 1983 seasons.

CHARLES MANN
Defensive End—Washington Redskins

Born April 12, 1961, at Sacramento, Calif.
Height, 6.06. Weight, 260.
High School—Sacramento, Calif., Valley.
Attended University of Nevada at Reno.

Selected by Oakland in 18th round (210th player selected) of 1983 USFL draft.
Selected by Washington in 3rd round (84th player selected) of 1983 NFL draft.
Signed by Washington Redskins, May 9, 1983.
Washington NFL, 1983 through 1985.
Games: 1983 (16), 1984 (16), 1985 (16). Total—48.
Pro statistics: Credited with one safety, 1983; recovered one fumble, 1984 and 1985.
Played in NFC Championship Game following 1983 season.
Played in NFL Championship Game following 1983 season.

LIONEL MANUEL JR.
Wide Receiver—New York Giants

Born April 13, 1962, at Rancho Cucamonga, Calif.
Height, 5.11. Weight, 175.
High School—La Puente, Calif., Bassett.
Attended Citrus College and University of The Pacific.

Selected by Los Angeles in 1984 USFL territorial draft.
Selected by New York Giants in 7th round (171st player selected) of 1984 NFL draft.
Signed by New York Giants, June 4, 1984.
On injured reserve with pulled hamstring, November 30 through December 27, 1985; activated, December 28, 1985.

| | | –PASS RECEIVING- | | | | –PUNT RETURNS- | | | | —TOTAL— | | |
Year Club	G.	P.C.	Yds.	Avg.	TD.	No.	Yds.	Avg.	TD.	TD.	Pts.	F.
1984—New York Giants NFL	16	33	619	18.8	4	8	62	7.8	0	4	24	2
1985—New York Giants NFL	12	49	859	17.5	5		None			5	30	1
Pro Totals—2 Years	28	82	1478	18.0	9	8	62	7.8	0	9	54	3

Additional pro statistics: Rushed three times for two yards, 1984.

MARCUS MAREK
Linebacker—Cleveland Browns

Born January 8, 1961 at Masury, O.
Height, 6.02. Weight, 224.
High School—Masury, O. Brookfield.
Attended Ohio State University.

Selected by Boston in 9th round (107th player selected) of 1983 USFL draft.
Signed by Boston Breakers, February 26, 1983.
Franchise transferred to New Orleans, October 18, 1983.
On developmental squad, June 24 through remainder of 1984 season.
Franchise transferred to Portland, November 13, 1984.
On developmental squad, March 1 through April 17, 1985; activated, April 18, 1985.
On developmental squad, April 25 through May 8, 1985; activated, May 9, 1985.
On developmental squad, May 18 through May 23, 1985; activated, May 24, 1985.
Released by Portland Breakers, July 31, 1985; signed as free agent by Chicago Bears, August 8, 1985.
Released by Chicago Bears, August 26, 1985; signed as free agent by Cleveland Browns, May 4, 1986.
On developmental squad for 1 game with New Orleans Breakers in 1984.
On developmental squad for 10 games with Portland Breakers in 1985.

| | | —INTERCEPTIONS— | | | |
Year Club	G.	No.	Yds.	Avg.TD.	
1983—Boston USFL	18	4	23	5.8	0
1984—New Orleans USFL	17	1	16	16.0	0
1985—Portland USFL	9	1	1	1.0	0
Pro Totals—3 Years	44	6	40	6.7	0

Additional pro statistics: Recovered three fumbles for 89 yards and a touchdown and credited with one sack for six yards, 1983; recovered six fumbles for eight yards, 1984; credited with one sack for three yards and recovered one fumble for one yard, 1985.

KENNETH MARGERUM
(Ken)
Wide Receiver—Chicago Bears

Born October 5, 1958, at Fountain Valley, Calif.
Height, 6.00. Weight, 180.
High School—Fountain Valley, Calif.
Received bachelor of arts degree in communications and psychology
from Stanford University.

Named as wide receiver on THE SPORTING NEWS College All-America Team, 1979.
Selected by Chicago in 3rd round (67th player selected) of 1981 NFL draft.
On physically unable to perform/reserve with knee injury, July 20 through entire 1984 season.

Year Club	——PASS RECEIVING——

Year Club	G.	P.C.	Yds.	Avg.	TD.
1981—Chicago NFL	16	39	584	15.0	1
1982—Chicago NFL	9	14	207	14.8	3
1983—Chicago NFL	15	21	336	16.0	2
1985—Chicago NFL	16	17	190	11.2	2
Pro Totals—4 Years	56	91	1317	14.5	8

Additional pro statistics: Rushed once for 11 yards and recovered one fumble, 1981; fumbled once, 1982, 1983 and 1985; rushed once for seven yards, 1983; rushed once for minus seven yards, 1985.
Played in NFC Championship Game following 1985 season.
Played in NFL Championship Game following 1985 season.

DANIEL CONSTANTINE MARINO JR.
(Dan)
Quarterback—Miami Dolphins
Born September 15, 1961, at Pittsburgh, Pa.
Height, 6.04. Weight, 214.
High School—Pittsburgh, Pa., Central Catholic.
Received bachelor of arts degree in communications from University of Pittsburgh.
Brother-in-law of Bill Maas, nose tackle-defensive end with Kansas City Chiefs.
Named THE SPORTING NEWS NFL Player of the Year, 1984.
Named to THE SPORTING NEWS NFL All-Star Team, 1984 and 1985.
Named THE SPORTING NEWS NFL Rookie of the Year, 1983.
Named as quarterback on THE SPORTING NEWS College All-America Team, 1981.
Established NFL records for completion percentage by rookie (58.45), 1983; most touchdowns passing, season (48), 1984; most passing yards gained, season (5,084), 1984; most passes completed, season (362), 1984; most games, 300 yards passing, season (9), 1984; most games, 400 yards passing, season (4), 1984.
Tied NFL record for most consecutive games, 400 yards passing (2), 1984.
Led NFL quarterbacks in passing with 108.9 points in 1984.
Selected by Los Angeles in 1st round (1st player selected) of 1983 USFL draft.
Selected by Miami in 1st round (27th player selected) of 1983 NFL draft.
Signed by Miami Dolphins, July 9, 1983.
Left Miami Dolphins camp voluntarily, July 25 through August 31, 1985.
Reported and granted roster exemption, September 1 through September 4, 1985; activated, September 5, 1985.
Selected by Kansas City Royals' organization in 4th round of free-agent draft, June 5, 1979.

Year Club		——————PASSING——————							——RUSHING——				—TOTAL—		
	G.	Att.	Cmp.	Pct.	Gain	T.P.	P.I.	Avg.	Att.	Gain	Avg.	TD.	TD.	Pts.	F.
1983—Miami NFL	11	296	173	58.4	2210	20	6	7.47	28	45	1.6	2	2	12	5
1984—Miami NFL	16	★564	★362	64.2	★5084	★48	17	★9.01	28	—7	—0.3	0	0	0	6
1985—Miami NFL	16	567	★336	59.3	★4137	★30	21	7.30	26	—24	—0.9	0	0	0	9
Pro Totals—3 Years	43	1427	871	61.0	11431	98	44	8.01	82	14	0.2	2	2	12	20

Quarterback Rating Points: 1983 (96.0), 1984 (108.9), 1985 (84.1). Total—96.4.
Additional pro statistics: Recovered two fumbles, 1983; recovered two fumbles and fumbled six times for minus three yards, 1984; recovered two fumbles and fumbled nine times for minus four yards, 1985.
Played in AFC Championship Game following 1984 and 1985 seasons.
Played in NFL Championship Game following 1984 season.
Played in Pro Bowl (NFL All-Star Game) following 1984 season.
Named to play in Pro Bowl following 1983 season; replaced due to injury by Bill Kenney.
Named to play in Pro Bowl following 1985 season; replaced due to injury by Ken O'Brien.

FRED D. MARION
Safety—New England Patriots
Born January 2, 1959, at Gainesville, Fla.
Height, 6.02. Weight, 191.
High School—Gainesville, Fla., Buchholz.
Attended University of Miami (Fla.).
Brother of Frank Marion, linebacker with Memphis Southmen (WFL) and New York Giants, 1975 and 1977 through 1983.
Selected by New England in 5th round (112th player selected) of 1982 NFL draft.

Year Club		——INTERCEPTIONS——			
	G.	No.	Yds.	Avg.	TD.
1982—New England NFL	9		None		
1983—New England NFL	16	2	4	2.0	0
1984—New England NFL	16	2	39	19.5	0
1985—New England NFL	16	7	★189	27.0	0
Pro Totals—4 Years	57	11	232	21.1	0

Additional pro statistics: Recovered one fumble, 1982 and 1984; recovered three fumbles for nine yards, 1985.
Played in AFC Championship Game following 1985 season.
Played in NFL Championship Game following 1985 season.
Played in Pro Bowl (NFL All-Star Game) following 1985 season.

CURT MARSH
Guard—Los Angeles Raiders
Born August 25, 1959, at Tacoma, Wash.
Height, 6.05. Weight, 275.
High School—Snohomish, Wash.
Attended University of Washington.

Selected by Oakland in 1st round (23rd player selected) of 1981 NFL draft.
On injured reserve with rib injury, September 2 through October 9, 1981; activated, October 10, 1981.
Franchise transferred to Los Angeles, May 7, 1982.
On injured reserve with back injury, August 30 through entire 1983 season.
On injured reserve with broken arm, August 20 through October 18, 1985; activated October 19, 1985.
Oakland NFL, 1981; Los Angeles Raiders NFL, 1982, 1984 and 1985.
Games: 1981 (11), 1982 (9), 1984 (16), 1985 (7). Total—43.
Pro statistics: Recovered one fumble, 1981.

DOUG MARSH
Tight End—St. Louis Cardinals
Born June 18, 1958, at Akron, O.
Height, 6.03. Weight, 240.
High School—Akron, O., Central.
Attended University of Michigan.

Selected by St. Louis in 2nd round (33rd player selected) of 1980 NFL draft.
On injured reserve with knee injury, September 1 through October 1, 1981; activated, October 2, 1981.
On injured reserve with dislocated hip, October 28 through remainder of 1981 season.

		—PASS RECEIVING—			
Year Club	G.	P.C.	Yds.	Avg.	TD.
1980—St. Louis NFL	16	22	269	12.2	4
1981—St. Louis NFL	4	6	80	13.3	1
1982—St. Louis NFL	8	5	83	16.6	0
1983—St. Louis NFL	16	32	421	13.2	8
1984—St. Louis NFL	16	39	608	15.6	5
1985—St. Louis NFL	16	37	355	9.6	1
Pro Totals—6 Years	76	141	1816	12.9	19

Additional pro statistics: Fumbled once, 1980, 1981 and 1983; rushed once for minus five yards, 1984.

HENRY H. MARSHALL
Wide Receiver—Kansas City Chiefs
Born August 9, 1954, at Broxton, Ga.
Height, 6.02. Weight, 213.
High School—Dalzell, S.C., Hillcrest.
Attended University of Missouri.

Selected by Kansas City in 3rd round (79th player selected) of 1976 NFL draft.
On injured reserve with knee injury, November 25 through remainder of 1981 season.
On injured reserve with broken arm, December 7 through remainder of 1983 season.
On injured reserve with separated shoulder, November 5 through December 12, 1985; activated, December 13, 1985.

		—RUSHING—				PASS RECEIVING				—TOTAL—		
Year Club	G.	Att.	Yds.	Avg.	TD.	P.C.	Yds.	Avg.	TD.	TD.	Pts.	F.
1976—Kansas City NFL	14	5	101	20.2	1	28	443	15.8	2	3	18	1
1977—Kansas City NFL	14	7	11	1.6	0	23	445	19.3	4	4	24	2
1978—Kansas City NFL	16	1	—5	—5.0	0	26	433	16.7	2	2	12	0
1979—Kansas City NFL	16	2	34	17.0	1	21	332	15.8	1	2	12	0
1980—Kansas City NFL	16	3	22	7.3	0	47	799	17.0	6	6	36	0
1981—Kansas City NFL	12	3	69	23.0	0	38	620	16.3	4	4	24	2
1982—Kansas City NFL	9	3	25	8.3	0	40	549	13.7	3	3	18	0
1983—Kansas City NFL	13		None			50	788	15.8	6	6	36	0
1984—Kansas City NFL	16		None			62	912	14.7	4	4	24	2
1985—Kansas City NFL	11		None			25	446	17.8	0	0	0	1
Pro Totals—10 Years	137	24	257	10.7	2	360	5767	16.0	32	34	204	8

Additional pro statistics: Returned one kickoff for no yards, 1976; returned six punts for 51 yards, 1978; attempted one pass with one interception, 1981; attempted one pass with no completions, 1982.

LEONARD ALLEN MARSHALL
Defensive End—New York Giants
Born October 22, 1961, at Franklin, La.
Height, 6.03. Weight, 285.
High School—Franklin, La.
Attended Louisiana State University.
Brother of Chris Marshall, linebacker at Tulane University; and related
to Eddie Robinson, head coach at Grambling State University; Ernie Ladd,
defensive lineman with San Diego Chargers, Houston Oilers and Kansas City Chiefs,
1961 through 1968; and Warren Wells, wide receiver with Detroit Lions and Oakland
Raiders, 1964 and 1967 through 1970.

Selected by Tampa Bay in 10th round (109th player selected) of 1983 USFL draft.
Selected by New York Giants in 2nd round (37th player selected) of 1983 NFL draft.
Signed by New York Giants, June 13, 1983.
New York Giants NFL, 1983 through 1985.
Games: 1983 (14), 1984 (16), 1985 (16). Total—46.
Pro statistics: Credited with one safety, 1983; intercepted one pass for three yards, 1985.
Played in Pro Bowl (NFL All-Star Game) following 1985 season.

WILBER BUDDYHIA MARSHALL
Linebacker—Chicago Bears
Born April 18, 1962, at Titusville, Fla.
Height, 6.01. Weight, 225.
High School—Titusville, Fla., Astronaut.
Attended University of Florida.

Selected by Tampa Bay in 1984 USFL territorial draft.
Selected by Chicago in 1st round (11th player selected) of 1984 NFL draft.
Signed by Chicago Bears, June 19, 1984.
Chicago NFL, 1984 and 1985.
Games: 1984 (15), 1985 (16). Total—31.
Pro statistics: Intercepted four passes for 23 yards, ran two yards with lateral on kickoff return and recovered one fumble for eight yards, 1985.
Played in NFC Championship Game following 1984 and 1985 seasons.
Played in NFL Championship Game following 1985 season.

BRENT MARTIN
Center—Atlanta Falcons
Born June 5, 1963, at Madera, Calif.
Height, 6.03. Weight, 255.
High School—Madera, Calif.
Attended Stanford University.

Selected by Oakland in 1985 USFL territorial draft.
Selected by Atlanta in 10th round (257th player selected) of 1985 NFL draft.
Signed by Atlanta Falcons, July 19, 1985.
On injured reserve with back injury, August 20 through entire 1985 season.

CHARLES M. MARTIN
Defensive End—Green Bay Packers
Born August 31, 1959, at Canton, Ga.
Height, 6.04. Weight, 270.
High School—Canton, Ga., Cherokee.
Attended Livingston University.

Selected by Birmingham in 15th round (173rd player selected) of 1983 USFL draft.
Signed by Birmingham Stallions, January 22, 1983.
On developmental squad, March 26 through April 9, 1983; activated, April 10, 1983.
On developmental squad, June 17 through July 1, 1983; activated, July 2, 1983.
Released by Birmingham Stallions, February 13, 1984; signed as free agent by Green Bay Packers, July 7, 1984.
On developmental squad for 4 games with Birmingham Stallions in 1983.
Birmingham USFL, 1983; Green Bay NFL, 1984 and 1985.
Games: 1983 (14), 1984 (16), 1985 (16). Total NFL—32. Total Pro—46.
USFL statistics: Recovered one fumble, 1983.
NFL statistics: Recovered one fumble, 1985.

CHRISTOPHER MARTIN
(Chris)
Linebacker—Minnesota Vikings
Born December 19, 1960, at Huntsville, Ala.
Height, 6.02. Weight, 230.
High School—Huntsville, Ala., J. O. Johnson.
Attended Auburn University.

Selected by Birmingham in 1983 USFL territorial draft.
Signed as free agent by New Orleans Saints, May 5, 1983.
On injured reserve with ankle injury, December 17 through remainder of 1983 season.
Released by New Orleans Saints, August 27, 1984; awarded on waivers to Minnesota Vikings, August 28, 1984.
New Orleans NFL, 1983; Minnesota NFL, 1984 and 1985.
Games: 1983 (15), 1984 (16), 1985 (12). Total—43.
Pro statistics: Recovered one fumble for eight yards and a touchdown, 1984.

DERRICK ROY MARTIN
Defensive Back—San Francisco 49ers
Born May 31, 1957, at Los Angeles, Calif.
Height, 6.00. Weight, 185.
High School—Compton, Calif.
Attended Arizona State University and San Jose State University.

Signed as free agent by Toronto Argonauts, April, 1980.
On injured list, July 23 through July 29, 1980; activated, July 30, 1980.
Released by Toronto Argonauts, September 7, 1980; re-signed by Argonauts, October 12, 1980.
Released by Toronto Argonauts, June 28, 1981; signed as free agent by Dallas Cowboys, July 2, 1981.
Released by Dallas Cowboys, August 3, 1981; signed as free agent by San Diego Chargers, January 14, 1982.
Released by San Diego Chargers, August 6, 1982; signed by Oakland Invaders, November 9, 1982.
Protected in merger of Oakland Invaders and Michigan Panthers, December 6, 1984.
Granted free agency, August 1, 1985; signed by San Francisco 49ers for 1986, December 20, 1985.

		INTERCEPTIONS				-PUNT RETURNS-				—KICKOFF RET.—				—TOTAL—		
Year	Club	G.	No.	Yds.	Avg.	TD.	No.	Yds.	Avg.	TD.	No.	Yds.	Avg.	TD.	TD.	Pts.	F.
1980—Toronto CFL		11	2	12	6.0	0	4	17	4.3	0	0	112	18.7	0	0	0	0
1983—Oakland USFL		18	2	72	36.0	*1	None				None				1	6	0
1984—Oakland USFL		18	3	123	41.0	1	None				None				1	6	0
1985—Oakland USFL		18	6	41	6.8	0	None				None				0	0	0
CFL Totals—1 Year		11	2	12	6.0	0	4	17	4.3	0	6	112	18.7	0	0	0	0
USFL Totals—3 Years		54	11	236	21.5	2	0	0	0.0	0	0	0	0.0	0	2	12	0
Pro Totals—4 Years		65	13	248	19.1	2	4	17	4.3	0	6	112	18.7	0	2	12	0

Additional pro statistics: Recovered one fumble, 1983.
Played in USFL Championship Game following 1985 season.

DOUG MARTIN
Defensive End—Minnesota Vikings
Born May 22, 1957, at Fairfield, Calif.
Height, 6.03. Weight, 255.
High School—Fairfield, Calif., Armijo.
Attended University of Washington.
Brother of George Martin, defensive end with New York Giants.

Selected by Minnesota in 1st round (9th player selected) of 1980 NFL draft.
Placed on did not report list, August 15, 1980; activated, September 13, 1980.
Granted free agency, February 1, 1984.
Placed on did not report list, August 14 through August 17, 1984; re-signed by Vikings, August 18, 1984.
Granted roster exemption, August 21 through August 31, 1984; activated, September 1, 1984.
Minnesota NFL, 1980 through 1985.
Games: 1980 (11), 1981 (16), 1982 (9), 1983 (16), 1984 (13), 1985 (16). Total—81.
Pro statistics: Recovered one fumble, 1981; intercepted one pass for no yards, 1982; recovered two fumbles, 1983;
recovered two fumbles for 29 yards, 1985.

ED MARTIN
Linebacker—Indianapolis Colts
Born March 29, 1962, at Evanston, Ill.
Height, 6.04. Weight, 220.
High School—Evanston, Ind., Township.
Attended Indiana State University.

Selected by Pittsburgh in 6th round (120th player selected) of 1984 USFL draft.
Selected by Dallas in 7th round (193rd player selected) of 1984 NFL draft.
USFL rights traded by Pittsburgh Maulers to Los Angeles Express for draft choices, June 1, 1984.
Signed by Los Angeles Express, June 1, 1984.
Granted roster exemption, June 1 through June 14, 1984; activated, June 15, 1984.
On physically unable to perform/active, February 18 through February 27, 1985; activated, February 28, 1985.
On developmental squad, February 28 through March 21, 1985; activated, March 22, 1985.
Released by Los Angeles Express, April 22, 1985; signed as free agent by Dallas Cowboys, June 10, 1985.
Released by Dallas Cowboys, August 5, 1985; signed as free agent by Indianapolis Colts, March 24, 1986.
On developmental squad for 3 games with Los Angeles Express in 1985.
Los Angeles USFL, 1984 and 1985.
Games: 1984 (2), 1985 (5). Total—7.

ERIC MARTIN
Wide Receiver—New Orleans Saints
Born November 8, 1961, at Van Vleck, Tex.
Height, 6.01. Weight, 195.
High School—Van Vleck, Tex.
Attended Louisiana State University.

Named as wide receiver on THE SPORTING NEWS College All-America Team, 1983.
Selected by Portland in 1985 USFL territorial draft.
Selected by New Orleans in 7th round (179th player selected) of 1985 NFL draft.
Signed by New Orleans Saints, June 21, 1985.

		PASS RECEIVING				-PUNT RETURNS-				—KICKOFF RET.—				—TOTAL—		
Year	Club	G.	P.C.	Yds.	Avg.	TD.	No.	Yds.	Avg.	TD.	No.	Yds.	Avg.	TD.	TD.	Pts.	F.
1985—New Orleans NFL		16	35	522	14.9	4	8	53	6.6	0	15	384	25.6	0	4	24	1

Additional pro statistics: Rushed twice for minus one yard, 1985.

GEORGE DWIGHT MARTIN
Defensive End—New York Giants
Born February 16, 1953, at Greenville, S. C.
Height, 6.04. Weight, 255.
High School—Fairfield, Calif., Armijo.
Attended University of Oregon.
Brother of Doug Martin, defensive end with Minnesota Vikings.

Established NFL record for touchdowns by down lineman, career (5).
Selected by New York Giants in 11th round (262nd player selected) of 1975 NFL draft.
New York Giants NFL, 1975 through 1985.
Games: 1975 (14), 1976 (14), 1977 (10), 1978 (16), 1979 (16), 1980 (16), 1981 (16), 1982 (9), 1983 (14), 1984 (16), 1985 (16).
Total—157.
Pro statistics: Recovered two fumbles, 1976; intercepted one pass for 30 yards and one touchdown, 1977; recovered

one fumble, 1977, 1980, 1984 and 1985; ran 83 yards with blocked field goal for a touchdown, 1978; recovered three fumbles, 1979; caught one pass for four yards and a touchdown, 1980; recovered three fumbles for 28 yards and two touchdowns, 1981; intercepted one pass for 56 yards and a touchdown, 1985.

MICHAEL MARTIN
(Mike)
Wide Receiver—Cincinnati Bengals
Born November 18, 1960, at Washington, D.C.
Height, 5.10. Weight, 186.
High School—Washington, D.C., Eastern.
Attended University of Illinois.

Selected by Chicago in 1983 USFL territorial draft.
Selected by Cincinnati in 8th round (221st player selected) of 1983 NFL draft.
Signed by Cincinnati Bengals, May 19, 1983.
On injured reserve with broken fibula, November 17 through remainder of 1983 season.

Year Club	G.	PASS RECEIVING				-PUNT RETURNS-				—KICKOFF RET.—				—TOTAL—		
		P.C.	Yds.	Avg.	TD.	No.	Yds.	Avg.	TD.	No.	Yds.	Avg.	TD.	TD.	Pts.	F.
1983—Cincinnati NFL	10	2	22	11.0	0	23	227	9.9	0	1	19	19.0	0	0	0	2
1984—Cincinnati NFL	15	11	164	14.9	0	24	376	*15.7	0	19	386	20.3	0	0	0	4
1985—Cincinnati NFL	16	14	187	13.4	0	32	268	8.4	0	48	1104	23.0	0	0	0	4
Pro Totals—3 Years	41	27	373	13.8	0	79	871	11.0	0	68	1509	22.2	0	0	0	10

Additional pro statistics: Rushed twice for 21 yards, 1983; rushed once for three yards and recovered two fumbles, 1984.

ROBBIE L. MARTIN
Wide Receiver—Indianapolis Colts
Born December 3, 1958, at Los Angeles, Calif.
Height, 5.08. Weight, 177.
High School—Villa Park, Calif.
Attended California Poly State University at San Luis Obispo.

Traded by Detroit Lions to Indianapolis Colts for running back Alvin Moore, July 25, 1985.
Selected by Pittsburgh in 4th round (100th player selected) of 1981 NFL draft.
Released by Pittsburgh Steelers, August 24, 1981; claimed on waivers by Detroit Lions, August 26, 1981.
On injured reserve with knee injury, September 13 through October 28, 1983; activated, October 29, 1983.

Year Club	G.	PASS RECEIVING				-PUNT RETURNS-				—KICKOFF RET.—				—TOTAL—		
		P.C.	Yds.	Avg.	TD.	No.	Yds.	Avg.	TD.	No.	Yds.	Avg.	TD.	TD.	Pts.	F.
1981—Detroit NFL	16		None			52	450	8.7	1	25	509	20.4	0	1	6	3
1982—Detroit NFL	9	1	18	18.0	0	26	275	10.6	0	16	268	16.8	0	0	0	3
1983—Detroit NFL	10		None			15	183	12.2	*1	8	140	17.5	0	1	6	3
1984—Detroit NFL	14	1	9	9.0	0	25	210	8.4	0	10	144	14.4	0	0	0	5
1985—Indianapolis NFL	16	10	128	12.8	0	40	443	11.1	1	32	638	19.9	0	1	6	5
Pro Totals—5 Years	65	12	155	12.9	0	158	1561	9.9	3	91	1699	18.7	0	3	18	19

Additional pro statistics: Recovered two fumbles, 1981; recovered one fumble, 1982 and 1983; rushed once for 14 yards and recovered four fumbles, 1984; rushed once for 23 yards, 1985.

ROD MARTIN
Linebacker—Los Angeles Raiders
Born April 7, 1954, at Welch, W. Va.
Height, 6.02. Weight, 225.
High School—Los Angeles, Calif., Hamilton.
Attended Los Angeles City College and University of Southern California.
Brother of Ricky Martin, wide receiver with Winnipeg Blue Bombers
and Pittsburgh Maulers, 1982 through 1984.

Named to THE SPORTING NEWS NFL All-Star Team, 1983.
Selected by Oakland in 12th round (317th player selected) of 1977 NFL draft.
Traded with defensive back Steve Jackson by Oakland Raiders to San Francisco 49ers for future considerations, August 30, 1977.
Released by San Francisco 49ers, September 14, 1977; signed as free agent by Oakland Raiders, November 7, 1977.
Franchise transferred to Los Angeles, May 7, 1982.

Year Club	—INTERCEPTIONS—					Year Club	—INTERCEPTIONS—				
	G.	No.	Yds.	Avg.	TD.		G.	No.	Yds.	Avg.	TD.
1977—Oakland NFL	1		None			1982—L.A. Raiders NFL	9	3	60	20.0	*1
1978—Oakland NFL	15		None			1983—L.A. Raiders NFL	16	4	81	20.3	*2
1979—Oakland NFL	16		None			1984—L.A. Raiders NFL	16	2	31	15.5	1
1980—Oakland NFL	16	2	15	7.5	0	1985—L.A. Raiders NFL	16	1	16	16.0	0
1981—Oakland NFL	16	1	7	7.0	0	Pro Totals—9 Years	121	13	210	16.2	4

Additional pro statistics: Recovered one fumble, 1979; recovered two fumbles for 42 yards and a touchdown, 1980; recovered three fumbles, 1981; returned one kickoff for no yards, 1983; recovered one fumble for 77 yards and a touchdown and credited with one safety, 1984; recovered three fumbles for three yards and fumbled once, 1985.
Played in AFC Championship Game following 1977, 1980 and 1983 seasons.
Played in NFL Championship Game following 1980 and 1983 seasons.
Played in Pro Bowl (NFL All-Star Team) following 1983 and 1984 seasons.

EUGENE RAYMOND MARVE
Linebacker—Buffalo Bills
Born August 14, 1960, at Flint, Mich.
Height, 6.02. Weight, 240.
High School—Flint, Mich., Northern.
Attended Saginaw Valley State College.

Selected by Buffalo in 3rd round (59th player selected) of 1982 NFL draft.
Buffalo NFL, 1982 through 1985.
Games: 1982 (9), 1983 (16), 1984 (16), 1985 (14). Total—55.
Pro statistics: Intercepted one pass for no yards, 1982; recovered one fumble, 1982 and 1985; recovered three fumbles, 1984.

MICKEY MARVIN
Guard—Los Angeles Raiders
Born October 5, 1955, at Hendersonville, N.C.
Height, 6.04. Weight, 265.
High School—Hendersonville, N.C., Brevard.
Attended University of Tennessee.

Selected by Oakland in 4th round (112th player selected) of 1977 NFL draft.
On injured reserve with knee injury, September 12 through December 6, 1979; activated, December 7, 1979.
Franchise transferred to Los Angeles, May 7, 1982.
Oakland NFL, 1977 through 1981; Los Angeles Raiders NFL, 1982 through 1985.
Games: 1977 (8), 1978 (14), 1979 (2), 1980 (16), 1981 (16), 1982 (9), 1983 (14), 1984 (9), 1985 (15). Total—103.
Pro statistics: Recovered one fumble, 1978, 1980, 1981 and 1984.
Played in AFC Championship Game following 1977, 1980 and 1983 seasons.
Played in NFL Championship Game following 1980 and 1983 seasons.

RICHARD RAY MASSIE
(Rick)
Wide Receiver—Denver Broncos
Born January 16, 1960, at Paris, Ky.
Height, 6.00. Weight, 185.
High School—Paris, Ky., Bourbon County.
Received bachelor of arts degree in education from University of Kentucky in 1983.

Signed as free agent by Calgary Stampeders, March 27, 1984.
Selected by Denver in 2nd round (46th player selected) of 1984 NFL supplemental draft.
Released by Calgary Stampeders, August 18, 1984; re-signed by Stampeders, September 16, 1984.
On injured reserve, October 14 through remainder of 1984 season.
Released by Calgary Stampeders, June 20, 1985; signed by Denver Broncos, February 6, 1986.

		——PASS RECEIVING——			
Year	Club	G.	P.C.	Yds.	Avg. TD.
1984—Calgary CFL		9	15	233	15.5 0

BRUCE MARTIN MATHISON
Quarterback—Buffalo Bills
Born April 25, 1959, at Superior, Wis.
Height, 6.03. Weight, 203.
High School—Superior, Wis.
Attended University of Nebraska.

Selected by Boston in 1983 USFL territorial draft.
Selected by San Diego in 10th round (272nd player selected) of 1983 NFL draft.
Signed by San Diego Chargers, May 26, 1983.
Released by San Diego Chargers, September 2, 1985; signed as free agent by Buffalo Bills, September 10, 1985.

			——————PASSING——————								——RUSHING——				—TOTAL—		
Year	Club	G.	Att.	Cmp.	Pct.	Gain	T.P.	P.I.	Avg.	Att.	Yds.	Avg.	TD.	TD.	Pts.	F.
1983—San Diego NFL		1	5	3	60.0	41	0	1	8.20	1	0	0.0	0	0	0	1
1984—San Diego NFL		2			None							None		0	0	0
1985—Buffalo NFL		10	228	113	49.6	1635	4	14	7.17	27	231	8.6	1	1	6	8
Pro Totals—3 Years		13	233	116	49.8	1676	4	15	7.19	28	231	8.3	1	1	6	9

Quarterback Rating Points: 1985 (53.5).
Additional pro statistics: Recovered two fumbles and fumbled eight times for minus nine yards, 1985.

TREVOR ANTHONY MATICH
Center—New England Patriots
Born October 9, 1961, at Sacramento, Calif.
Height, 6.04. Weight, 270.
High School—Sacramento, Calif., Rio Americano.
Attended Brigham Young University.

Selected by Houston in 10th round (139th player selected) of 1985 USFL draft.
Selected by New England in 1st round (28th player selected) of 1985 NFL draft.
Signed by New England Patriots, July 30, 1985.
On injured reserve with ankle injury, October 12 through remainder of 1985 season.
New England NFL, 1985.
Games: 1985 (1).

RONALD ANTHONY MATTES
(Ron)
Offensive Tackle—Seattle Seahawks
Born August 8, 1963, at Shenandoah, Pa.
Height, 6.06. Weight, 289.
High School—Ashland, Pa., North Schuylkill.
Attended University of Virginia.

Selected by Orlando in 1985 USFL territorial draft.
Selected by Seattle in 7th round (193rd player selected) of 1985 NFL draft.
Signed by Seattle Seahawks, July 19, 1985.
On injured reserve with back injury, August 27 through entire 1985 season.

ALLAMA MATTHEWS
Tight End—Atlanta Falcons
Born August 24, 1961, at Jacksonville, Fla.
Height, 6.02. Weight, 230.
High School—Jacksonville, Fla., Andrew Jackson.
Attended Vanderbilt University.

Selected by Philadelphia in 12th round (137th player selected) of 1983 USFL draft.
Selected by Atlanta in 12th round (322nd player selected) of 1983 NFL draft.
Signed by Atlanta Falcons, May 16, 1983.
On injured reserve with neck injury, October 9 through remainder of 1984 season.
Released by Atlanta Falcons, October 19, 1985; re-signed by Falcons, October 24, 1985.

| | | —PASS RECEIVING— | | | |
Year Club	G.	P.C.	Yds.	Avg.	TD.
1983—Atlanta NFL	15	3	37	12.3	0
1984—Atlanta NFL	6	1	7	7.0	0
1985—Atlanta NFL	15	7	57	8.1	1
Pro Totals—3 Years	36	11	101	9.2	1

Additional pro statistics: Recovered one fumble, 1983; returned one kickoff for three yards, 1984; returned one kickoff for 11 yards, 1985.

BRUCE MATTHEWS
Offensive Tackle—Houston Oilers
Born August 8, 1961, at Arcadia, Calif.
Height, 6.04. Weight, 280.
High School—Arcadia, Calif.
Received degree in industrial engineering from University of Southern California in 1983.
Son of Clay Matthews Sr., end with San Francisco 49ers, 1950 and 1953 through 1955;
brother of Clay Matthews Jr., linebacker with Cleveland Browns.

Named as guard on THE SPORTING NEWS College All-America Team, 1982.
Selected by Los Angeles in 1983 USFL territorial draft.
Selected by Houston in 1st round (9th player selected) of 1983 NFL draft.
Signed by Houston Oilers, July 24, 1983.
Houston NFL, 1983 through 1985.
Games: 1983 (16); 1984 (16), 1985 (16). Total—48.
Pro statistics: Recovered three fumbles, 1985.

WILLIAM CLAY MATTHEWS JR.
(Known by middle name.)
Linebacker—Cleveland Browns
Born March 15, 1956, at Palo Alto, Calif.
Height, 6.02. Weight, 235.
High Schools—Arcadia, Calif. and Winnetka, Ill., New Trier East.
Received bachelor of science degree in business administration from
University of Southern California in 1978; attending Southern Cal for master's in business administration.
Son of Clay Matthews Sr., end with San Francisco 49ers, 1950 and 1953 through 1955;
brother of Bruce Matthews, offensive tackle with Houston Oilers.

Named to THE SPORTING NEWS NFL All-Star Team, 1984.
Named as linebacker on THE SPORTING NEWS College All-America Team, 1977.
Selected by Cleveland in 1st round (12th player selected) of 1978 NFL draft.
On injured reserve with broken ankle, September 16 through December 30, 1982; activated, December 31, 1982.

| | | —INTERCEPTIONS— | | | |
Year Club	G.	No.	Yds.	Avg.	TD.
1978—Cleveland NFL	15	1	5	5.0	0
1979—Cleveland NFL	16	1	30	30.0	0
1980—Cleveland NFL	14	1	6	6.0	0
1981—Cleveland NFL	16	2	14	7.0	0
1982—Cleveland NFL	2		None		
1983—Cleveland NFL	16		None		
1984—Cleveland NFL	16		None		
1985—Cleveland NFL	14		None		
Pro Totals—8 Years	109	5	55	11.0	0

Additional pro statistics: Recovered two fumbles, 1979; recovered one fumble, 1980 and 1984; recovered two fumbles for 16 yards, 1981; recovered one fumble for 15 yards, 1985.
Played in Pro Bowl (NFL All-Star Game) following 1985 season.

BRETT DERRELL MAXIE
Defensive Back—New Orleans Saints
Born January 13, 1962, at Dallas, Tex.
Height, 6.02. Weight, 190.
High School—Dallas, Tex., James Madison.
Attended Texas Southern University.

Signed as free agent by New Orleans Saints, June 21, 1985.
Released by New Orleans Saints, September 2, 1985; re-signed by Saints, September 3, 1985.
New Orleans NFL, 1985.
Games: 1985 (16).
Pro statistics: Recovered one fumble, 1985.

VERNON LEROY MAXWELL
Linebacker—Detroit Lions
Born October 25, 1961, at Birmingham, Ala.
Height, 6.02. Weight, 238.
High School—Los Angeles, Calif., Verbum Dei.
Attended Arizona State University.

Named as linebacker on THE SPORTING NEWS College All-America Team, 1982.
Selected by Arizona in 1983 USFL territorial draft.
Selected by Baltimore in 2nd round (29th player selected) of 1983 USFL draft.
Signed by Baltimore Colts, July 21, 1983.
Franchise transferred to Indianapolis, March 31, 1984.
Traded by Indianapolis Colts to San Diego Chargers for 5th round pick in 1986 draft, August 1, 1985.
Released by San Diego Chargers, August 27, 1985; signed as free agent by Detroit Lions, October 25, 1985.
Baltimore NFL, 1983; Indianapolis NFL, 1984; Detroit NFL, 1985.
Games: 1983 (16), 1984 (16), 1985 (9). Total—41.
Pro statistics: Intercepted one pass for 31 yards, 1983; recovered two fumbles, 1983 and 1984.

MARK MAY
Offensive Tackle—Washington Redskins
Born November 2, 1959, at Oneonta, N.Y.
Height, 6.06. Weight, 295.
High School—Oneonta, N.Y.
Attended University of Pittsburgh.

Outland Trophy winner, 1980.
Named as offensive tackle on THE SPORTING NEWS College All-America Team, 1980.
Selected by Washington in 1st round (20th player selected) of 1981 NFL draft.
Washington NFL, 1981 through 1985.
Games: 1981 (16), 1982 (9), 1983 (15), 1984 (16), 1985 (16). Total—72.
Pro statistics: Recovered one fumble, 1983 and 1985.
Played in NFC Championship Game following 1982 and 1983 seasons.
Played in NFL Championship Game following 1982 and 1983 seasons.

STAFFORD EARL MAYS
Defensive End—St. Louis Cardinals
Born March 13, 1958, at Lawrence, Kan.
Height, 6.02. Weight, 255.
High School—Tacoma, Wash., Lincoln.
Attended Mt. Hood Junior College and received degree in sociology
from University of Washington in 1981.

Selected by St. Louis in 9th round (225th player selected) of 1980 NFL draft.
St. Louis NFL, 1980 through 1985.
Games: 1980 (16), 1981 (16), 1982 (8), 1983 (16), 1984 (16), 1985 (16). Total—88.
Pro statistics: Recovered one fumble, 1981 and 1982; recovered two fumbles, 1983.

HOWARD JEROME McADOO
Linebacker—Los Angeles Rams
Born January 14, 1962, at Harbor City, Calif.
Height, 6.02. Weight, 230.
High School—Rolling Hills, Calif.
Attended Michigan State University.

Selected by Cleveland in 11th round (305th player selected) of 1983 NFL draft.
Signed by Cleveland Browns, May 11, 1983.
Released by Cleveland Browns, August 29, 1983; signed by Pittsburgh Maulers, November 12, 1983.
On developmental squad, February 24 through April 4, 1984; activated, April 5, 1984.
Franchise disbanded, October 25, 1984.
Selected by Portland Breakers in USFL dispersal draft, December 6, 1984.
On developmental squad, April 20 through May 8, 1985; activated, May 9, 1985.
Released by Portland Breakers, July 31, 1985; signed as free agent by Los Angeles Rams, March 22, 1986.
On developmental squad for 6 games with Pittsburgh Maulers in 1984.
On developmental squad for 3 games with Los Angeles Express in 1985.
Pittsburgh USFL, 1984; Portland USFL, 1985.
Games: 1984 (12), 1985 (16). Total—28.
Pro statistics: Credited with ½ sack for 4½ yards and recovered two fumbles, 1985.

KEN H. McALISTER
Linebacker—Kansas City Chiefs
Born April 15, 1960, at Oakland, Calif.
Height, 6.05. Weight, 220.
High School—Oakland, Calif.
Attended University of San Francisco (did not play college football).

Signed as free agent by Seattle Seahawks, April 30, 1982.

Released by Seattle Seahawks, September 14, 1983; signed as free agent by San Francisco 49ers, November 23, 1983.

Released by San Francisco 49ers, December 30, 1983; signed as free agent by Kansas City Chiefs, February 1, 1984.

On injured reserve with knee injury, August 19 through entire 1985 season.

Seattle NFL, 1982; Seattle (2)-San Francisco (4) NFL, 1983; Kansas City NFL, 1984.

Games: 1982 (9), 1983 (6), 1984 (15). Total—30.

Pro statistics: Returned two kickoffs for 41 yards and recovered one fumble, 1982; returned three kickoffs for 59 yards, 1983; intercepted two passes for 33 yards and recovered one fumble, 1984.

REESE McCALL II
Tight End
Born June 16, 1956, at Bessemer, Ala.
Height, 6.06. Weight, 245.
High School—Bessemer, Ala., Jess Lanier.
Received bachelor of science degree in physical education from
Auburn University in 1978.

Selected by Baltimore in 1st round (25th player selected) of 1978 NFL draft.

On inactive list, September 12 and September 19, 1982.

On reserve/did not report, August 14 through August 17, 1983.

Traded by Baltimore Colts to Tampa Bay Buccaneers for future draft pick, August 18, 1983.

Released by Tampa Bay Buccaneers, August 29, 1983; awarded on waivers to Detroit Lions, August 30, 1983.

Granted free agency, February 1, 1986; withdrew qualifying offer, May 14, 1986.

Year Club		G.	P.C.	Yds.	Avg.	TD.
			—PASS RECEIVING—			
1978—Baltimore NFL		16	11	160	14.5	1
1979—Baltimore NFL		14	37	536	14.5	4
1980—Baltimore NFL		16	18	322	17.9	5
1981—Baltimore NFL		16	21	314	15.0	2
1982—Baltimore NFL		7	2	6	3.0	0
1983—Detroit NFL		16	1	6	6.0	0
1984—Detroit NFL		16	3	15	5.0	0
1985—Detroit NFL		16	1	7	7.0	0
Pro Totals—8 Years		117	94	1366	14.5	12

Additional pro statistics: Returned one punt for 37 yards and ran five yards with blocked punt for a touchdown, 1978; recovered one fumble, 1978 and 1980; fumbled once, 1978 through 1980; recovered two fumbles, 1979.

MICHAEL ANTHONY McCLEARN
(Mike)
Offensive Tackle—Washington Redskins
Born January 7, 1961, at Newburgh, N.Y.
Height, 6.04. Weight, 274.
High School—Montgomery, N.Y., Valley Central.
Attended Temple University.

Selected by Philadelphia in 1983 USFL territorial draft.

Selected by Cleveland in 8th round (209th player selected) of 1983 NFL draft.

Signed by Cleveland Browns, May 11, 1983.

Released by Cleveland Browns, August 16, 1983; signed by Philadelphia Stars, September 19, 1983.

On developmental squad, February 24 through March 9, 1984; activated, March 10, 1984.

On developmental squad, April 28 through May 11, 1984; activated, May 12, 1984.

On developmental squad, May 18 through June 1, 1984; activated, June 2, 1984.

On developmental squad, June 21 through remainder of 1984 season.

Franchise transferred to Baltimore, November 1, 1984.

Released injured by Baltimore Stars, February 18, 1985; signed as free agent by Washington Redskins, March 6, 1985.

On injured reserve with dislocated fingers, August 30 through entire 1985 season.

On developmental squad for 7 games with Philadelphia Stars in 1984.

Philadelphia USFL, 1984.

Games: 1984 (9).

Played in USFL Championship Game following 1984 season.

MIKE McCLOSKEY
Tight End—Houston Oilers
Born February 2, 1961, at Philadelphia, Pa.
Height, 6.05. Weight, 246.
High School—Philadelphia, Pa., Father Judge.
Attended Penn State University.

Selected by Philadelphia in 1983 USFL territorial draft.

Selected by Houston in 4th round (88th player selected) of 1983 NFL draft.

Signed by Houston Oilers, June 22, 1983.

Year	Club	G.	P.C.	Yds.	Avg.	TD.
1983—Houston NFL		16	16	137	8.6	1
1984—Houston NFL		15	9	152	16.9	1
1985—Houston NFL		16	4	29	7.3	1
Pro Totals—3 Years		47	29	318	11.0	3

Additional pro statistics: Returned one kickoff for 11 yards, 1983; recovered one fumble, 1985.

MILT McCOLL
Linebacker—San Francisco 49ers
Born August 28, 1959, at Oak Park, Ill.
Height, 6.06. Weight, 230.
High School—Covina, Calif., South Hills.
Received degree in human biology from Stanford University and studied
at Stanford's overseas campus at Cliveden, England, 1980;
and currently attending medical school at Stanford University.
Son of Bill McColl, end with Chicago Bears, 1952 through 1959.

Signed as free agent by San Francisco 49ers, July 1, 1981.
On injured reserve with pulled hamstring, October 22 through November 17, 1983; activated, November 18, 1983.
San Francisco NFL, 1981 through 1985.
Games: 1981 (16), 1982 (9), 1983 (12), 1984 (16), 1985 (16). Total—69.
Pro statistics: Intercepted one pass for 22 yards, 1981; recovered one fumble for 28 yards and a touchdown, 1985.
Played in NFC Championship Game following 1981 and 1984 seasons.
Member of San Francisco 49ers for NFC Championship Game following 1983 season; did not play.
Played in NFL Championship Game following 1981 and 1984 seasons.

PHILIP JOSEPH McCONKEY
(Phil)
Wide Receiver—New York Giants
Born February 24, 1957, at Buffalo, N.Y.
Height, 5.10. Weight, 170.
High School—Buffalo, N.Y., Caniaius.
Attended U.S. Naval Academy.

Signed as free agent by New York Giants, May 6, 1983.
On military reserve, August 29 through entire 1983 season.
On injured reserve with broken ribs, November 26 through remainder of 1984 season.

Year	Club		PASS RECEIVING				-PUNT RETURNS-				—KICKOFF RET.—				—TOTAL—		
		G.	P.C.	Yds.	Avg.	TD.	No.	Yds.	Avg.	TD.	No.	Yds.	Avg.	TD.	TD.	Pts.	F.
1984—N.Y. Giants NFL		13	8	154	19.3	0	46	306	6.7	0	28	541	19.3	0	1	6	2
1985—N.Y. Giants NFL		16	25	404	16.2	1	53	442	8.3	0	12	234	19.5	0	1	6	1
Pro Totals—2 Years		29	33	558	16.9	1	99	748	7.6	0	40	775	19.4	0	2	12	3

Additional pro statistics: Recovered kickoff in end zone for a touchdown and recovered one fumble, 1984; recovered two fumbles, 1985.

JAMES McDONALD
Tight End—Los Angeles Rams
Born March 29, 1961, at Long Beach, Calif.
Height, 6.05. Weight, 240.
High School—Long Beach, Calif., Polytechnic.
Attended University of Southern California.

Signed as free agent by Los Angeles Rams, May 20, 1983.
Released by Los Angeles Rams, September 2, 1985; awarded on waivers to Detroit Lions, September 3, 1985.
Traded by Detroit Lions to Los Angeles Rams for conditional 12th round pick in 1987 draft, October 15, 1985.
On injured reserve with knee injury, December 21 through remainder of 1985 season.

Year	Club	G.	P.C.	Yds.	Avg.	TD.
1983—L.A. Rams NFL		16	1	1	1.0	1
1984—L.A. Rams NFL		16	4	55	13.8	0
1985—Det.(6)-Rams(9) NFL		15	5	81	16.2	0
Pro Totals—3 Years		47	10	137	13.7	1

PAUL McDONALD
Quarterback—Cleveland Browns
Born February 23, 1958, at Montebello, Calif.
Height, 6.02. Weight, 185.
High School—La Puente, Calif., Bishop Amat.
Received business degree from University of Southern California and
attending Case Western Reserve for master's degree in business.

Selected by Cleveland in 4th round (109th player selected) of 1980 NFL draft.

Year	Club		PASSING							RUSHING				—TOTAL—		
		G.	Att.	Cmp.	Pct.	Gain	T.P.	P.I.	Avg.	Att.	Yds.	Avg.	TD.	TD.	Pts.	F.
1980—Cleveland NFL		15				None				3	2	0.7	0	0	0	2
1981—Cleveland NFL		12	57	35	61.4	463	4	2	8.12	2	0	0.0	0	0	0	4
1982—Cleveland NFL		9	149	73	49.0	993	5	8	6.66	7	−13	−1.9	0	0	0	3

Year Club		PASSING							RUSHING				TOTAL		
	G.	Att.	Cmp.	Pct.	Gain	T.P.	P.I.	Avg.	Att.	Yds.	Avg.	TD.	TD.	Pts.	F.
1983—Cleveland NFL	16	68	32	47.1	341	1	4	5.01	3	17	5.7	0	0	0	1
1984—Cleveland NFL	16	493	271	55.0	3472	14	23	7.04	22	4	0.2	1	1	6	16
1985—Cleveland NFL	16				None						None		0	0	0
Pro Totals—6 Years	84	767	411	53.6	5269	24	37	6.87	37	10	0.3	1	1	6	26

Quarterback Rating Points: 1981 (95.8), 1982 (59.5), 1983 (42.6), 1984 (67.3). Total—65.7.

Additional pro statistics: Fumbled twice for minus nine yards, 1980; recovered one fumble, 1983; caught one pass for minus four yards, recovered five fumbles and fumbled 16 times for minus five yards, 1984.

REGINALD LEE McELROY
(Reggie)
Offensive Tackle—New York Jets
Born March 4, 1960, at Beaumont, Tex.
Height, 6.06. Weight, 270.
High School—Beaumont, Tex., Charlton Pollard.
Received degree in physical education from West Texas State University.

Selected by New York Jets in 2nd round (51st player selected) of 1982 NFL draft.
On injured reserve with knee injury, August 24 through entire 1982 season.
Granted free agency, February 1, 1985; re-signed by Jets, September 10, 1985.
Granted roster exemption, September 10 through September 13, 1985; activated, September 14, 1985.
New York Jets NFL, 1983 through 1985.
Games: 1983 (16), 1984 (16), 1985 (13). Total—45.
Pro statistics: Returned one kickoff for seven yards, 1983.

VANN WILLIAM McELROY
Safety—Los Angeles Raiders
Born January 13, 1960, at Birmingham, Ala.
Height, 6.02. Weight, 195.
High School—Uvalde, Tex.
Received bachelor of business administration degree in marketing management
from Baylor University in 1983.

Selected by Los Angeles Raiders in 3rd round (64th player selected) of 1982 NFL draft.
On inactive list, September 12 and September 19, 1982.

Year Club		INTERCEPTIONS			
	G.	No.	Yds.	Avg.	TD.
1982—L.A. Raiders NFL	7		None		
1983—L.A. Raiders NFL	16	8	68	8.5	0
1984—L.A. Raiders NFL	16	4	42	10.5	0
1985—L.A. Raiders NFL	12	2	23	11.5	0
Pro Totals—4 Years	51	14	133	9.5	0

Additional pro statistics: Intercepted one pass for no yards, 1982; recovered three fumbles for five yards, 1983; recovered four fumbles for 12 yards, 1984; recovered one fumble, 1985.
Played in AFC Championship Game following 1983 season.
Played in NFL Championship Game following 1983 season.
Played in Pro Bowl (NFL All-Star Game) following 1983 and 1984 seasons.

PAUL McFADDEN
Placekicker—Philadelphia Eagles
Born September 24, 1961, at Cleveland, O.
Height, 5.11. Weight, 163.
High School—Euclid, O.
Received bachelor of science degree in general administration
from Youngstown State University in 1984.

Selected by Chicago in 9th round (174th player selected) of 1984 USFL draft.
Selected by Philadelphia in 12th round (312th player selected) of 1984 NFL draft.
Signed by Philadelphia Eagles, July 15, 1984.

Year Club		PLACE KICKING				
	G.	XP.	XPM.	FG.	FGA.	Pts.
1984—Philadelphia NFL	16	26	1	★30	★37	116
1985—Philadelphia NFL	16	29	0	25	30	104
Pro Totals—2 Years	32	55	1	55	67	220

BUFORD LAMAR McGEE
Running Back—San Diego Chargers
Born August 16, 1960, at Durant, Miss.
Height, 6.00. Weight, 206.
High School—Durant, Miss.
Received bachelor of science degree in business from University of Mississippi in 1984.

Selected by Birmingham in 1984 USFL territorial draft.
Selected by San Diego in 11th round (286th player selected) of 1984 NFL draft.
Signed by San Diego Chargers, June 2, 1984.
On injured reserve with hamstring injury, September 3 through October 4, 1985; activated, October 5, 1985.

Year Club	G.		RUSHING			PASS RECEIVING				TOTAL		
		Att.	Yds.	Avg.	TD.	P.C.	Yds.	Avg.	TD.	TD.	Pts.	F.
1984—San Diego NFL	16	67	226	3.4	4	9	76	8.4	2	6	36	1
1985—San Diego NFL	11	42	181	4.3	3	3	15	5.0	0	3	18	4
Pro Totals—2 Years	27	109	407	3.7	7	12	91	7.6	2	9	54	5

	KICKOFF RETURNS				
Year Club	G.	No.	Yds.	Avg.	TD.
1984—San Diego NFL	16	14	315	22.5	0
1985—San Diego NFL	11	7	135	19.3	0
Pro Totals—2 Years	27	21	450	21.4	0

Additional pro statistics: Recovered one fumble, 1984; recovered two fumbles, 1985.

MARK ALLEN McGRATH
Wide Receiver—Washington Redskins
Born December 17, 1957, at San Diego, Calif.
Height, 5.11. Weight, 175.
High School—Seattle, Wash., Shorecrest.
Received degree in criminal justice from Montana State University.

Signed as free agent by Seattle Seahawks, May 5, 1980.
On injured reserve with knee injury, August 19 through entire 1980 season.
On injured reserve with broken hand, October 13 through remainder of 1981 season.
Released by Seattle Seahawks, September 6, 1982; signed as free agent by Washington Redskins, April 5, 1983.
On injured reserve with separated shoulder, September 8 through December 15, 1983; activated, December 16, 1983.
Released by Washington Redskins, August 22, 1984; re-signed by Redskins, September 19, 1984.
On injured reserve with thigh injury, August 20 through November 20, 1985; activated after clearing procedural waivers, November 22, 1985.

		PASS RECEIVING			
Year Club	G.	P.C.	Yds.	Avg.	TD.
1981—Seattle NFL	6	4	47	11.8	0
1983—Washington NFL	2	1	6	6.0	0
1984—Washington NFL	13	10	118	11.8	1
1985—Washington NFL	5		None		
Pro Totals—4 Years	26	15	171	11.4	1

Member of Washington Redskins for NFC and NFL Championship Games following 1983 season; did not play.

KELI SCOTT McGREGOR
Tight End—Indianapolis Colts
Born January 23, 1963, at Primghar, Ia.
Height, 6.06. Weight, 250.
High School—Lakewood, Colo.
Received bachelor of arts degree in microbiology
from Colorado State University in 1985.

Selected by Los Angeles in 13th round (182nd player selected) of 1985 USFL draft.
Selected by Denver in 4th round (110th player selected) of 1985 NFL draft.
Signed by Denver Broncos, July 3, 1985.
Released by Denver Broncos, September 16, 1985; signed as free agent by Indianapolis Colts, November 6, 1985.
On injured reserve with finger injury, December 17 through remainder of 1985 season.
Denver (2)-Indianapolis (6) NFL, 1985.
Games: 1985 (8).

LAWRENCE McGREW
(Larry)
Linebacker—New England Patriots
Born July 23, 1957, at Berkeley, Calif.
Height, 6.05. Weight, 233.
High School—Berkeley, Calif.
Attended Contra Costa Junior College and received degree in speech communications from
University of Southern California in 1980.

Selected by New England in 2nd round (45th player selected) of 1980 NFL draft.
On injured reserve with knee and elbow injuries, December 19 through remainder of 1980 season.
On injured reserve with knee injury, August 31 through entire 1981 season.
New England NFL, 1980 and 1982 through 1985.
Games: 1980 (11), 1982 (8), 1983 (16), 1984 (16), 1985 (13). Total—64.
Pro statistics: Intercepted one pass for three yards and recovered one fumble, 1983; intercepted one pass for no yards and recovered two fumbles, 1985.
Played in AFC Championship Game following 1985 season.
Played in NFL Championship Game following 1985 season.

—DID YOU KNOW—

That the Cleveland Browns have never beaten the Steelers at Pittsburgh's Three Rivers Stadium since the facility opened in 1970? A 10-9 loss on November 3 last season dropped the Browns' record there to 0-16.

CURTIS McGRIFF
Defensive End—New York Giants
Born May 17, 1958, at Donaldsonville, Ga.
Height, 6.05. Weight, 276.
High School—Cottonwood, Ala.
Attended University of Alabama.

Signed as free agent by New York Giants, June 9, 1980.
On injured reserve with knee injury, December 1 through remainder of 1980 season.
On injured reserve with knee injury, December 8 through remainder of 1981 season.
On injured reserve with knee injury, October 26 through remainder of 1983 season.
New York Giants NFL, 1980 through 1985.
Games: 1980 (13), 1981 (14), 1982 (9), 1983 (8), 1984 (16), 1985 (16). Total—76.
Pro statistics: Recovered one fumble for three yards, 1985.

PAT McINALLY
Punter—Cincinnati Bengals
Born May 7, 1953, at Villa Park, Calif.
Height, 6.06. Weight, 212.
High School—Villa Park, Calif.
Received degree from Harvard University.

Named to THE SPORTING NEWS NFL All-Star Team, 1981.
Selected by Cincinnati in 5th round (120th player selected) of 1975 NFL draft.
Missed entire 1975 season due to leg injury.

| | | —PASS RECEIVING— | | | | | | —PUNTING— | | | |
Year	Club	G.	P.C.	Yds.	Avg.TD.		Year	Club	G.	No.	Avg.	Blk.
1976—Cincinnati NFL		14		None			1976—Cincinnati NFL		14	76	39.5	0
1977—Cincinnati NFL		14	17	258	15.2	3	1977—Cincinnati NFL		14	67	41.8	1
1978—Cincinnati NFL		16	15	189	12.6	0	1978—Cincinnati NFL		16	91	*43.1	0
1979—Cincinnati NFL		16	1	24	24.0	0	1979—Cincinnati NFL		16	89	41.3	2
1980—Cincinnati NFL		16	18	269	14.9	2	1980—Cincinnati NFL		16	83	40.8	*2
1981—Cincinnati NFL		16	6	68	11.3	0	1981—Cincinnati NFL		16	72	*45.4	1
1982—Cincinnati NFL		9		None			1982—Cincinnati NFL		9	31	38.7	0
1983—Cincinnati NFL		16		None			1983—Cincinnati NFL		16	67	41.9	*2
1984—Cincinnati NFL		16		None			1984—Cincinnati NFL		16	67	42.3	0
1985—Cincinnati NFL		16		None			1985—Cincinnati NFL		16	57	42.3	1
Pro Totals—10 Years		149	57	808	14.2	5	Pro Totals—10 Years		149	700	41.8	9

Additional pro statistics: Recovered two fumbles, fumbled once, rushed once for four yards and attempted one pass with one completion for four yards, 1977; rushed once for 18 yards, 1979; rushed once for no yards, recovered one fumble and fumbled twice, 1980; rushed once for minus 27 yards, 1981; attempted two passes with two completions for 77 yards, 1984; attempted one pass with no completions and rushed once for minus two yards, 1985.
Played in AFC Championship Game following 1981 season.
Played in NFL Championship Game following 1981 season.
Played in Pro Bowl (NFL All-Star Game) following 1981 season.

MICHAEL D. McINNIS
Defensive End—Atlanta Falcons
Born March 22, 1962, at Jackson, Miss.
Height, 6.05. Weight, 270.
High School—Jackson, Miss., Lanier.
Attended University of Arkansas at Pine Bluff.

Selected by Philadelphia in 6th round (118th player selected) of 1984 USFL draft.
On developmental squad, February 24 through May 17, 1984; activated, May 18, 1984.
Selected by Atlanta in 2nd round (37th player selected) of 1984 NFL supplemental draft.
On injured reserve, June 23 through remainder of 1984 season.
Franchise transferred to Baltimore, November 1, 1984.
On developmental squad, February 21 through April 5, 1985; activated, April 6, 1985.
On developmental squad, April 7, 1985.
Traded by Baltimore Stars to Portland Breakers for draft choice, April 9, 1985.
On developmental squad, April 9 through April 17, 1985; activated April 18, 1985.
On developmental squad, May 30 through July 30, 1985.
Released by Portland Breakers, July 31, 1985; signed as free agent by Atlanta Falcons, May 6, 1986.
On developmental squad for 12 games with Philadelphia Stars in 1984.
On developmental squad for 7 games with Baltimore Stars and 5 games with Portland Breakers in 1985.
Philadelphia USFL, 1984; Portland USFL, 1985.
Games: 1984 (5), 1985 (6). Total—11.
Pro statistics: Credited with one sack for eight yards, 1984.

GUY MAURICE McINTYRE
Guard—San Francisco 49ers
Born Feburary 17, 1961, at Thomasville, Ga.
Height, 6.03. Weight, 264.
High School—Thomasville, Ga.
Attended University of Georgia.
Cousin of Lomas Brown, offensive tackle with Detroit Lions.

Selected by Jacksonville in 1984 USFL territorial draft.
Selected by San Francisco in 3rd round (73rd player selected) of 1984 NFL draft.

Signed by San Francisco 49ers, May 8, 1984.
San Francisco NFL, 1984 and 1985.
Games: 1984 (15), 1985 (15). Total—30.
Pro statistics: Returned one kickoff for no yards, 1984; recovered one fumble in end zone for a touchdown, 1985.
Played in NFC Championship Game following 1984 season.
Played in NFL Championship Game following 1984 season.

RICK E. McIVOR
Quarterback—St. Louis Cardinals
Born September 26, 1960, at Fort Davis, Tex.
Height, 6.04. Weight, 210.
High School—Fort Stockton, Tex.
Attended University of Texas.

Selected by Houston in 1984 USFL territorial draft.
Selected by St. Louis in 3rd round (80th player selected) of 1984 NFL draft.
Signed by St. Louis Cardinals, July 16, 1984.

				PASSING						RUSHING				TOTAL	
Year	Club	G.	Att.	Cmp.	Pct.	Gain	T.P.	P.I.	Avg.	Att.	Yds.	Avg.	TD.	TD.	Pts.	F.
1984—St. Louis NFL		4	4	0	0.0	0	0	0	0.0	3	5	1.7	0	0	0	0
1985—St. Louis NFL		2			None						None			0	0	0
Pro Totals—2 Years		6	4	0	0.0	0	0	0	0.0	3	5	1.7	0	0	0	0

Quarterback Rating Points: 1984 (39.6).

RALEIGH McKENZIE
Guard—Washington Redskins
Born February 8, 1963, at Knoxville, Tenn.
Height, 6.02. Weight, 262.
High School—Knoxville, Tenn., Austin-East.
Received bachelor of science degree from University of Tennessee in 1985.
Twin brother of Reggie McKenzie, linebacker with Los Angeles Raiders.

Selected by Washington in 11th round (290th player selected) of 1985 NFL draft.
Signed by Washington Redskins, June 20, 1985.
Washington NFL, 1985.
Games: 1985 (6).

REGINALD McKENZIE
(Reggie)
Linebacker—Los Angeles Raiders
Born February 8, 1963, at Knoxville, Tenn.
Height, 6.01. Weight, 240.
High School—Knoxville, Tenn., Austin-East.
Attended University of Tennessee.
Twin brother of Raleigh McKenzie, guard with Washington Redskins.

Selected by Los Angeles Raiders in 10th round (275th player selected) of 1985 NFL draft.
Signed by Los Angeles Raiders, June 26, 1985.
Los Angeles Raiders NFL, 1985.
Games: 1985 (16).
Pro statistics: Recovered one fumble, 1985.

ODIS McKINNEY JR.
Safety—Los Angeles Raiders
Born May 19, 1957, at Detroit, Mich.
Height, 6.02. Weight, 190.
High School—Reseda, Calif.
Attended Los Angeles Valley Junior College and University of Colorado.

Selected by New York Giants in 2nd round (37th player selected) of 1978 NFL draft.
Traded by New York Giants to Oakland Raiders for 8th round pick in 1981 draft, May 26, 1980.
Franchise transferred to Los Angeles, May 7, 1982.
Released by Los Angeles Raiders, August 27, 1985; awarded on waivers to Kansas City Chiefs, August 28, 1985.
Released by Kansas City Chiefs, October 8, 1985; signed as free agent by Los Angeles Raiders, October 18, 1985.

		INTERCEPTIONS			
Year	Club	G.	No.	Yds.	Avg.	TD.
1978—N.Y. Giants NFL		14	1	11	11.0	0
1979—N.Y. Giants NFL		15	1	25	25.0	0
1980—Oakland NFL		16	3	22	7.3	0
1981—Oakland NFL		16	3	38	12.7	0
1982—L.A. Raiders NFL		9		None		
1983—L.A. Raiders NFL		16	1	0	0.0	0
1984—L.A. Raiders NFL		16	1	0	0.0	0
1985—KC (5)-Raid. (10) NFL		15	1	22	22.0	0
Pro Totals—8 Years		117	11	118	10.7	0

Additional pro statistics: Recovered one fumble, 1978, 1979, 1981, 1984 and 1985; fumbled once, 1979, 1980 and 1984; recovered one fumble for four yards and returned one punt for no yards, 1980; returned one kickoff for no yards, 1984.
Played in AFC Championship Game following 1980 and 1983 seasons.
Played in NFL Championship Game following 1980 and 1983 seasons.

DENNIS LEWIS McKINNON
Wide Receiver—Chicago Bears
Born August 22, 1961, at Quitman, Ga.
Height, 6.01. Weight, 185.
High School—Miami, Fla., South Miami Senior.
Received bachelor of arts degree in criminology from Florida State University in 1983.

Signed as free agent by Chicago Bears, May 4, 1983.
Expected to miss 1986 season due to knee injury.

		PASS RECEIVING				-PUNT RETURNS-				—KICKOFF RET.—				—TOTAL—		
Year	Club	G.	P.C.	Yds.	Avg.	TD.	No.	Yds.	Avg.	TD.	No.	Yds.	Avg.	TD.	TD.	Pts.	F.
1983—Chicago NFL		16	20	326	16.3	4	34	316	9.3	*1	2	42	21.0	0	5	30	2
1984—Chicago NFL		12	29	431	14.9	3	5	62	12.4	0		None			3	18	1
1985—Chicago NFL		14	31	555	17.9	7	4	44	11.0	0	1	16	16.0	0	7	42	1
Pro Totals—3 Years		42	80	1312	16.4	14	43	422	9.8	1	3	58	19.3	0	15	90	4

Additional pro statistics: Recovered one fumble, 1983; rushed twice for 12 yards, 1984; rushed once for no yards, 1985.

Played in NFC Championship Game following 1984 and 1985 seasons.
Played in NFL Championship Game following 1985 season.

DENNIS N. McKNIGHT
Center-Guard—San Diego Chargers
Born September 12, 1959, at Dallas, Tex.
Height, 6.03. Weight, 273.
High School—Staten Island, N.Y., Wagner.
Received degree from Drake University in 1981.

Signed as free agent by Cleveland Browns, May 3, 1981.
Released by Cleveland Browns, August 18, 1981; signed as free agent by San Diego Chargers, March 30, 1982.
On inactive list, September 12 and September 19, 1982.
San Diego NFL, 1982 through 1985.
Games: 1982 (7), 1983 (16), 1984 (16), 1985 (16). Total—55.
Pro statistics: Recovered two fumbles, 1983 and 1984.

DANA McLEMORE
Cornerback-Kick Returner—San Francisco 49ers
Born July 1, 1960, at Los Angeles, Calif.
Height, 5.10. Weight, 183.
High School—Los Angeles, Calif., Venice.
Attended University of Hawaii.

Selected by San Francisco in 10th round (269th player selected) of 1982 NFL draft.
On inactive list, September 12, 1982.

			-PUNT RETURNS-				—KICKOFF RET.—				—TOTAL—		
Year	Club	G.	No.	Yds.	Avg.	TD.	No.	Yds.	Avg.	TD.	TD.	Pts.	F.
1982—San Francisco NFL		8	7	156	22.3	1	16	353	22.1	0	1	6	0
1983—San Francisco NFL		14	31	331	10.7	*1	30	576	19.2	0	1	6	0
1984—San Francisco NFL		16	45	521	11.6	1	3	80	26.7	0	2	12	1
1985—San Francisco NFL		16	38	258	6.8	0	4	76	19.0	0	0	0	5
Pro Totals—4 Years		54	121	1266	10.5	3	53	1085	20.5	0	4	24	6

Additional pro statistics: Intercepted two passes for 54 yards and a touchdown, 1984; intercepted one pass for no yards and recovered two fumbles, 1985.

Played in NFC Championship Game following 1983 and 1984 seasons.
Played in NFL Championship Game following 1984 season.

MICHAEL JAMES McLEOD
(Mike)
Defensive Back—Green Bay Packers
Born May 4, 1958, at Bozeman, Mont.
Height, 6.00. Weight, 180.
High School—Cheyenne, Wyo., East.
Received bachelor of science degree in political science degree from Montana State University and received degree in law from University of Alberta.

Signed as free agent by Edmonton Eskimos, March 15, 1980.
On injured list, June 23 through August 13, 1980; activated, August 14, 1980.
Released by Edmonton Eskimos, August 27, 1980; signed as free agent by Green Bay Packers, September 25, 1984.
On injured reserve with cracked rib and bruised kidney, November 2 through remainder of 1985 season.

			INTERCEPTIONS				-PUNT RETURNS-				—KICKOFF RET.—				—TOTAL—		
Year	Club	G.	No.	Yds.	Avg.	TD.	No.	Yds.	Avg.	TD.	No.	Yds.	Avg.	TD.	TD.	Pts.	F.
1980—Edmonton CFL		6	1	21	21.0	0	15	97	6.5	0		None			0	0	0
1981—Edmonton CFL		16	5	31	6.2	0		None			1	25	25.0	0	0	0	0
1982—Edmonton CFL		16	1	22	22.0	0	5	58	11.6	0	1	0	0.0	0	0	0	0
1983—Edmonton CFL		16	4	52	13.0	0		None				None			0	0	0
1984—Edmonton CFL		7	1	0	0.0	0	11	145	13.2	0		None			0	0	1
1984—Green Bay NFL		12	1	0	0.0	0		None				None			0	0	0
1985—Green Bay NFL		8		None				None				None			0	0	0
CFL Totals—5 Years		61	12	126	10.5	0	31	300	9.7	0	2	25	12.5	0	0	0	1
NFL Totals—2 Years		20	1	0	0.0	0	0	0	0.0	0	0	0	0.0	0	0	0	0
Pro Totals—7 Years		81	13	126	9.7	0	31	300	9.7	0	2	25	12.5	0	0	0	1

Additional CFL statistics: Recovered two fumbles, 1981; recovered one fumble for two yards, 1983.
Additional NFL statistics: Recovered one fumble, 1984.
Played in CFL Championship Game following 1980 through 1982 seasons.

JAMES ROBERT McMAHON
(Jim)
Quarterback—Chicago Bears
Born August 21, 1959, at Jersey City, N.J.
Height, 6.01. Weight, 187.
High School—Roy, Utah.
Attended Brigham Young University.

Selected by Chicago in 1st round (5th player selected) of 1982 NFL draft.
On injured reserve with lacerated kidney, November 9 through remainder of 1984 season.

Year Club	G.	Att.	Cmp.	Pct.	Gain	T.P.	P.I.	Avg.	Att.	Yds.	Avg.	TD.	TD.	Pts.	F.
			PASSING							RUSHING				TOTAL	
1982—Chicago NFL	8	210	120	57.1	1501	9	7	7.15	24	105	4.4	1	1	6	1
1983—Chicago NFL	14	295	175	59.3	2184	12	13	7.40	55	307	5.6	2	3	18	4
1984—Chicago NFL	9	143	85	59.4	1146	8	2	8.01	39	276	7.1	2	2	12	1
1985—Chicago NFL	13	313	178	56.9	2392	15	11	7.64	47	252	5.4	3	4	24	4
Pro Totals—4 Years	44	961	558	58.1	7223	44	33	7.52	165	940	5.7	8	10	60	10

Quarterback Rating Points: 1982 (80.1), 1983 (77.6), 1984 (97.8), 1985 (82.6). Total—83.0.
Additional pro statistics: Punted once for 59 yards, 1982; caught one pass for 18 yards and a touchdown, punted once for 36 yards and recovered three fumbles, 1983; caught one pass for 42 yards, 1984; caught one pass for 13 yards and a touchdown, 1985.
Played in NFC Championship Game following 1985 season.
Played in NFL Championship Game following 1985 season.
Played in Pro Bowl (NFL All-Star Game) following 1985 season.

STEVE DOUGLAS McMICHAEL
Defensive Tackle—Chicago Bears
Born October 17, 1957, at Houston, Tex.
Height, 6.02. Weight, 260.
High School—Freer, Tex.
Attended University of Texas.

Selected by New England in 3rd round (73rd player selected) of 1980 NFL draft.
On injured reserve with back injury, November 3 through remainder of 1980 season.
Released by New England Patriots, August 24, 1981; signed as free agent by Chicago Bears, October 15, 1981.
New England NFL, 1980; Chicago NFL, 1981 through 1985.
Games: 1980 (6), 1981 (10), 1982 (9), 1983 (16), 1984 (16), 1985 (16). Total—73.
Pro statistics: Recovered one fumble, 1981 and 1985; recovered one fumble for 64 yards, 1982; recovered two fumbles, 1983; credited with one safety, 1985.
Played in NFC Championship Game following 1984 and 1985 seasons.
Played in NFL Championship Game following 1985 season.

LEWIS LORANDO McMILLAN
(Randy)
Fullback—Indianapolis Colts
Born December 17, 1958, at Havre de Grace, Md.
Height, 6.00. Weight, 212.
High School—Belair, Md., North Hartford.
Attended Hartford Community College and University of Pittsburgh.

Selected by Baltimore in 1st round (12th player selected) of 1981 NFL draft.
Franchise transferred to Indianapolis, March 31, 1984.

Year Club	G.	Att.	Yds.	Avg.	TD.	P.C.	Yds.	Avg.	TD.	TD.	Pts.	F.
		RUSHING				PASS RECEIVING				TOTAL		
1981—Baltimore NFL	16	149	597	4.0	3	50	466	9.3	1	4	24	1
1982—Baltimore NFL	9	101	305	3.0	1	15	90	6.0	0	1	6	1
1983—Baltimore NFL	16	198	802	4.1	5	24	195	8.1	1	6	36	5
1984—Indianapolis NFL	16	163	705	4.3	5	19	201	10.6	0	5	30	1
1985—Indianapolis NFL	15	190	858	4.5	7	22	115	5.2	0	7	42	0
Pro Totals—5 Years	72	801	3267	4.1	21	130	1067	8.2	2	23	138	8

Additional pro statistics: Recovered one fumble, 1982; recovered three fumbles, 1983.

AUDREY GLENN McMILLIAN
Defensive Back—Houston Oilers
Born August 13, 1962, at Carthage, Tex.
Height, 6.00. Weight, 190.
High School—Carthage, Tex.
Received bachelor of science degree in industrial distribution
from Purdue University in 1985.

Selected by Houston in 1985 USFL territorial draft.
Selected by New England in 3rd round (84th player selected) of 1985 NFL draft.
Signed by New England Patriots, July 1, 1985.
Released by New England Patriots, September 2, 1985; awarded on waivers to Houston Oilers, September 3, 1985.
Houston NFL, 1985.
Games: 1985 (16).

SEAN McNANIE
Defensive End—Buffalo Bills
Born September 9, 1961, at Mundelein, Ill.
Height, 6.05. Weight, 265.
High School—Mundelein, Ill.
Attended Arizona State University and San Diego State University.

Selected by Oakland in 2nd round (30th player selected) of 1984 USFL draft.
Selected by Buffalo in 3rd round (79th player selected) of 1984 NFL draft.
Signed by Buffalo Bills, June 1, 1984.
Buffalo NFL, 1984 and 1985.
Games: 1984 (15), 1985 (16). Total—31.

DONALD McNEAL
(Don)
Cornerback—Miami Dolphins
Born May 6, 1958, at Atmore, Ala.
Height, 5.11. Weight, 192.
High School—Atmore, Ala., Escambia County.
Received bachelor of science degree in social welfare
from University of Alabama.
Cousin of Mike Williams, running back with Atlanta Falcons.

Named as cornerback on THE SPORTING NEWS College All-America Team, 1979.
Selected by Miami in 1st round (21st player selected) of 1980 NFL draft.
On injured reserve with wrist injury, December 11 through remainder of 1980 season.
On injured reserve with Achilles tendon injury, August 29 through entire 1983 season.
On injured reserve with knee injury, August 19 through October 18, 1985; activated, October 19, 1985.

		—INTERCEPTIONS—			
Year Club	G.	No.	Yds.	Avg.	TD.
1980—Miami NFL	13	5	17	3.4	0
1981—Miami NFL	12		None		
1982—Miami NFL	9	4	42	10.5	*1
1984—Miami NFL	11	3	41	13.7	1
1985—Miami NFL	10		None		
Pro Totals—5 Years	55	12	100	8.3	2

Additional pro statistics: Recovered one fumble, 1980 and 1981; recovered two fumbles for five yards, 1984.
Played in AFC Championship Game following 1982, 1984 and 1985 seasons.
Played in NFL Championship Game following 1982 and 1984 seasons.

FREEMAN McNEIL
Running Back—New York Jets
Born April 22, 1959, at Jackson, Miss.
Height, 5.11. Weight, 212.
High School—Wilmington, Calif., Banning.
Attended University of California at Los Angeles.

Selected by New York Jets in 1st round (3rd player selected) of 1981 NFL draft.
On injured reserve with foot injury, October 10 through November 13, 1981; activated, November 14, 1981.
On injured reserve with separated shoulder, September 27 through November 10, 1983; activated, November 11, 1983.
On injured reserve with broken ribs, December 6 through remainder of 1984 season.

		—RUSHING—				PASS RECEIVING				—TOTAL—		
Year Club	G.	Att.	Yds.	Avg.	TD.	P.C.	Yds.	Avg.	TD.	TD.	Pts.	F.
1981—New York Jets NFL	11	137	623	4.5	2	18	171	9.5	1	3	18	5
1982—New York Jets NFL	9	151	*786	*5.2	6	16	187	11.7	1	7	42	7
1983—New York Jets NFL	9	160	654	4.1	1	21	172	8.2	3	4	24	4
1984—New York Jets NFL	12	229	1070	4.7	5	25	294	11.8	1	6	36	4
1985—New York Jets NFL	14	294	1331	4.5	3	38	427	11.2	2	5	30	9
Pro Totals—5 Years	55	971	4464	4.6	17	118	1251	10.6	8	25	150	29

Additional pro statistics: Attempted one pass with one completion for five yards and a touchdown, 1983; recovered one fumble, 1983 and 1984.
Played in AFC Championship Game following 1982 season.
Played in Pro Bowl (NFL All-Star Game) following 1982 and 1985 seasons.
Named to Pro Bowl following 1984 season; replaced due to injury by Greg Bell.

MARK ANTHONY McNEIL
Defensive Back—Los Angeles Rams
Born August 25, 1961, at San Antonio, Tex.
Height, 6.00. Weight, 195.
High School—San Antonio, Tex., Sam Houston.
Attended University of Nevada at Las Vegas, Mt. San Antonio College and University of Houston.

Signed as free agent by San Antonio Gunslingers, April 6, 1985.
On developmental squad, April 6 through April 10, 1985; activated, April 11, 1985.
Released by San Antonio Gunslingers, July 23, 1985; signed as free agent by Los Angeles Rams, March 21, 1986.
On developmental squad for 1 game with San Antonio Gunslingers in 1985.
San Antonio USFL, 1985.
Games: 1985 (6).

BRUCE EDWARD McNORTON
Cornerback—Detroit Lions
Born February 28, 1959, at Daytona Beach, Fla.
Height, 5.11. Weight, 175.
High School—Daytona Beach, Fla., Spruce Creek.
Received bachelor of arts degree in social work from Georgetown (Ky.) College in 1982.
Selected by Detroit in 4th round (96th player selected) of 1982 NFL draft.
On injured reserve with knuckle injury, September 10 through December 10, 1982; activated, December 11, 1982.

		—INTERCEPTIONS—			
Year Club	G.	No.	Yds.	Avg.	TD.
1982—Detroit NFL..................	4		None		
1983—Detroit NFL..................	16	7	30	4.3	0
1984—Detroit NFL..................	16	2	0	0.0	0
1985—Detroit NFL..................	16	2	14	7.0	0
Pro Totals—4 Years............	52	11	44	4.0	0

MILES GREGORY McPHERSON
Defensive Back
Born March 30, 1960, at Queens, N.Y.
Height, 5.11. Weight, 191.
High School—Malverne, N.Y.
Attended University of New Haven.
Brother of Donald McPherson, quarterback at Syracuse University;
and Mark McPherson, professional middleweight boxer.
Selected by Los Angeles Rams in 10th round (256th player selected) of 1982 NFL draft.
Released by Los Angeles Rams, September 6, 1982; signed as free agent by San Diego Chargers, November 24, 1982.
On injured reserve with broken collarbone, December 12 through remainder of 1983 season.
On injured reserve with knee injury, September 28 through November 9, 1984; actiivated, November 10, 1984.
On injured reserve with knee injury, August 20 through September 17, 1985.
Released by San Diego Chargers, September 18, 1985; re-signed by Chargers, October 24, 1985.
Released by San Diego Chargers, May 9, 1986.
San Diego NFL, 1982 through 1985.
Games: 1982 (6), 1983 (11), 1984 (9), 1985 (9). Total—35.
Pro statistics: Intercepted one pass for no yards, returned five kickoffs for 77 yards and fumbled once, 1983; recovered one fumble, 1984 and 1985; intercepted one pass for 30 yards, 1985.

DAN McQUAID
Offensive Tackle—Washington Redskins
Born October 4, 1960, at Cortland, Calif.
Height, 6.07. Weight, 278.
High School—Clarksburg, Calif., Delta.
Attended University of Nevada at Las Vegas.
Selected by New Jersey in 16th round (318th player selected) of 1984 USFL draft.
Signed as free agent by Los Angeles Rams, May 4, 1984.
On injured reserve with back injury, August 21 through entire 1984 season.
Traded by Los Angeles Rams to Washington Redskins for 4th round pick in 1986 draft, August 24, 1985.
Washington NFL, 1985.
Games: 1985 (16).

ANTHONY McSWAIN
(Chuck)
Running Back—Los Angeles Raiders
Born February 21, 1961, at Rutherford, N.C.
Height, 6.00. Weight, 191.
High School—Forest City, N.C., Chase.
Attended Clemson University.
Brother of Rod McSwain, cornerback with New England Patriots.
Selected by Washington in 1983 USFL territorial draft.
Selected by Dallas in 5th round (135th player selected) of 1983 NFL draft.
Signed by Dallas Cowboys, May 26, 1983.
On injured reserve with torn tendon in finger, September 26 through remainder of 1983 season.
Released by Dallas Cowboys, August 16, 1985; signed as free agent by Los Angeles Raiders, March 21, 1986.

		KICKOFF RETURNS			
Year Club	G.	No.	Yds.	Avg.	TD.
1983—Dallas NFL	1	1	17	17.0	0
1984—Dallas NFL	15	20	403	20.2	0
Pro Totals—2 Years............	16	21	420	20.0	0

Additional pro statistics: Fumbled twice, 1984.

RODNEY McSWAIN
(Rod)
Cornerback—New England Patriots

Born January 28, 1962, at Caroleen, N.C.
Height, 6.01. Weight, 198.
High School—Forest City, N.C., Chase.
Attended Clemson University.
Brother of Chuck McSwain, running back with Los Angeles Raiders.

Selected by Washington in 1984 USFL territorial draft.
Selected by Atlanta in 3rd round (63rd player selected) of 1984 NFL draft.
Signed by Atlanta Falcons, May 16, 1984.
Traded by Atlanta Falcons to New England Patriots for 8th round pick in 1985 draft, August 27, 1984.
New England NFL, 1984 and 1985.
Games: 1984 (15), 1985 (16). Total—31.
Pro statistics: Recovered one fumble, 1984; intercepted one pass for no yards, 1985.
Played in AFC Championship Game following 1985 season.
Played in NFL Championship Game following 1985 season.

MICHAEL LEE MEADE
(Mike)
Fullback—Detroit Lions

Born February 12, 1960, at Dover, Del.
Height, 5.11. Weight, 224.
High School—Dover, Del.
Received bachelor of science degree in business management
from Penn State University in 1982.

Selected by Green Bay in 5th round (126th player selected) of 1982 NFL draft.
On injured reserve with broken leg, November 24 through remainder of 1982 season.
Released by Green Bay Packers, August 27, 1984; awarded on waivers to Detroit Lions, August 28, 1984.

		—RUSHING—				PASS RECEIVING				—TOTAL—		
Year Club	G.	Att.	Yds.	Avg.	TD.	P.C.	Yds.	Avg.	TD.	TD.	Pts.	F.
1982—Green Bay NFL	2	14	42	3.0	0	3	—5	—1.7	0	0	0	0
1983—Green Bay NFL	16	55	201	3.7	1	16	110	6.9	2	3	18	2
1984—Detroit NFL	15		None				None			0	0	1
1985—Detroit NFL	16	3	18	6.0	0	2	21	10.5	0	0	0	0
Pro Totals—4 Years	49	72	261	3.6	1	21	126	6.0	2	3	18	3

Additional pro statistics: Returned two kickoffs for 31 yards, 1982; recovered one fumble, 1983; returned four kickoffs for 32 yards, 1984.

DARRYL SCOTT MEADOWS
Safety—New York Jets

Born February 15, 1961, at Cincinnati, O.
Height, 6.01. Weight, 199.
High School—Cincinnati, O., LaSalle.
Attended University of Toledo.

Signed as free agent by Houston Oilers, June 2, 1983.
Released by Houston Oilers, August 29, 1983; re-signed by Oilers, September 2, 1983.
Released by Houston Oilers, October 2, 1984; re-signed by Oilers, October 12, 1984.
Released by Houston Oilers, August 20, 1985; signed as free agent by New York Jets, April 23, 1986.
Houston NFL, 1983 and 1984.
Games: 1983 (16), 1984 (13). Total—29.

JOHNNY MEADS
Linebacker—Houston Oilers

Born June 25, 1961, at Labadieville, La.
Height, 6.02. Weight, 225.
High School—Napoleonville, La., Assumption.
Attended Nicholls State University.

Selected by New Orleans in 3rd round (55th player selected) of 1984 USFL draft.
Selected by Houston in 3rd round (58th player selected) of 1984 NFL draft.
Signed by Houston Oilers, July 17, 1984.
On injured reserve with knee injury, October 8 through remainder of 1985 season.
Houston NFL, 1984 and 1985.
Games: 1984 (16), 1985 (5). Total—21.

TIMOTHY FREDERICK MEAMBER
(Tim)
Linebacker—Minnesota Vikings

Born October 29, 1962, at Yreka, Calif.
Height, 6.03. Weight, 228.
High School—Yreka, Calif.
Attended University of Washington.

Selected by Portland in 1985 USFL territorial draft.

USFL rights traded with rights to defensive end Ron Holmes by Portland Breakers to Baltimore Stars for rights to defensive end Kenny Neil, February 13, 1985.
Selected by Minnesota in 3rd round (60th player selected) of 1985 NFL draft.
Signed by Minnesota Vikings, August 12, 1985.
On injured reserve with hernia, September 12 through November 1, 1985; activated, November 2, 1985.
On injured reserve with knee injury, December 7 through remainder of 1985 season.
Minnesota NFL, 1985.
Games: 1985 (4).

KARL BERNARD MECKLENBURG
Defensive End-Linebacker—Denver Broncos
Born September 1, 1960, at Seattle, Wash.
Height, 6.03. Weight, 250.
High School—Edina, Minn., West.
Attended Augustana College (S.D.) and received bachelor of
science degree in biology from University of Minnesota in 1983.
Brother of Eric Mecklenburg, linebacker at University of Colorado.

Selected by Chicago in 21st round (246th player selected) of 1983 USFL draft.
Selected by Denver in 12th round (310th player selected) of 1983 NFL draft.
Signed by Denver Broncos, May 14, 1983.

| | | —INTERCEPTIONS— | | | |
Year Club	G.	No.	Yds.	Avg.	TD.
1983—Denver NFL	16	None			
1984—Denver NFL	16	2	105	52.5	0
1985—Denver NFL	16	None			
Pro Totals—3 Years	48	2	105	52.5	0

Additional pro statistics: Recovered one fumble, 1984 and 1985.
Played in Pro Bowl (NFL All-Star Game) following 1985 season.

LANCE ALAN MEHL
Name pronounced Mell.
Linebacker—New York Jets
Born February 14, 1958, at Bellaire, O.
Height, 6.03. Weight, 235.
High School—Bellaire, O.
Received bachelor of science degree in industrial arts education from
Pennsylvania State University in 1980.
Selected by New York Jets in 3rd round (69th player selected) of 1980 NFL draft.

| | | —INTERCEPTIONS— | | | |
Year Club	G.	No.	Yds.	Avg.	TD.
1980—New York Jets NFL	14	None			
1981—New York Jets NFL	15	3	17	5.7	0
1982—New York Jets NFL	9	2	38	19.0	0
1983—New York Jets NFL	16	7	57	8.1	1
1984—New York Jets NFL	16	None			
1985—New York Jets NFL	16	3	33	11.0	0
Pro Totals—6 Years	86	15	145	9.7	1

Additional pro statistics: Recovered one fumble, 1981 through 1984; fumbled once, 1985.
Played in AFC Championship Game following 1982 season.
Played in Pro Bowl (NFL All-Star Game) following 1985 season.

GREGORY PAUL MEISNER
(Greg)
Nose Tackle—Los Angeles Rams
Born April 23, 1959, at New Kensington, Pa.
Height, 6.03. Weight, 253.
High School—New Kensington, Pa., Valley.
Received bachelor of arts degree in psychology from University of Pittsburgh in 1981.
Selected by Los Angeles in 3rd round (63rd player selected) of 1981 NFL draft.
On non-football injury list with head injuries suffered in bar fight, August 18 through October 23, 1981; activated, October 24, 1981.
On injured reserve with knee injury, December 16 through remainder of 1982 season.
Granted free agency, February 1, 1985; re-signed by Rams, September 18, 1985.
Granted roster exemption, September 18 and September 19, 1985; activated, September 20, 1985.
Los Angeles Rams NFL, 1981 through 1985.
Games: 1981 (9), 1982 (6), 1983 (16), 1984 (16), 1985 (14). Total—61.
Pro statistics: Returned one kickoff for 17 yards, 1981; recovered one fumble, 1984.
Played in NFC Championship Game following 1985 season.

—DID YOU KNOW—

That in a November 11, 1984 victory over the Buffalo Bills, New England running back Tony Collins rushed four times for one net yard but scored on two one-yard touchdown runs?

GUIDO A. MERKENS
Quarterback-Wide Receiver—New Orleans Saints

Born August 14, 1955, at San Antonio, Tex.
Height, 6.01. Weight, 195.
High School—San Antonio, Tex., Edison.
Received bachelor of science degree in physical education from
Sam Houston State University in 1976.

Signed as free agent by Houston Oilers, June, 1978.
Released by Houston Oilers, August 29, 1978; re-signed by Oilers, September 22, 1978.
On injured reserve with knee injury, August 26 through November 12, 1980; re-signed after clearing procedural waivers, November 14, 1980.
Released by Houston Oilers, December 13, 1980; signed as free agent by New Orleans Saints, December 15, 1980.

		–PASS RECEIVING–				–PUNT RETURNS–				—TOTAL—		
Year Club	G.	P.C.	Yds.	Avg.	TD.	No.	Yds.	Avg.	TD.	TD.	Pts.	F.
1978—Houston NFL	12	1	6	6.0	0	13	132	10.2	0	0	0	3
1979—Houston NFL	16	3	44	14.7	1	2	6	3.0	0	1	6	1
1980—Houston (3)-N. Orl. (1) NFL	4		None				None			0	0	0
1981—New Orleans NFL	16	29	458	15.8	1	1	—12	—12.0	0	1	6	1
1982—New Orleans NFL	9		None				None			0	0	1
1983—New Orleans NFL	16		None				None			0	0	0
1984—New Orleans NFL	16		None				None			0	0	0
1985—New Orleans NFL	16	3	61	20.3	1		None			1	6	0
Pro Totals—8 Years	105	36	569	15.8	3	16	126	7.9	0	3	18	6

		–––––––––PASSING–––––––––						
Year Club	G.	Att.	Cmp.	Pct.	Gain	T.P.	P.I.	Avg.
1978—Houston NFL	12			None				
1979—Houston NFL	16			None				
1980—Houston (3)-New Orleans (1) NFL	4			None				
1981—New Orleans NFL	16	2	1	50.0	20	0	0	10.00
1982—New Orleans NFL	9	49	18	36.7	186	1	2	3.80
1983—New Orleans NFL	16			None				
1984—New Orleans NFL	16			None				
1985—New Orleans NFL	16	1	1	100.0	7	1	0	7.00
Pro Totals—8 Years	105	52	20	38.5	213	2	2	4.10

Quarterback Rating Points: 1981 (85.4), 1982 (38.1), 1985 (135.4). Total—48.1.
Additional pro statistics: Returned two kickoffs for 22 yards, 1979; recovered one fumble, 1979 and 1980; returned two kickoffs for 38 yards, rushed twice for minus one yard and recovered three fumbles, 1981; rushed nine times for 30 yards, 1982; rushed once for 16 yards and punted four times for a 36.0 average, 1983; returned one kickoff for no yards and rushed once for minus two yards, 1985.
Played in AFC Championship Game following 1978 and 1979 seasons.

RICHARD CASEY MERRILL
(Known by middle name.)
Defensive End—New York Giants

Born July 16, 1957, at Oakland, Calif.
Height, 6.04. Weight, 260.
High School—Danville, Calif., Monte Vista.
Received bachelor of arts degree in history from University of California at Davis in 1979.

Selected by Cincinnati in 5th round (113th player selected) of 1979 NFL draft.
Released by Cincinnati Bengals, August 27, 1979; signed as free agent by Green Bay Packers, September 11, 1979.
On injured reserve with knee injury, December 12 through remainder of 1979 season.
Released by Green Bay Packers, October 5, 1983; signed as free agent by New York Giants, October 13, 1983.
Granted free agency, February 1, 1985; re-signed by Giants, October 2, 1985.
Granted roster exemption, October 2 through October 11, 1985; activated, October 12, 1985.
Green Bay NFL, 1979 through 1982; Green Bay (5)-New York Giants (10) NFL, 1983; New York Giants NFL, 1984 and 1985.
Games: 1979 (13), 1980 (16), 1981 (16), 1982 (9), 1983 (15), 1984 (16), 1985 (11). Total—96.
Pro statistics: Recovered one fumble, 1980; recovered three fumbles, 1981.

SAM MERRIMAN
Linebacker—Seattle Seahawks

Born May 5, 1961, at Tucson, Ariz.
Height, 6.03. Weight, 225.
High School—Tucson, Ariz., Amphitheater.
Attended University of Idaho.

Selected by Arizona in 12th round (143rd player selected) of 1983 USFL draft.
Selected by Seattle in 7th round (177th player selected) of 1983 NFL draft.
Signed by Seattle Seahawks, May 22, 1983.
Seattle NFL, 1983 through 1985.
Games: 1983 (16), 1984 (16), 1985 (14). Total—46.
Pro statistics: Recovered one fumble, 1983; recovered blocked punt in end zone for a touchdown, 1985.
Played in AFC Championship Game following 1983 season.

MICHAEL LAMAR MERRIWEATHER
(Mike)
Linebacker—Pittsburgh Steelers
Born November 26, 1960, at Albans, N.Y.
Height, 6.02. Weight, 215.
High School—Vallejo, Calif.
Received bachelor of arts degree in history from University of the Pacific in 1982.
Selected by Pittsburgh in 3rd round (70th player selected) of 1982 NFL draft.

Year Club	G.	No.	Yds.	Avg.	TD.
1982—Pittsburgh NFL.............	9		None		
1983—Pittsburgh NFL.............	16	3	55	18.3	1
1984—Pittsburgh NFL.............	16	2	9	4.5	0
1985—Pittsburgh NFL.............	16	2	36	18.0	*1
Pro Totals—4 Years...........	57	7	100	14.3	2

Additional pro statistics: Returned one punt for three yards, 1982; recovered two fumbles, 1983; recovered one fumble, 1984; fumbled once, 1985.
Played in AFC Championship Game following 1984 season.
Played in Pro Bowl (NFL All-Star Game) following 1984 and 1985 seasons.

PETER HENRY METZELAARS
(Pete)
Tight End—Buffalo Bills
Born May 24, 1960, at Three Rivers, Mich.
Height, 6.07. Weight, 240.
High School—Portage, Mich., Central.
Received bachelor of science degree in economics from Wabash College in 1982.
Selected by Seattle in 3rd round (75th player selected) of 1982 NFL draft.
On injured reserve with knee injury, October 17 through November 30, 1984; activated, December 1, 1984.
Traded by Seattle Seahawks to Buffalo Bills for wide receiver Byron Franklin, August 20, 1985.

Year Club	G.	P.C.	Yds.	Avg.	TD.
1982—Seattle NFL....................	9	15	152	10.1	0
1983—Seattle NFL....................	16	7	72	10.3	1
1984—Seattle NFL....................	9	5	80	16.0	0
1985—Buffalo NFL....................	16	12	80	6.7	1
Pro Totals—4 Years...........	50	39	384	9.8	2

Additional pro statistics: Recovered one fumble and fumbled twice, 1982; returned one kickoff for no yards, 1983; fumbled once, 1984; recovered one fumble for two yards, 1985.
Played in AFC Championship Game following 1983 season.

JOHN DOUGLAS MEYER
Defensive End—Los Angeles Rams
Born May 28, 1959, at Phoenix, Ariz.
Height, 6.06. Weight, 256.
High School—Phoenix, Ariz., Alhambra.
Attended Scottsdale Community College, Glendale Community College
and Arizona State University.
Selected by Pittsburgh in 2nd round (43rd player selected) of 1982 NFL draft.
On injured reserve with knee injury, September 7 through entire 1982 season.
On physically unable to perform/active with knee injury, July 15 through August 15, 1983.
On physically unable to perform/reserve with knee injury, August 16 through entire 1983 season.
Released by Pittsburgh Steelers after failing physical, July 15, 1984; signed as free agent by Los Angeles Rams, May 20, 1985.
On injured reserve with knee injury, July 18 through entire 1985 season.

RICHARD JAMES MIANO
Name pronounced Mee-AN-oh.
(Rich)
Safety—New York Jets
Born September 3, 1962, at Newton, Mass.
Height, 6.00. Weight, 200.
High School—Honolulu, Haw., Kaiser.
Attended University of Hawaii.
Selected by Denver in 9th round (132nd player selected) of 1985 USFL draft.
Selected by New York Jets in 6th round (166th player selected) of 1985 NFL draft.
Signed by New York Jets, July 16, 1985.
Released by New York Jets, September 2, 1985; re-signed by Jets, September 3, 1985.

Year Club	G.	No.	Yds.	Avg.	TD.
1985—N.Y. Jets NFL	16	2	9	4.5	0

ROBERT ANTHONY MICHO
(Bob)
Tight End—San Diego Chargers

Born March 7, 1962, at Omaha, Neb.
Height, 6.03. Weight, 240.
High School—Austin, Tex., L.C. Anderson.
Attended University of Texas.

Selected by Houston in 1984 USFL territorial draft.
Selected by Denver in 10th round (272nd player selected) of 1984 NFL draft.
Signed by Denver Broncos, May 12, 1984.
On injured reserve with toe injury, August 13 through November 7, 1984.
Awarded on procedural waivers to San Diego Chargers, November 9, 1984.
On injured reserve with foot injury, August 26 through entire 1985 season.
San Diego NFL, 1984.
Games: 1984 (6).

FRANKLIN MIDDLETON JR.
(Frank)
Running Back—Tampa Bay Buccaneers

Born October 28, 1960, at Savannah, Ga.
Height, 5.11. Weight, 201.
High School—Savannah, Ga., Sol C. Johnson.
Attended Florida A&M University.

Selected by Tampa Bay in 1983 USFL territorial draft.
Signed as free agent by Seattle Seahawks, April 28, 1983.
Released by Seattle Seahawks, July 25, 1983; signed as free agent by Tampa Bay Bandits, September 30, 1983.
Released by Tampa Bay Bandits, January 17, 1984; signed as free agent by Indianapolis Colts, June 21, 1984.
Released by Indianapolis Colts, October 16, 1985; signed as free agent by Tampa Bay Buccaneers, March 22, 1986.

		—RUSHING—				—KICKOFF RET.—				—TOTAL—		
Year Club	G.	Att.	Yds.	Avg.	TD.	No.	Yds.	Avg.	TD.	TD.	Pts.	F.
1984—Indianapolis NFL	16	92	275	3.0	1	15	112	7.5	1	2	12	2
1985—Indianapolis NFL	5	13	35	2.7	1	5	54	10.8	0	1	6	0
Pro Totals—2 Years	21	105	310	3.0	2	20	166	8.3	1	3	18	2

Additional pro statistics: Returned one kickoff for 11 yards and recovered two fumbles, 1984; returned one kickoff for 20 yards, 1985.

KELVIN BERNARD MIDDLETON
Defensive Back—Pittsburgh Steelers

Born September 8, 1961, at Macon, Ga.
Height, 5.11. Weight, 185.
High School—Macon, Ga., Southwest.
Attended Wichita State University.

Signed as free agent by Los Angeles Raiders, May 4, 1983.
Released by Los Angeles Raiders, August 16, 1983; signed by Oklahoma Outlaws, October 18, 1983.
Protected in merger of Oklahoma Outlaws and Arizona Wranglers, December 6, 1984.
On developmental squad, June 14 through June 20, 1985; activated, June 21, 1985.
Granted free agency, August 1, 1985; signed by Pittsburgh Steelers, May 29, 1986.
On developmental squad for 1 game with Arizona Outlaws in 1985.

		—INTERCEPTIONS—			
Year Club	G.	No.	Yds.	Avg.	TD.
1984—Oklahoma USFL	18	6	33	5.5	0
1985—Arizona USFL	16	3	64	21.3	0
Pro Totals—2 Years	34	9	97	10.8	0

Additional pro statistics: Credited with 4½ sacks for 36½ yards and recovered two fumbles for two yards, 1984; credited with one sack for four yards, 1985.

BRYAN MILLARD
Name pronounced Mill-ARD.
Offensive Tackle—Seattle Seahawks

Born December 2, 1960, at Sioux City, Ia.
Height, 6.05. Weight, 282.
High School—Dumas, Tex.
Attended University of Texas.

Selected by New Jersey in 12th round (142nd player selected) of 1983 USFL draft.
Signed by New Jersey Generals, February 4, 1983.
On injured reserve with knee injury, April 18 through remainder of 1983 season.
On developmental squad, May 6 through May 10, 1984; activated, May 11, 1984.
Granted free agency, July 15, 1984; signed as free agent by Seattle Seahawks, July 31, 1984.
On injured reserve with knee injury, December 8 through remainder of 1984 season.
On developmental squad for 1 game with New Jersey Generals in 1984.
New Jersey USFL, 1983 and 1984; Seattle NFL, 1984 and 1985.
Games: 1983 (7), 1984 USFL (17), 1984 NFL (14), 1985 (16). Total USFL—24. Total NFL—30. Total Pro—54.

KEITH MILLARD

Name pronounced Mill-ARD.

Defensive End—Minnesota Vikings

Born March 18, 1962, at Pleasanton, Calif.
Height, 6.06. Weight, 260.
High School—Pleasanton, Calif., Foothill.
Attended Washington State University.

Selected by Arizona in 1st round (5th player selected) of 1984 USFL draft.
Selected by Minnesota in 1st round (13th player selected) of 1984 NFL draft.
USFL rights traded by Arizona Wranglers to Jacksonville Bulls for 1st round pick in 1985 draft, July 5, 1984.
Signed by Jacksonville Bulls, July 5, 1984.
On developmental squad, March 2 through March 8, 1985; activated, March 9, 1985.
On suspended list, May 23 through May 29, 1985; reinstated, May 30, 1985.
Released by Jacksonville Bulls, August 5, 1985; signed by Minnesota Vikings, August 6, 1985.
On developmental squad for 1 game with Jacksonville Bulls in 1985.
Jacksonville USFL, 1985; Minnesota NFL, 1985.
Games: 1985 USFL (17), 1985 NFL (16). Total Pro—33.
USFL statistics: Credited with 12 sacks for 86½ yards and recovered one fumble, 1985.
NFL statistics: Recovered one fumble, 1985.

MATT G. MILLEN

Linebacker—Los Angeles Raiders

Born March 12, 1958, at Hokendauqua, Pa.
Height, 6.02. Weight, 245.
High School—Whitehall, Pa.
Received bachelor of business administration degree in marketing from
Pennsylvania State University in 1980.
Nephew of Andy Tomasic, back with Pittsburgh Steelers, 1942 and 1946 and
pitcher with New York Giants, 1949.

Selected by Oakland in 2nd round (43rd player selected) of 1980 NFL draft.
Franchise transferred to Los Angeles, May 7, 1982.

| | | —INTERCEPTIONS— | | | |
Year Club	G.	No.	Yds.	Avg.	TD.
1980—Oakland NFL	16	2	17	8.5	0
1981—Oakland NFL	16		None		
1982—L.A. Raiders NFL	9	3	77	25.7	0
1983—L.A. Raiders NFL	16	1	14	14.0	0
1984—L.A. Raiders NFL	16		None		
1985—L.A. Raiders NFL	16		None		
Pro Totals—6 Years	89	6	108	18.0	0

Additional pro statistics: Recovered one fumble, 1981; returned one kickoff for 13 yards and recovered two fumbles, 1982; returned two kickoffs for 19 yards, 1983.
Played in AFC Championship Game following 1980 and 1983 seasons.
Played in NFL Championship Game following 1980 and 1983 seasons.

BRETT MILLER

Offensive Tackle—Atlanta Falcons

Born October 2, 1958 at Lynwood, Calif.
Height, 6.07. Weight, 290.
High School—Glendale, Calif.
Attended Glendale Community College and University of Iowa.

Selected by Washington in 5th round (57th player selected) of 1983 USFL draft.
Selected by Atlanta in 5th round (129th player selected) of 1983 NFL draft.
Signed by Atlanta Falcons, May 25, 1983.
On injured reserve with sprained ankle, November 12 through December 9, 1985; activated, December 10, 1985.
Atlanta NFL, 1983 through 1985.
Games: 1983 (16), 1984 (15), 1985 (12). Total—43.

DANIEL SCOTT MILLER

(Dan)

Placekicker—St. Louis Cardinals

Born December 30, 1960, at West Palm Beach, Fla.
Height, 5.10. Weight, 172.
High School—Clewiston, Fla.
Received bachelor of business administration degree in accounting from University of Miami (Fla.).

Selected by Washington in 11th round (281st player selected) of 1982 NFL draft.
On inactive list, September 12, 1982.
Released by Washington Redskins, September 15, 1982; signed as free agent by New England Patriots, November 24, 1982.
Released by New England Patriots, December 10, 1982; signed as free agent by Baltimore Colts, December 15, 1982.
Released by Baltimore Colts, August 29, 1983; signed by Jacksonville Bulls, September 28, 1983.
Released by Jacksonville Bulls, March 13, 1984; awarded on waivers to Birmingham Stallions, March 14, 1984.
Released by Birmingham Stallions, July 17, 1985; signed as free agent by Atlanta Falcons, July 24, 1985.
Released by Atlanta Falcons, August 26, 1985; signed as free agent by St. Louis Cardinals, March 21, 1986.

Year Club	G.	XP.	XPM.	FG.	FGA.	Pts.
1982—NE (2)-Bal (3) NFL.	5	9	1	6	11	27
1984—Jx(3)-Br(15) USFL...	18	*69	5	13	20	108
1985—Birmingham USFL.	18	49	3	19	28	†108
Pro Totals—3 Years.......	41	127	9	38	59	243

†Includes one 2-point conversion.

MIKE MILLER
Wide Receiver—New Orleans Saints
Born December 29, 1959, at Flint, Mich.
Height, 5.11. Weight, 182.
High School—Flint, Mich.
Attended University of Tennessee.

Selected by New Jersey in 1983 USFL territorial draft.
Selected by Green Bay in 4th round (104th player selected) of 1983 NFL draft.
Signed by Green Bay Packers, June 29, 1983.
Released by Green Bay Packers, August 29, 1983; awarded on waivers to New York Giants, August 30, 1983.
Released by New York Giants, August 13, 1984; signed as free agent by Cleveland Browns, July 15, 1985.
Released by Cleveland Browns, August 5, 1985; signed as free agent by New Orleans Saints and placed on reserve/future list, November 29, 1985.
Activated from reserve/future list, December 4, 1985.

			——PASS RECEIVING——		
Year Club	G.	P.C.	Yds.	Avg.	TD.
1983—New York Giants NFL	13	7	170	24.3	0
1985—New Orleans NFL........	3			None	
Pro Totals—2 Years............	16	7	170	24.3	0

Additional pro statistics: Rushed once for two yards and returned two kickoffs for 31 yards, 1983.

SHAWN MILLER
Nose Tackle—Los Angeles Rams
Born March 14, 1961, at Ogden, Utah.
Height, 6.04. Weight, 255.
High School—Ogden, Utah, Weber.
Attended Utah State University.

Signed as free agent by Los Angeles Rams, May 5, 1984.
Released by Los Angeles Rams, August 27, 1984; re-signed by Rams, August 28, 1984.
On injured reserve with back injury, November 9 through remainder of 1984 season.
Los Angeles Rams NFL, 1984 and 1985.
Games: 1984 (8), 1985 (16). Total—24.
Pro statistics: Returned one kickoff for 10 yards, 1985.
Played in NFC Championship Game following 1985 season.

JAMES ANTHONY MILLS
(Jim)
Offensive Tackle—Denver Broncos
Born September 23, 1961, at Vancouver, B.C., Canada.
Height, 6.09. Weight, 281.
High School—Richmond, B.C., Canada.
Attended University of Hawaii.

Selected by Los Angeles in 6th round (67th player selected) of 1983 USFL draft.
Selected by Baltimore in 9th round (225th player selected) of 1983 NFL draft.
Signed by Baltimore Colts, May 25, 1983.
On injured reserve with knee injury, October 25 through remainder of 1983 season.
Franchise transferred to Indianapolis, March 31, 1984.
On injured reserve with shoulder injury, August 20 through entire 1985 season.
Granted free agency, February 1, 1986; re-signed by Colts and traded to Denver Broncos for draft choice, May 19, 1986.
Baltimore NFL, 1983; Indianapolis NFL, 1984.
Games: 1983 (7), 1984 (14). Total—21.

RICHARD MILOT
(Rich)
Linebacker—Washington Redskins
Born May 28, 1957, at Coraopolis, Pa.
Height, 6.04. Weight, 237.
High School—Coraopolis, Pa., Moon.
Received bachelor of business administration degree in marketing from
Pennsylvania State University in 1979.

Selected by Washington in 7th round (182nd player selected) of 1979 NFL draft.
On injured reserve with knee injury, October 20 through November 20, 1981; activated, November 21, 1981.

Year Club	G.	No.	Yds.	Avg.TD.
1979—Washington NFL	14		None	
1980—Washington NFL	16	4	—8	—2.0 0
1981—Washington NFL	11		None	
1982—Washington NFL	9		None	
1983—Washington NFL	16	2	20	10.0 0
1984—Washington NFL	14	3	42	14.0 0
1985—Washington NFL	16	2	33	16.5 0
Pro Totals—7 Years	96	11	87	7.9 0

—INTERCEPTIONS—

Additional pro statistics: Recovered one fumble, 1980; recovered one fumble for 18 yards and fumbled once, 1981.
Played in NFC Championship Game following 1982 and 1983 seasons.
Played in NFL Championship Game following 1982 and 1983 seasons.

FRANKY LyDALE MINNIFIELD
(Frank)
Cornerback—Cleveland Browns
Born January 1, 1960, at Lexington, Ky.
Height, 5.09. Weight, 180.
High School—Lexington, Ky., Henry Clay.
Attended University of Louisville.
Related to Dirk Minniefield, guard with Cleveland Cavaliers.

Selected by Chicago in 3rd round (30th player selected) of 1983 USFL draft.
Signed by Chicago Blitz, January 28, 1983.
On injured reserve with knee injury, March 8 through remainder of 1983 season.
Franchise transferred to Arizona, September 30, 1983.
On developmental squad, March 4 through March 21, 1984; activated, March 22, 1984.
On developmental squad, April 27 through May 6, 1984; activated, May 7, 1984.
Signed by Cleveland Browns, May 20, 1984.
Released by Arizona Wranglers, August 23, 1984.
Cleveland Browns contract approved by NFL, August 25, 1984.
Granted roster exemption, August 25 through August 30, 1984; activated, August 31, 1984.
On developmental squad for 3 games with Arizona Wranglers in 1984.

Year Club	G.	No.	Yds.	Avg.TD.
1983—Chicago USFL	1		None	
1984—Arizona USFL	15	4	74	18.5 1
1984—Cleveland NFL	15	1	26	26.0 0
1985—Cleveland NFL	16	1	3	3.0 0
USFL Totals—2 Years	16	4	74	18.5 1
NFL Totals—2 Years	31	2	29	14.5 0
Pro Totals—4 Years	47	6	103	17.2 1

—INTERCEPTIONS—

Additional USFL statistics: Recovered two fumbles for minus six yards, 1984.
Additional NFL statistics: Recovered two fumbles for 10 yards, 1984; recovered one fumble for six yards, 1985.
Played in USFL Championship Game following 1984 season.

CEDRIC ALWYN MINTER
Running Back—New York Jets
Born November 13, 1958, at Charleston, S.C.
Height, 5.10. Weight, 200.
High School—Boise, Ida., Borah.
Received degree in special and elementary education from Boise State University.

Signed as free agent by Toronto Argonauts, March, 1981.
Granted free agency, March 1, 1984; signed by New York Jets, April 26, 1984.
On injured reserve with pulled quadricep, October 26 through November 23, 1984; activated, November 24, 1984.
Released by New York Jets, October 2, 1985; re-signed by Jets, March 25, 1986.

Year Club	G.	RUSHING Att.	Yds.	Avg.	TD.	PASS RECEIVING P.C.	Yds.	Avg.	TD.	TOTAL TD.	Pts.	F.
1981—Toronto CFL	15	182	815	4.5	3	28	371	13.3	0	3	22	2
1982—Toronto CFL	16	120	563	4.7	7	61	828	13.6	5	12	76	1
1983—Toronto CFL	14	107	599	5.6	5	38	444	11.7	3	8	48	1
1984—New York Jets NFL	8	34	136	4.0	1	10	109	10.9	1	2	12	1
1985—New York Jets NFL	3	8	23	2.9	0	1	13	13.0	0	0	0	0
CFL Totals—3 Years	45	409	1977	4.8	15	127	1643	12.9	8	23	146	4
NFL Totals—2 Years	11	42	159	3.8	1	11	122	11.1	1	2	12	1
Pro Totals—5 Years	56	451	2136	4.7	16	138	1765	12.8	9	25	158	5

Year Club	G.	PUNT RETURNS No.	Yds.	Avg.	TD.	KICKOFF RET. No.	Yds.	Avg.TD.
1981—Toronto CFL	15	3	41	13.7	0	11	266	22.0 0
1982—Toronto CFL	16	3	42	14.0	0	12	227	18.9 0
1983—Toronto CFL	14		None				None	
1984—New York Jets NFL	8	4	44	11.0	0	10	224	22.4 0
1985—New York Jets NFL	3	2	25	12.5	0	1	14	14.0 0
CFL Totals—3 Years	45	6	83	13.8	0	23	493	21.4 0
NFL Totals—2 Years	11	6	69	11.5	0	11	238	21.6 0
Pro Totals—5 Years	56	12	152	12.7	0	34	731	21.5 0

Additional pro statistics: Attempted one pass with one completion for 22 yards and a touchdown and recovered two fumbles, 1981; attempted one pass with no completions, 1982.
Played in CFL Championship Game following 1982 and 1983 seasons.

DEAN MARTIN MIRALDI
Offensive Tackle—Denver Broncos
Born April 8, 1958, at Culver City, Calif.
Height, 6.05. Weight, 285.
High School—Rosemead, Calif.
Attended California State University at Long Beach and University of Utah.

Selected by Philadelphia in 2nd round (55th player selected) of 1981 NFL draft.
On injured reserve with pulled hamstring, September 1 through entire 1981 season.
On inactive list, September 12 and September 19, 1982.
On injured reserve with knee injury, November 19 through December 23, 1982; activated, December 24, 1982.
Released by Philadelphia Eagles, August 20, 1985; signed as free agent by Denver Broncos, August 26, 1985.
Philadelphia NFL, 1982 through 1984; Denver NFL, 1985.
Games: 1982 (1), 1983 (13), 1984 (16), 1985 (10). Total—40.

JOHN C. MISKO
Punter—New York Jets
Born October 1, 1954, at Highland Park, Mich.
Height, 6.05. Weight, 207.
High School—Porterville, Calif.
Attended Porterville Junior College and Oregon State University.

Signed as free agent by Buffalo Bills, June, 1980.
Released by Buffalo Bills, August 26, 1980; claimed on procedural waivers by New York Jets, February 19, 1981.
Released by New York Jets, August 25, 1981; signed as free agent by Los Angeles Rams, March 15, 1982.
Released by Los Angeles Rams, September 6, 1982; re-signed by Rams, September 7, 1982.
Released by Los Angeles Rams, August 7, 1985; awarded on waivers to New York Jets, August 8, 1985.
Released by New York Jets, August 8, 1985; re-signed by Jets, March 25, 1986.

		——PUNTING——			
Year Club		G.	No.	Avg.	Blk.
1982—L.A. Rams NFL		9	45	43.6	1
1983—L.A. Rams NFL		16	82	40.3	1
1984—L.A. Rams NFL		16	74	38.7	0
Pro Totals—3 Years		41	201	40.4	2

LEONARD BOYD MITCHELL
Offensive Tackle—Philadelphia Eagles
Born October 12, 1958, at Houston, Tex.
Height, 6.07. Weight, 295.
High School—Houston, Tex., Booker T. Washington.
Attended University of Houston.

Named as defensive tackle on THE SPORTING NEWS College All-America Team, 1980.
Selected by Philadelphia in 1st round (27th player selected) of 1981 NFL draft.
Philadelphia NFL, 1981 through 1985.
Games: 1981 (16), 1982 (9), 1983 (10), 1984 (16), 1985 (16). Total—67.

LYVONIA ALBERT MITCHELL
(Stump)
Running Back—St. Louis Cardinals
Born March 15, 1959, at St. Mary's, Ga.
Height, 5.09. Weight, 188.
High School—St. Mary's, Ga., Camden County.
Attended The Citadel.

Established NFL record for most yards, combined kick returns, season (1,737), 1981; most kickoff returns, rookie season (55), 1981; most combined kick returns, game, 13 vs. Atlanta Falcons, October 10, 1981.
Selected by St. Louis in 9th round (226th player selected) of 1981 NFL draft.

		——RUSHING——				PASS RECEIVING				—TOTAL—		
Year Club	G.	Att.	Yds.	Avg.	TD.	P.C.	Yds.	Avg.	TD.	TD.	Pts.	F.
1981—St. Louis NFL	16	31	175	5.6	0	6	35	5.8	1	2	12	3
1982—St. Louis NFL	9	39	189	4.8	1	11	149	13.5	0	1	6	3
1983—St. Louis NFL	15	68	373	5.5	3	7	54	7.7	0	3	18	5
1984—St. Louis NFL	16	81	434	5.4	9	26	318	12.2	2	11	66	6
1985—St. Louis NFL	16	183	1006	*5.5	7	47	502	10.7	3	10	60	6
Pro Totals—5 Years	72	402	2177	5.4	20	97	1058	10.9	6	27	162	23

		—PUNT RETURNS—				—KICKOFF RET.—			
Year Club	G.	No.	Yds.	Avg.	TD.	No.	Yds.	Avg.	TD.
1981—St. Louis NFL	16	42	445	10.6	1	55	*1292	23.5	0
1982—St. Louis NFL	9	27	165	6.1	0	16	364	22.8	0
1983—St. Louis NFL	15	38	337	8.9	0	36	778	21.6	0
1984—St. Louis NFL	16	38	333	8.8	0	35	804	23.0	0
1985—St. Louis NFL	16	11	97	8.8	0	19	345	18.2	0
Pro Totals—5 Years	72	156	1377	8.8	1	161	3583	22.3	0

Additional pro statistics: Recovered one fumble, 1982 and 1983; recovered two fumbles, 1984 and 1985; attempted one pass with one completion for 20 yards, 1984; attempted two passes with one completion for 31 yards, 1985.

TIMOTHY MOFFETT
(Tim)
Wide Receiver—Los Angeles Raiders
Born February 8, 1962, at Laurel, Miss.
Height, 6.01. Weight, 175.
High School—Taylorsville, Miss.
Attended University of Mississippi.

Selected by Birmingham in 1985 USFL territorial draft.
Selected by Los Angeles Raiders in 3rd round (79th player selected) of 1985 NFL draft.
Signed by Los Angeles Raiders, July 16, 1985.

		——PASS RECEIVING——				
Year	Club	G.	P.C.	Yds.	Avg.	TD.
1985—L.A. Raiders NFL.........		13	5	90	18.0	0

Additional pro statistics: Fumbled once, 1985.

RALF MOJSIEJENKO
Name pronounced Mose-YEN-ko.
Punter—San Diego Chargers
Born January 28, 1963, at Salzgitter Lebenstadt, West Germany.
Height, 6.03. Weight, 198.
High School—Bridgman, Mich.
Attended Michigan State University.

Named as punter on THE SPORTING NEWS College All-America Team, 1983.
Selected by Jacksonville in 9th round (118th player selected) of 1985 USFL draft.
Selected by San Diego in 4th round (96th player selected) of 1985 NFL draft.
Signed by San Diego Chargers, July 23, 1985.

		——PUNTING——			
Year	Club	G.	No.	Avg.	Blk.
1985—San Diego NFL		16	68	42.4	0

Additional pro statistics: Rushed once for no yards and fumbled once for 13-yard loss, 1985.

ROBIN GABRIEL MONACO
(Rob)
Offensive Tackle—St. Louis Cardinals
Born September 5, 1961, at Hamden, Conn.
Height, 6.03. Weight, 283.
High School—Hamden, Conn.
Received bachelor of arts degree in psychology and geology
from Vanderbilt University in 1985.

Selected by Memphis in 1985 USFL territorial draft.
Selected by St. Louis in 8th round (212th player selected) of 1985 NFL draft.
Signed by St. Louis Cardinals, July 21, 1985.
On injured reserve with torn thigh muscle, October 18 through remainder of 1985 season.
St. Louis NFL, 1985.
Games: 1985 (6).

MATTHEW L. MONGER
(Matt)
Linebacker—New York Jets
Born November 15, 1961, at Denver, Colo.
Height, 6.01. Weight, 235.
High School—Miami, Okla.
Received bachelor of science degree in marketing
from Oklahoma State University in 1985.

Selected by New York Jets in 8th round (208th player selected) of 1985 NFL draft.
Signed by New York Jets, July 23, 1985.
New York Jets NFL, 1985.
Games: 1985 (15).
Pro statistics: Recovered two fumbles, 1985.

ART MONK
Wide Receiver—Washington Redskins
Born December 5, 1957, at White Plains, N.Y.
Height, 6.03. Weight, 209.
High School—White Plains, N.Y.
Attended Syracuse University.

Established NFL record for most pass receptions, season (106), 1984.
Named to THE SPORTING NEWS NFL All-Star Team, 1984 and 1985.
Selected by Washington in 1st round (18th player selected) of 1980 NFL draft.
On injured reserve with broken foot, January 7, 1983 through remainder of 1982 season playoffs.
On injured reserve with knee injury, September 2 through September 29, 1983; activated, September 30, 1983.

Year Club	G.	RUSHING				PASS RECEIVING				TOTAL		
		Att.	Yds.	Avg.	TD.	P.C.	Yds.	Avg.	TD.	TD.	Pts.	F.
1980—Washington NFL	16		None			58	797	13.7	3	3	18	0
1981—Washington NFL	16	1	−5	−5.0	0	56	894	16.0	6	6	36	0
1982—Washington NFL	9	7	21	3.0	0	35	447	12.8	1	1	6	3
1983—WashingtonNFL	12	3	−19	−6.3	0	47	746	15.9	5	5	30	0
1984—Washington NFL	16	2	18	9.0	0	*106	1372	12.9	7	7	42	0
1985—Washington NFL	15	7	51	7.3	0	91	1226	13.5	2	2	12	2
Pro Totals—6 Years	84	20	66	3.3	0	393	5482	13.9	24	24	144	5

Additional pro statistics: Returned one kickoff for 10 yards, 1980; attempted one pass with one completion for 46 yards, 1983; fumbled once, 1984.

Played in NFC Championship Game following 1983 season.

Played in NFL Championship Game following 1983 season.

Played in Pro Bowl (NFL All-Star Game) following 1984 and 1985 seasons.

CARL MONROE

Running Back-Kick Returner—San Francisco 49ers

Born February 20, 1960, at Pittsburgh, Pa.

Height, 5.08. Weight, 180.

High School—San Jose, Calif., William C. Overfelt.

Attended Gavilan College and University of Utah.

Selected by Philadelphia in 23rd round (272nd player selected) of 1983 USFL draft.

Signed as free agent by San Francisco 49ers, April 28, 1983.

Released by San Francisco 49ers, August 29, 1983; re-signed by 49ers, September 1, 1983.

On injured reserve with broken foot, October 4 through December 29, 1983; activated, December 30, 1983.

Year Club	G.	RUSHING				PASS RECEIVING				TOTAL		
		Att.	Yds.	Avg.	TD.	P.C.	Yds.	Avg.	TD.	TD.	Pts.	F.
1983—San Francisco NFL	5	10	23	2.3	0	2	61	30.5	0	0	0	0
1984—San Francisco NFL	16	3	13	4.3	0	11	139	12.6	1	1	6	2
1985—San Francisco NFL	14		None			10	51	5.1	0	1	6	0
Pro Totals—3 Years	35	13	36	2.8	0	23	251	10.9	1	2	12	2

			KICKOFF RETURNS			
Year Club	G.	No.	Yds.	Avg.	TD.	
1983—San Francisco NFL	5	8	152	19.0	0	
1984—San Francisco NFL	16	27	561	20.8	0	
1985—San Francisco NFL	14	28	717	25.6	1	
Pro Totals—3 Years	35	63	1430	22.7	1	

Played in NFC Championship Game following 1983 and 1984 seasons.

Played in NFL Championship Game following 1984 season.

JOSEPH C. MONTANA

(Joe)

Quarterback—San Francisco 49ers

Born June 11, 1956, at Monongahela, Pa.

Height, 6.02. Weight, 195.

High School—Monongahela, Pa., Ringgold.

Received bachelor of business administration degree in marketing from University of Notre Dame in 1978.

Established NFL records for highest passer rating, career (92.6); highest completion percentage, career (63.3); lowest interception percentage, career (2.61); most consecutive 300-yard games, season (5), 1982.

Selected by San Francisco in 3rd round (82nd player selected) of 1979 NFL draft.

Year Club	G.	PASSING							RUSHING				TOTAL		
		Att.	Cmp.	Pct.	Gain	T.P.	P.I.	Avg.	Att.	Yds.	Avg.	TD.	TD.	Pts.	F.
1979—San Francisco NFL	16	23	13	56.5	96	1	0	4.17	3	22	7.3	0	0	0	1
1980—San Francisco NFL	15	273	176	*64.5	1795	15	9	6.58	32	77	2.4	2	2	12	4
1981—San Francisco NFL	16	488	311	*63.7	3565	19	12	7.31	25	95	3.8	2	2	12	2
1982—San Francisco NFL	9	*346	213	61.6	2613	17	11	7.55	30	118	3.9	1	1	6	4
1983—San Francisco NFL	16	515	332	64.5	3910	26	12	7.59	61	284	4.7	2	2	12	3
1984—San Francisco NFL	16	432	279	64.6	3630	28	10	8.40	39	118	3.0	2	2	12	4
1985—San Francisco NFL	15	494	303	*61.3	3653	27	13	7.39	42	153	3.6	3	3	18	5
Pro Totals—7 Years	103	2571	1627	63.3	19262	133	67	7.49	232	867	3.7	12	12	72	23

Quarterback Rating Points: 1979 (80.9), 1980 (87.8), 1981 (88.2), 1982 (87.9), 1983 (94.6), 1984 (102.9), 1985 (91.3). Total—92.6.

Additional pro statistics: Recovered one fumble, 1979 and 1980; recovered two fumbles and fumbled four times for minus two yards, 1982; recovered two fumbles and fumbled four times for minus three yards, 1984; recovered three fumbles and fumbled five times for minus 11 yards, 1985.

Played in NFC Championship Game following 1981, 1983 and 1984 seasons.

Played in NFL Championship Game following 1981 and 1984 seasons.

Played in Pro Bowl (NFL All-Star Game) following 1981, 1983 and 1984 seasons.

Named to play in Pro Bowl following 1985 season; replaced due to injury by Jim McMahon.

CLEOTHA MONTGOMERY
(Cle)
Wide Receiver—Los Angeles Raiders

Born July 1, 1956, at Greenville, Miss.
Height, 5.08. Weight, 180.
High School—Greenville, Miss.
Attended Abilene Christian University.
Brother of Wilbert Montgomery, running back with Detroit Lions.

Signed as free agent by Washington Redskins, May, 1978.
Released by Washington Redskins, July 17, 1978; signed as free agent by Denver Broncos, May, 1980.
Released by Denver Broncos, August 26, 1980; signed as free agent by Cincinnati Bengals, September 19, 1980.
Released by Cincinnati Bengals, September 1, 1981; signed as free agent by Cleveland Browns, September 10, 1981.
Released by Cleveland Browns, October 9, 1981; signed as free agent by Oakland Raiders, December 16, 1981.
Franchise transferred to Los Angeles, May 7, 1982.
Released by Los Angeles Raiders, September 6, 1982; re-signed by Raiders, September 7, 1982.
On injured reserve with knee injury, October 1 through remainder of 1985 season.

		—PUNT RETURNS—				—KICKOFF RET.—				—TOTAL—		
Year Club	G.	No.	Yds.	Avg.	TD.	No.	Yds.	Avg.	TD.	TD.	Pts.	F.
1980—Cincinnati NFL	14	31	223	7.2	0	44	843	19.2	0	0	0	3
1981—Cleveland (4)-Oakland (1) NFL	5	17	121	7.1	0	17	382	22.5	0	0	0	2
1982—Los Angeles Raiders NFL	9	None				17	312	18.4	0	0	0	0
1983—Los Angeles Raiders NFL	14	None				21	464	22.1	0	0	0	1
1984—Los Angeles Raiders NFL	16	14	194	13.9	1	26	555	21.3	0	1	6	1
1985—Los Angeles Raiders NFL	4	8	84	10.5	0	7	150	21.4	0	0	0	0
Pro Totals—6 Years	62	70	622	8.9	1	132	2706	20.5	0	1	6	7

Additional pro statistics: Rushed once for 12 yards and recovered two fumbles, 1980; recovered one fumble, 1981 and 1984; recovered two fumbles, 1982; rushed twice for seven yards and caught two passes for 29 yards, 1983; rushed once for one yard, 1984.
Played in AFC Championship Game following 1983 season.
Played in NFL Championship Game following 1983 season.

WILBERT MONTGOMERY
Running Back—Detroit Lions

Born September 16, 1954, at Greenville, Miss.
Height, 5.10. Weight, 195.
High School—Greenville, Miss.
Attended Jackson State University and Abilene Christian University.
Brother of Cle Montgomery, wide receiver with Los Angeles Raiders.

Selected by Philadelphia in 6th round (154th player selected) of 1977 NFL draft.
On did not report list, August 20, 1985.
Traded by Philadelphia Eagles to Detroit Lions for linebacker Garry Cobb, August 21, 1985.
On injured reserve with knee injury, October 30 through remainder of 1985 seson.

		——RUSHING——				PASS RECEIVING				—TOTAL—		
Year Club	G.	Att.	Yds.	Avg.	TD.	P.C.	Yds.	Avg.	TD.	TD.	Pts.	F.
1977—Philadelphia NFL	14	45	183	4.1	2	3	18	6.0	0	3	18	4
1978—Philadelphia NFL	14	259	1220	4.7	9	34	195	5.7	1	10	60	6
1979—Philadelphia NFL	16	338	1512	4.5	9	41	494	12.0	5	14	84★14
1980—Philadelphia NFL	12	193	778	4.0	8	50	407	8.1	2	10	60	3
1981—Philadelphia NFL	15	286	1402	4.9	8	49	521	10.6	2	10	60	6
1982—Philadelphia NFL	8	114	515	4.5	7	20	258	12.9	2	9	54	3
1983—Philadelphia NFL	5	29	139	4.8	0	9	53	5.9	0	0	0	1
1984—Philadelphia NFL	16	201	789	3.9	2	60	501	8.4	0	2	12	5
1985—Detroit NFL	7	75	251	3.3	0	7	55	7.9	0	0	0	0
Pro Totals—9 Years	107	1540	6789	4.4	45	273	2502	9.2	12	58	348	42

		KICKOFF RETURNS			
Year Club	G.	No.	Yds.	Avg.	TD.
1977—Philadelphia NFL	14	23	619	★26.9	1
1978—Philadelphia NFL	14	6	154	25.7	0
1979—Philadelphia NFL	16	1	6	6.0	0
1980—Philadelphia NFL	12	1	23	23.0	0
1981—Philadelphia NFL	15	None			
1982—Philadelphia NFL	8	1	12	12.0	0
1983—Philadelphia NFL	5	None			
1984—Philadelphia NFL	16	None			
1985—Detroit NFL	7	None			
Pro Totals—9 Years	107	32	814	25.4	1

Additional pro statistics: Recovered two fumbles, 1979, 1981 and 1982; recovered one fumble, 1980, 1984 and 1985; attempted one pass with no completions, 1980; attempted two passes with no completions, 1984.
Played in NFC Championship Game following 1980 season.
Played in NFL Championship Game following 1980 season.
Played in Pro Bowl (NFL All-Star Game) following 1978 and 1979 seasons.

—DID YOU KNOW—

That when the Chicago Bears and New England Patriots met in Super Bowl XX, it was the first time either team played in a league title game in 22 seasons?

MAX MONTOYA JR.
Guard—Cincinnati Bengals
Born May 12, 1956, at Montebello, Calif.
Height, 6.05. Weight, 275.
High School—La Puente, Calif.
Attended Mt. San Jacinto Junior College and University of California at Los Angeles.

Selected by Cincinnati in 7th round (168th player selected) of 1979 NFL draft.
Cincinnati NFL, 1979 through 1985.
Games: 1979 (11), 1980 (16), 1981 (16), 1982 (9), 1983 (16), 1984 (16), 1985 (16). Total—100.
Pro statistics: Recovered one fumble, 1981.
Played in AFC Championship Game following 1981 season.
Played in NFL Championship Game following 1981 season.

WARREN MOON
Quarterback—Houston Oilers
Born November 18, 1956, at Los Angeles, Calif.
Height, 6.03. Weight, 210.
High School—Los Angeles, Calif., Hamilton.
Attended University of Washington.

Tied NFL record for most fumbles, season (17), 1984.
Signed as free agent by Edmonton Eskimos, March, 1978.
USFL rights traded by Memphis Showboats to Los Angeles Express for future draft pick, August 30, 1983.
Granted free agency, March 1, 1984; signed by Houston Oilers, March 1, 1984.

Year Club	G.	Att.	Cmp.	Pct.	Gain	T.P.	P.I.	Avg.	Att.	Yds.	Avg.	TD.	TD.	Pts.	F.
				PASSING						RUSHING			TOTAL		
1978—Edmonton CFL	15	173	89	51.4	1112	5	7	6.43	30	114	3.8	1	1	6	1
1979—Edmonton CFL	16	274	149	54.4	2382	20	12	8.69	56	150	2.7	2	2	12	1
1980—Edmonton CFL	16	331	181	54.7	3127	25	11	9.45	55	352	6.4	3	3	18	0
1981—Edmonton CFL	15	378	237	62.7	3959	27	12	10.47	50	298	6.0	3	3	18	1
1982—Edmonton CFL	16	562	333	59.3	5000	36	16	8.90	54	259	4.8	4	4	24	1
1983—Edmonton CFL	16	664	380	57.2	5648	31	19	8.51	85	527	6.2	3	3	18	7
1984—Houston NFL	16	450	259	57.6	3338	12	14	7.42	58	211	3.6	1	1	6	*17
1985—Houston NFL	14	377	200	53.1	2709	15	19	7.19	39	130	3.3	0	0	0	12
CFL Totals—6 Years	94	2382	1369	57.5	21228	144	77	8.91	330	1700	5.2	16	16	96	11
NFL Totals—2 Years	30	827	459	55.5	6047	27	33	7.31	97	341	3.5	1	1	6	29
Pro Totals—8 Years	124	3209	1828	57.0	27275	171	110	8.50	427	2041	4.8	17	17	102	40

Quarterback Rating Points: 1984 (76.9), 1985 (68.5). Total—73.1.
Additional CFL statistics: Recovered one fumble, 1982.
Additional NFL statistics: Recovered seven fumbles and fumbled 17 times for minus one yard, 1984; recovered five fumbles and fumbled 12 times for minus eight yards, 1985.
Played in CFL Championship Game following 1978 through 1982 seasons.

ALVIN MOORE
Running Back—Detroit Lions
Born May 3, 1959, at Randolph, Ariz.
Height, 6.00. Weight, 194.
High School—Coolidge, Ariz.
Attended Arizona State University.
Related to Lee Roy Selmon, defensive end with Tampa Bay Buccaneers, 1976 through 1984; and Dewey Selmon, linebacker with Tampa Bay Buccaneers and San Diego Chargers, 1976 through 1982.

Selected by Arizona in 1983 USFL territorial draft.
Selected by Baltimore in 7th round (169th player selected) of 1983 NFL draft.
Signed by Baltimore Colts, May 22, 1983.
Franchise transferred to Indianapolis, March 31, 1984.
Traded by Indianapolis Colts to Detroit Lions for wide receiver Robbie Martin, July 25, 1985.

Year Club	G.	Att.	Yds.	Avg.	TD.	P.C.	Yds.	Avg.	TD.	TD.	Pts.	F.
			RUSHING				PASS RECEIVING				TOTAL	
1983—Baltimore NFL	15	57	205	3.6	1	6	38	6.3	0	1	6	0
1984—Indianapolis NFL	13	38	127	3.3	2	9	52	5.8	0	2	12	3
1985—Detroit NFL	16	80	221	2.8	4	19	154	8.1	1	5	30	5
Pro Totals—3 Years	44	175	553	3.2	7	34	244	7.2	1	8	48	8

Year Club	G.	No.	Yds.	Avg.	TD.
		KICKOFF RETURNS			
1983—Baltimore NFL	15	2	40	20.0	0
1984—Indianapolis NFL	13	2	19	9.5	0
1985—Detroit NFL	16	13	230	17.7	0
Pro Totals—3 Years	44	17	289	17.0	0

Additional pro statistics: Attempted one pass with no completions, 1984 and 1985; recovered one fumble, 1985.

BOOKER THOMAS MOORE
Fullback—Buffalo Bills
Born June 23, 1959, at Flint, Mich.
Height, 5.11. Weight, 224.
High School—Flint, Mich., Southwestern.
Attended Pennsylvania State University.

Selected by Buffalo in 1st round (28th player selected) of 1981 NFL draft.
On non-football injury list with Guillian Barre syndrome, August 18 through entire 1981 season.

Year	Club	G.	Att.	Yds.	Avg.	TD.	P.C.	Yds.	Avg.	TD.	TD.	Pts.	F.
				RUSHING				PASS RECEIVING				TOTAL	
1982—Buffalo NFL		5	16	38	2.4	0	1	8	8.0	0	0	0	2
1983—Buffalo NFL		15	60	275	4.6	0	34	199	5.9	1	1	6	1
1984—Buffalo NFL		15	24	84	3.5	0	33	172	5.2	0	0	0	4
1985—Buffalo NFL		16	15	23	1.5	1	7	44	6.3	0	1	6	1
Pro Totals—4 Years		51	115	420	3.7	1	75	423	5.6	1	2	12	8

Additional pro statistics: Recovered one fumble, 1983 and 1984; returned three kickoff for 31 yards, 1985.

DANA MOORE
Punter-Placekicker—Philadelphia Eagles
Born September 7, 1961, at Baton Rouge, La.
Height, 5.11. Weight, 185.
High School—Baton Rouge, La., Belaire.
Attended Mississippi State University.

Selected by New Jersey in 18th round (214th player selected) of 1983 USFL draft.
Signed by New Jersey Generals, January 21, 1983.
Released by New Jersey Generals, March 2, 1983; signed as free agent by Washington Federals, March 26, 1983.
On injured reserve with knee injury, March 27 through remainder of 1984 season.
Franchise transferred to Orlando, October 12, 1984.
Granted free agency, November 30, 1984; signed by San Francisco 49ers, April 16, 1985.
Released by San Francisco 49ers, August 20, 1985; signed as free agent by Philadelphia Eagles, February 19, 1986.

			PUNTING	
Year	Club	G.	No.	Avg.	Blk.
1983—Washington USFL		15	86	40.5	....
1984—Washington USFL		5	26	36.1	....
Pro Totals—2 Years		20	112	39.5	....

Additional pro statistics: Successful on one of three field goal attempts and ran once for minus eight yards, 1983; recovered one fumble and fumbled once, 1984.

DERLAND PAUL MOORE
Nose Tackle—New Orleans Saints
Born October 7, 1951, at Malden, Mo.
Height, 6.04. Weight, 273.
High School—Poplar Bluff, Mo.
Attended University of Oklahoma.

Selected by New Orleans in 2nd round (29th player selected) of 1973 NFL draft.
On injured reserve with knee injury, November 29 through remainder of 1977 season.
On injured reserve with knee and ankle injuries, November 27 through remainder of 1984 season.
On injured reserve with foot injury, September 3 through November 13, 1985; activated after clearing procedural waivers, November 15, 1985.
Released by New Orleans Saints, April 24, 1986; re-signed by Saints, May 13, 1986.
New Orleans NFL, 1973 through 1985.
Games: 1973 (13), 1974 (14), 1975 (14), 1976 (14), 1977 (10), 1978 (15), 1979 (15), 1980 (16), 1981 (16), 1982 (9), 1983 (16), 1984 (12), 1985 (6). Total—170.
Pro statistics: Recovered one fumble, 1973, 1980, 1981 and 1982; intercepted one pass for no yards and returned one kickoff for 14 yards, 1973; recovered two fumbles, 1977; recovered one fumble for six yards, 1978.

MACK MOORE
Defensive End—Miami Dolphins
Born March 4, 1959, at Monroe, La.
Height, 6.04. Weight, 258.
High School—Monroe, La.
Attended City College of San Francisco and received degree from Texas A & M University.

Selected by Miami in 6th round (152nd player selected) of 1981 NFL draft.
Signed as free agent by British Columbia Lions, June 10, 1981.
Granted free agency, March 1, 1985; signed by Miami Dolphins, July 20, 1985.
British Columbia CFL, 1981 through 1984; Miami NFL, 1985.
Games: 1981 (16), 1982 (12), 1983 (16), 1984 (16), 1985 (16). Total CFL—60. Total Pro—76.
Pro statistics: Recovered two fumbles, 1982; recovered four fumbles, 1983; recovered one fumble, 1984.
Played in CFL Championship Game following 1983 season.
Played in AFC Championship Game following 1985 season.

MALCOLM G. MOORE
Wide Receiver—San Diego Chargers
Born June 24, 1961, at San Fernando, Calif.
Height, 6.05. Weight, 205.
High School—San Fernando, Calif.
Attended University of Southern California.

Selected by Los Angeles in 1984 USFL territorial draft.
Signed by Los Angeles Express, January 19, 1984.
Selected by Dallas in 2nd round (54th player selected) of 1984 NFL supplemental draft.
Released by Los Angeles Express, February 11, 1985; signed by Dallas Cowboys, March 20, 1985.
Released by Dallas Cowboys, August 5, 1985; signed as free agent by San Diego Chargers, March 10, 1986.

Year Club		G.	P.C.	Yds.	Avg.	TD.
		—PASS RECEIVING—				
1984—Los Angeles USFL		17	31	354	11.4	0

Additional pro statistics: Fumbled once, 1984.

NATHANIEL MOORE
(Nat)
Wide Receiver—Miami Dolphins

Born September 19, 1951, at Tallahassee, Fla.
Height, 5.09. Weight, 188.
High School—Miami, Fla., Edison.
Attended Tennessee-Martin College, Miami-Dade (South) Community College and University of Florida.
Cousin of Ken Johnson, running back with New York Giants, 1979.

Named to THE SPORTING NEWS AFC All-Star Team, 1977.
Selected by Jacksonville Sharks in 5th round of 1974 WFL draft.
Selected by Miami in 3rd round (78th player selected) of 1974 NFL draft.
On physically unable to perform/active with knee injury, July 30 through August 23, 1982; activated, August 24, 1982.
Granted free agency, February 1, 1984; re-signed by Dolphins, August 12, 1985.
Granted roster exemption, August 12 through August 22, 1985; activated, August 23, 1985.

Year Club		G.	Att.	Yds.	Avg.	TD.	P.C.	Yds.	Avg.	TD.	TD.	Pts.	F.
			—RUSHING—				PASS RECEIVING				—TOTAL—		
1974—Miami NFL		13	3	16	5.3	0	37	605	16.4	2	2	12	1
1975—Miami NFL		14	8	69	8.6	0	40	705	17.6	4	4	24	1
1976—Miami NFL		9	4	36	9.0	0	33	625	18.9	4	4	24	1
1977—Miami NFL		14	14	89	6.4	1	52	765	14.7	*12	*13	78	0
1978—Miami NFL		16	4	−3	−0.8	0	48	645	13.4	10	10	60	1
1979—Miami NFL		16	3	22	7.3	0	48	840	17.5	6	6	36	1
1980—Miami NFL		16	1	3	3.0	0	47	564	12.0	7	7	42	1
1981—Miami NFL		13	1	3	3.0	0	26	452	17.4	2	2	12	0
1982—Miami NFL		9		None			8	82	10.3	1	1	6	0
1983—Miami NFL		16		None			39	558	14.3	6	6	36	1
1984—Miami NFL		16	1	3	3.0	0	43	573	13.3	6	6	36	2
1985—Miami NFL		15	1	11	11.0	0	51	701	13.7	7	7	42	0
Pro Totals—12 Years		167	40	249	6.2	1	472	7115	15.1	67	68	408	9

Year Club		G.	No.	Yds.	Avg.	TD.	No.	Yds.	Avg.	TD.
			—PUNT RETURNS—				—KICKOFF RET.—			
1974—Miami NFL		13	9	136	15.1	0	22	587	26.7	0
1975—Miami NFL		14	8	80	10.0	0	9	243	27.0	0
1976—Miami NFL		9	8	72	9.0	0	2	28	14.0	0
1977—Miami NFL		14		None				None		
1978—Miami NFL		16	1	11	11.0	0		None		
1979—Miami NFL		16		None				None		
1980—Miami NFL		16		None				None		
1981—Miami NFL		13		None				None		
1982—Miami NFL		9		None				None		
1983—Miami NFL		16		None				None		
1984—Miami NFL		16		None				None		
1985—Miami NFL		15		None				None		
Pro Totals—12 Years		167	26	299	11.5	0	33	858	26.0	0

Additional pro statistics: Completed one pass for 31 yards, 1974; recovered one fumble, 1974, 1975, 1977 and 1980; attempted one pass with no completions, 1980.
Played in AFC Championship Game following 1982, 1984 and 1985 seasons.
Played in NFL Championship Game following 1982 and 1984 seasons.
Played in Pro Bowl (NFL All-Star Game) following 1977 season.

STEPHEN ELLIOTT MOORE
(Steve)
Guard-Offensive Tackle—New England Patriots

Born October 1, 1960, at Memphis, Tenn.
Height, 6.04. Weight, 285.
High School—Memphis, Tenn., Fairley.
Attended Tennessee State University.
Brother of Jeffrey B. Moore, wide receiver with Los Angeles Rams, 1980 and 1981.

Selected by Birmingham in 4th round (37th player selected) of 1983 USFL draft.
Selected by New England in 3rd round (80th player selected) of 1983 NFL draft.
Signed by New England Patriots, May 25, 1983.
New England NFL, 1983 through 1985.
Games: 1983 (4), 1984 (16), 1985 (16). Total—36.
Played in AFC Championship Game following 1985 season.
Played in NFL Championship Game following 1985 season.

EMERY MATTHEW MOOREHEAD
Tight End—Chicago Bears

Born March 22, 1954, at Evanston, Ill.
Height, 6.02. Weight, 220.
High School—Evanston, Ill.
Received bachelor of arts degree in communications from University of Colorado in 1977.

Selected by New York Giants in 6th round (153rd player selected) of 1977 NFL draft.
On injured reserve with bruised kidney, November 27 through remainder of 1979 season.
Traded by New York Giants to Denver Broncos for 8th round pick in 1981 draft, May 23, 1980.
Released by Denver Broncos, September 1, 1980; re-signed by Broncos, September 2, 1980.
Released by Denver Broncos, August 3, 1981; claimed on waivers by Chicago Bears, August 4, 1981.
Released by Chicago Bears, August 29, 1981; re-signed by Bears after clearing procedural waivers, October 21, 1981.

| | | —RUSHING— | | | | PASS RECEIVING | | | | —TOTAL— | | |
Year Club	G.	Att.	Yds.	Avg.	TD.	P.C.	Yds.	Avg.	TD.	TD.	Pts.	F.
1977—New York Giants NFL	13	1	5	5.0	0	12	143	11.9	1	1	6	0
1978—New York Giants NFL	10		None			3	45	15.0	0	0	0	0
1979—New York Giants NFL	13	36	95	2.6	0	9	62	6.9	0	0	0	0
1980—Denver NFL	16	2	7	3.5	0		None			0	0	0
1981—Chicago NFL	9		None				None			0	0	0
1982—Chicago NFL	9	2	3	1.5	0	30	363	12.1	5	5	30	0
1983—Chicago NFL	16	5	6	1.2	0	42	597	14.2	3	3	18	0
1984—Chicago NFL	16	1	—2	—2.0	0	29	497	17.1	1	1	6	0
1985—Chicago NFL	15		None			35	481	13.7	1	1	6	0
Pro Totals—9 Years	117	47	114	2.4	0	160	2188	13.7	11	11	66	0

Additional pro statistics: Returned four punts for 65 yards (16.3 average), 1977; returned two punts for 52 yards (26.0 average), 1978; returned one kickoff for 16 yards, 1979; returned one kickoff for 18 yards, 1980; returned 23 kickoffs for 476 yards (20.7 average), 1981.
Played in NFC Championship Game following 1984 and 1985 seasons.
Played in NFL Championship Game following 1985 season.

ERIC MORAN
Offensive Tackle—Houston Oilers
Born June 10, 1960, at Spokane, Wash.
Height, 6.05. Weight, 280.
High School—Pleasanton, Calif., Foothill.
Attended University of Washington.
Son of Jim Moran, defensive tackle with New York Giants, 1964 through 1967;
and brother of Rich Moran, center-guard with Green Bay Packers.

Selected by Oakland in 16th round (186th player selected) of 1983 USFL draft.
Selected by Dallas in 10th round (273rd player selected) of 1983 NFL draft.
USFL rights traded by Oakland Invaders to Los Angeles Express for rights to defensive tackle Brian Douglas and linebacker Randy McClanahan, May 2, 1983.
Signed by Los Angeles Express, June 9, 1983.
Released injured by Los Angeles Express, February 15, 1984; signed by Dallas Cowboys, April 27, 1984.
Released by Dallas Cowboys, August 27, 1984; signed as free agent by Houston Oilers, September 5, 1984.
Los Angeles USFL, 1983; Houston NFL, 1984 and 1985.
Games: 1983 (3), 1984 (8), 1985 (15). Total NFL—23. Total Pro—26.

RICHARD JAMES MORAN
(Rich)
Center-Guard—Green Bay Packers
Born March 19, 1962, at Boise, Ida.
Height, 6.02. Weight, 272.
High School—Pleasanton, Calif., Foothill.
Received degree in marketing from San Diego State University in 1985.
Son of Jim Moran, defensive tackle with New York Giants, 1964 through 1967;
and brother of Eric Moran, offensive tackle with Houston Oilers.

Selected by Arizona in 4th round (57th player selected) of 1985 USFL draft.
Selected by Green Bay in 3rd round (71st player selected) of 1985 NFL draft.
Signed by Green Bay Packers, July 24, 1985.
Green Bay NFL, 1985.
Games: 1985 (16).

MICHAEL KARL MORGAN
(Known by middle name.)
Nose Tackle—Tampa Bay Buccaneers
Born February 23, 1961, at Houma, La.
Height, 6.01. Weight, 255.
High School—Houma, La., Vandebilt Catholic.
Attended University of California at Los Angeles.

Selected by Arizona in 21st round (242nd player selected) of 1983 USFL draft.
Signed as free agent by Saskatchewan Roughriders, May 2, 1983.
Released by Saskatchewan Roughriders, June 26, 1984; signed as free agent by Tampa Bay Buccaneers, July 10, 1984.
Released by Tampa Bay Buccaneers, August 27, 1984; re-signed by Buccaneers, September 5, 1984.
Released by Tampa Bay Buccaneers, October 19, 1984; re-signed by Buccaneers, October 26, 1984.
Saskatchewan CFL, 1983; Tampa Bay NFL, 1984 and 1985.
Games: 1983 (16), 1984 (13), 1985 (16). Total NFL—29. Total Pro—45.
CFL statistics: Recovered one fumble, 1983.
NFL statistics: Recovered two fumbles, 1985.

STANLEY DOUGLAS MORGAN
Wide Receiver—New England Patriots

Born February 17, 1955, at Easley, S. C.
Height, 5.11. Weight, 181.
High School—Easley, S. C.
Received bachelor of science degree in education from University of Tennessee in 1979.

Selected by New England in 1st round (25th player selected) of 1977 NFL draft.

Year Club	G.	Att.	RUSHING Yds.	Avg.	TD.	P.C.	PASS RECEIVING Yds.	Avg.	TD.	TD.	TOTAL Pts.	F.
1977—New England NFL	14	1	10	10.0	0	21	443	*21.1	3	3	18	0
1978—New England NFL	16	2	11	5.5	0	34	820	24.1	5	5	30	6
1979—New England NFL	16	7	39	5.6	0	44	1002	*22.8	*12	13	78	1
1980—New England NFL	16	4	36	9.0	0	45	991	*22.0	6	6	36	0
1981—New England NFL	13	2	21	10.5	0	44	1029	*23.4	6	6	36	2
1982—New England NFL	9	2	3	1.5	0	28	584	20.9	3	3	18	0
1983—New England NFL	16	1	13	13.0	0	58	863	14.9	2	2	12	5
1984—New England NFL	13			None		38	709	18.7	5	5	30	0
1985—New England NFL	15	1	0	0.0	0	39	760	19.5	5	5	30	1
Pro Totals—9 Years	128	20	133	6.7	0	351	7201	20.5	47	48	288	15

Year Club	G.	PUNT RETURNS No.	Yds.	Avg.	TD.
1977—New England NFL	14	16	220	13.8	0
1978—New England NFL	16	32	335	10.5	0
1979—New England NFL	16	29	289	10.0	1
1980—New England NFL	16		None		
1981—New England NFL	13	15	116	7.7	0
1982—New England NFL	9		None		
1983—New England NFL	16		None		
1984—New England NFL	13		None		
1985—New England NFL	15		None		
Pro Totals—9 Years	128	92	960	10.4	1

Additional pro statistics: Returned one kickoff for 17 yards, 1978; returned one kickoff for 12 yards, 1979; recovered one fumble for three yards, 1980; recovered two fumbles, 1981 and 1983.
Played in AFC Championship Game following 1985 season.
Played in NFL Championship Game following 1985 season.
Played in Pro Bowl (NFL All-Star Game) following 1979 and 1980 seasons.

LARRY MORIARTY
Running Back—Houston Oilers

Born April 24, 1958, at Santa Barbara, Calif.
Height, 6.01. Weight, 240.
High School—Santa Barbara, Calif., Dos Pueblos.
Attended Santa Barbara City Junior College and University of Notre Dame.
Cousin of Pat Moriarty, running back with Cleveland Browns, 1979; and Tom Moriarty,
safety with Atlanta Falcons, Pittsburgh Steelers, Michigan Panthers and
Pittsburgh Maulers, 1977 through 1981, 1983 and 1984.

Selected by Chicago in 1983 USFL territorial draft.
Selected by Houston in 5th round (114th player selected) of 1983 NFL draft.
Signed by Houston Oilers, July 14, 1983.
On did not report list, August 20 through August 29, 1985.
Granted roster exemption, August 30 through September 6, 1985; activated, September 7, 1985.

Year Club	G.	Att.	RUSHING Yds.	Avg.	TD.	P.C.	PASS RECEIVING Yds.	Avg.	TD.	TD.	TOTAL Pts.	F.
1983—Houston NFL	16	65	321	4.9	3	4	32	8.0	0	3	18	1
1984—Houston NFL	14	189	785	4.2	6	31	206	6.6	1	7	42	5
1985—Houston NFL	15	106	381	3.6	3	17	112	6.6	0	3	18	2
Pro Totals—3 Years	45	360	1487	4.1	12	52	350	6.7	1	13	78	8

Additional pro statistics: Returned two kickoffs for 25 yards and recovered one fumble, 1983; attempted one pass with one completion for 16 yards and recovered two fumbles, 1984.

MICHAEL HENRY MOROSKI
(Mike)
Quarterback—San Francisco 49ers

Born September 4, 1957, at Bakersfield, Calif.
Height, 6.04. Weight, 200.
High School—Novato, Calif.
Received bachelor of arts degree in agricultural economics from University of California at Davis.

Selected by Atlanta in 6th round (154th player selected) of 1979 draft.
On injured reserve with broken collarbone, September 14 through December 18, 1981; activated, December 19, 1981.
USFL rights traded by Los Angeles Express to Denver Gold for rights to wide receiver Billy Waddy, January 21, 1984.
Released by Atlanta Falcons, August 20, 1985; awarded on waivers to San Francisco 49ers, August 21, 1985.
Released by San Francisco 49ers, September 1, 1985; signed as free agent by Houston Oilers, September 11, 1985.
Released by Houston Oilers, October 16, 1985; signed as free agent by Los Angeles Raiders, October 23, 1985.

Released by Los Angeles Raiders, October 25, 1985; signed as free agent by Houston Oilers, November 21, 1985. Released by Houston Oilers, December 18, 1985; signed as free agent by San Francisco 49ers, April 7, 1986.

Year Club	G.	Att.	Cmp.	Pct.	Gain	T.P.	P.I.	Avg.	Att.	Yds.	Avg.	TD.	TD.	Pts.	F.
				PASSING						RUSHING			TOTAL		
1979—Atlanta NFL	2	15	8	53.3	97	0	0	6.47	3	31	10.3	1	1	6	1
1980—Atlanta NFL	3	3	2	66.7	24	0	0	8.00		None			0	0	0
1981—Atlanta NFL	3	26	12	46.2	132	0	1	5.08	3	17	5.7	0	0	0	0
1982—Atlanta NFL	9	13	10	76.9	87	1	0	6.69		None			0	0	2
1983—Atlanta NFL	16	70	45	64.3	575	2	4	8.21	2	12	6.0	0	0	0	2
1984—Atlanta NFL	16	191	102	53.4	1207	2	9	6.32	21	98	4.7	0	0	0	6
1985—Houston NFL	5	34	20	58.4	249	1	1	7.32	2	2	1.0	0	0	0	0
Pro Totals—7 Years	54	352	199	56.5	2371	6	15	6.74	31	160	5.2	1	1	6	9

Quarterback Rating Points: 1979 (73.5), 1980 (91.0), 1981 (45.9), 1982 (119.7), 1983 (75.6), 1984 (56.8), 1985 (79.2). Total—65.0.

Additional pro statistics: Recovered two fumbles, 1984.

KYLE DOUGLAS MORRELL

Name pronounced More-EL.

Safety—Minnesota Vikings

Born October 9, 1963, at Scottsdale, Ariz.
Height, 6.01. Weight, 189.
High School—Bountiful, Utah, Viewmont.
Attended Brigham Young University.

Selected by Minnesota in 4th round (106th player selected) of 1985 NFL draft.
Signed by Minnesota Vikings, August 7, 1985.
On injured reserve with knee injury, August 27 through entire 1985 season.

DAVE MORRILL

Nose Tackle—Cleveland Browns

Born April 27, 1963, at Dayton, O.
Height, 6.02. Weight, 260.
High School—Centerville, O.
Attended Ohio State University.

Selected by New Jersey in 1985 USFL territorial draft.
Signed as free agent by Cleveland Browns, May 6, 1985.
On injured reserve with knee injury, August 27 through entire 1985 season.

DWAINE MORRIS

Defensive Tackle—Philadelphia Eagles

Born August 24, 1963, at Independence, La.
Height, 6.02. Weight, 260.
High School—Greensburg, La.
Attended University of Southwestern Louisiana.

Signed as free agent by Philadelphia Eagles, July 22, 1985.
On injured reserve with hip injury, September 13 through remainder of 1985 season.
Philadelphia NFL, 1985.
Games: 1985 (1).

JOSEPH MORRIS

(Joe)

Running Back—New York Giants

Born September 15, 1960, at Fort Bragg, N.C.
Height, 5.07. Weight, 195.
High Schools—Southern Pines, N.C. and Ayer, Mass.
Attended Syracuse University.
Brother of Jamie Morris, running back at University of Michigan.

Selected by New York Giants in 2nd round (45th player selected) of 1982 NFL draft.

Year Club	G.	Att.	Yds.	Avg.	TD.	P.C.	Yds.	Avg.	TD.	TD.	Pts.	F.
		RUSHING				PASS RECEIVING				TOTAL		
1982—New York Giants NFL	5	15	48	3.2	1	8	34	4.3	0	1	6	1
1983—New York Giants NFL	15	35	145	4.1	0	2	1	0.5	1	1	6	2
1984—New York Giants NFL	16	133	510	3.8	4	12	124	10.3	0	4	24	1
1985—New York Giants NFL	16	294	1336	4.5	*21	22	212	9.6	0	*21	126	6
Pro Totals—4 Years	52	477	2039	4.3	26	44	371	8.4	1	27	162	10

Year Club	G.	No.	Yds.	Avg.	TD.
		KICKOFF RETURNS			
1982—New York Giants NFL	5		None		
1983—New York Giants NFL	15	14	255	18.2	0
1984—New York Giants NFL	16	6	69	11.5	0
1985—New York Giants NFL	16	2	25	12.5	0
Pro Totals—4 Years	52	22	349	15.9	0

Additional pro statistics: Recovered one fumble, 1982 and 1983; recovered two fumbles, 1985.
Played in Pro Bowl (NFL All-Star Game) following 1985 season.

RANDALL MORRIS
Running Back—Seattle Seahawks
Born April 22, 1961, at Anniston, Ala.
Height, 6.00. Weight, 190.
High School—Long Beach, Calif., Polytechnic.
Attended University of Tennessee.
Brother of Thomas Morris, safety with Tampa Bay Buccaneers, 1982 and 1983.
Selected by Memphis in 1984 USFL territorial draft.
Selected by Seattle in 10th round (270th player selected) of 1984 NFL draft.
Signed by Seattle Seahawks, May 18, 1984.
On injured reserve with neck injury, August 28 through September 27, 1984; activated, September 28, 1984.

		—RUSHING—				PASS RECEIVING				—TOTAL—		
Year Club	G.	Att.	Yds.	Avg.	TD.	P.C.	Yds.	Avg.	TD.	TD.	Pts.	F.
1984—Seattle NFL	10	58	189	3.3	0	9	61	6.8	0	0	0	2
1985—Seattle NFL	16	55	236	4.3	0	6	14	2.3	0	0	0	4
Pro Totals—2 Years	26	113	425	3.8	0	15	75	5.0	0	0	0	6

		KICKOFF RETURNS			
Year Club	G.	No.	Yds.	Avg.	TD.
1984—Seattle NFL	10	8	153	19.1	0
1985—Seattle NFL	16	31	636	20.5	0
Pro Totals—2 Years	26	39	789	20.2	0

Additional pro statistics: Recovered one fumble, 1984; attempted one pass with no completions, 1985.

GUY WALKER MORRISS
Center-Guard—New England Patriots
Born May 13, 1951, at Colorado City, Tex.
Height, 6.04. Weight, 255.
High School—Arlington, Tex., Sam Houston.
Received bachelor of science degree in physical education from Texas Christian University in 1973.
Selected by Philadelphia in 2nd round (28th player selected) of 1973 NFL draft.
Released by Philadelphia Eagles, March 5, 1984; signed as free agent by New England Patriots, July 31, 1984.
Philadelphia NFL, 1973 through 1983; New England NFL, 1984 and 1985.
Games: 1973 (14), 1974 (14), 1975 (14), 1976 (13), 1977 (16), 1978 (16), 1979 (16), 1980 (16), 1981 (16), 1982 (9), 1983 (16), 1984 (16), 1985 (16). Total—190.
Pro statistics: Recovered one fumble, 1973; fumbled twice and recovered two fumbles for minus 10 yards, 1974; fumbled twice and recovered one fumble, 1975; fumbled once, 1977 and 1983; fumbled twice for minus eight yards, 1981.
Played in NFC Championship Game following 1980 season.
Played in AFC Championship Game following 1985 season.
Played in NFL Championship Game following 1980 and 1985 seasons.

JAMES MORRISSEY
(Jim)
Linebacker—Chicago Bears
Born December 24, 1962, at Flint, Mich.
Height, 6.03. Weight, 215.
High School—Flint, Mich., Powers.
Attended Michigan State University.
Selected by Baltimore in 8th round (106th player selected) of 1985 USFL draft.
Selected by Chicago in 11th round (302nd player selected) of 1985 NFL draft.
Signed by Chicago Bears, June 26, 1985.
Released by Chicago Bears, September 2, 1985; re-signed by Bears, September 10, 1985.
Chicago NFL, 1985.
Games: 1985 (15).
Played in NFC Championship Game following 1985 season.
Played in NFL Championship Game following 1985 season.

STEVEN BRYAN MORSE
(Steve)
Running Back—Pittsburgh Steelers
Born May 28, 1963, at Mobile, Ala.
Height, 5.11. Weight, 214.
High School—Mobile, Ala., John S. Shaw.
Received bachelor of science degree in chemical engineering
from University of Virginia in 1985.
Signed as free agent by Pittsburgh Steelers, June 10, 1985.
Released by Pittsburgh Steelers, September 2, 1985; re-signed by Steelers, September 3, 1985.

		—RUSHING—				PASS RECEIVING				—TOTAL—		
Year Club	G.	Att.	Yds.	Avg.	TD.	P.C.	Yds.	Avg.	TD.	TD.	Pts.	F.
1985—Pittsburgh NFL	16	8	17	2.1	0	None				0	0	0

Additional pro statistics: Recovered one fumble, 1985.

DONALD HOWARD MOSEBAR
(Don)
Center—Los Angeles Raiders
Born September 11, 1961, at Yakima, Calif.
Height, 6.06. Weight, 270.
High School—Visalia, Calif., Mount Whitney.
Attended University of Southern California.

Selected by Los Angeles in 1983 USFL territorial draft.
Selected by Los Angeles Raiders in 1st round (26th player selected) of 1983 NFL draft.
Signed by Los Angeles Raiders, August 29, 1983.
Granted roster exemption, August 29, 1983; activated, September 9, 1983.
On injured reserve with back injury, November 8 through remainder of 1984 season.
Los Angeles Raiders NFL, 1983 through 1985.
Games: 1983 (14), 1984 (10), 1985 (16). Total—40.
Played in AFC Championship Game following 1983 season.
Played in NFL Championship Game following 1983 season.

MARK DeWAYNE MOSELEY
Placekicker—Washington Redskins
Born March 12, 1948, at Lanesville, Tex.
Height, 6.00. Weight, 205.
High School—Livingston, Tex.
Attended Texas A&M University and Stephen F. Austin College.

Established NFL records for most consecutive field goals (23), 1981-82; highest field goal percentage, season (95.24), 1982; most points scored by kicker, season (161), 1983.
Named to THE SPORTING NEWS NFC All-Star Team, 1979.
Named THE SPORTING NEWS NFL Player of the Year, 1982.
Selected by Philadelphia in 14th round (346th player selected) of 1970 NFL draft.
Placed on waivers by Philadelphia Eagles and signed by Houston Oilers as free agent, September 13, 1971.
Released by Houston Oilers, 1973; signed as free agent by Washington Redskins, February 1, 1974.

		PLACE KICKING							PLACE KICKING			
Year Club	G.	XP.	XPM.	FG.	FGA.	Pts.	Year Club	G.	XP.	XPM.	FG.	FGA.	Pts.
1970—Philadelphia NFL ...	14	25	3	14	25	67	1979—Washington NFL	16	39	0	*25	*33	114
1971—Houston NFL	12	25	2	16	26	73	1980—Washington NFL	16	27	3	18	33	81
1972—Houston NFL	1	2	0	1	2	5	1981—Washington NFL	16	38	4	19	30	95
1974—Washington NFL	13	27	2	17	30	81	1982—Washington NFL	9	16	3	*20	21	76
1975—Washington NFL	14	37	2	16	25	85	1983—Washington NFL	16	*62	1	33	*47	*161
1976—Washington NFL	14	31	1	*22	34	97	1984—Washington NFL	16	48	3	24	31	120
1977—Washington NFL	14	19	0	*21	*37	82	1985—Washington NFL	16	31	2	22	34	97
1978—Washington NFL	16	30	1	19	30	87	Pro Totals—15 Years	203	457	27	288	438	1321

Additional pro statistics: Punted 10 times for 35.0 average and recovered one fumble, 1970.
Played in NFC Championship Game following 1982 and 1983 seasons.
Played in NFL Championship Game following 1982 and 1983 seasons.
Played in Pro Bowl (NFL All-Star Game) following 1979 and 1982 seasons.

MARTIN MOSS
Defensive End
Born December 16, 1958, at San Diego, Calif.
Height, 6.04. Weight, 252.
High School—San Diego, Calif., Lincoln.
Received bachelor of arts degree in sociology from
University of California at Los Angeles in 1982.

Selected by Detroit in 8th round (208th player selected) of 1982 NFL draft.
On injured reserve with shoulder injury, October 10 through December 4, 1985; activated after clearing procedural waivers, December 6, 1985.
Granted free agency with no qualifying offer, February 1, 1986.
Detroit NFL, 1982 through 1985.
Games: 1982 (5), 1983 (15), 1984 (16), 1985 (6). Total—42.

WALTER STEPHEN MOTT III
(Steve)
Center—Detroit Lions
Born March 24, 1961, at New Orleans, La.
Height, 6.03. Weight, 265.
High School—Marrero, La., Archbishop Shaw.
Attended University of Alabama.

Selected by Birmingham in 1983 USFL territorial draft.
Selected by Detroit in 5th round (121st player selected) of 1983 NFL draft.
Signed by Detroit Lions, June 1, 1983.
On physically unable to perform/active with knee injury, July 22 through August 8, 1984; activated, August 9, 1984.
On injured reserve with dislocated ankle, October 8 through remainder of 1984 season.
Detroit NFL, 1983 through 1985.
Games: 1983 (13), 1984 (6), 1985 (16). Total—35.
Pro statistics: Fumbled once, 1983; recovered one fumble, 1985.

ZEKE MOWATT
Tight End—New York Giants
Born March 5, 1961, at Wauchula, Fla.
Height, 6.03. Weight, 238.
High School—Wauchula, Fla., Hardee County.
Attended Florida State University.

Selected by Tampa Bay in 1983 USFL territorial draft.
Signed as free agent by New York Giants, June 1, 1983.
On injured reserve with knee injury, August 31 through entire 1985 season.

Year Club	G.	P.C.	Yds.	Avg.	TD.
1983—New York Giants NFL	16	21	280	13.3	1
1984—New York Giants NFL	16	48	698	14.5	6
Pro Totals—2 Years............	32	69	978	14.2	7

ALEX MOYER III
Linebacker—Miami Dolphins
Born October 25, 1963, at Detroit, Mich.
Height, 6.01. Weight, 221.
High School—Delafield, Wis., St. John's Military.
Attended Northwestern University.

Selected by Birmingham in 7th round (100th player selected) of 1985 USFL draft.
Selected by Miami in 3rd round (83rd player selected) of 1985 NFL draft.
Signed by Miami Dolphins, July 19, 1985.
On injured reserve with thigh injury, September 4 through October 18, 1985; activated, October 19, 1985.
Miami NFL, 1985.
Games: 1985 (10).
Pro statistics: Intercepted one pass for four yards and recovered one fumble, 1985.
Played in AFC Championship Game following 1985 season.

PAUL STEWART MOYER
Safety—Seattle Seahawks
Born July 26, 1961, at Villa Park, Calif.
Height, 6.01. Weight, 201.
High School—Villa Park, Calif.
Attended Fullerton College and Arizona State University.

Signed as free agent by Seattle Seahawks, April 28, 1983.
On injured reserve with shoulder injury, September 11 through October 17, 1985; activated, October 18, 1985.

Year Club	G.	No.	Yds.	Avg.	TD.
1983—Seattle NFL..................	16	1	19	19.0	1
1984—Seattle NFL..................	16		None		
1985—Seattle NFL..................	11		None		
Pro Totals—3 Years............	43	1	19	19.0	1

Additional pro statistics: Recovered three fumbles, 1983.
Played in AFC Championship Game following 1983 season.

CALVIN SALEEM MUHAMMAD
(Formerly known as Calvin Vincent Rainey.)
Wide Receiver—Washington Redskins
Born December 10, 1958, at Jacksonville, Fla.
Height, 5.11. Weight, 190.
High School—Jacksonville, Fla., William M. Raines.
Attended Texas Southern University.

Signed by Toronto Argonauts, April 10, 1980.
Selected by Oakland in 12th round (322nd player selected) of 1980 NFL draft.
On injured list, July 8 through entire 1980 season.
Released by Toronto Argonauts, June 29, 1981; signed by Oakland Raiders, July, 1981.
On injured reserve with knee injury, August 15 through entire 1981 season.
Franchise transferred to Los Angeles, May 7, 1982.
On injured reserve with dislocated shoulder, August 28 through October 2, 1984; activated, October 3, 1984.
Traded by Los Angeles Raiders to Washington Redskins for 4th round pick in 1985 draft, October 3, 1984.
On injured reserve with sprained ankle, November 27 through remainder of 1985 season.

Year Club	G.	P.C.	Yds.	Avg.	TD.
1982—L.A. Raiders NFL.........	8	3	92	30.7	1
1983—L.A. Raiders NFL.........	15	13	252	19.4	2
1984—Washington NFL..........	10	42	729	17.4	4
1985—Washington NFL..........	12	9	116	12.9	1
Pro Totals—4 Years............	45	67	1189	17.7	8

Additional pro statistics: Fumbled twice, 1983; recovered two fumbles and fumbled once, 1984.
Played in AFC Championship Game following 1983 season.
Played in NFL Championship Game following 1983 season.

MICHAEL RENE MULARKEY
(Mike)
Tight End—Minnesota Vikings
Born November 19, 1961, at Miami, Fla.
Height, 6.04. Weight, 233.
High School—Fort Lauderdale, Fla., Northeast.
Attended University of Florida.

Selected by Tampa Bay in 1983 USFL territorial draft.
Selected by San Francisco in 9th round (229th player selected) of 1983 NFL draft.
Signed by San Francisco 49ers, June 1, 1983.
Released by San Francisco 49ers, August 29, 1983; awarded on waivers to Minnesota Vikings, August 30, 1983.
On injured reserve with ankle injury, September 30 through remainder of 1983 season.

		—PASS RECEIVING—			
Year Club	G.	P.C.	Yds.	Avg.	TD.
1983—Minnesota NFL............	3	None			
1984—Minnesota NFL............	16	14	134	9.6	2
1985—Minnesota NFL............	15	13	196	15.1	1
Pro Totals—3 Years............	34	27	330	12.2	3

Additional pro statistics: Recovered one fumble and fumbled once, 1984; ran nine yards with lateral on kickoff return, 1985.

MARK ALAN MULLANEY
Defensive End—Minnesota Vikings
Born April 30, 1953, at Denver, Colo.
Height, 6.06. Weight, 245.
High School—Denver, Colo., George Washington.
Received degree in humanities and social science from Colorado State University.

Selected by Minnesota in 1st round (25th player selected) of 1975 NFL draft.
On injured reserve with broken collarbone, September 30 through December 4, 1983; activated, December 5, 1983.
On injured reserve with nerve damage in neck, November 23 through remainder of 1984 season.
Minnesota NFL, 1975 through 1985.
Games: 1975 (14), 1976 (12), 1977 (14), 1978 (15), 1979 (16), 1980 (16), 1981 (15), 1982 (9), 1983 (7), 1984 (7), 1985 (15). Total—140.
Pro statistics: Recovered two fumbles for three yards, 1976; recovered one fumble, 1978, 1980, 1981 and 1983; intercepted one pass for 15 yards and recovered two fumbles, 1985.
Played in NFC Championship Game following 1976 and 1977 seasons.
Played in NFL Championship Game following 1976 season.

DAVLIN MULLEN
Cornerback—New York Jets
Born February 17, 1960, at McKeesport, Pa.
Height, 6.01. Weight, 177.
High School—Clairton, Pa.
Attended Western Kentucky University.

Selected by New York Jets in 8th round (217th player selected) of 1983 NFL draft.
On injured reserve with turf toe, September 3 through October 9, 1985; activated after clearing procedural waivers, October 11, 1985.

		INTERCEPTIONS				–PUNT RETURNS–				—KICKOFF RET.—				—TOTAL—		
Year Club	G.	No.	Yds.	Avg.	TD.	No.	Yds.	Avg.	TD.	No.	Yds.	Avg.	TD.	TD.	Pts.	F.
1983—New York Jets NFL	11	None				2	13	6.5	0	3	57	19.0	0	0	0	1
1984—New York Jets NFL	15	1	25	25.0	0	1	8	8.0	0	2	34	17.0	0	0	0	0
1985—New York Jets NFL	11	3	14	4.7	0	None				None				0	0	0
Pro Totals—3 Years.......	37	4	39	9.8	0	3	21	7.0	0	5	91	18.2	0	0	0	1

TONY V. MUMFORD
Running Back—St. Louis Cardinals
Born June 14, 1963, at Philadelphia, Pa.
Height, 6.00. Weight, 215.
High School—Pine Hill, N.J., Overbrook Regional.
Attended Penn State University.
Cousin of Lloyd Mumford, defensive back with Miami Dolphins
and Baltimore Colts, 1969 through 1978.

Selected by Baltimore in 1985 USFL territorial draft.
Selected by New England in 12th round (328th player selected) of 1985 NFL draft.
Signed by New England Patriots, July 19, 1985.
Released by New England Patriots, August 28, 1985; signed as free agent by St. Louis Cardinals, November 20, 1985.
St. Louis NFL, 1985.
Games: 1985 (2).
Pro statistics: Returned one kickoff for 19 yards and fumbled once, 1985.

MIKE MUNCHAK
Guard—Houston Oilers
Born March 5, 1960, at Scranton, Pa.
Height, 6.03. Weight, 286.
High School—Scranton, Pa., Central.
Received bachelor of business administration degree from Penn State University in 1982.

Selected by Houston in 1st round (8th player selected) of 1982 NFL draft.
On injured reserve with broken ankle, November 24 through December 23, 1982; activated, December 24, 1982.
Houston NFL, 1982 through 1985.
Games: 1982 (4), 1983 (16), 1984 (16), 1985 (16). Total—52.
Pro statistics: Recovered two fumbles for three yards, 1985.
Played in Pro Bowl (NFL All-Star Game) following 1984 and 1985 seasons.

MICHAEL ANTHONY MUNOZ
(Known by middle name.)
Offensive Tackle—Cincinnati Bengals
Born August 19, 1958, at Ontario, Calif.
Height, 6.06. Weight, 278.
High School—Ontario, Calif., Chaffey.
Received bachelor of science degree in public administration from
University of Southern California in 1980.
Named to THE SPORTING NEWS NFL All-Star Team, 1981, 1984 and 1985.
Selected by Cincinnati in 1st round (3rd player selected) of 1980 NFL draft.
Cincinnati NFL, 1980 through 1985.
Games: 1980 (16), 1981 (16), 1982 (9), 1983 (16), 1984 (16), 1985 (16). Total—89.
Pro statistics: Caught one pass for minus six yards, 1980; caught one pass for one yard and a touchdown and recovered one fumble, 1984; caught one pass for one yard, 1985.
Played in AFC Championship Game following 1981 season.
Played in NFL Championship Game following 1981 season.
Played in Pro Bowl (NFL All-Star Game) following 1981 and 1983 through 1985 seasons.

DAVID MICHAEL MURPHY
(Dave)
Wide Receiver—Pittsburgh Steelers
Born September 11, 1963, at Pittsburgh, Pa.
Height, 6.02. Weight, 195.
High School—Mechanicsburg, Pa., Cumberland Valley.
Received bachelor of science degree in marketing management
from Juniata College in 1985.
Signed as free agent by Pittsburgh Steelers, June 20, 1985.
On injured reserve with knee injury, August 20 through entire 1985 season.

MARK STEVEN MURPHY
Safety—Green Bay Packers
Born April 22, 1958, at Canton, O.
Height, 6.02. Weight, 199.
High School—Canton, O., Glen Oaks.
Received bachelor of science degree in business administration from West Liberty State College.
Signed as free agent by Green Bay Packers, April 25, 1980.
On injured reserve with broken hand, August 14 through December 17, 1980; activated after clearing procedural waivers, December 19, 1980.

Year Club	G.	No.	Yds.	Avg.	TD.
		—INTERCEPTIONS—			
1980—Green Bay NFL............	1	None			
1981—Green Bay NFL............	16	3	57	19.0	0
1982—Green Bay NFL............	9	None			
1983—Green Bay NFL............	16	None			
1984—Green Bay NFL............	16	1	4	4.0	0
1985—Green Bay NFL............	15	2	50	25.0	*1
Pro Totals—6 Years............	73	6	111	18.5	1

Additional pro statistics: Recovered two fumbles, 1981; recovered one fumble, 1983 and 1985; recovered one fumble for two yards and fumbled once, 1984; returned one punt for four yards, 1985.

EDWARD PETER MURRAY
(Ed)
Placekicker—Detroit Lions
Born August 29, 1956, at Halifax, Nova Scotia.
Height, 5.10. Weight, 175.
High School—Victoria, British Columbia, Spectrum.
Received bachelor of science degree in education from Tulane University in 1980.
Cousin of Mike Rogers, center with Edmonton Oilers of NHL.
Selected by Detroit in 7th round (166th player selected) of 1980 NFL draft.
On suspended list, September 10 through November 19, 1982; reinstated, November 20, 1982.

Year Club	G.	XP.	XPM.	FG.	FGA.	Pts.
		—PLACE KICKING—				
1980—Detroit NFL..............	16	35	1	*27	*42	116
1981—Detroit NFL..............	16	46	0	25	35	*121
1982—Detroit NFL..............	7	16	0	11	12	49
1983—Detroit NFL..............	16	38	0	25	32	113
1984—Detroit NFL..............	16	31	0	20	27	91
1985—Detroit NFL..............	16	31	2	26	31	109
Pro Totals—6 Years.......	87	197	3	134	179	599

Played in Pro Bowl (NFL All-Star Game) following 1980 season.

GREG NARON
Guard—Philadelphia Eagles
Born October 21, 1963, at Guilford County, N.C.
Height, 6.04. Weight, 270.
High School—Randleman, N.C.
Attended University of North Carolina.

Selected by Baltimore in 1985 USFL territorial draft.
Selected by Philadelphia in 4th round (93rd player selected) of 1985 NFL draft.
Signed by Philadelphia Eagles, July 28, 1985.
On injured reserve with knee injury, September 3 through entire 1985 season.

JOSEPH ANDREW NASH
(Joe)
Nose Tackle—Seattle Seahawks
Born October 11, 1960, at Boston, Mass.
Height, 6.03. Weight, 250.
High School—Dorchester, Mass., Boston College High.
Received bachelor of arts degree in sociology from Boston College in 1982.

Signed as free agent by Seattle Seahawks, April 30, 1982.
On inactive list, September 12 and September 19, 1982.
Seattle NFL, 1982 through 1985.
Games: 1982 (7), 1983 (16), 1984 (16), 1985 (16). Total—55.
Pro statistics: Recovered three fumbles (including one in end zone for a touchdown), 1984.
Played in AFC Championship Game following 1983 season.
Played in Pro Bowl (NFL All-Star Game) following 1984 season.

TONY CURTIS NATHAN
Running Back—Miami Dolphins
Born December 14, 1956, at Birmingham, Ala.
Height, 6.00. Weight, 206.
High School—Birmingham, Ala., Woodlawn.
Attended University of Alabama.

Named as punt returner on THE SPORTING NEWS AFC All-Star Team, 1979.
Selected by Miami in 3rd round (61st player selected) of 1979 NFL draft.

		—RUSHING—				PASS RECEIVING				—TOTAL—		
Year Club	G.	Att.	Yds.	Avg.	TD.	P.C.	Yds.	Avg.	TD.	TD.	Pts.	F.
1979—Miami NFL	16	16	68	4.3	0	17	213	12.5	2	3	18	8
1980—Miami NFL	16	60	327	5.5	1	57	588	10.3	5	6	36	9
1981—Miami NFL	13	147	782	*5.3	5	50	452	9.0	3	8	48	2
1982—Miami NFL	8	66	233	3.5	1	16	114	7.1	0	1	6	2
1983—Miami NFL	16	151	685	4.5	3	52	461	8.9	1	4	24	2
1984—Miami NFL	16	118	558	4.7	1	61	579	9.5	2	3	18	3
1985—Miami NFL	16	143	667	4.7	5	72	651	9.0	1	6	36	7
Pro Totals—7 Years	101	701	3320	4.7	16	325	3058	9.4	14	31	186	33

		—PUNT RETURNS—				—KICKOFF RET.—		
Year Club	G.	No.	Yds.	Avg.	TD.	No.	Yds.	Avg.TD.
1979—Miami NFL	16	28	306	10.9	1	45	1016	22.6 0
1980—Miami NFL	16	23	178	7.7	0	5	102	20.4 0
1981—Miami NFL	13		None				None	
1982—Miami NFL	8		None				None	
1983—Miami NFL	16		None				None	
1984—Miami NFL	16		None				None	
1985—Miami NFL	16		None				None	
Pro Totals—7 Years	101	51	484	9.5	1	50	1118	22.4 0

Additional pro statistics: Recovered one fumble, 1980, 1984 and 1985; attempted one pass with no completions, 1980; recovered two fumbles and attempted one pass with no completions, 1981; attempted two passes with one completion for 15 yards and one touchdown, 1982; attempted four passes with three completions for 46 yards and returned three kickoffs for 15 yards, 1983.
Played in AFC Championship Game following 1982, 1984 and 1985 seasons.
Played in NFL Championship Game following 1982 and 1984 seasons.

ROBERT NEAL
(Speedy)
Fullback—Miami Dolphins
Born August 26, 1962, at Key West, Fla.
Height, 6.02. Weight, 254.
High School—Key West, Fla.
Attended University of Miami (Fla.).

Selected by Tampa Bay in 4th round (77th player selected) of 1984 USFL draft.
Selected by Buffalo in 3rd round (82nd player selected) of 1984 NFL draft.
Signed by Buffalo Bills, July 19, 1984.
Released by Buffalo Bills, August 20, 1985; signed as free agent by Miami Dolphins, May 21, 1986.

		—RUSHING—				PASS RECEIVING				—TOTAL—		
Year Club	G.	Att.	Yds.	Avg.	TD.	P.C.	Yds.	Avg.	TD.	TD.	Pts.	F.
1984—Buffalo NFL	12	49	175	3.6	1	9	76	8.4	0	1	6	0

RENALDO NEHEMIAH
Wide Receiver—San Francisco 49ers
Born March 24, 1959, at Newark, N.J.
Height, 6.01. Weight, 183.
High School—Scotch Plains, N.J., Fanwood.
Attended University of Maryland.

Signed as free agent by San Francisco 49ers, April 16, 1982.
On injured reserve with back injury, August 20 through entire 1985 season.

		——PASS RECEIVING——				
Year	Club	G.	P.C.	Yds.	Avg.	TD.
1982—San Francisco NFL		8	8	161	20.1	1
1983—San Francisco NFL		16	17	236	13.9	1
1984—San Francisco NFL		16	18	357	19.8	2
Pro Totals—3 Years...........		40	43	754	17.5	4

Additional pro statistics: Rushed once for minus one yard, 1982; fumbled once, 1983.
Played in NFC Championship Game following 1983 and 1984 seasons.
Played in NFL Championship Game following 1984 season.

CHARLES LaVERNE NELSON
(Chuck)
Placekicker—Minnesota Vikings
Born February 23, 1960, at Seattle, Wash.
Height, 5.11. Weight, 175.
High School—Everett, Wash.
Attended University of Washington.

Named as placekicker on THE SPORTING NEWS College All-America Team, 1982.
Selected by Chicago in 23rd round (270th player selected) of 1983 USFL draft.
Selected by Los Angeles Rams in 4th round (87th player selected) of 1983 NFL draft.
Signed by Los Angeles Rams, July 13, 1983.
Released by Los Angeles Rams, August 27, 1984; signed as free agent by Buffalo Bills, October 30, 1984.
Released by Buffalo Bills, August 19, 1985; signed as free agent by Minnesota Vikings, March 18, 1986.

		——PLACE KICKING——					
Year	Club	G.	XP.	XPM.	FG.	FGA.	Pts.
1983—L. A. Rams NFL		12	33	*4	5	11	48
1984—Buffalo NFL..............		7	14	0	3	5	23
Pro Totals—2 Years.......		19	47	4	8	16	71

Additional pro statistics: Recovered one fumble, 1983.

CURTIS SHANE NELSON
(Known by middle name.)
Linebacker—San Diego Chargers
Born May 25, 1955, at Mathis, Tex.
Height, 6.00. Weight, 238.
High School—Mathis, Tex.
Attended Blinn Junior College and Baylor University.

Signed as free agent by Buffalo Bills, June, 1977.
On injured reserve with knee injury, November 6 through December 10, 1981; activated, December 11, 1981.
On injured reserve with knee injury, December 18 through remainder of 1981 season.
On injured reserve with knee injury, September 14 through remainder of 1982 season.
Released by Buffalo Bills after failing physical, August 30, 1983; signed as free agent by San Diego Chargers, February 26, 1985.
On injured reserve with ruptured Achilles tendon, September 2 through entire 1985 season.

		——INTERCEPTIONS——				
Year	Club	G.	No.	Yds.	Avg.	TD.
1977—Buffalo NFL...................		14		None		
1978—Buffalo NFL...................		16	3	69	23.0	0
1979—Buffalo NFL...................		16	1	13	13.0	0
1980—Buffalo NFL...................		16		None		
1981—Buffalo NFL...................		10		None		
1982—Buffalo NFL...................		1		None		
Pro Totals—6 Years...........		73	4	82	20.5	0

Additional pro statistics: Recovered two fumbles, 1977 and 1980; recovered one fumble, 1978 and 1979.

COACHING RECORD
Assistant freshman coach at Cornell University, 1984.

—DID YOU KNOW—

That Washington rookie Barry Wilburn cost teammate Darrell Green two touchdowns on punt returns in consecutive games last season? On December 8 at Philadelphia, Wilburn was penalized for an illegal block that nullified an 89-yard run by Green. On December 15 vs. Cincinnati, Wilburn was called for unneccessary roughness and Green lost a 77-yard touchdown run.

DARRIN MILO NELSON
Running Back—Minnesota Vikings
Born January 2, 1959, at Sacramento, Calif.
Height, 5.09. Weight, 185.
High School—Downey, Calif., Pius X.
Received bachelor of science degree in urban and environmental planning
from Stanford University in 1981.
Brother of Kevin Nelson, running back with Los Angeles Express, 1984 and 1985;
cousin of Ozzie Newsome, tight end with Cleveland Browns; and
Carlos Carson, wide receiver with Kansas City Chiefs.
Selected by Minnesota in 1st round (7th player selected) of 1982 NFL draft.

Year Club	G.	Att.	Yds.	Avg.	TD.	P.C.	Yds.	Avg.	TD.	TD.	Pts.	F.
			RUSHING			PASS RECEIVING				TOTAL		
1982—Minnesota NFL	7	44	136	3.1	0	9	100	11.1	0	0	0	2
1983—Minnesota NFL	15	154	642	4.2	1	51	618	12.1	0	1	6	5
1984—Minnesota NFL	15	80	406	5.1	3	27	162	6.0	1	4	24	4
1985—Minnesota NFL	16	200	893	4.5	5	43	301	7.0	1	6	36	7
Pro Totals—4 Years	53	478	2077	4.3	9	130	1181	9.1	2	11	66	18

Year Club	G.	No.	Yds.	Avg.	TD.	No.	Yds.	Avg.	TD.
		PUNT RETURNS				KICKOFF RET.			
1982—Minnesota NFL	7		None			6	132	22.0	0
1983—Minnesota NFL	15		None			18	445	24.7	0
1984—Minnesota NFL	15	23	180	7.8	0	39	891	22.8	0
1985—Minnesota NFL	16	16	133	8.3	0	3	51	17.0	0
Pro Totals—4 Years	53	39	313	8.0	0	66	1519	23.0	0

Additional pro statistics: Recovered one fumble, 1983; recovered three fumbles, 1984; recovered two fumbles for 16 yards, 1985.

DERALD LAWRENCE NELSON
(Derrie)
Linebacker—San Diego Chargers
Born February 8, 1958, at York, Neb.
Height, 6.02. Weight, 234.
High School—Fairmont, Neb.
Attended University of Nebraska.
Nephew of Bob Cerv, outfielder-first baseman with New York Yankees,
Kansas City A's and Houston Colt .45s, 1951 through 1962;
and cousin of Eric Swanson, rookie wide receiver with St. Louis Cardinals.
Selected by Dallas in 4th round (108th player selected) of 1981 NFL draft.
Released by Dallas Cowboys, August 14, 1981; signed as free agent by Cleveland Browns, August 21, 1981.
Released by Cleveland Browns, August 24, 1981; signed as free agent by San Diego Chargers, March 30, 1982.
On injured reserve with hip pointer, August 31 through entire 1982 season.
On injured reserve with finger nerve injury, August 20 through November 7, 1984; activated after clearing procedural waivers, November 9, 1984.
San Diego NFL, 1983 through 1985.
Games: 1983 (15), 1984 (6), 1985 (16). Total—37.
Pro statistics: Ran 21 yards with blocked punt for a touchdown, 1983.

EDMUND CLAU-VON NELSON
Defensive End-Defensive Tackle—Pittsburgh Steelers
Born April 30, 1960, at Live Oak, Fla.
Height, 6.03. Weight, 278.
High School—Tampa, Fla., C. Leon King.
Received bachelor of science degree in personnel management
and industrial relations from Auburn University.
Selected by Pittsburgh in 7th round (172nd player selected) of 1982 NFL draft.
On injured reserve with calf injury, November 15 through remainder of 1985 season.
Pittsburgh NFL, 1982 through 1985.
Games: 1982 (8), 1983 (16), 1984 (16), 1985 (6). Total—46.
Pro statistics: Recovered one fumble, 1982.
Played in AFC Championship Game following 1984 season.

KARL NELSON
Offensive Tackle—New York Giants
Born June 14, 1960, at DeKalb, Ill.
Height, 6.06. Weight, 285.
High School—DeKalb, Ill.
Attended Iowa State University.
Selected by Tampa Bay in 4th round (44th player selected) of 1983 USFL draft.
Selected by New York Giants in 3rd round (70th player selected) of 1983 NFL draft.
Signed by New York Giants, June 13, 1983.
On injured reserve with foot injury, August 23 through entire 1983 season.
New York Giants NFL, 1984 and 1985.
Games: 1984 (16), 1985 (16). Total—32.
Pro statistics: Recovered one fumble, 1985.

LEE MARTIN NELSON
Safety—St. Louis Cardinals
Born January 30, 1954, at Kissimmee, Fla.
Height, 5.10. Weight, 185.
High School—Melbourne, Fla.
Attended Pensacola Junior College and Florida State University.

Selected by St. Louis in 15th round (420th player selected) of 1976 NFL draft.
On injured reserve, November 22 through remainder of 1977 season.
Released by St. Louis Cardinals, September 2, 1985; re-signed by Cardinals, September 11, 1985.

Year Club	G.	No.	Yds.	Avg.	TD.	No.	Yds.	Avg.	TD.	TD.	Pts.	F.
			-INTERCEPTIONS-				—KICKOFF RET.—				—TOTAL—	
1976—St. Louis NFL	14			None		1	43	43.0	0	0	0	0
1977—St. Louis NFL	10	4	37	9.3	0	3	68	22.7	0	0	0	0
1978—St. Louis NFL	16	1	—3	—3.0	0	3	58	19.3	0	0	0	0
1979—St. Louis NFL	16			None				None		0	0	0
1980—St. Louis NFL	16			None		1	29	29.0	0	0	0	0
1981—St. Louis NFL	15			None				None		0	0	0
1982—St. Louis NFL	8	1	7	7.0	0			None		0	0	0
1983—St. Louis NFL	16	1	8	8.0	0			None		0	0	0
1984—St. Louis NFL	16			None				None		0	0	0
1985—St. Louis NFL	13			None		3	49	16.3	0	0	0	1
Pro Totals—10 Years	141	7	49	7.0	0	11	247	22.5	0	0	0	1

Additional pro statistics: Recovered one fumble, 1976, 1979 and 1980; returned one punt for four yards, 1977; returned four punts for 88 yards, 1979; returned one punt for five yards, 1980; recovered two fumbles, 1981; recovered four fumbles for 36 yards and a touchdown, 1983; returned two punts for 14 yards, 1985.

ROBERT LEE NELSON
(Bob)
Linebacker—Los Angeles Raiders
Born June 30, 1953, at Stillwater, Minn.
Height, 6.04. Weight, 235.
High School—Stillwater, Minn.
Received bachelor of science degree in education from University of Nebraska.

Selected by Buffalo in 2nd round (42nd player selected) of 1975 NFL draft.
Missed most of 1975 season due to leg injury (on active roster for 3 games but did not play).
Played out option with Buffalo Bills; signed as free agent by Oakland Raiders, March, 1978.
On injured reserve, August 11 through entire 1978 season.
Released by Oakland Raiders, August 21, 1979; signed as free agent by San Francisco 49ers, November 2, 1979.
On injured reserve with broken arm, November 14 through remainder of 1979 season.
Released by San Francisco 49ers after failing physical, July 19, 1980; signed as free agent by Oakland Raiders, July 25, 1980.
On injured reserve with shoulder injury, October 8 through November 26, 1980; activated, November 27, 1980.
On injured reserve with knee injury, August 25 through entire 1981 season.
Franchise transferred to Los Angeles, May 7, 1982.
On injured reserve with knee injury, November 23 through remainder of 1984 season.
On injured reserve with knee injury, August 20 through entire 1985 season.
Buffalo NFL, 1976 and 1977; San Francisco NFL, 1979; Oakland NFL, 1980; Los Angeles Raiders NFL, 1982 through 1984.
Games: 1976 (14), 1977 (11), 1979 (1), 1980 (9), 1982 (9), 1983 (16), 1984 (12). Total—72.
Pro statistics: Recovered one fumble, 1976 and 1983; returned one kickoff for 10 yards, 1977; intercepted one pass for no yards, 1980.
Played in AFC Championship Game following 1980 and 1983 seasons.
Played in NFL Championship Game following 1980 and 1983 seasons.

ROBERT WILLIAM NELSON
(Bob)
Defensive Tackle—Tampa Bay Buccaneers
Born March 3, 1959, at Baltimore, Md.
Height, 6.03. Weight, 256.
High School—Baltimore, Md., Patapsco.
Attended University of Miami (Fla.).

Selected by Miami in 5th round (120th player selected) of 1982 NFL draft.
Released by Miami Dolphins, September 6, 1982; signed by Chicago Blitz, November 30, 1983.
Traded with running back Kevin McLee and 12th round picks in 1984 and 1985 drafts by Chicago Blitz to Arizona Wranglers for rights to guard Bruce Branch, January 13, 1983.
Franchise transferred to Chicago, September 30, 1983.
Traded by Chicago Blitz to Oklahoma Outlaws for guard Terry Crouch, January 19, 1984.
Not protected in merger of Oklahoma Outlaws and Arizona Wranglers; selected by Jacksonville Bulls in USFL dispersal draft, December 6, 1984.
Granted free agency, August 1, 1985; signed by Tampa Bay Buccaneers, August 6, 1985.
Released by Tampa Bay Buccaneers, September 2, 1985; re-signed by Buccaneers, March 21, 1986.
Arizona USFL, 1983; Oklahoma USFL, 1984; Jacksonville USFL, 1985.
Games: 1983 (18), 1984 (18), 1985 (18). Total—54.
Pro statistics: Credited with six sacks for 44 yards, 1983; recovered two fumbles and credited with 6½ sacks for 43 yards, 1984; credited with 5½ sacks for 37 yards, 1985.

STEVEN LEE NELSON
(Steve)
Linebacker—New England Patriots
Born April 26, 1951, at Farmington, Minn.
Height, 6.02. Weight, 230.
High School—Anoka, Minn.
Attended Augsburg College and received bachelor of science degree in education
from North Dakota State University in 1974.

Named to THE SPORTING NEWS NFL All-Star Team, 1980.
Selected by New England in 2nd round (34th player selected) of 1974 NFL draft.
On injured reserve with knee injury, November 16 through remainder of 1976 season.
On injured reserve with separated shoulder, October 2 through October 30, 1981; activated, October 31, 1981.
On injured reserve with broken thumb, September 28 through November 24, 1983; activated, November 25, 1983.

Year Club	G.	No.	Yds.	Avg.TD.
1974—New England NFL	11			None
1975—New England NFL	14	2	8	4.0 0
1976—New England NFL	10	2	32	16.0 0
1977—New England NFL	13			None
1978—New England NFL	14	5	104	20.8 0
1979—New England NFL	15	1	18	18.0 0
1980—New England NFL	16	3	37	12.3 0
1981—New England NFL	12	1	9	9.0 0
1982—New England NFL	9			None
1983—New England NFL	8	1	6	6.0 0
1984—New England NFL	16	1	0	0.0 0
1985—New England NFL	15			None
Pro Totals—12 Years	153	16	214	13.4 0

Additional pro statistics: Recovered one fumble, 1974, 1977, 1979, 1980 and 1983; recovered three fumbles, 1976 and 1985; recovered four fumbles, 1978.
Played in AFC Championship Game following 1985 season.
Played in NFL Championship Game following 1985 season.
Played in Pro Bowl (NFL All-Star Game) following 1980, 1984 and 1985 seasons.

EDWARD KENNETH NEWMAN
(Ed)
Guard—Miami Dolphins
Born June 4, 1951, at Woodbury, N.Y.
Height, 6.02. Weight, 255.
High School—Syosset, N.Y.
Attended Florida Atlantic University and received bachelor of science degree
in psychology from Duke University.

Selected by Miami in 6th round (156th player selected) of 1973 NFL draft.
On injured reserve with knee injury, November 23 through remainder of 1978 season.
On injured reserve with knee injury, December 31 through remainder of 1982 season.
On injured reserve with knee injury, August 19 through entire 1985 season.
Miami NFL, 1973 through 1984.
Games: 1973 (11), 1974 (14), 1975 (14), 1976 (14), 1977 (14), 1978 (12), 1979 (16), 1980 (16), 1981 (16), 1982 (8), 1983 (16), 1984 (16). Total—167.
Pro statistics: Recovered one fumble, 1974, 1976 and 1978; recovered two fumbles, 1980.
Played in AFC Championship Game following 1973 and 1984 seasons.
Played in NFL Championship Game following 1973 and 1984 seasons.
Played in Pro Bowl (NFL All-Star Game) following 1981, 1983 and 1984 seasons.
Named to Pro Bowl following 1982 season; replaced due to injury by Bob Kuechenberg.

HARRY KENT NEWSOME JR.
Punter—Pittsburgh Steelers
Born January 25, 1963, at Cheraw, S.C.
Height, 6.00. Weight, 187.
High School—Cheraw, S.C.
Attended Wake Forest University.

Selected by New Jersey in 15th round (213th player selected) of 1985 USFL draft.
Selected by Pittsburgh in 8th round (214th player selected) of 1985 NFL draft.
Signed by Pittsburgh Steelers, July 26, 1985.

Year Club	G.	No.	Avg.	Blk.
1985—Pittsburgh NFL	16	78	39.6	1

OZZIE NEWSOME
Tight End—Cleveland Browns
Born March 16, 1956, at Muscle Shoals, Ala.
Height, 6.02. Weight, 232.
High School—Leighton, Ala., Colbert County.
Received bachelor of science degree in recreation and park management from University of Alabama.
Cousin of Darrin Nelson, running back with Minnesota Vikings, and Kevin Nelson,
running back with Los Angeles Express, 1984 and 1985.

Established NFL record for most pass receptions by tight end, career (502).
Named to THE SPORTING NEWS NFL All-Star Team, 1984.
Named to THE SPORTING NEWS AFC All-Star Team, 1979.
Named as wide receiver on THE SPORTING NEWS College All-America Team, 1977.
Selected by Cleveland in 1st round (23rd player selected) of 1978 NFL draft.

Year Club	—PASS RECEIVING—				
	G.	P.C.	Yds.	Avg.	TD.
1978—Cleveland NFL..............	16	38	589	15.5	2
1979—Cleveland NFL..............	16	55	781	14.2	9
1980—Cleveland NFL..............	16	51	594	11.6	3
1981—Cleveland NFL..............	16	69	1002	14.5	6
1982—Cleveland NFL..............	8	49	633	12.9	3
1983—Cleveland NFL..............	16	89	970	10.9	6
1984—Cleveland NFL..............	16	89	1001	11.2	5
1985—Cleveland NFL..............	16	62	711	11.5	5
Pro Totals—8 Years...........	120	502	6281	12.5	39

Additional pro statistics: Returned two punts for 29 yards, rushed 13 times for 96 yards and two touchdowns and fumbled once, 1978; rushed once for six yards, 1979; rushed twice for 13 yards and fumbled twice, 1980; rushed twice for 20 yards, 1981; recovered one fumble, 1985.
Played in Pro Bowl (NFL All-Star Game) following 1981, 1984 and 1985 seasons.

TIMOTHY ARTHUR NEWSOME
(Timmy)
Fullback—Dallas Cowboys
Born May 17, 1958, at Ahoskie, N. C.
Height, 6.01. Weight, 235.
High School—Ahoskie, N. C.
Received bachelor of arts degree in business administration from
Winston-Salem State University in 1980.

Selected by Dallas in 6th round (162nd player selected) of 1980 NFL draft.

Year Club	——RUSHING——					PASS RECEIVING				—TOTAL—		
	G.	Att.	Yds.	Avg.	TD.	P.C.	Yds.	Avg.	TD.	TD.	Pts.	F.
1980—Dallas NFL	16	25	79	3.2	2	4	43	10.8	0	2	12	0
1981—Dallas NFL	15	13	38	2.9	0		None			0	0	1
1982—Dallas NFL	9	15	98	6.5	1	6	118	19.7	1	2	12	1
1983—Dallas NFL	16	44	185	4.2	2	18	250	13.9	4	6	36	0
1984—Dallas NFL	15	66	268	4.1	5	26	263	10.1	0	5	30	3
1985—Dallas NFL	14	88	252	2.9	2	46	361	7.8	1	3	18	2
Pro Totals—6 Years...................................	85	251	920	3.7	12	100	1035	10.4	6	18	108	7

Year Club	KICKOFF RETURNS				
	G.	No.	Yds.	Avg.	TD.
1980—Dallas NFL	16	12	293	24.4	0
1981—Dallas NFL	15	12	228	19.0	0
1982—Dallas NFL	9	5	74	14.8	0
1983—Dallas NFL	16	1	28	28.0	0
1984—Dallas NFL	15		None		
1985—Dallas NFL	14		None		
Pro Totals—6 Years...........	85	30	623	20.8	0

Additional pro statistics: Recovered two fumbles, 1980; recovered one fumble, 1982.
Played in NFC Championship Game following 1980 through 1982 seasons.

VINCENT KARL NEWSOME
(Vince)
Safety—Los Angeles Rams
Born January 22, 1961, at Braintree, Wash.
Height, 6.01. Weight, 179.
High School—Vacaville, Calif.
Attended University of Washington.

Selected by Oakland in 4th round (42nd player selected) of 1983 USFL draft.
Selected by Los Angeles Rams in 4th round (97th player selected) of 1983 NFL draft.
Signed by Los Angeles Rams, May 22, 1983.

Year Club	——INTERCEPTIONS——				
	G.	No.	Yds.	Avg.	TD.
1983—L.A. Rams NFL..............	16		None		
1984—L.A. Rams NFL..............	16	1	31	31.0	0
1985—L.A. Rams NFL..............	16	3	20	6.7	0
Pro Totals—3 Years...........	48	4	51	12.8	0

Additional pro statistics: Recovered one fumble, 1985.
Played in NFC Championship Game following 1985 season.

MIKE A. NEWTON
Running Back—Washington Redskins
Born May 14, 1962, at London, England.
Height, 5.11. Weight, 227.
High School—Brooklyn, N.Y., South Shore.
Attended Southern Connecticut State University.

Signed as free agent by Washington Redskins, May 6, 1985.
On injured reserve with knee injury, July 22 through entire 1985 season.

TIMOTHY REGINALD NEWTON
(Tim)
Nose Tackle—Minnesota Vikings

Born March 23, 1963, at Orlando, Fla.
Height, 6.00. Weight, 302.
High School—Orlando, Fla., Jones.
Attended University of Florida.

Selected by Tampa Bay in 1985 USFL territorial draft.
Selected by Minnesota in 6th round (164th player selected) of 1985 NFL draft.
Signed by Minnesota Vikings, June 17, 1985.
Minnesota NFL, 1985.
Games: 1985 (16).
Pro statistics: Intercepted two passes for 63 yards, recovered one fumble and fumbled once, 1985.

MARK STEPHEN NICHOLS
Wide Receiver—Detroit Lions

Born October 29, 1959, at Bakersfield, Calif.
Height, 6.02. Weight, 208.
High School—Bakersfield, Calif.
Attended Bakersfield Junior College and San Jose State University.

Selected by Detroit in 1st round (16th player selected) of 1981 NFL draft.
On injured reserve with broken foot, December 25 through remainder of 1982 season.
On injured reserve with knee injury, December 21 through remainder of 1985 season.

| | | —PASS RECEIVING— | | | |
Year Club	G.	P.C.	Yds.	Avg.	TD.
1981—Detroit NFL	12	10	222	22.2	1
1982—Detroit NFL	7	8	146	18.3	2
1983—Detroit NFL	16	29	437	15.1	1
1984—Detroit NFL	15	34	744	21.9	1
1985—Detroit NFL	14	36	592	16.4	4
Pro Totals—5 Years	64	117	2141	18.3	9

Additional pro statistics: Rushed three times for 50 yards and returned four kickoffs for 74 yards, 1981; fumbled once, 1981 and 1985; rushed once for three yards, 1982; rushed once for 13 yards and fumbled twice, 1983; rushed three times for 27 yards and recovered one fumble, 1984; rushed once for 15 yards, 1985.

RICKY ANTONIO NICHOLS
Wide Receiver—Indianapolis Colts

Born July 27, 1962, at Norfolk, Va.
Height, 5.10. Weight, 180.
High School—Chesapeake, Va., Great Bridge.
Attended East Carolina University.

Selected by Portland in 7th round (93rd player selected) of 1985 USFL draft.
Selected by Indianapolis in 8th round (200th player selected) of 1985 NFL draft.
Signed by Indianapolis Colts, July 8, 1985.
On injured reserve with groin injury, August 27 through November 17, 1985; activated, November 18, 1985.
Indianapolis NFL, 1985.
Games: 1985 (3).

SCOTT STEPHEN NICOLAS
Linebacker—Cleveland Browns

Born August 7, 1960, at Wichita Falls, Tex.
Height, 6.03. Weight, 226.
High School—Clearwater, Fla.
Received bachelor of business administration degree in marketing
from University of Miami (Fla.) in 1982.

Selected by Cleveland in 12th round (310th player selected) of 1982 NFL draft.
Cleveland NFL, 1982 through 1985.
Games: 1982 (9), 1983 (16), 1984 (16), 1985 (16). Total—57.
Pro statistics: Returned two kickoffs for 16 yards and fumbled once for minus 14 yards, 1982; returned two kickoffs for 29 yards, 1983; recovered one fumble, 1984 and 1985; returned one kickoff for 12 yards, 1984; returned one kickoff for nine yards, 1985.

TORRAN BLAKE NIXON
(Tory)
Cornerback—San Francisco 49ers

Born February 24, 1962, at Eugene, Ore.
Height, 5.11. Weight, 186.
High School—Phoenix, Ariz., Shadow Mountain.
Attended Univeristy of Arizona, Phoenix College and San Diego State University.

Selected by Arizona in 1st round (2nd player selected) of 1985 USFL draft.
Selected by Washington in 2nd round (33rd player selected) of 1985 NFL draft.
Signed by Washington Redskins, August 1, 1985.
Traded by Washington Redskins to San Francisco 49ers for 6th round pick in 1986 draft, September 2, 1985.
San Francisco NFL, 1985.
Games: 1985 (16).

BRIAN DAVID NOBLE
Linebacker—Green Bay Packers
Born September 6, 1962, at Anaheim, Calif.
Height, 6.03. Weight, 237.
High School—Anaheim, Calif.
Attended Fullerton College and Arizona State University.

Selected by Arizona in 1985 USFL territorial draft.
Selected by Green Bay in 5th round (125th player selected) of 1985 NFL draft.
Signed by Green Bay Packers, July 19, 1985.
Green Bay NFL, 1985.
Games: 1985 (16).

FALANIKO NOGA
First name pronounced Fah-lah-NEE-koh.
Linebacker—St. Louis Cardinals
Born March 2, 1962, at American Samoa.
Height, 6.01. Weight, 235.
High School—Honolulu, Haw., Farrington.
Attended University of Hawaii.
Brother of Pete Noga, linebacker, and Al Noga, defensive tackle,
both at University of Hawaii.

Selected by Oakland in 10th round (192nd player selected) of 1984 USFL draft.
Selected by St. Louis in 8th round (201st player selected) of 1984 NFL draft.
Signed by St. Louis Cardinals, July 16, 1984.
St. Louis NFL, 1984 and 1985.
Games: 1984 (16), 1985 (16). Total—32.
Pro statistics: Recovered one fumble, 1984; recovered two fumbles, 1985.

KEITH NORD
Safety—Minnesota Vikings
Born March 13, 1957, at Minneapolis, Minn.
Height, 6.00. Weight, 188.
High School—Minneapolis, Minn., Minnetonka.
Received degree in marketing from St. Cloud State University in
1979; and attending University of Minnesota for master's degree.

Signed as free agent by Minnesota Vikings, May 26, 1979.
On injured reserve with torn Achilles tendon, September 20 through remainder of 1983 season.
On physically unable to perform/reserve with Achilles tendon injury, August 8 through entire 1984 season.
Minnesota NFL, 1979 through 1983 and 1985.
Games: 1979 (16), 1980 (16), 1981 (16), 1982 (9), 1983 (3), 1985 (16). Total—76.
Pro statistics: Returned three punts for 11 yards, 1979; recovered one fumble, 1979, 1981 and 1982; fumbled once, 1979; returned one kickoff for 70 yards and a touchdown and recovered three fumbles, 1980; returned 14 kickoffs for 229 yards and fumbled twice, 1981; returned three kickoffs for 43 yards, 1982; intercepted one pass for no yards, 1983.

CHRIS COOPER NORMAN
Punter—Denver Broncos
Born May 25, 1962, at Albany, Ga.
Height, 6.02. Weight, 198.
High School—Albany, Ga., Dougherty.
Attended University of South Carolina.

Signed as free agent by Denver Broncos, May 2, 1984.

| | | ——PUNTING—— | | |
Year Club	G.	No.	Avg.	Blk.
1984—Denver NFL	16	96	40.1	0
1985—Denver NFL	16	92	40.9	★2
Pro Totals—2 Years	32	188	40.5	2

Additional pro statistics: Recovered one fumble and fumbled once, 1984 and 1985; rushed once for no yards and attempted one pass with no completions, 1985.

SCOTT ALLAN NORWOOD
Placekicker—Buffalo Bills
Born July 17, 1960, at Alexandria, Va.
Height, 6.00. Weight, 206.
High School—Alexandria, Va., Thomas Jefferson.
Received bachelor of business administration degree in management from James Madison University.

Signed as free agent by Atlanta Falcons, May 5, 1982.
Released by Atlanta Falcons, August 30, 1982; signed by Birmingham Stallions, January 4, 1983.
On developmental squad, March 15 through March 25, 1984.
On injured reserve with knee injury. March 26 through remainder of 1984 season.
Released by Birmingham Stallions, February 18, 1985; signed as free agent by Buffalo Bills, March 22, 1985.
On developmental squad for 2 games with Birmingham Stallions in 1984.

Year Club	G.	XP.	XPM.	FG.	FGA.	Pts.
1983—Birmingham USFL.	18	34	1	25	34	109
1984—Birmingham USFL.	3	4	0	3	4	13
1985—Buffalo NFL..............	16	23	0	13	17	62
USFL Totals—2 Years...	21	38	1	28	38	122
NFL Totals—1 Year.......	16	23	0	13	17	62
Pro Totals—3 Years.......	37	61	1	41	55	184

Additional pro statistics: Caught one pass for no yards and recovered one fumble, 1983.

JAY McKINLEY NOVACEK
Wide Receiver—St. Louis Cardinals
Born October 24, 1962, at Martin, S.D.
Height, 6.04. Weight, 217.
High School—Gothenburg, Neb.
Received bachelor of science degree in industrial education
from University of Wyoming in 1986.
Selected by Houston in 5th round (69th player selected) of 1985 USFL draft.
Selected by St. Louis in 6th round (158th player selected) of 1985 NFL draft.
Signed by St. Louis Cardinals, July 21, 1985.
St. Louis NFL, 1985.
Games: 1985 (16).
Pro statistics: Caught one pass for four yards and returned one kickoff for 20 yards, 1985.

TERENCE JOHN NUGENT
(Terry)
Quarterback—Tampa Bay Buccaneers
Born December 5, 1961, at Merced, Calif.
Height, 6.04. Weight, 218.
High School—Elk Grove, Calif.
Received bachelor of science degree in physical education from Colorado State University in 1985.
Selected by Denver in 1984 USFL territorial draft.
Selected by Cleveland in 6th round (158th player selected) of 1984 NFL draft.
Signed by Cleveland Browns, June 14, 1984.
Active for 16 games with Cleveland Browns in 1984; did not play.
Released by Cleveland Browns, August 27, 1985; signed as free agent by Tampa Bay Buccaneers, May 20, 1986.

FREDDIE JOE NUNN
Linebacker—St. Louis Cardinals
Born April 9, 1962, at Noxubee County, Miss.
Height, 6.04. Weight, 228.
High School—Louisville, Miss., Nanih Waiya.
Attended University of Mississippi.
Selected by Birmingham in 1985 USFL territorial draft.
Selected by St. Louis in 1st round (18th player selected) of 1985 NFL draft.
Signed by St. Louis Cardinals, August 5, 1985.
St. Louis NFL, 1985.
Games: 1985 (16).
Pro statistics: Recovered two fumbles, 1985.

BART STEVEN OATES
Center—New York Giants
Born December 16, 1958, at Mesa, Ariz.
Height, 6.03. Weight, 267.
High School—Albany, Ga.
Received bachelor's degree in accounting from Brigham Young University.
Brother of Brad Oates, offensive tackle with St. Louis Cardinals, Detroit Lions,
Kansas City Chiefs, Cincinnati Bengals, Green Bay Packers and Philadelphia Stars,
1976 through 1981, 1983 and 1984.
Named as center on THE SPORTING NEWS USFL All-Star Team, 1983.
Selected by Philadelphia in 2nd round (17th player selected) of 1983 USFL draft.
Signed by Philadelphia Stars, January 24, 1983.
On developmental squad, April 28 through May 5, 1983; activated, May 6, 1983.
Franchise transferred to Baltimore, November 1, 1984.
Released by Baltimore Stars, August 27, 1985; signed as free agent by New York Giants, August 28, 1985.
On developmental squad for 1 game with Philadelphia Stars in 1983.
Philadelphia USFL, 1983 and 1984; Baltimore USFL, 1985; New York Giants NFL, 1985.
Games: 1983 (17), 1984 (17), 1985 USFL (18), 1985 NFL (16). Total USFL—52. Total Pro—68.
USFL statistics: Rushed once for five yards and recovered two fumbles, 1984; recovered one fumble for four yards, 1985.
NFL statistics: Recovered two fumbles, 1985.
Played in USFL Championship Game following 1983 through 1985 seasons.

VICTOR HUGO OATIS
Wide Receiver—Miami Dolphins
Born January 6, 1959, at Monroe, La.
Height, 6.00. Weight, 177.
High School—Winnsboro, La.
Received degree in drafting technology from Northwestern (La.) State University.

Selected by Philadelphia in 19th round (224th player selected) of 1983 USFL draft.
Selected by Philadelphia in 6th round (147th player selected) of 1983 NFL draft.
Signed by Philadelphia Eagles, May 13, 1983.
Released by Philadelphia Eagles, August 22, 1983; awarded on waivers to Baltimore Colts, August 24, 1983.
Franchise transferred to Indianapolis, March 31, 1984.
On injured reserve with thigh injury, August 27 through entire 1984 season.
Traded by Indianapolis Colts to Cleveland Browns for draft choice, May 16, 1985.
Released by Cleveland Browns, August 5, 1985; awarded on waivers to Miami Dolphins, August 6, 1985.
Released by Miami Dolphins, August 19, 1985; re-signed by Dolphins, March 6, 1986.

		—PASS RECEIVING—			
Year Club	G.	P.C.	Yds.	Avg.	TD.
1983—Baltimore NFL	9	6	93	15.5	0

RONNIE ALEXANDER O'BARD
Cornerback
Born June 11, 1958, at San Diego, Calif.
Height, 5.09. Weight, 190.
High School—Spring Valley, Calif., Monte Vista.
Attended University of Idaho, Grossmont College and Brigham Young University.

Signed as free agent by San Diego Chargers, May 20, 1984.
Released on injured waivers with dislocated thumb, August 27, 1984; signed as free agent by Arizona Outlaws, November 29, 1984.
Released by Arizona Outlaws, January 19, 1985; signed as free agent by San Diego Chargers, April 26, 1985.
Released by San Diego Chargers, August 28, 1985; re-signed by Chargers, September 3, 1985.
Released by San Diego Chargers, May 9, 1986.
Played for San Diego Sharks in California Football League, 1982 and 1983.
San Diego NFL, 1985.
Games: 1985 (16).

KENNETH JOHN O'BRIEN JR.
(Ken)
Quarterback—New York Jets
Born November 27, 1960, at Long Island, N.Y.
Height, 6.04. Weight, 210.
High School—Sacramento, Calif., Jesuit.
Attended California State University at Sacramento and received degree in
political science from University of California at Davis in 1983.

Led NFL quarterbacks in passing with 96.2 points in 1985.
Selected by Oakland in 6th round (66th player selected) of 1983 USFL draft.
Selected by New York Jets in 1st round (24th player selected) of 1983 NFL draft.
Signed by New York Jets, July 21, 1983.
Active for 16 games with New York Jets in 1983; did not play.

Year Club	G.	—————PASSING—————							—RUSHING—				—TOTAL—		
		Att.	Cmp.	Pct.	Gain	T.P.	P.I.	Avg.	Att.	Yds.	Avg.	TD.	TD.	Pts.	F.
1984—N.Y. Jets NFL	10	203	116	57.1	1402	6	7	6.91	16	29	1.8	0	0	0	4
1985—N.Y. Jets NFL	16	488	297	60.9	3888	25	8	7.97	25	58	2.3	0	0	0	14
Pro Totals—3 Years	26	691	413	59.8	5290	31	15	7.66	41	87	2.1	0	0	0	18

Quarterback Rating Points: 1984 (74.0), 1985 (96.2). Total—89.7.
Additional pro statistics: Recovered two fumbles, 1984; recovered four fumbles, 1985.
Played in Pro Bowl (NFL All-Star Game) following 1985 season.

MICHAEL LOUIS OBROVAC
(Mike)
Offensive Tackle—Green Bay Packers
Born October 11, 1955, at Canton, O.
Height, 6.06. Weight, 275.
High School—Canton, O., McKinley.
Attended Bowling Green State University.

Signed as free agent by Toronto Argonauts, April, 1978.
Released by Toronto Argonauts, June 15, 1978; re-signed by Argonauts, March, 1979.
On injured list, July 6 through September 12, 1980; activated, September 12, 1980.
Granted free agency, March 1, 1981; signed as free agent by Cincinnati Bengals, March 10, 1981.
Left Cincinnati Bengals camp voluntarily, August 13, 1981; returned, August 23, 1981.
On injured reserve with knee injury, October 9 through December 8, 1981; activated, December 9, 1981.
On injured reserve with knee injury, August 28 through entire 1984 season.
Placed on retired list, July 24, 1985.
Traded by Cincinnati Bengals to Green Bay Packers for 11th round pick in 1986 draft, September 4, 1985.
Granted roster exemption, September 4 through September 15, 1985.
Released by Green Bay Packers, September 16, 1985; re-signed by Packers, February 28, 1986.

Toronto CFL, 1979 and 1980; Cincinnati, NFL, 1981 through 1983.
Games: 1979 (16), 1980 (7), 1981 (6), 1982 (9), 1983 (10). Total CFL—23. Total NFL—25. Total Pro—48.
Played in AFC Championship Game following 1981 season.
Played in NFL Championship Game following 1981 season.

CLIFTON LOUIS ODOM
(Cliff)
Linebacker—Indianapolis Colts

Born September 15, 1958, at Beaumont, Tex.
Height, 6.02. Weight, 233.
High School—Beaumont, Tex., French.
Attended University of Texas at Arlington.

Selected by Cleveland in 3rd round (72nd player selected) of 1980 NFL draft.
On injured reserve with knee injury, November 3 through remainder of 1980 season.
Released by Cleveland Browns, August 18, 1981; signed as free agent by Oakland Raiders, March 1, 1982.
Franchise transferred to Los Angeles, May 7, 1982.
Released by Los Angeles Raiders, August 10, 1982; signed as free agent by Baltimore Colts, August 12, 1982.
Released by Baltimore Colts, September 6, 1982; re-signed by Colts, September 7, 1982.
Franchise transferred to Indianapolis, March 31, 1984.
Cleveland NFL, 1980; Baltimore NFL, 1982 and 1983; Indianapolis NFL, 1984 and 1985.
Games: 1980 (8), 1982 (8), 1983 (15), 1984 (16), 1985 (16). Total—63.
Pro statistics: Recovered one fumble, 1984; recovered two fumbles, 1985.

ROBERT BRUCE OLDERMAN
(Bob)
Guard—Kansas City Chiefs

Born June 5, 1962, at Brookville, Pa.
Height, 6.04. Weight, 262.
High School—Atlanta, Ga., Marist.
Attended University of Virginia.

Selected by Orlando in 1985 USFL territorial draft.
Selected by Kansas City in 4th round (99th player selected) of 1985 NFL draft.
Signed by Kansas City Chiefs, July 19, 1985.
Kansas City NFL, 1985.
Games: 1985 (16).

HUBERT OLIVER
(Hubie)
Fullback—Indianapolis Colts

Born November 12, 1957, at Elyria, O.
Height, 5.10. Weight, 212.
High School—Elyria, O.
Attended University of Arizona.

Selected by Philadelphia in 10th round (275th player selected) of 1981 NFL draft.
On injured reserve with knee injury, September 7 through December 9, 1982; activated, December 10, 1982.
On injured reserve with knee injury, December 22 through remainder of 1982 season.
Released by Philadelphia Eagles, September 9, 1985; signed as free agent by Indianapolis Colts, May 12, 1986.
Active for 2 games with Philadelphia Eagles in 1982; did not play.

Year Club	G.	Att.	Yds.	Avg.	TD.	P.C.	Yds.	Avg.	TD.	TD.	Pts.	F.
			—RUSHING—				PASS RECEIVING			—TOTAL—		
1981—Philadelphia NFL	13	75	329	4.4	1	10	37	3.7	0	1	6	1
1983—Philadelphia NFL	16	121	434	3.6	1	49	421	8.6	2	3	18	5
1984—Philadelphia NFL	16	72	263	3.7	0	32	142	4.4	0	0	0	0
1985—Philadelphia NFL	1	1	3	3.0	0	1	4	4.0	0	0	0	0
Pro Totals—5 Years	46	269	1029	3.8	2	92	604	6.6	2	4	24	6

Additional pro statistics: Recovered two fumbles, 1983; recovered one fumble, 1984.

NEAL OLKEWICZ
Linebacker—Washington Redskins

Born January 30, 1957, at Phoenixville, Pa.
Height, 6.00. Weight, 233.
High School—Phoenixville, Pa.
Received bachelor of arts degree in law enforcement from University of Maryland in 1979.

Signed as free agent by Washington Redskins, May 7, 1979.
On injured reserve with knee injury, December 10 through remainder of 1981 season.

Year Club	G.	No.	Yds.	Avg.	TD.
		—INTERCEPTIONS—			
1979—Washington NFL	16	1	4	4.0	0
1980—Washington NFL	12		None		
1981—Washington NFL	14	2	22	11.0	1
1982—Washington NFL	9		None		
1983—Washington NFL	16	1	14	14.0	0
1984—Washington NFL	16		None		
1985—Washington NFL	16	1	21	21.0	0
Pro Totals—7 Years	99	5	61	12.2	1

Additional pro statistics: Recovered one fumble, 1980 and 1985; recovered three fumbles, 1982; recovered two fumbles, 1983 and 1984.

Played in NFC Championship Game following 1982 and 1983 seasons.

Played in NFL Championship Game following 1982 and 1983 seasons.

KENNETH ROBERT OLSON
(Ken)
Placekicker—San Francisco 49ers

Born September 15, 1959, at Washington, D.C.
Height, 5.11. Weight, 190.
High School—Camp Springs, Md., Crossland.
Received degree in physical education from Salisbury State College.

Signed as free agent by Chicago Blitz, October 21, 1982.

Released by Chicago Blitz, February 20, 1983; signed as free agent by Washington Federals, April 10, 1983.

On developmental squad, April 23 and April 24, 1983.

Released by Washington Federals, April 25, 1983; signed as free agent by San Antonio Gunslingers, December 26, 1983.

Released by San Antonio Gunslingers, January 24, 1984; signed as free agent by Arizona Outlaws, January 6, 1985.

Released by Arizona Outlaws, February 11, 1985; signed as free agent by San Diego Chargers, April 12, 1985.

Released by San Diego Chargers, June 10, 1985; signed as free agent by San Francisco 49ers, May 15, 1986.

On developmental squad for 1 game with Washington Federals in 1983.

		——PLACE KICKING——					
Year	Club	G.	XP.	XPM.	FG.	FGA.	Pts.
1983—Washington USFL...		2	3	1	0	1	3

TERRY ORR
Tight End—Washington Redskins

Born September 27, 1961, at Savannah, Ga.
Height, 6.03. Weight, 227.
High School—Abilene, Tex., Cooper.
Received bachelor of science degree in speech communications
from University of Texas in 1985.

Selected by San Antonio in 1985 USFL territorial draft.

Selected by Washington in 10th round (263rd player selected) of 1985 NFL draft.

Signed by Washington Redskins, July 18, 1985.

On injured reserve with ankle injury, August 20 through entire 1985 season.

KEITH ORTEGO
Wide Receiver—Chicago Bears

Born August 30, 1963, at Eunice, La.
Height, 6.00. Weight, 180.
High School—Eunice, La.
Attended McNeese State University.

Signed as free agent by Chicago Bears, May 3, 1985.

On injured reserve with knee injury, August 19 through November 6, 1985; activated after clearing procedural waivers, November 8, 1985.

		——PUNT RETURNS——				
Year	Club	G.	No.	Yds.	Avg.TD.	
1985—Chicago NFL		7	17	158	9.3	0

Played in NFC Championship Game following 1985 season.

Played in NFL Championship Game following 1985 season.

VINCENT LEE OSBY
(Vince)
Linebacker—Cleveland Browns

Born July 8, 1961, at Los Angeles, Calif.
Height, 5.11. Weight, 222.
High School—Lynwood, Calif.
Attended Pasadena City College and University of Illinois.

Signed as free agent by San Diego Chargers, May 20, 1984.

Released by San Diego Chargers, August 27, 1984; re-signed by Chargers, August 28, 1984.

On injured reserve with hamstring injury, August 26 through October 9, 1985; activated after clearing procedural waivers, October 11, 1985.

On injured reserve with ankle injury, October 24 through November 22, 1985; activated, November 23, 1985.

Released by San Diego Chargers, May 9, 1986; awarded on waivers to Cleveland Browns, May 23, 1986.

San Diego NFL, 1984 and 1985.

Games: 1984 (16), 1985 (7). Total—23.

Pro statistics: Recovered one fumble for 46 yards, 1985.

—DID YOU KNOW—

That the Chargers' Ed White broke former teammate Mick Tinglehoff's record for games played by an offensive lineman when he played in his 241st game in 1985?

CHRIS DONALD OSSWALD
Center-Guard—Washington Redskins
Born November 13, 1962, at Dover, Dela.
Height, 6.04. Weight, 268.
High School—Schofield, Wis., D.C. Everest.
Attended University of Wisconsin.

Signed as free agent by Washington Redskins, May 13, 1985.
On injured reserve with ankle injury, August 20 through entire 1985 season.

LOUIS BYRON OUBRE III
Named pronounced OO-bray.
Guard—Philadelphia Eagles
Born May 15, 1958, at New Orleans, La.
Height, 6.04. Weight, 270.
High School—New Orleans, La., St. Augustine.
Received degree in accounting from University of Oklahoma.

Selected by New Orleans in 5th round (112th player selected) of 1981 NFL draft.
On injured reserve with shoulder separation, August 5 through entire 1981 season.
On physically unable to perform/reserve with Achilles tendon injury, August 28 through October 29, 1985.
Released by New Orleans Saints, October 30, 1985; signed as free agent by Philadelphia Eagles, May 7, 1986.
New Orleans NFL, 1982 through 1984.
Games: 1982 (9), 1983 (16), 1984 (12). Total—37.

DENNIS RAY OWENS
Nose Tackle—New England Patriots
Born February 24, 1960, at Clinton, N.C.
Height, 6.01. Weight, 258.
High School—Clinton, N.C.
Attended North Carolina State University.

Signed as free agent by New England Patriots, May 13, 1982.
Released by New England Patriots, September 2, 1985; re-signed by Patriots, September 3, 1985.
New England NFL, 1982 through 1985.
Games: 1982 (9), 1983 (16), 1984 (16), 1985 (14). Total—55.
Pro statistics: Recovered one fumble, 1982 and 1984; recovered one fumble for four yards, 1983.
Played in AFC Championship Game following 1985 season.
Played in NFL Championship Game following 1985 season.

MEL TYRAE OWENS
Linebacker—Los Angeles Rams
Born December 7, 1958, at Detroit, Mich.
Height, 6.02. Weight, 224.
High School—DeKalb, Ill.
Received bachelor of arts degree in political science from University of Michigan in 1981.

Selected by Los Angeles in 1st round (9th player selected) of 1981 NFL draft.
Los Angeles Rams NFL, 1981 through 1985.
Games: 1981 (16), 1982 (7), 1983 (16), 1984 (16), 1985 (16). Total—71.
Pro statistics: Recovered two fumbles, 1983 and 1984; intercepted one pass for minus four yards, 1984; recovered two fumbles for 14 yards, 1985.
Played in NFC Championship Game following 1985 season.

DAVID WADE PACELLA
(Dave)
Guard—Pittsburgh Steelers
Born February 7, 1960, at Swickley, Pa.
Height, 6.02. Weight, 266.
High School—Reading, Pa.
Received bachelor of arts degree in liberal arts from University of Maryland.

Selected by Washington in 1983 USFL territorial draft.
Signed by Washington Federals, January 26, 1983.
Granted free agency, July 15, 1984; signed by Philadelphia Eagles, August 22, 1984.
Released by Philadelphia Eagles, May 7, 1985; signed as free agent by New York Jets, June 21, 1985.
On injured reserve with knee injury, August 14 through October 22, 1985.
Released by New York Jets, October 23, 1985; signed as free agent by Pittsburgh Steelers, May 13, 1986.
Washington USFL, 1983 and 1984; Philadelphia NFL, 1984.
Games: 1983 (18), 1984 USFL (18), 1984 NFL (16). Total USFL—36. Total Pro—52.
Pro statistics: Recovered one fumble, 1983; recovered two fumbles, 1984.

—DID YOU KNOW—
That when Occidental College running back Vance Mueller was selected in the fourth round by the Raiders, he was the first player selected by the NFL from that school since quarterback Jack Kemp was picked 29 years ago?

MICHAEL JONATHAN PAGEL
(Mike)
Quarterback—Cleveland Browns
Born September 13, 1960, at Douglas, Ariz.
Height, 6.02. Weight, 207.
High School—Phoenix, Ariz., Washington.
Attended Arizona State University.
Brother of Karl Pagel, outfielder-first baseman with Chicago Cubs and Cleveland Indians, 1978, 1979 and
1981 through 1983; and minor league coach, Cleveland Indians' organization, 1984.

Selected by Baltimore in 4th round (84th player selected) of 1982 NFL draft.
Franchise transferred to Indianapolis, March 31, 1984.
Granted free agency, February 1, 1986; re-signed by Colts and traded to Cleveland Browns for 7th round pick in
1987 draft, May 22, 1986.

			PASSING						RUSHING				TOTAL	
Year Club	G.	Att.	Cmp.	Pct.	Gain	T.P.	P.I.	Avg.	Att.	Yds.	Avg.	TD.	TD.	Pts.	F.
1982—Baltimore NFL	9	221	111	50.2	1281	5	7	5.80	19	82	4.3	1	1	6	9
1983—Baltimore NFL	15	328	163	49.7	2353	12	17	7.17	54	441	8.2	0	0	0	4
1984—Indianapolis NFL	11	212	114	53.8	1426	8	8	6.73	26	149	5.7	1	1	6	4
1985—Indianapolis NFL	16	393	199	50.6	2414	14	15	6.14	25	160	6.4	2	2	12	6
Pro Totals—4 Years	51	1154	587	50.9	7474	39	47	6.48	124	832	6.7	4	4	24	23

Quarterback Rating Points: 1982 (62.4), 1983 (64.0), 1984 (71.8), 1985 (65.8). Total—65.8.
Additional pro statistics: Recovered three fumbles and fumbled nine times for minus four yards, 1982; recovered
one fumble, 1984; recovered two fumbles and caught one pass for six yards, 1985.

ANTHONY R. PAIGE
(Tony)
Fullback—New York Jets
Born October 14, 1962, at Washington, D.C.
Height, 5.10. Weight, 220.
High School—Hyattsville, Md., DeMatha Catholic.
Received degree in broadcasting from Virginia Tech.

Selected by Pittsburgh in 1984 USFL territorial draft.
Selected by New York Jets in 6th round (149th player selected) of 1984 NFL draft.
Signed by New York Jets, May 29, 1984.

		RUSHING				PASS RECEIVING				TOTAL	
Year Club	G.	Att.	Yds.	Avg.	TD.	P.C.	Yds.	Avg.	TD.	TD.	Pts.	F.
1984—New York Jets NFL	16	35	130	3.7	7	6	31	5.2	1	8	48	1
1985—New York Jets NFL	16	55	158	2.9	8	18	120	6.7	2	10	60	1
Pro Totals—2 Years	32	90	288	3.2	15	24	151	6.3	3	18	108	2

Additional pro statistics: Returned three kickoffs for seven yards, 1984; recovered one fumble, 1985.

STEPHONE PAIGE
Wide Receiver—Kansas City Chiefs
Born October 15, 1961, at Long Beach, Calif.
Height, 6.02. Weight, 191.
High School—Long Beach, Calif., Polytechnic.
Attended Saddleback College and Fresno State University.

Established NFL record for pass reception yards, game (309), against San Diego Chargers, December 22, 1985.
Selected by Oakland in 1983 USFL territorial draft.
Signed as free agent by Kansas City Chiefs, May 9, 1983.

		PASS RECEIVING				KICKOFF RET.—				TOTAL	
Year Club	G.	P.C.	Yds.	Avg.	TD.	No.	Yds.	Avg.	TD.	TD.	Pts.	F.
1983—Kansas City NFL	16	30	528	17.6	6		None			6	36	1
1984—Kansas City NFL	16	30	541	18.0	4	27	544	20.1	0	4	24	0
1985—Kansas City NFL	16	43	943	*21.9	10	2	36	18.0	0	10	60	0
Pro Totals—3 Years	48	103	2012	19.5	20	29	580	20.0	0	20	120	1

Additional pro statistics: Recovered one fumble, 1983; rushed three times for 19 yards, 1984; rushed once for 15
yards, 1985.

JEFFREY FRANKLIN PAINE
(Jeff)
Linebacker—Kansas City Chiefs
Born August 19, 1961, at Garland, Tex.
Height, 6.02. Weight, 224.
High School—Richardson, Tex.
Attended Texas A&M University.

Selected by San Antonio in 1984 USFL territorial draft.
Selected by Kansas City in 5th round (134th player selected) of 1984 NFL draft.
Signed by Kansas City Chiefs, July 9, 1984.
On injured reserve with knee injury, September 17 through October 18, 1985; activated, October 19, 1985.
Kansas City NFL, 1984 and 1985.
Games: 1984 (14), 1985 (12). Total—26.

IRVIN LEE PANKEY
(Irv)
Offensive Tackle—Los Angeles Rams
Born February 15, 1958, at Aberdeen, Md.
Height, 6.04. Weight, 267.
High School—Aberdeen, Md.
Attended Pennsylvania State University.

Selected by Los Angeles in 2nd round (50th player selected) of 1980 NFL draft.
On injured reserve with torn Achilles tendon, August 16 through entire 1983 season.
Los Angeles Rams NFL, 1980 through 1985.
Games: 1980 (16), 1981 (13), 1982 (9), 1984 (16), 1985 (16). Total—70.
Pro statistics: Recovered two fumbles and returned one kickoff for no yards, 1981; recovered one fumble, 1985.
Played in NFC Championship Game following 1985 season.

WILLIAM PARIS
(Bubba)
Offensive Tackle—San Francisco 49ers
Born October 6, 1960, at Louisville, Ky.
Height, 6.06. Weight, 299.
High School—Louisville, Ky., DeSales.
Received degree from University of Michigan in 1982.

Selected by San Francisco in 2nd round (29th player selected) of 1982 NFL draft.
On injured reserve with knee injury, September 6 through entire 1982 season.
San Francisco NFL, 1983 through 1985.
Games: 1983 (16), 1984 (16), 1985 (16). Total—48.
Pro statistics: Recovered one fumble, 1984.
Played in NFC Championship Game following 1983 and 1984 seasons.
Played in NFL Championship Game following 1984 season.

ANDREW JAMES PARKER
(Andy)
Tight End—Los Angeles Raiders
Born September 8, 1961, at Redlands, Calif.
Height, 6.05. Weight, 240.
High Schools—Dana Point, Calif., Dana Hills and Encinitas, Calif., San Dieguito.
Received bachelor of science degree in physical education
from University of Utah in 1984.

Selected by Philadelphia in 5th round (100th player selected) 1984 USFL draft.
Selected by Los Angeles Raiders in 5th round (127th player selected) of 1984 NFL draft.
Signed by Los Angeles Raiders, June 19, 1984.
On injured reserve with back injury, November 3 through remainder of 1984 season.
Los Angeles Raiders NFL, 1984 and 1985.
Games: 1984 (9), 1985 (16). Total—25.

RICK U. PARROS
Running Back—Seattle Seahawks
Born June 14, 1958, at Brooklyn, N. Y.
Height, 5.11. Weight, 200.
High School—Salt Lake City, Utah, Granite.
Attended Utah State University.

Selected by Denver in 4th round (107th player selected) of 1980 NFL draft.
On injured reserve with knee injury, July 25 through entire 1980 season.
On injured reserve with neck injury, October 28 through remainder of 1983 season.
Placed on injured waivers with shoulder injury, August 27 through November 18, 1985; awarded on procedural waivers to Seattle Seahawks, November 20, 1985.

| | | —RUSHING— | | | | PASS RECEIVING | | | | —TOTAL— | | |
Year Club	G.	Att.	Yds.	Avg.	TD.	P.C.	Yds.	Avg.	TD.	TD.	Pts.	F.
1981—Denver NFL	16	176	749	4.3	2	25	216	8.6	1	3	18	6
1982—Denver NFL	9	77	277	3.6	1	37	259	7.0	2	3	18	3
1983—Denver NFL	6	30	96	3.2	1	12	126	10.5	2	3	18	3
1984—Denver NFL	15	46	208	4.5	2	6	25	4.2	0	2	12	0
1985—Denver NFL	4	8	19	2.4	0	1	27	27.0	0	0	0	1
Pro Totals—5 Years	50	337	1349	4.0	6	81	653	8.1	5	11	66	13

Additional pro statistics: Recovered one fumble, 1981 and 1983.

JEFFREY THOMAS PARTRIDGE
(Jeff)
Punter—Cincinnati Bengals
Born September 13, 1961, at Orange, Calif.
Height, 6.01. Weight, 175.
High School—Tustin, Calif.
Attended Golden West Junior College and University of Washington.
Brother of Rick Partridge, punter with Denver Broncos.

Signed by Los Angeles Express, January 10, 1983.

Released by Los Angeles Express, February 27, 1983; re-signed by Express, March 16, 1983.
Released by Los Angeles Express, August 1, 1985; signed as free agent by Cincinnati Bengals, February 13, 1986.

Year Club	G.	No.	Avg.	Blk.
1983—Los Angeles USFL	16	87	42.2	....
1984—Los Angeles USFL	18	77	39.8	....
1985—Los Angeles USFL	18	73	41.4	....
Pro Totals—3 Years	52	237	41.2	....

Additional pro statistics: Recovered one fumble and attempted one pass with one completion for minus three yards, 1984; attempted one pass with no completions, 1985.

RICHARD BLAKE PARTRIDGE
(Rick)
Punter—Denver Broncos
Born August 26, 1957, at Orange, Calif.
Height, 6.01. Weight, 175.
High School—Tustin, Calif.
Attended Golden West Junior College and received bachelor of science degree
in accounting from University of Utah in 1979.
Brother of Jeff Partridge, punter with Cincinnati Bengals.

Selected by Green Bay in 8th round (208th player selected) of 1979 NFL draft.
Released by Green Bay Packers, August 23, 1979; signed as free agent by New Orleans Saints, September 20, 1979.
Traded by New Orleans Saints to San Diego Chargers for 8th round pick in 1981 draft, August 31, 1980.
Released by San Diego Chargers, August 17, 1981; signed as free agent by Baltimore Colts, May 5, 1982.
Released by Baltimore Colts, August 10, 1982; signed by Denver Gold, February 4, 1983.
Released by Denver Gold, February 27, 1983; signed as free agent by Michigan Panthers, April 26, 1983.
Released by Michigan Panthers, June 7, 1983; signed as free agent by Memphis Showboats, October 24, 1983.
Traded by Memphis Showboats to New Jersey Generals for draft choice, January 28, 1985.
Granted free agency with option not exercised, July 31, 1985; awarded on waivers to Baltimore Stars, August 1, 1985.
Released by Baltimore Stars, August 2, 1985; signed as free agent by Denver Broncos, April 23, 1986.

Year Club	G.	No.	Avg.	Blk.
1979—New Orleans NFL	13	57	40.9	0
1980—San Diego NFL	16	60	39.1	1
1983—Michigan USFL	6	23	39.3	....
1984—Memphis USFL	18	80	41.3	....
1985—New Jersey USFL	18	66	41.4	....
NFL Totals—2 Years	29	117	40.0	1
USFL Totals—3 Years	42	169	41.1	....
Pro Totals—5 Years	71	286	40.6	....

Additional NFL statistics: Rushed three times for no yards and recovered three fumbles, 1980.
Additional USFL statistics: Recovered one fumble and attempted one pass with no completions, 1983; fumbled twice, 1984; attempted one pass with one interception, rushed three times for 16 yards and a touchdown and recovered two fumbles, 1985.
Played in AFC Championship Game following 1980 season.

JOEL PATTEN
Offensive Tackle—Dallas Cowboys
Born February 7, 1958, at Augsburg, Germany.
Height, 6.06. Weight, 240.
High School—Fairfax, Va., Robinson.
Received bachelor of science degree in history education from Duke University.

Signed as free agent by Cleveland Browns, May 7, 1980.
On injured reserve with groin injury, September 6 through November 6, 1980; activated, November 7, 1980.
On injured reserve with knee injury, August 24 through entire 1981 season.
Released by Cleveland Browns, September 8, 1982.
USFL rights traded by Michigan Panthers to Washington Federals for past consideration, February 8, 1983.
Signed by Washington Federals, February 8, 1983.
On developmental squad, May 4 through June 2, 1984; activated, June 3, 1984.
Franchise transferred to Orlando, October 12, 1984.
Released by Orlando Renegades, August 26, 1985; signed as free agent by Dallas Cowboys, March 21, 1986.
On developmental squad for 4 games with Washington Federals in 1984.
Cleveland NFL, 1980; Washington USFL, 1983 and 1984; Orlando USFL, 1985.
Games: 1980 (16), 1983 (18), 1984 (14), 1985 (18). Total NFL—16. Total USFL—32. Total Pro—48.
Pro statistics: Recovered two fumbles, 1983.

ELVIS VERNELL PATTERSON
Defensive Back—New York Giants
Born October 21, 1960, at Bryan, Tex.
Height, 5.11. Weight, 188.
High School—Houston, Tex., Jack Yates.
Attended University of Kansas.

Selected by Jacksonville in 10th round (207th player selected) of 1984 USFL draft.
Signed as free agent by New York Giants, May 3, 1984.

Year Club	G.	No.	Yds.	Avg.	TD.
1984—N.Y. Giants NFL	15		None		
1985—N.Y. Giants NFL	16	6	88	14.7	*1
Pro Totals—2 Years...........	31	6	88	14.7	1

Additional pro statistics: Recovered one fumble, 1985.

MARK LESTER PATTISON
Wide Receiver—Los Angeles Raiders
Born December 13, 1961, at Seattle, Wash.
Height, 6.02. Weight, 190.
High School—Seattle, Wash., Roosevelt.
Received degree in political science from University of Washington.

Selected by Portland in 1985 USFL territorial draft.
Selected by Los Angeles Raiders in 7th round (199th player selected) of 1985 NFL draft.
Signed by Los Angeles Raiders, June 29, 1985.
On injured reserve with hamstring injury, August 27 through entire 1985 season.

WHITNEY PAUL
Linebacker—New Orleans Saints
Born October 8, 1955, at Galveston, Tex.
Height, 6.03. Weight, 215.
High School—Galveston, Tex., Ball.
Attended University of Colorado.
Related to Alton Alexis, wide receiver with Cleveland Browns.

Selected by Kansas City in 10th round (277th player selected) of 1976 NFL draft.
Traded by Kansas City Chiefs to New Orleans Saints for 7th round pick in 1983 draft, July 31, 1982.

Year Club	G.	No.	Yds.	Avg.	TD.
1976—Kansas City NFL.........	14		None		
1977—Kansas City NFL.........	14	1	6	6.0	0
1978—Kansas City NFL.........	16	3	21	7.0	0
1979—Kansas City NFL.........	15	1	28	28.0	0
1980—Kansas City NFL.........	12	1	0	0.0	0
1981—Kansas City NFL.........	15	2	30	15.0	0
1982—New Orleans NFL.........	9	1	14	14.0	0
1983—New Orleans NFL........	16	2	3	1.5	0
1984—New Orleans NFL........	16		None		
1985—New Orleans NFL........	14		None		
Pro Totals—10 Years.........	141	11	102	9.3	0

Additional pro statistics: Recovered one fumble, 1976; recovered two fumbles, 1977; returned one kickoff for no yards, recovered one fumble and fumbled once, 1978; recovered three fumbles, 1979; recovered two fumbles for 32 yards and a touchdown, 1980; recovered one fumble for 47 yards and a touchdown, 1981.

WALTER JERRY PAYTON
Running Back—Chicago Bears
Born July 25, 1954, at Columbia, Miss.
Height, 5.10. Weight, 202.
High School—Columbia, Miss.
Received bachelor of arts degree in communications and special education from Jackson State University.
Brother of Eddie Payton, kick returner with Cleveland Browns, Detroit Lions, Kansas City Chiefs,
Toronto Argonauts and Minnesota Vikings, 1977 through 1982; nephew of Rickey Young,
running back with San Diego Chargers and Minnesota Vikings, 1975 through 1983.

Established NFL records for most yards gained, rushing, game (275), November 20, 1977, against Minnesota Vikings; most rushing yards, career (14,860); most rushing attempts, career (3,371); most combined yards, career (19,338); most combined attempts, career (3,831); most consecutive combined 2,000-yard seasons (3), 1983 through 1985; most games, 100 yards rushing, career (73); most seasons, 1,000 yards rushing (9).
Tied NFL record for most consecutive games, 100 yards rushing (9), 1985.
Named NFC Player of the Year by THE SPORTING NEWS, 1976 and 1977.
Named to THE SPORTING NEWS NFL All-Star Team, 1980, 1984 and 1985.
Named to THE SPORTING NEWS NFC All-Star Team, 1976 through 1979.
Selected by Chicago in 1st round (4th player selected) of 1975 NFL draft.
USFL rights traded by Birmingham Stallions to Chicago Blitz for rights to quarterback Phil Kessel and a draft pick, January 23, 1984.

Year Club	G.	—RUSHING— Att.	Yds.	Avg.	TD.	PASS RECEIVING P.C.	Yds.	Avg.	TD.	—TOTAL— TD.	Pts.	F.
1975—Chicago NFL..............................	13	196	679	3.5	7	33	213	6.5	0	7	42	9
1976—Chicago NFL..............................	14	*311	1390	4.5	13	15	149	14.9	0	13	78	10
1977—Chicago NFL..............................	14	*339	*1852	*5.5	*14	27	269	10.0	0	*16	96	11
1978—Chicago NFL..............................	16	*333	1395	4.2	11	50	480	9.6	0	11	66	5
1979—Chicago NFL..............................	16	*369	1610	4.4	14	31	313	10.1	2	16	96	7
1980—Chicago NFL..............................	16	317	1460	4.6	6	46	367	8.0	1	7	42	5
1981—Chicago NFL..............................	16	339	1222	3.6	6	41	379	9.2	2	8	48	9
1982—Chicago NFL..............................	9	148	596	4.0	1	32	311	9.7	0	1	6	3
1983—Chicago NFL..............................	16	314	1421	4.5	6	53	607	11.5	2	8	48	5
1984—Chicago NFL..............................	16	381	1684	4.4	11	45	368	8.2	0	11	66	5
1985—Chicago NFL..............................	16	324	1551	4.8	9	49	483	9.9	2	11	66	6
Pro Totals—11 Years......................	162	3371	14860	4.4	98	422	3939	9.3	11	109	654	75

| | | —PASSING— | | | | | | | —KICKOFF RET.— | | | |
Year Club	G.	Att.	Cmp.	Pct.	Gain	T.P.	P.I.	Avg.	No.	Yds.	Avg.	TD.
1975—Chicago NFL	13	1	0	00.0	0	0	1	0.00	14	444	*31.7	0
1976—Chicago NFL	14				None				1	0	0.0	0
1977—Chicago NFL	14				None				2	95	47.5	0
1978—Chicago NFL	16				None						None	
1979—Chicago NFL	16	1	1	100.0	54	1	0	54.00			None	
1980—Chicago NFL	16	3	0	00.0	0	0	0	0.00			None	
1981—Chicago NFL	16	2	0	00.0	0	0	0	0.00			None	
1982—Chicago NFL	9	3	1	33.3	39	1	0	13.00			None	
1983—Chicago NFL	16	6	3	50.0	95	3	2	15.83			None	
1984—Chicago NFL	16	8	3	37.5	47	2	1	5.88			None	
1985—Chicago NFL	16	5	3	60.0	96	1	0	19.20			None	
Pro Totals—11 Years	162	29	11	37.9	331	8	4	11.41	17	539	31.7	0

Additional pro statistics: Punted once for 39 yards, 1975; recovered one fumble, 1975, 1982, 1984 and 1985; recovered five fumbles, 1977; recovered two fumbles, 1978, 1979 and 1983; recovered three fumbles, 1980 and 1981.
Played in NFC Championship Game following 1984 and 1985 seasons.
Played in NFL Championship Game following 1985 season.
Played in Pro Bowl (NFL All-Star Game) following 1976 through 1980 and 1983 through 1985 seasons.

WAYNE LAMAR PEACE
Quarterback—San Diego Chargers
Born November 3, 1961, at Gainesville, Fla.
Height, 6.02. Weight, 215.
High School—Lakeland, Fla.
Received business administration degree in marketing from University of Florida.
Selected by Tampa Bay in 1984 USFL territorial draft.
Signed by Tampa Bay Bandits, February 7, 1984.
Selected by Cincinnati in 1st round (7th player selected) of 1984 NFL supplemental draft.
Traded by Tampa Bay Bandits to Portland Breakers for two draft choices, February 6, 1985.
Left Portland Breakers voluntarily, February 8, 1985 (rights reverted to Tampa Bay Bandits).
Released by Tampa Bay Bandits, February 15, 1985; signed by Cincinnati Bengals, February 21, 1985.
Released by Cincinnati Bengals, August 12, 1985; awarded on waivers to Miami Dolphins, August 13, 1985.
Left Miami Dolphins camp voluntarily, August 19, 1985; signed as free agent by San Diego Chargers, April 15, 1986.

| | | —PASSING— | | | | | | | —RUSHING— | | | | —TOTAL— | | |
Year Club	G.	Att.	Cmp.	Pct.	Gain	T.P.	P.I.	Avg.	Att.	Yds.	Avg.	TD.	TD.	Pts.	F.
1984—Tampa Bay USFL	8	43	18	41.9	215	1	4	5.00	6	35	5.8	0	0	0	1

Quarterback Rating Points: 1984 (26.8).

JOE PELLEGRINI
Guard-Center—Atlanta Falcons
Born April 8, 1957, at Boston, Mass.
Height, 6.04. Weight, 264.
High School—Braintree, Mass., Archbishop Williams.
Received bachelor of science degree in geological
engineering from Harvard University in 1979.
Signed as free agent by New York Jets, May 5, 1981.
On injured reserve with back injury, August 25 through entire 1981 season.
Released by New York Jets, August 27, 1984; signed as free agent by Atlanta Falcons, September 4, 1984.
USFL rights traded by Jacksonville Bulls to New Jersey Generals for past considerations, February 6, 1985.
On injured reserve with leg injury, September 2 through October 31, 1985; activated, November 1, 1985.
On injured reserve with sprained ankle, December 6 through remainder of 1985 season.
New York Jets NFL, 1982 and 1983; Atlanta NFL, 1984 and 1985.
Games: 1982 (9), 1983 (16), 1984 (15), 1985 (5). Total—45.
Pro statistics: Recovered one fumble, 1983.
Member of New York Jets for AFC Championship Game following 1982 season; did not play.

SCOTT JOHN PELLUER
Linebacker—New Orleans Saints
Born April 26, 1959, at Yakima, Wash.
Height, 6.02. Weight, 227.
High School—Bellevue, Wash., Interlake.
Received degree in secondary education from Washington State University.
Step-son of Jim Harryman, Athletic Director at Bellevue Community College;
brother of Steve Pelluer, quarterback with Dallas Cowboys;
and brother of Arnie Pelluer, linebacker at Stanford University.
Selected by Dallas in 4th round (91st player selected) of 1981 NFL draft.
Released by Dallas Cowboys, August 31, 1981; claimed on waivers by New Orleans Saints, September 1, 1981.
On inactive list, September 12, 1982.
On injured reserve with knee injury, December 11 through remainder of 1985 season.
New Orleans NFL, 1981 through 1985.
Games: 1981 (16), 1982 (6), 1983 (16), 1984 (16), 1985 (11). Total—65.
Pro statistics: Recovered one fumble, 1981 and 1985.

STEVEN CARL PELLUER
(Steve)
Quarterback—Dallas Cowboys

Born July 29, 1962, at Yakima, Wash.
Height, 6.04. Weight, 210.
High School—Bellevue, Wash., Interlake.
Attended University of Washington.
Step-son of Jim Harryman, Athletic Director at Bellevue Community College;
brother of Scott Pelluer, linebacker with New Orleans Saints;
and brother of Arnie Pelluer, linebacker at Stanford University.

Selected by Oakland in 6th round (110th player selected) of 1984 USFL draft.
Selected by Dallas in 5th round (113th player selected) of 1984 NFL draft.
Signed by Dallas Cowboys, July 7, 1984.

Year Club	G.	PASSING Att.	Cmp.	Pct.	Gain	T.P.	P.I.	Avg.	RUSHING Att.	Yds.	Avg.	TD.	TOTAL TD.	Pts.	F.
1984—Dallas NFL	1			None						None			0	0	0
1985—Dallas NFL	2	8	5	62.5	47	0	0	5.88	3	—2	—0.7	0	0	0	0
Pro Totals—2 Years	3	8	5	62.5	47	0	0	5.88	3	—2	—0.7	0	0	0	0

Quarterback Rating Points: 1985 (78.6).

JAIRO A. PENARANDA
Name pronounced Hi-row Penya-rahnda.
Fullback—Philadelphia Eagles

Born June 15, 1958, at Barranquilla, Columbia.
Height, 6.00. Weight, 217.
High School—Burbank, Calif., John Burroughs.
Attended Los Angeles Valley College and University of California at Los Angeles.

Selected by Los Angeles in 12th round (328th player selected) of 1981 NFL draft.
Released by Los Angeles Rams, September 6, 1982; signed by Arizona Wranglers, November 11, 1982.
Released by Arizona Wranglers, February 7, 1983; signed as free agent by Oakland Invaders, February 17, 1983.
Selected by Memphis Showboats in 13th round (78th player selected) of USFL expansion draft, September 6, 1983.
On developmental squad, April 12 through April 17, 1984; activated, April 18, 1984.
On developmental squad, April 25 through April 30, 1984.
Released by Memphis Showboats May 1, 1984; signed as free agent by San Francisco 49ers, May 12, 1984.
On injured reserve with ankle injury, August 27 through September 4, 1984.
Released by San Francisco 49ers, September 5, 1984; signed as free agent by Philadelphia Eagles, November 27, 1985.
On developmental squad for 2 games with Memphis Showboats in 1984.

Year Club	G.	RUSHING Att.	Yds.	Avg.	TD.	PASS RECEIVING P.C.	Yds.	Avg.	TD.	TOTAL TD.	Pts.	F.
1981—Los Angeles NFL	16		None				None			0	0	0
1983—Oakland USFL	18	10	28	2.8	0	7	42	6.0	0	0	0	2
1984—Memphis USFL	8	19	53	2.8	0	3	16	5.3	1	1	6	0
1985—Philadelphia NFL	4		None				None			0	0	0
NFL Totals—2 Years	20	0	0	0.0	0	0	0	0.0	0	0	0	0
USFL Totals—2 Years	26	29	81	2.8	0	10	58	5.8	1	1	6	2
Pro Totals—4 Years	46	29	81	2.8	0	10	58	5.8	1	1	6	2

Additional pro statistics: Returned two kickoffs for nine yards, 1984.

COACHING RECORD

Assistant coach, Memphis Showboats USFL, 1985.

JESSE ANDREW PENN II
Linebacker—Dallas Cowboys

Born September 6, 1962, at Martinsville, Va.
Height, 6.03. Weight, 217.
High School—Martinsville, Va.
Attended Virginia Tech.

Selected by New Jersey in 1st round (5th player selected) of 1985 USFL draft.
Selected by Dallas in 2nd round (44th player selected) of 1985 NFL draft.
Signed by Dallas Cowboys, May 9, 1985.
Dallas NFL, 1985.
Games: 1985 (16).
Pro statistics: Returned blocked punt 46 yards for a touchdown and recovered one fumble, 1985.

GEORGE EVANS PEOPLES
Running Back

Born August 25, 1960, at Tampa, Fla.
Height, 6.00. Weight, 215.
High School—Tampa, Fla., King.
Attended Auburn University.

Selected by Dallas in 8th round (216th player selected) of 1982 NFL draft.
Released by Dallas Cowboys, August 29, 1983; awarded on waivers to New England Patriots, August 30, 1983.
Released by New England Patriots, August 27, 1984; signed as free agent by Tampa Bay Buccaneers, November 6, 1984.

Released by Tampa Bay Buccaneers, September 2, 1985; re-signed by Buccaneers, December 13. 1985.
Granted free agency with no qualifying offer, February 1, 1986.

		—RUSHING—				PASS RECEIVING			—TOTAL—		
Year Club	G.	Att.	Yds.	Avg.	TD.	P.C. Yds.	Avg.	TD.	TD.	Pts.	F.
1982—Dallas NFL	8	7	22	3.1	0	None			0	0	0
1983—New England NFL	16		None			None			0	0	0
1984—Tampa Bay NFL	6	1	2	2.0	0	None			0	0	0
1985—Tampa Bay NFL	2		None			None			0	0	0
Pro Totals—4 Years	32	8	24	3.0	0	0	0	0.0	0	0	0	0

Additional pro statistics: Recovered one fumble, 1982 and 1983.
Played in NFC Championship Game following 1982 season.

EDWARD JOSEPH PEROT
Name pronounced Pay-row.
(Pete)
Guard—New Orleans Saints
Born April 28, 1957, at Natchitoches, La.
Height, 6.02. Weight, 261.
High School—Natchitoches, La., St. Mary's.
Attended Northwestern Louisiana State University.

Selected by Philadelphia in 2nd round (48th player selected) of 1979 NFL draft.
On injured reserve with shoulder injury, August 29 through entire 1983 season.
Granted free agency, February 1, 1985; signing rights released by Philadelphia Eagles, May 7, 1985.
Signed as free agent by New Orleans Saints, August 19, 1985.
Released by New Orleans Saints, September 2, 1985; re-signed by Saints, September 24, 1985.
On injured reserve with bruised calf, November 15 through remainder of 1985 season.
Philadelphia NFL, 1979 through 1982 and 1984; New Orleans NFL, 1985.
Games: 1979 (14), 1980 (16), 1981 (16), 1982 (9), 1984 (12), 1985 (7). Total—74.
Played in NFC Championship Game following 1980 season.
Played in NFL Championship Game following 1980 season.

JESSE BENNETT PERRIN
(Benny)
Safety—St. Louis Cardinals
Born October 20, 1959, at Orange County, Calif.
Height, 6.02. Weight, 175.
High School—Decatur, Ala.
Attended University of Alabama.

Selected by St. Louis in 3rd round (65th player selected) of 1982 NFL draft.
On injured reserve with knee injury, November 20 through remainder of 1985 season.

		—INTERCEPTIONS—			
Year Club	G.	No.	Yds.	Avg.	TD.
1982—St. Louis NFL	9	1	35	35.0	0
1983—St. Louis NFL	16	4	50	12.5	0
1984—St. Louis NFL	16	4	22	5.5	0
1985—St. Louis NFL	7		None		
Pro Totals—4 Years	48	9	107	11.9	0

Additional pro statistics: Recovered two fumbles for 32 yards and a touchdown, attempted one pass with one completion for four yards and rushed once for no yards, 1983; attempted one pass with one completion for no yards and recovered two fumbles for 16 yards, 1984; recovered one fumble, 1985.

WILLIAM PERRY
Defensive Tackle—Chicago Bears
Born December 16, 1962, at Aiken, S.C.
Height, 6.02. Weight, 308.
High School—Aiken, S.C.
Attended Clemson University.
Brother of Michael Perry, defensive tackle at Clemson University.

Selected by Orlando in 1985 USFL territorial draft.
Selected by Chicago in 1st round (22nd player selected) of 1985 NFL draft.
Signed by Chicago Bears, August 5, 1985.
Chicago NFL, 1985.
Games: 1985 (16).
Pro statistics: Rushed five times for seven yards and two touchdowns, caught one pass for four yards and a touchdown and recovered two fumbles for 66 yards, 1985.
Played in NFC Championship Game following 1985 saeson.
Played in NFL Championship Game following 1985 season.

—DID YOU KNOW—

That the Pittsburgh Steelers have had different starting quarterbacks in each of their past four opening-day games? In 1982, the starter was Terry Bradshaw; in '83, Cliff Stoudt; in '84, David Woodley and in '85, Mark Malone.

JAMES T. PERRYMAN
(Jim)
Safety—Buffalo Bills
Born December 23, 1960, at Oakland, Calif.
Height, 6.00. Weight, 175.
High School—Pittsburgh, Pa., South Hills.
Received degree from Millikin University.

Signed as free agent by Denver Gold, January 10, 1983.
Released by Denver Gold, February 2, 1983; signed as free agent by Pittsburgh Maulers, October 5, 1983.
Released by Pittsburgh Maulers, February 16, 1984; re-signed by Maulers, May 2, 1984.
On developmental squad, May 2 through May 9, 1984; activated, May 10, 1984.
Franchise disbanded, October 25, 1984; selected by Oakland Invaders in USFL dispersal draft, December 6, 1984.
Released by Oakland Invaders, January 28, 1985; signed as free agent by Buffalo Bills, March 21, 1985.
Released by Buffalo Bills, August 27, 1985; re-signed by Bills, October 12, 1985.
On developmental squad for 1 game with Pittsburgh Maulers in 1984.
Pittsburgh USFL, 1984; Buffalo NFL, 1985.
Games: 1984 (12), 1985 (11). Total—23.

ANTHONY LEMONT PETERS
(Tony)
Safety—Washington Redskins
Born April 28, 1953, at Oklahoma City, Okla.
Height, 6.01. Weight, 190.
High School—Pauls Valley, Okla.
Attended Northeastern Oklahoma A&M and University of Oklahoma.

Selected by Cleveland in 4th round (82nd player selected) of 1975 NFL draft.
Left Cleveland Browns' camp in contract dispute, August 1, 1979.
Traded by Cleveland Browns to Washington Redskins for 5th round pick in 1980 draft and 4th and 10th round picks in 1981 draft, August 17, 1979.
Suspended indefinitely, September 2, 1983, with drug charges pending.
Suspended November 18, 1983 for remainder of 1983 season; reinstated, May 15, 1984.
On injured reserve with abdominal strain, November 17 through remainder of 1984 season.

| | | —INTERCEPTIONS— | | | |
Year Club	G.	No.	Yds.	Avg.	TD.
1975—Cleveland NFL	14	1	0	0.0	0
1976—Cleveland NFL	14		None		
1977—Cleveland NFL	14	2	29	14.5	0
1978—Cleveland NFL	16	2	7	3.5	0
1979—Washington NFL	16	1	−4	−4.0	0
1980—Washington NFL	16	4	59	14.8	0
1981—Washington NFL	16	3	0	0.0	0
1982—Washington NFL	9	1	14	14.0	0
1984—Washington NFL	8		None		
1985—Washington NFL	10	2	21	10.5	0
Pro Totals—10 Years	133	16	126	7.9	0

Additional pro statistics: Recovered one fumble for 10 yards, 1975; returned one punt for no yards, 1979; fumbled once, 1979 and 1980; returned one kickoff for five yards, 1981; recovered one fumble, 1981, 1982 and 1984.
Played in NFC Championship Game following 1982 season.
Played in NFL Championship Game following 1982 season.
Played in Pro Bowl (NFL All-Star Game) following 1982 season.

KURT DAVID PETERSEN
Guard—Dallas Cowboys
Born June 17, 1957, at St. Louis, Mo.
Height, 6.04. Weight, 278.
High School—St. Louis, Mo., Lutheran North.
Received bachelor of science degree in industrial
engineering from University of Missouri in 1980.

Selected by Dallas in 4th round (105th player selected) of 1980 NFL draft.
Dallas NFL, 1980 through 1985.
Games: 1980 (16), 1981 (16), 1982 (9), 1983 (14), 1984 (13), 1985 (16). Total—84.
Pro statistics: Recovered one fumble, 1980 and 1985; recovered two fumbles for three yards, 1981; recovered two fumbles, 1982.
Played in NFC Championship Game following 1980 through 1982 seasons.

GERARD PAUL PHELAN
Name pronounced FAY-lin.
Wide Receiver—New England Patriots
Born January 20, 1963, at Winningboro, N.J.
Height, 6.00. Weight, 190.
High School—Radnor, Pa., Archbishop Carroll.
Received degree in finance from Boston College in 1985.

Selected by New Jersey in 1985 USFL territorial draft.
Selected by New England in 4th round (108th player selected) of 1985 NFL draft.
Signed by New England Patriots, July 22, 1985.
On injured reserve with knee injury, August 19 through entire 1985 season.

JOE PHILLIPS
Wide Receiver—Washington Redskins
Born April 12, 1963, at Franklin, Ky.
Height, 5.09. Weight, 188.
High School—Franklin, Ky., Simpson.
Attended University of Kentucky.

Signed as free agent by Washington Redskins, May 2, 1985.
Released by Washington Redskins, September 2, 1985; re-signed by Redskins, November 20, 1985.
Released by Washington Redskins, November 22, 1985; re-signed by Redskins, November 27, 1985.
Washington NFL, 1985.
Games: 1985 (4).

REGGIE PHILLIPS
Defensive Back—Chicago Bears
Born December 12, 1960, at Houston, Tex.
Height, 5.10. Weight, 170.
High School—Houston, Tex., Jack Yates.
Attended Southern Methodist University.

Selected by Houston in 1985 USFL territorial draft.
Selected by Chicago in 2nd round (49th player selected) of 1985 NFL draft.
Signed by Chicago Bears, July 9, 1985.
Chicago NFL, 1985.
Games: 1985 (16).
Pro statistics: Recovered one fumble, 1985.
Played in NFC Championship Game following 1985 season.
Played in NFL Championship Game following 1985 season.

BILL PICKEL
Name pronounced Pick-ELL.
Defensive Tackle—Los Angeles Raiders
Born November 5, 1959, at Queens, N.Y.
Height, 6.05. Weight, 260.
High Schools—Milford, Conn.; and Brooklyn, N.Y., St. Francis.
Attended Rutgers University.
Brother of Chris Pickel, linebacker at Rutgers University.

Selected by New Jersey in 1983 USFL territorial draft.
Selected by Los Angeles Raiders in 2nd round (54th player selected) of 1983 NFL draft.
Signed by Los Angeles Raiders, May 26, 1983.
Los Angeles Raiders NFL, 1983 through 1985.
Games: 1983 (16), 1984 (16), 1985 (16). Total—48.
Pro statistics: Recovered one fumble, 1983.
Played in AFC Championship Game following 1983 season.
Played in NFL Championship Game following 1983 season.

CLAY FLOYD PICKERING
Wide Receiver—Cincinnati Bengals
Born June 2, 1961, at Jacksonville, Fla.
Height, 6.05. Weight, 215.
High School—Akron, O., Archbishop.
Attended University of Maine.

Signed as free agent by Cincinnati Bengals, May 20, 1984.
Released by Cincinnati Bengals, August 27, 1984; re-signed by Bengals, August 28, 1984.
On injured reserve with pulled hamstring, September 21 through remainder of 1984 season.
On injured reserve with pulled hamstring, September 3 through December 19, 1985; activated, December 20, 1985.
Cincinnati NFL, 1984 and 1985.
Games: 1984 (3), 1985 (1). Total—4.

RAYMON EARL PINNEY JR.
(Ray)
Offensive Tackle-Center—Pittsburgh Steelers
Born June 29, 1954, at Seattle, Wash.
Height, 6.04. Weight, 265.
High School—Seattle, Wash., Shorecrest.
Received bachelor of arts degree in finance from University of Washington.

Named as offensive tackle on THE SPORTING NEWS USFL All-Star Team, 1983 and 1985.
Selected by Pittsburgh in 2nd round (37th player selected) of 1976 NFL draft.
On injured reserve with stomach injury, August 22 through entire 1979 season.
Granted free agency, February 1, 1983.
USFL rights traded by Denver Gold to Michigan Panthers for future draft pick, April 26, 1983.
Signed by Michigan Panthers, April 27, 1983.
On developmental squad, April 27 through April 30, 1983; activated, May 1, 1983.
Protected in merger of Michigan Panthers and Oakland Invaders, December 6, 1984.
Released by Oakland Invaders, August 13, 1985; re-signed by Pittsburgh Steelers, September 13, 1985.
Granted roster exemption, September 13 through September 15, 1985; activated, September 16, 1985.
Pittsburgh NFL, 1976 through 1978, 1980 through 1982 and 1985; Michigan USFL, 1983 and 1984; Oakland USFL, 1985.

Games: 1976 (14), 1977 (14), 1978 (13), 1980 (16), 1981 (16), 1982 (9), 1983 (10), 1984 (18), 1985 USFL (18), 1985 NFL (15). Total NFL—97. Total USFL—46. Total Pro—143.

NFL statistics: Recovered one fumble, 1978; caught one pass for one yard and a touchdown, 1981; caught one pass for three yards and a touchdown, 1982.

USFL statistics: Caught one pass for two yards and a touchdown, 1983; caught one pass for three yards and a touchdown, 1985.

Played in AFC Championship Game following 1976 and 1978 seasons.

Played in NFL Championship Game following 1978 season.

Played in USFL Championship Game following 1983 and 1985 seasons.

MIKE PITTS
Defensive End—Atlanta Falcons
Born September 25, 1960, at Baltimore, Md.
Height, 6.05. Weight, 277.
High School—Baltimore, Md., Polytechnic.
Attended University of Alabama.
Cousin of Rick Porter, running back with Baltimore Stars.

Named as defensive end on THE SPORTING NEWS College All-America Team, 1982.

Selected by Birmingham in 1983 USFL territorial draft.

Selected by Atlanta in 1st round (16th player selected) of 1983 NFL draft.

Signed by Atlanta Falcons, July 16, 1983.

On injured reserve with knee injury, December 6 through remainder of 1984 season.

Atlanta NFL, 1983 through 1985.

Games: 1983 (16), 1984 (14), 1985 (16). Total—46.

Pro statistics: Recovered one fumble for 26 yards, 1983; recovered two fumbles, 1984; intercepted one pass for one yard, recovered one fumble for six yards and fumbled once, 1985.

RONALD DWAYNE PITTS
(Ron)
Cornerback—Buffalo Bills
Born October 14, 1962, at Detroit, Mich.
Height, 5.10. Weight, 180.
High School—Orchard Park, N.Y.
Received degree in communications from
University of California at Los Angeles in 1985.
Son of Elijah Pitts, running back with Green Bay Packers, Los Angeles Rams and New Orleans Saints, 1961 through 1971; scout, Green Bay Packers, 1972; and assistant coach with Los Angeles Rams, 1973 through 1977; Houston Oilers, 1981 through 1983; Hamilton Tiger-Cats, 1984 and Buffalo Bills, 1978 through 1980 and since 1985.

Selected by Buffalo in 7th round (169th player selected) of 1985 NFL draft.

Signed by Buffalo Bills, July 30, 1985.

On injured reserve with foot injury, August 19 through entire 1985 season.

MICHAEL RICORDO PLEASANT
Wide Receiver—Los Angeles Rams
Born August 16, 1955, at Muskogee, Okla.
Height, 6.02. Weight, 193.
High School—Muskogee, Okla.
Received degree in special education and physical education
from University of Oklahoma in 1978.

Signed as free agent by Oakland Raiders, May 10, 1981.

Released by Oakland Raiders, August 13, 1981; signed as free agent by Los Angeles Rams, July 1, 1982.

Released by Los Angeles Rams, August 31, 1982; signed as free agent by San Diego Chargers, April 20, 1983.

On injured reserve with pulled hamstring, August 27 through entire 1983 season.

Released by San Diego Chargers, August 14, 1984; signed as free agent by Los Angeles Rams for 1985, November 13, 1984.

Signed for 1984 season, November 14, 1984.

On injured reserve with leg injury, August 17 through entire 1985 season.

Los Angeles Rams NFL, 1984.

Games: 1984 (5).

Pro statistics: Returned two kickoffs for 48 yards, 1984.

REGINALD LECARNO PLEASANT
(Reggie)
Cornerback—Tampa Bay Buccaneers
Born May 2, 1962, at Sumter, S.C.
Height, 5.10. Weight, 175.
High School—Sumter, S.C., Furman.
Attended Clemson University.

Selected by Orlando in 1985 USFL territorial draft.

Selected by Atlanta in 6th round (152nd player selected) of 1985 NFL draft.

Signed by Atlanta Falcons, June 11, 1985.

Released by Atlanta Falcons, August 27, 1985; re-signed by Falcons, September 16, 1985.

Released by Atlanta Falcons, October 8, 1985; signed as free agent by Tampa Bay Buccaneers, March 17, 1986.

Atlanta NFL, 1985.

Games: 1985 (3).

KURT ALAN PLOEGER
Name pronounced PLEW-ger.
Defensive End—Dallas Cowboys
Born December 1, 1962, at Iowa Falls, Ia.
Height, 6.05. Weight, 259.
High School—LeSueur, Minn.
Received bachelor of science degree from Gustavus Adolphus College in 1985.

Selected by Dallas in 6th round (144th player selected) of 1985 NFL draft.
Signed by Dallas Cowboys, July 14, 1985.
On injured reserve with thigh injury, August 2 through entire 1985 season.

ARTHUR SCOTT PLUNKETT
(Art)
Offensive Tackle—New England Patriots
Born March 8, 1959, at Chicago, Ill.
Height, 6.07. Weight, 262.
High Schools—Arlington Heights, Ill., Arlington and Salt Lake City, Utah, Skyline.
Attended University of Nevada at Las Vegas.

Selected by Los Angeles in 8th round (216th player selected) of 1981 NFL draft.
On injured reserve with back injury, August 24 through October 26, 1981; claimed on procedural waivers by St. Louis Cardinals, October 28, 1981.
Released by St. Louis Cardinals, September 3, 1985, signed as free agent by New England Patriots, September 11, 1985.
St. Louis NFL, 1981 through 1984; New England NFL, 1985.
Games: 1981 (8), 1982 (9), 1983 (16), 1984 (16), 1985 (15). Total—64.
Played in AFC Championship Game following 1985 season.
Played in NFL Championship Game following 1985 season.

JAMES WILLIAM PLUNKETT JR.
(Jim)
Quarterback—Los Angeles Raiders
Born December 5, 1947, at San Jose, Calif.
Height, 6.02. Weight, 220.
High Schools—San Jose, Calif., Overfeldt and James Lick.
Attended Stanford University.

Tied NFL record for longest completed passing play from scrimmage when he threw a 99-yard touchdown pass to wide receiver Cliff Branch against Washington Redskins, October 2, 1983.
Heisman Trophy winner, 1970.
Named THE SPORTING NEWS College Football Player of the Year, 1970.
Named as quarterback on THE SPORTING NEWS College All-America Team, 1970.
Named THE SPORTING NEWS AFC Rookie of the Year, 1971.
Selected by New England in 1st round (1st player selected) of 1971 NFL draft.
Traded by New England Patriots to San Francisco 49ers for quarterback Tom Owen and four draft choices (two 1st round selections in 1976 plus 1st and 2nd round picks in 1977), April 5, 1976.
Released by San Francisco 49ers, August 28, 1978; signed as free agent by Oakland Raiders, September 12, 1978.
Franchise transferred to Los Angeles, May 7, 1982.
On injured reserve with pulled abdominal muscle, October 13 through November 11, 1984; activated, November 12, 1984.
On injured reserve with dislocated shoulder, September 23 through remainder of 1985 season.
Active for 14 games with Oakland Raiders in 1978; did not play.

Year Club	G.	Att.	Cmp.	Pct.	Gain	T.P.	P.I.	Avg.	Att.	Yds.	Avg.	TD.	TD.	Pts.	F.
				PASSING						RUSHING			TOTAL		
1971—New England NFL..........	14	328	158	48.2	2158	19	16	6.58	45	210	4.7	0	0	0	6
1972—New England NFL..........	14	355	169	47.6	2196	8	25	6.19	36	230	6.4	1	1	6	6
1973—New England NFL..........	14	376	193	51.3	2550	13	17	6.78	44	209	4.8	5	5	30	6
1974—New England NFL..........	14	352	173	49.1	2457	19	22	6.98	30	161	5.4	2	2	12	4
1975—New England NFL..........	5	92	36	39.1	571	3	7	6.21	4	7	1.8	1	1	6	2
1976—San Francisco NFL..........	12	243	126	51.9	1592	13	16	6.55	19	95	5.0	0	0	0	1
1977—San Francisco NFL..........	14	248	128	51.6	1693	9	14	6.83	28	71	2.5	1	1	6	2
1979—Oakland NFL..................	4	15	7	46.7	89	1	1	5.93	3	18	6.0	0	0	0	0
1980—Oakland NFL..................	13	320	165	51.6	2299	18	16	7.18	28	141	5.0	2	2	12	9
1981—Oakland NFL..................	9	179	94	52.5	1045	4	9	5.84	12	38	3.2	1	1	6	3
1982—L.A. Raiders NFL..........	9	261	152	58.2	2035	14	15	7.80	15	6	0.4	0	0	0	4
1983—L.A. Raiders NFL..........	14	379	230	60.7	2935	20	18	7.74	26	78	3.0	0	0	0	7
1984—L.A. Raiders NFL..........	8	198	108	54.5	1473	6	10	7.44	16	14	0.9	1	1	6	2
1985—L.A. Raiders NFL..........	3	103	71	68.9	803	3	3	7.80	5	12	2.4	0	0	0	6
Pro Totals—15 Years	147	3449	1810	52.5	23896	150	189	6.93	311	1290	4.1	14	14	84	58

Quarterback Rating Points: 1971 (68.6), 1972 (46.1), 1973 (66.0), 1974 (63.8), 1975 (39.9), 1976 (62.8), 1977 (62.2), 1979 (60.1), 1980 (72.8), 1981 (56.7), 1982 (77.3), 1983 (82.7), 1984 (67.6), 1985 (89.6). Total—66.1.
Additional pro statistics: Recovered one fumble, 1972 through 1974, 1981, 1982 and 1984; recovered two fumbles, 1977 and 1980; fumbled three times for minus six yards, 1981; fumbled four times for minus seven yards, 1982; recovered three fumbles, 1983; recovered one fumble and fumbled six times for minus five yards, 1985.
Played in AFC Championship Game following 1980 and 1983 seasons.
Played in NFL Championship Game following 1980 and 1983 seasons.

JOHNNIE EDWARD POE
Cornerback—New Orleans Saints
Born August 29, 1959, at St. Louis, Mo.
Height, 6.01. Weight, 194.
High School—East St. Louis, Ill., Lincoln.
Attended University of Missouri.
Selected by New Orleans in 6th round (144th player selected) of 1981 NFL draft.

			—INTERCEPTIONS—		
Year Club	G.	No.	Yds.	Avg.	TD.
1981—New Orleans NFL........	15	1	0	0.0	0
1982—New Orleans NFL........	9		None		
1983—New Orleans NFL........	16	7	146	20.9	1
1984—New Orleans NFL........	16	1	16	16.0	0
1985—New Orleans NFL........	16	3	63	21.0	*1
Pro Totals—5 Years...........	72	12	225	18.8	2

Additional pro statistics: Recovered one fumble for 10 yards and returned one punt for two yards, 1981; recovered one fumble, 1982 and 1985; recovered two fumbles, 1983; fumbled once, 1985.

FRANK EDWARD POKORNY
Wide Receiver—Pittsburgh Steelers
Born May 13, 1963, at Uniontown, Pa.
Height, 6.00. Weight, 198.
High School—Monaca, Pa., Center.
Received bachelor of science degree in business administration
from Youngstown State University in 1986.
Signed as free agent by Pittsburgh Steelers, May 15, 1985.
On injured reserve with separated shoulder, August 25 through November 28, 1985; activated after clearing procedural waivers, November 30, 1985.
Pittsburgh NFL, 1985.
Games: 1985 (4).

FRANK POLLARD
Running Back—Pittsburgh Steelers
Born June 15, 1957, at Clifton, Tex.
Height, 5.10. Weight, 223.
High School—Meridian, Tex.
Attended Baylor University.
Selected by Pittsburgh in 11th round (305th player selected) of 1980 NFL draft.

		——RUSHING——				PASS RECEIVING				—TOTAL—		
Year Club	G.	Att.	Yds.	Avg.	TD.	P.C.	Yds.	Avg.	TD.	TD.	Pts.	F.
1980—Pittsburgh NFL..............................	16	4	16	4.0	0		None			0	0	1
1981—Pittsburgh NFL..............................	14	123	570	4.6	2	19	156	8.2	0	2	12	5
1982—Pittsburgh NFL..............................	9	62	238	3.8	2	6	39	6.5	0	2	12	3
1983—Pittsburgh NFL..............................	16	135	608	4.5	4	16	127	7.9	0	4	24	5
1984—Pittsburgh NFL..............................	15	213	851	4.0	6	21	186	8.9	0	6	36	9
1985—Pittsburgh NFL..............................	16	233	991	4.3	3	24	250	10.4	0	3	18	2
Pro Totals—6 Years..................................	86	770	3274	4.3	17	86	758	8.8	0	17	102	25

		KICKOFF RETURNS			
Year Club	G.	No.	Yds.	Avg.	TD.
1980—Pittsburgh NFL.............	16	22	494	22.5	0
1981—Pittsburgh NFL.............	14		None		
1982—Pittsburgh NFL.............	9		None		
1983—Pittsburgh NFL.............	16		None		
1984—Pittsburgh NFL.............	15		None		
1985—Pittsburgh NFL.............	16		None		
Pro Totals—6 Years...........	86	22	494	22.5	0

Additional pro statistics: Returned one punt for five yards, 1980; recovered one fumble, 1983 and 1985; recovered two fumbles, 1984.
Played in AFC Championship Game following 1984 season.

TOM POLLEY
Name pronounced PAUL-ee.
Linebacker—Philadelphia Eagles
Born February 17, 1962, at Minneapolis, Minn.
Height, 6.03. Weight, 235.
High School—St. Louis Park, Minn.
Attended Normandale Community College and University of Nevada at Las Vegas.
Selected by Arizona in 1985 USFL territorial draft.
Selected by Philadelphia in 8th round (205th player selected) of 1985 NFL draft.
Signed by Philadelphia Eagles, July 22, 1985.
On injured reserve with neck injury, August 27 through October 2, 1985; activated after clearing procedural waivers, October 4, 1985.
On injured reserve with neck injury, October 18 through remainder of 1985 season.
Philadelphia NFL, 1985.
Games: 1985 (2).

DAVID PONDER
Defensive Lineman—Buffalo Bills
Born June 27, 1962, at Cairo, Ga.
Height, 6.03. Weight, 250.
High School—Cairo, Ga.
Attended Florida State University.

Signed as free agent by Dallas Cowboys, May 3, 1984.
Released by Dallas Cowboys, August 27, 1984; re-signed by Cowboys, March 21, 1985.
Released by Dallas Cowboys, October 26, 1985; signed as free agent by Los Angeles Raiders, November 21, 1985.
Released by Los Angeles Raiders, November 23, 1985; signed as free agent by Buffalo Bills, May 6, 1986.
Dallas NFL, 1985.
Games: 1984 (4).

NATHAN POOLE
Running Back—Denver Broncos
Born December 17, 1956, at Alexander City, Ala.
Height, 5.09. Weight, 212.
High School—Alexander City, Ala., Benjamin Russell.
Received degree in business management from University of Louisville.

Selected by Cincinnati in 10th round (250th player selected) of 1979 NFL draft.
Released by Cincinnati Bengals, August 10, 1981; signed as free agent by Toronto Argonauts, August 18, 1981.
Released by Toronto Argonauts, August 29, 1981; signed as free agent by Denver Broncos, April 16, 1982.
Released by Denver Broncos, August 20, 1984; signed by Chicago Blitz, October 27, 1984.
Franchise disbanded, November 20, 1984; signed as free agent by Seattle Seahawks, May 8, 1985.
Released by Seattle Seahawks, August 19, 1985; signed as free agent by Denver Broncos, December 3, 1985.

			—RUSHING—				PASS RECEIVING				—TOTAL—		
Year Club	G.	Att.	Yds.	Avg.	TD.	P.C.	Yds.	Avg.	TD.		TD.	Pts.	F.
1979—Cincinnati NFL	16	1	—3	—3.0	0	1	—10	—10.0	0		0	0	2
1980—Cincinnati NFL	16	5	6	1.2	0	2	—4	—2.0	0		0	0	1
1981—Toronto CFL	1	6	33	5.5	0	1	4	4.0	0		0	0	0
1982—Denver NFL	9	7	36	5.1	0		None				0	0	0
1983—Denver NFL	16	81	246	3.0	4	20	184	9.2	0		4	24	1
1985—Denver NFL	3	4	12	3.0	0		None				0	0	0
NFL Totals—5 Years	60	98	297	3.0	4	23	170	7.4	0		4	24	4
CFL Total—1 Year	1	6	33	5.5	0	1	4	4.0	0		0	0	0
Pro Totals—6 Years	61	104	330	3.2	4	24	174	7.3	0		4	24	4

		KICKOFF RETURNS			
Year Club	G.	No.	Yds.	Avg.	TD.
1979—Cincinnati NFL	16	7	128	18.3	0
1980—Cincinnati NFL	16	1	8	8.0	0
1981—Toronto CFL	1		None		
1982—Denver NFL	9	1	0	0.0	0
1983—Denver NFL	16		None		
1985—Denver NFL	3		None		
NFL Totals—5 Years	60	9	136	15.1	0
CFL Total—1 Year	1	0	0	0.0	0
Pro Totals—6 Years	61	9	136	15.1	0

Additional pro statistics: Recovered two fumbles, 1979; recovered one fumble, 1980 and 1983.

TRACY RANDOLPH PORTER
Wide Receiver—New Orleans Saints
Born June 1, 1959, at Baton Rouge, La.
Height, 6.02. Weight, 202.
High School—Baton Rouge, La., Southern University Laboratory.
Received bachelor of science degree in finance from Louisiana State University.

Selected by Detroit in 4th round (99th player selected) of 1981 NFL draft.
Traded by Detroit Lions to Baltimore Colts for 10th round pick in 1984 draft, August 29, 1983.
Franchise transferred to Indianapolis, March 31, 1984.
On injured reserve with leg injury, August 20 through September 1, 1985.
Released by Indianapolis Colts, September 2, 1985; signed as free agent by New Orleans Saints, May 9, 1986.

		——PASS RECEIVING——			
Year Club	G.	P.C.	Yds.	Avg.	TD.
1981—Detroit NFL	12	3	63	21.0	1
1982—Detroit NFL	8	9	124	13.8	0
1983—Baltimore NFL	16	28	384	13.7	0
1984—Indianapolis NFL	16	39	590	15.1	2
Pro Totals—4 Years	52	79	1161	14.7	3

Additional pro statistics: Attempted one pass with no completions, 1982; recovered one fumble and fumbled twice, 1984.

—DID YOU KNOW—
That Ron Jaworski's 99-yard touchdown pass to Mike Quick against Atlanta last November 10 was just the sixth pass of that distance in NFL history?

KENNETH F. POTTER
(Ken)
Kicker—Los Angeles Raiders
Born August 23, 1962, at Pomona, Calif.
Height, 6.02. Weight, 195.
High School—La Verne, Calif., Damien.
Received bachelor of arts degree in economics from University of California at Los Angeles.

Signed as free agent by Portland Breakers, April 12, 1985.
On developmental squad, April 20 through April 24, 1985.
Released by Portland Breakers, April 25, 1985; signed as free agent by Los Angeles Rams, June 26, 1985.
Released by Los Angeles Rams, August 17, 1985; signed as free agent by Los Angeles Raiders, April 21, 1986.
On developmental squad for 1 game with Portland Breakers in 1985.
Portland USFL, 1985.
Games: 1985 (1).

VINCENT SHAWN POTTS
(Known by middle name.)
Wide Receiver—Buffalo Bills
Born September 9, 1960, at Kalamazoo, Mich.
Height, 5.10. Weight, 166.
High School—Kalamazoo, Mich., Hackett.
Attended Bowling Green State University.

Signed as free agent by Cleveland Browns, May 24, 1983.
Released by Cleveland Browns, August 22, 1983; signed by Pittsburgh Maulers, November 10, 1983.
On developmental squad, April 5 through April 19, 1984; activated, April 20, 1984.
Traded by Pittsburgh Maulers to Chicago Blitz for draft choice, May 1, 1984.
Franchise disbanded, November 20, 1984.
Selected by Houston Gamblers in USFL dispersal draft, December 6, 1984.
On developmental squad, February 21 through March 6, 1985; activated, March 7, 1985.
On developmental squad, May 26 through May 31, 1985; activated, June 1, 1985.
Granted free agency with option not exercised, August 2, 1985; signed by Buffalo Bills, May 6, 1986.
On developmental squad for 2 games with Pittsburgh Maulers in 1984.
On developmental squad for 2 games with Houston Gamblers in 1985.

		PASS RECEIVING				—KICKOFF RET.—				—TOTAL—		
Year	Club	G.	P.C.	Yds.	Avg.	TD.	No.	Yds.	Avg.	TD.	TD.	Pts.	F.
1984—Pittsburgh(8)-Chicago(7) USFL		15	11	153	13.9	1	None				1	6	0
1985—Houston USFL		13	8	50	6.3	1	6	101	16.8	0	1	6	0
Pro Totals—2 Years		28	19	203	10.7	2	6	101	16.8	0	2	12	0

Additional pro statistics: Returned two punts for three yards, 1984; rushed once for two yards, 1985.

KARL ALANZO POWE
Name pronounced Poe.
Wide Receiver—Dallas Cowboys
Born January 17, 1962, at Mobile, Ala.
Height, 6.02. Weight, 175.
High School—Prichard, Ala., Mattie T. Blount.
Attended Alabama State University.

Selected by Birmingham in 1985 USFL territorial draft.
Selected by Dallas in 7th round (178th player selected) of 1985 NFL draft.
Signed by Dallas Cowboys, July 2, 1985.

		—PASS RECEIVING—				
Year	Club	G.	P.C.	Yds.	Avg.	TD.
1985—Dallas NFL		15	14	237	16.9	0

Additional pro statistics: Returned one kickoff for 17 yards and fumbled once, 1985.

MARVIN POWELL
Offensive Tackle—Tampa Bay Buccaneers
Born August 30, 1955, at Fort Bragg, N. C.
Height, 6.05. Weight, 270.
High School—Fayetteville, N. C., 71st.
Received bachelor of arts degree in speech and political science from
University of Southern California in 1977 and attending New York Law School.

Named as offensive tackle on THE SPORTING NEWS College All-America Team, 1976.
Named to THE SPORTING NEWS AFC All-Star Team, 1979.
Named to THE SPORTING NEWS NFL All-Star Team, 1981.
Selected by New York Jets in 1st round (4th player selected) of 1977 NFL draft.
Placed on did not report list, August 19 through September 9, 1985.
Reported and granted roster exemption, September 10 through September 13, 1985; activated, September 14, 1985.
Placed on waivers by New York Jets, May 6, 1985; waivers recalled by Jets and traded to Tampa Bay Buccaneers for conditional 8th round pick in 1987 draft, May 19, 1986.
New York Jets NFL, 1977 through 1985.
Games: 1977 (11), 1978 (14), 1979 (16), 1980 (15), 1981 (14), 1982 (8), 1983 (16), 1984 (16), 1985 (14). Total—124.
Pro statistics: Recovered one fumble, 1978 and 1980.
Played in AFC Championship Game following 1982 season.
Played in Pro Bowl (NFL All-Star Game) following 1979 through 1982 seasons.
Named to Pro Bowl following 1983 season; replaced due to law school by Henry Lawrence.

PHILIP MAURICE POZDERAC
Name pronounced Poz-DEH-rick.
(Phil)
Offensive Tackle—Dallas Cowboys
Born December 19, 1959, at Cleveland, O.
Height, 6.09. Weight, 282.
High School—Garfield Heights, O.
Received bachelor of business administration degree in finance
from University of Notre Dame in 1982.

Selected by Dallas in 5th round (137th player selected) of 1982 NFL draft.
Dallas NFL, 1982 through 1985.
Games: 1982 (7), 1983 (16), 1984 (15), 1985 (14). Total—52.
Pro statistics: Caught one pass for one yard, 1984.
Member of Dallas Cowboys for NFC Championship Game following 1982 season; did not play.

TROY DEAN PRATER
(Known by middle name.)
Defensive End—Buffalo Bills
Born September 28, 1958, at Altus, Okla.
Height, 6.04. Weight, 256.
High School—Wichita Falls, Tex., Rider.
Attended Oklahoma State University.

Selected by Cleveland in 10th round (271st player selected) of 1981 NFL draft.
Released by Cleveland Browns, August 24, 1981; signed as free agent by Kansas City Chiefs, May 10, 1982.
On commissioner's exempt list, November 20 through November 23, 1982.
On non-football injury list with knee injury, November 24 through remainder of 1982 season.
USFL rights traded with running back Darrell Smith, defensive tackle Mike Perko and placekicker Rex Robinson by Chicago Blitz to Boston Breakers for rights to quarterback Greg Landry, August 11, 1982.
USFL rights traded by New Orleans Breakers to Chicago Blitz for future draft pick, January 26, 1984.
Released by·Kansas City Chiefs, August 27, 1984; signed as free agent by Buffalo Bills, September 12, 1984.
Released by Buffalo Bills, August 30, 1985; re-signed by Bills, September 3, 1985.
Kansas City NFL, 1982 and 1983; Buffalo NFL, 1984 and 1985.
Games: 1982 (2), 1983 (16), 1984 (13), 1985 (16). Total—47.
Pro statistics: Recovered one fumble, 1983.

GUY TYRONE PRATHER
Name pronounced PRAY-ther.
Linebacker—Green Bay Packers
Born March 28, 1958, at Gaithersburg, Md.
Height, 6.02. Weight, 230.
High School—Gaithersburg, Md.
Received bachelor of science degree in accounting from Grambling State University in 1980.

Signed as free agent by Dallas Cowboys, May, 1980.
Released by Dallas Cowboys, August 19, 1980; signed as free agent by Green Bay Packers, January 16, 1981.
Green Bay NFL, 1981 through 1985.
Games: 1981 (16), 1982 (9), 1983 (16), 1984 (16), 1985 (16). Total—73.
Pro statistics: Recovered one fumble, 1982 and 1984; returned one kickoff for seven yards. 1984; rushed once for no yards and fumbled once, 1985.

LARRY THOMAS PRIDEMORE JR.
(Tom)
Safety—Atlanta Falcons
Born April 29, 1956, at Oak Hill, W. Va.
Height, 5.11. Weight, 186.
High School—Ansted, W. Va.
Received bachelor of science degree in business management from
West Virginia University.

Former member of West Virginia House of Delegates.
Selected by Atlanta in 9th round (236th player selected) of 1978 NFL draft.
Released by Atlanta Falcons, August 22, 1978; re-signed by Falcons, August 30, 1978.

Year Club	G.	-INTERCEPTIONS- No.	Yds.	Avg.	TD.	-KICKOFF RET.- No.	Yds.	Avg.	TD.	-TOTAL- TD.	Pts.	F.
1978—Atlanta NFL	16	1	0	0.0	0	4	71	17.8	0	0	0	0
1979—Atlanta NFL	16	2	20	10.0	0	9	111	12.3	0	0	0	0
1980—Atlanta NFL	16	2	2	1.0	0	3	39	13.0	0	0	0	0
1981—Atlanta NFL	16	2	221	31.6	1	None				1	6	0
1982—Atlanta NFL	9	1	28	28.0	0	None				0	0	0
1983—Atlanta NFL	16	4	56	14.0	0	None				0	0	0
1984—Atlanta NFL	16	2	0	0.0	0	None				0	0	0
1985—Atlanta NFL	16	2	45	22.5	0	None				0	0	0
Pro Totals—8 Years	121	21	372	17.7	1	16	221	13.8	0	1	6	0

Additional pro statistics: Recovered three fumbles for minus seven yards, 1978; recovered one fumble for 33 yards, 1979; recovered two fumbles, 1980, 1982 and 1984; recovered three fumbles for 24 yards and returned one punt for no yards, 1981; rushed once for seven yards, 1984; rushed once for 48 yards, 1985.

MICHAEL ROBERT PRIOR
(Mike)
Defensive Back—Tampa Bay Buccaneers

Born November 14, 1963, at Chicago Heights, Ill.
Height, 6.00. Weight, 200.
High School—Chicago Heights, Ill., Marion Catholic.
Received degree in business administration
from Illinois State University in 1985.

Selected by Memphis in 4th round (60th player selected) of 1985 USFL draft.
Selected by Tampa Bay in 7th round (176th player selected) of 1985 NFL draft.
Signed by Tampa Bay Buccaneers, June 10, 1985.
Selected by Baltimore Orioles' organization in 18th round of free-agent draft, June 4, 1984.
Selected by Los Angeles Dodgers' organization in 4th round of free-agent draft, June 3, 1985.

		-PUNT RETURNS-				—KICKOFF RET.—				—TOTAL—		
Year Club	G.	No.	Yds.	Avg.	TD.	No.	Yds.	Avg.	TD.	TD.	Pts.	F.
1985—Tampa Bay NFL	16	13	105	8.1	0	10	131	13.1	0	0	0	4

Additional pro statistics: Recovered three fumbles, 1985.

JOE PROKOP
Punter—New York Jets

Born July 7, 1960, at St. Paul, Minn.
Height, 6.03. Weight, 225.
High School—White Bear Lake, Minn.
Attended California State Poly University at Pomona.

Signed as free agent by Los Angeles Rams, June 20, 1984.
Released by Los Angeles Rams, July 16, 1984.
USFL rights traded by Los Angeles Express to Houston Gamblers for past considerations, November 12, 1984.
Signed by Houston Gamblers, November 12, 1984.
Released by Houston Gamblers, January 28, 1985; signed as free agent by San Antonio Gunslingers, February 5, 1985.
Released by San Antonio Gunslingers, February 12, 1985; signed as free agent by New York Giants, June 21, 1985.
Released by New York Giants, August 26, 1985; signed as free agent by Green Bay Packers, September 4, 1985.
Released by Green Bay Packers, November 5, 1985; signed as free agent by New York Jets, March 25, 1986.

		——PUNTING——		
Year Club	G.	No.	Avg.	Blk.
1985—Green Bay NFL	9	56	39.5	0

ANDREW PROVENCE
Defensive End—Atlanta Falcons

Born March 8, 1961, at Savannah, Ga.
Height, 6.03. Weight, 267.
High School—Savannah, Ga., Benedictine.
Attended University of South Carolina.

Selected by Washington in 1983 USFL territorial draft.
Selected by Atlanta in 3rd round (75th player selected) of 1983 NFL draft.
Signed by Atlanta Falcons, May 30, 1983.
Atlanta NFL, 1983 through 1985.
Games: 1983 (16), 1984 (16), 1985 (16). Total—48.
Pro statistics: Recovered one fumble for 26 yards, 1983; recovered one fumble, 1984.

MICHAEL PRUITT
(Mike)
Fullback—Kansas City Chiefs

Born April 3, 1954, at Chicago, Ill.
Height, 6.00. Weight, 225.
High School—Chicago, Ill., Wendell Phillips.
Received bachelor of arts degree in business administration from Purdue University.

Named to THE SPORTING NEWS AFC All-Star Team, 1979.
Selected by Cleveland in 1st round (7th player selected) of 1976 NFL draft.
On injured reserve with knee injury, November 2 through November 29, 1984; activated, November 30, 1984.
Released by Cleveland Browns, September 2, 1985; signed as free agent by Buffalo Bills, September 17, 1985.
Released by Buffalo Bills, October 21, 1985; signed as free agent by Kansas City Chiefs, October 23, 1985.

		—————RUSHING—————				PASS RECEIVING				—TOTAL—		
Year Club	G.	Att.	Yds.	Avg.	TD.	P.C.	Yds.	Avg.	TD.	TD.	Pts.	F.
1976—Cleveland NFL	13	52	138	2.7	0	8	26	3.3	0	0	0	4
1977—Cleveland NFL	13	47	205	4.4	1	3	12	4.0	0	1	6	1
1978—Cleveland NFL	16	135	560	4.1	5	20	112	5.6	0	5	30	3
1979—Cleveland NFL	16	264	1294	4.9	9	41	372	9.1	2	11	66	6
1980—Cleveland NFL	16	249	1034	4.2	6	63	471	7.5	0	6	36	9
1981—Cleveland NFL	16	247	1103	4.5	7	63	442	7.0	1	8	48	5
1982—Cleveland NFL	9	143	516	3.6	3	22	140	6.4	0	3	18	4
1983—Cleveland NFL	15	293	1184	4.0	10	30	157	5.2	2	12	72	4
1984—Cleveland NFL	10	163	506	3.1	6	5	29	5.8	0	6	36	1
1985—Buff.(4)-K.C.(9) NFL	13	112	390	3.5	2	7	43	6.1	0	2	12	0
Pro Totals—10 Years	137	1707	6930	4.1	49	262	1804	6.9	5	54	324	37

Additional pro statistics: Returned six kickoffs for 106 yards, 1976; returned six kickoffs for 131 yards, 1977; recovered two fumbles, 1978 and 1981 through 1983; recovered one fumble, 1984.
Played in Pro Bowl (NFL All-Star Game) following 1979 and 1980 seasons.

PHILLIP DAVID PUZZUOLI

Name pronounced Pa-ZOOL-ee.

(Dave)

Nose Tackle—Cleveland Browns

Born January 12, 1961, at Greenwich, Conn.
Height, 6.03. Weight, 260.
High School—Stamford, Conn., Catholic.
Attended University of Pittsburgh.

Selected by Tampa Bay in 8th round (85th player selected) of 1983 USFL draft.
Selected by Cleveland in 6th round (149th player selected) of 1983 NFL draft.
Signed by Cleveland Browns, May 31, 1983.
Cleveland NFL, 1983 through 1985.
Games: 1983 (16), 1984 (16), 1985 (16). Total—48.
Pro statistics: Recovered one fumble for two yards, 1983; recovered one fumble, 1984; returned two kickoffs for eight yards, 1985.

MICHAEL ANTHONY QUICK

(Mike)

Wide Receiver—Philadelphia Eagles

Born May 14, 1959, at Hamlet, N.C.
Height, 6.02. Weight, 190.
High School—Rockingham, N.C., Richmond.
Attended Fork Union Military Academy and North Carolina State University.

Named to THE SPORTING NEWS NFL All-Star Team, 1985.
Tied NFL record for longest passing play from scrimmage when he caught a 99-yard touchdown pass from quarterback Ron Jaworski against Atlanta Falcons, November 10, 1985.
Selected by Philadelphia in 1st round (20th player selected) of 1982 NFL draft.
On did not report list, August 20 through September 1, 1985.
Reported and granted roster exemption, September 2 through September 4, 1985; activated, September 5, 1985.

| | | ——PASS RECEIVING—— | | | |
Year Club	G.	P.C.	Yds.	Avg.	TD.
1982—Philadelphia NFL	9	10	156	15.6	1
1983—Philadelphia NFL	16	69	*1409	20.4	13
1984—Philadelphia NFL	14	61	1052	17.2	9
1985—Philadelphia NFL	16	73	1247	17.1	11
Pro Totals—4 Years............	55	213	3864	18.1	34

Additional pro statistics: Recovered one fumble, 1982 and 1985; fumbled once, 1983 and 1985; rushed once for minus five yards, 1984.
Played in Pro Bowl (NFL All-Star Game) following 1983 through 1985 seasons.

FRED QUILLAN

Center—San Francisco 49ers

Born January 27, 1956, at Portland, Ore.
Height, 6.05. Weight, 266.
High School—Portland, Ore., Central Catholic.
Attended University of Oregon.

Selected by San Francisco in 7th round (175th player selected) of 1978 NFL draft.
San Francisco NFL, 1978 through 1985.
Games: 1978 (14), 1979 (16), 1980 (16), 1981 (16), 1982 (9), 1983 (14), 1984 (16), 1985 (16). Total—117.
Pro statistics: Returned one kickoff for eight yards, 1978; fumbled twice for minus 34 yards, 1979; fumbled once for minus 42 yards, 1980; fumbled once, 1981; recovered one fumble, 1983.
Played in NFC Championship Game following 1981, 1983 and 1984 seasons.
Played in NFL Championship Game following 1981 and 1984 seasons.
Played in Pro Bowl (NFL All-Star Game) following 1984 and 1985 seasons.

DAVID RACKLEY

Cornerback—New Orleans Saints

Born February 2, 1961, at Miami, Fla.
Height, 5.09. Weight, 170.
High School—Miami, Fla., Jackson.
Attended Miami Dade Junior College and Texas Southern University.

Signed by Los Angeles Express, March 30, 1984.
On developmental squad, March 30 through remainder of 1984 season.
Released by Los Angeles Express, February 4, 1985; signed as free agent by San Diego Chargers, April 12, 1985.
Released by San Diego Chargers, July 29, 1985; signed as free agent by New Orleans Saints, August 12, 1985.
On injured reserve with hamstring injury, September 2 through October 2, 1985; activated after clearing procedural waivers, October 4, 1985.
On injured reserve with hamstring injury, November 21 through remainder of 1985 season.
On developmental squad for 13 games with Los Angeles Express in 1984.
New Orleans NFL, 1985.
Games: 1985 (7).
Pro statistics: Returned one kickoff for 63 yards, 1985.

GEORGE JOSEPH RADACHOWSKY JR.
Defensive Back—Indianapolis Colts
Born September 7, 1962, at Danbury, Conn.
Height, 5.11. Weight, 178.
High School—Danbury, Conn.
Attended Boston College.

Selected by Philadelphia in 5th round (84th player selected) of 1984 USFL draft.
Selected by Los Angeles Rams in 7th round (188th player selected) of 1984 NFL draft.
Signed by Los Angeles Rams, July 9, 1984.
Traded by Los Angeles Rams to Indianapolis Colts for 11th round pick in 1985 draft, August 27, 1984.
Released by Indianapolis Colts, September 30, 1985; re-signed by Colts, April 1, 1986.
Indianapolis NFL, 1984 and 1985.
Games: 1984 (16), 1985 (3). Total—19.
Pro statistics: Returned one kickoff for no yards and fumbled once, 1984.

JOHN RADE
Name pronounced RAY-dee.
Linebacker—Atlanta Falcons
Born August 31, 1960, at Ceres, Calif.
Height, 6.01. Weight, 220.
High School—Sierra Vista, Ariz., Buena.
Attended Modesto Junior College and Boise State University.

Signed as free agent by Boston Breakers, February 10, 1983.
Released by Boston Breakers, February 12, 1983.
Selected by Atlanta in 8th round (215th player selected) of 1983 NFL draft.
Signed by Atlanta Falcons, May 16, 1983.
On injured reserve with pinched nerve in neck, October 24 through remainder of 1984 season.
Atlanta NFL, 1983 through 1985.
Games: 1983 (16), 1984 (7), 1985 (16). Total—39.
Pro statistics: Recovered two fumbles for 16 yards and a touchdown, 1983; recovered one fumble, 1984; intercepted two passes for 42 yards and a touchdown, 1985.

J. SCOTT RADECIC
Name pronounced RADD-ah-seck.

(Known by middle name.)
Linebacker—Kansas City Chiefs
Born June 14, 1962, at Pittsburgh, Pa.
Height, 6.03. Weight, 246.
High School—Pittsburgh, Pa., Brentwood.
Attended Penn State University.

Selected by Philadelphia in 1984 USFL territorial draft.
Selected by Kansas City in 2nd round (34th player selected) of 1984 NFL draft.
Signed by Kansas City Chiefs, July 12, 1984.

		—INTERCEPTIONS—			
Year Club	G.	No.	Yds.	Avg.	TD.
1984—Kansas City NFL..........	16	2	54	27.0	1
1985—Kansas City NFL..........	16	1	21	21.0	0
Pro Totals—2 Years............	32	3	75	25.0	1

Additional pro statistics: Recovered one fumble, 1985.

WAYNE R. RADLOFF
Center-Guard—Atlanta Falcons
Born May 17, 1961, at London, England.
Height, 6.05. Weight, 265.
High School—Winter Haven, Fla.
Attended University of Georgia.

Named center on THE SPORTING NEWS USFL All-Star Team, 1984.
Selected by Michigan in 2nd round (15th player selected) of 1983 USFL draft.
Signed by Michigan Panthers, January 22, 1983.
On developmental squad, April 4 through April 9, 1983; activated, April 10, 1983.
Not protected an merger of Michigan Panthers and Oakland Invaders; not selected in USFL dispersal draft, December 6, 1984.
Signed as free agent by Atlanta Falcons, March 1, 1985.
On developmental squad for 1 game with Michigan Panthers in 1983.
Michigan USFL, 1983 and 1984; Atlanta NFL, 1985.
Games: 1983 (17), 1984 (18), 1985 (16). Total USFL—35. Total Pro—51.
Pro statistics: Recovered one fumble, 1983.
Played in USFL Championship Game following 1983 season.

—DID YOU KNOW—

That when kicker John Lee was selected by the Cardinals in round two in the 1986 NFL draft, he was the highest picked kicker since Russell Erxleben was drafted by New Orleans in round one in 1979?

THOMAS MICHAEL RAFFERTY
(Tom)
Center—Dallas Cowboys

Born August 2, 1954, at Syracuse, N. Y.
Height, 6.03. Weight, 264.
High School—Manlius, N. Y.
Received bachelor of science degree in physical education from Penn State University; attending University of Dallas for master's degree.

Selected by Dallas in 4th round (119th player selected) of 1976 NFL draft.
Dallas NFL, 1976 through 1985.
Games: 1976 (13), 1977 (14), 1978 (16), 1979 (16), 1980 (16), 1981 (16), 1982 (9), 1983 (16), 1984 (16), 1985 (16). Total—148.
Pro statistics: Fumbled once, 1977; recovered one fumble, 1979 and 1981; recovered one fumble for six yards, 1980; fumbled twice for minus 30 yards, 1981; recovered two fumbles, 1982, 1984 and 1985; caught one pass for eight yards, 1983.
Played in NFC Championship Game following 1977, 1978 and 1980 through 1982 seasons.
Played in NFL Championship Game following 1977 and 1978 seasons.

DANIEL PAUL RAINS
(Dan)
Linebacker—Chicago Bears

Born April 26, 1956, at Rochester, Pa.
Height, 6.01. Weight, 220.
High School—Hopewell, Pa.
Received bachelor of science degree in criminology from University of Cincinnati.

Signed as free agent by Philadelphia Eagles, May 10, 1978.
Released by Philadelphia Eagles, July 15, 1978; signed as free agent by Chicago Bears, May 14, 1982.
On injured reserve with hernia, July 29 through December 23, 1982; re-signed after clearing procedural waivers, December 25, 1982.
On injured reserve with knee injury, August 19 through entire 1985 season.
Chicago NFL, 1982 through 1984.
Games: 1982 (1), 1983 (15), 1984 (16). Total—32.
Pro statistics: Returned two kickoffs for 11 yards and recovered one fumble, 1983.
Played in NFC Championship Game following 1984 season.

DANIEL RAY RALPH
(Dan)
Defensive Tackle—St. Louis Cardinals

Born March 9, 1961, at Denver, Colo.
Height, 6.04. Weight, 260.
High School—Northglenn, Colo.
Attended University of Colorado and University of Oregon.

Selected by Arizona in 7th round (129th player selected) of 1984 USFL draft.
Selected by Atlanta in 6th round (163rd player selected) of 1984 NFL draft.
Signed by Atlanta Falcons, June 23, 1984.
Released by Atlanta Falcons, August 24, 1984; signed as free agent by St. Louis Cardinals, November 6, 1984.
On injured reserve with back injury, August 19 through entire 1985 season.
St. Louis NFL, 1984.
Games: 1984 (6).

DERRICK KENT RAMSEY
Tight End—New England Patriots

Born December 23, 1956, at Hastings, Fla.
Height, 6.05. Weight, 235.
High Schools—Hastings, Fla.; and Camden, N.J.
Attended University of Kentucky.

Selected by Oakland in 5th round (136th player selected) of 1978 NFL draft.
Franchise transferred to Los Angeles, May 7, 1982.
Traded by Los Angeles Raiders to New England Patriots for tight end Don Hasselbeck, September 13, 1983.

Year Club		PASS RECEIVING				—KICKOFF RET.—				—TOTAL—		
	G.	P.C.	Yds.	Avg.	TD.	No.	Yds.	Avg.	TD.	TD.	Pts.	F.
1978—Oakland NFL	16		None			7	125	17.9	0	0	0	0
1979—Oakland NFL	16	13	161	12.4	3		None			3	18	0
1980—Oakland NFL	16	5	117	23.4	0	1	10	10.0	0	0	0	0
1981—Oakland NFL	16	52	674	13.0	4		None			4	24	2
1982—Los Angeles Raiders NFL	9		None				None			0	0	0
1983—L. A. Raid. (2)-N. E. (14) NFL	16	24	335	14.0	6		None			6	36	0
1984—New England NFL	16	66	792	12.0	7		None			7	42	0
1985—New England NFL	16	28	285	10.2	1		None			1	6	1
Pro Totals—8 Years	121	188	2364	12.6	21	8	135	16.9	0	21	126	3

Additional pro statistics: Recovered one fumble, 1980 and 1981.
Played in AFC Championship Game following 1980 and 1985 seasons.
Played in NFL Championship Game following 1980 and 1985 seasons.

THOMAS LLOYD RAMSEY
(Tom)
Quarterback—New England Patriots
Born July 9, 1961, at Encino, Calif.
Height, 6.01. Weight, 188.
High School—Granada Hills, Calif., Kennedy.
Received bachelor of science degree in sociology
from University of California at Los Angeles in 1983.

Selected by Los Angeles in 5th round (49th player selected) of 1983 USFL draft.
Signed by Los Angeles Express, February 10, 1983.
Selected by New England in 10th round (267th player selected) of 1983 NFL draft.
On developmental squad, July 2 through remainder of 1983 season.
Traded by Los Angeles Express to Oakland Invaders for 3rd round pick in 1985 draft, March 29, 1984.
On developmental squad, March 30 through April 28, 1984; activated, April 29, 1984.
Released by Oakland Invaders, July 17, 1984; signed by New England Patriots, July 25, 1984.
On injured reserve with thumb injury, August 21 through entire 1984 season.
Released by New England Patriots, September 11, 1985; re-signed by Patriots, October 17, 1985.
On developmental squad for 1 game with Los Angeles Express in 1983.
On developmental squad for 4 games with Oakland Invaders in 1984.
Active for 11 games with New England Patriots in 1985; did not play.

			—PASSING—					—RUSHING—				—TOTAL—		
Year Club	G.	Att.	Cmp.	Pct.	Gain	T.P.	P.I.	Avg.	Att.	Yds.	Avg.	TD.	TD.	Pts.	F.
1983—Los Angeles USFL............	17	307	160	52.1	1975	13	14	6.43	28	80	2.9	1	1	6	4
1984—L.A. (5)-Oak. (5) USFL	10	91	54	59.3	512	2	7	5.63	8	38	4.8	0	0	0	1
Pro Totals—3 Years...........	27	398	214	53.8	2487	15	21	6.25	36	118	3.3	1	1	6	5

USFL Quarterback Rating Points: 1983 (67.1), 1984 (50.3). Total—63.6.
Member of New England Patriots for AFC Championship Game following 1985 season; did not play.
Member of New England Patriots for NFL Championship Game following 1985 season; did not play.

EASON LLOYD RAMSON
Tight End—Buffalo Bills
Born April 30, 1956, at Sacramento, Calif.
Height, 6.02. Weight, 234.
High School—Sacramento, Calif., Christian Brothers.
Attended Washington State University.

Selected by Green Bay in 12th round (312th player selected) of 1978 NFL draft.
Released by Green Bay Packers, August 15, 1978; signed as free agent by St. Louis Cardinals, August 24, 1978.
On injured reserve with groin injury, August 27 through September 11, 1979.
Released by St. Louis Cardinals, September 12, 1979; signed as free agent by San Francisco 49ers, December 6, 1979.
On injured reserve with knee injury, September 19 through October 23, 1981; activated, October 24, 1981.
Traded by San Francisco 49ers to Denver Broncos for 5th round pick in 1984 draft, April 10, 1984.
On injured reserve with fractured finger, August 13 through September 25, 1984.
Released by Denver Broncos, September 26, 1984; signed as free agent by Houston Oilers, July 10, 1985.
Released by Houston Oilers, August 6, 1985; signed as free agent by Buffalo Bills, August 12, 1985.
Released by Buffalo Bills, August 28, 1985; re-signed by Bills, August 30, 1985.

		—PASS RECEIVING—			
Year Club	G.	P.C.	Yds.	Avg.	TD.
1978—St. Louis NFL.................	15	23	238	10.3	1
1979—San Francisco NFL	2		None		
1980—San Francisco NFL	16	21	179	8.5	2
1981—San Francisco NFL	11	4	45	11.3	0
1982—San Francsico NFL	9	2	27	13.5	0
1983—San Francisco NFL	16	17	125	7.4	1
1985—Buffalo NFL..................	16	37	369	10.0	1
Pro Totals—7 Years...........	85	104	983	9.5	5

Additional pro statistics: Rushed twice for eight yards and recovered one fumble, 1978; returned one kickoff for 18 yards and rushed twice for minus two yards, 1980; returned one kickoff for 12 yards, 1981; returned two kickoffs for 20 yards, 1982; rushed once for three yards and fumbled twice, 1983; fumbled once, 1985.
Played in NFC Championship Game following 1981 and 1983 seasons.
Played in NFL Championship Game following 1981 season.

JOE RAMUNNO
Guard-Offensive Tackle—Chicago Bears
Born February 1, 1962, at Steamboat Springs, Colo.
Height, 6.03. Weight, 265.
High School—Steamboat Springs, Colo.
Attended University of Wyoming.

Signed as free agent by Chicago Bears, May 8, 1985.
On injured reserve with back injury, August 19 through entire 1985 season.

—DID YOU KNOW—
That on three different occasions, the Raiders' Fulton Walker returned seven punts in a game in 1985?

ERNEST TATE RANDLE

(Known by middle name.)

Safety—Indianapolis Colts

Born August 15, 1959, at Fredricksburg, Tex.
Height, 6.00. Weight, 196.
High School—Fort Stockton, Tex.,
Received bachelor of science degree in physical education and health from Texas Tech University.

Selected by Miami in 8th round (220th player selected) of 1982 NFL draft.
Released by Miami Dolphins, September 6, 1982; re-signed by Dolphins, September 7, 1982.
Released by Miami Dolphins, September 8, 1982; claimed on waivers by Houston Oilers, September 10, 1982.
On inactive list, September 12 and September 19, 1982.
Released by Houston Oilers, September 20, 1983; signed as free agent by Baltimore Colts, October 11, 1983.
Franchise transferred to Indianapolis, March 31, 1984.

Year Club	G.	No.	Yds.	Avg.	TD.
		—INTERCEPTIONS—			
1982—Houston NFL	7		None		
1983—Hou.(2)-Bal.(10) NFL	12	1	41	41.0	0
1984—Indianapolis NFL	16	3	66	22.0	0
1985—Indianapolis NFL	16	1	0	0.0	0
Pro Totals—4 Years	51	5	107	21.4	0

Additional pro statistics: Recovered two fumbles, 1984; recovered two fumbles for 14 yards and credited with one safety, 1985.

ERVIN RANDLE

Linebacker—Tampa Bay Buccaneers

Born October 12, 1962, at Hearne, Tex.
Height, 6.01. Weight, 250.
High School—Hearne, Tex.
Attended Baylor University.

Selected by San Antonio in 1985 USFL territorial draft.
Selected by Tampa Bay in 3rd round (64th player selected) of 1985 NFL draft.
Signed by Tampa Bay Buccaneers, July 18, 1985.
Tampa Bay NFL, 1985.
Games: 1985 (16).
Pro statistics: Intercepted one pass for no yards and recovered two fumbles, 1985.

RANDY ROBERT RASMUSSEN

Guard-Center—Pittsburgh Steelers

Born September 27, 1960, at Minneapolis, Minn.
Height, 6.01. Weight, 253.
High School—St. Paul, Minn., Irondale.
Received bachelor of applied studies degree in business and marketing from
University of Minnesota in 1984.

Selected by Chicago in 12th round (241st player selected) of 1984 USFL draft.
Selected by Pittsburgh in 8th round (220th player selected) of 1984 NFL draft.
Signed by Pittsburgh Steelers, June 18, 1984.
On injured reserve with knee injury, August 20 through October 2, 1985; activated after clearing procedural waivers, October 4, 1985.
Pittsburgh NFL, 1984 and 1985.
Games: 1984 (16), 1985 (11). Total—27.
Played in AFC Championship Game following 1984 season.

GERARD LEO RAYMOND

(Gerry)

Guard—New Orleans Saints

Born June 6, 1959, at Lewiston, Me.
Height, 6.03. Weight, 265.
High School—Lewiston, Me.
Received bachelor of science degree from Boston College.

Named as guard on THE SPORTING NEWS USFL All-Star Team, 1984.
Selected by New York Giants in 4th round (102nd player selected) of 1982 NFL draft.
Released by New York Giants, September 6, 1982; awarded on waivers to Baltimore Colts, September 7, 1982.
On inactive list, September 12 and September 19, 1982.
Released by Baltimore Colts, November 24, 1982; signed by Boston Breakers, December 22, 1982.
Franchise transferred to New Orleans, October 18, 1983.
Franchise transferred to Portland, November 13, 1984.
On developmental squad, June 7 through July 30, 1985.
Released by Portland Breakers, July 31, 1985; signed as free agent by New Orleans Saints, May 17, 1986.
On developmental squad for 3 games with Portland Breakers in 1985.
Active for 1 game with Baltimore Colts in 1982; did not play.
Baltimore NFL, 1982; Boston USFL, 1983; New Orleans USFL, 1984; Portland USFL, 1985.
Games: 1983 (18), 1984 (18), 1985 (15). Total—51.
Pro statistics: Recovered one fumble, 1983.

GARY PHILLIP REASONS
Linebacker—New York Giants
Born February 18, 1962, at Crowley, Tex.
Height, 6.04. Weight, 234.
High School—Crowley, Tex.
Received bachelor of science degree in business administration
from Northwestern State University.

Selected by New Jersey in 2nd round (26th player selected) of 1984 USFL draft.
USFL rights traded by New Jersey Generals to Tampa Bay Bandits for rights to linebacker Jim LeClair, January 30, 1984.
Selected by New York Giants in 4th round (105th player selected) of 1984 NFL draft.
Signed by New York Giants, July 12, 1984.

		—INTERCEPTIONS—			
Year Club	G.	No.	Yds.	Avg.TD.	
1984—N.Y. Giants NFL	16	2	26	13.0	0
1985—N.Y. Giants NFL	16	1	10	10.0	0
Pro Totals—2 Years	32	3	36	12.0	0

Additional pro statistics: Recovered three fumbles, 1984.

GLEN HERRSCHER REDD
Linebacker—New Orleans Saints
Born June 17, 1958, at Ogden, Utah.
Height, 6.01. Weight, 233.
High School—Ogden, Utah.
Attended Brigham Young University.

Selected by New Orleans in 6th round (166th player selected) of 1981 NFL draft.
On physically unable to perform/active with eye injury, July 27 through August 17, 1982; activated, August 18, 1982.
On injured reserve with broken arm, August 31 through entire 1982 season.
New Orleans NFL, 1981 and 1983 through 1985.
Games: 1981 (16), 1983 (16), 1984 (16), 1985 (16). Total—64.
Pro statistics: Intercepted one pass for seven yards, 1984; intercepted one pass for 25 yards and recovered two fumbles, 1985.

BARRY REDDEN
Fullback—Los Angeles Rams
Born July 21, 1960, at Sarasota, Fla.
Height, 5.10. Weight, 205.
High School—Sarasota, Fla.
Received degree in psychology from University of Richmond in 1982.

Selected by Los Angeles Rams in 1st round (14th player selected) of 1982 NFL draft.

		—RUSHING—				PASS RECEIVING				—TOTAL—		
Year Club	G.	Att.	Yds.	Avg.	TD.	P.C.	Yds.	Avg.	TD.	TD.	Pts.	F.
1982—Los Angeles Rams NFL	9	8	24	3.0	0	4	16	4.0	0	0	0	2
1983—Los Angeles Rams NFL	15	75	372	5.0	2	4	30	7.5	0	2	12	2
1984—Los Angeles Rams NFL	14	45	247	5.5	0	4	39	9.8	0	0	0	0
1985—Los Angeles Rams NFL	14	87	380	4.4	0	16	162	10.1	0	0	0	1
Pro Totals—4 Years	52	215	1023	4.8	2	28	247	8.8	0	2	12	5

		KICKOFF RETURNS			
Year Club	G.	No.	Yds.	Avg.TD.	
1982—L.A. Rams NFL	9	22	502	22.8	0
1983—L.A. Rams NFL	15	19	358	18.8	0
1984—L.A. Rams NFL	14	23	530	23.0	0
1985—L.A. Rams NFL	14		None		
Pro Totals—4 Years	52	64	1390	21.7	0

Additional pro statistics: Recovered one fumble, 1982.
Played in NFC Championship Game following 1985 season.

ANDRE DARNELL REED
Wide Receiver—Buffalo Bills
Born January 29, 1964, at Allentown, Pa.
Height, 6.00. Weight, 186.
High School—Allentown Pa., Louis E. Dieruff.
Attended Kutztown State College.

Selected by Orlando in 3rd round (39th player selected) of 1985 USFL draft.
Selected by Buffalo in 4th round (86th player selected) of 1985 NFL draft.
Signed by Buffalo Bills, July 19, 1985.

		—PASS RECEIVING—			
Year Club	G.	P.C.	Yds.	Avg.TD.	
1985—Buffalo NFL	16	48	637	13.3	4

Additional pro statistics: Rushed three times for minus one yard and a touchdown, returned five punts for 12 yards, recovered two fumbles and fumbled once, 1985.

DOUG REED
Defensive End—Los Angeles Rams
Born July 16, 1960, at San Diego, Calif.
Height, 6.03. Weight, 262.
High School—San Diego, Calif., Abraham Lincoln.
Attended San Diego City College and San Diego State University.

Selected by Los Angeles in 17th round (193rd player selected) of 1983 USFL draft.
Selected by Los Angeles Rams in 4th round (111th player selected) of 1983 NFL draft.
Signed by Los Angeles Rams, June 3, 1983.
On injured reserve with leg injury, August 29 through entire 1983 season.
Los Angeles Rams NFL, 1984 and 1985.
Games: 1984 (9), 1985 (16). Total—25.
Pro statistics: Recovered one fumble for two yards, 1984.
Played in NFC Championship Game following 1985 season.

BOOKER TED REESE
Defensive End—San Francisco 49ers
Born September 20, 1959, at Jacksonville, Fla.
Height, 6.06. Weight, 260.
High School—Jacksonville, Fla., Ribault.
Attended Bethune-Cookman College.

Selected by Tampa Bay in 2nd round (32nd player selected) of 1982 NFL draft.
On inactive list, September 12, 1982.
Traded by Tampa Bay Buccaneers to Los Angeles Rams for 12th round pick in 1985 draft, September 4, 1984.
On non-football injury list with drug problem, September 29 through November 1, 1984; activated, November 2, 1984.
Released by Los Angeles Rams, September 19, 1985; signed as free agent by San Francisco 49ers, March 12, 1986.
Tampa Bay NFL, 1982 and 1983; Tampa Bay (1)-Los Angeles Rams (9) NFL, 1984; Los Angeles Rams NFL, 1985.
Games: 1982 (7), 1983 (16), 1984 (10), 1985 (2). Total—35.
Pro statistics: Intercepted two passes for 11 yards, 1983.

KEN REEVES
Offensive Tackle-Guard—Philadelphia Eagles
Born October 4, 1961, at Pittsburg, Tex.
Height, 6.05. Weight, 268.
High School—Pittsburg, Tex.
Attended Texas A&M University.

Selected by Houston in 1985 USFL territorial draft.
Selected by Philadelphia in 6th round (156th player selected) of 1985 NFL draft.
Signed by Philadelphia Eagles, July 23, 1985.
Philadelphia NFL, 1985.
Games: 1985 (15).
Pro statistics: Recovered one fumble, 1985.

FRANK MICHAEL REICH
Name pronounced Rike.
Quarterback—Buffalo Bills
Born December 4, 1961, at Freeport, N.Y.
Height, 6.03. Weight, 208.
High School—Lebanon, Pa., Cedar Crest.
Received bachelor of science degree in finance from University of Maryland in 1984.

Selected by Tampa Bay in 1985 USFL territorial draft.
Selected by Buffalo in 3rd round (57th player selected) of 1985 NFL draft.
Signed by Buffalo Bills, August 1, 1985.
On injured reserve with Achilles heel injury, September 3 to December 5, 1985; activated, December 6, 1985.
Buffalo NFL, 1985.
Games: 1985 (1).
Pro statistics: Attempted one pass with one completion for 19 yards, 1985.

MIKE REICHENBACH
Linebacker—Philadelphia Eagles
Born September 14, 1961, at Fort Meade, Md.
Height, 6.02. Weight, 235.
High School—Bethlehem, Pa., Liberty.
Attended East Stroudsburg University.

Signed as free agent by Philadelphia Eagles, June 18, 1984.
Released by Philadelphia Eagles, August 27, 1984; re-signed by Eagles, September 25, 1984.
Philadelphia NFL, 1984 and 1985.
Games: 1984 (12), 1905 (16). Total—28.
Pro statistics: Recovered two fumbles, 1984; intercepted one pass for 10 yards, 1985.

BRUCE MICHAEL REIMERS
Offensive Tackle—Cincinnati Bengals
Born September 18, 1960, at Algona, Ia.
Height, 6.07. Weight, 280.
High School—Humboldt, Ia.
Attended Iowa State University.

Selected by Los Angeles in 7th round (136th player selected) of 1984 USFL draft.
Selected by Cincinnati in 8th round (204th player selected) of 1984 NFL draft.
Signed by Cincinnati Bengals, June 20, 1984.
Cincinnati NFL, 1984 and 1985.
Games: 1984 (15), 1985 (14). Total—29.

JOHNNY REMBERT
Linebacker—New England Patriots
Born January 19, 1961, at Hollandale, Miss.
Height, 6.03. Weight, 234.
High School—Arcadia, Fla., DeSoto.
Attended Cowley County Community College and Clemson University.

Selected by Washington in 1983 USFL territorial draft.
Selected by New England in 4th round (101st player selected) of 1983 NFL draft.
Signed by New England Patriots, May 16, 1983.
On injured reserve with knee injury, August 28 through November 2, 1984; activated, November 3, 1984.
New England NFL, 1983 through 1985.
Games: 1983 (15), 1984 (7), 1985 (16). Total—38.
Pro statistics: Recovered one fumble, 1983; recovered three fumbles for nine yards (including one in end zone for a touchdown), 1985.
Played in AFC Championship Game following 1985 season.
Played in NFL Championship Game following 1985 season.

MICHAEL RAY RENFRO
(Mike)
Wide Receiver—Dallas Cowboys
Born June 19, 1955, at Fort Worth, Tex.
Height, 6.00. Weight, 188.
High School—Fort Worth, Tex., Arlington Heights.
Received degree in business management from Texas Christian University.
Son of Ray Renfro, back with Cleveland Browns, 1952 through 1963 and
assistant coach with Detroit Lions and Dallas Cowboys, 1965 and 1968 through 1972.

Selected by Houston in 4th round (98th player selected) of 1978 NFL draft.
On injured reserve with knee injury, December 5 through remainder of 1978 season.
On injured reserve with pulled hamstring, November 27 through remainder of 1981 season.
On injured reserve with hepatitis, August 30 through September 29, 1983; activated, September 30, 1983.
On injured reserve with knee injury, November 28 through remainder of 1983 season.
Traded with 2nd round pick in 1984 draft and 5th round pick in 1985 draft by Houston Oilers to Dallas Cowboys for wide receiver Butch Johnson and 2nd round pick in 1984 draft, April 13, 1984.

		—PASS RECEIVING—			
Year Club	G.	P.C.	Yds.	Avg.	TD.
1978—Houston NFL	14	26	339	13.0	2
1979—Houston NFL	15	16	323	20.2	2
1980—Houston NFL	16	35	459	13.1	1
1981—Houston NFL	12	39	451	11.6	1
1982—Houston NFL	9	21	295	14.0	3
1983—Houston NFL	9	23	316	13.7	2
1984—Dallas NFL	16	35	583	16.7	2
1985—Dallas NFL	16	60	955	15.9	8
Pro Totals—8 Years	107	255	3721	14.6	21

Additional pro statistics: Rushed once for nine yards, 1978; fumbled once, 1978, 1979 and 1983; rushed once for 12 yards, 1980; recovered two fumbles for 12 yards and fumbled twice, 1981; rushed once for three yards, 1983; attempted two passes with one completion for 49 yards and a touchdown, 1984; recovered one fumble and fumbled three times, 1985.
Played in AFC Championship Game following 1979 season.

FUAD REVEIZ
Placekicker—Miami Dolphins
Born February 24, 1963, at Bogota, Columbia.
Height, 5.11. Weight, 222.
High School—Miami, Fla., Sunset.
Attended University of Tennessee.
Brother of Carlos Reveiz, placekicker at University of Tennessee.

Selected by Memphis in 1985 USFL territorial draft.
Selected by Miami in 7th round (195th player selected) of 1985 NFL draft.
Signed by Miami Dolphins, July 20, 1985.

		—PLACE KICKING—				
Year Club	G.	XP.	XPM.	FG.	FGA.	Pts.
1985—Miami NFL	16	50	2	22	27	116

Played in AFC Championship Game following 1985 season.

EDWARD RANNELL REYNOLDS
(Ed)
Linebacker—New England Patriots
Born September 23, 1961, at Stuttgart, West Germany.
Height, 6.05. Weight, 230.
High School—Ridgeway, Va., Drewry Mason.
Received bachelor of science degree in elementary education from University of Virginia in 1983.

Signed as free agent by New England Patriots, May 10, 1983.
Released by New England Patriots, August 29, 1983; re-signed by Patriots, September 28, 1983.
Released by New England Patriots, August 27, 1984; re-signed by Patriots, August 28, 1984.
On injured reserve with knee injury, September 11 through October 11, 1985; activated, October 12, 1985.
New England NFL, 1983 through 1985.
Games: 1983 (12), 1984 (16), 1985 (12). Total—40.
Pro statistics: Recovered two fumbles, 1983.
Played in AFC Championship Game following 1985 season.
Played in NFL Championship Game following 1985 season.

GEORGE RHYMES
(Buster)
Wide Receiver—Minnesota Vikings
Born January 27, 1962, at Miami, Fla.
Height, 6.01. Weight, 212.
High School—Miami, Fla., Northwestern.
Attended University of Oklahoma.

Established NFL record for most kickoff return yards, season (1,345), 1985.
Selected by San Antonio in 1985 USFL territorial draft.
Selected by Minnesota in 4th round (85th player selected) of 1985 NFL draft.
Signed by Minnesota Vikings, July 31, 1985.

		PASS RECEIVING				—KICKOFF RET.—				—TOTAL—		
Year	Club	G.	P.C.	Yds.	Avg.	TD.	No.	Yds.	Avg.	TD.	TD.	Pts.	F.
1985—Minnesota NFL		15	5	124	24.8	0	*53	*1345	25.4	0	0	0	2

Additional pro statistics: Recovered two fumbles, 1985.

ALLEN TROY RICE
Running Back—Minnesota Vikings
Born April 5, 1962, at Houston, Tex.
Height, 5.10. Weight, 198.
High School—Houston, Tex., Klein.
Attended Wharton County Junior College, Ranger Junior College and Baylor University.

Selected by Houston in 1984 USFL territorial draft.
Selected by Minnesota in 5th round (140th player selected) of 1984 NFL draft.
Signed by Minnesota Vikings, July 20, 1984.

			——RUSHING——				PASS RECEIVING				—TOTAL—		
Year	Club	G.	Att.	Yds.	Avg.	TD.	P.C.	Yds.	Avg.	TD.	TD.	Pts.	F.
1984—Minnesota NFL		14	14	58	4.1	1	4	59	14.8	1	2	12	1
1985—Minnesota NFL		14	31	104	3.4	3	9	61	6.8	1	4	24	0
Pro Totals—2 Years		28	45	162	3.6	4	13	120	9.2	2	6	36	1

Additional pro statistics: Returned three kickoffs for 34 yards and recovered two fumbles, 1984; returned four kickoffs for 70 yards and recovered one fumble, 1985.

JERRY LEE RICE
Wide Receiver—San Francisco 49ers
Born October 13, 1962, at Starkville, Miss.
Height, 6.02. Weight, 200.
High School—Crawford, Miss., B.L. Moor.
Attended Mississippi Valley State University.

Named as wide receiver on THE SPORTING NEWS College All-America Team, 1984.
Selected by Birmingham in 1st round (1st player selected) of 1985 USFL draft.
Selected by San Francisco in 1st round (16th player selected) of 1985 NFL draft.
Signed by San Francisco 49ers, July 23, 1985.

		——PASS RECEIVING——				
Year	Club	G.	P.C.	Yds.	Avg.	TD.
1985—San Francisco NFL		16	49	927	18.9	3

Additional pro statistics: Rushed six times for 26 yards and a touchdown, returned one kickoff for six yards and fumbled once, 1985.

—DID YOU KNOW—

That San Diego's Gary Anderson in 1985 became the first player in pro football history to rush for 100 yards in a game in two leagues in the same year? Anderson did it with the Tampa Bay Bandits of the United States Football League in the spring and with the Chargers in the fall.

HOWARD GLENN RICHARDS JR.
Guard—Dallas Cowboys
Born August 7, 1959, at St. Louis, Mo.
Height, 6.06. Weight, 260.
High School—St. Louis, Mo., Southwest.
Attended University of Missouri.
Nephew of Ernie McMillan, offensive tackle with St. Louis Cardinals and
Green Bay Packers, 1961 through 1975; assistant coach, Green Bay Packers, 1977 through 1983;
scout, St. Louis Cardinals, 1984; and offensive line coach, St. Louis Cardinals, 1985.

Selected by Dallas in 1st round (26th player selected) of 1981 NFL draft.
On injured reserve with torn tendon in thigh, November 17 through remainder of 1984 season.
On physically unable to perform/active with knee injury, August 20 through October 22, 1985; activated, October 23, 1985.
Dallas NFL, 1981 through 1985.
Games: 1981 (16), 1982 (8), 1983 (16), 1984 (11), 1985 (7). Total—58.
Pro statistics: Recovered one fumble, 1984.
Played in NFC Championship Game following 1981 and 1982 seasons.

ALBERT JOSEPH RICHARDSON
(Al)
Linebacker—New Orleans Saints
Born November 15, 1960, at New Orleans, La.
Height, 6.00. Weight, 240.
High School—Baton Rouge, La., Robert E. Lee.
Received degree in general business from Louisiana State University.

Selected by Tampa Bay in 12th round (133rd player selected) of 1983 USFL draft.
Signed as free agent by Denver Broncos, May 3, 1983.
Released by Denver Broncos after failing physical with broken wrist, May 13, 1983; signed as free agent by Tampa Bay Buccaneers, February 9, 1984.
Released by Tampa Bay Buccaneers, August 27, 1984; signed as free agent by Tampa Bay Bandits, October 15, 1984.
Released by Tampa Bay Bandits, August 2, 1985; signed as free agent by New Orleans Saints, May 13, 1986.
Tampa Bay USFL, 1985.
Games: 1985 (18).

ALPETTE RICHARDSON
(Al)
Linebacker—Atlanta Falcons
Born September 23, 1957, at Abbeville, Ala.
Height, 6.03. Weight, 222.
High School—Miami, Fla., Central.
Attended Georgia Tech.
Cousin of Huey Richardson, linebacker at University of Florida.

Selected by Atlanta in 8th round (201st player selected) of 1980 NFL draft.
On injured reserve with broken shoulder blade, October 6 through remainder of 1983 season.

| | | —INTERCEPTIONS— | | | |
Year Club	G.	No.	Yds.	Avg.	TD.
1980—Atlanta NFL	16	7	139	19.9	0
1981—Atlanta NFL	16	1	9	9.0	0
1982—Atlanta NFL	8		None		
1983—Atlanta NFL	5	1	38	38.0	0
1984—Atlanta NFL	16		None		
1985—Atlanta NFL	16		None		
Pro Totals—6 Years	77	9	186	20.7	0

Additional pro statistics: Recovered three fumbles (one in end zone for a touchdown), 1980; recovered three fumbles, 1984.

ERIC RICHARDSON
Wide Receiver—Buffalo Bills
Born April 18, 1962, at San Francisco, Calif.
Height, 6.01. Weight, 183.
High School—Novato, Calif.
Attended Monterey Peninsula College and San Jose State University.

Selected by Oakland in 1984 USFL territorial draft.
Selected by Buffalo in 2nd round (41st player selected) of 1984 NFL draft.
Signed by Buffalo Bills, May 17, 1984.
On injured reserve with knee injury, August 28 through entire 1984 season.

| | | —PASS RECEIVING— | | | |
Year Club	G.	P.C.	Yds.	Avg.	TD.
1985—Buffalo NFL	16	12	201	16.8	0

Additional pro statistics: Returned three kickoffs for 69 yards, 1985.

MICHAEL CALVIN RICHARDSON
(Mike)
Cornerback—Chicago Bears
Born May 23, 1961, at Compton, Calif.
Height, 6.00. Weight, 188.
High School—Compton, Calif.
Attended Arizona State University.

Named as defensive back on THE SPORTING NEWS College All-America Team, 1981 and 1982.
Selected by Arizona in 1983 USFL territorial draft.
Selected by Chicago in 2nd round (33rd player selected) of 1983 NFL draft.
Signed by Chicago Bears, July 20, 1983.

		—INTERCEPTIONS—			
Year Club	G.	No.	Yds.	Avg.TD.	
1983—Chicago NFL	16	5	9	1.8	0
1984—Chicago NFL	15	2	7	3.5	0
1985—Chicago NFL	14	4	174	43.5	*1
Pro Totals—3 Years	45	11	190	17.3	1

Additional pro statistics: Returned one kickoff for 17 yards and recovered two fumbles for seven yards, 1983; recovered one fumble, 1984; recovered one fumble for four yards and fumbled once, 1985.
Played in NFC Championship Game following 1984 and 1985 seasons.
Played in NFL Championship Game following 1985 season.

ROBBERT LEE RIDDICK
(Robb)
Running Back—Buffalo Bills
Born April 26, 1957, at Quakertown, Pa.
Height, 6.00. Weight, 195.
High School—Perkasie, Pa., Pennridge.
Attended Millersville State College.
Cousin of Will Lewis, cornerback with New Jersey Generals; and
Tim Lewis, defensive back with Green Bay Packers.

Selected by Buffalo in 9th round (241st player selected) of 1981 NFL draft.
On injured reserve with ankle injury, September 3 through October 16, 1981; activated, October 17, 1981.
On injured reserve with knee injury, September 7 through entire 1982 season.
On injured reserve with knee injury, August 19 through entire 1985 season.

		—RUSHING—				PASS RECEIVING				—TOTAL—		
Year Club	G.	Att.	Yds.	Avg.	TD.	P.C.	Yds.	Avg.	TD.	TD.	Pts.	F.
1981—Buffalo NFL	10	3	29	9.7	0	None				0	0	1
1983—Buffalo NFL	16	4	18	4.5	0	3	43	14.3	0	0	0	7
1984—Buffalo NFL	16	3	3	1.0	0	23	276	12.0	0	0	0	1
Pro Totals—3 Years	42	10	50	5.0	0	26	319	12.3	0	0	0	9

		—PUNT RETURNS—				—KICKOFF RET.—			
Year Club	G.	No.	Yds.	Avg.	TD.	No.	Yds.	Avg.TD.	
1981—Buffalo NFL	10	4	48	12.0	0	14	257	18.4	0
1983—Buffalo NFL	16	42	241	5.7	0	28	568	20.3	0
1984—Buffalo NFL	16	None				None			
Pro Totals—3 Years	42	46	289	6.3	0	42	825	19.6	0

Additional pro statistics: Recovered one fumble, 1983.

GERALD ANTONIO RIGGS
Running Back—Atlanta Falcons
Born November 6, 1960, at Tullos, La.
Height, 6.01. Weight, 230.
High School—Las Vegas, Nev., Bonanza.
Attended Arizona State University.

Selected by Atlanta in 1st round (9th player selected) of 1982 NFL draft.

		—RUSHING—				PASS RECEIVING				—TOTAL—		
Year Club	G.	Att.	Yds.	Avg.	TD.	P.C.	Yds.	Avg.	TD.	TD.	Pts.	F.
1982—Atlanta NFL	9	78	299	3.8	5	23	185	8.0	0	5	30	1
1983—Atlanta NFL	14	100	437	4.4	8	17	149	8.8	0	8	48	7
1984—Atlanta NFL	15	353	1486	4.2	13	42	277	6.6	0	13	78	11
1985—Atlanta NFL	16	*397	1719	4.3	10	33	267	8.1	0	10	60	0
Pro Totals—4 Years	54	928	3941	4.2	36	115	878	7.6	0	36	216	19

		KICKOFF RETURNS			
Year Club	G.	No.	Yds.	Avg.TD.	
1982—Atlanta NFL	9	None			
1983—Atlanta NFL	14	17	330	19.4	0
1984—Atlanta NFL	15	None			
1985—Atlanta NFL	16	None			
Pro Totals—4 Years	54	17	330	19.4	0

Additional pro statistics: Recovered one fumble, 1983; recovered two fumbles, 1984.
Played in Pro Bowl (NFL All-Star Game) following 1985 season.

AVON RILEY
Linebacker—Houston Oilers
Born February 10, 1958, at Savannah, Ga.
Height, 6.03. Weight, 236.
High School—Savannah, Ga.
Attended College of the Canyons and University of California at Los Angeles.

Selected by Houston in 9th round (243rd player selected) of 1981 NFL draft.
Houston NFL, 1981 through 1985.
Games: 1981 (16), 1982 (9), 1983 (16), 1984 (16), 1985 (15). Total—72.
Pro statistics: Returned one kickoff for 51 yards and recovered one fumble for six yards, 1981; returned one kickoff for 27 yards, 1982; intercepted one pass for no yards, ran 26 yards with lateral on kickoff return and recovered three fumbles for four yards, 1983; intercepted one pass for 14 yards and recovered one fumble, 1985.

ERIC RILEY
Cornerback—Denver Broncos
Born August 15, 1962, at Fort Myers, Fla.
Height, 6.00. Weight, 170.
High School—Fort Myers, Fla.
Attended Florida State University.

Selected by Tampa Bay in 1985 USFL territorial draft.
USFL rights traded with rights to running back Cedric Jones and placekicker Bobby Raymond by Tampa Bay Bandits to Jacksonville Bulls for rights to running back Marck Harrison, center Dan Turk and tight end Ken Whisenhunt, January 3, 1985.
Selected by Denver in 8th round (222nd player selected) of 1985 NFL draft.
Signed by Denver Broncos, July 18, 1985.
On injured reserve with concussion, August 20 through entire 1985 season.

DAVE BRIAN RIMINGTON
Center—Cincinnati Bengals
Born May 22, 1960, at Omaha, Neb.
Height, 6.03. Weight, 288.
High School—Omaha, Neb., South.
Received degree from University of Nebraska.

Outland Trophy winner, 1981 and 1982.
Named as center on THE SPORTING NEWS College All-America Team, 1982.
Selected by Boston in 1983 USFL territorial draft.
Selected by Cincinnati in 1st round (25th player selected) of 1983 NFL draft.
Signed by Cincinnati Bengals, June 6, 1983.
Cincinnati NFL, 1983 through 1985.
Games: 1983 (12), 1984 (16), 1985 (16). Total—44.
Pro statistics: Recovered one fumble and fumbled once, 1983; recovered three fumbles, 1985.

BILL RING
Running Back—San Francisco 49ers
Born December 13, 1956, at Des Moines, Iowa.
Height, 5.10. Weight, 205.
High School—Belmont, Calif., Carlmont.
Attended College of San Mateo and received degree in finance from Brigham Young University in 1980.

Signed as free agent by Pittsburgh Steelers, May 7, 1980.
Released by Pittsburgh Steelers, August 25, 1980; signed as free agent by San Francisco 49ers, April 14, 1981.
On injured reserve with lacerated finger, August 17 through September 17, 1981; activated after clearing procedural waivers, September 19, 1981.
Released by San Francisco 49ers, September 22, 1981; re-signed by 49ers, October 7, 1981.
On injured reserve with stress fracture in leg, November 15 through December 13, 1985; activated, December 14, 1985.

| | | —RUSHING— | | | | PASS RECEIVING | | | | —TOTAL— | | |
Year Club	G.	Att.	Yds.	Avg.	TD.	P.C.	Yds.	Avg.	TD.	TD.	Pts.	F.
1981—San Francisco NFL	12	22	106	4.8	0	3	28	9.3	1	1	6	1
1982—San Francisco NFL	8	48	183	3.8	1	13	94	7.2	0	1	6	1
1983—San Francisco NFL	16	64	254	4.0	2	23	182	7.9	0	2	12	1
1984—San Francisco NFL	16	38	162	4.3	3	3	10	3.3	0	3	18	0
1985—San Francisco NFL	10	8	23	2.9	1	2	14	7.0	0	1	6	0
Pro Totals—5 Years	62	180	728	4.0	7	44	328	7.5	1	8	48	3

| KICKOFF RETURNS | | | | | |
Year Club	G.	No.	Yds.	Avg.	TD.
1981—San Francisco NFL	12	10	217	21.7	0
1982—San Francisco NFL	8	6	145	24.2	0
1983—San Francisco NFL	16	4	68	17.0	0
1984—San Francisco NFL	16	1	27	27.0	0
1985—San Francisco NFL	10		None		
Pro Totals—5 Years	62	21	457	21.8	0

Additional pro statistics: Recovered one fumble, 1981, 1982 and 1985; recovered two fumbles, 1983.
Played in NFC Championship Game following 1981, 1983 and 1984 seasons.
Played in NFL Championship Game following 1981 and 1984 seasons.

ALAN RISHER
Quarterback—Tampa Bay Buccaneers
Born May 6, 1961, at New Orleans, La.
Height, 6.02. Weight, 190.
High School—Slidell, La., Salem.
Attended Louisiana State University.

Selected by Arizona in 15th round (170th player selected) of 1983 USFL draft.
Signed by Arizona Wranglers, February 2, 1983.
Protected in merger of Arizona Wranglers and Oklahoma Outlaws, December 6, 1984.
On developmental squad, March 3 and March 4, 1985.
Released by Arizona Outlaws, March 5, 1985; signed as free agent by Tampa Bay Buccaneers, May 9, 1985.
On developmental squad for 1 game with Arizona Outlaws in 1985.
Active for 1 game with Arizona Outlaws in 1985; did not play.

Year Club	G.	PASSING Att.	Cmp.	Pct.	Gain	T.P.	P.I.	Avg.	RUSHING Att.	Yds.	Avg.	TD.	TOTAL TD.	Pts.	F
1983—Arizona USFL	16	424	236	55.7	2672	20	16	6.30	57	231	4.1	0	0	0	1
1984—Arizona USFL	18	103	63	61.2	722	3	7	7.01	6	45	7.5	0	0	0	
1985—Tampa Bay NFL	16	None							1	10	10.0	0	0	0	
USFL Totals—3 Years	34	527	299	56.7	3394	23	23	6.44	63	276	4.4	0	0	0	1
NFL Totals—1 Year	16	0	0	0.0	0	0	0	0.00	1	10	10.0	0	0	0	
Pro Totals—4 Years	50	527	299	56.7	3394	23	23	6.44	64	286	4.5	0	0	0	1

Quarterback Rating Points: 1983 (74.6), 1984 (63.7). Total—72.5.
Additional pro statistics: Recovered seven fumbles and caught one pass for nine yards, 1983; recovered one fumble, 1984.
Played in USFL Championship Game following 1984 season.

CODY LEWIS RISIEN
Name pronounced Rise-un.
Offensive Tackle—Cleveland Browns
Born March 22, 1957, at Bryan, Tex.
Height, 6.07. Weight, 280.
High School—Houston, Tex., Cypress Fairbanks.
Received bachelor of science degree in building construction from Texas A&M University in 1982.

Selected by Cleveland in 7th round (183rd player selected) of 1979 NFL draft.
On injured reserve with knee injury, August 27 through entire 1984 season.
On injured reserve with knee injury, September 27 through October 22, 1985; activated, October 23, 1985.
Cleveland NFL, 1979 through 1983 and 1985.
Games: 1979 (15), 1980 (16), 1981 (16), 1982 (9), 1983 (16), 1985 (12). Total—84.

JAMES ALEXANDER RITCHER
(Jim)
Guard—Buffalo Bills
Born May 21, 1958, at Berea, O.
Height, 6.03. Weight, 265.
High School—Granger, O., Highland.
Attended North Carolina State University.

Named as center on THE SPORTING NEWS College All-America Team, 1979.
Outland Trophy winner, 1979.
Selected by Buffalo in 1st round of (16th player selected) 1980 NFL draft.
Buffalo NFL, 1980 through 1985.
Games: 1980, (14), 1981 (14), 1982 (9), 1983 (16), 1984 (14), 1985 (16). Total—83.

RONALD EUGENE RIVERA
(Ron)
Linebacker—Chicago Bears
Born January 7, 1962, at Fort Ord, Calif.
Height, 6.03. Weight, 239.
High School—Seaside, Calif.
Attended University of California at Berkeley.

Named as linebacker on THE SPORTING NEWS College All-America Team, 1983.
Selected by Oakland in 1984 USFL territorial draft.
Selected by Chicago in 2nd round (44th player selected) of 1984 NFL draft.
Signed by Chicago Bears, July 2, 1984.
Chicago NFL, 1984 and 1985.
Games: 1984 (15), 1985 (16). Total—31.
Pro statistics: Intercepted one pass for four yards and recovered one fumble for five yards and a touchdown, 1985.
Played in NFC Championship Game following 1984 and 1985 seasons.
Played in NFL Championship Game following 1985 season.

CARL ROACHES
Kick Returner-Wide Receiver
Born October 2, 1953, at Houston, Tex.
Height, 5.08. Weight, 170.
High School—Houston, Tex., Smiley.
Received bachelor of science degree in industrial education from Texas A&M University.

Selected by Tampa Bay in 14th round (377th player selected) of 1976 NFL draft.
Released by Tampa Bay Buccaneers, September, 1976; signed as free agent by Saskatchewan Roughriders, March, 1977.
Released by Saskatchewan Roughriders, August, 1977; signed as free agent by Houston Oilers, June 12, 1980.
Granted free agency, February 1, 1985; withdrew qualifying offer, June 26, 1985.
Signed by New Orleans Saints, August 8, 1985.
Released by New Orleans Saints, August 19, 1985; re-signed by Saints, October 16, 1985.
On injured reserve with rib injury, November 8 through remainder of 1985 season.
Granted free agency, February 1, 1986; withdrew qualifying offer, May 13, 1986.

| Year | Club | G. | –PUNT RETURNS– | | | | —KICKOFF RET.— | | | | —TOTAL— | | |
			No.	Yds.	Avg.	TD.	No.	Yds.	Avg.	TD.	TD.	Pts.	F.
1977—Saskatchewan CFL		3	2	12	6.0	0		None			0	0	0
1980—Houston NFL		16	47	384	8.2	0	37	746	20.2	0	0	0	6
1981—Houston NFL		16	39	296	7.6	0	28	769	27.5	*1	1	6	0
1982—Houston NFL		9	19	104	5.5	0	21	441	21.0	0	0	0	1
1983—Houston NFL		16	20	159	8.0	0	34	641	18.9	*1	1	6	3
1984—Houston NFL		16	26	152	5.8	0	30	679	22.6	0	0	0	1
1985—New Orleans NFL		3	4	21	5.3	0	4	76	19.0	0	0	0	1
CFL Totals—1 Year		3	2	12	6.0	0	0	0	0.0	0	0	0	0
NFL Totals—6 Years		76	155	1116	7.2	0	154	3352	21.8	2	2	12	12
Pro Totals—7 Years		79	157	1128	7.2	0	154	3352	21.8	2	2	12	12

Additional pro statistics: Recovered three fumbles, 1980; recovered one fumble, 1982 through 1984; caught four passes for 69 yards, 1984.
Played in Pro Bowl (NFL All-Star Game) following 1981 season.

JAMES ELBERT ROBBINS
(Tootie)
Offensive Tackle—St. Louis Cardinals
Born June 2, 1958, at Windsor, N.C.
Height, 6.05. Weight, 302.
High School—Bertie County, N.C.
Attended East Carolina University.

Selected by St. Louis in 4th round (90th player selected) of 1982 NFL draft.
St. Louis NFL, 1982 through 1985.
Games: 1982 (9), 1983 (13), 1984 (16), 1985 (12). Total—50.
Pro statistics: Recovered one fumble, 1983 and 1985.

RANDY ROBBINS
Cornerback—Denver Broncos
Born September 14, 1962, at Casa Grande, Ariz.
Height, 6.02. Weight, 189.
High School—Casa Grande, Ariz., Union.
Attended University of Arizona.

Selected by Arizona in 1984 USFL territorial draft.
Selected by Denver in 4th round (89th player selected) of 1984 NFL draft.
Signed by Denver Broncos, July 6, 1984.
On injured reserve with fractured forearm, August 20 through October 15, 1985; activated, October 16, 1985.

| Year | Club | G. | —INTERCEPTIONS— | | | |
			No.	Yds.	Avg.	TD.
1984—Denver NFL		16	2	62	31.0	1
1985—Denver NFL		10	1	3	3.0	0
Pro Totals—2 Years		26	3	65	21.7	1

Additional pro statistics: Recovered one fumble, 1984.

WILLIAM HAROLD ROBERTS
Offensive Tackle—New York Giants
Born August 5, 1962, at Miami, Fla.
Height, 6.05. Weight, 280.
High School—Miami, Fla., Carol City.
Attended Ohio State University.
Cousin of Reggie Sandilands, wide receiver with Memphis Showboats, 1984.

Selected by New Jersey in 1984 USFL territorial draft.
Selected by New York Giants in 1st round (27th player selected) of 1984 NFL draft.
Signed by New York Giants, June 4, 1984.
On injured reserve with knee injury, July 20 through entire 1985 season.
New York Giants NFL, 1984.
Games: 1984 (11).
Pro statistics: Recovered one fumble, 1984.

JOHN TERAN ROBERTSON
Offensive Tackle—Indianapolis Colts
Born September 26, 1961, at Eden, N.C.
Height, 6.05. Weight, 270.
High School—Eden, N.C., Morehead.
Received bachelor of science degree in industrial technology from
East Carolina University in 1984.

Selected by Memphis in 10th round (205th player selected) of 1984 USFL draft.
Selected by Philadelphia in 11th round (284th player selected) of 1984 NFL draft.
Signed by Philadelphia Eagles, May 25, 1984.
On injured reserve with back injury, August 27 through September 19, 1984.
Released by Philadelphia Eagles, September 20, 1984; re-signed by Eagles for 1985, October 22, 1984.
Released by Philadelphia Eagles, August 20, 1985; signed as free agent by Indianapolis Colts, March 24, 1986.

EUGENE ROBINSON
Cornerback—Seattle Seahawks
Born May 28, 1963, at Hartford, Conn.
Height, 6.00. Weight, 180.
High School—Hartford, Conn., Weaver.
Attended Colgate University.

Selected by New Jersey in 1985 USFL territorial draft.
Signed as free agent by Seattle Seahawks, May 15, 1985.

		—INTERCEPTIONS—			
Year Club	G.	No.	Yds.	Avg.	TD.
1985—Seattle NFL	16	2	47	23.5	0

Additional pro statistics: Returned one kickoff for 10 yards, 1985.

FRED LEE ROBINSON
Defensive End—San Diego Chargers
Born October 22, 1961, at Miami, Fla.
Height, 6.05. Weight, 240.
High School—Miami, Fla., Jackson.
Attended Navarro College and University of Miami (Fla.).
Cousin of James Bell, defensive back at University of Louisville.

Selected by Washington in 2nd round (24th player selected) of 1984 USFL draft.
Selected by Tampa Bay in 8th round (198th player selected) of 1984 NFL draft.
Released by Tampa Bay Buccaneers, August 20, 1984; signed as free agent by San Diego Chargers, August 22, 1984.
Released by San Diego Chargers, August 27, 1984; re-signed by Chargers, August 28, 1984.
San Diego NFL, 1984 and 1985.
Games: 1984 (16), 1985 (16). Total—32.
Pro statistics: Recovered one fumble, 1985.

JERRY DEWAYNE ROBINSON
Linebacker—Los Angeles Raiders
Born December 18, 1956, at San Francisco, Calif.
Height, 6.02. Weight, 225.
High School—Santa Rosa, Calif., Cardinal Newman.
Attended University of California at Los Angeles.

Named as linebacker on THE SPORTING NEWS College All-America Team, 1978.
Selected by Philadelphia in 1st round (21st player selected) of 1979 NFL draft.
On did not report list, August 20 through September 25, 1985.
Reported and granted roster exemption, September 26 through October 7, 1985; activated, October 8, 1985.
Traded by Philadelphia Eagles to Los Angeles Raiders for 2nd round pick in 1986 draft, September 30, 1985.

		—INTERCEPTIONS—			
Year Club	G.	No.	Yds.	Avg.	TD.
1979—Philadelphia NFL	16		None		
1980—Philadelphia NFL	16	2	13	6.5	0
1981—Philadelphia NFL	15	1	3	3.0	0
1982—Philadelphia NFL	9	3	19	6.3	0
1983—Philadelphia NFL	16		None		
1984—Philadelphia NFL	15		None		
1985—L.A. Raiders NFL	11		None		
Pro Totals—7 Years	98	6	35	5.8	0

Pro statistics: Recovered two fumbles, 1979, 1981 and 1983; recovered four fumbles for 59 yards and one touchdown and fumbled once, 1980; recovered one fumble, 1984.
Played in NFC Championship Game following 1980 season.
Played in NFL Championship Game following 1980 season.
Played in Pro Bowl (NFL All-Star Game) following 1981 season.

MARK LEON ROBINSON
Safety—Kansas City Chiefs
Born September 13, 1962, at Washington, D.C.
Height, 5.10. Weight, 206.
High School—Silver Spring, Md., John F. Kennedy.
Attended Penn State University.
Brother of Eric Robinson, running back with Washington Federal, 1983 and 1984.

Selected by Philadelphia in 1984 USFL territorial draft.
Selected by Kansas City in 4th round (90th player selected) of 1984 NFL draft.
Signed by Kansas City Chiefs, July 12, 1984.
On injured reserve with sprained ankle, September 3 through October 11, 1985; activated, October 12, 1985.
Kansas City NFL, 1984 and 1985.
Games: 1984 (16), 1985 (11). Total—27.
Pro statistics: Intercepted one pass for 20 yards and recovered one fumble, 1985.

MELVIN DELL ROBINSON
(Bo)
Tight End—New England Patriots

Born May 27, 1956, at LaMesa, Tex.
Height, 6.02. Weight, 235.
High School—LaMesa, Tex.
Attended West Texas State University.

Selected by Detroit in 3rd round (67th player selected) of 1979 NFL draft.
Released by Detroit Lions, August 31, 1981; signed as free agent by Atlanta Falcons, September 9, 1981.
On injured reserve with broken arm, September 1 through September 30, 1983; activated, October 1, 1983.
Released by Atlanta Falcons, August 27, 1984; awarded on waivers to New England Patriots, August 28, 1984.
On injured reserve with groin injury, September 2 through entire 1985 season.

		—RUSHING—				PASS RECEIVING				—TOTAL—	
Year Club	G.	Att.	Yds.	Avg.	TD.	P.C.	Yds.	Avg.	TD.	TD.	Pts. F.
1979—Detroit NFL	14	87	302	3.5	2	14	118	8.4	0	2	12 3
1980—Detroit NFL	14	3	2	0.7	0		None			0	0 0
1981—Atlanta NFL	15	9	24	2.7	0		None			0	0 0
1982—Atlanta NFL	9	19	108	5.7	0	7	55	7.9	2	2	12 0
1983—Atlanta NFL	12	3	9	3.0	0	12	100	8.3	0	0	0 1
1984—New England NFL	16		None			4	32	8.0	1	1	6 0
Pro Totals—6 Years	80	121	445	3.7	2	37	305	8.2	3	5	30 4

Additional pro statistics: Returned one punt for eight yards, 1979; recovered one fumble, 1979 and 1984; returned three kickoffs for 38 yards, 1984.

SHELTON ROBINSON
Linebacker—Seattle Seahawks

Born September 14, 1960, at Goldsboro, N.C.
Height, 6.03. Weight, 233.
High School—Pikeville, N.C., Aycock.
Received bachelor of science degree in industrial relations from
University of North Carolina in 1982.

Signed as free agent by Seattle Seahawks, April 30, 1982.
Seattle NFL, 1982 through 1985.
Games: 1982 (9), 1983 (16), 1984 (16), 1985 (15). Total—56.
Pro statistics: Intercepted one pass for 18 yards and recovered four fumbles for 21 yards and two touchdowns, 1983; recovered four fumbles for three yards, 1984; recovered one fumble for six yards, 1985.
Played in AFC Championship Game following 1983 season.

STACY ROBINSON
Wide Receiver—New York Giants

Born February 19, 1962, at St. Paul, Minn.
Height, 5.11. Weight, 186.
High School—St. Paul, Minn., Central.
Attended Prairie View A&M University and North Dakota State University.

Selected by Portland in 3rd round (34th player selected) of 1985 USFL draft.
Selected by New York Giants in 2nd round (46th player selected) of 1985 NFL draft.
Signed by New York Giants, July 17, 1985.
On injured reserve with broken hand, September 4 through November 29, 1985; activated, November 30, 1985.
New York Giants NFL, 1985.
Games: 1985 (4).

REGINALD HENRY ROBY
(Reggie)
Punter—Miami Dolphins

Born July 30, 1961, at Waterloo, Ia.
Height, 6.02. Weight, 243.
High School—Waterloo, Ia., East.
Attended University of Iowa.
Brother of Mike Roby, first baseman-outfielder in
San Francisco Giants' organization, 1967 and 1968.

Named to THE SPORTING NEWS NFL All-Star Team, 1984.
Led NFL in net punting average with 38.1 in 1984.
Selected by Chicago in 16th round (187th player selected) of 1983 USFL draft.
Selected by Miami in 6th round (167th player selected) of 1983 NFL draft.
Signed by Miami Dolphins, July 9, 1983.

		—PUNTING—		
Year Club	G.	No.	Avg.	Blk.
1983—Miami NFL	16	74	43.1	1
1984—Miami NFL	16	51	44.7	0
1985—Miami NFL	16	59	43.7	0
Pro Totals—3 Years	48	184	43.8	1

Played in AFC Championship Game following 1984 and 1985 seasons.
Played in NFL Championship Game following 1984 season.
Played in Pro Bowl (NFL All-Star Game) following 1984 season.

JAMES KYLE ROCKFORD
(Jim)
Defensive Back—Indianapolis Colts
Born September 5, 1961, at Bloomington, Ill.
Height, 5.10. Weight, 180.
High School—Springfield, Ill., Griffin.
Received bachelor of science degree in industrial recreation from University of Oklahoma in 1985.

Selected by San Antonio in 1985 USFL territorial draft.
Selected by Tampa Bay in 12th round (316th player selected) of 1985 USFL draft.
Signed by Tampa Bay Buccaneers, June 6, 1985.
Released by Tampa Bay Buccaneers, August 29, 1985; signed as free agent by San Diego Chargers, October 8, 1985.
Released by San Diego Chargers, October 18, 1985; signed as free agent by Indianapolis Colts, April 22, 1986.
San Diego NFL, 1985.
Games: 1985 (1).

CHRIS ROCKINS
Safety—Cleveland Browns
Born May 18, 1962, at Sherman, Tex.
Height, 6.00. Weight, 195.
High School—Sherman, Tex.
Attended Oklahoma State University.

Selected by Oklahoma in 1984 USFL territorial draft.
Selected by Cleveland in 2nd round (48th player selected) of 1984 NFL draft.
Signed by Cleveland Browns, May 17, 1984.
Cleveland NFL, 1984 and 1985.
Games: 1984 (16), 1985 (16). Total—32.
Pro statistics: Intercepted one pass for no yards, 1984; intercepted one pass for eight yards, 1985.

RODERICK DEL RODGERS
(Known by middle name.)
Running Back
Born June 22, 1960, at Tacoma, Wash.
Height, 5.10. Weight, 202.
High School—Salinas, Calif., North.
Attended University of Utah.

Selected by Green Bay in 3rd round (71st player selected) of 1982 NFL draft.
On injured reserve with neck injury, August 29 through entire 1983 season.
On injured reserve with broken fibula, August 12 through entire 1985 season.
Granted free agency with no qualifying offer, February 1, 1986.

		—RUSHING—			PASS RECEIVING				—TOTAL—		
Year Club	G.	Att.	Yds.	Avg.	TD.	P.C.	Yds.	Avg.	TD.	TD.	Pts.	F.
1982—Green Bay NFL	9	46	175	3.8	1	3	23	7.7	0	3	18	2
1984—Green Bay NFL	14	25	94	3.8	0	5	56	11.2	0	1	6	1
Pro Totals—2 Years	23	71	269	3.8	1	8	79	9.9	0	4	24	3

		KICKOFF RETURNS		
Year Club	G.	No.	Yds.	Avg.TD.
1982—Green Bay NFL	9	20	436	21.8 0
1984—Green Bay NFL	14	39	843	21.6 *1
Pro Totals—2 Years	23	59	1279	21.7 1

Additional pro statistics: Recovered two fumbles in end zone for two touchdowns, 1982.

DONALD LAVERT ROGERS
(Don)
Safety—Cleveland Browns
Born September 17, 1962, at Texarkana, Ark.
Height, 6.01. Weight, 206.
High School—Sacramento, Calif., Norte del Rio.
Attended University of California at Los Angeles.
Brother of Reggie Rogers, linebacker at University of Washington.

Named as defensive back on THE SPORTING NEWS College All-America Team, 1983.
Selected by San Antonio in 1st round (21st player selected) of 1984 USFL draft.
Selected by Cleveland in 1st round (18th player selected) of 1984 NFL draft.
USFL rights traded by San Antonio Gunslingers to Arizona Wranglers for draft pick, May 2, 1984.
Signed by Cleveland Browns, May 24, 1984.

		—INTERCEPTIONS—		
Year Club	G.	No.	Yds.	Avg.TD.
1984—Cleveland NFL	15	1	39	39.0 0
1985—Cleveland NFL	16	1	3	3.0 0
Pro Totals—2 Years	31	2	42	21.0 0

DOUGLAS KEITH ROGERS
(Doug)
Defensive End—San Francisco 49ers
Born June 23, 1960, at Chico, Calif.
Height, 6.05. Weight, 270.
High School—Bakersfield, Calif., Highland.
Received bachelor of arts degree in communications and sociology from
Stanford University in 1982.

Selected by Atlanta in 2nd round (36th player selected) of 1982 NFL draft.
Released by Atlanta Falcons, September 13, 1983; awarded on waivers to New England Patriots, September 14, 1983.
On physically unable to perform/reserve with shoulder and foot injuries, August 15 through October 21, 1985.
Released by New England Patriots, October 22, 1985; signed as free agent by San Francisco 49ers, May 15, 1986.
Atlanta NFL, 1982: Atlanta (2)-New England (10) NFL, 1983; New England NFL, 1984.
Games: 1982 (9), 1983 (12), 1984 (12). Total—33.

GEORGE WASHINGTON ROGERS JR.
Running Back—Washington Redskins
Born December 8, 1958, at Duluth, Ga.
Height, 6.02. Weight, 229.
High School—Duluth, Ga.
Attended University of South Carolina.

Heisman Trophy winner, 1980.
Named as running back on THE SPORTING NEWS College All-America Team, 1980.
Tied NFL record for most 100-yard games, rushing by rookie (9), 1981.
Named THE SPORTING NEWS NFL Rookie of the Year, 1981.
Named to THE SPORTING NEWS NFL All-Star Team, 1981.
Selected by New Orleans in 1st round (1st player selected) of 1981 NFL draft.
On inactive list, September 19, 1982.
Traded with 5th, 10th and 11th round picks in 1985 draft by New Orleans Saints to Washington Redskins for 1st round pick in 1985 draft, April 26, 1985.

		——RUSHING——				PASS RECEIVING				—TOTAL—		
Year Club	G.	Att.	Yds.	Avg.	TD.	P.C.	Yds.	Avg.	TD.	TD.	Pts.	F.
1981—New Orleans NFL	16	*378	*1674	4.4	13	16	126	7.9	0	13	78	13
1982—New Orleans NFL	6	122	535	4.4	3	4	21	5.3	0	3	18	4
1983—New Orleans NFL	13	256	1144	4.5	5	12	69	5.8	0	5	30	8
1984—New Orleans NFL	16	239	914	3.8	2	12	76	6.3	0	2	12	2
1985—Washington NFL	15	231	1093	4.7	7	4	29	7.3	0	7	42	9
Pro Totals—5 Years	66	1226	5360	4.4	30	48	321	6.7	0	30	180	36

Additional pro statistics: Recovered one fumble, 1981 and 1984; recovered two fumbles, 1983 and 1985.
Played in Pro Bowl (NFL All-Star Game) following 1981 and 1982 seasons.

JAMES ROGERS
(Jimmy)
Running Back—San Francisco 49ers
Born June 29, 1955, at Forrest City, Ark.
Height, 5.10. Weight, 194.
High School—Forrest City, Ark.
Attended University of Oklahoma.

Signed as free agent by Chicago Bears, July 19, 1979.
Released by Chicago Bears, August 13, 1979; signed as free agent by Edmonton Eskimos, March, 1980.
Released by Edmonton Eskimos, July 2, 1980; signed as free agent by New Orleans Saints, July 10, 1980.
Released by New Orleans Saints, August 26, 1985; signed as free agent by San Francisco 49ers for 1986, December 17, 1985.

		——RUSHING——				PASS RECEIVING				—TOTAL—		
Year Club	G.	Att.	Yds.	Avg.	TD.	P.C.	Yds.	Avg.	TD.	TD.	Pts.	F.
1980—New Orleans NFL	16	80	366	4.6	1	27	267	9.9	2	3	18	6
1981—New Orleans NFL	15	9	37	4.1	0	2	12	6.0	0	0	0	3
1982—New Orleans NFL	9	60	178	3.0	2	4	17	4.3	0	2	12	0
1983—New Orleans NFL	16	26	80	3.1	0		None			0	0	2
1984—New Orleans NFL	16		None				None			0	0	0
Pro Totals—5 Years	72	175	661	3.8	3	33	296	9.0	2	5	30	11

		KICKOFF RETURNS			
Year Club	G.	No.	Yds.	Avg.	TD.
1980—New Orleans NFL	16	41	930	22.7	0
1981—New Orleans NFL	15	28	621	22.2	0
1982—New Orleans NFL	9	1	24	24.0	0
1983—New Orleans NFL	16	7	103	14.7	0
1984—New Orleans NFL	16		None		
Pro Totals—5 Years	72	77	1678	21.8	0

Additional pro statistics: Recovered two fumbles, 1980; recovered one fumble, 1981 and 1983.

JEFFREY CHARLES ROHRER
(Jeff)
Linebacker—Dallas Cowboys
Born December 25, 1958, at Inglewood, Calif.
Height, 6.02. Weight, 230.
High School—Manhattan Beach, Calif., Mira Costa.
Received bachelor of science degree in administrative sciences from
Yale University in 1982.

Selected by Dallas in 2nd round (53rd player selected) of 1982 NFL draft.
Dallas NFL, 1982 through 1985.
Games: 1982 (8), 1983 (16), 1984 (16), 1985 (15). Total—55.
Pro statistics: Recovered one fumble for five yards and fumbled once, 1984.
Played in NFC Championship Game following 1982 season.

JAMES JOHN ROMANO
(Jim)
Center—Houston Oilers
Born September 7, 1959, at Glen Cove, N.Y.
Height, 6.03. Weight, 255.
High School—Glen Head, N.Y., North Shore.
Received bachelor of arts degree in commercial recreation from
Penn State University in 1982.

Selected by Los Angeles Raiders in 2nd round (37th player selected) of 1982 NFL draft.
On injured reserve with pulled hamstring, September 20 through remainder of 1983 season.
Traded by Los Angeles Raiders to Houston Oilers for 3rd and 6th round draft picks in 1985 draft, October 9, 1984.
Los Angeles Raiders NFL, 1982 and 1983; Los Angeles Raiders (6)-Houston (8) NFL, 1984; Houston NFL, 1985.
Games: 1982 (5), 1983 (1), 1984 (14), 1985 (16). Total—36.
Pro statistics: Fumbled once for minus 11 yards, 1984.

CHARLES MICHAEL ROMES
Cornerback—Buffalo Bills
Born December 16, 1954, at Verdun, France.
Height, 6.01. Weight, 190.
High School—Durham, N. C., Hillside.
Attended Lake City Junior College and North Carolina Central University.

Selected by Buffalo in 12th round (309th player selected) of 1977 NFL draft.

		——INTERCEPTIONS——			
Year Club	G.	No.	Yds.	Avg.	TD.
1977—Buffalo NFL	14		None		
1978—Buffalo NFL	16	2	95	47.5	1
1979—Buffalo NFL	16	1	0	0.0	0
1980—Buffalo NFL	16	2	41	20.5	0
1981—Buffalo NFL	16	4	113	28.3	0
1982—Buffalo NFL	9	1	8	8.0	0
1983—Buffalo NFL	16	2	27	13.5	0
1984—Buffalo NFL	16	5	130	26.0	0
1985—Buffalo NFL	16	7	56	8.0	0
Pro Totals—9 Years	135	24	470	19.6	1

Additional pro statistics: Returned one kickoff for 18 yards, 1977; fumbled once, 1977, 1978 and 1981; recovered two fumbles, 1978; ran 76 yards with blocked field goal for a touchdown and recovered one fumble for minus 10 yards, 1979; recovered two fumbles for 11 yards, 1981; recovered one fumble, 1984 and 1985.

WILLIE DEAN ROSBOROUGH
Defensive End—Washington Redskins
Born January 9, 1961, at Los Angeles, Calif.
Height, 6.04. Weight, 243.
High School—Simi Valley, Calif.
Attended University of Washington.

Signed as free agent by Philadelphia Stars, January 25, 1983.
On developmental squad, July 1 through July 4, 1983; activated, July 5, 1983.
On developmental squad, February 24 through March 1, 1984; activated, March 2, 1984.
On developmental squad, March 10 through March 16, 1984; activated, March 17, 1984.
On developmental squad, April 7 through May 11, 1984; activated, May 12, 1984.
Franchise transferred to Baltimore, November 1, 1984.
Released by Baltimore Stars, February 18, 1985; awarded on waivers to Portland Breakers, February 19, 1985.
On developmental squad, March 22 through March 31, 1984; activated, April 1, 1985.
Released by Portland Breakers, April 10, 1985; signed as free agent by Washington Redskins, May 16, 1985.
On injured reserve wih knee injury, August 7 through entire 1985 season.
On developmental squad for 1 game with Philadelphia Stars in 1983.
On developmental squad for 7 games with Philadelphia Stars in 1984.
On developmental squad for 1 game with Portland Breakers in 1985.
Philadelphia USFL, 1983 and 1984; Portland USFL, 1985.
Games: 1983 (17), 1984 (10), 1985 (5). Total—32.
Pro statistics: Recovered two fumbles, intercepted one pass for one yard and credited with five sacks for 19 yards, 1983; recovered one fumble, 1984; credited with one sack for 10 yards, 1985.
Played in USFL Championship Game following 1983 and 1984 seasons.

DONOVAN ROSE
Defensive Back—Miami Dolphins
Born March 9, 1957, at Norfolk, Va.
Height, 6.01. Weight, 190.
High School—Norfolk, Va., Norview.
Attended Hampton Institute.

Signed as free agent by Kansas City Chiefs, May 10, 1980.
Released by Kansas City Chiefs, September 1, 1980; re-signed by Chiefs after clearing procedural waivers, October 25, 1980.
Released by Kansas City Chiefs, August 25, 1981; signed as free agent by Toronto Argonauts, September 5, 1981.
Traded by Toronto Argonauts to Winnipeg Blue Bombers for draft choice, October 10, 1983.
Traded by Winnipeg Blue Bombers to Toronto Argonauts for draft choice, January 7, 1984.
Traded with 1985 draft choice by Toronto Argonauts to Winnipeg Blue Bombers for defensive back Paul Bennett, June 13, 1984.
Traded by Winnipeg Blue Bombers to Hamilton Tiger-Cats for draft choice, July 2, 1985.
Granted free agency, March 1, 1986; signed as free agent by Miami Dolphins, April 2, 1986.

| | | —INTERCEPTIONS— | | | |
Year Club	G.	No.	Yds.	Avg.	TD.
1980—Kansas City NFL	7		None		
1981—Toronto CFL	8		None		
1982—Torono CFL	9	1	34	34.0	0
1983—Tor (5)-Wpg (3) CFL	8	4	98	24.5	1
1984—Winnipeg CFL	16	8	39	4.9	0
1985—Hamilton CFL	13	6	151	25.2	0
NFL Totals—1 Year	7	0	0	0.0	0
CFL Totals—5 Years	54	19	322	16.9	1
Pro Totals—6 Years	61	19	322	16.9	1

Additional pro statistics: Returned six kickoffs for 122 yards, returned two punts for 33 yards and recovered two fumbles for four yards, 1981; recovered one fumble for 28 yards, 1983; recovered one fumble, 1984.

JOSEPH HAROLD ROSE
(Joe)
Tight End—Miami Dolphins
Born June 24, 1957, at Marysville, Calif.
Height, 6.03. Weight, 230.
High School—Marysville, Calif.
Received bachelor of arts degree in social science from University of California in 1980.
Cousin of Rod Scurry, pitcher with New York Yankees.

Selected by Miami in 7th round (185th player selected) of 1980 NFL draft.
On injured reserve with separated shoulder, October 12 through November 16, 1984; activated, November 17, 1984.

| | | —PASS RECEIVING— | | | |
Year Club	G.	P.C.	Yds.	Avg.	TD.
1980—Miami NFL	16	13	149	11.5	0
1981—Miami NFL	16	23	316	13.7	2
1982—Miami NFL	9	16	182	11.4	2
1983—Miami NFL	16	29	345	11.9	3
1984—Miami NFL	9	12	195	16.3	2
1985—Miami NFL	16	19	306	16.1	4
Pro Totals—6 Years	82	112	1493	13.3	13

Additional pro statistics: Recovered one fumble and returned one kickoff for five yards, 1981.
Played in AFC Championship Game following 1982, 1984 and 1985 seasons.
Played in NFL Championship Game following 1982 and 1984 seasons.

TED ROSNAGLE
Safety—Minnesota Vikings
Born September 29, 1961, at Pasadena, Calif.
Height, 6.03. Weight, 202.
High School—Tustin, Calif.
Attended Fullerton College and Portland State University.

Selected by Memphis in 7th round (147th player selected) of 1984 USFL draft.
USFL rights released by Memphis Showboats, January 26, 1984; USFL rights awarded to Arizona Wranglers, January 27, 1984.
Signed as free agent by Toronto Argonauts, February 19, 1984.
Released by Toronto Argonauts, July 15, 1984; signed as free agent by Seattle Seahawks, July 26, 1984.
Released by Seattle Seahawks, August 7, 1984; signed as free agent by Minnesota Vikings, April 21, 1985.
On injured reserve with knee injury, September 12 through November 22, 1985; activated, November 23, 1985.
Toronto CFL, 1984; Minnesota NFL, 1985.
Games: 1984 (1), 1985 (6). Total—7.

DANIEL RICHARD ROSS
(Dan)
Tight End—Seattle Seahawks
Born February 9, 1957, at Malden, Mass.
Height, 6.04. Weight, 235.
High School—Everett, Mass.
Received bachelor of science degree in criminal law from Northeastern University.

Named as tight end on THE SPORTING NEWS USFL All-Star Team, 1984.
Selected by Cincinnati in 2nd round (30th player selected) of 1979 NFL draft.
USFL rights traded with rights to offensive tackle Pat Staub by Philadelphia Stars to Boston Breakers for rights to quarterback Tim Cowan and 4th round pick in 1984 draft, February 18, 1983.
Signed by Boston Breakers, February 25, 1983, for contract to take effect after being granted free agency, February 1, 1984.
Franchise transferred to New Orleans, October 18, 1983.
Franchise transferred to Portland, November 13, 1984.
On developmental squad, May 9 through May 16, 1985; activated, May 17, 1985.
Released by Portland Breakers, July 31, 1985; re-signed by Bengals, August 29, 1985.
Granted roster exemption, August 29 through September 2, 1985; activated, September 3, 1985.
Traded by Cincinnati Bengals to Seattle Seahawks for 4th round pick in 1986 draft, October 15, 1985.
On developmental squad for 1 game with Portland Breakers in 1985.

			—PASS RECEIVING—			
Year Club	G.	P.C.	Yds.	Avg.	TD.	
1979—Cincinnati NFL	16	41	516	12.6	1	
1980—Cincinnati NFL	16	56	724	12.9	4	
1981—Cincinnati NFL	16	71	910	12.8	5	
1982—Cincinnati NFL	9	47	508	10.8	3	
1983—Cincinnati NFL	16	42	483	11.5	3	
1984—New Orleans USFL	18	65	833	12.8	2	
1985—Portland USFL	17	41	522	12.7	5	
1985—Cin.(6)-Sea.(10) NFL	16	16	135	8.4	2	
NFL Totals—6 Years	89	273	3276	12.0	18	
USFL Totals—2 Years	35	106	1355	12.8	7	
Pro Totals—8 Years	124	379	4631	12.2	25	

Additional NFL statistics: Recovered one fumble for four yards, 1979; fumbled once, 1980, 1982 and 1985; recovered one fumble for three yards and fumbled three times, 1981; recovered one fumble, 1985.
Additional USFL statistics: Scored one 2-point conversion, 1984; fumbled once, 1985.
Played in AFC Championship Game following 1981 season.
Played in NFL Championship Game following 1981 season.
Played in Pro Bowl (NFL All-Star Game) following 1982 season.

KEVIN LESLEY ROSS
Cornerback—Kansas City Chiefs
Born January 16, 1962, at Camden, N.J.
Height, 5.09. Weight, 180.
High School—Paulsboro, N.J.
Attended Temple University.

Selected by Philadelphia in 1984 USFL territorial draft.
Selected by Kansas City in 7th round (173rd player selected) of 1984 NFL draft.
Signed by Kansas City Chiefs, June 21, 1984.

		—INTERCEPTIONS—			
Year Club	G.	No.	Yds.	Avg.	TD.
1984—Kansas City NFL	16	6	124	20.7	1
1985—Kansas City NFL	16	3	47	15.7	0
Pro Totals—2 Years	32	9	171	19.0	1

Additional pro statistics: Recovered one fumble, 1984 and 1985.

PETER JOSEPH ROSTOSKY
(Pete)
Offensive Tackle—Pittsburgh Steelers
Born July 29, 1961, at Monongahela, Pa.
Height, 6.04. Weight, 260.
High School—Elizabeth, Pa., Forward.
Attended University of Connecticut.

Signed as free agent by Pittsburgh Steelers, May 10, 1983.
On injured reserve with knee injury, August 16 through entire 1983 season.
On injured reserve with knee injury, August 14 through October 22, 1984; activated after clearing procedural waivers, October 24, 1984.
Pittsburgh NFL, 1984 and 1985.
Games: 1984 (8), 1985 (16). Total—24.
Played in AFC Championship Game following 1984 season.

JAMES PETER ROURKE
(Jim)
Offensive Tackle—New Orleans Saints
Born February 10, 1957, at Weymouth, Mass.
Height, 6.05. Weight, 263.
High School—Dorchester, Mass., Boston College High.
Received bachelor of arts degree in sociology from Boston College in 1979.

Selected by Oakland in 9th round (238th player selected) of 1979 NFL draft.
Released by Oakland Raiders, August 27, 1979; signed as free agent by Kansas City Chiefs, February 16, 1980.
Released by Kansas City Chiefs, August 24, 1981; re-signed by Chiefs, September 29, 1981.

Released by Kansas City Chiefs, August 29, 1985; signed as free agent by New Orleans Saints, September 25, 1985.
Kansas City NFL, 1980 through 1984; New Orleans NFL, 1985.
Games: 1980 (15), 1981 (12), 1982 (9), 1983 (11), 1984 (13), 1985 (13). Total—73.
Pro statistics: Returned two kickoffs for no yards, 1981.

CURTIS LAMAR ROUSE
Guard-Offensive Tackle—Minnesota Vikings
Born July 13, 1960, at Augusta, Ga.
Height, 6.03. Weight, 318.
High School—Augusta, Ga., Lucy C. Laney.
Attended University of Tennessee at Chattanooga.

Selected by Minnesota in 11th round (286th player selected) of 1982 NFL draft.
Minnesota NFL, 1982 through 1985.
Games: 1982 (5), 1983 (16), 1984 (16), 1985 (16). Total—53.
Pro statistics: Recovered two fumbles, 1983; returned two kickoffs for 22 yards, 1984; recovered one fumble, 1984 and 1985.

LEE ROUSON
Running Back—New York Giants
Born October 18, 1962, at Elizabeth City, N.C.
Height, 6.01. Weight, 210.
High School—Greensboro, N.C., Page.
Attended Colorado University.
Cousin of Johnny Walton, quarterback with San Antonio Wings (WFL), Philadelphia Eagles and Boston-New Orleans Breakers, 1975, 1976, 1978, 1979, 1983 and 1984; and head coach at Elizabeth City State University, 1980 through 1982.

Selected by New Jersey in 1st round (11th player selected) of 1985 USFL draft.
Selected by New York Giants in 8th round (213th player selected) of 1985 NFL draft.
Signed by New York Giants, July 2, 1985.
On injured reserve with hamstring injury, September 2 through December 13, 1985; activated, December 14, 1985.
New York Giants NFL, 1985.
Games: 1985 (2).
Pro statistics: Rushed once for one yard and returned two kickoffs for 35 yards, 1985.

MIKE ROZIER
Running Back—Houston Oilers
Born March 1, 1961, at Camden, N.J.
Height, 5.10. Weight, 198.
High School—Camden, N.J., Wilson.
Attended Coffeyville Community College and University of Nebraska.

Named THE SPORTING NEWS College Football Player of the Year, 1983.
Heisman Trophy winner, 1983.
Named as running back on THE SPORTING NEWS College All-America Team, 1983.
Selected by Pittsburgh in 1st round (1st player selected) of 1984 USFL draft.
Signed by Pittsburgh Maulers, January 3, 1984.
On developmental squad, May 18 through June 15, 1984; activated, June 16, 1984.
Selected by Houston in 1st round (2nd player selected) of 1984 NFL supplemental draft.
Franchise disbanded, October 25, 1984.
Personal services contract assigned to Baltimore Stars, November 1, 1984.
Signed as free agent with Jacksonville Bulls, February 1, 1985.
Granted roster exemption, February 1 through February 13, 1985; activated, February 14, 1985.
Granted free agency, July 1, 1985; signed by Houston Oilers, July 1, 1985.
On developmental squad for 4 games with Pittsburgh Maulers in 1984.

| Year Club | G. | ——RUSHING—— | | | | PASS RECEIVING | | | | —TOTAL— | | |
		Att.	Yds.	Avg.	TD.	P.C.	Yds.	Avg.	TD.	TD.	Pts.	F.
1984—Pittsburgh USFL	14	223	792	3.6	3	32	259	8.1	0	3	18	8
1985—Jacksonville USFL	18	320	1361	4.3	12	50	366	7.3	3	15	90	10
1985—Houston NFL	14	133	462	3.5	8	9	96	10.7	0	8	48	3
USFL Totals—2 Years	32	543	2153	4.0	15	82	625	7.6	3	18	108	18
NFL Totals—1 Year	14	133	462	3.5	8	9	96	10.7	0	8	48	3
Pro Totals—3 Years	46	676	2615	3.9	23	91	721	7.9	3	26	156	21

Additional USFL statistics: Recovered eight fumbles, 1984; recovered four fumbles, 1985.
Additional NFL statistics: Recovered three fumbles, 1985.

ROBIN JAMES RUBICK
(Rob)
Tight End—Detroit Lions
Born September 27, 1960, at Newberry, Mich.
Height, 6.03. Weight, 234.
High School—Newberry, Mich.
Received degree in physical educaton from Grand Valley State College.
Nephew of Tom Villemure, head basketball coach at Grand Valley State College.

Selected by Detroit in 12th round (326th player selected) of 1982 NFL draft.
On physically unable to perform/active with back injury, July 27 through October 16, 1985; activated, October 17, 1985.

Year Club	G.	P.C.	Yds.	Avg.	TD.
1982—Detroit NFL	7	None			
1983—Detroit NFL	16	10	81	8.1	1
1984—Detroit NFL	16	14	188	13.4	1
1985—Detroit NFL	9	2	33	16.5	0
Pro Totals—4 Years	48	26	302	11.6	2

Additional pro statistics: Rushed once for one yard and a touchdown, 1982.

BEN RUDOLPH
Defensive End—New York Jets
Born August 29, 1957, at Evergreen, Ala.
Height, 6.05. Weight, 271.
High School—Fairhope, Ala.
Attended California State University at Long Beach.

Selected by New York Jets in 3rd round (60th player selected) of 1981 NFL draft.
On injured reserve with knee injury, January 5, 1983 through remainder of 1982 season playoffs.
Signed by Los Angeles Express, January 30, 1984, for contract to take effect after being granted free agency, February 1, 1985.
Released by Los Angeles Express, August 1, 1985; re-signed by Jets, August 5, 1985.
New York Jets NFL, 1981 through 1985; Los Angeles USFL, 1985.
Games: 1981 (15), 1982 (9), 1983 (16), 1984 (16), 1985 USFL (18), 1985 NFL (16). Total NFL—72. Total Pro—90.
NFL statistics: Returned one kickoff for eight yards, 1981; recovered one fumble, 1983 and 1984.
USFL statistics: Credited with eight sacks for 45½ yards and recovered one fumble, 1985.

KENNETH F. RUETTGERS
Name pronounced RUTT-gers.
(Ken)
Offensive Tackle—Green Bay Packers
Born August 20, 1962, at Bakersfield, Calif.
Height, 6.05. Weight, 267.
High School—Bakersfield, Calif., Garces Memorial.
Received bachelor of business administration degree from University of Southern California in 1985.

Selected by Green Bay in 1st round (7th player selected) of 1985 NFL draft.
Signed by Green Bay Packers, August 12, 1985.
Green Bay NFL, 1985.
Games: 1985 (15).

MAX CULP RUNAGER
Punter—San Francisco 49ers
Born March 24, 1956, at Greenwood, S.C.
Height, 6.01. Weight, 189.
High School—Orangeburg, S.C., Wilkinson.
Received bachelor of science degree in health and physical education from University of South Carolina.

Selected by Philadelphia in 8th round (211th player selected) of 1979 NFL draft.
Released by Philadelphia Eagles, September 28, 1983; re-signed by Eagles, October 26, 1983.
Released by Philadelphia Eagles, August 27, 1984; signed as free agent by San Francisco 49ers, September 12, 1984.

Year Club	G.	No.	Avg.	Blk.
1979—Philadelphia NFL	16	74	39.6	1
1980—Philadelphia NFL	16	75	39.3	1
1981—Philadelphia NFL	15	63	40.7	0
1982—Philadelphia NFL	9	44	40.5	0
1983—Philadelphia NFL	12	59	41.7	0
1984—San Francisco NFL	14	56	41.8	1
1985—San Francisco NFL	16	86	39.8	1
Pro Totals—7 Years	98	457	40.4	4

Additional pro statistics: Recovered one fumble and fumbled once, 1979; rushed once for six yards, 1983; rushed once for minus five yards, 1984.
Played in NFC Championship Game following 1980 and 1984 seasons.
Played in NFL Championship Game following 1980 and 1984 seasons.

ROBERT JEFFREY RUSH
(Bob)
Center—Kansas City Chiefs
Born February 27, 1955, at Santa Monica, Calif.
Height, 6.05. Weight, 270.
High School—Clarksville, Tenn., Northwest.
Received bachelor of arts degree in sociology from Memphis State University.

Named center on THE SPORTING NEWS College All-America Team, 1976.
Selected by San Diego in 1st round (24th player selected) of 1977 NFL draft.
On injured reserve with knee injury, July 19 through entire 1978 season.
Traded by San Diego Chargers to Kansas City Chiefs for 3rd round pick in 1985 draft and 5th round pick in 1986 draft, July 11, 1983.

San Diego NFL, 1977 and 1979 through 1982; Kansas City NFL, 1983 through 1985.
Games: 1977 (14), 1979 (16), 1980 (15), 1981 (16), 1982 (9), 1983 (15), 1984 (16), 1985 (16). Total—117.
Pro statistics: Fumbled twice for minus 35 yards, 1980; fumbled twice and recovered one fumble, 1983.
Played in AFC Championship Game following 1980 and 1981 seasons.

RUSTY RUSSELL
Offensive Tackle—Los Angeles Raiders
Born August 16, 1963, at Orangeburg, S.C.
Height, 6.05. Weight, 295.
High School—Orangeburg, S.C., Wilkinson.
Attended University of South Carolina.
Cousin of Rufus Bess, cornerback with Minnesota Vikings.

Selected by Washington in 1984 USFL territorial draft.
Selected by Philadelphia in 3rd round (60th player selected) of 1984 NFL draft.
Signed by Philadelphia Eagles, June 19, 1984.
On injured reserve with broken foot, August 28 through October 17, 1984; activated, October 18, 1984.
Released by Philadelphia Eagles, August 20, 1985; signed as free agent by Los Angeles Raiders for 1986, November 1, 1985.
Philadelphia NFL, 1984.
Games: 1984 (1).

JEFFREY RONALD RUTLEDGE
(Jeff)
Quarterback—New York Giants
Born January 22, 1957, at Birmingham, Ala.
Height, 6.01. Weight, 195.
High School—Birmingham, Ala., Banks.
Received degree in business education from University of Alabama.
Son of Paul E. (Jack) Rutledge, minor league infielder, 1950 through 1952.

Selected by Los Angeles in 9th round (246th player selected) of 1979 NFL draft.
On injured reserve with mononucleosis, October 22 through remainder of 1980 season.
On injured reserve with broken thumb, November 2 through remainder of 1981 season.
Traded by Los Angeles Rams to New York Giants for 4th round pick in 1983 draft, September 5, 1982.
Active for 9 games with New York Giants in 1982; did not play.

Year Club	G.	PASSING Att.	Cmp.	Pct.	Gain	T.P.	P.I.	Avg.	RUSHING Att.	Yds.	Avg.	TD.	TOTAL TD.	Pts.	F.
1979—Los Angeles NFL.............	3	32	13	40.6	125	1	4	3.91	5	27	5.4	0	0	0	0
1980—Los Angeles NFL.............	1	4	1	25.0	26	0	0	6.50	None				0	0	0
1981—Los Angeles NFL.............	4	50	30	60.0	442	3	4	8.84	5	—3	—0.6	0	0	0	0
1983—New York Giants NFL	4	174	87	50.0	1208	3	8	6.94	7	27	3.9	0	0	0	6
1984—New York Giants NFL	16	1	1	100.0	9	0	0	9.00	None				0	0	0
1985—New York Giants NFL	16			None					2	—6	—3.0	0	0	0	1
Pro Totals—7 Years...........	44	261	132	50.6	1810	7	16	6.98	19	45	2.4	0	0	0	7

Quarterback Rating Points: 1979 (23.0), 1980 (54.2), 1981 (75.6), 1983 (59.3), 1984 (104.2). Total—56.7.
Member of Los Angeles Rams for NFC and NFL Championship Game following 1979 season; did not play.

JAMES JOSEPH RYAN
(Jim)
Linebacker—Denver Broncos
Born May 18, 1957, at Camden, N.J.
Height, 6.01. Weight, 215.
High School—Pennsauken, N.J., Bishop Eustace.
Received bachelor of administration degree in management from College of William & Mary in 1979
and received master's degree in business administration from University of Denver.

Signed as free agent by Denver Broncos, May 12, 1979.
Denver NFL, 1979 through 1985.
Games: 1979 (16), 1980 (16), 1981 (16), 1982 (9), 1983 (15), 1984 (16), 1985 (16). Total—104.
Pro statistics: Recovered one fumble, 1979, 1983, 1984 and 1985; intercepted one pass for 21 yards and returned one kickoff for no yards, 1980; returned one kickoff for two yards, 1981; intercepted one pass for 13 yards, 1984.

PATRICK LEE RYAN
(Pat)
Quarterback—New York Jets
Born September 16, 1955, at Hutchinson, Kan.
Height, 6.03. Weight, 210.
High School—Oklahoma City, Okla., Putnam.
Received degree in transportation from University of Tennessee in 1978.

Selected by New York Jets in 11th round (281st player selected) of 1978 NFL draft.

Year Club	G.	PASSING Att.	Cmp.	Pct.	Gain	T.P.	P.I.	Avg.	RUSHING Att.	Yds.	Avg.	TD.	TOTAL TD.	Pts.	F.
1978—New York Jets NFL........	2	14	9	64.3	106	0	2	7.57	None				0	0	0
1979—New York Jets NFL........	1	4	2	50.0	13	0	1	3.25	None				0	0	1
1980—New York Jets NFL........	14			None					None				0	0	0
1981—New York Jets NFL........	15	10	4	40.0	48	1	1	4.80	3	—5	—1.7	0	0	0	0
1982—New York Jets NFL........	9	18	12	66.7	146	2	1	8.11	1	—1	—1.0	0	0	0	0

Year	Club	G.	Att.	Cmp.	—PASSING— Pct.	Gain	T.P.	P.I.	Avg.	—RUSHING— Att.	Yds.	Avg.	TD.	—TOTAL— TD.	Pts.
1983—New York Jets NFL		16	40	21	52.5	259	2	2	6.48	4	23	5.8	0	0	†1
1984—New York Jets NFL		16	285	156	54.7	1939	14	14	6.80	23	92	4.0	0	0	†1
1985—New York Jets NFL		16	9	6	66.7	95	0	0	10.56	3	—5	—1.7	0	0	0
Pro Totals—8 Years		89	380	210	55.3	2606	19	21	6.86	34	104	3.1	0	0	2

†Scored one extra point.
Quarterback Rating Points: 1978 (47.6), 1979 (17.7), 1981 (49.2), 1982 (105.1), 1983 (68.6), 1984 (72.0), 1985 (101.6)
Total—70.5.
Additional pro statistics: Recovered one fumble, 1983 and 1984.
Member of New York Jets for AFC Championship Game following 1982 season; did not play.

HARVEY SALEM
Offensive Tackle—Houston Oilers
Born January 15, 1961, at Berkeley, Calif.
Height, 6.06. Weight, 285.
High School—El Cerrito, Calif.
Received degree from University of California at Berkeley.
Named as offensive tackle on THE SPORTING NEWS College All-America Team, 1982.
Selected by Oakland in 1983 USFL territorial draft.
Selected by Houston in 2nd round (30th player selected) of 1983 NFL draft.
Signed by Houston Oilers, July 14, 1983.
Houston NFL, 1983 through 1985.
Games: 1983 (16), 1984 (16), 1985 (14). Total—46.

JEROME ELI SALLY
Nose Tackle—New York Giants
Born February 24, 1959, at Chicago, Ill.
Height, 6.03. Weight, 270.
High School—Maywood, Ill., Proviso East.
Received bachelor of science degree in industrial engineering from University of Missouri.
Signed as free agent by New Orleans Saints, May 27, 1982.
Released by New Orleans Saints, August 31, 1982; signed as free agent by New York Giants, December 1, 1982.
New York Giants NFL, 1982 through 1985.
Games: 1982 (4), 1983 (16), 1984 (16), 1985 (16). Total—52.
Pro statistics: Recovered one fumble, 1983; returned one kickoff for four yards, 1985.

BRIAN SCOTT SALONEN
Name pronounced Suh-LOW-nen.
Linebacker—Dallas Cowboys
Born July 29, 1961, at Glasgow, Mont.
Height, 6.03. Weight, 227.
High School—Great Falls, Mont.
Attended University of Montana.
Brother of Brad Salonen, tight end at University of Montana.
Selected by Houston in 9th round (188th player selected) of 1984 USFL draft.
Selected by Dallas in 10th round (278th player selected) of 1984 NFL draft.
Signed by Dallas Cowboys, June 7, 1984.
Dallas NFL, 1984 and 1985.
Games: 1984 (16), 1985 (16). Total—32.
Pro statistics: Returned two kickoffs for 30 yards and recovered one fumble, 1984.

LAWRENCE SAMPLETON
Tight End—Miami Dolphins
Born September 25, 1959, at Waelder, Tex.
Height, 6.05. Weight, 233.
High School—Seguin, Tex.
Attended University of Texas.
Selected by Philadelphia in 2nd round (47th player selected) of 1982 NFL draft.
Released by Philadelphia Eagles, September 2, 1985; signed as free agent by Miami Dolphins, March 26, 1986.

Year	Club	G.	—PASS RECEIVING— P.C.	Yds.	Avg.	TD.
1982—Philadelphia NFL		9	1	24	24.0	0
1983—Philadelphia NFL		7	2	28	14.0	0
1984—Philadelphia NFL		16			None	
Pro Totals—3 Years		32	3	52	17.3	0

—DID YOU KNOW—

That Darrin Nelson last season became the first Vikings running back since Chuck Foreman in 1975 to post consecutive 100-yard rushing games? On November 3 against Detroit, Nelson carried 25 times for 122 yards and followed up with a 21-146 performance against Green Bay on November 10.

CLINTON BERNARD SAMPSON
(Clint)
Wide Receiver—Denver Broncos
Born January 4, 1961, at Los Angeles, Calif.
Height, 5.11. Weight, 183.
High School—Los Angeles, Calif., Crenshaw.
Attended Mt. San Antonio College and received degree in public administration
and business management from San Diego State University in 1983.

Selected by Boston in 3rd round (35th player selected) of 1983 USFL draft.
Selected by Denver in 3rd round (60th player selected) of 1983 NFL draft.
Signed by Denver Broncos, July 13, 1983.
On injured reserve with concussion, October 26 through November 19, 1984; activated, November 20, 1984.

| | | | —PASS RECEIVING— | | |
Year Club	G.	P.C.	Yds.	Avg.	TD.
1983—Denver NFL	16	10	200	20.0	3
1984—Denver NFL	12	9	123	13.7	1
1985—Denver NFL	16	26	432	16.6	4
Pro Totals—3 Years	44	45	755	16.8	8

Additional pro statistics: Fumbled once, 1984.

RONALD F. SAMS JR.
(Ron)
Guard—New York Jets
Born April 12, 1961, at Bridgeville, Pa.
Height, 6.03. Weight, 255.
High School—McDonald, Pa., South Fayette.
Attended University of Pittsburgh.

Selected by Green Bay in 6th round (160th player selected) of 1983 NFL draft.
On injured reserve with torn hamstring, August 29 through October 15, 1983; activated by Green Bay Packers after clearing procedural waivers, October 17, 1983.
On injured reserve with neck injury, November 18 through remainder of 1983 season.
Released by Green Bay Packers, August 27, 1984; awarded on waivers to Minnesota Vikings, August 28, 1984.
Granted free agency, February 1, 1985; withdrew qualifying offer, August 22, 1985.
Signed by New York Jets, April 23, 1986.
Green Bay NFL, 1983; Minnesota NFL, 1984.
Games: 1983 (3), 1984 (12). Total—15.
Pro statistics: Fumbled once for minus 17 yards, 1984.

ERIC DOWNER SANDERS
Offensive Tackle—Atlanta Falcons
Born October 22, 1958, at Reno, Nev.
Height, 6.07. Weight, 280.
High School—Reno, Nev., Wooster.
Attended University of Nevada at Reno.

Selected by Atlanta in 5th round (136th player selected) of 1981 NFL draft.
On injured reserve with knee injury, November 10 through remainder of 1984 season.
Atlanta NFL, 1981 through 1985.
Games: 1981 (16), 1982 (9), 1983 (15), 1984 (10), 1985 (16). Total—66.
Pro statistics: Recovered one fumble, 1982; recovered one fumble for minus 23 yards, 1985.

EUGENE SANDERS
(Gene)
Offensive Tackle—Tampa Bay Buccaneers
Born November 10, 1956, at New Orleans, La.
Height, 6.03. Weight, 275.
High School—Harvey, La., West Jefferson.
Attended University of Washington and received degree in educational curriculum
and instructions from Texas A&M University.

Selected by Tampa Bay in 8th round (217th player selected) of 1979 NFL draft.
On injured reserve with wrist injury, October 11 through November 7, 1980; activated, November 8, 1980.
On injured reserve with pinched nerve in shoulder, September 20 through remainder of 1985 season.
Tampa Bay NFL, 1979 through 1985.
Games: 1979 (16), 1980 (11), 1981 (16), 1982 (4), 1983 (12), 1984 (16), 1985 (2). Total—77.
Pro statistics: Recovered one fumble, 1983.
Played in NFC Championship Game following 1979 season.

THOMAS SANDERS
Running Back—Chicago Bears
Born January 4, 1962, at Giddings, Tex.
Height, 5.11. Weight, 203.
High School—Giddings, Tex.
Attended Texas A&M University.

Selected by Houston in 1985 USFL territorial draft.
Selected by Chicago in 9th round (250th player selected) of 1985 NFL draft.

Signed by Chicago Bears, July 10, 1985.

Year Club	G.	Att.	RUSHING Yds.	Avg.	TD.	PASS RECEIVING P.C. Yds. Avg. TD.	TOTAL TD. Pts. F.
1985—Chicago NFL	15	25	104	4.2	1	1 9 9.0 0	1 6 1

Additional pro statistics: Returned one kickoff for 10 yards, 1985.
Played in NFC Championship Game following 1985 season.
Played in NFL Championship Game following 1985 season.

LUCIUS M. SANFORD
Linebacker—Buffalo Bills
Born February 14, 1956, at Milledgville, Ga.
Height, 6.02. Weight, 220.
High School—Atlanta, Ga., West Fulton.
Received bachelor of science degree in industrial management from
Georgia Tech in 1978.

Named as linebacker on THE SPORTING NEWS College All-America Team, 1977.
Selected by Buffalo in 4th round (89th player selected) of 1978 NFL draft.
On injured reserve with knee injury, October 31 through remainder of 1984 season.
On injured reserve with hamstring injury, September 3 through October 11, 1985; activated, October 12, 1985.

Year Club	G.	No.	INTERCEPTIONS Yds.	Avg.	TD.
1978—Buffalo NFL	16	1	41	41.0	0
1979—Buffalo NFL	16	2	44	22.0	0
1980—Buffalo NFL	16		None		
1981—Buffalo NFL	16		None		
1982—Buffalo NFL	9		None		
1983—Buffalo NFL	16	2	39	19.5	0
1984—Buffalo NFL	8		None		
1985—Buffalo NFL	11		None		
Pro Totals—8 Years	108	5	124	24.8	0

Additional pro statistics: Recovered one fumble, 1978, 1981, 1983 and 1985; ran 25 yards with blocked punt for a touchdown, 1979; recovered blocked punt in end zone for a touchdown and recovered two fumbles for minus one yard, 1980; recovered two fumbles for 46 yards and a touchdown, 1984.

JESSE SAPOLU
Name pronounced SA-pole-low.
Guard-Center—San Francisco 49ers
Born March 10, 1961, at Laie, Western Samoa.
Height, 6.04. Weight, 260.
High School—Honolulu, Haw., Farrington.
Attended University of Hawaii.

Selected by Oakland in 17th round (199th player selected) of 1983 USFL draft.
Selected by San Francisco in 11th round (289th player selected) of 1983 NFL draft.
Signed by San Francisco 49ers, July 10, 1983.
On physically unable to perform/active with fractured foot, July 19 through August 12, 1984.
On physically unable to perform/reserve with fractured foot, August 13 through November 7, 1984; activated, November 8, 1984.
On injured reserve with fractured foot, November 16 through remainder of 1984 season.
On injured reserve with broken foot, August 12 through entire 1985 season.
San Francisco NFL, 1983 and 1984.
Games: 1983 (16), 1984 (1). Total—17.
Played in NFC Championship Game following 1983 season.

JOHN WESLEY SAWYER
Tight End—Denver Broncos
Born July 26, 1953, at Brookhaven, Miss.
Height, 6.02. Weight, 230.
High School—Baker, La.
Attended University of Southern Mississippi.

Selected by Houston in 11th round (271st player selected) of 1975 NFL draft.
Claimed on waivers from Houston Oilers by Seattle Seahawks, September 14, 1977.
Released by Seattle Seahawks, October 28, 1978; re-signed by Seahawks, November 8, 1978.
On injured reserve with hamstring injury, August 21 through entire 1979 season.
Released by Seattle Seahawks, July 23, 1983; signed as free agent by Washington Redskins, July 28, 1983.
Released by Washington Redskins, October 27, 1983; signed as free agent by Denver Broncos, November 3, 1983.
USFL rights traded by New Orleans Breakers to Los Angeles Express for rights to defensive back Jeff Orlando, January 13, 1984.
On injured reserve with knee injury, November 10 through remainder of 1984 season.
On injured reserve with broken hand, August 20 through entire 1985 season.

Year Club	G.	PASS RECEIVING P.C. Yds.	Avg.	TD.	Year Club	G.	PASS RECEIVING P.C. Yds.	Avg.	TD.
1975—Houston NFL	8	7 144	20.6	1	1981—Seattle NFL	16	21 272	13.0	0
1976—Houston NFL	14	18 208	11.5	1	1982—Seattle NFL	7	8 92	11.5	0
1977—Seattle NFL	14	10 105	10.5	0	1983—Wash(7)-Den(7) NFL...	14	3 42	14.0	0
1978—Seattle NFL	11	9 101	11.2	0	1984—Denver NFL	10	17 122	7.2	0
1980—Seattle NFL	16	36 410	11.4	0	Pro Totals—9 Years	110	129 1496	11.6	2

Additional pro statistics: Fumbled once, 1975, 1977, 1978, 1980 and 1983; recovered one fumble and punted once for 32 yards, 1976; returned one kickoff for eight yards, 1981; returned one kickoff for 15 yards, 1983; recovered two fumbles, 1984.

MIKE SAXON
Punter—Dallas Cowboys
Born July 10, 1962, at Arcadia, Calif.
Height, 6.03. Weight, 187.
High School—Arcadia, Calif.
Attended Pasadena City College and San Diego State University.

Selected by Arizona in 13th round (265th player selected) of 1984 USFL draft.
Selected by Detroit in 11th round (300th player selected) of 1984 NFL draft.
Signed by Detroit Lions, May 29, 1984.
Released by Detroit Lions, August 27, 1984; signed by Arizona Wranglers, November 7, 1984.
Released by Arizona Wranglers, February 11, 1985; signed as free agent by Dallas Cowboys, March 27, 1985.

		——PUNTING——		
Year Club	G.	No.	Avg.	Blk.
1985—Dallas NFL	16	81	41.9	1

MARK ALLEN SCHELLEN
Running Back—Houston Oilers
Born August 5, 1961, at Omaha, Neb.
Height, 5.09. Weight, 233.
High School—Waterloo, Neb.
Attended University of Nebraska at Omaha and University of Nebraska at Lincoln.

Selected by New Orleans in 2nd round (32nd player selected) of 1984 USFL draft.
Signed by New Orleans Breakers, January 16, 1984.
Selected by San Francisco in 3rd round (80th player selected) of 1984 NFL supplemental draft.
Franchise transferred to Portland, November 13, 1984.
Released by Portland Breakers, February 4, 1985.
NFL rights traded by San Francisco 49ers to San Diego Chargers for draft choice, May 20, 1985.
Signed by San Diego Chargers, May 20, 1985.
On injured reserve with thigh injury, August 20 through entire 1985 season.
Released by San Diego Chargers, May 9, 1986; waivers recalled and traded by San Diego Chargers to Houston Oilers for conditional pick in 1987 draft, May 21, 1986.

		——RUSHING——				PASS RECEIVING				—TOTAL—		
Year Club	G.	Att.	Yds.	Avg.	TD.	P.C.	Yds.	Avg.	TD.	TD.	Pts.	F.
1984—New Orleans USFL	18	99	392	4.0	4	22	122	5.6	0	4	24	7

Additional USFL statistics: Recovered one fumble, 1984.

BRUCE DANIEL SCHOLTZ
Linebacker—Seattle Seahawks
Born September 26, 1958, at La Grange, Tex.
Height, 6.06. Weight, 240.
High School—Austin, Tex., Crockett.
Attended University of Texas.

Selected by Seattle in 2nd round (33rd player selected) of 1982 NFL draft.

		——INTERCEPTIONS——			
Year Club	G.	No.	Yds.	Avg.	TD.
1982—Seattle NFL	9	1	31	31.0	1
1983—Seattle NFL	16	1	8	8.0	0
1984—Seattle NFL	16	1	15	15.0	0
1985—Seattle NFL	16		None		
Pro Totals—4 Years	57	3	54	18.0	1

Additional pro statistics: Recovered one fumble, 1982 through 1985.
Played in AFC Championship Game following 1983 season.

TURK LEROY SCHONERT
Quarterback—Atlanta Falcons
Born January 15, 1957, at Torrance, Calif.
Height, 6.01. Weight, 190.
High School—Anaheim, Calif., Servite.
Attended Stanford University.

Selected by Chicago in 9th round (242nd player selected) of 1980 NFL draft.
Released by Chicago Bears, August 25, 1980; claimed on waivers by Cincinnati Bengals, August 26, 1980.
USFL rights traded by Oakland Invaders to Jacksonville Bulls for rights to running back Ted McKnight, linebacker Mark Jerue and 1st and 5th round picks in 1984 draft, October 24, 1983.
On injured reserve with separated shoulder, December 5 through remainder of 1984 season.
Granted free agency, February 1, 1985; re-signed by Bengals, April 4, 1985.
Traded by Cincinnati Bengals to Atlanta Falcons for 3rd round pick in 1986 draft, April 4, 1986.
Active for 16 games with Cincinnati Bengals in 1980; did not play.

		——PASSING——							——RUSHING——				—TOTAL—		
Year Club	G.	Att.	Cmp.	Pct.	Gain	T.P.	P.I.	Avg.	Att.	Yds.	Avg.	TD.	TD.	Pts.	F.
1981—Cincinnati NFL	4	19	10	52.6	166	0	0	8.74	7	41	5.9	0	0	0	1

Year Club	G.	Att.	Cmp.	Pct.	Gain	T.P.	P.I.	Avg.	Att.	Yds.	Avg.	TD.	TD.	Pts.	F.
				PASSING						RUSHING			TOTAL		
1982—Cincinnati NFL	2	1	1	100.0	6	0	0	6.00	3	−8	−2.7	0	0	0	1
1983—Cincinnati NFL	9	156	92	59.0	1159	2	5	7.43	29	117	4.0	2	2	12	6
1984—Cincinnati NFL	8	117	78	66.7	945	4	7	8.08	13	77	5.9	1	1	6	2
1985—Cincinnati NFL	7	51	33	64.7	460	1	0	9.02	8	39	4.9	0	0	0	3
Pro Totals—6 Years	30	344	214	62.2	2736	7	12	7.95	60	266	4.4	3	3	18	13

Quarterback Rating Points: 1981 (82.3), 1982 (91.7), 1983 (73.1), 1984 (77.8), 1985 (100.1). Total—79.1.

Additional pro statistics: Recovered one fumble, 1982; recovered four fumbles, 1983; recovered two fumbles and fumbled three times for minus two yards, 1985.

Member of Cincinnati Bengals for AFC and NFL Championship Games following 1981 season; did not play.

ADAM SCHREIBER
Guard—New Orleans Saints
Born February 20, 1962, at Galveston, Tex.
Height, 6.04. Weight, 270.
High School—Huntsville, Ala., Butler.
Attended University of Texas.

Selected by Houston in 1984 USFL territorial draft.
Selected by Seattle in 9th round (243rd player selected) of 1984 NFL draft.
Signed by Seattle Seahawks, June 20, 1984.
Released by Seattle Seahawks, August 27, 1984; re-signed by Seahawks, October 10, 1984.
Released by Seattle Seahawks, August 29, 1985; signed as free agent by New Orleans Saints, November 20, 1985.
Seattle NFL, 1984; New Orleans NFL, 1985.
Games: 1984 (6), 1985 (1). Total—7.

JAY BRIAN SCHROEDER
Name pronounced SCHRAY-der.
Quarterback—Washington Redskins
Born June 28, 1961, at Milwaukee, Wis.
Height, 6.04. Weight, 215.
High School—Pacific Palisades, Calif.
Attended University of California at Los Angeles.

Selected by Washington in 3rd round (83rd player selected) of 1984 NFL draft.
Active for 16 games with Washington Redskins in 1984; did not play.

Year Club	G.	Att.	Cmp.	Pct.	Gain	T.P.	P.I.	Avg.	Att.	Yds.	Avg.	TD.	TD.	Pts.	F.
				PASSING						RUSHING			TOTAL		
1985—Washington NFL	9	209	112	53.6	1458	5	5	6.98	17	30	1.8	0	0	0	5

Quarterback Rating Points: 1985 (73.8).

Additional pro statistics: Punted four times for 33.0 average, recovered one fumble and fumbled five times for minus three yards, 1985.

RECORD AS BASEBALL PLAYER
Led Carolina League batters in strikeouts with 172 in 1982.
Led South Atlantic League batters in strikeouts with 142 in 1981.
Received reported $100,000 bonus to sign with Toronto Blue Jays, 1979.

Year Club	League	Pos.	G.	AB.	R.	H.	2B.	3B.	HR.	RBI.	B.A.	PO.	A.	E.	F.A.
1979—Utica†	NYP	Pion.					(Did not play)								
1980—Medicine Hat‡	Pion.	OF	52	171	27	40	6	2	2	21	.234	93	6	5	.952
1981—Florence	S. Atl.	3B-OF	131	417	51	85	17	1	10	47	.204	112	101	28	.884
1982—Kinston	Carol.	OF	132	435	59	95	17	1	15	55	.218	178	17	15	.929
1983—Kinston§	Carol.	C-OF-1B	92	281	30	58	9	2	9	43	.206	519	53	20	.966

Selected by Toronto Blue Jays' organization in 1st round (third player selected) of free-agent draft, June 5, 1979.
†On temporary inactive list, June 30, 1979 through remainder of season.
‡On temporary inactive list, August 14 to September 3, 1980.
§Released, February 28, 1984.

ERIC JON SCHUBERT
Placekicker—New York Giants
Born May 28, 1962, at Abington, Pa.
Height, 5.08. Weight, 193.
High School—Wanaque, N.J., Lakeland Regional.
Attended University of Pittsburgh.

Selected by Pittsburgh in 1984 USFL territorial draft.
Signed by Pittsburgh Maulers, May 17, 1984.
Franchise disbanded, October 25, 1984; not selected in USFL dispersal draft, December 6, 1984.
Signed as free agent by New Jersey Generals, January 21, 1985.
Released by New Jersey Generals, February 18, 1985; signed as free agent by New England Patriots, April 16, 1985.
Released by New England Patriots, August 12, 1985; signed as free agent by New York Giants, August 20, 1985.
Released by New York Giants, August 26, 1985; re-signed by Giants, November 1, 1985.

Year Club	G.	XP.	XPM.	FG.	FGA.	Pts.
			PLACE KICKING			
1984—Pittsburgh USFL	6	4	2	4	10	16
1985—N.Y. Giants NFL	8	26	1	10	13	56
Pro Totals—2 Years	14	30	3	14	23	72

COACHING RECORD
Assistant coach at Lakeland Regional High School, Wanaque, N.J., 1985.

JEFF JOHN SCHUH
Linebacker—Cincinnati Bengals
Born May 22, 1958, at Crystal, Minn.
Height, 6.03. Weight, 234.
High School—Plymouth, Minn., Armstrong.
Attended North Hennepin Junior College and University of Minnesota.

Selected by Cincinnati in 7th round (176th player selected) of 1981 NFL draft.
Left Cincinnati Bengals camp voluntarily, July 22, 1981; returned, July 29, 1981.
Released by Cincinnati Bengals, August 31, 1981; re-signed by Bengals, September 1, 1981.
On injured reserve with toe injury, January 9 through remainder of 1981 season playoffs.
Cincinnati NFL, 1981 through 1985.
Games: 1981 (16), 1982 (9), 1983 (16), 1984 (16), 1985 (16). Total—73.
Pro statistics: Recovered one fumble, 1981 and 1985; intercepted one pass for no yards, 1984.

JOHN SCHUHMACHER
Guard—Houston Oilers
Born September 23, 1955, at Salem, Ore.
Height, 6.03. Weight, 277.
High School—Arcadia, Calif.
Attended University of Southern California.

Selected by Houston in 12th round (322nd player selected) of 1978 NFL draft.
On injured reserve with back injury, August 27 through entire 1979 season.
On injured reserve with back injury, August 26 through entire 1980 season.
On injured reserve with knee injury, September 6 through remainder of 1983 season.
Houston NFL, 1978 and 1981 through 1985.
Games: 1978 (11), 1981 (16), 1982 (9), 1983 (1), 1984 (16), 1985 (16). Total—69.
Pro statistics: Recovered one fumble, 1981.
Played in AFC Championship Game following 1978 season.

CHRISTOPHER SCHULTZ
(Chris)
Offensive Tackle—Dallas Cowboys
Born February 16, 1960, at Burlington, Ont., Canada.
Height, 6.08. Weight, 288.
High School—Burlington, Ont., Canada, Aldershot.
Attended University of Arizona.

Selected by Arizona in 1983 USFL territorial draft.
Selected by Dallas in 7th round (189th player selected) of 1983 NFL draft.
Signed by Dallas Cowboys, May 26, 1983.
On injured reserve with knee injury, August 21 through entire 1984 season.
Dallas NFL, 1983 and 1985.
Games: 1983 (5), 1985 (16). Total—21.

JODY SCHULZ
Linebacker—Philadelphia Eagles
Born August 17, 1960, at Easton, Md.
Height, 6.04. Weight, 235.
High School—Upper Marlboro, Md., Queen Anne.
Attended Chowan College and East Carolina University.

Selected by Washington in 14th round (165th player selected) of 1983 USFL draft.
Selected by Philadelphia in 2nd round (46th player selected) of 1983 NFL draft.
Signed by Philadelphia Eagles, May 24, 1983.
On injured reserve with knee injury, November 23 through remainder of 1983 season.
On injured reserve with knee injury, August 20 through entire 1985 season.
Philadelphia NFL, 1983 and 1984.
Games: 1983 (6), 1984 (15). Total—21.

CARLOS B. SCOTT
Center-Offensive Tackle—St. Louis Cardinals
Born July 2, 1960, at Hempstead, Tex.
Height, 6.04. Weight, 285.
High School—Waller, Tex.
Attended University of Texas at El Paso.

Selected by Arizona in 18th round (215th player selected) of 1983 USFL draft.
Selected by St. Louis in 7th round (184th player selected) of 1983 NFL draft.
Signed by St. Louis Cardinals, July 13, 1983.
St. Louis NFL, 1983 through 1985.
Games: 1983 (13), 1984 (16), 1985 (16). Total—45.
Pro statistics: Fumbled once, 1985.

CHRISTOPHER STERLING SCOTT
(Chris)
Defensive End—Indianapolis Colts
Born December 11, 1961, at Berea, O.
Height, 6.05. Weight, 271.
High School—Berea, O.
Attended Purdue University.

Selected by Indianapolis in 3rd round (66th player selected) of 1984 NFL draft.
Indianapolis NFL, 1984 and 1985.
Games: 1984 (14), 1985 (16). Total—30.

CHUCK SCOTT
Wide Receiver—Los Angeles Rams
Born May 24, 1963, at Jacksonville, Fla.
Height, 6.02. Weight, 202.
High School—Maitland, Fla., Lake Howell.
Attended Vanderbilt University.

Named as tight end on THE SPORTING NEWS College All-America Team, 1983.
Selected by Memphis in 1985 USFL territorial draft.
Selected by Los Angeles Rams in 2nd round (50th player selected) of 1985 NFL draft.
Signed by Los Angeles Rams, July 26, 1985.
On injured reserve with rotator cuff injury, September 2 through entire 1985 season.

EDWARD SCOTT
Defensive Back—Los Angeles Raiders
Born February 15, 1961, at New Orleans, La.
Height, 5.10. Weight, 182.
High School—New Orleans, La., Carver.
Received bachelor of arts degree in political science from Grambling State University.

Selected by New Orleans in 1984 USFL territorial draft.
Signed by Los Angeles Express, February 6, 1984.
Rights officially traded by New Orleans Breakers to Los Angeles Express for draft choices, March 19, 1984.
On developmental squad, March 19 through May 10, 1984; activated, May 11, 1984.
Released by Los Angeles Express, August 1, 1985; awarded on waivers to Baltimore Stars, August 2, 1985.
Released by Baltimore Stars, August 2, 1985; signed as free agent by Los Angeles Raiders, May 3, 1986.
On developmental squad for 7 games with Los Angeles Express in 1984.

Year Club	G.	No.	Yds.	Avg.TD.	
1984—Los Angeles USFL........	10			None	
1985—Los Angeles USFL........	16	2	36	18.0	0
Pro Totals—2 Years............	26	2	36	18.0	0

Additional pro statistics: Recovered two fumbles, 1985.

EDWARD SCOTT
(Ed)
Wide Receiver—Tampa Bay Buccaneers
Born December 29, 1962, at Oakland, Calif.
Height, 6.00. Weight, 190.
High School—San Diego, Calif., Clairemont.
Attended Idaho State University.

Signed as free agent by Denver Gold, January 15, 1985.
Released by Denver Gold, January 21, 1985; signed as free agent by Tampa Bay Buccaneers, May 9, 1985.

LINDSAY EUGENE SCOTT
Wide Receiver—Atlanta Falcons
Born December 6, 1960, at Jesup, Ga.
Height, 6.01. Weight, 197.
High School—Jesup, Ga., Wayne County.
Attended University of Georgia.

Selected by New Orleans in 1st round (13th player selected) of 1982 NFL draft.
Released by New Orleans Saints, November 12, 1985; signed as free agent by Atlanta Falcons, February 18, 1986.

Year Club	G.	P.C.	Yds.	Avg.	TD.
1982—New Orleans NFL........	8	17	251	14.8	0
1983—New Orleans NFL........	16	24	274	11.4	0
1984—New Orleans NFL........	16	21	278	13.2	1
1985—New Orleans NFL........	9	7	61	8.7	0
Pro Totals—4 Years............	49	69	864	12.5	1

Additional pro statistics: Rushed once for minus four yards, 1982; fumbled once, 1983 and 1984.

MALCOLM SCOTT
Tight End—New Orleans Saints
Born July 10, 1961, at New Orleans, La.
Height, 6.04. Weight, 240.
High School—New Orleans, La., St. Augustine.
Attended Louisiana State University.

Selected by Birmingham in 12th round (140th player selected) of 1983 USFL draft.
Selected by New York Giants in 5th round (124th player selected) of 1983 NFL draft.
Signed by New York Giants, June 13, 1983.
Released by New York Giants, July 20, 1984; signed as free agent by New Orleans Saints, May 9, 1986.

		——PASS RECEIVING——				
Year	Club	G.	P.C.	Yds.	Avg.	TD.
1983—N. Y. Giants NFL		16	17	206	12.1	0

RANDOLPH CHARLES SCOTT
(Randy)
Linebacker—Green Bay Packers
Born January 31, 1959, at Decatur, Ga.
Height, 6.01. Weight, 220.
High School—Decatur, Ga., Columbia.
Received degree in marketing from University of Alabama.

Signed as free agent by Green Bay Packers, May 19, 1981.
On injured reserve with knee injury, September 6 through November 17, 1983; activated; November 18, 1983.
Green Bay NFL, 1981 through 1985.
Games: 1981 (16), 1982 (9), 1983 (6), 1984 (16), 1985 (16). Total—63.
Pro statistics: Intercepted one pass for 12 yards, 1983; intercepted two passes for 50 yards and recovered five fumbles for 31 yards, 1985.

VICTOR RAMONE SCOTT
Cornerback—Dallas Cowboys
Born June 1, 1962, at East St. Louis, Ill.
Height, 6.00. Weight, 196.
High School—East St. Louis, Ill.
Attended University of Colorado.

Selected by Denver in 1984 USFL territorial draft.
Selected by Dallas in 2nd round (40th player selected) of 1984 NFL draft.
Signed by Dallas Cowboys, June 27, 1984.

		——INTERCEPTIONS——				
Year	Club	G.	No.	Yds.	Avg.	TD.
1984—Dallas NFL		16	1	5	5.0	0
1985—Dallas NFL		16	2	26	13.0	*1
Pro Totals—2 Years		32	3	31	10.3	1

Additional pro statistics: Recovered two fumbles, 1984; fumbled once, 1985.

WILLIE LOUIS SCOTT JR.
Tight End—Kansas City Chiefs
Born February 13, 1959, at Newberry, S.C.
Height, 6.04. Weight, 254.
High School—Newberry, S.C.
Received bachelor of science degree in health education
from University of South Carolina in 1981.

Selected by Kansas City in 1st round (14th player selected) of 1981 NFL draft.

		——PASS RECEIVING——				
Year	Club	G.	P.C.	Yds.	Avg.	TD.
1981—Kansas City NFL		16	5	72	14.4	1
1982—Kansas City NFL		9	8	49	6.1	1
1983—Kansas City NFL		16	29	247	8.5	6
1984—Kansas City NFL		15	28	253	9.0	3
1985—Kansas City NFL		16	5	61	12.2	0
Pro Totals—5 Years		72	75	682	9.1	11

Additional pro statistics: Recovered one fumble, 1982; rushed once for one yard, 1983; returned one kickoff for nine yards, 1984.

WILLIAM CHARLES SCRIBNER
(Bucky)
Punter—Seattle Seahawks
Born July 11, 1960, at Lawrence, Kan.
Height, 6.00. Weight, 202.
High School—Lawrence, Kan.
Attended Pratt Community College and received bachelor of
arts degree in personnel administration from Kansas University.

Selected by Green Bay in 11th round (299th player selected) of 1983 NFL draft.
Released by Green Bay Packers, September 4, 1985; signed as free agent by Seattle Seahawks, May 14, 1986.

Year Club	G.	No.	Avg.	Blk.
1983—Green Bay NFL	16	69	41.6	1
1984—Green Bay NFL	16	85	42.3	0
Pro Totals—2 Years	32	154	42.0	1

Additional pro statistics: Attempted one pass with no completions, 1984.

JOHN SCULLY
Guard—Atlanta Falcons

Born August 2, 1958, at Huntington, N.Y.
Height, 6.06. Weight, 255.
High School—Huntington, N.Y., Holy Family.
Received bachelor of arts degree in sociology from University of Notre Dame in 1980.
Brother-in-law of Tom Thayer, guard with Chicago Bears.

Named as center on THE SPORTING NEWS College All-America Team, 1980.
Selected by Atlanta in 4th round (109th player selected) of 1981 NFL draft.
On injured reserve with broken leg, October 29 through remainder of 1985 season.
Atlanta NFL, 1981 through 1985.
Games: 1981 (16), 1982 (9), 1983 (16), 1984 (16), 1985 (8). Total—65.
Pro statistics: Returned one kickoff for no yards, 1982; recovered one fumble, 1984.

SAMUEL RICARDO SEALE
(Sam)
Cornerback—Los Angeles Raiders

Born October 6, 1962, at Barbados, West Indies.
Height, 5.09. Weight, 180.
High School—Orange, N.J.
Attended Western State College.

Selected by Memphis in 15th round (309th player selected) of 1984 USFL draft.
Selected by Los Angeles Raiders in 8th round (224th player selected) of 1984 NFL draft.
Signed by Los Angeles Raiders, June 6, 1984.
Los Angeles Raiders NFL, 1984.
Games: 1984 (12).

Year Club	G.	No.	Yds.	Avg.	TD.
1984—L.A. Raiders NFL	12		None		
1985—L.A. Raiders NFL	16	23	482	21.0	0
Pro Totals—2 Years	28	23	482	21.0	0

Additional pro statistics: Intercepted one pass for 38 yards and a touchdown, 1985.

BILL SEARCEY
Offensive Tackle-Guard—San Diego Chargers

Born March 3, 1959, at Savannah, Ga.
Height, 6.01. Weight, 281.
High School—Savannah, Ga., Benedictine Military Academy.
Attended University of Alabama.

Signed as free agent by Detroit Lions, May 4, 1981.
Traded by Detroit Lions to Miami Dolphins for conditional draft pick, August 12, 1981.
Released by Miami Dolphins, August 17, 1981; signed as free agent by Detroit Lions, May 2, 1982.
Released by Detroit Lions, July 30, 1982; signed by Birmingham Stallions, December 6, 1982.
On developmental squad, May 3 through May 13, 1983; activated, May 14, 1983.
On developmental squad, May 23 through June 4, 1983; activated, June 5, 1983.
Selected by Houston Gamblers in 3rd round (14th player selected) of USFL expansion draft, September 6, 1983.
On developmental squad, February 24 through March 4, 1984; activated, March 5, 1984.
On developmental squad, March 16 through March 27, 1984.
On injured reserve, March 28 through May 15, 1984.
Released by Houston Gamblers, May 16, 1984; signed as free agent by New Orleans Breakers, July 11, 1984.
Franchise transferred to Portland, November 13, 1984.
Released by Portland Breakers, January 25, 1985; signed as free agent by San Diego Chargers, May 7, 1985.
On injured reserve with knee injury, September 2 through November 6, 1985; activated after clearing procedural waivers, November 8, 1985.
On injured reserve with knee injury, November 23 through remainder of 1985 season.
On developmental squad for 3 games with Birmingham Stallions in 1983.
On developmental squad for 3 games with Houston Gamblers in 1984.
Birmingham USFL, 1983; Houston USFL, 1984; San Diego NFL, 1985.
Games: 1983 (5), 1984 (2), 1985 (1). Total USFL—7. Total Pro—8.

JAMES EDWARD SEAWRIGHT
Linebacker—Buffalo Bills

Born March 30, 1962, at Greenville, S.C.
Height, 6.02. Weight, 219.
High School—Simpsonville, S.C., Hillcrest.
Attended University of South Carolina.

Selected by Los Angeles in 1985 USFL territorial draft.
Selected by Buffalo in 11th round (282nd player selected) of 1985 NFL draft.
Signed by Buffalo Bills, July 19, 1985.
On injured reserve with dislocated kneecap, September 2 through entire 1985 season.

ROBIN BRUNO SENDLEIN
Linebacker—Miami Dolphins

Born December 1, 1958, at Las Vegas, Nev.
Height, 6.03. Weight, 225.
High School—Las Vegas, Nev., Western.
Attended University of Texas.

Selected by Minnesota in 2nd round (45th player selected) of 1981 NFL draft.
Traded with 2nd round pick in 1986 draft by Minnesota Vikings to Miami Dolphins for rights to wide receiver Anthony Carter, August 15, 1985.
Minnesota NFL, 1981 through 1984; Miami NFL 1985.
Games: 1981 (16), 1982 (9), 1983 (16), 1984 (15), 1985 (16). Total—72.
Pro statistics: Recovered one fumble, 1981.
Played in AFC Championship Game following 1985 season.

JOSE RAFAEL SEPTIEN (MICHEL)
(Known by middle name.)

Name pronounced Rah-fay-EL Sep-tee-EN.
Placekicker—Dallas Cowboys

Born December 12, 1953, at Mexico City, Mex.
Height, 5.10. Weight, 180.
High School—Mexico City, Mex., Colegio Vista Hernosa.
Received degree from University of Southwestern Louisiana.
Son of Carlos Septien, member of two Mexican World Cup Soccer teams.

Named to THE SPORTING NEWS NFL All-Star Team, 1981.
Selected by New Orleans in 10th round (258th player selected) of 1977 NFL draft.
Released by New Orleans Saints, August 31, 1977; signed as free agent by Los Angeles Rams, September 14, 1977.
Released by Los Angeles Rams, August 26, 1978; signed as free agent by Dallas Cowboys, August 30, 1978.

			——PLACE KICKING——				
Year	Club	G.	XP.	XPM.	FG.	FGA.	Pts.
1977—Los Angeles NFL....		14	32	3	18	30	86
1978—Dallas NFL		16	★46	1	16	26	94
1979—Dallas NFL		16	40	4	19	29	97
1980—Dallas NFL		16	★59	1	11	17	92
1981—Dallas NFL		16	40	0	★27	35	★121
1982—Dallas NFL		9	28	0	10	14	58
1983—Dallas NFL		16	57	2	22	27	123
1984—Dallas NFL		16	33	1	23	29	102
1985—Dallas NFL		16	42	1	19	28	99
Pro Totals—9 Years.......		135	377	13	165	235	872

Additional pro statistics: Recovered two fumbles for 18 yards, 1980; punted two times for 31.0 average 1981.
Played in NFC Championship Game following 1978 and 1980 through 1982 seasons.
Played in NFL Championship Game following 1978 season.
Played in Pro Bowl (NFL All-Star Game) following 1981 season.

FRANK SEURER
Quarterback—Kansas City Chiefs

Born August 16, 1962, at Huntington Beach, Calif.
Height, 6.02. Weight, 195.
High School—Huntington Beach, Calif., Edison.
Attended University of Kansas.

Selected by Los Angeles in 5th round (94th player selected) of 1984 USFL draft.
Signed by Los Angeles Express, January 16, 1984.
Selected by Seattle in 3rd round (76th player selected) of 1984 NFL supplemental draft.
Released by Los Angeles Express, July 22, 1985; signed by Seattle Seahawks, July 25, 1985.
Released by Seattle Seahawks, August 20, 1985; signed as free agent by Kansas City Chiefs, April 14, 1986.

			————PASSING————							——RUSHING——				—TOTAL—		
Year	Club	G.	Att.	Cmp.	Pct.	Gain	T.P.	P.I.	Avg.	Att.	Yds.	Avg.	TD.	TD.	Pts.	F.
1984—Los Angeles USFL............		7	132	64	48.5	658	3	8	4.98	11	32	2.9	0	0	0	1
1985—Los Angeles USFL............		13	242	120	49.6	1479	7	18	6.11	16	96	6.0	0	0	0	3
Pro Totals—2 Years...........		20	374	184	49.2	2137	10	26	5.71	27	128	4.7	0	0	0	4

Quarterback Rating Points: 1984 (45.6), 1985 (47.5). Total—46.7.
Additional pro statistics: Recovered two fumbles for six yards, 1984; recovered one fumble, 1985.

STEVEN EDWARD SEWELL
(Steve)
Running Back—Denver Broncos

Born April 2, 1963, at San Francisco, Calif.
Height, 6.03. Weight, 210.
High School—San Francisco, Calif., Riordan.
Attended University of Oklahoma.

Selected by Los Angeles in 1st round (16th player selected) of 1985 USFL draft.
Selected by Denver in 1st round (26th player selected) of 1985 NFL draft.
Signed by Denver Broncos, July 22, 1985.

Year Club		RUSHING				PASS RECEIVING				TOTAL	
	G.	Att.	Yds.	Avg.	TD.	P.C.	Yds.	Avg.	TD.	TD.	Pts. F
1985—Denver NFL	16	81	275	3.4	4	24	224	9.3	1	5	30

Additional pro statistics: Returned one kickoff for 29 yards, attempted one pass with no completions and recov ered one fumble, 1985.

STANLEY SHAKESPEARE
Wide Receiver—Cleveland Browns
Born February 5, 1963, at Boynton Beach, Fla.
Height, 6.00. Weight, 180.
High School—Lake Worth, Fla.
Attended University of Miami (Fla.).

Selected by Orlando in 1985 USFL territorial draft.
Signed as free agent by Cleveland Browns, May 6, 1985.
On injured reserve with injured cheekbone, August 20 through entire 1985 season.

LUIS ERNESTO SHARPE JR.
Offensive Tackle—St. Louis Cardinals
Born June 16, 1960, at Havana, Cuba.
Height, 6.04. Weight, 260.
High School—Detroit, Mich., Southwestern.
Attended University of California at Los Angeles.

Named as offensive tackle on THE SPORTING NEWS College All-America Team, 1981.
Selected by St. Louis in 1st round (16th player selected) of 1982 NFL draft.
Granted free agency, February 1, 1985.
USFL rights traded by Houston Gamblers to Memphis Showboats for draft picks, April 18, 1985.
Signed by Memphis Showboats, April 18, 1985.
Released by Memphis Showboats, August 25, 1985; re-signed by Cardinals, August 31, 1985.
Granted roster exemption, August 31 through September 2, 1985; activated, September 3, 1985.
St. Louis NFL, 1982 through 1985; Memphis USFL, 1985.
Games: 1982 (9), 1983 (16), 1984 (16), 1985 USFL (10), 1985 NFL (16). Total NFL—57. Total Pro—67.
Pro statistics: Recovered one fumble, 1982 and 1984; rushed once for 11 yards and recovered two fumbles, 1983.

JOSEPH LESLIE SHEARIN
(Joe)
Guard—Tampa Bay Buccaneers
Born April 16, 1960, at Dallas, Tex.
Height, 6.04. Weight, 250.
High School—Dallas, Tex., Woodrow Wilson.
Received degree in radio and television from University of Texas.

Selected by Los Angeles Rams in 7th round (181st player selected) of 1982 NFL draft.
On injured reserve with neck injury, September 7 through entire 1982 season.
Released by Los Angeles Rams, August 27, 1985; signed as free agent by Tampa Bay Buccaneers, September 25, 1985.
Los Angeles Rams NFL, 1983 and 1984; Tampa Bay NFL, 1985.
Games: 1983 (16), 1984 (15), 1985 (10). Total—41.

DONNIE SHELL
Safety—Pittsburgh Steelers
Born August 26, 1952, at Whitmire, S. C.
Height, 5.11. Weight, 197.
High School—Whitmire, S. C.
Received bachelor of science degree in health and physical education from South Carolina State in 1974 and received master's degree in guidance and counseling from South Carolina State.

Named to THE SPORTING NEWS AFC All-Star Team, 1979.
Named to THE SPORTING NEWS NFL All-Star Team, 1980.
Signed as free agent by Pittsburgh Steelers, 1974.

Year Club	INTERCEPTIONS				Year Club	INTERCEPTIONS			
	G.	No.	Yds.	Avg.TD.		G.	No.	Yds.	Avg.TD.
1974—Pittsburgh NFL	14	1	0	0.0	0	1981—Pittsburgh NFL............	14	5	52	10.4	0
1975—Pittsburgh NFL	14	1	29	29.0	0	1982—Pittsburgh NFL............	9	5	27	5.4	0
1976—Pittsburgh NFL	14	1	4	4.0	0	1983—Pittsburgh NFL............	16	5	18	3.6	0
1977—Pittsburgh NFL	12	3	14	4.7	0	1984—Pittsburgh NFL............	16	7	61	8.7	1
1978—Pittsburgh NFL............	16	3	21	7.0	0	1985—Pittsburgh NFL............	16	4	40	10.0	0
1979—Pittsburgh NFL............	16	5	10	2.0	0	Pro Totals—12 Years.........	173	47	411	8.7	1
1980—Pittsburgh NFL............	16	7	135	19.3	0					

Additional pro statistics: Recovered one fumble, 1974, 1975, 1976, 1982 and 1983; caught two passes for 39 yards, 1975; recovered five fumbles for 21 yards and one touchdown and returned one punt for six yards, 1978; recovered two fumbles, 1979, 1981 and 1985; recovered one fumble for seven yards, 1980.
Played in AFC Championship Game following 1974 through 1976, 1978, 1979 and 1984 seasons.
Played in NFL Championship Game following 1974, 1975, 1978 and 1979 seasons.
Played in Pro Bowl (NFL All-Star Game) following 1978 through 1982 seasons.

TODD ANDREW SHELL
Linebacker—San Francisco 49ers
Born June 24, 1962, at Mesa, Ariz.
Height, 6.04. Weight, 225.
High School—Mesa, Ariz., Mountain View.
Attended Brigham Young University.

Selected by Denver in 3rd round (51st player selected) of 1984 USFL draft.
Selected by San Francisco in 1st round (24th player selected) of 1984 NFL draft.
Signed by San Francisco 49ers, June 12, 1984.

Year Club	G.	No.	Yds.	Avg.TD.	
			INTERCEPTIONS		
1984—San Francisco NFL	16	3	81	27.0	1
1985—San Francisco NFL	15	1	33	33.0	0
Pro Totals—2 Years............	31	4	114	28.5	1

Additional pro statistics: Recovered one fumble, 1984 and 1985.
Played in NFC Championship Game following 1984 season.
Played in NFL Championship Game following 1984 season.

TIMOTHY THOMAS SHERWIN
(Tim)
Tight End—Indianapolis Colts
Born May 4, 1958, at Troy, N.Y.
Height, 6.06. Weight, 245.
High School—Watervliet, N.Y.
Received bachelor of arts degree in sociology from Boston College in 1981.

Selected by Baltimore in 4th round (94th player selected) of 1981 NFL draft.
Franchise transferred to Indianapolis, March 31, 1984.
On injured reserve with knee injury, November 6 through remainder of 1985 season.

Year Club	G.	P.C.	Yds.	Avg.	TD.
			PASS RECEIVING		
1981—Baltimore NFL	16	2	19	9.5	0
1982—Baltimore NFL	9	21	280	13.3	0
1983—Baltimore NFL	15	25	358	14.3	0
1984—Indianapolis NFL	16	11	169	15.4	0
1985—Indianapolis NFL	8	5	64	12.8	0
Pro Totals—5 Years............	64	64	890	13.9	0

Additional pro statistics: Recovered one fumble for a touchdown, 1982; returned one kickoff for two yards, 1984; fumbled once, 1985.

JOSEPH MICHAEL SHIELD
(Joe)
Quarterback—New England Patriots
Born June 26, 1962, at Brattleboro, Vt.
Height, 6.01. Weight, 185.
High School—Worcester, Mass., Academy.
Received degree in English literature from Trinity College in 1985.

Selected by New Jersey in 14th round (200th player selected) of 1985 USFL draft.
Selected by Green Bay in 11th round (294th player selected) of 1985 NFL draft.
Signed by Green Bay Packers, July 17, 1985.
Released by Green Bay Packers, September 24, 1985; signed as free agent by New England Patriots, April 1, 1986.
Active for 3 games with Green Bay Packers in 1985; did not play.

MIKE SHINER
Offensive Tackle—Los Angeles Rams
Born January 27, 1961, at Palo Alto, Calif.
Height, 6.08. Weight, 262.
High School—Sunnyvale, Calif., Fremont.
Attended University of Notre Dame.

Selected by Chicago in 1984 USFL territorial draft.
Signed by Los Angeles Rams for 1985, November 13, 1984.
On injured reserve with calf injury, August 20 through entire 1985 season.

JACKIE RENARDO SHIPP
Linebacker—Miami Dolphins
Born March 19, 1962, at Muskogee, Okla.
Height, 6.02. Weight, 236.
High School—Stillwater, Okla., C.E. Donart.
Attended Oklahoma University.

Selected by Oklahoma in 1984 USFL territorial draft.
Selected by Miami in 1st round (14th player selected) of 1984 NFL draft.
Signed by Miami Dolphins, July 14, 1984.
Miami NFL, 1984 and 1985.
Games: 1984 (16), 1985 (16). Total—32.

Pro statistics: Intercepted one pass for seven yards and recovered two fumbles, 1985.
Played in AFC Championship Game following 1984 and 1985 seasons.
Played in NFL Championship Game following 1984 season.

GEORGE EDWARD SHORTHOSE
Wide Receiver-Kick Returner—Kansas City Chiefs
Born December 22, 1961, at Stanton, Calif.
Height, 6.00. Weight, 198.
High School—Jefferson City, Mo.
Attended University of Missouri.

Selected by New Jersey in 3rd round (35th player selected) of 1985 USFL draft.
Selected by Miami in 6th round (145th player selected) of 1985 NFL draft.
Signed by Miami Dolphins, July 14, 1985.
Released by Miami Dolphins, August 26, 1985; re-signed by Dolphins, September 17, 1985.
Released by Miami Dolphins, September 21, 1985; signed as free agent by Kansas City Chiefs, December 4, 1985.
Kansas City NFL, 1985.
Games: 1985 (3).
Pro statistics: Returned one kickoff for 11 yards, 1985.

MICKEY CHARLES SHULER
Tight End—New York Jets
Born August 21, 1956, at Harrisburg, Pa.
Height, 6.03. Weight, 231.
High School—Enola, Pa., East Pennsboro.
Received degree in health and physical education from Pennsylvania State University.

Selected by New York Jets in 3rd round (61st player selected) of 1978 NFL draft.
On injured reserve with shoulder separation, September 1 through November 13, 1981; activated, November 14, 1981.

| | | —PASS RECEIVING— | | | |
Year Club	G.	P.C.	Yds.	Avg.	TD.
1978—N.Y. Jets NFL	16	11	67	6.1	3
1979—N.Y. Jets NFL	16	16	225	14.1	3
1980—N.Y. Jets NFL	16	22	226	10.3	2
1981—N.Y. Jets NFL	6		None		
1982—N.Y. Jets NFL	9	8	132	16.5	3
1983—N.Y. Jets NFL	16	26	272	10.5	1
1984—N.Y. Jets NFL	16	68	782	11.5	6
1985—N.Y. Jets NFL	16	76	879	11.6	7
Pro Totals—8 Years...........	111	227	2583	11.4	25

Additional pro statistics: Fumbled once, 1978 through 1980, 1984 and 1985; returned one kickoff for 12 yards, 1978; returned one kickoff for 15 yards, 1979; returned two kickoffs for 25 yards, 1980; returned one kickoff for three yards, 1983; returned one kickoff for no yards, 1984; recovered one fumble, 1985.
Played in AFC Championship Game following 1982 season.

MARK SHUMATE
Defensive Tackle—Green Bay Packers
Born March 30, 1960, at Poynette, Wis.
Height, 6.05. Weight, 265.
High School—Poynette, Wis.
Attended University of Wisconsin.

Selected by Kansas City in 10th round (257th player selected) of 1983 NFL draft.
Released by Kansas City Chiefs, August 22, 1983; signed as free agent by Edmonton Eskimos, May 3, 1984.
Released by Edmonton Eskimos, August 28, 1984; signed as free agent by New York Jets, May 10, 1985.
Released by New York Jets, September 2, 1985; re-signed by Jets, September 3, 1985.
Released by New York Jets, October 2, 1985; signed as free agent by Green Bay Packers, October 8, 1985.
Released by Green Bay Packers, November 9, 1985; re-signed by Packers, February 28, 1986.
Edmonton CFL, 1984; New York Jets (4)-Green Bay (4) NFL, 1985.
Games: 1984 (8), 1985 (8). Total—16.

ERIC SCOTT SIEVERS
Tight End—San Diego Chargers
Born November 9, 1958, at Urbana, Ill.
Height, 6.03. Weight, 235.
High School—Arlington, Va., Washington & Lee.
Attended University of Maryland.

Selected by San Diego in 4th round (107th player selected) of 1981 NFL draft.

| | | —PASS RECEIVING— | | | |
Year Club	G.	P.C.	Yds.	Avg.	TD.
1981—San Diego NFL	16	22	276	12.5	3
1982—San Diego NFL	9	12	173	14.4	1
1983—San Diego NFL	16	33	452	13.7	3
1984—San Diego NFL	14	41	438	10.7	3
1985—San Diego NFL	16	41	438	10.7	6
Pro Totals—5 Years...........	71	149	1777	11.9	16

Additional pro statistics: Returned two kickoffs for four yards, 1981; recovered one fumble and fumbled once, 198 and 1984; returned one kickoff for 17 yards, 1982; returned one kickoff for six yards and rushed once for minus seven yards, 1983; returned one kickoff for three yards, 1985.

Played in AFC Championship Game following 1981 season.

ANTHONY EARL SIMMONS
(Tony)
Defensive End—San Diego Chargers
Born December 18, 1962, at Oakland, Calif.
Height, 6.04. Weight, 270.
High School—Oakland, Calif., McClymonds.
Attended University of Tennessee.

Selected by Memphis in 1985 USFL territorial draft.
Selected by San Diego in 12th round (318th player selected) of 1985 NFL draft.
Signed by San Diego Chargers, July 10, 1985.
San Diego NFL, 1985.
Games: 1985 (13).

JOHN CHRISTOPHER SIMMONS
Cornerback—Cincinnati Bengals
Born December 1, 1958, at Little Rock, Ark.
Height, 5.11. Weight, 192.
High School—Little Rock, Ark., Parkview.
Attended Southern Methodist University.

Selected by Cincinnati in 3rd round (64th player selected) of 1981 NFL draft.
On injured reserve with shoulder injury, September 1 through October 8, 1981; activated, October 9, 1981.
On injured reserve with dislocated shoulder, September 7 through December 24, 1982; activated, December 25, 1982.
Released by Cincinnati Bengals, August 29, 1983; re-signed by Bengals, August 31, 1983.
On injured reserve with knee injury, September 3 through October 18, 1985; activated, October 19, 1985.

		-PUNT RETURNS-				—KICKOFF RET.—				—TOTAL—		
Year Club	G.	No.	Yds.	Avg.	TD.	No.	Yds.	Avg.	TD.	TD.	Pts.	F.
1981—Cincinnati NFL	11	5	24	4.8	0	1	10	10.0	0	0	0	1
1982—Cincinnati NFL	2		None				None			0	0	0
1983—Cincinnati NFL	16	25	173	6.9	0	14	317	22.6	0	0	0	4
1984—Cincinnati NFL	16	12	98	8.2	0	1	15	15.0	0	1	6	0
1985—Cincinnati NFL	9		None				None			0	0	0
Pro Totals—5 Years	54	42	295	7.0	0	16	342	21.4	0	1	6	5

Additional pro statistics: Recovered one fumble, 1981; recovered three fumbles, 1983; intercepted two passes for 43 yards and a touchdown, 1984.
Played in AFC Championship Game following 1981 season.
Played in NFL Championship Game following 1981 season.

PHILLIP SIMMS
(Phil)
Quarterback—New York Giants
Born November 3, 1956, at Lebanon, Ky.
Height, 6.03. Weight, 216.
High School—Louisville, Ky., Southern.
Attended Morehead State University.

Selected by New York Giants in 1st round (7th player selected) of 1979 NFL draft.
On injured reserve with separated shoulder, November 18 through December 25, 1981; activated, December 26, 1981.
On injured reserve with knee injury, August 30 through entire 1982 season.
On injured reserve with dislocated thumb, October 13 through remainder of 1983 season.

		——PASSING——							——RUSHING——				—TOTAL—		
Year Club	G.	Att.	Cmp.	Pct.	Gain	T.P.	P.I.	Avg.	Att.	Yds.	Avg.	TD.	TD.	Pts.	F.
1979—N.Y. Giants NFL	12	265	134	50.6	1743	13	14	6.58	29	166	5.7	1	1	6	9
1980—N.Y. Giants NFL	13	402	193	48.0	2321	15	19	5.77	36	190	5.3	1	1	6	6
1981—N.Y. Giants NFL	10	316	172	54.4	2031	11	9	6.43	19	42	2.2	0	0	0	7
1983—N.Y. Giants NFL	2	13	7	53.8	130	0	1	10.00		None			0	0	0
1984—N.Y. Giants NFL	16	533	286	53.7	4044	22	18	7.59	42	162	3.9	0	0	0	8
1985—N.Y. Giants NFL	16	495	275	55.6	3829	22	20	7.74	37	132	3.6	0	0	0	*16
Pro Totals—6 Years	69	2024	1067	52.7	14098	83	81	6.97	163	692	4.2	2	2	12	46

Quarterback Rating Points: 1979 (65.9), 1980 (58.9), 1981 (74.2), 1983 (56.6), 1984 (78.1), 1985 (78.6). Total—72.1.
Additional pro statistics: Fumbled nine times for minus two yards, 1979; recovered two fumbles, 1980 and 1981; fumbled six times for minus five yards, 1980; fumbled seven times for minus 15 yards, 1981; caught one pass for 13 yards, recovered four fumbles and fumbled eight times for minus five yards, 1984; recovered five fumbles and fumbled 16 times for minus 22 yards, 1985.
Played in Pro Bowl (NFL All-Star Game) following 1985 season.

RONALD BERNARD SIMPKINS
(Ron)
Linebacker—Cincinnati Bengals
Born April 2, 1958, at Detroit, Mich.
Height, 6.01. Weight, 235.
High School—Detroit, Mich., Western.
Received bachelor of general studies degree from University of Michigan in 1980.

Selected by Cincinnati in 7th round (167th player selected) of 1980 NFL draft.
On injured reserve with pulled hamstring, August 31 through entire 1981 season.
Released by Cincinnati Bengals, September 6, 1982; re-signed by Bengals, September 14, 1982.
On inactive list, September 19, 1982.
Cincinnati NFL, 1980 and 1982 through 1985.
Games: 1980 (16), 1982 (5), 1983 (15), 1984 (16), 1985 (16). Total—68.
Pro statistics: Returned three kickoffs for eight yards and fumbled once, 1980; recovered one fumble, 1980, 1983 and 1984; recovered one fumble for four yards, 1985.

KEITH EDWARD SIMPSON
Cornerback—Seattle Seahawks
Born March 9, 1956, at Memphis, Tenn.
Height, 6.01. Weight, 195.
High School—Memphis, Tenn., Hamilton.
Attended Memphis State University.

Named as cornerback on THE SPORTING NEWS College All-America Team, 1977.
Selected by Seattle in 1st round (9th player selected) of 1978 NFL draft.

Year Club	G.	No.	Yds.	Avg.	TD.	Year Club	G.	No.	Yds.	Avg.	TD.
		INTERCEPTIONS						INTERCEPTIONS			
1978—Seattle NFL	13	2	40	20.0	1	1983—Seattle NFL	14	4	39	9.8	0
1979—Seattle NFL	15	4	72	18.0	0	1984—Seattle NFL	15	4	138	34.5	*2
1980—Seattle NFL	16	3	15	5.0	0	1985—Seattle NFL	15		None		
1981—Seattle NFL	12	2	34	17.0	0	Pro Totals—8 Years	108	19	338	17.8	3
1982—Seattle NFL	8		None								

Additional pro statistics: Recovered one fumble, 1978 and 1981; recovered one fumble for three yards, 1980; recovered two fumbles, 1983 and 1984; fumbled once, 1983.
Played in AFC Championship Game following 1983 season.

DARRYL LEON SIMS
Defensive End—Pittsburgh Steelers
Born July 23, 1961, at Winston-Salem, N.C.
Height, 6.03. Weight, 264.
High School—Bridgeport, Conn., Basick.
Attended University of Wisconsin.

Selected by Jacksonville in 1985 USFL territorial draft.
Selected by Pittsburgh in 1st round (20th player selected) of 1985 NFL draft.
Signed by Pittsburgh Steelers, July 18, 1985.
Pittsburgh NFL, 1985.
Games: 1985 (16).

KENNETH W. SIMS
(Ken)
Defensive End—New England Patriots
Born October 31, 1959, at Kosse, Tex.
Height, 6.05. Weight, 271.
High School—Groesbeck, Tex.
Attended University of Texas.

Named as defensive end on THE SPORTING NEWS College All-America Team, 1981.
Selected by New England in 1st round (1st player selected) of 1982 NFL draft.
On injured reserve with broken leg, December 3 through remainder of 1985 season.
New England NFL, 1982 through 1985.
Games: 1982 (9), 1983 (5), 1984 (16), 1985 (13). Total—43.
Pro statistics: Recovered two fumbles, 1985.

CURT EDWARD SINGER
Offensive Tackle—Seattle Seahawks
Born November 4, 1961, at Aliquippa, Pa.
Height, 6.05. Weight, 264.
High School—Aliquippa, Pa., Hopewell.
Attended University of Tennessee.

Selected by Memphis in 1984 USFL territorial draft.
Selected by Washington in 6th round (167th player selected) of 1984 NFL draft.
Signed by Washington Redskins, June 26, 1984.
Released by Washington Redskins, August 27, 1984; re-signed by Redskins, August 28, 1984.
On injured reserve with back injury, August 30 through entire 1984 season.
Released by Washington Redskins, August 20, 1985; signed as free agent by Seattle Seahawks, April 15, 1986.

MICHAEL SINGLETARY
(Mike)
Linebacker—Chicago Bears
Born October 9, 1958, at Houston, Tex.
Height, 6.00. Weight, 230.
High School—Houston, Tex., Worthing.
Received bachelor of arts degree in management from Baylor University.

Named to THE SPORTING NEWS NFL All-Star Team, 1984 and 1985.

Named as linebacker on THE SPORTING NEWS College All-America Team, 1980.
Selected by Chicago in 2nd round (38th player selected) of 1981 NFL draft.
Placed on did not report list, August 10 and August 20, 1985.
Granted roster exemption, August 21 through August 25, 1985; activated, August 26, 1985.
Chicago NFL, 1981 through 1985.
Games: 1981 (16), 1982 (9), 1983 (16), 1984 (16), 1985 (16). Total—73.
Pro statistics: Intercepted one pass for minus three yards, 1981; recovered one fumble, 1982 and 1984; intercepted one pass for no yards and recovered four fumbles for 15 yards, 1983; intercepted one pass for four yards, 1984; intercepted one pass for 23 yards and recovered three fumbles for 11 yards, 1985.
Played in NFC Championship Game following 1984 and 1985 seasons.
Played in NFL Championship Game following 1985 season.
Played in Pro Bowl (NFL All-Star Game) following 1983 through 1985 seasons.

PAUL ANTHONY SKANSI
Wide Receiver—Seattle Seahawks
Born January 11, 1961, at Tacoma, Wash.
Height, 5.11. Weight, 190.
High School—Gig Harbor, Wash., Peninsula.
Attended University of Washington.

Selected by Michigan in 4th round (39th player selected) of 1983 USFL draft.
Selected by Pittsburgh in 5th round (133rd player selected) of 1983 NFL draft.
Signed by Pittsburgh Steelers, June 5, 1983.
Released by Pittsburgh Steelers, August 27, 1984; signed as free agent by Seattle Seahawks, October 25, 1984.
Released by Seattle Seahawks, September 2, 1985; re-signed by Seahawks, October 2, 1985.

		PASS RECEIVING			-PUNT RETURNS-				—KICKOFF RET.—				—TOTAL—		
Year Club	G.	P.C.	Yds.	Avg.	TD.	No.	Yds.	Avg.	TD.	No.	Yds.	Avg.	TD.	TD.	Pts.	F.
1983—Pittsburgh NFL	15	3	39	13.0	0	43	363	8.4	0	None				0	0	5
1984—Seattle NFL	7	7	85	12.1	0	16	145	9.1	0	None				0	0	0
1985—Seattle NFL	12	21	269	12.8	1	31	312	10.1	0	19	358	18.8	0	1	6	1
Pro Totals—3 Years	34	31	393	12.7	1	90	820	9.1	0	19	358	18.8	0	1	6	6

Additional pro statistics: Recovered two fumbles, 1983; recovered one fumble, 1985.

HARRY GORDON SKIPPER
Cornerback—Cleveland Browns
Born February 4, 1960, at Baxley, Ga.
Height, 5.11. Weight, 175.
High School—Baxley, Ga., Appling County.
Received bachelor of arts degree in broadcast journalism from University of South Carolina in 1983.

Selected by Washington in 1983 USFL territorial draft.
Signed as free agent by Montreal Concordes, March 3, 1983.
Granted free agency, March 1, 1986; signed by Cleveland Browns, April 18, 1986.

		—INTERCEPTIONS—		
Year Club	G.	No.	Yds.	Avg.TD.
1983—Montreal CFL	15	10	*198	19.8	1
1984—Montreal CFL	16	8	*253	31.6	*2
1985—Montreal CFL	16	7	121	17.3	0
Pro Totals—3 Years	47	25	572	22.9	3

Additional pro statistics: Recovered three fumbles and fumbled once, 1983; recovered two fumbles for minus six yards with one touchdown and fumbled once, 1984; recovered two fumbles, 1985.

BOB SLATER
Defensive Tackle—Washington Redskins
Born November 14, 1960, at Pawhuska, Okla.
Height, 6.04. Weight, 265.
High School—Mason, Okla.
Received degree in business from University of Oklahoma in 1984.

Selected by Oklahoma in 1984 USFL territorial draft.
Selected by Washington in 2nd round (31st player selected) of 1984 NFL draft.
Signed by Washington Redskins, July 16, 1984.
On injured reserve with knee injury, August 28 through entire 1984 season.
On physically unable to perform/reserve with knee injury, August 20 through entire 1985 season.

JACKIE RAY SLATER
Offensive Tackle—Los Angeles Rams
Born May 27, 1954, at Jackson, Miss.
Height, 6.04. Weight, 271.
High School—Jackson, Miss., Wingfield.
Received bachelor of arts degree from Jackson State University;
attending Livingston University for master's degree in physical education.

Selected by Los Angeles in 3rd round (86th player selected) of 1976 NFL draft.
On injured reserve with knee injury, October 17 through remainder of 1984 season.
Los Angeles Rams NFL, 1976 through 1985.
Games: 1976 (14), 1977 (14), 1978 (16), 1979 (16), 1980 (15), 1981 (11), 1982 (9), 1983 (16), 1984 (7), 1985 (16). Total—134.

Pro statistics: Recovered one fumble, 1978, 1980 and 1985; recovered one fumble for 13 yards, 1983.
Played in NFC Championship Game following 1976, 1978, 1979 and 1985 seasons.
Played in NFL Championship Game following 1979 season.
Played in Pro Bowl (NFL All-Star Game) following 1983 and 1985 seasons.

TONY TYRONE SLATON
Center—Los Angeles Rams
Born April 12, 1961, at Merced, Calif.
Height, 6.04. Weight, 265.
High School—Merced, Calif.
Received bachelor of science degree from University of Southern California in 1984.

Selected by Los Angeles in 1984 USFL territorial draft.
Selected by Buffalo in 6th round (155th player selected) of 1984 NFL draft.
Signed by Buffalo Bills, June 1, 1984.
Released by Buffalo Bills, August 20, 1984; signed as free agent by Los Angeles Rams, August 23, 1984.
On injured reserve with strained abdominal muscles, September 21 through remainder of 1984 season.
Released by Los Angeles Rams, August 20, 1985; re-signed by Rams, September 19, 1985.
Active for 3 games with Los Angeles Rams in 1984; did not play.
Los Angeles Rams NFL, 1985.
Games: 1985 (13).
Pro statistics: Returned one kickoff for 18 yards and recovered one fumble, 1985.
Played in NFC Championship Game following 1985 season.

FREDRICK SMALL
(Fred)
Linebacker—Pittsburgh Steelers
Born July 15, 1963, at Los Angeles, Calif.
Height, 5.11. Weight, 227.
High School—Los Angeles, Calif., John C. Fremont.
Attended University of Washington.

Selected by Portland in 1985 USFL territorial draft.
Selected by Pittsburgh in 9th round (241st player selected) of 1985 NFL draft.
Signed by Pittsburgh Steelers, July 19, 1985.
Pittsburgh NFL, 1985.
Games: 1985 (16).

DONALD FREDERICK SMEREK
(Don)
Defensive Tackle—Dallas Cowboys
Born December 20, 1957, at Waterford, Mich.
Height, 6.07. Weight, 265.
High School—Henderson, Nev., Basic.
Received degree in physical education from University of Nevada at Reno.

Signed as free agent by Dallas Cowboys, May, 1980.
On injured reserve with rib injury entire 1980 season.
On injured reserve with knee injury, September 19 through remainder of 1981 season.
USFL rights traded by San Antonio Gunslingers to Michigan Panthers for rights to wide receiver Stanley Washington, October 13, 1983.
On injured reserve with shoulder injury, September 10 through October 25, 1985; activated, October 26, 1985.
Dallas NFL, 1981 through 1985.
Games: 1981 (2), 1982 (7), 1983 (15), 1984 (16), 1985 (10). Total—50.
Played in NFC Championship Game following 1982 season.

FREDERICK C. SMERLAS
(Fred)
Nose Tackle—Buffalo Bills
Born April 8, 1957, at Waltham, Mass.
Height, 6.03. Weight, 270.
High School—Waltham, Mass.
Attended Boston College.

Selected by Buffalo in 2nd round (32nd player selected) of 1979 NFL draft.
On injured reserve with knee injury, November 29 through remainder of 1979 season.
Buffalo NFL, 1979 through 1985.
Games: 1979 (13), 1980 (16), 1981 (16), 1982 (9), 1983 (16), 1984 (16), 1985 (16). Total—102.
Pro statistics: Recovered three fumbles for 23 yards and one touchdown, 1979; recovered one fumble for 17 yards, 1981; recovered two fumbles, 1982 and 1984; intercepted one pass for 25 yards, 1984; recovered one fumble, 1985.
Played in Pro Bowl (NFL All-Star Game) following 1980 through 1983 seasons.

AARON CLAYTON SMITH
Linebacker—Denver Broncos
Born August 10, 1962, at Los Angeles, Calif.
Height, 6.02. Weight, 223.
High School—Playa Del Rey, Calif., St. Bernard.
Received bachelor of science degree in health education
and sociology from Utah State University in 1984.
Brother of Al Smith, linebacker at Utah State University.

Selected by Jacksonville in 9th round (187th player selected) of 1984 USFL draft.
Selected by Denver in 6th round (159th player selected) of 1984 NFL draft.
Signed by Denver Broncos, June 7, 1984.
On injured reserve with knee injury, November 5 through remainder of 1984 season.
On injured reserve with knee injury, August 26 through entire 1985 season.
Denver NFL, 1984.
Games: 1984 (10).
Pro statistics: Returned one kickoff for two yards and fumbled once, 1984.

ALLANDA SMITH
Safety—Washington Redskins
Born March 7, 1962, at Houston, Tex.
Height, 6.02. Weight, 190.
High School—Houston, Tex., Booker T. Washington.
Attended Texas Christian University.

Selected by Washington in 1st round (8th player selected) of the 1984 USFL draft.
Rights traded by Washington Federals to Los Angeles Express for draft choice, February 29, 1984.
Signed by Los Angeles Express, March 2, 1984.
Granted roster exemption, March 2, 1984; activated, March 30, 1984.
Selected by Minnesota in 1st round (13th player selected) of 1984 NFL supplemental draft.
Released by Los Angeles Express, May 30, 1985; signed by Minnesota Vikings, May 31, 1985.
On injured reserve with ankle injury, August 20 through October 6, 1985.
Released by Minnesota Vikings, October 7, 1985; signed as free agent by Washington Redskins, April 16, 1986.
Los Angeles USFL, 1984 and 1985.
Games: 1984 (13), 1985 (10). Total—23.
Additional pro statistics: Returned lateral on interception for 19 yards, 1985.

BILLY RAY SMITH JR.
Linebacker—San Diego Chargers
Born August 10, 1961, at Fayetteville, Ark.
Height, 6.03. Weight, 231.
High School—Plano, Tex.
Attended University of Arkansas.
Son of Billy Ray Smith, Sr., defensive tackle with Los Angeles Rams, Pittsburgh
Steelers and Baltimore Colts, 1957 through 1962 and 1964 through 1970.

Named as defensive end on THE SPORTING NEWS College All-America Team, 1981 and 1982.
Selected by Oakland in 1st round (7th player selected) of 1983 USFL draft.
Selected by San Diego in 1st round (5th player selected) of 1983 NFL draft.
Signed by San Diego Chargers, May 19, 1983.
On injured reserve with back injury, December 20 through remainder of 1985 season.

| | | —INTERCEPTIONS— | | | |
Year Club	G.	No.	Yds.	Avg.TD.	
1983—San Diego NFL	16		None		
1984—San Diego NFL	16	3	41	13.7	0
1985—San Diego NFL	15	1	0	0.0	0
Pro Totals—3 Years............	47	4	41	10.3	0

Additional pro statistics: Returned one kickoff for 10 yards and recovered one fumble, 1983; recovered three fumbles, 1984 and 1985.

BRUCE BERNARD SMITH
Defensive End—Buffalo Bills
Born June 18, 1963, at Norfolk, Va.
Height, 6.04. Weight, 279.
High School—Norfolk, Va., Booker T. Washington.
Attended Virginia Tech.

Outland Trophy winner, 1984.
Selected by Baltimore in 1985 USFL territorial draft.
Signed by Buffalo Bills, February 28, 1985.
Selected by Buffalo in 1st round (1st player selected) of 1985 NFL draft.
Buffalo NFL, 1985.
Games: 1985 (16).
Pro statistics: Rushed once for no yards and recovered four fumbles, 1985.

BYRON KEITH SMITH
Defensive End—Indianapolis Colts
Born December 21, 1962, at Los Angeles, Calif.
Height, 6.05. Weight, 272.
High School—Canoga Park, Calif.
Attended University of California.

Selected by Oakland in 1984 USFL territorial draft.
Signed by Oakland Invaders, January 10, 1984.
Released by Oakland Invaders, February 20, 1984; signed as free agent by Saskatchewan Roughriders, March 19, 1984.
Selected by Indianapolis in 3rd round (66th player selected) of 1984 NFL supplemental draft.
On retired list with torn thigh muscle, June 3 through August 28, 1984.
Released by Saskatchewan Roughriders, August 29, 1984; signed by Indianapolis Colts, October 3, 1984.

Granted roster exemption, October 3 through October 14, 1984.
Released by Indianapolis Colts, October 15, 1984; re-signed by Colts, November 28, 1984.
Indianapolis NFL, 1984 and 1985.
Games: 1984 (3), 1985 (16). Total—19.

CARL DOUGLAS SMITH
(Doug)
Center—Los Angeles Rams
Born November 25, 1956, at Columbus, O.
Height, 6.03. Weight, 253.
High School—Columbus, O., Northland.
Received bachelor of science degree in education from Bowling Green State University in 1978
and attending California State University at Fullerton for master's degree in exercise physiology.
Signed as free agent by Los Angeles Rams, May 16, 1978.
On injured reserve with knee injury, September 28 through remainder of 1979 season.
On injured reserve with knee injury, October 30 through remainder of 1980 season.
On injured reserve with concussion, December 14 through remainder of 1985 season.
Los Angeles Rams NFL, 1978 through 1985.
Games: 1978 (16), 1979 (4), 1980 (8), 1981 (16), 1982 (9), 1983 (14), 1984 (16), 1985 (13). Total—96.
Pro statistics: Recovered one fumble, 1978 and 1985; returned one kickoff for eight yards, 1978; fumbled once, 1981
and 1983; recovered two fumbles, 1982.
Played in NFC Championship Game following 1978 season.
Played in Pro Bowl (NFL All-Star Game) following 1984 season.
Named to play in Pro Bowl following 1985 season; replaced due to injury by Fred Quillan.

DENNIS SMITH
Safety—Denver Broncos
Born February 3, 1959, at Santa Monica, Calif.
Height, 6.03. Weight, 200.
High School—Santa Monica, Calif.
Attended University of Southern California.
Selected by Denver in 1st round (15th player selected) of 1981 NFL draft.

| | | | —INTERCEPTIONS— | | |
Year Club	G.	No.	Yds.	Avg.	TD.
1981—Denver NFL	16	1	65	65.0	0
1982—Denver NFL	8	1	29	29.0	0
1983—Denver NFL	14	4	39	9.8	0
1984—Denver NFL	15	3	13	4.3	0
1985—Denver NFL	13	3	46	15.3	0
Pro Totals—5 Years	66	12	192	16.0	0

Additional pro statistics: Recovered two fumbles, 1981; recovered one fumble for 64 yards and a touchdown, 1984.
Played in Pro Bowl (NFL All-Star Game) following 1985 season.

DONALD LOREN SMITH
(Don)
Defensive End—Buffalo Bills
Born May 9, 1957, at Oakland, Calif.
Height, 6.05. Weight, 270.
High School—Tarpon Springs, Fla.
Received bachelor of science degree in education from University of Miami in 1979.
Named as defensive lineman on THE SPORTING NEWS College All-America Team, 1978.
Selected by Atlanta in 1st round (17th player selected) of 1979 NFL draft.
Granted free agency, February 1, 1985; re-signed by Falcons and traded to Buffalo Bills for 6th round pick in 1986
draft, August 20, 1985.
Granted roster exemption, August 20 through August 22, 1985; activated, August 23, 1985.
Atlanta NFL, 1979 through 1984; Buffalo NFL, 1985.
Games: 1979 (16), 1980 (16), 1981 (16), 1982 (9), 1983 (15), 1984 (16), 1985 (16). Total—104.
Pro statistics: Recovered one fumble for five yards, 1979; recovered three fumbles for two yards, 1981; recovered
three fumbles, 1982; recovered two fumbles, 1984 and 1985.

—DID YOU KNOW—
That when Washington's George Rogers (104 yards) and John Riggins (103) each rushed for more than 100 yards in the Redskins' 27-10 triumph over St. Louis on October 7, it marked the first time in the club's 54-year history that two runners had hit the 100-yard plateau in the same game? Ironically, Keith Griffin (164) and Rogers (124) accomplished the feat again four weeks later against Atlanta.

DOUGLAS ARTHUR SMITH
(Doug)
Defensive End—Houston Oilers
Born June 6, 1960, at Mesic, N.C.
Height, 6.04. Weight, 285.
High School—Bayboro, N.C., Pamlico Central.
Attended Auburn University.

Named as defensive tackle on THE SPORTING NEWS USFL All-Star Team, 1985.
Selected by Birmingham in 1984 USFL territorial draft.
Selected by Houston in 2nd round (29th player selected) of 1984 NFL draft.
Signed by Birmingham Stallions, August 2, 1984.
On developmental squad, March 2 through March 7, 1985; activated, March 8, 1985.
Released by Birmingham Stallions, October 7, 1985; signed by Houston Oilers, October 10, 1985.
Granted roster exemption, October 10, 1985.
On developmental squad for 1 game with Birmingham Stallions in 1985.
Birmingham USFL, 1985; Houston NFL, 1985.
Games: 1985 USFL (17), 1985 NFL (11). Total Pro—28.
USFL statistics: Credited with five sacks and recovered one fumble, 1985.

GARY LOVELL SMITH
Guard—Cincinnati Bengals
Born January 27, 1960, at Bitburg Air Force Base, Germany.
Height, 6.02. Weight, 265.
High School—Hampton, Va., Kecoughtan.
Attended Virginia Polytechnic Institute and State University.

Signed as free agent by Pittsburgh Steelers, May 13, 1982.
Released by Pittsburgh Steelers, September 6, 1982; signed as free agent by Philadelphia Stars, October 5, 1982.
Released by Philadelphia Stars, February 27, 1983; awarded on procedural waivers to Baltimore Colts, May 5, 1983.
Released by Baltimore Colts, August 29, 1983; signed as free agent by Pittsburgh Maulers, October 7, 1983.
Released by Pittsburgh Maulers, February 20, 1984; signed as free agent by Cincinnati Bengals, May 20, 1984.
Released by Cincinnati Bengals, August 27, 1985; re-signed by Bengals, February 21, 1986.
Cincinnati NFL, 1984.
Games: 1984 (8).

JAMES ARTHUR SMITH
(Jim)
Wide Receiver—Los Angeles Raiders
Born July 20, 1955, at Harvey, Ill.
Height, 6.02. Weight, 205.
High School—Blue Island, Ill., Eisenhower.
Attended University of Michigan.

Named as wide receiver on THE SPORTING NEWS USFL All-Star Team, 1985.
Named as wide receiver on THE SPORTING NEWS College All-America Team, 1976.
Selected by Pittsburgh in 3rd round (75th player selected) of 1977 NFL draft.
On injured reserve with broken leg, November 26 through remainder of 1980 season.
On inactive list, September 19, 1982.
Granted free agency, February 1, 1983.
USFL rights traded by Michigan Panthers to Birmingham Stallions for 3rd round pick in 1984 draft, April 5, 1983.
Signed by Birmingham Stallions, April 6, 1983.
On developmental squad, June 17 through June 24, 1983; activated, June 25, 1983.
On developmental squad, June 3 through June 6, 1985; activated, June 7, 1985.
Granted free agency, July 31, 1985; re-signed by Steelers and traded to Los Angeles Raiders for 5th round pick in 986 draft, August 31, 1985.
Granted roster exemption, August 31 through September 6, 1985; activated, September 7, 1985.
On injured reserve with hamstring injury, October 19 through remainder of 1985 season.
On developmental squad for 1 game with Birmingham Stallions in 1983 and 1985.

Year Club	G.	PASS RECEIVING				-PUNT RETURNS-				—KICKOFF RET.—				—TOTAL—		
		P.C.	Yds.	Avg.	TD.	No.	Yds.	Avg.	TD.	No.	Yds.	Avg.	TD.	TD.	Pts.	F.
977—Pittsburgh NFL	14	4	80	20.0	0	36	294	8.2	0	16	381	23.8	0	0	0	3
978—Pittsburgh NFL	9	6	83	13.8	2	9	65	7.2	0	1	16	16.0	0	2	12	1
979—Pittsburgh NFL	15	17	243	14.3	2	16	146	9.1	0	None				2	12	1
980—Pittsburgh NFL	12	37	711	19.2	9	7	28	4.0	0	None				9	54	1
981—Pittsburgh NFL	15	29	571	19.7	7	30	204	6.8	0	None				7	42	1
982—Pittsburgh NFL	8	17	387	22.8	4	None				None				4	24	1
983—Birmingham USFL	12	51	756	14.8	3	None				None				3	18	0
984—Birmingham USFL	18	89	*1481	16.6	8	None				None				8	†50	0
985—Birmingham USFL	17	87	1322	15.2	*20	None				None				21	126	2
985—L.A. Raiders NFL	6	3	28	9.3	1	None				None				1	6	0
NFL Totals—7 Years	79	113	2103	18.6	25	98	737	7.5	0	17	397	23.4	0	25	150	8
USFL Totals—3 Years	47	227	3559	15.7	31	0	0	0.0	0	0	0	0.0	0	32	194	2
Pro Totals—10 Years	126	340	5662	16.7	56	98	737	7.5	0	17	397	23.4	0	57	344	10

†Includes one 2-point conversion.
Additional NFL statistics: Rushed once for 12 yards, 1979; recovered one fumble, 1979 through 1981; rushed once or 15 yards, 1981.
Additional USFL statistics: Rushed five times for 39 yards, 1983; rushed twice for minus five yards, 1984; ran 22 ards with lateral for a touchdown and recovered two fumbles, 1985.
Played in AFC Championship Game following 1978 and 1979 seasons.
Played in NFL Championship Game following 1978 and 1979 seasons.

JAMES WADDELL SMITH
Wide Receiver—Indianapolis Colts
Born August 24, 1955, at New Orleans, La.
Height, 6.02. Weight, 180.
High School—Los Angeles, Calif., Manual Arts.
Attended Southwest Los Angeles Junior College and
received bachelor of science degree in communications from University of Kansas.

Selected by Kansas City in 8th round (215th player selected) of 1977 NFL draft.
Released by Kansas City Chiefs, September 5, 1977; signed as free agent by Edmonton Eskimos, September 1, 1977.
USFL rights traded with linebacker Ben Apuna by Chicago Blitz to Washington Federals for rights to quarterbac Vince Evans, December 27, 1983.
Granted free agency, March 1, 1984; signed by Los Angeles Raiders, March 15, 1984.
Released by Los Angeles Raiders, August 27, 1984; signed as free agent by Dallas Cowboys, September 6, 1984.
Released by Dallas Cowboys, October 13, 1984; signed as free agent by Houston Oilers, July 10, 1985.
Released by Houston Oilers, August 19, 1985; signed as free agent by Indianapolis Colts, August 27, 1985.
Released by Indianapolis Colts, September 2, 1985; re-signed by Colts, May 27, 1986.

| | | RUSHING | | | | PASS RECEIVING | | | | TOTAL | | |
Year Club	G.	Att.	Yds.	Avg.	TD.	P.C.	Yds.	Avg.	TD.	TD.	Pts.	F
1977—Edmonton CFL	6	None				19	253	13.3	2	2	12	
1978—Edmonton CFL	16	1	19	19.0	0	58	875	15.1	9	9	54	
1979—Edmonton CFL	16	1	26	26.0	1	*74	*1214	16.4	*13	*14	84	
1980—Edmonton CFL	12	2	—1	—5.0	0	30	482	16.1	4	4	24	
1981—Edmonton CFL	16	3	84	28.0	0	65	1077	16.6	9	9	†56	
1982—Edmonton CFL	14	4	40	10.0	0	41	729	17.8	7	7	42	
1983—Edmonton CFL	13	None				55	887	16.1	7	7	42	
1984—Dallas NFL	2	1	—5	—5.0	0	1	7	7.0	0	0	0	
CFL Totals—7 Years	93	11	168	15.3	1	342	5517	16.1	51	52	314	
NFL Totals—1 Year	2	1	—5	—5.0	0	1	7	7.0	0	0	0	
Pro Totals—8 Years	95	12	163	13.6	1	343	5524	16.1	51	52	314	

†Includes 2-point conversion.

Additional CFL statistics: Attempted two passes with one completion for 36 yards and a touchdown, 1979; recovered one fumble, 1979 through 1983; attempted one pass with one completion for 27 yards and a touchdown, 1982; attempted one pass with no completions, 1983.
Played in CFL Championship Game following 1978, 1979, 1981 and 1982 seasons.

JEFF K. SMITH
Running Back-Kick Returner—Kansas City Chiefs
Born March 22, 1962, at Wichita, Kan.
Height, 5.09. Weight, 201.
High School—Wichita, Kan., Southeast.
Attended University of Nebraska.

Selected by Baltimore in 7th round (101st player selected) of 1985 USFL draft.
Selected by Kansas City in 10th round (267th player selected) of 1985 NFL draft.
Signed by Kansas City Chiefs, July 18, 1985.
On injured reserve with sprained ankle, December 4 through remainder of 1985 season.

| | | RUSHING | | | | PASS RECEIVING | | | | TOTAL | | |
Year Club	G.	Att.	Yds.	Avg.	TD.	P.C.	Yds.	Avg.	TD.	TD.	Pts.	F
1985—Kansas City NFL	13	30	118	3.9	0	18	157	8.7	2	2	12	1

| | | KICKOFF RETURNS | | |
Year Club	G.	No.	Yds.	Avg.TD.
1985—Kansas City NFL	13	33	654	19.8 0

Additional pro statistics: Recovered one fumble, 1985.

JOHN THOMAS SMITH
(J. T.)
Wide Receiver-Kick Returner—St. Louis Cardinals
Born October 29, 1955, at Leonard, Tex.
Height, 6.02. Weight, 185.
High School—Leonard, Tex., Big Spring.
Attended North Texas State University.

Named as punt returner on THE SPORTING NEWS NFL All-Star Team, 1980.
Signed as free agent by Washington Redskins, May, 1978.
Released by Washington Redskins, September 21, 1978; signed as free agent by Kansas City Chiefs, November 7, 1978.
On inactive list, September 19, 1982.
On injured reserve with knee injury, August 30 through October 13, 1983; activated, October 14, 1983.
On injured reserve with separated shoulder, December 10 through remainder of 1984 season.
Released by Kansas City Chiefs, August 26, 1985; signed as free agent by St. Louis Cardinals, September 17, 1985.

| | PASS RECEIVING | | | | PUNT RETURNS | | | | KICKOFF RET. | | | TOTAL | | |
Year Club	G.	P.C.	Yds.	Avg.	TD.	No.	Yds.	Avg.	TD.	No.	Yds.	Avg.	TD.	Pts.	F.
1978—Wash(6)-KC(6) NFL	12					4	33	8.3	0	1	18	18.0	0	0	0
1979—Kansas City NFL	16	33	444	13.5	3	58	*612	10.6	2	None			5	30	
1980—Kansas City NFL	16	46	655	14.2	2	40	*581	*14.5	*2	None			4	24	
1981—Kansas City NFL	16	63	852	13.5	2	50	528	10.6	0	None			2	12	

Year Club	G.	PASS RECEIVING			-PUNT RETURNS-			−KICKOFF RET.−			−TOTAL−		
		P.C.	Yds.	Avg. TD.	No.	Yds.	Avg. TD.	No.	Yds.	Avg. TD.	TD.	Pts.	F.
1982—Kansas City NFL........	5	10	168	16.8 1	3	26	8.7 0	None			1	6	0
1983—Kansas City NFL........	9	7	85	12.1 0	26	210	8.1 0	1	5	5.0 0	0	0	0
1984—Kansas City NFL........	15	8	69	8.6 0	39	332	8.5 0	19	391	20.6 0	0	0	1
1985—St. Louis NFL.............	14	43	581	13.5 1	26	283	10.9 0	4	59	14.8 0	1	6	3
Pro Totals—8 Years.......	103	210	2854	13.6 9	246	2605	10.6 4	25	473	18.9 0	13	78	10

Additional pro statistics: Recovered one fumble for one yard, 1979; recovered two fumbles, 1980; recovered one fumble for 19 yards, 1981; rushed three times for 36 yards, 1985.
Played in Pro Bowl (NFL All-Star Game) following 1980 season.

LANCE SMITH
Guard—St. Louis Cardinals
Born January 1, 1963, at Kannapolis, N.C.
Height, 6.02. Weight, 262.
High School—Kannapolis, N.C., A.L. Brown.
Attended Louisiana State University.
Selected by Portland in 1985 USFL territorial draft.
Selected by St. Louis in 3rd round (72nd player selected) of 1985 NFL draft.
Signed by St. Louis Cardinals, July 21, 1985.
St. Louis NFL, 1985.
Games: 1985 (14).
Pro statistics: Recovered one fumble, 1985.

LEONARD PHILLIP SMITH
Safety—St. Louis Cardinals
Born September 2, 1960, at New Orleans, La.
Height, 5.11. Weight, 202.
High School—Baton Rouge, La., Robert E. Lee.
Attended McNeese State University.
Selected by Boston in 2nd round (14th player selected) of 1983 USFL draft.
Selected by St. Louis in 1st round (17th player selected) of 1983 NFL draft.
Signed by St. Louis Cardinals, May 3, 1983.

Year Club	G.	——INTERCEPTIONS——		
		No.	Yds.	Avg.TD.
1983—St. Louis NFL................	16	None		
1984—St. Louis NFL................	12	2	31	15.5 1
1985—St. Louis NFL................	16	2	73	36.5 0
Pro Totals—3 Years...........	44	4	104	26.0 1

Additional pro statistics: Returned one kickoff for 19 yards, 1983; recovered one fumble, 1984; returned five kickoffs for 68 yards and recovered three fumbles and fumbled once, 1985.

LUCIOUS IRVIN SMITH
Cornerback
Born January 17, 1957, at Columbus, Ga.
Height, 5.10. Weight, 190.
High School—San Diego, Calif., Kearny.
Attended San Diego State University and California State University at Fullerton.
Signed as free agent by Los Angeles Rams, May 5, 1980.
Traded with 5th round pick in 1985 draft by Los Angeles Rams to Kansas City Chiefs for quarterback Steve Fuller, August 19, 1983.
Released by Kansas City Chiefs, August 27, 1984; signed as free agent by Buffalo Bills, September 14, 1984.
Released by Buffalo Bills, October 9, 1984; signed as free agent by San Diego Chargers, October 17, 1984.
On injured reserve with knee injury, October 8 through remainder of 1985 season.
Granted free agency, February 1, 1986; withdrew qualifying offer, April 20, 1986.
Los Angeles Rams NFL, 1980 through 1982; Kansas City NFL, 1983; Buffalo (4)-San Diego (9) NFL, 1984; San Diego NFL, 1985.
Games: 1980 (16), 1981 (16), 1982 (8), 1983 (16), 1984 (13), 1985 (5). Total—74.
Pro statistics: Recovered two fumbles, 1980; recovered one fumble, 1981 and 1983; intercepted three passes for 99 yards and a touchdown, 1983; intercepted one pass for seven yards, returned one punt for no yards and fumbled once, 1984.

MARK SMITH
Wide Receiver—Indianapolis Colts
Born April 4, 1962, at Fayetteville, N.C.
Height, 6.00. Weight, 180.
High School—Fayetteville, N.C., E.E. Smith.
Attended University of North Carolina.
Selected by Philadelphia in 1984 USFL territorial draft.
Selected by Washington in 7th round (195th player selected) of 1984 NFL draft.
Signed by Washington Redskins, May 16, 1984.
Released by Washington Redskins, August 14, 1984; signed by Baltimore Stars, November 26, 1984.
Released by Baltimore Stars, January 28, 1985; signed as free agent by Indianapolis Colts, March 29, 1985.
On injured reserve with ankle injury, August 20 through entire 1985 season.

MICHAEL WAYNE SMITH
(Mike)
Cornerback—Miami Dolphins
Born October 24, 1962, at Houston, Tex.
Height, 6.00. Weight, 171.
High School—Houston, Tex., Booker T. Washington.
Attended University of Texas at El Paso.

Selected by Arizona in 4th round (49th player selected) of 1985 USFL draft.
Selected by Miami in 4th round (91st player selected) of 1985 NFL draft.
Signed by Miami Dolphins, May 30, 1985.
Released by Miami Dolphins, October 5, 1985; re-signed by Dolphins, November 13, 1985.
Miami NFL, 1985.
Games: 1985 (7).
Played in AFC Championship Game following 1985 season.

PHILLIP KEITH SMITH
(Phil)
Wide Receiver—Philadelphia Eagles
Born April 28, 1961, at Los Angeles, Calif.
Height, 6.03. Weight, 190.
High School—Gardena, Calif., Junipero Serra.
Received degree in public administration from San Diego State University.

Selected by Arizona in 11th round (122nd player selected) of 1983 USFL draft.
Selected by Baltimore in 4th round (85th player selected) of 1983 NFL draft.
Signed by Baltimore Colts, May 19, 1983.
On non-football injury list with sinus condition, November 1 through remainder of 1983 season.
Franchise transferred to Indianapolis, March 31, 1984.
Released by Indianapolis Colts, July 28, 1985; signed as free agent by Philadelphia Eagles, February 26, 1986.

		KICKOFF RETURNS			
Year Club	G.	No.	Yds.	Avg.	TD.
1983—Baltimore NFL	1		None		
1984—Indianapolis NFL	16	32	651	20.3	*1
Pro Totals—2 Years...........	17	32	651	20.3	1

Additional pro statistics: Rushed twice for minus 10 yards and fumbled once, 1984.

RICKY SMITH
Cornerback—Miami Dolphins
Born July 20, 1960, at Quincy, Fla.
Height, 6.00. Weight, 182.
High School—Quincy, Fla., James A. Shanks.
Received bachelor of science degree in human services from
Alabama State University in 1982.

Selected by New England in 6th round (141st player selected) on 1982 NFL draft.
Traded by New England Patriots to Washington Redskins for 7th round pick in 1985 draft, September 11, 1984.
Released by Washington Redskins, July 29, 1985; awarded on waivers to Indianapolis Colts, July 30, 1985.
Released by Indianapolis Colts, September 2, 1985; signed as free agent by Miami Dolphins for 1986, December 20, 1985.

		—PUNT RETURNS—				—KICKOFF RET.—				—TOTAL—		
Year Club	G.	No.	Yds.	Avg.	TD.	No.	Yds.	Avg.	TD.	TD.	Pts.	F.
1982—New England NFL.................................	9	16	139	8.7	0	24	567	23.6	*1	1	6	3
1983—New England NFL.................................	16	38	398	10.5	0	42	916	21.8	0	0	0	11
1984—N.E. (1)-Wash. (11) NFL.........................	12			None		1	22	22.0	0	0	0	0
Pro Totals—3 Years....................................	37	54	537	9.9	0	67	1505	22.5	1	1	6	14

Additional pro statistics: Recovered two fumbles, 1982; recovered six fumbles, 1983; intercepted one pass for 37 yards, 1984.

ROBERT BENJAMIN SMITH
Defensive End—Minnesota Vikings
Born December 3, 1962, at Bogalusa, La.
Height, 6.05. Weight, 245.
High School—Bogalusa, La.
Attended Grambling State University.

Selected by New Orleans in 1984 USFL territorial draft.
USFL rights traded by New Orleans Breakers to Arizona Wranglers for defensive end Junior Ah You and past considerations, January 9, 1984.
Signed by Arizona Wranglers, January 9, 1984.
On developmental squad, February 24 through April 20, 1984.
On injured reserve with knee injury, April 21 through June 25, 1984; activated, June 26, 1984.
Selected by Minnesota in 2nd round (40th player selected) of 1984 NFL supplemental draft.
Not protected in merger of Arizona Wranglers and Oklahoma Outlaws, December 6, 1984; signed by Minnesota Vikings, March 21, 1985.
On developmental squad for 8 games with Arizona Wranglers in 1984.
On developmental squad for USFL Championship Game following 1984 season.
Minnesota NFL, 1985.
Games: 1985 (16).

STEPHEN BRIAN SMITH
(Steve)
Quarterback—San Diego Chargers

Born December 19, 1962, at Flint, Mich.
Height, 6.00. Weight, 200.
High Schools—Swartz Creek, Mich.; and Grand Blanc., Mich.
Received bachelor of arts degree in education from University of Michigan.

Selected by Michigan in 1984 USFL territorial draft.
Signed as free agent by Montreal Concordes, March 7, 1984.
Selected by San Diego in 2nd round (34th player selected) of 1984 NFL supplemental draft.
Released by Montreal Concordes, July 1, 1985; awarded on waivers to Ottawa Rough Riders, July 2, 1985.
Released by Ottawa Rough Riders, August 11, 1985; signed by San Diego Chargers, April 17, 1986.

Year Club	G.	Att.	Cmp.	Pct.	Gain	T.P.	P.I.	Avg.	Att.	Yds.	Avg.	TD.	TD.	Pts.	F.
					PASSING						RUSHING			TOTAL	
1984—Montreal CFL	16	45	19	42.2	263	3	7	5.84	15	104	6.9	0	1	6	1
1985—Ottawa CFL	2	1	0	0.0	0	0	0	0.00	5	45	9.0	0	0	0	0
Pro Totals—2 Years	18	46	19	41.3	263	3	7	5.72	20	149	7.5	0	1	6	1

Additional CFL statistics: Caught three passes for 45 yards and a touchdown, 1984; caught three passes for 18 yards, 1985.

TIM SMITH
Wide Receiver—Houston Oilers

Born March 20, 1957, at Tucson, Ariz.
Height, 6.02. Weight, 206.
High School—San Diego, Calif., St. Augustine.
Attended University of Nebraska.

Selected by Houston in 3rd round (79th player selected) of 1980 NFL draft.
On injured reserve with broken finger, September 1 through November 26, 1981; activated, November 27, 1981.

Year Club	G.	P.C.	Yds.	Avg.	TD.
			PASS RECEIVING		
1980—Houston NFL	16	2	21	10.5	0
1981—Houston NFL	4	2	37	18.5	0
1982—Houston NFL	9		None		
1983—Houston NFL	16	83	1176	14.2	6
1984—Houston NFL	16	69	1141	16.5	4
1985—Houston NFL	16	46	660	14.3	2
Pro Totals—6 Years	77	202	3035	15.0	12

Additional pro statistics: Returned one kickoff for no yards, 1980; fumbled once, 1980, 1983 and 1985; ran seven yards with lateral on kickoff return, 1982; rushed twice for 16 yards, 1983; recovered one fumble, 1984 and 1985; punted once for 26 yards, 1985.

WAYNE LESTER SMITH
Cornerback—St. Louis Cardinals

Born May 9, 1957, at Chicago, Ill.
Height, 6.00. Weight, 170.
High School—Chicago, Ill., Harper.
Attended University of Wisconsin at LaCrosse, Loop Junior College and received bachelor
of arts degree in sociology and management from Purdue University in 1980.

Selected by Detroit in 11th round (278th player selected) of 1980 NFL draft.
Released by Detroit Lions, December 7, 1982; claimed on waivers by St. Louis Cardinals, December 8, 1982.
On injured reserve with knee injury, December 16 through remainder of 1982 season.

Year Club	G.	No.	Yds.	Avg.	TD.
			INTERCEPTIONS		
1980—Detroit NFL	16	1	23	23.0	0
1981—Detroit NFL	16		None		
1982—Det. (5)-St.L. (1) NFL	6	1	10	10.0	0
1983—St. Louis NFL	16	2	3	1.5	0
1984—St. Louis NFL	16	4	35	8.8	0
1985—St. Louis NFL	16		None		
Pro Totals—6 Years	86	8	71	8.9	0

Additional pro statistics: Recovered two fumbles, 1980; recovered one fumble for four yards, 1981; recovered one fumble, 1983 and 1985; recovered three fumbles for 12 yards, 1984.

RAY MICHAEL SNELL
Guard

Born February 24, 1958, at Baltimore, Md.
Height, 6.04. Weight, 265.
High School—Hyattsville, Md., Northwestern.
Attended University of Wisconsin.

Named as guard on THE SPORTING NEWS College All-America Team, 1979.
Selected by Tampa Bay in 1st round (22nd player selected) of 1980 NFL draft.
On injured reserve with knee injury, September 13 through November 18, 1982; activated, November 19, 1982.
Traded by Tampa Bay Buccaneers to Pittsburgh Steelers for guard Steve Courson, July 30, 1984.
On injured reserve with knee injury, January 4, 1985 through remainder of 1984 season playoffs.

Released by Pittsburgh Steelers, October 18, 1985; signed as free agent by Detroit Lions, October 31, 1985.
On injured reserve with broken facial bone, November 13 through remainder of 1985 season.
Granted free agency with no qualifying offer, February 1, 1986.
Tampa Bay NFL, 1980 through 1983; Pittsburgh NFL, 1984; Pittsburgh (5)-Detroit (2) NFL, 1985.
Games: 1980 (13), 1981 (16), 1982 (7), 1983 (9), 1984 (13), 1985 (7). Total—65.
Pro statistics: Recovered one fumble, 1984.

BRYAN SOCHIA

Name pronounced So-SHAY.

Nose Tackle—Houston Oilers

Born July 21, 1961, at Massena, N.Y.
Height, 6.03. Weight, 254.
High School—Brasher Falls, N.Y., St. Lawrence Central.
Attended Northwestern Oklahoma State University.

Signed as free agent by Houston Oilers, June 2, 1983.
On injured reserve with knee and ankle injuries, August 29 through September 26, 1983; activated after clearing procedural waivers, September 27, 1983.
Houston NFL, 1983 through 1985.
Games: 1983 (12), 1984 (16), 1985 (16). Total—44.

KURT SOHN

Name pronounced Sewn.

Wide Receiver—New York Jets

Born June 26, 1957, at Ithaca, N.Y.
Height, 5.11. Weight, 180.
High School—Huntington, N.Y.
Attended Nassau Community College, North Carolina State and Fordham University.

Signed as free agent by Los Angeles Rams, May 29, 1980.
Released by Los Angeles Rams, August 18, 1980; signed as free agent by New York Jets, June 16, 1981.
On injured reserve with knee injury, August 19 through remainder of 1983 season.
On physically unable to perform/active with knee injury, July 14 through August 12, 1984; activated, August 13, 1984.
On injured reserve with knee injury, October 26 through November 29, 1984; activated, November 30, 1984.

Year Club	G.	PASS RECEIVING				PUNT RETURNS				KICKOFF RET.				TOTAL		
		P.C.	Yds.	Avg.	TD.	No.	Yds.	Avg.	TD.	No.	Yds.	Avg.	TD.	TD.	Pts.	F.
1981—New York Jets NFL....	16		None			13	66	5.1	0	26	528	20.3	0	0	0	5
1982—New York Jets NFL....	9		None				None			15	299	19.9	0	0	0	0
1984—New York Jets NFL....	5	2	28	14.0	0		None				None			0	0	0
1985—New York Jets NFL....	15	39	534	13.7	4	16	149	9.3	0	3	7	2.3	0	4	24	0
Pro Totals—4 Years.......	45	41	562	13.7	4	29	215	7.4	0	44	834	19.0	0	4	24	5

Additional pro statistics: Recovered two fumbles, 1981; rushed once for 12 yards, 1985.
Played in AFC Championship Game following 1982 season.

RONALD MATTHEW SOLT

(Ron)

Guard—Indianapolis Colts

Born May 19, 1962, at Bainebridge, Md.
Height, 6.03. Weight, 275.
High School—Wilkes-Barre, Pa., James M. Coughlin.
Attended University of Maryland.

Selected by Washington in 1984 USFL territorial draft.
Selected by Indianapolis in 1st round (19th player selected) of 1984 NFL draft.
Signed by Indianapolis Colts, August 11, 1984.
On injured reserve with knee injury, December 17 through remainder of 1985 season.
Indianapolis NFL, 1984 and 1985.
Games: 1984 (16), 1985 (15). Total—31.
Pro statistics: Recovered one fumble, 1984.

ROBERT DONNELL SOWELL JR.

Cornerback—Miami Dolphins

Born June 23, 1961, at Columbus, O.
Height, 5.11. Weight, 175.
High School—Columbus, O., Mifflin.
Attended Howard University.

Signed as free agent by Miami Dolphins, July 3, 1983.
Played semi-pro football with Twin Cities Cougars in 1981.
On injured reserve with knee injury, November 13 through remainder of 1985 season.
Miami NFL, 1983 through 1985.
Games: 1983 (16), 1984 (16), 1985 (10). Total—42.
Pro statistics: Returned one punt for no yards, 1983; recovered one fumble, 1983 and 1984; intercepted one pass for seven yards, 1984.
Played in AFC Championship Game following 1984 season.
Played in NFL Championship Game following 1984 season.

JOHN STEPHEN SPAGNOLA
Tight End—Philadelphia Eagles
Born August 1, 1957, at Bethlehem, Pa.
Height, 6.04. Weight, 240.
High School—Bethlehem, Pa., Catholic.
Received bachelor of arts degree in political science from Yale University in 1980.

Selected by New England in 9th round (245th player selected) of 1979 NFL draft.
Released by New England Patriots, August 20, 1979; signed as free agent by Philadelphia Eagles, August 27, 1979.
On injured reserve with back injury, August 30 through entire 1983 season.

Year Club	G.	P.C.	Yds.	Avg.	TD.
1979—Philadelphia NFL	16	2	24	12.0	0
1980—Philadelphia NFL	16	18	193	10.7	3
1981—Philadelphia NFL	11	6	83	13.8	0
1982—Philadelphia NFL	9	26	313	12.0	2
1984—Philadelphia NFL	16	65	701	10.8	1
1985—Philadelphia NFL	16	64	772	12.1	5
Pro Totals—6 Years	84	181	2086	11.5	11

Additional pro statistics: Recovered one fumble, 1979 through 1981; returned one kickoff for no yards, 1980; ▪mbled twice, 1980 and 1984; fumbled once, 1985.
Played in NFC Championship Game following 1980 season.
Played in NFL Championship Game following 1980 season.

GARY L. SPANI
Name pronounced SPAIN-ee.
Linebacker—Kansas City Chiefs
Born January 9, 1956, at Satanta, Kan.
Height, 6.02. Weight, 228.
High School—Manhattan, Kan.
Attended Kansas State University.

Selected by Kansas City in 3rd round (58th player selected) of 1978 NFL draft.
On injured reserve with knee injury, August 30 through October 13, 1983; activated, October 14, 1983.
Kansas City NFL, 1978 through 1985.
Games: 1978 (14), 1979 (16), 1980 (16), 1981 (16), 1982 (8), 1983 (10), 1984 (14), 1985 (14). Total—108.
Pro statistics: Recovered one fumble for six yards, 1978; recovered one fumble, 1979 and 1982; intercepted one pass r 47 yards and a touchdown and recovered four fumbles for 16 yards and one touchdown, 1980; recovered two mbles for 91 yards and one touchdown, 1981; recovered one fumble for five yards, 1983.

TIM SPENCER
Running Back—San Diego Chargers
Born December 10, 1960, at Martins Ferry, O.
Height, 6.01. Weight, 220.
High School—St. Clairsville, O., Richland.
Attended Ohio State University.

Selected by Chicago in 1st round (2nd player selected) of 1983 USFL draft.
Signed by Chicago Blitz, January 7, 1983.
Selected by San Diego in 11th round (307th player selected) of 1983 NFL draft.
Franchise transferred to Arizona, September 30, 1983.
Not protected in merger of Arizona Wranglers and Oklahoma Outlaws; selected by Memphis Showboats in USFL dispersal draft, December 6, 1984.
On developmental squad, February 21 through March 8, 1985; activated, March 9, 1985.
Granted free agency, August 1, 1985; signed by San Diego Chargers, August 2, 1985.
On developmental squad for 2 games with Memphis Showboats in 1985.

Year Club	G.	Att.	Yds.	Avg.	TD.	P.C.	Yds.	Avg.	TD.	TD.	Pts.	F.
1983—Chicago USFL	18	300	1157	3.9	6	38	362	9.5	2	8	48	2
1984—Arizona USFL	18	227	1212	5.3	17	46	589	12.8	2	19	114	3
1985—Memphis USFL	16	198	789	4.0	3	14	96	6.9	0	3	18	3
1985—San Diego NFL	16	124	478	3.9	10	11	135	12.3	0	10	60	1
USFL Totals—3 Years	52	725	3158	4.4	26	98	1047	10.7	4	30	180	8
NFL Totals—1 Year	16	124	478	3.9	10	11	135	12.3	0	10	60	1
Pro Totals—4 Years	68	849	3636	4.3	36	109	1182	10.8	4	40	240	9

Additional USFL statistics: Attempted one pass with no completions, 1983; recovered one fumble, 1983 and 1985.
Played in USFL Championship Game following 1984 season.

TODD LAMONT SPENCER
Running Back
Born July 20, 1962, at Portland, Ore.
Height, 6.00. Weight, 217.
High School—El Cerrito, Calif.
Received bachelor of science degree in economics from University of Southern California.
Son of Thad Spencer, former heavyweight boxer.

Selected by Los Angeles in 1984 USFL territorial draft.
Signed as free agent by Pittsburgh Steelers, June 15, 1984.
On injured reserve with knee injury, October 19 through remainder of 1984 season.
Granted free agency with option not exercised, February 1, 1986.

Year Club	G.	Att.	Yds.	Avg.	TD.	P.C.	Yds.	Avg.	TD.	TD.	Pts.	F
			RUSHING			PASS RECEIVING				TOTAL		
1984—Pittsburgh NFL	7	1	0	0.0	0	0	0	0.0	0	0	0	5
1985—Pittsburgh NFL	16	13	56	4.3	0	3	25	8.3	0	0	0	3
Pro Totals—2 Years	23	14	56	4.0	0	3	25	8.3	0	0	0	8

Year Club		G.	No.	Yds.	Avg.	TD.
			KICKOFF RETURNS			
1984—Pittsburgh NFL		7	18	373	20.7	0
1985—Pittsburgh NFL		16	27	617	22.9	0
Pro Totals—2 Years		23	45	990	22.0	0

Additional pro statistics: Recovered two fumbles, 1984; recovered one fumble, 1985.

KIRK EDWARD SPRINGS
Safety—New York Jets
Born August 16, 1958, at Cincinnati, O.
Height, 6.00. Weight, 197.
High School—Cincinnati, O., Woodward.
Attended Miami (O.) University.

Signed as free agent by Seattle Seahawks, May 7, 1980.
Released by Seattle Seahawks, August 2, 1980; signed as free agent by New York Jets, February 11, 1981.
Released by New York Jets, August 31, 1981; re-signed by Jets, October 13, 1981.

Year Club	G.	No.	Yds.	Avg.	TD.	No.	Yds.	Avg.	TD.	No.	Yds.	Avg.	TD.	TD.	Pts.	F
		INTERCEPTIONS				-PUNT RETURNS-				—KICKOFF RET.—				—TOTAL—		
1981—N.Y. Jets NFL	10	2	5	2.5	0	None				None				0	0	
1982—N.Y. Jets NFL	9	1	0	0.0	0	None				None				0	0	
1983—N.Y. Jets NFL	16	None				23	287	12.5	*1	16	364	22.8	0	1	6	
1984—N.Y. Jets NFL	16	1	13	13.0	0	28	247	8.8	0	23	521	22.7	0	0	0	
1985—N.Y. Jets NFL	16	None				14	147	10.5	0	10	227	22.7	0	0	0	
Pro Totals—5 Years	67	4	18	4.5	0	65	681	10.5	1	49	1112	22.7	0	1	6	

Additional pro statistics: Recovered two fumbles, 1981 and 1985; recovered one fumble, 1983; recovered two fumbles for four yards, 1984.
Played in AFC Championship Game following 1982 season.

RONALD EDWARD SPRINGS
(Ron)
Running Back—Tampa Bay Buccaneers
Born November 4, 1956, at Williamsburg, Va.
Height, 6.02. Weight, 224.
High School—Williamsburg, Val., Lafayette.
Attended Coffeyville Junior College and Ohio State University.

Selected by Dallas in 5th round (136th player selected) of 1979 NFL draft.
Released by Dallas Cowboys, September 2, 1985; signed as free agent by Tampa Bay Buccaneers, September 1, 1985.

Year Club	G.	Att.	Yds.	Avg.	TD.	P.C.	Yds.	Avg.	TD.	TD.	Pts.	F
			RUSHING			PASS RECEIVING				TOTAL		
1979—Dallas NFL	16	67	248	3.7	2	25	251	10.0	1	3	18	
1980—Dallas NFL	15	89	326	3.7	6	15	212	14.1	1	7	42	
1981—Dallas NFL	16	172	625	3.6	10	46	359	7.8	2	12	72	
1982—Dallas NFL	9	59	243	4.1	2	17	163	9.6	2	4	24	
1983—Dallas NFL	16	149	541	3.6	7	73	589	8.1	1	8	48	
1984—Dallas NFL	16	68	197	2.9	1	46	454	9.9	3	4	24	
1985—Tampa Bay NFL	12	16	54	3.4	0	3	44	14.7	0	0	0	
Pro Totals—7 Years	100	620	2234	3.6	28	225	2072	9.2	10	38	228	1

Year Club		G.	No.	Yds.	Avg.	TD.
			KICKOFF RETURNS			
1979—Dallas NFL		16	38	780	20.5	0
1980—Dallas NFL		15	None			
1981—Dallas NFL		16	None			
1982—Dallas NFL		9	None			
1983—Dallas NFL		16	1	13	13.0	0
1984—Dallas NFL		16	None			
1985—Tampa Bay NFL		12	5	112	22.4	0
Pro Totals—7 Years		100	44	905	20.6	0

Additional pro statistics: Attempted three passes with one completion for 30 yards and one touchdown and recovered two fumbles, 1979; recovered four fumbles for 11 yards and attempted one pass with one interception, 1981; recovered one fumble, 1982; attempted two passes with one completion for 15 yards and a touchdown and recovered three fumbles, 1983; attempted one pass with no completions, 1984.
Played in NFC Championship Game following 1980 through 1982 seasons.

—DID YOU KNOW—

That in Green Bay's 43-10 victory over Detroit on October 6, Packers receiver Phillip Epps caught two passes for 37 yards—both for touchdowns—but teammate James Lofton caught 10 passes for 151 yards without a TD?

JACK STEVE SQUIREK
Linebacker—Los Angeles Raiders
Born February 16, 1959, at Cleveland, O.
Height, 6.04. Weight, 235.
High School—Cleveland, O., Cuyahoga Heights.
Attended University of Illinois.

Selected by Los Angeles Raiders in 2nd round (35th player selected) of 1982 NFL draft.
On injured reserve with broken jaw, August 28 through September 28, 1984; activated, September 29, 1984.
Los Angeles Raiders NFL, 1982 through 1985.
Games: 1982 (9), 1983 (16), 1984 (12), 1985 (16). Total—53.
Pro statistics: Recovered one fumble, 1982 and 1984; intercepted one pass for three yards, 1985.
Played in AFC Championship Game following 1983 season.
Played in NFL Championship Game following 1983 season.

JOHNNY LEE STALLWORTH
(John)
Wide Receiver—Pittsburgh Steelers
Born July 15, 1952, at Tuscaloosa, Ala.
Height, 6.02. Weight, 202.
High School—Tuscaloosa, Ala.
Received bachelor of science degree in business from Alabama A&M University in 1974;
and received master's degree in business administration from Alabama A&M University.

Named to THE SPORTING NEWS AFC All-Star Team, 1979.
Selected by Pittsburgh in 4th round (82nd player selected) of 1974 NFL draft.
On injured reserve with cracked fibula, September 17 through October 31, 1980; activated, November 1, 1980.
On injured reserve with broken foot, November 13 through remainder of 1980 season.
On injured reserve with pulled hamstring, October 7 through November 3, 1983; activated, November 4, 1983.

		——RUSHING——				PASS RECEIVING				—TOTAL—		
Year Club	G.	Att.	Yds.	Avg.	TD.	P.C.	Yds.	Avg.	TD.	TD.	Pts.	F.
1974—Pittsburgh NFL	13	1	—9	—9.0	0	16	269	16.8	1	1	6	0
1975—Pittsburgh NFL	11			None		20	423	21.2	4	4	24	0
1976—Pittsburgh NFL	8			None		9	111	12.3	2	3	18	0
1977—Pittsburgh NFL	14	6	47	7.8	0	44	784	17.8	7	7	42	1
1978—Pittsburgh NFL	16			None		41	798	19.5	9	9	54	2
1979—Pittsburgh NFL	16			None		70	*1183	16.9	8	8	48	4
1980—Pittsburgh NFL	3			None		9	197	21.9	1	1	6	0
1981—Pittsburgh NFL	16	1	17	17.0	0	63	1098	17.4	5	5	30	4
1982—Pittsburgh NFL	9	1	9	9.0	0	27	441	16.3	7	7	42	2
1983—Pittsburgh NFL	4			None		8	100	12.5	0	0	0	0
1984—Pittsburgh NFL	16			None		80	1395	17.4	11	11	66	1
1985—Pittsburgh NFL	16			None		75	937	12.5	5	5	30	0
Pro Totals—12 Years	142	9	64	7.1	0	462	7736	16.7	60	61	366	14

Additional pro statistics: Recovered one fumble, 1975 and 1978; advanced one lateral for 47 yards and a touchdown, 1976; recovered three fumbles, 1979.
Played in AFC Championship Game following 1974 through 1976, 1978, 1979 and 1984 seasons.
Played in NFL Championship Game following 1974, 1975, 1978 and 1979 seasons.
Played in Pro Bowl (NFL All-Star Game) following 1979, 1982 and 1984 seasons.

SYLVESTER STAMPS
Running Back—Atlanta Falcons
Born February 24, 1961, at Vicksburg, Miss.
Height, 5.07. Weight, 166.
High School—Vicksburg, Miss.
Attended Jackson State University.

Selected by Birmingham in 18th round (370th player selected) of 1984 USFL draft.
Signed by Birmingham Stallions, January 12, 1984.
Released by Birmingham Stallions, February 8, 1984; signed as free agent by Atlanta Falcons, May 2, 1984.
On injured reserve with hamstring injury, November 29 through remainder of 1984 season.
Released by Atlanta Falcons, September 2, 1985; re-signed by Falcons, December 6, 1985.
Released by Atlanta Falcons, December 7, 1985; re-signed by Falcons, December 10, 1985.

		——RUSHING——				PASS RECEIVING				—TOTAL—		
Year Club	G.	Att.	Yds.	Avg.	TD.	P.C.	Yds.	Avg.	TD.	TD.	Pts.	F.
1984—Atlanta NFL	10	3	15	5.0	0	4	48	12.0	0	0	0	2
1985—Atlanta NFL	2			None				None		0	0	0
Pro Totals—2 Years	12	3	15	5.0	0	4	48	12.0	0	0	0	2

	KICKOFF RETURNS				
Year Club	G.	No.	Yds.	Avg.	TD.
1984—Atlanta NFL	10	19	452	23.8	0
1985—Atlanta NFL	2	4	89	22.3	0
Pro Totals—2 Years	12	23	541	23.5	0

—DID YOU KNOW—
That Rich Camarillo of New England and the Eagles' Mike Horan both tied for the longest punt last season with a 75-yarder?

L. SCOTT STANKAVAGE

(Known by middle name.)

Quarterback—Denver Broncos

Born July 5, 1962, at Philadelphia, Pa.
Height, 6.01. Weight, 192.
High School—Buckingham, Pa., Central Bucks East.
Received bachelor of science degree in business administration
from University of North Carolina in 1984.

Selected by Philadelphia in 1984 USFL territorial draft.
Signed as free agent by Denver Broncos, May 2, 1984.
Released by Denver Broncos, August 20, 1984; re-signed by Broncos, September 5, 1984.
Released by Denver Broncos, November 13, 1984; re-signed by Broncos, December 27, 1984.
Released by Denver Broncos, August 20, 1985; re-signed by Broncos, August 27, 1985.
Released by Denver Broncos, September 2, 1985; re-signed by Broncos, February 6, 1986.

Year Club	G.	Att.	Cmp.	Pct.	Gain	T.P.	P.I.	Avg.	Att.	Yds.	Avg.	TD.	TD.	Pts.	F.
				—PASSING—					—RUSHING—				—TOTAL—		
1984—Denver NFL	1	18	4	22.2	58	0	1	3.22		None			0	0	0

Quarterback Rating Points: 1984 (17.4).
Additional pro statistics: Recovered one fumble, 1984.

WALTER STANLEY

Wide Receiver-Kick Returner—Green Bay Packers

Born November 5, 1962, at Chicago, Ill.
Height, 5.09. Weight, 180.
High School—Chicago, Ill., South Shore.
Attended University of Colorado and Mesa College (Colo.).

Selected by Memphis in 4th round (54th player selected) of 1985 USFL draft.
Selected by Green Bay in 4th round (98th player selected) of 1985 NFL draft.
Signed by Green Bay Packers, July 19, 1985.

Year Club	G.	No.	Yds.	Avg.	TD.	No.	Yds.	Avg.	TD.	TD.	Pts.	F.
		-PUNT RETURNS-				—KICKOFF RET.—				—TOTAL—		
1985—Green Bay NFL	13	14	179	12.8	0	9	212	23.6	0	0	0	2

ROHN TAYLOR STARK

(First name pronounced Ron).

Punter—Indianapolis Colts

Born May 4, 1959, at Minneapolis, Minn.
Height, 6.03. Weight, 199.
High School—Pine River, Minn.
Attended United States Air Force Academy Prep School and received degree
in finance from Florida State University.

Established NFL record for highest average, punting, career, 300 or more attempts (45.16).
Named as punter on The Sporting News College All-America Team, 1981.
Led NFL in punting yards with 4,124 in 1983.
Selected by Baltimore in 2nd round (34th player selected) of 1982 NFL draft.
Franchise transferred to Indianapolis, March 31, 1984.

Year Club	G.	No.	Avg.	Blk.
		—PUNTING—		
1982—Baltimore NFL	9	46	44.4	0
1983—Baltimore NFL	16	91	*45.3	0
1984—Indianapolis NFL	16	*98	44.7	0
1985—Indianapolis NFL	16	78	*45.9	*2
Pro Totals—4 Years	57	313	45.2	2

Additional pro statistics: Rushed once for eight yards, 1982 and 1983; attempted one pass with no completions, 1982, 1983 and 1985; fumbled once, 1982; rushed twice for no yards and attempted one pass with one interception, 1984; recovered one fumble, 1984 and 1985.
Played in Pro Bowl (NFL All-Star Game) following 1985 season.

STEPHEN DALE STARRING

First name pronounced Steff-in.

Wide Receiver-Kick Returner—New England Patriots

Born July 30, 1961, at Baton Rouge, La.
Height, 5.10. Weight, 172.
High School—Vinton, La.
Received degree in physical education from McNeese State University in 1985.

Selected by Washington in 3rd round (28th player selected) of 1983 USFL draft.
Selected by New England in 3rd round (74th player selected) of 1983 NFL draft.
Signed by New England Patriots, May 16, 1983.

Year Club	G.	P.C.	Yds.	Avg.	TD.	No.	Yds.	Avg.	TD.	TD.	Pts.	F.
		-PASS RECEIVING-				-PUNT RETURNS-				—TOTAL—		
1983—New England NFL	15	17	389	22.9	2		None			2	12	1
1984—New England NFL	16	46	657	14.3	4	10	73	7.3	0	4	24	1
1985—New England NFL	16	16	235	14.7	0	2	0	0.0	0	0	0	4
Pro Totals—3 Years	47	79	1281	16.2	6	12	73	6.1	0	6	36	6

KICKOFF RETURNS

Year Club	G.	No.	Yds.	Avg.TD.
1983—New England NFl	15		None	
1984—New England NFL	16		None	
1985—New England NFL	16	48	1012	21.1 0
Pro Totals—3 Years	47	48	1012	21.1 0

Additional pro statistics: Recovered one fumble for eight yards and rushed twice for minus 16 yards, 1984; recovered one fumble, 1985.
Played in AFC Championship Game following 1985 season.
Played in NFL Championship Game following 1985 season.

WILLIAM ANTHONY STEELS
(Known by middle name.)
Running Back—Buffalo Bills
Born January 8, 1959, at Sacramento, Calif.
Height, 5.09. Weight, 200.
High Schools—Riverside, Calif., John W. North; Jacksonville, Ark.; and Zoragoza, Spain.
Received bachelor of science degree in physical education from University of Nebraska.

Signed as free agent by Philadelphia Eagles, May 8, 1982.
Released by Philadelphia Eagles, August 16, 1982; signed by Boston Breakers, January 24, 1983.
On developmental squad, March 27 through March 30, 1983; activated, March 31, 1983.
On developmental squad, April 15 through April 27, 1983; activated, April 28, 1983.
Franchise transferred to New Orleans, October 18, 1983.
Franchise transferred to Portland, November 13, 1984.
Released by Portland Breakers, December 18, 1984; awarded on waivers to Orlando Renegades, December 26, 1984.
Released by Orlando Renegades, February 18, 1985; signed as free agent by San Diego Chargers, April 26, 1985.
Released by San Diego Chargers, October 18, 1985; awarded on waivers to Buffalo Bills, October 21, 1985.
On developmental squad for 4 games with Boston Breakers in 1983.

		—RUSHING—				PASS RECEIVING				—TOTAL—		
Year Club	G.	Att.	Yds.	Avg.	TD.	P.C.	Yds.	Avg.	TD.	TD.	Pts.	F.
1983—Boston USFL	15	55	237	4.3	1	20	148	7.4	3	4	24	4
1984—New Orleans USFL	18	37	141	3.8	0	14	66	4.7	0	0	0	3
1985—San Diego (6)-Buffalo (9) NFL	15	10	38	3.8	0	2	9	4.5	0	0	0	2
USFL Totals—2 Years	33	92	378	4.1	1	34	214	6.3	3	4	24	7
NFL Totals—1 Year	15	10	38	3.8	0	2	9	4.5	0	0	0	2
Pro Totals—3 Years	48	102	416	4.1	1	36	223	6.2	3	4	24	9

		—PUNT RETURNS—				—KICKOFF RET.—			
Year Club	G.	No.	Yds.	Avg.	TD.	No.	Yds.	Avg.TD.	
1983—Boston USFL	15	8	45	5.6	0	13	204	15.7	0
1984—New Orleans USFL	18		None			14	173	12.4	0
1985—San Diego (6)-Buffalo (9) NFL	15		None			30	561	18.7	0
USFL Totals—2 Years	33	8	45	5.6	0	27	377	14.0	0
NFL Totals—1 Year	15	0	0	0.0	0	30	561	18.7	0
Pro Totals—3 Years	48	8	45	5.6	0	57	938	16.5	0

Additional USFL statistics: Recovered three fumbles, 1984.
Additional NFL statistics: Recovered two fumbles, 1985.

JOHN STEEVENS
Center-Guard—San Francisco 49ers
Born December 8, 1960, at Claremont, Calif.
Height, 6.04. Weight, 265.
High School—Claremont, Calif.
Attended Citrus College and Fresno State University.

Signed as free agent by New England Patriots, February 25, 1985.
Released by New England Patriots, May 30, 1985; signed as free agent by San Francisco 49ers, July 20, 1985.
On injured reserve with knee injury, August 17 through entire 1985 season.

DEAN STEINKUHLER
Name pronounced Stine-cooler.
Guard—Houston Oilers
Born January 27, 1961, at Burr, Neb.
Height, 6.03. Weight, 273.
High School—Sterling, Neb.
Attended University of Nebraska.

Outland Trophy winner, 1983.
Named as guard on THE SPORTING NEWS College All-America Team, 1983.
Selected by Arizona in 6th round (116th player selected) of 1984 USFL draft.
Signed by Houston Oilers, April 30, 1984.
Selected officially by Houston in 1st round (2nd player selected) of 1984 NFL draft.
On injured reserve with knee injury, November 5 through remainder of 1984 season.
On injured reserve with knee injury, October 11 through December 19, 1985; activated, December 20, 1985.
Active for 6 games with Houston Oilers in 1985; did not play.
Houston NFL, 1984.
Games: 1984 (10).

MICHAEL IVER STENSRUD
(Mike)
Nose Tackle—Houston Oilers
Born February 19, 1956, at Forest City, Iowa.
Height, 6.05. Weight, 280.
High School—Lake Mills, Iowa.
Received degree in agricultural administration from Iowa State University.

Selected by Houston in 2nd round (31st player selected) of 1979 NFL draft.
On injured reserve with knee injury, September 21 through November 16, 1979; activated, November 17, 1979.
Houston NFL, 1979 through 1985.
Games: 1979 (6), 1980 (16), 1981 (16), 1982 (9), 1983 (16), 1984 (16), 1985 (16). Total—95.
Pro statistics: Recovered one fumble, 1981 through 1985; intercepted one pass for no yards, 1985.
Played in AFC Championship Game following 1979 season.

HAL FRANKLIN STEPHENS
Defensive End—Kansas City Chiefs
Born April 14, 1961, at Whiteville, N.C.
Height, 6.04. Weight, 252.
High School—Whiteville, N.C.
Attended East Carolina University.

Selected by Memphis in 4th round (80th player selected) of 1984 USFL draft.
USFL rights traded by Memphis Showboats to Oakland Invaders for running back Jack Holmes, January 30, 1984.
Selected by Los Angeles Rams in 5th round (133rd player selected) of 1984 NFL draft.
Signed by Los Angeles Rams, July 9, 1984.
On injured reserve with ankle injury, August 21 through entire 1984 season.
Released by Los Angeles Rams, August 27, 1985; signed as free agent by Detroit Lions, November 14, 1985.
Released by Detroit Lions, November 21, 1985; signed as free agent by Kansas City Chiefs, December 11, 1985.
Detroit (1)-Kansas City (1) NFL, 1985.
Games: 1985 (2).

DWIGHT EUGENE STEPHENSON
Center—Miami Dolphins
Born November 20, 1957, at Murfreesboro, N.C.
Height, 6.02. Weight, 255.
High School—Hampton, Va.
Attended University of Alabama.

Named to THE SPORTING NEWS NFL All-Star Team, 1984 and 1985.
Selected by Miami in 2nd round (48th player selected) of 1980 NFL draft.
Miami NFL, 1980 through 1985.
Games: 1980 (16), 1981 (16), 1982 (9), 1983 (16), 1984 (16), 1985 (16). Total—89.
Pro statistics: Recovered one fumble, 1980 and 1984.
Played in AFC Championship Game following 1982, 1984 and 1985 seasons.
Played in NFL Championship Game following 1982 and 1984 seasons.
Played in Pro Bowl (NFL All-Star Game) following 1983 through 1985 seasons.

MARK STEVENSON
Guard-Center—Detroit Lions
Born February 24, 1956, at Waukegan, Ill.
Height, 6.03. Weight, 285.
High School—Rock Island, Ill.
Attended University of Missouri and Western Illinois University.

Signed as free agent by Seattle Seahawks, May 15, 1979.
Released by Seattle Seahawks after failing physical, July 15, 1979; signed as free agent by Chicago Bears, May 7, 1982.
Released by Chicago Bears, July 27, 1982; signed by Chicago Blitz, January 26, 1983.
On injured reserve with knee injury, April 13 through remainder of 1983 season.
Franchise transferred to Arizona, September 30, 1983.
Played with Chicago Fire of American Football Association, 1981.
On reserve/non-football injury with knee injury, February 20 through April 19, 1984; activated, April 20, 1984.
On developmental squad, April 20 through May 11, 1984.
On injured reserve with knee injury, May 12 through remainder of 1984 season.
Protected in merger of Arizona Wranglers and Oklahoma Outlaws, December 6, 1984.
Traded by Arizona Outlaws to Memphis Showboats for defensive back Bryan Howard, January 21, 1985.
Released injured by Memphis Showboats, February 18, 1985; signed as free agent by San Diego Chargers, April 26, 1985.
Released by San Diego Chargers, August 26, 1985; signed as free agent by Detroit Lions, December 7, 1985.
On developmental squad for 3 games with Arizona Wranglers in 1984.
Chicago USFL, 1983; Detroit NFL, 1985.
Games: 1983 (6), 1985 (2). Total—8.

—DID YOU KNOW—
That when the Chargers picked James FitzPatrick in the first round in the 1986 NFL draft, he became the 15th offensive lineman selected from Southern California in round one since 1968?

ARTHUR BARRY STILL
(Art)
Defensive End—Kansas City Chiefs
Born December 5, 1955, at Camden, N.J.
Height, 6.07. Weight, 257.
High School—Camden, N.J.
Received bachelor of arts degree in general studies from University of Kentucky in 1978.
Named as defensive end on THE SPORTING NEWS College All-America Team, 1977.
Named to THE SPORTING NEWS NFL All-Star Team, 1980.
Selected by Kansas City in 1st round (2nd player selected) of 1978 NFL draft.
On injured reserve with knee injury, September 23 through October 30, 1981; activated, October 31, 1981.
On injured reserve with knee injury, November 5 through remainder of 1985 season.
Kansas City NFL, 1978 through 1985.
Games: 1978 (16), 1979 (16), 1980 (16), 1981 (11), 1982 (9), 1983 (15), 1984 (16), 1985 (9). Total—108.
Pro statistics: Recovered one fumble, 1978, 1980, 1981 and 1983; recovered one fumble for 13 yards, 1979; recovered
ne fumble for four yards, 1982; recovered one fumble for three yards, 1984; recovered two fumbles, 1985.
Played in Pro Bowl (NFL All-Star Game) following 1980 through 1982 and 1984 seasons.

KENNETH LEE STILLS
(Ken)
Defensive Back—Green Bay Packers
Born September 6, 1963, at Oceanside, Calif.
Height, 5.10. Weight, 185.
High School—Oceanside, Calif., El Camino.
Attended El Camino College and University of Wisconsin.
Selected by Jacksonville in 1985 USFL territorial draft.
Selected by Green Bay in 8th round (209th player selected) of 1985 NFL draft.
Signed by Green Bay Packers, July 19, 1985.
Released by Green Bay Packers, September 2, 1985; re-signed by Packers, October 30, 1985.
Green Bay NFL, 1985.
Games: 1985 (8).
Pro statistics: Returned one kickoff for 14 yards, 1985.

GREG SCOTT STORR
Linebacker—New Orleans Saints
Born October 16, 1960, at Reading, Pa.
Height, 6.02. Weight, 225.
High School—West Lawn, Pa., Wilson.
Received bachelor of science degree in speech and
communications from Boston College in 1982.
Selected by Minnesota in 6th round (147th player selected) of 1982 NFL draft.
On non-football injury list with shoulder separation, July 29 through entire 1982 season.
Released by Minnesota Vikings, August 29, 1983; signed by New Orleans Breakers, October 26, 1983.
On injured reserve, February 20 through March 28, 1984; activated, March 29, 1984.
On developmental squad, March 29 through April 13, 1984; activated, April 14, 1984.
Franchise transferred to Portland, November 13, 1984.
Released by Portland Breakers, July 31, 1985; signed as free agent by New Orleans Saints, May 17, 1986.
On developmental squad for 2 games with New Orleans Breakers in 1984.
New Orleans USFL, 1984; Portland USFL, 1985.
Games: 1984 (11), 1985 (18). Total—29.
Pro statistics: Recovered one fumble, 1984; intercepted one pass for 11 yards, credited with three sacks for 19
yards and returned one kickoff for two yards, 1985.

JEFF OWEN STOVER
Defensive End—San Francisco 49ers
Born May 22, 1958, at Corning, Calif.
Height, 6.05. Weight, 275.
High School—Corning, Calif., Union.
Attended University of Oregon.
Signed as free agent by San Francisco 49ers, April 20, 1982.
On injured reserve with knee injury, September 4 through November 15, 1984; activated, November 16, 1984.
San Francisco NFL, 1982 through 1985.
Games: 1982 (9), 1983 (16), 1984 (6), 1985 (16). Total—47.
Pro statistics: Recovered one fumble, 1982, 1983 and 1985.
Played in NFC Championship Game following 1983 and 1984 seasons.
Played in NFL Championship Game following 1984 season.

STEPHEN MICHAEL STRACHAN
(Steve)
Running Back—Los Angeles Raiders
Born March 22, 1963, at Everett, Mass.
Height, 6.01. Weight, 221.
High School—Burlington, Mass.
Received bachelor of science degree in finance from Boston College in 1985.
Selected by Los Angeles Raiders in 11th round (303rd player selected) of 1985 NFL draft.

Signed by Los Angeles Raiders, June 28, 1985.
Released by Los Angeles Raiders, August 27, 1985; re-signed by Raiders, September 23, 1985.
On injured reserve with hamstring injury, October 23 through remainder of 1985 season.
Los Angeles Raiders NFL, 1985.
Games: 1985 (4).
Pro statistics: Rushed twice for one yard, 1985.

TIMOTHY T. STRACKA
(Tim)
Tight End—Chicago Bears
Born September 27, 1959, at Madison, Wis.
Height, 6.03. Weight, 225.
High School—Madison, Wis., West.
Received bachelor of business administration degree in finance and risk
management from University of Wisconsin in 1983.

Selected by Cleveland in 6th round (145th player selected) of 1983 NFL draft.
On injured reserve with neck injury, August 29 through October 5, 1984; activated, October 6, 1984.
On injured reserve with broken ankle, November 14 through remainder of 1984 season.
Left Cleveland Browns camp voluntarily and released, July 30, 1985; signed as free agent by Chicago Bears, April 6, 1986.

		—PASS RECEIVING—			
Year Club	G.	P.C.	Yds.	Avg.	TD.
1983—Cleveland NFL..............	13	1	12	12.0	0
1984—Cleveland NFL..............	6	1	15	15.0	0
Pro Totals—2 Years...........	19	2	27	13.5	0

THOMAS STRAUTHERS
(Tom)
Defensive End—Philadelphia Eagles
Born April 6, 1961, at Wesson, Miss.
Height, 6.04. Weight, 265.
High School—Brookhaven, Miss.
Attended Jackson State University.

Selected by Oakland in 21st round (247th player selected) of 1983 USFL draft.
Selected by Philadelphia in 10th round (258th player selected) of 1983 NFL draft.
Signed by Philadelphia Eagles, June 15, 1983.
On injured reserve with broken hand, August 16 through November 23, 1983; activated by Philadelphia Eagles after clearing procedural waivers, November 25, 1983.
Philadelphia NFL, 1983 through 1985.
Games: 1983 (4), 1984 (16), 1985 (16). Total—36.
Pro statistics: Returned one kickoff for 12 yards, 1984.

RICHARD GENE STRENGER
(Rich)
Offensive Tackle—Detroit Lions
Born March 10, 1960, at Port Washington, Wis.
Height, 6.07. Weight, 276.
High School—Grafton, Wis.
Received bachelor of science degree in literature science and art from University of Michigan in 1983.

Selected by Michigan in 1983 USFL territorial draft.
Selected by Detroit in 2nd round (40th player selected) of 1983 NFL draft.
Signed by Detroit Lions, July 4, 1983.
On injured reserve with knee injury, September 4 through remainder of 1984 season.
Detroit NFL, 1983 through 1985.
Games: 1983 (16), 1984 (1), 1985 (13). Total—30.

DONALD JOSEPH STROCK
(Don)
Quarterback—Miami Dolphins
Born November 27, 1950, at Pottstown, Pa.
Height, 6.05. Weight, 220.
High School—Pottstown, Pa., Owen J. Roberts.
Received bachelor of science degree in distributive direction from
Virginia Technical University in 1973.
Brother of Dave Strock, former kicker with Houston Oilers, Miami Dolphins,
Florida Blazers, Shreveport Steamer and Washington Redskins.

Selected by Miami in 5th round (111th player selected) of 1973 NFL draft.
On did not report list, August 16 through September 4, 1983.
Reported and granted roster exemption, September 5, 1983; activated, September 9, 1983.
Member of Miami Dolphins' taxi squad, 1973.

		—————PASSING—————							—RUSHING—				—TOTAL—		
Year Club	G.	Att.	Cmp.	Pct.	Gain	T.P.	P.I.	Avg.	Att.	Yds.	Avg.	TD.	TD.	Pts.	F.
1974—Miami NFL......................	1			None					1	—7	—7.0	0	0	0	0
1975—Miami NFL......................	6	45	26	57.8	230	2	2	5.11	6	38	6.3	1	1	6	1

Year Club	G.	PASSING Att.	Cmp.	Pct.	Gain	T.P.	P.I.	Avg.	RUSHING Att.	Yds.	Avg.	TD.	TOTAL TD.	Pts.	F.
1976—Miami NFL	4	47	21	44.7	359	3	2	7.64	2	13	6.5	1	1	6	1
1977—Miami NFL	4	4	2	50.0	12	0	1	3.00	None				0	0	0
1978—Miami NFL	16	135	72	53.3	825	12	6	6.11	10	23	2.3	0	0	0	4
1979—Miami NFL	16	100	56	56.0	830	6	6	8.30	3	18	6.0	0	0	0	3
1980—Miami NFL	16	62	30	48.4	313	1	5	5.05	1	—3	—3.0	0	0	0	1
1981—Miami NFL	16	130	79	60.8	901	6	8	6.93	14	—26	—1.9	0	0	0	0
1982—Miami NFL	9	55	30	54.5	306	2	5	5.56	3	—9	—3.0	0	0	0	1
1983—Miami NFL	15	52	34	65.4	403	4	1	7.75	6	—16	—2.7	0	0	0	0
1984—Miami NFL	16	6	4	66.7	27	0	0	4.50	2	—5	—2.5	0	0	0	1
1985—Miami NFL	16	9	7	77.8	141	1	0	15.67	2	—6	—3.0	0	0	0	0
Pro Totals—12 Years	135	645	361	56.0	4347	37	36	6.74	50	20	0.4	2	2	12	12

Quarterback Rating Points: 1975 (67.9), 1976 (74.6), 1977 (16.7), 1978 (83.3), 1979 (78.3), 1980 (35.1), 1981 (71.1), 1982 (44.8), 1983 (106.5), 1984 (76.4), 1985 (155.8). Total—72.5.

Additional pro statistics: Recovered one fumble, 1975, 1978 and 1983; fumbled four times for minus five yards, 1978; fumbled once for minus three yards, 1982; fumbled once for minus two yards, 1984.

Played in AFC Championship Game following 1982, 1984 and 1985 seasons.

Played in NFL Championship Game following 1982 and 1984 seasons.

VINCE STROTH
Offensive Tackle—San Francisco 49ers

Born November 25, 1960, at San Jose, Calif.

Height, 6.03. Weight, 259.

High School—San Jose, Calif., Bellarmine.

Attended Brigham Young University.

Selected by Arziona in 13th round (146th player selected) of 1983 USFL draft.

Signed by Arizona Wranglers, January 27, 1983.

On developmental squad, March 4 through March 31, 1983; activated, April 1, 1983.

Franchise transferred to Chicago, September 30, 1983.

Franchise disbanded, November 20, 1984.

Selected by New Jersey Generals in USFL dispersal draft, December 6, 1984.

Granted free agency, August 1, 1985; signed by San Francisco 49ers, December 18, 1985.

On developmental squad for 4 games with Arizona Wranglers in 1983.

Arizona USFL 1983; Chicago USFL, 1984; New Jersey USFL, 1985; San Francisco NFL, 1985.

Games: 1983 (14), 1984 (6), 1985 USFL (18), 1985 NFL (1). Total USFL—38. Total Pro—39.

Pro statistics: Returned two kickoffs for 25 yards and recovered one fumble for four yards, 1984.

JAMES STUCKEY
(Jim)
Defensive End—San Francisco 49ers

Born June 21, 1958, at Cayce, S.C.

Height, 6.04. Weight, 251.

High School—Columbia, S.C., Airport.

Attended Clemson University.

Named as defensive end on THE SPORTING NEWS College All-America Team, 1979.

Selected by San Francisco in 1st round (20th player selected) of 1980 NFL draft.

Released by San Francisco 49ers, October 18, 1985, re-signed by 49ers, October 24, 1985.

San Francisco NFL, 1980 through 1985.

Games: 1980 (16), 1981 (15), 1982 (9), 1983 (16), 1984 (16), 1985 (15). Total—87.

Pro statistics: Credited with one safety, 1980; recovered one fumble, 1981, 1982 and 1985.

Played in NFC Championship Game following 1981, 1983 and 1984 seasons.

Played in NFL Championship Game following 1981 and 1984 seasons.

MARK WAYNE STUDAWAY
Defensive End—Tampa Bay Buccaneers

Born September 20, 1960, at Memphis, Tenn.

Height, 6.03. Weight, 269.

High School—Memphis, Tenn., South Side.

Attended University of Tennessee.

Selected by Memphis in 1984 USFL territorial draft.

Selected by Houston in 4th round (85th player selected) of 1984 NFL draft.

Signed by Houston Oilers, July 7, 1984.

On injured reserve with knee injury, October 12 through remainder of 1984 season.

Released by Houston Oilers, August 30, 1985; signed as free agent by Tampa Bay Buccaneers, November 5, 1985.

Houston NFL, 1984; Tampa Bay NFL, 1985.

Games: 1984 (6), 1985 (6). Total—12.

DAVID DERALD STUDDARD
(Dave)
Offensive Tackle—Denver Broncos

Born November 22, 1955, at San Antonio, Tex.

Height, 6.04. Weight, 260.

High School—Pearsall, Tex.

Received degree in physical education from University of Texas.

Brother of Les Studdard, center with Kansas City Chiefs and Houston Oilers, 1982 and 1983; nephew of Howard Fest, guard with Cincinnati Bengals and Tampa Bay Buccaneers, 1968 through 1976.

Selected by Baltimore in 9th round (245th player selected) of 1978 NFL draft.
Released by Baltimore Colts, August 30, 1978; signed as free agent by Denver Broncos, January 31, 1979.
Denver NFL, 1979 through 1985.
Games: 1979 (16), 1980 (16), 1981 (16), 1982 (9), 1983 (16), 1984 (16), 1985 (16). Total—105.
Pro statistics: Caught one pass for two yards and a touchdown, 1979; recovered one fumble, 1980 and 1983; caught one pass for 10 yards, 1981; returned two kickoffs for eight yards, 1983; caught one pass for minus four yards, 1984; recovered two fumbles, 1985.

JOHN SCOTT STUDWELL
(Known by middle name.)
Linebacker—Minnesota Vikings
Born August 27, 1954, at Evansville, Ind.
Height, 6.02. Weight, 230.
High School—Evansville, Ind., Harrison.
Attended University of Illinois.
Selected by Minnesota in 9th round (250th player selected) of 1977 NFL draft.

		—INTERCEPTIONS—			
Year Club	G.	No.	Yds.	Avg.	TD.
1977—Minnesota NFL............	14	1	4	4.0	0
1978—Minnesota NFL............	13		None		
1979—Minnesota NFL............	14	1	18	18.0	0
1980—Minnesota NFL............	16	1	4	4.0	0
1981—Minnesota NFL............	16		None		
1982—Minnesota NFL............	8	1	3	3.0	0
1983—Minnesota NFL............	16		None		
1984—Minnesota NFL............	16	1	20	20.0	0
1985—Minnesota NFL............	14	2	20	10.0	0
Pro Totals—9 Years...........	127	7	69	9.9	0

Additional pro statistics: Recovered one fumble for six yards and returned one kickoff for no yards, 1979; recovered one fumble, 1980, 1982 and 1983; recovered three fumbles, 1981.
Played in NFC Championship Game following 1977 season.

MATTHEW JEROME SUHEY
(Matt)
Fullback—Chicago Bears
Born July 7, 1958, at Bellefonte, Pa.
Height, 5.11. Weight, 217.
High School—State College, Pa.
Received bachelor of science degree in marketing from Penn State University in 1980.
Grandson of Bob Higgins, end with Canton Bulldogs, 1920 and 1921, and son of Steve Suhey,
guard with Pittsburgh Steelers, 1948 and 1949.
Selected by Chicago in 2nd round (46th player selected) of 1980 NFL draft.

		—RUSHING—				PASS RECEIVING				—TOTAL—		
Year Club	G.	Att.	Yds.	Avg.	TD.	P.C.	Yds.	Avg.	TD.	TD.	Pts.	F.
1980—Chicago NFL	16	22	45	2.0	0	7	60	8.6	0	0	0	1
1981—Chicago NFL	15	150	521	3.5	3	33	168	5.1	0	3	18	3
1982—Chicago NFL	9	70	206	2.9	3	36	333	9.3	0	3	18	2
1983—Chicago NFL	16	149	681	4.6	4	49	429	8.8	1	5	30	5
1984—Chicago NFL	16	124	424	3.4	4	42	312	7.4	2	6	36	6
1985—Chicago NFL	16	115	471	4.1	1	33	295	8.9	1	2	12	2
Pro Totals—6 Years....................................	88	630	2348	3.7	15	200	1597	8.0	4	19	114	19

		KICKOFF RETURNS			
Year Club	G.	No.	Yds.	Avg.	TD.
1980—Chicago NFL	16	19	406	21.4	0
1981—Chicago NFL	15		None		
1982—Chicago NFL	9		None		
1983—Chicago NFL	16		None		
1984—Chicago NFL	16		None		
1985—Chicago NFL	16		None		
Pro Totals—6 Years..........	88	19	406	21.4	0

Additional pro statistics: Returned one punt for four yards, 1980; recovered three fumbles, 1981; recovered one fumble, 1982 and 1985; attempted one pass with one completion for 74 yards and a touchdown, 1983; attempted one pass with no completions and recovered two fumbles, 1984.
Played in NFC Championship Game following 1984 and 1985 seasons.
Played in NFL Championship Game following 1985 season.

CARL JEFFERY SULLIVAN
Defensive End—San Francisco 49ers
Born April 30, 1962, at San Jose, Calif.
Height, 6.04. Weight, 230.
High School—San Francisco, Calif., Abraham Lincoln.
Attended City College of San Francisco and San Jose State University.
Selected by Oakland in 1984 USFL territorial draft.
Signed by Oakland Invaders, January 14, 1984.
Released by Oakland Invaders, February 20, 1984; re-signed by Invaders, March 23, 1984.

On developmental squad, April 16 through May 10, 1984; activated, May 11, 1984.
On developmental squad, May 25 through June 7, 1984; activated, June 8, 1984.
Not protected in merger of Oakland Invaders and Michigan Panthers; selected by Oakland Invaders in USFL dispersal draft, December 6, 1984.
Released by Oakland Invaders, August 2, 1985; signed as free agent by San Francisco 49ers, April 8, 1986.
On developmental squad for 6 games with Oakland Invaders in 1984.
Oakland USFL, 1984 and 1985.
Games: 1984 (8), 1985 (18). Total—26.
Pro statistics: Credited with one sack for five yards and recovered fumble in end zone for a touchdown, 1984; recovered two fumbles, 1985.
Played in USFL Championship Game following 1985 season.

IVORY ULYSSES SULLY
Defensive Back—Tampa Bay Buccaneers
Born June 20, 1957, at Salisbury, Md.
Height, 6.00. Weight, 201.
High School—Leonia, N.J.
Received degree in physical education from University of Delaware.

Signed as free agent by Los Angeles Rams, June, 1979.
On injured reserve with ankle injury, August 14 through October 18, 1979; re-signed after clearing procedural waivers, October 20, 1979.
Released by Los Angeles Rams, October 31, 1979; re-signed by Rams, November 7, 1979.
Granted free agency, February 1, 1985; re-signed by Rams and traded to Tampa Bay Buccaneers for 8th round pick on 1986 draft, August 1, 1985.
Los Angeles Rams NFL, 1979 through 1984; Tampa Bay NFL, 1985.
Games: 1979 (6), 1980 (16), 1981 (16), 1982 (9), 1983 (16), 1984 (16), 1985 (16). Total—95.
Played in NFC Championship Game following 1979 season.
Played in NFL Championship Game following 1979 season.
Pro statistics: Returned four kickoffs for 36 yards, recovered two fumbles and fumbled once, 1980 and 1981; returned three kickoffs for 31 yards, 1981; returned five kickoffs for 84 yards, 1982; recovered one fumble, 1983, 1984 and 1985; credited with one safety and returned one kickoff for three yards, 1984; intercepted one pass for 20 yards, 1985.

DONALD O. SUMMERS
(Don)
Tight End—Green Bay Packers
Born February 22, 1961, at Grants Pass, Ore.
Height, 6.04. Weight, 230.
High Schools—Eagle Point, Ore., and Medford, Ore.
Attended Oregon Tech and Boise State University.

Signed as free agent by Oakland Invaders, January 8, 1984.
Released by Oakland Invaders, January 30, 1984; signed as free agent by Denver Broncos, May 2, 1984.
Released by Denver Broncos, August 26, 1985; re-signed by Broncos, September 17, 1985.
Released by Denver Broncos, October 4, 1985; signed as free agent by Green Bay Packers, May 2, 1986.

		—PASS RECEIVING—			
Year Club	G.	P.C.	Yds.	Avg.	TD.
1984—Denver NFL	16	3	32	10.7	0
1985—Denver NFL	2		None		
Pro Totals—2 Years	18	3	32	10.7	0

Additional pro statistics: Recovered one fumble, 1984.

JOHN WESLEY SWAIN
Cornerback—Pittsburgh Steelers
Born September 4, 1959, at Miami, Fla.
Height, 6.01. Weight, 195.
High School—Miami, Fla., Carol City.
Received degree in sociology from University of Miami (Fla.).

Selected by Minnesota in 4th round (101st player selected) of 1981 NFL draft.
Released by Minnesota Vikings, September 2, 1985; awarded on waivers to Miami Dolphins, September 3, 1985.
Released by Miami Dolphins, October 19, 1985; signed as free agent by Pittsburgh Steelers, October 22, 1985.

		—INTERCEPTIONS—		
Year Club	G.	No.	Yds.	Avg.TD.
1981—Minnesota NFL	12	2	18	9.0 0
1982—Minnesota NFL	9	2	20	10.0 0
1983—Minnesota NFL	14	6	12	2.0 0
1984—Minnesota NFL	15	2	20	10.0 0
1985—Mia. (6)-Pitt. (9) NFL..	15	2	4	2.0 0
Pro Totals—5 Years	65	14	74	5.3 0

Additional pro statistics: Recovered one fumble, 1981 and 1984.

KARL VANCE SWANKE
Offensive Tackle-Center—Green Bay Packers
Born December 29, 1957, at Elmhurst, Ill.
Height, 6.06. Weight, 262.
High School—Newington, Conn.
Attended Boston College.

Selected by Green Bay in 6th round (143rd player selected) of 1980 NFL draft.
On injured reserve with knee injury, September 29 through remainder of 1981 season.
On injured reserve with knee injury, December 29 through remainder of 1982 season.
On injured reserve with knee injury, December 18 through remainder of 1985 season.
Green Bay NFL, 1980 through 1985.
Games: 1980 (16), 1981 (4), 1982 (8), 1983 (16), 1984 (15), 1985 (15). Total—74.
Pro statistics: Caught one pass for two yards and a touchdown 1981; recovered one fumble, 1982; recovered two fumbles, 1983.

CALVIN EUGENE SWEENEY
Wide Receiver—Pittsburgh Steelers
Born January 12, 1955, at Riverside, Calif.
Height, 6.02. Weight, 190.
High School—Riverside, Calif., Perris Union.
Attended Riverside Junior College, University of California at Riverside and received
business degree from University of Southern California.

Selected by Pittsburgh in 4th round (110th player selected) of 1979 NFL draft.
On injured reserve with foot injury, August 13 through entire 1979 season.
Released by Pittsburgh Steelers, September 1, 1980; re-signed by Steelers, September 8, 1980.
On injured reserve with pulled hamstring, September 4 through October 18, 1984; activated, October 19, 1984.

		——PASS RECEIVING——			
Year Club	G.	P.C.	Yds.	Avg.	TD.
1980—Pittsburgh NFL	15	12	282	23.5	1
1981—Pittsburgh NFL	14	2	53	26.5	0
1982—Pittsburgh NFL	7	5	50	10.0	0
1983—Pittsburgh NFL	16	39	577	14.8	5
1984—Pittsburgh NFL	9	2	25	12.5	0
1985—Pittsburgh NFL	16	16	234	14.6	0
Pro Totals—6 Years	77	76	1221	16.1	6

Additional pro statistics: Returned three kickoffs for 42 yards, 1980; fumbled once, 1981; rushed once for minus two yards, 1983; recovered one fumble, 1985.
Played in AFC Championship Game following 1984 season.

JAMES JOSEPH SWEENEY
(Jim)
Guard-Center—New York Jets
Born August 8, 1962, at Pittsburgh, Pa.
Height, 6.04. Weight, 266.
High School—Pittsburgh, Pa., Seton LaSalle.
Attended University of Pittsburgh.

Selected by Pittsburgh in 1984 USFL territorial draft.
Selected by New York Jets in 2nd round (37th player selected) of 1984 NFL draft.
Signed by New York Jets, July 12, 1984.
New York Jets NFL, 1984 and 1985.
Games: 1984 (10), 1985 (16). Total—26.

DENNIS NEAL SWILLEY
Center—Minnesota Vikings
Born June 28, 1955, at Bossier City, La.
Height, 6.03. Weight, 245.
High School—Pine Bluff, Ark.
Attended Texas A&M University and received degree in interior
design/architectural design from North Texas State University.

Selected by Minnesota in 2nd round (55th player selected) of 1977 NFL draft.
On reserve/retired list entire 1984 season.
Minnesota NFL, 1977 through 1983 and 1985.
Games: 1977 (14), 1978 (14), 1979 (16), 1980 (16), 1981 (16), 1982 (9), 1983 (16), 1985 (16). Total—117.
Pro statistics: Returned one kickoff for no yards and fumbled once, 1977; recovered one fumble, 1979, 1982 and 1985.
Played in NFC Championship Game following 1977 season.

DARRYL VICTOR TALLEY
Linebacker—Buffalo Bills
Born July 10, 1960, at Cleveland, O.
Height, 6.04. Weight, 227.
High School—East Cleveland, O., Shaw.
Received degree in physical education from West Virginia University.
Brother of John Talley, quarterback at West Virginia University.

Named as linebacker on THE SPORTING NEWS College All-America Team, 1982.
Selected by New Jersey in 2nd round (24th player selected) of 1983 USFL draft.
Selected by Buffalo in 2nd round (39th player selected) of 1983 NFL draft.
Signed by Buffalo Bills, June 14, 1983.
Buffalo NFL, 1983 through 1985.
Games: 1983 (16), 1984 (16), 1985 (16). Total—48.
Pro statistics: Returned two kickoffs for nine yards and recovered two fumbles for six yards, 1983; recovered one fumble and intercepted one pass for no yards, 1984.

ROBERT STANLEY TALLEY
(Stan)
Punter—Cleveland Browns

Born September 5, 1958, at Dallas, Tex.
Height, 6.05. Weight, 225.
High School—Torrance, Calif., West Torrance.
Attended El Camino Junior College and received degree in marketing
from Texas Christian University in 1982.

Named punter on THE SPORTING NEWS USFL All-Star Team, 1985.
Led USFL in punting yardage with 3,825 in 1983 and 4,569 in 1984.
Signed as free agent by Atlanta Falcons, May 5, 1981.
Released by Atlanta Falcons, August 23, 1981; signed as free agent by New Orleans Saints, May 6, 1982.
Released by New Orleans Saints, September 6, 1982; signed by Oakland Invaders, January 11, 1983.
Protected in merger of Oakland Invaders and Michigan Panthers, December 6, 1984.
Released by Oakland Invaders, August 28, 1985; signed as free agent by Cleveland Browns, April 21, 1986.

			——PUNTING——		
Year	Club	G.	No.	Avg.	Blk.
1983—Oakland USFL		18	87	*44.0	....
1984—Oakland USFL		18	*110	41.5	....
1985—Oakland USFL		18	66	*44.3	....
Pro Totals—3 Years		54	263	43.0	....

Additional pro statistics: Fumbled twice and rushed once for no yards, 1983; recovered one fumble, 1984.
Played in USFL Championship Game following 1985 season.

STEVE TASKER
Kick Returner—Houston Oilers

Born April 10, 1962, at Leoti, Kan.
Height, 5.09. Weight, 185.
High School—Leoti, Kan., Wichita County.
Attended Dodge City Community College and Northwestern University.

Selected by Houston in 9th round (226th player selected) of 1985 NFL draft.
Signed by Houston Oilers, June 14, 1985.
On injured reserve with knee injury, October 23 through remainder of 1985 season.

			——RUSHING——				PASS RECEIVING				—TOTAL—		
Year	Club	G.	Att.	Yds.	Avg.	TD.	P.C.	Yds.	Avg.	TD.	TD.	Pts.	F.
1985—Houston NFL		7	2	16	8.0	0	2	19	9.5	0	0	0	0

			KICKOFF RETURNS			
Year	Club	G.	No.	Yds.	Avg.	TD.
1985—Houston NFL		7	17	447	26.3	0

MOSIULA TATUPU
(Mosi)
Fullback—New England Patriots

Born April 26, 1955, at Pago Pago, American Samoa
Height, 6.00. Weight, 227.
High School—Honolulu, Haw., Punahou.
Attended University of Southern California.
Son of Mosi Tatupu, former Samoan boxing champ; and cousin of Terry Tautolo,
linebacker with Philadelphia Eagles, San Francisco 49ers, Detroit Lions and Miami Dolphins,
1976 through 1984; and John Tautolo, offensive tackle with Portland Breakers, 1985.

Selected by New England in 8th round (215th player selected) of 1978 NFL draft.

			——RUSHING——				PASS RECEIVING				—TOTAL—		
Year	Club	G.	Att.	Yds.	Avg.	TD.	P.C.	Yds.	Avg.	TD.	TD.	Pts.	F.
1978—New England NFL		16	3	6	2.0	0	None				0	0	0
1979—New England NFL		16	23	71	3.1	0	2	9	4.5	0	0	0	0
1980—New England NFL		16	33	97	2.9	3	4	27	6.8	0	3	18	0
1981—New England NFL		16	38	201	5.3	2	12	132	11.0	1	3	18	2
1982—New England NFL		9	30	168	5.6	0	None				0	0	0
1983—New England NFL		16	106	578	5.5	4	10	97	9.7	1	5	30	1
1984—New England NFL		16	133	553	4.2	4	16	159	9.9	0	4	24	4
1985—New England NFL		16	47	152	3.2	2	2	16	8.0	0	2	12	1
Pro Totals—8 Years		121	413	1826	4.4	15	46	440	9.6	2	17	102	8

Additional pro statistics: Returned one kickoff for 17 yards, 1978; returned three kickoffs for 15 yards, 1979;
recovered three fumbles, 1981; recovered one fumble, 1983 through 1985; returned one kickoff for nine yards, 1984.
Played in AFC Championship Game following 1985 season.
Played in NFL Championship Game following 1985 season.

TERRY WAYNE TAUSCH
Offensive Tackle-Guard—Minnesota Vikings

Born February 5, 1959, at New Braunfels, Tex.
Height, 6.05. Weight, 270.
High School—New Braunfels, Tex.
Received bachelor of business administration degree in marketing from
University of Texas in 1981.

Named as offensive tackle on THE SPORTING NEWS College All-America Team, 1981.
Selected by Minnesota in 2nd round (39th player selected) of 1982 NFL draft.
Minnesota NFL, 1982 through 1985.
Games: 1982 (2), 1983 (10), 1984 (16), 1985 (16). Total—44.

JOHNNY TAYLOR
Linebacker—Atlanta Falcons
Born June 21, 1960, at Seattle, Wash.
Height, 6.04. Weight, 235.
High School—Garfield, Wash.
Attended Wenatchee Valley Junior College and University of Hawaii.

Signed as free agent by Atlanta Falcons, May 2, 1984.
Released by Atlanta Falcons, August 21, 1984; re-signed by Falcons after clearing procedural waivers, December 6, 1984.
Atlanta NFL, 1984 and 1985.
Games: 1984 (2), 1985 (15). Total—17.
Pro statistics: Recovered one fumble, 1985.

KENNETH DANIEL TAYLOR
(Ken)
Cornerback—Chicago Bears
Born September 2, 1963, at San Jose, Calif.
Height, 6.01. Weight, 185.
High School—San Jose, Calif., Yerba Buena.
Attended Oregon State University.

Signed as free agent by Chicago Bears, May 3, 1985.

| | | -INTERCEPTIONS- | | | | -PUNT RETURNS- | | | | —TOTAL— | | |
Year Club	G.	No.	Yds.	Avg.	TD.	No.	Yds.	Avg.	TD.	TD.	Pts.	F.
1985—Chicago NFL	16	3	28	9.3	0	25	198	7.9	0	0	0	3

Additional pro statistics: Returned one kickoff for 18 yards and recovered one fumble, 1985.
Played in NFC Championship Game following 1985 season.
Played in NFL Championship Game following 1985 season.

LAWRENCE TAYLOR
Linebacker—New York Giants
Born February 4, 1959, at Williamsburg, Va.
Height, 6.03. Weight, 243.
High School—Williamsburg, Va., Lafayette.
Attended University of North Carolina.

Named to THE SPORTING NEWS NFL All-Star Team, 1981 and 1983 through 1985.
Named as linebacker on THE SPORTING NEWS College All-America Team, 1980.
Selected by New York Giants in 1st round (2nd player selected) of 1981 NFL draft.

| | | ——INTERCEPTIONS—— | | | |
Year Club	G.	No.	Yds.	Avg.	TD.
1981—N.Y. Giants NFL	16	1	1	1.0	0
1982—N.Y. Giants NFL	9	1	97	97.0	*1
1983—N.Y. Giants NFL	16	2	10	5.0	0
1984—N.Y. Giants NFL	16	1	—1	—1.0	0
1985—N.Y. Giants NFL	16			None	
Pro Totals—5 Years	73	5	107	21.4	1

Additional pro statistics: Recovered one fumble for four yards, 1981; fumbled once, 1981 and 1983; recovered two fumbles for three yards, 1983; recovered two fumbles for 25 yards, 1985.
Played in Pro Bowl (NFL All-Star Game) following 1981 through 1985 seasons.

LENNY MOORE TAYLOR
Wide Receiver—Indianapolis Colts
Born February 15, 1961, at Miami, Fla.
Height, 5.10. Weight, 179.
High School—Miami, Fla., Southridge.
Attended University of Tennessee.

Selected by Memphis in 1984 USFL territorial draft.
Selected by Green Bay at 12th round (313th player selected) of 1984 NFL draft.
Signed by Green Bay Packers, June 29, 1984.
On injured reserve with neck injury, August 21 through November 19, 1984; activated after clearing procedural waivers, November 21, 1984.
Released by Green Bay Packers, August 26, 1985; signed as free agent by Indianapolis Colts, May 12, 1986.
Green Bay NFL, 1984.
Games: 1984 (2).
Pro statistics: Caught one pass for eight yards, 1984.

ROBERT EARL TAYLOR
(Rob)
Offensive Tackle—Tampa Bay Buccaneers
Born November 14, 1960, at St. Charles, Ill.
Height, 6.06. Weight, 281.
High School—Kettering, O., Fairmont East.
Received degree in electrical engineering from Northwestern University.

Selected by Philadelphia in 12th round (328th player selected) of 1982 NFL draft.
Released by Philadelphia Eagles, August 23, 1982; claimed on waivers by Baltimore Colts, August 25, 1982.
Released by Baltimore Colts, September 6, 1982; signed as free agent by Chicago Blitz, October 4, 1982.
Franchise transferred to Arizona, September 30, 1983.
Protected in merger of Arizona Wranglers and Oklahoma Outlaws, December 6, 1984.
Granted free agency, November 30, 1984; signed by Birmingham Stallions, January 23, 1985 (Arizona did not exercise right of first refusal).
Traded by Birmingham Stallions to Houston Gamblers for defensive end Malcolm Taylor, February 12, 1985.
On developmental squad, February 21 through March 2, 1985; activated, March 3, 1985.
Released by Houston Gamblers, July 31, 1985; awaded on waivers to Baltimore Stars, August 1, 1985.
Released by Baltimore Stars, August 2, 1985; signed as free agent by Tampa Bay Buccaneers, March 26, 1986.
On developmental squad for 1 game with Houston Gamblers in 1985.
Chicago USFL, 1983 and 1984; Houston USFL, 1985.
Games: 1983 (18), 1984 (18), 1985 (16). Total—52.
Pro statistics: Recovered one fumble, 1983.
Played in USFL Championship Game following 1984 season.

TERRY TAYLOR
Cornerback—Seattle Seahawks
Born July 18, 1961, at Warren, O.
Height, 5.10. Weight, 188.
High School—Youngstown, O., Rayen.
Attended Southern Illinois University.
Cousin of Walter Poole, running back with Chicago Blitz
and Houston Gamblers, 1983 and 1984.

Selected by Chicago in 2nd round (25th player selected) of 1984 USFL draft.
Selected by Seattle in 1st round (22nd player selected) of 1984 NFL draft.
Signed by Seattle Seahawks, July 10, 1984.

		—INTERCEPTIONS—			
Year Club	G.	No.	Yds.	Avg.	TD.
1984—Seattle NFL	16	3	63	21.0	0
1985—Seattle NFL	16	4	75	18.8	*1
Pro Totals—2 Years	32	7	138	19.7	1

Additional pro statistics: Returned blocked punt for 15 yards and a touchdown, 1985.

JIMMY DEWAYNE TEAL
Wide Receiver—Buffalo Bills
Born August 18, 1962, at Lufkin, Tex.
Height, 5.10. Weight, 170.
High School—Diboll, Tex.
Attended Texas A&M University.

Selected by Houston in 1985 USFL territorial draft.
Selected by Buffalo in 5th round (130th player selected) of 1985 NFL draft.
Signed by Buffalo Bills, July 19, 1985.
On injured reserve with hamstring injury, September 3 through December 5, 1985; activated, December 6, 1985.
Buffalo NFL, 1985.
Games: 1985 (3).
Pro statistics: Caught one pass for 24 yards and returned one kickoff for 20 yards, 1985.

WILLIE TEAL
Cornerback—Minnesota Vikings
Born December 20, 1957, at Texarkana, Tex.
Height, 5.10. Weight, 195.
High School—Texarkana, Tex., Liberty Eylau.
Attended Louisiana State University.

Selected by Minnesota in 2nd round (30th player selected) of 1980 NFL draft.
On injured reserve with knee injury, September 12 through December 19, 1980; activated, December 20, 1980.

		—INTERCEPTIONS—			
Year Club	G.	No.	Yds.	Avg.	TD.
1980—Minnesota NFL	1	None			
1981—Minnesota NFL	16	4	23	5.8	0
1982—Minnesota NFL	9	4	15	3.8	0
1983—Minnesota NFL	16	3	26	8.7	0
1984—Minnesota NFL	11	1	53	53.0	1
1985—Minnesota NFL	16	3	6	2.0	0
Pro Totals—6 Years	69	15	123	8.2	1

Additional pro statistics: Recovered three fumbles for five yards, 1983; returned one punt for no yards and fumbled once, 1984; recovered two fumbles for 65 yards and a touchdown, 1985.

THOMAS ALLEN THAYER
(Tom)
Guard-Center—Chicago Bears
Born August 16, 1961, at Joliet, Ill.
Height, 6.04. Weight, 261.
High School—Joliet, Ill., Catholic.
Received bachelor of arts degree in communications and public relations
from University of Notre Dame.
Brother-in-law of John Scully, guard with Atlanta Falcons.

Selected by Chicago in 1983 USFL territorial draft.
Signed by Chicago Blitz, April 26, 1983.
Selected by Chicago in 4th round (91st player selected) of 1983 NFL draft.
Franchise transferred to Arizona, September 30, 1983.
Protected in merger of Arizona Wranglers and Oklahoma Outlaws, December 6, 1984.
On developmental squad, March 3 through March 10, 1985; activated, March 11, 1985.
Granted free agency, July 15, 1985; signed by Chicago Bears, July 19, 1985.
On developmental squad for 1 game with Arizona Outlaws in 1985.
Chicago USFL, 1983 and 1984; Arizona USFL, 1985; Chicago NFL, 1985.
Games 1983 (10), 1984 (18), 1985 USFL (17), 1985 NFL (16). Total USFL—45. Total Pro—61.
USFL statistics: Recovered two fumbles, 1985.
Played in USFL Championship Game following 1984 season.
Played in NFC Championship Game following 1985 season.
Played in NFL Championship Game following 1985 season.

JOSEPH ROBERT THEISMANN
(Joe)
Quarterback—Washington Redskins
Born September 9, 1949, at New Brunswick, N.J.
Height, 6.00. Weight, 198.
High School—South River, N.J.
Received bachelor of arts degree in sociology from University of Notre Dame in 1971.

Named to THE SPORTING NEWS NFL All-Star Team, 1983.
Selected by Miami in 4th round (99th player selected) of 1971 NFL draft.
Traded by Miami Dolphins to Washington Redskins for the Redskins' 1st round draft choice in 1976, January 25, 1974.
On injured reserve with broken leg, November 19 through remainder of 1985 season.
Selected by Minnesota Twins' organization in 39th round of free-agent draft, June 8, 1971.

Year Club	G.	Att.	Cmp.	Pct.	Gain	T.P.	P.I.	Avg.	Att.	Yds.	Avg.	TD.	TD.	Pts.	F.
1971—Toronto CFL	14	278	148	53.2	2440	17	21	8.78	81	564	7.0	1	1	8	5
1972—Toronto CFL	6	127	77	60.6	1157	10	13	9.11	21	147	7.0	1	1	6	0
1973—Toronto CFL	14	274	157	57.3	2496	13	13	9.11	70	343	4.9	1	1	6	9
1974—Washington NFL	9	11	9	81.8	145	1	0	13.18	3	12	4.0	1	1	6	0
1975—Washington NFL	14	22	10	45.5	96	1	3	4.36	3	34	11.3	0	0	0	0
1976—Washington NFL	14	163	79	48.5	1036	8	10	6.36	17	97	5.7	1	1	6	2
1977—Washington NFL	14	182	84	46.2	1097	7	9	6.03	29	149	5.1	1	1	6	0
1978—Washington NFL	16	390	187	47.9	2593	13	18	6.65	37	177	4.8	1	1	6	8
1979—Washington NFL	16	395	233	59.0	2797	20	13	7.08	46	181	3.9	4	4	24	3
1980—Washington NFL	16	454	262	57.7	2962	17	16	6.52	29	175	6.0	3	3	18	6
1981—Washington NFL	16	496	293	59.1	3568	19	20	7.19	36	177	4.9	2	2	12	7
1982—Washington NFL	9	252	161	63.9	2033	13	9	8.07	31	150	4.8	0	0	0	4
1983—Washington NFL	16	459	276	60.1	3714	29	11	8.09	37	234	6.3	1	1	6	1
1984—Washington NFL	16	477	283	59.3	3391	24	13	7.11	62	314	5.1	1	1	6	7
1985—Washington NFL	11	301	167	55.5	1774	8	16	5.89	25	115	4.6	2	2	12	4
CFL Totals—3 Years	34	679	382	56.3	6093	40	47	8.97	172	1054	6.1	3	3	20	14
NFL Totals—12 Years	167	3602	2044	56.7	25206	160	138	7.00	355	1815	5.1	17	17	102	42
Pro Totals—15 Years	201	4281	2426	56.7	31299	200	185	7.31	527	2869	5.4	20	20	122	56

NFL Quarterback Rating Points: 1974 (149.1), 1975 (33.6), 1976 (59.9), 1977 (58.0), 1978 (61.6), 1979 (84.0), 1980 (75.1), 1981 (77.3), 1982 (91.3), 1983 (97.0), 1984 (86.6), 1985 (59.6). Total—77.3.
Additional CFL statistics: Scored one single, kicked one conversion, punted three times for 182 yards and returned one punt for seven yards, 1971; recovered three fumbles, 1973.
Additional NFL statistics: Returned 15 punts for 157 yards, 1974; returned two punts for five yards, 1975; recovered one fumble, 1976 and 1981; recovered three fumbles and fumbled eight times for minus 26 yards, 1978; recovered two fumbles and fumbled three times for minus four yards, 1979; fumbled six times for minus two yards, 1980; recovered one fumble and fumbled four times for minus 21 yards, 1982; recovered six fumbles and fumbled seven times for five yards, 1984; punted once for one yard, 1985.
Played in CFL Championship Game following 1971 season.
Played in NFC Championship Game following 1982 and 1983 seasons.
Played in NFL Championship Game following 1982 and 1983 seasons.
Played in Pro Bowl (NFL All-Star Game) following 1982 and 1983 seasons.

—DID YOU KNOW—

That only six players have scored more than 100 career touchdowns in the National Football League? In 1985, Chicago's Walter Payton became the sixth, joining Jim Brown, Lenny Moore, Don Hutson, Franco Harris and John Riggins.

RAY CHARLES THIELEMANN

Name pronounced TEEL-munn.

(R. C.)

Guard—Washington Redskins

Born August 12, 1955, at Houston, Tex.
Height, 6.04. Weight, 262.
High School—Houston, Tex., Spring Woods.
Attended University of Arkansas.

Selected by Atlanta in 2nd round (36th player selected) of 1977 NFL draft.
On injured reserve with shoulder separation, September 13 through October 12, 1979; activated, October 13, 1979.
On injured reserve with shoulder injury, December 13 through remainder of 1979 season.
On did not report list, August 16 through August 24, 1983.
Reported and granted exemption, August 25, 1983; activated, September 1, 1983.
Granted free agency, February 1, 1985; re-signed by Falcons and traded to Washington Redskins for wide receiver Charlie Brown, August 26, 1985.
Granted roster exemption, August 26 through August 29, 1985; activated, August 30, 1985.
On injured reserve with knee injury, October 2 through remainder of 1985 season.
Atlanta NFL, 1977 through 1984; Washington NFL, 1985.
Games: 1977 (14), 1978 (16), 1979 (11), 1980 (16), 1981 (16), 1982 (9), 1983 (16), 1984 (16), 1985 (3). Total—117.
Pro statistics: Recovered one fumble, 1977, 1983 and 1984; recovered two fumbles, 1978 through 1981.
Played in Pro Bowl (NFL All-Star Game) following 1981 through 1983 seasons.

BENJAMIN THOMAS JR.

(Ben)

Defensive End—New England Patriots

Born July 2, 1961, at Ashburn, Ga.
Height, 6.04. Weight, 280.
High School—Ashburn, Ga., Turner County.
Attended Auburn University.

Selected by Birmingham in 1985 USFL territorial draft.
Selected by New England in 2nd round (56th player selected) of 1985 NFL draft.
Signed by New England Patriots, July 24, 1985.
New England NFL, 1985.
Games: 1985 (15).
Played in AFC Championship Game following 1985 season.
Played in NFL Championship Game following 1985 season.

CALVIN LEWIS THOMAS

Fullback—Chicago Bears

Born January 7, 1960, at St. Louis, Mo.
Height, 5.11. Weight, 245.
High School—St. Louis, Mo., McKinley.
Attended University of Illinois.

Signed as free agent by Chicago Bears, May 21, 1982.
On inactive list, September 12, 1982.

Year Club	G.	RUSHING Att.	Yds.	Avg.	TD.	PASS RECEIVING P.C.	Yds.	Avg.	TD.	TOTAL TD.	Pts.	F.
1982—Chicago NFL	6	5	4	0.8	0	None				0	0	1
1983—Chicago NFL	13	8	25	3.1	0	2	13	6.5	0	0	0	0
1984—Chicago NFL	16	40	186	4.7	1	9	39	4.3	0	1	6	1
1985—Chicago NFL	14	31	125	4.0	4	5	45	9.0	0	4	24	0
Pro Totals—4 Years	49	84	340	4.0	5	16	97	6.1	0	5	30	2

Additional pro statistics: Recovered one fumble, 1984.
Played in NFC Championship Game following 1984 and 1985 seasons.
Played in NFL Championship Game following 1985 season.

CHUCK THOMAS

Center-Guard—Atlanta Falcons

Born February 24, 1960, at Houston, Tex.
Height, 6.03. Weight, 277.
High School—Houston, Tex., Stratford.
Attended University of Oklahoma.

Selected by San Antonio in 1985 USFL territorial draft.
Selected by Houston in 8th round (199th player selected) of 1985 NFL draft.
Signed by Houston Oilers, July 13, 1985.
Released by Houston Oilers, September 2, 1985; signed as free agent by Atlanta Falcons, November 22, 1985.
Atlanta NFL, 1985.
Games: 1985 (4).

KELLY SCOTT THOMAS

Offensive Tackle—Miami Dolphins

Born September 9, 1960, at Lynwood, Calif.
Height, 6.06. Weight, 270.
High School—La Mirada, Calif.
Attended University of Southern California.

Selected by Los Angeles in 1983 USFL territorial draft.
Selected by Tampa Bay in 4th round (99th player selected) of 1983 NFL draft.
Signed by Tampa Bay Buccaneers, May 20, 1983.
Traded by Tampa Bay Buccaneers to Washington Redskins for cornerback Anthony Washington, August 2, 1985.
On injured reserve with back injury, August 20 through September 1, 1985.
Released by Washington Redskins, September 2, 1985; signed as free agent by Miami Dolphins, March 6, 1986.
Tampa Bay NFL, 1983 and 1984.
Games: 1983 (14), 1984 (10). Total—24.

ROBERT RANDALL THOMAS
(Bob)
Placekicker
Born August 7, 1952, at Rochester, N.Y.
Height, 5.10. Weight, 175.
High School—Rochester, N. Y., McQuaid Jesuit.
Received bachelor of arts degree in government from
University of Notre Dame in 1974; and received law degree from Loyola University Law School.

Selected by Los Angeles in 15th round (388th player selected) of 1974 NFL draft.
Released by Los Angeles Rams, September, 1974; signed by Jacksonville Sharks (WFL), 1974.
Released by Jacksonville Sharks (WFL), 1974.
Claimed on waivers from Los Angeles Rams by Chicago Bears, February 26, 1975.
On injured reserve with pulled hamstring, September 16 through remainder of 1981 season.
Released by Chicago Bears, September 6, 1982; signed as free agent by Detroit Lions, September 10, 1982.
Released by Detroit Lions, November 20, 1982; signed as free agent by Chicago Bears, December 20, 1982.
Released by Chicago Bears, September 2, 1985; signed as free agent by San Diego Chargers, September 12, 1985.
Granted free agency, February 1, 1986; withdrew qualifying offer, April 7, 1986.

| Year—Club | | —PLACE KICKING— | | | | |
	G.	XP.	XPM.	FG.	FGA.	Pts.
1975—Chicago NFL............	14	18	4	13	23	57
1976—Chicago NFL............	14	27	3	12	25	63
1977—Chicago NFL............	14	27	3	14	27	69
1978—Chicago NFL............	16	26	2	17	22	77
1979—Chicago NFL............	16	34	3	16	27	82
1980—Chicago NFL............	16	35	2	13	18	74
1981—Chicago NFL............	2	2	1	2	3	8
1982—Det (2)-Chi (2) NFL	4	9	0	10	12	39
1983—Chicago NFL............	16	35	3	14	25	77
1984—Chicago NFL............	16	35	2	22	28	101
1985—San Diego NFL........	15	51	4	18	28	105
Pro Totals—11 Years.....	143	299	27	151	238	752

Played in NFC Championship Game following 1984 season.

SEAN THOMAS
Defensive Back—Atlanta Falcons
Born April 12, 1962, at Sacramento, Calif.
Height, 5.11. Weight, 190.
High School—Sacramento, Calif., Luther Burbank.
Attended Sacramento City College and Texas Christian University.

Selected by Arizona in 1st round (15th player selected) of 1985 USFL draft.
Selected by Cincinnati in 3rd round (70th player selected) of 1985 NFL draft.
Signed by Cincinnati Bengals, May 30, 1985.
Released by Cincinnati Bengals, September 2, 1985; re-signed by Bengals, September 3, 1985.
Released by Cincinnati Bengals, October 8, 1985; signed as free agent by Atlanta Falcons, November 13, 1985.
Cincinnati (5)-Atlanta (6) NFL, 1985.
Games: 1985 (11).

ARLAND LEE THOMPSON
Guard—Minnesota Vikings
Born September 19, 1957, at Lockney, Tex.
Height, 6.04. Weight, 265.
High School—Plainview, Tex.
Attended Baylor University.

Selected by Chicago in 4th round (103rd player selected) of 1980 NFL draft.
Released by Chicago Bears, September 1, 1980; signed as free agent by Denver Broncos, December 5, 1980.
Released by Denver Broncos, August 25, 1981; signed as free agent by Green Bay Packers, October 14, 1981.
Released by Green Bay Packers, August 23, 1982; awarded on waivers to Baltimore Colts, August 25, 1982.
Released by Baltimore Colts, December 2, 1982; signed by Denver Gold, March 16, 1983.
On developmental squad, March 16 through May 3, 1983; activated, May 4, 1983.
On injured reserve, May 10 through remainder of 1983 season.
Awarded on procedural waivers to Arizona Wranglers, August 2, 1983.
Franchise transferred to Chicago, September 30, 1983.
Traded with wide receiver Wally Henry by Chicago Blitz to San Antonio Gunslingers for rights to tight end Robert Fisher and future draft pick, November 14, 1983.
On developmental squad, May 11 through May 16, 1985; activated, May 17, 1985.
On developmental squad, May 30 through June 11, 1985; activated, June 12, 1985.
Released by San Antonio Gunslingers, July 23, 1985; signed as free agent by Minnesota Vikings, May 2, 1986.
On developmental squad for 7 games with Denver Gold in 1983.

On developmental squad for 3 games with San Antonio Gunslingers in 1985.
Denver NFL, 1980; Green Bay NFL, 1981; Baltimore NFL, 1982; Denver USFL, 1983; San Antonio USFL, 1984 and 1985.
Games: 1980 (2), 1981 (10), 1982 (3), 1983 (1), 1984 (18), 1985 (14). Total NFL—15. Total USFL—33. Total Pro—48.
Pro statistics: Recovered one fumble, 1981.

BRODERICK THOMPSON
Defensive Tackle—Dallas Cowboys
Born August 14, 1960, at Birmingham, Ala.
Height, 6.05. Weight, 280.
High School—Cerritos, Calif., Richard Gahr.
Attended Cerritos College and University of Kansas.

Signed as free agent by Dallas Cowboys, April 28, 1983.
Released by Dallas Cowboys, August 2, 1983; signed as free agent by San Antonio Gunslingers, November 12, 1983.
Traded with 1st round pick in 1984 draft by San Antonio Gunslingers to Chicago Blitz for rights to quarterback Bob Gagliano, January 3, 1984.
Released by Chicago Blitz, January 31, 1984; signed as free agent by Los Angeles Express, February 10, 1984.
Released by Los Angeles Express, February 13, 1984; signed as free agent by Los Angeles Rams, May 4, 1984.
Released by Los Angeles Rams, August 21, 1984; signed as free agent by Portland Breakers, January 23, 1985.
Released by Portland Breakers, July 31, 1985; awarded on waivers to Memphis Showboats, August 1, 1985.
Released by Memphis Showboats, August 2, 1985; signed as free agent by Dallas Cowboys, August 3, 1985.
Portland USFL, 1985; Dallas NFL, 1985.
Games: 1985 USFL (18), 1985 NFL (11). Total Pro—29.

EMMUEL LEE THOMPSON
Defensive Back—Philadelphia Eagles
Born November 15, 1959, at Houston, Tex.
Height, 5.11. Weight, 182.
High School—Houston, Tex., Booker T. Washington.
Attended Texas A&I University.

Signed as free agent by Denver Broncos, April 30, 1982.
Released by Denver Broncos, July 29, 1982; signed by Birmingham Stallions, January 17, 1983.
On reserve/did not report, January 23 through February 7, 1984; activated, February 8, 1984.
Released by Birmingham Stallions, February 20, 1984; signed as free agent by San Antonio Gunslingers, March 10, 1984.
On developmental squad, March 10 through March 27, 1984.
Released by San Antonio Gunslingers, March 28, 1984; signed as free agent by Hamilton Tiger-Cats, April 26, 1984.
Released by Hamilton Tiger-Cats, June 24, 1984; signed as free agent by Green Bay Packers, July 2, 1984.
Released by Green Bay Packers, August 27, 1984; signed as free agent by Pittsburgh Maulers, October 9, 1984.
Franchise disbanded, October 25, 1984; not selected in USFL dispersal draft, December 6, 1984.
Signed as free agent by San Antonio Gunslinger, January 8, 1985.
Traded by San Antonio Gunslingers to Jacksonville Bulls for past consideration, January 16, 1985.
Released by Jacksonville Bulls, January 28, 1985; signed as free agent by Buffalo Bills, March 21, 1985.
Released by Buffalo Bills, August 6, 1985; signed as free agent by Philadelphia Eagles, May 7, 1986.
On developmental squad for 3 games with San Antonio Gunslingers in 1984.

		—INTERCEPTIONS—			
Year Club	G.	No.	Yds.	Avg.	TD.
1983—Birmingham USFL	17	5	24	4.8	0

LAWRENCE DONNELL THOMPSON
(Known by middle name.)
Defensive End—Indianapolis Colts
Born October 27, 1958, at Lumberton, N.C.
Height, 6.05. Weight, 263.
High School—Lumberton, N.C.
Attended University of North Carolina.

Selected by Baltimore in 1st round (18th player selected) of 1981 NFL draft.
On physically unable to perform/active with shoulder injury, July 24 through August 22, 1982; activated, August 23, 1982.
Franchise transferred to Indianapolis, March 31, 1984.
Placed on suspended list, August 12 through September 11, 1984.
On non-football injury list with shoulder and back injuries, September 12 through October 11, 1984; activated, October 12, 1984.
Baltimore NFL, 1981 through 1983; Indianapolis NFL, 1984 and 1985.
Games: 1981 (13), 1982 (9), 1983 (14), 1984 (10), 1985 (15). Total—61.
Pro statistics: Recovered one fumble, 1981; credited with one safety, 1983; recovered one fumble for nine yards, 1985.

LEONARD IRWIN THOMPSON
Wide Receiver—Detroit Lions
Born July 28, 1952, at Oklahoma City, Okla.
Height, 5.11. Weight, 192.
High School—Tucson, Ariz., Pueblo.
Attended Arizona Western College and Oklahoma State University.

Selected by Detroit in 8th round (194th player selected) of 1975 NFL draft.
On physically unable to perform/active with foot injury, July 29 through August 30, 1982; activated, August 31, 1982.
Placed on did not report list, August 20 through August 27, 1984.

Reported and granted roster exemption, August 28 through August 31, 1984; activated, September 1, 1984.

		—RUSHING—				PASS RECEIVING				—TOTAL—		
Year Club	G.	Att.	Yds.	Avg.	TD.	P.C.	Yds.	Avg.	TD.	TD.	Pts.	F.
1975—Detroit NFL	14	1	—12	—12.0	0		None			0	0	2
1976—Detroit NFL	14	1	0	0.0	0	3	52	17.3	0	0	0	0
1977—Detroit NFL	14	31	91	2.9	1	7	42	6.0	0	2	12	0
1978—Detroit NFL	16	1	7	7.0	0	10	167	16.7	4	4	24	2
1979—Detroit NFL	15	5	24	4.8	0	24	451	18.8	2	2	12	3
1980—Detroit NFL	16	6	61	10.2	0	19	511	26.9	3	3	18	1
1981—Detroit NFL	16	10	75	7.5	1	30	550	18.3	3	4	24	1
1982—Detroit NFL	9	2	16	8.0	0	17	328	19.3	4	4	24	1
1983—Detroit NFL	13	4	72	18.0	1	41	752	18.3	3	4	24	2
1984—Detroit NFL	16	3	—7	—2.3	0	50	773	15.5	6	6	36	1
1985—Detroit NFL	16		None			51	736	14.4	5	5	30	0
Pro Totals—11 Years	159	64	327	5.1	3	252	4362	17.3	30	34	204	12

		KICKOFF RETURNS			
Year Club	G.	No.	Yds.	Avg.	TD.
1975—Detroit NFL	14	12	271	22.6	0
1976—Detroit NFL	14	5	86	17.2	0
1977—Detroit NFL	14	5	84	16.8	0
1978—Detroit NFL	16	8	207	25.9	0
1979—Detroit NFL	15	6	151	25.2	0
1980—Detroit NFL	16		None		
1981—Detroit NFL	16		None		
1982—Detroit NFL	9		None		
1983—Detroit NFL	13		None		
1984—Detroit NFL	16		None		
1985—Detroit NFL	16		None		
Pro Totals—11 Years	159	36	799	22.2	0

Additional pro statistics: Recovered one fumble, 1976, 1981, 1983 and 1984; ran two yards with blocked punt for a touchdown and attempted one pass with no completions, 1977; returned three punts for 19 yards and recovered four fumbles, 1978; returned nine punts for 117 yards, 1979; recovered two fumbles, 1980.

WILLIS HOPE THOMPSON
(Weegie)
Wide Receiver—Pittsburgh Steelers
Born March 21, 1961, at Pensacola, Fla.
Height, 6.06. Weight, 210.
High School—Midlothian, Va.
Received bachelor of science degree in management from Florida State University in 1984.

Selected by Tampa Bay in 1984 USFL territorial draft.
USFL rights traded with rights to quarterback Kelly Lowrey by Tampa Bay Bandits to Jacksonville Bulls for rights to wide receiver Mark Militello and running back Mike Grayson, January 4, 1984.
Selected by Pittsburgh in 4th round (108th player selected) of 1984 NFL draft.
Signed by Pittsburgh Steelers, July 22, 1984.

		—PASS RECEIVING—			
Year Club	G.	P.C.	Yds.	Avg.	TD.
1984—Pittsburgh NFL	16	17	291	17.1	3
1985—Pittsburgh NFL	16	8	138	17.3	1
Pro Totals—2 Years	32	25	429	17.2	4

Additional pro statistics: Fumbled once, 1984.
Played in AFC Championship Game following 1984 season.

DONALD KEVIN THORP
(Don)
Nose Tackle—Chicago Bears
Born July 10, 1962, at Chicago, Ill.
Height, 6.04. Weight, 260.
High School—Buffalo Grove, Ill.
Received bachelor of arts degree in finance from University of Illinois.

Named as defensive lineman on THE SPORTING NEWS College All-America Team, 1983.
Selected by Chicago in 1984 USFL territorial draft.
Selected by New Orleans in 6th round (156th player selected) of 1984 NFL draft.
Signed by New Orleans Saints, June 21, 1984.
On injured reserve with neck injury, October 9 through remainder of 1984 season.
Released by New Orleans Saints, August 26, 1985; signed as free agent by Chicago Bears, February 12, 1986.
New Orleans NFL, 1984.
Games: 1984 (5).

CLIFFORD RAY THRIFT
(Cliff)
Linebacker—Chicago Bears
Born May 3, 1956, at Dallas, Tex.
Height, 6.01. Weight, 230.
High School—Purcell, Okla.
Attended East Central (Okla.) University.

Selected by San Diego in 3rd round (73rd player selected) of 1979 NFL draft.
On injured reserve with ruptured tricep, October 28 through December 30, 1981; activated, December 31, 1981.
On injured reserve with pulled hamstring, September 5 through November 11, 1983; activated, November 12, 1983.
Released by San Diego Chargers, July 9, 1985; awarded on waivers to Chicago Bears, July 10, 1985.

Year Club	G.	—INTERCEPTIONS— No.	Yds.	Avg.	TD.
1979—San Diego NFL	16	None			
1980—San Diego NFL	15	1	0	0.0	0
1981—San Diego NFL	7	None			
1982—San Diego NFL	9	2	16	8.0	0
1983—San Diego NFL	6	None			
1984—San Diego NFL	16	• None			
1985—Chicago NFL	16	None			
Pro Totals—7 Years	85	3	16	5.3	0

Additional pro statistics: Returned one kickoff for 11 yards, 1979; recovered two fumbles, 1979 and 1982; recovered one fumble, 1980.
Played in AFC Championship Game following 1980 and 1981 seasons.
Played in NFC Championship Game following 1985 season.
Played in NFL Championship Game following 1985 season.

DENNIS LEE THURMAN
Safety—Dallas Cowboys
Born April 13, 1956, at Los Angeles, Calif.
Height, 5.11. Weight, 179.
High School—Santa Monica, Calif.
Received degree in journalism from University of Southern California.
Brother of Junior Thurman, safety at University of Southern California.
Selected by Dallas in 11th round (306th player selected) of 1978 NFL draft.

Year Club	G.	—INTERCEPTIONS— No.	Yds.	Avg.	TD.
1978—Dallas NFL	16	2	35	17.5	0
1979—Dallas NFL	16	1	0	0.0	0
1980—Dallas NFL	16	5	114	22.8	1
1981—Dallas NFL	16	9	187	20.8	0
1982—Dallas NFL	9	3	75	25.0	*1
1983—Dallas NFL	16	6	49	8.2	0
1984—Dallas NFL	16	5	81	16.2	1
1985—Dallas NFL	16	5	21	4.2	*1
Pro Totals—8 Years	121	36	562	15.6	4

Additional pro statistics: Returned three kickoffs for 42 yards, returned one punt for no yards and fumbled twice, 1978; recovered two fumbles, 1978 and 1983; recovered one fumble, 1979, 1981, 1982 and 1984; recovered two fumbles for 14 yards, 1980; returned one kickoff for 17 yards, 1982; recovered fumble in end zone for a touchdown, 1983.
Played in NFC Championship Game following 1978 and 1980 through 1982 seasons.
Played in NFL Championship Game following 1978 season.

JOHN TICE
Tight End—New Orleans Saints
Born June 22, 1960, at Bayshore, N.Y.
Height, 6.05. Weight, 243.
High School—Central Islip, N.Y.
Attended University of Maryland.
Brother of Mike Tice, tight end with Seattle Seahawks.
Selected by Washington in 1983 USFL territorial draft.
Selected by New Orleans in 3rd round (65th player selected) of 1983 NFL draft.
Signed by New Orleans Saints, July 6, 1983.
On injured reserve with ankle injury, November 19 through remainder of 1984 season.

Year Club	G.	—PASS RECEIVING— P.C.	Yds.	Avg.	TD.
1983—New Orleans NFL	16	7	33	4.7	1
1984—New Orleans NFL	10	6	55	9.2	1
1985—New Orleans NFL	16	24	266	11.1	2
Pro Totals—3 Years	42	37	354	9.6	4

Additional pro statistics: Recovered two fumbles, 1983; recovered one fumble, 1985.

MICHAEL PETER TICE
(Mike)
Tight End—Seattle Seahawks
Born February 2, 1959, at Bayshore, N.Y.
Height, 6.07. Weight, 250.
High School—Central Islip, N.Y.
Attended University of Maryland.
Brother of John Tice, tight end with New Orleans Saints.
Signed as free agent by Seattle Seahawks, April 30, 1981.
On injured reserve with fractured ankle, October 15 through December 6, 1985; activated, December 7, 1985.

Year Club	—PASS RECEIVING—				
	G.	P.C.	Yds.	Avg.	TD.
1981—Seattle NFL	16	5	47	9.4	0
1982—Seattle NFL	9	9	46	5.1	0
1983—Seattle NFL	15		None		
1984—Seattle NFL	16	8	90	11.3	3
1985—Seattle NFL	9	2	13	6.5	0
Pro Totals—5 Years	65	24	196	8.2	3

Additional pro statistics: Recovered one fumble, 1982 and 1983; returned two kickoffs for 28 yards, 1983; returned one kickoff for 17 yards, 1985.
Played in AFC Championship Game following 1983 season.

PATRICK LEE TILLEY
(Pat)
Wide Receiver—St. Louis Cardinals
Born February 15, 1953, at Shreveport, La.
Height, 5.10. Weight, 178.
High School—Shreveport, La., Fair Park.
Received bachelor of arts degree in sociology from Louisiana Tech University.

Selected by St. Louis in 4th round (114th player selected) of 1976 NFL draft.
On injured reserve with groin injury, December 17 through remainder of 1980 season.

Year Club		-PASS RECEIVING-				-PUNT RETURNS-				—TOTAL—		
	G.	P.C.	Yds.	Avg.	TD.	No.	Yds.	Avg.	TD.	TD.	Pts.	F.
1976—St. Louis NFL	13	26	407	15.7	1	15	146	9.7	0	1	6	2
1977—St. Louis NFL	14	5	64	12.8	0	13	111	8.5	0	0	0	1
1978—St. Louis NFL	16	62	900	14.5	3	2	8	4.0	0	3	18	1
1979—St. Louis NFL	16	57	938	16.5	6		None			6	36	0
1980—St. Louis NFL	14	68	966	14.2	6		None			6	36	0
1981—St. Louis NFL	16	66	1040	15.8	3		None			3	18	1
1982—St. Louis NFL	9	36	465	12.9	2		None			2	12	0
1983—St. Louis NFL	16	44	690	15.7	5		None			5	30	1
1984—St. Louis NFL	16	52	758	14.6	5		None			5	30	1
1985—St. Louis NFL	16	49	726	14.8	6	1	—1	—1.0	0	6	36	0
Pro Totals—10 Years	146	465	6954	15.0	37	31	264	8.5	0	37	222	7

Additional pro statistics: Recovered one fumble, 1977, 1980 and 1983; rushed once for 32 yards, 1978.
Named to play in Pro Bowl (NFL All-Star Game) following 1980 season; replaced due to injury by Wallace Francis.

ANDRE BERNARD TIPPETT
Linebacker—New England Patriots
Born December 27, 1959, at Birmingham, Ala.
Height, 6.03. Weight, 241.
High School—Newark, N.J., Barringer.
Attended Ellsworth Community College and received bachelor of liberal arts degree from
University of Iowa in 1983.
Cousin of Andre Williams, linebacker at Delaware State College.

Named to THE SPORTING NEWS NFL All-Star Team, 1985.
Selected by New England in 2nd round (41st player selected) of 1982 NFL draft.
New England NFL, 1982 through 1985.
Games: 1982 (9), 1983 (15), 1984 (16), 1985 (16). Total—56.
Pro statistics: Recovered one fumble, 1982 and 1983; recovered four fumbles for 25 yards and a touchdown, 1985.
Played in AFC Championship Game following 1985 season.
Played in NFL Championship Game following 1985 season.
Played in Pro Bowl (NFL All-Star Game) following 1984 and 1985 seasons.

GLEN WESTON TITENSOR
Name pronounced TIGHT-en-sir.
Guard—Dallas Cowboys
Born February 21, 1958, at Bellflower, Calif.
Height, 6.04. Weight, 264.
High School—Garden Grove, Calif., Bolsa Grande.
Attended University of California at Los Angeles and Brigham Young University.

Selected by Dallas in 3rd round (81st player selected) of 1981 NFL draft.
Dallas NFL, 1981 through 1985.
Games: 1981 (16), 1982 (4), 1983 (15), 1984 (15), 1985 (16). Total—66.
Pro statistics: Recovered one fumble, 1981.
Played in NFC Championship Game following 1981 season.
Member of Dallas Cowboys for NFC Championship Game following 1982 season; did not play.

RICHARD TODD
Quarterback—New Orleans Saints
Born November 19, 1953, at Birmingham, Ala.
Height, 6.02. Weight, 212.
High School—Mobile, Ala., Davidson.
Received bachelor of science degree in physical education from University of Alabama.

Established NFL record for most completions, game (42), September 21, 1980, vs. San Francisco 49ers.

Selected by New York Jets in 1st round (6th player selected) of 1976 NFL draft.
On injured reserve with broken collarbone, November 21 through remainder of 1978 season.
Traded by New York Jets to New Orleans Saints for 1st round pick in 1984 draft, February 18, 1984.

		—————————PASSING—————————							—————RUSHING—————				—TOTAL—		
Year	Club	G.	Att.	Cmp.	Pct.	Gain	T.P.	P.I.	Avg.	Att.	Yds.	Avg.	TD.	TD.	Pts.	F.
1976—N.Y. Jets NFL		13	162	65	40.1	870	3	12	5.37	28	107	3.8	1	1	6	5
1977—N.Y. Jets NFL		12	265	133	50.2	1863	11	17	7.03	24	46	1.9	2	2	12	4
1978—N.Y. Jets NFL		5	107	60	56.1	849	6	10	7.93	14	18	1.3	0	0	0	1
1979—N.Y. Jets NFL		15	334	171	51.2	2660	16	22	7.96	36	93	2.6	5	5	30	7
1980—N.Y. Jets NFL		16	479	264	55.1	3329	17	★30	6.95	49	330	6.7	5	5	30	10
1981—N.Y. Jets NFL		16	497	279	56.1	3231	25	13	6.50	32	131	4.1	0	0	0	5
1982—N.Y. Jets NFL		9	261	153	58.6	1961	14	8	7.51	13	—5	—0.4	1	1	6	4
1983—N.Y. Jets NFL		16	518	308	59.5	3478	18	26	6.71	35	101	2.9	0	0	0	5
1984—New Orleans NFL		15	312	161	51.6	2178	11	19	6.98	28	111	4.0	0	0	0	9
1985—New Orleans NFL		2	32	16	50.0	191	3	4	5.97			None		0	0	0
Pro Totals—10 Years		119	2967	1610	54.3	20610	124	161	6.95	259	932	3.6	14	14	84	50

Quarterback Rating Points: 1976 (33.4), 1977 (60.6), 1978 (61.8), 1979 (66.4), 1980 (62.4), 1981 (81.8), 1982 (87.3), 1983 (70.3), 1984 (60.6), 1985 (60.3). Total—67.8.
Additional pro statistics: Recovered two fumbles, 1976 and 1981; fumbled once for minus three yards, 1978; recovered four fumbles and fumbled seven times for minus 10 yards, 1979; recovered three fumbles and fumbled 10 times for minus three yards, 1980; caught one pass for one yard, 1981; fumbled four times for minus six yards, 1982; recovered one fumble, 1983; recovered three fumbles and fumbled nine times for minus 16 yards, 1984.
Played in AFC Championship Game following 1982 season.

JEFFREY MARK TOEWS

Name pronounced Taves.

(Jeff)

Guard-Center—Miami Dolphins

Born November 4, 1957, at San Jose, Calif.
Height, 6.03. Weight, 255.
High School—San Jose, Calif., Del Mar.
Attended University of Washington.
Brother of Loren Toews, linebacker with Pittsburgh Steelers, 1973 through 1983.

Named as offensive tackle on THE SPORTING NEWS College All-America Team, 1978.
Selected by Miami in 2nd round (53rd player selected) of 1979 NFL draft.
On injured reserve, December 7 through remainder of 1980 season.
On injured reserve with knee injury, November 18 through remainder of 1985 season.
Miami NFL, 1979 through 1985.
Games: 1979 (11), 1980 (7), 1981 (9), 1982 (9), 1983 (8), 1984 (16), 1985 (11). Total—71.
Pro statistics: Recovered one fumble, 1985.
Played in AFC Championship Game following 1982 and 1984 seasons.
Played in NFL Championship Game following 1982 and 1984 seasons.

ALVIN TOLES

Linebacker—New Orleans Saints

Born March 23, 1963, at Barnesville, Ga.
Height, 6.01. Weight, 211.
High School—Forsyth, Ga., Mary Persons.
Attended University of Tennessee.

Selected by Memphis in 1985 USFL territorial draft.
Selected by New Orleans in 1st round (24th player selected) of 1985 NFL draft.
Signed by New Orleans Saints, July 10, 1985.
New Orleans NFL, 1985.
Games: 1985 (16).

MIKE TOMCZAK

Name pronounced Tom-zak.

Quarterback—Chicago Bears

Born October 23, 1962, at Calumet City, Ill.
Height, 6.01. Weight, 195.
High School—Calumet City, Ill., Thornton Fractional North.
Attended Ohio State University.

Selected by New Jersey in 1985 USFL territorial draft.
Signed as free agent by Chicago Bears, May 9, 1985.

		—————————PASSING—————————							—————RUSHING—————				—TOTAL—		
Year	Club	G.	Att.	Cmp.	Pct.	Gain	T.P.	P.I.	Avg.	Att.	Yds.	Avg.	TD.	TD.	Pts.	F.
1985—Chicago NFL		6	6	2	33.3	33	0	0	5.50	2	3	1.5	0	0	0	1

Quarterback Rating Points: 1985 (52.8).
Additional pro statistics: Recovered one fumble and fumbled once for minus 13 yards, 1985.
Member of Chicago Bears for NFC Championship Game following 1985 season; did not play.
Played in NFL Championship Game following 1985 season.

AL LEE TOON JR.
Wide Receiver—New York Jets
Born April 30, 1963, at Newport News, Va.
Height, 6.04. Weight, 200.
High School—Newport News, Va., Menchville.
Attended University of Wisconsin.

Selected by Jacksonville in 1985 USFL territorial draft.
Selected by New York Jets in 1st round (10th player selected) of 1985 NFL draft.
Signed by New York Jets, September 11, 1985.
Granted roster exemption, September 11 through September 13, 1985; activated, September 14, 1985.

		——PASS RECEIVING——				
Year	Club	G.	P.C.	Yds.	Avg.	TD.
1985—N.Y. Jets NFL		15	46	662	14.4	3

Additional pro statistics: Rushed once for five yards, 1985.

STACEY J. TORAN
Safety—Los Angeles Raiders
Born November 10, 1961, at Indianapolis, Ind.
Height, 6.02. Weight, 200.
High School—Indianapolis, Ind., Broad Ripple.
Received degree from University of Notre Dame in 1984.

Selected by Chicago in 1984 USFL territorial draft.
Selected by Los Angeles Raiders in 6th round (168th player selected) of 1984 NFL draft.
Signed by Los Angeles Raiders, June 2, 1984.
Los Angeles Raiders NFL, 1984 and 1985.
Games: 1984 (16), 1985 (16). Total—32.
Pro statistics: Intercepted one pass for 76 yards and a touchdown, 1985.

THOMAS JEFFREY TOTH
(Tom)
Offensive Tackle—New England Patriots
Born May 23, 1962, at Chicago, Ill.
Height, 6.05. Weight, 275.
High School—Orland Park, Ill., Carl Sandberg.
Attended Western Michigan University.

Selected by Oakland in 7th round (95th player selected) of 1985 USFL draft.
Selected by New England in 4th round (102nd player selected) of 1985 NFL draft.
Signed by New England Patriots, July 19, 1985.
On injured reserve with ankle injury, August 15 through entire 1985 season.

JOSEPH RAY TOWNSELL
(Jojo)
Wide Receiver—New York Jets
Born November 4, 1960, at Reno, Nev.
Height, 5.09. Weight, 180.
High School—Reno, Nev., Hug.
Received degree in sociology from University of California at Los Angeles in 1982.

Selected by Los Angeles in 6th round (72nd player selected) of 1983 USFL draft.
Selected by New York Jets in 3rd round (78th player selected) of 1983 NFL draft.
Signed by Los Angeles Express, June 3, 1983.
Released by Los Angeles Express, August 1, 1985; signed by New York Jets, August 5, 1985.

		——PASS RECEIVING——				
Year	Club	G.	P.C.	Yds.	Avg.	TD.
1983—Los Angeles USFL		5	21	326	15.5	3
1984—Los Angeles USFL		18	58	889	15.3	7
1985—Los Angeles USFL		16	47	777	16.5	6
1985—N.Y. Jets NFL		16	12	187	15.6	0
USFL Totals—3 Years		39	126	1992	15.8	16
NFL Total—1 Year		16	12	187	15.6	0
Pro Totals—4 Years		55	138	2179	15.8	16

Additional USFL statistics: Returned one kickoff for eight yards, 1983; rushed eight times for 19 yards, 1984; fumbled twice, 1984 and 1985; rushed twice for nine yards, returned eight punts for 33 yards and recovered one fumble, 1985.
Additional NFL statistics: Returned six punts for 65 yards, returned two kickoffs for 42 yards, recovered one fumble and fumbled once, 1985.

ANDRE TOWNSEND
Defensive End-Nose Tackle—Denver Broncos
Born October 8, 1962, at Chicago, Ill.
Height, 6.03. Weight, 265.
High School—Aberdeen, Miss.
Attended University of Mississippi.

Selected by Birmingham in 1984 USFL territorial draft.

Selected by Denver in 2nd round (46th player selected) of 1984 NFL draft.
Signed by Denver Broncos, June 18, 1984.
Denver NFL, 1984 and 1985.
Games: 1984 (16), 1085 (16). Total—32.
Pro statistics: Recovered one fumble, 1984 and 1985.

GREG TOWNSEND
Defensive End—Los Angeles Raiders
Born November 3, 1961, at Los Angeles, Calif.
Height, 6.03. Weight, 250.
High School—Compton, Calif., Dominguez.
Attended Long Beach City College and Texas Christian University.

Selected by Oakland in 7th round (79th player selected) of 1983 USFL draft.
Selected by Los Angeles Raiders in 4th round (110th player selected) of 1983 NFL draft.
Signed by Los Angeles Raiders, July 7, 1983.
Los Angeles Raiders NFL, 1983 through 1985.
Games: 1983 (16), 1984 (16), 1985 (16). Total—48.
Pro statistics: Recovered one fumble for 66 yards and a touchdown, 1983; recovered one fumble, 1985.
Played in AFC Championship Game following 1983 season.
Played in NFL Championship Game following 1983 season.

MARK JOSEPH TRAYNOWICZ
Name pronounced TRAY-no-witz.
Guard—Buffalo Bills
Born November 20, 1962, at Omaha, Neb.
Height, 6.05. Weight, 272.
High School—Bellevue, Neb., West.
Received degree in civil engineering from University of Nebraska in 1985.

Selected by Houston in 1st round (9th player selected) of 1985 USFL draft.
Selected by Buffalo in 2nd round (29th player selected) of 1985 NFL draft.
Signed by Buffalo Bills, July 20, 1985.
Buffalo NFL, 1985.
Games: 1985 (14).
Pro statistics: Recovered one fumble, 1985.

TRAVIS TYRONE TUCKER
Tight End—Cleveland Browns
Born September 19, 1963, at Brooklyn, N.Y.
Height, 6.03. Weight, 227.
High School—Brooklyn, N.Y., South Shore.
Attended Southern Connecticut State University.

Selected by Cleveland in 11th round (287th player selected) of 1985 NFL draft.
Signed by Cleveland Browns, July 11, 1985.

Year Club	—PASS RECEIVING—				
	G.	P.C.	Yds.	Avg.	TD.
1985—Cleveland NFL	16	2	20	10.0	0

ANTHONY IVAN TUGGLE
Defensive Back—Pittsburgh Steelers
Born September 13, 1963, at Baton Rouge, La.
Height, 6.01. Weight, 211.
High School—Baker, La.
Attended Southern University and Nicholls State University.

Selected by Los Angeles in 5th round (64th player selected) of 1985 USFL draft.
Selected by Cincinnati in 4th round (97th player selected) of 1985 NFL draft.
Signed by Cincinnati Bengals, July 21, 1985.
Released by Cincinnati Bengals, August 27, 1985; signed as free agent by Pittsburgh Steelers, December 11, 1985.
Pittsburgh NFL, 1985.
Games: 1985 (2).
Pro statistics: Returned one kickoff for eight yards, 1985.

MANU'ULA ASOVALU TUIASOSOPO
Name pronounced Tooey-ahso-sopo.

In Samoan, first name means, "Happy Bird".

(Manu)
Defensive Tackle—San Francisco 49ers
Born August 30, 1957, at Los Angeles, Calif.
Height, 6.03. Weight, 262.
High School—Long Beach, Calif., St. Anthony.
Attended University of California at Los Angeles.

Cousin of Terry Tautolo, linebacker with Philadelphia Eagles, San Francisco 49ers, Detroit Lions and
Miami Dolphins, 1976 through 1984; John Tautolo, offensive tackle with Portland Breakers, 1985;
Frank Manumaleuga, linebacker with Kansas City Chiefs and Oakland Invaders, 1979 through 1981, 1983 and 1984;
and Jack Thompson, quarterback with Cincinnati Bengals and Tampa Bay Buccaneers, 1979 through 1984;
related to Matt Elisara, nose tackle with Denver Gold and Oakland Invaders, 1983.

Selected by Seattle in 1st round (18th player selected) of 1979 NFL draft.
On physically unable to perform/active with knee injury, July 30 through August 15, 1982; activated, August 16, 1982.
Traded by Seattle Seahawks to San Francisco 49ers for 4th round pick in 1984 draft and 10th round pick in 1985 draft, April 4, 1984.
Seattle NFL, 1979 through 1983; San Francisco NFL, 1984 and 1985.
Games: 1979 (16), 1980 (16), 1981 (16), 1982 (9), 1983 (16), 1984 (16), 1985 (15). Total—104.
Pro statistics: Recovered one fumble, 1980 and 1982; recovered three fumbles, 1981; recovered two fumbles for six yards, 1984.
Played in AFC Championship Game following 1983 season.
Played in NFC Championship Game following 1984 season.
Played in NFL Championship Game following 1984 season.

MARK PULEMAU TUINEI
Name pronounced TWO-e-nay.
Center—Dallas Cowboys
Born March 31, 1960, at Nanakuli, Oahu, Haw.
Height, 6.05. Weight, 270.
High School—Honolulu, Haw., Punahou.
Attended University of California at Los Angeles and University of Hawaii.
Brother of Tom Tuinei, defensive end with Edmonton Eskimos.

Selected by Boston in 19th round (227th player selected) of 1983 USFL draft.
Signed as free agent by Dallas Cowboys, April 28, 1983.
Dallas NFL, 1983 through 1985.
Games: 1983 (10), 1984 (16), 1985 (16). Total—42.

WILLIE TULLIS
Cornerback—New Orleans Saints
Born April 5, 1958, at Newville, Ala.
Height, 6.00. Weight, 190.
High School—Headland, Ala.
Attended University of Southern Mississippi and Troy State University.

Selected by Houston in 8th round (217th player selected) of 1981 NFL draft.
Released by Houston Oilers, September 3, 1985; signed as free agent by New Orleans Saints, September 17, 1985.

		INTERCEPTIONS			–PUNT RETURNS–			—KICKOFF RET.—				—TOTAL—		
Year Club	G.	No.	Yds.	Avg. TD.	No.	Yds.	Avg. TD.	No.	Yds.	Avg.	TD.	TD.	Pts.	F.
1981—Houston NFL	16		None		2	29	14.5 0	32	779	24.3	★1	1	6	0
1982—Houston NFL	9		None			None		5	91	18.2	0	0	0	0
1983—Houston NFL	16	5	65	13.0 0		None		1	16	16.0	0	0	0	0
1984—Houston NFL	16	4	48	12.0 0		None			None			0	0	1
1985—New Orleans NFL	14	2	22	11.0 0	17	141	8.3 0	23	470	20.4	0	0	0	
Pro Totals—5 Years	71	11	135	12.3 0	19	170	8.9 0	61	1356	22.2	1	1	6	2

Additional pro statistics: Recovered one fumble, 1984.

DANIEL ANTHONY TURK
(Dan)
Center—Pittsburgh Steelers
Born June 25, 1962, at Milwaukee, Wis.
Height, 6.04. Weight, 259.
High School—Milwaukee, Wis., James Madison.
Attended Drake University and University of Wisconsin.

Selected by Jacksonville in 1985 USFL territorial draft.
USFL rights traded with rights to running back Marck Harrison and tight end Ken Whisenhunt by Jacksonville Bulls to Tampa Bay Bandits for rights to running back Cedric Jones, kicker Bobby Raymond and defensive back Eric Riley, January 3, 1985.
Selected by Pittsburgh in 4th round (101st player selected) of 1985 NFL draft.
Signed by Pittsburgh Steelers, July 19, 1985.
On injured reserve with broken wrist, September 16 through remainder of 1985 season.
Pittsburgh NFL, 1985.
Games: 1985 (1).

DARYL TURNER
Wide Receiver—Seattle Seahawks
Born December 15, 1961, at Wadley, Ga.
Height, 6.03. Weight, 198.
High School—Flint, Mich., Southwestern.
Attended Michigan State University.

Selected by Michigan in 1984 USFL territorial draft.
Selected by Seattle in 2nd round (49th player selected) of 1984 NFL draft.
Signed by Seattle Seahawks, May 16, 1984.

	—PASS RECEIVING—				
Year Club	G.	P.C.	Yds.	Avg.	TD.
1984—Seattle NFL	16	35	715	20.4	10
1985—Seattle NFL	16	34	670	19.7	★13
Pro Totals—2 Years	32	69	1385	20.1	23

JIMMY LEE TURNER
Cornerback—Cincinnati Bengals

Born June 15, 1959, at Sherman, Tex.
Height, 6.00. Weight, 187.
High School—Sherman, Tex.
Attended University of California at Los Angeles.

Selected by Philadelphia in 7th round (80th player selected) of 1983 USFL draft.
Selected by Cincinnati in 3rd round (81st player selected) of 1983 NFL draft.
Signed by Cincinnati Bengals, May 31, 1983.
Cincinnati NFL, 1983 through 1985.
Games: 1983 (16), 1984 (16), 1985 (16). Total—48.
Pro statistics: Intercepted one pass for four yards and recovered one fumble, 1984; intercepted one pass for 40 yards, 1985.

JOHN TURNER JR.
Cornerback—Minnesota Vikings

Born February 22, 1956, at Miami, Fla.
Height, 6.00. Weight, 199.
High School—Miami, Fla., Norland.
Received bachelor of science degree in physical education from University of Miami (Fla.) in 1978.

Selected by Minnesota in 2nd round (48th player selected) of 1978 NFL draft.
Traded by Minnesota Vikings to San Diego Chargers for offensive tackle Billy Shields, August 10, 1984. (Shields did not report and was returned in exchange for 3rd round pick in 1985 draft, September 3, 1984.)
Left San Diego Chargers camp voluntarily, August 13 through August 20, 1984.
Returned and granted roster exemption, August 21 and August 22, 1984; activated, August 23, 1984.
Released by San Diego Chargers, August 27, 1985; signed as free agent by Minnesota Vikings, September 12, 1985.

| | | | —INTERCEPTIONS— | | |
Year Club	G.	No.	Yds.	Avg.	TD.
1978—Minnesota NFL	14	1	15	15.0	0
1979—Minnesota NFL	16	2	48	24.0	0
1980—Minnesota NFL	16	6	22	3.7	0
1981—Minnesota NFL	13		None		
1982—Minnesota NFL	9	2	43	21.5	*1
1983—Minnesota NFL	16	6	37	6.2	0
1984—San Diego NFL	15	2	43	21.5	0
1985—Minnesota NFL	15	5	62	12.4	0
Pro Totals—8 Years	114	24	270	11.3	1

Additional pro statistics: Returned one punt for no yards and fumbled once, 1979; recovered one fumble, 1980 and 1984; recovered one fumble for 35 yards, 1982; recovered two fumbles for 24 yards, 1983.

KEENA TURNER
Linebacker—San Francisco 49ers

Born October 22, 1958, at Chicago, Ill.
Height, 6.02. Weight, 219.
High School—Chicago, Ill., Vocational.
Attended Purdue University.

Selected by San Francisco in 2nd round (39th player selected) of 1980 NFL draft.

| | | | —INTERCEPTIONS— | | |
Year Club	G.	No.	Yds.	Avg.	TD.
1980—San Francisco NFL	16	2	15	7.5	0
1981—San Francisco NFL	16	1	0	0.0	0
1982—San Francisco NFL	9		None		
1983—San Francisco NFL	15		None		
1984—San Francisco NFL	16	4	51	12.8	0
1985—San Francisco NFL	15		None		
Pro Totals—6 Years	87	7	66	9.4	0

Additional pro statistics: Recovered three fumbles, 1981; recovered one fumble, 1983; returned two fumbles for 65 yards and a touchdown, 1985.
Played in NFC Championship Game following 1981, 1983 and 1984 seasons.
Played in NFL Championship Game following 1981 and 1984 seasons.
Played in Pro Bowl (NFL All-Star Game) following 1984 season.

MAURICE ANTOINE TURNER
Running Back—Minnesota Vikings

Born September 10, 1960, at Salt Lake City, Utah.
Height, 5.11. Weight, 200.
High School—Layton, Utah.
Received bachelor of arts degree in business administration from Utah State University.

Selected by Minnesota in 12th round (325th player selected) of 1983 NFL draft.
Released by Minnesota Vikings, August 29, 1983.
USFL rights traded by Houston Gamblers to Oakland Invaders for rights to wide receiver Perry Parmelee, October 28, 1983.
Signed by Oakland Invaders, November 20, 1983.
Released by Oakland Invaders, February 9, 1984; re-signed by Minnesota Vikings after clearing procedural waivers, May 10, 1984.

Released by Minnesota Vikings, August 29, 1984; re-signed by Vikings, September 12, 1984.
Released by Minnesota Vikings, November 15, 1985; signed as free agent by Green Bay Packers, November 21, 1985.
Released by Green Bay Packers, December 11, 1985; signed as free agent by Minnesota Vikings, March 19, 1986.
Minnesota NFL, 1984; Minnesota (10)-Green Bay (3) NFL, 1985.
Games: 1984 (13), 1985 (13). Total—26.
Pro statistics: Returned two kickoffs for 21 yards, 1984; returned four kickoffs for 61 yards, 1985.

THOMAS WILLIAM TURNURE
Name pronounced Tur-NEWER.
(Tom)
Center-Guard—Detroit Lions
Born July 9, 1957, at Seattle, Wash.
Height, 6.04. Weight, 250.
High School—Seattle, Wash., Roosevelt.
Received bachelor of science degree in economics from University of Washington in 1980.

Selected by Detroit in 3rd round (57th player selected) of 1980 NFL draft.
On injured reserve with knee injury, September 23 through remainder of 1980 season.
Granted free agency, February 1, 1984; signed by Michigan Panthers, June 15, 1984.
Granted roster exemption, June 15, 1984; activated, June 18, 1984.
Protected in merger of Michigan Panthers and Oakland Invaders, December 6, 1984.
Granted free agency, August 1, 1985; re-signed by Lions, November 15, 1985.
Detroit NFL, 1980 through 1982; Michigan USFL, 1984; Oakland USFL, 1985; Detroit NFL, 1985.
Games: 1980 (3), 1981 (16), 1982 (9), 1984 (2), 1985 USFL (18), 1985 NFL (6). Total NFL—34. Total USFL—20. Total Pro—54.
Played in USFL Championship Game following 1985 season.

WENDELL AVERY TYLER
Running Back—San Francisco 49ers
Born May 20, 1955, at Shreveport, La.
Height, 5.10. Weight, 207.
High School—Los Angeles, Calif., Crenshaw.
Attended University of California at Los Angeles.

Selected by Los Angeles in 3rd round (79th player selected) of 1977 NFL draft.
On injured reserve with knee injury, September 12 through remainder of 1978 season.
On non-football injury list with hip injury, September 3 through October 23, 1980; activated, October 24, 1980.
On injured reserve with dislocated elbow, December 6 through remainder of 1980 season.
Traded with defensive tackle Cody Jones and 3rd round pick in 1983 draft by Los Angeles Rams to San Francisco 49ers for 2nd and 4th round picks in 1983 draft, April 25, 1983.

| | | —RUSHING— | | | | PASS RECEIVING | | | | —TOTAL— | | |
Year Club	G.	Att.	Yds.	Avg.	TD.	P.C.	Yds.	Avg.	TD.	TD.	Pts.	F.
1977—Los Angeles Rams NFL	14	61	317	5.2	3	1	3	3.0	0	3	18	0
1978—Los Angeles Rams NFL	2	14	45	3.2	0	2	17	8.5	0	0	0	2
1979—Los Angeles Rams NFL	16	218	1109	*5.1	9	32	308	9.6	1	10	60	9
1980—Los Angeles Rams NFL	4	30	157	5.2	0	2	8	4.0	0	0	0	1
1981—Los Angeles Rams NFL	15	260	1074	4.1	12	45	436	9.7	5	17	102	11
1982—Los Angeles Rams NFL	9	137	564	4.1	9	38	375	9.9	4	13	78	*10
1983—San Francisco NFL	14	176	856	4.9	4	34	285	8.4	2	6	36	7
1984—San Francisco NFL	16	246	1262	5.1	7	28	230	8.2	2	9	54	13
1985—San Francisco NFL	13	171	867	5.1	6	20	154	7.7	2	8	48	6
Pro Totals—9 Years	103	1313	6251	4.8	50	202	1816	9.0	16	66	396	59

| | | KICKOFF RETURNS | | | |
Year Club	G.	No.	Yds.	Avg.	TD.
1977—L.A. Rams NFL	14	24	523	21.8	0
1978—L.A. Rams NFL	2	2	31	15.5	0
1979—L.A. Rams NFL	16	1	16	16.0	0
1980—L.A. Rams NFL	4		None		
1981—L.A. Rams NFL	15		None		
1982—L.A. Rams NFL	9		None		
1983—San Francisco NFL	14		None		
1984—San Francisco NFL	16		None		
1985—San Francisco NFL	13		None		
Pro Totals—9 Years	103	27	570	21.1	0

Additional pro statistics: Recovered one fumble, 1978, 1979 and 1982; recovered two fumbles, 1984 and 1985.
Played in NFC Championship Game following 1979, 1983 and 1984 seasons.
Played in NFL Championship Game following 1979 and 1984 seasons.
Played in Pro Bowl (NFL All-Star Game) following 1984 season.

TIMOTHY G. TYRRELL
Name pronounced Tuhr-RELL.
(Tim)
Running Back—Atlanta Falcons
Born February 19, 1961, at Chicago, Ill.
Height, 6.01. Weight, 201.
High School—Hoffman Estates, Ill., James B. Conant.
Attended William Rainey Harper College and Northern Illinois University.

Selected by Chicago in 1984 USFL territorial draft.
Signed as free agent by Atlanta Falcons, May 2, 1984.
Released by Atlanta Falcons, August 27, 1984; re-signed by Falcons, October 3, 1984,
Atlanta NFL, 1984 and 1985.
Games: 1984 (11), 1985 (16). Total—27.
Pro statistics: Returned one kickoff for no yards and recovered three fumbles, 1984; returned one kickoff for 13 yards and fumbled once, 1985.

KEITH VAN HORNE
Offensive Tackle—Chicago Bears
Born November 6, 1957, at Mt. Lebanon, Pa.
Height, 6.07. Weight, 276.
High School—Fullerton, Calif.
Received bachelor of arts degree in broadcast journalism from University of Southern California.
Brother of Pete Van Horne, first baseman in Chicago Cubs' organization, 1977.

Named as offensive tackle on THE SPORTING NEWS College All-America Team, 1980.
Selected by Chicago in 1st round (11th player selected) of 1981 NFL draft.
Chicago NFL, 1981 through 1985.
Games: 1981 (14), 1982 (9), 1983 (14), 1984 (14), 1985 (16). Total—67.
Pro statistics: Recovered one fumble, 1981 and 1982.
Played in NFC Championship Game following 1984 and 1985 seasons.
Played in NFL Championship Game following 1985 season.

NORWOOD JACOB VANN JR.
Linebacker—Los Angeles Rams
Born February 18, 1962, at Philadelphia, Pa.
Height, 6.01. Weight, 225.
High School—Warsaw, N.C., James Kenan.
Attended East Carolina University.

Selected by Los Angeles Rams in 10th round (253rd player selected) of 1984 NFL draft.
On injured reserve with knee injury, October 21 through December 20, 1985; activated, December 21, 1985.
Los Angeles Rams NFL, 1984 and 1985.
Games: 1984 (16), 1985 (8). Total—24.
Pro statistics: Credited with one safety and recovered two fumbles, 1984; recovered one fumble, 1985.
Played in NFC Championship Game following 1985 season.

JEFFREY ALOYSIUS VAN NOTE
(Jeff)
Center—Atlanta Falcons
Born February 7, 1946, at South Orange, N. J.
Height, 6.02. Weight, 264.
High School—Bardstown, Ky., St. Joseph Prep.
Received bachelor of arts degree in history and political science from
University of Kentucky in 1969.

Selected by Atlanta NFL in 11th round (262nd player selected) of 1969 AFL-NFL draft.
Played in Continental Football League with Huntsville, 1969.
Atlanta NFL, 1969 through 1985.
Games: 1969 (1), 1970 (14), 1971 (14), 1972 (14), 1973 (14), 1974 (14), 1975 (14), 1976 (10), 1977 (14), 1978 (16), 1979 (16), 1980 (16), 1981 (16), 1982 (9), 1983 (16), 1984 (16), 1985 (16). Total—230.
Pro statistics: Recovered one fumble, 1970, 1972 and 1981; fumbled once, 1971 and 1975; recovered one fumble for 6 yards, 1979; fumbled once for minus 20 yards, 1981.
Played in Pro Bowl (NFL All-Star Game) following 1974, 1975 and 1979 through 1982 seasons.

BRAD ALAN VAN PELT
Linebacker—Los Angeles Raiders
Born April 5, 1951, at Owosso, Mich.
Height, 6.05. Weight, 235.
High School—Owosso, Mich.
Attended Michigan State University.

Named to THE SPORTING NEWS NFC All-Star Team, 1978 and 1979.
Named as safety on THE SPORTING NEWS College All-America Team, 1972.
Selected by New York Giants in 2nd round (40th player selected) of 1973 NFL draft.
Traded by New York Giants to Minnesota Vikings for running back Tony Galbreath, July 12, 1984.
Placed on did not report list, August 21 through October 2, 1984.
Granted roster exemption, October 3 through October 8, 1984.
Traded by Minnesota Vikings to Los Angeles Raiders for 6th round pick in 1985 draft and 2nd round pick in 1986 draft, October 9, 1984.
Granted roster exemption, October 9 through October 14, 1984; activated, October 15, 1984.
Selected by Detroit Tigers' organization in 10th round of free-agent draft, June 5, 1969.
Selected by California Angels' organization in 13th round of free-agent draft, June 6, 1972.
Selected by St. Louis Cardinals' organization in secondary phase of free-agent draft, January 10, 1973.
Selected by Cleveland Indians' organization in secondary phase of free-agent draft, January 9, 1974.

Year	Club	G.	No.	Yds.	Avg.TD.
1973—N.Y. Giants NFL		5			None
1974—N.Y. Giants NFL		12	2	22	11.0 0
1975—N.Y. Giants NFL		14	3	8	2.7 0
1976—N.Y. Giants NFL		14	2	13	6.5 0
1977—N.Y. Giants NFL		14	2	9	4.5 0
1978—N.Y. Giants NFL		14	3	32	10.7 0
1979—N.Y. Giants NFL		16			None
1980—N.Y. Giants NFL		15	3	3	1.0 0

Year	Club	G.	No.	Yds.	Avg.TD.
1981—N.Y. Giants NFL		14	1	10	10.0 0
1982—N.Y. Giants NFL		9			None
1983—N.Y. Giants NFL		16	2	7	3.5 0
1984—L.A. Raiders NFL		9	1	9	9.0 0
1985—L.A. Raiders NFL		16	1	22	22.0 0
Pro Totals—13 Years		168	20	135	6.8 0

Additional pro statistics: Recovered two fumbles, 1974, 1981 and 1982; recovered one fumble, 1977; recovered one fumble for 42 yards and caught one pass for 20 yards, 1979; recovered three fumbles for 46 yards, 1980.
Played in Pro Bowl (NFL All-Star Game) following 1976 through 1980 seasons.

ELTON ALVIN VEALS
Running Back—San Francisco 49ers
Born March 26, 1961, at Baton Rouge, La.
Height, 5.11. Weight, 230.
High School—Baton Rouge, La., Istrouma.
Attended Merritt College and Tulane University.

Selected by New Orleans in 1984 USFL territorial draft.
Selected by Pittsburgh in 11th round (303rd player selected) of 1984 NFL draft.
Signed by Pittsburgh Steelers, May 19, 1984.
Released by Pittsburgh Steelers, August 25, 1985; signed as free agent by San Francisco 49ers, February 9, 1986.

			—RUSHING—				PASS RECEIVING				—TOTAL—		
Year	Club	G.	Att.	Yds.	Avg.	TD.	P.C.	Yds.	Avg.	TD.	TD.	Pts.	F.
1984—Pittsburgh NFL		15	31	87	2.8	0		None			0	0	0

Additional pro statistics: Returned four kickoffs for 40 yards and recovered one fumble, 1984.
Played in AFC Championship Game following 1984 season.

GARIN LEE VERIS
Name pronounced GARR-in VAIR-is.
Defensive End—New England Patriots
Born February 27, 1963, at Chillicothe, O.
Height, 6.04. Weight, 255.
High School—Chillicothe, O.
Attended Stanford University.

Selected by Oakland in 1985 USFL territorial draft.
Selected by New England in 2nd round (48th player selected) of 1985 NFL draft.
Signed by New England Patriots, July 25, 1985.
New England NFL, 1985.
Games: 1985 (16).
Pro statistics: Recovered two fumbles, 1985.
Played in AFC Championship Game following 1985 season.
Played in NFL Championship Game following 1985 season.

DAVID VERSER
Wide Receiver—Tampa Bay Buccaneers
Born March 1, 1958, at Kansas City, Kan.
Height, 6.01. Weight, 200.
High School—Kansas City, Kan., Sumner.
Attended University of Kansas.

Selected by Cincinnati in 1st round (10th player selected) of 1981 NFL draft.
Traded conditionally by Cincinnati Bengals to Green Bay Packers for draft choice, August 26, 1985.
Released by Green Bay Packers, September 2, 1985; signed as free agent by Tampa Bay Buccaneers for 1986 December 6, 1985.
Signed for 1985 season, December 11, 1985.

			—RUSHING—				PASS RECEIVING				—TOTAL—		
Year	Club	G.	Att.	Yds.	Avg.	TD.	P.C.	Yds.	Avg.	TD.	TD.	Pts.	F.
1981—Cincinnati NFL		16	2	11	5.5	0	6	161	26.8	2	2	12	2
1982—Cincinnati NFL		9	1	1	1.0	0	4	98	24.5	1	1	6	0
1983—Cincinnati NFL		13	2	31	15.5	0	7	82	11.7	0	0	0	0
1984—Cincinnati NFL		11	2	5	2.5	0	6	113	18.8	0	0	0	0
1985—Tampa Bay NFL		1			None			None			0	0	1
Pro Totals—5 Years		50	7	48	6.9	0	23	454	19.7	3	3	18	3

			KICKOFF RETURNS			
Year	Club	G.	No.	Yds.	Avg.TD.	
1981—Cincinnati NFL		16	29	691	23.8	0
1982—Cincinnati NFL		9	16	320	20.0	0
1983—Cincinnati NFL		13	13	253	19.5	0
1984—Cincinnati NFL		11	3	46	15.3	0
1985—Tampa Bay NFL		1	4	61	15.3	0
Pro Totals—5 Years		50	65	1371	21.1	0

Played in AFC Championship Game following 1981 season.
Played in NFL Championship Game following 1981 season.

THOMAS VIGORITO
(Tom)
Wide Receiver—Miami Dolphins

Born October 23, 1959, at Passaic, N.J.
Height, 5.10. Weight, 190.
High School—Wayne, N.J., DePaul.
Received bachelor of science degree in human resources from University of Virginia.

Selected by Miami in 5th round (138th player selected) of 1981 NFL draft.
On injured reserve with knee injury, September 6 through remainder of 1983 season.
On physically unable to perform/active with knee injury, July 19 through August 20, 1984.
On physically unable to perform/reserve with knee injury, August 21 through entire 1984 season.
On injured reserve with torn hamstring, September 13 through October 23, 1985; activated after clearing procedural waivers, October 25, 1985.

| Year Club | G. | —RUSHING— | | | | PASS RECEIVING | | | | —TOTAL— | | |
		Att.	Yds.	Avg.	TD.	P.C.	Yds.	Avg.	TD.	TD.	Pts.	F.
1981—Miami NFL	16	35	116	3.3	1	33	237	7.2	2	4	24	1
1982—Miami NFL	9	19	99	5.2	1	24	186	7.8	0	2	12	2
1983—Miami NFL	1		None			1	7	7.0	0	0	0	0
1985—Miami NFL	9		None			1	9	9.0	0	0	0	3
Pro Totals—4 Years	35	54	215	4.0	2	59	439	7.4	2	6	36	6

| Year Club | G. | —PUNT RETURNS— | | | | —KICKOFF RET.— | | | |
		No.	Yds.	Avg.	TD.	No.	Yds.	Avg.	TD.
1981—Miami NFL	16	36	379	10.5	1	4	84	21.0	0
1982—Miami NFL	9	20	192	9.6	1		None		
1983—Miami NFL	1	1	62	62.0	0		None		
1985—Miami NFL	9	22	197	9.0	0		None		
Pro Totals—4 Years	35	79	830	10.5	2	4	84	21.0	0

Additional pro statistics: Recovered one fumble, 1982; recovered two fumbles, 1985.
Played in AFC Championship Game following 1982 and 1985 seasons.
Played in NFC Championship Game following 1982 season.

SCOTT VIRKUS
Defensive End—Buffalo Bills

Born September 7, 1959, at Palo Alto, Calif.
Height, 6.05. Weight, 279.
High School—Rochester, N.Y., Greece Olympia.
Attended City College of San Francisco and Purdue University.

Signed as free agent by Buffalo Bills, May 12, 1983.
Released by Buffalo Bills, September 12, 1984; awarded on waivers to New England Patriots, September 13, 1984.
Released by New England Patriots, November 7, 1984; signed as free agent by Pittsburgh Steelers, December 6, 1984.
Released by Pittsburgh Steelers after failing physical, December 7, 1984; signed as free agent by Indianapolis Colts, December 11, 1984.
Released by Indianapolis Colts, August 20, 1985; re-signed by Colts, September 11, 1985.
Released by Indianapolis Colts, May 5, 1986; signed as free agent by Buffalo Bills, May 19, 1986.
Played semi-pro football with North Tonawanda Cougars in 1982.
Buffalo NFL, 1983; Buffalo (2)-New England (5)-Indianapolis (1) NFL, 1984; Indianapolis NFL, 1985.
Games: 1983 (15), 1984 (8), 1985 (15). Total—38.

LIONEL VITAL
Running Back—Washington Redskins

Born July 15, 1963, at Loreauville, La.
Height, 5.09. Weight, 195.
High School—Loreauville, La.
Attended Nichols State University.

Selected by Arizona in 13th round (187th player selected) of 1985 USFL draft.
Selected by Washington in 7th round (185th player selected) of 1985 NFL draft.
Signed by Washington Redskins, July 18, 1985.
On injured reserve with hamstring injury, August 20 through entire 1985 season.

TIMOTHY GENE VOGLER
(Tim)
Center—Buffalo Bills

Born October 2, 1956, at Troy, O.
Height, 6.01. Weight, 267.
High School—Covington, O.
Attended Ohio State University.

Signed as free agent by Buffalo Bills, May 5, 1979.
On injured reserve with broken hand, August 28 through October 5, 1979; activated, October 6, 1979.
On injured reserve with hamstring injury, November 29 through remainder of 1980 season.
Buffalo NFL, 1979 through 1985.
Games: 1979 (10), 1980 (10), 1981 (14), 1982 (6), 1983 (16), 1984 (16), 1985 (14). Total—86.
Pro statistics: Returned one kickoff for no yards, 1980; recovered one fumble, 1985.

BRIAN E. VOGT
Defensive End—Cleveland Browns
Born August 16, 1962, at Cincinnati, O.
Height, 6.02. Weight, 282.
High School—Norwood, O.
Received bachelor of arts degree in arts and marketing from Findlay College in 1985.

Signed as free agent by Cleveland Browns, July 25, 1985.
On injured reserve with back injury, August 20 through entire 1985 season.

MICHAEL WADE
Wide Receiver—Cincinnati Bengals
Born February 4, 1961, at Waukegan, Ill.
Height, 5.09. Weight, 194.
High School—North Chicago, Ill.
Attended Iowa State University.

Selected by Michigan in 19th round (393rd player selected) of 1984 USFL draft.
Signed by Michigan Panthers, January 11, 1984.
Released by Michigan Panthers, February 8, 1984; signed as free agent by Denver Broncos, May 2, 1984.
Released by Denver Broncos, August 20, 1984; signed as free agent by Calgary Stampeders, October 5, 1984.
Released by Calgary Stampeders, July 2, 1985; signed as free agent by Cincinnati Bengals, July 22, 1985.
Released by Cincinnati Bengals, August 19, 1985; re-signed by Bengals, February 18, 1986.

		—PASS RECEIVING—			
Year	Club	G.	P.C.	Yds.	Avg. TD.
1984—Calgary CFL		3	5	56	11.2 0

Additional CFL statistics: Rushed once for 20 yards, returned one kickoff for 12 yards and fumbled once, 1984.

HENRY CARL WAECHTER
Defensive Tackle—Chicago Bears
Born February 13, 1959, at Epworth, Ia.
Height, 6.05. Weight, 275.
High School—Epworth, Ia., Western Dubuque.
Attended Waldorf Junior College and received business degree from University of Nebraska.

Selected by Chicago in 7th round (173rd player selected) of 1982 NFL draft.
Released by Chicago Bears, August 29, 1983; signed as free agent by Baltimore Colts, September 28, 1983.
Franchise transferred to Indianapolis, March 31, 1984.
Released by Indianapolis Colts, September 19, 1984; signed as free agent by Chicago Bears, December 5, 1984.
Released by Chicago Bears, September 2, 1985; re-signed by Bears, September 3, 1985.
Chicago NFL, 1982; Baltimore NFL, 1983; Indianapolis (1)-Chicago (2) NFL, 1984; Chicago NFL, 1985.
Games: 1982 (9), 1983 (11), 1984 (3), 1985 (13). Total—36.
Pro statistics: Credited with one safety, 1985.
Played in NFC Championship Game following 1984 and 1985 seasons.
Played in NFL Championship Game following 1985 season.

DANIEL WRIGHT WAGONER
(Dan)
Defensive Back—Atlanta Falcons
Born December 12, 1959, at High Point, N.C.
Height, 5.10. Weight, 180.
High School—High Point, N.C., T. Wingate Andrews.
Received degree in business administration from University of Kansas.

Selected by Detroit in 9th round (231st player selected) of 1982 NFL draft.
On injured reserve with pulled hamstring, August 30 through December 23, 1982; re-signed after clearing procedural waivers, December 25, 1982.
Released by Detroit Lions, September 8, 1984.
USFL rights traded by Chicago Blitz to Orlando Renegades for rights to running back Reggie Evans, October 12, 1984.
Signed as free agent by Minnesota Vikings, October 31, 1984.
Released by Minnesota Vikings, August 9, 1985; signed as free agent by Atlanta Falcons, September 18, 1985.
Detroit NFL, 1982 and 1983; Detroit (1)-Minnesota (4) NFL, 1984; Atlanta NFL, 1985.
Games: 1982 (1), 1983 (14), 1984 (5), 1985 (14). Total—34.
Pro statistics: Returned 13 kickoffs for 262 yards (20.2 avg.) and recovered one fumble, 1985.

STAN WALDEMORE
Offensive Lineman—New York Jets
Born February 20, 1955, at Newark, N. J.
Height, 6.04. Weight, 269.
High School—Newark, N. J., Essex Catholic.
Received degree in construction management from University of Nebraska in 1978.

Selected by Atlanta in 3rd round (70th player selected) of 1978 NFL draft.
Released by Atlanta Falcons, September 1, 1978; signed as free agent by New York Jets, October 10, 1978.
Released by New York Jets, August 21, 1979; re-signed by Jets, August 28, 1979.
On injured reserve with knee injury, September 29 through remainder of 1983 season.
On injured reserve with knee injury, Sepember 3 through entire 1985 season.
New York Jets NFL, 1978 through 1984.

Games: 1978 (4), 1979 (16), 1980 (16), 1981 (16), 1982 (9), 1983 (4), 1984 (14). Total—79.
Pro statistics: Fumbled once for minus three yards, 1980; recovered one fumble, 1982 and 1984.
Played in AFC Championship Game following 1982 season.

BYRON BURNEIL WALKER
Wide Receiver—Seattle Seahawks
Born July 28, 1960, at Scott Air Force Base, Ill.
Height, 6.04. Weight, 190.
High School—Warner Robins, Ga.
Attended The Citadel.

Signed as free agent by Seattle Seahawks, April 30, 1982.

Year Club	—PASS RECEIVING—				
	G.	P.C.	Yds.	Avg.	TD.
1982—Seattle NFL..................	9	10	156	15.6	2
1983—Seattle NFL..................	16	12	248	20.7	2
1984—Seattle NFL..................	16	13	236	18.2	1
1985—Seattle NFL..................	16	19	285	15.0	2
Pro Totals—4 Years...........	57	54	925	17.1	7

Additional pro statistics: Returned blocked field goal attempt 56 yards for a touchdown, recovered one fumble and fumbled once, 1985.
Played in AFC Championship Game following 1983 season.

DWIGHT GERARD WALKER
Wide Receiver—New Orleans Saints
Born January 10, 1959, at Metairie, La.
Height, 5.10. Weight, 185.
High School—Metairie, La., East Jefferson.
Attended Nicholls State University.

Selected by Cleveland in 4th round (87th player selected) of 1982 NFL draft.
On non-football injury list with bruised heart muscle, September 2 through September 27, 1984; activated, September 28, 1984.
Released by Cleveland Browns, September 2, 1985; signed as free agent by New Orleans Saints, March 6, 1986.

Year Club		—RUSHING—				PASS RECEIVING				—TOTAL—		
	G.	Att.	Yds.	Avg.	TD.	P.C.	Yds.	Avg.	TD.	TD.	Pts.	F.
1982—Cleveland NFL.............................	9		None			8	136	17.0	0	0	0	2
1983—Cleveland NFL.............................	16	19	100	5.3	0	29	273	9.4	1	1	6	1
1984—Cleveland NFL.............................	11	1	—8	—8.0	0	10	122	12.2	0	0	0	1
Pro Totals—3 Years................................	36	20	92	4.6	0	47	531	11.3	1	1	6	4

Year Club		—PUNT RETURNS—				—KICKOFF RET.—			
	G.	No.	Yds.	Avg.	TD.	No.	Yds.	Avg.	TD.
1982—Cleveland NFL..	9	19	101	5.3	0	13	295	22.7	0
1983—Cleveland NFL..	16	3	26	8.7	0	29	627	21.6	0
1984—Cleveland NFL..	11	6	50	8.3	0		None		
Pro Totals—3 Years..	36	28	177	6.3	0	42	922	22.0	0

Additional pro statistics: Recovered two fumbles, 1982; attempted three passes with one completion for 25 yards, intercepted once and recovered three fumbles, 1983.

FULTON LUTHER WALKER JR.
Safety—Los Angeles Raiders
Born April 30, 1958, at Martinsburg, W. Va.
Height, 5.11. Weight, 196.
High School—Martinsburg, W. Va.
Received bachelor of science degree in physical
education from University of West Virginia in 1981.

Established NFL record for most punt return yards, season (692), 1985.
Named as kick returner to THE SPORTING NEWS NFL All-Star Team, 1983.
Selected by Miami in 6th round (154th player selected) of 1981 NFL draft.
On injured reserve with broken thumb, August 28 through September 27, 1984; activated, September 28, 1984.
Released by Miami Dolphins, September 21, 1985; signed as free agent by Los Angeles Raiders, September 26, 1985.

Year Club		INTERCEPTIONS				—PUNT RETURNS—				—KICKOFF RET.—				—TOTAL—		
	G.	No.	Yds.	Avg.	TD.	No.	Yds.	Avg.	TD.	No.	Yds.	Avg.	TD.	TD.	Pts.	F.
1981—Miami NFL..................	16	1	0	0.0	0	5	50	10.0	0	38	932	24.5	⋆1	1	6	4
1982—Miami NFL..................	9	3	54	18.0	0		None			20	433	21.7	0	0	0	0
1983—Miami NFL..................	15	1	7	7.0	0	8	86	10.8	0	36	962	⋆26.7	0	0	0	1
1984—Miami NFL..................	12		None			21	169	8.0	0	29	617	21.3	0	0	0	2
1985—Mia (2)-Raid (13) NFL	15		None			⋆62	⋆692	11.2	0	21	467	22.2	0	0	0	5
Pro Totals—5 Years.......	67	5	61	12.2	0	96	997	10.4	0	144	3411	23.7	1	1	6	12

Additional pro statistics: Recovered two fumbles, 1981 and 1985; recovered one fumble, 1983.
Played in AFC Championship Game following 1982 and 1984 seasons.
Played in NFL Championship Game following 1982 and 1984 seasons.

LaQUENTIN ANTONIO WALKER
(Quentin)
Running Back—St. Louis Cardinals
Born August 27, 1961, at Teaneck, N.J.
Height, 6.01. Weight, 200.
High School—Teaneck, N.J.
Attended University of Virginia.

Selected by Washington in 1984 USFL territorial draft.
Selected by St. Louis in 7th round (185th player selected) of 1984 NFL draft.
Signed by St. Louis Cardinals, July 16, 1984.
On injured reserve with leg injury, August 28 through September 27, 1984; activated, September 28, 1984.
On injured reserve with broken ankle, October 26 through remainder of 1984 season.
On injured reserve with fractured wrist, August 26 through entire 1985 season.
St. Louis NFL, 1984.
Games: 1984 (3).

RICHARD WALKER
(Rick)
Tight End—Washington Redskins
Born May 28, 1955, at Santa Ana, Calif.
Height, 6.04. Weight, 235.
High School—Santa Ana, Calif., Valley.
Attended Santa Ana Junior College and University of California at Los Angeles.

Selected by Cincinnati in 4th round (85th player selected) of 1977 NFL draft.
Released by Cincinnati Bengals, August 27, 1979; re-signed by Bengals, October 9, 1979.
Released by Cincinnati Bengals, August 26, 1980; signed as free agent by Washington Redskins, September 12, 1980.

| | | —PASS RECEIVING— | | | |
Year Club	G.	P.C.	Yds.	Avg.	TD.
1977—Cincinnati NFL	6	1	13	13.0	0
1978—Cincinnati NFL	15	12	126	10.5	2
1979—Cincinnati NFL	10	1	14	14.0	1
1980—Washington NFL	15	10	88	8.8	1
1981—Washington NFL	16	11	112	10.2	1
1982—Washington NFL	9	12	92	7.7	1
1983—Washington NFL	16	17	168	9.9	2
1984—Washington NFL	16	5	52	10.4	1
1985—Washington NFL	16	1	8	8.0	0
Pro Totals—9 Years	119	70	673	9.6	9

Additional pro statistics: Fumbled once, 1978 and 1980; recovered two fumbles and rushed once for minus eight yards, 1980; rushed once for five yards, 1981; recovered one fumble, 1981 and 1984; rushed twice for 11 yards, 1982; rushed twice for 10 yards, 1983; rushed once for two yards, 1984; rushed three times for 16 yards, 1985.
Played in NFC Championship Game following 1982 and 1983 seasons.
Played in NFL Championship Game following 1982 and 1983 seasons.

WESLEY DARCEL WALKER
Wide Receiver—New York Jets
Born May 26, 1955, at San Bernardino, Calif.
Height, 6.00. Weight, 179.
High School—Carson, Calif.
Attended University of California.

Selected by New York Jets in 2nd round (33rd player selected) of 1977 NFL draft.
On injured reserve with knee injury, October 31 through remainder of 1979 season.
On injured reserve with thigh injury, October 11 through November 14, 1980; activated, November 15, 1980.
Placed on did not report list, August 20 through August 26, 1984.
Reported and granted roster exemption, August 27 through August 31, 1984; activated, September 1, 1984.
On injured reserve with knee injury, September 3 through October 4, 1985; activated, October 5, 1985.

| | | —RUSHING— | | | | PASS RECEIVING | | | | —TOTAL— | | |
Year Club	G.	Att.	Yds.	Avg.	TD.	P.C.	Yds.	Avg.	TD.	TD.	Pts.	F.
1977—New York Jets NFL	14	3	25	8.3	0	35	740	*21.1	3	3	18	2
1978—New York Jets NFL	16	1	—3	—3.0	0	48	*1169	*24.4	8	8	48	2
1979—New York Jets NFL	9		None			23	569	24.7	5	5	30	0
1980—New York Jets NFL	11		None			18	376	20.9	1	1	6	0
1981—New York Jets NFL	13		None			47	770	16.4	9	9	54	0
1982—New York Jets NFL	9		None			39	620	15.9	6	6	36	0
1983—New York Jets NFL	16		None			61	868	14.2	7	7	42	0
1984—New York Jets NFL	12	1	1	1.0	0	41	623	15.2	7	7	42	0
1985—New York Jets NFL	12		None			34	725	21.3	5	5	†32	1
Pro Totals—9 Years	112	5	23	4.6	0	346	6460	18.7	51	51	308	5

†Credited with one safety.
Additional pro statistics: Recovered one fumble, 1978 and 1985.
Played in AFC Championship Game following 1982 season.
Played in Pro Bowl (NFL All-Star Game) following 1978 and 1982 seasons.

DARNELL WALL
Defensive End—Washington Redskins
Born April 27, 1961, at Washington, D.C.
Height, 6.06. Weight, 280.
High School—Washington, D.C., Calvin Coolidge.
Attended Virginia Union University.
Brother of Charles Chisley, wide receiver with Washington Federals, 1983.
Selected by Oakland in 5th round (67th player selected) of 1985 USFL draft.
Signed by Oakland Invaders, January 23, 1985.
Released injured by Oakland Invaders, February 11, 1985; re-signed by Invaders, February 21, 1985.
On developmental squad, February 21 through entire 1985 season.
Released by Oakland Invaders, August 2, 1985; signed as free agent by Washington Redskins, May 8, 1986.
On developmental squad for 18 games with Oakland Invaders in 1985.
On developmental squad for USFL Championship Game following 1985 season.

EVERSON COLLINS WALLS
Cornerback—Dallas Cowboys
Born December 28, 1959, at Dallas, Tex.
Height, 6.01. Weight, 194.
High School—Dallas, Tex., L.V. Berkner.
Received bachelor of arts degree in accounting from Grambling State University in 1981.
Cousin of Ralph Anderson, back with Pittsburgh Steelers and New England Patriots,
1971 through 1973; and Herkie Walls, wide receiver-kick returner with Tampa Bay Buccaneers.
Established NFL record for most seasons leading league in interceptions (3).
Signed as free agent by Dallas Cowboys, May, 1981.

		—INTERCEPTIONS—			
Year Club	G.	No.	Yds.	Avg.	TD.
1981—Dallas NFL	16	*11	133	12.1	0
1982—Dallas NFL	9	*7	61	8.7	0
1983—Dallas NFL	16	4	70	17.5	0
1984—Dallas NFL	16	3	12	4.0	0
1985—Dallas NFL	16	*9	31	3.4	0
Pro Totals—5 Years	73	34	307	9.0	0

Additional pro statistics: Recovered one fumble, 1981; fumbled once, 1982; recovered one fumble for four yards, 1985.
Played in NFC Championship Game following 1981 and 1982 seasons.
Played in Pro Bowl (NFL All-Star Game) following 1981 through 1983 and 1985 seasons.

McCUREY HERCULES WALLS
(Herkie)
Wide Receiver-Kick Returner—Tampa Bay Buccaneers
Born July 18, 1961, at Garland, Tex.
Height, 5.08. Weight, 160.
High School—Garland, Tex.
Attended University of Texas.
Cousin of Everson Walls, cornerback with Dallas Cowboys.
Selected by Boston in 12th round (134th player selected) of 1983 USFL draft.
Selected by Houston in 7th round (170th player selected) of 1983 NFL draft.
Signed by Houston Oilers, July 6, 1983.
On injured reserve with dislocated finger, August 16 through September 24, 1985.
Released by Houston Oilers, September 25, 1985; re-signed by Oilers, November 9, 1985.
Granted free agency, February 1, 1986; withdrew qualifying offer, April 9, 1986.
Signed by Tampa Bay Buccaneers, May 27, 1986.

		—RUSHING—				PASS RECEIVING				—TOTAL—		
Year Club	G.	Att.	Yds.	Avg.	TD.	P.C.	Yds.	Avg.	TD.	TD.	Pts.	F.
1983—Houston NFL	16	5	44	8.8	0	12	276	23.0	1	1	6	0
1984—Houston NFL	14	4	20	5.0	0	18	291	16.2	1	1	6	0
1985—Houston NFL	6		None			1	7	7.0	0	0	0	0
Pro Totals—3 Years	36	9	64	7.1	0	31	574	18.5	2	2	12	0

		KICKOFF RETURNS			
Year Club	G.	No.	Yds.	Avg.	TD.
1983—Houston NFL	16	9	110	12.2	0
1984—Houston NFL	14	15	289	19.3	0
1985—Houston NFL	6	12	234	19.5	0
Pro Totals—3 Years	36	36	633	17.6	0

JOSEPH FOLLMANN WALTER JR.
(Joe)
Offensive Tackle—Cincinnati Bengals
Born June 18, 1963, at Dallas, Tex.
Height, 6.06. Weight, 290.
High School—Garland, Tex., North.
Attended Texas Tech University.
Selected by Denver in 1985 USFL territorial draft.

— 423 —

Selected by Cincinnati in 7th round (181st player selected) of 1985 NFL draft.
Signed by Cincinnati Bengals, July 15, 1985.
Cincinnati NFL, 1985.
Games: 1985 (14).

MICHAEL DAVID WALTER
(Mike)
Linebacker—San Francisco 49ers
Born November 30, 1960, at Salem, Ore.
Height, 6.03. Weight, 238.
High School—Eugene, Ore., Sheldon.
Attended University of Oregon.

Selected by Los Angeles in 20th round (240th player selected) of 1983 USFL draft.
Selected by Dallas in 2nd round (50th player selected) of 1983 NFL draft.
Signed by Dallas Cowboys, July 7, 1983.
Released by Dallas Cowboys, August 27, 1984; awarded on waivers to San Francisco 49ers, August 28, 1984.
Dallas NFL, 1983; San Francisco NFL, 1984 and 1985.
Games: 1983 (15), 1984 (16), 1985 (14). Total—45.
Pro statistics: Intercepted one pass for no yards, 1985.
Played in NFC Championship Game following 1984 season.
Played in NFL Championship Game following 1984 season.

DALE JAMES WALTERS
Punter—San Diego Chargers
Born June 21, 1961, at Dighton, Kan.
Height, 6.00. Weight, 210.
High School—Grand Prairie, Tex.
Received bachelor of arts degree in sports management from Rice University.

Selected by Houston in 1984 USFL territorial draft.
Signed by Houston Gamblers, January 21, 1984.
Released by Houston Gamblers, May 15, 1985; signed as free agent by Washington Redskins, June 12, 1985.
Released by Washington Redskins, August 20, 1985; signed as free agent by San Diego Chargers, April 20, 1986.

		——PUNTING——		
Year Club	G.	No.	Avg.	Blk.
1984—Houston USFL	18	64	41.0	....
1985—Houston USFL	12	38	39.5	....
Pro Totals—2 Years	30	102	40.4	....

Additional pro statistics: Attempted one pass with no completions, rushed once for 18 yards and recovered two fumbles, 1984; fumbled once, 1984 and 1985; recovered two fumbles for three yards, 1985.

DANNY EUGENE WALTERS
Cornerback—San Diego Chargers
Born November 4, 1960, at Prescott, Ark.
Height, 6.01. Weight, 180.
High School—Chicago, Ill., Percy L. Julian.
Attended University of Arkansas.

Selected by New Jersey in 11th round (123rd player selected) of 1983 USFL draft.
Selected by San Diego in 4th round (95th player selected) of 1983 NFL draft.
Signed by San Diego Chargers, July 9, 1983.
On injured reserve with knee injury, November 15 through remainder of 1984 season.

		——INTERCEPTIONS——			
Year Club	G.	No.	Yds.	Avg.	TD.
1983—San Diego NFL	16	7	55	7.9	0
1984—San Diego NFL	8		None		
1985—San Diego NFL	16	5	71	14.2	0
Pro Totals—3 Years	40	12	126	10.5	0

Additional pro statistics: Recovered one fumble, 1985.

CHRISTOPHER B. WALTMAN
(Chris)
Tight End—Dallas Cowboys
Born November 25, 1961, at Rochester, Minn.
Height, 6.07. Weight, 255.
High School—Elgin, Minn., Millville.
Attended Oregon State University.

Signed as free agent by Dallas Cowboys, May 2, 1985.
On injured reserve with neck injury, August 20 through entire 1985 season.

—DID YOU KNOW—
That the Chicago Bears' 46 points scored in Super Bowl XX were the most ever by one team in Super Bowl history?

CHRISTOPHER LAMAR WARD
(Chris)
Offensive Tackle—San Francisco 49ers
Born December 16, 1955, at Cleveland, O.
Height, 6.03. Weight, 267.
High School—Dayton, O., Patterson Cooperative.
Attended Ohio State University.

Named as offensive tackle on THE SPORTING NEWS College All-America Team, 1977.
Selected by New York Jets in 1st round (4th player selected) of 1978 NFL draft.
Released by New York Jets, August 29, 1984; signed as free agent by New Orleans Saints, September 3, 1984.
Released by New Orleans Saints, August 5, 1985; signed as free agent by San Francisco 49ers, March 10, 1986.
New York Jets NFL, 1978 through 1983; New Orleans NFL, 1984.
Games: 1978 (16), 1979 (16), 1980 (14), 1981 (16), 1982 (9), 1983 (16), 1984 (13). Total—100.
Played in AFC Championship Game following 1982 season.

CURT WARNER
Running Back—Seattle Seahawks
Born March 18, 1961, at Wyoming, W. Va.
Height, 5.11. Weight, 205.
High School—Pineville, W. Va.
Attended Penn State University.

Selected by Philadelphia in 1983 USFL territorial draft.
Selected by Seattle in 1st round (3rd player selected) of 1983 NFL draft.
Signed by Seattle Seahawks, June 29, 1983.
On injured reserve with knee injury, September 5 through remainder of 1984 season.
Selected by Philadelphia Phillies' organization in 32nd round of free-agent draft, June 5, 1979.

		—RUSHING—				PASS RECEIVING				—TOTAL—		
Year Club	G.	Att.	Yds.	Avg.	TD.	P.C.	Yds.	Avg.	TD.	TD.	Pts.	F.
1983—Seattle NFL	16	335	1449	4.3	13	42	325	7.7	1	14	84	6
1984—Seattle NFL	1	10	40	4.0	0	1	19	19.0	0	0	0	0
1985—Seattle NFL	16	291	1094	3.8	8	47	307	6.5	1	9	54	8
Pro Totals—3 Years	33	636	2583	4.1	21	90	651	7.2	2	23	138	14

Additional pro statistics: Recovered two fumbles, 1983 and 1985.
Played in AFC Championship Game following 1983 season.
Played in Pro Bowl (NFL All-Star Game) following 1983 season.

DON WARREN
Tight End—Washington Redskins
Born May 5, 1956, at Bellingham, Wash.
Height, 6.04. Weight, 242.
High School—Covina, Calif., Royal Oak.
Attended Mt. San Antonio Junior College and San Diego State University.

Selected by Washington in 4th round (103rd player selected) of 1979 NFL draft.

	—PASS RECEIVING—				
Year Club	G.	P.C.	Yds.	Avg.	TD.
1979—Washington NFL	16	26	303	11.7	0
1980—Washington NFL	13	31	323	10.4	0
1981—Washington NFL	16	29	335	11.6	1
1982—Washington NFL	9	27	310	11.5	0
1983—Washington NFL	13	20	225	11.3	2
1984—Washington NFL	16	18	192	10.7	0
1985—Washington NFL	16	15	163	10.9	1
Pro Totals—7 Years	99	166	1851	11.2	4

Additional pro statistics: Recovered one fumble, 1979 and 1985; fumbled once, 1980; rushed once for five yards, 1985.
Played in NFC Championship Game following 1982 and 1983 seasons.
Played in NFL Championship Game following 1982 and 1983 seasons.

FRANK WILLIAM WARREN III
Defensive End—New Orleans Saints
Born September 14, 1959, at Birmingham, Ala.
Height, 6.04. Weight, 278.
High School—Birmingham, Ala., Phillips.
Attended Auburn University.

Selected by New Orleans in 3rd round (57th player selected) of 1981 NFL draft.
New Orleans NFL, 1981 through 1985.
Games: 1981 (16), 1982 (9), 1983 (16), 1984 (16), 1985 (16). Total—73.
Pro statistics: Recovered one fumble, 1981 and 1983; intercepted one pass for six yards, 1983; recovered one fumble for 50 yards and a touchdown and returned blocked field goal attempt 42 yards for a touchdown, 1985.

CHRIS WASHINGTON
Linebacker—Tampa Bay Buccaneers
Born March 6, 1962, at Jackson, Miss.
Height, 6.04. Weight, 230.
High School—Chicago, Ill., Percy L. Julian.
Attended Iowa State University

Selected by Washington in 3rd round (49th player selected) of 1984 USFL draft.
Selected by Tampa Bay in 6th round (142nd player selected) of 1984 NFL draft.
Signed by Tampa Bay Buccaneers, June 5, 1984.
Tampa Bay NFL, 1984 and 1985.
Games: 1984 (16), 1985 (16). Total—32.
Pro statistics: Recovered one fumble, 1985.

JOE DAN WASHINGTON
Running Back—Atlanta Falcons
Born September 24, 1953, at Crockett, Tex.
Height, 5.10. Weight, 179.
High School—Port Arthur, Tex., Lincoln.
Received bachelor of arts degree in public relations from University of Oklahoma.

Named as running back on THE SPORTING NEWS College All-America Team, 1974.
Selected by San Diego in 1st round (4th player selected) of 1976 NFL draft.
Missed entire 1976 season due to injury.
Traded with 5th round pick in 1979 draft by San Diego Chargers to Baltimore Colts for running back Lydell Mitchell, August 23, 1978.
Traded by Baltimore Colts to Washington Redskins for 2nd round pick in 1981 draft, April 28, 1981.
On injured reserve with knee injury, September 7 through November 19, 1982; activated, November 20, 1982.
On injured reserve with knee injury, September 29 through November 27, 1984; activated, November 28, 1984.
Traded with 2nd round pick in 1985 draft and 1st round pick in 1986 draft by Washington Redskins to Atlanta Falcons for 2nd round pick in 1985 draft and 2nd and 6th round picks in 1986 draft, April 30, 1985.

		—————RUSHING—————				PASS RECEIVING				—TOTAL—		
Year Club	G.	Att.	Yds.	Avg.	TD.	P.C.	Yds.	Avg.	TD.	TD.	Pts.	F.
1977—San Diego NFL	13	62	217	3.5	0	31	244	7.9	0	0	0	1
1978—Baltimore NFL	16	240	956	4.0	0	45	377	8.4	1	2	12	12
1979—Baltimore NFL	15	242	884	3.7	4	*82	750	9.1	3	7	42	8
1980—Baltimore NFL	16	144	502	3.5	1	51	494	9.7	3	4	24	5
1981—Washington NFL	14	210	916	4.4	4	70	558	8.0	3	7	42	8
1982—Washington NFL	7	44	190	4.3	1	19	134	7.1	1	2	12	2
1983—Washington NFL	15	145	772	5.3	0	47	454	9.7	6	6	36	2
1984—Washington NFL	7	56	192	3.4	1	13	74	5.7	0	1	6	3
1985—Atlanta NFL	16	52	210	4.0	1	37	328	8.9	1	2	12	1
Pro Totals—9 Years	119	1195	4839	4.0	12	395	3413	8.6	18	31	186	42

		—PUNT RETURNS—				—KICKOFF RET.—			
Year Club	G.	No.	Yds.	Avg.	TD.	No.	Yds.	Avg.TD.	
1977—San Diego NFL	13		None				None		
1978—Baltimore NFL	16	7	37	5.3	0	19	499	26.3	*1
1979—Baltimore NFL	15		None			1	1	1.0	0
1980—Baltimore NFL	16		None				None		
1981—Washington NFL	14		None				None		
1982—Washington NFL	7		None				None		
1983—Washington NFL	15		None			1	16	16.0	0
1984—Washington NFL	7		None				None		
1985—Atlanta NFL	16		None				None		
Pro Totals—9 Years	119	7	37	5.3	0	21	516	24.6	0

Additional pro statistics: Attempted one pass with one completion for 32 yards and one touchdown, 1977; attempted four passes with two completions for 80 yards and two touchdowns and recovered two fumbles, 1978; attempted one pass with one interception and recovered two fumbles for four yards, 1979; attempted two passes with one completion for 32 yards, 1981; attempted one pass with one completion for 35 yards, 1982; attempted one pass with no completions, 1983 and 1984; recovered one fumble, 1985.
Played in NFC Championship Game following 1982 and 1983 seasons.
Played in NFL Championship Game following 1983 season.
Member of Washington Redskins for NFL Championship Game following 1982 season; did not play.
Played in Pro Bowl (NFL All-Star Game) following 1979 season.

LIONEL WASHINGTON
Cornerback—St. Louis Cardinals
Born October 21, 1960, at New Orleans, La.
Height, 6.00. Weight, 188.
High School—Lutcher, La.
Received degree in sports administration from Tulane University.

Selected by Tampa Bay in 20th round (229th player selected) of 1983 USFL draft.
Selected by St. Louis in 4th round (103rd player selected) of 1983 NFL draft.
Signed by St. Louis Cardinals, May 6, 1983.
On injured reserve with broken fibula, September 16 through November 21, 1985; activated, November 22, 1985.

Year Club	—INTERCEPTIONS— G.	No.	Yds.	Avg.	TD.
1983—St. Louis NFL	16	8	92	11.5	0
1984 St. Louis NFL	15	5	42	8.4	0
1985—St. Louis NFL	5	1	48	48.0	*1
Pro Totals—3 Years	36	14	182	13.0	1

Additional pro statistics: Recovered one fumble, 1983 and 1984.

RONNIE CARROLL WASHINGTON
Linebacker—Atlanta Falcons
Born July 29, 1963, at Monroe, La.
Height, 6.01. Weight, 236.
High School—Monroe, La., Richwood.
Attended Northeast Louisiana University.

Selected by Arizona in 1st round (13th player selected) of 1985 USFL draft.
Selected by Atlanta in 8th round (215th player selected) of 1985 NFL draft.
Signed by Atlanta Falcons, July 18, 1985.
Atlanta NFL, 1985.
Games: 1985 (16).
Additional pro statistics: Returned one kickoff for no yards, recovered one fumble and fumbled once, 1985.

SAMUEL LEE WASHINGTON JR.
(Sam)
Cornerback—Cincinnati Bengals
Born March 7, 1960, at Tampa, Fla.
Height, 5.09. Weight, 180.
High School—Tampa, Fla., Tampa Bay Tech.
Received bachelor of science degree in health, physical education and recreation
from Mississippi Valley State University in 1982.

Signed as free agent by Pittsburgh Steelers, May 5, 1982.
On injured reserve with knee injury, August 31 through December 7, 1982; re-signed after clearing procedural waivers, December 9, 1982.
Released by Pittsburgh Steelers, October 24, 1985; signed as free agent by Cincinnati Bengals, October 29, 1985.

Year Club	—INTERCEPTIONS— G.	No.	Yds.	Avg.	TD.
1982—Pittsburgh NFL	4		None		
1983—Pittsburgh NFL	16	1	25	25.0	0
1984—Pittsburgh NFL	14	6	138	23.0	*2
1985—Pitt. (7)-Cinc. (8) NFL.	15		None		
Pro Totals—4 Years	49	7	163	23.3	2

Pro statistics: Returned three kickoffs for 34 yards and recovered one fumble, 1985.
Played in AFC Championship Game following 1984 season.

ANDRE WATERS
Cornerback—Philadelphia Eagles
Born March 10, 1962, at Belle Glade, Fla.
Height, 5.11. Weight, 182.
High School—Pahokee, Fla.
Received degree in business administration from Cheyney State College.

Signed as free agent by Philadelphia Eagles, June 20, 1984.

Year Club	KICKOFF RETURNS G.	No.	Yds.	Avg.	TD.
1984—Philadelphia NFL	16	13	319	24.5	*1
1985—Philadelphia NFL	16	4	74	18.5	0
Pro Totals—2 Years	32	17	393	23.1	1

Additional pro statistics: Recovered one fumble and fumbled once, 1984 and 1985; returned one punt for 23 yards, 1985.

BOBBY LAWRENCE WATKINS
Cornerback—Detroit Lions
Born May 31, 1960, at Cottonwood, Ida.
Height, 5.10. Weight, 184.
High School—Dallas, Tex., Bishop Dunne.
Attended Southwest Texas State University.

Selected by Detroit in 2nd round (42nd player selected) of 1982 NFL draft.

Year Club	—INTERCEPTIONS— G.	No.	Yds.	Avg.	TD.
1982—Detroit NFL	9	5	22	4.4	0
1983—Detroit NFL	16	4	48	12.0	0
1984—Detroit NFL	16	6	0	0.0	0
1985—Detroit NFL	16	5	15	3.0	0
Pro Totals—4 Years	57	20	85	4.3	0

Additional pro statistics: Recovered one fumble, 1982; recovered three fumbles for six yards and fumbled once, 1983; recovered two fumbles, 1985.

STEPHEN ROSS WATSON
(Steve)
Wide Receiver—Denver Broncos
Born May 28, 1957, at Baltimore, Md.
Height, 6.04. Weight, 195.
High School—Wilmington, Del., St. Mark's.
Received degree in parks administration from Temple University.

Signed as free agent by Denver Broncos, May 12, 1979.

		—PASS RECEIVING—			
Year Club	G.	P.C.	Yds.	Avg.	TD.
1979—Denver NFL	16	6	83	13.8	0
1980—Denver NFL	16	6	146	24.3	0
1981—Denver NFL	16	60	1244	20.7	*13
1982—Denver NFL	9	36	555	15.4	2
1983—Denver NFL	16	59	1133	19.2	5
1984—Denver NFL	16	69	1170	17.0	7
1985—Denver NFL	16	61	915	15.0	5
Pro Totals—7 Years	105	297	5246	17.7	32

Additional pro statistics: Returned one kickoff for five yards and recovered one fumble, 1980; rushed twice for six yards and recovered two fumbles, 1981; rushed once for minus four yards, 1982; fumbled once, 1982 and 1983; rushed three times for 17 yards, 1983.

Played in Pro Bowl (NFL All-Star Game) following 1981 season.

FRANK WATTELET
Safety—New Orleans Saints
Born October 25, 1958, at Paola, Kan.
Height, 6.00. Weight, 185.
High School—Abilene, Kan.
Attended University of Kansas.

Signed as free agent by New Orleans Saints, May 27, 1981.
Released by New Orleans Saints after failing physical, July 15, 1981; re-signed by Saints, July 17, 1981.

		—INTERCEPTIONS—			
Year Club	G.	No.	Yds.	Avg.	TD.
1981—New Orleans NFL	16	3	16	5.3	0
1982—New Orleans NFL	9		None		
1983—New Orleans NFL	16	2	33	16.5	0
1984—New Orleans NFL	16	2	52	26.0	1
1985—New Orleans NFL	16	2	0	0.0	0
Pro Totals—5 Years	73	9	101	11.2	1

Additional pro statistics: Recovered one fumble, 1981 and 1982; returned one kickoff for four yards and recovered three fumbles for six yards, 1983; recovered two fumbles for 22 yards and a touchdown, 1984; recovered one fumble for four yards and rushed twice for 42 yards, 1985.

TED WATTS
Cornerback—New York Giants
Born May 29, 1958, at Tarpon Springs, Fla.
Height, 6.00. Weight, 190.
High School—Tarpon Springs, Fla., Tarpon.
Attended Texas Tech University.

Named as defensive back on THE SPORTING NEWS College All-America Team. 1980.
Selected by Oakland in 1st round (21st player selected) of 1981 NFL draft.
Franchise transferred to Los Angeles, May 7, 1982.
Traded by Los Angeles Raiders to New York Giants for 4th round pick in 1986 draft, August 31, 1985.

		-INTERCEPTIONS-				-PUNT RETURNS-				—TOTAL—		
Year Club	G.	No.	Yds.	Avg.	TD.	No.	Yds.	Avg.	TD.	TD.	Pts.	F.
1981—Oakland NFL	16	1	12	12.0	0	35	284	8.1	1	1	6	3
1982—Los Angeles Raiders NFL	9	1	0	0.0	0		None			0	0	0
1983—Los Angeles Raiders NFL	16	1	13	13.0	0		None			0	0	0
1984—Los Angeles Raiders NFL	16	1	0	0.0	0		None			0	0	0
1985—New York Giants NFL	16	1	0	0.0	0		None			0	0	0
Pro Totals—5 Years	73	5	25	5.0	0	35	284	8.1	1	1	6	3

Additional pro statistics: Recovered two fumbles for one yard, 1981; recovered one fumble, 1983.
Played in AFC Championship Game following 1983 season.
Played in NFL Championship Game following 1983 season.

DAVID BENJAMIN WAYMER JR.
(Dave)
Cornerback—New Orleans Saints
Born July 1, 1958, at Brooklyn, N.Y.
Height, 6.01. Weight, 188.
High School—Charlotte, N.C., West.
Received bachelor of arts degree in economics from University of Notre Dame in 1980.

Selected by New Orleans in 2nd round (41st player selected) of 1980 NFL draft.

Year Club		G.	No.	Yds.	Avg.	TD.
				—INTERCEPTIONS—		
1980—New Orleans NFL		16		None		
1981—New Orleans NFL		16	4	54	13.5	0
1982—New Orleans NFL		9		None		
1983—New Orleans NFL		16		None		
1984—New Orleans NFL		16	4	9	2.3	0
1985—New Orleans NFL		16	6	49	8.2	0
Pro Totals—6 Years		89	14	112	8.0	0

Additional pro statistics: Returned three punts for 29 yards, 1980; fumbled once, 1980 and 1985; recovered two fumbles, 1980, 1981 and 1982; recovered three fumbles, 1983.

CLARENCE WEATHERS
Wide Receiver-Punt Returner—Cleveland Browns
Born January 10, 1962, at Green's Pond, S.C.
Height, 5.09. Weight, 170.
High School—Fort Pierce, Fla.
Attended Delaware State College.
Brother of Robert Weathers, running back with New England Patriots.

Signed as free agent by New England Patriots, July 20, 1983.
On injured reserve with broken foot, August 28 through October 19, 1984; activated, October 20, 1984.
Released by New England Patriots, September 2, 1985; awarded on waivers to Cleveland Browns, September 3, 1985.

Year Club	G.	P.C.	Yds.	Avg.	TD.	No.	Yds.	Avg.	TD.	TD.	Pts.	F.
		-PASS RECEIVING-				-PUNT RETURNS-				—TOTAL—		
1983—New England NFL	16	19	379	19.9	3	4	1	0.3	0	3	18	2
1984—New England NFL	9	8	115	14.4	2	1	7	7.0	0	2	12	0
1985—Cleveland NFL	13	16	449	28.1	3	28	218	7.8	0	3	18	3
Pro Totals—3 Years	38	43	943	21.9	8	33	226	6.8	0	8	48	5

Additional pro statistics: Returned three kickoffs for 58 yards and rushed once for 28 yards, 1985; recovered one fumble, 1983 and 1985; returned one kickoff for 17 yards and rushed once for 18 yards, 1985.

CURTIS WEATHERS
Linebacker—Cleveland Browns
Born September 16, 1956, at Memphis, Tenn.
Height, 6.05. Weight, 230.
High School—Memphis, Tenn., Bishop Byrne.
Received degree in political science from University of Mississippi in 1979.

Selected by Cleveland in 9th round (241st player selected) of 1979 NFL draft.
On injured reserve with knee and hamstring injuries, September 26 through November 2, 1980; activated, November 3, 1980.
On injured reserve with dislocated thumb, December 9 through remainder of 1981 season.
On injured reserve with knee injury, September 7 through November 18, 1982; activated, November 19, 1982.
Cleveland NFL, 1979 through 1985.
Games: 1979 (16), 1980 (10), 1981 (13), 1982 (7), 1983 (16), 1984 (16), 1985 (16). Total—94.
Pro statistics: Caught one pass for 14 yards, fumbled once and returned one kickoff for no yards, 1979; intercepted one pass for nine yards, 1985.

ROBERT JAMES WEATHERS
Running Back—New England Patriots
Born September 13, 1960, at Westfield, N.Y.
Height, 6.02. Weight, 222.
High School—Fort Pierce, Fla.
Attended Arizona State University.
Brother of Clarence Weathers, wide receiver-punt returner with Cleveland Browns .

Selected by New England in 2nd round (40th player selected) of 1982 NFL draft.
On injured reserve with knee injury, September 13 through December 7, 1984; activated, December 8, 1984.

Year Club	G.	Att.	Yds.	Avg.	TD.	P.C.	Yds.	Avg.	TD.	TD.	Pts.	F.
		——RUSHING——				PASS RECEIVING				—TOTAL—		
1982—New England NFL	6	24	83	3.5	1	3	24	8.0	0	1	6	1
1983—New England NFL	15	73	418	5.7	1	23	212	9.2	0	1	6	4
1984—New England NFL	2		None				None			0	0	0
1985—New England NFL	16	41	174	4.2	1	2	18	9.0	0	1	6	0
Pro Totals—4 Years	39	138	675	4.9	3	28	254	9.1	0	3	18	5

Additional pro statistics: Returned three kickoffs for 68 yards, 1983; returned one kickoff for 18 yards, 1985.
Played in AFC Championship Game following 1985 season.
Played in NFL Championship Game following 1985 season.

MICHAEL LEWIS WEBSTER
(Mike)
Center—Pittsburgh Steelers
Born March 18, 1952, at Tomahawk, Wis.
Height, 6.01. Weight, 258.
High School—Rhinelander, Wis.
Attended University of Wisconsin.

Named to THE SPORTING NEWS NFL All-Star Team, 1980, 1981 and 1983.
Named to THE SPORTING NEWS AFC All-Star Team, 1978 and 1979.
Selected by Pittsburgh in 5th round (125th player selected) of 1974 NFL draft.
Pittsburgh NFL, 1974 through 1985.
Games: 1974 (14), 1975 (14), 1976 (14), 1977 (14), 1977 (14), 1978 (16), 1980 (16), 1981 (16), 1982 (9), 1983 (16), 1984 (16), 1985 (16). Total—177.
Pro statistics: Fumbled twice, 1976; recovered two fumbles for two yards, 1979; recovered two fumbles, 1983; recovered one fumble, 1985.
Played in AFC Championship Game following 1974 through 1976, 1978, 1979 and 1984 seasons.
Played in NFL Championship Game following 1974, 1975, 1978 and 1979 seasons.
Played in Pro Bowl (NFL All-Star Game) following 1978 through 1985 seasons.

CLAYTON CHARLES WEISHUHN
Name pronounced Why-SOON.
Linebacker—New England Patriots
Born October 7, 1959, at San Angelo, Tex.
Height, 6.02. Weight, 220.
High School—Wall, Tex.
Received bachelor of science degree in physical education from
Angelo State University in 1982.

Selected by New England in 3rd round (60th player selected) of 1982 NFL draft.
On injured reserve with knee injury, September 5 through remainder of 1984 season.
On injured reserve with knee injury, August 19 through entire 1985 season.
New England NFL, 1982 through 1984.
Games: 1982 (9), 1983 (16), 1984 (1). Total—26.
Pro statistics: Recovered one fumble, 1982; ran 27 yards with lateral on interception for a touchdown and recovered three fumbles, 1983.

HERB DOYAN WELSH
Defensive Back—New York Giants
Born January 12, 1961, at Los Angeles, Calif.
Height, 5.11. Weight, 180.
High School—Downey, Calif., Warren.
Attended Cerritos College and University of California at Los Angeles.

Selected by Portland in 10th round (135th player selected) of 1985 USFL draft.
Selected by New York Giants in 12th round (326th player selected) of 1985 NFL draft.
Signed by New York Giants, July 9, 1985.

		—INTERCEPTIONS—			
Year	Club	G.	No.	Yds.	Avg.TD.
1985—N.Y. Giants NFL		16	2	8	4.0 0

RAIMUND WERSCHING
Name pronounced WERE-shing.
(Ray)
Placekicker—San Francisco 49ers
Born August 21, 1950, at Mondsee, Austria.
Height, 5.11. Weight, 215.
High School—Downey, Calif., Earl Warren.
Attended Cerritos College and received bachelor of science degree in
accounting from University of California at Berkeley.

Tied NFL records for most field goals, game, no misses (6) vs. New Orleans Saints, October 16, 1983; most extr points, no misses, season (56), 1984.
Signed as free agent by Atlanta Falcons, 1971.
Released by Atlanta Falcons, 1971; signed as free agent by San Diego Chargers, 1973.
Released by San Diego Chargers, September 6, 1976; re-signed by Chargers, October 16, 1976.
Released by San Diego Chargers, August, 1977; signed as free agent by San Francisco 49ers, October 11, 1977.
On injured reserve with hip injury, September 12 through October 9, 1981; activated, October 10, 1981.

Year Club	G.	XP.	XPM.	FG.	FGA.	Pts.	Year Club	G.	XP.	XPM.	FG.	FGA.	Pts
1973—San Diego NFL	14	13	2	11	25	46	1980—San Fran. NFL	16	33	*6	15	19	
1974—San Diego NFL	14	0	0	5	11	15	1981—San Fran. NFL	12	30	0	17	23	
1975—San Diego NFL	14	20	1	12	24	56	1982—San Fran. NFL	9	23	2	12	17	
1976—San Diego NFL	9	14	2	4	8	26	1983—San Fran. NFL	16	51	0	25	30	1
1977—San Fran. NFL	10	23	0	10	17	53	1984—San Fran. NFL	16	56	0	25	35	*1
1978—San Fran. NFL	16	24	1	15	23	69	1985—San Fran. NFL	16	*52	1	13	21	
1979—San Fran. NFL	16	32	3	20	24	92	Pro Totals—13 Years	178	371	18	184	277	9

Additional pro statistics: Recovered one fumble, 1985.
Played in NFC Championship Game following 1981, 1983 and 1984 seasons.
Played in NFL Championship Game following 1981 and 1984 seasons.

CURTIS BERNARD WEST
(Known by middle name.)
Linebacker—Detroit Lions
Born March 13, 1958, at Conroe, Tex.
Height, 6.00. Weight, 220.
High School—Conroe, Tex.
Attended North Texas State University.

Signed by Saskatchewan Roughriders, July 20, 1981.
Traded by Saskatchewan Roughriders to Hamilton Tiger-Cats, July 25, 1981.
Traded by Hamilton Tiger-Cats to Saskatchewan Roughriders, August 9, 1981.
Released by Saskatchewan Roughriders, June 17, 1983.
USFL rights traded by Oakland Invaders to Washington Federals for rights to defensive tackle Chris Riehm, October 26, 1983.
Signed by Washington Federals, December 3, 1983.
On developmental squad, February 24 through March 23, 1984; activated, March 24, 1984.
On developmental squad, April 13 through April 15, 1984; activated, April 16, 1984.
On developmental squad, May 10 through June 7, 1984; activated, June 8, 1984.
Franchise transferred to Orlando, October 12, 1984.
Released by Orlando Renegades, February 18, 1985; re-signed by Renegades, February 21, 1985.
On developmental squad, February 28 through March 7, 1985.
Released by Orlando Renegades, March 8, 1985; re-signed by Renegades, March 20, 1985.
Released by Orlando Renegades, August 1, 1985; signed as free agent by Detroit Lions, March 6, 1986.
On developmental squad for 9 games with Washington Federals in 1984.
On developmental squad for 1 game with Orlando Renegades in 1985.
Hamilton (2)-Saskatchewan (2) CFL, 1981; Saskatchewan CFL, 1982; Washington USFL, 1984; Orlando USFL, 1985.
Games: 1981 (4), 1982 (11), 1984 (9), 1985 (14). Total CFL—15. Total USFL—23. Total Pro—38.
CFL statistics: Recovered one fumble, 1981.
USFL statistics: Credited with one sack for one yard, 1984.

EDWARD LEE WEST III
(Ed)
Tight End—Green Bay Packers
Born August 2, 1961, at Colbert County, Ala.
Height, 6.01. Weight, 242.
High School—Leighton, Ala., Colbert County.
Attended Auburn University.

Selected by Birmingham in 1984 USFL territorial draft.
Signed as free agent by Green Bay Packers, May 3, 1984.
Released by Green Bay Packers, August 27, 1984; re-signed by Packers, August 30, 1984.

| | | —PASS RECEIVING— | | | |
Year Club	G.	P.C.	Yds.	Avg.	TD.
1984—Green Bay NFL	16	6	54	9.0	4
1985—Green Bay NFL	16	8	95	11.9	1
Pro Totals—2 Years	32	14	149	10.6	5

Additional pro statistics: Rushed once for two yards and a touchdown and recovered one fumble, 1984; rushed once for no yards and fumbled once, 1985.

DWIGHT WHEELER
Center-Offensive Tackle—Los Angeles Raiders
Born January 13, 1955, at Memphis, Tenn.
Height, 6.03. Weight, 274.
High School—Memphis, Tenn., Manassas.
Attended Tennessee State University.

Selected by New England in 4th round (102nd player selected) of 1978 NFL draft.
On injured reserve with broken leg, September 13 through remainder of 1978 season.
On injured reserve with ankle injury, December 12 through remainder of 1979 season.
Released by New England Patriots, August 27, 1984; signed as free agent by Los Angeles Raiders, November 8, 1984.
Released by Los Angeles Raiders, November 12, 1984; re-signed by Raiders, November 15, 1984.
Released by Los Angeles Raiders, September 2, 1985; re-signed by Raiders, March 20, 1986.
New England NFL, 1978 through 1983; Los Angeles Raiders NFL, 1984.
Games: 1978 (2), 1979 (13), 1980 (16), 1981 (16), 1982 (9), 1983 (16), 1984 (4). Total—76.
Pro statistics: Returned one kickoff for no yards, 1978; fumbled once for minus 14 yards, 1979; fumbled once for minus 41 yards, 1980.

KENNETH MOORE WHISENHUNT
(Ken)
Tight End—Atlanta Falcons
Born February 28, 1962, at Atlanta, Ga.
Height, 6.02. Weight, 233.
High School—Augusta, Ga., Richmond.
Attended Georgia Tech.

Selected by Jacksonville in 1985 USFL territorial draft.
USFL rights traded with rights to running back Marck Harrison and center Dan Turk by Jacksonville Bulls to

Tampa Bay Bandits for rights to kicker Bobby Raymond, running back Cedric Jones and defensive back Eric Riley, January 3, 1985.
Selected by Atlanta in 12th round (313th player selected) of 1985 NFL draft.
Signed by Atlanta Falcons, July 18, 1985.

		—PASS RECEIVING—			
Year	Club	G.	P.C.	Yds.	Avg. TD.
1985—Atlanta NFL		16	3	48	16.0 0

Additional pro statistics: Rushed once for three yards, returned four kickoffs for 33 yards and recovered one fumble, 1985.

BRADLEY DEE WHITE
(Brad)
Defensive Tackle—Indianapolis Colts

Born August 18, 1958, at Rexburg, Idaho.
Height, 6.02. Weight, 253.
High School—Idaho Falls, Idaho, Skyline.
Attended University of Tennessee.

Selected by Tampa Bay in 12th round (310th player selected) of 1981 NFL draft.
Released by Tampa Bay Buccaneers, August 27, 1984; signed as free agent by Indianapolis Colts, August 31, 1984.
Tampa Bay NFL, 1981 through 1983; Indianapolis NFL, 1984 and 1985.
Games: 1981 (16), 1982 (9), 1983 (16), 1984 (15), 1985 (16). Total—72.

CHARLES RAYMOND WHITE
Running Back—Los Angeles Rams

Born January 22, 1958, at Los Angeles, Calif.
Height, 5.10. Weight, 190.
High School—San Fernando, Calif.
Attended University of Southern California.

Heisman Trophy winner, 1979.
Named as running back on THE SPORTING NEWS College All-America Team, 1979.
Named THE SPORTING NEWS College Player of the Year, 1979.
Selected by Cleveland in 1st round (27th player selected) of 1980 NFL draft.
On injured reserve with broken ankle, August 16 through entire 1983 season.
On physically unable to perform/active with ankle injury, July 19 through August 11, 1984; activated, August 12, 1984.
On injured reserve with ankle and back injuries, November 30 through remainder of 1984 season.
Released by Cleveland Browns, June 4, 1985; signed as free agent by Los Angeles Rams, July 9, 1985.
Released by Los Angeles Rams, September 2, 1985; re-signed by Rams, September 3, 1985.

			—RUSHING—				PASS RECEIVING				—TOTAL—		
Year	Club	G.	Att.	Yds.	Avg.	TD.	P.C.	Yds.	Avg.	TD.	TD.	Pts.	F.
1980—Cleveland NFL		14	86	279	3.2	5	17	153	9.0	1	6	36	1
1981—Cleveland NFL		16	97	342	3.5	1	27	219	8.1	0	1	6	8
1982—Cleveland NFL		9	69	259	3.8	3	34	283	8.3	0	3	18	2
1984—Cleveland NFL		10	24	62	2.6	0	5	29	5.8	0	0	0	0
1985—Los Angeles Rams NFL		16	70	310	4.4	3	1	12	12.0	0	3	18	3
Pro Totals—5 Years		65	346	1252	3.6	12	84	696	8.3	1	13	78	14

			KICKOFF RETURNS		
Year	Club	G.	No.	Yds.	Avg.TD.
1980—Cleveland NFL		14	1	20	20.0 0
1981—Cleveland NFL		16	12	243	20.3 0
1982—Cleveland NFL		9		None	
1984—Cleveland NFL		10	5	80	16.0 0
1985—L. A. Rams NFL		16	17	300	17.6 0
Pro Totals—5 Years		65	35	643	18.4 0

Additional pro statistics: Recovered one fumble, 1980; recovered three fumbles, 1981; returned one punt for no yards, 1985.
Played in NFC Championship Game following 1985 season.

CRAIG C. WHITE
Wide Receiver—New England Patriots

Born October 8, 1961, at St. Joseph, Mo.
Height, 6.01. Weight, 194.
High Schools—Decatur, Ill.; Stephen; and Lawrence, Kan.
Attended University of Missouri.

Selected by Houston in 7th round (148th player selected) of 1984 USFL draft.
Selected by Buffalo in 11th round (299th player selected) of 1984 NFL draft.
Signed by Buffalo Bills, July 9, 1984.
Released by Buffalo Bills, August 27, 1984; re-signed by Bills, August 28, 1984.
On non-football injury list with foot injury, July 21 and July 22, 1985.
Released by Buffalo Bills, July 23, 1985; signed As free agent by New England Patriots, May 10, 1986.

		—PASS RECEIVING—			
Year	Club	G.	P.C.	Yds.	Avg. TD.
1984—Buffalo NFL		14	4	28	7.0 0

Additional pro statistics: Returned one kickoff for five yards, 1984.

EDWARD ALVIN WHITE
(Ed)
Offensive Tackle—San Diego Chargers
Born April 4, 1947, at La Mesa, Calif.
Height, 6.02. Weight, 284.
High Schools—La Mesa, Calif., Helix and Indio, Calif.
Received degree in landscape architecture from University of California at Berkeley.

Named to THE SPORTING NEWS NFC All-Star Team, 1975 and 1976.
Selected by Minnesota NFL in 2nd round (39th player selected) of 1969 AFL-NFL draft.
Traded by Minnesota Vikings to San Diego Chargers for past considerations, July 29, 1978 (past considerations were awarding of White's rights to Chargers for running back Rickey Young).
Minnesota NFL, 1969 through 1977; San Diego NFL, 1978 through 1985.
Games: 1969 (14), 1970 (14), 1971 (14), 1972 (14), 1973 (14), 1974 (13), 1975 (13), 1976 (13), 1977 (13), 1978 (15), 1979 (16), 1980 (16), 1981 (16), 1982 (9), 1983 (16), 1984 (15), 1985 (16). Total—241.
Pro statistics: Ran three yards with a lateral from a rushing play, 1972; recovered one fumble, 1973, 1976, 1980 and 1983.
Played in NFC Championship Game following 1973, 1974, 1976 and 1977 seasons.
Played in AFC Championship Game following 1980 and 1981 seasons.
Played in NFL Championship Game following 1969, 1973, 1974 and 1976 seasons.
Played in AFL-NFL Championship Game following 1969 season.
Played in Pro Bowl (NFL All-Star Game) following 1975 through 1977 and 1979 seasons.

JAMES WHITE
Defensive End—Cleveland Browns
Born July 5, 1962, at Rayville, La.
Height, 6.03. Weight, 245.
High School—Rayville, La.
Attended Louisiana State University.

Selected by Portland in 1985 USFL territorial draft.
Signed as free agent by Cleveland Browns, May 6, 1985.
On injured reserve with knee injury, August 20 through November 20, 1985; activated after clearing procedural waivers, November 22, 1985.
Released by Cleveland Browns, November 26, 1985; re-signed by Browns, April 17, 1986.
Active for 1 game with Cleveland Browns in 1985; did not play.

RANDY LEE WHITE
Defensive Tackle—Dallas Cowboys
Born January 15, 1953, at Wilmington, Del.
Height, 6.04. Weight, 272.
High School—Wilmington, Del., Thomas McKean.
Attended University of Maryland.

Outland Trophy winner, 1974.
Named as defensive end on THE SPORTING NEWS College All-America Team, 1974.
Named to THE SPORTING NEWS NFC All-Star Team, 1978 and 1979.
Named to THE SPORTING NEWS NFL All-Star Team, 1980, 1981, 1983 and 1985.
Selected by Dallas in 1st round (2nd player selected) of 1975 NFL draft.
Placed on did not report list, August 21 through August 26, 1984.
Reported and granted roster exemption, August 27 through September 2, 1984; activated, September 3, 1984.
Dallas NFL, 1975 through 1985.
Games: 1975 (14), 1976 (14), 1977 (14), 1978 (16), 1979 (15), 1980 (16), 1981 (16), 1982 (9), 1983 (16), 1984 (16), 1985 (16). Total—162.
Pro statistics: Recovered two fumbles, 1975 and 1977; recovered one fumble, 1976, 1979, 1982 and 1983; returned one kickoff for 15 yards, 1978.
Played in NFC Championship Game following 1975, 1977, 1978 and 1980 through 1982 seasons.
Played in NFL Championship Game following 1975, 1977 and 1978 seasons.
Played in Pro Bowl (NFL All-Star Game) following 1977 and 1979 through 1985 seasons.
Named to play in Pro Bowl following 1978 season; replaced due to injury by Doug English.

REGINALD HOWARD WHITE
(Reggie)
Defensive End—Philadelphia Eagles
Born December 19, 1962, at Chattanooga, Tenn.
Height, 6.05. Weight, 285.
High School—Chattanooga, Tenn., Howard.
Attended University of Tennessee.

Named as defensive end on THE SPORTING NEWS USFL All-Star Team, 1985.
Named as defensive end on THE SPORTING NEWS College All-America Team, 1983.
Selected by Memphis in 1984 USFL territorial draft.
Signed by Memphis Showboats, January 15, 1984.
On developmental squad, March 9 through March 23, 1984; activated, March 24, 1984.
Selected by Philadelphia in 1st round (4th player selected) of 1984 NFL supplemental draft.
Released by Memphis Showboats, September 19, 1985; signed by Philadelphia Eagles, September 21, 1985.
Granted roster exemption, September 21 through September 26, 1985; activated, September 27, 1985.
On developmental squad for 2 games with Memphis Showboats in 1984.
Memphis USFL, 1984 and 1985; Philadelphia NFL, 1985.
Games: 1984 (16), 1985 USFL (18), 1985 NFL (13). Total USFL—34. Total Pro—47.

USFL statistics: Credited with 12 sacks for 84 yards and recovered one fumble, 1984; credited with 11½ sacks for 93½ yards, credited with one safety and recovered one fumble for 20 yards and a touchdown, 1985. NFL statistics: Recovered two fumbles, 1985.

SAMMY WHITE
Wide Receiver—Minnesota Vikings
Born March 16, 1954, at Winnsboro, La.
Height, 5.11. Weight, 200.
High School—Monroe, La., Richwood.
Received degree in education from Grambling State University.
Related to Jimmie Giles, tight end with Tampa Bay Buccaneers.
Named THE SPORTING NEWS NFC Rookie of the Year, 1976.
Selected by Minnesota in 2nd round (54th player selected) of 1976 NFL draft.
On injured reserve with groin injury, August 27 through November 14, 1985; activated, November 15, 1985.

		—RUSHING—				PASS RECEIVING				—TOTAL—		
Year Club	G.	Att.	Yds.	Avg.	TD.	P.C.	Yds.	Avg.	TD.	TD.	Pts.	F.
1976—Minnesota NFL	14	5	—10	—2.0	0	51	906	17.8	10	10	60	3
1977—Minnesota NFL	14		None			41	760	18.5	★9	9	54	2
1978—Minnesota NFL	16	5	30	6.0	0	53	741	14.0	9	9	54	1
1979—Minnesota NFL	15	1	6	6.0	0	42	715	17.0	4	4	24	1
1980—Minnesota NFL	16	4	65	16.3	0	53	887	16.7	5	5	30	0
1981—Minnesota NFL	16	2	—1	—0.5	0	66	1001	15.2	3	3	18	1
1982—Minnesota NFL	7		None			29	503	17.3	5	5	30	0
1983—Minnesota NFL	11	1	7	7.0	0	29	412	14.2	4	4	24	0
1984—Minnesota NFL	13		None			21	399	19.0	1	1	6	1
1985—Minnesota NFL	6		None			8	76	9.5	0	0	0	0
Pro Totals—10 Years	128	18	97	5.4	0	393	6400	16.3	50	50	300	9

		—PUNT RETURNS—				—KICKOFF RET.—		
Year Club	G.	No.	Yds.	Avg.	TD.	No.	Yds.	Avg.TD.
1976—Minnesota NFL	14	3	45	15.0	0	9	173	19.2 0
1977—Minnesota NFL	14		None			7	113	16.1 0
1978—Minnesota NFL	16	1	0	0.0	0	3	50	16.7 0
1979—Minnesota NFL	15		None				None	
1980—Minnesota NFL	16		None				None	
1981—Minnesota NFL	16	1	0	0.0	0		None	
1982—Minnesota NFL	7		None				None	
1983—Minnesota NFL	11		None				None	
1984—Minnesota NFL	13		None				None	
1985—Minnesota NFL	6		None				None	
Pro Totals—10 Years	128	5	45	9.0	0	19	336	17.7 0

Additional pro statistics: Recovered two fumbles, 1976; recovered one fumble, 1977 and 1980.
Played in NFC Championship Game following 1976 and 1977 seasons.
Played in NFL Championship Game following 1976 season.
Played in Pro Bowl (NFL All-Star Game) following 1976 and 1977 seasons.

WILFORD DANIEL WHITE
(Danny)
Quarterback—Dallas Cowboys
Born February 9, 1952, at Mesa, Ariz.
Height, 6.03. Weight, 193.
High School—Mesa, Ariz., Westwood.
Attended Arizona State University.
Son of Wilford White, halfback with Chicago Bears, 1951 and 1952.
Selected by Dallas in 3rd round (53rd player selected) of 1974 NFL draft.
Played in World Football League with Memphis Southmen, 1974 and 1975.
Signed by Dallas Cowboys after World Football League folded, April 15, 1976.
Selected by Cleveland Indians' organization in 39th round of free-agent draft, June 5, 1973.
Selected by Houston Astros' organization in secondary phase of free-agent draft, January 9, 1974.
Selected by Cleveland Indians' organization in secondary phase of free-agent draft, June 5, 1974.
Selected by Cleveland Indians' organization in secondary phase of free-agent draft, January 9, 1975.

		—PASSING—							—RUSHING—				—TOTAL—		
Year Club	G.	Att.	Cmp.	Pct.	Gain	T.P.	P.I.	Avg.	Att.	Yds.	Avg.	TD.	TD.	Pts.	F.
1974—Memphis WFL	....	155	79	51.0	1190	11	9	7.68	24	103	4.3	0	0	0	....
1975—Memphis WFL	....	195	104	53.3	1445	10	8	7.41	23	116	5.0	0	0	1	....
1976—Dallas NFL	14	20	13	65.0	213	2	2	10.65	6	17	2.8	0	0	0	0
1977—Dallas NFL	14	10	4	40.0	35	0	1	3.50	1	—2	—2.0	0	0	0	0
1978—Dallas NFL	16	34	20	58.8	215	0	1	6.32	5	7	1.4	0	0	0	2
1979—Dallas NFL	16	39	19	48.7	267	1	2	6.85	1	25	25.0	0	0	0	1
1980—Dallas NFL	16	436	260	59.6	3287	28	25	7.54	27	114	4.2	1	1	6	8
1981—Dallas NFL	16	391	223	57.0	3098	22	13	7.92	38	104	2.7	0	0	0	★14
1982—Dallas NFL	9	247	156	63.2	2079	16	12	8.42	17	91	5.4	0	0	0	★10
1983—Dallas NFL	16	533	334	62.7	3980	29	23	7.47	18	31	1.7	4	5	30	10
1984—Dallas NFL	14	233	126	54.1	1580	11	11	6.78	6	21	3.5	0	0	0	2
1985—Dallas NFL	14	450	267	59.3	3157	21	17	7.02	22	44	2.0	1	2	12	6
WFL Totals—2 Years	....	350	183	52.3	2635	21	17	7.53	47	219	4.7	0	0	0	....
NFL Totals—10 Years	145	2393	1422	59.4	17911	130	107	7.48	141	452	3.2	6	8	48	53
Pro Totals—12 Years	....	2743	1605	58.5	20546	151	124	7.49	188	671	3.6	6	8	48	....

NFL Quarterback Rating Points: 1976 (94.4), 1977 (10.4), 1978 (65.3), 1979 (58.6), 1980 (80.8), 1981 (87.5), 1982 (91.1), 1983 (85.6), 1984 (71.5), 1985 (80.6). Total—82.0.

Year Club	G.	No.	Avg.	Blk.	Year Club	G.	No.	Avg.	Blk.
		PUNTING					PUNTING		
1974—Memphis WFL	....	80	40.9	0	1982—Dallas NFL	9	37	41.7	0
1975—Memphis WFL	....	41	*45.1	0	1983—Dallas NFL	16	38	40.6	1
1976—Dallas NFL	14	70	38.4	2	1984—Dallas NFL	14	82	38.4	0
1977—Dallas NFL	14	80	39.6	1	1985—Dallas NFL	14	1	43.0	0
1978—Dallas NFL	16	76	40.5	1	WFL Totals—2 Years	....	121	42.3	0
1979—Dallas NFL	16	76	41.7	0	NFL Totals—10 Years	145	610	40.3	5
1980—Dallas NFL	16	71	40.9	0	Pro Totals—12 Years	....	731	40.6	5
1981—Dallas NFL	16	79	40.8	0					

Additional WFL statistics: Scored one action point, 1975.
Additional NFL statistics: Recovered one fumble, 1977; recovered two fumbles and fumbled twice for minus eight yards, 1978; recovered one fumble for 15 yards and caught one pass for minus nine yards, 1980; recovered eight fumbles and fumbled 14 times for minus 34 yards, 1981; recovered two fumbles, 1982; caught one pass for 15 yards and a touchdown and recovered four fumbles, 1983; recovered one fumble and fumbled twice for minus three yards, 1984; caught one pass for 12 yards and a touchdown, recovered two fumbles and fumbled six times for minus six yards, 1985.
Played in NFC Championship Game following 1977, 1978 and 1980 through 1982 seasons.
Played in NFL Championship Game following 1977 and 1978 seasons.
Played in Pro Bowl (NFL All-Star Game) following 1982 season.

BARRY T. WILBURN
Cornerback—Washington Redskins
Born December 9, 1963, at Memphis, Tenn.
Height, 6.03. Weight, 186.
High School—Memphis, Tenn., Melrose.
Attended University of Mississippi.

Selected by Washington in 8th round (219th player selected) of 1985 NFL draft.
Signed by Washington Redskins, July 18, 1985.
Washington NFL, 1985.
Games: 1985 (16).
Pro statistics: Intercepted one pass for 10 yards and recovered one fumble, 1985.

MIKE WILCHER
Linebacker—Los Angeles Rams
Born March 20, 1960, at Washington, D.C.
Height, 6.03. Weight, 240.
High School—Washington, D.C., Eastern.
Attended University of North Carolina.

Selected by Philadelphia in 1983 USFL territorial draft.
Selected by Los Angeles Rams in 2nd round (36th player selected) of 1983 NFL draft.
Signed by Los Angeles Rams NFL, June 16, 1983.
Los Angeles Rams NFL, 1983 through 1985.
Games: 1983 (15), 1984 (15), 1985 (16). Total—46.
Pro statistics: Intercepted one pass for no yards, 1985.
Played in NFC Championship Game following 1985 season.

JAMES CURTIS WILDER
Running Back—Tampa Bay Buccaneers
Born May 12, 1958, at Sikeston, Mo.
Height, 6.03. Weight, 225.
High School—Sikeston, Mo.
Attended Northeastern Oklahoma A&M and University of Missouri.

Established NFL records for most rushing attempts, season (407), 1984; most combined attempts, season (496), 1984.
Tied NFL record for most rushing attempts, game (43) vs. Green Bay Packers, September 30, 1984.
Selected by Tampa Bay in 2nd round (34th player selected) of 1981 NFL draft.
On injured reserve with broken ribs, November 15 through remainder of 1983 season.

Year Club	G.	RUSHING Att.	Yds.	Avg.	TD.	PASS RECEIVING P.C.	Yds.	Avg.	TD.	TOTAL TD.	Pts.	F.
1981—Tampa Bay NFL	16	107	370	3.5	4	48	507	10.6	1	5	30	3
1982—Tampa Bay NFL	9	83	324	3.9	3	53	466	8.8	1	4	24	5
1983—Tampa Bay NFL	10	161	640	4.0	4	57	380	6.7	2	6	36	1
1984—Tampa Bay NFL	16	*407	1544	3.8	13	85	685	8.1	0	13	78	10
1985—Tampa Bay NFL	16	365	1300	3.6	10	53	341	6.4	0	10	60	9
Pro Totals—5 Years	67	1123	4178	3.7	34	296	2379	8.0	4	38	228	28

Additional pro statistics: Returned one kickoff for 19 yards, 1981; recovered one fumble, 1981 and 1985; recovered one fumble for three yards, 1982; attempted one pass with one completion for 16 yards and a touchdown and recovered four fumbles, 1984.
Played in Pro Bowl (NFL All-Star Game) following 1984 season.

REGGIE WAYMAN WILKES
Linebacker—Atlanta Falcons
Born May 27, 1956, at Pine Bluff, Ark.
Height, 6.04. Weight, 240.
High School—Atlanta, Ga., Southwest.
Received bachelor of science degree in biology from Georgia Tech in 1978; attending
Morehouse School of Medicine and University of Pennsylvania Medical School (exchange program).
Cousin of Jamaal Wilkes, forward with Golden State Warriors,
Los Angeles Lakers and Los Angeles Clippers, 1974-75 through 1985-86.
Selected by Philadelphia in 3rd round (66th player selected) of 1978 NFL draft.
Traded by Philadelphia Eagles to Atlanta Falcons for 7th round pick in 1986 draft, April 17, 1986.
Philadelphia NFL, 1978 through 1985.
Games: 1978 (16), 1979 (16), 1980 (16), 1981 (14), 1982 (9), 1983 (14), 1984 (14), 1985 (16). Total—115.
Pro statistics: Recovered six fumbles, 1978; intercepted two passes for no yards and recovered two fumbles, 1979;
intercepted one pass for no yards, 1980; intercepted two passes for 18 yards and scored extra point on pass reception,
1981; recovered one fumble, 1982; intercepted one pass for six yards, 1984.
Played in NFC Championship Game following 1980 season.
Played in NFL Championship Game following 1980 season.

JIMMY RAY WILKS
Defensive End—New Orleans Saints
Born March 12, 1958, at Los Angeles, Calif.
Height, 6.05. Weight, 265.
High School—Pasadena, Calif.
Attended Pasadena Community College and San Diego State University.
Selected by New Orleans in 12th round (305th player selected) of 1981 NFL draft.
On inactive list, September 19, 1982.
New Orleans NFL, 1981 through 1985.
Games: 1981 (16), 1982 (8), 1983 (16), 1984 (16), 1985 (16). Total—72.
Pro statistics: Recovered two fumbles, 1981; recovered one fumble, 1983 and 1984.

GERALD WILLIAM WILLHITE
Running Back—Denver Broncos
Born May 30, 1959, at Sacramento, Calif.
Height, 5.10. Weight, 200.
High School—Rancho Cordova, Calif., Cordova.
Attended American River Junior College and San Jose State University.
Brother of Kevin Willhite, running back, and Randy Willhite,
defensive back, both at University of Oregon.
Selected by Denver in 1st round (21st player selected) of 1982 NFL draft.
On injured reserve with pulled hamstring, August 30 through October 27, 1983; activated, October 28, 1983.

Year Club		G.	—RUSHING—				PASS RECEIVING				—TOTAL—		
		G.	Att.	Yds.	Avg.	TD.	P.C.	Yds.	Avg.	TD.	TD.	Pts.	F.
1982—Denver NFL		9	70	347	5.0	2	26	227	8.7	0	2	12	5
1983—Denver NFL		8	43	188	4.4	3	14	153	10.9	1	4	24	0
1984—Denver NFL		16	77	371	4.8	2	27	298	11.0	0	2	12	3
1985—Denver NFL		15	66	237	3.6	3	35	297	8.5	1	4	24	2
Pro Totals—4 Years		48	256	1143	4.5	10	102	975	9.6	2	12	72	10

Year Club		G.	—PUNT RETURNS—				—KICKOFF RET.—			
		G.	No.	Yds.	Avg.	TD.	No.	Yds.	Avg.TD.	
1982—Denver NFL		9	6	63	10.5	0	17	337	19.8	0
1983—Denver NFL		8	None				None			
1984—Denver NFL		16	20	200	10.0	0	4	109	27.3	0
1985—Denver NFL		15	16	169	10.6	0	2	40	20.0	0
Pro Totals—4 Years		48	42	432	10.3	0	23	486	21.1	0

Additional pro statistics: Attempted two passes with no completions and one interception, 1982; attempted one pass
with no completions, 1983; attempted two passes with one completion for 20 yards and recovered two fumbles, 1984;
attempted three passes with no completions, 1985.

BYRON WILLIAMS
Wide Receiver—New York Giants
Born October 31, 1960, at Texarkana, Tex.
Height, 6.02. Weight, 180.
High School—Texarkana, Tex., Liberty Eylau.
Attended University of Texas at Arlington.
Selected by Denver in 21st round (249th player selected) of 1983 USFL draft.
Selected by Green Bay in 10th round (253rd player selected) of 1983 NFL draft.
Signed by Green Bay Packers, May 25, 1983.
Released by Green Bay Packers, August 29, 1983; signed as free agent by Philadelphia Eagles, September 13, 1983.
Released by Philadelphia Eagles, September 29, 1983; signed as free agent by New York Giants, October 27, 1983.
Active for 2 games with Philadelphia Eagles in 1983; did not play.

Year Club	G.	P.C.	Yds.	Avg.	TD.
1983—Phi (0)-NYG (5) NFL..	5	20	346	17.3	1
1984—N.Y. Giants NFL	16	24	471	19.6	2
1985—N.Y. Giants NFL	16	15	280	18.7	0
Pro Totals—3 Years...........	37	59	1097	18.6	3

————PASS RECEIVING————

Additional pro statistics: Fumbled once, 1983; rushed twice for 18 yards and recovered one fumble, 1985.

DARRYL EUGENE WILLIAMS
(Dokie)
Wide Receiver—Los Angeles Raiders
Born August 25, 1960, at Oceanside, Calif.
Height, 5.11. Weight, 180.
High School—Oceanside, Calif., El Camino.
Received degree in political science from University of California at Los Angeles.

Selected by Oakland in 8th round (90th player selected) of 1983 USFL draft.
Selected by Los Angeles Raiders in 5th round (138th player selected) of 1983 NFL draft.
Signed by Los Angeles Raiders, July 6, 1983.

Year Club	G.	PASS RECEIVING				—KICKOFF RET.—				—TOTAL—		
		P.C.	Yds.	Avg.	TD.	No.	Yds.	Avg.	TD.	TD.	Pts.	F.
1983—Los Angeles Raiders NFL	16	14	259	18.5	3	5	88	17.6	0	3	18	2
1984—Los Angeles Raiders NFL	16	22	509	23.1	4	24	621	25.9	0	4	24	0
1985—Los Angeles Raiders NFL	16	48	925	19.3	5	1	19	19.0	0	5	30	0
Pro Totals—3 Years.....................	48	84	1693	20.2	12	30	728	24.3	0	12	72	2

Member of Los Angeles Raiders for AFC Championship Game following 1983 season; did not play.
Played in NFL Championship Game following 1983 season.

DERWIN DAWAYNE WILLIAMS
Wide Receiver—New England Patriots
Born May 6, 1961, at Brownwood, Tex.
Height, 6.00. Weight, 170.
High School—Brownwood, Tex.
Attended University of New Mexico.

Selected by New England in 7th round (192nd player selected) of 1984 NFL draft.
On injured reserve with concussion, August 27 through entire 1984 season.
On injured reserve with knee injury, January 4, 1986 through remainder of 1985 season playoffs.

————PASS RECEIVING————

Year Club	G.	P.C.	Yds.	Avg.	TD.
1985—New England NFL.......	16	9	163	18.1	0

EDWARD EUGENE WILLIAMS
(Ed)
Linebacker—New England Patriots
Born August 9, 1961, at Odessa, Tex.
Height, 6.04. Weight, 244.
High School—Odessa, Tex., Ector.
Attended University of Texas.

Selected by San Antonio in 1984 USFL territorial draft.
Selected by New England in 2nd round (43rd player selected) of 1984 NFL draft.
Signed by New England Patriots, July 13, 1984.
New England NFL, 1984 and 1985.
Games: 1984 (14), 1985 (13). Total—27.
Played in AFC Championship Game following 1985 season.
Played in NFL Championship Game following 1985 season.

ERIC MICHAEL WILLIAMS
Defensive Tackle—Detroit Lions
Born February 24, 1962, at Stockton, Calif.
Height, 6.04. Weight, 260.
High School—Stockton, Calif., St. Mary's.
Attended Washington State University.
Son of Roy Williams, 2nd round selection of Detroit Lions in 1962 NFL draft.

Selected by New Jersey in 1st round (19th player selected) of 1984 USFL draft.
Selected by Detroit in 3rd round (62nd player selected) of 1984 NFL draft.
Signed by Detroit Lions, July 21, 1984.
On injured reserve with cracked cervical disc, December 4 through remainder of 1985 season.
Detroit NFL, 1984 and 1985.
Games: 1984 (12), 1985 (12). Total—24.
Pro statistics: Recovered one fumble, 1985.

ERIC THOMAS WILLIAMS
Safety—Pittsburgh Steelers
Born February 21, 1960, at Raleigh, N.C.
Height, 6.01. Weight, 187.
High School—Garner, N.C.
Attended North Carolina State University.

Selected by Philadelphia in 21st round (248th player selected) of 1983 USFL season.
Signed by Pittsburgh Steelers, June 1, 1983.
On injured reserve with sprained ankle, September 20 through remainder of 1983 season.

		—INTERCEPTIONS—			
Year Club	G.	No.	Yds.	Avg.TD.	
1983—Pittsburgh NFL	3	None			
1984—Pittsburgh NFL	16	3	49	16.3	0
1985—Pittsburgh NFL	14	4	47	11.8	0
Pro Totals—3 Years	33	7	96	13.7	0

Additional pro statistics: Recovered one fumble for six yards, 1984.
Played in AFC Championship Game following 1984 season.

GARDNER WILLIAMS
Defensive Back—Los Angeles Raiders
Born December 11, 1961, at Washington, D.C.
Height, 6.02. Weight, 199.
High School—Oakland, Calif., Bishop O'Dowd.
Received bachelor of arts degree in business administration from St. Mary's (Calif.) College in 1984.
Son of Howie Williams, defensive back with Oakland Raiders, 1964 through 1969.

Selected by Michigan in 18th round (369th player selected) of 1984 USFL draft.
Selected by Los Angeles Raiders in 11th round (282nd player selected) of 1984 NFL draft.
Signed by Los Angeles Raiders, June 13, 1984.
Released by Los Angeles Raiders, August 27, 1984; signed as free agent by Detroit Lions, October 18, 1984.
Released by Detroit Lions, November 9, 1984; signed as free agent by San Francisco 49ers, April 16, 1985.
Released by San Francisco 49ers, August 12, 1985; signed as free agent by Los Angeles Raiders, March 10, 1986.
Detroit NFL, 1984.
Games: 1984 (3).

GEORGE VAN WILLIAMS
(Known by middle name.)
Running Back—New York Giants
Born March 15, 1959, at Johnson City, Tenn.
Height, 6.00. Weight, 210.
High School—Johnson City, Tenn., All-Science.
Attended East Tennessee State University and Carson-Newman College.

Selected by Buffalo in 4th round (93rd player selected) of 1982 NFL draft.
On injured reserve with knee injury, September 7 through entire 1982 season.
Released by Buffalo Bills, September 17, 1985; signed as free agent by New York Giants, April 20, 1986.

		—RUSHING—				PASS RECEIVING				—TOTAL—		
Year Club	G.	Att.	Yds.	Avg.	TD.	P.C.	Yds.	Avg.	TD.	TD.	Pts.	F.
1983—Buffalo NFL	16	3	11	3.7	0	None				0	0	2
1984—Buffalo NFL	16	18	51	2.8	0	5	46	9.2	1	1	6	1
1985—Buffalo NFL	2	None				1	7	7.0	0	0	0	0
Pro Totals—3 Years	34	21	62	3.0	0	6	53	8.8	1	1	6	3

		KICKOFF RETURNS			
Year Club	G.	No.	Yds.	Avg.TD.	
1983—Buffalo NFL	16	22	494	22.5	0
1984—Buffalo NFL	16	39	820	21.0	0
1985—Buffalo NFL	2	1	20	20.0	0
Pro Totals—3 Years	34	62	1334	21.5	0

Additional pro statistics: Returned one punt for no yards, 1983; recovered one fumble, 1983 and 1984.

GREG WILLIAMS
Safety—Washington Redskins
Born August 1, 1959, at Greenville, Miss.
Height, 5.11. Weight, 185.
High School—Greenville, Miss., Christian Academy.
Attended Mississippi Delta Junior College and Mississippi State University.

Signed as free agent by Washington Redskins, May 12, 1982.
Washington NFL, 1982 through 1985.
Games: 1982 (9), 1983 (16), 1984 (16), 1985 (16). Total—57.
Pro statistics: Returned one punt for nine yards and one kickoff for two yards, 1982; intercepted two passes for 25 yards, returned one kickoff for six yards and recovered four fumbles for four yards, 1983; recovered one fumble, 1984 and 1985; returned one punt for no yards, 1984.
Played in NFC Championship Game following 1982 and 1983 seasons.
Played in NFL Championship Game following 1982 and 1983 seasons.

JAMES HENRY WILLIAMS
(Jimmy)
Linebacker—Detroit Lions
Born November 15, 1960, at Washington, D.C.
Height, 6.03. Weight, 230.
High School—Washington, D.C., Woodrow Wilson.
Attended University of Nebraska.
Brother of Toby Williams, defensive end with New England Patriots.

Selected by Detroit in 1st round (15th player selected) of 1982 NFL draft.
On injured reserve with broken foot, December 20 through remainder of 1982 season.
Detroit NFL, 1982 through 1985.
Games: 1982 (6), 1983 (16), 1984 (16), 1985 (16). Total—54.
Pro statistics: Intercepted one pass for four yards, 1982; recovered one fumble, 1983 through 1985.

JAMIE WILLIAMS
Tight End—Houston Oilers
Born February 25, 1960, at Vero Beach, Fla.
Height, 6.04. Weight, 232.
High School—Davenport, Ia., Central.
Attended University of Nebraska.

Selected by Boston in 1983 USFL territorial draft.
Selected by New York Giants in 3rd round (63rd player selected) of 1983 NFL draft.
Signed by New York Giants, June 30, 1983.
Released by New York Giants, August 29, 1983; signed as free agent by St. Louis Cardinals, September 13, 1983.
Released by St. Louis Cardinals, October 5, 1983; signed as free agent by Tampa Bay Buccaneers, January 25, 1984.
USFL rights traded by New Orleans Breakers to New Jersey Generals for past consideration, March 26, 1984.
Released by Tampa Bay Buccaneers, May 8, 1984; awarded on waivers to Houston Oilers, May 21, 1984.

		—PASS RECEIVING—			
Year Club	G.	P.C.	Yds.	Avg.	TD.
1983—St. Louis NFL................	1		None		
1984—Houston NFL................	16	41	545	13.3	3
1985—Houston NFL................	16	39	444	11.4	1
Pro Totals—3 Years...........	33	80	989	12.4	4

Additional pro statistics: Returned one kickoff for no yards, recovered one fumble and fumbled twice, 1984; returned two kickoffs for 21 yards and fumbled once, 1985.

JOEL WILLIAMS
First name pronounced Jo-EL.
Linebacker—Atlanta Falcons
Born December 13, 1956, at Miami, Fla.
Height, 6.01. Weight, 225.
High School—Miami, Fla., North.
Attended Peru College and received bachelor of business administration degree
from University of Wisconsin at LaCrosse in 1979.
Cousin of Bobby Rusley, linebacker at University of Louisville.

Signed as free agent by Miami Dolphins, July 12, 1979.
Released by Miami Dolphins, August 27, 1979; claimed on waivers by Atlanta Falcons, August 28, 1979.
On injured reserve with knee injury, December 19 through remainder of 1981 season.
USFL rights released by Birmingham Stallions, August 16, 1983; rights awarded on waivers to Pittsburgh Maulers, August 17, 1983.
Traded by Atlanta Falcons to Philadelphia Eagles for 2nd round pick in 1984 draft, August 21, 1983.
Granted free agency, February 1, 1985; re-signed by Eagles, October 23, 1985.
Granted roster exemption, October 23 through November 3, 1985; activated, November 4, 1985.
Traded by Philadelphia Eagles to Atlanta Falcons for 5th round pick in 1986 draft, April 29, 1986.
Atlanta NFL, 1979 through 1982; Philadelphia NFL, 1983 through 1985.
Games: 1979 (16), 1980 (16), 1981 (10), 1982 (9), 1983 (16), 1984 (16), 1985 (7). Total—90.
Pro statistics: Intercepted two passes for 55 yards, recovered three fumbles for 42 yards and one touchdown and credited with one safety, 1980; intercepted one pass for 25 yards and recovered two fumbles for 57 yards and a touchdown, 1981; recovered one fumble, 1982 and 1983; recovered two fumbles, 1984.

JOHN ALAN WILLIAMS
Running Back—Seattle Seahawks
Born October 26, 1960, at Muskegon, Mich.
Height, 5.11. Weight, 205.
High School—Muskegon, Mich., Reeths Puffer.
Attended University of Wisconsin.

Selected by Michigan in 14th round (159th player selected) of 1983 USFL draft.
Signed by Michigan Panthers, January 12, 1983.
Protected in merger of Michigan Panthers and Oakland Invaders, December 6, 1984.
Released by Oakland Invaders, July 31, 1985; signed as free agent by Dallas Cowboys, August 12, 1985.
Released by Dallas Cowboys, October 29, 1985; signed as free agent by Seattle Seahawks, November 6, 1985.
On injured reserve with ankle injury, December 7 through remainder of 1985 season.

		—RUSHING—				PASS RECEIVING				—TOTAL—		
Year Club	G.	Att.	Yds.	Avg.	TD.	P.C.	Yds.	Avg.	TD.	TD.	Pts.	F.
1983—Michigan USFL.....................	18	153	624	4.1	12	8	80	10.0	1	13	78	3

Year Club	G.	Att.	Yds.	Avg.	TD.	P.C.	Yds.	Avg.	TD.	TD.	Pts.	F.
			RUSHING				PASS RECEIVING				TOTAL	
1984—Michigan USFL	18	197	984	5.0	8	25	218	8.7	0	8	48	4
1985—Oakland USFL	18	186	857	4.6	9	13	136	10.5	1	10	60	2
1985—Dallas(8)-Seattle(2) NFL	10	14	42	3.0	0			None		0	0	3
USFL Totals—3 Years	54	536	2465	4.6	29	46	434	9.4	2	31	186	9
NFL Totals—1 Year	10	14	42	3.0	0	0	0	0.0	0	0	0	3
Pro Totals—4 Years	64	550	2507	4.6	29	46	434	9.4	2	31	186	12

KICKOFF RETURNS

Year Club	G.	No.	Yds.	Avg.	TD.
1983—Michigan USFL	18	12	290	24.2	0
1984—Michigan USFL	18	3	77	25.7	0
1985—Oakland USFL	18		None		
1985—Dal.(8)-Sea.(2) NFL	10	6	129	21.5	0
USFL Totals—3 Years	54	15	367	24.5	0
NFL Totals—1 Year	10	6	129	21.5	0
Pro Totals—4 Years	64	21	496	23.6	0

Additional USFL statistics: Recovered one fumble, 1983 and 1984; attempted two passes with no completions, 1985.
Additional NFL statistics: Recovered two fumbles, 1985.
Played in USFL Championship Game following 1983 and 1985 seasons.

JONATHAN WILLIAMS
(Jon)
Running Back—New England Patriots
Born June 1, 1961, at Somerville, N.J.
Height, 5.09. Weight, 209.
High School—Somerville, N.J.
Attended Penn State University.

Selected by Philadelphia in 1984 USFL territorial draft.
Selected by New England in 3rd round (70th player selected) of 1984 NFL draft.
Signed by New England Patriots, July 13, 1984.
On injured reserve with knee injury, November 3 through remainder of 1984 season.
On injured reserve with knee injury, July 26 through entire 1985 season.

KICKOFF RETURNS

Year Club	G.	No.	Yds.	Avg.	TD.
1984—New England NFL	9	23	461	20.0	0

KEVIN J. WILLIAMS
Cornerback—Washington Redskins
Born November 28, 1961, at San Diego, Calif.
Height, 5.09. Weight, 169.
High School—San Diego, Calif., Crawford.
Attended San Diego City College and Iowa State University.

Selected by Los Angeles in 1st round (38th player selected) of 1985 USFL draft.
Signed as free agent by Washington Redskins, May 13, 1985.
Released by Washington Redskins, August 27, 1985; re-signed by Redskins, October 2, 1985.
Washington NFL, 1985.
Games: 1985 (12).

LAWRENCE RICHARD WILLIAMS II
(Larry)
Offensive Tackle-Guard—Cleveland Browns
Born July 3, 1963, at Orange, Calif.
Height, 6.05. Weight, 269.
High School—Santa Ana, Calif., Mater Dei.
Received bachelor of arts degree in American studies (journalism) and business
from University of Notre Dame in 1985.

Selected by Portland in 10th round (136th player selected) of 1985 USFL draft.
Selected by Cleveland in 10th round (259th player selected) of 1985 NFL draft.
Signed by Cleveland Browns, July 15, 1985.
On injured reserve with wrist injury, August 20 through entire 1985 season.

LEE ERIC WILLIAMS
Defensive End—San Diego Chargers
Born October 15, 1962, at Fort Lauderdale, Fla.
Height, 6.06. Weight, 270.
High School—Fort Lauderdale, Fla., Stranahan.
Received degree in business administration from Bethune-Cookman College.

Selected by Tampa Bay in 1984 USFL territorial draft.
USFL rights traded with rights to defensive tackle Dewey Forte by Tampa Bay Bandits to Los Angeles Express for draft choice, March 2, 1984.
Signed by Los Angeles Express, March 6, 1984.
Granted roster exemption, March 6 through March 15, 1984; activated, March 16, 1984.

Selected by San Diego in 1st round (6th player selected) of 1984 NFL supplemental draft.
Released by Los Angeles Express, October 20, 1984; signed by San Diego Chargers, October 22, 1984.
Granted roster exemption, October 22 through October 28, 1984; activated, October 29, 1984.
Los Angeles USFL, 1984; San Diego NFL, 1984 and 1985.
Games: 1984 USFL (14), 1984 NFL (8), 1985 (16). Total NFL—24. Total Pro—38.
USFL statistics: Credited with 13 sacks for 92 yards, 1984.
NFL statistics: Intercepted one pass for 66 yards and a touchdown, 1984; intercepted one pass for 17 yards and recovered one fumble for two yards, 1985.

LESTER WILLIAMS
Nose Tackle—New England Patriots
Born January 19, 1959, at Miami, Fla.
Height, 6.03. Weight, 272.
High School—Miami, Fla., Carol City.
Attended University of Miami (Fla.).

Named as defensive end on THE SPORTING NEWS College All-America Team, 1981.
Selected by New England in 1st round (27th player selected) of 1982 NFL draft.
On injured reserve with broken arm, October 17 through remainder of 1984 season.
On injured reserve with knee injury, September 3 through October 17, 1985; activated, October 18, 1985.
New England NFL, 1982 through 1985.
Games: 1982 (9), 1983 (15), 1984 (7), 1985 (9). Total—40.
Pro statistics: Recovered one fumble, 1982 and 1984.
Played in AFC Championship Game following 1985 season.
Played in NFL Championship Game following 1985 season.

MICHAEL WILLIAMS
(Mike)
Running Back—Atlanta Falcons
Born July 16, 1961, at Atmore, Ala.
Height, 6.02. Weight, 225.
High School—Atmore, Ala., Escambia County.
Attended Northeast Mississippi Junior College and Mississippi College.
Cousin of Don McNeal, cornerback with Miami Dolphins.

Selected by Birmingham in 7th round (77th player selected) of 1983 USFL draft.
Selected by Philadelphia in 4th round (89th player selected) of 1983 NFL draft.
Signed by Philadelphia Eagles, May 26, 1983.
Released by Philadelphia Eagles, August 20, 1985; signed as free agent by Atlanta Falcons, April 3, 1986.

		—RUSHING—			PASS RECEIVING				—TOTAL—		
Year Club	G.	Att.	Yds.	Avg.	TD.	P.C.	Yds.	Avg.	TD.	TD.	Pts.	F.
1983—Philadelphia NFL	15	103	385	3.7	0	17	142	8.4	0	0	0	1
1984—Philadelphia NFL	16	33	83	2.5	0	7	47	6.7	0	0	0	1
Pro Totals—2 Years	31	136	468	3.4	0	24	189	7.9	0	0	0	2

Additional pro statistics: Returned three kickoffs for 59 yards, 1983.

NEWTON DENNIS WILLIAMS
Running Back—Indianapolis Colts
Born May 10, 1959, at Charlotte, N.C.
Height, 5.10. Weight, 204.
High School—Charlotte, N.C., North Mecklenburg.
Received bachelor of science degree in telecommunications
and broadcast management from Arizona State University.

Selected by San Francisco in 5th round (139th player selected) of 1982 NFL draft.
Released by San Francisco 49ers, September 6, 1982; re-signed by 49ers, September 9, 1982.
On injured reserve with shoulder injury, December 16 through remainder of 1982 season.
Released by San Francisco 49ers, August 16, 1983; awarded on waivers to Baltimore Colts, August 18, 1983.
Franchise transferred to Indianapolis, March 31, 1984.
On injured reserve with ankle injury, August 22 through entire 1984 season.
Released by Indianapolis Colts, September 5, 1985; re-signed by Colts, May 2, 1986.

		—RUSHING—			PASS RECEIVING				—TOTAL—		
Year Club	G.	Att.	Yds.	Avg.	TD.	P.C.	Yds.	Avg.	TD.	TD.	Pts.	F.
1982—San Francisco NFL	6	None				None				0	0	0
1983—Baltimore NFL	16	28	77	2.8	0	4	46	11.5	0	0	0	0
Pro Totals—2 Years	22	28	77	2.8	0	4	46	11.5	0	0	0	0

OLIVER LAVELL WILLIAMS JR.
Wide Receiver—Indianapolis Colts
Born October 17, 1960, at Chicago, Ill.
Height, 6.03. Weight, 191.
High School—Gardena, Calif., Serra.
Attended Los Angeles Harbor Junior College and University of Illinois.
Brother of David Williams, rookie wide receiver with Chicago Bears;
and Steven Williams, wide receiver at University of Illinois.

Selected by Chicago in 1983 USFL territorial draft.
Selected by Chicago in 12th round (313th player selected) of 1983 NFL draft.
Signed by Chicago Bears, May 12, 1983.
On injured reserve with back injury, August 16 through September 19, 1983.

Released by Chicago Bears, September 20, 1983; signed by Chicago Blitz, November 21, 1983.
Released by Chicago Blitz, February 14, 1984; re-signed by Blitz, February 17, 1984.
On developmental squad, February 24 through March 13, 1984.
Released by Chicago Blitz, March 14, 1984; signed as free agent by St. Louis Cardinals, July 17, 1984.
Released by St. Louis Cardinals, August 27, 1984; signed as free agent by Arizona Outlaws, January 6, 1985.
Released by Arizona Outlaws, February 11, 1985; signed as free agent by San Antonio Gunslingers, February 19, 1985.
Released by San Antonio Gunslingers, March 20, 1985; signed as free agent by Indianapolis Colts, March 29, 1985.
On injured reserve with back injury, August 27 through October 30, 1985; activated after clearing procedural waivers, November 1, 1985.
On developmental squad for 3 games with Chicago Blitz in 1984.

Year Club	G.	P.C.	Yds.	Avg.	TD.
1985—San Antonio USFL........	2	1	16	16.0	0
1985—Indianapolis NFL.........	8	9	175	19.4	1
Pro Totals—2 Years............	10	10	191	19.1	1

Additional USFL statistics: Returned five punts for five yards and returned eight kickoffs for 181 yards, 1985.
Additional NFL statistics: Returned three kickoffs for 44 yards, recovered one fumble and fumbled twice, 1985.

PERRY LAMAR WILLIAMS
Cornerback—New York Giants
Born May 12, 1961, at Hamlet, N.C.
Height, 6.02. Weight, 203.
High School—Hamlet, N.C., Richmond County.
Attended North Carolina State University.

Selected by Washington in 7th round (76th player selected) of 1983 USFL draft.
Selected by New York Giants in 7th round (178th player selected) of 1983 NFL draft.
Signed by New York Giants, June 13, 1983.
On injured reserve with foot injury, August 17 through entire 1983 season.

Year Club	G.	No.	Yds.	Avg.	TD.
1984—N.Y. Giants NFL	16	3	7	2.3	0
1985—N.Y. Giants NFL	16	2	28	14.0	0
Pro Totals—2 Years............	32	5	35	7.0	0

Additional pro statistics: Recovered one fumble, 1984 and 1985.

RALPH WILLIAMS
Wide Receiver—Green Bay Packers
Born April 6, 1960, at Cincinnati, O.
Height, 6.02. Weight, 195.
High School—Cincinnati, O., Aiken.
Attended Miami University (O).

Signed as free agent by Green Bay Packers, June 21, 1985.
On injured reserve with broken thumb, August 19 through entire 1985 season.

RALPH WILLIAMS
Offensive Tackle—New Orleans Saints
Born March 27, 1958, at Monroe, La.
Height, 6.03. Weight, 270.
High School—Monroe, La., West.
Attended Southern University.

Signed as free agent by Houston Oilers, May 16, 1981.
On injured reserve with back injury, August 31 through entire 1981 season.
On inactive list, September 19, 1982.
On commissioner's exempt list, November 19 through November 23, 1982; activated, November 24, 1982.
Released by Houston Oilers, August 29, 1983; re-signed by Oilers, September 21, 1983.
Released by Houston Oilers, October 17, 1983; signed by San Antonio Gunslingers, November 27, 1983.
Released by San Antonio Gunslingers, July 23, 1985; signed as free agent by New Orleans Saints, July 30, 1985.
Houston NFL, 1982 and 1983; San Antonio USFL, 1984 and 1985; New Orleans NFL, 1985.
Games: 1982 (7), 1983 (1), 1984 (18), 1985 USFL (18), 1985 NFL (16). Total NFL—24. Total USFL—16. Total Pro—60.
Pro statistics: Recovered one fumble, 1984.

REGINALD WILLIAMS
(Reggie)
Linebacker—Cincinnati Bengals
Born September 19, 1954, at Flint, Mich.
Height, 6.00. Weight, 228.
High School—Flint, Mich., Southwestern.
Received bachelor of arts degree in psychology from Dartmouth College.

Selected by Cincinnati in 3rd round (82nd player selected) of 1976 NFL draft.

| Year Club | G. | —INTERCEPTIONS— | | |
		No.	Yds.	Avg.TD.
1976—Cincinnati NFL	14	1	17	17.0	0
1977—Cincinnati NFL	14	3	67	22.3	1
1978—Cincinnati NFL	16	1	11	11.0	0
1979—Cincinnati NFL	12	2	5	2.5	0
1980—Cincinnati NFL	14	2	8	4.0	0
1981—Cincinnati NFL	16	4	33	8.3	0
1982—Cincinnati NFL	9	1	20	20.0	0
1983—Cincinnati NFL	16		None		
1984—Cincinnati NFL	16	2	33	16.5	0
1985—Cincinnati NFL	16		None		
Pro Totals—10 Years	143	16	194	12.1	1

Additional pro statistics: Recovered blocked punt in end zone for a touchdown, recovered two fumbles and returned one punt for no yards, 1977 and 1980; fumbled once, 1977 and 1980; recovered one fumble for 30 yards, 1978; recovered one fumble, 1979 and 1980; recovered three fumbles, 1981, recovered four fumbles and credited with one safety, 1982; recovered four fumbles for 59 yards and a touchdown, 1983; recovered four fumbles for four yards, 1985.
Played in AFC Championship Game following 1981 season.
Played in NFL Championship Game following 1981 season.

ROBERT ANTHONY WILLIAMS
Safety

Born September 26, 1962, at Chicago, Ill.
Height, 5.11. Weight, 202.
High School—Chicago, Ill., Dunbar Vocational.
Attended Eastern Illinois University.

Signed as free agent by Pittsburgh Steelers, June 10, 1984.
On injured reserve with knee injury, August 14 through December 6, 1984; activated after clearing procedural waivers, December 7, 1984.
On injured reserve with knee injury, August 20 through entire 1985 season.
Granted free agency with option not exercised, February 1, 1986.
Pittsburgh NFL, 1984.
Games: 1984 (2).
Played in AFC Championship Game following 1984 season.

ROBERT JERRY WILLIAMS
(Ben)
Defensive End—Buffalo Bills

Born September 1, 1954, at Yazoo City, Miss.
Height, 6.03. Weight, 266.
High School—Yazoo City, Miss.
Attended University of Mississippi.

Selected by Buffalo in 3rd round (78th player selected) of 1976 NFL draft.
Buffalo NFL, 1976 through 1985.
Games: 1976 (13), 1977 (14), 1978 (16), 1979 (16), 1980 (16), 1981 (16), 1982 (9), 1983 (16), 1984 (15), 1985 (16). Total—147.
Pro statistics: Recovered one fumble, 1976, 1977, 1980, 1981 and 1982; intercepted one pass for no yards and credited with one safety, 1981; intercepted one pass for 20 yards, 1982; returned three kickoffs for 56 yards and recovered two fumbles, 1983.
Played in Pro Bowl (NFL All-Star Game) following 1982 season.

TOBIAS WILLIAMS
(Toby)
Defensive End—New England Patriots

Born November 19, 1959, at Washington, D.C.
Height, 6.03. Weight, 265.
High School—Washington, D.C., Woodrow Wilson.
Received bachelor of arts degree in criminal justice from University of Nebraska in 1983.
Brother of Jimmy Williams, linebacker with Detroit Lions.

Selected by Boston in 1983 USFL territorial draft.
Selected by New England in 10th round (265th player selected) of 1983 NFL draft.
Signed by New England Patriots, May 25, 1983.
On injured reserve with knee injury, October 18 through remainder of 1985 season.
New England NFL, 1983 through 1985.
Games: 1983 (16), 1984 (16), 1985 (5). Total—37.
Pro statistics: Recovered one fumble, 1984.

VAUGHN AARON WILLIAMS
Defensive Back—San Francisco 49ers

Born December 14, 1961, at Denver, Colo.
Height, 6.02. Weight, 193.
High School—Denver, Colo., George Washington.
Attended Stanford University.

Selected by Oakland in 1984 USFL territorial draft.
Signed as free agent by San Francisco 49ers, May 10, 1984.

On injured reserve with pulled hamstring, August 27 through September 27, 1984.
Released by San Francisco 49ers, September 28, 1984; signed as free agent by Indianapolis Colts, October 10, 1984.
Released by Indianapolis Colts, August 27, 1985; signed as free agent by San Francisco 49ers, February 19, 1986.
Indianapolis NFL, 1984.
Games: 1984 (10).

CARLTON WILLIAMSON
Safety—San Francisco 49ers
Born June 12, 1958, at Atlanta, Ga.
Height, 6.00. Weight, 204.
High School—Atlanta, Ga., Brown.
Received degree in urban science from University of Pittsburgh in 1981.

Selected by San Francisco in 3rd round (65th player selected) of 1981 NFL draft.
On injured reserve with fractured fibula, August 30 through October 21, 1983; activated, October 22, 1983.

| | | | —INTERCEPTIONS— | | |
Year Club	G.	No.	Yds.	Avg.	TD.
1981—San Francisco NFL	16	4	44	11.0	0
1982—San Francisco NFL	8		None		
1983—San Francisco NFL	9	4	51	12.8	0
1984—San Francisco NFL	15	2	42	21.0	0
1985—San Francisco NFL	16	3	137	45.7	*1
Pro Totals—5 Years............	64	13	274	21.1	1

Additional pro statistics: Recovered two fumbles for three yards, 1981.
Played in NFC Championship Game following 1981, 1983 and 1984 seasons.
Played in NFL Championship Game following 1981 and 1984 seasons.
Played in Pro Bowl (NFL All-Star Game) following 1984 and 1985 seasons.

KEITH WILLIS
Defensive End—Pittsburgh Steelers
Born July 29, 1959, at Newark, N.J.
Height, 6.01. Weight, 254.
High School—Newark, N.J., Malcolm X. Shabazz.
Attended Northwestern University.

Signed as free agent by Pittsburgh Steelers, April 30, 1982.
Pittsburgh NFL, 1982 through 1985.
Games: 1982 (9), 1983 (14), 1984 (12), 1985 (16). Total—51.
Pro statistics: Recovered one fumble, 1983 and 1984.
Played in AFC Championship Game following 1984 season.

LARRY RAY WILLIS
Wide Receiver—Denver Broncos
Born July 13, 1963, at Santa Monica, Calif.
Height, 5.10. Weight, 170.
High School—Santa Monica, Calif.
Attended Taft College and Fresno State University.

Selected by Oakland in 1985 USFL territorial draft.
Signed as free agent by Denver Broncos, May 3, 1985.
On injured reserve with hand injury, August 20 through entire 1985 season.

OTIS MITCHELL WILLIS
(Mitch)
Defensive Tackle—Los Angeles Raiders
Born March 16, 1962, at Dallas, Tex.
Height, 6.07. Weight, 280.
High School—Arlington, Tex., Lamar.
Received bachelor of business administration degree from Southern Methodist University in 1984.

Selected by San Antonio in 4th round (68th player selected) of 1984 USFL draft.
Selected by Los Angeles Raiders in 7th round (183rd player selected) of 1984 NFL draft.
Signed by Los Angeles Raiders, June 15, 1984.
On injured reserve with shoulder injury, August 27 through entire 1984 season.
On injured reserve with knee injury, September 7 through October 4, 1985; activated, October 5, 1985.
Los Angeles Raiders NFL, 1985.
Games: 1985 (11).

BONNIE RAY WILMER
(Known by middle name.)
Defensive Back—New Orleans Saints
Born June 27, 1962, at Pineville, La.
Height, 6.02. Weight, 190.
High School—Marksville, La.
Attended Louisiana Tech University.

Signed as free agent by Seattle Seahawks, May 3, 1984.
Released by Seattle Seahawks, August 27, 1984; re-signed by Seahawks, October 10, 1984.

Released by Seattle Seahawks, November 12, 1984; signed as free agent by Memphis Showboats, December 10, 1984.
Released by Memphis Showboats, February 12, 1985; re-signed by Seahawks, June 21, 1985.
Released by Seattle Seahawks, August 19, 1985; signed as free agent by New Orleans Saints, May 15, 1986.
Seattle NFL, 1984.
Games: 1984 (3).

BRENARD KENRIC WILSON
Defensive Back—Philadelphia Eagles

Born August 15, 1955, at Daytona Beach, Fla.
Height, 6.00. Weight, 185.
High School—Daytona Beach, Fla., Father Lopez.
Received bachelor of science degree in economics and business administration
from Vanderbilt University.

Signed as free agent by Philadelphia Eagles, May, 1978.
Released by Philadelphia Eagles, August 28, 1978; re-signed by Eagles, December 28, 1978.
On injured reserve with broken foot, December 4 through remainder of 1979 season

Year Club	G.	No.	Yds.	Avg.	TD.
			—INTERCEPTIONS—		
1979—Philadelphia NFL	14	4	70	17.5	0
1980—Philadelphia NFL	16	6	79	13.2	0
1981—Philadelphia NFL	15	5	73	14.6	0
1982—Philadelphia NFL	8	1	0	0.0	0
1983—Philadelphia NFL	16		None		
1984—Philadelphia NFL	16	1	28	28.0	0
1985—Philadelphia NFL	16		None		
Pro Totals—7 Years	101	17	250	14.7	0

Additional pro statistics: Recovered one fumble, 1979 and 1982; returned two kickoffs for no yards, 1979; recovered one fumble for two yards, 1985.
Played in NFC Championship Game following 1980 season.
Played in NFL Championship Game following 1980 season.

CHARLES WADE WILSON
(Known by middle name.)
Quarterback—Minnesota Vikings

Born February 1, 1959, at Greenville, Tex.
Height, 6.03. Weight, 210.
High School—Commerce, Tex.
Attended East Texas State University.

Selected by Minnesota in 8th round (210th player selected) of 1981 NFL draft.
On inactive list, September 12, 1982.
On commissioner's exempt list, November 20 through December 7, 1982; activated, December 8, 1982.
Active for 4 games with Minnesota Vikings in 1982; did not play.

Year Club	G.	Att.	Cmp.	Pct.	Gain	T.P.	P.I.	Avg.	Att.	Yds.	Avg.	TD.	TD.	Pts.	F.
				—PASSING—					—RUSHING—				—TOTAL—		
1981—Minnesota NFL	3	13	6	46.2	48	0	2	3.69		None			0	0	2
1983—Minnesota NFL	1	28	16	57.1	124	1	2	4.43	3	—3	—1.0	0	0	0	1
1984—Minnesota NFL	8	195	102	52.3	1019	5	11	5.23	9	30	3.3	0	0	0	2
1985—Minnesota NFL	4	60	33	55.0	404	3	3	6.73		None			0	0	0
Pro Totals—5 Years	16	296	157	53.0	1595	9	18	5.39	12	27	2.3	0	0	0	5

Quarterback Rating Points: 1981 (16.4), 1983 (50.3), 1984 (52.5), 1985 (71.8). Total—53.3.
Additional pro statistics: Recovered one fumble, 1981.

DARRYAL E. WILSON
Wide Receiver—New England Patriots

Born September 19, 1960, at Florence, Ala.
Height, 6.00. Weight, 182.
High School—Bristol, Va., Virginia.
Attended University of Tennessee.

Selected by New Jersey in 1983 USFL territorial draft.
Selected by New England in 2nd round (47th player selected) of 1983 NFL draft.
Signed by New England Patriots, June 3, 1983.
On injured reserve with knee injury, November 4 through remainder of 1983 season.
On physically unable to perform/reserve with knee injury, August 14 through entire 1984 season.
On physically unable to perform/reserve with knee injury, August 15 through entire 1985 season.
New England NFL, 1983.
Games: 1983 (9).

DAVID CARLTON WILSON
(Dave)
Quarterback—New Orleans Saints

Born April 27, 1959, at Anaheim, Calif.
Height, 6.03. Weight, 210.
High School—Anaheim, Calif., Katella.
Attended Fullerton Junior College and University of Illinois.

Selected by New Orleans in NFL supplementary draft, July 7, 1981; Saints forfeited 1st round pick in 1982 draft.
On injured reserve with knee injury, August 15 through entire 1982 season.
On injured reserve with elbow injury, November 15 through remainder of 1985 season.

Year Club	G.	Att.	Cmp.	Pct.	Gain	T.P.	P.I.	Avg.	Att.	Yds.	Avg.	TD.	TD.	Pts.	F.
			PASSING							RUSHING			TOTAL		
1981—New Orleans NFL............	11	159	82	51.6	1058	1	11	6.65	5	1	0.2	0	0	0	4
1983—New Orleans NFL............	8	112	66	58.9	770	5	7	6.88	5	3	0.6	1	1	6	5
1984—New Orleans NFL............	5	93	51	54.8	647	7	4	6.96	3	—7	—2.3	0	0	0	2
1985—New Orleans NFL............	10	293	145	49.5	1843	11	15	6.29	18	7	0.4	0	0	0	6
Pro Totals—4 Years..........	34	657	344	52.4	4318	24	37	6.57	31	4	0.1	1	1	6	1?

Quarterback Rating Points: 1981 (46.1), 1983 (68.7), 1984 (83.9), 1985 (60.7). Total—62.1.
Additional pro statistics: Recovered three fumbles and fumbled four times for minus eight yards, 1981; recovered one fumble and fumbled six times for minus 23 yards, 1985.

DONALD ALLEN WILSON
(Don)
Safety—Buffalo Bills
Born July 21, 1961, at Washington, D.C.
Height, 6.02. Weight, 190.
High School—Washington, D.C., Cardoza.
Attended Ellsworth Junior College and North Carolina State University.

Signed as free agent by Buffalo Bills, May 16, 1984.

Year Club	G.	No.	Yds.	Avg.	TD.	No.	Yds.	Avg.	TD.	TD.	Pts.	F.
			PUNT RETURNS				KICKOFF RET.				TOTAL	
1984—Buffalo NFL..............................	16	33	297	9.0	1	34	576	16.9	0	1	6	3
1985—Buffalo NFL..............................	16	16	161	10.1	0	22	465	21.1	0	1	6	5
Pro Totals—2 Years......................	32	49	458	9.3	1	56	1041	18.6	0	2	12	8

Additional pro statistics: Recovered one fumble for 40 yards, 1984; intercepted two passes for 23 yards and recovered one fumble for 61 yards and a touchdown, 1985.

EARL WILSON
Defensive End—San Diego Chargers
Born September 13, 1958, at Long Branch, N.J.
Height, 6.04. Weight, 268.
High School—Atlantic City, N.J.
Attended University of Kentucky.

Signed as free agent by Toronto Argonauts, August 1, 1982.
Granted free agency, March 1, 1985; signed by San Diego Chargers, April 10, 1985.
Toronto CFL, 1982 through 1984; San Diego NFL, 1985.
Games: 1982 (11), 1983 (16), 1984 (14), 1985 (16). Total CFL—41. Total Pro—57.
CFL statistics: Intercepted three passes for eight yards, 1982; recovered two fumbles, 1984.
NFL statistics: Recovered one fumble, 1985.

MARC DOUGLAS WILSON
Quarterback—Los Angeles Raiders
Born February 15, 1957, at Bremerton, Wash.
Height, 6.06. Weight, 205.
High School—Seattle, Wash., Shorecrest.
Received bachelor of arts degree in economics from Brigham Young University in 1980.

Selected by Oakland in 1st round (15th player selected) of 1980 NFL draft.
Franchise transferred to Los Angeles, May 7, 1982.
On injured reserve with dislocated shoulder, November 7 through December 30, 1983; activated, December 31 1983.

Year Club	G.	Att.	Cmp.	Pct.	Gain	T.P.	P.I.	Avg.	Att.	Yds.	Avg.	TD.	TD.	Pts.	F.
			PASSING							RUSHING			TOTAL		
1980—Oakland NFL....................	2	5	3	60.0	31	0	0	6.20	1	3	3.0	0	0	0	0
1981—Oakland NFL....................	13	366	173	47.3	2311	14	19	6.31	30	147	4.9	2	2	12	8
1982—L.A. Raiders NFL.............	8	2	1	50.0	4	0	0	2.00		None			0	0	0
1983—L.A. Raiders NFL.............	10	117	67	57.3	864	8	6	7.38	13	122	9.4	0	0	0	4
1984—L.A. Raiders NFL.............	16	282	153	54.3	2151	15	17	7.63	30	56	1.9	1	1	6	1?
1985—L.A. Raiders NFL.............	16	388	193	49.7	2608	16	21	6.72	24	98	4.1	2	2	12	8
Pro Totals—5 Years..........	65	1160	590	50.9	7969	53	63	6.87	98	426	4.3	5	5	30	31

Quarterback Rating Points: 1980 (77.9), 1981 (58.8), 1982 (56.3), 1983 (82.0), 1984 (71.7), 1985 (62.7). Total—66.0.
Additional pro statistics: Recovered two fumbles and fumbled eight times for minus three yards, 1981; recovered one fumble, 1983; recovered three fumbles and fumbled 11 times for minus 11 yards, 1984; recovered two fumbles and fumbled eight times for minus four yards, 1985.
Played in AFC Championship Game following 1983 season.
Member of Oakland Raiders for AFC Championship Game following 1980 season; did not play.
Played in NFL Championship Game following 1983 season.
Member of Oakland Raiders for NFL Championship Game following 1980 season; did not play.

MICHAEL RUBEN WILSON
(Mike)
Wide Receiver—San Francisco 49ers
Born December 19, 1958, at Los Angeles, Calif.
Height, 6.03. Weight, 215.
High School—Carson, Calif.
Attended Washington State University.

Selected by Dallas in 9th round (246th player selected) of 1981 NFL draft.
Released by Dallas Cowboys, August 24, 1981; signed as free agent by San Francisco 49ers, August 27, 1981.
On injured reserve with broken finger, September 9 through November 19, 1982; activated, November 20, 1982.

			—PASS RECEIVING—			
Year Club	G.	P.C.	Yds.	Avg.	TD.	
1981—San Francisco NFL	16	9	125	13.9	1	
1982—San Francisco NFL	6	6	80	13.3	1	
1983—San Francisco NFL	15	30	433	14.4	0	
1984—San Francisco NFL	13	17	245	14.4	1	
1985—San Francisco NFL	16	10	165	16.5	2	
Pro Totals—5 Years...........	66	72	1048	14.6	5	

Additional pro statistics: Returned four kickoffs for 67 yards and recovered one fumble, 1981; fumbled once, 1983; returned one kickoff for 14 yards, 1984.
Played in NFC Championship Game following 1981, 1983 and 1984 seasons.
Played in NFL Championship Game following 1981 and 1984 seasons.

OTIS RAY WILSON
Linebacker—Chicago Bears
Born September 15, 1957, at New York, N.Y.
Height, 6.02. Weight, 231.
High School—Brooklyn, N.Y., Thomas Jefferson.
Attended Syracuse University and University of Louisville.

Named as linebacker on THE SPORTING NEWS College All-America Team, 1979.
Selected by Chicago in 1st round (19th player selected) of 1980 NFL draft.

		—INTERCEPTIONS—			
Year Club	G.	No.	Yds.	Avg.	TD.
1980—Chicago NFL	16	2	4	2.0	0
1981—Chicago NFL	15		None		
1982—Chicago NFL	9	2	39	19.5	⋆1
1983—Chicago NFL	16	1	6	6.0	0
1984—Chicago NFL	15		None		
1985—Chicago NFL	16	3	35	11.7	⋆1
Pro Totals—6 Years...........	87	8	84	10.5	2

Additional pro statistics: Fumbled once, 1980; recovered three fumbles for 31 yards, 1981; recovered two fumbles and credited with one safety, 1985.
Played in NFC Championship Game following 1984 and 1985 seasons.
Played in NFL Championship Game following 1985 season.
Played in Pro Bowl (NFL All-Star Game) following 1985 season.

STANLEY T. WILSON
Running Back—Cincinnati Bengals
Born August 23, 1961, at Los Angeles, Calif.
Height, 5.10. Weight, 210.
High School—Banning, Calif.
Attended University of Oklahoma.

Selected by New Jersey in 1983 USFL territorial draft.
Selected by Cincinnati in 9th round (248th player selected) of 1983 NFL draft.
Signed by Cincinnati Bengals, May 19, 1983.
On non-football injury list with drug problem, August 23 through September 20, 1984; activated, September 21, 1984.
On injured reserve with dislocated shoulder, October 1 through October 31, 1984.
On NFL suspended list with drug problem, November 1 through remainder of 1984 season and 1985 season; reinstated, May 9, 1986.

		—RUSHING—				PASS RECEIVING				—TOTAL—		
Year Club	G.	Att.	Yds.	Avg.	TD.	P.C.	Yds.	Avg.	TD.	TD.	Pts.	F.
1983—Cincinnati NFL...................	10	56	267	4.8	1	12	107	8.9	1	2	12	4
1984—Cincinnati NFL...................	1	17	74	4.4	0	2	15	7.5	0	0	0	0
Pro Totals—2 Years...................	11	73	341	4.7	1	14	122	8.7	1	2	12	4

		KICKOFF RETURNS			
Year Club	G.	No.	Yds.	Avg.	TD.
1983—Cincinnati NFL.............	10	7	161	23.0	0
1984—Cincinnati NFL.............	1		None		
Pro Totals—2 Years...........	11	7	161	23.0	0

Additional pro statistics: Recovered two fumbles, 1983.

STEVEN ANTHONY WILSON
(Steve)
Cornerback—Denver Broncos

Born August 24, 1957, at Los Angeles, Calif.
Height, 5.10. Weight, 195.
High School—Durham, N.C., Northern.
Received bachelor of business administration degree in marketing from Howard University in 1979.
Son of (Touchdown) Tommy Wilson, halfback with Los Angeles Rams, Cleveland Browns
and Minnesota Vikings, 1956 through 1963.
Signed as free agent by Dallas Cowboys, May 6, 1979.
Released by Dallas Cowboys, August 14, 1979; re-signed by Cowboys, August 29, 1979.
Released by Dallas Cowboys, September 6, 1982; signed as free agent by Denver Broncos, September 14, 1982.

		INTERCEPTIONS				-PUNT RETURNS-				—KICKOFF RET.—				—TOTAL—		
Year	Club	G.	No.	Yds.	Avg.	TD.	No.	Yds.	Avg.	TD.	No.	Yds.	Avg.	TD.	TD.	Pts.	F
1979—Dallas NFL		16		None			35	236	6.7	0	19	328	17.3	0	0	0
1980—Dallas NFL		16	4	82	20.5	0		None			7	139	19.9	0	0	0
1981—Dallas NFL		16	2	0	0.0	0		None			2	32	16.0	0	0	0
1982—Denver NFL		8	2	22	11.0	0		None			6	123	20.5	0	0	0
1983—Denver NFL		16	5	91	18.2	0		None			24	485	20.2	0	0	0
1984—Denver NFL		15	4	59	14.8	0	1	0	0.0	0		None			0	0
1985—Denver NFL		14	3	8	2.7	0		None				None			0	0
Pro Totals—7 Years		101	20	262	13.1	0	36	236	6.6	0	58	1107	19.1	0	0	0

Additional pro statistics: Recovered one fumble, 1979, 1981 and 1984; caught three passes for 76 yards, 197▌
recovered one fumble for two yards, 1985.
Played in NFC Championship Game following 1980 and 1981 seasons.

WAYNE MacARTHUR WILSON
Fullback—New Orleans Saints

Born September 4, 1957, at Montgomery County, Md.
Height, 6.03. Weight, 218.
High School—Ellicott, Md., Howard.
Received degree in recreation from Shepherd College.
Selected by Houston in 12th round (324th player selected) of 1979 NFL draft.
Released by Houston Oilers, August 29, 1979; signed as free agent by New Orleans Saints, September 11, 1979.

			——RUSHING——				PASS RECEIVING				—TOTAL—		
Year	Club	G.	Att.	Yds.	Avg.	TD.	P.C.	Yds.	Avg.	TD.	TD.	Pts.	F
1979—New Orleans NFL		14	5	26	5.2	0		None			0	0	
1980—New Orleans NFL		15	63	188	3.0	1	31	241	7.8	1	2	12	3
1981—New Orleans NFL		16	44	137	3.1	1	31	384	12.4	4	5	30	
1982—New Orleans NFL		8	103	413	4.0	3	25	175	7.0	2	5	30	4
1983—New Orleans NFL		14	199	787	4.0	9	20	178	8.9	2	11	66	6
1984—New Orleans NFL		14	74	261	3.5	1	33	314	9.5	3	4	24	2
1985—New Orleans NFL		16	168	645	3.8	1	38	228	6.0	2	3	18	2
Pro Totals—7 Years		97	656	2457	3.7	16	178	1520	8.5	14	30	180	1▌

			KICKOFF RETURNS			
Year	Club	G.	No.	Yds.	Avg.	TD.
1979—New Orleans NFL		14	11	230	20.9	0
1980—New Orleans NFL		15	9	159	17.7	0
1981—New Orleans NFL		16	31	722	23.3	0
1982—New Orleans NFL		8	7	192	27.4	0
1983—New Orleans NFL		14	9	239	26.6	0
1984—New Orleans NFL		14	1	23	23.0	0
1985—New Orleans NFL		16		None		
Pro Totals—7 Years		97	68	1565	23.0	0

Additional pro statistics: Recovered one fumble, 1979, 1981, 1982 and 1985; recovered two fumbles, 1980.

WILLIAM MIKE WILSON
(Known by middle name.)
Offensive Tackle—Cincinnati Bengals

Born May 28, 1955, at Norfolk, Va.
Height, 6.05. Weight, 271.
High School—Gainesville, Ga., Johnson.
Attended University of Georgia.
Selected by Cincinnati in 4th round (103rd player selected) of 1977 NFL draft.
Signed by Toronto Argonauts, May, 1977.
Released by Toronto Argonauts, July 6, 1978; signed by Cincinnati Bengals, July 6, 1978; activated, October 13, 1978
Placed on physically unable to perform list with knee injury, July 6, 1978.
Toronto CFL, 1977; Cincinnati NFL, 1978 through 1985.
Games: 1977 (16), 1978 (9), 1979 (16), 1980 (16), 1981 (16), 1982 (9), 1983 (16), 1984 (16), 1985 (16). Total NFL—11▌
Total Pro—130.
Played in AFC Championship Game following 1981 season.
Played in NFL Championship Game following 1981 season.

SAMMY WINDER
Running Back—Denver Broncos
Born July 15, 1959, at Madison, Miss.
Height, 5.11. Weight, 203.
High School—Madison, Miss., Ridgeland.
Attended University of Southern Mississippi.
Selected by Denver in 5th round (131st player selected) of 1982 NFL draft.

		——RUSHING——				PASS RECEIVING			—TOTAL—		
ear Club	G.	Att.	Yds.	Avg.	TD.	P.C.	Yds.	Avg.	TD.	TD.	Pts.	F.
'82—Denver NFL	8	67	259	3.9	1	11	83	7.5	0	1	6	1
'83—Denver NFL	14	196	757	3.9	3	23	150	6.5	0	3	18	7
'84—Denver NFL	16	296	1153	3.9	4	44	288	6.5	2	6	36	5
'85—Denver NFL	14	199	714	3.6	8	31	197	6.4	0	8	48	4
Pro Totals—4 Years	52	758	2883	3.8	16	109	718	6.6	2	18	108	17

Additional pro statistics: Recovered one fumble, 1982 and 1985; recovered two fumbles, 1984; attempted one pass ith no completions, 1985.
Played in Pro Bowl (NFL All-Star Game) following 1984 season.

BLAKE LEO WINGLE
Guard—Green Bay Packers
Born April 17, 1960, at Pottsville, Calif.
Height, 6.02. Weight, 260.
High School—Oxnard, Calif., Rio Mesa.
Attended Ventura College, California Poly State University at San Luis Obispo and received degree in College of letters and sciences from University of California at Los Angeles.
Selected by Pittsburgh in 9th round (244th player selected) of 1983 NFL draft.
Released by Pittsburgh Steelers, October 5, 1985; signed as free agent by Green Bay Packers, November 20, 1985.
Pittsburgh NFL, 1983 and 1984; Pittsburgh (3)-Green Bay (2) NFL, 1985.
Games: 1983 (16), 1984 (15), 1985 (5). Total—36.
Member of Pittsburgh Steelers for AFC Championship Game following 1984 season; did not play.

RICHARD ALLEN WINGO
(Rich)
Linebacker
Born July 16, 1956, at Elkhart, Ind.
Height, 6.01. Weight, 230.
High School—Elkhart, Ind., Central.
Received bachelor of science degree in education from University of Alabama in 1979.
Selected by Green Bay in 7th round (184th player selected) of 1979 NFL draft.
On injured reserve with back injury, September 2 through remainder of 1980 season.
On injured reserve with knee injury, December 9, 1982 through January 4, 1983; activated, January 5, 1983.
On injured reserve with separated shoulder, August 12 through entire 1985 season.
Granted free agency, February 1, 1986; withdrew qualifying offer, May 19, 1986.

	——INTERCEPTIONS——			
Year Club	G.	No.	Yds.	Avg.TD.
1979—Green Bay NFL	16	2	13	6.5 0
1981—Green Bay NFL	16	1	38	38.0 0
1982—Green Bay NFL	5	1	0	0.0 0
1983—Green Bay NFL	16		None	
1984—Green Bay NFL	16		None	
Pro Totals—5 Years	69	4	51	12.8 0

Additional pro statistics: Recovered one fumble, 1979; scored extra point on pass reception, 1981.

KELLEN BOSWELL WINSLOW
Tight End—San Diego Chargers
Born November 5, 1957, at St. Louis, Mo.
Height, 6.05. Weight, 242.
High School—East St. Louis, Ill.
Attended University of Missouri.

Tied NFL record for most touchdowns, pass receptions, game (5), November 22, 1981, against Oakland Raiders.
Named as tight end on THE SPORTING NEWS College All-America Team, 1978.
Named to THE SPORTING NEWS NFL All-Star Team, 1980 and 1981.
Selected by San Diego in 1st round (13th player selected) of 1979 NFL draft.
On injured reserve with broken leg, October 19 through remainder of 1979 season.
Left San Diego Chargers voluntarily and granted roster exemption, September 3 through September 9, 1984; ctivated, September 10, 1984.
On injured reserve with knee injury, October 23 through remainder of 1984 season.
On physically unable to perform/active with knee injury, August 20 through October 17, 1985; activated, October 3, 1985.

	——PASS RECEIVING——						——PASS RECEIVING——			
ear Club	G.	P.C.	Yds.	Avg.	TD.	Year Club	G.	P.C.	Yds.	Avg.	TD.
'79—San Diego NFL	7	25	255	10.2	2	1983—San Diego NFL	16	88	1172	13.3	8
'80—San Diego NFL	16	*89	1290	14.5	9	1984—San Diego NFL	7	55	663	12.1	2
'81—San Diego NFL	16	*88	1075	12.2	10	1985—San Diego NFL	10	25	318	12.7	0
'82—San Diego NFL	9	54	721	13.4	6	Pro Totals—7 Years	81	424	5494	13.0	37

Additional pro statistics: Fumbled once, 1979, 1982 and 1984; fumbled twice, 1980 and 1981; attempted two pass with no completions, 1981; recovered two fumbles, 1981 and 1983; attempted one pass with no completions, 198 fumbled three times, 1983.

Played in AFC Championship Game following 1980 and 1981 seasons.

Played in Pro Bowl (NFL All-Star Game) following 1980 through 1983 seasons.

DENNIS EDWARD WINSTON
Linebacker—Pittsburgh Steelers
Born October 25, 1955, at Forrest City, Ark.
Height, 6.00. Weight, 241.
High School—Marianna, Ark., Robert E. Lee.
Attended University of Arkansas.
Cousin of Clifford Brooks, back with Cleveland Browns, Philadelphia Eagles,
New York Jets and Buffalo Bills, 1972 through 1976.

Selected by Pittsburgh in 5th round (132nd player selected) of 1977 NFL draft.
Traded by Pittsburgh Steelers to New Orleans Saints for 6th round pick in 1982 draft, April 27, 1982.
Left New Orleans Saints camp voluntarily, October 1, 1985.
Released by New Orleans Saints, October 9, 1985; signed as free agent by Pittsburgh Steelers, October 15, 1985.

| | | | —INTERCEPTIONS— | | | |
Year	Club	G.	No.	Yds.	Avg.	TD.
1977—Pittsburgh NFL		13	2	7	3.5	0
1978—Pittsburgh NFL		16		None		
1979—Pittsburgh NFL		16	3	48	16.0	1
1980—Pittsburgh NFL		14		None		
1981—Pittsburgh NFL		14	1	1	1.0	0
1982—New Orleans NFL		9	2	—2	—1.0	0
1983—New Orleans NFL		16	3	21	7.0	0
1984—New Orleans NFL		16	2	90	45.0	★2
1985—N.O.(2)-Pitt.(10) NFL...		12		None		
Pro Totals—9 Years		126	13	165	12.7	3

Additional pro statistics: Recovered one fumble, 1978, 1983 and 1984; recovered three fumbles, 1979; recovere blocked punt in end zone for a touchdown, recovered four fumbles and returned one kickoff for 13 yards, 198 recovered two fumbles, 1982; fumbled once, 1983; ran eight yards with lateral from interception, 1985.

Played in AFC Championship Game following 1978 and 1979 seasons.

Played in NFL Championship Game following 1978 and 1979 seasons.

BLAISE WINTER
Defensive End—Indianapolis Colts
Born January 31, 1962, at Blauvelt, N.Y.
Height, 6.03. Weight, 295.
High School—Orangeburg, N.Y., Tappan Zee.
Attended Syracuse University.

Selected by New Jersey in 1984 USFL territorial draft.
Selected by Indianapolis in 2nd round (35th player selected) of 1984 NFL draft.
Signed by Indianapolis Colts, July 27, 1984.
On injured reserve with shoulder injury, August 27 through entire 1985 season.
Indianapolis NFL, 1984.
Games: 1984 (16).
Pro statistics: Recovered one fumble, 1984.

LARRY WINTERS
Defensive Back—New York Giants
Born February 14, 1960, at Marbury, Md.
Height, 6.01. Weight, 210.
High Schools—LaPlata, Md.; and Fork Union, Va., Military.
Attended University of North Carolina and St. Paul's College.

Signed as free agent by New York Giants, May 7, 1985.
On injured reserve with pinched nerve, August 26 through entire 1985 season.

JEFFREY ROLLAND WISKA
(Jeff)
Guard—Cleveland Browns
Born October 17, 1959, at Detroit, Mich.
Height, 6.03. Weight, 265.
High School—Redford, Mich., Catholic Central.
Received bachelor of arts degree in business management
from Michigan State University in 1982.

Selected by New York Giants in 7th round (186th player selected) of 1982 NFL draft.
On injured reserve with knee injury, August 9 through entire 1982 season.
Released by New York Giants, August 23, 1983; signed by Michigan Panthers, November 27, 1983.
Protected in merger of Michigan Panthers and Oakland Invaders, December 6, 1984.
Granted free agency, August 1, 1985; signed by Cleveland Browns, April 20, 1986.
Michigan USFL, 1984; Oakland USFL, 1985.
Games: 1984 (18), 1985 (18). Total—36.
Pro statistics: Recovered two fumbles, 1985.
Played in USFL Championship Game following 1985 season.

LEO JOSEPH WISNIEWSKI
Nose Tackle—Indianapolis Colts
Born November 6, 1959, at Hancock, Mich.
Height, 6.01. Weight, 259.
High School—Pittsburgh, Pa., Fox Chapel.
Received bachelor of arts degree in speech communications from Penn State University.

Selected by Baltimore in 2nd round (28th player selected) of 1982 NFL draft.
On injured reserve with knee injury, September 7 through November 18, 1982; activated, November 19, 1982.
Franchise transferred to Indianapolis, March 31, 1984.
On injured reserve with knee injury, December 4 through remainder of 1984 season.
On injured reserve with knee injury, August 20 through entire 1985 season.
Baltimore NFL, 1982 and 1983; Indianapolis NFL, 1984.
Games: 1982 (7), 1983 (15), 1984 (14). Totals—36.
Pro statistics: Recovered two fumbles, 1983; recovered one fumble, 1984.

JOHN JOSEPH WITKOWSKI
Quarterback—Detroit Lions
Born June 18, 1962, at Flushing, N.Y.
Height, 6.01. Weight, 205.
High School—Lindenhurst, N.Y.
Received bachelor of arts degree in economics from Columbia University in 1984.

Selected by Philadelphia in 7th round (138th player selected) of 1984 USFL draft.
Selected by Detroit in 6th round (160th player selected) of 1984 NFL draft.
Signed by Detroit Lions, June 10, 1984.
Released by Detroit Lions, September 2, 1985; re-signed by Lions, March 6, 1986.

			PASSING						RUSHING			TOTAL		
Year	Club	G.	Att.	Cmp.	Pct.	Gain	T.P.	P.I.	Avg.	Att.	Yds.	Avg. TD.	TD.	Pts. F.
1984—Detroit NFL		3	34	13	38.2	210	0	0	6.18	7	33	4.7 0	0	0 1

Quarterback Rating Points: 1984 (59.7).

MARK STEVEN WITTE
Name pronounced WIT-ee.
Tight End—Tampa Bay Buccaneers
Born December 3, 1959, at Corpus Christi, Tex.
Height, 6.03. Weight, 240.
High School—San Marcos, Tex.
Attended North Texas State University.

Selected by Denver in 7th round (81st player selected) of 1983 USFL draft.
Selected by Tampa Bay in 11th round (297th player selected) of 1983 NFL draft.
Signed by Tampa Bay Buccaneers, June 1, 1983.

		PASS RECEIVING			
Year	Club	G.	P.C.	Yds.	Avg. TD.
1983—Tampa Bay NFL		16	2	15	7.5 0
1984—Tampa Bay NFL		16		None	
1985—Tampa Bay NFL		16	3	28	9.3 0
Pro Totals—3 Years		48	5	43	8.6 0

Additional pro statistics: Recovered one fumble, 1984 and 1985.

CRAIG ALAN WOLFLEY
Guard—Pittsburgh Steelers
Born May 19, 1958, at Buffalo, N.Y.
Height, 6.01. Weight, 260.
High School—Orchard Park, N.Y.
Received bachelor of science degree in speech communication from Syracuse University in 1980.
Brother of Ronnie Wolfley, running back with St. Louis Cardinals.

Selected by Pittsburgh in 5th round (138th player selected) of 1980 NFL draft.
On injured reserve with pulled hamstring, October 5 through November 18, 1984; activated, November 19, 1984.
Pittsburgh NFL, 1980 through 1985.
Games: 1980 (16), 1981 (16), 1982 (9), 1983 (14), 1984 (9), 1985 (13). Total—77.
Pro statistics: Recovered two fumbles, 1982; recovered one fumble, 1983 and 1985.
Played in AFC Championship Game following 1984 season.

RONALD PAUL WOLFLEY
(Ron)
Running Back—St. Louis Cardinals
Born October 14, 1962, at Blasdel, N.Y.
Height, 6.00. Weight, 222.
High School—Hamburg, N.Y., Frontier Central.
Attended West Virginia University.
Brother of Craig Wolfley, guard with Pittsburgh Steelers.

Selected by Birmingham in 1985 USFL territorial draft.
Selected by St. Louis in 4th round (104th player selected) of 1985 NFL draft.
Signed by St. Louis Cardinals, July 21, 1985.

Year	Club	G.	Att.	Yds.	Avg.	TD.	P.C.	Yds.	Avg.	TD.	TD.	Pts.
			—RUSHING—				PASS RECEIVING				—TOTAL	
1985—St. Louis NFL		16	24	64	2.7	0	2	18	9.0	0	0	0

KICKOFF RETURNS

Year	Club	G.	No.	Yds.	Avg.TD.	
1985—St. Louis NFL		16	13	234	18.0	0

GEORGE IVORY WONSLEY
Running Back—Indianapolis Colts

Born November 23, 1960, at Moss Point, Miss.
Height, 6.00. Weight, 217.
High School—Moss Point, Miss.
Attened Mississippi State University.
Brother of Otis Wonsley, running back with Washington Redskins; Nathan Wonsley, running back
at University of Mississippi; Leroy Wonsley, running back at Winston Salem State University;
and Josea Wonsley, running back at Lenoir-Rhyne College.
Selected by New Jersey in 1984 USFL territorial draft.
Selected by Indianapolis in 4th round (103rd player selected) of 1984 NFL draft.
Signed by Indianapolis Colts, May 24, 1984.

Year	Club	G.	Att.	Yds.	Avg.	TD.	P.C.	Yds.	Avg.	TD.	TD.	Pts.
			—RUSHING—				PASS RECEIVING				—TOTAL	
1984—Indianapolis NFL		14	37	111	3.0	0	9	47	5.2	0	0	0
1985—Indianapolis NFL		16	138	716	5.2	6	30	257	8.6	0	6	36
Pro Totals—2 Years		30	175	827	4.7	6	39	304	7.8	0	6	36

Additional pro statistics: Returned four kickoffs for 52 yards, 1984.

OTIS WONSLEY
Running Back—Washington Redskins

Born August 13, 1957, at Pascagoula, Miss.
Height, 5.10. Weight, 214.
High School—Moss Point, Miss.
Received degree in physical education from Alcorn State University.
Brother of George Wonsley, running back with Indianapolis Colts; Nathan Wonsley, running back
at University of Mississippi; Leroy Wonsley, running back at Winston Salem State University;
and Josea Wonsley, running back at Lenoir-Rhyne College.
Selected by New York Giants in 9th round (229th player selected) of 1980 NFL draft.
Released by New York Giants, September 1, 1980; signed as free agent by Washington Redskins, April 6, 1981.
On injured reserve with knee injury, December 18 through remainder of 1981 season.

Year	Club	G.	Att.	Yds.	Avg.	TD.	P.C.	Yds.	Avg.	TD.	TD.	Pts.
			—RUSHING—				PASS RECEIVING				—TOTAL	
1981—Washington NFL		15	3	11	3.7	0	1	5	5.0	0	0	0
1982—Washington NFL		9	11	36	3.3	0	1	1	1.0	1	1	6
1983—Washington NFL		16	25	88	3.5	0	None				0	0
1984—Washington NFL		16	18	38	2.1	4	None				4	24
1985—Washington NFL		16	4	8	2.0	0	None				0	0
Pro Totals—5 Years		72	61	181	3.0	4	2	6	3.0	1	5	30

KICKOFF RETURNS

Year	Club	G.	No.	Yds.	Avg.TD.	
1981—Washington NFL		15	6	124	20.7	0
1982—Washington NFL		9	1	14	14.0	0
1983—Washington NFL		16	2	36	18.0	0
1984—Washington NFL		16		None		
1985—Washington NFL		16	2	26	13.0	0
Pro Totals—5 Years		72	11	200	18.2	0

Additional pro statistics: Recovered one fumble, 1982 and 1983.
Played in NFC Championship Game following 1982 and 1983 seasons.
Played in NFL Championship Game following 1982 and 1983 seasons.

KENNETH EMIL WOODARD
(Ken)
Linebacker—Denver Broncos

Born January 22, 1960, at Detroit, Mich.
Height, 6.01. Weight, 218.
High School—Detroit, Mich., Martin Luther King.
Attended Tuskegee Institute.
Selected by Denver in 10th round (274th player selected) of 1982 NFL draft.
Denver NFL, 1982 through 1985.
Games: 1982 (9), 1983 (16), 1984 (16), 1985 (16). Total—57.
Pro statistics: Recovered one fumble, 1983; intercepted one pass for 27 yards and a touchdown, 1984; intercepte
one pass for 18 yards, 1985.

— 452 —

RAYMOND LEE WOODARD
(Ray)
Defensive End—Denver Broncos

Born August 20, 1961, at Corrigan, Tex.
Height, 6.06. Weight, 267.
High School—Corrigan, Tex., Corrigan-Camden.
Attended University of Texas.

Selected by Houston in 1984 USFL territorial draft.
Selected by San Diego in 8th round (199th player selected) of 1984 NFL draft.
Signed by San Diego Chargers, June 27, 1984.
On injured reserve with dislocated shoulder, August 13 through entire 1984 season.
Released by San Diego Chargers, August 14, 1985; signed as free agent by Denver Broncos, March 18, 1986.

DAVID EUGENE WOODLEY
Quarterback—Pittsburgh Steelers

Born October 25, 1958, at Shreveport, La.
Height, 6.02. Weight, 210.
High School—Shreveport, La., Byrd.
Attended Louisiana State University.

Selected by Miami in 8th round (214th player selected) of 1980 NFL draft.
Granted free agency, February 1, 1984; re-signed by Dolphins and traded to Pittsburgh Steelers for 3rd round pick in 1984 draft, February 21, 1984.

Year Club	G.	Att.	Cmp.	Pct.	Gain	T.P.	P.I.	Avg.	Att.	Yds.	Avg.	TD.	TD.	Pts.	F.
1980—Miami NFL	13	327	176	53.8	1850	14	17	5.66	55	214	3.9	3	3	18	3
1981—Miami NFL	15	366	191	52.2	2470	12	13	6.75	63	272	4.3	4	4	24	9
1982—Miami NFL	9	179	98	54.7	1080	5	8	6.03	36	207	5.8	2	3	18	2
1983—Miami NFL	5	89	43	48.3	528	3	4	5.93	19	78	4.1	0	0	0	4
1984—Pittsburgh NFL	7	156	85	54.5	1273	8	7	8.16	11	14	1.3	0	0	0	5
1985—Pittsburgh NFL	9	183	94	51.4	1357	6	14	7.42	17	71	4.2	2	2	12	8
Pro Totals—6 Years	58	1300	687	52.8	8558	48	63	6.58	201	856	4.3	11	12	72	31

Quarterback Rating Points: 1980 (63.2), 1981 (69.7), 1982 (63.4), 1983 (59.6), 1984 (79.9), 1985 (54.8). Total—65.8.
Additional pro statistics: Recovered two fumbles and fumbled nine times for minus 21 yards, 1981; caught one pass for 15 yards and a touchdown and recovered three fumbles, 1982; caught one pass for six yards, 1983; recovered two fumbles and fumbled five times for minus four yards, 1984; recovered two fumbles, 1985.
Played in AFC Championship Game following 1982 season.
Member of Pittsburgh Steelers for AFC Championship Game following 1984 season; did not play.
Played in NFL Championship Game following 1982 season.

DWAYNE DONZELL WOODRUFF
Cornerback—Pittsburgh Steelers

Born February 18, 1957, at Bowling Green, Ky.
Height, 6.00. Weight, 198.
High School—New Richmond, O.
Received bachelor of science degree in commerce from University of Louisville in 1979.

Selected by Pittsburgh in 6th round (161st player selected) of 1979 NFL draft.
USFL rights traded with rights to quarterback Jeff Hostetler by Pittsburgh Maulers to Arizona Wranglers for a draft pick, May 2, 1984.
On injured reserve with dislocated elbow, October 15 through November 14, 1985; activated, November 15, 1985.

		—INTERCEPTIONS—		
Year Club	G.	No.	Yds.	Avg. TD.
1979—Pittsburgh NFL	16	1	31	31.0 0
1980—Pittsburgh NFL	16	1	0	0.0 0
1981—Pittsburgh NFL	16	1	17	17.0 0
1982—Pittsburgh NFL	9	5	53	10.6 0
1983—Pittsburgh NFL	15	3	85	28.3 0
1984—Pittsburgh NFL	16	5	56	11.2 1
1985—Pittsburgh NFL	12	5	80	16.0 0
Pro Totals—7 Years	100	21	322	15.3 1

Additional pro statistics: Recovered one fumble and fumbled once, 1981; recovered one fumble for 65 yards and a touchdown, 1984.
Played in AFC Championship Game following 1979 and 1984 seasons.
Played in NFL Championship Game following 1979 season.

RICK L. WOODS
Defensive Back—Pittsburgh Steelers

Born November 16, 1959, at Boise, Ida.
Height, 6.01. Weight, 195.
High School—Boise, Ida.
Attended Boise State University.

Selected by Pittsburgh in 4th round (97th player selected) of 1982 NFL draft.
On injured reserve with elbow injury, December 9, 1982 through January 6, 1983; activated, January 7, 1983.

Year Club		-INTERCEPTIONS-				-PUNT RETURNS-				—TOTAL—		
	G.	No.	Yds.	Avg.	TD.	No.	Yds.	Avg.	TD.	TD.	Pts.	F.
1982—Pittsburgh NFL	5	1	12	12.0	0	13	142	10.9	0	0	0	2
1983—Pittsburgh NFL	15	5	53	10.6	0	5	46	9.2	0	1	6	0
1984—Pittsburgh NFL	15	2	0	0.0	0	6	40	6.7	0	0	0	0
1985—Pittsburgh NFL	16		None			13	46	3.5	0	0	0	0
Pro Totals—4 Years	51	8	65	8.1	0	37	274	7.4	0	1	6	2

Additional pro statistics: Recovered two fumbles, 1982; recovered two fumbles for 38 yards and a touchdown, 1983. Played in AFC Championship Game following 1984 season.

HAROLD WOOLFOLK
(Butch)
Running Back—Houston Oilers
Born March 1, 1960, at Milwaukee, Wis.
Height, 6.01. Weight, 212.
High School—Westfield, N.J.
Received bachelor of science degree in physical therapy
from University of Michigan in 1982.

Tied NFL record for most rushing attempts, game (43) vs. Philadelphia Eagles, November 20, 1983.
Selected by New York Giants in 1st round (18th player selected) of 1982 NFL draft.
Traded by New York Giants to Houston Oilers for 3rd round pick in 1985 draft, March 21, 1985.

Year Club		——RUSHING——				PASS RECEIVING				—TOTAL—		
	G.	Att.	Yds.	Avg.	TD.	P.C.	Yds.	Avg.	TD.	TD.	Pts.	F.
1982—New York Giants NFL	9	112	439	3.9	2	23	224	9.7	2	4	24	5
1983—New York Giants NFL	16	246	857	3.5	4	28	368	13.1	0	4	24	8
1984—New York Giants NFL	15	40	92	2.3	1	9	53	5.9	0	1	6	1
1985—Houston NFL	16	103	392	3.8	1	80	814	10.2	4	5	30	5
Pro Totals—4 Years	56	501	1780	3.6	8	140	1459	10.4	6	14	84	19

Year Club		KICKOFF RETURNS			
	G.	No.	Yds.	Avg.	TD.
1982—N.Y. Giants NFL	9	20	428	21.4	0
1983—N.Y. Giants NFL	16	2	13	6.5	0
1984—N.Y. Giants NFL	15	14	232	16.6	0
1985—Houston NFL	16		None		
Pro Totals—4 Years	56	36	673	18.7	0

Additional pro statistics: Recovered one fumble, 1982 through 1984; recovered two fumbles, 1985.

RONALD J. WOOTEN
(Ron)
Guard—New England Patriots
Born June 28, 1959, at Cape Cod, Mass.
Height, 6.04. Weight, 273.
High School—Kinston, N.C.
Received bachelor of science degree in chemistry
from University of North Carolina in 1982.

Selected by New England in 6th round (157th player selected) of 1981 NFL draft.
On injured reserve with back injury, August 31 through entire 1981 season.
New England NFL, 1982 through 1985.
Games: 1982 (9), 1983 (16), 1984 (16), 1985 (14). Total—55.
Played in AFC Championship Game following 1985 season.
Played in NFL Championship Game following 1985 season.

STEVE WRAY
Quarterback—Miami Dolphins
Born January 29, 1960, at Nuremburg, West Germany.
Height, 6.02. Weight, 215.
High School—Plainfield, Ind.
Attended Franklin College.

Signed as free agent by Seattle Seahawks, April 28, 1983.
On injured reserve with ankle injury, August 29 through entire 1983 season.
Released by Seattle Seahawks, August 27, 1984.
USFL rights traded with rights to kicker Marco Morales by Memphis Showboats to Denver Gold for rights to linebacker John Harper and defensive back Rod Perry, January 3, 1985.
USFL rights traded by Denver Gold to Birmingham Stallions for future considerations, January 25, 1985.
Signed by Birmingham Stallions, January 29, 1985.
Released by Birmingham Stallions, February 18, 1985; signed as free agent by Indianapolis Colts, March 28, 1985.
Released by Indianapolis Colts, August 14, 1985; signed as free agent by Miami Dolphins, March 6, 1986.

BRET JOSEPH WRIGHT
Punter—Detroit Lions
Born January 5, 1962, at Hammond, La.
Height, 6.03. Weight, 210.
High School—Ponchatoula, La.
Received degree in constructional drafting from Southeastern Louisiana University.

Selected by New York Jets in 8th round (217th player selected) of 1984 NFL draft.
Released by New York Jets, August 21, 1984; re-signed by Jets, May 7, 1985.
Released by New York Jets, August 7, 1985; signed as free agent by Detroit Lions, March 6, 1986.

ERIC WRIGHT
Cornerback—San Francisco 49ers
Born April 18, 1959, at St. Louis, Mo.
Height, 6.01. Weight, 185.
High School—East St. Louis, Ill., Assumption.
Attended University of Missouri.

Named to THE SPORTING NEWS NFL All-Star Team, 1985.
Selected by San Francisco in 2nd round (40th player selected) of 1981 NFL draft.
On inactive list, September 19, 1982.
On injured reserve with pulled abdomen, December 24 through remainder of 1985 season playoffs.

		—INTERCEPTIONS—			
Year Club	G.	No.	Yds.	Avg.	TD.
1981—San Francisco NFL	16	3	26	8.7	0
1982—San Francisco NFL	7	1	31	31.0	0
1983—San Francisco NFL	16	7	★164	23.4	★2
1984—San Francisco NFL	16	2	0	0.0	0
1985—San Francisco NFL	16	1	0	0.0	0
Pro Totals—5 Years............	71	14	221	15.8	2

Additional pro statistics: Recovered two fumbles, 1981; recovered one fumble, 1983.
Played in NFC Championship Game following 1981, 1983 and 1984 seasons.
Played in NFL Championship Game following 1981 and 1984 seasons.
Played in Pro Bowl (NFL All-Star Game) following 1984 season.
Named to play in Pro Bowl following 1985 season; replaced due to injury by Gary Green.

FELIX CARL WRIGHT
Defensive Back—Cleveland Browns
Born June 22, 1959, at Carthage, Mo.
Height, 6.02. Weight, 190.
High School—Carthage, Mo.
Received bachelor of science degree in physical education and history
from Drake University in 1981.

Signed as free agent by Houston Oilers, May 17, 1982.
Released by Houston Oilers, August 23, 1982; signed as free agent by Hamilton Tiger-Cats, October 24, 1982.
Granted free agency, March 1, 1985; signed by Cleveland Browns, May 6, 1985.

		—INTERCEPTIONS—			
Year Club	G.	No.	Yds.	Avg.	TD.
1982—Hamilton CFL	2	2	32	16.0	0
1983—Hamilton CFL	12	6	140	23.3	1
1984—Hamilton CFL	16	7	100	14.3	1
1985—Cleveland NFL..............	16	2	11	5.5	0
CFL Totals—3 Years	30	15	272	18.1	2
NFL Totals—1 Year...........	16	2	11	5.5	0
Pro Totals—4 Years............	46	17	283	16.6	2

Additional CFL statistics: Returned one punt for three yards, 1982; returned seven punts for 36 yards, recovered
three fumbles for 10 yards and fumbled twice, 1983; recovered two fumbles, 1984.
Additional NFL statistics: Recovered two fumbles, 1985.

JAMES WILLIE WRIGHT
(Jim)
Tight End—Denver Broncos
Born September 1, 1956, at Fort Hood, Tex.
Height, 6.03. Weight, 240.
High School—Brenham, Tex.
Attended Blinn Junior College and received bachelor of science
degree in psychology from Texas Christian University in 1978.

Selected by Atlanta in 7th round (179th player selected) of 1978 NFL draft.
On injured reserve with knee injury, August 13 through remainder of 1979 season.
Released by Atlanta Falcons, August 26, 1980; signed as free agent by Denver Broncos, December 15, 1980.
On injured reserve with shoulder and neck injuries, October 21 through remainder of 1983 season.

		—PASS RECEIVING—			
Year Club	G.	P.C.	Yds.	Avg.	TD.
1978—Atlanta NFL	15	2	26	13.0	0
1980—Denver NFL	1		None		
1981—Denver NFL	16	3	22	7.3	1
1982—Denver NFL	9	9	120	13.3	1
1983—Denver NFL	6	13	134	10.3	0
1984—Denver NFL	16	11	118	10.7	1
1985—Denver NFL	16	28	246	8.8	1
Pro Totals—7 Years............	79	66	666	10.1	4

Additional pro statistics: Returned two kickoffs for 31 yards, 1978; rushed once for 11 yards and recovered one
fumble for one yard, 1981; rushed once for minus four yards, 1982; rushed once for minus 11 yards and fumbled twice,
1983; recovered one fumble, 1985.

LOUIS DONNEL WRIGHT
Cornerback—Denver Broncos
Born January 31, 1953, at Gilmer, Tex.
Height, 6.03. Weight, 200.
High School—Bakersfield, Calif.
Attended Arizona State University, Bakersfield College and San Jose State University.
Named to THE SPORTING NEWS NFL All-Star Team, 1984.
Named to THE SPORTING NEWS AFC All-Star Team, 1977 through 1979.
Selected by Denver in 1st round (17th player selected) of 1975 NFL draft.
On injured reserve with calf injury, November 28 through remainder of 1981 season.

		—INTERCEPTIONS—						—INTERCEPTIONS—		
Year Club	G.	No.	Yds.	Avg.TD.	Year Club	G.	No.	Yds.	Avg.TD
1975—Denver NFL	11	2	9	4.5	0	1981—Denver NFL	8		None	
1976—Denver NFL	14		None		1982—Denver NFL	9	2	18	9.0
1977—Denver NFL	14	3	128	*42.7	*1	1983—Denver NFL	16	6	50	8.3
1978—Denver NFL	16	2	2	1.0	0	1984—Denver NFL	16	1	1	1.0
1979—Denver NFL	16	2	20	10.0	0	1985—Denver NFL	15	5	44	8.8
1980—Denver NFL	15		None		Pro Totals—11 Years	150	23	272	11.8

Additional pro statistics: Recovered one fumble for four yards, 1975; fumbled once, 1975, 1978 and 1983; recovered one fumble, 1976 and 1982; ran one lateral 32 yards, 1976; recovered two fumbles, 1978; recovered one fumble for yards and a touchdown, 1979; recovered one fumble for minus five yards, 1981; returned one punt for no yards and recovered one fumble for 40 yards, 1983; recovered two fumbles for 27 yards and a touchdown, 1984; returned blocked field goal attempt for 60 yards and a touchdown, 1985.
Played in AFC Championship Game following 1977 season.
Played in NFL Championship Game following 1977 season.
Played in Pro Bowl (NFL All-Star Game) following 1977 through 1979, 1983 and 1985 seasons.

RANDALL STEVEN WRIGHT
(Randy)
Quarterback—Green Bay Packers
Born January 12, 1961, at St. Charles, Ill.
Height, 6.02. Weight, 194.
High School—St. Charles, Ill.
Received degree in communications from University of Wisconsin.
Selected by Memphis in 9th round (188th player selected) of 1984 USFL draft.
USFL rights released by Memphis Showboats, February 7, 1984.
Selected by Green Bay in 6th round (153rd player selected) of 1984 NFL draft.
Signed by Green Bay Packers, June 30, 1984.
On injured reserve with knee injury, December 12 through remainder of 1984 season.

		—————PASSING—————							——RUSHING——				—TOTAL—	
Year Club	G.	Att.	Cmp.	Pct.	Gain	T.P.	P.I.	Avg.	Att.	Yds.	Avg.	TD.	TD.	Pts. P
1984—Green Bay NFL	8	62	27	43.5	310	2	6	5.00	8	11	1.4	0	0	0
1985—Green Bay NFL	5	74	39	52.7	552	2	4	7.46	8	8	1.0	0	0	0
Pro Totals—2 Years	13	136	66	48.5	862	4	10	6.34	16	19	1.2	0	0	0

Quarterback Rating Points: 1984 (30.4), 1985 (63.6). Total—47.8.
Additional pro statistics: Recovered one fumble, 1984; recovered two fumbles and fumbled five times for minus si yards, 1985.

TIMOTHY JON WRIGHTMAN
(Tim)
Tight End—Chicago Bears
Born March 27, 1960, at Harbor City, Calif.
Height, 6.03. Weight, 236.
High School—San Pedro, Calif., Mary Star of the Sea.
Attended University of California at Los Angeles.
Selected by Chicago in 3rd round (62nd player selected) of 1982 NFL draft.
Signed by Chicago Blitz, August 5, 1982.
USFL rights subsequently traded by Arizona Wranglers to Chicago Blitz for rights to quarterback Dan Manucc October 22, 1982.
On injured reserve with knee injury, March 3 through May 5, 1983; activated, May 6, 1983.
Franchise transferred to Arizona, September 30, 1983.
On reserve/non-football injury with knee injury, February 20 through April 20, 1984; activated, April 21, 1984.
On developmental squad, April 21 through remainder of 1984 season.
Granted free agency, November 30, 1984; signed by Chicago Bears, March 21, 1985.
On developmental squad for 10 games with Arizona Wranglers in 1984.

	—PASS RECEIVING—				
Year Club	G.	P.C.	Yds.	Avg.	TD.
1983—Chicago USFL	9	6	86	14.3	0
1985—Chicago NFL	16	24	407	17.0	1
Pro Totals—2 Years	25	30	493	16.4	1

On developmental squad for USFL Championship Game following 1984 season.
Played in NFC Championship Game following 1985 season.
Played in NFL Championship Game following 1985 season.

ANTHONY LEON WROTEN
(Tony)
Tight End—Tampa Bay Buccaneers
Born October 8, 1962, at Fort Dix, N.J.
Height, 6.03. Weight, 225.
High School—Renton, Wash., Hazen.
Attended University of Washington.

Selected by Portland in 1985 USFL territorial draft.
Signed as free agent by Tampa Bay Buccaneers, May 9, 1985.
On injured reserve with knee injury, August 20 through entire 1985 season.

GEORGE ANTHONY YARNO
Offensive Tackle—Tampa Bay Buccaneers
Born August 12, 1957, at Spokane, Wash.
Height, 6.02. Weight, 265.
High Schools—Anchorage, Ala., East; and Spokane, Wash., Joel E. Ferris.
Received bachelor of arts degree in criminal justice from Washington State University in 1979.
Brother of John Yarno, center with Seattle Seahawks and Denver Gold, 1977 through 1982 and 1984.

Signed as free agent by Tampa Bay Buccaneers, May 10, 1979.
USFL rights traded by Houston Gamblers to Denver Gold for rights to defensive back John Holt and defensive end Clenzie Pierson, September 23, 1983.
Signed by Denver Gold, October 17, 1983, to contract to take effect after being granted free agency, February 1, 1984.
Released by Denver Gold, July 31, 1985; re-signed by Buccaneers, August 13, 1985.
On injured reserve with knee injury, October 28 through November 28, 1985; activated, November 29, 1985.
Tampa Bay NFL, 1979 through 1983; Denver USFL, 1984 and 1985; Tampa Bay NFL, 1985.
Games: 1979 (15), 1980 (16), 1981 (16), 1982 (9), 1983 (14), 1984 (18), 1985 USFL (18), 1985 NFL (12). Total NFL—82. Total USFL—36. Total Pro—118.
NFL statistics: Returned one kickoff for 14 yards, 1982; kicked one extra point, 1983.
USFL statistics: Recovered two fumbles, 1984; recovered one fumble, 1985.
Played in NFC Championship Game following 1979 season.

ANTHONY RICARDO YOUNG
Safety—Indianapolis Colts
Born October 8, 1963, at Columbia, S.C.
Height, 5.11. Weight, 187.
High School—Pemberton, N.J., Township.
Attended Temple University.

Selected by Baltimore in 1985 USFL territorial draft.
Selected by Indianapolis in 3rd round (61st player selected) of 1985 NFL draft.
Signed by Indianapolis Colts, August 10, 1985.
Indianapolis NFL, 1985.
Games: 1985 (14).
Pro statistics: Recovered four fumbles for 28 yards and a touchdown, intercepted one pass for no yards and returned two kickoffs for 15 yards, 1985.

FREDD YOUNG
Linebacker—Seattle Seahawks
Born November 14, 1961, at Dallas, Tex.
Height, 6.01. Weight, 220.
High School—Dallas, Tex., Woodrow Wilson.
Attended New Mexico State University.

Selected by Arizona in 1984 USFL territorial draft.
Selected by Seattle in 3rd round (76th player selected) of 1984 NFL draft.
Signed by Seattle Seahawks, May 17, 1984.
Seattle NFL, 1984 and 1985.
Games: 1984 (16), 1985 (16). Total—32.
Pro statistics: Recovered one fumble for 13 yards, 1985.
Played in Pro Bowl (NFL All-Star Game) following 1984 and 1985 seasons.

GLEN YOUNG
Wide Receiver-Kick Returner—Cleveland Browns
Born October 11, 1960, at Greenwood, Miss.
Height, 6.02. Weight, 205.
High School—Greenwood, Miss.
Attended Mississippi State University.

Selected by Oakland in 2nd round (18th player selected) of 1983 USFL draft.
Selected by Philadelphia in 3rd round (62nd player selected) of 1983 NFL draft.
Signed by Philadelphia Eagles, May 13, 1983.
Released by Philadelphia Eagles, August 27, 1984; awarded on waivers to St. Louis Cardinals, August 28, 1984.
Released by St. Louis Cardinals, September 5, 1984; signed as free agent by Cleveland Browns, November 14, 1984.
Active for 1 game with St. Louis Cardinals in 1984; did not play.

		PASS RECEIVING				–PUNT RETURNS–				—KICKOFF RET.—				—TOTAL—		
Year	Club	G.	P.C.	Yds.	Avg.	TD.	No.	Yds.	Avg.	TD.	No.	Yds.	Avg.	TD.	TD.	Pts.	F.
1983—Philadelphia NFL		16	3	125	41.7	1	14	93	6.6	0	26	547	21.0	0	1	6	2

Year Club		PASS RECEIVING				-PUNT RETURNS-			-KICKOFF RET.-			-TOTAL-		
	G.	P.C.	Yds.	Avg.	TD.	No.	Yds.	Avg.	No.	Yds.	Avg.	TD.	TD.	Pts.	F.
1984—St.L. (0)-Cle. (2) NFL ...	2	1	47	47.0	0		None		5	134	26.8	0	0	0	0
1985—Cleveland NFL............	15	5	111	22.2	1		None		35	898	25.7	0	1	6	1
Pro Totals—3 Years.......	33	9	283	31.4	2	14	93	6.6	66	1579	23.9	0	2	12	3

Additional pro statistics: Recovered one fumble, 1983.

LONNIE YOUNG
Defensive Back—St. Louis Cardinals
Born July 18, 1963, at Flint, Mich.
Height, 6.01. Weight, 182.
High School—Flint, Mich., Beecher.
Received degree in communications from Michigan State University in 1985.

Selected by New Jersey in 8th round (112th player selected) of 1985 USFL draft.
Selected by St. Louis in 12th round (325th player selected) of 1985 NFL draft.
Signed by St. Louis Cardinals, July 15, 1985.

Year Club		—INTERCEPTIONS—			
	G.	No.	Yds.	Avg.	TD.
1985—St. Louis NFL.................	16	3	0	0.0	0

Additional pro statistics: Recovered one fumble, 1985.

MICHAEL DAVID YOUNG
(Mike)
Wide Receiver—Los Angeles Rams
Born February 2, 1962, at Hanford, Calif.
Height, 6.01. Weight, 185.
High School—Visalia, Calif., Mount Whitney.
Attended University of California at Los Angeles.

Selected by Memphis in 1985 USFL territorial draft.
Selected by Los Angeles Rams in 6th round (161st player selected) of 1985 NFL draft.
Signed by Los Angeles Rams, July 23, 1985.

Year Club		—PASS RECEIVING—			
	G.	P.C.	Yds.	Avg.	TD.
1985—L.A. Rams NFL.............	15	14	157	11.2	0

Additional pro statistics: Fumbled once, 1985.
Played in NFC Championship Game following 1985 season.

ROYNELL YOUNG
Cornerback—Philadelphia Eagles
Born December 1, 1957, at New Orleans, La.
Height, 6.01. Weight, 185.
High School—New Orleans, La., Cohen.
Attended Alcorn State University.

Selected by Philadelphia in 1st round (23rd player selected) of 1980 NFL draft.
On injured reserve with strained abdominal muscles, October 12 through November 15, 1984; activated, November 16, 1984.

Year Club		—INTERCEPTIONS—			
	G.	No.	Yds.	Avg.	TD.
1980—Philadelphia NFL	16	4	27	6.8	0
1981—Philadelphia NFL	13	4	35	8.8	0
1982—Philadelphia NFL	9	4	0	0.0	0
1983—Philadelphia NFL	16	1	0	0.0	0
1984—Philadelphia NFL	7		None		
1985—Philadelphia NFL	14	1	0	0.0	0
Pro Totals—6 Years............	75	14	62	4.4	0

Additional pro statistics: Returned one kickoff for 18 yards and recovered two fumbles, 1983.
Played in NFC Championship Game following 1980 season.
Played in NFL Championship Game following 1980 season.
Played in Pro Bowl (NFL All-Star Game) following 1981 season.

STEVE YOUNG
Quarterback—Tampa Bay Buccaneers
Born November 11, 1961, at Salt Lake City, Utah.
Height, 6.02. Weight, 200.
High School—Greenwich, Conn.
Attended Brigham Young University.

Named as quarterback on THE SPORTING NEWS College All-America Team, 1983.
Selected by Los Angeles in 1st round (10th player selected) of 1984 USFL draft.
Signed by Los Angeles Express, March 5, 1984.
Granted roster exemption, March 5, 1984; activated, March 30, 1984.
Selected by Tampa Bay in 1st round (1st player selected) of 1984 NFL supplemental draft.
On developmental squad, March 31 through April 15, 1985; activated, April 16, 1985.
Released by Los Angeles Express, September 9, 1985; signed by Tampa Bay Buccaneers, September 10, 1985.
Granted roster exemption, September 10 through September 22, 1985; activated, September 23, 1985.

On developmental squad for 3 games with Los Angeles Express in 1985.

Year Club	G.	Att.	Cmp.	Pct.	Gain	T.P.	P.I.	Avg.	Att.	Yds.	Avg.	TD	TD	Pts	F.
				PASSING							RUSHING			TOTAL	
1984—Los Angeles USFL............	12	310	179	57.7	2361	10	9	7.62	79	515	6.5	7	7	†48	7
1985—Los Angeles USFL............	13	250	137	54.8	1741	6	13	6.96	56	368	6.6	2	2	12	7
1985—Tampa Bay NFL	5	138	72	52.2	935	3	8	6.78	40	233	5.8	1	1	6	4
USFL Totals—2 Years.......	25	560	316	56.4	4102	16	22	7.33	135	883	6.5	9	9	60	14
NFL Totals—1 Year..........	5	138	72	52.2	935	3	8	6.78	40	233	5.8	1	1	6	4
Pro Totals—3 Years...........	30	698	388	55.6	5037	19	30	7.22	175	1116	6.4	10	10	66	18

†Includes three 2-point conversions.
USFL Quarterback Rating Points: 1984 (80.6), 1985 (63.1). Total—73.1.
NFL Quarterback Rating Points: 1985 (56.9).
Additional USFL statistics: Recovered four fumbles, 1984; recovered one fumble and fumbled seven times for minus 11 yards, 1985.
Additional NFL statistics: Recovered one fumble and fumbled four times for minus one yard, 1985.

TYRONE DONNIVE YOUNG
Wide Receiver—New Orleans Saints
Born April 29, 1960, at Ocala, Fla.
Height, 6.06. Weight, 192.
High School—Ocala, Fla., Forest.
Attended University of Florida.

Selected by Tampa Bay in 1983 USFL territorial draft.
Signed as free agent by New Orleans Saints, May 20, 1983.
On injured reserve with knee injury, August 28 through entire 1985 season.

Year Club	G.	P.C.	Yds.	Avg.	TD.
		PASS RECEIVING			
1983—New Orleans NFL........	16	7	85	12.1	3
1984—New Orleans NFL........	16	29	597	20.6	3
Pro Totals—2 Years............	32	36	682	18.9	6

Additional pro statistics: Fumbled once, 1984.

CARL AUGUST ZANDER JR.
Linebacker—Cincinnati Bengals
Born April 12, 1963, at Mendham, N.J.
Height, 6.02. Weight, 235.
High School—Mendham, N.J., West Morris.
Attended University of Tennessee.

Selected by Memphis in 1985 USFL territorial draft.
Selected by Cincinnati in 2nd round (43rd player selected) of 1985 NFL draft.
Signed by Cincinnati Bengals, July 21, 1985.
Cincinnati NFL, 1985.
Games: 1985 (16).
Pro statistics: Returned one kickoff for 19 yards and recovered one fumble for 34 yards, 1985.

LUIS FERNANDO ZENDEJAS
Placekicker—Minnesota Vikings
Born October 22, 1961, at Mexico City, Mexico.
Height, 5.09. Weight, 186.
High School—Chico, Calif., Don Antonio Lugo.
Attended Arizona State University.
Brother of Joaquin Zendejas, placekicker with New England Patriots, 1983; brother of Max Zendejas, rookie placekicker with Dallas Cowboys; brother of Alan Zendejas, placekicker at Arizona State University; cousin of Tony Zendejas, placekicker with Houston Oilers; and cousin of Martin Zendejas, placekicker at University of Nevada at Reno.

Selected by Arizona in 1985 USFL territorial draft.
Signed by Arizona Outlaws, January 22, 1985.
Released by Arizona Outlaws, June 24, 1985; signed as free agent by Atlanta Falcons, July 20, 1985.
Released by Atlanta Falcons, July 29, 1985; signed as free agent by Minnesota Vikings, March 6, 1986.

Year Club	G.	XP.	XPM.	FG.	FGA.	Pts.
		PLACE KICKING				
1985—Arizona USFL...........	18	36	*5	24	33	108

TONY ZENDEJAS
Placekicker—Houston Oilers
Born March 15, 1960, at Curimeo Michucan, Mexico.
Height, 5.08. Weight, 160.
High School—Chino, Calif.
Attended University of Nevada at Reno.
Brother of Martin Zendejas, placekicker at University of Nevada at Reno;
cousin of Joaquin Zendejas, placekicker with New England Patriots, 1983;
cousin of Max Zendejas, rookie placekicker with Dallas Cowboys;
cousin of Luis Zendejas, placekicker with Minnesota Vikings;
and cousin of Alan Zendejas, placekicker at Arizona State University.

Tied NFL record for most field goals, 50 or more yards, game (2), against San Diego Chargers, November 24, 1985.

Named as kicker on THE SPORTING NEWS USFL All-Star Team, 1984 and 1985.
Selected by Los Angeles in 5th round (90th player selected) of 1984 USFL draft.
Signed by Los Angeles Express, February 21, 1984.
Selected by Washington in 1st round (27th player selected) of 1984 NFL supplemental draft.
Granted free agency, July 1, 1985; signed by Washington Redskins, July 3, 1985.
Traded by Washington Redskins to Houston Oilers for 5th round pick in 1987 draft, August 27, 1985.

			——PLACE KICKING——				
Year	Club	G.	XP.	XPM.	FG.	FGA.	Pts.
1984—Los Angeles USFL...		18	33	0	21	30	96
1985—Los Angeles USFL...		18	22	1	*26	*34	100
1985—Houston NFL............		14	29	2	21	27	92
USFL Totals—2 Years...		36	55	1	47	64	196
NFL Totals—1 Year......		14	29	2	21	27	92
Pro Totals—3 Years.......		50	84	3	68	91	288

Additional NFL statistics: Attempted one pass with one completion for minus seven yards and recovered one fumble, 1985.

GARY WAYNE ZIMMERMAN
Offensive Tackle-Guard—Minnesota Vikings
Born December 13, 1961, at Fullerton, Calif.
Height, 6.06. Weight, 264.
High School—Walnut, Calif.
Attended University of Oregon.

Named as offensive tackle on THE SPORTING NEWS USFL All-Star Team, 1984 and 1985.
Selected by Los Angeles in 2nd round (36th player selected) of 1984 USFL draft.
Signed by Los Angeles Express, February 13, 1984.
Granted roster exemption, February 13 through February 23, 1984; activated, February 24, 1984.
Selected by New York Giants in 1st round (3rd player selected) of 1984 NFL supplemental draft.
NFL rights traded by New York Giants to Minnesota Vikings for two 2nd round picks in 1986 draft, April 29, 1986.
Released by Los Angeles Express, May 19, 1986; signed by Minnesota Vikings, May 21, 1986.
Los Angeles USFL, 1984 and 1985.
Games: 1984 (17), 1985 (17). Total—34.
Pro statistics: Returned one kickoff for no yards, recovered two fumbles and fumbled once, 1984.

JAMES ARTHUR ZORN
(Jim)
Quarterback—Green Bay Packers
Born May 10, 1953, at Whittier, Calif.
Height, 6.02. Weight, 200.
High School—Cerritos, Calif., Gahr.
Attended Cerritos College and California Poly State University—Pomona.

Signed as free agent by Dallas Cowboys, 1975.
Released by Dallas Cowboys, September 19, 1975; signed as free agent by Seattle Seahawks, January 8, 1976.
Released by Seattle Seahawks, September 2, 1985; signed as free agent by Green Bay Packers, September 24, 1985.

			——————PASSING——————							—RUSHING—				—TOTAL—	
Year	Club	G.	Att.	Cmp.	Pct.	Gain	T.P.	P.I.	Avg.	Att.	Yds.	Avg.	TD.	TD.	Pts.	F
1976—Seattle NFL......................		14	*439	208	47.4	2571	12	*27	5.86	52	246	4.7	4	4	24	
1977—Seattle NFL......................		10	251	104	41.4	1687	16	19	6.72	25	141	5.6	1	1	6	
1978—Seattle NFL......................		16	443	248	56.0	3283	15	20	7.41	59	290	4.9	6	6	36	1
1979—Seattle NFL......................		16	505	285	56.4	3661	20	18	7.25	46	279	6.1	2	2	12	
1980—Seattle NFL......................		16	488	276	56.6	3346	17	20	6.86	44	214	4.9	1	1	6	1
1981—Seattle NFL......................		13	397	236	59.4	2788	13	9	7.02	30	140	4.7	1	1	6	
1982—Seattle NFL......................		9	245	126	51.4	1540	7	11	6.29	15	113	7.5	1	1	6	
1983—Seattle NFL......................		16	205	103	50.2	1166	7	7	5.69	30	71	2.4	1	1	6	
1984—Seattle NFL......................		16	17	7	41.2	80	0	2	4.71	7	−3	−0.4	0	0	0	
1985—Green Bay NFL................		13	123	56	45.5	794	4	6	6.46	10	9	0.9	0	0	0	
Pro Totals—10 Years........		139	3113	1649	53.0	20916	111	139	6.72	318	1500	4.7	17	17	102	5

Quarterback Rating Points: 1976 (49.2), 1977 (54.3), 1978 (72.2), 1979 (77.6), 1980 (72.4), 1981 (82.3), 1982 (62.1), 1983 (64.8), 1984 (16.4), 1985 (57.4). Total—67.5.

Additional pro statistics: Recovered three fumbles, 1976 and 1978; recovered one fumble, 1977; fumbled 11 times for minus 18 yards, 1978; recovered four fumbles and fumbled 12 times for minus 13 yards, 1980; caught one pass for 2 yards, recovered one fumble and fumbled five times for minus three yards, 1982; recovered two fumbles and fumbled three times for minus one yard, 1985.
Played in AFC Championship Game following 1983 season.

Additional Active Players

GLENN THATCHER HYDE
Center-Guard—Seattle Seahawks
Born March 14, 1951, at Boston, Mass.
Height, 6.03. Weight, 252.
High School—Lexington, Mass.
Received bachelor of science degree in physical education and health from
University of Pittsburgh in 1974.

Signed as free agent by Atlanta Falcons, 1974.
Traded by Atlanta Falcons to Washington Redskins for 8th round pick in 1976 draft, March 10, 1975.
Released by Washington Redskins, September 5, 1975; signed as free agent by Charlotte Hornets (WFL), September, 1975.
Signed as free agent by New England Patriots after World Football League folded, 1976.
Played in World Football League with Chicago Fire, 1974.
Released by New England Patriots, September 6, 1976; signed as free agent by Denver Broncos, September 28, 1976.
Released by Denver Broncos, August 29, 1978; re-signed by Broncos, September 8, 1978.
Traded by Denver Broncos to Baltimore Colts for 8th round pick in 1983 draft, September 6, 1982.
Released by Baltimore Colts, December 7, 1982.
USFL rights traded by Washington Federals to Denver Gold for 1984 draft choice, December 14, 1982.
Signed by Denver Gold, December 20, 1982.
On developmental squad, May 22 through May 24, 1983; activated, May 25, 1983.
Traded with defensive end Larry White by Denver Gold to Chicago Blitz for wide receiver Neil Balholm, tight end Mike Hirn, defensive end Bill Purifoy, linebacker Orlando Flanagan and rights to tight end Peter Holohan, December 28, 1983.
Franchise disbanded, November 20, 1984; not selected in USFL dispersal draft, December 6, 1984.
Signed as free agent by Denver Broncos, December 13, 1984.
Granted free agency, February 1, 1985 when not tendered qualifying offer; re-signed by Broncos, April 9, 1985.
Released by Denver Broncos, November 22, 1985; signed as free agent by Seattle Seahawks, June 2, 1986.
On developmental squad for 1 game with Denver Gold in 1983.
Active for 1 game with Denver Broncos in 1984; did not play.
Chicago WFL, 1974; Charlotte WFL, 1975; Denver NFL, 1976 through 1981, 1984 and 1985; Baltimore NFL, 1982; Denver USFL, 1983; Chicago USFL, 1984.
Games: 1974 (10), 1975 (1), 1976 (11), 1977 (14), 1978 (15), 1979 (16), 1980 (16), 1981 (16), 1982 (5), 1983 (17), 1984 USFL (18), 1985 (11). Total WFL—11. Total NFL—104. Total USFL—35. Total Pro—150.
Pro statistics: Returned one kickoff for 15 yards, 1977.
Played in AFC Championship Game following 1977 season.
Played in NFL Championship Game following 1977 season.

COACHING RECORD
Player-coach, Denver USFL, June 2 through remainder of 1983 season.

LOUIS BERNARD JACKSON
Running Back—Los Angeles Rams
Born January 27, 1958, at Fresno, Calif.
Height, 5.11. Weight, 195.
High School—Fresno, Calif., Roosevelt.
Attended California Poly State University at San Luis Obispo.

Selected by New York Giants in 7th round (168th player selected) of 1981 NFL draft.
Released by New York Giants, September 2, 1982; signed by Oakland Invaders, January 26, 1983.
Released by Oakland Invaders, February 7, 1983; re-signed by Invaders, February 9, 1983.
On developmental squad, March 18 through April 9, 1983; activated, April 10, 1983.
On developmental squad, March 16 through March 29, 1984; activated, March 30, 1984.
On developmental squad, May 4 through May 24, 1984; activated, May 25, 1984.
Not protected in merger of Oakland Invaders and Michigan Panthers, December 6, 1984.
Signed as free agent by Portland Breakers, January 22, 1985.
Granted free agency, November 30, 1984; signed by Portland Breakers, January 23, 1985.
Released by Portland Breakers, July 31, 1985; signed as free agent by Los Angeles Rams, May 22, 1986.
On developmental squad for 3 games with Oakland Invaders in 1983.
On developmental squad for 5 games with Oakland Invaders in 1984.

—DID YOU KNOW—

That Matt Cavanaugh made only two starts in three seasons as a backup quarterback to Joe Montana in San Francisco? In 1984, Cavanaugh led the 49ers to a 21-9 victory over the Philadelphia Eagles; in '85, Cavanaugh led the Niners to a 24-13 win over the Eagles. Cavanaugh was traded to the Eagles last April.

		RUSHING				PASS RECEIVING				−TOTAL−		
Year Club	G.	Att.	Yds.	Avg.	TD.	P.C.	Yds.	Avg.	TD.	TD.	Pts.	F.
1981—N.Y. Giants NFL	11	27	68	2.5	1	3	25	8.3	0	1	6	1
1983—Oakland USFL	15	82	273	3.3	0	29	294	10.1	1	1	6	3
1984—Oakland USFL	13	38	144	3.8	0	19	133	7.0	0	0	0	3
1985—Portland USFL	18	73	296	4.1	0	24	257	10.7	2	2	12	6
NFL Totals—1 Year	11	27	68	2.5	1	3	25	8.3	0	1	6	1
USFL Totals—3 Years	46	193	713	3.7	0	72	684	9.5	3	3	18	12
Pro Totals—4 Years	57	220	781	3.6	1	75	709	9.5	3	4	24	13

		KICKOFF RETURNS			
Year Club	G.	No.	Yds.	Avg.TD.	
1981—N.Y. Giants NFL	11			None	
1983—Oakland USFL	15			None	
1984—Oakland USFL	13			None	
1985—Portland USFL	18	26	638	24.5	0
NFL Totals—1 Year	11	0	0	0.0	0
USFL Totals—3 Years	46	26	638	24.5	0
Pro Totals—4 Years	57	26	638	24.5	0

Additional pro statistics: Attempted one pass with no completions and returned 11 kickoffs for 215 yards, 1983; recovered three fumbles and returned one kickoff for six yards, 1984; attempted two passes with one completion for 17 yards with one touchdown and one interception and recovered two fumbles, 1985.

JUNIOR MILLER
Tight End—Dallas Cowboys
Born November 26, 1957, at Midland, Tex.
Height, 6.04. Weight, 240.
High School—Midland, Tex., Robert E. Lee.
Attended University of Nebraska.

Named as tight end on THE SPORTING NEWS College All-America Team, 1979.
Selected by Atlanta in 1st round (7th player selected) of 1980 NFL draft.
Placed on did not report list, August 14 through August 19, 1984.
Reported and granted roster exemption, August 20 through August 23, 1984; activated, August 24, 1984.
Traded by Atlanta Falcons to New Orleans Saints for 6th round pick in 1985 draft, August 26, 1984.
Granted free agency, February 1, 1985; withdrew qualifying offer, August 22, 1985.
Signed by Dallas Cowboys, May 30, 1986.

		PASS RECEIVING		
Year Club	G.	P.C.	Yds.	Avg. TD.
1980—Atlanta NFL	16	46	584	12.7 9
1981—Atlanta NFL	16	32	398	12.4 3
1982—Atlanta NFL	9	20	221	11.1 1
1983—Atlanta NFL	15	16	125	7.8 0
1984—New Orleans NFL	15	8	81	10.1 1
Pro Totals—5 Years	71	122	1409	11.5 14

Additional pro statistics: Rushed twice for minus two yards and fumbled twice, 1980; recovered one fumble, 1982; fumbled once, 1982 and 1983; rushed once for two yards, 1983.
Played in Pro Bowl (NFL All-Star Game) following 1980 and 1981 seasons.

WILLIAM SUTTON
(Mickey)
Cornerback—Los Angeles Rams
Born August 28, 1961, at Greenville, Miss.
Height, 5.09. Weight, 170.
High School—Union City, Calif., Logan.
Attended University of Montana.

Signed as free agent by Hamilton Tiger-Cats, April 15, 1983.
Released by Hamilton Tiger-Cats, July 25, 1983; signed by Pittsburgh Maulers, September 2, 1983.
Franchise disbanded, October 25, 1984.
Selected by Birmingham Stallions in USFL dispersal draft, December 6, 1984.
Granted free agency, August 1, 1985; signed by Los Angeles Rams, May 17, 1986.

		INTERCEPTIONS				−KICKOFF RET.−				−TOTAL−	
Year Club	G.	No.	Yds.	Avg.	TD.	No.	Yds.	Avg.	TD.	TD.	Pts.
1983—Hamilton CFL	1			None				None		0	0
1984—Pittsburgh USFL	17	1	16	16.0	0	9	232	25.8	0	1	6
1985—Birmingham USFL	17	2	30	15.0	0	15	244	16.3	0	0	0
CFL Totals—1 Year	1	0	0	0.0	0	0	0	0.0	0	0	0
USFL Totals—2 Years	34	3	46	15.3	0	24	476	19.8	0	1	6
Pro Totals—3 Years	35	3	46	15.3	0	24	476	19.8	0	1	6

Additional CFL statistics: Recovered one fumble, 1983.
Additional USFL statistics: Recovered one fumble for 44 yards and a touchdown, 1984; returned one punt for four yards and recovered four fumbles, 1985.

—DID YOU KNOW—
That the Steelers had only four fair catches on punt returns in 1985?

RICHARD KEITH UECKER

(Known by middle name.)

Guard-Offensive Tackle—Green Bay Packers

Born June 29, 1960, at Hollywood, Fla.

Height, 6.05. Weight, 270.

High School—Hollywood, Fla., Hollywood Hills.

Attended Auburn University.

Selected by Denver in 9th round (243rd player selected) of 1982 NFL draft.
On injured reserve with Achilles tendon injury, August 14 through October 21, 1984.
Awarded on procedural waivers to Green Bay Packers, October 23, 1984.
On injured reserve with knee injury, November 2 through remainder of 1985 season.
Denver NFL, 1982 and 1983; Green Bay NFL, 1984 and 1985.
Games: 1982 (5), 1983 (16), 1984 (6), 1985 (7). Total—34.
Pro statistics: Returned one kickoff for 12 yards and fumbled once, 1982; recovered one fumble, 1985.

BENJAMIN MICHAEL UTT

(Ben)

Guard—Indianapolis Colts

Born June 13, 1959, at Richmond, Calif.

Height, 6.05. Weight, 276.

High School—Vidalia, Ga.

Received bachelor of science degree in industrial management from Georgia Tech in 1982.

Signed as free agent by Dallas Cowboys, May, 1981.
Released by Dallas Cowboys, August 14, 1981; signed as free agent by Baltimore Colts, January 18, 1982.
Franchise transferred to Indianapolis, March 31, 1984.
Baltimore NFL, 1982 and 1983; Indianapolis NFL, 1984 and 1985.
Games: 1982 (9), 1983 (16), 1984 (16), 1985 (16). Total—57.
Pro statistics: Recovered one fumble, 1984.

RANDY LEE VAN DIVIER

Guard—Los Angeles Raiders

Born June 5, 1958, at Anaheim, Calif.

Height, 6.05. Weight, 265.

High School—Anaheim, Calif.

Attended University of Washington.

Selected by Baltimore in 3rd round (68th player selected) of 1981 NFL draft.
Released by Baltimore Colts, September 6, 1982; signed as free agent by Los Angeles Raiders, November 19, 1982.
Released by Los Angeles Raiders, August 29, 1983.
USFL rights traded with rights to tight end John Thompson by Denver Gold to Oakland Invaders for rights to
quarterback Steve DeBerg, October 7, 1983.
Signed by Oakland Invaders, November 30, 1983.
On developmental squad, February 24 through March 8, 1984; activated, March 9, 1984.
Not protected in merger of Oakland Invaders and Michigan Panthers; selected by New Jersey Generals in USFL
dispersal draft, December 6, 1984.
Released by New Jersey Generals, February 11, 1985; signed as free agent by Portland Breakers, March 12, 1985.
On developmental squad, March 12 through March 31, 1985; activated, April 1, 1985.
Released by Portland Breakers, April 2, 1985; re-signed by Portland Breakers, April 27, 1985.
Released by Portland Breakers, June 26, 1985; re-signed by Los Angeles Raiders, July 6, 1985.
On injured reserve with broken leg, August 20 through entire 1985 season.
On developmental squad for 2 games with Oakland Invaders in 1984.
On developmental squad for 2 games with Portland Breakers in 1985.
Active for 5 games with Los Angeles Raiders in 1982; did not play.
Baltimore NFL, 1981; Los Angeles Raiders NFL, 1982; Oakland USFL, 1984; Portland USFL, 1985.
Games: 1981 (16), 1984 (16), 1985 (9). Total USFL—32. Total Pro—41.
Pro statistics: Caught one pass for no yards, 1984.

ADDITIONAL PLAYER TRANSACTIONS

The following player transactions involve players in the Register occurring after May 20, 1986.

ACHICA, GEORGE—Released by New York Jets after failing physical, May 21, 1986.

ADICKES, MARK—Signed by Kansas City Chiefs, June 3, 1986.

ANTHONY, TYRONE—Awarded on waivers to Chicago Bears, May 30, 1986.

BAKER, KEITH—Released by Philadelphia Eagles, May 27, 1986; signed as free agent by
San Francisco 49ers, May 31, 1986.

FAUROT, RON—Released by San Diego Chargers after failing physical, May 30, 1986.

HERKENHOFF, MATT—Kansas City Chiefs withdrew qualifying offer, May 30, 1986.

HICKS, DWIGHT—San Francisco 49ers withdrew qualifying offer, June 5, 1986.

HOLLY, BOB—Atlanta Falcons withdrew qualifying offer, June 6, 1986.

SEARCEY, BILL—Released by San Diego Chargers after failing physical, May 30, 1986.

WASHINGTON, JOE—Atlanta Falcons withdrew qualifying offer, June 6, 1986.

NFL Head Coaches

LEEMAN BENNETT
Tampa Bay Buccaneers

Born June 20, 1938, at Paducah, Ky.
High School—Paducah, Ky., Tilghman.
Received bachelor of science degree from University of Kentucky in 1961.

COACHING RECORD

Assistant coach at University of Kentucky, 1961, 1962 and 1965.
In Military Service, 1963 and 1964.
Assistant coach at University of Pittsburgh, 1966.
Assistant coach at University of Cincinnati, 1967 and 1968.
Assistant coach at United States Naval Academy, 1969.
Assistant coach, St. Louis Cardinals NFL, 1970 and 1971.
Assistant coach, Detroit Lions NFL, 1972.
Assistant coach, Los Angeles Rams NFL, 1973 through 1976.

Year Club	Pos.	W.	L.	T.
1977—Atlanta NFL	†Second	7	7	0
1978—Atlanta NFL	†Second	9	7	0
1979—Atlanta NFL	†Third	6	10	0
1980—Atlanta NFL	†First	12	4	0
1981—Atlanta NFL	†Second	7	9	0
1982—Atlanta NFL	‡§Fourth	5	4	0
1985—Tampa Bay NFL	xFifth	2	14	0
Pro Totals—7 Years		48	55	0

†Western Division (National Conference).
‡Tied for position.
§National Conference.
xCentral Division (National Conference).

PLAYOFF RECORD

Year Club	W.	L.
1978—Atlanta NFL	1	1
1980—Atlanta NFL	0	1
1982—Atlanta NFL	0	1
Pro Totals—3 Years	1	3

1978—Won conference playoff game from Philadelphia, 14-13; lost conference playoff game to Dallas, 27-20.
1980—Lost conference playoff game to Dallas, 30-27.
1982—Lost conference playoff game to Minnesota, 30-24.

RAYMOND EMMETT BERRY
New England Patriots

Born February 27, 1933, at Corpus Christi, Tex.
High School—Paris, Tex.
Attended Schreiner Institute and received bachelor of arts degree from
Southern Methodist University in 1955.

Played wide receiver.
Inducted into Pro Football Hall of Fame, 1973.
Named to THE SPORTING NEWS NFL Western Conference All-Star Team, 1957 through 1960.
Selected (as future choice) by Baltimore in 20th round of 1954 NFL draft.

| Year Club | —PASS RECEIVING— | | | | | Year Club | —PASS RECEIVING— | | | |
	G.	P.C.	Yds.	Avg.	TD.		G.	P.C.	Yds.	Avg.	TD
1955—Baltimore NFL	12	13	205	15.8	0	1962—Baltimore NFL	14	51	687	13.5	‡
1956—Baltimore NFL	12	37	601	16.2	2	1963—Baltimore NFL	9	44	703	16.0	‡
1957—Baltimore NFL	12	47	*800	17.0	6	1964—Baltimore NFL	12	43	663	15.4	6
1958—Baltimore NFL	12	*56	794	14.2	*9	1965—Baltimore NFL	14	58	739	12.7	7
1959—Baltimore NFL	12	*66	*959	14.5	*14	1966—Baltimore NFL	14	56	786	14.0	‡
1960—Baltimore NFL	12	*74	*1298	17.5	10	1967—Baltimore NFL	7	11	167	15.2	‡
1961—Baltimore NFL	12	75	873	11.6	0	Pro Totals—13 Years	154	631	9275	14.7	6‡

Additional pro statistics: Returned two kickoffs for 27 yards, 1955; fumbled once, 1962.
Played in NFL Championship Game following 1958, 1959 and 1964 seasons.
Played in Pro Bowl (NFL All-Star Game) following 1958, 1959, 1961, 1963 and 1964 seasons.

COACHING RECORD

Assistant coach, Dallas Cowboys NFL, 1968.
Assistant coach at University of Arkansas, 1970 through 1972.
Assistant coach, Detroit Lions NFL, 1973 through 1975.
Assistant coach, Cleveland Browns NFL, 1976 and 1977.
Assistant coach, New England Patriots NFL, 1978 through 1981.
Training camp assistant coach, Minnesota Vikings NFL, 1984.

Year	Club	Pos.	W.	L.	T.
1984—New England NFL†		‡Second	4	4	0
1985—New England NFL		‡§Second	11	5	0
	Pro Totals—2 Years....................................		15	9	0

†Replaced Ron Meyer, October 25, 1984 with 5-3 record and in third place.
‡Eastern Division (American Conference).
§Tied for position.

PLAYOFF RECORD

Year	Club	W.	L.
1985—New England NFL....................................		3	1

1985—Won wild-card playoff game from New York Jets, 26-14; won conference playoff game from Los Angeles Raiders, 27-20; won conference championship game from Miami, 31-14; lost NFL championship game (Super Bowl XX) to Chicago, 46-10.

HENRY CHARLES BULLOUGH
(Hank)
Buffalo Bills

Born January 24, 1934, at Scranton, Pa.
High School—Canton, O., Timken Vocational.
Received bachelor of science degree in physical education
from Michigan State University.
Father of Shane Bullough, linebacker at Michigan State University.

Played offensive guard.
Selected by Green Bay in 5th round of 1954 NFL draft.
Green Bay NFL, 1955 and 1958.
In Military Service, 1956 and 1957.

COACHING RECORD

Assistant coach at Michigan State University, 1959 through 1970.
Assistant coach, Baltimore Colts NFL, 1970 through 1972.
Assistant coach, New England Patriots NFL, 1973 through 1979.
Assistant coach, Cincinnati Bengals NFL, 1980 through 1983.
Named head coach USFL Pittsburgh Maulers, May, 1984 (franchise folded in October, 1984 before season started).
Assistant coach, Buffalo Bills NFL, 1985.

Year	Club	Pos.	W.	L.	T.
1978—New England NFL†		......	0	1	0
1985—Buffalo NFL‡		§Fifth	2	10	0
	Pro Totals—2 Years................................		2	11	0

†Named co-coach with Ron Erhardt replacing suspended head coach Chuck Fairbanks for final regular season game, December 18, 1978.
‡Replaced Kay Stephenson, October 1, 1985, with 0-4 record and in fifth place.
§Eastern Division (American Conference).

JEROME MONAHAN BURNS
(Jerry)
Minnesota Vikings

Born January 24, 1927, at Detroit, Mich.
High School—Detroit, Mich., Catholic Central.
Received degree in physical education from University of Michigan.

Assistant coach at University of Hawaii, 1951.
Assistant coach at Whittier College, 1952.
Head coach at St. Mary of Redford High School, Detroit, Mich., 1953.
Assistant coach at University of Iowa, 1954 through 1960.
Assistant coach, Green Bay Packers NFL, 1966 and 1967.
Assistant coach, Minnesota Vikings NFL, 1968 through 1985.

Year	Club	Pos.	W.	L.	T.
1961—Iowa		†‡Seventh	5	4	0
1962—Iowa		†‡Fifth	4	5	0
1963—Iowa		†Eighth	3	3	2
1964—Iowa		†‡Ninth	3	6	0
1965—Iowa		†Tenth	1	9	0
	College Totals—5 Years.........................		16	27	2

†Big 10 Conference.
‡Tied for position.

DONALD DAVID CORYELL
(Don)
San Diego Chargers

Born October 17, 1924, at Seattle, Wash.
High School—Seattle, Wash., Lincoln.
Received bachelor of arts degree in 1950 and master of arts degree in 1951 from
University of Washington.

COACHING RECORD

Named NFL Coach of the Year by THE SPORTING NEWS, 1974.
Assistant coach at Punahou Academy, Honolulu, 1951.
Head coach at Farrington High School, Honolulu, 1952.
Assistant coach at University of Washington, 1953 and 1954.
Head coach and athletic director at Fort Ord, Calif., 1956.
Assistant coach at University of Southern California, 1960.

Year	Club	Pos.	W.	L.	T.	Year	Club	Pos.	W.	L.	T.
1955—	Wenatchee Valley JC	†First	7	0	1	1973—	St. Louis NFL	zFourth	4	9	1
1957—	Whittier	‡First	6	2	1	1974—	St. Louis NFL	zxFirst	10	4	0
1958—	Whittier	‡First	9	1	0	1975—	St. Louis NFL	zFirst	11	3	0
1959—	Whittier	‡First	8	2	0	1976—	St. Louis NFL	zxSecond	10	4	0
1961—	San Diego State	§xThird	7	2	1	1977—	St. Louis NFL	zThird	7	7	0
1962—	San Diego State	§First	8	2	0	1978—	San Diego NFLa	bxSecond	8	4	0
1963—	San Diego State	§xFirst	7	2	0	1979—	San Diego NFL	bFirst	12	4	0
1964—	San Diego State	§Second	8	2	0	1980—	San Diego NFL	bxFirst	11	5	0
1965—	San Diego State	§Third	8	2	0	1981—	San Diego NFL	bxFirst	10	6	0
1966—	San Diego State	§First	11	0	0	1982—	San Diego NFL	cxFourth	6	3	0
1967—	San Diego State	§First	10	1	0	1983—	San Diego NFL	bxFourth	6	10	0
1968—	San Diego State	....	9	0	1	1984—	San Diego NFL	bFifth	7	9	0
1969—	San Diego State	yFirst	11	0	0	1985—	San Diego NFL	bxThird	8	8	0
1970—	San Diego State	yxFirst	9	2	0						
1971—	San Diego State	yxFourth	6	5	0	College Totals—16 Years			134	24	4
1972—	San Diego State	yFirst	10	1	0	Pro Totals—13 Years			110	76	1

†Washington State Junior College Conference
‡Southern California Intercollegiate Athletic Conference.
§California Collegiate Athletic Association.
xTied for postion.
yPacific Coast Athletic Association.
zEastern Division (National Conference.).
aReplaced Tommy Prothro, September 25, 1978 with 1-3 record and tied for fourth place; St. Louis received third-round pick in 1980 draft from San Diego as compensation.
bWestern Division (American Conference.).
cAmerican Conference.

PLAYOFF RECORD

Year	Club	W.	L.
1974—	St. Louis NFL	0	1
1975—	St. Louis NFL	0	1
1979—	San Diego NFL	0	1
1980—	San Diego NFL	1	1
1981—	San Diego NFL	1	1
1982—	San Diego NFL	1	1
	Pro Totals—6 Years	3	6

1974—Lost conference playoff game to Minnesota, 30-14.
1975—Lost conference playoff game to Los Angeles, 35-23.
1979—Lost conference playoff game to Houston, 17-14.
1980—Won conference playoff game from Buffalo, 20-14; lost conference championship game to Oakland, 34-27.
1981—Won conference playoff game in overtime from Miami, 41-38; lost conference championship game to Cincinnati, 27-7.
1982—Won conference playoff game from Pittsburgh, 31-28; lost conference playoff game to Miami, 34-13.

COLLEGIATE BOWL GAME RECORD

Year	Club	W.	L.
1966—	San Diego State	1	0
1967—	San Diego State	1	0
1969—	San Diego State	1	0
	Totals—3 Years	3	0

1966—Won Camellia Bowl from Montana State, 28-7.
1967—Won Camellia Bowl from San Francisco State, 27-6.
1969—Won Pasadena Bowl from Boston University, 28-7.

MICHAEL KELLER DITKA
(Mike)
Chicago Bears

Born October 18, 1939, at Carnegie, Pa.
High School—Aliquippa, Pa.
Attended University of Pittsburgh.

Played tight end.
Named as end on THE SPORTING NEWS College All-America Team, 1960.
Named NFL Rookie of the Year by THE SPORTING NEWS, 1961.
Named to THE SPORTING NEWS NFL Western Conference All-Star Team, 1961 through 1965.
Selected by Chicago in 1st round of 1961 NFL draft.
Traded by Chicago Bears to Philadelphia Eagles for quarterback Jack Concannon and a 1968 draft choice, April 26, 1967.
Traded by Philadelphia Eagles to Dallas Cowboys for receiver Dave McDaniels, January 18, 1969.

—PASS RECEIVING—					—PASS RECEIVING—				
Year Club	G.	P.C.	Yds.	Avg. TD.	Year Club	G.	P.C.	Yds.	Avg. TD.
1961—Chicago NFL	14	56	1076	19.2 12	1968—Philadelphia NFL	11	13	111	8.5 2
1962—Chicago NFL	14	58	904	15.6 5	1969—Dallas NFL	12	17	268	15.8 3
1963—Chicago NFL	14	59	794	13.5 8	1970—Dallas NFL	14	8	98	12.3 0
1964—Chicago NFL	14	75	897	12.0 5	1971—Dallas NFL	14	30	360	12.0 1
1965—Chicago NFL	14	36	454	12.6 2	1972—Dallas NFL	14	17	198	11.6 1
1966—Chicago NFL	14	32	378	11.8 2	Pro Totals—12 Years	158	427	5812	13.6 43
1967—Philadelphia NFL	9	26	274	10.5 2					

Additional pro statistics: Recovered one fumble for a touchdown, 1962 and 1964; fumbled once, 1969; rushed twice for two yards, returned three kickoffs for 30 yards and recovered one fumble, 1971.
Played in NFC Championship Game following 1970 through 1972 seasons.
Played in NFL Championship Game following 1963, 1970 and 1971 seasons.
Played in Pro Bowl (NFL All-Star Game) following 1961 through 1965 seasons.

COACHING RECORD

Named NFL Coach of the Year by THE SPORTING NEWS, 1985.
Assistant coach, Dallas Cowboys NFL, 1973 through 1981.

Year Club	Pos.	W.	L.	T.
1982—Chicago NFL	†‡Eleventh	3	6	0
1983—Chicago NFL	‡§Second	8	8	0
1984—Chicago NFL	§First	10	6	0
1985—Chicago NFL	§First	15	1	0
Pro Totals—4 Years		36	21	0

†National Conference.
‡Tied for position.
§Central Division (National Conference).

PLAYOFF RECORD

Year Club	W.	L.
1984—Chicago NFL	1	1
1985—Chicago NFL	3	0
Pro Totals—2 Years	4	1

1984—Won conference playoff game from Washington, 23-19; lost conference championship game to San Francisco, 23-0.
1985—Won conference playoff game from New York Giants, 21-0; won conference championship game from Los Angeles Rams, 24-0; won NFL championship game (Super Bowl XX) from New England, 46-10.

RODNEY DOUGLAS DOWHOWER
(Rod)
Indianapolis Colts
Born April 15, 1943, at Ord, Neb.
High School—Santa Barbara, Calif.
Attended Santa Barbara City Junior College, received bachelor of arts degree in social science from San Diego State University and master's degree in history from U.S. International University, both in 1971.

Signed as free agent by San Francisco 49ers, 1965.
On taxi squad during entire 1965 season.
Released by San Francisco 49ers, August, 1966.

COACHING RECORD

Graduate assistant at San Diego State University, 1966 and 1967.
Assistant coach at San Diego State University, 1968 through 1972.
Assistant coach, St. Louis Cardinals NFL, 1973, 1983 and 1984.
Assistant coach at University of California at Los Angeles, 1974 and 1975.
Assistant coach at Boise State University, 1976.
Assistant coach at Stanford University, 1977 and 1978.
Assistant coach, Denver Broncos NFL, 1980 through 1982.

Year Club	Pos.	W.	L.	T.
1979—Stanford	†Sixth	5	5	1
1985—Indianapolis NFL	‡ Fourth	5	11	0
College Totals—1 Year		5	5	1
Pro Totals—1 Year		5	11	0

†Pacific 10.
‡Eastern Division (American Conference).

THOMAS RAYMOND FLORES
(Tom)
Los Angeles Raiders
Born March 21, 1937, at Fresno, Calif.
High School—Sanger, Calif.
Attended Fresno City College and received bachelor of arts degree in education from University of the Pacific in 1958.

Played quarterback.
Threw six touchdown passes in a game, December 22, 1963.

Drafted by Calgary Stampeders, 1958.
Released by Calgary Stampeders, 1958; signed as free agent by Washington Redskins, 1959.
Released by Washington Redskins, 1959; signed as free agent by Oakland Raiders, 1960.
Traded with offensive end Art Powell and 2nd round draft choice by Oakland AFL to Buffalo AFL for quarterback Daryle Lamonica, offensive end Glenn Bass and 3rd and 5th round draft choices, 1967.
Released by Buffalo, signed by Kansas City, 1969.
On Kansas City Chiefs' taxi squad entire 1970 season.

Year Club	G.	—————PASSING—————							———RUSHING———				—TOTAL—		
		Att.	Cmp.	Pct.	Gain	T.P.	P.I.	Avg.	Att.	Yds.	Avg.	TD.	TD.	Pts.	F.
1960—Oakland AFL	14	252	136	*54.0	1738	12	12	6.90	19	123	6.5	3	3	18	
1961—Oakland AFL	14	366	190	51.9	2176	15	19	5.95	23	36	1.6	1	1	6	
1962—Oakland AFL					Missed entire season because of illness.										
1963—Oakland AFL	14	247	113	45.7	2101	20	13	8.51	12	2	0.2	0	0	0	
1964—Oakland AFL	14	200	98	49.0	1389	7	14	6.95	11	64	5.8	0	0	0	
1965—Oakland AFL	14	269	122	45.3	1593	14	11	5.92	11	32	2.9	0	0	0	
1966—Oakland AFL	14	306	151	49.4	2638	24	14	8.62	5	50	10.0	1	1	6	
1967—Buffalo AFL	13	64	22	34.4	260	0	8	4.06	None				0	0	
1968—Buffalo AFL	1	5	3	60.0	15	0	1	3.00	None				0	0	
1969—Buf.-K.C. AFL	13	6	3	50.0	49	0	0	8.17	1	0	0.0	0	0	0	
Pro Totals—10 Years	111	1715	838	48.9	11959	92	92	6.97	82	307	3.7	5	5	30	

Played in AFL All-Star Game following 1966 season.

COACHING RECORD

Freshman coach at University of the Pacific, 1959.
Assistant coach, Buffalo Bills NFL, 1971.
Assistant coach, Oakland Raiders NFL, 1972 through 1978.

Year Club	Pos.	W.	L.	T.
1979—Oakland NFL	†‡Third	9	7	0
1980—Oakland NFL	†‡First	11	5	0
1981—Oakland NFL	†Fourth	7	9	0
1982—L.A. Raiders NFL	§First	8	1	0
1983—L.A. Raiders NFL	†First	12	4	0
1984—L.A. Raiders NFL	†Third	11	5	0
1985—L.A. Raiders NFL	‡ First	12	4	0
Pro Totals—7 Years		70	35	0

†Western Division (American Conference).
‡Tied for position.
§American Conference.

PLAYOFF RECORD

Year Club	W.	L.
1980—Oakland NFL	4	0
1982—Los Angeles Raiders NFL	1	1
1983—Los Angeles Raiders NFL	3	0
1984—Los Angeles Raiders NFL	0	1
1985—Los Angeles Raiders NFL	0	1
Pro Totals—5 Years	8	3

1980—Won conference playoff game from Houston, 27-7; won conference playoff game from Cleveland, 14-12; won conference championship game from San Diego, 34-27; won NFL championship game (Super Bowl XV) from Philadelphia, 27-10.
1982—Won conference playoff game from Cleveland, 27-10; lost conference playoff game to New York Jets, 17-14.
1983—Won conference playoff game from Pittsburgh, 38-10; won conference championship game from Seattle, 30-14; won NFL championship game (Super Bowl XVIII) from Washington, 38-9.
1984—Lost wild-card playoff game to Seattle, 13-7.
1985—Lost conference playoff game to New England, 27-20.

JOE JACKSON GIBBS
Washington Redskins

Born November 25, 1940, at Mocksville, N. C.
High School—Sante Fe, Calif., Spring.
Attended Cerritos Junior College, received bachelor of science degree in physical education from San Diego State University in 1964 and received master's degree from San Diego State in 1966.

COACHING RECORD

Named NFL Coach of the Year by THE SPORTING NEWS, 1982 and 1983.
Graduate assistant at San Diego State University, 1964 and 1965.
Assistant coach at San Diego State University, 1966.
Assistant coach at Florida State University, 1967 and 1968.
Assistant coach at University of Southern California, 1969 and 1970.
Assistant coach at University of Arkansas, 1971 and 1972.
Assistant coach, St. Louis Cardinals NFL, 1973 through 1977.
Assistant coach, Tampa Bay Buccaneers NFL, 1978.
Assistant coach, San Diego Chargers NFL, 1979 and 1980.

—DID YOU KNOW—

That the Chicago Bears scored 256 more points than the Buffalo Bills in 1985?

Year	Club	Pos.	W.	L.	T.
1981—	Washington NFL	†Fourth	8	8	0
1982—	Washington NFL	‡First	8	1	0
1983—	Washington NFL	†First	14	2	0
1984—	Washington NFL	†First	11	5	0
1985—	Washington NFL	†§ First	10	6	0
Pro Totals—5 Years			51	22	0

†Eastern Division (National Conference).
‡National Conference.
§Tied for position.

PLAYOFF RECORD

Year	Club	W.	L.
1982—	Washington NFL	4	0
1983—	Washington NFL	2	1
1984—	Washington NFL	0	1
Pro Totals—3 Years		6	2

1982—Won conference playoff game from Detroit, 31-7; won conference playoff game from Minnesota, 21-7; won conference championship game from Dallas, 31-17; won NFL championship game (Super Bowl XVII) from Miami, 27-17.
1983—Won conference playoff game from Los Angeles Rams, 51-7; won conference championship game from San Francisco, 24-21; lost NFL championship game (Super Bowl XVIII) to Los Angeles Raiders, 38-9.
1984—Lost conference playoff game to Chicago, 23-19.

JERRY MICHAEL GLANVILLE
Houston Oilers
Born October 14, 1941, at Detroit, Mich.
High School—Reading, O.
Attended Montana State University and received bachelor of science degree from Northern Michigan University in 1964 and master's degree in art western from Western Kentucky University in 1966.

COACHING RECORD

Assistant coach at Central Catholic High School, Lima, O., 1963 and 1964.
Assistant coach at Reading High School, Reading, O., 1965.
Assistant coach at Northern Michigan University, 1966.
Assistant coach at Western Kentucky University, 1967.
Assistant coach at Georgia Tech, 1968 through 1973.
Assistant coach, Detroit Lions NFL, 1974 through 1976.
Assistant coach, Atlanta Falcons NFL, 1977 through 1982.
Assistant coach, Buffalo Bills NFL, 1983.
Assistant coach, Houston Oilers NFL, 1984 and 1985.

Year	Club	Pos.	W.	L.	T.
1985—	Houston NFL†	‡Fourth	0	2	0

†Replaced Hugh Campbell, December 9, 1985, with 5-9 record and in fifth place.
‡Central Division (American Conference).

ALVIS FORREST GREGG
(Known by middle name.)
Green Bay Packers
Born October 18, 1933, at Birthright, Tex.
High School—Sulphur Springs, Tex.
Received bachelor of science degree in physical education from Southern Methodist University in 1959.
Father of Forrest Gregg Jr., assistant coach with Green Bay Packers.

Played offensive tackle.
Inducted into Pro Football Hall of Fame, 1977.
Named to THE SPORTING NEWS NFL Western Conference All-Star Teams, 1959, 1962, 1963, 1965 and 1967.
Selected by Green Bay in 2nd round of 1956 NFL draft.
Military service, 1957.
Released by Green Bay Packers and signed as free agent by Dallas Cowboys, 1971.
Green Bay NFL, 1956 and 1958 through 1970; Dallas NFL, 1971.
Games: 1956 (11), 1958 (12), 1959 (12), 1960 (12), 1961 (14), 1962 (14), 1963 (14), 1964 (14), 1965 (14), 1966 (14), 1967 (14), 1968 (14), 1969 (14), 1970 (14), 1971 (6). Total—193.
Pro statistics: Recovered one fumble, 1958, 1965 and 1967; recovered two fumbles, 1963 and 1968; returned two kickoffs for 21 yards, 1970.
Played in NFL Championship Game following 1960 through 1962 and 1965 through 1967 seasons.
Played in AFL-NFL Championship Games following 1966 and 1967 seasons.
Played in Pro Bowl (NFL All-Star Game) following 1960 through 1964 and 1966 through 1968 seasons.

COACHING RECORD

Assistant coach, Green Bay Packers NFL, 1969 and 1970.
Assistant coach, San Diego Chargers NFL, 1972 and 1973.
Assistant coach, Cleveland Browns NFL, 1974.

Year Club	Pos.	W.	L.	T.
1975—Cleveland NFL	†Fourth	3	11	0
1976—Cleveland NFL	‖Third	9	5	0
1977—Cleveland NFL‡	†Fourth	6	7	0
1979—Toronto CFL	§Fourth	5	11	0
1980—Cincinnati NFL	†Fourth	6	10	0
1981—Cincinnati NFL	First	12	4	0
1982—Cincinnati NFL	xySecond	7	2	0
1983—Cincinnati NFL	†Third	7	9	0
1984—Green Bay NFL	zSecond	8	8	0
1985—Green Bay NFL	zSecond	8	8	0
NFL Totals—9 Years		66	64	0
CFL Totals—1 Year		5	11	0
Pro Totals—10 Years		71	75	0

†Central Division (American Conference).
‡Replaced by interim coach Dick Modzelewski, December 12, 1977.
§Eastern Conference.
xAmerican Conference.
yTied for position.
zCentral Division (National Conference).

PLAYOFF RECORD

Year Club	W.	L.
1981—Cincinnati NFL	2	1
1982—Cincinnati NFL	0	1
Pro Totals—2 Years	2	2

1981—Won conference playoff game from Buffalo, 28-21; won conference championship game from San Diego, 27-7; lost NFL championship game (Super Bowl XVI) to San Francisco, 26-21.
1982—Lost conference playoff game to New York Jets, 44-17.

DANIEL E. HENNING
(Dan)
Atlanta Falcons
Born June 21, 1942, at Bronx, N.Y.
High School—Fresh Meadows, N.Y., St. Francis Prep.
Attended College of William & Mary.
Father of Dan Henning, Jr., quarterback at University of Maryland.

Played quarterback.
Signed as free agent by San Diego Chargers, February 19, 1964.
Released by San Diego Chargers, September 1, 1964; re-signed by Chargers, December 2, 1964.
Released by San Diego Chargers, August 2, 1965; re-signed by Chargers, July 2, 1966.
Released by San Diego Chargers, August 25, 1966; re-signed and placed on taxi squad for 1966 season.
Released by San Diego Chargers, August 29, 1967.
Active for 1 game with San Diego Chargers in 1966; did not play.
Played with Springfield, Mass., of Atlantic Coast Football League, 1964.
Played with Norfolk Neptunes of Continental Football League, 1965 and 1967.

COACHING RECORD
Assistant coach at Homer L. Ferguson High School, Newport News, Va., 1967.
Assistant coach at Florida State University, 1968 through 1970 and 1974.
Assistant coach at Virginia Tech, 1971 and 1973.
Assistant coach, Houston Oilers NFL, 1972.
Assistant coach, New York Jets NFL, 1976 through 1978.
Assistant coach, Miami Dolphins NFL, 1979 and 1980.
Assistant coach, Washington Redskins NFL, 1981 and 1982.

Year Club	Pos.	W.	L.	T.
1983—Atlanta NFL	†Fourth	7	9	0
1984—Atlanta NFL	†Fourth	4	12	0
1985—Atlanta NFL	†Fourth	4	12	0
Pro Totals—3 Years		15	33	0

†Western Division (National Conference).

CHARLES ROBERT KNOX SR.
(Chuck)
Seattle Seahawks
Born April 27, 1932, at Sewickley, Pa.
High School—Sewickley, Pa.
Received bachelor of arts degree in history from Juniata College in 1954.
Father of Chuck Knox Jr., running back at University of Arizona.

COACHING RECORD
Named NFL Coach of the Year by THE SPORTING NEWS, 1973, 1980 and 1984.
Assistant coach at Juniata College, 1954.
Assistant coach at Tyrone (Pa.) High School, 1955.
Head coach at Ellwood City (Pa.) High School, 1956 through 1958 (Won 10, Lost 16, Tied 2).

Assistant coach at Wake Forest University, 1959 and 1960.
Assistant coach at University of Kentucky, 1961 and 1962.
Assistant coach, New York Jets AFL, 1963 through 1966.
Assistant coach, Detroit Lions NFL, 1967 through 1972.

Year Club	Pos.	W.	L.	T.
1973—Los Angeles NFL	†First	12	2	0
1974—Los Angeles NFL	†First	10	4	0
1975—Los Angeles NFL	†First	12	2	0
1976—Los Angeles NFL	†First	10	3	1
1977—Los Angeles NFL	†First	10	4	0
1978—Buffalo NFL	‡§Fourth	5	11	0
1979—Buffalo NFL	‡Fourth	7	9	0

Year Club	Pos.	W.	L.	T.
1980—Buffalo NFL	‡First	11	5	0
1981—Buffalo NFL	‡Third	10	6	0
1982—Buffalo NFL	x§Eighth	4	5	0
1983—Seattle NFL	ySecond	9	7	0
1984—Seattle NFL	ySecond	12	4	0
1985—Seattle NFL	y§Third	8	8	0
Pro Totals—13 Years		120	70	1

†Western Division (National Conference).
‡Eastern Division (American Conference).
§Tied for position.
xAmerican Conference.
yWestern Division (American Conference).

PLAYOFF RECORD

Year Club	W.	L.
1973—Los Angeles NFL	0	1
1974—Los Angeles NFL	1	1
1975—Los Angeles NFL	1	1
1976—Los Angeles NFL	1	1
1977—Los Angeles NFL	0	1
1980—Buffalo NFL	0	1
1981—Buffalo NFL	1	1
1983—Seattle NFL	2	1
1984—Seattle NFL	1	1
Pro Totals—9 Years	7	9

1973—Lost conference playoff game to Dallas, 27-16.
1974—Won conference playoff game from Washington, 19-10; lost conference championship game to Minnesota, 14-10.
1975—Won conference playoff game from St. Louis, 35-23; lost conference championship game to Dallas, 37-7.
1976—Won conference playoff game from Dallas, 14-12; lost conference championship game to Minnesota, 24-13.
1977—Lost conference playoff game to Minnesota, 14-7.
1980—Lost conference playoff game to San Diego, 20-14.
1981—Won conference playoff game from New York Jets, 31-27; lost conference playoff game to Cincinnati, 28-21.
1983—Won wild-card playoff game from Denver, 31-7; won conference playoff game from Miami, 27-20; lost conference championship game to Los Angeles Raiders, 30-14.
1984—Won wild-card playoff game from Los Angeles Raiders, 13-7; lost conference playoff game to Miami, 31-10.

THOMAS WADE LANDRY
(Tom)
Dallas Cowboys

Born September 11, 1924, at Mission, Tex.
High School—Mission, Tex.
Received bachelor of business administration degree from University of Texas in 1949
and bachelor of science degree in industrial engineering from University of Houston.
Played defensive back.
Selected in 4th round from New York AAFC by New York Giants NFL in AAFC-NFL merger, 1950.

Year Club	G.	-INTERCEPTIONS-				-PUNTING-			-TOTAL-		
		No.	Yds.	Avg.	TD.	No.	Avg.	Blk.	TD.	Pts.	F.
1949—New York AAFC	13	1	44	44.0	0	51	44.1	★2	0	0	..
1950—New York Giants NFL	12	2	0	0.0	0	58	36.8	1	1	6	0
1951—New York Giants NFL	10	8	121	15.1	★2	15	42.5	0	3	18	0
1952—New York NFL	12	8	99	12.4	0	82	41.0	1	2	12	5
1953—New York NFL	12	3	55	18.3	0	44	40.3	0	0	0	1
1954—New York NFL	12	8	71	8.9	0	64	42.5	0	0	0	1
1955—New York NFL	12	2	14	7.0	0	★75	40.3	1	0	0	0
AAFC Totals—1 Year	13	1	44	44.0	0	51	44.1	2	0	0	..
NFL Totals—6 Years	70	31	360	11.6	3	338	40.4	3	6	36	7
Pro Totals—7 Years	83	32	404	12.6	3	389	40.9	5	6	36	..

Year Club	G.	-PUNT RETURNS-				-KICKOFF RET.-		
		No.	Yds.	Avg.	TD.	No.	Yds.	Avg.TD.
1949—New York AAFC	13	3	52	17.3	0	2	39	19.5 0
1950—New York Giants NFL	12	None				None		
1951—New York Giants NFL	10	1	0	0.0	0	1	0	0.0 0
1952—New York NFL	12	10	88	8.8	0	1	20	20.0 0
1953—New York NFL	12	1	5	5.0	0	2	38	19.0 0
1954—New York NFL	12	None				None		
1955—New York NFL	12	None				None		
AAFC Totals—1 Year	13	3	52	17.3	0	2	39	19.5 0
NFL Totals—6 Years	70	12	93	7.8	0	4	58	14.5 0
Pro Totals—7 Years	83	15	145	9.7	0	6	97	16.2 0

Additional AAFC statistics: Rushed 29 times for 91 yards and caught six passes for 109 yards, 1949.
Additional NFL statistics: Rushed seven times for 40 yards and a touchdown, 1952; attempted 47 passes with 11

completions for 172 yards, one touchdown and seven interceptions, 1952; recovered two fumbles for 41 yards and one touchdown, 1950; recovered one fumble for nine yards and a touchdown, 1951; recovered two fumbles, 1952; recovered one fumble, 1953 and 1955; recovered two fumbles for 14 yards, 1954.
Played in Pro Bowl (NFL All-Star Game) following 1954 season.

COACHING RECORD

Named NFL Coach of the Year by THE SPORTING NEWS, 1966.
Player-coach for New York Giants NFL, 1954 and 1955.
Assistant coach for New York Giants NFL, 1956 through 1959.

Year	Club	Pos.	W.	L.	T.	Year	Club	Pos.	W.	L.	T.
1960—	Dallas NFL	†Seventh	0	11	1	1974—	Dallas NFL	yThird	8	6	0
1961—	Dallas NFL	‡Sixth	4	9	1	1975—	Dallas NFL	ySecond	10	4	0
1962—	Dallas NFL	‡Fifth	5	8	1	1976—	Dallas NFL	yFirst	11	3	0
1963—	Dallas NFL	‡Fifth	4	10	0	1977—	Dallas NFL	yFirst	12	2	0
1964—	Dallas NFL	‡Fifth	5	8	1	1978—	Dallas NFL	yFirst	12	4	0
1965—	Dallas NFL	§‡Second	7	7	0	1979—	Dallas NFL	y§First	11	5	0
1966—	Dallas NFL	‡First	10	3	1	1980—	Dallas NFL	y§First	12	4	0
1967—	Dallas NFL	xFirst	9	5	0	1981—	Dallas NFL	yFirst	12	4	0
1968—	Dallas NFL	xFirst	12	2	0	1982—	Dallas NFL	zSecond	6	3	0
1969—	Dallas NFL	xFirst	11	2	1	1983—	Dallas NFL	ySecond	12	4	0
1970—	Dallas NFL	yFirst	10	4	0	1984—	Dallas NFL	y§Second	9	7	0
1971—	Dallas NFL	yFirst	11	3	0	1985—	Dallas NFL	y§First	10	6	0
1972—	Dallas NFL	ySecond	10	4	0						
1973—	Dallas NFL	§yFirst	10	4	0		Pro Totals—26 Years		233	132	6

†Western Conference.
‡Eastern Conference.
§Tied for position.
xCapitol Division (Eastern Conference).
yEastern Division (National Conference).
zNational Conference.

PLAYOFF RECORD

Year	Club	W.	L.	Year	Club	W.	L.
1965—	Dallas NFL	0	1	1976—	Dallas NFL	0	1
1966—	Dallas NFL	0	1	1977—	Dallas NFL	3	0
1967—	Dallas NFL	1	1	1978—	Dallas NFL	2	1
1968—	Dallas NFL	1	1	1979—	Dallas NFL	0	1
1969—	Dallas NFL	0	2	1980—	Dallas NFL	2	1
1970—	Dallas NFL	2	1	1981—	Dallas NFL	1	1
1971—	Dallas NFL	3	0	1982—	Dallas NFL	2	1
1972—	Dallas NFL	1	1	1983—	Dallas NFL	0	1
1973—	Dallas NFL	1	1	1985—	Dallas NFL	0	1
1975—	Dallas NFL	2	1		Pro Totals—19 Years	21	18

1965—Lost Playoff Bowl to Baltimore, 35-3.
1966—Lost NFL championship game to Green Bay, 34-27.
1967—Won conference playoff game from Cleveland, 52-14; lost NFL championship game to Green Bay, 21-17.
1968—Lost conference playoff game to Cleveland, 31-20; won Playoff Bowl from Minnesota, 17-13.
1969—Lost conference playoff game to Cleveland, 38-14; lost Playoff Bowl to Los Angeles, 31-0.
1970—Won conference playoff game from Detroit, 5-0; won conference championship game from San Francisco, 17-10; lost NFL championship game (Super Bowl V) to Baltimore, 16-13.
1971—Won conference playoff game from Minnesota, 20-12; won conference championship game from San Francisco, 14-3; won NFL championship game (Super Bowl VI) from Miami, 24-3.
1972—Won conference playoff game from San Francisco, 30-28; lost conference championship game to Washington, 26-3.
1973—Won conference playoff game from Los Angeles, 27-16; lost conference championship game to Minnesota, 27-10.
1975—Won conference playoff game from Minnesota, 17-14; won conference championship game from Los Angeles, 37-7; lost NFL championship game (Super Bowl X) to Pittsburgh, 21-17.
1976—Lost conference playoff game to Los Angeles, 14-12.
1977—Won conference playoff game from Chicago, 37-7; won conference championship game from Minnesota, 23-6; won NFL championship game (Super Bowl XII) from Denver, 27-10.
1978—Won conference playoff game from Atlanta, 27-20; won conference championship game from Los Angeles, 28-0; lost NFL championship game (Super Bowl XIII) to Pittsburgh, 35-31.
1979—Lost conference playoff game to Los Angeles, 21-19.
1980—Won conference playoff game from Los Angeles, 34-13; won conference playoff game from Atlanta, 30-27; lost conference championship game to Philadelphia, 20-7.
1981—Won conference playoff game from Tampa Bay, 38-0; lost conference championship game to San Francisco, 28-27.
1982—Won conference playoff game from Tampa Bay, 30-17; won conference playoff game from Green Bay, 37-26; lost conference championship game to Washington, 31-17.
1983—Lost wild-card playoff game to Los Angeles Rams, 24-17.
1985—Lost conference playoff game to Los Angeles Rams, 20-0.

JOHN MACKOVIC
Kansas City Chiefs
Born October 1, 1943, at Barberton, O.
High School—Barberton, O.
Received bachelor of arts degree in Spanish from Wake Forest University in 1964.
COACHING RECORD
Graduate assistant at Miami University (Ohio), 1965.

Assistant coach at Barberton High School, Barberton, O., 1966.
Freshman coach at Army, 1967 and 1968.
Assistant coach at San Jose State University, 1969 and 1970.
Assistant coach at Army, 1971 and 1972.
Assistant coach at University of Arizona, 1973 through 1976.
Assistant coach at Purdue University, 1977.
Assistant coach, Dallas Cowboys NFL, 1981 and 1982.

Year Club	Pos.	W.	L.	T.
1978—Wake Forest	†Sixth	1	10	0
1979—Wake Forest	†‡Second	8	4	0
1980—Wake Forest	†‡Fourth	5	6	0
1983—Kansas City NFL	‡§Fourth	6	10	0
1984—Kansas City NFL	§Fourth	8	8	0
1985—Kansas City NFL	§Fifth	6	10	0
College Totals—3 Years		14	20	0
Pro Totals—3 Years		20	28	0

†Atlantic Coast Conference.
‡Tied for position.
§Western Division (American Conference).

COLLEGIATE BOWL GAME RECORD

Year Club	W.	L.
1979—Wake Forest	0	1

1979—Lost Tangerine Bowl to Louisiana State, 34-10.

JAMES ERNEST MORA
(Jim)
New Orleans Saints
Born May 24, 1935, at Los Angeles, Calif.
High School—Los Angeles, Calif., University.
Received bachelor of arts degree in physical education from Occidental College
in 1957; received master's degree in education from
University of Southern California in 1967.
Played in U.S. Marines at Quantico in 1957 and at Camp Lejeune in 1958 and 1959.

COACHING RECORD

Named THE SPORTING NEWS USFL Coach of the Year, 1984.
Assistant coach at Occidental College, 1960 through 1963.
Assistant coach at Stanford University, 1967.
Assistant coach at University of Colorado, 1968 through 1973.
Assistant coach at University of California at Los Angeles, 1974.
Assistant coach at University of Washington, 1975 through 1977.
Assistant coach, Seattle NFL, 1978 through 1981.
Assistant coach, New England NFL, 1982.

Year Club	Pos.	W.	L.	T.
1964—Occidental	†Third	5	4	0
1965—Occidental	†First	8	1	0
1966—Occidental	†Fourth	5	4	0
1983—Philadelphia USFL	‡First	15	3	0
1984—Philadelphia USFL	§First	16	2	0
1985—Baltimore USFL	xFourth	10	7	1
College Totals—3 Years		18	9	0
Pro Totals—3 Years		41	12	1

†Southern California Intercollegiate Conference.
‡Atlantic Division.
§Atlantic Division (Eastern Conference).
xEastern Conference.

PLAYOFF RECORD

Year Club	W.	L.
1983—Philadelphia USFL	1	1
1984—Philadelphia USFL	3	0
1985—Baltimore USFL	3	0
Pro Totals—3 Years	7	1

1983—Won divisional playoff game from Chicago, 44-38 (OT); lost USFL championship game to Michigan, 24-22.
1984—Won conference playoff game from New Jersey, 28-7; won conference championship game from Birmingham,
20-10; won USFL championship game from Arizona, 23-3.
1985—Won conference playoff game from New Jersey, 20-17; won conference championship game from Birmingham,
28-14; won USFL championship game from Oakland, 28-24.

CHARLES HENRY NOLL
(Chuck)
Pittsburgh Steelers
Born January 5, 1932, at Cleveland, O.
High School—Cleveland, O., Benedictine.
Received bachelor of science degree in education from University of Dayton in 1953.

Played linebacker and offensive guard.
Selected by Cleveland in 21st round of 1953 NFL draft.

Year Club	G.	INTERCEPTIONS				—KICKOFF RET.—				—TOTAL—		
		No.	Yds.	Avg.	TD.	No.	Yds.	Avg.	TD.	TD.	Pts.	F.
1953—Cleveland NFL	12	None				1	2	2.0	0	0	0	0
1954—Cleveland NFL	12	None				None				0	0	0
1955—Cleveland NFL	12	5	74	14.8	1	None				1	8	0
1956—Cleveland NFL	12	1	13	13.0	0	None				1	6	0
1957—Cleveland NFL	5	None				None				0	0	0
1958—Cleveland NFL	12	None				None				0	0	0
1959—Cleveland NFL	12	2	5	2.5	0	1	20	20.0	0	0	0	0
Pro Totals—7 Years	77	8	92	11.5	1	2	22	11.0	0	2	14	0

Additional pro statistics: Recovered two fumbles for 10 yards, 1954; credited with one safety, 1955; recovered one fumble for 39 yards and a touchdown, 1956.
Played in NFL Championship Game following 1953 through 1955 seasons.

COACHING RECORD

Assistant coach, Los Angeles Chargers AFL, 1960.
Assistant coach, San Diego Chargers AFL, 1961 through 1965.
Assistant coach, Baltimore Colts NFL, 1966 through 1968.

Year Club	Pos.	W.	L.	T.	Year Club	Pos.	W.	L.	T.
1969—Pittsburgh NFL	†Fourth	1	13	0	1978—Pittsburgh NFL	‡First	14	2	0
1970—Pittsburgh NFL	‡Third	5	9	0	1979—Pittsburgh NFL	‡First	12	4	0
1971—Pittsburgh NFL	‡Second	6	8	0	1980—Pittsburgh NFL	‡Third	9	7	0
1972—Pittsburgh NFL	‡First	11	3	0	1981—Pittsburgh NFL	‡Second	8	8	0
1973—Pittsburgh NFL	†§First	10	4	0	1982—Pittsburgh NFL	x§Fourth	6	3	0
1974—Pittsburgh NFL	‡First	10	3	1	1983—Pittsburgh NFL	†First	10	6	0
1975—Pittsburgh NFL	‡First	12	2	0	1984—Pittsburgh NFL	‡First	9	7	0
1976—Pittsburgh NFL	‡§First	10	4	0	1985—Pittsburgh NFL	‡§Second	7	9	0
1977—Pittsburgh NFL	‡First	9	5	0	Pro Totals—17 Years		149	97	1

†Century Division (Eastern Conference).
‡Central Division (American Conference).
§Tied for position.
xAmerican Conference.

PLAYOFF RECORD

Year Club	W.	L.
1972—Pittsburgh NFL	1	1
1973—Pittsburgh NFL	0	1
1974—Pittsburgh NFL	3	0
1975—Pittsburgh NFL	3	0
1976—Pittsburgh NFL	1	1
1977—Pittsburgh NFL	0	1
1978—Pittsburgh NFL	3	0
1979—Pittsburgh NFL	3	0
1982—Pittsburgh NFL	0	1
1983—Pittsburgh NFL	0	1
1984—Pittsburgh NFL	1	1
Pro Totals—11 Years	15	7

1972—Won conference playoff game from Oakland, 13-7; lost conference championship game to Miami, 21-17.
1973—Lost conference playoff game to Oakland, 33-14.
1974—Won conference playoff game from Buffalo, 32-14; won conference championship game from Oakland, 24-13; won NFL championship game (Super Bowl IX) from Minnesota, 16-6.
1975—Won conference playoff game from Baltimore, 28-10; won conference championship game from Oakland, 16-10; won NFL championship game (Super Bowl X) from Dallas, 21-17.
1976—Won conference playoff game from Baltimore, 40-14; lost conference championship game to Oakland, 24-7.
1977—Lost conference playoff game to Denver, 34-21.
1978—Won conference playoff game from Denver, 33-10; won conference championship game from Houston, 34-5; won NFL championship game (Super Bowl XIII) from Dallas, 35-31.
1979—Won conference playoff game from Miami, 34-14; won conference championship game from Houston, 27-13; won NFL championship game (Super Bowl XIV) from Los Angeles, 31-19.
1982—Lost conference playoff game to San Diego, 31-28.
1983—Lost conference playoff game to Los Angeles Raiders, 38-10.
1984—Won conference playoff game from Denver, 24-17; lost conference championship game to Miami, 45-28.

DUANE CHARLES PARCELLS
(Bill)
New York Giants

Born August 22, 1941, at Englewood, N.J.
High School—Oradell, N.J., River Dell.
Received bachelor of arts degree in education from Wichita State University in 1964.

COACHING RECORD

Assistant coach at Hastings College, 1964.
Assistant coach at Wichita State University, 1965.
Assistant coach at West Point, 1966 through 1969.
Assistant coach at Florida State University, 1970 through 1972.
Assistant coach at Vanderbilt University, 1973 and 1974.
Asstant coach at Texas Tech University, 1975 through 1977.
Assistant coach, New England Patriots, NFL, 1980.

Assistant coach, New York Giants NFL, 1981 and 1982.

Year	Club	Pos.	W.	L.	T.
1978—	Air Force	....	3	8	0
1983—	New York Giants NFL	†Fifth	3	12	1
1984—	New York Giants NFL	†‡Second	9	7	0
1985—	New York Giants NFL	†‡First	10	6	0
	College Totals—1 Year		3	8	0
	Pro Totals—3 Years		22	25	1

†Eastern Division (National Conference).
‡Tied for position.

PLAYOFF RECORD

Year	Club	W.	L.
1984—	New York Giants NFL	1	1
1985—	New York Giants NFL	1	1
	Pro Totals—2 Years	2	2

1984—Won wild-card playoff game from Los Angeles Rams, 16-10; lost conference playoff game to San Francisco, 21-10.
1985—Won wild-card playoff game from San Francisco, 17-3; lost conference playoff game to Chicago, 21-0.

DANIEL EDWARD REEVES
(Dan)
Denver Broncos
Born January 19, 1944, at Rome, Ga.
High School—Americus, Ga.
Attended University of South Carolina.

Played running back.
Named to THE SPORTING NEWS NFL Eastern Conference All-Star Team, 1966.
Signed as free agent by Dallas NFL, 1965.

Year	Club	G.	Att.	Yds.	Avg.	TD.	P.C.	Yds.	Avg.	TD.	TD.	Pts.	F.
			RUSHING				PASS RECEIVING				TOTAL		
1965—	Dallas NFL	13	33	102	3.1	2	9	210	23.3	1	3	18	0
1966—	Dallas NFL	14	175	757	4.3	8	41	557	13.6	8	*16	96	6
1967—	Dallas NFL	14	173	603	3.5	5	39	490	12.6	6	11	66	7
1968—	Dallas NFL	4	40	178	4.5	4	7	84	12.0	1	5	30	0
1969—	Dallas NFL	13	59	173	2.9	4	18	187	10.4	1	5	30	2
1970—	Dallas NFL	14	35	84	2.4	2	12	140	11.7	0	2	12	4
1971—	Dallas NFL	14	17	79	4.6	0	3	25	8.3	0	0	0	1
1972—	Dallas NFL	14	3	14	4.7	0	None				0	0	0
	Pro Totals—8 Years	100	535	1990	3.7	25	129	1693	13.1	17	42	252	20

Year	Club	G.	Att.	Cmp.	Pct.	Gain	T.P.	P.I.	Avg.	No.	Yds.	Avg.	TD.
			PASSING							KICKOFF RET.			
1965—	Dallas NFL	13	2	1	50.0	11	0	0	5.50	2	45	22.5	0
1966—	Dallas NFL	14	6	3	50.0	48	0	0	8.00	3	56	18.7	0
1967—	Dallas NFL	14	7	4	57.1	195	2	1	27.86	None			
1968—	Dallas NFL	4	4	2	50.0	43	0	0	10.75	None			
1969—	Dallas NFL	13	3	1	33.3	35	0	1	11.67	None			
1970—	Dallas NFL	14	3	1	33.3	14	0	1	4.67	None			
1971—	Dallas NFL	14	5	2	40.0	24	0	1	4.80	None			
1972—	Dallas NFL	14	2	0	00.0	0	0	0	0.00	None			
	Pro Totals—8 Years	100	32	14	43.8	370	2	4	11.56	5	101	20.2	0

Additional pro statistics: Returned two punts for minus one yard, 1966.
Played in NFC Championship Game following 1970 and 1971 seasons.
Played in NFL Championship Game following 1966, 1967, 1970 and 1971 seasons.

COACHING RECORD

Player-coach, Dallas Cowboys NFL, 1970 and 1971.
Assistant coach, Dallas Cowboys NFL, 1972 and 1974 through 1980.

Year	Club	Pos.	W.	L.	T.
1981—	Denver NFL	†‡First	10	6	0
1982—	Denver NFL	§12th	2	7	0
1983—	Denver NFL	†‡Second	9	7	0
1984—	Denver NFL	†First	13	3	0
1985—	Denver NFL	†Second	11	5	0
	Pro Totals—5 Years		45	28	0

†Western Division (American Conference).
‡Tied for position.
§American Conference.

PLAYOFF RECORD

Year	Club	W.	L.
1983—	Denver NFL	0	1
1984—	Denver NFL	0	1
	Pro Totals—2 Years	0	2

1983—Lost wild-card playoff game to Seattle, 31-7.
1984—Lost conference playoff game to Pittsburgh, 24-17.

JOHN ALEXANDER ROBINSON
Los Angeles Rams
Born July 25, 1935, at Chicago, Ill.
High School—San Mateo, Calif.
Received bachelor of science degree in education from University of Oregon in 1958.

COACHING RECORD
Assistant coach at University of Oregon, 1960 through 1971.
Assistant coach at University of Southern California, 1972 through 1974.
Assistant coach, Oakland Raiders NFL, 1975.

Year Club	Pos.	W.	L.	T.
1976—Southern California	†First	11	1	0
1977—Southern California	†‡Second	8	4	0
1978—Southern California	§First	12	1	0
1979—Southern California	§First	11	0	1
1980—Southern California	§Third	8	2	1
1981—Southern California	‡§Second	9	3	0
1982—Southern California	§x.....	8	3	0
1983—Los Angeles Rams NFL	ySecond	9	7	0
1984—Los Angeles Rams NFL	ySecond	10	6	0
1985—Los Angeles Rams NFL	yFirst	11	5	0
College Totals—7 Years		67	14	2
Pro Totals—3 Years		30	18	0

†Pacific-8 Conference.
‡Tied for position.
§Pacific-10 Conference.
xIneligible for conference title.
yWestern Division (National Conference).

PLAYOFF RECORD
Year Club	W.	L.
1983—Los Angeles Rams NFL	1	1
1984—Los Angeles Rams NFL	0	1
1985—Los Angeles Rams NFL	1	1
Pro Totals—3 Years	2	3

1983—Won wild-card playoff game from Dallas, 24-17; lost conference playoff game to Washington, 51-7.
1984—Lost wild-card game to New York Giants, 16-13.
1985—Won conference playoff game from Dallas, 20-0; lost conference championship game to Chicago, 24-0.

COLLEGIATE BOWL GAME RECORD
Year Club	W.	L.
1976—Southern California	1	0
1977—Southern California	1	0
1978—Southern California	1	0
1979—Southern California	1	0
1981—Southern California	0	1
Totals—5 Years	4	1

1976—Won Rose Bowl from Michigan, 14-6.
1977—Won Bluebonnet Bowl from Texas A&M, 47-28.
1978—Won Rose Bowl from Michigan, 17-10.
1979—Won Rose Bowl from Ohio State, 17-16.
1981—Lost Fiesta Bowl to Penn State, 26-10.

DARRYL D. ROGERS
Detroit Lions
Born May 28, 1935, at Los Angeles, Calif.
High School—Long Beach, Calif., Jordan.
Attended Long Beach City College and received bachelor of arts degree
in 1957 and master's degree in physical education in
1964, both from Fresno State University.

Signed as free agent by Los Angeles Rams, April, 1959.
Released by Los Angeles Rams, August, 1959.
In U.S. Marine Corps, 1958 and 1959.

COACHING RECORD
Named College Coach of the Year by THE SPORTING NEWS, 1978.
Assistant coach at Fresno City College, 1961 through 1964.

Year Club	Pos.	W.	L.	T.	Year Club	Pos.	W.	L.	T.
1965—Hayward State	†§.....	3	7	0	1977—Michigan State	zThird	7	3	1
1966—Fresno State	‡xSecond	7	3	0	1978—Michigan State	‡zFirst	8	3	0
1967—Fresno State	‡xSecond	3	8	0	1979—Michigan State	‡zSeventh	5	6	0
1968—Fresno State	xFirst	7	4	0	1980—Arizona State	aFourth	7	4	0
1969—Fresno State	‡yFifth	6	4	0	1981—Arizona State	‡aSecond	9	2	0
1970—Fresno State	yThird	8	4	0	1982—Arizona State	‡aThird	10	2	0
1971—Fresno State	yThird	6	5	0	1983—Arizona State	‡aSixth	6	4	1
1972—Fresno State	‡yThird	6	4	1	1984—Arizona State	aSixth	5	6	0
1973—San Jose State	ySecond	5	4	2	1985—Detroit NFL	bcThird	7	9	0
1974—San Jose State	‡ySecond	8	3	1	College Totals—20 Years		129	84	7
1975—San Jose State	yFirst	9	2	0	Pro Totals—1 Year		7	9	0
1976—Michigan State	‡zSeventh	4	6	1					

†Ineligible for conference title.
‡Tied for position.
§Far Western Conference.
xCalifornia Collegiate Athletic Association.
yPacific Coast Athletic Association.
zBig 10 Conference.
aPacific-10 Conference.
bCentral Division (National Conference).
cTied for position.

COLLEGIATE BOWL GAME RECORD

Year Club	W.	L.
1968—Fresno State	0	1
1971—Fresno State	0	1
1982—Arizona State	1	0
Totals—3 Years	1	2

1968—Lost Camelia Bowl to Humboldt State, 29-14.
1971—Lost Mercy Bowl to California State-Fullerton, 17-14.
1982—Won Fiesta Bowl from Oklahoma, 32-21.

JAMES DAVID RYAN
(Buddy)
Philadelphia Eagles
Born February 17, 1934, at Frederick, Okla.
High School—Frederick, Okla.
Received bachelor of arts degree in education from Oklahoma State University
in 1957; and received master's degree in education
from Middle Tennessee State University in 1966.

Served in Korea.
Played on Fourth Army Championship team in Japan for two years.
Discharged as master sergeant.

COACHING RECORD
Head Coach and Athletic Director at Gainesville High School, Gainesville, Tex., 1957 through 1959.
Assistant coach at Marshall High School, Marshall, Tex., 1960.
Assistant coach at University of Buffalo, 1961 through 1965.
Assistant coach at Vanderbilt University, 1966.
Assistant coach at University of The Pacific, 1967.
Assistant coach, New York Jets NFL, 1968 through 1975.
Assistant coach, Minnesota Vikings NFL, 1976 and 1977.
Assistant coach, Chicago Bears NFL, 1978 through 1985.

MARTIN EDWARD SCHOTTENHEIMER
(Marty)
Cleveland Browns
Born September 23, 1943, at Canonsburg, Pa.
High School—McDonald, Pa.
Received bachelor of arts degree in English from University of Pittsburgh in 1964.

Played linebacker.
Selected by Buffalo in 7th round of 1965 AFL draft.
Released by Buffalo Bills and signed with Boston Patriots, 1969.
Traded by New England Patriots to Pittsburgh Steelers for offensive tackle Mike Haggerty and a draft choice,
July 10, 1971.
Released by Pittsburgh Steelers, 1971.

Year Club		INTERCEPTIONS			Year Club		INTERCEPTIONS		
	G.	No.	Yds.	Avg.TD.		G.	No.	Yds.	Avg.TD.
1965—Buffalo AFL	14		None		1970—Boston NFL	12		None	
1966—Buffalo AFL	14	1	20	20.0 0	AFL Totals—5 Years	67	6	133	22.2 1
1967—Buffalo AFL	14	3	88	29.3 1	NFL Totals—1 Year	12	0	0	0.0 0
1968—Buffalo AFL	14	1	22	22.0 0	Pro Totals—6 Years	79	6	133	22.2 1
1969—Boston AFL	11	1	3	3.0 0					

Additional pro statistics: Returned one kickoff for 13 yards, 1969; returned one kickoff for eight yards, 1970.
Played in AFL Championship Game following 1965 and 1966 seasons.
Played in AFL All-Star Game following 1965 season.

COACHING RECORD
Assistant coach, Portland WFL, 1974.
Assistant coach, New York Giants NFL, 1975 through 1977.
Assistant coach, Detroit Lions NFL, 1978 and 1979.
Assistant coach, Cleveland Browns NFL, 1980 through 1984.

Year Club	Pos.	W.	L.	T.
1984—Cleveland NFL†	‡Third	4	4	0
1985—Cleveland NFL	‡First	8	8	0
Pro Totals—2 Years		12	12	0

†Replaced Sam Rutigliano, October 22, 1984 with 1-7 record and in third place.
‡Central Division (American Conference).

Year	Club	W.	I..
1985—Cleveland NFL		0	1

1985—Lost conference playoff game to Miami, 24-21.

DONALD FRANCIS SHULA
(Don)
Miami Dolphins

Born January 4, 1930, at Painesville, O.
High School—Painesville, O., Harvey.
Received bachelor of arts degree in sociology from John Carroll University in 1951.
Father of David Shula, assistant coach with Miami Dolphins,
and Mike Shula, quarterback at University of Alabama.

Played defensive back.
Selected by Cleveland in 9th round of 1951 NFL draft.
Traded with quarterback Harry Agganis, defensive backs Bert Rechichar and Carl Taseff, end Gern Nagler, guards Elmer Willhoite, Ed Sharkey and Art Spinney and tackles Dick Batten and Stu Sheetz by Cleveland NFL to Baltimore NFL for linebacker Tom Catlin, guard Herschel Forester, halfback John Petitbon and tackles Don Colo and Mike McCormack, March 25, 1953.
Sold by Baltimore NFL to Washington NFL, 1957.

Year	Club	—INTERCEPTIONS— G.	No.	Yds.	Avg.TD.	Year	Club	—INTERCEPTIONS— G.	No.	Yds.	Avg.TD.
1951—Cleveland NFL		12	4	23	5.8	0	1956—Baltimore NFL	12	1	2	2.0	0
1952—Cleveland NFL		5		None		1957—Washington NFL	11	3	48	16.0	0
1953—Baltimore NFL		12	3	46	15.3	0	Pro Totals—7 Years	73	21	267	12.7	0
1954—Baltimore NFL		12	5	84	16.8	0						
1955—Baltimore NFL		9	5	64	12.8	0						

Additional pro statistics: Returned one kickoff for six yards, 1951; caught one pass for six yards, 1953; rushed twice for three yards, 1954; recovered one fumble, 1953; recovered two fumbles for 26 yards, 1955; recovered one fumble for six yards and returned one kickoff for no yards, 1956.
Played in NFL Championship Game following 1951 and 1952 seasons.

COACHING RECORD

Named NFL Coach of the Year by THE SPORTING NEWS, 1964, 1968, 1970 and 1972.
Assistant coach at University of Virginia, 1958.
Assistant coach at University of Kentucky, 1959.
Assistant coach, Detroit Lions NFL, 1960 through 1962.

Year	Club	Pos.	W.	L.	T.	Year	Club	Pos.	W.	L.	T
1963—Baltimore NFL		†Third	8	6	0	1975—Miami NFL		§xFirst	10	4	0
1964—Baltimore NFL		†First	12	2	0	1976—Miami NFL		§Third	6	8	0
1965—Baltimore NFL		†Second	10	3	1	1977—Miami NFL		§xFirst	10	4	0
1966—Baltimore NFL		†Second	9	5	0	1978—Miami NFL		§xFirst	11	5	0
1967—Baltimore NFL		†Second	11	1	2	1979—Miami NFL		§First	10	6	0
1968—Baltimore NFL		‡First	13	1	0	1980—Miami NFL		§Third	8	8	0
1969—Baltimore NFL		‡Second	8	5	1	1981—Miami NFL		§First	11	4	1
1970—Miami NFL		§Second	10	4	0	1982—Miami NFL		yxSecond	7	2	0
1971—Miami NFL		§First	10	3	1	1983—Miami NFL		§First	12	4	0
1972—Miami NFL		§First	14	0	0	1984—Miami NFL		§First	14	2	0
1973—Miami NFL		§First	12	2	0	1985—Miami NFL		§First	12	4	0
1974—Miami NFL		§First	11	3	0	Pro Totals—23 Years			239	86	6

†Western Conference.
‡Coastal Division (Western Conference).
§Eastern Division (American Conference).
xTied for position.
yAmerican Conference.

PLAYOFF RECORD

Year	Club	W.	L.	Year	Club	W.	L.
1964—Baltimore NFL	0	1	1978—Miami NFL		0	1
1965—Baltimore NFL	1	1	1979—Miami NFL		0	1
1966—Baltimore NFL	1	0	1981—Miami NFL		1	1
1968—Baltimore NFL	2	1	1982—Miami NFL		3	1
1970—Miami NFL	0	1	1983—Miami NFL		0	1
1971—Miami NFL	2	1	1984—Miami NFL		2	1
1972—Miami NFL	3	0	1985—Miami NFL		1	1
1973—Miami NFL	3	0	Pro Totals—16 Years		18	13
1974—Miami NFL	0	1				

1964—Lost NFL championship game to Cleveland, 27-0.
1965—Lost conference playoff game to Green Bay, 13-10; won Playoff Bowl from Dallas, 35-3.
1966—Won Playoff Bowl from Philadelphia, 20-14.
1968—Won conference playoff game from Minnesota, 24-14; won NFL championship game from Cleveland, 34-0; lost AFL-NFL playoff game (Super Bowl III) to New York Jets, 16-7.
1970—Lost conference playoff game to Oakland, 21-14.
1971—Won conference playoff game from Kansas City, 27-24; won conference playoff game from Baltimore, 21-0; lost NFL championship game (Super Bowl VI) to Dallas, 24-3.
1972—Won conference playoff game from Cleveland, 20-14; won conference championship game from Pittsburgh, 21-17; won NFL championship game (Super Bowl VII) from Washington, 14-7.
1973—Won conference playoff game from Cincinnati, 34-16; won conference championship game from Oakland, 27-10; won NFL championship game (Super Bowl VIII) from Minnesota, 24-7.

1974—Lost conference playoff game to Oakland, 28-26.
1978—Lost conference playoff game to Houston, 17-9.
1979—Lost conference playoff game to Pittsburgh, 34-14.
1981—Lost conference playoff game in overtime to San Diego, 41-38.
1982—Won conference playoff game from New England, 28-13; won conference playoff game from San Diego, 34-13; won conference championship game from New York Jets, 14-0; lost NFL championship game (Super Bowl XVII) to Washington, 27-17.
1983—Lost conference playoff game to Seattle, 27-20.
1984—Won conference playoff game from Seattle, 31-10; won conference championship game from Pittsburgh, 45-28; lost NFL championship game (Super Bowl XIX) to San Francisco, 38-16.
1985—Won conference playoff game from Cleveland, 24-21; lost conference championship game to New England, 31-14.

EUGENE CLIFTON STALLINGS
(Gene)
St. Louis Cardinals
Born March 2, 1935, at Paris, Tex.
High School—Paris, Tex.
Attended Texas A&M University.

COACHING RECORD
Student assistant coach, freshman team at Texas A&M University, 1957.
Assistant coach at University of Alabama, 1958 through 1964.
Assistant coach, Dallas Cowboys NFL, 1972 through 1985.

Year	Club	Pos.	W.	L.	T.
1965—Texas A&M		†‡Seventh	3	7	0
1966—Texas A&M		†Fourth	4	5	1
1967—Texas A&M		†First	7	4	0
1968—Texas A&M		†‡Sixth	3	7	0
1969—Texas A&M		†‡Sixth	3	7	0
1970—Texas A&M		†Eighth	2	9	0
1971—Texas A&M		†Fourth	5	6	0
College Totals—7 Years			27	45	1

†Southwest Conference.
‡Tied for position.

COLLEGIATE BOWL GAME RECORD

Year	Club	W.	L.
1967—Texas A&M		1	0

1967—Won Cotton Bowl from Alabama, 20-16.

WILLIAM ERNEST WALSH
(Bill)
San Francisco 49ers
Born November 30, 1931, at Los Angeles, Calif.
High School—Los Angeles, Calif., Hayward.
Attended San Mateo Junior College and received bachelor of arts degree
and master's degree in education from San Jose State in 1959.

COACHING RECORD
Named THE SPORTING NEWS NFL Coach of the Year, 1981.
Assistant coach at Monterey Peninsula College, 1955.
Assistant coach at San Jose State University, 1956.
Head coach at Washington Union High, Fremont, Calif., 1957 through 1959.
Assistant coach at University of California, 1960 through 1962.
Assistant coach at Stanford University, 1963 through 1965.
Assistant coach, Oakland Raiders AFL, 1966.
Assistant coach, Cincinnati Bengals AFL, 1968 and 1969.
Assistant coach, Cincinnati Bengals NFL, 1970 through 1975.
Assistant coach, San Diego Chargers NFL, 1976.

Year	Club	Pos.	W.	L.	T.
1967—San Jose CoFL		†Second	7	5	0
1977—Stanford		‡§Second	9	3	0
1978—Stanford		xFourth	8	4	0
1979—San Francisco NFL		yFourth	2	14	0
1980—San Francisco NFL		yThird	6	10	0
1981—San Francisco NFL		yFirst	13	3	0
1982—San Francisco NFL		z§11th	3	6	0
1983—San Francisco NFL		yFirst	10	6	0
1984—San Francisco NFL		yFirst	15	1	0
1985—San Francisco NFL		ySecond	10	6	0
College Totals—2 Years			17	7	0
Pro Totals—7 Years			59	46	0

†Continental League.
‡Pacific Eight Conference.
§Tied for position.
xPacific Ten Conference.
yWestern Division (National Conference).
zNational Conference.

PLAYOFF RECORD

Year Club	W.	L.
1981—San Francisco NFL	3	0
1983—San Francisco NFL	1	1
1984—San Francisco NFL	3	0
1985—San Francisco NFL	0	1
Pro Totals—4 Years	7	2

1981—Won conference playoff game from New York Giants, 38-34; won conference championship game from Dallas, 28-27; won NFL championship game (Super Bowl XVI) from Cincinnati, 26-21.
1983—Won conference playoff game from Detroit, 24-23; lost conference championship game to Washington, 24-21.
1984—Won conference playoff game from New York Giants, 21-10; won conference championship game from Chicago, 23-0; won NFL championship game (Super Bowl XIX) from Miami, 38-16.
1985—Lost wild-card playoff game to New York Giants, 17-3.

COLLEGIATE BOWL GAME RECORD

Year Club	W.	L.
1977—Stanford	1	0
1978—Stanford	1	0
Totals—2 Years	2	0

1977—Won Sun Bowl from Louisiana State, 24-14.
1978—Won Bluebonnet Bowl from Georgia, 25-22.

JOSEPH FRANK WALTON
(Joe)
New York Jets
Born December 15, 1935, at Beaver Falls, Pa.
High School—Beaver Falls, Pa.
Received bachelor of arts degree in history from University of Pittsburgh in 1957.
Son of Frank Walton, guard with Boston Redskins, 1934 and 1935;
and Washington Redskins, 1944 and 1945; assistant coach, Pittsburgh Steelers, 1946.

Played tight end.
Named end on THE SPORTING NEWS College All-America Team, 1956.
Selected by Washington in 2nd round of 1957 NFL draft.

Year Club	G.	P.C.	Yds.	Avg.	TD.
1957—Washington NFL	12	3	57	19.0	0
1958—Washington NFL	12	32	532	16.6	5
1959—Washington NFL	9	21	317	15.1	3
1960—Washington NFL	12	27	401	14.9	3
1961—N.Y. Giants NFL	12	36	544	15.1	2
1962—N.Y. Giants NFL	14	33	406	12.3	9
1963—N.Y. Giants NFL	12	26	371	14.3	6
Pro Totals—7 Years	83	178	2628	14.8	28

Additional pro statistics: Intercepted one pass for 55 yards, 1957; fumbled once, 1958, 1959, 1961 and 1962; recovered one fumble for four yards, 1960.

COACHING RECORD

Scout for New York Giants NFL, 1967 and 1968.
Assistant coach, New York Giants NFL, 1969 through 1973.
Assistant coach, Washington Redskins NFL, 1974 through 1980.
Assistant coach, New York Jets NFL, 1981 and 1982.

Year Club	Pos.	W.	L.	T.
1983—New York Jets NFL	†‡Fourth	7	9	0
1984—New York Jets NFL	†Third	7	9	0
1985—New York Jets NFL	†‡Second	11	5	0
Pro Totals—3 Years		25	23	0

†Eastern Division (American Conference).
‡Tied for position.

PLAYOFF RECORD

Year Club	W.	L.
1985—New York Jets NFL	0	1

1985—Lost wild-card playoff game to New England, 26-14.

SAMUEL DAVID WYCHE
(Sam)
Cincinnati Bengals
Born January 5, 1945, at Atlanta, Ga.
High School—Atlanta, Ga., North Fulton.
Received bachelor of arts degree in business administration from Furman University
in 1966 and received master's degree from University of South Carolina.
Brother of Joseph (Bubba) Wyche, former quarterback with Saskatchewan Roughriders,
Detroit Wheels, Chicago Fire and Shreveport Steamer.

Played quarterback.
Played in Continental Football League with Wheeling Ironmen, 1966.
Signed as free agent by Cincinnati AFL, 1968.
Traded by Cincinnati Bengals to Washington Redskins for running back Henry Dyer, May 5, 1971.
Traded by Washington Redskins to Detroit Lions for quarterback Bill Cappelman, August 17, 1974.
Released by Detroit Lions, September 2, 1975; signed as free agent by St. Louis Cardinals, 1976.
Released by St. Louis Cardinals, September 23, 1976; signed as free agent by Buffalo Bills, October 26, 1976.
Member of Washington Redskins' taxi squad, 1973.
Active for 7 games with Buffalo Bills in 1976; did not play.

Year Club	G.	Att.	Cmp.	Pct.	Gain	T.P.	P.I.	Avg.	Att.	Yds.	Avg.	TD.	TD.	Pts.	F.
				—PASSING—					—RUSHING—				—TOTAL—		
1966—Wheeling CoFL	....	18	9	50.0	101	0	1	5.61	5	—11	—2.2	0	0	0	0
1968—Cincinnati AFL	3	55	35	63.6	494	2	2	8.98	12	74	6.2	0	0	0	2
1969—Cincinnati AFL	7	108	54	50.0	838	7	4	7.76	12	107	8.9	1	1	6	1
1970—Cincinnati NFL	13	57	26	45.6	411	3	2	7.21	19	118	6.2	2	2	12	3
1971—Washington NFL	1			None					1	4	4.0	0	0	0	0
1972—Washington NFL	7			None						None			0	0	0
1974—Detroit NFL	14	1	0	00.0	0	0	1	0.00	1	0	0.0	0	0	0	0
1976—St. Louis NFL	1	1	1	100.0	5	0	0	5.00		None			0	0	0
AFL Totals—2 Years	10	163	89	54.9	1332	9	6	8.17	24	181	7.5	1	1	6	3
NFL Totals—5 Years	36	59	27	45.8	416	3	3	7.05	21	122	5.8	2	2	12	3
Pro Totals—7 Years	46	222	116	52.3	1748	12	9	7.87	45	303	6.7	3	3	18	6

Additional CoFL statistics: Intercepted three passes for nine yards, 1966.
Additional AFL statistics: Caught one pass for five yards, 1968.
Additional NFL statistics: Recovered one fumble for minus one yard, 1970.
Played in NFL Championship Game following 1972 season.

COACHING RECORD

Graduate assistant at University of South Carolina, 1967.
Assistant coach, San Francisco 49ers NFL, 1979 through 1982.

Year Club	Pos.	W.	L.	T.
1983—Indiana	†‡Eighth	3	8	0
1984—Cincinnati NFL	§Second	8	8	0
1985—Cincinnati NFL	§‡Second	7	9	0
College Totals—1 Year		3	8	0
Pro Totals—2 Years		15	17	0

†Big Ten Conference.
‡Tied for position.
§Central Division (American Conference).

Recently Retired Coach

HAROLD PETER GRANT
(Bud)
Born May 20, 1927, at Superior, Wis.
High School—Superior, Wis., Central.
Attended University of Minnesota.

Played offensive end.
Selected by Philadelphia in 1st round of 1950 NFL draft.

Year Club	G.	P.C.	Yds.	Avg.	TD.
		—PASS RECEIVING—			
1951—Philadelphia NFL	12		None		
1952—Philadelphia NFL	12	56	997	17.8	7
1953—Winnipeg CFL	16	*68	922	13.5	5
1954—Winnipeg CFL	16	*49	752	15.3	5
1955—Winnipeg CFL	16	36	556	15.4	2
1956—Winnipeg CFL	16	*63	*970	15.3	1
NFL Totals—2 Years	24	56	997	17.8	7
CFL Totals—4 Years	64	216	3200	14.8	13
Pro Totals—6 Years	88	272	4197	15.4	20

Additional NFL statistics: Returned one punt for nine yards, 1951; fumbled four times, 1952.
Additional CFL statistics: Intercepted four passes, rushed once for nine yards and returned two punts for four yards, 1953; intercepted one pass for five yards and fumbled three times, 1954; fumbled once, 1955 and 1956; intercepted two passes for six yards, returned one punt for five yards and returned one kickoff for 29 yards, 1956.

COACHING RECORD

Named NFL Coach of the Year by THE SPORTING NEWS, 1969.

Year Club	Pos.	W.	L.	T.
1957—Winnipeg CFL	†Second	12	4	0
1958—Winnipeg CFL	†First	13	3	0
1959—Winnipeg CFL	†First	12	4	0
1960—Winnipeg CFL	†First	14	2	0
1961—Winnipeg CFL	†First	13	3	0
1962—Winnipeg CFL	†First	11	5	0
1963—Winnipeg CFL	†Fourth	7	9	0
1964—Winnipeg CFL	†Fifth	1	14	1
1965—Winnipeg CFL	†Second	11	5	0
1966—Winnipeg CFL	†Second	8	7	1
1967—Minnesota NFL	‡Fourth	3	8	3
1968—Minnesota NFL	‡First	8	6	0
1969—Minnesota NFL	‡First	12	2	0
1970—Minnesota NFL	§First	12	2	0
1971—Minnesota NFL	§First	11	3	0
1972—Minnesota NFL	§Third	7	7	0

Year Club	Pos.	W.	L.	T.
1973—Minnesota NFL	§First	12	2	0
1974—Minnesota NFL	§First	10	4	0
1975—Minnesota NFL	§First	12	2	0
1976—Minnesota NFL	§First	11	2	1
1977—Minnesota NFL	§xFirst	9	5	0
1978—Minnesota NFL	§xFirst	8	7	1
1979—Minnesota NFL	§Third	7	9	0
1980—Minnesota NFL	§xFirst	9	7	0
1981—Minnesota NFL	§Fourth	7	9	0
1982—Minnesota NFL	yxFourth	5	4	0
1983—Minnesota NFL	§xSecond	8	8	0
1985—Minnesota NFL	§xThird	7	9	0
CFL Totals—10 Years		102	56	2
NFL Totals—18 Years		158	96	5
Pro Totals—28 Years		260	152	7

†Western Conference.
‡Century Division (Western Conference).
§Central Division (National Conference).
xTied for position.
yNational conference.

PLAYOFF RECORD

Year Club	W.	L.	Year Club	W.	L.
1957—Winnipeg CFL	3	2	1973—Minnesota NFL	2	1
1958—Winnipeg CFL	3	1	1974—Minnesota NFL	2	1
1959—Winnipeg CFL	3	0	1975—Minnesota NFL	0	1
1960—Winnipeg CFL	1	2	1976—Minnesota NFL	2	1
1961—Winnipeg CFL	3	0	1977—Minnesota NFL	1	1
1962—Winnipeg CFL	3	1	1978—Minnesota NFL	0	1
1965—Winnipeg CFL	3	2	1980—Minnesota NFL	0	1
1966—Winnipeg CFL	1	2	1982—Minnesota NFL	1	1
1968—Minnesota NFL	0	2	NFL Totals—12 Years	10	13
1969—Minnesota NFL	2	1	CFL Totals—8 Years	20	10
1970—Minnesota NFL	0	1			
1971—Minnesota NFL	0	1	Pro Totals—20 Years	30	23

1957—Won conference playoff game from Calgary, 15-3 (after 13-13 tie); won conference championship series from Edmonton, two games to one (19-7, 4-5, 17-2); lost CFL championship game to Hamilton, 32-7.
1958—Won conference championship series from Edmonton, two games to one (30-7, 7-30, 23-7); won CFL championship game from Hamilton, 35-28.
1959—Won conference championship series from Edmonton, two games to none (19-11, 16-8); won CFL championship game from Hamilton, 21-7.
1960—Lost conference championship series to Edmonton, two games to one (22-16, 5-10, 2-4).
1961—Won conference championship series from Calgary, two games to none (14-1, 43-14); won CFL championship game from Hamilton, 21-14.
1962—Won conference championship series from Calgary, two games to one (14-20, 19-11, 12-7); won CFL championship game from Hamilton, 28-27.
1965—Won conference playoff game from Saskatchewan, 15-9; won conference championship series from Calgary, two games to one (9-27, 15-11, 19-2); lost CFL championship game to Hamilton, 22-16.
1966—Won conference playoff game from Edmonton, 16-8; lost conference championship series to Saskatchewan, two games to none (7-14, 19-21).
1968—Lost conference playoff game to Baltimore, 24-14; lost Playoff Bowl to Dallas, 17-13.
1969—Won conference playoff game from Los Angeles, 23-20; won NFL championship game from Cleveland, 27-7; lost AFL-NFL playoff game (Super Bowl IV) to Kansas City, 23-7.
1970—Lost conference playoff game to San Francisco, 17-14.
1971—Lost conference playoff game to Dallas, 20-12.
1973—Won conference playoff game from Washington, 27-20; won conference championship game from Dallas, 27-10; lost NFL championship game (Super Bowl VIII) to Miami, 24-7.
1974—Won conference playoff game from St. Louis, 30-14; won conference championship game from Los Angeles, 14-10; lost NFL championship game (Super Bowl IX) to Pittsburgh, 16-6.
1975—Lost conference playoff game to Dallas, 17-14.
1976—Won conference playoff game from Washington, 35-20; won conference championship game from Los Angeles, 24-13; lost NFL championship game (Super Bowl XI) to Oakland, 32-14.
1977—Won conference playoff game from Los Angeles, 14-7; lost conference championship game to Dallas, 23-6.
1978—Lost conference playoff game to Los Angeles, 34-10.
1980—Lost conference playoff game to Philadelphia, 31-16.
1982—Won conference playoff game from Atlanta, 30-24; lost conference playoff game to Washington, 21-7.

NBA RECORD

Sea.—Team	G.	Min.	FGA	FGM	Pct.	FTA	FTM	Pct.	Reb.	Ast.	PF	Disq.	Pts.	Avg.
1949-50—Minneapolis	35	....	115	42	.365	17	1	.412	....	19	36	....	91	2.6
1950-51—Minneapolis	61	....	184	53	.288	83	52	.627	115	71	106	0	159	2.6
NBA Totals	96	....	299	95	.318	100	53	.530	....	90	142	....	250	2.6

Member of NBA championship team, 1949-50.

Recently Retired Players

JULIUS THOMAS ADAMS
Born April 26, 1948, at Macon, Ga.
Height, 6.03. Weight, 270.
High School—Macon, Ga., Ballard.
Attended Texas Southern University.
Selected by New England in 2nd round (27th player selected) of 1971 NFL draft.
On injured reserve with fractured shoulder blade, September 8 through remainder of 1978 season.
Released by New England Patriots, September 2, 1985; re-signed by Patriots, September 3, 1985.
New England NFL, 1971 through 1985.
Games: 1971 (14), 1972 (11), 1973 (14), 1974 (14), 1975 (9), 1976 (14), 1977 (14), 1978 (1), 1979 (16), 1980 (16), 1981 (16), 1982 (9), 1983 (16), 1984 (16), 1985 (16). Total—196.
Pro statistics: Recovered one fumble, 1972, 1973, 1979, 1982 and 1983; recovered two fumbles for 12 yards, 1985.
Played in AFC Championship Game following 1985 season.
Played in NFL Championship Game following 1985 season.

LYLE MARTIN ALZADO
Name pronounced Al-ZAY-doe.
Born April 3, 1949, at Brooklyn, N. Y.
Height, 6.03. Weight, 260.
High School—Cedarhurst, N. Y., Lawrence.
Received bachelor of arts degree in special education from Yankton College in 1971.
Named to THE SPORTING NEWS AFC All-Star Team, 1977 and 1978.
Selected by Denver in 4th round (79th player selected) of 1971 NFL draft.
Traded by Denver Broncos to Cleveland Browns for 2nd and 5th round picks in 1980 draft and 3rd round pick in 981 draft, August 12, 1979.
Traded by Cleveland Browns to Oakland Raiders for 8th round pick in 1982 draft, April 28, 1982.
Franchise transferred to Los Angeles, May 7, 1982.
On injured reserve with ruptured Achilles tendon, November 21 through remainder of 1985 season.
Denver NFL, 1971 through 1978; Cleveland NFL, 1979 through 1981; Los Angeles Raiders NFL, 1982 through 1985.
Games: 1971 (12), 1972 (14), 1973 (14), 1974 (14), 1975 (14), 1976 (1), 1977 (14), 1978 (16), 1979 (15), 1980 (16), 1981 (15), 982 (9), 1983 (15), 1984 (16), 1985 (11). Total—196.
Pro statistics: Recovered five fumbles for six yards, 1972; recovered one fumble, 1973, 1979, 1981, 1983 and 1984; ecovered two fumbles, 1974; recovered three fumbles for 14 yards, 1975; recovered three fumbles for one yard, 1977; redited with one safety, 1978, 1983 and 1985; recovered one fumble for seven yards, 1982; recovered one fumble in end one for a touchdown, 1985.
Played in AFC Championship Game following 1977 and 1983 seasons.
Played in NFL Championship Game following 1977 and 1983 seasons.
Played in Pro Bowl (NFL All-Star Game) following 1977 and 1978 seasons.

RUSSELL DEAN BOLINGER
(Russ)
Born September 10, 1954, at Wichita, Kan.
Height, 6.05. Weight, 255.
High School—Lompoc, Calif.
Attended University of California at Riverside and California State University at Long Beach.
Selected by Detroit in 3rd round (68th player selected) of 1976 NFL draft.
Traded by Detroit Lions to Los Angeles Rams for 5th round pick in 1983 draft, April 26, 1983.
On injured reserve with knee injury, August 16 through remainder of 1978 season.
Granted free agency, February 1, 1985; signed by Memphis Showboats, April 12, 1985.
Granted free agency, August 1, 1985; re-signed by Rams, August 5, 1985.
On injured reserve with broken arm, October 1 through December 13, 1985; activated, December 14, 1985.
Detroit NFL, 1976, 1977 and 1979 through 1982; Los Angeles Rams NFL, 1983 through 1985; Memphis USFL, 1985.
Games: 1976 (12), 1977 (14), 1979 (16), 1980 (16), 1981 (16), 1982 (9), 1983 (16), 1984 (16), 1985 USFL (10), 1985 NFL (6). otal NFL—121. Total Pro—131.
Pro statistics: Caught one pass for minus one yard, 1979; recovered one fumble, 1980; recovered two fumbles, 1981.
Member of Los Angeles Rams for NFC Championship Game following 1985 season; did not play.

WILLIAM FRANK CURRIER
(Bill)
Born January 5, 1955, at Glen Burnie, Md.
Height, 6.00. Weight, 196.
High School—Glen Burnie, Md.
Received bachelor of science degree in physical education from University of South Carolina.
Selected by Houston in 9th round (232nd player selected) of 1977 NFL draft.
Released by Houston Oilers, August 26, 1980; signed as free agent by New England Patriots, September 3, 1980.
Traded by New England Patriots to New York Giants for 11th round pick in 1982 draft, August 31, 1981.
On injured reserve with back injury, August 29 through October 18, 1984; activated, October 19, 1984.
On injured reserve with back injury, September 28 through remainder of 1985 season.
Released by New York Giants after failing physical, May 22, 1986.

Year	Club	G.	No.	Yds.	Avg.	TD.
1977—Houston NFL		14	2	0	0.0	0
1978—Houston NFL		14	1	8	8.0	0
1979—Houston NFL		16		None		
1980—New England NFL		16		None		
1981—N.Y. Giants NFL		16	3	2	0.7	0
1982—N.Y. Giants NFL		9	1	0	0.0	0
1983—N.Y. Giants NFL		15	2	37	18.5	1
1984—N.Y. Giants NFL		9	1	7	7.0	0
1985—N.Y. Giants NFL		2	1	9	9.0	0
Pro Totals—9 Years		111	11	63	5.7	1

Additional pro statistics: Recovered two fumbles, 1977 and 1978; recovered one fumble, 1979, 1981 and 1983; returned six kickoffs for 98 yards, 1980.

Played in AFC Championship Game following 1978 and 1979 seasons.

JOSEPH MICHAEL DeLAMIELLEURE

Name pronounced Deh-Lah-meh-LURE.

(Joe)

Born March 16, 1951, at Detroit, Mich.
Height, 6.03. Weight, 260.
High School—Center Line, Mich., St. Clement.
Received bachelor of science degree in criminal justice from Michigan State University in 1973.
Uncle of Jeff DeLamielleure, safety at Cornell University.

Named to THE SPORTING NEWS AFC All-Star Team, 1975 through 1979.
Named to THE SPORTING NEWS NFL All-Star Team, 1980.
Named as guard on THE SPORTING NEWS College All-America Team, 1972.
Selected by Buffalo in 1st round (26th player selected) of 1973 NFL draft.
On did not report list, August 18 through August 31, 1980.
Traded by Buffalo Bills to Cleveland Browns for 2nd round pick in 1981 draft and 3rd round pick in 1982 draft September 1, 1980.
Released by Cleveland Browns, August 12, 1985; signed as free agent by Buffalo Bills, September 17, 1985.
Placed on retired list, November 26, 1985.
Buffalo NFL, 1973 through 1979 and 1985; Cleveland NFL, 1980 through 1984.
Games: 1973 (14), 1974 (14), 1975 (14), 1976 (14), 1977 (14), 1978 (16), 1979 (16), 1980 (16), 1981 (16), 1982 (9), 1983 (16) 1984 (16), 1985 (10). Total—185.
Pro statistics: Recovered one fumble, 1973, 1974, 1977, 1978 and 1984; recovered two fumbles, 1976.
Played in Pro Bowl (NFL All-Star Game) following 1975 through 1980 seasons.

LOWELL DOUGLAS ENGLISH

(Doug)

Born August 25, 1953, at Dallas, Tex.
Height, 6.05. Weight, 258.
High School—Dallas, Tex., Bryan Adams.
Received bachelor of social and behavioral science degree from University of Texas.

Selected by Detroit in 2nd round (38th player selected) of 1975 NFL draft.
On reserve-retired list entire 1980 season.
Reinstated, June 29, 1981.
On injured reserve with ruptured disc, November 13 through remainder of 1985 season.
Detroit NFL, 1975 through 1979 and 1981 through 1985.
Games: 1975 (14), 1976 (7), 1977 (14), 1978 (14), 1979 (16), 1981 (16), 1982 (9), 1983 (15), 1984 (16), 1985 (10) Total—131.
Pro statistics: Recovered one fumble, 1976, 1977, 1982 and 1984; credited with one safety, 1977 and 1979; recovered two fumbles, 1979; recovered three fumbles for 20 yards, 1981; credited with two safeties, 1983.
Played in Pro Bowl (NFL All-Star Game) following 1978 and 1981 through 1983 seasons.

ROBERT E. JACKSON

Born April 1, 1953, at Charlotte, N. C.
Height, 6.05. Weight, 260.
High School—Huntersville, N. C., North Mecklenberg.
Received bachelor of science degree in economics from Duke University.

Signed as free agent by Cleveland Browns, 1975.
Cleveland NFL, 1975 through 1985.
Games: 1975 (14), 1976 (14), 1977 (14), 1978 (16), 1979 (16), 1980 (14), 1981 (16), 1982 (9), 1983 (16), 1984 (16), 1985 (15) Total—160.
Pro statistics: Recovered one fumble, 1975 and 1984; recovered two fumbles for three yards, 1976; returned one kickoff for 21 yards and recovered two fumbles, 1977; returned one kickoff for 19 yards, 1978; returned one kickoff fc 18 yards, 1979; returned one kickoff for no yards, 1980.

ROBERT HENRY PRATT JR.

Born May 25, 1951, at Richmond, Va.
Height, 6.04. Weight, 250.
High School—Richmond, Va., St. Christopher's.
Received bachelor of science degree in business administration from
University of North Carolina in 1974.

Selected by Baltimore in 3rd round (67th player selected) of 1974 NFL draft.
Traded by Baltimore Colts to Seattle Seahawks for 5th round pick in 1984 draft, July 12, 1982.
Baltimore NFL, 1974 through 1981; Seattle NFL, 1982 through 1985.
Games: 1974 (13), 1975 (14), 1976 (14), 1977 (14), 1978 (16), 1979 (16), 1980 (16), 1981 (15), 1982 (9), 1983 (15), 1984 (10), 1985 (12). Total—170.
Pro statistics: Returned four kickoffs for 64 yards, 1975; returned one kickoff for 21 yards, 1976; recovered one fumble for 21 yards and one touchdown, 1977; recovered one fumble, 1981 through 1983 and 1985; fumbled once, 1981; caught one pass for 30 yards, 1984.
Played in AFC Championship Game following 1983 season.

JOHN RIGGINS

Born August 4, 1949, at Centralia, Kan.
Height, 6.02. Weight, 240.
High School—Centralia, Kan.
Attended University of Kansas.
Brother of Frank Riggins, outfielder in California Angels' organization, 1969 through 1972.
Established NFL records for most touchdowns and most rushing touchdowns, season (24), 1983.
Selected by New York Jets in 1st round (6th player selected) of 1971 NFL draft.
Played out option with New York Jets in 1975 and signed as free agent by Washington Redskins, June 10, 1976.
On injured reserve, December 6 through remainder of 1977 season.
Left Washington Redskins camp voluntarily and placed on left camp-retired list, July 31, 1980; reinstated, May 25, 1981.
Released by Washington Redskins, March 19, 1986.

Year Club	G.	—————RUSHING—————				PASS RECEIVING				—TOTAL—		
		Att.	Yds.	Avg.	TD.	P.C.	Yds.	Avg.	TD.	TD.	Pts.	F.
1971—New York Jets NFL	14	180	769	4.3	1	36	231	6.4	2	3	18	6
1972—New York Jets NFL	12	207	944	4.6	7	21	230	11.0	1	8	48	2
1973—New York Jets NFL	11	134	482	3.6	4	23	158	6.9	0	4	24	6
1974—New York Jets NFL	10	169	680	4.0	5	19	180	9.5	2	7	42	3
1975—New York Jets NFL	14	238	1005	4.2	8	30	363	12.1	1	9	54	5
1976—Washington NFL	14	162	572	3.5	3	21	172	8.3	1	4	24	6
1977—Washington NFL	5	68	203	3.0	0	7	95	13.6	2	2	12	0
1978—Washington NFL	15	248	1014	4.1	5	31	299	9.6	0	5	30	7
1979—Washington NFL	16	260	1153	4.4	9	28	163	5.8	3	12	72	5
1981—Washington NFL	15	195	714	3.7	13	6	59	9.8	0	13	78	1
1982—Washington NFL	8	*177	553	3.1	3	10	50	5.0	0	3	18	2
1983—Washington NFL	15	375	1347	3.6	*24	5	29	5.8	0	*24	144	5
1984—Washington NFL	14	327	1239	3.8	*14	7	43	6.1	0	14	84	7
1985—Washington NFL	12	176	677	3.8	8	6	18	3.0	0	8	48	3
Pro Totals—14 Years	175	2916	11352	3.9	104	250	2090	8.4	12	116	696	58

Additional pro statistics: Recovered two fumbles for minus seven yards, 1971; recovered one fumble, 1973, 1975, 1976 and 1978; recovered two fumbles, 1974; attempted one pass with no completions, 1983 and 1985.
Played in NFC Championship Game following 1982 and 1983 seasons.
Played in NFL Championship Game following 1982 and 1983 seasons.
Played in Pro Bowl (NFL All-Star Game) following 1975 season.

LEE ROY SELMON

Born October 20, 1954, at Eufaula, Okla.
Height, 6.03. Weight, 250.
High School—Eufaula, Okla.
Received degree in special education from University of Oklahoma.
Brother of Dewey Selmon, linebacker with Tampa Bay Buccaneers and
San Diego Chargers, 1976 through 1982; and Lucious Selmon,
assistant coach at University of Oklahoma; and related to Alvin Moore, running back on Detroit Lions.
Named as defensive end on THE SPORTING NEWS College All-America Team, 1975.
Outland Trophy winner, 1975.
Named to THE SPORTING NEWS NFC All-Star Team, 1978 and 1979.
Named to THE SPORTING NEWS NFL All-Star Team, 1980.
Selected by Tampa Bay in 1st round (1st player selected) of 1976 NFL draft.
On injured reserve with knee injury, December 5 through remainder of 1978 season.
On injured reserve with back injury, July 25 through entire 1985 season.
Tampa Bay NFL, 1976 through 1984.
Games: 1976 (8), 1977 (14), 1978 (16), 1979 (16), 1980 (16), 1981 (14), 1982 (9), 1983 (14), 1984 (16). Total—121.
Pro statistics: Recovered two fumbles, 1977, 1980 and 1984; recovered two fumbles for 29 yards and one touchdown, 1979; recovered one fumble, 1982; recovered one fumble for four yards, 1983.
Played in NFC Championship Game following 1979 season.
Named to play in Pro Bowl (NFL All-Star Game) following 1979 season; replaced due to injury by Al Baker.
Played in Pro Bowl (NFL All-Star Game) following 1980 through 1984 seasons.

WILLIAM DEAN SHIELDS
(Billy)

Born August 23, 1953, at Vicksburg, Miss.
Height, 6.08. Weight, 284.
High School—Birmingham, Ala., Banks.
Attended Georgia Tech.
Selected by San Diego in 6th round (136th player selected) of 1975 NFL draft.

Traded by San Diego Chargers to Minnesota Vikings for safety John Turner, August 10, 1984.
Placed on did not report list, August 10 through September 2, 1984.
Returned to San Diego Chargers in exchange for 3rd round pick in 1985 draft, September 3, 1984.
Granted roster exemption, September 3 through September 18, 1984.
Released by San Diego Chargers, September 19, 1984; signed as free agent by San Francisco 49ers, September 27 1984.
Traded by San Francisco 49ers to New York Jets for 6th round pick in 1986 draft, August 2, 1985.
On injured reserve with knee injury, September 3 through November 7, 1985; activated, November 8, 1985.
Released by New York Jets, December 5, 1985; awarded on waivers to Kansas City Chiefs, December 6, 1985.
Granted free agency with no qualifying offer, February 1, 1986.
San Diego NFL, 1975 through 1983; San Francisco NFL, 1984; New York Jets (3)-Kansas City (2) NFL, 1985.
Games: 1975 (11), 1976 (14), 1977 (13), 1978 (16), 1979 (16), 1980 (16), 1981 (16), 1982 (9), 1983 (16), 1984 (10), 1985 (5 Total—142.
Pro statistics: Recovered one fumble, 1978 and 1979; recovered two fumbles, 1980.
Played in AFC Championship Game following 1980 and 1981 seasons.
Played in NFC Championship Game following 1984 season.
Played in NFL Championship Game following 1984 season.

BILLY RAY SIMS

Born September 18, 1955, at St. Louis, Mo.
Height, 6.00. Weight, 212.
High School—Hooks, Tex.
Received bachelor of arts degree in recreational therapy from University of Oklahoma in 1980.

Heisman Trophy winner, 1978.
Named THE SPORTING NEWS College Player of the Year, 1978.
Named as running back on THE SPORTING NEWS College All-America Team, 1978 and 1979.
Named THE SPORTING NEWS NFL Rookie of the Year, 1980.
Selected by Detroit in 1st round (1st player selected) of 1980 NFL draft.
On did not report list, September 6 through September 9, 1982; activated, September 10, 1982.
Signed by Houston Gamblers, July 1, 1983, for contract to take effect after being granted free agency, February 1984.
USFL rights subsequently traded by New Jersey Generals to Houston Gamblers for 1st round pick in 1984 dra and future draft picks, October 7, 1983.
Signed by Detroit Lions, December 16, 1983, and Gamblers contract was subsequently voided in court, Februar 10, 1984.
On injured reserve with knee injury, October 24 through remainder of 1984 season.
On physically unable to perform/reserve with knee injury, August 20 through entire 1985 season.

Year Club	G.	Att.	RUSHING Yds.	Avg.	TD.	PASS RECEIVING P.C.	Yds.	Avg.	TD.	—TOTAL— TD.	Pts.
1980—Detroit NFL	16	313	1303	4.2	*13	51	621	12.2	3	*16	96
1981—Detroit NFL	14	296	1437	4.9	13	28	451	16.1	2	15	90
1982—Detroit NFL	9	172	639	3.7	4	34	342	10.1	0	4	24
1983—Detroit NFL	13	220	1040	4.7	7	42	419	10.0	0	7	42
1984—Detroit NFL	8	130	687	5.3	5	31	239	7.7	0	5	30
Pro Totals—5 Years	60	1131	5106	4.5	42	186	2072	11.1	5	47	282

Additional pro statistics: Recovered one fumble, 1980 and 1982; recovered three fumbles, 1981; recovered fo fumbles, 1983; recovered two fumbles, 1984.
Played in Pro Bowl (NFL All-Star Game) following 1980 through 1982 seasons.

FREDDIE SOLOMON

Born January 11, 1953, at Sumter, S. C.
Height, 5.11. Weight, 185.
High School—Sumter, S. C.
Received degree in physical education from University of Tampa in 1975.
Related to Roland Solomon, defensive back with Dallas Cowboys,
Buffalo Bills and Denver Broncos, 1980 and 1981.

Selected by Miami in 2nd round (36th player selected) of 1975 NFL draft.
Traded with defensive back Vern Roberson and a 1st and 5th round pick in 1978 draft from Miami Dolphins to San Francisco 49ers for running back Delvin Williams, April 17, 1978.

Year Club	G.	Att.	RUSHING Yds.	Avg.	TD.	PASS RECEIVING P.C.	Yds.	Avg.	TD.	—TOTAL— TD.	Pts.	F.
1975—Miami NFL	14	4	87	21.8	0	22	339	15.4	2	3	18	2
1976—Miami NFL	10	4	60	15.0	1	27	453	16.8	2	4	24	0
1977—Miami NFL	13	6	43	7.2	0	12	181	15.1	1	2	12	2
1978—San Francisco NFL	16	14	70	5.0	1	31	458	14.8	2	3	18	5
1979—San Francisco NFL	15	6	85	14.2	1	57	807	14.2	7	8	48	3
1980—San Francisco NFL	16	8	56	7.0	0	48	658	13.7	8	10	60	5
1981—San Francisco NFL	15	9	43	4.8	0	59	969	16.4	8	8	48	3
1982—San Francisco NFL	9	1	—4	—4.0	0	19	323	17.0	3	3	18	2
1983—San Francisco NFL	13	1	3	3.0	0	31	662	21.4	4	4	24	1
1984—San Francisco NFL	14	6	72	12.0	1	40	737	18.4	10	11	66	0
1985—San Francisco NFL	16	2	4	2.0	0	25	259	10.4	1	1	6	1
Pro Totals—11 Years	151	61	519	8.5	4	371	5846	15.8	48	57	342	24

Year Club	G.	—PUNT RETURNS— No.	Yds.	Avg.	TD.	—KICKOFF RET.— No.	Yds.	Avg.TD.	
1975—Miami NFL	14	26	320	12.3	1	17	348	20.5	0
1970—Miami NFL	10	13	205	15.8	1	1	12	12.0	0
1977—Miami NFL	13	32	285	8.9	0	10	273	27.3	1
1978—San Francisco NFL	16	9	35	3.9	0	None			
1979—San Francisco NFL	15	23	142	6.2	0	None			
1980—San Francisco NFL	16	27	298	11.0	*2	4	61	15.3	0
1981—San Francisco NFL	15	29	173	6.0	0	None			
1982—San Francisco NFL	9	13	122	9.4	0	None			
1983—San Francisco NFL	13	5	34	6.8	0	None			
1984—San Francisco NFL	14	None				None			
1985—San Francisco NFL	16	None				None			
Pro Totals—11 Years	151	177	1614	9.1	4	32	694	21.7	1

Additional pro statistics: Recovered two fumbles for two yards, 1975; attempted one pass with no completions, 1976, 1980 and 1985; attempted 10 passes with five completions for 85 yards and one interception, recovered four fumbles and fumbled five times for minus two yards, 1978; attempted one pass with one completion for 12 yards, 1979; recovered two fumbles, 1979 and 1981; recovered five fumbles, 1980; attempted one pass with one completion for 25 yards, 1981; recovered one fumble, 1982 and 1983.
Played in NFC Championship Game following 1981, 1983 and 1984 seasons.
Played in NFL Championship Game following 1981 and 1984 seasons.

JAN STENERUD

Name pronounced Yon STEN-uh-rood.
Born November 26, 1942, at Fetsund, Norway.
Height, 6.02. Weight, 190.
High School—Lillestrom, Norway.
Received bachelor of science degree in commerce from Montana State University.

Established NFL records for most 100-point seasons, career (7); most field goals made, career (373); highest field goal percentage, game, five attempts (1.000), November 2, 1969 and December 7, 1969, against Buffalo Bills.
Established AFL career record for highest field goal percentage, 70.3.
Named as placekicker on THE SPORTING NEWS College All-America Team, 1966.
Named to THE SPORTING NEWS AFL All-Star Team, 1968 and 1969.
Named to THE SPORTING NEWS AFC All-Star Team, 1970 and 1975.
Selected by Kansas City in 3rd round of 1966 AFL Red Shirt draft.
Released by Kansas City Chiefs, August 26, 1980; signed as free agent by Green Bay Packers, November 25, 1980.
Granted free agency, February 1, 1984; re-signed by Packers and traded to Minnesota Vikings for 7th round pick in 1985 draft, July 17, 1984.

Year Club	G.	XP.XPM.FG.FGA.Pts.				
1967—Kansas City AFL	14	45	0	*21	*36	108
1968—Kansas City AFL	14	39	1	30	40	129
1969—Kansas City AFL	14	38	0	27	35	119
1970—Kansas City NFL	14	26	0	*30	42	116
1971—Kansas City NFL	14	32	0	26	44	110
1972—Kansas City NFL	14	32	0	21	36	95
1973—Kansas City NFL	14	21	2	24	38	93
1974—Kansas City NFL	14	24	2	17	24	75
1975—Kansas City NFL	14	30	1	*22	32	96
1976—Kansas City NFL	14	27	6	21	38	90
1977—Kansas City NFL	14	27	1	8	18	51
1978—Kansas City NFL	16	25	1	20	30	85
1979—Kansas City NFL	16	28	1	12	23	64
1980—Green Bay NFL	4	3	0	3	5	12
1981—Green Bay NFL	16	35	1	22	24	101
1982—Green Bay NFL	9	25	2	13	18	64
1983—Green Bay NFL	16	52	0	21	26	115
1984—Minnesota NFL	16	30	1	20	23	90
1985—Minnesota NFL	16	41	2	15	26	86
Pro Totals—19 Years	263	580	21	373	558	1699

Additional pro statistics: Fumbled once, recovered two fumbles and punted once for 28 yards, 1976.
Played in AFL Championship Game following 1969 season.
Played in AFL-NFL Championship Game following 1969 season.
Played in AFL All-Star Game following 1968 and 1969 seasons.
Played in Pro Bowl (NFL All-Star Game) following 1970, 1971, 1975 and 1984 seasons.

STEVE ALAN WILSON

Born May 19, 1954, at Fort Sill, Okla.
Height, 6.04. Weight, 270.
High School—Macon, Ga., Southwest.
Received degree in business administration from University of Georgia.

Selected by Tampa Bay in 5th round (154th player selected) of 1976 NFL draft.
On injured reserve with hand injury, December 9 through remainder of 1983 season.
On injured reserve with fractured rib, September 6 through November 21, 1985; activated, November 22, 1985.
Tampa Bay NFL, 1976 through 1985.
Games: 1976 (12), 1977 (14), 1978 (16), 1979 (16), 1980 (15), 1981 (15), 1982 (8), 1983 (10), 1984 (16), 1985 (5). Total—127.
Pro statistics: Recovered two fumbles, 1978; recovered one fumble, 1980, 1982 and 1983; fumbled once, 1983 and 1984.
Played in NFC Championship Game following 1979 season.

—DID YOU KNOW—

That the 62 points scored by the Jets against Tampa Bay on November 17 were the single-game high in 1985?

CHARLE EDWARD YOUNG

Born February 5, 1951, at Fresno, Calif.
Height, 6.04. Weight, 234.
High School—Fresno, Calif., Edison.
Received bachelor of arts degree from University of Southern California.

Named to THE SPORTING NEWS NFC All-Star Team, 1974 and 1975.
Named as tight end on THE SPORTING NEWS College All-America Team, 1972.
Selected by Philadelphia in 1st round (6th player selected) of 1973 NFL draft.
Traded by Philadelphia Eagles to Los Angeles Rams for quarterback Ron Jaworski, March 10, 1977.
Traded with 3rd and 4th round picks in 1980 draft by Los Angeles Rams to San Francisco 49ers for 3rd round pick
in 1980 draft and 3rd round pick in 1983 draft, April 28, 1980.
Released by San Francisco 49ers, July 21, 1983; signed as free agent by Seattle Seahawks, July 27, 1983.
Granted free agency with no qualifying offer, February 1, 1986.

Year Club	G.	RUSHING Att.	Yds.	Avg.	TD.	PASS RECEIVING P.C.	Yds.	Avg.	TD.	TOTAL TD.	Pts.	F.
1973—Philadelphia NFL	14	4	24	6.0	1	55	854	15.5	6	7	42	0
1974—Philadelphia NFL	14	6	38	6.3	0	63	696	11.0	3	3	18	4
1975—Philadelphia NFL	14	2	1	0.5	0	49	659	13.4	3	3	18	0
1976—Philadelphia NFL	14	1	6	6.0	0	30	374	12.5	0	0	0	1
1977—Los Angeles NFL	14	None				5	35	7.0	1	1	6	0
1978—Los Angeles NFL	16	2	6	3.0	0	18	213	11.8	0	0	0	0
1979—Los Angeles NFL	15	None				13	144	11.1	2	2	12	2
1980—San Francisco NFL	16	None				29	325	11.2	2	2	12	0
1981—San Francisco NFL	16	None				37	400	10.8	5	5	30	0
1982—San Francisco NFL	9	None				22	189	8.6	0	0	0	0
1983—Seattle NFL	16	None				36	529	14.7	2	2	12	0
1984—Seattle NFL	15	1	5	5.0	0	33	337	10.2	1	1	6	1
1985—Seattle NFL	14	None				28	351	12.5	2	2	12	1
Pro Totals—13 Years	187	16	80	5.0	1	418	5106	12.2	27	28	168	12

Additional pro statistics: Recovered one fumble, 1973, 1975, 1979 and 1983; returned one kickoff for 14 yards, 1980.
Played in NFC Championship Game following 1979 and 1981 seasons.
Played in AFC Championship Game following 1983 season.
Member of Los Angeles Rams for NFC Championship Game following 1978 season; did not play.
Played in NFL Championship Game following 1981 season.
Member of Los Angeles Rams for NFL Championship Game following 1979 season; did not play.
Played in Pro Bowl (NFL All-Star Game) following 1973 through 1975 seasons.